The SAT Prep Black Book

"The Most Effective SAT Strategies Ever Published"

Third Edition

By Patrick Barrett

The best way out is always through.
Robert Frost

Dedication

The first SAT Prep Black Book came out over a decade ago, and I didn't know then whether *anybody*, anywhere, would want to read it. Since that time, hundreds of thousands of students all over the world have used Black Books to get ready for tests like the SAT, ACT, and GRE.

Standardized testing can be a stressful, daunting experience, and it has been incredibly gratifying to help so many students navigate that process—to show people that they're capable of more than they thought, and that even intimidating obstacles can be overcome.

I'd like to dedicate this book to the people who made all of this possible: the readers of Black Books like this one.

Thank you so much for your support.

Additional Resources Online

All you need to prepare for the SAT is this Black Book and real SAT practice tests from the College Board. (See "Only Work with Questions from the College Board!" on page 16 of this Black Book for more on the importance of working with real SAT questions written by the College Board, and where to find them.)

But if you'd like more from me—including sample videos and updates related to test preparation, admissions, and the college experience—please check out the following channels:

SATprepVideos.com

This is where you can sign up for the e-mail newsletter and check out sample videos of question walkthroughs to see the training in this book applied to real SAT practice questions in real time.

YouTube.com/QuestPrep

Here you can find sample videos from the online video courses, as well as videos about other aspects of test prep and admissions.

Facebook.com/QuestPreparation

This is the main place to find updates and articles related to test prep, higher education, and—everyone's favorite—miscellany.

Instagram.com/Quest.Prep

Basically the same deal as Facebook above, but, you know, more pictures.

QuestPrep.com

This is the place to find all the basic info and FAQs about Quest Prep—from books and video courses to one-on-one tutoring.

Job Interviews Podcast

This is our podcast where we interview people about their education, work, and life experiences.

The right conversation can be life-changing, especially when it involves learning from someone else's choices, regrets, successes, and mistakes. Unfortunately, these kinds of profound, helpful conversations are hard to come by—you're lucky if you have 2 or 3 of them as a young adult, and lots of people never even get to have a single one. *Job Interviews* is here to fill that void with honest, real, direct advice about school and careers from real people with real experiences.

We conduct thorough, lively, funny interviews (or at least, we think they're funny) with people in a wide variety of careers from a wide variety of backgrounds. We find out about the work and school choices they made, how it all worked out for them, and what they would recommend to a young person in their field. You get the benefit of their life experiences without having to spend years learning hard lessons. Every single episode—just like every single life—includes twists, unexpected insights, and useful, concrete, actionable ideas you can start applying in your own quest, right now. We made this podcast to be the kind of resource that we wish had been available for us. We hope you like it, and we hope it helps you.

You can find *Job Interviews* wherever you get your podcasts.

Table of Contents

PLEASE Read This First!!!

> *Victorious warriors win first and then go to war, while defeated warriors go to war first and then seek to win.*
> Sun Tzu

Yeah, so… this book is hundreds of pages long.

You may be wondering if I expect you to read all of it, or if reading *any* of it is really going to help you at all. At least, that's what I'd be wondering if I were you. Most SAT prep books are pretty long, and pretty useless.

So let me explain a few things that will hopefully help set your mind at ease.

First, you should know that I've helped hundreds of thousands of people all over the globe prepare for standardized tests since before there was Instagram, or the Nintendo Wii, or touchscreens in most cars. But instead of focusing on memorizing concepts from the classroom like math formulas and obscure definitions—which is what most test prep resources teach—my preferred approach to standardized testing has always been based on understanding how a test is designed, and then thinking strategically about how to exploit the weaknesses of that design. (Different tests have different weaknesses, but any multiple-choice test that's designed to be given to huge numbers of people and provide reliable data must follow certain design rules, and those rules always introduce weaknesses that we can take advantage of.)

I also think about testing from the standpoint of performance, not just theory. In my publications, I strive to explain all aspects of test-taking with an eye towards helping you figure out how to *implement* what I'm teaching you—everything from dealing with testing anxiety and time management, all the way down to explaining why an individual answer choice is right or wrong, and determining what lessons you can draw from a mistake that will help you on future questions.

My personal tutoring clients pay me hundreds of dollars per hour and only come to me through word of mouth. In other words, I only have tutoring clients because previous clients recommend me to their friends and family.

So, in short: my approach to the SAT is likely to be actually helpful to you, instead of just wasting your time with mindless repetition of stuff you've already heard, which probably didn't help the first time you heard it anyway.

And here's more good news…

You Probably Don't Need to Read This Whole Super Long Book to Raise Your Score Significantly.

This Black Book has lots of pages, and it's structured so that certain kinds of ideas are repeated and demonstrated in different ways throughout the text. For example, my walkthroughs of real SAT questions show the specific application of generalized ideas that appear in the training sections of this book. Some people only skim the generalized training, and then dive right into the walkthroughs. Some people only focus on the training parts of the book and don't read many walkthroughs. And even if you're really into the walkthroughs, you'll probably decide on your own that they're so repetitive you don't need to read all of them. (I didn't set out to make the walkthroughs repetitive on my own; it's just that they're based on real SAT questions, and the SAT is a very repetitive test, so there's not much I can do to keep the walkthroughs from touching on the same concepts over and over again.)

So you may be wondering why I bothered to write such a long book—if most readers don't need to read the whole thing, then why does the whole thing exist?

The reason is that different readers will benefit from different aspects of the book… and I know from years of experience that a sizable number of readers actually *want* to understand every single aspect of the SAT, and will welcome the chance to digest this Black Book in its entirety.

Choosing Which Parts of this Black Book to Read, and in What Order

This book consists of a few different types of material, which can be loosely grouped as follows:

- General articles on topics like managing your time (in preparation and on test day), when and how to guess, and so on.
- Complete training on the two sections of the SAT (Reading and Writing, and Math)
- Detailed walkthroughs of every SAT question from four official SAT Practice Tests released by the College Board in the current format of the test, showing you how the training from the rest of this Black Book can actually be implemented on test day against real SAT questions (for more on which practice tests to use, see "Only Work with Questions from the College Board!" on page 16).

You can choose your own path through the ideas in this book, based on your needs and your learning style. Here are two examples of ways that readers in my test audience have reported going through it:

- If you're new to the SAT in general, then you'd probably be better off reading this Black Book basically in order from this point on—starting with the general training, then moving on to the training for individual parts of the SAT, and finishing with the walkthroughs, so you can see the ideas from the training in action.

- If you're satisfied that you completely understand how to handle some parts of the test and you're just looking for help on other parts, then you can consider getting right to work on your problem areas—but I'd advise you to come back to the other parts of the book later on, because they might help you get even better at the areas you currently consider to be your strongest. And when you decide that you really want to maximize your overall SAT score and give yourself the best possible chances in your college admissions campaign, then you'll want to be sure to check out these particular articles on overall prepping and test strategy:

  - The Importance of Details: Avoiding "Careless Errors" (page 14)
  - Only Work with Questions from the College Board! (page 16)
  - Setting (the Right) Goals (page 26)
  - How to Train for the SAT—Mastering the Ideas in this Black Book (page 27)
  - Where to Find "Missing Points" (page 28)
  - Guessing on the SAT (page 33)
  - Time Management On Test Day (page 36)
  - Reading Graphs, Charts, Tables, and Other Figures (page 48)
  - How The Digital SAT Impacts Our Approach (page 54)

My only somewhat firm recommendation on how to digest this Black Book is that you make sure you look through the training for a section of the SAT *before* you read the corresponding walkthroughs, because that will make it easier for you to make sure you get the maximum benefit from the walkthroughs. My question walkthroughs are much more thorough than the ones provided by the College Board itself, and they draw on concepts that aren't obvious to an untrained test-taker, but that are spelled out in the training sections.

At the same time, if you feel like you fully understand how a particular kind of question should be attacked, then there's no reason to go through every single walkthrough for that question type in this Black Book. As I mentioned, the SAT is incredibly repetitive (that's part of what makes it standardized, in fact), which means the walkthroughs can start to feel repetitive once you really understand the test.

Keep an open mind!

If you want me to be on your team for the SAT, then you have to give us both a fighting chance. That means reading this book with an open mind, looking carefully at the many example solutions to get an idea of how the principles taught in this book apply to real College Board questions, going to www.SATprepVideos.com to watch the free video demonstrations, and—above all—sticking with it when you run into difficulties. I've done my part to help you beat the test by laying bare exactly how the SAT works and exactly where it's vulnerable. Now it's up to you to read the battle plan and mount your attack.

Even though there are a variety of effective ways you could choose to tackle this material, as I explained above, *you won't get the full benefit of this book if you don't pay attention to what you read!*

Stick with it!

I can guarantee you that you will encounter real test questions that *seem* to violate the rules and patterns I talk about in this book. This is a normal part of the process—everyone, including myself, occasionally runs into a question that seems to break the rules.

When this happens, it's always because the test-taker has made a mistake.

So it's crucial that we remember that SAT questions must always follow a set of predictable rules, no matter how much any particular question might seem to break those rules. It will be tempting to think, "Oh, I guess this one math question requires me to know advanced trig, even though the Black Book said that would never happen," or "Well, I guess this reading question requires me to think about symbolism, even though that's supposed to be impossible on the SAT." As soon as you go down that road—as soon as you stop playing by the rules of the test and start treating the SAT like something it's not—your score will suffer.

So don't do that :)

Using Real SAT Practice Tests

The SAT Prep Black Book that you're reading right now will teach you all the rules, patterns, and design principles of real SAT questions, and will show you hundreds of solutions for real SAT questions, but you'll only be able to practice these ideas with real SAT Practice Tests from the College Board.

I want to make sure I mention this up-front because some readers think it's okay to work with practice questions from test prep companies like Kaplan, Barron's, et cetera. See "Only Work with Questions from the College Board!" on page 16 of this Black Book for an in-depth examination of all the reasons why those fake questions should be avoided.

Don't Believe Me? Don't Worry.

As you read this book, you may encounter advice that surprises you, or that contradicts "conventional wisdom" in test preparation (if there is such a thing).

Don't worry. This book contains walkthroughs for all the questions in linear SAT Practice Tests #1 – 4 from the College Board's website (as opposed to the tests in the Bluebook app, or the physical Blue Book—for more on this distinction, see "Only Work with Questions from the College Board!" on page 16 of this Black Book). That means you'll be able to read along as I give detailed, practical, non-obvious explanations for every real SAT question in those four tests, using the ideas in this Black Book. You'll see for yourself that the advice in this book can be successfully and consistently applied to real SAT practice questions.

Remember that the true test of SAT prep advice from *any* source, myself included, is whether that advice can be used successfully against real SAT practice questions from the College Board.

Using this Black Book to Prepare for the PSAT

On a question-by-question basis, the SAT and the PSAT are essentially the same: any question, passage, or figure that appears on either test could conceivably appear on the other. This makes it pretty easy for you to prepare for the PSAT and the SAT at the same time, because practically speaking, they're the same test.

So the best way to prepare for the PSAT is simply to use this book to prepare for the SAT as you normally would.

A Note on Repetition

There's a good chance that you will feel like parts of this book are repetitive. You're right—they are. This is because the SAT is a very, very repetitive test, which means that my discussions of how different questions and sections work will often involve repeating myself to some extent.

I've found that the best way for students to understand this test, and how it differs from classroom tests, is to reinforce all the basic information about the test until it becomes second nature. If you finish this Black Book and you're so familiar with the SAT that basic information about the test feels obvious and boring because you've heard it several times in a variety of situations, then that means you're probably in a good position to do really well on the test. Spending the extra time to read through this book will probably save you dozens and dozens of hours of practice and re-testing that would be necessary with a different approach to test prep—and it will get you a better score besides. So I think it's worth it to hear me mention key aspects of the test's design more than once.

About My Writing Style...

You may have already noticed that I use an informal, conversational writing style in this Black Book. I do this because my students tend to find that style much easier to read and digest than a formal "textbook" style.

This means I might do a few things your English teacher wouldn't love, such as starting sentences with conjunctions like "and" or "but." Most teachers will tell you not to do that in formal writing, even though famous and respected authors like John Locke, W. E. B. DuBois, and Jane Austen did it all the time.

You'll also find that many of my sentences would be unacceptable if they appeared in an SAT Writing question. Don't worry about that, though; as we'll discuss in the training for those questions, you'll find that most writers don't strictly follow all the College Board's grammar and punctuation rules in real life.

So I don't think of my Black Books as examples of formal writing (see? I just started a sentence with a conjunction again... and now I'm putting an ellipsis inside parentheses... and I'm not sure how to punctuate the end of this sentence, so I might just go all out and resort to multiple exclamation points and a smiley face!!!!! ☺). I prefer to write in a way that feels less like a textbook and more like a conversation, while still making sure my meaning is clear. In my experience, students find this approach much more engaging and ultimately much more effective—which is the whole point.

Part 1: The Secrets of SAT Success

In this part of the Black Book, we'll cover the most important concepts that underlie effective SAT preparation. Unfortunately, these are things that most untrained test-takers never realize, which causes them to spend more time than necessary on their SAT preparation... and come away with very little to show for all that effort.

The rest of this Black Book will build on these critical concepts; you'll see them at work in all of my training and walkthroughs.

In this part of the Black Book, you'll learn the following:

- why the SAT isn't designed like a regular high school test
- how the College Board manages to create difficult questions based on relatively simple concepts
- why some people do better in school than they do on the SAT, or vice-versa
- why there can only be one valid answer for each SAT question
- some fundamental errors that keep most untrained test-takers from ever approaching the SAT correctly
- how everyday experiences in high school can set you up with the wrong expectations on test day
- how to react when it seems like a question has more than one good answer
- important differences between classroom discussions and the analysis you'll need to use on the SAT
- why it's so important to see each SAT question as a system of ideas
- why any detail can potentially reveal the best way to answer a question, no matter how insignificant it seems to an untrained test-taker
- and more...

The "Big Secrets" of the SAT: Simplicity, Repetition, Weirdness, and Details

> *There are no secrets that time does not reveal.*

Jean Racine

Before we get into all the strategies and advice for specific areas of the test, I want to start out by sharing something very important with you: the "secret" of the SAT.

Here it is: the SAT frustrates so many test-takers because it asks about basic things in very strange (but repetitive) ways.

The simple reason so many people struggle with the test is that they're looking at it in completely the wrong way.

Let's examine why this is.

Imagine you're the College Board. Colleges use your test scores to help figure out which applicants to admit, and they only trust your test because it consistently provides them with reliable measurements. So how do you go about making a test that can be given to millions of students a year and still compare them all in a meaningful way, despite the wide variations in their backgrounds and abilities?

You can't just make a super-difficult test, because that won't really provide useful information to the colleges who rely on you. For example, you can't just focus the math test on advanced ideas from calculus and statistics, because many of the test-takers have never taken those subjects—and, even if they had, the results from your test wouldn't really tell the colleges anything that wasn't already reflected in students' transcripts. You also can't make a test that relies on subjective, opinion-based interpretation of literature, because then the test results won't correlate to anything meaningful on a large scale, and colleges won't be able to rely on the data from your test.

So, if you're the College Board, you need to design the SAT so it avoids advanced concepts and arbitrary interpretation. Otherwise, your test will be useless for colleges, because colleges want to use a test that measures something meaningful about every applicant in the same way every time. In other words, you have to test *basic* ideas in an *objective* way, rather than testing *advanced* ideas in a *subjective* way.

But then you have another problem: if you give a traditional objective test of basic ideas to millions of college-bound, motivated students, a lot of them are going to do really well on it—and then your results will be useless for a different reason, because there will be so many high scores that the data won't help colleges to make distinctions between applicants in their admissions decisions.

So how do you solve this problem?

The College Board solves this problem by combining basic ideas in weird (but repetitive and predictable) ways. The result is that doing well on the SAT involves the ability to look at a new test question and then figure out how it follows the rules that all SAT questions of that type must follow. And that's what this book will teach you to do.

This is why there are so many people who do so well in advanced classes in high school but have a relatively hard time with the SAT: the SAT tests simpler stuff in a stranger way. It basically requires a totally different skill-set from high school or college. (You may be wondering why some students do well on both the SAT and school. These people are just good at both skill-sets. It's a bit like being good at both football and wrestling: there's enough of an overlap that some people are naturally good at both, but enough of a difference that many people struggle with one or the other. Or both.)

Now that you know the SAT's big secret, the rest of this Black Book—and the SAT itself—will probably make a lot more sense to you. This book is basically a road map to all the weird things the SAT does. It will teach you how to navigate the SAT's bizarre design, and how to exploit the many weaknesses inherent in that design.

Certainty and the SAT

I've spent more hours than I can count helping my students raise their SAT scores, and all of that time has made me realize that there's a serious problem blocking most SAT-takers from realizing their full potential.

It's not a problem that has to do with strategy, memorization, timing, focus, or anything like that. This problem is at the root of the very nature of the SAT itself. And if you don't come to terms with it, your score can only be mediocre at best.

The problem is that the SAT only gives you one correct answer choice for each question, and this correct answer choice is totally, definitively, incontrovertibly the correct answer—there are no arguments to be made against it (once we know the test's rules).

But a lot of untrained test-takers never realize this. In this book, I talk a lot about all the specific ways that the SAT is different from tests you take in high school. But I really want to emphasize this one difference, because it will affect every single thing you do as you prepare for the test. So I'm saying it again—read closely:

Multiple-choice SAT questions always have ONE, and only ONE, correct answer. Furthermore, the issue of which answer choice is the correct one is absolutely beyond disagreement. As surely as 2 and 2 make 4—and not 5 or 3—every single multiple-choice SAT question has exactly one correct answer choice. And you can find it with total certainty once you know the SAT's rules, which is what you'll learn in this Black Book.

A Real-Life Example

Why is this such a big deal, you ask?

Imagine this common high school situation, which you've probably been through yourself. Your history teacher is going over the answers to a multiple-choice test with your class. It's a test he wrote himself, and he wrote it just for your class. And as he's going through the test, he tells you that the answer to number 9 is choice (D). Half the class groans—they all marked (B). One of the students who marked (B) raises her hand and makes a convincing argument that she should get credit for marking (B). She explains that if you read the question a certain way, (B) and (D) are equally good answers. The teacher, who wants to be open-minded and fair, reconsiders the question, and decides that it's poorly written. In light of the student's argument, he can understand why (B) might have looked like the right answer. And, because he's fair, he announces that he'll give equal credit for both (B) and (D).

That sort of thing happens every day in high schools all across the country. It's the natural result of a system in which teachers have to write their own classes' exams, and don't have enough time to proof-read them or even test them out on sample classes in advance. Inevitably, some poorly written questions get past the teacher. The teacher corrects the problem later by giving credit as necessary, or throwing questions out, or whatever.

What message does this send to students? Unfortunately, students come to believe that the answers to *all* tests are open to discussion and debate, that *all* questions are written by stressed-out teachers who work with specific students in mind, that *all* questions are potentially flawed and open to interpretation.

Then, when these students take the SAT, things get crazy. They can never settle on anything, because they've been taught that the proper approach to a multiple-choice test is to look for any way at all to bend every answer until it's correct. They mark wrong answers left and right—usually they manage to eliminate one or two choices, and then the rest all seem equally correct, so they take a stab at each question and move on to the next, never really being certain of anything.

Most of these untrained test-takers are wrong way more often than they think.

And the worst part is that they never even realize what's holding them back.

Two Key Realizations

If you're going to do well on the SAT, you have to realize two things.

First, you have to know that the SAT is a totally objective test, and that every single question has only one right answer, as we've discussed. The SAT is written by teams of people; before a question appears on the SAT, it's been thoroughly reviewed and tested by experts. No matter how much it might seem otherwise, every multiple-choice question on the SAT has only one right answer that follows the rules of the test.

Once you come to accept that, the second thing you have to realize is that you—specifically YOU, the person reading this—can find the answer to every SAT question if you learn what to look for. You can. And with the right training and practice, you will.

So let's wrap this whole thing up nice and simple:

1. The only way to do really well on the SAT is to mark the correct answer to most or all of the questions on the test.

2. The only reliable way to mark the correct answer consistently is to be able to identify it consistently.

3. Before you can identify the correct answer consistently, you have to know and believe that there will always be one correct answer for every question—if you're open to the possibility that more than one choice could be acceptable, you won't be strict about eliminating answers by using the rules and patterns of the test.

4. Most untrained test-takers never realize this, and as a result they never maximize their performance. Instead, they treat the SAT like a regular high school test, which is a huge mistake for the reasons we just discussed.

Now that we've established this important concept, we have to talk about something that comes up often in testing situations…

What to Do When it Looks Like There Might be Two Right Answers to a Question

Even though you know there can only be one valid answer to a real SAT question, there will be times when you think more than one choice might be correct. It happens to everybody. It happens to me, and it will happen to you. When it does happen, you must immediately recognize that you've done something wrong—you misread a key word, you left off a minus sign, something like that.

There are two ways to fix this situation. One way is to cut your losses and go on to the next question, planning to return to the difficult question later on, when your head has cleared. This is what I usually do, and we cover it in more detail in "Time Management On Test Day," which starts on page 36 of this Black Book.

The second way is to keep working on the difficult question. Try and figure out what might be causing the confusion while the question is still fresh in your mind, and resolve the issue right then and there. I'm not such a big fan of this approach because I tend to find that things are clearer to me when I return to a question after skipping it. But some people find that moving on without answering a question just means they have to familiarize themselves with it all over again when they come back, and they prefer to stay focused on a particular question until they either find the right answer or decide to guess on it.

To see which type of person you are, just do what comes naturally, and experiment a little bit with both approaches in your practice sessions—then check your results and see which approach yields more total correct answers per section.

The Importance of Details: Avoiding "Careless Errors"

You will make all kinds of mistakes; but as long as you are generous and true, and also fierce, you cannot hurt the world or even seriously distress her.

Winston Churchill

As you go through the test-taking strategies in this Black Book, one thing will become very clear to you: at every turn, the SAT is obsessed with details in a way that high school and college courses typically are not.

Finding the right answer to an SAT Reading and Writing question often relies on recognizing the significance of a single word in a passage that an untrained test-taker would easily overlook. An SAT Math question involving algebra and fractions might have the reciprocal and the opposite of the right answer as two of the wrong answer choices. And so on.

This means that doing extremely well on the SAT isn't just a matter of knowing the proper strategies (though that's a big part of it, of course!). It's also a matter of being almost fanatically obsessed with the tiniest details. In fact, I would say that in most cases the biggest difference between someone who scores a 600 on a section of the SAT and someone who scores an 800 isn't that the 800-scorer is any smarter or any more knowledgeable, but that she's much more diligent about paying attention to details.

This strong orientation to detail is exactly the opposite of what most teachers in most high schools reward in their classes. Generally speaking, teachers are more interested in things like participation, an ability to defend your position, and a willingness to think of the big picture, especially in humanities classes. On the SAT, those things rarely come in handy. What matters on the SAT is your ability to execute relatively simple strategies over and over again on a variety of questions without missing small details that would normally go overlooked in a classroom discussion.

For this reason, the attitude that most test-takers typically have towards so-called "careless errors"—which is that they don't really matter as long as you basically understand what the question is about—is very destructive when you take the SAT.

I'd even say that most test-takers could improve their scores by at least 50 to 100 points per section—usually more—if they would just eliminate these kinds of errors completely. But most people don't take these small mistakes seriously, and they don't know a reliable way to separate right answers from wrong answers anyway. So they usually end up making the same kinds of small errors, often without realizing it, no matter how much they practice.

Why are Careless Errors so Easy to Make on the SAT?

As always, when we try to figure out why the SAT is the way it is, we have to remember why the test exists in the first place: colleges and universities find the data from the test to be useful when they're evaluating applicants. This is only possible because the test questions are written according to specific rules and patterns that don't change, and because the test uses the multiple-choice format, which limits student responses and allows the grading to be objective, in the sense that a test-taker either marks the correct answer to a question, or she doesn't, with no gray area in between.

Here's the kicker: the multiple-choice format itself, and the SAT's rules and patterns specifically, would be useless for the purpose of making fine, meaningful distinctions among millions of test-takers unless the questions were written in a very detail-oriented way.

In other words, the College Board has to be obsessed with details because otherwise its data would be useless.

So the questions on the SAT are extremely nit-picky in a way that most test-takers never really encounter in a high school classroom.

How Can We Pay Attention to Details and Avoid Careless Mistakes?

When we get into the walkthroughs of real SAT questions later in this book, you'll notice that I always talk about each question as a system of ideas. Instead of just explaining how the right answer satisfies the prompt, I also talk about the patterns we can see in the wrong answers, and about how the wrong answers relate to the right answer. I do this for a variety of reasons, but one of the biggest reasons is that being aware of how the parts of a question interact with one another is one of the best ways to verify that an answer choice is right. If the choice you like makes sense within the larger context of the test's design, then you can have more confidence in your decisions and a greater degree of certainty that you haven't made a mistake.

On the other hand, most of the time when people do make a mistake on the test, it's because they haven't considered the question in its entirety. Instead, they catch a couple of phrases or concepts, make an unwarranted assumption or a faulty calculation, see an answer choice that reflects their mistake, and then move on to the next question without reconsidering their decisions.

So please do us both a favor and take a lesson from the way I think carefully about parts of each question that most people might consider irrelevant. I do that with good reason, as we'll see in the walkthroughs later in this book.

Part 2: When to Use College Board Materials... And When Not To

In this part of the Black Book, I'll explain why it's so important to work with real SAT questions from the College Board... but also important to ignore the College Board's own "explanations" of those real SAT questions (you'll see why I put the word "explanations" in quotation marks like that, too). Finally, if you've already run out of official questions from the College Board, I'll give you some ideas of other sources you can use in a pinch.

Among other things, you'll learn the following:

- why it's so important to practice with questions that follow the same rules as the questions you'll see on test day
- what really holds most people back from scoring as high as they should (it isn't subject-matter knowledge!)
- where we can find real test questions from the College Board
- which College Board practice tests correspond to the walkthroughs in this book
- some common differences between questions from the College Board and questions from other companies
- why it makes no sense to practice with "harder" questions than you'll see on test day
- why the College Board's "explanations" are often unhelpful for most test-takers who need them
- the elements of a good explanation for an official SAT question
- the most important part of using real SAT questions in your training
- why your analysis of an SAT question should always be directed at diagnosing similar situations on test day
- how the College Board's "explanations" of SAT Math questions often ignore the techniques that high-scorers actually use
- how the College Board's "explanations" of SAT Reading and Writing questions use circular reasoning to avoid revealing too much
- how to use the walkthroughs in this Black Book
- why you should read the entire walkthrough when you use this Black Book to help you with an SAT question
- why my walkthroughs are more thorough than you'll need to be on test day, and what to do on test day instead
- why you probably won't run out of practice material if you use the College Board's materials wisely
- which other practice materials to use—and which to avoid—if you do feel like you need more practice questions
- and more...

Only Work with Questions from the College Board!

One must learn by doing the thing.

Sophocles

Three of the most important themes in this book, which are reflected on almost every level of my SAT advice, are the following:

- SAT questions are written according to specific rules and patterns, and…
- …beating the SAT means learning to exploit the inherent weaknesses of those rules and patterns, because…
- …most of the problems that most people have on the SAT are the result of poor test-taking skills, not of deficiencies in subject-matter knowledge.

I'll expand on these ideas in the rest of this Black Book, but for right now I want to impress something upon you that is extremely, extremely important: it's absolutely critical that you practice with real SAT questions written by the actual College Board itself, and not with any other kind of practice test, or practice questions.

Only the real questions written by the actual College Board are guaranteed to behave like the questions you'll see on test day. Questions written by other companies (Kaplan, Barron's, or anybody else) are simply not guaranteed to behave like the real thing. In some cases, the differences are obvious, and, frankly, shocking. Some companies write fake practice SAT Reading and Writing questions in which the passive voice is the difference between a right answer and a wrong answer; some fake SAT Math questions rely on math formulas the real SAT doesn't test. And so on. As you might imagine, practicing with questions like that won't help your score—in fact, it's likely to bring your score down.

Fake practice questions that break the rules of the real test will encourage you to develop bad test-taking habits, and will keep you from being able to develop good habits. For our purposes, then, fake SAT questions written by any company except the College Board are basically useless. If you want to learn how to beat the SAT, you should work with real SAT questions.

Where to Find Real Practice SAT Questions

As we just discussed, you should only practice with real SAT practice questions from the College Board—but there are actually three main sets of those questions, and it's worth spending a moment to clarify the differences from one set to the next.

Digital SAT Practice Tests in the Bluebook App

The current SAT is delivered in an adaptive digital format—that is, almost everyone will take the test on a computer, and how well you do on the first module of each section determines the difficulty level of the second module (at least as far as the College Board defines "difficulty"—for more on this, see "How The Digital SAT Impacts Our Approach" on page 54).

The College Board offers a free app called "Bluebook" that simulates this adaptive digital test-taking experience. You can search for the app online, or, if you prefer, you can find a link to the app at QuestPrep.com/Practice (note that at the time of this writing, the College Board's Bluebook app is only available on tablets, laptops, and desktops—not smartphones).

That app gives you access to six complete, full-length digital SAT practice tests. You will definitely want to use the app to take one or more practice tests before test day, for two critical reasons:

- practicing with real test questions is crucial for your success, as discussed here and elsewhere in this Black Book, and
- you want to be completely comfortable with the digital testing interface before test day, and the only way to do that is to practice answering real SAT questions on the College Board's Bluebook app.

This Black Book contains complete walkthroughs for four real SAT practice tests from the College Board; the tests in the Bluebook app *are not* the tests that correspond to the walkthroughs later in this book! Those walkthroughs later in this book correspond to the first four linear SAT practice tests available from the College Board's website—let's talk about those now.

Linear SAT Practice Tests

These are called "linear" practice tests because they aren't the adaptive, digital tests—they're just normal PDF documents, like paper tests. One of the intended advantages of the adaptive tests is that they're supposed to be more efficient than linear tests; they can assess test-takers with fewer questions. Conversely, these linear "paper" tests are less efficient than the adaptive versions, which means these tests have more questions and take more time than their linear counterparts, as you can see in the table below.

Test Format	Reading and Writing		Math		Total	
Adaptive Digital SAT	64 minutes	54 questions	70 minutes	44 questions	134 minutes	98 questions
Linear "Paper" SAT	78 minutes	66 questions	86 minutes	54 questions	164 minutes	120 questions

These tests are available online directly from the College Board's website, or you can find those same tests at QuestPrep.com/Practice. The first four of these linear SAT practice tests from the College Board's website are the four tests that correspond to the walkthroughs later in this book, so you absolutely need access to these tests if you want to get the most out of this book—again, you can find those tests on the College Board's website, or at QuestPrep.com/Practice.

SAT Practice Tests in the College Board's Physical Blue Book

The College Board publication *The Official Digital SAT Study Guide*, also known as the "Blue Book," contains four SAT practice tests as well—*but these are not the same as the practice tests in the Bluebook app, or the practice tests on the College Board's website!*

In my opinion, the College Board made a weird decision about the practice tests they would include in the Blue Book (which is kind of a polite way to say they made a bad decision). Instead of just including the same linear SAT practice tests available for free in PDF form on their website, they decided to sort of approximate the experience of taking the digital test, just in paper format. So these tests in the Blue Book have the same number of questions as the adaptive digital test, *not* as the linear "paper" tests available in PDF form from the College Board's website. The College Board decided to present tests 1 and 3 in the physical Blue Book as though someone taking the digital test had scored *lower* on the first module and gotten an *easier* second module, and they decided to present tests 2 and 4 in the physical Blue Book as though someone taking the digital test had scored *higher* on the first module and gotten a *harder* second module.

(This is explained by the College Board on page 317 of their physical Blue Book, in a section called "About These Practice Tests.")

The result of this decision is that practice tests 1 and 3 in the physical Blue Book are *easier* SAT practice tests, and practice tests 2 and 4 in the physical Blue Book are *harder* SAT practice tests! This is *incredibly* important, and many test-takers will overlook the one page in the physical Blue Book that explains this difference, and they will get confused about why two of the practice tests seemed easier, and the other two seemed harder.

Which Questions, Exactly, You Should Use

We just established that there are three main sources of real SAT practice questions from the College Board:

- 4 digital practice tests, free in the Bluebook app (these are the digital tests)
- 4 linear PDF tests, free from the College Board's website or QuestPrep.com/Practice (these are the PDF tests)
- 4 paper practice tests, available in the College Board's physical Blue Book (these are the book tests)

There's one more important fact to know about these tests that we didn't cover yet: they're not all the same on a question-by-question basis, but they all come from the same pool of questions . That means that some questions from each of the three sources above might appear on a test from either or both of the other sources; in some cases, entire modules or sections are the same.

(Before we go any further, let me point out that you don't have to understand and memorize every detail we're about to discuss; this explanation gets a little nitpicky and detail-oriented. In a moment, we'll break down the takeaway from this section, which is the only part you need to remember. I'm just including the following explanation because some readers will want to understand the logic behind the conclusions in this section.)

In no particular order:

- The first module of each section from the book tests is identical to the first module of each section from the digital tests.
- The second module of each section from the book tests is identical to the *lower*-scoring module from the digital tests for tests 1 and 3, and identical to the *higher*-scoring module from the digital tests for tests 2 and 4.
- The second module of each section from the book tests is different from the *higher*-scoring module from the digital tests for tests 1 and 3, and different from the *lower*-scoring module from the digital tests for tests 2 and 4.
- Many questions from the PDF tests appear throughout the different modules of the digital tests and the book tests, but the PDF tests are largely different from the digital tests and the book tests.

We have two main goals in our practice:

1. Get comfortable using the training from the SAT Prep Black Book to find correct answers to real SAT questions.
2. Become familiar with the digital interface that the College Board uses to deliver the digital SAT.

The first goal above is *by far* the most important, and it will be the focus of nearly all of your SAT preparation. But the second goal above is important, too. With these two ideas in mind, let's get to this section's major takeaway.

The Takeaway

The walkthroughs in this Black Book correspond to the first four linear tests mentioned above, which are available for free in PDF format from the College Board's website, and also from QuestPrep.com/Practice. Those four PDF tests are the main practice tests you will use in your preparation; anytime this book mentions a question from a practice SAT test, it's referring to those four PDF tests. Download those PDF tests (and print them out, if you feel like it) and make sure you have access to them as you work through the training and walkthroughs in this book. You will use these four PDF tests to practice and master the training in this Black Book.

The digital tests in the Bluebook app are the only way to simulate the actual digital test-taking experience you will have on test day, so you will need to practice with that app—that way, when you sit down on test day, you won't run into anything unexpected related to the testing software. It's important to be able to navigate back and forth among the questions, check to make sure you answered everything, and so on. It's also incredibly important to become proficient with the provided calculator—in fact, a whole section of this book is dedicated to that topic, entitled "Special Technique: Using The Surprisingly Powerful Digital SAT Calculator" on page 280 of this Black Book.

After you've gotten comfortable with the training in this Black Book and practiced sufficiently with the PDF tests—but before test day—you should take at least one full digital practice SAT on the Bluebook app (or more, if you have the time). You should simulate testing conditions as much as you reasonably can: take the test in one sitting, in a quiet room without distractions, etc. Because of the issues discussed earlier, it's likely that you'll see questions on the digital test that you already encountered in your training, depending on how many of the walkthroughs you read in this Black Book, and how much of the PDF tests you work through in your training. Since you may have already seen some of those questions, your scores on the digital practice tests could be slightly inflated; that doesn't really matter either way, though, because your primary goal in taking those digital practice tests is to get comfortable using the Bluebook app.

So make sure you have access to the paper tests for the bulk of your training and preparation as you work through this Black Book, and then make sure you spend as much time as you need to poking around the Bluebook app before test day to get completely comfortable with it—including taking at least one full-length digital practice test on that Bluebook app before test day.

What about the physical Blue Book?

I don't recommend following any of the training advice in the College Board's physical Blue Book—as we've already discussed and will continue to discuss, most mainstream test prep basically rehashes academic, classroom-style lessons that aren't really helpful on standardized tests, and the Blue Book is no different. We shouldn't be surprised, really, that the College Board doesn't give away the secrets to beating the SAT, because if they just told everybody how to beat the test, then the test wouldn't have much value anymore.

So I don't recommend that you follow the test prep advice in the Blue Book. The only value in the book would be the real practice tests—and for earlier versions of the SAT, I would have said you should definitely get a copy of the Blue Book just to get those tests.

But the physical Blue Book for the digital SAT basically just provides a more limited version of the first four free digital tests in the Bluebook app. Since you can get the Bluebook app and its digital practice tests for free, there isn't really any advantage to using the physical Blue Book. If you'd like to have a physical copy of real SAT practice questions that you can carry around with you, then feel free to get a copy of the Blue book, but it isn't a necessary part of your preparation.

Also, the tests in the physical Blue Book don't correspond to the walkthroughs later in this Black Book; again, those walkthroughs correspond to the free PDF tests available on the College Board's website, or at QuestPrep.com/Practice.

So the physical Blue Book doesn't really have any particular advantage over the digital tests, or the PDF tests. There's nothing wrong with getting a copy of the physical Blue Book if you want one, so I'm not going to tell you *not* to do it—just be aware that the test prep advice in that book isn't very effective, and that book doesn't contain any practice tests that you can't get for free in the Bluebook app.

What About "Harder" Questions?

One of the most common objections to the idea of using real SAT practice questions in general is that some companies (most notably Barron's) are known for writing practice questions that are "harder" than real test questions—the argument is that working with more difficult questions will make the real test seem like a breeze in comparison.

Unfortunately, this approach is too clever for its own good! It overlooks the nature of difficulty on the SAT. If the "harder" practice questions from a third-party company were hard *in the same way that "hard" SAT questions are hard,* then using them might be a good idea. But those fake questions are harder in a way that makes them totally unlike real questions, so they're a waste of time.

When a third-party company writes fake questions to be hard, it does so by incorporating skills that a high-school student would need to use in advanced classes: complicated math concepts, subtle literary analysis, and so on. But these skills have no place on the SAT, because the SAT limits itself to very basic ideas, and tries to fool you by asking you about basic things in weird ways.

So if you want to raise your SAT score, the skill you need to develop is the ability to look at real SAT questions, figure out whatever basic thing they actually want you to do, and then do it. That's what this Black Book teaches you. In fact, the more familiar you become with the SAT, the more you'll see that "hard" official SAT questions aren't really any different from "easy" ones when you get right down to it. This is why it's pointless to use fake questions, even if they're supposed to be more challenging.

Whenever students ask if they should use "harder" questions to get ready for the SAT, I always answer with this analogy: it's true that performing on the flying trapeze is harder than making an omelet, but getting better at the trapeze won't make your omelets any better, because the two things have nothing in common. Just because something is harder doesn't mean it's helpful.

I really can't stress this enough: if you're serious about raising your score, then you need to practice with real SAT questions written by the College Board, because real test questions are what you'll see on test day.

I sometimes have students who ignore this part of my SAT advice, and the results are never good. Seriously. Trust me on this. Only use questions from the College Board.

Why it's so Important for Me to "Re-Explain" Questions from the College Board

| *Whatever is worth doing at all is worth doing well.*
Philip Stanhope

You may have realized by now that the College Board already provides "explanations" for every official practice question in their released practice tests, and that this Black Book also contains explanations for the same official practice questions. You may also be asking yourself why I'd bother writing out a ton of in-depth explanations for questions that already have "explanations" by the College Board.

On top of that, you may have noticed that I just put the word "explanations" in quotation marks every time I referred to "explanations" written by the College Board. And you may be wondering what's up with all of that.

Actually, it relates to a very important question that underlies our entire method of preparation: what's the purpose of practicing with official test questions from the College Board, and how do the official practice questions you work on relate to the questions that you'll see on test day?

The questions that you see on test day won't be word-for-word repetitions of the questions in the official SAT Practice Tests from the College Board, but the questions on test-day *will* follow the exact same design principles as the official practice questions. They'll observe the same rules and patterns, and they'll try to trick you in the same ways, even if that's not immediately obvious to an untrained test-taker.

That means you'll miss out on the true value of practicing with real SAT questions from the College Board *unless you analyze them effectively afterwards.* You'll never see any one specific practice question from one real SAT test on another real SAT test, but you *will* see lots of other questions that follow the same underlying principles as the questions you practice with. So your analysis of your practice sessions needs to get into those underlying principles, or your preparation won't be nearly as effective as it could be.

For these reasons, a good explanation of an official SAT practice question should point out 5 things:

1. Specifically why the right answer is right—what attributes does it have that you can expect to find in other right answers that you'll see on test day?

2. Specifically why the wrong answers are wrong, and which attributes you'll see again in the wrong answers on test day

3. The fastest and easiest way that you could have arrived at the right answer to the question

4. The attributes of the question that will appear in other questions on test day, so you can exploit them when you see them in the future

5. The tricks that the College Board tried to play on untrained test-takers when it constructed the question, and how we can avoid falling for similar tricks on test day

In general, the College Board's own "explanations" don't address these issues. Instead, they typically provide some kind of limited or circular statement about Reading and Writing questions, and a relatively formulaic approach for Math questions. The College Board occasionally provides more detailed explanations for some questions, but, for the most part, the College Board's explanations do almost nothing to help you learn the deeper lessons from a practice question, and then apply them to future questions—which makes sense, really, because if the College Board fully explained how SAT questions actually work, it would be working against its own interests.

This is why it's necessary for me to provide my own explanations for the College Board's practice questions. My explanations address the elements above so that you can learn what you should actually do on test day.

You can see what I'm talking about if you skim through the College Board's SAT practice question "explanations." But I'll provide a few examples of what I'm talking about below, to make sure we're on the same page.

College Board Explanations on the Reading and Writing Section

The College Board's explanations for its Reading questions are often circular, essentially boiling down to a statement like "Choice (A) is right because it's the right answer, while the other choices are wrong because they're not right." Instead of trying to help you understand what the College Board considers to be correct, or why the SAT is constructed the way it is, this type of "explanation" generally adds nothing to your understanding.

One example of this kind of non-explanation can be found in the College Board's "explanation" for question 11 from section 1, module 2 of SAT Practice Test #1. The prompt for that question asks us "how the Lord Chancellor respond[s] to the crowd," and the correct answer says that "he describes the crowd as being united, even though the crowd clearly appears otherwise." The "explanation" for the question *does* mention some of the relevant parts of the text, such as the crowd shouting "Bread!" or "Taxes!", and it does say "the text… presents [the crowd] as not knowing what they really want," but the explanation fails to provide a clear connection between people shouting different things and the right answer to the question; it also describes the crowd "as not knowing what they really want" without directly quoting the relevant text to show how we know this is true—as you'll see in the SAT Reading training later in this book, all correct answers to SAT Reading questions must be based on specific words and phrases in the relevant text. The explanation says the Lord Chancellor observes that the crowd is "shouting with "unanimity," or total agreement" but that "clearly, this isn't the case"—again, instead of spelling out *how* we know "this isn't the case," which is the whole point of the explanation, the College Board's explanation basically just says that the Lord Chancellor's comment is "clearly" not accurate. If this were "clear[]," no explanation would be necessary.

The explanation concludes by basically telling us that the three wrong answer choices are wrong because the statements they make aren't true—which wouldn't help anyone who picked one of those choices—and the explanation don't use the text itself as supporting evidence, which is the most important part of any discussion of real SAT questions. In other words, the "explanation" just tells us that the wrong answers are wrong, without, for the most part, explaining *why* the College Board thinks those answers are wrong, or what we might be able to learn about those answers that we could expect to find in the wrong answers to future SAT questions.

On the other hand, the walkthrough for that question later in this Black Book actually makes a clear, specific connection between the requirements of the prompt, the relevant phrases in the provided text, and the corresponding statements in the correct answer choice. Of course, that walkthrough also explains what's wrong with the other choices from a test-taking standpoint, using words and phrases from the provided text as supporting evidence. (Take a look at the walkthrough on page 124 of this Black Book to see what I mean).

College Board Explanations on the Math Section

When the College Board "explains" an SAT Math question, it generally avoids the kind of non-formulaic approaches that high-scoring test-takers would actually use on the question; in fact, the College Board rarely explains alternative approaches for its Math questions. And while the College Board's "explanations" sometimes address the idea that errors in reading or calculation might lead to a wrong answer, they don't address what most of those errors actually involve, nor tell you how to look out for them in the future.

For an example, consider the College Board's "explanation" to question 15 from section 2, module 1 of SAT Practice Test #1. The College Board explanation for that question generates the equation $y = a(b)^{\frac{x}{k}}$, which involves 5 variables and a fractional exponent, from nowhere, with no explanation as to how a test-taker might come up with something similar on their own for a future question. Then the explanation simply walks the reader through the algebraic solution to the question, where the test-taker must know which value to plug in for each of those variables. The only comment on the wrong answer choices is the idea that each one "is incorrect and may result from conceptual or calculation errors," which is a true statement about any wrong answer choice to any question, and is completely unhelpful. There's no mention of other ways to approach the question, and no mention of the features of the prompt and the answer choices that a trained test-taker would notice when deciding how to solve the problem. There's also no description of the specific miscalculations that could lead a test-taker to any of the wrong answer choices.

This sort of "explanation" usually only makes sense to a test-taker who already knows how to answer the question… but that kind of test-taker doesn't need an explanation for the question. Meanwhile, a test-taker who found the question difficult would probably only be *more* confused and intimidated after reading the College Board's unnecessarily complex explanation.

In contrast, my walkthrough for that question (which appears on page 314 in this Black Book) provides two solutions for this question, and each solution is expressed in plain English—with detailed explanations of each step in the process, so students who didn't already know how to answer a question like this one could actually learn how to apply similar solutions on their own. Whereas the College Board explanation seems to approach this question in the most complex and formal way possible, my explanation shows that we can solve this problem by just doubling a given number the right number of times. (Most SAT Math walkthroughs in this Black Book provide two or more solutions to help you learn that there are multiple ways to approach most SAT Math questions). Finally, I explain a plausible reason that an untrained test taker might end up choosing each of the three wrong answers, so that readers can learn the kinds of mistakes they'll need to look out for on test day.

Three Important Notes on the Question Walkthroughs in this Book

Before we move on, let's talk about three important ideas related to the walkthroughs in this book.

Look at the Sample Walkthroughs!

I've included a sample diagram and explanation for each type of walkthrough at the beginning of each walkthrough section. These diagrams explain how the walkthroughs are organized, and show you how the walkthrough reflects the ideal thought process as you attack each question according to the training in this Black Book. While the walkthroughs are designed so that each one can stand on its own, you'll get more out of each walkthrough if you take a few seconds to look at the sample layouts first.

- The sample diagrams for my SAT Reading and Writing walkthroughs are on page 96 and 98.
- The sample diagram for my SAT Math walkthroughs is on page 298.

Read the Entire Walkthrough!

If you're going to look up a walkthrough in this book for a particular question from an SAT Practice Test, then be sure to read the whole thing, including any introductory text explaining the key concepts involved in the question, and any notes at the end of the walkthrough! If you just read part of the walkthrough, you may not realize many of the key details of the question that will actually be useful to you on test day.

My Walkthroughs are More Thorough Than You'll Need to be on Test Day!

My walkthroughs often go into a lot of detail, but that doesn't mean that applying these techniques on test day should take you a long time! Remember that the point of my walkthrough is to show you everything of importance that's going on in the question, so you can understand how the SAT really works—but even though the discussion of a particular question might go on for a full page or more, we could often have chosen the correct answer in 10 seconds or less on test day, and pretty much always in 30 seconds or less, if all we were trying to do was to answer the question and not thoroughly dissect it as part of our training.

Remember that on test day, you don't have to explain to someone every single aspect of what's going on in each question the way we do in this book; you just have to find the correct answer in the way that's quickest and most comfortable for you. In the Math walkthroughs, for example, we might look at 2 or 3 different ways to answer one question—but you won't need to find multiple solutions to these questions on test day. We're just looking at a lot of different ways to show you that multiple approaches can be successful, so you can find which one works best for you.

My purpose in this Black Book is to communicate the ideal thought process when encountering a new SAT question, so I often need to go into great detail. But your purpose on test day is to find the correct answer with total certainty as quickly and easily as possible, so you should focus on that goal. In time, you'll find that a lot of the thoughts I spell out on the page in a walkthrough become second-nature for you, so that you don't even consciously register them for more than a split second as you work through a question.

"But What if I Run Out of Practice Materials?!"

If you're totally on board with the idea that the real SAT Practice Tests available from the College Board are all you need for your preparation, and you have no interest in other practice materials, then you can probably skip this section. But if you're curious about the pros and cons of other practice material options, read on.

As discussed in "Only Work with Questions from the College Board!" on page 16 of this Black Book, the training and walkthroughs in this Black Book are intended to be used along with the first four real PDF practice tests available from the College Board's website (and also from QuestPrep.com/Practice). Also, you should plan to take at least one full digital practice SAT using the College Board's Bluebook app before test day, to make sure you have a chance to get completely comfortable with that software ahead of time (even though some of the questions in those digital tests also appear in the PDF tests you'll see in your training).

These tests available for free from the College Board should be more than enough practice for students preparing for the SAT according to the methods in this Black Book, as long as they review their practice work properly as we discuss in "How to Train for the SAT—Mastering the Ideas in this Black Book" on page 27. But I occasionally hear from students who want more real tests to practice with—sometimes because they had already used all the available tests from the College Board before reading my book, and sometimes because they just wanted the security of knowing more practice materials were available for them.

This is a bit tricky. As we've already discussed, you should only work with real SAT Practice Tests written by the College Board, because only practice materials from the College Board are guaranteed to follow all the subtle, important standards used to make the SAT. Working with practice materials created by other companies means you won't get a chance to practice all the SAT-specific techniques that work on real questions—and you'll also pick up habits that work on the fake questions, but WON'T work on test day.

So my first bit of advice for you if you've already gone through all the SAT Practice Tests from the College Board is to go back through those same practice tests again. Take a second look (and maybe a third and fourth look—yes, really) at all of those questions, especially the ones you missed on your first attempt, and really re-analyze each one—thinking about what makes the right answer right, what makes the wrong answers wrong, what you need to know to choose the correct answer, how you could find that information quickly, and so on.

After that, if you *insist* on using other practice materials—which, again, really shouldn't be necessary for just about anybody, and, again, isn't really something I recommend—then here's a list of your various practice material options, and the pros and cons of each one, listed in order from most acceptable to least acceptable.

Previous Generation SAT Practice Tests

You can find ten real practice tests from the previous generation of the SAT at QuestPrep.com/Practice, and you should also be able to find old copies of the College Board's "Blue Book" from even earlier versions of the SAT. These older editions contain a number of official practice tests from previous generations of the SAT, depending on the year and the specific book.

- Pros: The skills required to answer SAT Reading questions on these tests are highly similar to the skills you need to beat SAT Reading questions on the current version of the SAT—that is, careful, literal reading of the text on the page, with no interpretation, assumptions, or outside knowledge (the biggest difference is probably that older tests included passages that were more than a page long and came with around ten questions each, while the current digital SAT uses passages that are only a paragraph or two long, with one question each). The math from these older tests is also pretty similar to the math on the digital SAT. Some question types from these tests are nearly identical to question types on the digital SAT, while others aren't identical, but are still fairly similar. The differences between these older SAT tests and the current digital SAT won't cause you to develop habits that will hurt you on test day.

- Cons: The structure and format of these older tests (number of sections, number of questions per section, etc.) is different from the current structure and format of the SAT, so the timing of each section won't be the same as it will be on test day. These old tests also include some obviously different question types, like "Best Evidence" or even Analogies questions, depending on the age of the test. Ignore any old, obviously different question types that don't appear on the current version of the SAT. Further, the Writing section on the 2004-2016 version of the test isn't very useful practice for current SAT Writing questions.

ACT Practice Tests

The SAT and ACT are definitely not identical tests, but they're pretty similar in a lot of ways.

- Pros: The ACT Reading section is pretty similar to the previous generation SAT Reading section described above, and the ACT Math section is pretty similar to the SAT Math section. If you practice with those materials, you *will* be using questions written by a creator of a nationally standardized test—it just won't be the College Board.

- Cons: The ACT is a different test from the SAT, made by a different organization. The standards on the two tests overlap somewhat, but they aren't exactly the same. You may pick up some habits that work well against ACT questions but that aren't as effective against SAT questions. Some questions on the ACT Science section are actually more similar to questions that could appear on the SAT than a lot of people realize, but some incorporate ideas that aren't relevant to the digital SAT; it's not really a good idea to use practice questions from the ACT Science section to prepare for anything other than the ACT Science section. Some ACT English questions are fairly similar to the SAT Writing questions on the digital SAT, but ACT English questions test some different grammar concepts from the ones that appear on the SAT, and ACT English questions can test issues related to style, while SAT Writing questions can't.

AP Practice Tests

The AP English Tests and AP Math Tests are somewhat similar to the SAT Reading Test and SAT Math Tests, respectively.

- Pros: These tests follow some roughly similar standards to the standards used to create the SAT, because they were also created by the College Board, but AP tests aren't really directly comparable to the SAT.
- Cons: AP tests rely on advanced subject matter knowledge in a way that the digital SAT doesn't, which can lead to habits that might hurt you on test day (or at best waste your preparation time).

Third-Party Practice Tests

These are the worst practice questions you could use, because the companies that write them don't necessarily understand the way the real SAT is designed, and they have no incentive to develop questions that consistently adhere to the College Board's rules and standards.

- Pros: None to speak of.
- Cons: These tests may seem to imitate the real SAT on the surface, especially to untrained test-takers, which can make it even harder for those test-takers to realize the important differences that can exist between these tests and the real SAT. I would strongly advise you to stay far away from practice materials written by third-party companies. In theory, I suppose it's conceivable that a third-party company could create practice questions that followed the same rules as the actual SAT, but I've never seen it done. There are plenty of other question sources earlier in this list, and I'd be willing to trust any of them before I used practice questions from a third-party company.

What About Practice Materials From Khan Academy?

The College Board has an official relationship with Khan Academy, and Khan Academy offers a free "Official Digital SAT" online course. A lot of test-takers will assume that any "Official" preparation material that's officially connected to the College Board must be a good resource to use. Of course, as we discussed in "Only Work with Questions from the College Board!" on page 16, this assumption isn't valid—the test prep advice in the College Board's "Blue Book" is fairly unhelpful, and we shouldn't assume that any other SAT prep materials from (or connected to) the College Board will be any different.

The Khan Academy Official Digital SAT course has two main components:

- Training materials (articles and videos)
- Practice questions (quizzes and tests, as well as individual questions embedded in some training materials)

The practice questions in the Khan Academy course are not official SAT practice questions from the College Board! They are closer to the real thing than anything you're likely to find in other third-party practice materials, but they aren't official questions.

The course is divided into a Reading and Writing course and a Math course.

- The Digital SAT Reading and Writing course is… not great. The SAT Reading training doesn't sufficiently tie correct answers to specific words and phrases in the text, and some techniques it teaches depend on test-takers rephrasing and summarizing ideas from the provided text in their own words—which leads to exactly the kind of interpretation and assumptions that will make wrong answer choices appealing to test-takers, intentionally or otherwise. Not many people can rephrase or summarize a provided text without accidentally altering its meaning slightly (or more than slightly), and the people who can already do this well are probably already reading and thinking precisely enough to score high on the SAT, and don't need the course. In general, the approaches taught in the SAT Reading training would be easy to apply incorrectly in a way that would lead test-takers to wrong answer choices. The SAT Writing training is better, although probably a little more formal, academic, and technical than it needs to be.
- The Digital SAT Math course is better than the Reading and Writing course. It does cover the math concepts that you need to know for the SAT Math section in a way that is fairly faithful to the way they actually appear in real SAT Math questions. But it rarely (if ever) shows more than one solution to a question, and it basically ignores the absurd power of the built-in graphing calculator that you'll be able to use on test day (as discussed in the section called "Special Technique: Using The Surprisingly Powerful Digital SAT Calculator" on page 280 of this Black Book). Sometimes that math training will walk you through an algebraic solution that would take most test-takers multiple minutes to think of and then execute,

without ever mentioning that you can just enter the relevant equation directly into the provided calculator and find the answer instantly.

So the problems with the SAT Reading and Writing course have more to do with what's *in* the training leading to bad habits that are likely to hurt your score, while the problem with the SAT Math course have more to do with what's *missing* from the training that would save you a ton of time and effort on test day.

You can probably guess by now that I don't recommend using this video course. Some parts of the course certainly have merit, but those parts are mixed in with other content that could create problems for the reasons mentioned above; a test-taker who needed the course wouldn't be able to tell the difference, and a test-taker who could tell the difference wouldn't need the course.

(I feel compelled to offer an aside—Khan Academy in general contains tons of useful, valuable academic content outside of SAT prep, and has accomplished really impressive things as a free educational resource used by millions of people across the world. I'm not being critical of Khan Academy; I'm just pointing out some issues with its SAT prep, specifically, so that you can best understand the pros and cons of the different resources available to you.)

Conclusion

So now you've read my take on all the most common alternatives to real SAT practice materials. But I want to make it absolutely clear, one more, time, that *I don't actually recommend using any of them if you can possibly avoid it.* There are real, official, full-length SAT tests available *for free* from the College Board's website and QuestPrep.com/Practice. Those practice tests should be more than enough for almost anyone.

If you've already done those practice tests, you can still review them, using some of the drills and exercises that we'll discuss in "How to Train for the SAT—Mastering the Ideas in this Black Book" on page 27. The key to doing your absolute best on the SAT isn't to churn out as many hours of mindless practice as you can; it's to review your practice until you understand every mistake you've ever made from the College Board's perspective, so you can avoid those issues in the future.

Part 3: Goals and Training

Now we'll talk about the right way to set goals during your SAT training, and then we'll arm you with a bunch of ideas for scheduling your time, and creative exercises that are far more effective than just taking practice tests over and over again.

In this part of the Black Book, you'll learn the following:

- the key skillsets you need to have to be able to pull off a perfect SAT score (or any other score you want)
- what you actually need to do in order to get better at the SAT
- how to set goals that will make progress both easier to achieve and easier to track
- the approach I recommend for mastering the ideas in this Black Book
- how to focus on the critical step that usually comes before you stop making mistakes
- what to fix in your approach before you start worrying about time management on test day
- the best order of attack for most people to use when training for the different sections of the SAT
- why you potentially shouldn't attack your weak areas first, especially if you need to hit a specific target score
- why mindlessly taking a lot of practice tests doesn't help most people as much as they expect
- a variety of unusual drills and exercises that will help you understand how the SAT really works
- how to arrange your preparation schedule (that is, if you even need a schedule in the first place)
- why you probably shouldn't put your faith in diagnostics, even if they come from the College Board
- and more…

Setting (the Right) Goals

The secret of all victory lies in the organization of the non-obvious.

Marcus Aurelius

At some point, most of my tutoring clients ask me what I think is the highest possible score they can hope for on the SAT. Sometimes they frame it in terms of their previous scores—"If I already have a 1260, can I possibly bring that up to a 1500?"

The answer to this question is simple on the surface, but there are actually many other issues surrounding this question that you want to make sure you consider.

But let's start with the simple stuff first.

If you can read American English pretty well, and if you know the basic principles of arithmetic, geometry, algebra, and trig, then there's no reason why you can't *eventually* make a 1600, or any other score you want, because every question on the SAT relies on your ability to read and understand American English and/or to use relatively basic math principles.

Please read that last sentence carefully… especially the word "eventually!" I'm absolutely not saying that a person whose highest score so far is an 1100 can just snap her fingers and make a 1600 overnight. What I'm saying is that the SAT is a test of basic skills, and if we have those basic skills then there's no reason, in theory, why we shouldn't be able to answer every question correctly, once we're familiar with the design of the test.

Of course, raising an SAT score significantly is going to take some effort, in just about every case. Approaching the SAT in the right way isn't necessarily *difficult*, but it is definitely *different* from the way you would approach tests in high school or college. If you want to raise your score a lot, then you'll really have to try to think like the test—which, again, is not an extremely difficult thing to do, but will take some consistent conscious effort on your part.

(By the way, if you don't read American English very well, check out "Advice for Non-Native Speakers of American English" on page 526 of this Black Book. And if you don't know the basic concepts of arithmetic, geometry, algebra, and trig, then review the SAT Math Toolbox, which starts on page 243.)

Getting Better at the SAT

We should think of the SAT as a test that asks us to do basically the same things over and over again.

And over again.

And over again, again. And then again.

For this reason, once you have a handle on the concepts spelled out in this book, getting better at the SAT isn't a matter of *learning* anything further—it's a matter of *improving your accuracy* in the application of principles you already know.

So once you know the basics, it's a bit like improving your free-throws in basketball, or practicing for a piano recital, or even getting better at a video game. It's more an exercise in improving your technical execution, and less an exercise in broadening your intellect.

(Of course, this metaphor doesn't hold up completely. There are some SAT questions—most notably on the Math section—that will reward you for thinking a bit creatively. But the way we attack the test should always rely on the basic concepts and strategies described in this Black Book. The simple fact remains that the difference between a 600 and an 800 on a given section nearly always comes down to better strategy, execution, and accuracy, and not to more knowledge or intelligence.)

How to Set Goals

The most popular way to set an SAT goal is usually to target a particular score. That can work fine, of course, but it's not the way I like to do it.

Instead, I recommend that you target particular levels of accuracy in particular skillsets, and then let the scores rise on their own as a consequence of your improved abilities.

In other words, rather than say, "I want to try to get a 600 in the Reading and Writing section on my next practice test," say something like, "I want to go an entire section without missing a single question in which I know the meanings of all the words." Then try to achieve that standard of execution (which, by the way, would lead to a score much higher than 600 for most test-takers). Or, in the Math section, set a goal like "I want to go an entire practice test without making a 'careless' mental error," or "I want to make sure I understand at least one wrong answer choice with each question that I answer," and so on.

If you set these kinds of task-based goals, rather than score-based goals, your improvement will generally be more meaningful and lasting, and it will come more quickly and easily.

How to Train for the SAT—Mastering the Ideas in this Black Book

After questions about the structure of the test itself, the most common question I get has to do with the right way to "study" for the SAT. People want to know the best order for tackling the different parts of the test, what kind of schedule they should follow, whether they should take a practice SAT on the day before the real test—all kinds of stuff.

The short answer to all of these questions is that there really is no single best way to tackle the material in this Black Book, because no two students will have the same exact needs when it comes to prepping. Different people will have different strengths and weaknesses, different schedules, different target scores, different starting points, different attention spans, and so on. So I'm not going to tell you exactly how to manage your preparation schedule. Instead, I'm going to give you guidelines and important considerations for you to weigh on your own, and then it'll be up to you to piece those things together in a way that works well for you.

So we'll handle it in this order:

- the recommended skill progression
- guidelines for the order in which you tackle different parts of the test
- ideas for drills and exercises
- general notes on scheduling

Let's get started.

The Recommended Skill Progression

Most people measure their progress by the scores they make on practice tests, but I don't advise that, at least not in the beginning. I'd rather see you measure your progress in terms of your overall understanding of the SAT. This is a subjective measurement, to be sure, but it's actually a lot more reliable than practice test results when you're just starting out.

So your first goal is to get a general grasp of the mechanics of each part of the test. You do this by reading the relevant portion of this Black Book, following along with some or all of the sample solutions in the walkthroughs, and checking out the free videos at www.SATprepVideos.com until you feel like you can understand the reasoning behind most or all of the test.

After you have a grasp of the foundation of the test, your next goal is to understand the mistakes you make when you look at questions on your own (whether we're talking about practice tests, practice sections, or just individual questions—more on that below). In other words, at this stage your main goal isn't really to keep from making mistakes; it's simply to *understand* your mistakes *after you make them*. You want to figure out what the mistake was, of course, but you also want to figure out why it happened, and what you should have noticed in the question that would have kept you from making the mistake in the first place, or would have allowed you to catch it and correct it after it was made. This is why I spend so much time in this Black Book talking about each question as a system of concepts and relationships, and explaining the ways that right answers differ from wrong answers, and the relationships that typically exist among them. Those are the things you want to get in the habit of noticing when you look at an SAT question, because if those things seem to be in order then you've probably understood the question correctly.

Once you have a solid grasp of the reasons you're making mistakes and the things you could do to avoid them, your next goal is actually eliminating those mistakes—either by avoiding them in the first place, or by noticing them after they happen and then correcting them. This is where it really helps to be aware of the test's rules and patterns, particularly when it comes to answer choices. At this stage, your goal is to make sure that you never miss a question as a result of a mistake on your part—you want to get to a point where the only reason you ever miss a question is that it might involve a word, grammar principle, or math concept that you were unfamiliar with, and that you can't work around. In other words, your goal is to eliminate so-called "careless mistakes."

When you have essentially eliminated careless mistakes, you'll probably be at a point where your scores on practice tests are more than satisfactory. If not, you need to think carefully about what's causing you to miss the remaining questions, and how to fix those issues. (But be careful here—too many people jump to the incorrect conclusion that they missed an SAT Math question, for example, because they didn't know the right formula, when they may have simply misread the prompt, a figure, or an answer choice.)

You may also have to think about timing issues at this stage in your progression, though most people who get to a point where they've eliminated "careless errors" find that timing is no longer a concern. If timing is still an issue, review "Time Management On Test Day" on page 36 of this Black Book, and remember that your goal on the test isn't to do a lot of work very quickly—it's to streamline and reduce the amount of work that goes into answering each question in the first place.

The Order of Attack

I pretty much always recommend that students start with the Reading and Writing section, because it's typically the part of the test where it's easiest to start noticing how the SAT uses rules and patterns to make questions predictable and objective even when they might seem not to be. It's also a good introduction to the extreme importance of reading carefully and paying attention to details on the whole test.

There are really only two reasons I might recommend not starting with the Reading and Writing section. One would be if you already consistently answered all questions on that section correctly. The other reason would be if you really wanted to work on SAT Math AND you just didn't have enough time before your test date to start with Reading and Writing questions. In all other situations, though, I'd start with Reading and Writing, even if that isn't the part of the test that bothers you most. It's the foundation for the rest of the SAT.

When you feel like you understand the Reading and Writing questions, you can move on to the Math section. As I mention many times in this book, the Math section combines relatively basic concepts and presents them in strange ways, so we have to learn how to look at a Math question and figure out which basic concepts are involved, and then use those concepts to answer the question. After you've learned how the College Board uses consistent rules to make Reading and Writing questions formulaic and objective, it's easier to see similar rules at work in the Math questions, and then combine that understanding with the subject matter knowledge required by the Math section—which is usually at least a little familiar for most test-takers, since most test-takers have had classes in algebra, geometry, and basic trigonometry.

Where to Find "Missing Points"

Most test-takers have some idea of a target score that will make them competitive for their target schools, or for certain scholarship programs, and those target scores are usually somewhere in the range of 1200 to 1600, depending on the student's goals and situation (of course, there are some people whose target scores might be different).

Most people try to hit their target scores by improving in the areas where they're weakest, and that's certainly understandable. But I would recommend that you also consider working to improve the areas where you're *strongest* first, for 2 reasons:

1. People often feel more comfortable working on their strong areas, so there can be less stress.

2. The mistakes you're making in your strong areas are more likely to be things related to "careless errors," or things you can correct with minimal effort.

So if you find yourself short of your goal score, it might be a good idea to focus first on making your strong areas even stronger, rather than struggling to bring your weak areas up.

But what if you need to meet a target score within a single section?

Some test-takers don't just need to reach a certain overall score; sometimes schools or programs are looking for a score on either the Reading and Writing or Math section to meet particular cutoffs. But you can still use the strategy of improving on your strong areas even in these situations, because every section has different question types, and most students are naturally more comfortable with some questions types than others. I would recommend focusing on your preferred question types until you're basically perfect at answering them before going on to question types that you don't like as much.

Drills and Exercises

Most people get ready for the SAT or PSAT the same way they'd get ready for a school test: they try to memorize stuff, and then they do a lot of practice questions. After you've read the sections of this Black Book that deal with the way SAT questions work, you'll understand why this approach won't really help most people. The SAT isn't a test of advanced knowledge, so memorizing obscure definitions and math formulas won't do much. And it doesn't repeat test items exactly, so taking tons of practice tests—without thorough review and analysis afterward—on the assumption that you'll see the exact same questions on test day is also a bad idea.

(This, by the way, is why you probably know so many people who work so hard on the SAT or PSAT and have so little to show for it. They're getting ready for the test as though it were a final exam in a geometry class, and that's not what it is.)

Of course, that raises an important question: if you're not supposed to get ready for the SAT by memorizing stuff and doing a million practice questions, then what are you supposed to do instead?

You're supposed to try to *understand* the test instead. When you understand how the SAT works—really, truly understand it—you'll find that it's a relatively basic test, and that you really don't need to spend a hundred hours getting ready for it. (If you're going for a perfect 1600, then you will probably need to spend a bit more time than the average person—but we'll talk about that later, in "The Nature of Elite Scores" on page 524).

You come to understand the SAT by thinking about how the test is designed and why it's designed that way, so that you can eventually see it the same way the College Board sees it. And you get to that point by thinking about the things that we talk about in this book, and by making a conscious and intentional effort to apply them to a sufficient sample of real test questions.

This process may incidentally involve a little memorization—you'll want to remember what kinds of patterns to look for, for example. And it will also involve a certain amount of practice as you learn to use these ideas against real SAT questions. But our ultimate goal is to see the SAT as a coherent, predictable system of rules and patterns we understand, instead of having to say, "I've done 8 practice tests, but my score just isn't improving."

Ultimately, you want to realize that the SAT tests the same underlying principles according to the same rules and patterns on every test, but that each individual SAT question will appear unique to people who don't know how the test works. And you want to be able to identify the ways that an individual question follows those rules and patterns, so that you can "decode" each question and mark the answer that the College Board will reward.

Now let's talk about some different options for getting to that point. Here are four of my favorite exercises. I've given them ridiculous names to help them stick in your head, and to emphasize that they're different from just mindlessly taking practice tests.

1. The Semi-Structured Stare-And-Ponder

The Semi-Structured Stare-And-Ponder is a great way to begin to appreciate how the SAT is actually designed. You start out by learning the general idea of how a certain question type works by reading the relevant portions of this Black Book and looking at a good number of the walkthroughs in here. Then you find a question of the same type in a real SAT practice test from the College Board.

And then you stare at the question.

And you ponder it.

You try to figure out how that question is doing the kinds of things that I talk about in this Black Book. You think carefully about the wording, the answer choices, all that stuff. Ultimately, your goal is to understand the College Board's motivation for writing the question in that way—why the right answer is right, why the wrong answers are wrong, and why the College Board thinks the wrong answers would be appealing to different types of test-takers who might make different types of mistakes.

When you feel you've stared at a particular question and pondered it long enough, you move on to another one, and stare at it (and ponder it, too). You look for the same types of design elements and relationships, with the same ultimate goal of seeing the question through the College Board's eyes, and being able to explain every aspect of the question's design.

Then you move on to the next question. Or you eat a sandwich, or go for a walk or something—when staring and pondering in a semi-structured way gets boring, you stop. You come back to it later, when you're interested to see how much more of the SAT you can figure out. Ideally, the process is relaxed, with no real consideration of time. You're just letting the ideas rattle around in your head, and letting your brain get used to looking for them in real SAT questions. You don't get frustrated if you can't see how something works. You're just getting used to a new way of looking at test questions in a low-pressure setting.

Of course, when you actually take the test, you won't want to approach it in this way. That goes without saying. But that shouldn't stop you from pondering all the different aspects of the test in this kind of relaxed way as a part of your preparation, because the more you do this kind of thing, the more quickly you'll be able to analyze and diagnose real test questions in the future. Let things percolate a bit and you may be surprised what you start to notice in the future.

2. Practice-and-a-Postie

The word "postie" here is short for the phrase "post mortem," which in this case refers to the idea of analyzing a test or a practice session after the fact. I included the word "postie" in the name of this exercise because I really, really want to emphasize that if you don't make a serious analysis of your practice work after you finish it, then you're really wasting the time you spend practicing.

So basically you start out by doing parts of a practice test, or even an entire practice test. You can do these practice sections with or without time limits, as you see fit (of course, the actual SAT will have a time limit, so you'll want to practice with a time limit at some point, but it might not be beneficial in the beginning).

I wouldn't recommend that you use practice sections or full practice tests until you've made some progress in understanding the rules and patterns of individual SAT questions—otherwise, you'll just end up wasting lots of time and getting frustrated when you miss a lot of questions and don't understand why.

I also wouldn't recommend that you do practice tests or sections without doing a full post-mortem on them, in which you go through all the questions and try to understand the following things:

- why the College Board wrote each question the way it did
- what you could have done to answer the question correctly as quickly and directly as possible
- what lessons you can learn from that question that might be applicable to future questions

This post-mortem step is absolutely critical if you want to make a serious improvement on the SAT, but it's something that most people completely ignore, or do only halfway.

Since the whole point of your practice sessions is to prepare you to do well on test day, the most important thing you can learn from any question is how to recognize its rules and patterns at work *in future questions.* In other words, as weird as it may sound, the actual answer to a particular practice question doesn't really matter that much; what matters is whether the question can teach us how to answer *future questions on test day.* So it's much better to miss a practice question and learn something from it than to get lucky on a practice question and not learn anything.

And if you don't really sit and think about the questions you've missed, you're going to keep missing similar questions in the future—maybe not questions that seem similar on the surface (there may not even be any that seem similar on the surface), but you'll definitely miss questions with similar fundamentals, and there will probably be a lot of them.

So please make sure you give some serious thought to the questions you answer in practice sessions after you finish them. Otherwise, the time you spend doing them is basically wasted. (By the way, if you do a good job on your post-mortems you should find that you dramatically reduce the amount of practice that you need to reach your goal, so you save yourself a ton of time in the long run.)

3. The Shortcut Search

In this exercise, which can be part of a post-mortem or just an exercise on its own, you look at some real SAT questions for which you already know the answers. It's best to do this with questions you've already practiced with, as opposed to just looking at the answer key for questions you haven't tried to answer yet, so you can save questions you haven't seen for a different practice session.

Our goal with this exercise is not to figure out the right answer to a question, but to figure out the fastest and easiest way to arrive at that answer with certainty, using the various SAT-specific rules and patterns that you learn in this Black Book.

4. WWMIR?

This abbreviation stands for "What Would Make It Right?" In this drill, you go through each answer choice in a question and ask yourself what would have to change about the question for that choice to be the correct one. If a Math question asks for the value of x in a given equation, and one wrong answer choice is the value of y from that equation, then the answer to "WWMIR" is something like "if the College Board had asked for the value of y." Similarly, the answer to "WWMIR" for an SAT Writing question might be something like "if this noun had been singular instead of plural." Forcing yourself to try to re-imagine the questions in ways that would make the wrong answers right will help reinforce your understanding of how right and wrong answers work for particular parts of the SAT.

Things To Think About For Scheduling

As I mentioned above, years of working with a wide variety of students have left me convinced that there is no single best schedule for every test-taker. In fact, I think it would be closer to the truth to say that no two test-takers would probably have the exact same optimal preparation schedule. So now that we've talked about general ideas to use in your preparation, let's talk about the things you'll need to think about when you schedule that preparation.

Do You Like To Get An Early Start, Or Are You An Adrenaline Junkie?

Imagine that you're in a history class, and the teacher announces a massive research assignment that will be due in 2 months. There are two general reactions to a situation like this: some people rush home and start working on it right away, and some people already know that they'll pull a couple of all-nighters right before it's due and knock it out like that. I find that the same general tendencies exist when it comes to test prep. If you'd get started on a 2-month project when the due date is still 2 months away, then you should probably start as early as possible on your test preparation. If you're more of a last-minute person, then you're probably more of a last-minute prepper, too. I've seen both approaches work out very well tons of times, as long as the test-taker was comfortable with the particular approach and had been successful with similar timelines on other projects.

How Long Can You Stand To Stare At The Same Page?

Some people have longer attention spans than others, and some are just naturally more interested in the SAT than others. If you really can't manage more than 10 to 30 minutes of sustained attention to the test at a time, then you'll probably want to do shorter and more frequent bouts of preparation. On the other hand, if you're the kind of person who can easily spend 2 hours thinking about the SAT without wanting to scream, then it may make more sense for you to do an hour or two each weekend and largely ignore the test during the week. The most important aspect of this question is whether you're consistent in your efforts, and whether your understanding steadily improves.

What Kind of Score Increase Do You Need?

This one is probably obvious: the bigger the score increase you need, the earlier you'll want to start prepping. You may end up needing less time than you think, but it's better to have the extra time and not need it, than the other way around.

How Much Free Time do You Have?

Again, fairly obvious: the less free time you have in your schedule, the earlier you need to start prepping in order to accommodate a particular amount of prep time. (But again, one potential wrinkle in this part of the discussion is the fact that the actual amount of prep time you need may be significantly more or significantly less than you'd expect at the outset.)

How Many Questions/Sections/Tests Do You Need To Do?

This may come as a surprise, but there is no magic number of practice questions that will guarantee you hit your target score. Based on my fairly wide experience, I would say that over 99% of people do need to do some kind of actual practice work with the ideas in this

Black Book—it's very rare that a person is able to implement the strategies on test day with full effectiveness after merely reading about them. So you'll want to do some number of practice questions or sections. The operative question is "how many?"

And the issue is one of quality, not quantity. Most people will assume (very incorrectly) that if they simply do a certain number of questions they're guaranteed to improve. But that really isn't the case, because of the unique way in which the SAT is designed. It's much more important to try to *understand* a representative sample of questions than it is to crank out a million repetitions simply for its own sake. If you can look at a single real SAT practice test and really, thoroughly understand what the College Board is doing in that whole test, and why, and how you can use the strategies in this book to beat that test, then you're ready.

Do You Even Need a Schedule?

Finally, I'd like to close by pointing out that a specific test-prep schedule might not even be ideal for you in the first place. In my experience, students are often very bad at predicting how long it will take them to master a particular skill on the SAT, because the SAT is so different from traditional tests. You may pick up SAT Reading and Writing very quickly and take longer to build good SAT Math skills, or the other way around, and there may not be any correlation between those lengths of time and your academic strengths. Or you might rapidly build up good test-taking instincts for all the question types, and then have a difficult time eliminating your "careless mistakes," and spend weeks perfecting that. You may be full of enthusiasm and excitement one week, and then suddenly find yourself with no time at all the next week. And so on. An overly rigid schedule may prevent you from adapting to these kinds of situations, or to others.

My general "scheduling" advice, then, is simple. If I were you, I would try to start prepping as early as you can, even if that just means flipping absent-mindedly through this Black Book in the very beginning. The earlier you start, the more gradual the prep can be, and the more likely it is to stick. At the same time, I'd recommend prepping in ways that you find mentally engaging, and taking breaks when it gets boring and counter-productive. After every practice section or full-length practice test, I would *strongly* recommend a serious post-mortem.

And that's basically it. Modify it and make it your own as you see fit.

Be Careful with Diagnostics, Even from the College Board!

A lot of test-takers try to assess their weaknesses with some kind of diagnostic test, often from a tutor or test prep company. In fact, even the score report you get from the College Board after taking the SAT or PSAT provides a breakdown of your supposed strengths and weaknesses based on which questions you missed.

In my opinion, you want to be very careful when you consider this kind of feedback, because it overlooks the fact that there are many, many reasons that a test-taker might miss any given SAT question, and those reasons might not have anything to do with someone's idea of the question's "type."

For instance, you might miss a Reading and Writing question because you don't know some of the words in the question, or you might miss it because you misread the question, or because you were in a hurry and didn't have time to consider the question carefully enough. You might miss a Math question for any of the same reasons, or because you made a simple mistake in the arithmetic component of an algebra question, or because you keyed something into the calculator incorrectly. But diagnostic reports on multiple-choice tests can't measure your *reasons* for missing things—they can only try to classify each question into types, and then assume that people who miss a question are bad at answering questions of that type, without considering all the other reasons a question might have been missed.

So I rarely pay any attention to such diagnostic reports, and I don't encourage my students to worry about them in most scenarios. The only limited exception I would make would be in an extreme case. For example, if you miss every single question on a diagnostic that involves a chart, graph, or other figure, and you don't miss any other questions on the entire test, then there's a good chance that you do need to work on your approach to questions involving figures.

But outside of those kinds of rare situations, I'd recommend that you pay more attention to your own feelings about where your weak areas are, as long as you're trying to diagnose those weaknesses honestly. For instance, it's tempting to look at an SAT Math question you missed that involves circles, and assume that you missed it because you're not good with circles. But if you pay close attention to how you tried to answer the question, then you may realize that you actually missed it because you eliminated two of the answer choices without good reason, or you didn't notice a word in the prompt. Either way, the experience of looking back over a question you missed and trying to figure out why the correct answer is correct, and how you might have arrived at that correct answer if you had looked at the question differently, is far more helpful than accepting a diagnostic report at face value.

Part 4: Guessing and Time-Management on Test Day

This part of the Black Book will explore the key factors that should impact your decisions about how to invest every second on test day. We'll start with a detailed discussion of the right way to think about guessing on test day (which is very important!), and then we'll build on that and have a broader discussion about using your time in the most effective way possible.

In this part of the Black Book, you'll learn the following:

- why just marking your best guess for every question isn't a good strategy
- why you should never forget your training—whether a question seems simple, impossible, or anything in between
- why you shouldn't worry about being stumped a few times on test day
- how the SAT is designed to punish most people's guessing instincts
- the right way to think about guessing, so it can help your score instead of getting in the way
- key, section-specific considerations to keep in mind when you get stuck on different kinds of SAT questions
- the two types of guessing on the SAT, and why the one you probably haven't heard of might be better for you
- the important implications of viewing time as an investment on test day
- how quickly a trained test-taker can generally answer a real SAT question
- why and how you should approach each section of the SAT in multiple passes
- easily overlooked test-taking mistakes that can cost you points and undo your hard work
- how to diagnose any remaining issues with time management
- why skipping questions sooner may be the key to raising your score
- why you should never worry about the average amount of time you spend on each question
- and more…

Guessing on the SAT

If things go wrong, don't go with them.

Roger Babson

It's important for us to talk about the correct approach to guessing on the SAT, because most untrained test-takers go about it in ways that don't help their scores as much as possible.

Let's start with the most basic relevant fact: the SAT has no wrong-answer penalty. In other words, the test doesn't take any points away from you if you answer a question incorrectly, instead of just leaving it blank.

With that in mind, you should always mark an answer to every question on a section before time runs out, even if you're just randomly choosing an answer. It can't hurt you, and there's a chance it could help.

Most untrained test-takers realize this on their own…

…and that's about where they stop thinking about SAT guessing altogether, unfortunately.

As a result, most people develop the habit of just putting down their "best guess" right away on any question they can't answer. For most untrained test-takers, this eventually bleeds into a general approach of marking down their first hunch on any question they see.

Even though this approach is very popular, it can still be a huge mistake, lowering your score for the following reasons:

- It ignores the fact that every official SAT question has a correct answer that's inarguable and totally predictable once you know how the test actually works.

- It ignores the SAT's habit of intentionally misleading people who only partially understand a question.

Let's explore those reasons in more detail, because it's very important to understand them if you're going to maximize your score.

Every Real Multiple-choice SAT Question has Exactly One Correct Answer.

Remember that every right answer on the SAT must be inarguable, and that there's always exactly one correct answer, and that the correct answer is undeniably right, according to the rules of the test—no matter how strange this idea might seem to an untrained test-taker.

If you forget this fundamental idea, you may end up being tempted to abandon your training when you face a challenging question that you can't quite figure out right away. You might let yourself decide that this one question is the exception, and that two or three of the answers are all equally valid in this one case. Then you might start to doubt or abandon the strategies you've learned as you go through the rest of the test, causing you to end up with a much worse score than you could have achieved if you'd stuck to the rules.

So if you find yourself guessing on something, you have to remember that it's NOT because there's something wrong with the question that makes it impossible to answer with certainty, and it's NOT because the strategies you learn in this Black Book don't work. If you find yourself wanting to guess on a question, it's because there's something about this question that you just aren't seeing. It might be a word you don't really know, or it might be a math concept that you've forgotten, or a complicated sentence you don't quite understand. It might even just be that you're getting flustered and forgetting something important about how the question must work.

That's fine—it happens at least a few times to every single person who takes the SAT. And the way the test is designed, you can be totally stumped a few times and still get an elite score. There's no need to beat yourself up about being unable to figure out a question. Just make sure you don't lose faith in your training simply because you're unable to execute that training sometimes.

So, for a trained test-taker, guessing should NEVER be the first instinct on a standardized test. You need to maintain a disciplined approach to every real SAT question you encounter, because that's the only way to make sure you attack each question using the principles in this Black Book—which, in turn, is the most effective way to maximize your score.

At this point, I know it might still be difficult to adjust to the fact that every real SAT question must follow certain rules you can learn, because it's so tempting to say that a difficult question "just doesn't follow the rules." But once you do adjust to the right way of thinking about the test, you'll have the comfort of knowing you can't really be surprised on test day—you can only be momentarily confused from looking at something the wrong way. We'll see more proof of this as we proceed with your training, and in the walkthroughs later in this book.

Of course, if you've been trying to figure out a tough SAT question and you've got no idea what to do, then you should eventually guess, rather than leave the question blank. But guessing is a last-ditch option, and it shouldn't change your mindset or mess up your overall game plan for the rest of the test. On top of that, there are specific ideas you should keep in mind if you have to guess on the SAT—and they're not things that most untrained test-takers ever think about.

That leads us into the other big problem with the normal approach to SAT guessing.

The SAT Is Designed to Lead You to Wrong Answers If You Don't Understand a Question.

As we'll see in more detail later on in this Black Book, the SAT is intentionally designed so that wrong answer choices often seem like the right answer to people who don't know how to approach a particular question. In other words, the very thing that keeps you from understanding a question in the first place is also the thing that's likely to attract you to a wrong answer if you decide to guess.

When untrained test-takers come to a question they're not sure about, they usually just put down the first choice that looks appealing to them, and move on to the next question—and this often means that they fall for a trap somewhere in the question, as we'll see in my walkthroughs of official SAT questions later on.

Instead of immediately guessing when a question can't be answered right away, a trained test-taker knows that she has to keep the design of the test in mind, and try to work around the issue that prevented her from immediately identifying the correct answer in the first place. This gives her a much better chance of correctly understanding how the question follows the rules and patterns of the SAT, which gives her a much better chance of answering the question correctly than she would have if she made a guess based on a poor understanding of the question.

Here are some of the kinds of things you can ask yourself when you can't figure out which choice is correct. I've broken them up by section. (Of course, we'll go into much more detail with instructions and examples of these ideas later in this book.)

Reading and Writing

- Did you misread or overlook a word or phrase in the prompt?
- Have you made a "real world" assumption that isn't actually supported by the text?
- Did you misread or overlook part of the provided text?
- Did you misread or overlook part of an answer choice?
- Did you try to answer based on outside knowledge, rather than what appears in the provided text?
- Is it possible that the question involves a grammar or punctuation rule you haven't considered? (SAT Writing questions only)

Math

- Did you misread the prompt, answer choices, or diagram?
- Did you make any calculation mistakes? (Remember that it's still possible to make a calculation mistake even when you use the calculator—you might mis-key, for example.)
- Could the question involve a math concept you haven't considered? (Remember that the question might involve concepts that are directly related to the concepts in the question and the answer choices—but the question can only require you to know a limited number of math concepts, as outlined in the Math Toolbox on page 243 of this Black Book.)

Very often, a trained test-taker will remember to refer to elements of her training like the ones I've sketched out above, and then actually be able to identify the mistake she made when she first saw the question. From there, it's often possible to identify the correct answer to the question, rather than try to make a misguided guess.

Of course, it can sometimes happen that a trained test-taker will be unable to figure out the correct answer to a question with total certainty, no matter how hard she tries. In those circumstances, she should still mark an answer before time runs out (since marking that answer can't hurt her score, and might help it)—but the best way to pick which choice you'll commit to may not be what you'd expect. This is a good time to talk about the different ways to guess on the SAT.

The Recommended Approach to Guessing on the SAT

These are the two main approaches to SAT guessing:

- Hunch guessing
- Constant guessing

Let's explore them in more detail.

Hunch Guessing: The Most Common Approach

Hunch guessing is exactly what it sounds like: choosing an answer based entirely on your subjective assessment of which choice feels right to you, using what you think you understand about the question. This approach tends to result in wrong answers for a lot of untrained test-takers, largely because it keeps them from working to understand how a difficult question follows the rules and patterns of the SAT, and because the College Board likes to include wrong answer choices that seem tempting to test-takers who don't fully understand the question.

But hunch guessing can be a useful strategy for some trained test-takers! There are two general types of test-takers who can benefit from hunch guessing:

- Test-takers who lack the confidence to know for sure that they're right, even though they're well-trained.

- Very high-performing trained test-takers who have developed reliable instincts about how the SAT works. These test-takers usually only feel the need to guess once or twice per section, and can often intuitively identify the correct answer to a tough question even if they feel like they've overlooked a key piece of the question that would make them certain.

In a moment, we'll talk about how you can find out whether you should employ hunch guessing or not.

Constant Guessing: The More Reliable Approach?

One way to avoid being influenced by the question and answer choices—and possibly picking the wrong answer as a result—is the technique of "constant" guessing. In this kind of guessing, once we've gone through our passes and answered every question we can handle with confidence, we then go back before time runs out and mark the same answer choice to every single skipped question. For example, we might mark all (A)s, or all (C)s. It doesn't matter which choice we pick; the goal is just to remove any kind of conscious interference from the process of guessing, and hope that random chance will cause us to get about 1/4 of our guesses right (since multiple choice questions on the SAT have four answer choices).

A lot of test-takers dislike constant guessing at first because it often involves marking down answers that seem like they must be wrong. But that's part of the process, and actually part of the rationale: when we use this approach, we're deliberately acknowledging that we don't understand the questions we're guessing on, and we're deliberately opening ourselves up to the possibility that certain answer choices might be correct, even if we don't understand why.

Guessing Wrap-Up

With hunch guessing, the hope is that a test-taker will somehow figure out the answer without understanding a question, and the result is often that the test-taker misses almost all the questions he guesses on; with constant guessing, the hope is that random chance will allow us to mark correct answers for a predictable fraction of the questions we can't figure out.

As we've discussed, different guessing approaches will work better for different test-takers. The following key factors will influence the best approach for you on test day:

- Your level of training and awareness of how the SAT works in general

- Your level of confidence in the choices that you mark as correct answers

- Whether your general intuitions about questions you don't fully understand tend to be reliable

Most untrained test-takers basically use the hunch-guessing approach on nearly every question, never even realizing that it's possible to know for sure which choice will be correct if we understand the rules and patterns of the SAT. This heavy reliance on hunch-guessing will nearly always result in a low-to-average score on any standardized test.

For most (but not all) trained test-takers, constant-guessing will result in at least as many correct answers as hunch-guessing will.

The only real way to know which approach is most likely to boost your score on test day is to experiment with each approach during your training, and see which one works best for you—that is, which one causes you to choose the correct answer more often when you guess.

A Critically Important Note On SAT Guessing

As we've discussed in other parts of this book, third-party questions from well-known test prep companies often break the actual rules and patterns of the real SAT, which can sometimes make it easier to hunch-guess your way to a correct answer on those fake questions. This is why it's EXTREMELY IMPORTANT that you test out your guessing strategy with real SAT questions written by the College Board, and NOT with third-party questions written by other companies!

Time Management On Test Day

> Time does not change us. It just unfolds us.
> Max Frisch

I recommend you read this section carefully, even if you feel like you don't need help with time management right now. My experience with students has shown me that everyone can improve their time management to some degree—no matter how good they think they already are when it comes to that aspect of testing performance—and improving your time management on test day is one of the fastest and easiest ways to raise your score.

We'll start by discussing the key underlying concept to keep in mind as you make decisions on test day. Then we'll go over the general process I recommend on test day in order to decide which question you should be answering at any given time. Finally, we'll discuss some other aspects of time management that might still be an issue after you've tried to implement everything else.

Remember That Time Is An Investment.

We always want to spend our time in the ways that are most likely to increase our score most efficiently. For example, we don't want to spend 90 seconds on a question that seems difficult to us if we could have spent those 90 seconds correctly answering 2 or 3 other questions that seem easier to us. If we have time to go back and try the harder question later, instead of just guessing on it, that's great—but we should take care of the ones we can answer more quickly first.

All of this leads to the following conclusions:

- We want to invest time in questions that we'll be able to answer correctly.
- We want to avoid working on questions that we'll end up having to guess on anyway.
- If we're not sure about an answer, we should use the guessing strategy that works best for us (for more on the issue of guessing on the SAT, see "Guessing on the SAT" on page 33 of this Black Book).

Now that we've discussed some key ideas underlying time management, let's talk about some ways we can apply them practically.

Answer Questions in the Order You Choose, Not in the Order They're Presented.

Most untrained test-takers answer questions in the order that the College Board chooses to present them, instead of prioritizing the questions they find easier. This is almost always a bad idea—sticking to the College Board's order can't possibly *help* your score, and the only way it could fail to *hurt* your score is if you're so good at the SAT that you know you'll finish every question quickly and correctly… in which case you wouldn't need to be reading this Black Book in the first place.

So instead of just accepting the order that the College Board chooses for its questions, we should decide on our own whether to answer each question as we first encounter it, or skip it for the moment. To help us make that decision, we should keep in mind the fundamentals of time management:

- Every question within a section has the same potential impact on your score.
- Working on a question and then having to guess on it is usually a waste of time.
- Getting a question wrong is also a waste of time.

When we first come to a question, we shouldn't assume that we have to try to answer it right away. We're the ones who decide what we'll work on next, not the College Board. Instead of just diving right in and trying to find a solution, we should read the question and decide quickly if we think we'll be able to find the correct answer with total confidence in a fairly short time. My general rule of thumb is that I give myself 10 seconds to see if I can figure out how to arrive at an answer in 30 seconds or less. In other words, I spend 10 seconds reading through the question and trying to figure out how I could solve it in under 30 seconds. If 10 seconds have gone by and I still have no idea how to attack the question, then I skip it for the moment. I can always come back to it later if I want to, and I'll definitely mark some kind of guess for the question if I can't figure out the answer before time expires, but it's silly to invest more time in the question now, when I could be working on other questions that would be quicker and easier for me. I always keep in mind that every question in the section has the same impact on my score, so I should ideally be working on the easiest unanswered question at any given moment.

Remember That SAT Questions Are Designed So Trained Test-Takers Can Answer Them Quickly—Usually In Under 30 Seconds.

As we've discussed in general, and as you'll see in more detail when we get into the section-specific training and walkthroughs, the SAT is actually a relatively simple and repetitive test once you understand its design. The SAT isn't interested in making us work out complicated solutions to advanced questions, because those kinds of skills are already measured in classroom settings or even on AP tests; instead, it's interested in seeing how quickly we can diagnose a question, identify the key information on the page, and apply the most efficient solution to arrive at the right answer. Questions are generally designed so that test-takers who know the unwritten rules of the test can answer them quickly. So if we know how the test works and we're still having a hard time answering a question, then we've probably misread or misunderstood some key element of the prompt, answer choices, or other information on the page; in these situations, continuing to spend a lot of time on the troublesome question is unlikely to yield results in the way that, say, spending more time on a complicated physics question in school might—in fact, spending more time is often the *only* way to arrive at the correct answer to a complicated question in a school setting which, again, is the opposite of how SAT questions tend to work.

In general, I find that trained test-takers can expect to work through a question in less than 30 seconds if all goes well—actually, students often find they can work through certain easier questions in 10 seconds or less. Of course, this doesn't mean that you're guaranteed to get a question wrong if you need more time, or that you should feel bad if you routinely take longer than 30 seconds to answer some questions. I'm just mentioning this idea to help you understand how the test is designed and what the rhythm of working through the questions efficiently can feel like.

All of this leads to the next idea, which is VERY important, and which most test-takers don't seem to realize:

Everyone Should Approach Each Section in Multiple Passes—Probably More than Two.

I've mentioned the idea of skipping questions if we don't think we'd be able to answer them with certainty, but there's a bit more to this idea than we've discussed so far.

A trained test-taker should approach a section of the SAT with the expectation of doing at least three or four passes through the section. This allows us to be fairly certain that we're not wasting time on questions that are more challenging for us when we could be scoring points on easier questions that we haven't seen yet.

Here's the basic idea—of course, you should feel free to modify this as you see fit, but this is roughly how I divide up the passes when I take a standardized test:

First Pass: Low-Hanging Fruit and Information-Gathering

I have two primary goals in mind the first time I go through a section of the SAT:

- I want to mark down correct answers for all the questions I feel I can work through pretty quickly and easily.
- I want to get an idea of what the harder questions look like.

I start the first pass by reading the first question on the section. If I can figure out a quick, easy way to attack the question and find the answer, then I do that—making EXTREMELY sure, as always, that I don't take the question for granted and fall for some kind of trick that causes me to mark the wrong answer. If I've looked at the first question for 10 seconds or so and I still don't feel like I have an idea of how to find the answer, then I skip it. I can always come back to it in a later pass if I want, or eventually guess on it.

After I handle the first question, either by finding the answer quickly and easily or by deciding to skip it for the moment, I go on to the second question, and repeat the process: if I look at the question for 10 seconds, and I think I can answer with total certainty by working on the question for another 30 seconds or less, then I do; if not, I skip it and save it for later.

I repeat this process until I've gone through every question on the section.

After the first pass, I've marked correct answers to all the questions that seemed pretty easy to me... and I've also put my eyes on *every single question on the section*, even if it was only to glance at the question and decide quickly that it was something that probably required more time than I wanted to spend on my first pass.

I'm going to use my knowledge of the various questions on the section when I do my next pass.

Second Pass: Questions that Require a Little More Thought

Keeping in mind what I saw during my first pass, I go back to the beginning of the section and find the first question that I skipped during my first pass. I read it a bit more carefully and think about it a bit more deliberately than I might have done on my first pass, when I was just trying to answer the questions that seemed obvious to me.

Just like on the first pass, I skip or answer each question, and I don't let myself get too bogged down on any one question; it's just that, now, I'm more willing to invest a few extra seconds trying to figure out how to approach a question than I was before. (Again, I'm NOT willing to spend several minutes on a single question at this point, because I know that the College Board never sets up a question in a way that would *require* a trained test-taker to work on the question for several minutes. I'm willing to spend more time analyzing the wording of a question, the relationships among the choices, and the other things we consider as trained test-takers, but I still know that when I figure out how to execute a solution, that solution will usually take less than 30 seconds per question.)

Unlike my first pass, though, I have some idea of what the other questions on the test look like when I go through my second pass, and I use that information to help me decide which questions I should skip again for a later pass, and which of the remaining questions seem easier to me. I let that knowledge guide me.

I always keep in mind that my goal at any given moment is to invest my time in the activities that are most likely to result in getting me the most points in the least time, which generally means answering the remaining questions that seem quickest and easiest to me, and making sure I don't make any careless errors.

When I've reached the end of my second pass, the only questions left unanswered are the ones that seem the most challenging, because I've now looked through the whole section twice and still decided not to attack them yet. Now it's time for the third pass.

Third Pass: Remain Upbeat and Remember Your Training

Most untrained test-takers would be very discouraged at the thought of focusing on the questions that seemed hardest initially, but we know two things that untrained test-takers don't know:

- The College Board generally makes questions seem challenging by using test-design principles that make the test seem harder than it is, not by writing questions that actually require advanced knowledge.

- On most days we can miss a handful of questions and still get an elite score if everything else is answered correctly. This means we never need to get flustered about a few questions that seem extra hard to us, as long as we're careful to answer all the other questions correctly. To put it another way, your score depends much more on how carefully you execute your training on the majority of questions that you find *less* intimidating, and much less on whether you're able to unravel the minority of questions you find *more* intimidating.

So on the third pass through the test, we need to keep in mind that our goal is basically to identify the unanswered questions that we're most likely to be able to answer correctly with a little extra attention and reflection in the time we have left. In general, these will be the questions that contain words and concepts that we're familiar with, as opposed to questions that include phrases we may not recognize—but it's important to keep in mind that you'll sometimes find you can work out the meaning of an unknown phrase if you stay calm and analyze the parts of the question that make sense to you. (For an example of how this can work, consider question 24 from section 2, module 2 of SAT Practice Test #3, which involves the phrase "standard deviation." Even if a test-taker is uncomfortable with that term, he might be able to work out roughly what it means and then answer the question correctly if he notices that the values in one set of numbers vary more from their average than the values in the other set do. See my walkthrough of that question on page 461, including my note on a way to attack the question if you don't know the term "standard deviation.")

By the time you start this third pass, you're likely to have used up half of your allotted time on the section, or maybe even three-quarters of it, or more. You may only have enough time to expect to answer a few more questions, so it's especially important to tackle the remaining questions in the order that you want. Start this pass on the question that seems like the one that's most likely to result in a correct answer in the shortest possible time, and then go on to the question that seems the next-most-likely to result in a right answer in the shortest possible time, and so on. If you feel like the last question on the test, for example, is likely to be the easiest remaining question to figure out, then start there.

At some point, you may be ready for a fourth pass, either because you've answered all the questions on the section, or you've decided that there are some questions on the section you just won't be able to answer with certainty before time runs out. This is when we might consider shifting our focus a little bit.

Review and Clean-Up Pass

I usually recommend you start your review pass through the section when you've answered all the questions that you think you can answer with certainty. On this last pass, the goal is to go back through all the questions you've answered and make sure that you haven't made any mistakes in the answers that you've marked. Be especially careful to check for all the little kinds of mistakes that the College Board likes to trick us into—stuff like misreading a word in a Reading and Writing passage, solving for the wrong variable on a Math question, and so on.

I often like to check my work by seeing if I can figure out the kinds of mistakes the College Board was trying to anticipate with the wrong answers that it included. If I can do that for a particular question, I can usually be pretty sure I've answered it correctly.

Of course, you should also have been very careful to avoid mistakes during the other passes, when you previously answered the questions, so this last pass usually shouldn't turn up too many mistakes. But we should always be on the lookout for mistakes, because we always need to remember that one of the College Board's main goals is to trick untrained test-takers into answering questions incorrectly even when they think they understand a question. Never forget that rigorous attention to detail—not advanced knowledge—is the main thing that separates top-scoring test-takers from everybody else!

After we've reviewed the questions we felt certain about, we may still have some questions on the section that are unanswered. In our last pass before time expires, we'll consider how to guess on those remaining questions.

Guessing Pass

If you find yourself still working on a section with only a few minutes left before time expires, then you'll want to make sure that you mark down an answer for every question on the section, even if you have to guess blindly on some of them—because that way you'll at least be giving yourself the chance to get lucky on the questions where you decide to guess. (Of course, if you've implemented the ideas in this Black Book and been diligent in your training, you probably won't find yourself guessing blindly at the end of a section—my point is just that you should always make sure to manage your time so that you've marked an answer for every question before time runs out, since there's no penalty for marking an incorrect answer on the SAT.)

There are two main ways to approach guessing on the SAT, and I cover them in "Guessing on the SAT" on page 33 of this Black Book. For now, the important thing to keep in mind is that, as trained test-takers, we need to make sure that we distinguish between questions whose answers we're certain about, and questions when we know we're guessing, so that we don't develop the mindset that the right answer to any SAT question is subjective or up for discussion. That way we can optimize our results from any guessing we need to do.

"Review Page" and "Mark for Review"

When you answer questions in the Bluebook app on test day, at the bottom of the application window you'll see a little box that tells you which question you're on, and how many questions are in the module: like "Question 4 of 27," for example. If you click on that box, another box appears that shows you a number for each question in the module. Numbers that correspond to questions you haven't answered yet will be inside a dotted-line box, while numbers that correspond to questions you've answered will be in a solid blue box. You can use this to see at a glance which questions you've answered, and which ones you haven't, and you can click on any number to navigate to that question. You can also click on "Go to Review Page" to navigate away from the question you're on, and see this same information displayed on a full page. All of this makes it easier for you to jump around to the questions you still need to work on as you go through the passes described above.

Also, when you look at the page for each question, immediately to the right of the question number is a little flag and the words "Mark for Review." You can click that flag to mark that question as a reminder to come back to it if you like, and then you'll see a little red flag next to the question number, in addition to the dotted-line box or the solid blue box. It's probably enough just to see that a question hasn't been answered to remind you that you need to come back and answer that question, but if you'd like to mark it, you can do that too.

Make it your Own and Remember What Counts.

As I mentioned earlier, you should feel free to modify this idea of approaching the test in passes, and make it your own. The key thing to remember is that you should always be investing your time in the activities that are most likely to improve your score in the least time, instead of mindlessly tackling whatever the College Board decides to throw at you next.

A Few More Things to Keep in Mind

Below, I'd like to address a few other important considerations when you approach the test in this way.

Don't Lose Track of Time.

As we've discussed, the idea of approaching the test in passes is an essential part of optimal test-taking, because it allows us to make sure we invest our time in ways that are most likely to get us more points. But we still have to make sure we move through each pass with an appropriate sense of urgency. Sometimes, finishing a pass can make us feel like we're done with the section overall, because we find ourselves considering how to answer the last few questions of the section much earlier than untrained test-takers will see them. But it's important to remember that we're not expecting to answer every question when we complete a pass! We're just looking for the easiest remaining questions on each pass, even though it might feel like we're completing the section multiple times. So we can't take breaks while we work through a section, even though it might be tempting to pause sometimes. When I finish one pass, I go right back to the questions that are still unanswered and start the next pass, and I repeat this process until time is called—even after I've finished answering the questions, I keep re-checking my work, because I know how important it is to make sure I avoid mistakes.

Mistakes Will Undo Your Hard Work. Don't Make Them.

You've probably noticed by now that I constantly remind you of the importance of avoiding small mistakes. This is because every wrong answer costs you in two ways:

- You lose the time you invested in the question, which you could have invested in a question you would have answered correctly.
- You lose the opportunity to mark a correct answer for the question you got wrong.

So when you're going through your passes, you want to make sure to remain thorough and diligent on the questions that you answer, because it doesn't help you to work on a question and get it wrong.

Similarly, you should take your final review and guessing passes seriously, because correcting a question that you'd previously marked wrong is just as valuable as marking a correct answer on a blank question.

Other Time-Management Issues

Up until now, we've been discussing general time-management strategies that apply to all trained test-takers. But you may still feel that you have other concerns when it comes to timing, and we'll address some of those now.

A lot of test-takers who are used to having timing issues on regular high school tests worry about having enough time on the SAT because they don't realize how different the SAT is from non-standardized tests. Then test day comes around, and untrained test-takers see questions that look strange to them, and they start to panic... none of which helps with their time-management issues.

But my first piece of advice for a student in this position is to put the issue of time-management aside until after you learn about everything else in this Black Book. You might very well find that you no longer have any issues with time-management after you adopt my approach to the SAT.

In most situations, test-takers who worry about time are using the wrong approach to the test in the first place. So they don't need to get quicker at the old approach—instead, they need to start using a method that's more efficient and, therefore, inherently faster. You'll learn a much more efficient approach in this Black Book; it takes less time and produces better results than the traditional approach that most untrained test-takers will use. It's like learning to use a lawn mower after you've been cutting the grass with scissors.

So, again, the first thing I'd recommend you do is ignore your timing issues at the beginning of your preparation, and see if they go away on their own as you come to understand how the test really works. They often do.

If they don't go away, though, there's still plenty of stuff we can try. Read on.

Reading Speed

Some test-takers are naturally slower at reading than others, but most people find they read fast enough for the SAT if they're approaching questions in the most efficient way. As a general rule of thumb, if you don't have problems with the speed of your reading in your classes in school, then you probably read fast enough to do very well on the SAT (assuming you're using the right strategies).

For what it's worth, most of us can make some kind of improvement on our reading speed just by making a conscious effort to read faster. I know that might sound simplistic, but it's true. If you constantly remind yourself to read faster, you'll find yourself reading faster. It's a bit like walking—most of us could walk noticeably faster if we just made a deliberate effort to do so.

If you have a serious issue with reading speed that can be diagnosed by a professional, then it might be a good idea to try to petition the College Board for extra time when you take the test.

Nerves

A lot of people get nervous at the thought of taking the SAT, and some people freeze up when they're nervous. If this kind of thing is affecting your time management, consider trying these two ways to address it. First, you can work on consciously channeling your nervousness into productive energy. Direct it toward making you read more carefully, or considering a new angle on a question that's troubling you, and so on. Second, you can recognize that the root of your nervousness is likely to be a feeling of frustration or even powerlessness when it comes to the SAT, which is probably tied to a lot of misconceptions about the SAT that we're clearing up in your training. The best way to beat that feeling is by learning how the test really works so you can see that it's actually not scary at all; it's just weird, and detail-oriented.

The idea of prepping for a test like the SAT can feel overwhelming. We can address this feeling by breaking up the task of preparing for the test from one giant challenge to a bunch of small tasks, and only thinking about tackling those individual tasks one at a time—most students find it much less intimidating to focus on just learning about guessing on the SAT, or learning how to read a frequency table, or other small, simple, specific tasks, compared to the more vague and opaque challenge of raising their SAT scores by a certain amount. So focus on the smaller task immediately in front of you, and you might feel more comfortable with this process.

You May Need to Work on Deciding to Skip Questions Faster.

If you're using the multiple-pass approach that I described in "Time Management On Test Day" on page 36 of this Black Book, but still having difficulties with time, then you may need to make a conscious effort to get better at recognizing when to skip a question during a pass. As I said in that discussion, my general recommendation is that students should move on to the next question if ten seconds have gone by and they still can't figure out how to attack the question they're looking at. You may want to play around with trying to make that decision even faster.

(To be clear, I don't try to *answer* the question in ten seconds. I'm just saying that I try to figure out what my approach is going to be within the first ten seconds of reading a question. For example, it might take me ten seconds to read a question, look at the answer choices, and think, "I could find the answer by graphing each answer choice and comparing the result to the text in the prompt." I haven't actually found the answer yet, but I know how to approach the question, and would probably do so right then, rather than saving the question for a later pass. This is an important distinction.)

If I can't see how I'm going to approach a question within the first ten seconds of reading it, I immediately forget about that question for the time being, and go on to the next one. I recommend you do the same thing. Remember that our goal is to invest our time in the easiest questions available.

Everyone runs into questions that just don't "click." This is a completely normal part of taking a standardized test, and you need to train yourself to act accordingly. So it's important to learn to skip questions as soon as you realize you can't work productively on them. There's no shame in it—in fact, working on questions in passes like this is a major part of smart, disciplined test-taking, even for people who get perfect SAT scores.

Don't Think about the Average Time per Question.

A lot of untrained test-takers try to maintain a constant pace throughout a given section, which ends up causing unnecessary worry and costing them points. These test-takers usually find the average amount of time allotted for each question by dividing the number of minutes for a section by the number of questions in the section. Then they mistakenly adopt this average-time-per-question as a guideline for how long they should spend on every single question, no matter what. As they go through the test, if they find a question they can answer quickly, they slow down a little so that the question still takes up roughly the average amount of time per question on that section; if they find a question that seems harder for them, they panic and rush because they still want to try to get it done in something close to the average amount of time per question on that section.

This approach might make sense if most of the questions on a given section were very similar to one another in terms of subject matter, difficulty, and complexity... but they aren't. Some questions will naturally take you 10 or 15 seconds to figure out with total certainty (especially as you get better at implementing the strategies in this Black Book, which you'll see in the training and question walkthroughs later on). In these situations, it would be silly to spend extra time staring at a question once you've checked your solution and made sure you're right. On the other hand, sometimes you'll misunderstand a question, or keep making a small mistake that causes you not to arrive at any of the answer choices, or you'll have some other issue on a question that might cause you to skip it twice and then finally be forced to guess on it, and you'll end up spending a total of two minutes or more on one question. For these kinds of questions, it makes no sense to try to cram all of that thinking into an arbitrary time limit.

So the smart way to approach the SAT is to realize that some questions take much less time than average, and some questions might take you more than a minute or two. You should try to handle every question as quickly as you can without sacrificing accuracy—whether that means solving it on your current pass, saving it for later, or finally deciding to skip it altogether and just guess. If you keep this attitude, you'll find that the questions you answer quickly will make up for the extra time you need for the occasional question that stumps you in the later passes.

Analyze and Adjust Your Performance.

If you're still having timing issues, you may need to do some analysis on the specific questions that are slowing you down. When you practice with real test questions, make note of the questions that take you a lot of time. Go back to them after your practice session is over, and try to identify the elements they have in common that made them take so long for you. All test-takers have different triggers that might cause them to spend more time than necessary on some questions, and your goal is to figure out what causes it to happen to you. You might think about issues like the following, just as examples:

- Do you have trouble reading the prompt carefully if it involves several lines of text?
- Do you re-check your work three or four times on each question, even after you're sure you haven't made a mistake?
- Do you panic when a question involves a figure?

Try to pinpoint the kinds of things that generally slow you down. Then do some untimed review of relevant practice questions from the College Board and really analyze and break down the aspect of solving those questions that takes you the most time, using the walkthroughs from this Black Book. Then, keep in mind what you've learned when you do your next timed practice, and try to modify the behavior that was costing you extra time before.

Breaking down your performance like this and thinking about how you react to different elements of official practice questions from the College Board can give you some insights into where you should focus as you try to increase your speed. For example, if you find that certain calculations take a lot of time for you to do by hand, consider using your calculator a little more; if you find that you're frequently re-reading blocks of text, focus on trying to absorb all the necessary information in one or two tries. You'll find that identifying the causes of your issues as precisely as you possibly can will make it a lot easier to figure out the likely solutions to your problems.

On the Reading and Writing Section, Remember that We Never Need to Memorize Every Detail in The Provided Text.

Some test-takers have a difficult time accepting the fact that the rules and patterns of the SAT prevent the College Board from writing questions that would require test-takers to remember and understand all the relevant text for a question at once. This causes them to spend much more time and energy than necessary on trying to keep the entire passage, prompt, and all the answer choices in their head simultaneously—when in reality it's more efficient and effective to identify the small portions of any individual passage that are actually relevant to a particular question, and then consider the answer choices one at a time. We'll see this process at work later on in the training for the Reading and Writing section, and in the walkthroughs for those questions.

On the Math Section, Remember that the College Board Rewards Us for Finding Informal Solutions.

Sometimes, a test-taker will waste time on a formal solution as though she were going to submit the work to a teacher, forgetting that the College Board will only grade her on the answer choice she picks. In fact, as we'll see in the walkthroughs in this Black Book, the fastest solutions to many questions don't involve formulas, or even written solutions at all.

If you find yourself writing out a lot of steps for most questions, then give yourself permission to be more efficient and informal, and focus on finding answers without doing so much writing. As we'll discuss in more detail later on, these solutions might involve analyzing the answer choices as part of the question, using the calculator, noticing a shortcut that's possible because of a figure, and so on.

Consider Petitioning the College Board for Accommodations.

If you've been working on implementing the ideas in this Black Book, and particularly in this section, but you're still feeling totally overwhelmed by the time limits on the SAT, then you may want to consider contacting the College Board for special timing accommodations. The requirements for getting these accommodations can change at any time (as can the nature of the accommodations themselves), so I won't discuss them here. If you're interested in more information on these accommodations, you can look them up on the College Board's website, or ask a teacher or guidance counselor for advice.

Part 5: Key Techniques for the Whole SAT

Before we discuss specific training for the different kinds of SAT questions, we'll briefly discuss a few concepts that will be relevant throughout the test.

In this part of the Black Book, you'll learn the following:

- how most people look at a set of answer choices, and why it holds them back
- a habit that will help you catch your mistakes (and answer questions more effectively in the first place)
- how a question's answer choices can often reveal SAT-specific shortcuts that untrained test-takers don't notice
- what the vertical scan is, why it's so useful on the SAT, and how to execute it
- the importance of understanding graphs, tables, and other figures, and the key rules for reading them
- how to read a wide range of figures that you might encounter on test day, and why it's so important to be familiar with them BEFORE test day
- the implications of the adaptive digital format of the SAT
- and more…

Always Consider Every Answer Choice!

When untrained test-takers think they've found the right answer to a question, they typically mark it immediately and then move on to the next question—even if the choice they've selected is the very first one in the set, and they haven't looked at the others at all. This is a very common way to go through the test, but it's a terrible habit to get into!

As we know by now, the College Board deliberately creates wrong answers that will appeal to people who've made a mistake in addressing the question—whether through misreading, miscalculating, or even just being nervous.

So as trained test-takers, we always want to make sure that we're giving ourselves every opportunity to assess what's really going on in a question… and to catch any mistakes we might make so we can correct them and get the high scores we deserve.

Catching Your Mistakes

One of the best ways to catch your mistakes on the SAT is to check *every* answer choice whenever you answer a question, even if you think you've already found the right answer.

When you read through the whole set of answer choices, you're giving yourself access to more information about the question, which is always helpful for a trained test-taker who understands how SAT questions are constructed. You might end up realizing that more than one of the choices seems like a valid answer at first—which we know can't be true on the SAT—in which case you know that you need to revisit the question and keep your training in mind so you can figure out which choice really is correct. (Or you might realize that some of the other choices fit hidden patterns that suggest the choice you like really *is* correct, in which case you can have even more confidence that you've answered the question correctly.) These are advantages that other test-takers won't have.

Finding the Easiest Approach to Any Question

As we'll see throughout this Black Book, trained test-takers can almost always use the relationships among a set of answer choices to help diagnose what's going on in a question before they even start thinking about which answer is likely to be correct. For example:

- On a Reading question, being aware of the options in the answer choices can help you zero in on the parts of the provided text that might be relevant to a question, allowing you to focus your energies effectively.

- On a Writing question, noticing the similarities and differences among the answer choices can help you realize which concepts are actually being tested by a question, while untrained test-takers might incorrectly focus on ideas that aren't relevant to finding the right answer at all.

- On a Math question, being aware of the relationships within a set of answer choices can help you identify solutions that might take less than 10 seconds and not even require any calculations, while untrained test-takers waste unnecessary time on a formal solution that will involve more steps, and have greater potential for error and frustration.

Every SAT Question is a System of Ideas

You'll see throughout this Black Book that we try to understand each question as a whole system of ideas—and that system includes all of the answer choices! When you read each answer choice, you're in a better position to see what's going on in the whole question: what kinds of mistakes the College Board hopes you'll make, what you need to focus on to find the correct answer in the most efficient way, and so on.

So remember to check every answer choice, even if you're sure you've found the right answer after the first choice or two! You'll understand questions better in the first place, which will allow you to attack them more quickly and more successfully; when you do make a mistake, you'll have a much better chance of catching it and correcting it.

On the next page, we'll explore one specialized way of considering every answer choice: the vertical scan.

The Vertical Scan: A Key Tactic for Trained Test-Takers

Before we get into the details of the different kinds of questions you'll encounter on test day in a few pages, I want to discuss a special technique that will often come in handy on the SAT (and, indeed, on most standardized multiple-choice tests). I call this technique the "vertical scan," and it can help you notice the similarities, differences, and other relationships within a set of answer choices more easily, and keep them clear in your head with less effort.

An Important Note Before We Get Started!

The vertical scan is just one way to get a quick, accurate impression of the similarities and differences among a set of answer choices. It doesn't have to be the only way you read the answer choices for a question, and you don't have to use it on every question (or *any* question, for that matter)! You'll probably run into a few situations in which the vertical scan gives you enough information to be able to answer a question with total certainty, but there will also be lots of times when you decide to scan the answer choices vertically *and* read them horizontally as well. I'm not suggesting that you never read horizontally on test day! I'm just giving you another tool for evaluating answer choices that a lot of untrained test-takers never think of.

How to Execute the Vertical Scan

Performing the vertical scan is relatively easy: we just mentally divide a set of answers choices into a few "columns" based on the similarities and differences that initially leap out at us, and then we proceed to read *down* each column, instead of reading or skimming *across* each choice as a separate row, which is what most untrained test-takers do when they read a set of answer choices.

An Example Using an SAT Writing Question

See the diagram below for a general demonstration of the difference between the way an untrained test-taker looks at a set of answer choices, and the way we analyze those answer choices with a vertical scan. These choices are taken from question 26 from section 1, module 1 of SAT Practice Test #2:

Normal Horizontal Reading and the Vertical Scan
(dashed arrows indicate reading direction)

Untrained / horizontal-only reading approach
A) prey, rather,
B) prey rather,
C) prey, rather;
D) prey; rather,

Trained / vertical scanning approach
A) prey, rather,
B) prey rather,
C) prey, rather;
D) prey; rather,

On the left side, we can see the answer choices more or less as they appear in the test booklet. Most untrained test-takers will just read them in sequence from left to right, and try to remember each item separately afterward. Their inner monologue while reading might be something like this: "Okay, the choices are prey-comma-rather-comma, prey-rather-comma, prey-comma-rather-semicolon, and prey-semicolon-rather-comma."

On the right side, we can see the same answer choices visualized as four rough "columns." When we scan down the columns, it's easier to note several things:

- In the first "column," we can see quickly that every choice uses the word "prey" (that is, no choice uses a word like the possessive noun "prey's," nor the plural noun "preys," as the first word in the choice).
- The second "column" shows us that two of the four choices have a comma after "prey," while one choice has a semicolon after "prey," and one choice has no punctuation after "prey."
- The third "column" shows us that every choice has the word "rather."
- The fourth "column" shows us that three of the four choice have a comma after the word "rather," while one has a semicolon after "rather."

Our inner monologue while we do a vertical scan on this question might sound something like this: "It looks like every choice starts with "prey," and then two choices have a comma after that, while one has a semicolon there, and one has no punctuation. After that, every choice has the word "rather," and then three choices end with a comma, and one ends with a semicolon."

When we use the vertical scan to look at the choices in this way, it becomes easier to realize which options the question is actually presenting to us. For example, in this question, we can see that if we figure out which punctuation (if any) should go after "prey," then we can eliminate two or three answers. (For a complete discussion of that question, take a look at the corresponding walkthrough on page 152 of this Black Book.)

An Example Using an SAT Math Question

Let's look at an example from the SAT Math section as well. The following choices are taken from question 11 from section 2, module 1 of SAT Practice Test #1:

Normal Horizontal Reading and the Vertical Scan

(dashed arrows indicate reading direction)

Untrained / horizontal-only reading approach	Trained / vertical scanning approach
A) $y = -1.9x - 10.1$	A) $y = -1.9x - 10.1$
B) $y = -1.9x + 10.1$	B) $y = -1.9x + 10.1$
C) $y = 1.9x - 10.1$	C) $y = 1.9x - 10.1$
D) $y = 1.9x + 10.1$	D) $y = 1.9x + 10.1$

Again, on the left side we see the answer choices as they appear in the test booklet. Most untrained test-takers will simply read the choices from left to right, as they're presented.

But on the right side we can see the same choices visually divided into columns. When we make a quick vertical scan of those columns, we can note the following things more easily:

- Every choice begins with $y =$.
- Two choices are followed by $-1.9x$, and two are followed by $1.9x$.
- Two choices are then followed by -10.1, and two are followed by $+10.1$.

This is helpful, because it lets us know that we can focus our attention on two issues:

1. whether or not $1.9x$ should be negative
2. whether 10.1 should be added to or subtracted from the right side of the equation

For a complete discussion of this question, take a look at its walkthrough on page 309 of this Black Book.

When to Use the Vertical Scan

We can use the vertical scan whenever we notice that the answer choices in a question are highly similar to each other, or whenever we want to reconsider the relationships among the answer choices in light of the answer-choice patterns we've been trained to notice on a particular type of question. (We'll discuss specific answer-choice patterns later, in the parts of this Black Book devoted to the different types of questions you'll see on test day.)

We'll generally find that sets of answer choices for Math questions and Writing questions are the most vulnerable to the vertical scan, because they're more likely to include answer choices that imitate each other visually, while SAT Reading questions tend to have wrong answers that differ from right answers in other ways.

Now that we've discussed how and when to use vertical scans, you may still be wondering *why* we'd want to use them. As it turns out, they're pretty helpful in a lot of scenarios…

Benefits of the Vertical Scan

We've already mentioned that vertical scans can help you note and keep track of the differences among a set of answer choices. But why is that a big deal in the first place?

Once you understand how the SAT actually works (which you'll learn as you continue to go through this Black Book), you'll find that one of the major challenges on test day is simply keeping track of all the relevant details in a question and making sure you never fall for the College Board's repeated tricks.

The vertical scan can help you overcome this challenge in several important ways:

- It can give you a simple way to notice all the options being presented to you, since you're directly comparing the answer choices to each other instead of evaluating each choice individually.
- It can help alert you to the mistakes the College Board is hoping you'll make, by calling your attention to the relationships among the answer choices.
- It can make some answer choice patterns more obvious. (We'll discuss the answer choice patterns for each question type in the corresponding training later in this book.)

The vertical scan can also help you figure out what you need to focus on to find the answer to the question, which may not always be obvious at first. This is often possible because the vertical scan makes it easier to notice relationships among the ideas represented in each answer choice in a set. For example, if the differences in a set of answer choices for an SAT Writing question all relate to whether particular words are singular or plural, then you know that the question is testing your understanding of things like subject-verb agreement, which might not have been obvious when you first read the relevant sentence. If the answer choices for an SAT Math question all differ from each other by a factor of 10, then we know that multiplying or dividing by 10 is probably a key element of the ideal approach to the question, which may not have otherwise been obvious.

Conclusion

By now, you can probably tell that the vertical scan is a very powerful tool in a lot of situations, whether as a stand-alone reading method in some questions, or in combination with the normal line-by-line method of reading answer choices. Keep this in mind as you continue your training. You'll see many more examples of its use in the question walkthroughs throughout this Black Book.

Reading Graphs, Charts, Tables, and Other Figures

The importance of careful reading on the SAT extends beyond passages, prompts, and answer choices. We also need to be able to read graphs, charts, tables, and a variety of other figures that can appear on the Math as well as the Reading and Writing section, because the College Board includes figures like these throughout the test.

By now, it should be no surprise that every figure on the SAT obeys certain rules and conventions—whether it's a scatterplot, a table, a dot plot, or some other kind of figure—because we know that the SAT is highly standardized.

You may already be comfortable with reading data from a variety of different kinds of figures in school or in your hobbies (for example, histograms are often encountered in photography, while line graphs and bar graphs come up in fantasy sports, and so on). If that's the case, then you'll probably find that you can understand the figures on the SAT relatively easily, and you just need to understand the test's extra rules and conventions in order to be ready to read figures on test day.

But many test-takers will find that at least some of the charts, graphs, and diagrams on the SAT are a little tricky to read at first. The College Board likes to present us with a variety of different figures, and most students will probably encounter at least one kind of figure on test day that they're not used to reading.

But there's no need to worry! Even the unusual figures on the SAT will always follow the rules we'll discuss in this section. So, as trained test-takers, we realize we can always answer data-related questions correctly if we keep the SAT's rules in mind, and read carefully.

In this section, we'll start out by discussing the rules we need to follow when reading figures on the SAT. Then, we'll review some types of figures that you might see on test day, in case you're not feeling confident with graphical representations of data in general.

Reading Figures Rule 1: No Judgment Calls or Outside Knowledge

Whenever the SAT asks us to answer a question based on data in a figure, the data in the figure will always clearly and directly support one correct answer choice, with no subjective interpretation on our part. We'll never run into a situation in which two different aspects of the data contradict each other and the only way to find the answer is to make a subjective decision that one aspect of the data is more important than the other one, or anything like that. The wording in the question, the wording in the figure, and the wording in the passage (if relevant) will always point to one clear, correct answer that follows the rules of the relevant section of the SAT (whether it's a Reading and Writing question or a Math question). On top of that, you'll never need any outside knowledge about a topic in the data; for example, if a question asks about a table showing the growth rates of populations of bacteria, you won't be required to know anything about the bacteria on your own in order to answer the question (although you may have to find some related information in the provided text, as we'll discuss below, and as you'll see in the question walkthroughs later in this Black Book).

For an example from a real SAT practice question, look at question 14 from section 1, module 1 of SAT Practice Test #1 from the College Board. That question provides a table with the number of films that four people from a certain era were involved in, and says that "so many films and associated records for this era have been lost that counts of those four figures' output should be taken as bare minimums rather than totals." We need to pick the answer choices that "uses data from the table" to give an example of this idea. The correct answer says that one of the people (who the table tells us acted in 66 films) actually "acted in far more than 66 films," and that another person (who the table tells us directed 58 films) actually "directed more than 58" films. This is a direct demonstration of the idea from the text that the numbers in the table "should be taken as bare minimums rather than totals," because it shows us that these two people worked on more movies than the table indicates. No other answer choice exemplifies this idea—no other choice describes a person working on more movies than the table says that person worked on. It's not the case that one answer choice says somebody directed three more movies than the tables says, and another answer choice says somebody acted in five more movies than the table says, and we have to make a judgment call about which one of those examples satisfies the requirements of the prompt "most effectively." Again, as we always see on every real SAT multiple-choice question, one answer choice is clearly right, and every other choice is clearly wrong, with no subjective judgment or opinion involved. Also, we don't need any outside knowledge—all the information required to answer the question is present in the table and the passage, and we don't need to have prior knowledge of movies, record-keeping, or anything else from the question to find the right answer. (For a detailed discussion of that question, see its walkthrough on page 107 of this Black Book.)

Reading Figures Rule 2: ALL Text and Labels are Important.

This might sound like an obvious piece of advice, but you'd be surprised how often untrained test-takers mistakenly think a question can't be answered because they don't realize they overlooked a label on a table, or because they misread the title of a graph, or something else along those lines.

Generally, you'll find that key phrases in the prompt or answer choices are nearly identical to phrases that appear in figures as labels, titles, headings, and other text elements. For this reason, it's very important that you notice all the text in a figure! Make a deliberate point of looking for text above, below, and to both sides of all figures, as well as within the figures themselves. We'll see examples of how important this can be throughout the walkthroughs in this Black Book.

Remember that figures on the SAT don't always look like figures we encounter in the classroom! Don't make the mistake of thinking that reading the labels of the *x*- and *y*-axes on a graph will always give you all the information you need to answer the question, even though that's often the case in science and math classes. There may be multiple labels on any axis, or there may be a label along the top or right side of a figure, or there may be sub-titles, or keys, or notes about scale, or other elements in the figure. If you don't notice a particular text element in a particular figure, you may not be able to answer a question about that figure with certainty—so get used to looking for important text even in places where you wouldn't normally see critical information in a classroom setting.

Reading Figures Rule 3: Be Sure to Use the Right Data.

Figures on the SAT often display a variety of different pieces of information, which means that a big part of answering a question about a figure is identifying the data you need, and ignoring the data that's not relevant. *Make sure you're looking in the right place when you answer a data-related question.*

Here are some examples of common mistakes that can lead untrained test-takers to consider the wrong data when they try to answer a question:

- A bar graph may use multiple shades of gray in a cluster of bars, leading an untrained test-taker to misread the key and pay attention to the wrong bar.
- An untrained test-taker may not realize her eyes have skipped to a different line of data when she tries to read a value off a table.
- An untrained test-taker may think a label applies to one bar in a figure when it actually applies to an adjacent bar.

So when you refer to a figure, make sure that the data you consider is actually the data that the question is asking about.

Again, I know this might sound obvious, but we have to remember that one of the College Board's most effective tactics, on either section, is to give untrained test-takers the opportunity to make *small, simple* mistakes without noticing them. As trained test-takers, we always have to look out for those potential small mistakes. One of the easiest ways to fall for a wrong answer is to look at the wrong data in a figure, because the College Board often includes wrong answers to data-based questions that would seem to be correct to test-takers who make a likely mistake in reading the relevant figure. Remember the importance of careful reading at all times!

For an example from a real SAT practice question, look at question 15 from section 1, module 2 of SAT Practice Test #1. That question asks for the two years from the table whose corresponding data is an example of the difference between employment in France and the United States described in the passage. Wrong answer choice (D) is the result we get if we accidentally use the years that are one line above the years in the correct answer. (For a detailed discussion of that question, see its walkthrough on page 127 in this book. Also, don't worry if you don't know anything about employment statistics in different countries—the passage for that question provides all the information you need to know to answer the question, which will always be the case on SAT Reading questions.)

Reading Figures Rule 4: It's Not Enough Just To Make A True Statement!

SAT Reading questions with figures will often ask for the choice that "best describes data" that supports a claim or hypothesis, or that completes an example from the passage. Sometimes an answer choice will make a true statement about the provided data, but that data won't satisfy the requirement in the prompt—it won't support the claim or hypothesis, or complete the example, or whatever the prompt wants the right answer to do.

So keep in mind that you can't just look for a choice that says something true about the provided data—that choice has to satisfy the requirements of the prompt!

For example, the passage in question 15 from section 1, module 1 of SAT Practice Test #1 ends with the claim that "plants of these species that grow in close proximity to other plants gain an advantage at an early developmental stage." The prompt asks for the choice that "describes data from the table that support the researchers' claim." Wrong answer choice (A) accurately describes the data in the provided table when it says that "for all five species, less than 75% of juvenile plants were growing in patches of vegetation"… but this accurate statement, by itself, doesn't tell us anything about the researchers' claim, so it can't be right. See my walkthrough of this question on page 108 of this Black Book for more details.

Reading Figures Rule 6: Get Comfortable with Figures on the SAT BEFORE Test Day.

Getting comfortable with reading figures on the SAT is like getting comfortable with any other part of the SAT: it's a little different from what you're used to in a classroom setting, but, once you learn how the test works and you get in some practice, you'll find that the stuff you need to do on the SAT is usually less complicated and more straightforward and predictable than stuff you have to do in school.

Remember that figures will appear in the Reading and Writing section as well as the Math section of the SAT, so you'll encounter a variety of SAT questions with figures as you prepare for the test. If you have trouble with any SAT practice questions that involve figures, review those questions carefully to understand why you got them wrong and what you could do to answer a similar question correctly in the future (and, of course, review the relevant walkthroughs in this Black Book).

Common Types of Figures

Now we'll discuss the different ways to read data from some of the most common types of figures you'll see on test day.

Tables

A table consists of rows and columns. A row is a horizontal grouping of individual boxes or "cells," and a column is a vertical grouping of cells. Each row or column has its own label. The label for a row is usually in the leftmost cell in that row. The label for a column is usually in the topmost cell in that column. The example table below shows the heights and vertical leaps of four students.

Cell   Column

Students' Heights And Vertical Leaps (m)				
Student Name	Susan	James	Derek	Lauren
Height (m)	1.67	1.78	1.61	1.72
Vertical Leap (m)	0.40	0.45	0.65	0.51

Row {

In the example above, the row labeled "Vertical Leap (m)" tells us the vertical leap, in meters, of each student in the table. The column labeled "Lauren" gives us the data for the student named Lauren.

The cell shared by a particular row and column—that is, the cell located at the intersection of that row and column—contains the numerical data that reflects the combination of the data in the labels for that row and column. In the example above, the row labeled "Vertical Leap (m)" intersects with the column labeled "Lauren" at the cell that contains the number "0.51." This tells us that the "Vertical Leap (m)" for "Lauren" is "0.51." In other words, the student named Lauren has a vertical leap of 0.51 meters.

Sub-groupings

Tables are often used to show a breakdown of data into certain groups or classes, especially through "sub-groupings." Sometimes we'll see multiple layers of labels on either the horizontal or vertical axis of the table, or on both axes. This indicates sub-groupings of data. The example table below shows us which types of lunches were served on which days in a school cafeteria over a 10-week period.

Type Of Lunch Served In Cafeteria Over 10-Week Period

	Hot Lunches			Cold Lunches		
Day Of Week	Pasta	Pizza	Tacos	Sandwich	Salad	Smoothie
Monday	2	3	0	1	4	0
Tuesday	1	2	2	3	0	2
Wednesday	1	3	1	2	2	1
Thursday	0	0	4	2	1	3
Friday	2	1	1	4	2	0
Total	6	9	8	12	9	6

In the table above, we can see the title, "Type Of Lunch Served In Cafeteria Over 10-Week Period," at the top. Below the title, we can see that the lunches are divided into two sub-groupings: "Hot Lunches" and "Cold Lunches." Under the "Hot Lunches" sub-grouping, we can see "Pasta," "Pizza," and "Tacos," while under the "Cold Lunches" sub-grouping, we can see "Sandwich," "Salad," and "Smoothie."

(For an example of these kinds of sub-groupings in a real SAT question, see question 8 from section 2, module 1 of SAT Practice Test #3 from the College Board. The label "Grade level" in that table has four sub-groupings: "Sixth," "Seventh," "Eighth," and "Total.")

Bar Graphs

A bar graph is just a different graphical representation of the same kind of information that can appear in a table. The bar graphs below show the information from the table above entitled "Students' Heights And Vertical Leaps (m)."

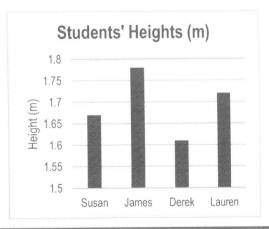

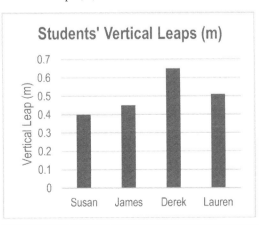

In both bar graphs, the vertical axis on the left shows the range of numerical values, and the horizontal axis along the bottom shows the different students whose data appears in the graph. For example, in the bar graph titled "Students' Vertical Leaps (m)," we can find Lauren's vertical leap by finding the bar labeled "Lauren," then seeing how far up Lauren's value travels against the numerical values on the left side of the graph. When we do that, we can see that Lauren's vertical leap is right around 0.5 m.

Multiple bars in a cluster

Sometimes a bar graph will use clusters of bars to show more than one type of data. The different bars in a cluster will often be color-coded according to a key or legend. The example below uses clusters of bars to combine the data from the two previous graphs:

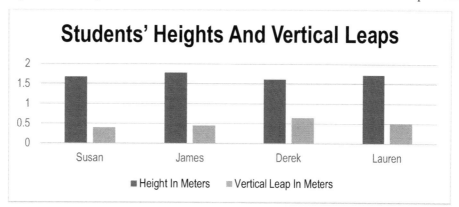

In the bar graph above, the key at the bottom tells us that the dark bar represents the student's height in meters, while the lighter bar represents the student's vertical leap in meters.

Line Graphs

Line graphs are often used to show the change in a data set over time. Typically, the horizontal axis shows different points in time—days, months, years, etc.—and the vertical axis shows the range of numerical values. The data is plotted as coordinate points on the graph, and the points are connected to form a line that shows how the data changes between the increments on the horizontal axis. The example line graph below shows the population of Kansas City from 1960 to 2010:

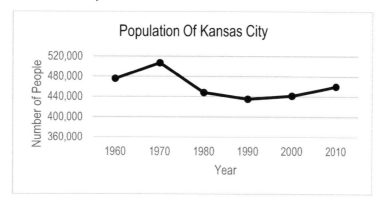

Multiple lines

Some line graphs track the changes in more than one variable. In situations with multiple lines, the lines will often involve different patterns of dots and dashes, explained in a key, so that it's easier to see which line represents which data. The line graph below shows the population of Kansas City, Boise, and Detroit from 1960 to 2010:

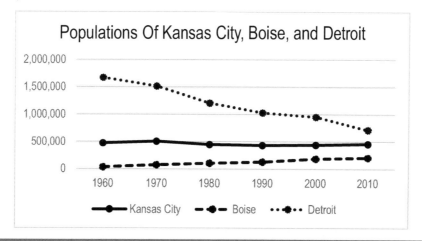

Frequency Tables

A frequency table shows how often a given value appears in a data set.

Data value	Frequency
7	1
8	2
9	4
10	3
11	2

The frequency table above expresses the values in the data set $7, 8, 8, 9, 9, 9, 9, 10, 10, 10, 11, 11$.

Histograms

A histogram is a special type of bar graph used to show how data is distributed in a set. It can be another way to express information similar to what we saw in the frequency table above.

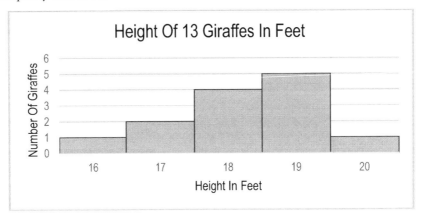

The histogram above shows us that, in a group of 13 giraffes,

- 1 is 16 feet tall
- 2 are 17 feet tall
- 4 are 18 feet tall
- 5 are 19 feet tall
- 1 is 20 feet tall.

For an example from a real SAT practice question, look at question 26 from section 2, module 2 of SAT Practice Test #2. That question includes two histograms entitled "Data Set A" and "Data Set B." For a detailed discussion of that question, see its walkthrough on page 408 in this book.

Dot Plots

Dot plots are fairly similar to histograms; they're a slightly different way to show how data is distributed. Let's go ahead and express the same data in the histogram above as a dot plot.

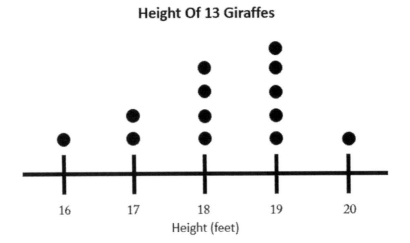

As you can see in the dot plot above, instead of having a labeled vertical axis, there's just one dot to represent each data point at a certain value—for example, 4 dots above the line labeled 18 to show that there are 4 giraffes that are 18 feet tall.

Scatterplots

A scatterplot is typically used to demonstrate the general relationship between two variables as that relationship is revealed in a population. A scatterplot is similar in some ways to what we see when we plot the points for a line graph, except that we don't connect the points in the scatterplot, and it's acceptable to have multiple points with the same x- and/or y-values. The example scatterplot below shows the relationship between height and age in a population of people. Each point represents the height and age of one person.

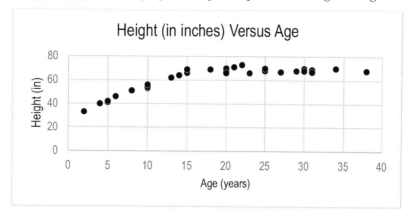

Line of best fit

A "line of best fit" or "trend line" is a line that can be drawn through a scatterplot to represent the overall trend of the data in the scatterplot. There's a mathematical formula for determining a line of best fit for a given dataset, but we'll never need that formula for the SAT. All we really need to know about a line of best fit on the SAT is that it's a line that travels more or less through the middle of the points in a scatterplot.

If we add a line of best fit to the scatterplot above, we get this:

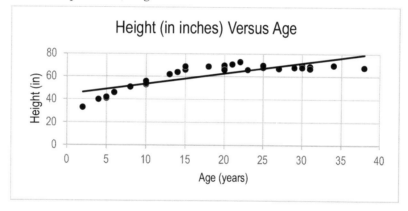

Conclusion

We've discussed the rules for reading figures on the SAT, and we've also discussed the more common types of figures that appear on the test. Remember that you may also see other figures that we haven't specifically discussed! The SAT likes to use unusual figures sometimes, so we can't know *exactly* what we'll see on test day. But any figures that do appear will follow the rules discussed in this section, and will have enough in common with the figures we've talked about that we'll always be able to read them carefully and figure out the answers to any relevant questions if we understand the above examples.

For more in-depth explanations of real figures in real SAT practice questions, see the walkthroughs later in this Black Book of questions involving figures.

How The Digital SAT Impacts Our Approach

At the time of this writing, the current version of the SAT is digital. In other words, almost all students will take the SAT on a computer or tablet, instead of on paper. This really doesn't have a huge impact on the way we will prepare for the test, but it does raise a few issues that we'll cover in this section.

The "Adaptive" SAT

The digital SAT is adaptive. The basic idea of an "adaptive" test is that the test-taker answers some number of questions, and then based on the test-taker's performance, the testing software will provide harder questions (for students who perform better on the first batch of questions) or easier questions (for students who perform worse on the first batch of questions).

The goal of adaptive testing is to produce more accurate results using fewer questions. One potential weakness with this kind of test design is that the "difficulty level" of a question can't be measured objectively—any one question will be more difficult for some test-takers than for others, and different test-takers will miss the same question for different reasons. But that doesn't really matter, because this is the format the College Board picked for the SAT, and we don't have any choice in the matter anyway, so I won't go on about the problems with adaptive testing.

On the SAT specifically, the adaptive format means that each section is divided into two modules. In other words, the SAT Reading and Writing section has a first module and a second module, and the SAT Math section has a first module and a second module.

For any one test, all test-takers get the same first module for each section. After they take that module, the software sees how well they did on that first module, and then uses that information to decide what to give the test-takers next. Test-takers who perform better on the first module will see more difficult questions in the second module (at least, in the College Board's opinion), and will have a chance to score higher, and test-takers who perform worse on the first module will see easier questions in the second module (again, in the College Board's opinion), and will have a lower score ceiling.

That means the "difficulty"—as imperfectly determined by the College Board—of the second half of each section will be determined by your performance on the first half of each section.

The big takeaway here is that none of this really has any particular impact on your strategy on test day. Our goal is still to answer as many questions correctly as we can within the time limit. It's still the case that getting more answers right gets you a higher score, and failing to answer as many questions correctly will get you a lower score.

Don't try to guess how well you did on the first module by analyzing the questions you see in the second module.

Some students might see questions on the second module that seem easy to them and think "Oh no! I must have done poorly on the first module, because these questions are too easy." But we shouldn't think that way, for several reasons:

- Difficulty is subjective. A question that the College Board thinks is difficult might not seem difficult to you.
- If you do well on the first module, it doesn't mean that every single question in the second module will be noticeably more difficult; the second module will still have a mix of harder questions and less hard questions.
- Very often, harder SAT Math questions *seem* simple on the surface, but you need to use your careful reading skills to determine what's really going on underneath. So an "easy" first impression doesn't necessarily indicate an easy question. Never assume a question is hard or easy, and treat each question with the same level of respect and carefulness.
- Even if you didn't do as well as you wanted on the first module—which, again, isn't something you can tell based on how hard the questions in the second module seem to you, as discussed above—how does that impact anything? No matter what, while you're taking the SAT, your goal is to get as many questions right as you can on the module you're currently working on. Whether you bombed the first module or aced it, your job is still to do your best on the second module. So plan to stay focused in practice—and on test day—on the questions in front of you, and use all the time you're given to answer as many questions correctly as you can, according to the training in this book.

Ultimately, when you get comfortable with the concepts in this Black Book, a lot of SAT questions *will* seem kind of easy to you—at least compared to the way they seem to untrained test-takers—because the SAT is a standardized test that does the same set of things over and over again, and once you know what those things are, real SAT questions can often feel fairly one-dimensional. Just make sure you're reading carefully and paying attention to details, as discussed throughout this Black Book, and don't get distracted trying to evaluate the apparent difficulty of any questions you see.

The Linear "Paper" Version Of The SAT

The College Board does offer a paper version of the current SAT as well. The paper version is linear—that is, not adaptive—as the adaptive format pretty much requires the use of software. Also, the linear paper version has 120 questions, whereas the adaptive digital version has 98 questions.

Whether you take the adaptive digital SAT or the linear paper SAT isn't a choice that you get to make as a test-taker; instead, it seems to be a logistical decision based on the availability of devices in any particular testing location. At the time of this writing, it seems that the large majority of test-takers will be taking the digital SAT on a computer or tablet, and that test-takers will only take the linear paper version when taking the digital version isn't possible.

So if you haven't heard otherwise, assume you're taking the digital SAT.

The main thing you need to know about the paper SAT is that the questions on the paper SAT follow the <u>exact same standards</u> as the questions on the digital SAT, and that any question that appears on either version could appear on the other version.

The reason that this matters to you is that the walkthroughs in this Black Book correspond to the questions in the first four linear paper practice SATs available for free in PDF format from the College Board's website, and also at QuestPrep.com/Practice (for more on this topic, see "Only Work with Questions from the College Board!" on page 16 of this Black Book).

The adaptive nature of the digital SAT would make it tricky to write or use corresponding walkthroughs for a variety of logistical reasons, so just basing the walkthroughs off of linear PDF tests, where you can immediately access any particular question without potentially having to answer a whole module ahead of time, makes more sense.

Using "paper" SAT practice questions to prepare is exactly as effective as using digital SAT practice questions to prepare, as far as learning how to choose the correct answers to real SAT questions is concerned, because the questions are the same—they're just delivered differently. The only drawback to practicing with the paper tests is that it doesn't give you the opportunity to get comfortable with the digital interface used in the College Board's Bluebook software that you'll see on test day—which we'll discuss in the next section.

Using The SAT's Digital Interface

As discussed above, almost all students will take the SAT on a computer using the College Board's Bluebook software. Any software will have its own little quirks, and you don't want any of Bluebook's quirks to have a negative impact on your score, so it's important for you to get comfortable with the SAT's digital interface <u>before</u> test day.

Fortunately, that's pretty easy, because you can download Bluebook for free and practice with it on many different kinds of devices. At the time of this writing, you can use Bluebook on most laptops, desktops, and tablets, but not on smartphones. But that could change at any time, and it's not my software anyway, so don't take my word for it—for all things Bluebook-related, head to the relevant page on the College Board's website, which at the time of this writing can be found here:

https://bluebook.collegeboard.org/students

You can also find a link to that software at QuestPrep.com/Practice.

Computer-based testing is widely used, and Bluebook's design is pretty straightforward, so most students will find the interface more-or-less familiar. Even so, let's point out a few things that are worth noticing:

- Every question has a "Mark for Review" button above the prompt. You can use this button to make note of questions you want to come back to for whatever reason.

- The bottom middle of every question screen has a button that says "Question (X) of (Y)," to indicate which question you're on out of however many questions are in the module. You can click this button to get an overview of all questions on the section—you can see which ones are answered, which ones are unanswered, and which ones you marked for review, as we just discussed. You'll also see a button to go to the "Review Page."

- At the end of each section you'll see a "Review Page," which is essentially the same as the screen you see when you click the button we just discussed in the previous bullet point. It lets you see which questions are answered, unanswered, and/or marked for review.

- There's a button to hide the clock in the top middle of each screen. By default, I recommend leaving the clock visible so you don't lose track of time.

- There's a button at the top right of each question showing the letters "ABC" with a line through them. You can click this button to toggle an option to show a button to the right of each answer choice that lets you cross out that answer choice. I recommend using this cautiously, especially in the beginning of your training, because a common mistake for untrained test-takers is to eliminate the right answer mistakenly early on, and then get confused when they have no basis for choosing with certainty from the remaining answer choices. For most test-takers, keeping all the choices visible—even ones you don't think are right—could increase the odds that you would catch a mistake like this and have a chance to fix it.

- You can annotate the text—that is, highlight it and/or take notes on it—but I don't recommend doing either of those things, whether you take the paper or digital SAT. Annotating involves interpretation, and on the SAT we must always pick answer choices based on the plain words on the page, and not on any subjective interpretation of those words. We'll discuss this idea more in the SAT Reading training starting on page 59 of this Black Book.

- SAT Math question screens in Bluebook have a "Reference" button in the top right, which provides a lot of formulas as well as some basic information that will be useful as you take the test. As we discuss throughout the SAT Math training starting on page 241, SAT Math is not primarily a test of applying formulas, but it can still be useful to be aware of the provided reference information.

- SAT Math question screens in Bluebook have a "Calculator" button in the top right, which you can use to access the Bluebook calculator. This calculator is *surprisingly* powerful and useful—so much so that we'll talk about it in its own article on page 280, entitled "Special Technique: Using The Surprisingly Powerful Digital SAT Calculator."

There a lot of other little things to explore in the interface—you can zoom in and out, shift the layout of the question screens, etc.—so again, I strongly recommend you get comfortable with the software at home. Download it and open a practice test when you're <u>not</u> actually answering questions so you can just kind of hit every button and find out what it all does. Get fully used to it before test day, so when you take the test for real you can focus all your attention on applying your training and finding wrong answers.

You should plan to take at least one full digital SAT practice test before test day on the Bluebook app—although almost all of your preparation and practice will use the real practice questions from the "paper" PDF practice tests mentioned above. For a more complete discussion of this topic, see "Only Work with Questions from the College Board!" on page 16 of this Black Book

Part 6: Reading And Writing Section Training And Walkthroughs

In this part of the book, we'll finally start tackling a specific section on the SAT, applying all of the training concepts we've discussed so far. Remember that prepping for the SAT Reading and Writing section lays the foundation for the entire SAT: reading carefully and paying attention to details that other people will overlook are the most important skills on both sections of the SAT.

In this part of the Black Book, you'll learn the following:

- the two major groups of questions on this section, and the "big secret" of doing well on each of them
- all about the specific types of questions within each group, and how to approach them
- why the College Board had to design SAT Reading and Writing questions the way they're designed
- the key role that literal reading plays throughout the SAT
- the difference between restatement and demonstration, and why both are critical on test day
- the four reasons why most untrained test-takers never realize how SAT Reading and Writing actually works
- how the College Board tries to trick us into thinking subjectively instead of objectively
- why it's so important to consider the precise meaning of each word we encounter
- the wrong answer choice types we consistently see on the SAT Reading and Writing section
- how to deal with text that's hard to follow
- how mentally removing "comma sandwiches" can help you understand a text better
- specific ideas to keep in mind for decoding the types of text you'll encounter on test day
- the recommended process for answering SAT Reading and Writing questions
- how to answer "most nearly mean" questions
- how to approach questions with figures and data
- how to remain objective when answering questions about the "main purpose" of a passage
- how to attack questions about paired passages without guessing what an author might say
- the specific grammatical rules that appear on the SAT—many of which might seem outdated to a lot of teachers
- the unwritten rules that shape this section
- the hidden patterns that often appear among answer choices, and how to use them on test day
- how to recognize intervening phrases and work around them
- how "parallelism" can help us determine which choice is correct
- how to apply all of these ideas to every Reading and Writing question in four official SAT Practice Tests
- and more…

SAT Reading And Writing Training

> *Education… has produced a vast population able to read but unable to distinguish what is worth reading.*
> G. M. Trevelyan

Overview and important reminders for the SAT Reading and Writing section

Students often tell me that Reading and Writing questions are their least favorite part of the SAT. A lot of people think these questions are too subjective to be part of a standardized test—they think that questions about literature can be answered in more than one way, so it's unfair for them to be part of a multiple-choice test.

Fortunately, this isn't the case. The right answer to an SAT Reading and Writing question is every bit as clear and definite as the right answer to an SAT Math question. In this section, I'll show you how trained test-takers identify those right answers.

But first, I want to say that again, because it's really important. I'll add some white space around it. And bold it and center it, even:

The right answer to an SAT Reading and Writing question is always as clear and definite and objectively correct as the right answer to an SAT Math question.

If the Reading and Writing questions depended on subjective opinion—rather than predictable, defined standards—then the SAT would produce meaningless results, because there would be no objective basis for rewarding one answer choice and punishing the others. And if the results from the SAT were meaningless, then colleges would stop using them.

You see, the main challenge with reading on the SAT is that it requires you to look at a passage in a way that's totally different from the approach you would use in an English class. In a typical English class, you're often rewarded for coming up with any interpretation of a passage that you possibly can; every interpretation that doesn't directly contradict the provided reading is welcomed with open arms.

But that approach clearly won't work for a multiple-choice question with only one correct answer—one choice has to be right, and the others have to be wrong. So on the SAT, you have to read everything as literally as you possibly can, without overlooking any phrases, or adding any of your own interpretation at all. (We'll get into this in a lot more detail below.)

After working with me, most of my students who didn't like SAT Reading and Writing at first end up changing their minds about these questions. Actually, they often end up thinking that the Reading and Writing questions are the easiest ones on the entire test, and I tend to agree with them.

The two broad question categories of the SAT Reading and Writing section

The questions on the SAT Reading and Writing section fall neatly into two distinct groups, each with its own rules and standards. One group of questions is based on reading comprehension; we'll call these Reading questions. The other group is based on the College Board's idea of acceptable grammar and punctuation; we'll call these Writing questions.

(Don't worry—it's very, very easy to tell Reading questions from Writing questions, so you shouldn't have any difficulty figuring out which strategies to apply to any particular question. An SAT Writing question will ask you which choice "conforms to the conventions of Standard English," and when you encounter one, you will have to pick the choice which follows the College Board's grammar and punctuation rules. An SAT Reading question is any question on the SAT Reading and Writing section that does *not* ask you which choice "conforms to the conventions of Standard English.")

So even though the College Board officially calls this the "Reading and Writing section," it's really more like two sections joined together—a Reading section and a Writing section. For this reason, we'll split our training into two sub-sections:

- one section for Reading questions, and
- one section for Writing questions.

We'll start with the Reading question training first, because the skills you'll need for those questions—careful reading and close attention to detail—are the two most important skills across the entire SAT.

SAT Reading Training

> *To pay attention, this is our endless and proper work.*
Mary Oliver

In this section, we will only discuss *SAT Reading questions*, specifically. In other words, the training in this section only applies to questions in the SAT Reading and Writing section that *don't* ask which choice "conforms to the conventions of Standard English."

(Again, SAT Reading and Writing questions that ask which choice "conforms to the conventions of Standard English" are SAT Writing questions; they follow their own rules and standards, which we will discuss in the next training section. That section is called "SAT Writing Training" and begins on page 75.)

Now let's dive in to the SAT Reading training.

The "Big Secret" of SAT Reading Questions

In order for the College Board to develop Reading questions that would function properly on a multiple-choice test, it had to overcome a pretty big problem: it needed a way to ask questions about a passage that weren't subjective, so that each question would only have one legitimate, objective correct answer. After all, the College Board has to use the multiple-choice format to make efficient grading of millions of tests possible, and you can't use that format effectively unless one choice for each question is clearly correct, and the other choices are clearly wrong—otherwise, each question would be up for debate, and colleges wouldn't be able to rely on the data generated by the test.

So the College Board had to find a way to eliminate interpretation from the process of answering questions about a text. This would allow the College Board to write questions that would ask students to talk about a text while still using the multiple choice format in a valid, meaningful way.

If you think about it, there are really only two ways you can possibly talk about a text without interpreting it—and these two ways of talking about a text are the big secret of SAT Reading questions. The correct answers to all Reading questions must do one or both of these things, and the incorrect answers must fail to do either of these things. I'll put them in italics, because they're really important:

- *directly restating the text without changing its meaning, and/or*
- *plainly demonstrating an idea that appears in the relevant text*

In other words, believe it or not, we'll find that the correct answer to every single SAT Reading question is spelled out somewhere right in the text in front of you.

Yes, really.

(At this point, if you've ever taken the SAT before, or ever had any kind of traditional SAT preparation, you're probably shaking your head angrily and cursing me for lying to you about the test. But trust me on this: the correct answers to SAT Reading questions are always restated or demonstrated by relevant ideas from the provided text directly on the screen in front of you, and the incorrect answers are always wrong because they fail to be restated or demonstrated by the text.)

Before we proceed, let me take a moment to give you concrete examples of how restatement and demonstration work on SAT Reading questions.

Restatement

Restatement refers to the idea that two separate pieces of text express the same idea using different words. For an example of this, let's start with the following phrase, which appears in question 10 from section 1, module 1 of SAT Practice Test #1:

> [Mother] was almost always there, ready to play with the children… she used to write stories for them…
> and she always made up funny pieces of poetry for their birthdays and for other great occasions.

That question asks "what is true about Mother." The correct answer is (C), the only one that directly restates an idea from the passage. That choice says "she creates stories and poems for her children," which directly restates "she used to write stories for them" and "she always made up funny pieces of poetry for their birthdays" from the quotation above.

The other choices are loosely connected to the text, and test-takers who don't read carefully might even think some of the other choices restate the text. But when we read the other choices carefully, we can find concrete reasons why each one fails to restate the text. (For a complete discussion of this question and its wrong answer choices, see its walkthrough on page 105 in this Black Book.)

Demonstration

The idea of demonstration is a little different from the idea of restatement, but both concepts involve careful reading and a focus on evaluating the literal meaning of a text, without interpretation. When a correct answer depends on demonstration, one of two things happens:

1. the correct answer provides an example or scenario that's exactly described in the text, or

2. the text provides an example or scenario that's exactly described in the correct answer

For an example of demonstration in a real SAT Reading question, look at question 3 from section 1, module 1 of SAT Practice Test #1. That question asks which word should go in the blank. The text provided with that question tells us about a "model" where "tribal nations and research institutions are equal partners," then says the following:

> A collaboration between the Crow Tribe and Montana State University (blank) this model: tribal citizens worked alongside scientists…

The right answer is choice (D), "exemplifies," even though nothing in the surrounding text specifically *restates* the idea that the "collaboration" is an "example" of anything. So how do we know that "exemplifies" is the correct answer?

Well, the text tells us about a "model" where "tribal nations and research institutions are equal partners." Then, it tells us about a "collaboration between the Crow Tribe and Montana State University" where "tribal citizens worked alongside scientists." This is a specific instance of the broad concept mentioned earlier—it *is* an example of "this model," so the text *demonstrates* the idea of "exemplif[ying]" something—that is, the "collaboration" "exemplifies" the "model" mentioned earlier, just as (D) requires. So (D) is demonstrated in the provided text, which means it's right. (For a complete discussion of this question, please see its walkthrough on page 101 in this Black Book.)

Again, a *restatement* of the word "exemplifies" might be a phrase like "illustrates this idea in action" or "provides an instance of this concept at work." But in this case, instead of restating the correct answer, the passage *demonstrated* the correct answer: it just described something that was an example of something else. This might seem a like a nitpicky distinction to make, but on certain challenging questions, understanding the difference between restatement and demonstration will help you find the portion of the relevant text that directly supports the correct answer.

Is That Really All There Is?

It might sound a little ridiculous to say that all SAT Reading questions avoid literary interpretation and focus on the literalist ideas of restatement and demonstration, but let's think about this from the College Board's standpoint:

1. The College Board needs the SAT to include multiple-choice questions about passages.
2. The College Board needs to avoid any ambiguity and interpretation in order for the SAT to fulfill its role as a legitimate, reliable standardized test.
3. The only way to discuss a text without interpreting it is to restate it or plainly demonstrate ideas from it.

All of this leads to one conclusion:

4. The College Board has designed the correct answers to SAT Reading questions so they restate elements of the text, or are demonstrated by elements of the text.

At this point, you might be wondering something very important: if SAT Reading questions really are as simple as I say, then how can so many intelligent people take the SAT every year without ever noticing that the correct answer to each question either says exactly the same thing as the text they're reading, or demonstrates an idea from the text in a literal way?

This is a very good question. There are four reasons why most test-takers never notice how Reading questions work, and you need to know them so you can prevent them from affecting you negatively:

1. Most test-takers aren't even looking for an answer choice to be stated directly in the text.

Most SAT-takers are used to analyzing everything they read the way an English teacher would want, so when they read the passages on the SAT they try to analyze them automatically. In other words, most test-takers wouldn't even notice if an answer choice was directly restated or demonstrated by the text, because it never occurs to them to look for that. This is just one more way in which the College Board tries to exploit your "classroom" instincts to disguise right answers.

2. The College Board deliberately phrases questions to make you think you should use subjective interpretation to find the answer.

If you've ever seen any real SAT Reading questions from the College Board, you've definitely seen that they use words and phrases like "most logical and precise," "most likely," "most effectively," and so on, like this:

> Based on the texts, how would the author of Text 2 most likely respond…

The College Board deliberately phrases questions in this way to mislead you, and get you to try to interpret the text. It wants you to think that two or three answer choices might all be pretty likely, but one of those is "most likely," and you have to figure out which one. So we have to learn to ignore the subjectivity in phrases like "most nearly," "most likely," etc. When I read a question like "which choice best states the main purpose of the text," I treat that question as though it said, "which is the only choice that restates or demonstrates an idea from the provided text?"

Here's a simple chart with some similar examples of how we should treat the prompt when it contains phrases that seem subjective to untrained test-takers:

When the prompt says...	...we should read it as...
"Which choice completes the text with the most logical and precise word or phrase?"	"Which is the only choice that is restated or demonstrated in the provided text?"
"How would the author of Text 2 most likely respond..."	"The author of Text 2 directly states which opinion?"
"Which choice completes the text with the most logical transition?"	"Which is the only choice that demonstrates the relationships in the provided text?"

3. We sometimes have to be extremely particular about the exact meanings of, and relationships between, the words in the prompt, the text, and in the answer choices.

The College Board is very picky about the specific meanings of phrases. As a result, test-takers who aren't used to being so picky often make the mistake of thinking that more than one answer choice can be restated or demonstrated by the passage. One clear example of this from a real SAT question can be found in question 6 from section 1, module 1, of SAT Practice Test #1. That question requires us to find the word in the answer choices that restates the idea of "rejecti[ng]" something. The correct answer is "repudiates," but one of the wrong answer choices is "recants." A lot of test-takers who are somewhat familiar with these two words will have a hard time choosing between them, because they both relate to the idea of not agreeing with something.

But the word "recants" specifically includes the idea of saying that you don't believe in something *that you used to believe in*. Without this concept, we can't use the word "recants." That provided text for question 6 doesn't demonstrate the idea of no longer believing in something one used to believe in, and this missing concept makes "recants" wrong. For a full explanation of that question, see its walkthrough on page 103.

So if you want to answer every Reading question correctly, you'll have to learn to *attack* every single phrase that you read, and you'll have to make sure you're only considering *exactly* what each word means, instead of working from your vague assumptions about what it "basically" means, or what you think it implies, as you might do in a Literature class. The College Board splits hairs when it comes to these things—and if you want to score high, then you'll have to learn to split them too.

4. Test-takers are sometimes mistaken about what words mean.

No matter how strong your vocabulary is, I promise you that there are some words that you use incorrectly—it happens to all of us. Sometimes the differences are subtle. For example, I once had a student who mistakenly thought that "shrewd" had a strong negative connotation. He correctly understood that it involved being clever and intelligent, but incorrectly thought that it indicated a certain type of calculating evil. For this reason, he didn't pick an answer choice with the word "shrewd," since he didn't see anything in the text that indicated negativity, and he missed the question. On the other hand, sometimes the differences are huge, and a little embarrassing—I always thought the word "pied" meant something like "renowned" or "famous," because of the story of the Pied Piper. But it actually describes something with patches of different colors. Needless to say, I drew a complete blank when a test question mentioned the word "pied" and my understanding of that word didn't match with anything on the page.

(Don't think that memorizing vocabulary words will help correct these mistakes—memorizing vocab might even contribute to making more of them, because test-takers' actual understanding of memorized vocabulary is often limited. For now, just know that you might be confronted with unknown vocabulary words at some point; for more on this topic, see ""What if I don't know the words?" on page 522.)

If you're looking at a question and none of the answer choices seems to be restated or demonstrated by the passage, then the bottom line is that you've made a mistake somewhere.

****

So those are the four major reasons that most test-takers never realize that the correct answers to SAT Reading questions function by directly restating the relevant portion of the text. I'll list them again briefly, for review:

1. Test-takers aren't even looking for these kinds of ideas in the first place.
2. The College Board deliberately misleads you by using subjective phrasing.
3. You have to be extremely particular about what words actually mean.
4. Sometimes you might have a flawed understanding of a word you think you know.

Now that we've covered the big secret of SAT Reading questions, which is that the correct answers to all SAT Reading questions must be spelled out on the page, you might be wondering what the wrong answers do.

Well, simply put, the wrong answers are the ones that *aren't* restated or demonstrated by the relevant text. And the ways that they fail to be restated or demonstrated are standardized, just like every other important detail of the test, so it can be very beneficial for us to know the various ways that wrong answers tend to relate back to the text on the SAT.

What Do Wrong Answers Do?

Broadly speaking, wrong answers are wrong because they fail to restate the relevant portion of the text or demonstrate an idea from it. But there are a handful of ways that the College Board creates these wrong answers—that is, there are certain common ways in which wrong answers fail to restate the passage exactly, or to be demonstrated by the passage. And it can be very helpful for us to know what those ways are.

But Wait! Before We Discuss Types of Wrong Answers…

Remember as you learn about these answer types that you won't need to classify each wrong answer choice—or any wrong answer choice—on test day, or even when you train for the test. Your only job is to pick the correct answer choice out of the set of provided answer choices, of course. But we're going to discuss these different types of wrong answer choices because knowing the standardized ways that the College Board tries to trick us will allow us to be ready for those tricks, and avoid falling for them.

In some instances, some of these wrong answer choice types might seem to overlap—there might be a specific answer choice that I see as one type of wrong answer choice, but you see as more of another type of answer choice, for example. That's fine! To some extent, the classifications will vary a little depending on the test-taker's perspective. We don't need to agree on the exact classification for each wrong answer on each test as long as we can reliably separate the right answers from the wrong answers.

A Hypothetical Example

For the purposes of illustration, we'll use a fake question and fake wrong answers. In other words, what you see below did NOT come from a real College Board source. It came from my head. But I constructed it in the same ways that the College Board constructs its wrong answers. And later, I'll demonstrate my methods in action against real questions from the College Board's SAT Practice Tests #1-4 (remember, you should only ever practice with real test questions from the College Board itself).

Okay, so let's pretend our fake sample question reads like this:

> According to the text, research suggests that Benjamin Franklin invented bifocals because…

And let's pretend that this appears in the text:

> …Researchers have shown that Benjamin Franklin's sister was visually impaired, which might explain the amount of energy that Franklin invested in the invention of bifocals…

(By the way, as far as I know, Benjamin Franklin's sister had nothing to do with the invention of bifocals. In fact, I don't even know if he had a sister. It's an example—just go with it.)

Here are some of the various wrong answer types we might see for a question like this.

Wrong answer type 1: Off by one or two words

This might be one of the most dangerous and sneaky types of wrong answer when it comes to trapping test-takers who know how the test works. For this type of wrong answer, the College Board provides a phrase that mirrors the text exactly—except for one or two words. Even when test-takers know they have to find answer choices that are restated or demonstrated by the passage, they can still fall for these kinds of wrong answers if they're not in the habit of constantly attacking every single word they read.

> Example:

> His sister had a congenital vision problem.

In this wrong answer, the ideas of "sister" and "had a vision problem" directly restate the phrase "Franklin's sister was visually impaired" from the fake citation. But the word "congenital" isn't reflected at all in the citation, so this answer choice would be wrong if this were a real SAT question. Remember that you have to look for a textual justification for every concept in every answer choice.

Wrong answer type 2: Barely relevant

This type of wrong answer is a statement that has almost nothing to do with the provided text. These wrong answers can be very tempting to a lot of test-takers, because they usually don't actually contradict the text—they just say something that might seem to make sense to an untrained test-taker. This wrong answer type exploits your natural tendency to give the benefit of the doubt to anything that doesn't directly contradict the text.

Example:

> He wanted to revolutionize the way society viewed glasses.

This wrong answer has almost nothing to do with anything mentioned in the citation. Once we know that the correct answer must be spelled out directly in the passage, it's usually pretty easy to eliminate these barely relevant choices from consideration—but for untrained test-takers, these kinds of answer choices can often be quite tempting.

Wrong answer type 3: Statements that would be valid literary interpretations in a classroom

The College Board frequently creates wrong answers that would be valid, defensible interpretations of the text in a literature class. Students often fall for these types of wrong answers if they're still mistakenly approaching the test in a subjective, interpretive way, instead of in the objective way that the College Board rewards. These types of wrong answers often involve character analysis, symbolism, or metaphor.

Example:

> Franklin loved his sister and wanted to make her life easier.

In this imaginary example, the answer choice reflects the fact that the text mentions Franklin's sister's eye problems as a motivation for the invention. But the answer choice adds some interpretation of Franklin's character when it speculates that Franklin was motivated by love for his sister and a desire to lighten her burden. While that would certainly be a plausible analysis of the passage in a literature class, it doesn't restate or demonstrate the passage, so it's a wrong answer. Since the text didn't mention Franklin loving his sister and inventing bifocals to make her life easier, we can't assume that he did—for all we know, she worked for him and he just wanted her to be able to do a better job, or he felt pressure from his parents to help her out, or who knows what else.

Wrong answer type 4: Plausible statements that aren't in the text

Another very common type of wrong answer is one that might seem like a plausible statement to a reader who already has a general familiarity with the subject, even though the statement itself isn't restated or demonstrated in the passage.

Example:

> He thought that improved vision would help his countrymen to be more productive with their work.

This imaginary example might tempt some untrained test-takers who have learned about Franklin in school, and know that he placed a lot of importance on productivity and effectiveness, even though the relevant text doesn't say anything about that at all. It's especially important to look out for this kind of wrong answer on SAT Reading questions related to science, history, or data, where you might be tempted to rely on your outside knowledge instead of focusing exclusively on the words on the page.

Wrong answer type 5: Direct contradiction

This type of wrong answer directly contradicts something in the citation.

Example:

> His sister's perfect vision served as an inspiration.

Here, the wrong answer choice contradicts the cited fact that the sister had poor vision. This imaginary example might fluster an untrained test-taker, because he wouldn't expect the College Board to use an answer choice that says exactly the opposite of what the text says. People who notice an answer choice like this one will likely get confused and wonder whether they read the passage wrong, then wonder whether they read the prompt or answer choice wrong, and then go back and carefully read everything all over again, while doubting themselves and wondering what they're missing. This kind of time-wasting response is probably exactly why the College Board includes answers choices like this in the first place.

Wrong answer type 6: Confused relationships

This type of wrong answer uses a lot of the ideas mentioned in the citation, but mixes up the relationships among them. The College Board includes these types of wrong answers because they want to trap people who remember major concepts from the passage but who don't bother to pay close attention to the way those concepts relate to each other—this is just one more example of the ways in which small details play a tremendously important role on the SAT.

Example:

> His sister invested in a cure for his vision problems.

This made-up example mentions the ideas of the sister, the investing, the vision problems, and the idea that the bifocals would correct those problems, but it mixes up the relationships among those ideas. Untrained test-takers who don't read carefully often fall for these types of wrong answers.

Wrong answer type 7: Wrong part of the passage

Some wrong answer choices for SAT Reading questions will restate or demonstrate an idea that *does* appear in the provided text, but that isn't relevant to the part of the text that the question asks about. For example, an SAT Reading question might include a passage with an underlined sentence, and then ask about the function of that underlined sentence. A wrong answer choice for such a question might describe the function of a *different* sentence—in this case, that answer choice would technically be demonstrated in the provided text, just in the wrong part of that text (that is, not in the underlined sentence that the prompt asks about).

This type of answer choice is hard to relate to the made-up Ben Franklin example we've been discussing without creating a whole made-up passage to go with it, so if you'd like to see it in action, take a look at the walkthrough for question 8 from section 1, module 1, of SAT Practice Test #1 on page 104 (choice (A) from that question is the example of this wrong answer type).

As trained test-takers, we always need to make sure that we're looking at the part of the passage that's relevant to the prompt when we pick an answer choice. This is especially true if we think that two choices both seem to restate the passage accurately—it may well be that one of them is restating the wrong part of the text, which makes it a wrong answer.

Conclusion

These wrong answer types, or combinations of them, will account for most of the wrong answers you'll encounter in SAT Reading questions. Basically, they all boil down to the idea that wrong answers provide information that differs from the information found in the relevant portion of the text, while the right answer for each question will restate concepts and relationships from the relevant part of the text, or be demonstrated by the relevant part of the text.

(Once again, bear in mind that you don't have to classify the wrong answer choices that you encounter on test day, or in practice! You only need to pick the correct answer. But we're discussing the types of wrong answer choices here because it will be harder for the College Board to trick you if you already know what kinds of tricky wrong answer choices will appear on the test.)

Now that we've explored the types of wrong answers we're likely to encounter on SAT Reading questions, we need to talk about how to read and digest the text provided with those questions.

How to approach the provided text on SAT Reading questions

The College Board likes to incorporate different types of writing in the passages that it uses for SAT Reading questions. When I say "different," I'm not only referring to the subject matter that appears in the section (such as literary, scientific, and historical texts)—I'm referring to broader differences in the kinds of passages you'll see:

- Some passages include excerpts from texts written anywhere from the 17th century to the 21st century.
- Some passages include excerpts from essays, novels, poems, or even plays.
- Some passages use short sentences and a style that we might think of as more "modern," while other passages use much longer sentences, and sometimes don't even follow the rules of punctuation and grammar that you'll need to know for the SAT Writing questions on this part of the SAT.

The result of this wide array of different writing styles is that most test-takers will find some passages harder to read than others. Most high school English classes don't ask their students to read such a wide variety of texts as carefully as the SAT requires, so I've found that it's helpful to give my students some specific tactics that will help them navigate any kind of text they'll see on test day.

We'll talk about the individual tactics first, and then we'll talk about how those tactics tend to be useful in different ways on the different kinds of passages we'll see from the College Board.

Key tactics:

1. Always focus on the easiest questions available, but don't make assumptions about any particular type of passage.

In "Everyone Should Approach Each Section in Multiple Passes—Probably More than Two." on page 37 of this Black Book, we discussed the importance of investing your time in questions that you find easier before you worry about questions that are harder for you.

But as you use this approach, it's important not to develop the bad habit of assuming that you should always skip certain types of passages or certain types of questions and save them for later passes! As you'll see during your training, and during the walkthroughs of real SAT questions later in this Black Book, the College Board can write questions that are straightforward and relatively obvious about any kind of passage… and it can also ask questions that are relatively complex and potentially confusing about any kind of passage. So if you get in the habit of avoiding all questions with figures for as long as possible, or automatically saving any questions involving poems for later, or something else along those lines, you'll probably miss out on the opportunity to tackle some easier questions in an early pass, which could cause you to rush through them later, and hurt your score.

2. Use the "bad connection" approach when you encounter parts of a sentence or paragraph that make no sense to you.

A lot of people dislike reading certain kinds of passages because they get frustrated when they don't understand what an author is saying. But, as trained test-takers, we have to remember that our goal on SAT Reading questions is NOT to understand every word or phrase in all provided text, because no real SAT question will require us to do that. Instead, our goal is always—and only—to try to understand *as much of a text as we need to* in order to figure out which choice is the only one that restates or demonstrates the relevant part of the passage.

So instead of focusing on the parts of a text that you don't understand, which is only likely to cause frustration, you may find that it's surprisingly effective just to ignore the confusing parts of a sentence or a paragraph, and think about the meanings of the parts you *do* understand. Believe it or not, this can often give you enough information to arrive at a correct answer with certainty; alternatively, it can put you in a position to make a very well-informed hunch guess, if you decide to use that kind of guessing. (See "Guessing on the SAT" on page 33 of this Black Book for more on the different approaches to SAT guessing.)

I often compare this approach to the experience of trying to have a phone conversation or a video chat with somebody when there's a bad connection between you—instead of clearly hearing everything the other person says, you can only hear bits and pieces, but those bits and pieces are often enough to allow you to understand most of what the other person is saying. Most high school students are pretty good at communicating in this way when they have to. I recommend you make a conscious attempt to view the challenging parts of a provided text in the same way: try to focus on the parts you understand better, and use them to figure out which answer choice meets the requirements in the prompt.

3. Don't be afraid to ignore the meanings of academic or technical expressions, especially.

Some scientific passages on the SAT will include academic-sounding phrases you've never heard before, which will intimidate a lot of untrained test-takers. As trained test-takers, we need to realize that we can often completely ignore the meanings of these technical expressions, even if they seem like they're extremely important to the passage. SAT Practice Test #1 includes phrases like "parasitic dodder plant," "magnetosensation," and "allergic histamine response." But you don't need to know the meanings of any of these phrases to answer the questions where they appear; we could literally ignore those words and phrases completely without any effect on our ability to find the right answer.

Things to keep in mind when reading literary excerpts

Literary excerpts on the SAT can sometimes include relatively long, relatively complex sentences, especially if they come from older sources. They may also involve expressions that don't make much sense to us, even if we think we understand the individual words that make up the expressions. For these reasons, we may need to be especially prepared to ignore or work around the parts of individual sentences that we don't understand, using the tactics described above.

But there's another difficult aspect of some literary passages: their narrative structures. Unlike the other types of passages on the SAT, the literary passages often depict a story or episode, and many untrained test-takers will feel a strong need to try to understand the structure and flow of the overall narrative. As trained test-takers, we need to remember that the College Board never asks us to understand every part of the provided text all at once; instead, it can only ask us questions based on individual words and phrases throughout that text. So if we can't understand the entire sequence of events in a literary passage, there's no need to panic—we may still be able to answer the relevant question with certainty if we just focus on the portions of the provided text that we can understand, and remember our training.

Things to keep in mind when reading academic passages

Academic passages on the SAT are generally modern in terms of style and grammar, which can make them feel more approachable in some ways than the other passages. On the other hand, many untrained test-takers might be intimidated by some of the phrases and concepts that appear in academic passages, because they might refer to scientific concepts or historical events that test-takers have never encountered before. Of course, as trained test-takers, we know that SAT Reading questions always provide the information we need to be able to answer them with complete certainty, so there's no need to panic if an academic passage discusses something unfamiliar.

We also know that technical terms can often be overlooked for SAT purposes because they end up not being relevant to the prompt or answer choices, as we discussed above, and as we'll see in the Reading walkthroughs on page 96 in this Black Book.

You might think that test-takers who aren't particularly strong in academic areas likes science and history would have a harder time with passages related to those areas than people who like those subjects in school would—but this isn't always the case! It sometimes happens that untrained test-takers who like science or history will look at a related passage on the SAT and assume they already know what it's trying to say, because the passage might discuss a topic that they've already read about in real life. This can be a very dangerous situation, because it can lead some test-takers to answer based on outside knowledge, which can cause them to pick answer choices that might seem like true statements in real life, even if they aren't restated or demonstrated directly in the passage.

Some of these passages can include figures; as trained test-takers, we need to remember to read any provided figures as carefully as we would read any other text associated with an SAT question. (See "Reading Graphs, Charts, Tables, and Other Figures" on page 48 of this Black Book for more on this.)

The general process for SAT Reading questions

Most SAT Reading questions can be answered with a fairly simple process, which we'll discuss now. After that, I'll show you how to tweak this process for the various SAT Reading question types you'll see on the test. (Actually, the process we'll use for *all* SAT Reading questions is basically the same, with a few minor, occasional modifications, but I'll present them as unique scenarios because most students have already been taught to see them that way by other tutors or books.)

Don't worry if this process feels uncomfortable or strange when you first read it. In later sections of this Black Book, we'll go through a lot of questions from real SAT Practice Tests together, and you can see these techniques in action for yourself. You can also watch the videos at www.SATprepVideos.com to get a feel for the process. (Remember that this section only discusses SAT Reading questions, not SAT Writing questions—that is, not questions that ask which choice "conforms to the conventions of Standard English." Those questions deal with grammar and punctuation, and we'll discuss those in the SAT Writing Training section starting on page 75.)

1. Read the question to figure out which question type you're trying to answer.

Answering different question types requires you to focus on different aspects of the provided text. Knowing which question type you're working with *before* you read any provided text will give you a hint about what to look out for as you read that text, so I recommend starting out by reading the actual question—that is, the specific sentence that ends with a question mark—which appears right above the answer choices. (We'll be discussing different question types at the end of this section.)

2. Read the provided text. Keep in mind the strategies from our earlier discussion on how to approach different types of passages.

Now that you know which type of question you're dealing with, keep in mind any special considerations for that question type as you read the provided text. We discussed some things to keep in mind for this step in the section called "How to approach the provided text on SAT Reading questions" on page 64.

3. Find three wrong answers, referring back to the provided text as needed.

Now that you've read the question and the relevant text, you can consider each answer choice—referring back to the provided text as needed—to see which choice meets the standards of restatement and demonstration for SAT Reading questions, and which choices fail to meet those standards.

It's generally easiest to find wrong answers first. For one thing, there are three times as many of them; for another, it's usually easier to identify ways that answer choices differ from the text than it is to feel confident that a choice says exactly the same thing as the text. Expect to find that most (and possibly all) of the wrong answers you find will fit into one of the types I talked about in "What Do Wrong Answers Do?" on page 62. (But remember that it's not really important to *classify* the wrong answers—it's only important to note that three of the choices aren't literally restated or demonstrated in the text, which means they must be wrong! The classifications we mentioned in the training are just tools to help you organize your thinking.)

If you end up not being able to eliminate three choices, then you're making some kind of mistake. It might be that you've misread the text or the question. It might be that your understanding of some of the words you read is slightly (or very) inaccurate. It's often the case that people who are left with 2 or 3 answer choices that seem to be restated or demonstrated by the text probably aren't being picky enough about sticking to *exactly* what each word on the page means to ensure an accurate restatement or demonstration.

If you end up eliminating all 4 answer choices from consideration, then you've probably misread or misunderstood one or more words in the question, passage, or answer choices.

4. Check the remaining answer choice.

See if the remaining answer choice is restated or demonstrated by concepts and relationships from the relevant text. Always keep in mind that the right answer is going to be restated or demonstrated somewhere *directly* on the page. You should NEVER try to justify an answer choice by making a broad inference from the overall passage that isn't actually directly supported by specific phrases from the text.

If the remaining answer choice meets this requirement, that's great—you've found the right answer. If you still can't identify one choice that's clearly restated or demonstrated by the passage (and three choices that aren't), then you'll need to consider whether to hunch-guess right away, or skip the question and save it for a later pass. For more on this aspect of SAT-taking, see "Guessing on the SAT" on page 33 of this Black Book, and "Time Management On Test Day" on page 36.

Closing thoughts on the SAT Reading process

And that's it, believe it or not—the process for SAT Reading questions typically isn't that complex.

As I noted above, the simple process we just went through applies to SAT Reading questions in general. But let's look at some specific, small adjustments we might make for different question types we'll encounter on this section.

What about Text Completion Questions?

Some SAT Reading questions will provide a short passage with a blank, and then ask which answer choice "completes the text with the most logical and precise word or phrase." We will refer to these as "Text Completion" questions.

Many untrained test-takers make the critical mistake of just choosing whichever answer choice "sounds best" to them—either the choice that sounds the most academic, or the most formal, or that seems to make the most sense, or that seems like it creates a statement that's probably true in real life. But we know that we can't select an answer choice for an SAT Reading question based on subjective reasons like these.

Instead—as always—we'll pick the answer choice that is restated or demonstrated by the relevant text. In this case, the "relevant text" is just the rest of the sentence (or sentences) in the question. I'm going to rephrase that and make it its own paragraph because it's the key to this question type; I think I'll even put a shaded box around it just to make sure we all know how important this idea is:

> Every Text Completion question contains a clue *right in the prompt sentence(s)* that lets you know which answer choice is right—the right answer will be restated or demonstrated by the clue that appears in the provided text.

You might be wondering how we find that clue. Well, it's not actually that hard, because the provided text is never that long, so there's not really a lot of room for it to hide, so to speak. The difficulty most untrained test-takers face isn't that they can't find the clue; it's that they don't even know they need to look for the clue in the first place, because they don't know about the relationship that must exist between the word in the blank and the rest of the text. This will all make a lot more sense once we look at an example, so let's do that.

A Made-up Example

This is going to be a made-up example of how this question type works, and of the kinds of tricks the College Board likes to play to make it more difficult for test-takers to find the right answer(s). The reason we're using a made-up example is that it lets us look at the mechanics of this question type in a slightly simplified format, and it also lets me modify the example to show you various presentations of this question type. We'll start with the simplest one.

> After the dog ate a large dinner, he was _____.

In the made-up example sentence above, the correct answer could be the word "full." In this case, the word "full" is demonstrated by the idea of the dog "[eating] a large dinner." So "ate a large dinner" is the clue in the sentence that tells us how we need to describe the dog in the phrase "he was _____."

(Notice that in real life, there would be nothing wrong with putting a word like "happy" or "tired" or "gassy" or "tiny" or almost any other word in that blank, because logically speaking, a dog could "be" almost anything after eating a large dinner, and his state doesn't have to depend on the fact that he just ate a large dinner—that's why many test-takers will talk themselves into choices like the ones I just mentioned. But only a word like "full" is actually demonstrated in the sentence—again, by the phrase "ate a large dinner"—which is why a word like "full" is required on the SAT in this situation.)

Now let's look at a twist that the College Board likes to put on this kind of question.

> After the dog ate a large dinner, he was no longer _____.

This sentence is exactly the same as the other one, except it adds the phrase "no longer" before the blank. Now the underlined word needs to describe something that a dog would *no longer* be after "[eating] a large dinner." Now a word like "hungry" would be the right answer—basically, a word that means the opposite of a word like "full," as we saw in the original version of the sentence.

Let's consider another spin the College Board might use on a sentence like this.

> The dog never got his dinner, so he was still _____.

This is another way to reverse the situation described in the original sentence. Now the blank needs to describe a dog who never got to eat dinner. Again, this is basically the opposite of the original description of the dog, so a word like "hungry" would be correct here.

Now let's take a look at another, still more complex example:

> The dog never got his dinner, so he didn't feel _____.

Notice that this sentence involves a sort of double-reversal—we have to figure out how the dog *wouldn't* feel if he *never* got his dinner. If a dog didn't get any dinner, he wouldn't feel full—so the right answer would be a word like "full."

At this point you're probably starting to get the idea—the right answer will be the word that is restated or demonstrated elsewhere in the sentence, but the College Board might use negating words and phrases like "never" or "not" or "no longer" (or other phrases, depending on the prompt sentence) to make it so the right answer is the *opposite* of that idea that appears elsewhere in the sentence—and it might even use *multiple* negating or modifying words or phrases to try to trip you up. It can be tricky, but once you know how it works, it's relatively one-dimensional. It just becomes a matter of reading very carefully and not mixing up the relationship between the underlined phrase and the key part (or parts) of the provided text. We'll see all of these ideas at work in the walkthroughs starting later in this Black Book.

(Notice that, in the above examples, I sort of came up with a word that could go in the blank. When we actually answer questions of this type, we don't spend time trying to guess what sort of word will go in the blank; we just consider the answer choices and determine which one satisfies the unwritten requirements of this question type. I just left out the step of analyzing hypothetical answer choices to keep this section simpler, and to illustrate more clearly the idea of the right answer being restated or demonstrated by a phrase in the sentence.)

Let's consider a real-life example. Question 2 from section 1, module 1 of SAT Practice Test #1 says that someone "continuously worked" to do something, then refers to that work using the phrase "this (blank) effort." The correct answer is "persistent." This answer choice creates the phrase "persistent effort," which is directly restated by the idea of "continuously work[ing]." So the right answer results in a phrase that is directly restated in the provided text, which is what we'll see in every question of this type. For a complete discussion of that question, see its walkthrough on page 100 of this Black Book.

All answer choices will be grammatically acceptable.

Sometimes test-takers will try to eliminate an answer choice for being the wrong part of speech, or for another grammar-related reason. In other words, if the blank must be a verb, an untrained test-taker might try to eliminate an answer choice for being a noun.

But for questions of this type, every answer choice will be grammatically acceptable—in other words, each choice will be the correct part of speech, and won't cause any grammatical problems in the sentence. We don't ever eliminate an answer choice for a question of this type for grammar reasons.

For example, question 1 from section 1, module 1 of SAT Practice Test #1 requires a verb form in the blank. Two answer choices ("demands" and "doubts") can also be used as nouns—but that doesn't factor into our analysis when we try to figure out which choice is correct. For a complete discussion of that question, see its walkthrough on page 100 of this Black Book.

Each choice on questions of this type will be grammatically acceptable, and figuring out the right answer will be based only on the meaning of each choice.

What about "Most Nearly Mean" Questions?

The SAT Reading section includes a variation on the Text Completion question called the "Most Nearly Mean" question. "Most Nearly Mean" questions are like Text Completion questions, except instead of a blank, they feature an underlined word. Then they provide four answer choices, each of which is a word or short phrase, and they ask which answer choice is the one that the underlined word or phrase "most nearly mean[s]," like this:

> As used in the text, what does the word "plotz" most nearly mean?

We can answer these questions by pretending that the underlined word or phrase is just a blank, and then treating it exactly like the Text Completion questions we just discussed: we figure out which answer choice is restated or demonstrated in the provided text. We don't even need to consider the underlined word in the original question.

(Note that some real College Board SAT practice tests include "Most Nearly Mean" questions, and some don't; this is a little unusual, but it doesn't really impact our training—as we just discussed, our approach to these questions is essentially identical to our approach to Text Completion questions, so as long as we practice that approach, we'll be ready for any Text Completion or "Most Nearly Mean" questions we encounter on test day.)

What about "Most Logically Completes" Questions?

Some SAT Reading questions will provide a short passage that ends with a blank, along with four answer choices that are relatively long phrases. The prompt will ask "which choice most logically completes the text?"

Like the "Most Nearly Mean" questions mentioned above, these "Most Logically Completes" questions basically function the same as Text Completion questions. On the surface, the two big differences between "Most Logically Completes" questions and Text Completion questions are the fact that the blank that appears in the provided text for "Most Logically Completes" questions always appears at the end of that text (rather than somewhere in the middle, as we see in Text Completion questions), and the answer choices are long phrases (instead of individual words, as we see in Text Completion questions). But we pick the answer choice using the same process—we eliminate all answer choices that aren't restated or demonstrated in the provided text, and we pick the one answer choice that is restated or demonstrated in the provided text.

Let's consider a real-life example. The provided text for question 17 from section 1, module 1 of SAT Practice Test #1 talks about the idea that some people think sauropods "evol[ved]… to such massive sizes" because of "high levels of atmospheric carbon dioxide." Then the text says that "there is no evidence of significant spikes in carbon dioxide levels coinciding with relevant periods in sauropod evolution…

suggesting that (blank)." The correct answer says that "the evolution of larger body sizes in sauropods did not depend on increased atmospheric carbon dioxide." That answer is exactly demonstrated by the idea in the provided text that "there is no evidence of significant spikes in carbon dioxide levels coinciding with relevant periods in sauropod evolution," where "relevant periods in sauropod evolution" refers to "the evolution of sauropods to such massive sizes" from earlier in the provided text. Notice that "the evolution of larger body sizes in sauropods" restates "the evolution of sauropods to such massive sizes," and "did not depend on increased atmospheric carbon dioxide" restates "there is no evidence of significant spikes in carbon dioxide levels coinciding." Again, the right answer is the only one demonstrated in the provided text. For a complete discussion of this question, see its walkthrough on page 109 of this Black Book.

What about General Passage Questions?

Some SAT Reading questions will provide a passage, and just ask for information from that passage. These are fairly straightforward; you'll just need to remember, as always, to answer based on the specific words and phrases that appear in the text, and not on any assumptions or interpretations.

Let's consider a real-life example. The provided text for question 10 from section 1, module 1 of SAT Practice Test #1 tells us about several different things that "Mother did." Then the prompt asks "according to the text, what is true about Mother?" The correct answer says "she creates stories and poems for her children." We know this answer choice is correct because it is directly, plainly restated in the provided text, which says "she used to write stories for [her children]" and "she always made up funny pieces of poetry" for them. Again, we can see that the correct answer is the only one that is plainly restated in the provided text. For a complete discussion of this question, see its walkthrough on page 105 of this Black Book.

What about "Data" Questions?

Some SAT Reading questions will provide a figure, a short passage, and some answer choices, and then ask which choice "describes data from the table that support the researchers' claim," or "most effectively uses data from the graph to complete the example," or something similar.

As we discussed earlier in "Reading Graphs, Charts, Tables, and Other Figures" on page 48, the current version of the SAT is designed to incorporate skills related to reading and understanding figures with data. These Data questions fundamentally function like any other SAT Reading question, in that they require us to find the answer choice that's restated or demonstrated in the provided text; what makes Data questions different is that their provided text will also include a figure we'll need to read.

(When we see questions that refer to figures, we want to keep in mind the basic concepts that we discussed in "Reading Graphs, Charts, Tables, and Other Figures" on page 48 in this Black Book, and combine them with our awareness of the other rules and patterns of SAT Reading questions in order to identify the choice that's exactly restated or demonstrated by what appears on the page.)

There are two main ideas we need to consider when we read an answer choice for a Data question. First, we need to make sure that the answer choice accurately describes the data. For example, a wrong answer choice might say that a certain value was the highest value in the table, when in reality some other value was higher, or it might say that some value stayed the same over the course of several years, when in fact it went up and down over that period. Any time we see an answer choice that makes an inaccurate statement about a provided figure, we know that choice is wrong, and we can eliminate it.

The second challenge is to determine whether the statement made in the answer choice fulfills the requirement in the prompt regarding the "claim," or "example," or "hypothesis" in the text. Many wrong answer choices will accurately describe the figure, but the statement they make won't fulfill the requirement in the prompt—they'll be irrelevant, or even directly contradict the idea in the prompt.

Let's consider a real-life example. Question 14 from section 1, module 1 of SAT Practice Test #1 provides a table that tells us how many projects different actors and directors were involved in over certain time periods. The passage tells us that due to "lost" "records," these numbers "should be taken as bare minimums rather than totals," and that "it's entirely possible, for example, that (blank)." The right answer, (C), tells us that one actress (who, according to the table, acted in 66 films) "acted in far more than 66 films," and a director (who, according to the table, directed 58 films) "directed more than 58." This idea that the people in the table actually did more work than the table reflects directly demonstrates the idea that the numbers in the table are "bare minimums," and that the real numbers could be more. So this answer choice accurately refers to the numbers in the table, and also demonstrates the idea from the passage that's relevant to the "example" mentioned in the prompt, exactly as the standards for this question type require. For a full discussion of this question, see its walkthrough on page 107 of this Black Book.

What about "Main Idea/Main Purpose" Questions?

You'll occasionally see a question that asks you to identify the "main idea" or "main purpose" of the provided text. These questions can basically be treated in the same way that any other SAT Reading question can: the correct answer choice will be the only choice that restates or demonstrates an idea from the relevant part of the text, and every wrong answer choice will fail to be restated or demonstrated in the relevant text.

As an example, consider question 10 from section 1, module 2 of SAT Practice Test #1. That question provides an excerpt from a poem by William Shakespeare, and asks for the "main idea of the text."

That text, which we're told is "addressed to a close friend as if he were physically present," says "I [hurry] to my bed… then my thoughts… [begin] a zealous pilgrimage to thee, and keep my drooping eyelids open wide." This exactly demonstrates the idea in the correct answer, which says "the speaker is thinking about the friend instead of immediately falling asleep"—notice that "my thoughts… [begin] a zealous pilgrimage to thee" directly demonstrates the idea that "the speaker is thinking about the friend," and "keep my drooping eyelids open wide" directly demonstrates not "immediately falling asleep"—someone whose "eyelids" are "open wide" is not asleep. So we can see that even when discussing the "main idea" of a poem by William Shakespeare, we still don't do any literary interpretation, and we still answer based on exactly what appears in the provided text. For a full discussion of this question, see its walkthrough on page 124 of this Black Book.

What about "Function and Structure" Questions?

Some SAT Reading and Writing questions ask you about the "function" of some (usually underlined) part of a text, or about the "overall structure" of the text. The correct answer will be the only choice that plainly describes the relevant text—that is, it will be the only choice that is directly demonstrated in the text.

We can see a real-life example of this kind of question in question 9 from section 1, module 1 of SAT Practice Test #1. The provided text for that question discusses a "study." The question asks for the "function" of the following text:

> Using data spanning from 1994 to 2010 for a set of US companies, the team compared over 29,000 annual earnings forecasts to the actual earnings later reported by those companies.

The correct answer is "to explain part of the methodology used in the team's study." This exactly describes the quoted text above, which explains an aspect of what the team did to conduct the study (and, in turn, the underlined text exactly *demonstrates* the idea expressed in the right answer choice). For a full discussion of this question, see its walkthrough on page 104 of this Black Book. For more on terms like "methodology" that appear in SAT Reading questions, see "A Few Important Terms Related To Studies and Experiments" on page 73 of this Black Book.

What about Quotation Questions?

Some questions will make a claim about some literary work, and then ask for a "quotation" from that work that "most effectively illustrates the claim." Each answer choice will be a quotation from the work in question. As you might guess by now, the right answer will be the one that plainly demonstrates whatever the "claim" in the prompt says, while none of the other answer choices will meet this requirement.

We can see an example of this kind of question in question 12 from section 1, module 2 of SAT Practice Test #1. That question says that in a certain novel, the author "portrays Alexandra Bergson as having a deep emotional connection to her natural surroundings." The right answer is a quotation from that novel that says "she had never known before how much the country meant to her… she had felt as if her heart were hiding down there, somewhere, with the quail and the plover and all the little wild things…." The idea that the "country meant" something to her, and that "her heart [was] hiding" in it directly demonstrates the idea of "a deep emotional connection to her natural surroundings," just as the claim in the prompt requires. For a full discussion of this question, see its walkthrough on page 125 of this Black Book.

What about Paired Passages?

Sometimes an SAT Reading question provides two short texts, and asks what the author of one text would say about something in the other text. Many untrained test-takers feel like they have to guess what the author would think, which seems kind of subjective and impossible; in reality, whatever the prompt asks you about must be something that the author in question has already expressed in the provided text, and—as always—you can just find the relevant text and pick the answer choice that is restated or demonstrated by that text.

We can see this idea in action in question 9 of section 1, module 2 of SAT Practice Test #1. That question provides us with two texts, and asks us what "the author of Text 2" would "most likely say about Text 1's characterization of the discovery involving EGR." Again, as trained test-takers, we know that we aren't expected to just guess here; we know it must be the case that the provided text contains the information we need.

When we check Text 1 to see its "characterization of the discovery involving EGR," we see that it says that "both humans and panther worms have a gene for early growth response (EGR) linked to regeneration," and that this is "an especially promising discovery." Now that we have this information, we can check Text 2 to see what that author thinks about someone calling this discovery "especially promising." When we do that, we see that the author mentions the discovery from Text 1 and the "excitement" it "caused," then says "however, as the team pointed out, the gene likely functions very differently in humans than it does in panther worms."

The correct answer says "Text 1's characterization of the discovery involving EGR" "is overly optimistic given additional observations from Srivastava and her team." So we can see that the right answer is pulled directly from what Text 2 says about the topic in the prompt; we don't have to wonder what that author "would most likely say" about someone calling that discovery "promising," because we can check to see what that author *actually* says in the provided text about people who are "excited[d]" about that discovery. For a full discussion of this question, see its walkthrough on page 123 of this Black Book.

What about Logical Transition Questions?

Some SAT Reading questions will provide a short passage with a blank and ask "which choice completes the text with the most logical transition." Each answer choice will be an example of what I call "transition words." (This isn't a formal grammatical concept—it's just an easy way to think about this idea in the context of the SAT.)

"Transition words" are just words (or short phrases) that indicate some type of relationship between the idea before the transition and the idea after the transition. Here are some examples of the kinds of words I'm talking about:

- likewise
- however
- nevertheless
- previously
- therefore
- for instance
- furthermore
- although

The SAT likes to ask us to select the transition that reflects the appropriate connection between the idea in the previous sentence and the idea in the sentence in question. For example, the SAT would consider this underlined transition word to be ACCEPTABLE:

> My brother likes to watch most sports on TV. However, he doesn't enjoy watching tennis.

In this case, the word "however" appropriately indicates that the second sentence provides information which is unexpected based on the information in the first sentence, or somehow opposed to the idea in the first sentence: the first sentence says my brother likes to watch most sports on TV, but the second sentence says he doesn't like to watch a particular sport.

But a transition word like the following would be UNACCEPTABLE on the SAT Reading and Writing section:

> *My brother likes to watch most sports on TV. Therefore, he doesn't enjoy watching tennis.

The word "therefore" would indicate that the information in the second sentence is the logical result of the information in the first sentence, but that isn't the case here. We always need to make sure that we choose the transition word that correctly demonstrates the relationship between the previous sentence and the given sentence.

For a real-life example of this question type, we can look at question 29 from section 1, module 1 of SAT Practice Test #1. The provided text for that question starts with this sentence:

> Although novels and poems are considered distinct literary forms, many authors have created hybrid works that incorporate elements of both.

The following sentence mentions "a verse novel," which it describes as "a book-length narrative complete with characters and a plot but conveyed in short, crisp lines of poetry rather than prose." So the first sentence tells us about "hybrid works" that "incorporate elements of both" "novels and poems," and the second sentence tells us about a particular "verse novel" that's "book-length" but conveyed in... poetry." The relationship required by the correct answer, "for example," is exactly demonstrated by the fact that the second sentence is an "example" of the idea expressed in the first sentence. For a full discussion of this question, see its walkthrough on page 116 of this Black Book.

What about "If True" Questions?

Some questions will present a short passage that contains a claim or hypothesis of some kind. The prompt will ask "which finding" from the answer choices, "if true," would either support or weaken that claim or hypothesis.

As always, the right answer will be the one that demonstrates the relevant idea from the text (or demonstrates the *opposite* of that idea, if we need to find the choice that "weakens" the statement in the passage). We'll need to read the text, find the claim or hypothesis we're being asked about, and figure out which answer choice demonstrates a concept from that claim or hypothesis.

We can see a real-life example of this question type in question 16 from section 1, module 2 of SAT Practice Test #1. The provided text for that question describes a study where a "computer model... categorize[s]" pottery fragments "as accurately as a team of expert archaeologists." The passage then says that "some archaeologists have expressed concern that they might be replaced by such computer models, but the researchers claim that outcome is highly unlikely." The claim that this "outcome" (that is, archaeologists being replaced by computer models) is "highly unlikely" is the one that we need to support.

The correct answer says that "categorizing pottery fragments limits the amount of time [archaeologists] can dedicate to other important tasks that only human experts can do." The idea of "important tasks that only human experts can do" exactly demonstrates that "computer models" "replac[ing]" "archaeologists" is "highly unlikely," because if "archaeologists" have "important tasks that only humans can do," they can't be "replaced by... computer models" (it must be the case that "computer models" can't do something that "only humans can do"). For a full discussion of this question, see its walkthrough on page 128 of this Black Book.

What about Notes Questions?

Some SAT Reading questions begin with the sentence "while researching a topic, a student has taken the following notes." That sentence is followed by a bulleted list of notes, and then a statement of some goal the student has: the student wants to explain something, or the student wants to compare one thing to another thing, or something similar. Finally, the question will ask which choice uses information from the notes to achieve that goal.

As we might expect, the right answer will be the only one that plainly achieves whatever "goal" is mentioned in the prompt. As we might also expect, we have to read very carefully and think very carefully about exactly what that "goal" is, and whether each answer choice achieves it.

We can see a real-life example of this question type in question 32 from section 1, module 1 of SAT Practice Test #1, which provides some notes about a "study" related to "pterosaurs." The prompt says "the student wants to present the study and its findings," so we know the right answer will be the only one that presents the study and its findings. Sure enough, the right answer says "in a 2021 study, Chinsamy-Turan determined that pterosaur jawbones… had few growth lines relative to the bones of fully grown pterosaurs and thus belonged to juveniles." This choice "presents" the study, as the stated "goal" requires, by providing basic information about it, and it tell us the "findings" of the study, as the stated "goal" also requires, when it says that "Chinsamy-Turan determined" that the "pterosaur jawbones… belonged to juveniles." For a full discussion of this question, see its walkthrough on page 118 of this Black Book.

These Notes questions involve a lot of text, but we can actually almost always skip the bulleted notes completely, and just answer based on the "goal" described in the prompt. If you encounter an idea in the answer choices and you're not sure how that idea relates to the "goal" from the prompt, it can occasionally be helpful to look back at the notes to clear up any confusion, but this usually isn't necessary. For example, in the question we just discussed, the goal is to "present the study and its findings." When we consider each answer choice, we can see that only (D) tells us about anything that could be called "findings," when it says what "Chinsamy-Turan determined." No other choice presents findings, so those choices must be wrong, which we can conclude without reading any of the provided notes.

"Unfamiliar"/ "Already Familiar"

This question type sometimes incorporates an added wrinkle by including in the goal the idea of presenting information to an audience that is either "unfamiliar" or "familiar" with a certain person. When this happens, we need to keep the following in mind:

- If the audience is *unfamiliar* with the person in question, we need to pick an answer choice that provides some basic information about that person. This is more or less what we would do in real life; if we know someone is unfamiliar with a certain person we're talking about, we would briefly introduce that person. For example, if we were going to mention Bugs Bunny to someone who didn't know anything about Bugs Bunny, we wouldn't say "I had a nightmare about Bugs Bunny." Instead, we would say something like "I had a nightmare about Bugs Bunny, a cartoon rabbit."

- If the audience is *familiar* with the topic in question, we should mention that topic without introducing it with basic information.

"Emphasize"

One more wrinkle that appears occasionally in "Notes" questions relates to the word "emphasize." When a "Notes" question asks you for the choice that "emphasizes" a certain idea, you may need to choose between an answer choice that does mention that idea, as the prompt requires—but also mentions another idea as well—and another choice that *only* mentions the idea that the prompt asks about. The correct answer will be the one that *only* mentions the idea that should be "emphasized," and doesn't bring up anything else; the choices that mention other ideas will be wrong. This demonstrates the idea of emphasizing something: when we emphasize an idea, we call extra attention to that specific idea, as opposed to bringing up one or more other topics at the same time.

We'll see these ideas at work in the walkthroughs starting on page 96.

Conclusion

At this point, we've discussed the best ways to approach every type of SAT Reading question. You now know everything you need to know to be able to answer any SAT Reading question that can appear on test day.

On the next page we'll discuss a few important terms related to studies and experiments that will definitely show up in your practice and on test day. After that, it'll be time for a quick review of your SAT Reading training before we continue with SAT Writing training, and then dive into SAT Reading and Writing question walkthroughs starting on page 96 of this Black Book. There, you'll be able to see all of these ideas at work against real practice SAT questions from the College Board.

A Few Important Terms Related To Studies and Experiments

A few terms related to experimental design come up frequently enough in SAT Reading questions that we should cover them briefly.

(To be clear, you don't need to have any deep understanding of the scientific method to get a great SAT score; you don't need to know what a control group is, or an independent variable, or anything else like that for this test. This article is just here because it's a good idea to have a precise understanding of these few terms, since that will probably help you answer a few questions on test day.)

We've discussed how getting a list of 1000 words like "ameliorate" and "refulgent" and then memorizing their definitions in hopes that this will help you on test day is a bad idea. It's a bad idea for several reasons, but the main one is that we have no way of knowing ahead of time of which challenging words will appear on test day in such a way that knowing their definitions will help your score.

In this brief section we will discuss a few words that *will* show up on test day—you might not see every one of these terms, but you will definitely see some of them, so it's worth it to take a minute and make sure we're clear on what these words mean.

Most test-takers are already fairly familiar with them, but we know that the SAT is a test of *details*, and if you don't think precisely about what these terms mean—and how they're different from each other—then you might have trouble with certain questions. Also, bear in mind that some of these terms have multiple meanings; we're going to discuss them here in the context of a scientific study or experiment.

Aim	The <u>aim</u> of an experiment is what the researcher wants to find out in creating and executing the experiment. This isn't the same as what the researcher thinks will happen, or what the researcher finds out once the study is finished. You can see a real SAT question that asks about the aim of a study in question 32 of section 1, module 2 of SAT Practice Test #2. The walkthrough for that question is on page 172 of this Black Book.
Hypothesis	A <u>hypothesis</u> is a statement of what a researcher thinks will happen in an experiment, or what a researcher thinks is true. The study or experiment tests the researcher's hypothesis. For our purposes, information that a researcher finds in a study or experiment can support the hypothesis—that is, tend to agree with the hypothesis, or show that the hypothesis is likely to be true. It can also weaken or undermine the hypothesis—that is, tend to disagree with the hypothesis, or show that the hypothesis isn't likely to be true. You can see a real SAT question that asks about a hypothesis in question 15 of section 1, module 2 of SAT Practice Test #3. The walkthrough for that question is on page 197 of this Black Book.
Methodology	The <u>methodology</u> of a study or experiment is what the researcher actually did to test the hypothesis—it's the method that the researcher used. (This isn't the same as reporting what happened once the experiment ended—that would be the findings of the experiment.) You can see a real SAT question that involves the methodology of a study in question 9 of section 1, module 1 of SAT Practice Test #1. The walkthrough for that question is on page 104 of this Black Book.
Findings	Findings are what the researcher finds out after the study or experiment ends. Usually the findings are the data that was found in the experiment, and/or descriptions of what happened in the experiment. (This isn't the same as the researcher's conclusion—we'll discuss that next.) You can see a real SAT question that involves the findings of a study in question 32 of section 1, module 1 of SAT Practice Test #1. The walkthrough for that question is on page 118 of this Black Book.
Conclusion	The conclusion is the researcher's interpretation of the findings of the experiment, which usually involves saying whether or not the findings of the experiment supported the hypothesis. You can see a real SAT question that asks about the conclusion of a study in question 14 of section 1, module 1 of SAT Practice Test #2. The walkthrough for that question is on page 145 of this Black Book.

A sample experiment

Let's imagine a simple experiment with all of the features mentioned above.

- Aim: A researcher wants to find out whether plants need water to be able to grow.

- Hypothesis: The researcher says that plants probably do need water to be able to grow.

- Methodology: The researcher creates two groups of identical plants; he waters one group but not the other.

- Findings: The group that wasn't watered didn't grow, but the group that was watered did grow.

- Conclusion: The researcher concludes that plants do need water to be able to grow.

Remember—you *will* see some or all of these terms on test day, so make sure you're completely comfortable with them, and that you think carefully about what they do and don't mean as you answer any questions where they appear.

A bonus term

There's one more scientific term that comes up often enough in SAT Reading questions that it's worth mentioning here.

Correlation	Correlation describes a relationship between two values. When values are correlated positively, they increase together. For example, the more time Sue works, the more money she makes—her time spent working and her income are positively correlated. When values are correlated negatively (or "inversely"), one increases when the other decreases. For example, the more time Josh spends at the mall, the less money he has—his time spent at the mall and the amount of money in his wallet are negatively correlated.

SAT Reading Quick Summary

This is a one-page summary of the major concepts you'll need to know for SAT Reading questions. Use it to evaluate your comprehension or jog your memory. For a more in-depth treatment of these ideas, see the rest of this section.

The Big Secret of SAT Reading Questions

SAT Reading questions require careful, literal reading. Our job is to find the answer choice that's restated or demonstrated by the relevant text. The answer to every question comes directly from the provided text. No interpretation whatsoever is involved.

SAT Reading Training Summary

SAT Reading questions are every question on the SAT Reading and Writing section that *do not* ask which choice "conforms to the conventions of Standard English." The rules for SAT Reading are simple; the challenging thing is making sure you follow them all the time, no matter what. Here they are:

- Correct answers are always directly restated or demonstrated in the text—no matter the kind of passage, and no matter the kind of question.
- Details are critical. The difference between right and wrong can be one word.
- There's always exactly one objectively right answer choice per question; other choices are objectively wrong. There aren't "good," "better," and "best," choices; there are only wrong choices and right choices.

SAT Reading questions may involve the following concepts:

- picking the answer choice that completes the text with a word or phrase that restates or demonstrates an idea from the provided text
- choosing the transition word that appropriately relates the given sentence to the previous sentence
- picking the choice that plainly describes the function of a part of the text, or the structure of the overall text
- picking the statement that is consistent with the information in a provided figure, and that also restates or demonstrates an idea from the relevant text
- picking the quotation that demonstrates the idea from the prompt
- picking the choice that uses information from provided notes to meet one or more requirements from the prompt

Here are the most common wrong-answer patterns you'll see on SAT Reading questions:

- Answer choice contains statements that might seem plausible, but aren't actually stated in the text.
- Answer choices may mention concepts from the text but confuses the relationships among them.
- Answer choice is barely relevant to the text.
- Answer choice directly contradicts the text.
- Answer choice could be an acceptable literary interpretation in a classroom discussion, but doesn't actually restate or demonstrate ideas present in the provided text.

The general SAT Reading process:

1. Read the question to determine its type.
2. Read the provided text.
3. Find three wrong answers, referring back to the text as needed.
4. Check whether the remaining choice meets the standards for a right answer to an SAT Reading question.

See the many walkthroughs of real SAT Reading and Writing questions starting on page 96 of this book for demonstrations of these principles.

SAT Writing Training

> *Thus I got into my bones the essential structure of the ordinary British sentence, which is a noble thing.*
> Winston Churchill

Now that we've covered SAT Reading questions, let's tackle SAT Writing questions. This training section specifically targets questions on the SAT Reading and Writing section that ask which choice "conforms to the conventions of Standard English." (For all other SAT Reading and Writing question types, please refer back to the SAT Reading training on page 59.)

In the last training section, we learned about the critical importance of careful reading and paying attention to details on the SAT. Those skills are every bit as important when we work on SAT Writing questions; we'll just be paying attention to different details, and applying our knowledge of the limited, standardized grammar and punctuation concepts that appear in the SAT Writing Toolbox starting on page 76 of this Black Book. Just as we learned to attack SAT Reading questions in a systematic and dependable way—even though they mostly ask us to do things we don't normally do in school—we can learn to beat SAT Writing questions by sticking to predictable, standardized strategies.

The "big secret" of SAT Writing questions

The big secret of SAT Writing questions is that they don't necessarily follow the rules and conventions that you normally encounter at school, at home, or online. Instead, these questions follow the rules that the College Board has decided they should follow, which might loosely be described as the rules that governed standard written American English in the mid-20th century. (We'll cover exactly what those rules are later in this section, in the SAT Writing Toolbox starting on page 76.)

Most untrained test-takers don't realize this. Whenever they come across a new SAT Writing question, they just try to identify the choice that sounds best to *them*, the way *they* would phrase things if they were writing or talking in their everyday lives.

This is a huge mistake. By now we should realize that the SAT doesn't care what seems right to you, or to me, or to anybody else who doesn't write the SAT. So instead of looking at an SAT question and answering based on what sounds good to *us*, we should be answering based on what the test consistently rewards. That's all. What you or I think sounds good or bad isn't important if it disagrees with the College Board's standards.

Let me say that again: when you're faced with an SAT Writing question, you should immediately ask yourself which answer satisfies the College Board's rules and patterns for that type of question.

When we talked about SAT Reading questions earlier in this Black Book, we said that one of the biggest reasons people struggle with those questions is that they're used to classroom discussions in which almost any interpretation of a text has some value, while SAT Reading questions only reward a literal reading of each text. Well, a lot of test-takers have a similar issue when it comes to SAT Writing questions, because most English teachers have very loose standards for grammar and punctuation. This means that most test-takers find the College Board penalizes them for things that their English teachers would accept.

For example, many people are taught in school that a comma can be placed almost anywhere in a sentence, whether to indicate that a reader would take a breath at that point in the sentence if it were being read out loud, or just to break up a lot of text, or for any number of other reasons. But SAT Writing questions don't reward us for using commas like that—instead, they have their own rigid rules about comma usage. Similarly, many test-takers might use pronouns in such a way that it can be unclear which specific nouns those pronouns refer to. But this usage is never acceptable on the SAT, because correct answers to SAT Writing questions must always leave no ambiguity about which pronoun refers to which noun. Again, we'll cover the College Board's rules for these things in the SAT Writing Toolbox starting on page 76.

(By the way, don't be nervous if you're not familiar with some of the technical grammatical terms we'll use in this section, like "conjunction," or "independent clause." In a few pages, I'll explain the terms that will help you understand how the SAT operates. And remember that the SAT itself will never require us to know the name of a grammatical concept in order to answer a question correctly; we just have to learn some rules, and then be able to recognize when these rules are being followed, and when they aren't.)

How to identify and attack SAT Writing questions

SAT Writing questions test rule-based concepts like proper verb conjugations, the proper use of punctuation, acceptable phrase placement, and so on. These questions test your ability to identify the form of a phrase or sentence that follows the SAT's rules for "Standard English."

You'll be able to identify these SAT Writing questions because they'll ask you which choice "conforms to the conventions of Standard English." That's important, so I'll repeat it in bold, with some eye-catching formatting:

SAT Writing questions will ask you which choice "conforms to the conventions of Standard English."

The training in this section only applies to those questions.

An individual SAT Writing question can cover multiple areas of grammar and punctuation, but don't worry—most questions will only cover one or two topics each, and we'll find that the topics tested on the SAT are relatively simple, completely predictable, and repetitive.

Since SAT Writing questions are all about picking the answer choice that follows the rules and patterns for ideal phrases and sentences as determined by the College Board, we'll need to do two things:

- learn the College Board's standards for grammar and punctuation, and
- get familiar with the way the College Board tests those standards in real SAT practice questions.

Once we've done this, we can answer any SAT Writing question that the College Board throws at us.

We'll take care of the first step by reviewing the SAT Writing Toolbox, which is a collection of all the major rules and patterns you'll need to know to understand the College Board's standards for grammar and punctuation. Once we've learned all the relevant information from that toolbox, we'll jump right in to the various test design elements that the College Board uses in SAT Writing questions.

SAT Writing Toolbox

Whether you feel totally comfortable with grammar and punctuation as general concepts, or you can't wait to be done with all your English classes and never read a book or write a sentence ever again, I *strongly* recommend that you read this entire toolbox *twice*.

(Even if you think you already have a perfect understanding of modern English grammar, I want to remind you gently that the College Board will probably disagree with you on at least a few issues—and the only thing that matters on SAT Writing questions is what the College Board thinks about grammar and punctuation.)

Remember—we need to be fully comfortable with the College Board's rules and standards for English grammar and punctuation, which aren't necessarily the same as the rules and standards that you're used to, or the rules and standards that your teachers prefer. Of course, the grammar rules on the SAT have much in common with the grammar rules that most people use, but we know by now that the SAT is a test of *details*, and there are a number of details we need to pay special attention to if we want to be able to pick the correct answer on SAT Writing questions consistently.

Also, because of the ways that different parts of a sentence interact with each other, there will be some overlap among the concepts we talk about, so don't worry if some of these ideas run together a little bit in your mind. As long as you can identify the right answer when you're practicing, you're in good shape.

If you're feeling confused at any point as you read through any one of these topics, just do your best and keep reading through the material. I'll follow up with examples when necessary, and the examples will tend to clear things up—because it's often a lot harder to understand a description of these issues than it is just to look at an example and see what we're talking about. So, again, just keep at it, even if things don't seem clear right away.

This is also a good time for me to bring up the importance of the question walkthroughs you'll see after this training. We'll cover a lot of stuff in this training section, but you'll really get the best sense of how to beat SAT Writing questions by using the official SAT Practice Tests to follow along with the walkthroughs in this Black Book. That way, you can see all of this material in action, which will really help you recognize these concepts when you see them on test day.

And after that, of course, the most important thing is always for you to do some real practice SAT Writing questions on your own once you've learned the material in this Black Book.

(Before we jump in, I'd like to reiterate that the SAT will never test you on specific grammatical terms like "participle," "pronoun," "conjugation," and so on, so don't worry if you can't keep those terms straight—or if you've never even heard of them. Instead, the SAT tests you on its principles of grammar and punctuation by having you choose the form of a phrase that it considers acceptable within the context of a passage. So you'll never see direct questions about grammatical terminology on the SAT—we only discuss these terms here to make the training and walkthroughs easier to understand.)

Important note:

In this section, I'll show you a lot of different sample sentences—some with errors, some without. To keep things clear, the examples with errors will have an asterisk (*) at the beginning of the example.

So if you see an example that begins with an asterisk (*), you'll know that it shows something you should *avoid* on SAT Writing questions.

Nouns

Nouns are the first parts of speech that babies learn, because nouns are the things you can point to. A baby can point to its mother and say, "mommy," because the word "mommy" describes an actual, physical thing. The most basic nouns are things you can point at like a baby would, such as the following:

- apple
- bicycle
- toy

- umbrella
- watch
- computer

- shoe
- train
- mall

- sign
- book
- car

Any object you can touch or point to is a noun.

But there are other types of nouns as well. Some nouns represent ideas, like "happiness" or "fatalism." These nouns are things that you can't point to. But don't worry—you can usually recognize them by their endings.

If a word ends in "-ness," "-ism," "-hood," "-ology," or anything similar, it's probably a noun, like "quickness," "cubism," "brotherhood," and "cardiology."

Nouns can be either **singular** or **plural**. The plural form of a noun is usually formed with the suffix "-s" or with the suffix "-es," but there are some special nouns that form their plurals differently. "Shoe," "box," and "mouse" are all singular nouns, and "shoes," "boxes," and "mice" are the plural forms of those nouns.

Verbs

Verbs are the second-most basic class of words. A verb is an action. Verbs are things you can do—the word *do*, itself, is a verb. Here are some examples of verbs:

- run
- do
- make
- swim
- cook
- imagine
- follow
- think

Verbs tell us the actions that nouns are doing:

I <u>run</u> far.

He <u>makes</u> noise.

They <u>cook</u> breakfast.

We <u>swim</u> nearby.

A verb takes different forms, called "conjugations," depending on who is doing the action described by the verb, and the time period of the action described by the verb. For the purposes of the SAT, we care about two aspects of a conjugation:

- whether a verb-form is singular or plural (which is called the verb's "number"), and
- whether a verb's action takes place in the present, past, or future (which is called the verb's "tense")

Singular versus plural verbs

Like nouns, verbs have singular and plural forms. Singular forms of verbs often end in "-s," while plural forms often do not.

Rhonda <u>drives</u> to the dentist.

My friends <u>drive</u> downtown.

In these sentences,

- The singular noun "Rhonda" requires the singular verb form "drives."
- The plural noun "friends" requires the plural verb form "drive."

Here's the verb "to speak" conjugated in the present tense. Note that the form used with the singular pronouns "he," "she," and "it" ends in "-s":

I speak	we speak
you speak	you speak
he/she/it speaks	they speak

In many cases, the singular and plural forms of a verb are identical, as we see in the following examples:

I like biscuits.

We like biscuits.

Both of these examples would be acceptable on the SAT because "like" can be both a singular verb-form and a plural verb-form, depending on the pronoun doing the action, which means it can be acceptably paired with both the singular pronoun "I" and the plural pronoun "we."

A verb must always agree in number with the noun or nouns that it modifies, as we see below:

Monica and Alex enjoy the theater.

The previous example would be acceptable on the SAT because "Monica and Alex" is a plural subject, and "enjoy" is a plural verb-form that modifies that plural subject. But the following example would be unacceptable on the SAT:

*Monica and Alex enjoys the theater.

This would be unacceptable on the SAT because "enjoys" is a singular verb-form that might seem, at first, like it correctly agrees with the singular noun "Alex." But in this sentence, "enjoys" actually has to agree with the plural noun phrase "Monica and Alex," because the sentence tells us that Monica and Alex *both* enjoy the theater, not Alex alone.

Mixing singular verbs with plural nouns (and plural verbs with singular nouns) is a common error in SAT Writing questions. Always check to see which noun a verb is supposed to agree with!

Tenses of verbs

As we discussed before, verbs describe actions. We have three basic **tenses** to describe when the action of a verb takes place: past, present, and future. We change the form of a verb to indicate its tense. Consider the following:

> I love my grandmother.

"Love" is a present-tense verb-form, indicating that the action of loving my grandmother is going on right now.

> I will love my children very much when I have them.

"Will love" is a future-tense verb-form that indicates the loving has not started yet, but will happen later.

> I loved my pet goldfish.

"Loved" is a past-tense verb-form, indicating that the act of loving has already finished.

On the SAT Writing Section, verb tenses should indicate actions in a sequence that's logically possible; if a question requires you to consider the tense of a verb, make sure you pick an answer choice that doesn't create an impossible sequence of events in the context of the passage. Similarly, any verb form you choose should be in the same tense as the other verbs in the provided text, unless some word or phrase specifies that the verb in question occurs in a different timeframe.

Verbs in "-ing" and "to" forms

The "–ing" and "to" forms of verbs can function as nouns:

> I like to sing.

> Singing entertains my marmot.

In the previous examples, "to sing" and "singing" both act like nouns:

- "to sing" is the object of the verb "like."
- "Singing" is the subject of the verb "entertains."

The "–ing" and "to" forms of verbs *aren't* conjugated, so they *can't* be the main verb in a sentence.

> *I to swim in my pool.

> *My sister jumping through a flaming hoop.

Neither example above is an acceptable sentence on the SAT, because neither contains a main verb—"to swim" and "jumping" aren't conjugated verb forms, so neither can be the main verb in a sentence.

The "-ing" form of a verb is called a "participle," and we'll discuss it more in the section called "Avoid dangling participles" on page 90.

The "to" form of a verb is called an "infinitive," and we'll discuss it more in the section called "Infinitive clauses" on page 85.

Misleading verb forms in the answer choices

Sometimes, the SAT uses a question's answer choices to try to confuse us about the proper form of a verb. There's a real-life example of this issue in question 19 from section 1, module 2 of SAT Practice Test #1, involving this phrase:

> The award-winning book is Harris's first novel, but her writing (blank) honored before.

The choices include three plural verb forms: two are different past-tense forms, and one is in the present tense. Many untrained test-takers will see those choices and think that they need to determine which tense is appropriate, and then they'll get stuck trying to figure that out. But, in reality, the noun that must agree with the verb is the singular noun "writing." This singular noun needs a singular verb form, and the only choice with a singular verb form is the correct answer, (C), "has been." Since the blank requires a singular verb form, and only one singular verb form appears in the answer choices, we don't need to think about the correct tense of the verb form at all.

For a complete discussion of this question, please see its walkthrough on page 130 in this Black Book.

Pronouns

Pronouns are a particular type of noun that we use to refer to a noun that has already been mentioned. These are pronouns:

- I
- you
- he
- she
- it
- we
- they
- me
- him
- her
- us
- them
- one
- who
- which
- that

(NOTE: The words "that" and "which" are special types of pronouns called "relative pronouns." Both words can also be used in other ways that aren't related to pronouns, depending on the context. Don't worry about those other usages right now—just know that the words "that" and "which" are often, but not always, pronouns.)

When we have a sentence like

> Thomas wants to know why he has to do the dishes.

the word "he" lets us know that we're still talking about the person that was recently mentioned. It would sound strange to say:

> Thomas wants to know why Thomas has to do the dishes.

So we use the pronoun "he" in place of the second "Thomas."

When a pronoun appears on the SAT, it must agree in number with the noun it's replacing:

> Last week I saw an antique car. I even got to sit in <u>it</u>.

In the above example, the singular pronoun "it" is correctly used to refer to the singular noun "car." Let's look at an example that breaks this rule, and would be UNACCEPTABLE on the SAT:

> *Last week I saw an antique car. I even got to sit in <u>them</u>.

The second sentence above incorrectly uses the plural pronoun "them" to refer to the singular noun "car."

Pronoun ambiguity

On the SAT Writing section, we can only use a pronoun if that pronoun could only be referring to a single, specific noun phrase. If an answer choice would make it unclear which noun a pronoun refers to, then that answer choice must be incorrect. We can see a real-life example of an SAT question involving pronoun ambiguity in question 25 from section 1, module 1 of SAT Practice Test #1.

Two of that question's answer choices are plural pronouns, and two are singular pronouns. But no singular noun appears before the blank in the provided text that the singular pronouns could logically refer to, so we know we can eliminate the two singular pronoun choices. Of the remaining choices, only one ((B), "themselves") makes it clear that the plural pronoun in the blank refers to the "turtle barnacles" doing the action in the sentence, and not to one of the other plural nouns in the sentence. For a complete discussion of that question, see its walkthrough on page 114 in this Black Book.

Possessives

Luckily, the SAT's rules for **possessives** are actually pretty simple, even if they arguably differ from today's common usage. There are three things you need to know if you want to form possessives on the SAT.

First, you need to know how possessive pronouns are formed. Most people are comfortable with these possessive pronouns:

- my
- his
- her

The ones that sometimes cause trouble tend to be these:

- your
- its
- whose
- their

People often mix up those possessive pronouns with the following contractions:

- The possessive pronoun "your" is confused with the contraction "you're," which is short for "you are."
- The possessive pronoun "its" is confused with the contraction "it's," which is short for "it is."
- The possessive pronoun "whose" is confused with the contraction "who's," which is short for "who is."
- The possessive pronoun "their" is confused with the contraction "they're," which is short for "they are."

So here's the rule to remember: *these possessive pronouns contain no apostrophes.* If you're in a position where you have to choose between "your" and "you're," or "its" and "it's," or "whose" and "who's," or "their" and "they're," remember that the form with the apostrophe is a contraction involving a form of the verb "to be," and the other form is possessive. Whenever you see these contractions in a sentence or an answer choice, imagine them in their "un-contracted" state, and you should be able to tell if they're appropriate:

- "You're" with an apostrophe can always be read as "you are"
- "It's" with an apostrophe can always be read as "it is"
- "Who's" with an apostrophe can always be read as "who is"
- "They're" with an apostrophe can always be read as "they are"

Many people are unsure about sentences like these:

> *She sat in the car and honked <u>it's</u> horn.

*<u>Who's</u> house is this?

But if we imagine the contractions in their "un-contracted" forms, the grammatical errors become a lot more obvious:

*She sat in the car and honked <u>it is</u> horn.

*<u>Who is</u> house is this?

When you get into the habit of reading "you're" as "you are," "it's" as "it is," "who's" as "who is," and "they're" as "they are," you won't be tricked by that kind of sentence.[1]

The **second** thing to remember about possessives is that a PLURAL noun ending in "-s" will ALWAYS form its possessive with a single apostrophe, and nothing more. Consider the following examples:

This toy belongs to the cats. It is the <u>cats'</u> toy.

Those are the <u>girls'</u> bikes. Those bikes belong to the girls.

That lawn mower belongs to the neighbors. It is the <u>neighbors'</u> lawn mower.

In each of these three situations, there's a plural noun that ends in "-s":

- cats
- girls
- neighbors

To form a possessive for each of those plural nouns, you just add an apostrophe, and don't change anything else:

- cats'
- girls'
- neighbors'

So that's the second rule: to form the possessive of a plural noun ending in "-s," just add an apostrophe to the end.

The **third** rule is that EVERY OTHER KIND OF NOUN forms its possessive with an apostrophe AND an "s." That's right: except for pronouns, and for plural nouns ending in "-s," every noun on the SAT forms its possessive with an apostrophe and an "s."

Here are a few examples of words that get an apostrophe and an "s" on the SAT to show possession. Note that some of these possessive forms differ from modern usage (including the things your teachers might write):

This ball belongs to my dog. It is my <u>dog's</u> ball.

The game belongs to the children. It is the <u>children's</u> game.

The abacus has wooden beads. They are the <u>abacus's</u> wooden beads.

The geese live on a pond. It is the <u>geese's</u> pond.

So let's do a quick review of the three possessive rules you need to know for the SAT:

1. Possessive pronouns like "your," "their," "whose," and "its" NEVER include apostrophes.
2. The possessive form of a plural noun ending in "-s" is formed by adding an apostrophe and nothing else.
3. The possessive form of EVERY OTHER KIND OF NOUN is formed by adding an apostrophe and an "s," no matter what letter or sound the base noun ends in.

Once you learn these rules and see them in action on some real SAT practice questions, they'll become second nature.

---

[1] One more bonus mistake: People sometimes confuse the word "there," which indicates a place, with the possessive pronoun "their," which indicates that something belongs to a group of people. In this case, the easiest thing to remember is probably that the word "there" has a spelling similar to the spellings of "here" and "where," and all of those words are related to physical positions.

So, one more time, just to be clear:

The word "their" is a possessive pronoun that indicates ownership: "They invited me to <u>their</u> house."

The word "they're" is always interchangeable with the phrase "they are": "They said <u>they're</u> going to decide tomorrow."

The word "there" has a similar spelling to "here" and "where," and indicates position: "The car isn't here; it's over <u>there</u>."

For a real-life example of a question involving possessives, take a look at question 21 from section 1, module 1 of SAT Practice Test #1. The relevant text says:

> … it is misleading to say that Watson and Crick discovered the double helix. (blank) findings were based on…

We need to choose from among "they're," "it's," "their," and "its" for the correct text in the underlined portion. When we look at the context, we see that the "findings" belong to "Watson and Crick." Since we're talking about the idea of "Watson and Crick" possessing something ("findings"), and since "Watson and Crick" is plural, we know that we need a plural possessive pronoun here. The only choice with a plural possessive pronoun is (C), "their," which is the correct answer. (For a more detailed discussion of that question, please take a look at its walkthrough on page 112 in this book.)

Singular vs plural

One of the broadest and most common issues that comes up in SAT Writing questions is choosing whether the singular or plural form of a noun, pronoun, or verb is appropriate. This can come up in a lot of ways, and you should learn to keep a sharp eye out for all of them.

This idea of the difference between singular and plural forms has already come up in this Toolbox in other situations, and we'll see more of it in the walkthroughs later in this Black Book—it's just such a common issue that I wanted to call it to your attention here. Always remember to be on the lookout for issues related to the difference between singular and plural forms of words, especially in the context of verbs and pronouns.

Conjunctions

Conjunctions are words that link ideas to each other, like the following:

- and
- yet
- or
- because
- but
- either
- nor
- neither

On the SAT Writing section, two or more ideas that are linked by a conjunction must appear in the same form. (This is one example of something called "parallelism," which we'll discuss later in "Special Technique: Considering Parallelism When Answering Writing Questions" on page 93.)

So the following sentence would be ACCEPTABLE in an SAT Writing question:

> Samantha likes singing, dancing, and acting.

In the above sentence, the words "singing," "dancing," and "acting" are connected by the conjunction "and," and they're all in the same form (the "-ing" form), so this would be an acceptable sentence in an SAT Writing question.

But the following sentence would be UNACCEPTABLE in an SAT Writing question:

> *Samantha likes singing, dancing, and to act.

In the above sentence, the phrases "singing," "dancing," and "to act" are all connected with the conjunction "and," but they're not all in the same form (one is in the "to" form, and two are in the "-ing" form), so this wouldn't be an acceptable sentence in an SAT Writing question.

Phrases

A phrase is a group of words that serves a particular function in a sentence; it usually functions like a part of speech.

A phrase can include one or more words.

Phrases are referred to by the functions they fulfill within their sentences. There are "noun phrases," "verb phrases," "prepositional phrases," "adverbial phrases," et cetera. Let's identify some of the phrases in the following sentence:

> The cat who lives next door likes my pineapple plant.

In the above sentence,

- "The cat" is a noun phrase.
- "lives next door" is a verb phrase.
- "the cat who lives next door" is a noun phrase that includes the noun phrase "the cat" and the verb phrase "lives next door."
- "likes my pineapple plant" is a verb phrase
- "my pineapple plant" is a noun phrase.

There are other phrases that could be said to exist in this sentence, but you get the idea.

Don't worry if this idea doesn't make a lot of sense right now! The SAT doesn't directly test your knowledge of phrases, or your ability to pull phrases out of a sentence. We're only covering this idea so that when I say, "the noun phrase such-and-such" in this toolbox and in the walkthroughs later in this book, you'll have some idea what I'm talking about.

Clauses

A clause is a group of words that includes a subject noun phrase, a verb phrase, and, if necessary, an object noun phrase. This is an example of a clause:

> This pizza recipe requires cheese.

In the clause above,

- "This pizza recipe" is the subject noun phrase.
- "requires" is the verb phrase.
- "cheese" is the object noun phrase.

Independent clauses

An independent clause can stand on its own as a complete sentence—in fact, the term "independent clause" means it can exist *independently* as a sentence, without "depending" on another clause. Here's an example of an independent clause:

> I collect wombats.

In the independent clause above, which CAN stand alone as a sentence,

- "I" is a noun phrase.
- "collect" is a verb phrase.
- There's no conjunction at the beginning of the sentence.
- The clause also includes the object noun phrase "wombats," but clauses in general don't require object phrases.

The following is really important, so I'm going to set it off with some fancy formatting to make it stand out:

Every grammatically acceptable sentence in an SAT Writing question must contain an independent clause.

Sometimes the sentence is just the independent clause on its own, and sometimes other things are added to the independent clause. A lot of SAT Writing questions involve the idea of combining multiple clauses in a sentence, and knowing which punctuation marks and/or words must separate those clauses, and which ones can't separate those clauses. Don't worry—the number of situations that can appear on test day are limited, and we'll learn them here in the toolbox and then get comfortable with them in the walkthroughs starting on page 96.

When two independent clauses appear right in a row, there are three different ways we can separate them.

Separating independent clauses with a period

One way to separate two consecutive independent clauses is with a period.

> I collect wombats. They're so fuzzy.

The two independent clauses above ("I collect wombats" and "they're so fuzzy") are separated with a period, which makes them two separate sentences. This is acceptable on the SAT.

Separating independent clauses with a semi-colon

Another way to separate two consecutive independent clauses is with a semi-colon.

> I collect wombats; they're so fuzzy.

The two independent clauses above are separated with a semi-colon, which makes them one sentence with two independent clauses. This is also acceptable on the SAT.

In SAT Writing questions, anywhere a period could be used to separate two sentences, a semi-colon is also acceptable, and vice-versa. The College Board considers semi-colons to be exactly like periods in the context of separating two sentences. Because of this, you will never have to choose between a period and a semi-colon to separate two sentences. This idea comes up a lot in SAT Writing questions, so make you sure you feel comfortable with it!

(In SAT Writing questions, the only other usage for semi-colons is to separate items in a complex list; this usage comes up less frequently, and we'll discuss it on page 86 in the section of this toolbox dedicated to semi-colons.)

Separating independent clauses with a colon

Another way to separate two consecutive independent clauses is with a colon, but this situation is slightly different, and doesn't come up as frequently.

| I collect wombats: I gather wombats from all walks of life, keeping them in a fully-functioning wombat town. |

The two independent clauses above are separated with a colon, which makes them one sentence with two independent clauses. This is also acceptable on the SAT, as long as the second independent clause somehow illustrates the idea in the first independent clause, or provides additional information or examples related to the idea in that first independent clause.

The College Board won't make you choose between separating two independent clauses with a period, semi-colon, or colon, but they might require you to choose between a colon and other alternative punctuation marks in a situation like the one just described. If an acceptable sentence containing an independent clause appears before the colon, and if the text after the colon illustrates or provides additional examples or information related to the independent clause that appears before the colon, then a colon will be acceptable.

(Note that, unlike a period or semi-colon in the uses described above, what appears after a colon doesn't *have* to contain an independent clause and be able to stand on its own as a sentence. Instead, a colon can still be used when what appears before the colon can stand on its own as a sentence, and what appears after the colon illustrates or provides further information or examples of what appears before the colon, *whether that text after the colon can stand on its own as a sentence or not.* We'll discuss this further in the section of this toolbox dedicated to colons on page 85.)

Let's make a little table summing up the ideas we just discussed:

Using Different Punctuation Marks To Separate Independent Clauses	
Period	This contains an independent clause and could be a sentence on its own. This also contains an independent clause and could be a sentence on its own.
Semicolon	This contains an independent clause and could be a sentence on its own; this also contains an independent clause and could be a sentence on its own.
Colon	This contains an independent clause, could be a sentence on its own, and sets up an illustration or example: this independent clause that could stand on its own is that illustration or example. -or- This contains an independent clause, could be a sentence on its own, and sets something up: this illustration or example that doesn't need to include an independent clause.

Separating independent clauses with a comma and a conjunction

We just discussed how it's acceptable in SAT Writing questions to separate two groups of words that both contain an independent clause—and can both stand on their own as sentences—with a period, a semi-colon, or a colon. It's NOT acceptable to use a comma to separate them, or to omit punctuation between them completely in this scenario.

When we have two consecutive groups of words that can both stand on their own as sentences and we put a comma between them, the result is called a "comma splice," and it's unacceptable on the SAT. You don't have to know the term "comma splice" as long as you know that we can't separate two groups of words that could each be sentences on their own with just a comma.

| *You sneezed on my sandwich, I hate when you do that. |

The above is a comma splice, because what appears before the comma can stand on its own as a sentence, and what appears after the comma can stand on its own as a sentence.

When we have two consecutive groups of words that can both stand on their own as sentences and we put no punctuation between them, the result is called a "run-on sentence," and it's unacceptable on the SAT. You don't have to know the term "run-on sentence" as long as you know that we can't just have two consecutive groups of words that could be sentences on their own with no punctuation appearing between them.

| *You sneezed on my sandwich I hate when you do that. |

The above is a run-on sentence, because it's two groups of words that can each stand on their own as sentences with no punctuation between them.

It IS okay to use a comma along with certain conjunctions in this situation. The conjunctions you'll most commonly see in this situation in an SAT Writing question are "and" and "but," but several other conjunctions may appear as well. We can use the word "FANBOYS" to remember them: For, And, Nor, But, Or, Yet, and So.

Go ahead and memorize those seven conjunctions if you feel like it, but the relevant conjunction in an SAT Writing question will almost always be "and" or "but."

> They wanted to go downtown, but the poodle wouldn't hear of it.

> We like to party, and we also like to invest in mutual funds.

Each sentence above contains two independent clauses. In each example, the independent clauses are underlined, and they are joined with a comma and a conjunction ("but" in the first sentence, and "and" in the second sentence). The following examples are UNACCEPTABLE in an SAT Writing question.

> *They wanted to go downtown but the poodle wouldn't hear of it.

> *We like to party, we also like to invest in mutual funds.

The first example uses the conjunction "but," but no comma appears before that conjunction. The second example uses a comma, but no conjunction appears after that comma (that second example is a comma splice, as mentioned above). If we use a comma and a conjunction to connect two independent clauses, both the comma and the conjunction must appear .

Dependent clauses

Above, we discussed independent clauses, which can stand on their own as sentences. A **dependent** clause is like an independent clause—it contains a noun phrase and a verb phrase—but the difference between them in SAT Writing questions is that a dependent clause can't stand on its own as a sentence, because it begins with a word like one of those listed here:

- after
- although
- as
- because
- before
- even if
- even though

- if
- in order that
- once
- provided that
- rather than
- since
- so

- so that
- than
- that
- though
- unless
- until
- where/wherever

- whether
- which/whichever
- while
- who/whom/whose
- whoever/whomever/whosever
- why

Most of the words and phrases in this list are **conjunctions** or **relative pronouns,** but you won't need to know those terms on test day, because the SAT Writing section doesn't require us to know the names of grammatical concepts. (You may remember that we called the words from that "FANBOYS" acronym "conjunctions" as well; those were "coordinating conjunction," while these are "subordinating conjunctions." You don't need to know those terms, but I'll make the distinction here in case you were wondering why we have two different lists that include something called "conjunctions.")

Again, you don't need to memorize these terms; just be aware that we might refer to a "conjunction" or a "relative pronoun" in the walkthroughs later in this book when we discuss real practice SAT questions, and that all you need to know is that those kinds of words often appear at the beginning of dependent clauses.

(Note that you don't need to memorize the above list; instead, you can just read through it a couple of times. After you start to work with real practice SAT Writing questions and read through the walkthroughs in this Black Book, you'll get comfortable with spotting dependent clauses.)

A dependent clause CANNOT stand on its own as a complete sentence, as we see in the following example:

> while now I only eat mushrooms from Japan

In the dependent clause above, which CANNOT stand alone as a sentence,

- "I" is a noun phrase.

- "Only eat" is a verb phrase.

- "While" is a conjunction.

- "Mushrooms from Japan" is another noun phrase, serving as the object of the verb "eat," but clauses don't have to include object nouns.

As mentioned above, a dependent clause can't stand on its own as a sentence—it has to be added to a sentence that includes an independent clause. There are basically two ways that can happen: the dependent clause can appear *before* the independent clause, or it can appear *after* the independent clause, and there's one important difference to keep in mind based on this distinction.

When the dependent clause appears *before* the independent clause, we separate the clauses with a comma:

> Because you keep honking at people, we have to leave town forever.

In the example above, "because you keep honking at people" is a dependent clause—a clause that *can't* stand on its own as a sentence—and it appears before the independent clause "we have to leave town forever." That means a comma *must* appear between them. When the dependent clause appears *after* the independent clause, no comma appears between them :

> We have to leave town forever because you keep honking at people.

In the example above, we've switched the order of the independent and dependent clauses from the previous example. Now the dependent clause appears *after* the independent clause, so we have to omit the comma.

The exception to this situation in SAT Writing questions is when the dependent clause begins with a form of "which" or "who." In that case, we include the comma:

> The explosion was caused by my great-aunt, who was making gravy.

In this example sentence, the dependent clause "who was making gravy" that appears after the independent clause "the explosion was caused by my great-aunt" begins with "who," so we separate that dependent clause from the independent clause with a comma.

Infinitive clauses

An infinitive clause begins with the infinitive form of a verb, like "to understand" or "to flip." Such a clause indicates some kind of purpose or intention, and it can appear before or after an independent clause. These are a kind of dependent clause, and we treat them just like the dependent clauses in the examples above—when they appear *before* an independent clause, we use a comma between the clauses, and when they appear *after* an independent clause, no comma is used between the clauses.

> I go on a run every morning to ensure that I'll feel sweaty the rest of the day.

In the sentence above, the infinitive clause "to ensure that I'll feel sweaty the rest of the day" expresses the purpose of the action in the independent clause "I go on a run every morning." The infinitive clause appears *after* the independent clause, so there's no comma between the clauses.

When the infinitive clause appears *before* an independent clause in an SAT Writing question, it must be separated from that clause with a comma:

> To guarantee the best possible results, she hid a lobster in the dashboard.

In the sentence above, the infinitive clause "to guarantee the best possible results" expresses the purpose of the action in the independent clause "she hid a lobster in the dashboard." Because that infinitive clause appeared before the independent clause, it needed to be separated from that independent clause with a comma.

Sentence fragments

For the purposes of the SAT Writing section, any group of words that doesn't include an independent clause is a **sentence fragment**. The SAT will never require you to know the phrase "sentence fragment" in order to answer a question correctly, but you *will* be required to avoid answer choices that would result in sentence fragments. Here are some examples of sentence fragments:

> *The very best time for some hot chocolate and a nap.

> *Although we were never able to agree about the best way to fry and eat an entire package of candy bars.

The first example above is a sentence fragment because it doesn't include a verb phrase. The second example above is a sentence fragment because it's a clause that starts with "although" (which makes it a dependent clause), and it doesn't also include an independent clause.

Colons, semicolons, and commas

You'll see several questions on test day that involve the proper use of colons, semicolons, and commas. The rules for using colons and semicolons in SAT Writing questions are fairly straightforward, so we'll cover them first. Commas, on the other hand, are used in a wider variety of ways on the test, and proper comma usage on the SAT differs from the usage that's allowed by most teachers. Since it will take us a little more time and effort to explore commas, we'll do that after we get colons and semicolons out of the way.

Colons in SAT Writing questions

A colon is used after an independent clause to introduce text that illustrates the idea in the independent clause using one or more examples, or that provides further explanation or illustration of the idea in the independent clause. Everything that appears in a sentence leading up to a colon must be able to stand on its own as a complete sentence. Everything that appears *after* the colon can either stand on its own as a sentence, or not; either possibility can be fine as long as what appears after the colon illustrates the idea that appears before the colon.

The following examples show ACCEPTABLE colon usage on the SAT because, in each case, the part of the sentence leading up to the colon could stand on its own as a complete sentence, and what comes after the colon is an example or further explanation related to the idea mentioned before the colon:

> I brought two of my favorite books on the train: *Anna Karenina* and *The Little Engine That Could.*

> Sarah hadn't really liked dogs before she met Mr. Scruffles: when she was in kindergarten, a neighbor's Cocker Spaniel tricked her out of a turkey sandwich, and she never got over it.

Semicolons in SAT Writing questions

A semicolon on the SAT has two acceptable uses. The first one is **joining two independent clauses** ; in other words, a semicolon can be used on the SAT anywhere a period is used between two complete sentences. This was discussed on page 82, but we'll revisit it here, because it comes up a lot in SAT Writing questions.

This usage results in a sentence that includes two groups of words that could each be sentences on their own, as in the following example:

> Some days are colder than others; I've always preferred days when it snows.

The example above is ACCEPTABLE on the SAT because a semi-colon is used to separate the independent clause "some days are colder than others" from the independent clause "I've always preferred days when it snows." It would also be correct to write the above this way:

> Some days are colder than others. I've always preferred days when it snows.

(When two groups of words that can each stand on their own as complete sentences appear next to each other, the SAT won't ask you to choose between a semi-colon and a period to go between them, because either choice would be correct.)

On the SAT Writing section, we can't use a semicolon to join an independent clause to a dependent clause, nor to join two dependent clauses to each other (for more on clauses, see page 82).

The second acceptable use of a semi-colon on the SAT is **separating items in a complex list of three or more things** . When an ordinary list of three or more items appears on the SAT, we can separate those items with commas. A complex list is one where at least one of the items on the list is a phrase that *already* includes a comma. When that happens, we can't separate the items from each other with commas as well, because it won't be clear whether any given comma separates one list item from another, or whether that comma is just part of a phrase that's an item on the list. So we need to separate the items from each other with a semi-colon, to avoid confusion, like this:

> My favorite foods are sushi, which I first tried in 2009; pizza, which I first tried in 2012; and spaetzle, which I first tried in 2020.

In the example above, the three things on the list are:

- "sushi, which I first tried in 2009"
- "pizza, which I first tried in 2012"
- "spaetzle, which I first tried in 2020"

Because each item contains a comma, we have to separate them from each other with semi-colons, not commas.

Commas in SAT Writing questions

Commas can appear in a variety of ways on test day. We should approach questions that involve comma placement with the attitude that it's correct to *omit* commas unless we have a specific, concrete reason to use one. In other words, if a phrase would be acceptable without a particular comma, then the College Board wants us to leave out that comma.

It's also very important that you read the walkthroughs at the end of this training section so you can see what these comma placement questions are actually like.

The acceptable comma usage that we need to be aware of in SAT Writing questions falls into the following main categories:

1. commas used to divide items in a list of three or more things (including the so-called "Oxford comma," which we'll discuss in a moment)

2. commas with quotations or speech

3. commas between clauses

4. "comma sandwiches," which show that the sandwiched phrase could be removed from a sentence without creating any grammatical issues or changing the meaning of the rest of the sentence

We'll discuss each of these uses in more detail now.

Commas in a list of three or more things

On the SAT, if we have a list of three or more items, then a comma is placed after each item, and the word "and" appears before the last item in the list. For example, the following sentence is ACCEPTABLE in an SAT Writing question:

> Thomasina had always liked falcons, ravens, eagles, and cardinals.

But the following sentence would be UNACCEPTABLE in an SAT Writing question, because it omits the comma before the word "and:"

> *Thomasina had always liked falcons, ravens, eagles and cardinals.

(You may have heard someone call the comma that appears before the word "and" in these kinds of lists the "Oxford comma." If you've never heard that term, don't worry about it—you don't need to know it on the SAT. I only mention it because it has become fashionable in the last few years to omit the Oxford comma in some types of writing. It's important to remember that the College Board REQUIRES the Oxford comma in SAT Writing questions, even if your teachers might prefer you to avoid it in school.)

Also note that the College Board doesn't want us to use both a comma and the word "and" if we're only dealing with a list of two items. In other words, if a list only includes two things, then we should join those two things with the word "and;" there should NOT be a comma before or after the "and" in that case.

> The robot in my dreams ate nuts and bolts.

In the list of two things above ("nuts and bolts"), we separated the two things on the list with the word "and" and nothing else.

Commas with quotations or statements

If a reported statement from a person or publication is enclosed in quotation marks and introduced by a word like "said," "commented," or "remarked," **and that reported statement can stand on its own as a sentence,** then a comma must be inserted before the space that comes before the opening quotation mark:

> The master said, "A gentleman knows neither sorrow nor fear."

But if the reported statement enclosed in quotation marks **can't stand on its own as a sentence,** then no comma appears:

> A gentleman is someone who the master says "knows neither sorrow nor fear."

Also, if a reported statement is preceded by a phrase like "said that" or "reported that," then no comma appears:

> The master said that "a gentleman knows neither sorrow nor fear."

Lastly, if a quotation appears in the middle of a sentence without ending punctuation of its own, then a comma appears before the closing quotation mark:

> My coach used to say, "defense wins championships," but he also said, "the best defense is a good offense," so I never really understood what he meant.

Commas between clauses

How commas should appear between clauses is discussed in the section of this toolbox on clauses, which can be found on page 82.

"Comma sandwiches"

"Comma sandwich" isn't a technical grammatical term. It's something I made up to help test-takers remember a useful concept. As the name implies, a "comma sandwich" is a phrase "sandwiched" between two commas (or between a comma and a period, if the end of the comma sandwich is also the end of the sentence). This particular type of phrase isn't a clause or a part of a list. Instead, it's a descriptive phrase that provides additional information about something in a sentence.

When a comma sandwich is used properly in an SAT Writing question, the entire sandwiched phrase can be removed, leaving behind a complete sentence, and without changing the meaning of the rest of the sentence.

Let's look at a couple of examples of this so you can actually see what I'm talking about. In these examples, I'll underline the "comma sandwich":

> The man next door, <u>who told us we could borrow his lawn mower,</u> was always very helpful.

In the above sentence, removing the comma sandwich gives us this:

> The man next door was always very helpful.

Here's another example. Imagine we start with this sentence:

> The orange shirt, <u>a favorite of mine,</u> isn't clean right now.

Removing the comma sandwich gives us this:

> The orange shirt isn't clean right now.

In each case, we see that, when the commas and the phrase between them are removed, what's left is still a complete sentence.

SAT Writing questions don't frequently test us on comma sandwiches directly, but being aware of these phrases can help us analyze sentences in the provided text and then identify the answer choice that follows the relevant standards for that question. We'll see this idea at work in the walkthroughs starting on page 96.

No comma sandwich when a profession is indicated immediately before a name

We'll sometimes find that a passage mentions a person's occupation immediately before the person's name, instead of after the person's name with the help of a phrase like "who is a." When the profession is mentioned immediately before the name, the SAT doesn't allow us to use a comma sandwich. So, for example, this sentence would be ACCEPTABLE in an SAT Writing question:

> We read about famous astronaut Buzz Aldrin in class.

When the profession is mentioned immediately after the name, a comma sandwich is needed:

> Buzz Aldrin, a famous astronaut, was the subject of an article we read.

(By the way, the comma sandwich above is an example of an "appositive." An **appositive** is a descriptive phrase that can't stand on its own, inserted after the phrase it's describing, usually in some kind of comma sandwich. You don't need to know the word "appositive" on test day, but you might run into it when reading an explanation for a test item. If you do, you can basically just remember that an appositive is a kind of comma sandwich.)

The same rule applies in other situations where two noun phrases appear in order, and the second noun phrase is an example of the first noun phrase. We can see a real-life example of this in question 27 from section 1, module 2, of SAT Practice Test #3. That question contains the phrase "chemical compound aluminum oxide." No comma appears between these phrases, because "aluminum oxide" is an example of a "chemical compound," just like "Buzz Aldrin" is an example of a "famous astronaut" in the example above. For a complete discussion of this question, see its walkthrough on page 204.

Comma sandwiches at the beginning or end of a sentence

If a sandwiched phrase appears at the very beginning of a sentence, then the initial comma is omitted, because we can't start a sentence with a comma.

> <u>Unlike most people</u>, I had never seen a car made of teeth.

The underlined comma sandwich above "unlike most people" has no comma at the beginning, because it appears at the beginning of the sentence.

Similarly, if a sandwiched phrase appears at the very end of a sentence, then the final comma is omitted, because we can't include a comma immediately next to a period, exclamation point, or question mark.

> I had never seen a car made of teeth, <u>unlike most people</u>.

When we move the comma sandwich from the previous example to the end of the sentence, the last comma doesn't appear, and instead the comma sandwich ends with the period.

Descriptive noun phrases

Sometimes, the provided text for an SAT Writing question will include a comma-separated noun phrase that describes another noun in an independent or dependent clause, but that isn't an independent or dependent clause itself. When this happens, that descriptive noun phrase should appear in a comma sandwich—that is, set off from the rest of the sentence with commas.

> My most prized possession is a t-shirt from 1997, <u>a relic of a forgotten age</u>.

In the example above, the underlined descriptive noun phrase "<u>a relic of a forgotten age</u>" describes the "t-shirt from 1997," and it's separated from that phrase by a comma. The following would be UNACCEPTABLE on the SAT:

> *My most prized possession is a t-shirt from 1997 <u>a relic of a forgotten age</u>.

Sometimes answer choices in an SAT Writing question will result in a noun phrase without these commas, which just seems to be floating there randomly in the sentence, with no clear connection to anything—but the right answer will put commas around that phrase, and it will be clear what that phrase refers to.

We can see an example of this idea in question 25 from section 1, module 1 of SAT Practice Test #2. The blank in that question coincides with the end of a quotation, immediately followed by the noun phrase "an apt assessment." The correct answer inserts a comma at the end of the quotation, which is immediately followed by the phrase "an apt assessment" to show that the author is calling the quotation "an apt assessment" of something. For a complete discussion of this question, see its walkthrough on page 151.

Other "punctuation sandwiches"

You may see the "comma sandwich" concept on the test with dashes or parentheses around the sandwiched phrase, instead of commas. These other "punctuation sandwiches" function just like "comma sandwiches" on the SAT.

> The most important thing to remember about rhinoceroses (other than their complicated ideas about narrative structure) is never to borrow money from them.

> I ran down that street—the street I grew up on—and I never looked back.

No commas after conjunction expressions (unless a comma sandwich is involved)

Some people will be tempted to use commas by default after conjunction phrases, especially "and," "unless," and "such as." But we're not allowed to use commas after these expressions on the SAT (unless the comma is part of a comma sandwich), so the following sentences would be UNACCEPTABLE in an SAT Writing question, for example:

> *The Senator picked up the phone <u>and,</u> ordered a sandwich.

> *<u>Unless,</u> this time will be different, I don't think playing canasta is a good idea.

> *Jerry has always had a problem with dogs, <u>such as,</u> Pomeranians and Malamutes.

Instead, these versions would be ACCEPTABLE on the SAT:

> The Senator picked up the phone and ordered a sandwich.

> Unless this time will be different, I don't think playing canasta is a good idea.

> Jerry has always had a problem with dogs, such as Pomeranians and Malamutes.

It's possible to insert a comma sandwich immediately after a conjunction expression—in that case, the comma appears there because of the comma sandwich, and not because of the conjunction:

> The Senator picked up the phone and, with tears in his eyes, ordered a sandwich.

No commas randomly inserted into phrases

Sometimes an SAT Writing question will include an answer choice that inserts a comma between a subject and its verb, like this:

> *The big dog, runs after the pickup truck.

In the example above, "the big dog" is the subject of the sentence, "runs" is the verb that describes the action done by "the big dog," and there's no reason to insert a comma between them.

Or an answer choice will insert a comma into the middle of a prepositional phrase, like this:

> *They fell into the trench in the middle of, the night.

In the example above, "of the night" is a prepositional phrase, and there's no reason for a comma to appear in that phrase.

Basically, the College Board wants you to look at a sentence like one of the two we just considered and have to ask yourself, "is there some reason a comma should be here?" And then you try to think about all the different rules related to commas, and then maybe you hesitate to remove this one in case there's some special case you're forgetting.

But if an answer choice involves sticking a comma randomly into the middle of a phrase, and you can't think of any reason that it should be there based on your knowledge of the SAT Writing Toolbox, then don't be shy about picking an answer choice that gets rid of that comma—as long as that answer choice follows all the relevant standards we discuss in this training, of course.

Dashes

A dash is a punctuation mark that looks like an elongated hyphen (—). In SAT Writing questions, dashes can be used in two scenarios:

1. to create a punctuation sandwich as described on page 88

2. to function as a colon would, by appearing after a group of words that could be a sentence on its own, and before an example or explanation of the concept expressed before the dash (see page 85 for a description of the proper usage of colons on the SAT)

Question marks

Occasionally, an SAT Writing question will include the option to end a sentence with a question mark.

Many native English speakers can kind of tell when a sentence is a question, and should end with a question mark, so please don't overthink this if it's not something you're having trouble with. But for the sake of training, we'll spell out when a question mark is appropriate in an SAT Writing question.

Generally speaking, SAT Writing questions on the SAT that involve the possibility of including a question mark will feature a two-word verb phrase—that is, a verb phrase with a helping verb and a main verb, like these:

> are running
>
> could think
>
> have driven

In a declarative sentence (that is, a sentence that isn't a question), we place the subject of the verb before the two-word verb phrase, like this:

> We are running.
>
> Jenna could think.
>
> They have driven.

In a question, we'll see the subject placed *after* the helping verb, *between* the two verb forms, like this:

> Are we running?
>
> Could Jenna think?
>
> Have they driven?

When we see word order like this on the SAT, and we have the option to end the sentence with a question mark, we know a question mark is appropriate.

(Note that this isn't the only way to ask a question in real life, but this is how this issue appears in SAT Writing questions.)

Avoid dangling participles

A participle is a special verb form. On the SAT, the participles we need to worry about are the ones that end in "-ing," like "jumping" or "contemplating," or "-ed," like "decided" or "celebrated." A phrase that begins with a participle can be called a "participial phrase." They're often—but not always—used at the beginning of a sentence. In either case, these phrases need to be separated from the phrase they modify by a comma.

When these participial phrases are used on the SAT, they are always understood to refer to the first noun phrase in the independent clause in the sentence. Consider this example, where the participial phrase is underlined and the noun phrase it describes is in bold:

> <u>Screaming for help,</u> **the mailman** ran away from the angry dog.

In the sentence above,

- "screaming" is a participle
- "screaming for help" is the participial phrase (beginning with the participle "screaming," an "-ing" word)
- "the mailman ran away from the angry dog" is the independent clause (remember that an independent clause has a subject noun phrase and main verb phrase, and can stand on its own as a sentence)

We know this participle was used correctly because the word "screaming" describes the word "mailman" (the first noun phrase in the independent clause) which is what makes sense in context. The following sentence, on the other hand, would be completely UNACCEPTABLE on the SAT:

> *<u>Screaming for help,</u> **the** dog chased the mailman down the street.

What's wrong with the above sentence? We still have a participial phrase ("screaming for help") and an independent clause ("the dog chased the mailman down the street"), but the problem is that the participle in this sentence can't describe the first noun phrase in the independent clause, which is "the dog." This sentence is no good because the dog can't scream. Only the mailman can scream.

As mentioned above, such a phrase can also begin with a verb form ending in "-ed":

<u>Blocked by the enormous radish,</u> **the hamster** accepted his fate.

In the example above, the participial phrase "blocked by the enormous radish" describes the first noun phrase in the sentence's independent clause, which is "the hamster."

This kind of participial phrase can also appear at the end of a sentence (again, the participial phrase is underlined, and the noun phrase it describes is in bold):

Edward Glarpington is a terrible physicist, <u>insisting that all matter is made up of tiny stuffed bears.</u>

Occasionally, a participial phrase like this will be preceded by a preposition, like "despite":

<u>Despite being in a state of hypnosis,</u> **Gerard** flipped the omelet pretty well.

Whether the participial phrase appears at the beginning or the end of the sentence, and whether it starts with another word or not, it still must describe the first noun phrase in the independent clause of the sentence where it appears. If that first noun phrase in the independent clause can't logically be described by the participial phrase, that sentence is unacceptable on the SAT.

When phrases like this are used incorrectly, the result is called a "dangling participle," because the phrase with the participle is just kind of hanging there with no clear connection to the text. You don't need to know the term "dangling participle" on test day, just like you don't need to know any other technical grammatical term on test day—you just have to be able to identify and avoid this kind of error.

Conclusion

That concludes the grammar and punctuation issues you'll need to know for SAT Writing questions. If you've only read them through once, I strongly recommend again that you go back through and read them one more time—the concepts will probably feel much more comfortable and familiar after that.

Next we'll discuss a couple of topics we should keep in mind so that we can answer SAT Writing questions correctly and consistently.

The Intervening Phrase

Answering SAT Writing questions pretty much always comes down to being able to keep track of the relationships among the different words and phrases in the provided text, and making sure you pick the choice that uses the correct forms of the relevant words, in the correct order, with the correct punctuation. As we've already discussed, the concepts that the College Board tests must be predictable and standardized, and we can know ahead of time what the College Board will consider to be "correct" by getting comfortable with all of the concepts in the SAT Writing Toolbox on page 76.

One way that the College Board tries to make this more challenging is by inserting phrases between words that need to agree with each other—like a subject and its verb—so that untrained test-takers will lose track of which relationships exist between which words in the sentence. The result might be that a test-taker forgets some piece of information that's vital for picking the right answer, like one of the following:

- which word in the sentence a verb is supposed to agree with

- which noun a pronoun refers to

- what tense a verb should be in

- whether a clause is dependent or independent

- whether a sentence contains an independent clause

We call these "intervening phrases" because they tend to appear between words that would otherwise be right next to each other, which would make their relationship to each other much clearer; but when the intervening phrase appears between them, their relationship can be much less obvious.

We can see a real-life example of this issue in question 26 from section 1, module 1 of SAT Practice Test #1, which includes this text:

> … landing on one of the good spaces (blank) a player…

The answer choices are all different forms of the verb "to allow." An untrained test-taker might just notice the plural noun "spaces" right before the blank, and decide that the correct answer should be a plural verb form to match the plural noun "spaces." But if we read from the beginning of the sentence and check to see which noun is actually doing the action "allow," we notice that the intervening phrase "on one of the good spaces" appears between the verb form in the blank and its actual subject. When we mentally remove that phrase, it becomes much easier to identify the actual subject of the verb, which is the word "landing."

"Landing" is singular, so the correct answer must be a singular verb form—and it turns out that only one verb form in the answer choices is singular, and that's the correct answer, "allows." For a full discussion of that question, see its walkthrough on page 114 of this Black Book.

The College Board loves to include these phrases, and sometimes uses them to create unreasonably long sentences in the hopes that you'll kind of get lost in all that text, and lose track of what needs to agree with what. But if we take the time to read the entire sentence carefully, and to watch out for these phrases, then we can always figure out which words and phrases are relevant to the blank, and which answer choice creates the relationships among those words and phrases that adhere to the rules and standards we discussed in the SAT Writing toolbox.

Special Technique: Considering Parallelism When Answering Writing Questions

The term "parallelism" means different things to different people in the context of standardized test prep. For our purposes, it just refers to the idea that sometimes, when we're trying to figure out the proper form of a given word, or the proper punctuation in a certain situation, it can be helpful to check the surrounding text to see if that text already contains a word or phrase that's playing the same role as the word or phrase in the blank. If it is, then the form of that word or phrase that already appears in the provided text can tell us the form that the text in the blank should take.

That might sound confusing, so let's look at an example.

Question 25 from section 1, module 2 of SAT Practice Test #1 includes the following text:

> The lock would increase the salinity of the lakes and (blank) a natural barrier of water...

Our options for the blank are the following:

- creates
- create
- creating
- created

At first, just from looking at this sentence, we might have trouble deciding which choice is correct. If the subject of the verb is the singular noun "lock," then it might seem like the singular verb form "creates" is correct.

But if we look at the rest of the sentence, we can see that it already includes a phrase that tells us something the lock does: "would increase." From there, we can tell that the sentence describes two things the lock "would" do: "increase the salinity of the lakes" and "(blank) a natural barrier of water." Once we notice this form of the verb "increase," we can recognize that the verb "to create" needs to be in the same form as "increase," because the word in the blank tells us another thing that the lock "would" do." With this in mind, we know that the right answer is "create," to match the form of the other verb, "increase," since that's the other thing in the text that the lock "would" do.

For a full discussion of this question, see its walkthrough later in this book on page 133.

Unfortunately, it's not possible to use this technique on every single question, simply because the SAT doesn't structure its texts in a way that makes that possible. Depending on the context, though, we might use this technique to determine the appropriate form of a verb, as we just discussed, or even the right punctuation for a phrase, as long as something in the surrounding text is similar, and there's an answer choice to match it.

I'm not recommending that you double-check every sentence in every passage for these kinds of parallel structures—that would take up a lot of time, for one thing, and parallelism doesn't come up that frequently. Instead, keep this parallelism idea in mind for situations where you're having a hard time coming with a clear reason to pick an answer—you might be able to find a clue in the surrounding text that helps you identify the right answer with certainty.

The General Process for Answering SAT Writing Questions

Now that we've learned all the relevant rules and standards for SAT Writing questions, let's take a look at the general process I recommend for answering this type of question.

1. Read the provided text.

Read the text to get an initial idea of the concepts that might be relevant to the blank. Don't worry too much about noticing every little detail, and don't try to memorize the text—we're going to take another look at it once we've read the prompt and answer choices.

2. Carefully read the prompt and answer choices. Consider doing a vertical scan to make sure you note the similarities and differences among the answer choices.

Read the prompt. It's true that every SAT Writing question has the same prompt, but reading the prompt only takes a second, and these questions will appear right before and right after SAT Reading questions—so taking a moment to read the prompt is a good chance to verify that you are, in fact, looking at an SAT Writing question, and it reinforces the habit of reading all the relevant text for every question, which is an important part of noticing details and avoiding mistakes on the whole SAT.

Next, carefully read the answer choices. Consider doing a vertical scan to get an even stronger idea of the possibilities being presented in the answer choices, and the mistakes the College Board thinks an untrained test-taker is likely to make. (See "The Vertical Scan: A Key Tactic for Trained Test-Takers" on page 45 of this Black Book for more on this kind of analysis, as well as the SAT Reading and Writing walkthroughs starting on page 96 for examples of this technique in action.)

3. Look for any of the relevant issues we discussed in the SAT Writing Toolbox.

Look at the words in each answer choice, and see how they relate to the words in the text surrounding the blank. Do pronouns clearly refer to a specific noun, and do they agree in number with the words they refer to? Are verbs in the right number and tense? If periods, semi-colons, and/or colons are involved, can the text before and/or after stand on its own as a sentence? Are possessives used appropriately, etc.?

During this process, make sure to look out for intervening phrases that might make it harder to tell which relationships must exist between different words and phrases in the provided text, as discussed in "The Intervening Phrase" on page 92.

4. Find the Right Answer, or Eliminate Three Wrong Answers.

Sometimes you can immediately see which concept the question is testing, and you can tell that a particular answer choice is correct, using the rules and standards you learned in your training. If not, you should still be able to start eliminating wrong answer choices based on what we learned in the SAT Writing toolbox. For example, you might be able to tell that an answer choice has a verb in the wrong tense, or a comma in the wrong place. No matter what, make sure to consider all the answer choices, and then identify the one correct choice that follows the rules and standards of acceptable SAT Writing sentences, and the three wrong choices that fail to follow those rules and standards.

5. Take a Second Look to Reconsider the Question, the Answer Choices, and the Passage.

Now that you've chosen a correct answer, take another look at the question, answer choices, and provided text to make sure you haven't overlooked or misread anything. Did you get confused by an intervening phrase? Did you notice the placement of each comma in each answer choice? Always remember that the SAT is trying to trick you into making a small mistake on every single question. Stay on your toes.

6. Mark Your Answer Choice, and Move On.

Once you've gone through the process and double-checked your answer, mark your choice and move on.

Conclusion

Now we've discussed all the relevant concepts for both SAT Reading questions and SAT Writing questions. On the next page we'll do a quick review of what we learned for SAT Writing questions, and then we'll see all of our SAT Reading and Writing training ideas at work against real SAT practice questions in the walkthroughs.

SAT Writing Quick Summary

This is a one-page summary of the major concepts you'll need to know for SAT Writing questions. Use it to evaluate your comprehension or jog your memory. For a more in-depth treatment of these ideas, see the rest of this section.

The Big Secret of SAT Writing Questions

SAT Writing questions reward you for applying the College Board's standards for grammar and punctuation, rather than relying on your own sense of what sounds "right" to you personally.

SAT Writing Training Summary

SAT Writing questions are every question on the SAT Reading and Writing section that ask which choice "conforms to the conventions of Standard English." Common issues for these kinds of questions include:

- agreement in tense and number between verbs and nouns
- proper use of commas, semicolons, and colons
- acceptable words and/or punctuation used to separate clauses

… and similar topics, all of which are covered in the SAT Writing Toolbox earlier in this section, on page 76.

Here's the general SAT Writing process:

1. Read the provided text.
2. Carefully read the prompt and the answer choices.
3. Look for any of the issues we discussed in the SAT Writing Toolbox.
4. Find the right answer, or eliminate three wrong answers.
5. Take another look at the question, answer choices, and provided text.
6. Mark your answer choice, and move on.

See the many walkthroughs of real SAT Reading and Writing questions starting on page 96 of this book for demonstrations of these principles. If you want a more detailed description of the SAT rules for grammar and punctuation, see the SAT Writing Toolbox from page 76 in this section.

Reading and Writing Question Walkthroughs

Since we've gone through all of the necessary training for the SAT Reading and Writing section, it's time to see that process in action against real SAT questions like the ones you'll encounter on test day. (Remember, I recommend that you only prepare with official practice questions, because those are the only questions that are guaranteed to play by the College Board's rules. For more on that, see "Only Work with Questions from the College Board!" on page 16 of this Black Book.)

We'll go through every question in linear SAT Practice Tests #1-4 (available for free from the College Board's website, or from QuestPrep.com/Practice) starting in just a couple of pages. But first, I'd like to take a second to explain how my walkthroughs for this section are set up. (By the way, if you'd like to see some video demonstrations of these ideas, go to www.SATprepVideos.com for a selection of demonstration videos that are free to readers of this book.)

The question walkthroughs in this book are laid out in a way that allows us to do the following:

- capture the ideal thought process for attacking individual questions, from initial assessment of the question through consideration of each answer choice

- make it easier to focus on specific pieces of information, while also allowing you to read the entire solution easily

- present the walkthroughs so they can stand on their own, while still making it easy to refer back to the relevant parts of the training for more details on key ideas if you want a refresher

- demonstrate how mechanical and repetitive real SAT questions are

Sample Reading Walkthrough

Since there are two major question groups on the SAT Reading and Writing section, each with its own process, there are two different layouts for the walkthroughs—one for each question group. Here's a diagram of an example walkthrough for SAT Reading questions, with the elements of the walkthrough explained on the next page:

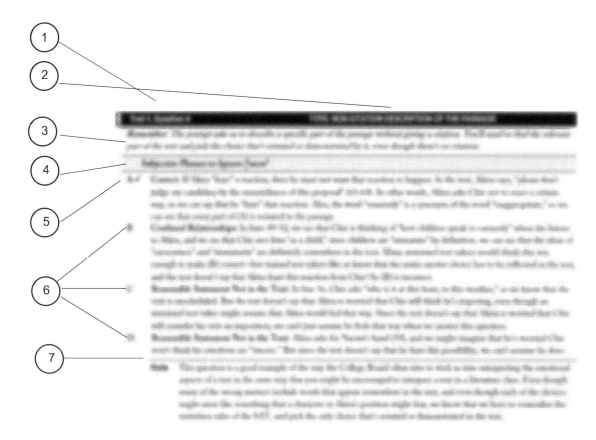

Explanation of SAT Reading Walkthrough Elements

The elements of the walkthrough are presented in a way that reflects the ideal mental process for approaching a new SAT Reading question. First, we quickly get a general impression of what's going on in the question, then we remind ourselves of what the question wants us to do, and finally we consider each answer choice and figure out which common SAT patterns it demonstrates:

1. This shows the test, module, and question number of the question being analyzed in the walkthrough. You can use this information to locate the relevant question in the College Board's free online linear practice tests, available from the College Board's website or from QuestPrep.com/Practice.

2. This indicates the type of question to help show you what kinds of associations a trained test-taker would initially make when reading this question's prompt. Remember that, regardless of question type, we always need to stay in the habit of answering every question based on a literal reading of the words and figures on the page, and we always pick the answer choice that's restated or demonstrated by the relevant text. Item 3 will tell you more about each type.

3. This italicized text is a quick reminder of the specific issues that are likely to come up in the question and how you should expect to tackle them, based on the question type identified in Item 2. See the description of Item 2 above for more.

4. This Item reminds us that we can ignore the kinds of subjective wording that the College Board often uses to try to fool untrained test-takers into interpreting the text. Remember that we should never try to interpret the text or read it subjectively, even though the College Board frequently uses phrases like "most likely" and "would probably." (See "2. The College Board deliberately phrases questions to make you think you should use subjective interpretation to find the answer." on page 60 for more on this idea.)

5. The correct answer will be noted with a checkmark icon, and the accompanying explanation will show exactly how the correct answer is restated or demonstrated by the relevant part of the passage.

6. The descriptions of the wrong answers will begin with a brief mention of the overall pattern being followed by the wrong answer, and then a lengthier explanation showing how the answer choice fails to meet the College Board's standards for this question type. (Remember to see "What Do Wrong Answers Do?" starting on page 62 of this Black Book for an explanation of these patterns.) Please keep in mind that you can still answer a question correctly without classifying or interpreting the wrong answers exactly the same way I do! Ultimately, all that matters is that you realize the wrong answers aren't restated or demonstrated in the relevant part of the text. If I decided to classify something as an example of the "confused relationships" pattern, and you think it's a better example of the "off by one or two words" pattern, for example, that's fine. The important thing is simply recognizing that the answer choice is wrong—I've just indicated these patterns here to help you see how I'm structuring my thinking as I approach a question.

7. If I feel that something is noteworthy about the question, but I can't fit that idea in the rest of the walkthrough, then I'll make a note of it at the end of the walkthrough. Be sure to pay attention to these notes when they appear, as they'll often contain useful information about what a particular question can teach us generally about future SAT questions.

Note that some walkthroughs are missing some of the Items in this list! If one of the Items above isn't relevant to a particular question, then it's omitted.

Remember that the ultimate goal of these walkthroughs is to help you see how I attack each question, and how I recommend you do the same. But, in the end, what matters most is that you develop an approach for SAT Reading questions that allows you to identify the one correct answer choice that's directly restated or demonstrated on the page, and the three wrong answer choices that aren't. Feel free to modify my approach as you see fit, as long as your modifications still bring you the results you want.

Sample Writing Walkthrough

Here's a diagram of an example walkthrough for SAT Writing questions, with the elements of the walkthrough explained on the next page:

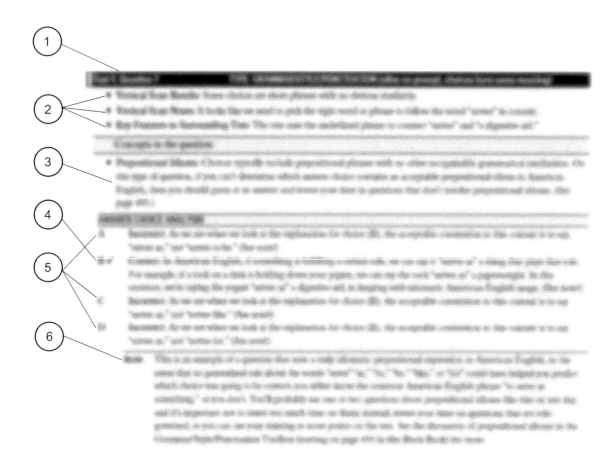

Explanation of SAT Writing Walkthrough Elements

The elements of the walkthrough are presented in an order that reflects "The General Process for Answering SAT Writing Questions" on page 94 of this Black Book, as we can see when referring to the diagram on the opposite page:

1. This shows the test, module, and question number of the question being analyzed in the walkthrough. You can use this information to locate the relevant question in the College Board's free online linear practice tests, available from the College Board's website or from QuestPrep.com/Practice.

2. This Item reflects the attributes of the question that a trained test-taker would notice upon first reading it:

   - the results of a vertical scan of the choices (see page 45 of this Black Book for more on that)
   - the relevant features of the surrounding text, which help us figure out the grammatical relationships that must exist between the right answer and the rest of the provided text

3. This Item reflects the concept(s) from the SAT Writing Toolbox that might be relevant to this question, based on the observations we made in Item 2.

4. The correct answer will be indicated with a check-mark icon, and the explanatory text will show how the correct answer follows the College Board's rules, as discussed in our training for SAT Writing questions.

5. For each of the three wrong answers, the walkthrough will explain how they fail to satisfy the College Board's requirements.

6. If I feel that something is noteworthy about the question but I can't fit that idea in the rest of the walkthrough, then I'll make a note of it at the end of the walkthrough. Be sure to pay attention to these notes when they appear, as they'll often contain useful information about what a particular question can teach us generally about future SAT questions.

Note that some walkthroughs are missing some of the items in this list! If one of the Items above isn't relevant to a particular question, then it's omitted.

Remember that the ultimate goal of these walkthroughs is to show you how I recommend you diagnose a question and evaluate the answer choices to find the correct answer. As always, you should feel free to modify this approach if you want, as long as your modifications still bring you the results you're looking for.

On the next page we'll dive in to a full set of SAT Reading and Writing walkthroughs for linear Practice Tests 1-4 from the College Board, available for free from the College Board's website or from QuestPrep.com/Practice.

TEST 1, MODULE 1

Test 1, Module 1, Question 1　　　　　　　　**TYPE: TEXT COMPLETION**

The prompt will be a short passage containing a blank. The correct answer will always be restated or demonstrated by key phrases in the provided text. See "What about Text Completion Questions?" on p. 66.

Subjective Phrases to Ignore: "most"

A　　Literary Interpretation: This choice will be tempting for untrained test-takers who read the sentence, conclude that Ochoa thinks people will one day live somewhere other than Earth, and think that picking this choice would make the sentence say something like "Ellen Ochoa <u>demands</u> that people do more research on living somewhere besides Earth." But that's not what this choice would say. Instead, it would say that Ochoa "demands" that people will need to live "in other environments than those found on Earth." The provided text doesn't restate or demonstrate the idea that Ochoa is demanding anything (or requiring anything, or insisting on anything, or doing anything else that would mean something like "demand[ing]"), and it's not even really clear what it would mean for Ochoa to "demand that humans will someday need" something. Since (A) doesn't restate or demonstrate any idea from the provided text, we know it's wrong.

B ✓　Correct: The provided text says that "although she doesn't have a definite idea of when it might happen," Ochoa "(blank) that humans will someday need to be able to live in other environments than those found on Earth." The text then refers back to this statement as "this conjecture." A "conjecture" is basically a statement that someone makes that they *think* is true, but that isn't conclusive. This choice would cause the text to say that Ochoa "<u>speculates</u> that humans will someday need to be able to live in other environments than those found on Earth." The idea that Ochoa is "speculat[ing]" about something that "might happen" exactly restates the idea of a "conjecture," so we know that (B) is correct.

C　　Direct Contradiction: This is pretty much the opposite of the right answer. As we saw in our discussion of (B), the text tells us that Ochoa thinks people living somewhere besides Earth "might happen," and thinking something might happen is the *opposite* of "doubt[ing]" that it will happen, as this choice would require. This choice might be tempting for test-takers who get confused about the word "although" and think that it tells us that Ochoa *doesn't* believe people will someday live in places other than Earth—as opposed to telling us that she thinks "it might happen," but she's just not sure when. See our discussion of (B) for more.

D　　Literary Interpretation: This choice could be tempting for test-takers who more or less follow the reasoning in our discussion of (B), but who don't think carefully about what the word "establishes" means. If Ochoa "establishe[d]" that people needed to live off of Earth one day, that would mean that this idea hadn't been proposed or thought of before, and that she was the first one to put it forward. This kind of detail doesn't appear in the provided text, which is enough for us to know that (D) must be wrong. Beyond that, to "establish[]" this idea would mean that the idea was something sure and definite, but this contradicts the provided text, which only says that Ochoa thinks "it might happen." For either of these reasons, (D) is wrong.

> **Note**　Choice (D) is a great example of an answer choice that might be fine in a classroom discussion, but is completely wrong on the SAT. Many high school students might think that there's no important difference between a person "speculating that…" something is the case and "establishing that…" something is the case—but on the SAT, that difference is very important! Always remember to think carefully about the specific meanings of the words in provided text, questions, and answer choices on the SAT.

Test 1, Module 1, Question 2　　　　　　　　**TYPE: TEXT COMPLETION**

The prompt will be a short passage containing a blank. The correct answer will always be restated or demonstrated by key phrases in the provided text. See "What about Text Completion Questions?" on p. 66.

Subjective Phrases to Ignore: "most"

A　　Literary Interpretation: This choice might be tempting for test-takers who read the provided text and see that Wauneka did something selfless to help other people, and then see a kind of association between benefiting other people and doing something "impartial." But being "impartial" just means that someone isn't biased one way or another; someone "promot[ing] public health" isn't necessarily "impartial" or not. Since nothing in the text tell us that Wauneka's "effort" was "impartial"—that is, not biased—this choice doesn't restate or demonstrate anything from the text, which means it must be wrong.

B　　Direct Contradiction: If anything, this choice is kind of the opposite of what needs to go in the blank. "Offhand" means something like "without any preparation or effort," which is definitely not the same as "continuously work[ing]." This choice isn't restated or demonstrated in the provided text, so it's wrong. See our discussion of (C) for more.

C ✓ **Correct:** The text says "Wauneka continuously worked," and then refers to "this (blank) effort." "Effort" restates the idea of "work[]," so we know the word in the blank, which describes "effort," must restate or demonstrate the idea of working "continuously." This choice would create the phrase "persistent effort," which pretty much exactly restates the idea of "continuous[] work[]." So (C) restates a relevant idea from the provided text, which means it's correct.

D **Literary Interpretation:** This choice will be tempting for some untrained test-takers who see that the provided text says that Wauneka "continuously worked," and then make a sort of general connection between the idea of working a lot and something being "mandatory." It's possible for a lot of work to be "mandatory," but work doesn't have to be "mandatory," and nothing in the provided text tells us that Wauneka *had* to do the work, or that she had no choice, or that someone made her, or anything else that would restate or demonstrate the idea of something being "mandatory." So (D) is wrong.

Test 1, Module 1, Question 3   **TYPE: TEXT COMPLETION**

The prompt will be a short passage containing a blank. The correct answer will always be restated or demonstrated by key phrases in the provided text. See "What about Text Completion Questions?" on p. 66.

Subjective Phrases to Ignore: "most"

A **Direct Contradiction:** As we'll see in our discussion of (D), this choice is basically the opposite of the right answer. The text describes a situation where "tribal nations and research institutions are equal partners," then describes a "collaboration" that "(blank) this model: tribal citizens worked alongside scientists…." "Tribal citizens work[ing] alongside scientists" is an example of "tribal nations and research institutions" being "equal partners," as described earlier in the text, but "circumvent" means something like "work around" or "avoid." The situation described in the second sentence is an *example* of the "model" described in the first sentence; it's not an instance of someone *avoiding* or working around that "model." So (A) is wrong—see our discussion of (D) for more.

B **Literary Interpretation:** As we saw in our discussion of (A), the provided text describes a "model" of "tribal nations and research institutions" being "equal partners," and tells us about a "collaboration between the Crow Tribe and Montana State University" that "(blank) this model." This choice might be tempting for test-takers who think "eclipses" sounds kind of academic and scientific, and therefore seems to fit the tone of the text—but this word would require the provided text to restate or demonstrate the idea that the "collaboration" in the second sentence somehow exceeded the "model" described in the first sentence: that it was bigger, or better, or made people forget all about the "model," or something else that would demonstrate or restate the idea of "eclipsing" something. Nothing like that appears in the text, so (B) is wrong.

C **Confused Relationships:** "Fabricates" would mean either to construct something, or to make up some idea that's not true or real. Nothing in the provided text restates or demonstrates either of these ideas, and this choice doesn't satisfy the reasoning we see in our analysis of the other answer choices. This choice might be tempting for test-takers who think that the "collaboration" somehow created the "model," but this idea doesn't appear in the text, so (C) can't be right. See the discussions of (A), (B), and (D) for more.

D ✓ **Correct:** As we saw in our discussions of (A) and (B), the provided text describes a "model" where "tribal nations and research institutions are equal partners." Then it says that a "collaboration between the Crow Tribe and Montana State University (blank) this model," and that as part of that collaboration "tribal citizens" worked with "scientists." Both the phrase "collaboration between the Crow Tribe and Montana State University" and the idea of "tribal citizens" working with "scientists" are examples of the "model" described in the first sentence, so the word "exemplifies" is explicitly demonstrated in the provided text—that is, the "collaboration" is an example of "tribal nations and research institutions" being "partners." This choice is directly demonstrated in the provided text, so we know it's correct.

Test 1, Module 1, Question 4   **TYPE: TEXT COMPLETION**

The prompt will be a short passage containing a blank. The correct answer will always be restated or demonstrated by key phrases in the provided text. See "What about Text Completion Questions?" on p. 66.

Subjective Phrases to Ignore: "most"

A ✓ **Correct:** The provided text describes "the parasitic dodder plant" doing something "at the same time as the host plant," and then refers to this idea with the phrase "this (blank)." The word "synchronization" describes multiple things happening at the same time, so this choice is exactly demonstrated in the provided text. That means (A) must be correct.

B **Literary Interpretation:** This choice will tempt some test-takers because they might reason that the dodder plant must wait around to flower "at the same time as the host plant," and this waiting around might be seen as kind of like "hibernation." But waiting around to do something isn't the same thing as hibernation! The word "hibernation" specifically refers to some kind of extended sleep, or period of dormancy, and the text doesn't describe anything like this—it doesn't say that the dodder plant goes into any kind of sleeping state, or anything along those lines. For all we know, the plant spends that time gathering nutrients, or growing, or who knows what else, while it waits to flower. The text doesn't tell us what the plant is doing during this time, so we can't just assume that it's "hibernat[ing]." Because this choice isn't restated or demonstrated in the provided text, we know it's wrong.

C   Confused Relationships: This choice will be tempting for test-takers who read the provided text and feel like the dodder plant waiting around to flower with its host is like a kind of "prediction," because the dodder plant waits for something that's going to happen in the future. This isn't really what a "prediction" is, but outside of that issue, if we look at how the word in the blank fits into the provided text, we can see that it would cause the sentence to refer to "this <u>prediction</u> with its host." The phrase "with its host" would mean that the host is also making the prediction, which doesn't really make sense in the provided text, and which also isn't restated or demonstrated in the provided text. So (C) must be wrong.

D   Barely Relevant: "Moderation" means something like "avoiding extremes," but nothing in the text restates or demonstrates this idea. This choice might be tempting because it sounds kind of scientific and might seem to fit the overall "tone" of the provided text, but as trained test-takers we know that this can never be our basis for choosing an answer choice on the SAT—we must always be able to point to the specific words and phrases that adhere to the relevant standards for that question type. There is no word or phrase in the provided text that restates or demonstrates the idea of "moderation," so we know (D) is wrong.

Note   The provided text for this question includes the phrase "parasitic dodder plant," which is exactly the kind of term that can be intimidating for untrained test-takers—they might think they need some kind of outside scientific knowledge to answer this question, or that other test-takers will know what a "parasitic dodder plant" is, or something else along those lines. But we don't need to know anything about this term to answer the question—all we have to do is understand that the plant in question does something "at the same time" as another plant, and that we can describe two things doing the same thing at the same time as "synchronization." Remember this on test day if you encounter an unknown and/or intimidating term: you don't need to understand every word in the provided text to be able to answer that question correctly. Instead, you only need to understand enough of that text to identify which choice follows the standards for the relevant question type.

Test 1, Module 1, Question 5   **TYPE: TEXT COMPLETION**

The prompt will be a short passage containing a blank. The correct answer will always be restated or demonstrated by key phrases in the provided text. See "What about Text Completion Questions?" on p. 66.

Subjective Phrases to Ignore: "most"

A   Literary Interpretation: The provided text tells us that "planetary formation" in binary star systems "should" be "nearly impossible," and tells us that it's "not surprising that the existence of planets" in those systems "has lacked (blank) explanation." Then it goes on to say that two people "shed light on the subject" by determining "a complex set of factors that could support planets' development." This choice will be tempting for a lot of untrained test-takers, because they'll read the provided text and come away with the basic idea that nobody really knows how these planets form, and those untrained test-takers will decide that it makes sense to say there's no "discernible explanation" for the way the planets form. But this is exactly the kind of vague conclusion we have to avoid when answering SAT questions! In order for "discernible" to be the correct answer, the text would have to restate or demonstrate the idea of an explanation that can't be discerned—that is, an explanation that can't be sensed, or perceived, or something else that could mean the same thing as not being "discernible." But that idea doesn't appear in the provided text, so (A) is wrong. See our discussion of (B) for more.

B ✓   Correct: As we saw in our discussion of (A), the text says that "planetary formation" in a certain situation "should" be "nearly impossible," then tells us that "the existence of planets in such systems has lacked (blank) explanation." The following sentence tells us that two people "shed light on the subject" by "determin[ing] a complex set of factors that could support planets' development." The phrase "has lacked" tells us that the blank in "(blank) explanation" describes the kind of explanation that this phenomenon <u>doesn't</u> have. The fact that "planetary formation" "in binary star systems" "should" be "nearly impossible," and that people have "shed light on the subject" by determining "a complex set of factors" that "could support planets' development" tells us that the explanation for "the existence of planets in such systems" is the *opposite* of "straightforward." (Note specifically that the phrase "complex set of factors" demonstrates the opposite of something "straightforward.") In other words, the provided text demonstrates the idea that the existence of those planets "lack[s] <u>straightforward</u> explanation," exactly as this choice requires. So (B) is demonstrated in the provided text, which means (B) is correct.

C   Direct Contradiction: This is close to the opposite of what should go in the blank, as we saw in our discussion of (B). This choice would cause the sentence to say that "the existence of planets in such systems has lacked <u>inconclusive</u> explanation." If that were the case, then any "explanation" would have to be "conclusive," but the text only tells us that the scientists "used modeling to determine a complex set of factors that *could* [emphasis added] support planets' development." Again, the text says that those factors *could* support planets' development, not that they conclusively *do* support their development, as this choice would require. In order for this choice to be correct, the text would specifically have to restate or demonstrate the idea of some kind of conclusive explanation for "planetary formation" in "binary star systems," or the absence of "inconclusive explanation[s]," neither of which is the case. So (C) is wrong.

D   **Barely Relevant:** This choice will tempt some test-takers, because real-life scientific discussions can often involve questions of bias—but there's nothing in the provided text that touches on the idea of anyone being biased for or against any particular idea or outcome. Since the idea of bias doesn't appear in the provided text, (D) must be wrong.

Test 1, Module 1, Question 6   **TYPE: TEXT COMPLETION**

The prompt will be a short passage containing a blank. The correct answer will always be restated or demonstrated by key phrases in the provided text. See "What about Text Completion Questions?" on p. 66.

Subjective Phrases to Ignore: "most"

A ✓ **Correct:** The provided text mentions how Harjo "(blank) television's tendency…" and then says that "this rejection is evident…." So we know that what Harjo does to "television's tendency" is a "rejection." This choice basically means "to deny or reject something." So (A), "repudiates," is directly restated in the text, which means it's correct.

B   **Literary Interpretation:** This choice will be tempting for some test-takers who read the text, understand that Harjo is doing something differently from the way others have done it, and feel like it makes sense to say that he's "proclaim[ing]" something about television, or culture, or something similar. But we can't ever pick an answer choice on the SAT because it just seems vaguely related to the provided text! We have to be able to point to specific words and phrases that restate or demonstrate the answer we choose. In order for us to say that Harjo "proclaims television's tendency" to do something, the text would have to talk about Harjo making some kind of statement about what television tends to do, which isn't the case. This choice would also cause the phrase "this rejection" to have nothing to refer back to. For either of these reasons, (B) is wrong.

C   **Barely Relevant:** We know that the correct answer to an SAT Reading question must restate or demonstrate ideas from the text. The word "foretells" describes someone predicting something that will happen in the future, but this idea doesn't appear in the provided text. This choice might tempt some test-takers who notice the discussion of the "past" along with what's "contemporary" and "current," but simply discussing different time periods isn't the same as "foretell[ing]" anything. So (C) is wrong.

D   **Literary Interpretation:** This choice will be very tempting for some test-takers who understand the reasoning from our discussion of (A), but who don't think precisely enough about the meaning of the word "recants." To recant something doesn't just mean to reject it, like "repudiates" from (A). Instead, it means you no longer believe in something *that you used to believe in*. This choice would require the provided text to mention that Harjo used to adhere to "television's tendency to situate Native characters in the distant past," but then he stopped, or something along those lines. But this idea doesn't appear in the text, so (D) is wrong.

Test 1, Module 1, Question 7   **TYPE: MAIN IDEA**

The prompt asks about the "main purpose" or "main idea" (or some similar phrase) of the text. The correct answer must be directly restated or demonstrated in the passage, with no interpretation. See "What about "Main Idea/Main Purpose" Questions?" on p.69.

Subjective Phrases to Ignore: "main"

A ✓ **Correct:** This passage starts by mentioning something that von Ahn was trying to do, then describing a problem he encountered, then telling how he "invented a simple security test." Then the passage tells us how this "reCAPTCHA test" worked. So every sentence relates to the invention of this test—either by providing context for why the test was needed, or how the test works, or what the benefits of the test are. Since every sentence in the passage connects to the idea in (A), we know (A) is correct.

B   **Literary Interpretation:** This choice will tempt some test-takers because the passage does mention "digital scanners," but it doesn't discuss how they work, as this choice would require. In order for this choice to be correct, the passage would have to include some kind of details about how digital scanners function—since the passage doesn't include that information, (B) is wrong.

C   **Literary Interpretation:** This choice will be tempting because the passage does mention the "book-digitizing project." But we can't say that the passage "calls attention" to that project, as this choice would require—the project is only mentioned in the context of explaining the reason for the reCAPTCHA test. The passage doesn't provide any details or information about the book project—why von Ahn decided to do it, how it turned out, or anything like that. (Contrast this with our discussion of (A) where we can see that every sentence in the passage is connected to the invention of reCAPTCHA.) Also, the phrase "call attention to" would require something in the passage that restated or demonstrated the idea of more people knowing about the book project, or thinking about it, or focusing on it, or something else related to the idea of "call[ing]" people's "attention" to this project. This doesn't appear, so (C) is wrong.

D   Literary Interpretation: Some test-takers will be tempted by this choice because they've seen reCAPTCHA out in the real world many times—but that's not a basis for choosing an answer choice on the SAT! We have to answer based on the provided text, and the provided text doesn't say anything about how popular reCAPTCHA is. So (D) is wrong.

The prompt asks about the "function" or "structure" of a part of the text. The correct answer must plainly and accurately describe the relevant text, with no interpretation. See "What about "Function and Structure" Questions?" on p. 70.

Subjective Phrases to Ignore: "best"

A   Wrong Part of the Passage: This choice will be tempting for some test-takers because it mentions "the physical setting of the scene," and the underlined text mentions "the landscape," which seems related to the "setting of the scene." But that underlined text doesn't mention any "detailed image," as this choice would require, nor does it describe any specific "physical" aspect of the scene at all—those details appear in the sentence *after* the underlined text ("the sugar-maples wavered like pyres of light," "a massing of grey orchards," and "the lingering green of an oak-grove"). Remember, we have to answer questions of this type based specifically on the underlined text; because this choice doesn't accurately describe that underlined text, we know it's wrong.

B   Literary Interpretation: This choice might be tempting for certain test-takers, because a lot of writing involves some kind of conflict, and a lot of high school students are taught in literature classes to interpret texts in ways that aren't based on what's directly present in the provided text—so those test-takers might read the provided text and decide that it could relate to some kind of "internal conflict." But the underlined text doesn't actually describe any conflict of any kind; on the contrary, it describes how Lily felt in tune with her surroundings, as we'll see in our discussion of (D). So (B) is wrong.

C   Confused Relationships: This choice is very close to being correct, except it mixes up which sentence says what, as we'll see in our discussion of (D). The underlined sentence describes how Lily feels connected to her surroundings, but "the next sentence" doesn't expand on this idea—that next sentence is just a physical description of Lily's surroundings, with no mention of Lily or her feelings whatsoever. So (C) is wrong. Instead, as we'll see in our discussion of (D), it is the *underlined* sentence that "expands on" an idea from the *previous* sentence—more on that below.

D ✓ Correct: The previous sentence tells us that Lily "could be keenly sensitive to a scene which was the fitting background for her own sensations," and this underlined sentence describes a specific instance of Lily being aware of a connection between her surroundings and her sensations—that is, it provides an "illustrat[ion]" of that idea, as this choice requires—with phrases like "the landscape... seemed an enlargement of her present mood," and "she found... herself in its calmness, its breadth, its long free reaches." So this choice exactly describes the text, and the text exactly demonstrates the ideas in this choice—which makes (D) correct.

The prompt asks about the "function" or "structure" of a part of the text. The correct answer must plainly and accurately describe the relevant text, with no interpretation. See "What about "Function and Structure" Questions?" on p. 70.

Subjective Phrases to Ignore: "best"

A   Wrong Part of the Passage: The sentence *following* the underlined sentence "summarize[s] the results of the team's analysis" by telling us what happened when there was greater "exposure to sunshine at work" in a particular situation. But the question asks about the underlined sentence, and the underlined text doesn't say anything about any results—it only tells us what data the team looked at, and which parts of that data were compared to each other. So (A) isn't restated or demonstrated by the relevant text, which means (A) is wrong.

B   Plausible but not in the Text: The first sentence tells us about "the study's findings" when it mentions that the "study...suggests that exposure to sunshine...can lead to overly optimistic behavior." But the underlined sentence doesn't include any example of people being exposed to sunshine, or of anyone being optimistic about anything, as the phrase "specific example" would require— so (B) must be wrong.

C ✓ Correct: The underlined text tells us that "the team" used "data from 1994 to 2010" and "compared over 29,000" earnings forecasts to the actual earnings that were later reported. This is a direct demonstration of explaining "part of the methodology used in the team's study"—that, is the way the team conducted the study. So this choice is demonstrated by the text, which means it's correct.

D   Plausible but not in the Text: This choice will be tempting for test-takers who assume that looking at data "spanning from 1994 to 2010" and "compar[ing] over 29,000" earnings forecasts to the actual reported earnings would be a "challenge," but the text never actually says that this was difficult, or harder than expected, or that there was any particular obstacle associated with this process, as the phrase "call out a challenge the team faced" would require. So we can't pick an answer choice that says the text mentions "a challenge," which means (D) is wrong.

The prompt asks for information from the passage. The answer must be restated or demonstrated by specific phrases in the text. See "What about General Passage Questions?" on p. 69.

A   Direct Contradiction: This is the opposite of what the text says—the only mention in the text of "ladies" "visit[ing]" Mother is that "Mother did not spend all her time… sitting dully at home waiting for dull ladies to pay [visits] to her." So Mother didn't wait around to be visited by ladies, and nothing in the text restates or demonstrates the idea that Mother wanted visits from more ladies, which means (A) must be wrong.

B   Off by One or Two Words: The text does say that Mother "always made up funny pieces of poetry for their birthdays and for other special occasions," but that's not the same as saying "birthdays are her favorite special occasion," as this choice would require. This choice will be tempting for untrained test-takers because in a classroom discussion, many students and teachers wouldn't think anything was wrong with reading the provided text and then describing birthdays as Mother's "favorite special occasion." But on the SAT we have to think about exactly what words mean—the word "favorite" means that you like something the most, and the text never actually tells us that Mother liked birthdays more than other special occasions, as the phrase "favorite special occasion" would require. So (B) is wrong.

C ✓ Correct: The text says that Mother "used to write stories for [the children]" and that she "made up funny pieces of poetry for their birthdays and for other great occasions." So the text specifically says that mother "creates stories and poems for her children," just as (C) requires, which means (C) is right.

D   Off by One or Two Words: This choice has the same problem that (B) has—just because the text describes mother doing something (in this case, "read[ing] to [her children]"), that doesn't mean that this activity is her "favorite." The text never tells us that Mother likes "reading to her children" more than any other activity, so we can't call reading "her favorite activity," as (D) would require. So (D) is wrong.

The prompt asks about the "main purpose" or "main idea" (or some similar phrase) of the text. The correct answer must be directly restated or demonstrated in the passage, with no interpretation. See "What about "Main Idea/Main Purpose" Questions?" on p.69.

Subjective Phrases to Ignore: "best"

A ✓ Correct: The prompt tells us that the speaker in the provided poem is addressing an "author." The poem says the author has a "mighty pen," and then goes on to describe a variety of things that author was able to do: "told of joy and mirth," "read the hearts and souls of men," "read" "the language of the flowers," and made "the little brook respond[] to thy call." All of this demonstrates "praise" for that writer, so the phrase "to praise a certain writer" is demonstrated in the text, as this choice would require. But this isn't enough for us to pick (A), because that's not all (A) says! Before we pick (A), we have to make sure that this entire answer choice is restated or demonstrated in the provided text—so let's see if we can do that. The rest of the choice tells us that the poem says the author is "especially perceptive regarding people and nature." The poem says the author has "read the hearts and souls of men as cradled from their birth." Reading men's "hearts and souls" is definitely an example of being "especially perceptive regarding people." The rest of the poem says the author "hast read" "the language of the flowers," which shows the author was "perceptive regarding… nature" as well. Each part of this answer choice is restated or demonstrated in the provided text, so (A) is correct.

B   Off by One or Two Words: This choice will be tempting for a lot of test-takers, because the poem mentions that the author has "read the hearts and souls of men," and also read "the language of the flowers," which might seem to describe "read[ing] extensively about a variety of topics," as this choice would require. But the text doesn't say the author has read <u>about</u> these topics; it says the author has read <u>the things themselves</u>. To "read" a flower or a person's soul isn't the same as reading *about* a flower or a person's soul. Reading something like a soul or a flower means seeing that thing and being able to gather some meaning or understanding about what's below its surface; this is what's described in the poem, but it's not what's mentioned in the answer choice, which only talks about reading *about* different topics—that is, reading books about those topics. Since the idea of reading *about* anything doesn't appear in the provided text, (B) must be wrong.

C   Literary Interpretation: This choice will be tempting for some test-takers because the provided text includes the phrase "with stroke of mighty pen," which might sound related to an author's "writing process" as mentioned in this answer choice. But the phrase "with stroke of mighty pen" doesn't demonstrate the idea of "call[ing] attention to a… careful and elaborately detailed writing process." The only part of the provided text that says anything about actual writing is the phrase "stroke of mighty pen," but that phrase doesn't include anything that could be called "careful" or "elaborately detailed;" in fact, it contains no details at all.

We can't pick a choice that mentions a "careful and elaborately detailed writing process" just because the provided text briefly mentions the "stroke" of a "pen." In order for (C) to be right, the text would have to include multiples details about the author's "writing process," and those details would have to show that the process was "careful": something about how the author always gets up at an exact time, or always writes in a certain place, or under certain conditions, or goes through some ritual before or after writing, and so on. But the text doesn't contain anything like that, so (C) is wrong.

D   **Barely Relevant:** Some untrained test-takers will want to pick this choice because they can imagine a pleasant "afternoon spent in nature" that includes details like "flowers" and a "little brook." But the provided text doesn't actually mention any particular "afternoon," or any memory of any specific time, nor does it state that the writer of the poem has ever spent any time whatsoever with the author the poem addresses. So (D) can't be right. Remember that we can't pick an answer choice just because we could imagine a scenario where that choice could be relevant to the provided text!

Test 1, Module 1, Question 12   TYPE: QUOTATION

The prompt will make a claim about a literary work, then ask which quotation "illustrates the claim." The right answer will plainly demonstrate the ideas in the provided claim. See "What about Quotation Questions?" on p. 70.

Subjective Phrases to Ignore: "most effectively"

A ✓   **Correct:** This choice says "you have not known what you are," which explicitly restates the idea of Whitman "directly" "address[ing]" the readers and telling them they "have not fully understood themselves." So (A) is right.

B   **Literary Interpretation:** In this choice, Whitman calls the readers "immense" and "interminable," which basically means something like "huge" and "endless." It's possible to not understand something "immense" and interminable, but this doesn't have to be the case—and saying that something is "immense" and "interminable" isn't the same as saying that this thing isn't "fully understood" by anyone in particular, as the prompt requires. This choice doesn't restate or demonstrate any idea from the prompt, so it's wrong.

C   **Barely Relevant:** This choice doesn't say anything about anyone understanding or not understanding anything, which the prompt requires; it simply says that Whitman should have gone "straight to" the readers, and talked to them and about them. Again, this doesn't restate or demonstrate anything from the prompt, so (C) is wrong.

D   **Off by One or Two Words:** This choice will be tempting for some test-takers, because the phrase "none has understood you" seems to restate the idea that the readers "have not fully understood themselves." In other words, those test-takers will reason that if "none has understood you," that must include the "you" that Whitman is addressing. But we can tell that (A) is the correct answer, and not (D), because the prompt asks for the quotation that says the readers "have not fully understood themselves," and only (A) specifically says that "you [the readers] have not known what you are." That statement from (A) restates the idea from the prompt, whereas the statement in (D) says that "none has understood you," which is a different idea from the readers not understanding themselves. Since (D) doesn't directly restate the idea from the prompt, (D) is wrong.

Note   The official explanation from the College Board for choice (D) completely ignores the statement "none has understood you" from that choice, and doesn't even attempt to explain why that statement doesn't make (D) correct. This is yet another example of how the College Board's official explanations for SAT questions are unhelpful and misleading—the College Board doesn't want to come right out and say "the correct answer has to say exactly what the prompt asks for, and (D) doesn't do that," because then the way to find right answers for real SAT questions would be too obvious. So the College Board's explanations avoid directly pointing out the specific details that make right answers right and wrong answers wrong, which means students who depend on those explanations are going to have a hard time maximizing their performance.

Test 1, Module 1, Question 13   TYPE: IF TRUE

The passage presents some claim or hypothesis. The prompt typically asks us to choose the "finding" that, "if true," would support or weaken the argument. Supporting statements will demonstrate the idea in the claim, and weakening statements will demonstrate the opposite of the idea in the claim. See "What about "If True" Questions?" on p. 71.

Subjective Phrases to Ignore: "most directly"

A ✓   **Correct:** This choice says Chambi "took... portraits of wealthy Peruvians," and also took pictures of "the people, sites and customs of Indigenous communities of the Andes." This demonstrates the idea of "captur[ing] diverse elements of Peruvian society," as the student claims in the provided text, because "diverse" means something like "including a variety of different versions of something"—in this case, "wealthy Peruvians" and "Indigenous communities of the Andes." This choice also says he "took... commissioned portraits" (which is an example of "representing... subjects with dignity" from the student's claim), and he "carefully document[ed]" his subjects (which is the same as "representing" them with "authenticity," because "documenting" something means recording it as it was). This choice demonstrates all the ideas from the student's claim in the provided text, so (A) is right.

B   Barely Relevant: The "student's claim" in the provided text tells us about the people Chambi photographed and the way he photographed them, but this choice doesn't tell us anything about the people in Chambi's images. The claim doesn't say anything about "technical" aspects of Chambi's work, or about his use of "light and shadow," as this choice requires. This choice doesn't restate or demonstrate anything related to the "student's claim," so (B) is wrong.

C   Wrong Part of the Passage: This choice tells us about when and where Chambi was "celebrated," which has nothing to do with the "student's claim" about the subjects of Chambi's photographs and how he "represent[ed]" them. This choice might tempt some test-takers because it seems to demonstrate the idea from the text that Chambi is a "renowned figure[]," but that statement isn't part of the "student's claim" from the second half of the provided text, which is what the prompt asks us about. So (C) is wrong.

D   Plausible but not in the Text: This choice just tells us that other Peruvian photographers have also photographed some of the subjects that Chambi photographed, but that information doesn't have any connection to the "student's claim" that Chambi's work captured different aspects of Peruvian society, or that he represents his subjects with "dignity and authenticity." This choice doesn't restate or demonstrate any idea from the "student's claim," so it can't be right. Some untrained test-takers will assume that the statement in this choice is probably true in real life, but as trained test-takers, we know this isn't a valid basis for picking an answer choice for an SAT Reading question.

Test 1, Module 1, Question 14	TYPE: DATA

The passage includes a figure. The question asks for the choice that uses data from the figure to accomplish a certain goal. The right answer will describe the data accurately and plainly accomplish the goal. See "What about "Data" Questions?" on p. 69.

Subjective Phrases to Ignore: "most"

A   Direct Contradiction: The provided text tells us that "many films and associated records... have been lost," and that the "counts" for the work of the people in the table "should be taken as bare minimums rather than totals." Then it says "it's entirely possible, for example, that (blank)." The phrase "for example" tells us that what goes in the blank must be an example of the "counts" in the table being "bare minimums"—in other words, that the real numbers can be more than what's listed in the table. This choice would cause the text to say that it's "possible" that "Dark Cloud" acted in "fewer films" than "Lillian St. Cyr, who is credited with 66 performances." The table tells us that Dark Cloud acted in 35 films, while St. Cyr acted in 66 movies, as this choice reflects. 35 films *is* "significantly fewer films" than the 66 films St. Cyr was in; this choice just describes the data in the table as it appears, rather than being an "example" of the real output of these "actors and filmmakers" being *higher* than what appears in the table. This is basically the opposite of what the prompt asks for. This choice doesn't restate or demonstrate the idea that lost films and records make the output in the table "bare minimums," and that real numbers are potentially higher than what appears in that table—so (A) is wrong. See the discussion of (C) for more.

B   Confused Relationships: This choice mentions "Edwin Carewe's 47 credited acting roles," and says that they were only from "films made after 1934." This will tempt some untrained test-takers who remember that the text says something about the data in the table being unreliable, and who notice that this choice mentions Carewe making films "after 1934," while the table says he was only active *until* 1934. But the text never tells us that the years these actors and filmmakers were active were incorrect; it only specifically tells us that "counts of" their "output should be taken as bare minimums"—in other words, they may have made more movies than what's listed in the table. But this choice says Carewe had "47 credited acting roles," just as the table says, which means this isn't an "example" of the real numbers of films exceeding what's in the table, as the prompt (along with the provided text) requires. So (B) is wrong.

C ✓ Correct: As we saw in our discussions of (A) and (B), the provided text tells us that "films" and "records" for the relevant era "have been lost," and that the numbers of films in the table are "bare minimums." The phrase "bare minimum[]" specifically describes the lowest possible number—that is, a situation where the real value could be higher than the listed value. This choice explicitly demonstrates that idea by causing the text to say that "it's entirely possible" that "Lillian St. Cyr acted in far more than 66 films and Edwin Carewe directed more than 58" (we can see that those numbers reflect what is listed in the provided table, so, again, saying that the real numbers could be higher than the numbers in the table demonstrates the idea from the provided text that those numbers in the table are "bare minimums"). This choice demonstrates an idea from the relevant text, so it's correct.

D   Direct Contradiction: This choice is basically the opposite of the correct answer; rather than describe a situation where the real number is *higher* than what appears in the table, this choice describes a situation where the real number is *lower* than what appears in the table—it says James Young Deer directed 33 films (instead of the 35 films listed in the table) and acted in 10 films (instead of the 33 films listed in the table). This choice would be tempting for test-takers who misread the word "minimum" as "maximum," and/or who misread the table in some way.

The passage includes a figure. The question asks for the choice that uses data from the figure to accomplish a certain goal. The right answer will describe the data accurately and plainly accomplish the goal. See "What about "Data" Questions?" on p. 69.

Subjective Phrases to Ignore: "best"

A   **Literary Interpretation:** This choice will be tempting, because it accurately describes the data in the table—but it doesn't "support the researchers' claim," as the prompt requires! We can read in the provided text that the "researchers' claim" is that "plants… that grow in close proximity to other plants gain an advantage." Nothing in the provided text tells us that "less than 75% of juvenile plants… growing in patches of vegetation" indicates any kind of advantage as described in the researchers' claim, so (A) doesn't satisfy the prompt and isn't correct. This choice will be tempting for some test-takers who notice that it makes an accurate statement about the data in the table and then try come up with some reason why this particular percentage could indicate that plants growing near other plants "gain an advantage," as the claim states—but again, that reason isn't actually present in the text.

B   **Direct Contradiction:** This choice directly contradicts the table, because *H. stoechas* actually has the *least* "number of juvenile plants growing in patches of vegetation," at 12, not the greatest as this choice claims. Beyond that, the text doesn't make any claim related to any individual species, or connect the idea of any one species having the most or fewest "juvenile plants growing in patches of vegetation" to the kind of "advantage" from the "researchers' claim." For either of these reasons, (B) is wrong.

C   **Direct Contradiction:** Like (B), this choice makes a statement that directly contradicts the table and the provided text—the text tells us that "if individual plants were randomly distributed," then "about 15%" would be "in patches of vegetation." The table includes a column labeled "percent found in patches of vegetation" which tells us that for all 5 species, more than 15% were found in patches of vegetation (in fact, that number for all 5 species is more than 50%). So this choice's claim that, for two of the species, "the percentage of juvenile plants growing in patches of vegetation was less than what would be expected if plants were randomly distributed" contradicts that information. Beyond that, if this statement *were* true, it would *discredit* the "researchers' claim," not "support" it, as the prompt requires. That claim is that "grow[ing] in close proximity to other plants" gives those plants an "advantage," but if there were *fewer* than expected young plants growing near other plants "in patches of vegetation," then that would indicate that close proximity to other plants was a *disadvantage*—which, again, is the opposite of the "researchers' claim." So (C) makes a statement that contradicts the provided text—and even if it didn't, the statement in (C) would contradict the "researchers' claim" if it *were* true. Either of these reasons makes (C) wrong.

D ✓   **Correct:** As we've seen in our discussion of the other answer choices, the provided text tells us that if plants were randomly distributed, "only about 15%" would be found growing "with other plants in patches of vegetation." That text also tells us that the researchers "claim that plants… that grow in close proximity to other plants gain an advantage." The prompt asks us for a choice that "describes data… that support the researchers' claim." First, this choice correctly describes the data in the table by saying that "the percentage of juvenile plants growing in patches of vegetation" was "higher than what would be expected if plants were randomly distributed." Again, the prompt says that if plants were randomly distributed, then "only about 15%" would be found "in patches of vegetation." But the table tells us that for each of the five plant species, more than 50% were in patches of vegetation. So this choice describes the data accurately. Second, the data "support the researchers' claim" because they show that a much higher percentage of plants appear in patches of vegetation than would be expected based on random chance, which demonstrates the idea that plants growing in patches "gain an advantage," as the "claim" requires—that "advantage" is why more plants are able to grow in those patches. This choice meets the requirements of the prompt, so it's correct.

The passage presents some claim or hypothesis. The prompt typically asks us to choose the "finding" that, "if true," would support or weaken the argument. Supporting statements will demonstrate the idea in the claim, and weakening statements will demonstrate the opposite of the idea in the claim. See "What about "If True" Questions?" on p. 71.

Subjective Phrases to Ignore: "most"

A   **Barely Relevant:** The prompt asks us which choice supports "the researchers' hypothesis," and the provided text tells us that this hypothesis is "that the plants depend on dissolving underlying rock with these acids." This choice says that "other species" in the same family live in areas with "more soil" but have "similar" "root structures." This doesn't support the hypothesis, because the presence of "more soil" doesn't tell us anything about whether these "other species" also use their roots to dissolve rock. We can't know whether these "other species" "depend on dissolving underlying rock" too, because this choice doesn't mention whether they dissolve rock—so this choice doesn't "support the researchers' hypothesis." Beyond that, what "other species" do doesn't necessarily tells us anything about what these two plants do—the hypothesis in the text relates to the two plants discussed in the passage, and what two "other species" in the same family do doesn't have any impact on that hypothesis. For any of these reasons, (A) is wrong.

B   Barely Relevant: This choice might be tempting for untrained test-takers, because it does discuss the two plants "secret[ing]... acids." But nothing in the provided text connects the idea of producing the two acids "in different proportions" to the idea that "the plants depend on dissolving underlying rock," as the researchers hypothesize. Simply mentioning a detail related to these plants secreting acid, as this choice does, isn't the same as supporting the idea that those plants depend on using those acids to dissolve rock, which is what the prompt requires. So (B) is wrong.

C ✓ Correct: "The researchers' hypothesis" in the provided text is that "the plants depend on dissolving underlying rock." The provided text also tells us that one result of the plants dissolving rock is that this "creates channels for continued growth." This choice describes a situation where "cracks in the surface" of rocks "are readily available," but those plants "carve new entry point into rocks" anyway. In other words, these rocks already contain cracks, which are "channels for continued growth" (one of the things that the text tells us these plants get from dissolving rock), but the plants still use their acids to dissolve rock and "carve new entry points." This supports the idea that "the plants depend on dissolving" the rock (since they do it even when "channels for continued growth" are already available), just as the hypothesis states. So this choice satisfies the prompt, which means it's correct.

D   Plausible but not in the Text: At first, this choice might seem similar to (C), and it might be difficult for some test-takers to choose between them. Both choices describes a situation where one of the reasons given in the provided text that the plants "dissolve underlying rock" is removed—for choice (C), that reason is the need to "create[] channels for continued growth," while for (D) that reason is to "release[] phosphates," since (D) describes a situation where the rocks don't have phosphates, but the plants still "thrive." But choice (C) is correct because it specifies that the plants "carve new entry points" anyway—that is, they still dissolve rock—while (D) only says that they "thrive." (D) doesn't tell us specifically whether those plants still dissolve rock when those rocks don't "contain phosphates," so this choice doesn't support the provided hypothesis that "plants depend on dissolving underlying rock." For all we know, those plants "thrive" without dissolving rock at all in the situation described in (D), since (D) doesn't specify otherwise; if that were true, then this situation would *contradict* the hypothesis, rather than support it. So (D) is wrong.

Test 1, Module 1, Question 17   **TYPE: MOST LOGICALLY COMPLETES**

The passage ends with a blank, and the answer choices are relatively long phrases. The right answer will restate or demonstrate an idea in the provided text. See "What about "Most Logically Completes" Questions?" on p. 68.

Subjective Phrases to Ignore: "most"

A   Direct Contradiction: This choice might be tempting for some test-takers because it mentions "different sauropod lineages," which restates the idea of "several sauropod lineages" from the text. But we can't pick an answer just because that choice includes a phrase that appears in the text! We have to make sure that all the ideas in an answer choice are restated and/or demonstrated in the text, with the same relationships among them that we see in the text. In this case, the text says that "there is no evidence of... spikes in carbon dioxide levels coinciding with... sauropod evolution." In other words, there's no evidence that changes in carbon dioxide level had any effect on any sauropod lineages whatsoever, so we can't say that "fluctuations in atmospheric carbon dioxide affected different sauropod lineages differently," or the same, or at all. So (A) directly contradicts that text, and it's wrong.

B ✓ Correct: As we just saw in our discussion of (A), the provided text tells us that "there is no evidence" that "spikes in carbon dioxide levels coincid[ed] with relevant periods in sauropod evolution." This choice demonstrates that idea by saying that "evolution of larger body sizes in sauropods did not depend on increased atmospheric carbon dioxide." "Evolution of larger body sizes" is an example of "sauropod evolution," and "did not depend on increased atmospheric carbon dioxide" restates "there is no evidence of... spikes in carbon dioxide levels coinciding." So (B) restates and/or demonstrates the ideas from the relevant text, which means it's correct. Notice that even if we had trouble completely understanding the second half of the provided text, the first half says "some researchers have attributed the evolution of sauropods to such massive sizes to... high levels of atmospheric carbon dioxide." The second half of the text begins with the word "however," which we know means that it must be introducing information that's opposed to the idea of sauropods reaching "massive sizes" because of "high levels" of "carbon dioxide"; that part of the text ends with "suggesting that (blank)." So again, we know from the word "however" that whatever goes in the blank must be the opposite of the idea of "the evolution of sauropods to such massive sizes" being caused by "high levels of atmospheric carbon dioxide," which is exactly what this choice says. Always remember that even if we don't completely understand every word or phrase in the provided text, we can often work around the parts we don't know and find the right answer anyway!

C   Direct Contradiction: This choice directly contradicts the provided text, which says "there is no evidence of... spikes in carbon dioxide levels coinciding with... sauropod evolution," and then specifically mentions the time "when the first large sauropods appeared" as well as "when sauropods reached their maximum known sizes" as examples of times when carbon dioxide levels did *not* coincide with sauropod evolution. Again, this is the opposite of what (C) says, so (C) is wrong.

D   Direct Contradiction: This choice will be tempting for test-takers who misread the text and think it says that high carbon dioxide levels kept the sauropods from getting bigger, rather than saying that no evidence shows that carbon dioxide levels coincided with sauropod evolution, as we saw in our discussion of the other choices. But this choice has the same basic problem that (A) and (C) have—it says there's a connection between sauropod size and "atmospheric carbon dioxide," which as we saw in our discussion of the other answer choices is the opposite of what the text says. So (D) is wrong.

Note Untrained test-takers who only focus on the first half of the text, which says that "some researchers... attributed" the "massive size" of sauropods to "high levels of carbon dioxide," will probably be tempted by either (A) or (C), and have a hard time choosing between them. Remember that if it seems like more than one answer choice is correct, then it must be the case that you're overlooking or misunderstanding some part of the provided text, the prompt, and/or an answer choice, because real SAT questions from the College Board can only ever have one inarguably correct answer choice. When it seems like more than one choice could be right, be sure to re-read the relevant text carefully, word by word, to find and fix your mistake—and if you're not making progress on the current question, consider moving on to the next question and coming back to the challenging question in a later pass.

Test 1, Module 1, Question 18	TYPE: MOST LOGICALLY COMPLETES

The passage ends with a blank, and the answer choices are relatively long phrases. The right answer will restate or demonstrate an idea in the provided text. See "What about "Most Logically Completes" Questions?" on p. 68.

Subjective Phrases to Ignore: "most"

A   Direct Contradiction: The sentence with the blank describes what "discussing philosophers whose views conflict with judges' views could" do. This choice says discussing these philosophers could let judges write opinions "without... consult[ing] philosophical works." But if the judges are "discussing" the "views" of "philosophers," then the judges *are* "consult[ing] philosophical works," which is the opposite of what (A) says. This choice contradicts the provided text (and also creates a paradox); the text never says anything about any situation where a judge doesn't "consult philosophical works," so we know (A) is wrong. (Note that it could be possible for the judges in question to "discuss[] philosophers," as the text says, "without... consult[ing] philosophical works," as this choice says, if they happen to have already memorized all those philosophical works and could "discuss[]" them without "consult[ing]" them. From that perspective, this choice wouldn't be directly contradicting the text, but it still wouldn't be restated or demonstrated in the text, either—as we just discussed, the passage never mentions any judge "discussing philosophers" but not "consult[ing] philosophical works," as this choice would require, so (A) is still wrong. Remember that we can't pick a choice just because the statement that choice makes could possibly true—that is, just because the passage doesn't *specifically* say that the statement in the answer choice is wrong. We have to pick the choice that the text *specifically* restates or demonstrates, as we'll see in our discussion of (B).)

B ✓ Correct: The text tells us that "judicial opinions... explain the reasoning behind [judges'] legal rulings." Then the text says that "the strongest judicial opinions" address "potential objections." "Views" that "conflict with judges' views" restates the idea of "potential objections," so what goes in the blank must restate the idea that "discussing philosophers whose views conflict with judges' views" would result in "strong[] judicial opinions." This choice says doing so would "help judges improve their arguments," which demonstrates the idea in the provided text that "judicial opinions" that "consider... objections" are better than the ones that don't—so (B) is correct. (Note that the text tells us that "opinions...explain... reasoning," and that "explaining reasoning" restates the word "argument"—so the text tells us directly that an "improve[d]... argument[]" is the same thing as a better "judicial opinion.")

C   Plausible but not in the Text: This choice will be tempting for untrained test-takers who read the provided text and come away with the idea that "discussing philosophers whose views conflict" with their own views is a good thing, and who feel like this choice also describes a good thing ("mak[ing] judicial opinions more comprehensible"), and who think that this is enough of a basis to pick this answer. But when the text says that something good happens, it's not enough to just pick an answer choice that also says something good happens; that good thing needs to be the same in the answer choice as it is in the text in order for that answer choice to be correct. In this case, the text says "consider[ing] and rebut[ting] potential objections" is what the "strongest judicial opinions" do, whereas this choice causes the text to say that judges "discussing philosophers whose views conflict" with their own views makes those opinions "more comprehensible to people without legal or philosophical training." But nothing in the provided text tells us that being "more comprehensible to people without legal or philosophical training" makes an opinion "strong[]," or even specifically describes any situation where these opinions are read by "people without legal or philosophical training." So we can't say that (C) demonstrates or restates an idea from the text. (Contrast this with the correct answer, (B), which would cause the text to say that "discussing philosophers whose views conflict" with the judges' views "improve[s] the argument." This restates the text, which tells us that "the strongest opinions" address "objections." See our discussion of (B) for more on this.)

D   Plausible but not in the Text: This choice is similar to (C), and is wrong for the same reason: it mentions something that probably seems kind of good to many test-takers—being "in line" with "broadly held" "views"—but nothing in the text says this is what "strong[]… opinions" do," or connects this idea to "discussing philosophers whose views conflict with judge's views." In fact, nothing in the text even mentions the idea of an opinion or view being "broadly held," or popular, or anything like that. So this choice doesn't restate or demonstrate ideas from the provided text, which means it's wrong.

- **Vertical Scan Results:** Each choice is a subject pronoun.
- **Vertical Scan Notes:** We need to determine whether the pronoun should be singular or plural, and which pronoun appropriately refers to the relevant noun in the provided text.
- **Key Features in Surrounding Text:** The blank tells us who "wanted a bag." The "customers" are the ones whom the "cashiers" "ask[ed]" about "want[ing] a bag," so the pronoun in the blank needs to refer to the plural third-person noun "customers."

Concepts in the question:

- **Pronouns:** Any pronoun in the correct answer choice must refer back to one specific phrase from the provided text. We can't use a pronoun on the SAT when it isn't clear what that pronoun refers to. (See page 78.)
- **Singular/Plural:** Choices include singular and plural versions of the same base word(s). Nouns, pronouns, and verbs must agree in number with the words they refer to or modify. (See page 81.)

ANSWER CHOICE ANALYSIS

A ✓   **Correct:** The underlined phrase refers to "customers," so the phrase needs to be plural and third person. This is the only choice that meets those requirements, so we know (A) is correct.

B   **Incorrect:** The underlined phrase refers to "customers," so the phrase needs to be plural and third person. This choice is *singular* and third person, so (B) is wrong.

C   **Incorrect:** The underlined phrase refers to "customers," so the phrase needs to be plural and third person. This choice can be plural, but it's in the *second* person, and there's nothing in the text to indicate that this text is addressed to the "customer" directly, as the word "you" would require. So (C) is wrong.

D   **Incorrect:** This choice has the same basic problem as (B), and is wrong for the same reasons.

> **Note**   A lot of untrained test-takers will feel like any one of these choices could work. But as trained test-takers, we know that any pronoun that appears in the correct answer to an SAT Writing question must clearly refer to a specific noun in the provided text. Only the plural pronoun "they" can refer to the plural noun "customers," whereas there's nothing in the provided text that (B), (C), or (D) could refer to—so they must be wrong, whether or not some people might think those options would sound okay in real life.

- **Vertical Scan Results:** Every answer choice includes the words "soul" and "positing," along with a quotation mark, with different punctuation marks appearing between the words "soul" and "positing."
- **Vertical Scan Notes:** We need to decide whether the right answer will include a comma, semi-colon, colon, or period.
- **Key Features in Surrounding Text:** The phrase "Epicurus defined… soul" can stand on its own as a sentence, but the phrase "positing that… absence" doesn't contain a main subject and verb phrase, so it can't stand on its own as a sentence. The phrase "positing that… absence" is a participial phrase that describes "Epicurus," the first noun in the sentence that contains the blank, so that phrase should be separated from the independent clause by a comma.

Concepts in the question:

- **Avoid Dangling Participles:** When a phrase starting with an -ing/-ed/-en word is joined to the main sentence by a comma, the first noun phrase in the independent clause of that sentence is described by the -ing/-ed/-en word. (See page 90.)
- **Independent and Dependent Clauses:** Choices would create and/or join clauses. An independent clause can stand on its own as a sentence, and a dependent clause can't. Remember rules for joining clauses related to periods, semi-colons, colons, commas, and conjunctions. (See page 82.)
- **Semicolons:** Semicolons can be used to separate two sets of words that could each stand on their own as complete sentences, or to separate items in a complex list. (See page 86.)

ANSWER CHOICE ANALYSIS

A ✓ Correct: This choice uses a comma to separate "Epicurus defined… soul," which can stand on its own as a sentence, and the participial phrase "positing that… absence," which describes "Epicurus," the first noun phrase in this sentence's independent clause. This satisfies our analysis above, so (A) is correct.

B Incorrect: What comes after the word "soul" isn't an example or explanation of what comes before the word soul, which means we can't have a colon after "soul." So (B) is wrong.

C Incorrect: What comes after the word "soul" can't stand on its own as a complete sentence, which means we can't have a semi-colon after "soul." So (C) is wrong.

D Incorrect: This choice has the same problem as (C)—what comes after the word "soul" can't stand on its own as a complete sentence, which means we can't have a period between "soul" and "positing." So (D) is wrong.

Test 1, Module 1, Question 21 — TYPE: SAT WRITING

- Vertical Scan Results: The answer choices are either possessive pronouns or contractions involving pronouns.
- Vertical Scan Notes: We need to decide whether the answer should be a possessive pronoun or a contraction involving a pronoun and a form of the verb "to be." We also need to decide whether the answer should be singular or plural.
- Key Features in Surrounding Text: The underlined phrase describes "findings." The word "findings" refers to what "Watson and Crick discovered," so we know that the "findings" belong to "Watson and Crick." That means the underlined phrase needs to be a possessive third-person plural pronoun.

Concepts in the question:

- Possessive and/or Plural: Choices include nouns ending in "-s," with or without an apostrophe before or after the "-s." The provided text will indicate which nouns should show ownership, and which shouldn't. (See page 79.)
- Singular/Plural: Choices include singular and plural versions of the same base word(s). Nouns, pronouns, and verbs must agree in number with the words they refer to or modify. (See page 81.)

ANSWER CHOICE ANALYSIS

A Incorrect: The underlined phrase needs to be a possessive third-person plural pronoun. This choice includes a third-person plural pronoun ("they"), but that pronoun isn't possessive; "they're" is the same in meaning as the phrase "they are," and if we inserted it into the provided text we would get "they are findings were based on…" which would result in one independent clause with two main verbs ("are" and "were"), and no acceptable punctuation to join them. Also, this choice would fail to indicate possession, as discussed in our analysis above. So (A) is wrong.

B Incorrect: This choice is similar to (A)—with the added problem that the pronoun is singular, not plural—and is wrong for the same reasons

C ✓ Correct: The underlined phrase needs to be a possessive third-person plural pronoun. This is the possessive form "their," which is both third-person and plural. This creates the phrase "their findings," which tells us that the "finding" belong to "Watson and Crick." So (C) is right.

D Incorrect: This choice is a possessive form, like the right answer (C) above, but this choice is *singular*, not plural like (C). There's nothing singular in the provided text that the "findings" could belong to, and that the pronoun "its" in this choice could refer to. So (D) is wrong.

Test 1, Module 1, Question 22 — TYPE: SAT WRITING

- Vertical Scan Results: Every choice includes the same four words with different comma placements in each choice.
- Vertical Scan Notes: We need to decide whether to include a comma after the profession "critic," after the name "Stina Chyn," and/or after the verb "claims."
- Key Features in Surrounding Text: The word "critic" is a profession which provides more information about "Stina Chyn." We know from our training that we don't include commas when a person's profession appears right before that person's name, so there shouldn't be a comma after "critic." "Stina Chyn" is a noun that's doing the verb "claims." There's no reason to place a comma between a noun and the action that noun is performing, so there shouldn't be a comma after "Chyn." Finally, the word "claims" comes before a quote that can't stand on its own as a sentence, and we know from our training that there shouldn't be a comma before a quote that can't stand on its own as a sentence.

Concepts in the question:

- Commas: Commas can be used between clauses, to form comma sandwiches, in a list of 3 or more items, and before reported speech. They can't appear for no reason. Review the training for the relevant details. (See page 86.)

Facebook.com/QuestPreparation   Youtube.com/QuestPrep

- **Quotations:** Commas may or may not need to appear before quotations, depending on whether the quotation can stand on its own as a sentence, and how the quotation is introduced. Review the training for the relevant details. (See page 87.)

A   Incorrect: As we discussed above, the correct answer shouldn't contain any commas, so this choice is wrong.

B   Incorrect: This choice has the same basic problem as (A).

C ✓   Correct: As we saw in our discussion above, the correct answer shouldn't contain any commas, so (C) is correct.

D   Incorrect: Like (A) and (B), this choice violates the reasoning we discussed above.

> **Note**   Some untrained test-takers will hesitate to pick the choice that includes no commas at all, because they'll feel like at least one of the commas in the answer choices should be there. But as trained test-takers, we know that we can only include commas (or any other punctuation) in an answer to an SAT Writing question when there is a specific reason from our training for that comma to appear. None of the commas in the answer choices meets that requirement, so we know the correct answer is the one without any commas. Remember this on test day, and don't second-guess yourself about excluding punctuation when there's no specific reason for that punctuation to appear.

Test 1, Module 1, Question 23   TYPE: SAT WRITING

- **Vertical Scan Results:** Each choice is a different version of the verb "to claim."
- **Vertical Scan Notes:** Two choices are participles, and one is an infinitive. Only one choice, (B), is a conjugated form of the verb "to claim."
- **Key Features in Surrounding Text:** The noun doing the action in the blank is the third-person plural noun "historians," so we need a third-person plural verb form in the blank.

Concepts in the question:

- **Independent and Dependent Clauses:** Choices would create and/or join clauses. An independent clause can stand on its own as a sentence, and a dependent clause can't. Remember rules for joining clauses related to periods, semi-colons, colons, commas, and conjunctions. (See page 82.)
- **Verb Tense/Conjugation:** Choices include different forms of the same verb. Look at the surrounding text to find the verb's subject. Also, look for other clues that could indicate the proper tense or form of the verb in the blank. (See page 77.)

A   Incorrect: This choice is a participle, and it would leave this sentence without a main verb, and without an independent clause. So (A) is wrong.

B ✓   Correct: This is the third-person plural verb form "claim," which appropriately modifies its third-person plural subject "historians." This is exactly what needs to go in the blank, as discussed above, because it provides the sentence with a main verb, and creates an acceptable independent clause. So (B) is right. (Note that "which occurs when… demand" is a dependent clause.)

C   Incorrect: This is a past-participle that, like (A), would leave the sentence without a main verb or an independent clause. So (C) is wrong.

D   Incorrect: This is the infinitive form "to claim" and it would create the same problem that (A) and (C) would create.

Test 1, Module 1, Question 24   TYPE: SAT WRITING

- **Vertical Scan Results:** Each choice starts with the word "food." Two choices have punctuation after the word "food," and one adds the word "while" after food.
- **Vertical Scan Notes:** We need to decide whether a colon, comma, or the word "while" should appear after "food," or whether "food" should stand on its own.
- **Key Features in Surrounding Text:** "Researchers studying… food" can stand on its own as a sentence. Also, the text that appears after the word "food" illustrates the reason "why some soil-dwelling roundworms in the Southern Hemisphere move in the opposite direction of Earth's magnetic field," as mentioned before the blank, which means there should be a colon after "food."

Concepts in the question:

- **Colons:** A colon can only be placed after a group of words that could be a sentence on its own. Everything after the colon must be a demonstration or example of the idea before the colon. (See page 85.)
- **Comma Splice:** A comma can't join two groups of words that could each be sentences on their own. (See page 83.)

- **Independent and Dependent Clauses:** Choices would create and/or join clauses. An independent clause can stand on its own as a sentence, and a dependent clause can't. Remember rules for joining clauses related to periods, semi-colons, colons, commas, and conjunctions. (See page 82.)

A ✓ Correct: This would cause everything leading up to "food" to be a sentence that can stand on its own, and everything after "food" to be an explanation of the idea mentioned before the colon. This is the exact situation that requires a colon in SAT Writing questions, so this choice is correct.

B Incorrect: This would create a comma splice, because everything before the comma could stand on its own as a sentence, and everything after the comma could also stand on its own as a sentence. So (B) is wrong.

C Incorrect: This choice, like (B) would create a comma splice—in this case, "Researchers... Northern Hemisphere" could stand on its own as a sentence, and "the magnetic field... sources" could also stand on its own as a sentence. So (C) is wrong.

D Incorrect: This choice has the same problem as (C), and is wrong for the same reason. (We could also think of it as a run-on sentence, since "researchers studying... food" can stand on its own as a sentence, and "in the Northern Hemisphere... sources" can also stand on its own as a sentence—but either way, the result of this choice is unacceptable in an SAT Writing question.)

Test 1, Module 1, Question 25   TYPE: SAT WRITING

- **Vertical Scan Results:** Each choice is a third-person pronoun; two are plural and two are singular. Two choices end with a version of "self," and two don't.
- **Vertical Scan Notes:** We need to decide whether the pronoun should be singular or plural, and whether it should end with a form of "self."
- **Key Features in Surrounding Text:** There's no singular noun before the underlined phrase that the underlined phrase could refer to. There are multiple plural nouns that the underlined phrase could refer to.

Concepts in the question:

- **Pronouns:** Any pronoun in the correct answer choice must refer back to one specific phrase from the provided text. We can't use a pronoun on the SAT when it isn't clear what that pronoun refers to. (See page 78.)
- **Singular/Plural:** Choices include singular and plural versions of the same base word(s). Nouns, pronouns, and verbs must agree in number with the words they refer to or modify. (See page 81.)

A Incorrect: This choice is wrong because there isn't any singular noun that appears before the underlined phrase that "it" from this choice could refer to. ("Barnacle" in the phrase "species of barnacle" is a singular noun, but this is part of the prepositional phrase "of barnacle" that describes "species," and isn't a physical object in the situation described in the sentence that the "turtle barnacles" could "attach" "to a sea turtle shell.")

B ✓ Correct: The pronoun in the blank must refer to a noun that already appeared in the sentence. All the nouns that this pronoun could refer to are plural, so the correct answer must be a plural pronoun—but that plural pronoun must somehow make it clear which plural noun it refers to. This choice ends with "-selves," which makes it clear that this pronoun is referring back to the "turtle barnacles" that are doing the "dissolv[ing]"—without including "-selves," this choice could refer to any of several different plural nouns in the sentence ("scientists," "species," "turtle barnacles," or "secretions"). Choice (B) avoids that ambiguity, so (B) is correct. See our discussion of (C) for more.

C Incorrect: As we saw in our discussion of (B), the pronoun in the blank must be plural. But "them" could refer to multiple plural nouns from the sentence, and we know that when pronouns appear in correct answer choices in SAT Writing questions, it must be clear what those pronouns refer to. It's not clear what "them" would refer to, so (C) is wrong.

D Incorrect: This choice has the same basic problem as (A), and is wrong for the same reason.

Test 1, Module 1, Question 26   TYPE: SAT WRITING

- **Vertical Scan Results:** Each choice is different form of the verb "to allow."
- **Vertical Scan Notes:** We need to decide whether the verb form should be singular or plural, and, if it should be plural, which form to use.
- **Key Features in Surrounding Text:** The intervening phrase "on one of the good spaces" appears right before the underlined phrase. If we remove that phrase, we're left with the phrase "landing (blank) a player to skip ahead...." With the intervening phrase removed, we can see that the subject of the verb in the underlined phrase is the singular noun "landing," which means that the correct answer must be a singular verb form.

Concepts in the question:

- **Intervening Phrase:** A distracting phrase appears between words that need to agree with each other grammatically. Identify pairs of words that need to agree with each other, and ignore phrases that appear between those words. (See page 92.)
- **Verb Tense/Conjugation:** Choices include different forms of the same verb. Look at the surrounding text to find the verb's subject. Also, look for other clues that could indicate the proper tense or form of the verb in the blank. (See page 77.)
- **Singular/Plural:** Choices include singular and plural versions of the same base word(s). Nouns, pronouns, and verbs must agree in number with the words they refer to or modify. (See page 81.)

ANSWER CHOICE ANALYSIS

A ✓ **Correct:** This is a singular verb form, which is appropriate because the verb doing the action in the blank is the singular noun "landing," as discussed above. So (A) is correct.

B **Incorrect:** This is a plural verb form, which is inappropriate because the verb doing the action is the singular noun "landing," as discussed above. So (B) is wrong.

C **Incorrect:** This choice has the same problem as (B), and is wrong for the same reason.

D **Incorrect:** This choice has the same problem as (B) and (C), and is wrong for the same reason.

> **Note** An untrained test-taker might read the provided sentence, not notice the intervening phrase "on one of the good spaces," think that the plural noun "spaces" was the subject of the verb in the underlined phrase, and then not be able to choose from among (B), (C), and (D). On the other hand, realizing that the subject of the verb in the blank is actually the singular noun "landing" makes it easy for us to choose the only singular verb form in the answer choices. Remember that the College Board loves to use intervening phrases (like "on one of the good spaces") to make it less clear which nouns and verbs need to agree with each other—so we always need to be on the lookout for this issue when answering SAT Writing questions.

Test 1, Module 1, Question 27   **TYPE: SAT WRITING**

- **Vertical Scan Results:** Every answer choice includes the words "equations" and "though" with different options for punctuation after each word.
- **Vertical Scan Notes:** We need to decide whether a comma, period, or no punctuation should appear after "equations," and we need to decide whether a comm, colon, or no punctuation should appear after "though."
- **Key Features in Surrounding Text:** "Hopper's subsequent… though" can stand on its own as a sentence, and everything that comes after "though" provides additional information about the idea expressed in the first half of that sentence.

Concepts in the question:

- **Colons:** A colon can only be placed after a group of words that could be a sentence on its own. Everything after the colon must be a demonstration or example of the idea before the colon. (See page 85.)
- **Comma Splice:** A comma can't join two groups of words that could each be sentences on their own. (See page 83.)
- **Independent and Dependent Clauses:** Choices would create and/or join clauses. An independent clause can stand on its own as a sentence, and a dependent clause can't. Remember rules for joining clauses related to periods, semi-colons, colons, commas, and conjunctions. (See page 82.)

ANSWER CHOICE ANALYSIS

A ✓ **Correct:** This is an appropriate use of a colon, because everything leading up to the colon can stand on its own as a sentence, and everything that comes after the colon is a further explanation of the idea expressed before the colon. This choice follows the College Board's standards for using colons, and it doesn't create any other problems—so (A) is correct.

B **Incorrect:** This would create a comma splice, because "Hopper's subsequent… though" can stand on its own as a sentence, and "as a… digital age" can stand on its own as a sentence. We can't separate two sentences with a comma, so (B) is wrong.

C **Incorrect:** This choice would make the word "though" part of the sentence "as a pioneering computer programmer, Hopper would help usher in the digital age." The word "though" indicates some kind of opposition to the idea that came before the sentence containing the word "though," but in this case, the sentence where "though" appears wouldn't demonstrate that relationship—in fact, the idea that Hopper "would help usher in the digital age" provides an *example* of how her "subsequent career would involve more than just equations," as the previous sentence would say. Since nothing in this sentence would oppose an idea from the previous sentence, the word "though" can't appear at the beginning of this sentence, which means (C) must be wrong.

D   Incorrect: This choice would result in a run-on sentence—that is, two groups of words that can each stand on their own as a sentence without any punctuation between them ("Hopper's subsequent… though" and "as a… digital age"). This violates the College Board's standards, so (D) is wrong.

- Vertical Scan Results: Each choice is a multi-word phrase that expresses a similar idea with different wording.
- Vertical Scan Notes: We have to decide which wording follows the College Board's standards.
- Key Features in Surrounding Text: Each answer choice is the independent clause of the sentence where it would appear. The underlined phrase is preceded by the participial phrase "upon recovering two years later." We know from our training that this participial phrase must logically describe the first noun phrase in the independent clause of the sentence where it appears—in this case, the first noun phrase in the correct answer choice.

Concepts in the question:

- Avoid Dangling Participles: When a phrase starting with an -ing/-ed/-en word is joined to the main sentence by a comma, the first noun phrase in the independent clause of that sentence is described by the -ing/-ed/-en word. (See page 90.)
- Independent and Dependent Clauses: Choices would create and/or join clauses. An independent clause can stand on its own as a sentence, and a dependent clause can't. Remember rules for joining clauses related to periods, semi-colons, colons, commas, and conjunctions. (See page 82.)

ANSWER CHOICE ANALYSIS

A ✓ Correct: This choice would cause "upon recovering two years later" to describe "Henry," since "Henry" is the first noun phrase in this choice. It makes sense for "Henry" to be the one "recovering two years later," so (A) is correct.

B   Incorrect: This choice would cause "upon recovering two years later" to describe "the reign of Henry," since "the reign of Henry" is the first noun phrase in this choice. We can't say that "the reign of Henry" is the one "recovering two years later"—Henry is recovering, not his reign—so (B) is wrong.

C   Incorrect: This choice has the same problem as (B)—it would cause "upon recovering two years later" to describe "Henry's reign," since "Henry's reign" is the first noun phrase in this choice. We can't say that "Henry's reign" is the one "recovering two years later," so (C) is wrong.

D   Incorrect: This choice would cause "upon recovering two years later" to describe "it," since "it" is the first noun phrase in this choice. We can't say that "it" is the one "recovering two years later"—Henry is recovering, not "it"—so (D) is wrong.

The choices are different transition phrases like "however," "instead of," or "for example." The right answer must reflect the relationship between the concepts before and after the blank. See "What about Logical Transition Questions?" on p. 71.

Subjective Phrases to Ignore: "most"

A   Direct Contradiction: The text tells us about "hybrid works" that incorporate elements of "both" "novels and poems." Then, after the underlined phrase, the text describes a "verse novel" that's a "book-length narrative… conveyed in… poetry." So what comes after the underlined phrase is an example of the idea described before the underlined phrase. But this phrase would indicate that there is some kind of difference or "contrast" between what comes before the underlined phrase and what comes after the underlined phrase. This contrast isn't demonstrated in the provided text—in fact, it's basically the opposite of what appears in the text—so (A) is wrong.

B   Confused Relationships: We saw in our discussion of (A) that what comes after the underlined phrase is an example of what comes before the underlined phrase. But this choice would say that what comes after the underlined phrase is some kind of result or consequence of what comes before that phrase; this idea isn't demonstrated in in the provided text, so (B) is wrong. This choice will be tempting for untrained test-takers who recognize that both halves of the sentence express similar ideas, and who think a word like "consequently" is fine to put between two similar ideas—but on an SAT Reading question, we can't pick an answer choice because it just seems "fine!" The correct answer must specifically restate or demonstrate ideas from the relevant text—as we'll see in our discussion of (D)—and that's not the case for (B).

C   Confused Relationships: This choice would reflect the idea that what comes after the underlined phrase is some kind of additional information beyond what was discussed before the underlined phrase—but that's not the case here, as we see in our discussion of the other answer choices. Instead, the text after the underlined phrase is an example of the idea expressed in the text before the underlined phrase. So (C) is wrong.

D ✓ Correct: As we saw in our discussion of (A), the text after the underlined phrase describes a "verse novel" "conveyed in... poetry," which is a direct example of the "hybrid works that incorporate both" "novels and poems" discussed in the first half of the sentence. This demonstrates the relationship required by (D) of the second half of the sentence being an "example" of what's discussed in the first half of the sentence—so (D) is correct.

Test 1, Module 1, Question 30 **TYPE: LOGICAL TRANSITION**

The choices are different transition phrases like "however," "instead of," or "for example." The right answer must reflect the relationship between the concepts before and after the blank. See "What about Logical Transition Questions?" on p. 71.

Subjective Phrases to Ignore: "most"

A Direct Contradiction: The text describes "wolves" who "at two weeks old" "can smell but cannot yet see or hear." Then it mentions "domesticated dogs," followed by the underlined phrase, and says they "can see, hear, and smell by the end of two weeks." So it tells us that wolves have one set of abilities at two weeks old, and dogs have a different set of abilities at two weeks old. This choice would require what comes after the underlined phrase to be the same idea as what comes before the underlined phrase, just expressed differently, but that's not the case here— before the underlined phrase, the text mentions one set of abilities that wolves have, and then after the underlined phrase, it mentions another set of abilities that dogs have. These are just two different ideas, not one idea expressed twice using "other words." So this is basically the opposite of the right answer, and (A) is wrong.

B Direct Contradiction: This choice indicates that what comes after the underlined phrase is an example of what comes before the underlined phrase—but as we saw in our discussion of (A), the information after the underlined phrase contrasts with the information before the underlined phrase, so (B) is wrong.

C ✓ Correct: This choice indicates that what follows the underlined phrase is different from what precedes the underlined phrase, which is exactly the case, as we saw in our discussion of (A)—the "wolves" "can smell but cannot yet see or hear," but the "dogs... can see, hear, and smell." So (C) is correct.

D Direct Contradiction: This choice would indicate that what comes after the underlined phrase is somehow appropriate based on the information before the underline phrase, or is the logical result of that information. But as we've already discussed, this isn't the case—the ideas before and after the underlined phrase are different from each other. So (D) is wrong.

Test 1, Module 1, Question 31 **TYPE: LOGICAL TRANSITION**

The choices are different transition phrases like "however," "instead of," or "for example." The right answer must reflect the relationship between the concepts before and after the blank. See "What about Logical Transition Questions?" on p. 71.

Subjective Phrases to Ignore: "most"

A Confused Relationships: This choice will be tempting for untrained test-takers who read the provided text and notice that the ideas expressed before the underlined phrase are basically the same as the ideas expressed after the underline phrase, and who think that "similarly" reflects this relationship. But the word "similarly" describes one idea that is *like* another idea, which isn't the case for the provided text: in these two sentences, *only one idea* is being discussed—the idea that "mathematicians" mostly used to work alone, but now they tend to work with other mathematicians. It would be okay to say something like "mathematicians tend to work alone; similarly, physicists also like to work alone," because that would be two distinct ideas that share some similarity. But it wouldn't be okay to say "mathematicians don't work alone as much anymore; similarly, they tend to work with other people now." This would basically be the same idea expressed twice, which isn't two "similar[]" ideas—it's two *identical* ideas. So (A) is wrong.

B Confused Relationships: This choice would indicate that what comes before the underlined phrase is the cause of what comes after the underlined phrase—but as we saw in our discussion of (A), the first sentence basically says that someone says mathematicians are working alone less frequently, and the second sentence just says again that this phenomenon is happening. So the first sentence isn't the cause of the second sentence, and (B) is wrong.

C Confused Relationships: This choice would be correct if the second sentence provided more insight or information into what's discussed in the first sentence, but that's not the case—see our discussion of (D) for more.

D ✓ Correct: The first sentence says "mathematicians have traditionally worked alone," but that there's been "a shift in the opposite direction." This choice would cause the second sentence to say that "increasingly, mathematicians are choosing to collaborate," and that this is a "trend illustrated by" more "mathematics publications credited to multiple authors." "Mathematicians" "choosing to collaborate" "increasingly" demonstrates the idea of a "trend" of more "mathematics publications credited to multiple authors," as well as "a shift in the opposite direction" from "mathematicians... work[ing] alone." The idea that "mathematicians are choosing to collaborate with their peers" "increasingly" is demonstrated in the text, so (D) is correct.

The passage presents a bulleted list of notes, then tells us a goal related to presenting that information. The correct answer will be the only one that demonstrates the ideas in the provided goal. See "What about Notes Questions?" on p. 71.

Subjective Phrases to Ignore: "most"

A   **Literary Interpretation:** The prompt says the student "wants to present the study and its findings," so the right answer must do both of these things. This choice mentions that "Chinsamy-Turan studied" something, but doesn't say what her "findings" were, as the prompt requires. This answer choice does mention that she was "initially unsure" of something, but "findings" aren't what we know or don't know at the beginning of a study—"findings" refers to what is found by the end of the study. This choice doesn't mention anything about what Chinsamy-Turan found out at the end of the study, so (A) is wrong.

B   **Literary Interpretation:** This choice has the same basic problem as (A)—it mentions a study, but doesn't mention "findings," as the prompt requires. To say the "jawbones… were the focus" of the study just tells us what the study was about; it doesn't tells us what anyone found out about the jawbones. Like (A), this choice doesn't mention "findings," so it's wrong.

C   **Literary Interpretation:** This choice has the same problem as (A) and (B)—it mentions the study, but not any "findings." Knowing that Chinsamy-Turan used certain techniques or that pterosaurs were "flying reptiles" from "millions of years ago" still doesn't tell us what Chinsamy-Turan found in her study. So (C) is wrong.

D ✓   **Correct:** This choice mentions "a 2021 study," and it tell us that Chinsamy-Turan "determined that pterosaur bones… had few growth lines… and thus belonged to juveniles." Since the choice mentions the study *and* tells what Chinsamy-Turan learned as a result of the study, we can say that it "present[s] the study and its findings," as the prompt requires. So (D) is right.

The passage presents a bulleted list of notes, then tells us a goal related to presenting that information. The correct answer will be the only one that demonstrates the ideas in the provided goal. See "What about Notes Questions?" on p. 71.

Subjective Phrases to Ignore: "most"

A   **Literary Interpretation:** The prompt says the student "wants to compare the two women's contributions to the March on Washington," so the right answer needs to demonstrate this goal in action. We can see that the provided notes mention two women named Anna Hedgeman and Daisy Bates. This choice mentions broadly that both women "contributed to the march," but only specifically describes what "Bates" did (she "delivered a brief but memorable address") with no mention of Hedgeman. We can't say this choice "compare[s]" the contributions of the two women if it doesn't even mention what one of the women contributed. So (A) is wrong.

B   **Literary Interpretation:** This choice tells us that Hedgeman "helped organize the march," which is one of the women's "contributions to the March on Washington," but the information about Bates is generalized, and doesn't mention what she did for the march: it says she "was a journalist and a school desegregation advocate." So, like choice (A), choice (B) only tells us one woman's contribution to the march—not both, as the prompt would require. That means (B) is wrong too.

C ✓   **Correct:** This is the only choice that tells us how both women "contribut[ed] to the March on Washington," as the prompt requires it says that "Hedgeman worked behind the scenes to make sure a woman speaker was included," and that "Bates was the sole woman to speak at the march." So (C) is correct. (Note that the word "although" makes the distinction between Hedgeman, who "worked behind the scenes," and "Bates," who spoke at the march, which demonstrates the idea of "compar[ing]," as required by the prompt.)

D   **Barely Relevant:** This choice provides general information about "African American women… [fighting] for civil rights," and it says that "one [woman] spoke at the march," but it doesn't specify what either Bates or Hedgeman did to contribute to the march, as the prompt requires—so (D) is wrong.

TEST 1, MODULE 2

The prompt will be a short passage containing a blank. The correct answer will always be restated or demonstrated by key phrases in the provided text. See "What about Text Completion Questions?" on p. 66.

Subjective Phrases to Ignore: "most"

A   **Plausible but not in the Text:** This choice will be tempting to untrained test-takers for a number of reasons. First of all, this choice creates what would be a generally okay-sounding in sentence in real life. Second, a lot of people will think that Lawrence sounds kind of smart, and will sort of convince themselves that people who are smart and artistic are probably skeptical about certain things. Third, there's nothing in the sentence that says he's <u>not</u> skeptical. This is *exactly* the kind of answer choice that test-takers who don't know the standards of the test will talk themselves into choosing on test day, and those test-takers will miss the question, and not understand why. This answer choice is also clearly wrong to someone who does know the standards of the test—this choice could only be correct if the provided text restated or demonstrated the idea that Lawrence didn't just believe everything he heard, that he didn't think things were true until he found out for himself, and/or that he demonstrated some other quality we could describe as "skeptical." The provided text doesn't restate or demonstrate that idea, so (A) is wrong.

B ✓ Correct: The provided text says that Lawrence "paid close attention to all the details." Paying attention to details exactly demonstrates the idea of being "observant," as this choice requires. This choice is demonstrated in the provided text, so (B) is correct.

C Plausible but not in the Text: Like (A), this choice seems like an okay sentence in real life—and a lot of test-takers will reason that because the word "critical" is connected to art in a lot of contexts, this choice kind of goes along with what the provided text is talking about, and could be the right answer. But as trained test-takers, we know that we can't pick a choice because it just sort of goes along with what appears on the page; we can only pick choices that are directly restated or demonstrated in the text. The provided text doesn't talk about any one criticizing anything—finding fault in something, evaluating anything, offering an opinion on anything, etc. So this choice isn't demonstrated or restated in the text, and it's wrong.

D Literary Interpretation: Untrained test-takers might see that Lawrence "capture[s]… beauty and vitality" and think that he's a good artist, so he's probably "confident." As always, though, we can only pick an answer choice because it's restated or demonstrated in the text. In this case, it's not enough to think that he's *probably* confident based on something that appears in the text; instead, the text must *tell us* or *show us* that he's confident through restatement and/or demonstration. The text doesn't say that Lawrence knew he was a great painter, or told people how talented he was, or anything else that we can point to that specifically lets us know that he was "confident"—so (D) is wrong.

Test 1, Module 2, Question 2   TYPE: TEXT COMPLETION

The prompt will be a short passage containing a blank. The correct answer will always be restated or demonstrated by key phrases in the provided text. See "What about Text Completion Questions?" on p. 66.

Subjective Phrases to Ignore: "most"

A Confused Relationships: Some test-takers will be tempted by this choice because ideas like "toxicity," "venom," and getting stung by a stingray might seem "disconcerting"—that is, upsetting or worrying. But there are a couple of problems with this way of thinking: for one, the text doesn't talk about anyone being upset or worried about anything, as the word "disconcerting" would require, and for another, the blank actually describes the "effect" of "age and sex" on the venom—it doesn't describe the venom or the toxicity itself. So (A) doesn't meet the standards for this question type, and it's wrong.

B Plausible but not in the Text: It's easy to imagine a situation in real life where scientists might test something to find out whether it's "acceptable," but we can't pick an answer choice based on whether we can imagine that it would be true in real life. Instead, we need to look in the provided text to see whether the idea in the answer choice is restated or demonstrated there—and in this case, it isn't. The blank describes the "effect on the toxicity," and there's no mention of an "effect on the toxicity" that would be okay or not okay, or that should be under or over a certain threshold, or anything else related to the idea of the "effect" being "acceptable." So (B) is wrong.

C Direct Contradiction: As we'll see in our discussion of (D), the text mentions that the scientists are trying to see whether "differences in these traits" (that is, "age and sex") "are associated with" "considerable variations" in the strength of the venom; "considerable variations" are the opposite of something being "imperceptible," because something "imperceptible" would be so small it couldn't be perceived, while something "considerable" would be big enough to make a difference. This choice is the opposite of what we see in the provided text, so it's wrong. Again, see the discussion of (D) below for more.

D ✓ Correct: The text tells us that the scientists are researching whether "differences in" "age and sex" "are associated" with "considerable variation in venom potency." The blank describes the word "effect" in a sentence that talks about the "effect" that "rays' age and sex" have on venom toxicity. The word "effect" restates the idea of the "differences" being "associated" with the "variations," the word "considerable" in the text directly restates "substantial" in this answer choice, and both describe the way those "traits" impact "venom potency." So "substantial effect" restates "considerable variations" "associated with," and (D) is right.

Test 1, Module 2, Question 3   TYPE: TEXT COMPLETION

The prompt will be a short passage containing a blank. The correct answer will always be restated or demonstrated by key phrases in the provided text. See "What about Text Completion Questions?" on p. 66.

Subjective Phrases to Ignore: "most"

A ✓   Correct: The blank describes "when a person's diaphragm contracts," and the next sentence refers to this idea as "these uncontrollable contractions." "Uncontrollable" from the text directly restates the idea of these "contractions" happening "involuntarily," as this choice requires, so (A) is right.

B   Wrong Part of the Passage: This choice will be tempting to some test-takers, because the text includes the idea that hiccups "may play an important role in helping infants." That sounds like a demonstration of something "beneficial[]," and it is—but the blank doesn't describe how hiccups affect infants! Instead, the blank describes the way someone's "diaphragm contracts," and as we saw in our discussion of (A), the text specifically tells us that those contractions are "uncontrollable." This choice doesn't restate or demonstrate an idea that's relevant to the blank, so (B) is wrong.

C   Plausible but not in the Text: A lot of test-takers will pick this answer choice because it's possible for hiccupping in real life to be "strenuous[]." But we can't pick an answer choice based on our real-life experiences with topics in the provided text—this choice can only be right if the text restates or demonstrates the idea that people are straining, or exerting, or somehow putting a lot of effort into hiccupping. That idea doesn't appear in the text, so (C) is wrong.

D   Barely Relevant: As we saw in our discussion of (A), the text describes the "contractions" as "uncontrollable"—it doesn't contain any mention of the idea of the contractions (or anything else) happening "smoothly," or evenly, or without incident, or anything similar. This choice might be tempting for test-takers who remembered the mention of "infants... breathing" and thought it would be good if infants breathed "smoothly"—but this idea doesn't appear in the text. So (D) is wrong.

Test 1, Module 2, Question 4	TYPE: TEXT COMPLETION

The prompt will be a short passage containing a blank. The correct answer will always be restated or demonstrated by key phrases in the provided text. See "What about Text Completion Questions?" on p. 66.

Subjective Phrases to Ignore: "most"

A   Plausible but not in the Text: The blank appears in the phrase "rarely (blank)," so we know the right answer will restate or demonstrate something that happens "rarely," according to the text. The text then describes "a world where artists create timeless works for exhibition and designers periodically produce new styles for the public to buy." The text also says that Okuma "challenges this view" because "her work can be seen in the Metropolitan Museum of Art and purchased through her online boutique." In other words, Okuma does something that "challenges" the idea expressed by "rarely (blank)," and by the idea of "artists" creating work "for exhibition" while designers "produc[e] new styles for the public to buy." The word "prevail" in this choice isn't related to any of these ideas, because nowhere in the text is there discussion of anyone winning anything, or succeeding against an opponent, or anything like that. This choice might be tempting for readers who notice that it would cause the text to say that "art and fashion rarely prevail," and who think that art and fashion are undervalued in real life, and that some people who make art and fashion have a difficult time, or something like that—but this idea doesn't appear in the text, and we can't pick an answer choice just because we think it would result in a phrase that matches our real-life opinions. So (A) is wrong.

B   Plausible but not in the Text: This choice has the same basic problem we saw in our discussion of (A)—whereas (A) basically means winning or being successful, (B) basically means giving in or losing, and neither concept appears anywhere in the text—there's no discussion of anyone "rarely succumb[ing]" to anything, just as there's no discussion of anyone "rarely prevail[ing]" over anything. So (B) is wrong just like (A) is wrong. This choice might be tempting for test-takers who feel like an artist whose work is in the Metropolitan Museum of Art must be determined and "rarely succumb" to adversity, or something—but that's not what the text says, so we can't pick (B) based on this idea.

C   Direct Contradiction: As we'll see in our discussion of (D), this is the opposite of the right answer—the text describes "art and fashion" doing different things: "artists" creating art "for exhibition" (that is, for people to look at, but not to buy), and designers "produc[ing]... styles for the public to buy." This demonstrates the idea of art and fashion "diverg[ing]," or being different from each other... but this choice would create the phrase "*rarely* diverge" (emphasis added)! We can't pick a choice that says two things "rarely diverge" when the text immediately goes on to describe them diverging. So this choice is the opposite of the right answer, and (C) is wrong. (Note that this choice might be tempting for test-takers who overlook the word "rarely.")

D ✓   Correct: As we saw in our discussion of (A), the text says that "fine art and fashion rarely (blank)" and then tells us about "artists" making art "for exhibition" and designers making "new styles for the public to buy." It then tells us about someone who "challenges this view," whose work "can be seen" in a museum and can also be "purchased." The phrase "rarely intersect" is exactly demonstrated by that text—if art and fashion "rarely intersect," then an example of that would be art being made "for exhibition" and fashion being made "for the public to buy," since these are two opposite scenarios. Also, a "challenge" to this "view" would be a person who demonstrates the opposite of that idea—that is, art and fashion not going in different directions, but instead coming together. In this case, that person is Okuma, whose work is on display in a museum and *also* available to buy. So the text demonstrates the idea that "art and fashion rarely intersect," which means (D) is correct.

Note The College Board loves to fluster test-takers when possible, and the phrase "Luiseño/ Shoshone-Bannock beadwork artist and designer Jamie Okuma" is an excellent example. This is basically just a string of nouns all in a row, and the first time you try to read it, you might think you overlooked a word or phrase somewhere because you feel like you can't make sense of it. But once you realize the College Board is basically just telling you that there's a person called Jamie Okuma, you can understand the text and move on with the question. Don't be intimidated by words or phrases that are unusual or hard to process at first—the College Board has to adhere to its own standards, which are pretty transparent and repetitive once you understand them, so it likes to throw in little wrinkles like this to try to make the questions a little harder. When you see a word or phrase like this on test day that's a little hard to grasp, just stay focused, keep reading, remember your training, and remember that all real SAT questions must follow the same standards.

The prompt will be a short passage containing a blank. The correct answer will always be restated or demonstrated by key phrases in the provided text. See "What about Text Completion Questions?" on p. 66.

Subjective Phrases to Ignore: "most"

A   **Barely Relevant:** This choice could be tempting to an untrained test-taker because the text discusses Shakespeare, and we might have a general association between Shakespeare and a character in a play "interject[ing]" a line. But that connection doesn't appear in the text, and the idea of "Elizabethan society" "interject[ing]" anything isn't restated or demonstrated anywhere. So we know (A) must be wrong. (This choice might also be tempting for test-takers who think "interject[]" can mean something like "force something on someone." But that's not what "interject[]" means—remember that on the SAT, we have to think very carefully about exactly what words actually do and don't mean in a way that is rarely necessary in a classroom situation .)

B   **Confused Relationships:** This choice will be tempting for test-takers who misread the text and think that "committed" refers to the word "rebellion"—that is, that this choice would cause the text to describe a "rebellion" "committed" by "the playwright's characters." But that's not what the text says! If we read more closely, we can see that the action of the verb in the blank is being done by "Elizabethan society" to "rigid expectations." Nothing in the text restates or demonstrates the idea of "Elizabethan society" carrying out or perpetrating "rigid expectations," and it's not even really clear what it would mean to "commit[]" "expectations." So (B) is wrong.

C   **Literary Interpretation:** A lot of test-takers will have a hard time choosing between this choice and the correct answer, (D). As always, the distinction comes down to restatement and demonstration. In a "real world" classroom context, almost no teacher or professor anywhere would find a problem with this word appearing in this sentence. But we know as trained test-takers that on the SAT, the correct answer must be restated or demonstrated in the provided text. For this choice, that would mean that the text would have to describe "Elizabethan society" "illustrat[ing]" "rigid expectations"—that is, the text would actually have to show "Elizabethan society" providing specific examples or illustrations of "rigid expectations." That could include phrases like "men always had to wear hats and women always had to wear gloves" or "it was absolutely forbidden for women to be in the park after 9 o'clock," or something else along those lines. But the text doesn't mention any examples like this. Note that simply including phrases like "rigid expectations" and "socially dictated gender roles" isn't the same as "illustrat[ing]" those ideas, as the examples I just provided would do. With all of this in mind, we know (C) is wrong.

D ✓   **Correct:** The text describes "rigid expectations (blank) by Elizabethan society," then refers back to "socially dictated... roles." "Society" "prescrib[ing]" something means "society" advising or requiring that someone do something, which is pretty much exactly demonstrated by the phrase "rigid expectations" and the idea of "socially dictated" "roles." So (D) appears directly in the text, which means it's right.

The prompt will be a short passage containing a blank. The correct answer will always be restated or demonstrated by key phrases in the provided text. See "What about Text Completion Questions?" on p. 66.

Subjective Phrases to Ignore: "most"

A   **Literary Interpretation:** This choice will be very tempting for test-takers who are somewhat familiar with the SAT's standards, but don't quite read carefully enough. The text mentions "such (blank) stimuli" and then says they "offer less relief" than something else. Someone who reads this without being careful about the relevant details might come away with the idea that the "stimuli" are somehow tricking people, or that they offer less relief than people think, and they're not what they seem, or something like that—but that's not what the text says! It just says the stimuli offer less relief than another option. So nothing in the text restates or demonstrates the idea that the stimuli are "deceptive," which means (A) is wrong.

B ✓ Correct: The phrase "such (blank) stimuli" refers back to the phrase "harmless applications of vibration or warming." The word "harmless" means the same thing as "innocuous," so this choice plainly restates the relevant text, which means (B) is correct.

C Literary Interpretation: This is the kind of choice that an untrained test-taker can easily find some justification for, but it doesn't meet the SAT's requirements for right answers on this question type. An untrained test-taker might decide that the "harmless applications" must be some new kind of treatment, or that "mild electric shock" must be a new treatment for this situation, or that we can call "vibration or warming" a kind of "novel stimuli" because the patient's body isn't used to them, or something... but the bottom line is that none of this is plainly stated in the provided text, so it can't be the basis for choosing the right answer on an SAT Reading question. The idea of anything being "novel," or new, isn't restated or demonstrated anywhere, which means (C) is wrong.

D Plausible but not in the Text: An untrained test-taker could easily make the argument that, in real life, vibration or warming are "impractical" ways to treat patients, because people might not have the equipment needed to produce those stimuli when they're out and about in their daily lives, or something like that. But this kind of argument has no basis on the SAT—we can only pick answers to questions like this one by basing them on the provided text, and that text doesn't say anything about whether any "stimuli" are "impractical" or not. So (D) is wrong.

Test 1, Module 2, Question 7	TYPE: TEXT COMPLETION

The prompt will be a short passage containing a blank. The correct answer will always be restated or demonstrated by key phrases in the provided text. See "What about Text Completion Questions?" on p. 66.

Subjective Phrases to Ignore: "most"

A Literary Interpretation: An untrained test-taker could easily do some literary interpretation to come up with a reason to select this choice as a way to describe a "province" on the "coast," "hundreds of kilometers" from the capital, that can only be reached "after a long overland journey." That interpretation would involve assuming that this "province" must be something small and unremarkable, so it probably isn't very noticeable and doesn't call much attention to itself, which would mean we could call it "unobtrusive." But again, this kind of analysis would require literary interpretation that goes beyond what's directly stated in the provided text; that text doesn't actually restate or demonstrate the idea that "Xoconochco's location" was "unobtrusive," so (A) is wrong. See the note below for a more in-depth discussion of the wrong answer choices for this question.

B Literary Interpretation: This choice has the same problem as (A), and is wrong for the same reasons—see the note below for a more in-depth discussion of the wrong answer choices for this question.

C Literary Interpretation: This choice has the same problem as (A), and is wrong for the same reasons—see the note below for a more in-depth discussion of the wrong answer choices for this question.

D ✓ Correct: The text says that Xoconochco was "hundreds of kilometers southeast of Tenochtitlan, the capital," and that you could only get to the capital from there "after a long overland journey." The word "peripheral" means something like "off to the side," or "away from the main area." Many test-takers will be familiar with this word from the phrase "peripheral vision," which describes seeing things out on the edge, outside of the main field of vision. The blank describes "Xoconochco's location within the empire," and (as discussed above) we're told that this "province" is very far away from the capital—this directly demonstrates that Xoconochco's location is "peripheral." So (D) is correct.

Note   When we read this text, we probably get an image in our minds of jungle, and dense forest, and wild areas, especially if we're at all familiar with the geography of the Aztec Empire. Because of that, an untrained test-taker could be very tempted to pick a word like "unobtrusive" or "concealed," based on the idea that Xoconochco might be surrounded by dense jungle and easy to overlook, or a word like "approximate," thinking that Xoconochco was so remote and overgrown that other people might not even be sure exactly where it was. But it's important to recognize that none of these ideas are present in the text! It doesn't matter what our personal associations are with the ideas that appear in the text, regardless of whether those associations are correct in the real world. Our answer choices must be based on specific words and phrases that appear in the provided text, and the text only states in different ways that Xoconochco is far away from the capital, Tenochtitlan, which makes (D) correct. (Here's a bonus way to know that (A) and (B) are wrong, for training purposes: note that the blank doesn't describe "Xoconochco"—it describes "Xoconochco's location within the empire," which isn't the same thing! So (A) and (B) would say that the province's location is "unobtrusive" or "concealed," not the city itself, so even if we overlooked the fact that the text doesn't say Xoconochco is "concealed" or "unobtrusive," we should notice that the blank doesn't even describe the province; it describes the province's *location*. Always make sure you understand how the blank fits into the sentence before you reason through the answer choices!)

The prompt asks about the "main purpose" or "main idea" (or some similar phrase) of the text. The correct answer must be directly restated or demonstrated in the passage, with no interpretation. See "What about "Main Idea/Main Purpose" Questions?" on p.69.

Subjective Phrases to Ignore: "best"

A ✓ Correct: The text says that Jane "went on with [her] day's business tranquilly." "Tranquil[]" means the same thing as "calm[]," so we know that Jane demonstrates "outward calmness," as this choice requires. The text also says that "vague suggestions kept wandering across [her] brain," and that she "kept involuntarily framing advertisements and pondering conjectures about new situations," and then refers to this "framing" and "pondering" as "these thoughts." In other words, there were "suggestions" and "thoughts" in her mind that "kept" "wandering" and coming "involuntarily," which demonstrates "internal restlessness," just as this choice also requires. Furthermore, the "calmness" and "restlessness" in the text demonstrate "contrast," just as this choice requires. So every part of this choice is demonstrated in the relevant text, which means it's correct.

B Direct Contradiction: This is the opposite of what the text says—the excerpt specifically says Jane kept thinking "of reasons why I should quit Thornfield." So (B) is wrong.

C Literary Interpretation: This choice will be tempting for untrained test-takers who don't read carefully, because they could read the provided text and come away with a general idea that Jane does her work, but isn't thrilled with her job—that is, that she has some associations with the job that are kind of positive and others that are kind of negative—and then they might read this choice that mentions both "challeng[es]" and "fulfill[ment]," and kind of think "yeah, that's pretty much what the text says," then mark this answer and move on. But the text doesn't actually say that Jane finds her work either "challenging" or "fulfilling!" It just says that she does her work "tranquilly," and then says she kept thinking about leaving and getting a new job—neither of which tells us anything about whether her current job is "challenging" or "fulfilling," as this choice would require. Neither half of this choice is demonstrated or restated in the text, so (C) is wrong.

D Off by One or Two Words: This choice will be very tempting as well, because it mentions "Jane's determination to secure employment outside of Thornfield Hall," and the text *does* include the idea of Jane wanting to "quit Thornfield" and find a job somewhere else. But the provided text doesn't restate or demonstrate the idea of "determination," as this choice would require! In fact, in the provided text, Jane says "these thoughts I did not think to check; they might germinate and bear fruit if they could." In other words, she didn't stop herself from having those thoughts, and she was fine with those thoughts turning into some kind of action. But simply not stopping yourself from thinking about something, and being okay with the idea of something potentially happening as a result, isn't the same as being "determine[d]" to make that thing happen. In order to restate or demonstrate the idea of "determination," the text would have to say something about Jane doing everything she could to get another job, or refusing to stop until she had a job somewhere else, or something else along those lines. But the text doesn't say that: it just says she couldn't stop thinking about having another job, and that if those thoughts turned into action, she was okay with that. So (D) is wrong.

The question will ask what the author of one passage would think about some aspect of the other passage. The answer must always be directly stated in the text, with no guessing or assumption from the test-taker. See "What about Paired Passages?" p. 70.

Subjective Phrases to Ignore: "most likely"

A Direct Contradiction: Text 1 describes the discovery "that both humans and panther worms have a gene for... (EGR)" as "especially promising." Text 2 mentions that "excitement," then says "however... the gene likely functions very differently in humans," and "how [EGR] operates in humans remains unclear." This choice directly contradicts Text 2, because this choice says "Srivastava and her team have identified how EGR functions in both humans and panther worms." Again, Text 2 says EGR is like a "switch" and "how this switch operates in humans remains unclear," while this choice claims "Srivastava" has "identified how EGR functions in... humans." So this is the opposite of what the text says, and (A) is wrong.

B ✓ Correct: As we saw in our discussion of (B), Text 1 calls a discovery related to EGR "especially promising," and Text 2 mentions this excitement, then says "however, as the team pointed out," the gene related to EGR "likely functions very differently in humans," and how it "operates in humans remains unclear." So Text 2 provides "additional observations from Srivastava and her team" about EGR that make it "unclear" whether the discovery mentioned in Text 1 will provide any benefit, which demonstrates the idea that calling the discovery "especially promising," as Text 1 does, is "overly optimistic," exactly as this choice requires. So (B) is demonstrated in the text, which means it's right.

C Direct Contradiction: This choice will be tempting for test-takers who don't read the question carefully enough, and think that it asks what the author of *Text 1* would say about the additional information about EGR in *Text 2*, instead of the other way around. If that were the case, this answer could seem to make sense, because Text 1 says the discovery related to EGR is "promising," but the information in Text 2 tells us that the discovery isn't really that promising—with this in mind, the author of Text 1 might call the author of Text 2's lack of excitement "unexpected." But again, that analysis is based on getting confused about which author is commenting on which text. Even without that misreading of the question, this choice could still be tempting, because it mentions that "Srivastava and her team's findings were generally met with enthusiasm," which *is* an idea that appears in Text 2 (that text says the team's "report[]… caused excitement"). But this question asks us what the author of Text 2 would say about "Text 1's characterization of the discovery," and Text 1 says the discovery is "promising." This choice would say that characterization was unexpected, because the "findings were generally met with enthusiasm." In other words, this choice would say that the "discovery involving EGR" being seen as "promising" was "unexpected" because the "findings were generally met with enthusiasm." But something "promising" being "met with enthusiasm" would be *expected*, not "unexpected." So (C) demonstrates the opposite of what appears in the text, and (C) is wrong.

D   Direct Contradiction: This choice is basically the opposite of the right answer. As we saw in our discussion of (B), "Text 1's characterization of the discovery involving EGR" is that it's "especially promising," but Text 2 tells us that the way EGR "operates in humans remains unclear"—this doesn't demonstrate the idea of something being "unfairly dismissive," as this choice would require. Being "unfairly dismissive" would mean downplaying something as unimportant or unremarkable when it really *is* important or remarkable—but again, in this case, the "promising discovery" from Text 1 turned out to be something whose actual impact "remains unclear," which means "dismiss[ing]" it isn't "unfair[]," as this choice would require. So (D) is wrong.

The prompt asks about the "main purpose" or "main idea" (or some similar phrase) of the text. The correct answer must be directly restated or demonstrated in the passage, with no interpretation. See "What about "Main Idea/Main Purpose" Questions?" on p.69.

A   Literary Interpretation: The text says the speaker goes "to… bed," but that "thoughts" keep the speaker's "drooping eyelids open wide." If the speaker's eyes are "open wide," then the speaker isn't asleep—so (A) can't be right. This choice will be tempting for many test-takers, because the language is old-fashioned and it might seem to describe a person sleeping and dreaming of a friend—but the clear detail of "eyelids open wide" lets us know definitively that the speaker isn't sleeping, and (A) must be wrong.

B   Literary Interpretation: The text mentions "a journey in my head," and that "my thoughts… [begin] a… pilgrimage" to the friend—but of these two phrases that might seem to be about taking a trip somewhere, one is specifically described as being "in my head," and the other says that "thoughts" are traveling, not the speaker—in either case, we can see that the speaker isn't physically traveling to the friend, as this choice would require. Beyond that, this choice would require a "plan[]" to go somewhere, but both mentions of going somewhere (again, only in the speaker's mind) are in the present tense—"begins a journey" and "[begin] a… pilgrimage." Plans are about what *will* happen *in the future*, by definition, not what's happening now. For either of these reasons, (B) is wrong.

C   Literary Interpretation: Like (A) and (B), this choice might be tempting because some test-takers will struggle with the old-fashioned language and misunderstand exactly what's being said. But even with that in mind, this text doesn't say anything whatsoever about "discuss[ing]" anything—there's no mention of talking, or listening, or conversation, or hearing anything said out loud, or anything remotely like that at all. Since the text doesn't mention anyone "discussi[ng]" anything, (C) can't be right.

D ✓   Correct: The speaker describes going "to my bed," and then "a journey in my head," and the speaker's "thoughts" beginning a "pilgrimage" to the friend—thoughts going to a person demonstrates the idea that "the speaker is thinking about the friend," as this choice requires. Then the text says that the "thoughts" about the friend "keep my drooping eyelids open wide"—that is, keep the speaker from "falling asleep," as this choice also requires. Every idea in this choice is demonstrated in the provided text, so this choice must be correct.

The prompt asks for information from the passage. The answer must be restated or demonstrated by specific phrases in the text. See "What about General Passage Questions?" on p. 69.

A   Confused Relationships: This choice will be tempting because it says "he asks about the meaning of the crowd's shouting," which is true—the text says "he kept repeating" the question "what can it all mean?" But this choice also says "he claims to know what the crowd wants," which isn't demonstrated or restated in the text—he says the crowd has "such unanimity," but that phrase doesn't indicate what they want; it just means that they all feel the same way. This choice is only partially restated or demonstrated in the provided text, so we know it must be wrong.

B   Literary Interpretation: The Lord Chancellor hears the people and asks "what can it all mean," but he never says anything about wanting to speak to the crowd, which is enough in itself to make this choice wrong. Beyond that, the crowd doesn't "ask[] to speak to the Sub-Warden," as this choice would also require. Instead, the text says "one man" asked "who roar for the Sub-Warden"; even if we're not sure whether this means that man is asking to speak to the Sub-Warden or not, we know that it's just this "one man" asking, and not the "crowd," as this choice would require. The text also specifically tells us that "everybody roared, but whether it was for the Sub-Warden, or not, did not clearly appear." So different people in the crowd were shouting for different things, and whether or not they wanted "to speak to the Sub-Warden" wasn't "clear[]," which is another reason we know (B) is wrong.

C   Barely Relevant: This choice is wrong because the Lord Chancellor doesn't even know what the "crowd's demands" are (we know this because he says "what can it all mean?" when he hears them shouting), and he doesn't "express sympathy" about anything. This choice will be tempting for some test-takers who think he expresses "annoy[ance]" at the crowd, but whether that's true or not, we know that (C) must still be wrong for the reasons we just discussed.

D ✓   Correct: This choice says "he describes the crowd as being united," and we can see in the text that he says their shouting has "such unanimity"—that is, that they all want the same thing, or feel the same way. This demonstrates the idea of him calling the crowd "united," as the first half of this choice requires. This choice also says "the crowd clearly appears otherwise" (that is, not united)—and the provided text tells us that "some were shouting "Bread!" and some "Taxes!", but no one seemed to know what it was they really wanted." If people are shouting for different things and nobody knew "what it was they really wanted," then the crowd is clearly not "united," just as the second half of this choice requires—so we can see that (D) is correct.

The prompt will make a claim about a literary work, then ask which quotation "illustrates the claim." The right answer will plainly demonstrate the ideas in the provided claim. See "What about Quotation Questions?" on p. 70.

Subjective Phrases to Ignore: "most effectively"

A ✓   Correct: The question asks for the choice that illustrates the idea of Alexandra "having a deep emotional connection to her natural surroundings." This choice mentions "how much the country meant to her," then describes "insects" "chirping... down in the long grass," and says Alexandra "felt as if her heart were hiding down there... with... all the little wild things." The idea that the country means a lot to her and that "her heart" was "hiding" in the "grass" with "the wild things" clearly demonstrates the "deep emotional connection" that the question asks for, so (A) is correct.

B   Literary Interpretation: This choice will tempt some untrained test-takers who don't read carefully enough, because the word "natural" appears in the question, and this choice mentions "poultry" and "hay"; some test-takers will reason that these are "natural" things. But the question actually asks about "natural surroundings," and these things aren't her surroundings—beyond that, the prompt asks about an "emotional connection," and this choice doesn't mention emotion or feelings at all. This choice just talks about Alexandra discussing farming matters with different people, and "learn[ing] a great deal." In a classroom setting we might imagine that what's described in this passage could be emotionally significant to Alexandra—but this text doesn't actually restate or demonstrate that idea; a person can talk about something and learn about something without "a deep emotional connection" to that thing. So we know (B) is wrong.

C   Literary Interpretation: This choice does describe Alexandra's "surroundings," as mentioned in the prompt—it tells us about "the howling of the wind," and "the highway," and "the dark country." But it doesn't say that Alexandra has any "emotional connection" to those surroundings. In fact, there's no mention of her emotions at all; there's just a description of her riding in a wagon alone down a highway at night in the country. This is exactly the kind of choice that will tempt untrained test-takers to try to interpret its imagery as being connected to certain emotions, but no idea like that actually appears in the text. This choice doesn't demonstrate the ideas mentioned in the prompt, so it's wrong.

D   Barely Relevant: Some untrained test-takers will read this answer choice and think that Alexandra being able to figure out the cost "to fatten each steer" and "guess the weight of a hog" are examples of her being connected to nature, and they'll pick this choice on that basis. But the prompt doesn't ask for a demonstration of Alexandra being "close to nature." Instead, it asks for a demonstration of her being "*emotional[ly]* connect[ed] to her *natural surroundings*" (emphasis added). Her understanding of fattening steers and ability to guess hog weights aren't examples of *emotional* connection, as the prompt would require—they're not described using any emotional terms—and steers and hogs aren't her "natural surroundings" anyway. So this choice doesn't demonstrate the ideas mentioned in the prompt, which means (D) is wrong.

The passage includes a figure. The question asks for the choice that uses data from the figure to accomplish a certain goal. The right answer will describe the data accurately and plainly accomplish the goal. See "What about "Data" Questions?" on p. 69.

Subjective Phrases to Ignore: "best"

A   Direct Contradiction: The prompt asks us to find the choice with data that "support the researchers' claim." We can read the provided text to see that the researchers "claim that two languages with very different spoken rates can nonetheless convey the same amount of information in a given amount of time," so this is the claim the data need to support. But we know this choice is wrong without even considering the claim, because it describes the data incorrectly—it says that "Thai and Hungarian have the lowest rates of speech," but we can see that the two languages with the lowest rates of speech are actually Thai (with 4.7 syllables per second) and *Vietnamese* (with 5.3 syllables per second). So we can rule out (A) and move on.

B ✓   Correct: As we saw in our discussion of (B), we need to find data that support the claim that "two languages with very different spoken rates can nonetheless convey the same amount of information in a given amount of time." This choice achieves that goal by mentioning "Vietnamese" and "Spanish," and explaining that Vietnamese is "spoken at a slower rate than Spanish" (we can see in the table that Spanish is spoken at the fastest rate, at 7.7 syllables per second, while Vietnamese is spoken at the second slowest rate, at 5.3 syllables per second—this meets the text's requirement for two languages "with very different spoken rates"), but that these two languages "convey[] information at approximately the same rate" (we can see in the table that Spanish conveys 42.0 bits per second of information, while Vietnamese conveys 42.5 bits per second of information —this meets the text's requirement for two languages that "convey the same amount of information in a given amount of time"). We can confirm the data by checking the provided table, and we can see that (B) is correct.

C   Direct Contradiction: We can eliminate this choice immediately for the same reason we eliminated (A)—it makes a false statement about the provided data. "The language that is spoken the fastest" is Spanish, at 7.7 syllables per second, but "the language that conveys information the fastest" is Vietnamese, at 42.5 bits per second. So again, we can rule out (C).

D   Direct Contradiction: This choice has the same basic problem as (A) and (C): it incorrectly describes the provided data. We can see in the table that Serbian conveys information at 39.1 bits per second, which is *more slowly* than Spanish does, at 42.0 bits per second—but this choice says the opposite is true. So (D) is wrong.

Note   SAT Reading questions about data will often include incorrect answer choices that describe the data accurately, but that don't satisfy the prompt. However, sometimes we can eliminate every wrong answer choice simply for making inaccurate statements about the data, as we just saw above. So before you start thinking about whether an answer choice in a data question satisfies the prompt, check first to see that it even describes the provided data accurately— you might be able to save yourself some time by quickly eliminating that answer choice, and moving on.

| Test 1, Module 2, Question 14 | TYPE: IF TRUE |

The passage presents some claim or hypothesis. The prompt typically asks us to choose the "finding" that, "if true," would support or weaken the argument. Supporting statements will demonstrate the idea in the claim, and weakening statements will demonstrate the opposite of the idea in the claim. See "What about "If True" Questions?" on p. 71.

Subjective Phrases to Ignore: "most strongly"

A ✓   Correct: This question asks for the choice that would "support their claim." We can read the text to find out that their claim (which appears after the phrase "have argued that") is that "experiencing awe… can… inspire us to act more altruistically." The prompt tells us that some participants had an "awe-inspiring experience" (looking at tall trees) and others didn't (they stared at a building), and then both sets of participants saw someone drop a box of pens. This choice said that people who had the awe-inspiring experience "helped the experimenter…more" than the other participants who didn't have the awe-inspiring experience. This demonstrates the idea in the claim that "experiencing awe" (in this case, looking at tall trees) can "enable" people "to act more altruistically" (in this case, "help[ing]" someone pick up pens). Notice specifically that "help[ing]" by "pick[ing] up significantly more pens" from this choice directly demonstrates "act[ing] more altruistically" from the provided text. So this choice demonstrates the ideas from the claim, which means (A) is correct.

B   Literary Interpretation: This choice might be tempting for an untrained test-taker, because someone could read this choice and reason that participants using "a greater number of positive words to describe the trees and the building" could be evidence that those people "experience[ed]" greater "awe" than people who didn't use so many positive words, and this choice says those participants who used more positive words were the ones who "helped the experimenter pick up the pens." So this could seem to be an example of "experiencing awe" "enabl[ing]" people "to act more altruistically," which might make it hard for some test-takers to choose between (A) and (B)—except we can't conclude that using "a greater number of positive words to describe the trees and the building" is the same as having "experienc[ed] awe," or that it specifically means experiencing *more awe* than people who used fewer positive words. We know we can't answer an SAT Reading question by making our own judgments about what's "awe-inspiring" and what isn't—instead, we have to depend on the provided text. In this case, that provided text tells us that "gaz[ing]" at the "trees" was the "awe-inspiring experience." So this choice describes a mix of people who had the awe-inspiring experience (looking at trees) and people who didn't (the ones who looked at the building) "help[ing] the experimenter pick up the pens." That means this choice talks about people "act[ing]… altruistically" whether they had the "awe-inspiring experience" or not, which means this choice doesn't demonstrate anything relevant to the "researchers' claim" that "experiencing awe" leads to "altruistic[]" behavior. So (B) is wrong.

C   Direct Contradiction: This choice does the opposite of the what the researchers "claim," according to the prompt. That claim says people who "experienc[e] awe" are more likely "to act altruistically." But this choice says the people who "report[ed]...a feeling of awe" were the ones "who did not help the experimenter pick up the pens." So this contradicts the provided text, which means (C) is wrong.

D   Barely Relevant: This choice talks about whether "participants... notice that the experimenter had dropped the pens," but just noticing whether something happened isn't altruistic (or not altruistic), as the text requires. This statement doesn't say anything about people "experiencing awe" and then "act[ing] more altruistically," as described in the researchers' claim, so this choice can't "support that claim," and it must be wrong.

Test 1, Module 2, Question 15   **TYPE: DATA**

The passage includes a figure. The question asks for the choice that uses data from the figure to accomplish a certain goal. The right answer will describe the data accurately and plainly accomplish the goal. See "What about "Data" Questions?" on p. 69.

Subjective Phrases to Ignore: "most effectively"

A ✓   Correct: The provided text ends with a blank, and the prompt asks us to "complete the statement." The sentence containing the blank says "this can be clearly seen by comparing the employment by sector in both countries in...." We can look at the previous sentence to see what "this" refers to, and when we do that we see that the previous sentence says "this transition happened at very different rates in the two countries." Once more we move one sentence back to see what "this transition" refers to, and we come to the first sentence of the passage, which tells us that "over the past two hundred years, the percentage... employed in the agricultural sector has declined in both France and the United States, while employment in the service sector... has risen." So the sentence with the blank refers to the idea that this shift in employment from being more agricultural to being more service-oriented happened at different rates in the U.S. and in France, and we need to find the choice whose data "clearly" show that difference. The sentence with the blank mentions "employment by sector," and we can see that the title of the graph includes that phrase. That graph includes columns for agriculture employment and services employment, both in the U.S. and in France, which is what the passage talks about, so we know that this is the data that's relevant to the question. This choice refers to the employment by sector in both countries in 1900 and 1950. When we look at the data for those years, we see that in 1900, the percentage of people employed in agriculture in France was 43, while the percentage of people employed in agriculture in the U.S. was 41; these numbers are pretty close to each other. However, in 1950, that percentage decreased to 32 in France, and to 14 in the U.S. So we see a drop of 11 percent in France, but 27 percent in the U.S. This shows the trend of moving away from agriculture jobs happening at different speeds in the two countries, because in the same 50 year period, the change in percentage was much larger in the U.S. than it was in France. Next, let's consider those percentages for service jobs—we see that in 1900, the percentage of people employed in service jobs in France was 28, while the percentage of people employed in service jobs in the U.S. was 31; again, these numbers are pretty similar. However, in 1950, that percentage increased to 35 in France, and more dramatically to 53 in the U.S. So we see a gain of only 7 percent in France, but 22 percent in the U.S. This demonstrates that the trend of moving toward service jobs was happening "at very different rates in the two countries," as the prompt requires, because in the same 50 year period, the change in percentage in both sectors was much larger in the U.S. than it was in France. Both sets of data from this choice demonstrate the trend described in the passage, so (A) is correct.

B   Direct Contradiction: If we repeat the analysis we just did for (A), we can see that employment in agriculture in France in 1800 was 64%, and in the U.S. was 68%, while by 2012 those numbers were 3% for France and 2% for the U.S. So the percentages for employment in agriculture in France and the U.S. were pretty similar to each other in 1800, and also in 2012. Let's check the numbers for service jobs: in France in 1800 the employment in service jobs was 14%, while in the U.S. that number was 13%. In France in 2012 the employment in service jobs was 76%, while that number in the U.S. was 80%. Again, we see that the percentages for each country in the same year were pretty similar in both agriculture and in services, so this choice doesn't demonstrate the idea from the prompt that employment in the U.S. and France shifted away from agriculture and toward service jobs at "different rates." That means (B) is wrong. See our discussion of (A) for more.

C   Direct Contradiction: Let's repeat our analysis that we did for choices (A) and (B)—we can see that employment in agriculture in France in 1900 was 43%, and in the U.S. was 41%, while by 2012 those numbers were 3% for France and 2% for the U.S. So the percentages for employment in agriculture in France and the U.S. were pretty similar to each other in 1900, and also in 2012. Let's check the numbers for service jobs: in France in 1900 the employment in service jobs was 28%, while in the U.S. that number was 31%. In France in 2012 the employment in service jobs was 76%, while that number in the U.S. was 80%. Again, we see that the percentages for each country in the same year were pretty similar in both agriculture and in services, so this choice doesn't demonstrate the idea from the prompt that employment in the U.S. and France shifted away from agriculture and toward service jobs at "different rates" either. That means (C) is wrong; again, see our discussion of (A) for more

---

D Direct Contradiction: We're almost done—we just need to check the numbers for this last answer choice. We can see that employment in agriculture in France in 1800 was 64%, and in the U.S. was 68%, while by 1900 those numbers were 43% for France and 41% for the U.S. So the percentages for employment in agriculture in France and the U.S. were pretty similar to each other in 1800, and also in 1900. Let's check the numbers for service jobs: in France in 1800 the employment in service jobs was 14%, while in the U.S. that number was 13%. In France in 1900 the employment in service jobs was 28%, while that number in the U.S. was 31. Once more, we see that the percentages for each country in the same year were pretty similar in both agriculture and in services, so this choice doesn't demonstrate the idea from the prompt that employment in the U.S. and France shifted away from agriculture and toward service jobs at "different rates." We can see that (D) is wrong; refer to our discussion of (A) for more. (Notice that the years from this choice are one line in the table above the years in correct answer (A); some untrained test-takers might pick (D) because they misread the graph and think 1800 and 1900 correspond to the data from 1900 and 1950. Always remember to read figures carefully on the SAT!)

Note The table also includes data for manufacturing jobs, but that information is irrelevant to the passage and the question. The College Board loves to include things that make it harder to notice the information you need to answer the question—like extra data in graphs, or repeated, unusual, multi-word phrases that are hard to understand the first time you read them, but that are actually fairly straightforward (as we saw in question 4 from earlier in this section). Don't get thrown off on test day if a table includes data you don't need! Just read all the relevant text and labels carefully, and focus on the information you need to answer the question. Also, notice that this question asks about things happening at "very different rates." Note that we didn't have to make a judgment call about what constitutes numbers being "very different" from each other; in the wrong answers, when numbers were similar to one another, they were within less than 7 percentage points, often within 2. When they were different, they were different by double digits. When the College Board asks us to find values that are very different from one another, we won't have to make judgment calls—the difference will be stark enough that only one choice can be correct, while the others are clearly wrong.

Test 1, Module 2, Question 16   **TYPE: IF TRUE**

The passage presents some claim or hypothesis. The prompt typically asks us to choose the "finding" that, "if true," would support or weaken the argument. Supporting statements will demonstrate the idea in the claim, and weakening statements will demonstrate the opposite of the idea in the claim. See "What about "If True" Questions?" on p. 71.

Subjective Phrases to Ignore: "most directly"

A Direct Contradiction: This choice asks us for the choice that supports the "researchers' claim." In order to find that claim, we need to check the provided text, which tells us that "researchers claim that outcome is highly unlikely." The previous sentence tells us that "that outcome" refers to the archaeologists being "replaced by… computer models." So we can see that the "claim" is that archaeologists being "replaced by… computer models" "is highly unlikely." This choice describes the model being "able to categorize…much more quickly than archaeologists." This is the opposite of what the question asks for—if the model works more quickly than the archaeologists, then that would support the idea that the model is better than the archaeologists, and the archaeologists *will* be replaced by the model. This is the opposite of the "claim" we're asked to support, so (A) is wrong.

B Confused Relationships: We're asked to find support for the claim that archaeologists won't be replaced by computer models. This choice describes something that neither the archaeologists nor the model were able to do. This choice will be tempting for some test-takers, because it describes the model not being able to do something—but in this case, the archaeologists couldn't do that thing either. So this choice doesn't support the claim, because it doesn't demonstrate any reason why archaeologists wouldn't be replaced by the computer model. Beyond that, this choice doesn't specify what portion of "the pottery fragments" either the model or the archaeologists were able to categorize, beyond simply saying neither group categorized "all" of them. For example, it's possible that the model categorized 99% of the fragments while the archaeologists only categorized 1% of the fragments, or vice-versa, or anything in between. This choice leaves open the possibility that one group did much better than the other, or that they both performed about the same, or a number of other possibilities—so its connection to the "claim" remains unclear. For either of these reasons, (B) is wrong.

C ✓ Correct: This choice describes "important tasks that only human experts can do." That phrase directly demonstrates the idea of computer models not being able to replace archaeologists, because if "only human experts can do" these "important tasks," then those humans can't be replaced by models—again, because the "tasks" are "important," and the models can't do them. This is exactly what the provided text and prompt require. So (C) is correct.

D Literary Interpretation: This might seem relevant to the claim, and it might be tempting to untrained test-takers, because those test-takers might think "well, if the archaeologists don't get dedicated training in sorting fragments, then maybe they could receive that training and get better at sorting than the models, and that would mean they won't get replaced." This isn't a terrible argument in real life, but it doesn't work on the SAT, because neither this choice nor the provided text actually says, specifically, that training archaeologists in categorizing fragments will lead to them being better at it than the models; also, neither this choice nor the text says anything about whether the archaeologists will receive any such training. Furthermore, the provided text tells us that sorting these fragments relies on "instinct developed over years of practice," so we know that at least some portion of the ability to sort fragments doesn't come from training anyway, but from experience. With all of this in mind, we can be sure that (D) is wrong.

| Test 1, Module 2, Question 17 | TYPE: MOST LOGICALLY COMPLETES |

The passage ends with a blank, and the answer choices are relatively long phrases. The right answer will restate or demonstrate an idea in the provided text. See "What about "Most Logically Completes" Questions?" on p. 68.

Subjective Phrases to Ignore: "most"

A ✓ Correct: The text tells us that veterans are a "small proportion of the total population of the United States," but that "they occupy a significantly higher proportion of the jobs in the civilian government." It goes on to say that one explanation for this situation might be that "military service familiarizes people with… structures that are also reflected in… civilian government," and that this "familiarity thus (blank)." This choice would say that "familiarity" with "structures… in… civilian government" makes jobs in government "appealing to military veterans." This is exactly what appears in the provided text: that text says that "a significantly higher proportion" of veterans are employed in "civilian government" (which demonstrates the idea of "civilian government jobs" being "especially appealing to military veterans" from this choice), and that an "explanation" for this situation is veterans being "familiarize[d]" with "structures" in "civilian government bureaucracy" (which restates the idea from this choice that "this familiarity" is what "makes" those "government jobs" "appealing"). So (A) is right.

B Barely Relevant: The text doesn't describe any "typical relationship between military service and subsequent career preferences" other than veterans getting government jobs, so it wouldn't make any sense to say that veterans getting government jobs "alters the typical relationship between military service" and veterans getting government jobs. This choice doesn't restate or demonstrate any ideas from the text, so it's wrong.

C Confused Relationships: This choice confuses the relationships among ideas in the text—it mentions "civilian government jobs" and also "military service," but the mention of "nonveterans" is unrelated to anything in the provided text. Nothing in the passage talks about what nonveterans should do, or says that anyone should join the military instead of trying for a job in civilian government. This choice will be tempting for test-takers who read the passage and conclude that it must be hard to get a job in government for people who aren't veterans, so nonveterans who want to work in government should join the military and then try to get a government job, after doing military service. But this has a couple of problems—for one thing, the text never says that it's hard to get a government job if you're not a veteran, just that proportionally more veterans tend to get government jobs. For another, this choice would cause the sentence to say that "this familiarity thus encourages nonveterans" who want government jobs to think about joining the military. Someone might reason that a counselor or government employee or something might "encourage" nonveterans to do something as they navigate their career paths, but it's not really clear what it would even mean for "familiarity" to "encourage[] nonveterans" to do something. For either of these reasons, (C) is wrong.

D Confused Relationships: The text describes veterans getting government jobs, but never mentions anything connected to the idea of "increas[ing] the number of… government jobs that require… military experience," and never even says that there are any jobs that "require… military experience." Also, like (C), this choice would create a sentence where "familiarity" is taking an action that doesn't even really make sense, because it would say that "familiarity… increases the number of… jobs…." This choice describes ideas that aren't present anywhere in the provided text, so it's wrong.

| Test 1, Module 2, Question 18 | TYPE: MOST LOGICALLY COMPLETES |

The passage ends with a blank, and the answer choices are relatively long phrases. The right answer will restate or demonstrate an idea in the provided text. See "What about "Most Logically Completes" Questions?" on p. 68.

Subjective Phrases to Ignore: "most"

A Direct Contradiction: The text tells us that many birds eat "carotenoids," which contribute to "feather coloration" and also "confer health benefits." It then tells us that carotenoids can create "deeply saturated colors" which are an "honest signal" of the bird's health. The text goes on to tell us that certain male tanager birds can "manipulate light" to create "the appearance of deeper saturation without the birds necessarily" eating a lot of carotenoids. This choice would say that "tanagers can engage in honest signaling without relying on carotenoid consumption," but the text told us that "honest signal[ing]" was when birds had "deeply saturated colors" *because* of carotenoid consumption. This choice basically says the opposite of what the text says, so it's wrong.

B Plausible but not in the Text: This choice will be tempting for test-takers who assume that "manipulat[ing] light" with "microstructures" to make tanager's look like they eat a lot of carotenoids, even if they really don't, must result in color saturation that's somehow less impressive or of lower quality than the "feather coloration" achieved by birds who actually eat a lot of carotenoids. This may be true in real life, for all we know, but nothing in the test restates or demonstrates this idea, and the "findings" in the text don't compare the "effective[ness]" of one kind of signal over another. So (B) is wrong.

C   Direct Contradiction: This choice directly contradicts the text, which says that "deeply saturated colors… communicate… an honest signal of a bird's overall fitness to potential mates," then describes how tanagers can develop similar colors in other ways. Beyond that, the "findings" described in the text just tell us about a way that birds can "creat[e] the appearance of deeper saturation," without mentioning anything that scientists don't understand or haven't determined, as this choice would require. So (C) is wrong.

D ✓   Correct: The text says that birds who eat lots of carotenoids are healthier, and that carotenoids also create "deeply saturated colors" which act as an "honest signal" of the bird's health. Then the text describes birds that can create "deeper saturation" *without* eating carotenoids; this wouldn't be an "honest signal," as described in the provided text, because in this case the bird has the appearance of eating healthy carotenoids without actually eating a lot of carotenoids and getting the corresponding health benefits. This would be an example of the bird's "appearance… function[ing] as a dishonest signal" of the bird's health, just as (D) says—so (D) is correct.

Test 1, Module 2, Question 19   TYPE: SAT WRITING

- Vertical Scan Results: The choices are different forms of the verb "to be."
- Vertical Scan Notes: Three options are plural forms, and one is singular. Some verb forms are present tense and some are past tense. We need to pick the form of the verb "to be" that's in agreement with its subject, and in the appropriate tense based on the surrounding text.
- Key Features in Surrounding Text: The blank is a verb whose action is being done by the singular noun "writing," so the right answer must be a singular verb form—only one choice meets this requirement, which means we can pick that choice without worrying about the tense of the verb.

Concepts in the question:

- Singular/Plural: Choices include singular and plural versions of the same base word(s). Nouns, pronouns, and verbs must agree in number with the words they refer to or modify. (See page 81.)
- Verb Tense/Conjugation: Choices include different forms of the same verb. Look at the surrounding text to find the verb's subject. Also, look for other clues that could indicate the proper tense or form of the verb in the blank. (See page 77.)

ANSWER CHOICE ANALYSIS

A   Incorrect: As we saw in our discussion above, we need a singular verb form—but this choice is plural. So (A) is wrong.

B   Incorrect: This choice has the same basic problem as (A), and is wrong for the same reasons.

C ✓   Correct: As we saw in our discussion above, we need a singular verb form, and this choice is the only one. So (C) is correct.

D   Incorrect: This choice has the same basic problem as (A) and (B), and is wrong for the same reason.

> **Note**   The blank requires a singular verb form, and only one answer choice is singular—once we noticed that, we could eliminate every wrong answer choice and be left with only the correct answer. The SAT likes to distract us with wrong answer choices that are subtly different from each other (like "were" and "have been") in the hopes that we'll get stuck trying to find some distinction between them—but once we realize the right answer has to be singular, we can eliminate them both and stop trying to figure out how they're different from one another. Keep this in mind on test day.

Test 1, Module 2, Question 20   TYPE: SAT WRITING

- Vertical Scan Results: The choices all include the word "out," and some choices also include a comma and/or the word "but."
- Vertical Scan Notes: We have to decide whether there should be a comma and/or the word "but" after the word "out."
- Key Features in Surrounding Text: Everything from the start of the provided text until the word "out" can stand on its own as a complete sentence. Everything after the blank can stand on its own as a complete sentence as well.

Concepts in the question:

- Commas: Commas can be used between clauses, to form comma sandwiches, in a list of 3 or more items, and before reported speech. They can't appear for no reason. Review the training for the relevant details. (See page 86.)
- Comma Splice: A comma can't join two groups of words that could each be sentences on their own. (See page 83.)

- **Independent and Dependent Clauses:** Choices would create and/or join clauses. An independent clause can stand on its own as a sentence, and a dependent clause can't. Remember rules for joining clauses related to periods, semi-colons, colons, commas, and conjunctions. (See page 82.)

ANSWER CHOICE ANALYSIS

A   Incorrect: This choice would add the conjunction "but" at the beginning of the second independent clause. But we know that on the SAT, if we use a conjunction like "but" to connect two independent clauses, then a comma must appear before the word "but." This choice is missing the comma, so (A) is wrong.

B ✓   Correct: Like (A), this choice adds the conjunction "but" after the first independent clause—but this choice *also* includes the comma that must appear before "but" when that word is used to join two independent clauses, so (B) is correct.

C   Incorrect: This choice would result in two complete sentences ("The Alvarez theory… out" and "it left… extinctions.") without any punctuation or conjunction between them, which we can't do on an SAT Writing question. So (C) is wrong.

D   Incorrect: This choice would create a comma splice, because it would connect two complete sentences ("The Alvarez theory… out" and "it left… extinctions.") with just a comma, which we can't do on an SAT Writing question. So (D) is wrong.

Test 1, Module 2, Question 21   TYPE: SAT WRITING

- **Vertical Scan Results:** Each choice is a different form of the verb "to force."
- **Vertical Scan Notes:** We need to figure out which form of the verb "to force" will agree with the surrounding text.
- **Key Features in Surrounding Text:** The sentence where the blank appears already has a main verb (in the phrase "those food sources may become"). The blank appears at the start of a comma-separated phrase that describes the first noun phrase in the independent clause (which is "those food sources"), so we need a participle in the blank.

Concepts in the question:

- **Avoid Dangling Participles:** When a phrase starting with an -ing/-ed/-en word is joined to the main sentence by a comma, the first noun phrase in the independent clause of that sentence is described by the -ing/-ed/-en word. (See page 90.)
- **Independent and Dependent Clauses:** Choices would create and/or join clauses. An independent clause can stand on its own as a sentence, and a dependent clause can't. Remember rules for joining clauses related to periods, semi-colons, colons, commas, and conjunctions. (See page 82.)

ANSWER CHOICE ANALYSIS

A   Incorrect: This choice is wrong for a few reasons—first, it's not the participle form we need, as discussed above. Second, if we were to conjugate the verb "to force," we would need to know which noun phrase it was modifying, but it's not clear which noun phrase that would be. Even if we knew which noun this conjugated verb was modifying, there would need to be a conjunction like "and" after the comma to join this phrase to the preceding independent clause. For any of these reasons, (A) is wrong.

B   Incorrect: The simplest way to understand why this choice is wrong is that the phrase "to force the monkeys to hunt…" would indicate that "the food sources" became unavailable *in order to* make the monkeys hunt. In other words, this choice would require the idea that the food sources intentionally did what they did for a certain purpose; this idea doesn't appear in the text, and also doesn't really make any sense. Beyond that, an infinitive clause like the one this choice would create shouldn't be separated from the independent clause with a comma, as we discussed in our training. For either reason, (B) is wrong.

C ✓   Correct: This choice creates the participial phrase "<u>forcing</u> the monkeys to hunt…" which describes the first noun phrase in this sentence's independent clause (that participial phrase tells us what "those food sources" do when they "become unavailable"). This conforms to the College Board's rules for participial phrases in SAT Writing question as we discussed in our training, so (C) is correct.

D   Incorrect: This choice is similar to (A), with the added problem of being in the past tense, without any indication in the surrounding text that the past tense is appropriate. So (D) is wrong too.

Test 1, Module 2, Question 22   TYPE: SAT WRITING

- **Vertical Scan Results:** The choices are short multi-word phrases with the same words in different orders. Two choices end in periods, and two choices end in question marks.
- **Vertical Scan Notes:** We need to decide whether the correct answer includes the wording "could the blueberries thrive" or "the blueberries could thrive," and we need to decide whether the correct answer should end with a period or a question mark.

- Key Features in Surrounding Text: The sentence after the sentence with the blank tells us that "Michel was determined to find out," which lets us know that the idea in the underlined phrase is something that's currently unknown. The only choice we're given to ensure the text includes some unknown idea for "Michel... to find out" is for the blank to contain a question.

Concepts in the question:

- Question Marks: Question marks in SAT Writing questions should appear at the end of sentences whose subject is placed between the words of a two-word verb phrase, like "will we go?" (See page 90.)

ANSWER CHOICE ANALYSIS

A   Incorrect: This choice is phrased like a question, with the subject "the blueberries" appearing after the helping verb "could," and before the verb form "thrive," which is appropriate for reasons discussed above—but a question must be punctuated with a question mark, not a period. So this choice is wrong.

B   Incorrect: This choice is phrased like a declarative statement, not a question, because the subject "the blueberries" appears before the two-word verb phrase "could thrive." This choice also doesn't end with a question mark. As we saw in our discussion above, we need an answer choice that expresses a question. So (B) is wrong.

C   Incorrect: This choice ends with a question mark, which is appropriate, given our discussion above—but it's phrased like a declarative statement, not a question, as we saw in our discussion of (B). So (C) is wrong.

D ✓ Correct: This choice is phrased like a question and it ends with a question mark, which is what we're looking for, as we discussed for (A) above. So (D) is right.

Test 1, Module 2, Question 23 — TYPE: SAT WRITING

- Vertical Scan Results: Each choice is a different form of the verb "to be."
- Vertical Scan Notes: We need to decide which tense and number of the verb "to be" is appropriate.
- Key Features in Surrounding Text: The noun doing the action of the verb is the singular noun "Paik." The sentence where the underlined phrase appears tells us that the action in that sentence is happening "today," so we know we need a present-tense verb form.

Concepts in the question:

- Singular/Plural: Choices include singular and plural versions of the same base word(s). Nouns, pronouns, and verbs must agree in number with the words they refer to or modify. (See page 81.)
- Verb Tense/Conjugation: Choices include different forms of the same verb. Look at the surrounding text to find the verb's subject. Also, look for other clues that could indicate the proper tense or form of the verb in the blank. (See page 77.)

ANSWER CHOICE ANALYSIS

A   Incorrect: As we saw in our discussion above, we need a present-tense verb form, but this verb is in the future tense. So (A) is wrong.

B   Incorrect: As we saw in our discussion above, we need a present-tense verb form, but this verb is in the past tense. So (B) is wrong. This choice might be tempting for test-takers who noticed that the text starts out talking about something from "1963," but who didn't also notice that the action of the underlined phrase is happening "today."

C   Incorrect: As we saw in our discussion above, we need a present-tense verb form, but this verb is in the past tense. So (C) is wrong. This choice might be tempting for the same reasons we discussed for choice (B) above.

D ✓ Correct: As we saw in our discussion above, we need a present-tense verb form. This is the only choice in the present tense, so we know (D) must be correct.

Test 1, Module 2, Question 24 — TYPE: SAT WRITING

- Vertical Scan Results: Each choice starts with the word "adjustments" and ends with the word "prior." Three choices include something between those two words—a comma, a period, or the word "and."
- Vertical Scan Notes: We have to decide which punctuation mark or word should appear between "adjustments" and "prior," or whether nothing should appear there.
- Key Features in Surrounding Text: Everything from the beginning of the sentence through the word "adjustments" can stand on its own as a sentence, and everything from the word "prior" through the end of the sentence can stand on its own as a sentence.

Concepts in the question:

- **Comma Splice:** A comma can't join two groups of words that could each be sentences on their own. (See page 83.)
- **Independent and Dependent Clauses:** Choices would create and/or join clauses. An independent clause can stand on its own as a sentence, and a dependent clause can't. Remember rules for joining clauses related to periods, semi-colons, colons, commas, and conjunctions. (See page 82.)

ANSWER CHOICE ANALYSIS

A **Incorrect:** This would result in two sets of words that can stand on their own as sentences ("The first… adjustments" and "prior to… days") having no punctuation, conjunction, or any other appropriate phrase to separate them. This violates the SAT's punctuation rules, so (A) is wrong.

B **Incorrect:** This choice creates a comma splice, because it would result in two sets of words that can stand on their own as sentences ("The first… adjustments" and "prior to… days") being separated by a comma. This violates the SAT's punctuation rules, so (B) is wrong.

C ✓ **Correct:** This choice separates two sets of words that can stand on their own as sentences ("The first… adjustments" and "prior to… days") with a period, which is appropriate according to the SAT's punctuation rules. So (C) is correct.

D **Incorrect:** This choice would insert the word "and" between two sets of words that can stand on their own as sentences ("The first… adjustments" and "prior to… days"). We know from our training that when we use a conjunction like "and" to join two independent clauses, a comma must appear before the word "and." This choice doesn't include that comma, so (D) is wrong.

Test 1, Module 2, Question 25 — TYPE: SAT WRITING

- **Vertical Scan Results:** Each choice is a different form of the verb "to create."
- **Vertical Scan Notes:** We have to pick whether a singular, plural, or participle form of the verb is appropriate.
- **Key Features in Surrounding Text:** The underlined phrase is a verb that's part of a sentence that includes the phrase "the lock would increase… and (blank)." So this verb is something that "the lock would" do, and it needs to be in the same form as the verb "increase."

Concepts in the question:

- **Parallelism:** The surrounding text includes phrasing and/or grammatical structures that should be mirrored by what appears in the blank. (See page 93.)
- **Verb Tense/Conjugation:** Choices include different forms of the same verb. Look at the surrounding text to find the verb's subject. Also, look for other clues that could indicate the proper tense or form of the verb in the blank. (See page 77.)

ANSWER CHOICE ANALYSIS

A **Incorrect:** This choice needs to be in the same form as the verb "increase," to express the idea of what the lock "would" do in addition to "increase." But this choice isn't in the same form as increase, and would cause the sentence to say the lock "would increase … and creates," which is incorrect in an SAT Writing question. So (A) is wrong.

B ✓ **Correct:** This choice is in the same form as the verb "increase," and would cause the sentence to say the lock "would increase… and create," which is correct. So (B) satisfies our analysis from above, and (B) is correct.

C **Incorrect:** This choice isn't in the same form as the verb "increase," and would cause the sentence to say the lock "would increase… and creating," which is incorrect in an SAT Writing question. So (C) doesn't satisfy our analysis from above, which means it's wrong.

D **Incorrect:** This choice isn't in the same form as the verb "increase," and would cause the sentence to say the lock "would increase… and created," which is incorrect in an SAT Writing question. So (D) doesn't satisfy our analysis from above, and it's wrong.

Note Some test-takers will struggle with this question, because they won't be sure which noun is doing the action "to create." Even when they realize that the noun is "lock," they might overlook "would" and think that they should pick the singular verb form "creates" to agree with the singular noun "lock." But when we think of parallelism, and we notice that the other verb phrase in this sentence is "would increase," we know that we need the form of "to create" that would come after "would." Keep this in mind on test day—pay attention to structures that are already in the text and are similar to the structures that appear in the blank.

Test 1, Module 2, Question 26 — TYPE: SAT WRITING

- **Vertical Scan Results:** Each choice is a longer phrase that uses similar words to express similar ideas.

- **Vertical Scan Notes:** Each choice expresses the idea of commercial plastics being associated with two problems in a slightly different way. We have to pick the one that satisfies the SAT's standards for this question type.
- **Key Features in Surrounding Text:** The blank comes right after the comma-separated participial phrase "despite being cheap, versatile, and easy to produce," so we know that the first noun phrase in this sentence's independent clause has to be the thing that's "cheap, versatile, and easy to produce."

Concepts in the question:

- **Avoid Dangling Participles:** When a phrase starting with an -ing/-ed/-en word is joined to the main sentence by a comma, the first noun phrase in the independent clause of that sentence is described by the -ing/-ed/-en word. (See page 90.)

ANSWER CHOICE ANALYSIS

A   **Incorrect:** The first noun phrase in the correct answer needs to be the thing that is described by the phrase "cheap, versatile, and easy to produce," as discussed above. That first noun phrase in this choice is "two problems," but "two problems" aren't what's "cheap, versatile, and easy to produce" in this sentence, so (A) is wrong.

B   **Incorrect:** This choice has the same problem as (B), and is wrong for the same reason.

C   **Incorrect:** The first noun phrase needs to be the thing that is described by the phrase "cheap, versatile, and easy to produce," as discussed above. This choice will be tempting, because if we don't read carefully, it looks like this choice starts with the noun phrase "commercial plastics.'" But it doesn't! This choice actually starts with the noun phrase "commercial plastics' two associated problems." As we saw in our discussions of (A) and (B), those "problems" can't be described as "cheap, versatile, and easy to produce," so (C) is wrong.

D ✓   **Correct:** The first noun phrase needs to be the thing that is described by the phrase "cheap, versatile, and easy to produce," as discussed above. This choice begins with the noun phrase "commercial plastics," which is appropriate because those are the things that are "cheap, versatile, and easy to produce." So (D) is correct.

Test 1, Module 2, Question 27   **TYPE: SAT WRITING**

- **Vertical Scan Results:** Each choice is the same three words with different with commas in different places.
- **Vertical Scan Notes:** We need to decide whether or not a comma should appear after "biologist" and/or after "Yuree Lee."
- **Key Features in Surrounding Text:** The word "biologist" is part of the phrase "plant cell biologist," which tells us the occupation of "Yuree Lee." We know from our training that when someone's occupation appears right before that person's name, there should be no comma between the name and occupation. The name "Yuree Lee" is the subject of the sentence, which does the action of the verb "showed," the word immediately after the blank. When the subject of the sentence is immediately followed by its verb, no comma should appear between them.

Concepts in the question:

- **Commas:** Commas can be used between clauses, to form comma sandwiches, in a list of 3 or more items, and before reported speech. They can't appear for no reason. Review the training for the relevant details. (See page 86.)

ANSWER CHOICE ANALYSIS

A   **Incorrect:** As we saw in our discussion above, there shouldn't be a comma after "biologist" or "Yuree Lee." This choice has a comma after "biologist," so it's wrong.

B   **Incorrect:** As we saw in our discussion above, there shouldn't be a comma after "biologist" or "Yuree Lee." This choice has a comma after "Yuree Lee," so it's wrong.

C ✓   **Correct:** As we saw in our discussion above, there shouldn't be a comma after "biologist" or "Yuree Lee." This choice doesn't have a comma in either position, so it's correct.

D   **Incorrect:** As we saw in our discussion above, there shouldn't be a comma after "biologist" or "Yuree Lee," But this choice has a comma in both of those places—so it's wrong.

Test 1, Module 2, Question 28   **TYPE: LOGICAL TRANSITION**

The choices are different transition phrases like "however," "instead of," or "for example." The right answer must reflect the relationship between the concepts before and after the blank. See "What about Logical Transition Questions?" on p. 71.

Subjective Phrases to Ignore: "most"

A   **Confused Relationships:** This choice would be appropriate if what came after the blank gave a specific example of the idea that came before the blank—for instance (see what I did there?) if the text after the blank said something like "if a spider were

---

climbing on a tree, its spatulae would bond to the atoms of the tree." But that's not what appears in the provided sentence, as we'll see in our discussion of (D), so (A) is wrong.

B   Direct Contradiction: This choice would indicate that what comes after the blank is something unexpected, given the earlier text, or something contrary to what comes before the blank. Instead, what appears after the blank tells us something that is made possible by the information that comes before the blank. So (B) is wrong.

C   Confused Relationships: This choice would be appropriate if what came after the blank was additional information that somehow resembles the information that came before the blank—for instance, if the text after the blank said that some other animal was also able to bond with things it touches. But this isn't the case—see our discussion of (D) for more.

D ✓ Correct: This choice is correct because the text before the blank describes how spiders' legs can "bond" to things, and the text after the blank describes how spiders are able to "cling to and climb on almost any surface." In other words, the text after the blank is the result or effect of the information before the blank. The provided text literally demonstrates that the text after the blank is a "result" of the text before the blank, so (D) is correct.

| Test 1, Module 2, Question 29 | TYPE: LOGICAL TRANSITION |

The choices are different transition phrases like "however," "instead of," or "for example." The right answer must reflect the relationship between the concepts before and after the blank. See "What about Logical Transition Questions?" on p. 71.

Subjective Phrases to Ignore: "most"

A ✓ Correct: This choice indicates that this third sentence introduces information that is somewhat unexpected, given the previous information. That relationship is demonstrated in the provided text, because the text before the blank tells us that "Sher-Gil was living in what must have seemed like an ideal city for a young artist" and that she was "studying" art and "mak[ing] a name for herself," but the text after the blank tells us that she "longed to return to her childhood home" anyway, because she believed "only there," "her art could truly flourish." The idea that she would want to leave "what... seemed like an ideal city" for a "young artist" like her is exactly the kind of unexpected information that the word "still" should introduce, so (A) is correct.

B   Direct Contradiction: This choice would make it seem like what comes after the blank is the logical result of what appears before the blank, but as we saw in our discussion of (A), that's the opposite of what's in the text: the information before the blank tells us that there are good things about where Sher-Gil was living, while the text after the blank tells us that Sher-Gil wanted to move back to her "home." So (B) is wrong.

C   Direct Contradiction: This choice would be appropriate if the text after the blank somehow reinforced or reiterated the ideas from before the text, but that's not the case—the text before the blank says Sher-Gil lived in a great place for a young artist and was doing well there, but the text after the blank says she "longed to return... home." So (C) is wrong.

D   Direct Contradiction: Like (B) and (C), this choice expresses an idea that is the opposite of what is demonstrated in the text. This choice would be appropriate if the text after the blank provided additional information to reinforce what came before the blank, but instead the text after the blank provides information that would be unexpected, based on the text before the blank. So (D) is wrong. See the discussions of the other answer choices for more.

| Test 1, Module 2, Question 30 | TYPE: LOGICAL TRANSITION |

The choices are different transition phrases like "however," "instead of," or "for example." The right answer must reflect the relationship between the concepts before and after the blank. See "What about Logical Transition Questions?" on p. 71.

Subjective Phrases to Ignore: "most"

A   Confused Relationships: The first sentence says that "activists across the state sold tea." The next sentence provides an example of this phenomenon by telling us that "the Woman's Suffrage Party" sold tea in San Francisco. Then the sentence containing the blank tells us about another "activist" "distribut[ing]" tea as well. This choice will be tempting, because the idea expressed after the blank is an "example" of an idea from the first sentence of the passage. But this choice would say that the idea in this sentence is an example of what was just stated in the *previous* sentence! That previous sentence tells us about "the Woman's Suffrage Party" selling tea in San Francisco. A woman "distribut[ing]" tea in Los Angeles isn't an "example" of women selling tea in San Francisco; it's just another event that was similar to the previously mentioned event, as we'll see in our discussion of (C). If the second sentence were removed, this choice could be correct—but that's not the case. So (A) is wrong.

B   Confused Relationships: This choice would require the text following this phrase to be some kind of logical ending or resolution of the ideas that appear before this phrase, but this isn't the case. Instead, the previous text describes an instance of women selling tea, and this text describes another instance of a woman "distribut[ing]" tea. Some test-takers will be tempted by this choice, because it's part of the last sentence of the passage, and that idea might seem to go along with the word "conclude." But that alone isn't enough to justify the use of the phrase "to conclude," and as trained test-takers we know that the right answer to questions of this type must be demonstrated in the provided text. Nothing in the provided text demonstrates the idea that the text after the blank is a "conclu[sion]" of anything. So (B) is wrong.

C ✓   Correct: As we saw in our discussion of (A), this choice is exactly right. The text right before the blank talks about "the Woman's Suffrage Party" selling tea in San Francisco, and the sentence containing the blank tells us about another "activist" in Los Angeles "distribut[ing]" tea as well. The text after the underlined phrase tells us about something "similar[]" to what appears in the text right before the underlined phrase, so (C) is correct.

D   Confused Relationships: This choice will be tempting for untrained test-takers, because as we saw in our discussion of (C), the text before the underlined phrase and the text after the underlined phrase express similar examples of what's mentioned in the first sentence. But this choice would only be appropriate if the text after the underlined phrase conveyed the *same* information as the text before the underlined phrase, just expressed differently. But saying that an activist in Los Angeles "distributed… Tea" isn't the *same* information as saying that "the Woman's Suffrage Party sold… Tea" in San Francisco. These are two different pieces of information in a row, which means we can't introduce the second one using the phrase "in other words." So (D) is wrong.

Test 1, Module 2, Question 31   **TYPE: NOTES**

The passage presents a bulleted list of notes, then tells us a goal related to presenting that information. The correct answer will be the only one that demonstrates the ideas in the provided goal. See "What about Notes Questions?" on p. 71.

Subjective Phrases to Ignore: "most"

A   Confused Relationships: The prompt asks us for the choice that "compare[s] the lengths of the two rail tunnels," but this choice doesn't even *mention* both rail tunnels—it only refers to one, so it can't be correct. This choice will be tempting for test-takers who don't read carefully, because they might think the two different places named in this choice refer to the two different rail tunnels, and they might think the comparative phrase "longer than 30 miles" is the comparison that the choice asks for—but as we just discussed, this isn't the case. So (A) is wrong.

B ✓   Correct: This choice mentions both tunnels ("Seikan" and "Channel") and their lengths ("33 miles long" and "31 miles long"), and compares those lengths by saying the Channel Tunnel is "slightly shorter" than the "Seikan Tunnel." This choice exactly demonstrates "compar[ing] the lengths of the two rail tunnels" as required by the prompt, so (B) is correct.

C   Confused Relationships: This choice has the same basic problem as (A)—the prompt asks for the choice that "compare[s] the lengths of the two rail tunnels," and this choice only talks about one of the tunnels. It's not possible to compare two tunnels by only mentioning one of the tunnels, so (C) is wrong. Also like (A), this choice may be tempting for test-takers who read too quickly and think that the two places named in this choice are the two different rail tunnels, although even in that case, this choice still doesn't contain the "compar[ison]" required by the prompt.

D   Confused Relationships: This choice will be tempting for untrained test-takers, because it does mention both rail tunnels—but the prompt doesn't ask for the choice that *mentions* both rail tunnels; instead, it specifically asks for the choice that "compare[s] the lengths of the two rail tunnels." This choice doesn't include any comparison, or mention anything about the tunnels' lengths, so we know it must be wrong.

Test 1, Module 2, Question 32   **TYPE: NOTES**

The passage presents a bulleted list of notes, then tells us a goal related to presenting that information. The correct answer will be the only one that demonstrates the ideas in the provided goal. See "What about Notes Questions?" on p. 71.

Subjective Phrases to Ignore: "most"

A   Literary Interpretation: The prompt asks for the choice that "provide[s] an explanation and example of 'flauna.'" This choice will be tempting for untrained test-takers, because it does provide an "explanation" of "flauna" when it tells us that "flauna" is "a combination of the words "flora" and "fauna."" But this choice doesn't give us any "example" of "flauna," so we know it's wrong.

B ✓   Correct: This choice gives us an explanation of the term "flauna" when it tells us the word is "a combination of the words "flora" and "fauna,"" and then it provides an example of this term when it mentions "a parrot with leaves for feathers." Notice that the phrase "such as" is a clue that what comes next is an example of what was just mentioned. This choice explicitly demonstrates the prompt's requirement of an "explanation" and "example" of "flauna," so we know it's correct.

C   Literary Interpretation: The prompt asks us to pick the choice that includes both an "explanation" and "example" of "flauna," but this choice doesn't actually do either of those. Some test-takers will think that the phrase "the subjects of his paintings" is an "explanation" of "flauna," but this phrase doesn't actually tell us what "flauna" refers to—and even if it did, this choice would still be missing the other requirement from the prompt, which was an "example" of "flauna." Again, we can see that (C) is wrong.

D   Literary Interpretation: This choice will also be tempting for untrained test-takers, because it does provide some information related to the term "flauna" that might seem to meet some of the requirements from the prompt. But the phrase "a term that…

Jon Ching… uses when describing his surreal artworks" is neither an explanation nor an example of "flauna." Simply knowing that Jon Ching uses this word to "describ[e] his… artworks" doesn't tell us what that word actually means, as an "explanation" would require, and it's not a specific "example" of "flauna" either. Beyond that, mentioning that "the subjects of *Nectar* and *Primaveral* are types of "flauna,'" isn't an example, because this choice doesn't tells us what those "subjects" are—for all we know, based on this choice, those subjects are cars, or sandwiches, or geometric shapes, or who knows what else. If we refer to the notes, we know that the subjects of those paintings are a "parrot" and a "leopard," but we have to pick an answer based on the information *in this choice*—and this choice doesn't include any "example[s]" of "flauna." So (D) is wrong.

Test 1, Module 2, Question 33   **TYPE: NOTES**

The passage presents a bulleted list of notes, then tells us a goal related to presenting that information. The correct answer will be the only one that demonstrates the ideas in the provided goal. See "What about Notes Questions?" on p. 71.

Subjective Phrases to Ignore: "most"

A   Plausible but not in the Text: The prompt asks for the choice that "emphasize[s] the uniqueness of Taylor's accomplishment." This choice provides some details about what Taylor did; this will be tempting for untrained test-takers who reason that few people, if any, probably "fled to St. Simons Island" and began working for the Union Army as Taylor did, and who decide that, based on that logic, we could call what's described in this choice an example of Taylor's "uniqueness." But nothing in this choice specifically says that this information makes Taylor "unique," or the only person to do something, or anything else like that. We know that the right answer to questions of this type on the SAT must specifically demonstrate the requirements of the prompt, and this choice doesn't do that. So (A) is wrong.

B   Plausible but not in the Text: This choice will be tempting to untrained test-takers for the same reason as (A)—most test-takers would think that Taylor's life experiences were probably "unique[]," which will lead them to conclude that this choice could be correct. But this choice also has the same problem as (A), which is that it doesn't specifically demonstrate anything that could be called "uniqueness." What matters here isn't what we, as test-takers, think is an example of "uniqueness." What matters is the answer choice specifically demonstrating the idea that something is "unique," which this choice doesn't do. So (B) is wrong. (See the explanation of (D) for more on demonstrating "uniqueness.")

C   Plausible but not in the Text: Again, like (A) and (B), this choice will be tempting for test-takers who assume that what it describes is something "unique[]"—that is, a book written by Taylor about her experiences during the Civil War still being available. But this choice has the same problem as (A) and (B): we can't pick a choice because *we* think that what the choice describes might be unique; we have to pick a choice that *specifically* demonstrates "uniqueness." This choice doesn't do that, so it's wrong—see the explanation of (D) for more.

D ✓ Correct: The prompt asks for the choice that "emphasize[s] the uniqueness of Taylor's accomplishment." In order to pick the right choice, we need to think carefully about what "uniqueness" means. Being "unique" means being one-of-a-kind—that is, being the only person who has some particular characteristic or distinction. This choice says "Taylor was the only Black woman to publish a Civil War memoir." The phrase "the only" tells us that Taylor was "unique[]" in doing what she did, just as the prompt requires. This is the only choice that demonstrates the idea that "Taylor's accomplishment" was "unique[]," as the prompt requires—not because *we* as test-takers think it's unique, but because the specific words on the page *tell us* it was unique, using the phrase "the only." So (D) is right.

TEST 2, MODULE 1

Test 2, Module 1, Question 1   **TYPE: TEXT COMPLETION**

The prompt will be a short passage containing a blank. The correct answer will always be restated or demonstrated by key phrases in the provided text. See "What about Text Completion Questions?" on p. 66.

Subjective Phrases to Ignore: "most"

A   Literary Interpretation: The text says that "Benito Juarez" was "one of the most (blank) figures in his country's history," followed by a colon. We know that the word in the blank will describe whatever comes after that colon. In this case, the text after the colon mentions "many significant accomplishments." So we need a word in the blank that would describe having "many significant accomplishments." But "unpredictable" would mean that he does things that are unexpected. This choice doesn't restate or demonstrate any idea from the provided text, so it's wrong. This choice might be tempting, because some test-takers could reason that Juarez being "from an Indigenous community" and becoming president would be "unpredictable," especially since the text says he was the "first" one to do that. But the blank describes what kind of figure he was "in his country's history," not whether him becoming president was something anyone predicted—and the provided text never actually says that him becoming president was a "surprise," or that "no one saw it coming," or anything like that. For all we know, he was the popular frontrunner and everyone expected him to win. Again, (A) is wrong.

B ✓ Correct: As we saw in our discussion of (A), we need to pick the choice that would describe having "many significant accomplishments." A person with "many significant accomplishments" as president would demonstrate the idea of an "important" figure "in his country's history," just as this choice requires. This choice is demonstrated in the provided text, so it's right.

C Plausible but not in the Text: Again, as we saw in our discussion of (A), we need the choice that restates the idea of having "many significant accomplishments." But this choice would mean that Juarez kept information hidden from people. Some untrained test-takers will be tempted by this choice because they assume that someone high up in government must know a lot of secrets—but that idea doesn't actually appear in the text, so we can't use it as a justification for picking an answer choice. We know that the right answer will always be restated or demonstrated by specific words or phrases in the provided text, which isn't the case here. So (C) is wrong.

D Direct Contradiction: If anything, this choice is the opposite of the right answer—as discussed above, the text tells us Juarez had "many significant accomplishments" as president, so we can't call him "ordinary," and nothing else in the provided text restates or demonstrates the idea that Juarez was just like everybody else, or that there was nothing special about him, as the word "ordinary" would require. This choice might be tempting for test-takers who have read, in other contexts, about certain important politicians starting out as "ordinary" citizens," or something like that—but again, that idea doesn't appear in the text, so we can't use it as a basis for picking an answer. That means (D) is wrong.

| Test 2, Module 1, Question 2 | TYPE: TEXT COMPLETION |

The prompt will be a short passage containing a blank. The correct answer will always be restated or demonstrated by key phrases in the provided text. See "What about Text Completion Questions?" on p. 66.

Subjective Phrases to Ignore: "most"

A Barely Relevant: The text tells us that "John Ashberry's poems" have "strange images, highly experimental syntax, and opaque subject matter," and says they "can be quite difficult to (blank)." This choice would cause the text to say that the poems are "difficult to delegate." It's not even really clear what it would mean to "delegate" a poem, because "delegat[ing]" means handing off a job or a responsibility to another person. But even if we're not sure what it would mean to "delegate" a poem, we can see that the provided text doesn't mention anything about giving someone a job to do, or anything like that—so (A) isn't restated or demonstrated in the text, which means it's wrong.

B Confused Relationships: This choice will be tempting for some test-takers, because it's possible to "compose" a poem—that is, to write a poem—and those test-takers might think this sentence is saying that it's hard for John Ashberry himself to write those poems. This is wrong for two reasons. For one, we don't know that the "strange images, highly experimental syntax, and opaque subject matter" in the poems are necessarily hard for Ashbery to *create*, based on the text—these characteristics might come very naturally to him, for all we know. For another, the provided text says, after the blank, that the poems "thus are the object of heated debate among scholars." The word "thus" makes it clear that the preceding phrase, "difficult to (blank)," is the reason the poems "are the object of heated debate among scholars." Poems being hard to "compose" wouldn't necessarily lead them to cause "heated debate among scholars," so this choice would cause the phrase "thus" to demonstrate a relationship in the text that doesn't exist. So (B) is wrong—keep all of this in mind as we discuss (C).

C ✓ Correct: The provided text says that Ashbery's poems have "strange images, highly experimental syntax, and opaque subject matter," which make them "difficult to (blank)" and "the object of heated debate among scholars." Aspects of the poems being "strange," "experimental," and "opaque" demonstrate the idea of the poems being "difficult to interpret," as this choice would require, and if the poems are difficult to "interpret," we would expect scholars to engage in "heated debate" about them—since scholars try to understand poems, "difficult[y]" "interpret[ing]" those poems would lead to "heated debate." This choice creates a phrase which is directly demonstrated in the provided text, so it's right.

D Literary Interpretation: This choice could be tempting for untrained test-takers for a couple of reasons. First, someone who's not reading carefully enough might read this choice as "pronounce," and think that unusual poetry as described in the given text might be hard to "pronounce"—but, of course, the word is renounce, not pronounce, so this explanation isn't viable. Second, someone might decide that Ashbery's poetry sounds like it wouldn't be very good, and they might think Ashbery would decide to "renounce" it—that is, say he no longer claims it as his work. But that explanation isn't any good either, because nothing in the provided text actually demonstrates or restates the idea of Ashbery abandoning his claim to his poems, and also because this choice would cause the sentence to say the poetry was "difficult to renounce"—that is, not that Ashbery would renounce the poetry, but that it would be *hard* for him to renounce it. So none of these explanations are supported by the text. Once more, since nothing in the text restates or demonstrates the idea of anyone "renounc[ing]" anything, (D) must be wrong.

The prompt will be a short passage containing a blank. The correct answer will always be restated or demonstrated by key phrases in the provided text. See "What about Text Completion Questions?" on p. 66.

Subjective Phrases to Ignore: "most"

A   Literary Interpretation: The text mentions a "sudden appearance and rapid diversification," and then calls that event "this (blank) change." This choice will tempt test-takers who assume that such a big change would cause some big problems, and/or who associate the content of this passage with the extinction of the dinosaurs, which was a "catastrophic" event. But nothing in the text describes anything bad happening, and the extinction of the dinosaurs isn't mentioned at all—since the text doesn't describe any negative event whatsoever, we can't call the change "catastrophic." So (A) must be wrong.

B   Plausible but not in the Text: As we saw in our discussion above, the word in the blank should complete the phrase "this (blank) change" so that it can refer back to a "sudden appearance and rapid diversification," as mentioned earlier in the sentence. This choice might be tempting for test-takers who think of fossils as hard to find, which would demonstrate being "elusive"—but this idea doesn't appear in the text, and the blank doesn't describe "fossil[s]" anyway. So (B) is wrong.

C ✓   Correct: Again, as discussed previously, the word in the blank must cause the phrase "this (blank) change" to refer back to a "sudden appearance and rapid diversification." The word "abrupt" is exactly demonstrated by something "sudden" and "rapid," so we know this choice must be correct.

D   Confused Relationships: This choice will be very tempting, because the word "imminent" describes something that is just about to happen, and the provided text talks about something that happened suddenly; some test-takers will feel like these are very closely-related ideas. In order for this choice to be correct, the phrase "this (blank) change" would have to be referring to a change that was *about* to happen, or could happen any second, or something like that—but the change in question happened "541 million years ago," which means the word "imminent" isn't supported by the text, and (D) is wrong.

The prompt will be a short passage containing a blank. The correct answer will always be restated or demonstrated by key phrases in the provided text. See "What about Text Completion Questions?" on p. 66.

Subjective Phrases to Ignore: "most"

A   Direct Contradiction: The text describes a "woman" from the "Bronze Age" who appeared to have had a "high position of power," and then says that "researchers" who think "that Bronze Age societies were ruled by men" might be persuaded by this "finding" to "(blank) that women may have also held leadership roles." This choice would cause the sentence to say that those researchers would basically give up on the idea that "women" had "leadership roles"—but that would contradict this "finding" that involved a "woman" who appeared to have a "high position of power," so (A) is wrong. See the discussion of (B) for more.

B ✓   Correct: As we saw in our discussion of (A), this choice should be something that "researchers who have argued that Bronze Age societies were ruled by men" would do to the idea that "women may have also held leadership roles" in the Bronze Age, in response to the discovery of a "woman" from that time who appeared to have a "high position of power." This choice would cause the sentence to say that those researchers would "concede," or admit, that "women may have also held leadership roles." The idea that those researchers "have argued that Bronze Age societies were ruled by men," but that they have now seen evidence of a powerful woman from that time, directly demonstrates the idea that they would "concede" that women "may have also held leadership roles"—that is, they would acknowledge the validity of an idea they had resisted previously. So (B) is right.

C   Literary Interpretation: This choice will be very tempting for test-takers who have some idea of how this kind of question works, but who don't read carefully enough. Someone who reads this passage quickly could get the sense that the "researchers" wouldn't believe a woman could have had a "high position of power," and that they would want to "refute" the idea that women could have "also held leadership roles"—that is, they would want to prove that this idea was false. But this text doesn't mention anywhere that anyone is trying to say that this theory about the "woman" whose skeleton was found is wrong, or logically flawed, or anything else that we could call "refut[ing]." Since the text doesn't restate or demonstrate the idea of anyone "refut[ing]" the idea of "women" holding "leadership roles," (C) can't be right.

D   Confused Relationships: Like (C), this choice could be tempting for test-takers who read the text too quickly and don't think carefully about what the sentence would actually say if we put this word in the blank, because the discussion of men and women in the Bronze Age, and who's in "power," sounds like it could go along with the idea of "Bronze Age" "men" "requir[ing]" that "women" do certain things. But the text never actually describes men making women do anything, and that's not what the sentence would say if we put this word in the blank, anyway. Instead, it would say that the "researchers" who argue that "Bronze Age societies were ruled by men" would "require that woman have also held leadership roles." It doesn't really make sense for someone to "require" that something in the past happened a certain way, because whatever that would be has already happened; it especially doesn't make sense for researchers who "argued" that men were in charge would "require" that women may have also been in charge. Again, it's not clear what this choice would even mean, but it's clear that the idea of the "researchers" "requir[ing]" anything isn't restated or demonstrated in the text, so (D) must be wrong.

Test 2, Module 1, Question 5 — TYPE: TEXT COMPLETION

The prompt will be a short passage containing a blank. The correct answer will always be restated or demonstrated by key phrases in the provided text. See "What about Text Completion Questions?" on p. 66.

Subjective Phrases to Ignore: "most"

A   **Barely Relevant:** The text describes an "accessory spleen" that some whales have, and then tells us that "its role isn't (blank)," and that "rather, the spleen may actively support...." So it basically says that the spleen isn't "(blank)," and that "rather," it "actively" does something. The word "rather" right after the blank lets us know that the spleen "actively support[ing]" something is the opposite of what goes in the blank. The word "replicable" means able to be copied or replicated, but the idea of being copied or replicated doesn't appear in the text, and being able to be copied or replicated isn't the opposite of doing something "actively." So (A) must be wrong.

B   **Literary Interpretation:** As we saw in our discussion of (A), the word "rather" tells us that the word in the blank should be something that's the opposite of "actively support[ing]" something. "Predetermined" means something like "decided ahead of time," but the text doesn't restate or demonstrate the idea of anything being decided ahead of time. Some untrained test-takers may attempt to interpret the text, and decide that the passage implies something about whether certain whales "develop[ing]" the "accessory spleen" is known or decided ahead of time or not, or something along those lines—but this wouldn't even actually cause the sentence to say that. Instead, this choice would cause the sentence to say that the "role" of the "spleen" "isn't predetermined." This idea isn't restated or demonstrated in the text, and this choice isn't the opposite of the spleen doing something "actively," so (B) is wrong too.

C   **Direct Contradiction:** This choice will definitely tempt test-takers who notice that the text says the "accessory spleen" is "seemingly functionless," and then decide that the phrase "isn't operative" restates the idea of being "seemingly functionless." But this choice wouldn't say that the spleen "isn't operative"—instead, it would say that the *spleen's role* "isn't operative," which isn't the same thing! It's not really clear what it would mean for a spleen's role not to be operative, or what it means for a "role" to "operat[e]," but it's not the same thing as the spleen itself not having a function—so this idea isn't restated or demonstrated in the text. Beyond that, this idea isn't the opposite of the spleen "actively" doing something, so this choice would cause the meaning of the word "rather" not to be demonstrated in the surrounding text (in fact, as we'll see in our discussion of (D), this choice is basically the opposite of what's demonstrated in the surrounding text, and what belongs in the blank). For either reason, (C) is wrong.

D ✓ **Correct:** As we've seen in our discussion of the other answer choices, the idea that comes after the word "rather" must be the opposite of the word that's in the blank. So the word in the blank must describe the opposite of doing something "actively." "Latent" basically means "dormant," or "not active." This is exactly the opposite of doing something "actively," so this choice demonstrates the relationship between the phrase containing the word "rather" and the idea that comes right before it; furthermore, the idea that something's role "isn't latent" restates the idea that it "actively" does something. So (D) is right.

Test 2, Module 1, Question 6 — TYPE: TEXT COMPLETION

The prompt will be a short passage containing a blank. The correct answer will always be restated or demonstrated by key phrases in the provided text. See "What about Text Completion Questions?" on p. 66.

Subjective Phrases to Ignore: "most"

A   **Direct Contradiction:** The provided text says "states taxes are (blank) other factors when considering an interstate move," and then tells us that "even significant differences" in state taxes "have almost no effect on most people's decisions," and that other things like "employment opportunities, housing availability, and climate are strong influences." This choice would cause the text to say that "state taxes are consistent with other factors when considering an interstate move," but that's the opposite of what we just saw in the passage—that passage tells us that "even significant differences" in state taxes "have almost no effect on most people's decisions," while other factors "are strong influences." So state taxes aren't "consistent with other factors," as this choice would require, and (A) is wrong.

B   **Literary Interpretation:** As we saw in our discussion of (A), the text demonstrates that "state taxes" aren't a big factor in people's decisions to move to a different state, while other "differences... are strong influences." This choice would cause the text to say that "state taxes are representative of other factors," which doesn't really make sense in context. This phrase would mean something like "state taxes" are typical examples of "other factors" like "employment opportunities, housing availability, and climate," which definitely isn't restated or demonstrated in the provided text—so it's wrong. This choice could be tempting for test-takers who don't think carefully about the specific result when we insert this phrase into the sentence, and who think it would cause the sentence to say something like "state taxes are one of the things people think about when deciding whether or not to move." But that's not what this choice would cause the text to say, and even if it did, that would be pretty much the opposite of what the text *does* say, as we saw in our discussion of (A). This is a great example of the importance of careful reading, because an untrained test-taker could take the word "representative" and come up with an argument for why it sort of goes along with some of the ideas present in the text—but when we actually read that text carefully, we can see that it doesn't fit at all, and can be eliminated.

C ✓ Correct: As we saw in our discussion of (A), the text says that "even significant differences in state taxation have almost no effect on most people's decisions," whereas "differences in employment opportunities, housing availability, and climate are strong influences." This exactly demonstrates the idea that "state taxes are <u>overshadowed by</u> other factors," as this choice requires—that is, the other factors are more important than the "state taxes." So (C) is right.

D Confused Relationships: A lot of test-takers will have a hard time picking between the right answer, (C), and this choice, because if we don't read them carefully, they both seem to say kind of the same thing—that state taxes aren't important "when considering an interstate move," and that "other factors" are. If we found ourselves in this position on test day, we would know that we need to step back, clear our heads, and take another look at everything, word by word. When we do that, we can see that inserting this choice would cause the text to say that "state taxes are <u>irrelevant to</u> other factors when considering an interstate move." It wouldn't say that "state taxes" are "irrelevant" to the *decision* to make an interstate move; it would say that "state taxes" are "irrelevant" to the "*other factors*" [emphasis added]. So, as we saw in our discussion of the other answer choices, the text demonstrates the idea that state taxes don't have a big impact on people's decisions to move to another state, while other factors do have a big impact. But *this* choice would cause the underlined phrase to say that state taxes don't have a big impact on *other factors* that people consider when deciding where to move. That idea doesn't appear elsewhere in the text, which means this choice wouldn't cause the underlined phrase to restate or demonstrate something from the provided text—so (D) must be wrong. This is exactly the kind of question where test-takers might feel *certain* that they've found a question with two viable answers, but we know from our training that we can always find a distinction that makes one answer right and the other choices wrong.

Test 2, Module 1, Question 7	TYPE: TEXT COMPLETION

The prompt will be a short passage containing a blank. The correct answer will always be restated or demonstrated by key phrases in the provided text. See "What about Text Completion Questions?" on p. 66.

Subjective Phrases to Ignore: "most"

A Literary Interpretation: The text says that "the author's claim" is "(blank), as it fails to account for several recent archaeological discoveries." The phrase "as it" tells us that the phrase "fails to account for several recent archaeological discoveries" is a demonstration of the idea that "the author's claim" is "(blank)." Beyond that, the provided text tells us what the "argument would need to address" "to be convincing," which demonstrates that the argument isn't "convincing" now. This choice will be tempting because it seems to say something bad about "the author's claim," but we can't just pick any choice that says something negative; instead, the right answer must restate or demonstrate the specific negative idea that appears in the text. This choice would call the claim "disorienting," which would require the text to specify that the claim was somehow confusing, or made people forget where they were relative to other things. An argument can "fail[] to account" for things, and fail to be "convincing," without "disorienting" people. This choice isn't restated or demonstrated in the text, so it's wrong.

B ✓ Correct: As we saw in our discussion of (A), the provided text says the "author's claim" "fails to account" for some things, and that it's not "convincing." This exactly demonstrates the idea that the argument is "tenuous"—that is, that the argument has problems, and that it's weak and ineffective. So (B) is right.

C Direct Contradiction: This choice is basically the opposite of the right answer, as we saw in our discussion of (B), although it will be tempting for test-takers who know that a real-life argument can be called "nuanced," and who think that this choice makes a sentence that would sound pretty good in a classroom setting. But we know that we can't pick an answer choice on the SAT because we think the sentence it creates would "sound good." We can only pick answer choices on the SAT that restate or demonstrate the relevant text, and nothing in the passage says that the "claim" is subtle, or deceptively clever, or anything else like "nuanced." So (C) is wrong.

D Literary Interpretation: Like (A), this choice will be tempting because the passage says something negative about the "claim"—that it "fails to account" for things, and that it's not "convincing"—and this choice also seems to say something negative about the "claim." But we can't pick an answer choice just because the text says something negative, and that answer choice also says something negative! We have to think about what that choice actually says, and whether that idea is restated or demonstrated in the text. When we do that, we notice that this choice requires the provided text to restate or demonstrate the idea that the claim is "unoriginal"—that is, that the author didn't come up with the "claim" himself, and that someone else came up with it first. But that idea doesn't appear in the text. Beyond that, a "claim" being "unoriginal" doesn't mean the claim wouldn't be "convincing," or that it would "fail[] to account" for anything, as the provided text would require—an unoriginal "claim" could be very convincing and account for all the latest "discoveries," for all we know; it would just need to be something that someone else already thought of. So this choice definitely isn't demonstrated in the provided text, which means it's wrong.

Test 2, Module 1, Question 8   TYPE: MAIN IDEA

The prompt asks about the "main purpose" or "main idea" (or some similar phrase) of the text. The correct answer must be directly restated or demonstrated in the passage, with no interpretation. See "What about "Main Idea/Main Purpose" Questions?" on p.69.

Subjective Phrases to Ignore: "best"

A   **Direct Contradiction:** As trained test-takers, we know that even the answers to "main purpose" questions will be based on specific words and phrases in the provided text, and not on any "overall impression" of the text that we get as readers. This choice will be tempting for many test-takers because of the word "retrace" in the provided poem, which seems to describe the "son" doing things that the speaker has already done. But there are a few problems with that—for one, it's not clear that "retrac[ing] the way" demonstrates "hav[ing]... accomplishments," as this choice would require—going the same way as another person isn't the same as having the same "accomplishments" as that person. For another, the poem specifically mentions the idea of the "son" soon "possessi[ng]" "great reaches" that are "unknown"—that is, that the speaker doesn't know anything about. This is the opposite of the child having "the same accomplishments" as the parent, because the parent doesn't even know what the child will end up doing. So the text doesn't' restate or demonstrate the idea of the parent having any "accomplishments," let alone the child having the "same" ones, and it *does* demonstrate the idea of the child doing things that are different from what the parent did (again, since they're "unknown" to the parent). With all of this in mind, we know (A) is wrong.

B   **Plausible but not in the Text:** This choice will be very tempting for untrained test-takers who notice that this poem is a parent addressing a child, and who know that in real life, "raising a child" often "involves" "struggles." But we can't answer a question on the SAT based on our own ideas of what happens in real life; we have to answer based on the text—and this text doesn't even mention anything about raising children at all, let alone specifying that "raising a child involves... struggles" of any kind. So (B) is wrong.

C   **Plausible but not in the Text:** Like (B), this choice will be tempting for untrained test-takers, because it seems to make a statement that would be true in real life, and that real-life parents would say to their children. But this poem doesn't actually include any "warn[ing]" whatsoever, nor does it actually say that any particular thing is "challeng[ing]." This choice is a great example of a statement that a student could make in an English classroom discussion without any pushback or correction from the teacher—but when we look at it from the perspective of the College Board, we can see that it actually mentions ideas that aren't demonstrated or restated anywhere in the provided text. So (C) is wrong.

D ✓   **Correct:** The speaker in the poem tells the "son" to "go forth," and that "great reaches... await... your possession." In other words, the speaker "encourage[s]" the child to go into the world to "possess[]" "great reaches," which is an example of having an "experience[]," as this choice requires. (Some test-takers will feel like understanding this part of the text requires some kind of literary interpretation, but "go[ing] forth" to do anything at all is an "experience," as this choice requires, even if we don't feel completely certain what it means to "possess[]" "great reaches.") Then the speaker says "my pilgrimage is through, but life is calling you!" The word "but" tells us that the phrase "life is calling you" is somehow opposed to the idea that the speaker's "pilgrimage is through"—in this case, that the "son's" pilgrimage isn't through, and that "life is calling" the son on a "pilgrimage." Since a pilgrimage is an "experience[]," this also demonstrates the idea of the "child... embrac[ing]... experiences," as this choice requires. Finally, telling the son to "go forth," and that something is "calling" him, demonstrates "encourag[ing]" the child to do something, as this choice also requires. This choice is demonstrated in the provided text, so it's right.

Test 2, Module 1, Question 9   TYPE: FUNCTION AND STRUCTURE

The prompt asks about the "function" or "structure" of a part of the text. The correct answer must plainly and accurately describe the relevant text, with no interpretation. See "What about "Function and Structure" Questions?" on p. 70.

Subjective Phrases to Ignore: "best"

A   **Confused Relationships:** This choice will be tempting because it mentions different concepts from the passage, but it confuses the relationships among those concepts. This choice mentions the "women" doing "work," just as the passage does, and the "range of personality traits" mentioned in this answer choice might seem to restate the idea that "people" "have their individual characters," as mentioned in the passage—but that statement was about "people" in general, and how "the trees" are like "people" in general; it's not a description of the "women" doing the "work" of collecting the syrup, as this choice would require. So this choice doesn't accurately describe the passage, which means it's wrong.

B   Literary Interpretation: This is exactly the kind of choice that an untrained test-taker will make an argument for, and end up choosing—even though it doesn't follow the College Board's standards for SAT Reading questions. The provided passage does describe people benefiting from their relationships with trees, because the people get the sap from the trees. Based on this, some untrained test-takers will reason that this choice basically describes the text as a whole, and they'll decide that, since the underlined sentence is part of that text, this choice should be fine to pick. But the prompt asks about "the function of the underlined sentence" specifically, and this sentence doesn't describe anyone benefiting from anything—in fact, it describes trees "yield[ing] up their life-blood," which is the opposite of benefitting from something. So (B) is wrong.

C   Confused Relationships: This choice will be tempting because the underlined sentence does comment on "human behavior," and the whole passage takes place in a "natural environment"—but nothing in the text demonstrates the "natural environment" "influenc[ing]" "human behavior" in any way, as this choice would require. The underlined sentence doesn't mention anything about people behaving differently because of some aspect of their natural surroundings, or anything like that. Remember that in order to pick an answer choice for an SAT Reading question, we have to be able to point to some specific word(s) or phrase(s) that justifies that choice; we can't ever answer based on some overall "impression" we have of the text. No word or phrase in the passage restates or demonstrates the idea of "human behavior" being "influenced by the natural environment," so (C) is wrong.

D ✓ Correct: The provided text says that "the women… test the trees," which directly demonstrates the idea of "the maple trees that the women evaluate," as mentioned in this choice—so we know that "the trees" mentioned in the underlined text are "the maple trees that the women evaluate" from this choice. The underlined text says that "the trees… have their individual characters," and that "some" are "ready to yield," while "others" are "more reluctant." This demonstrates the idea of "elaborat[ing] on an aspect of the maple trees," as this choice requires. This choice is exactly demonstrated by the underlined text, so (D) is right.

| Test 2, Module 1, Question 10 | TYPE: PAIRED PASSAGES |

The question will ask what the author of one passage would think about some aspect of the other passage. The answer must always be directly stated in the text, with no guessing or assumption from the test-taker. See "What about Paired Passages?" p. 70.

Subjective Phrases to Ignore: "most likely"

A ✓ Correct: We know that when an SAT Reading question asks us how someone from one text would react to an idea from another text, we don't have to speculate about what they would say—it will always be the case that the relevant text directly states how that person would feel about the topic in question. In this case, we need to find the choice that tells us what "Behrenfeld and colleagues" in Text 2 say about the "conventional wisdom" mentioned in Text 1. When we take a look at Text 1, we can see that the "conventional wisdom" is that "one species" of phytoplankton "should emerge after outcompeting the rest." So we need to look in Text 2 to see what "Behrenfeld and colleagues" say about phytoplankton competing with each other. The last sentence of that text tells us that "Behrenfeld's team" says that "direct competition among phytoplankton probably happens much less than previously thought." This exactly demonstrates the idea from this choice that "Behrenfeld and colleagues" in Text 2 would say that the "conventional wisdom" from Text 1 is "based on a misconception about phytoplankton species competing with one another"—that is, that the "conventional wisdom" assumes the phytoplankton compete with one another, but that "Behrenfeld's team" found that they probably compete "much less than previously thought." This choice is demonstrated in the two texts, so it's correct. (Notice how the idea of something happening differently from what was "previously thought" exactly demonstrates "a misconception.")

B   Plausible but not in the Text: This choice will be tempting for untrained test-takers because the idea of "routine replenishment of ocean nutrients prevent[ing] competition" sounds like something that's probably true in real life—but neither text actually mentions this idea, which is already enough for us to eliminate this answer choice. Beyond that, this choice specifically describes "prevent[ing] competition between phytoplankton species"—but "Behrenfeld's team" in Text 2 says "direct competition among phytoplankton probably happens much less than previously thought." So it *does* happen, just less than previously thought—which means "Behrenfeld and colleagues" wouldn't say that anything "prevents competition," as this choice would require. For either of these reasons, we know (B) is wrong.

C   Plausible but not in the Text: This choice mentions "compet[ing] with larger organisms," which is a concept that doesn't appear in either text—in fact, "larger organisms" aren't mentioned anywhere. So we know (C) can't be right. This choice will be tempting for untrained test-takers who try to use outside knowledge to create some scientific argument in favor of this answer choice, but as trained test-takers, we know that we always have to pick answer choices based on specific words and phrases in the relevant text, and not on our outside knowledge of the topics that appear in that text.

D   Confused Relationships: This choice mentions some ideas from the passages—like "ecologists," and "competition," and "phytoplankton," and "water density"—so (D) will be very tempting for untrained test-takers who don't read carefully, and fail to notice that this answer choice connects those ideas in ways that aren't reflected in the provided text. The provided text never "recommend[s]" that anyone do anything, and it also never says that "competition… is increased with water density." Either reason is enough to eliminate (D).

The prompt asks for information from the passage. The answer must be restated or demonstrated by specific phrases in the text. See "What about General Passage Questions?" on p. 69.

A ✓ Correct: The text says that "because Mars's atmosphere is only one percent as dense as Earth's, the air of Mars would not provide enough resistance" to keep a "standard helicopter" "aloft." The idea that "Mars's atmosphere is only one percent as dense as Earth's" exactly demonstrates that "Mars and Earth have different atmospheric conditions," and saying that "the air of Mars" wouldn't be "enough" to keep "a standard helicopter" "aloft" exactly demonstrates that "a helicopter built for Earth" couldn't "fly on Mars," as the prompt requires—again, "because Mars and Earth have different atmospheric conditions," as we just discussed. So (A) is exactly demonstrated in the provided text, which means it's right.

B Direct Contradiction: This choice will be tempting, because it mentions the idea of "large" "blades," which does appear in the provided text—but the text actually says that the helicopter with the "longer" "blades" is the one the team designed that *can* fly on Mars. So this choice is the opposite of what the text says, which means that it's wrong.

C Plausible but not in the Text: A lot of untrained test-takers will fall for this choice because they'll know that, in real life, gravity on Mars *is* "much weaker than the gravity of Earth." They'll feel like this must be relevant to the topic of the passage, and they'll decide that an answer choice that makes a real-life true statement can't be wrong. But this choice *is* wrong on the SAT, because the right answer must be based on specific words and phrases in the text, and the text never mentions gravity a single time. So the statement in this choice doesn't appear anywhere in the text, which means it must be wrong.

D Confused Relationships: Some untrained test-takers will have a hard time choosing between this choice and the correct answer, (A). As we saw in our discussion of (A), the text *does* say that the helicopter built for Mars had "longer" blades, which might imply that the problem with "standard helicopter[s]" is that they're "too small," as this choice says. But if this choice were accurate, that would mean that, in order to make a "helicopter built for Earth" able to fly on Mars, you would just need to make it bigger—which isn't what the text tells us. The text specifically tells us that the helicopter built for Mars has "longer blades"—not just that it's bigger in general. But it also tells us that those blades "rotate faster" than those of a standard helicopter—so even the bigger blades aren't actually sufficient for that helicopter to fly on Mars. And beyond all of that, the lack of bigger, faster blades isn't "why… a helicopter built for Earth" can't "fly on Mars"—these features are just one solution to the problem of making a helicopter that can fly on Mars. Instead, as we saw in our discussion of (A), the text tells us that the reason a "standard helicopter" can't fly on Mars is the difference in "atmospheric conditions." Again, different features on the helicopter (like "longer," "faster" "blades," for example) are ways to address that reason, but the actual situation that makes a "standard helicopter" "unable to fly on Mars" is the difference in atmosphere—not the size of the helicopter—as we saw in our discussion of (A). So (D) is wrong.

The prompt asks about the "main purpose" or "main idea" (or some similar phrase) of the text. The correct answer must be directly restated or demonstrated in the passage, with no interpretation. See "What about "Main Idea/Main Purpose" Questions?" on p.69.

Subjective Phrases to Ignore: "best"

A ✓ Correct: The text tells us about "jalis," and then tells us that "new technologies may have changed some aspects of the role," which directly restates that "there have been some changes in their role," as this choice requires. Then the text tells us that "jalis continue to be valued for knowing and protecting their peoples' stories," which directly restates the idea that "jalis continue to preserve their communities' histories," as this choice also requires. Every part of this choice exactly restates the provided text, so (A) is correct.

B Off by One or Two Words: The text does say that "jalis" "have often served as teachers," but it never says any of them "like teaching best," as this choice requires; in fact, the passage never says that jalis like anything in particular. This choice could be tempting for test-takers who know that, in real life, some people find teaching to be a rewarding job, and they like their students—but this idea doesn't appear in the text, so we can't pick an answer choice based on it. So (B) is wrong.

C Literary Interpretation: This choice will be tempting for test-takers who read that jalis are "keepers" of "family histories" as well as "records of important events." Those test-takers might imagine the jalis telling "entertaining" stories from these "histories," or about these "events," as this choice would require. This might happen in real life, for all we know, but the text never describes the jalis doing anything "entertaining" at all (nor doing anything for "centuries," which this choice would also require). So (C) must be wrong.

D Plausible but not in the Text: This choice sounds like it could be true in real life, and the passage comes close to saying what this choice says—but the text never actually says that "technology can now do" *any* of the things that "jalis used to be responsible for."

The text *does* say that "new technologies may have changed some aspects of the role today," but this isn't the same as saying that the technology itself "can now do" what jalis "used" to do. "New technologies" can "change[]… aspects" of jalis' "role" without actually replacing jalis in any capacity. Maybe jalis make presentations using computers, maybe they record events with cameras, maybe they connect with other jalis using the internet; these would all be examples of technology "chang[ing] some aspects of the role," without actually *doing* any "of the things jalis used to be responsible for." We don't know how they use technology, or what technology they use, because the text doesn't tell us; but it certainly doesn't tell us that the technology "can now do" things that jalis "used to be responsible for." So (D) is wrong.

The prompt asks about the "main purpose" or "main idea" (or some similar phrase) of the text. The correct answer must be directly restated or demonstrated in the passage, with no interpretation. See "What about "Main Idea/Main Purpose" Questions?" on p.69.

Subjective Phrases to Ignore: "best"

A ✓   **Correct:** The text tells us about the "Wigner crystal," and says that it "remained largely conjecture" until some researchers "captured an image of one." It then says that this image is "the first visual confirmation of the Wigner crystal." If the "Wigner crystal" was "largely conjecture" before—that is, it was just an idea that people talked about but hadn't ever actually seen or documented—and then "researchers" "captured an image of one," then that image would be "the most definitive evidence to date of the existence" of that crystal, just as this choice requires. Every idea in this choice is demonstrated in the passage, which means (A) is correct.

B   **Literary Interpretation:** This choice will be tempting because it does mention concepts from the passage, like "researchers" and "crystalline structures," but it also mentions ideas that don't appear in the passage. For example, the text never actually mentions that anything is "new" or "innovative"—for all we know, the process described in the passage has been around for a while, and this is just the first time someone used it to capture an image of the Wigner crystal. This choice also mentions the idea of "working with unusual crystalline structures" in general, but the only "crystalline structure" mentioned in the passage is the Wigner crystal, and the text never tells us that what appears in the passage is connected to any other such structure, as the phrase "unusual crystalline structures" would require. So (B) mentions ideas that aren't restated or demonstrated in the text, which means it's wrong.

C   **Off by One or Two Words:** A lot of test-takers will pick this choice, because the text does mention that graphene is one of the "components" that the "researchers" use "to capture an image of a Wigner crystal." But the text never says that graphene "is the most important of the components," which this choice would require—so we know that (C) must be wrong.

D   **Confused Relationships:** Like the other wrong answer choices, this one mentions ideas from the passage, but makes connections between those ideas that aren't demonstrated in the passage. The text does say that it took a long time for anyone to "acquire an image of a Wigner crystal," and it does mention that the crystal has a "honeycomb structure"—but it never tells us that the "honeycomb structure" is the thing that made it "difficult" to "acquire an image" of the "Wigner crystal"! This idea doesn't appear in the text, so we can't pick a choice that makes this statement. That means (D) is wrong.

The passage includes a figure. The question asks for the choice that uses data from the figure to accomplish a certain goal. The right answer will describe the data accurately and plainly accomplish the goal. See "What about "Data" Questions?" on p. 69.

Subjective Phrases to Ignore: "best"

A   **Direct Contradiction:** This question asks for "data… that support the researchers' conclusion," so we need to check the passage to see what the "researchers' conclusion" is. The passage says that "according to the researchers… there was a growing interest among CEOs in connecting with more departments in their companies." When we read this choice, we can see that it actually contradicts the data in the provided graph. That graph is entitled "Average Number of Individuals Reporting Directly to CEOs," and the key below tells us that the light columns reflect numbers for "managers" while the darker columns reflect numbers for "department leaders." This choice says that "the average numbers of managers and department leaders reporting directly to their CEO" was unchanged "from the 1991–1995 period to the 2001–2008 period." But we can see that both bars are larger in 2001-2008 than they were in 1991-1995—so this choice makes a statement that contradicts the data in the graph, which means it must be wrong.

B   **Direct Contradiction:** Like (A), this choice directly contradicts the data in the graph: we can see that the lighter column representing "managers" is largest in the 2001-2008 period, not the 1996-2001 period, as this choice would require. So (B) is wrong.

C   **Confused Relationships:** First and foremost, we can see that this choice describes the data accurately—the bar representing "department leaders reporting directly to their CEO" *is* larger than the bar representing "managers reporting directly to their

CEO" "in each of the three periods studied," just as this choice says. But describing the data accurately isn't the same as "support[ing] the researchers' conclusion," so we'll have to consider that aspect of the prompt next. This choice will be tempting for untrained test-takers, because the "researchers' conclusion" that we need to support is that "there was a growing interest among CEOs in connecting with more departments in their companies." Those untrained test-takers might see this choice's mention of the "average number of department leaders reporting directly to their CEO" being greater than something, and assume that must be a reference to the "growing interest" from the "conclusion." But as trained test-takers, we know that we have to think carefully about exactly what the provided text says. By definition, something that's "growing" has to increase *over time*. But "the average number of department leaders reporting directly to their CEO" being larger than "the average number of managers reporting directly to their CEO" in each time period from the graph *doesn't* show anything growing over time, as the phrase "growing interest" requires; it just shows that one number is consistently larger than another number, which could be true whether either of those numbers is growing, or shrinking, or staying the same. So the statement in this choice could be true whether "the average number of department leaders reporting directly to their CEO" were growing over time, or shrinking, or staying the same, which means this choice doesn't "support the researchers' conclusion" that "CEOs" had a "growing interest" "in connecting with more departments." That means (C) is wrong.

D ✓   Correct: This choice is correct: the "researchers' conclusion" is that "there was a growing interest among CEOs in connecting with more departments in their companies," and, as this choice points out, "the average number of department leaders reporting directly to their CEO rose over the three periods studied." The idea that the "average number... rose" directly demonstrates the idea of "growing," and "department leaders reporting directly to their CEO" directly demonstrates the idea of "CEOs" having an "interest" in "connecting with more departments in their companies." So (D) is correct.

Test 2, Module 1, Question 15	TYPE: IF TRUE

The passage presents some claim or hypothesis. The prompt typically asks us to choose the "finding" that, "if true," would support or weaken the argument. Supporting statements will demonstrate the idea in the claim, and weakening statements will demonstrate the opposite of the idea in the claim. See "What about "If True" Questions?" on p. 71.

Subjective Phrases to Ignore: "most directly"

A   Barely Relevant: The prompt asks for the choice that "undermines Foster's hypothesis," so we need to check the provided text for that hypothesis, and then find the choice that contradicts it. The passage talks about otters "damag[ing] the roots of eelgrass plants," then says that "Foster hypothesized that damage to eelgrass roots... benefits the meadow's health overall." This choice says that "eelgrass meadows are found near otter populations that are small and have only recently been reintroduced." To an untrained test-taker, this statement might seem relevant to the hypothesis. But the choice doesn't tell us how the "eelgrass meadows" are doing—we don't know whether they're in good health or bad, or doing better or worse compared to others; we only know that they were found near an otter population. The hypothesis says that otters damaging eelgrass roots "benefits the meadow's health overall," but this statement tells us nothing about the meadows' health, so it can't support or undermine that hypothesis. That means (A) is wrong.

B   Barely Relevant: The hypothesis described in the passage tells us about the impact of damage to eelgrass roots on those plants, and on the meadows where they live. The idea that there are other sites "not included in the study" where "large, well-established sea otter populations" live without "eelgrass meadows" has no effect on the hypothesis; nothing in the text or the hypothesis says otters *have* to live near eelgrass, it just describes what happens when otters *do* live near eelgrass. So (B) is wrong.

C ✓   Correct: The hypothesis in the passage says that "damage to eelgrass roots" (which we're told earlier in the passage can be caused by otters "digging for clams") ultimately "benefits the meadow's health overall." But this choice says that, "at several sites not included in the study, eelgrass meadows' health correlates negatively with the length of residence and size of otter populations." In other words, the more otters live near the meadows in these other sites, and the longer they live there, the worse the health of those meadows gets. This is the opposite of the hypothesis, which says that the "damage" that can be caused by otters digging for food "benefits the meadow's health." This choice contradicts the hypothesis, which means it "undermines" that hypothesis, as the prompt requires—so it's right.

D   Barely Relevant: This choice is similar to the right answer, (C), except this choice talks about the "health of plants unrelated to eelgrass," while choice (C) talks about "eelgrass meadows' health" specifically. The only plants that "Foster's hypothesis" talks about are "eelgrass plants," so the relative health of "plants unrelated to eelgrass" has no impact on that hypothesis. That means (D) is wrong.

Test 2, Module 1, Question 16	TYPE: MOST LOGICALLY COMPLETES

The passage ends with a blank, and the answer choices are relatively long phrases. The right answer will restate or demonstrate an idea in the provided text. See "What about "Most Logically Completes" Questions?" on p. 68.

A   Plausible but not in the Text: This choice might be tempting for test-takers who only focus on the last sentence of the passage, because this choice would seem to fit fairly well in that sentence in a typical classroom environment. But as trained test-takers, we know that's not enough of a justification for us to pick an answer choice—the correct answer must cause the text to restate or demonstrate another part of the provided text. This choice mentions "many other factors that motivated F. Scott to write," but the passage never mentions any "other factors that motivated" him. We might imagine in real life that there were many factors "that motivated F. Scott to write," but this idea doesn't appear in the text—so we know that (A) must be wrong.

B ✓ Correct: The passage says that "F. Scott Fitzgerald's writings were likely influenced in part by his marriage to Zelda Fitzgerald," which demonstrates a "contribution[] to literature" from Zelda, as this choice requires. The passage goes on to say that "many don't recognize Zelda as an author in her own right," and that she "authored several works herself," which are additional "contributions to literature" from Zelda, as this choice also requires. Given this information, "primarily view[ing] Zelda as an inspiration for F. Scott's writings" directly demonstrates the idea of "misrepresenting the full range of Zelda's contributions to literature," just as this choice says: this would "[]represent" her "range" of contributions as being "primarily... an inspiration," and not also a "writer." This choice accurately demonstrates an idea that appears elsewhere in the text, so it's right.

C   Barely Relevant: An untrained test-taker might speculate that people could "draw inaccurate conclusions" about how the Fitzgeralds "viewed each other's works," but the passage doesn't say anything about how they felt about each other's works—which means this choice isn't demonstrated in the passage, and it must be wrong.

D   Literary Interpretation: This choice will be tempting for test-takers who notice the idea from the passage that "F. Scott Fitzgerald's writings were likely influenced in part by his marriage," because writing about one's marriage must be somewhat "autobiographical," by definition. But this choice doesn't just say that F. Scott's writing was "autobiographical." It says that people read both F. Scott's *and* Zelda's works, not just in an "autobiographical light," but in an "*overly* autobiographical light [emphasis added]." The text never says anything about whether Zelda's works were "autobiographical" or not, and certainly never says people read either of their works in that "light" to too great an extent, as the word "overly" in this choice would require. So this choice must be wrong.

Test 2, Module 1, Question 17 **TYPE: MOST LOGICALLY COMPLETES**

The passage ends with a blank, and the answer choices are relatively long phrases. The right answer will restate or demonstrate an idea in the provided text. See "What about "Most Logically Completes" Questions?" on p. 68.

A   Direct Contradiction: The text mentions "*Testudo* tortoises" and says they "live alone and do not in engage in parental care," then says that "tortoise hatchlings showed a significant preference" for the "face-like" "image." This is the opposite of choice (A), which says "face-like stimuli" are perceived as "threatening by newborns of solitary species without parental care." Again, the "tortoise hatchlings," which are members of a "solitary species without parental care," "prefer[red]" the image—they didn't perceive it as "threatening," as this choice would require. So (A) is wrong.

B ✓ Correct: The passage says that "among social animals that care for their young," "newborns appear to show an innate attraction to faces and face-like stimuli." Then it says that *Testudo* tortoises "live alone and do not engage in parental care," and their hatchlings "showed a significant preference" for a "face-like" "image." In other words, all of the newborns mentioned in the passage, whether they were from a social species or not, and whether their species cared for their young or not, were "innate[ly] attract[ed]... to face-like stimuli." This demonstrates the idea from this choice that "researchers should not assume that an innate attraction to face-like stimuli" has anything to do with "social interaction or parental care." So (B) is right.

C   Direct Contradiction: The provided text specifically tells us that "among social animals that care for their young... newborns appear to show an innate attraction to faces and face-like stimuli." This choice directly contradicts that text by saying that this "attraction" is "learned rather than innate." so (C) is wrong.

D   Literary Interpretation: The text only talks about the preferences that "tortoise hatchlings" have for "face-like" "image[s]," and never mentions whether "adult *Testudo* tortoises" have any such preference—so we can't make a comparison between the strengths of their respective preferences, as this choice would require. Some test-takers will assume that this must be because the adults lack that preference, but that would be an *assumption* not based on anything in the provided text, and we can't pick answer choices to SAT Reading questions based on assumptions. This choice isn't restated or demonstrated in the passage, so it's wrong.

Test 2, Module 1, Question 18 **TYPE: MOST LOGICALLY COMPLETES**

The passage ends with a blank, and the answer choices are relatively long phrases. The right answer will restate or demonstrate an idea in the provided text. See "What about "Most Logically Completes" Questions?" on p. 68.

A ✓   Correct: The text says that "much of the collection's content predates the initial invasion," which is directly restated by the phrase "its content largely predates the invasion" from this answer choice. (Notice that the words "much" and "largely" in this context tell us that not *all* of the content "predates the initial invasion," which means that some of the content must be from "after the invasion," as this choice requires.) Beyond that, the statement from the text that "some of the poems contain inarguable references to beliefs and customs common in Spain during this era" demonstrates the idea that those poems must have been composed after "Aztec society" came into contact with Spain as a result of the "initial invasion," which means "*Cantares Mexicanos* also contains additions made after the invasion," as this choice requires. This choice is restated and demonstrated in the passage, so it's right.

B   Plausible but not in the Text: The passage tells us that "*Cantares Mexicanos*" is "in classical Nahuatl," which it says is "the principal language of the Aztec Empire." Although the text mentions Spain, it never mentions "the Spanish language" at all—so whether "those who compiled *Cantares Mexicanos*" knew any of "the Spanish language" isn't restated or demonstrated anywhere in the passage, which means this choice must be wrong. This statement certainly sounds like it *could* be true, but again, that idea isn't in the provided text, so we can't pick this choice.

C   Confused Relationships: The passage says that "some of the poems contain inarguable references to beliefs and customs common in Spain during this era," and this choice would make the next sentence say "thus, some scholars have concluded that <u>before the invasion by Spain, the poets of the Aztec Empire borrowed from the literary traditions of other societies.</u>" But the only mention of any non-Aztec influence on *Cantares Mexicanos* in the passage is from "Spain" during their invasion and occupation. The passage doesn't mention the impact of any "literary traditions" from "other societies" "before" that "invasion," or at any other time. This choice isn't demonstrated or restated in the text, so it's wrong.

D   Plausible but not in the Text: The passage talks about "Aztec society before the occupation of the empire by the army of Spain," then says that "nonetheless, some of the poems contain inarguable references to beliefs and customs common in Spain during this era." The word "nonetheless" tells us that this sentence contains some idea that is opposed to an idea from the previous sentences—whereas the previous sentence discussed "Aztec society before… Spain," this sentence must be talking about "the Aztec Empire" after being influenced by Spain. Furthermore, the word "inarguable" tells us that these "beliefs and customs" *did* come from Spain, as opposed to being a "coincidental resemblance," as this choice would require. Beyond that, nothing in the passage discusses the idea of "coincidental resemblance between the societies of Spain and the Aztec Empire," or of any coincidences of any kind. A lot of test-takers will like this choice because it sounds like it could be true in real life, but we know we can't pick an answer choice just because it could be true in real life. Once again, this choice isn't restated or demonstrated in the text, so we know (D) is wrong.

Test 2, Module 1, Question 19 — TYPE: MOST LOGICALLY COMPLETES

The passage ends with a blank, and the answer choices are relatively long phrases. The right answer will restate or demonstrate an idea in the provided text. See "What about "Most Logically Completes" Questions?" on p. 68.

A ✓   Correct: The passage says that "researchers" who were studying "the cognitive abilities" of monkeys "neglected to control for the physical difficulty of the tasks they used to evaluate the monkeys," and that monkeys performing tasks "requiring little dexterity… were judged by the same criteria" as "monkeys given physically demanding problems." The idea of monkeys being evaluated for "cognitive ability" using the "same criteria" whether their tasks were "physically demanding" or not demonstrates the idea of monkeys displaying "differences" in their performance for reasons that are unrelated "cognitive ability." In other words, the monkeys might perform worse on some tasks because the tasks were physically difficult, not because the monkeys lacked the cognitive ability to perform them—and if researchers "neglected to control for the physical difficulty of the tasks," as the passage says, the results "could suggest that there are differences in cognitive ability among the monkeys even though such differences may not actually exist," as this choice says—again, because monkeys might fail at some tasks due to the tasks' physical difficulty, not for cognitive reasons. This is exactly what (A) says, so this choice is right.

B   Direct Contradiction: As we saw in our discussion of (A), the passage tells us that the study might involve monkeys failing at tasks due to the physical difficulty of those tasks, not the tasks' cognitive difficulty, and that the researchers "neglected to control for the physical difficulty of the tasks." So it might seem like monkeys are failing for cognitive reasons when they're really failing for physical reasons—that means researchers wouldn't be able to be sure whether monkeys failed a task for cognitive reasons or physical reasons, which is the opposite of what the first half of this choice says. Furthermore, the study described in the prompt *would* tell researchers which "tasks the monkeys can perform," it would just make it unclear, when the monkeys failed, whether it was due to cognitive challenges or physical challenges—which is the opposite of what the second half of this choice says. So (B) is wrong.

C   Confused Relationships: This choice will be very tempting, because it could be a valid statement if the study described in the passage didn't have any flaws; in that case, it would say that a study of *C. imitator* monkeys without any flaws should only be seen as "indicative of the cognitive abilities" of that type of monkey. But the passage *does* point out a flaw in that study, so the results of this study shouldn't be "indicative of the cognitive abilities of *any* monkey species [emphasis added]," *including C. imitator*. So this statement contradicts the provided text. This choice could also be tempting for test-takers who overlook the phrase "other than *C. imitator*," because without that phrase, this choice would say that the flawed study described in the passage shouldn't be "taken as indicative of the cognitive abilities of any monkey species." But, again, that would ignore the phrase "other than *C. imitator*." When we read this choice in its entirety, and we note that the study was flawed (as described in the passage), we know that (C) must be wrong.

D   Plausible but not in the Text: This is the kind of choice that would be tempting for a test-taker who tries to use outside knowledge to answer SAT Reading questions. In real life, a potential problem with experiments on animals is that those experiments might require the animals to perform tasks in a laboratory setting that aren't similar to what that animal would "encounter[] in the wild," as this choice says. Also, the passage mentions two tasks ("sliding a panel" and "unscrewing a bottle and inserting a straw"), and neither one sounds like a problem a monkey would "encounter[] in the wild." But as we saw in our discussion of (A), there are flaws that make it unclear how much this study even tells us about "monkeys' cognitive abilities" in any context—so we can't say the study tells us more about "monkeys' cognitive abilities" in one situation than another—and just because the passage only mentions two tasks, that doesn't tell us that every task in the study was similar. For all we know, there were hundreds of tasks, and every other task besides the two mentioned in the passage took place in "wild" settings. So the passage doesn't demonstrate or restate the ideas in (D), which means (D) is wrong.

Test 2, Module 1, Question 20   TYPE: SAT WRITING

- Vertical Scan Results: Each choice is a different form of the verb "to enter."
- Vertical Scan Notes: We have to decide whether a participle ("having entered" or "entering"), infinitive (to enter), or conjugated form of "to enter" is appropriate.
- Key Features in Surrounding Text: When we read the surrounding text and notice the intervening phrase "inside African turquoise killifish eggs," we can mentally remove that phrase and realize that the underlined phrase is the action being done by the plural noun "embryos." We can also see that this sentence currently doesn't include a main verb.

Concepts in the question:

- **Independent and Dependent Clauses:** Choices would create and/or join clauses. An independent clause can stand on its own as a sentence, and a dependent clause can't. Remember rules for joining clauses related to periods, semi-colons, colons, commas, and conjunctions. (See page 82.)
- **Verb Tense/Conjugation:** Choices include different forms of the same verb. Look at the surrounding text to find the verb's subject. Also, look for other clues that could indicate the proper tense or form of the verb in the blank. (See page 77.)

ANSWER CHOICE ANALYSIS

A ✓   Correct: As we discussed above, the correct answer should be the action being done by "embryos." This choice would create the acceptable phrase "embryos… enter." This choice also solves the problem (noted above) of the sentence currently not including a main verb. So (A) is correct.

B   Incorrect: As we discussed above, the correct answer should be the action being done by "embryos." This choice would create the phrase "embryos… to enter," which would leave the first sentence without a main verb, and without an independent clause, which isn't acceptable on the SAT. So (B) is wrong.

C   Incorrect: This choice has the same basic problem as (B), and is wrong for the same reason.

D   Incorrect: This choice has the same basic problem as (B) and (C), and is wrong for the same reason

Test 2, Module 1, Question 21   TYPE: SAT WRITING

- Vertical Scan Results: Each choice is a different conjugation of the verb "to double."
- Vertical Scan Notes: We need to decide the appropriate tense of the verb " to double."
- Key Features in Surrounding Text: The only other conjugated verb phrase in the passage is "was… made," which consists of the past-tense helping verb "was" and the past participle "made." With nothing concrete in the provided text to tell us otherwise, we know the verb form in the correct answer choice should match this structure, and should also consist of a past-tense helping verb and a past participle.

Concepts in the question:

- Parallelism: The surrounding text includes phrasing and/or grammatical structures that should be mirrored by what appears in the blank. (See page 93.)
- Verb Tense/Conjugation: Choices include different forms of the same verb. Look at the surrounding text to find the verb's subject. Also, look for other clues that could indicate the proper tense or form of the verb in the blank. (See page 77.)

ANSWER CHOICE ANALYSIS

A   Incorrect: As we discussed above, the verb in the underlined phrase should consist of a past-tense helping verb and a past participle—but "has" is a present-tense helping verb, so (A) is wrong.

B ✓ Correct: As we discussed above, the verb in the underlined phrase should consist of a past tense helping verb and a past participle. "Had" is a past-tense helping verb, and "doubled" is a past participle, so (B) meets that requirement, which means it's right. Notice that we don't have to know the terms "helping verb" or "past participle" to answer this question; we just need to recognize that "had doubled" from this choice has the same structure as "was… made" from the provided text.

C   Incorrect: As we discussed above, the verb in the underlined phrase should consist of a past-tense helping verb and a past participle—but "doubles" is a present-tense form, so (C) is wrong.

D   Incorrect: As we discussed above, the verb in the underlined phrase should consist of a past-tense helping verb and a past participle—but "will double" is a future-tense form, so (D) is wrong.

Test 2, Module 1, Question 22   TYPE: SAT WRITING

- Vertical Scan Results: Each choice starts with "configurations" and ends with "TMAO." Some choices include either a comma, or a period, or the word "and" between those two words.
- Vertical Scan Notes: We need to decide what, if anything, should appear between "configurations" and "TMAO."
- Key Features in Surrounding Text: "The chemical… configurations" can stand on its own as a sentence, and "TMAO is found… fish" can also stand on its own as a sentence.

Concepts in the question:

- Comma Splice: A comma can't join two groups of words that could each be sentences on their own. (See page 83.)
- Independent and Dependent Clauses: Choices would create and/or join clauses. An independent clause can stand on its own as a sentence, and a dependent clause can't. Remember rules for joining clauses related to periods, semi-colons, colons, commas, and conjunctions. (See page 82.)

ANSWER CHOICE ANALYSIS

A ✓ Correct: This choice separates two sets of words that can stand on their own as sentences with a period, which follows the punctuation standards for the SAT. So (A) is correct.

B   Incorrect: This choice results in two sets of words that can stand on their own as sentences not being separated with any punctuation—also known as a "run-on sentence"—which violates the punctuation standards for the SAT. So (B) is wrong.

C   Incorrect: This choice separates two sets of words that can stand on their own as sentences with a comma, which creates a comma splice. This violates the punctuation standards for the SAT, so (C) is wrong.

D   Incorrect: This choice uses the conjunction "and" to separate two groups of words that could each stand on their own as sentences—but we know that on the SAT, when we use a conjunction like "and" to separate two independent clauses, a comma must appear before "and." That comma is missing, so (D) is wrong.

Test 2, Module 1, Question 23   TYPE: SAT WRITING

- Vertical Scan Results: Each choice is a different version of the verb "to experience"
- Vertical Scan Notes: We need to pick whether a past, present, or future tense version of "to experience" is appropriate, among other things.
- Key Features in Surrounding Text: The underlined phrase is a verb form that is separated from its subject by the intervening phrase "of Linda." When we remove that phrase we can see that the subject of the verb is "character." We can also see that every verb in the passage is in the present tense ("are," "connects," "prepares," "hears," "evoke"—note that "exiled" is an adjective in this context), and nothing in the passage indicates that the verb in the underlined phrase happens in a different timeframe—so we need a present-tense verb to go with the singular noun "character."

Concepts in the question:

- Parallelism: The surrounding text includes phrasing and/or grammatical structures that should be mirrored by what appears in the blank. (See page 93.)

- **Verb Tense/Conjugation:** Choices include different forms of the same verb. Look at the surrounding text to find the verb's subject. Also, look for other clues that could indicate the proper tense or form of the verb in the blank. (See page 77.)

A Incorrect: This is a past-tense verb, but as discussed above, we need a present-tense verb. So (A) is wrong.

B Incorrect: This has the same problem as (A), and is wrong for the same reasons.

C ✓ Correct: As discussed above, we need a present-tense verb that agrees with the singular subject "character." This choice meets those requirements, so (C) is right.

D Incorrect: This verb is in the future tense—but as we discussed above, we need a verb in the present tense. So (D) is wrong.

Note The word "synesthesia" appears in this passage. A lot of test-takers will be intimidated by this word, because they won't know what it means—but on this question, the meaning of the word "synesthesia" is completely irrelevant. The College Board loves to do whatever it can to fluster test-takers, and that definitely includes using unusual or challenging vocabulary, but the large majority of that vocabulary has no bearing on the right answer to the question, just like "synesthesia" in this question. So when you encounter challenging words on test day, don't let them throw you off—more often than not you can answer the question in front of you whether you're familiar with that challenging word or not.

Test 2, Module 1, Question 24   TYPE: SAT WRITING

- **Vertical Scan Results:** Each choice is the same two words with different punctuation.
- **Vertical Scan Notes:** We need to decide where (if anywhere) the apostrophe should appear in each word.
- **Key Features in Surrounding Text:** The sentence only mentions one "screw," and nothing in context states that there was more than one screw. Beyond that, a form that shows that the "screw" possesses the "threads" would connect the word "threads" to the sentence; otherwise "threads" is just a plural noun appearing after another plural noun with no grammatical connection to anything else. So "screw" should be both singular and possessive. Now let's consider "threads." The underlined phrase ends in a period, and if "threads" were in a possessive form, there wouldn't be anything after "threads" that could belong to "threads." Furthermore, nothing in the provided text says anything belonged to the "threads." So "threads" needs to be in a non-possessive form.

Concepts in the question:

- **Possessive and/or Plural:** Choices include nouns ending in "-s," with or without an apostrophe before or after the "-s." The provided text will indicate which nouns should show ownership, and which shouldn't. (See page 79.)

A Incorrect: This choice includes the singular possessive form "screw's," which fits our analysis above, but it also has the singular possessive form "thread's," which, as we just discussed, should be a non-possessive form. So (A) is wrong.

B Incorrect: This choice has the plural possessive form "screws'," which isn't appropriate, as we saw in our discussion above. So (B) is wrong.

C ✓ Correct: This choice includes the singular possessive form "screw's," and the non-possessive form "threads," which fits our analysis above. So (C) is right.

D Incorrect: This choice has the plural non-possessive form "screws" and the plural possessive form "threads'," neither of which satisfies our reasoning above. So (D) is wrong.

Test 2, Module 1, Question 25   TYPE: SAT WRITING

- **Vertical Scan Results:** Each choice has the word "materialism" followed by a quotation mark. Some choices include punctuation and/or the word "and" after "materialism."
- **Vertical Scan Notes:** We need to decide whether a comma, semi-colon, or no punctuation should appear after "materialism," as well as whether the word "and" should appear after "materialism."
- **Key Features in Surrounding Text:** The text from the beginning of the passage through the word "materialism" can stand on its own as a sentence. Everything after the word "materialism" *can't* stand on its own as a sentence, whether the word "and" is included or not. Everything after the word "materialism" is a noun phrase describing the quote in the given passage that appears immediately before that phrase.

Concepts in the question:

- **Commas:** Commas can be used between clauses, to form comma sandwiches, in a list of 3 or more items, and before reported speech. They can't appear for no reason. Review the training for the relevant details. (See page 86.)
- **Independent and Dependent Clauses:** Choices would create and/or join clauses. An independent clause can stand on its own as a sentence, and a dependent clause can't. Remember rules for joining clauses related to periods, semi-colons, colons, commas, and conjunctions. (See page 82.)
- **Descriptive Noun Phrase:** A comma-separated noun phrase describes the nearest phrase in the sentence where it appears. (See page 88.)
- **Semicolons:** Semicolons can be used to separate two sets of words that could each stand on their own as complete sentences, or to separate items in a complex list. (See page 86.)

ANSWER CHOICE ANALYSIS

A   Incorrect: We can't use a semi-colon after "materialism," because everything after "materialism" can't stand on its own as a sentence.

B   Incorrect: This choice has the same problem as (D) below, with the added problem of including the word "and." We know from our training that we use a comma to separate a descriptive noun phrase from the thing it describes, not the word "and." This choice could be tempting for test-takers who think that everything after "materialism" is an independent clause, rather than a descriptive noun phrase—although even in that case, there would also need to be a comma before "and."

C ✓ Correct: As we discussed above, everything after "materialism" is a noun phrase describing the quote in the passage; this descriptive phrase needs to be separated from the thing it describes by a comma. This choice includes that comma and doesn't create any other problems, so (C) is correct.

D   Incorrect: As we discussed above, everything after "materialism" is a noun phrase describing the quote in the passage; this descriptive phrase needs to be separated from the thing it describes by a comma. This choice is missing that comma, so it's wrong.

Test 2, Module 1, Question 26   TYPE: SAT WRITING

- **Vertical Scan Results:** Each choice is the same two words with different punctuation.
- **Vertical Scan Notes:** We have to decide whether a comma, semi-colon, or no punctuation should appear after "prey," and whether a comma or semi-colon should appear after "rather."
- **Key Features in Surrounding Text:** "To humans... prey" can stand on its own as a sentence, and "rather... approach" can stand on its own as a sentence.

Concepts in the question:

- **Commas:** Commas can be used between clauses, to form comma sandwiches, in a list of 3 or more items, and before reported speech. They can't appear for no reason. Review the training for the relevant details. (See page 86.)
- **Independent and Dependent Clauses:** Choices would create and/or join clauses. An independent clause can stand on its own as a sentence, and a dependent clause can't. Remember rules for joining clauses related to periods, semi-colons, colons, commas, and conjunctions. (See page 82.)
- **Semicolons:** Semicolons can be used to separate two sets of words that could each stand on their own as complete sentences, or to separate items in a complex list. (See page 86.)

ANSWER CHOICE ANALYSIS

A   Incorrect: This choice would create a comma splice, because it would separate two groups of words that can each stand on their own as sentences with a comma. So (A) is wrong.

B   Incorrect: This choice would results in two groups of words that can each stand on their own as sentences not having any punctuation, conjunction, or anything else separating them—so (B) is wrong.

C   Incorrect: In order for this choice to be correct, "to humans... prey, rather" would have to be a grammatically acceptable sentence in an SAT Writing question, but that's not the case. The word "rather" is an adverb that needs to introduce an idea that is somehow opposed to an idea from the previous independent clause. But this choice would put "rather" in the first independent clause of the passage, leaving no previous independent clause to make this relationship possible. So (C) is wrong—contrast this with our discussion of (D) below.

D ✓ Correct: This choice would separate two groups of words that can each stand on their own as sentences with a semi-colon, which is appropriate on the SAT Reading section. It would also place "rather" in the second independent clause, which appropriately indicates an opposition or difference between this independent clause and the previous independent clause. So (D) is right.

- Vertical Scan Results: Each choice is the same 5 words with different apostrophe placement.
- Vertical Scan Notes: We need to decide whether "playas" and "rocks" should be singular, plural, and/or possessive.
- Key Features in Surrounding Text: The passage only mentions one "playa." Also, we know the "sediment" belongs to the "playa," because if it didn't, then the word "sediment" would have no grammatical connection to the sentence up to the point where that word first appears. So "playa" should be in the possessive singular form. The provided text mentions multiple "rocks," and we know that the phrase "mysterious migration" belongs to the "rocks," because the text tells us that the rocks "move periodically from place to place, seemingly of their own volition." So "rocks" should be in the possessive plural form.

Concepts in the question:

- Possessive and/or Plural: Choices include nouns ending in "-s," with or without an apostrophe before or after the "-s." The provided text will indicate which nouns should show ownership, and which shouldn't. (See page 79.)

ANSWER CHOICE ANALYSIS

A   Incorrect: This choice uses the plural non-possessive form "playas" and the singular possessive form "rock's," neither of which satisfies our reasoning above. So (A) is wrong.

B   Incorrect: This choice uses the singular possessive form "playa's," which satisfies our reasoning above, but also uses the plural non-possessive form "rocks," which doesn't. So (B) is wrong.

C ✓ Correct: This choice uses the possessive singular form "playa's" and the possessive plural form "rocks'," both of which satisfy our reasoning above. So (C) is right.

D   Incorrect: This choice uses the possessive plural form "playas'," which contradicts our analysis above. So (D) is wrong.

- Vertical Scan Results: Each choice is the same word followed by different punctuation.
- Vertical Scan Notes: We need to decide whether a dash, colon, comma, or no punctuation should appear after "*Gingerbread.*"
- Key Features in Surrounding Text: The word "*Gingerbread*" is the subject of the clause where it appears, and it's immediately followed by its verb, "offers." There's no reason for any punctuation to appear between a subject and a verb with no word or phrase between them.

Concepts in the question:

- Colons: A colon can only be placed after a group of words that could be a sentence on its own. Everything after the colon must be a demonstration or example of the idea before the colon. (See page 85.)
- Commas: Commas can be used between clauses, to form comma sandwiches, in a list of 3 or more items, and before reported speech. They can't appear for no reason. Review the training for the relevant details. (See page 86.)

ANSWER CHOICE ANALYSIS

A   Incorrect: As we saw in our discussion above, there's no reason for any punctuation to appear between the noun "*Gingerbread*" and its verb "offers," but this choice would put a dash between those two words. So (A) is wrong.

B   Incorrect: This choice has the same basic problem as (A), and is wrong for the same reason.

C ✓ Correct: As we saw in our discussion above, there's no reason for any punctuation to appear between the noun "*Gingerbread*" and its verb "offers." So (C) is correct.

D   Incorrect: This choice has the same basic problem as (A) and (B), and is wrong for the same reason.

The passage presents a bulleted list of notes, then tells us a goal related to presenting that information. The correct answer will be the only one that demonstrates the ideas in the provided goal. See "What about Notes Questions?" on p. 71.

Subjective Phrases to Ignore: "most"

A   Barely Relevant: This choice doesn't even mention "microprobes," so it can't "explain an advantage of microprobes," as the prompt requires. This choice might be tempting for some test-takers because it does describe something that is done "successfully," which might sound like an "advantage," as the prompt requires. But being "successful[]" at something isn't the same as having an "advantage," and even if it were, this choice still doesn't mention "microprobes," as the prompt would require. So (A) is wrong.

B ✓ **Correct:** This choice mentions "microprobes," and says that they "could explore areas of Mars that are inaccessible to… rovers." The idea of "microprobes" doing something that "rovers" can't do specifically demonstrates an "advantage" of "microprobes," as the prompt requires. This choice exactly demonstrates the idea from the prompt, so (B) is right.

C **Literary Interpretation:** This choice doesn't "explain" any "advantage of microprobes," as the prompt would require. Some test-takers will be tempted by this choice, because they might reason that if "microprobes" are being considered as an alternative to "rovers," it must be because microprobes have some "advantages" over rovers. But this choice doesn't actually say why "microprobes have been proposed as an alternative." We need an answer choice that actually "explain[s] an advantage" that "microprobes" have, and this choice doesn't do that. So (C) is wrong. See the explanation of (B) for more.

D **Literary Interpretation:** This choice does provide some information about microprobes, but it doesn't tell us any "advantage" of microprobes, as the prompt requires. An "advantage of microprobes" must be some way that microprobes are better than another option, but this choice just tells us something that "both microprobes and rovers" can do. This isn't an "advantage," so (D) is wrong.

Test 2, Module 1, Question 30 **TYPE: NOTES**

The passage presents a bulleted list of notes, then tells us a goal related to presenting that information. The correct answer will be the only one that demonstrates the ideas in the provided goal. See "What about Notes Questions?" on p. 71.

Subjective Phrases to Ignore: "most"

A **Literary Interpretation:** This choice will be tempting, because it does mention *Paradise* and its author. But it doesn't "introduce" the reader to *Paradise*, as the prompt requires, because it doesn't tells us any information about *Paradise* whatsoever. Instead, this choice just tells us about the author of the book. This choice doesn't satisfy the requirements of the prompt, so it's wrong. See the explanation of (C) for more.

B **Literary Interpretation:** This choice does tell us a little about *Paradise* (that it's "a historical novel about colonial East Africa"), but it doesn't "introduce" us to the book's author, as the prompt requires; that is, it doesn't provide us with any information about him. So (B) is wrong.

C ✓ **Correct:** This choice provides some basic information about both *Paradise* (that it's "a much-praised historical novel about colonial East Africa") and its author, Abdulrazak Gurnah (that he's the "winner of the 2021 Nobel Prize in Literature"). This exactly demonstrates the requirements from the prompt of "introduc[ing] *Paradise*" to people "unfamiliar with the novel and its author," so (C) is right.

D **Literary Interpretation:** This choice will be very tempting for some test-takers, because it provides us with some information about *Paradise* and Abdulrazak Gurnah. But this choice doesn't actually tell us that Abdulrazak Gurnah wrote *Paradise!* So someone "unfamiliar with the novel and its author," as described in the prompt, wouldn't even know that Gurnah wrote the novel, based on this choice. So (D) is wrong.

> **Note** Answering this question correctly depends on thinking about what it means to "introduce" something to someone. To "introduce" a topic to someone who is unfamiliar with it is more than just mentioning that topic—it requires sharing some basic information about that thing. Only choice (C) provides basic information about both *Paradise* and its author, as the prompt requires.

Test 2, Module 1, Question 31 **TYPE: NOTES**

The passage presents a bulleted list of notes, then tells us a goal related to presenting that information. The correct answer will be the only one that demonstrates the ideas in the provided goal. See "What about Notes Questions?" on p. 71.

Subjective Phrases to Ignore: "most"

A **Off by One or Two Words:** The prompt asks for the choice that "emphasize[s] the relative sizes" of the "capitals' populations." This choice mentions the capitals and their populations, but doesn't mention anything about how the sizes of those populations relate to one another, as the word "relative" in the prompt requires. So (A) is wrong.

B **Off by One or Two Words:** This choice is basically the same as (A), and is wrong for the same reason.

C ✓ **Correct:** This choice mentions the capitals and their populations, like (A) and (B)—but it also specifically mentions that one "is larger than" the other. This demonstrates the idea of "emphasiz[ing]" their "relative sizes," as the prompt requires, so (C) is correct.

D **Confused Relationships:** This choice will be tempting for some test-takers, because it does mention populations and does make a comparison—but it compares each capital's population to the entire population of *its own country*, rather than comparing the populations of the two capitals to each other, as the prompt requires. Beyond that, it doesn't actually mention either capital directly—for either reason, (D) is wrong.

The passage presents a bulleted list of notes, then tells us a goal related to presenting that information. The correct answer will be the only one that demonstrates the ideas in the provided goal. See "What about Notes Questions?" on p. 71.

Subjective Phrases to Ignore: "most"

A   **Barely Relevant:** This choice mentions where some of the "knowledge" in the "House of Wisdom" came from, but it doesn't tell us "how the House of Wisdom preserved the world's knowledge." So (A) is wrong.

B   **Barely Relevant:** This choice provides some information about the "House of Wisdom"—when and where it was founded, and some people it employed—but that information doesn't tell us how "the world's knowledge" was "preserved" there. So (B) is wrong.

C   **Barely Relevant:** This choice mentions some specific authors, and says their works were "preserved" at the "House of Wisdom"— but simply mentioning that they were "preserved" isn't the same as saying *how* they were preserved, as the prompt requires! This choice doesn't tell us "how" the "knowledge" was "preserved," so (C) is wrong.

D ✓   **Correct:** This choice mentions "writings from different countries," which demonstrates the idea of "the world's knowledge," and says the "House of Wisdom... collected" those writings and "created paper versions... to be studied and shared." Making copies of "writings" is a way of "preserv[ing]" them, which means this choice actually demonstrates "how the House of Wisdom preserved the world's knowledge," as the prompt requires. So (D) is right.

The passage presents a bulleted list of notes, then tells us a goal related to presenting that information. The correct answer will be the only one that demonstrates the ideas in the provided goal. See "What about Notes Questions?" on p. 71.

Subjective Phrases to Ignore: "most"

A   **Confused Relationships:** This choice will be very tempting for a lot of test-takers because it summarizes a lot of the information in the notes. But the prompt asks for "a generalization about the kind of study" conducted by the researchers, not a specific statement about this study. So (A) is wrong—see the discussion of (D) for more.

B   **Direct Contradiction:** This is basically the opposite of what the prompt asks for; we're supposed to pick the choice that makes a "generalization about the kind of study" conducted by the researchers, but this choice is a very specific conclusion about this one study described in the notes. Rather than being broad and general, as the prompt requires, this choice is very narrow and specific. So (B) is wrong.

C   **Direct Contradiction:** This choice is fairly similar to (B); instead of making the kind of "generalization" described in the prompt, this choice provides some specific information about the study discussed in the provided notes.

D ✓   **Correct:** The prompt asks for "a generalization about the kind of study" described in the notes. A "generalization" is a broad statement that lacks specific details, and that's exactly what this choice demonstrates. Choice (D) tells us that "researchers have used statistical methods" to answer "questions of authorship" related to "music"; this statement describes the "kind of study" in the notes without mentioning any specific people or songs. Note that "researchers" using "statistical methods" comments on the "kind of study" that was done, as the prompt requires. So (D) satisfies the prompt, which means (D) is correct.

TEST 2, MODULE 2

The prompt will be a short passage containing a blank. The correct answer will always be restated or demonstrated by key phrases in the provided text. See "What about Text Completion Questions?" on p. 66.

Subjective Phrases to Ignore: "most"

A   **Literary Interpretation:** This choice will be tempting for a lot of test-takers, because the word "characterization" sounds like it would fit into a discussion of "literature." But we can't pick an answer choice for this question type just because we think it "fits" the subject matter! Instead, the right answer has to restate or demonstrate relevant ideas from the provided text, and nothing in this text even mentions any characters from any books, or anything else relevant to the idea of "characterization." So (A) is wrong.

B   **Literary Interpretation:** Like (A), this choice will be tempting because discussions of "literature" often include "interpretation." But the provided text doesn't say anything about finding meaning in any book, or trying to understand a text, or anything that could be called "interpretation." So (B) is wrong.

C ✓ **Correct:** The provided text says *The Mule Bone* was written by both "Hurston" and "Hughes," then describes them "working together." This both demonstrates and restates the idea of "collaboration," so (C) is correct.

D **Barely Relevant:** This choice will be tempting for test-takers who come up with some kind or argument about "literature" in real life not being very "commercial[]," or something along those lines, and feel like this choice would create a reasonable statement. But we know that the correct answer to SAT Reading questions must restate or demonstrate relevant ideas from the provided text, and nothing in the provided text describes anything related to business, or selling things, or anything else that could be called "commercial[]." So (D) must be wrong.

The prompt will be a short passage containing a blank. The correct answer will always be restated or demonstrated by key phrases in the provided text. See "What about Text Completion Questions?" on p. 66.

Subjective Phrases to Ignore: "most"

A **Literary Interpretation:** The text describes a "process" that's "considered (blank)" because of "environmental impact and... loss of material quality." The phrase "loss of material quality" clearly signals that whatever the "process" is "considered" must be something negative. The following sentence is introduced with the word "but," and described how a "chemist... helped develop a cleaner process" that produces something "desirable." The word "but" tells us this sentence introduces an idea that is somehow opposed to the previous idea, so we know that being "cleaner" and "desirable" is different from what the "process" described in the first sentence is. This choice says "resilient," which doesn't restate the idea of a "loss" of "quality," and isn't opposed to the idea of being "cleaner" and "desirable." So (A) is wrong. This choice will be tempting for some test-takers, because this passage discusses "recycling," which seems kind of related to the idea of something being "resilient"—but we can't pick an answer just because it seems "kind of related" to what appears in the provided text. We have to be able to point to specific words and phrases that restate or demonstrate the correct answer, and we can't do that with "resilient." So (A) is wrong.

B ✓ **Correct:** As we saw in our discussion of (A), the word in the blank describes a process that results in "loss of... quality," and that is somehow opposed to the idea of a "cleaner" process that makes something "desirable." This directly demonstrates the idea that the process is "inadequate," or not good enough—that process is associated with a "loss" of "quality," and is less clean than another process with a "desirable" result. So (B) is right.

C **Confused Relationships:** This choice will be tempting to some test-takers because it seems kind of vaguely related to the provided text. "Dynamic" basically means "changing," often in a positive way, so an untrained test-taker could argue that the text describes a positive change, because it mentions one kind of recycling that's not so great, and another one that's better—but the blank describes the *first* process, specifically, which (as we saw in our discussion of (A) and (B)) has some negative qualities that aren't restated or demonstrated by this choice. Beyond that, that first process isn't changing, as this choice would require—instead, a different, distinct process ("chemical" versus "mechanical") has been developed that's better than the first process. So (C) is wrong.

D **Direct Contradiction:** This choice is basically the opposite of the right answer (B)—as we saw in our discussion of that choice, the process described by the blank results in "loss of... quality," and is opposed to another process that's "cleaner" and makes something "desirable." So we can't call that first process "satisfactory," which means (D) is wrong

The prompt will be a short passage containing a blank. The correct answer will always be restated or demonstrated by key phrases in the provided text. See "What about Text Completion Questions?" on p. 66.

Subjective Phrases to Ignore: "most"

A **Confused Relationships:** The text says that "interruptions... have challenged an economist's assertion." Then it says that "the delays are unlikely to (blank) her projection entirely," but that they "will almost certainly extend its time frame." The word "but" in the phrase "but they will almost certainly extend its time frame" tells us that the idea of "extend[ing]" the "time frame" is somehow opposed to the phrase "(blank) her projection." Also, the word "entirely" in the phrase "unlikely to (blank)... entirely" tells us that the action in the blank *will* happen to some extent, just not "entirely." This choice would cause that second sentence to say that "the delays are unlikely to <u>dispute</u> her projection." It's not really clear what that would mean in this context, because "delays" can't really "dispute" something, but either way, we know this choice must be wrong because the idea of "disput[ing] her projection entirely" isn't opposed to "almost certainly extend[ing] its time frame," as the word "but" would require. This choice will be tempting for untrained test-takers who notice that the provided text describes someone whose "assertion" was "challenged," and who think that means "dispute" must be a good answer to pick. But the blank doesn't restate what happened to the "assertion"—instead, it says what the "delays are unlikely" to do to "her projection," and this choice doesn't make sense in that blank for the reasons we just discussed. So (A) is wrong.

B   Confused Relationships: This choice will be tempting for untrained test-takers who read the text and think that the economist was wrong, and should "withdraw" her "assertion." But this choice would cause the sentence to say "the delays are unlikely to <u>withdraw</u> her projection," rather than saying anything about the *economist* "withdraw[ing]" anything. Like (A), this would cause the "delays" to take an action that doesn't really make sense in the provided text, and beyond that, nothing in the provided text restates or demonstrates the idea of anyone "withdraw[ing]" anything, or taking anything back, or anything else along those lines. So (B) is wrong too.

C   Confused Relationships: This choice will be tempting for some test-takers who reason that if the "economist's assertion" was "challenged," the delays won't "<u>underscore</u> her projection"—in other words, they won't emphasize that the projection was important or appropriate. But this logic would ignore the word "entirely," which tells us that what's in the underlined phrase *does* happen to some extent—just not "entirely"—which isn't appropriate here, because the context doesn't provide any reason that the "interruptions" would "underscore" the "assertion" to some limited extent, as "unlikely to... entirely" would require. This choice would also fail to create the opposition required by the word "but" in the last sentence, because not "underscor[ing] her projection entirely" isn't in any way opposed to the idea of "extending its time frame." For either reason, (C) is wrong.

D ✓   Correct: This choice would cause the sentence to say that the "delays are unlikely to <u>invalidate</u> her projection entirely," but that they will "almost certainly extend its time frame." The word "invalidate" is appropriate here, because "unlikely to <u>invalidate</u>... entirely" tells us that the "delays" *will* "<u>invalidate</u> her projection" to some extent—this is demonstrated in the provided text, because her assertion involved "growth in sales... in the coming months," and the text says "the delays... will almost certainly extend" the assertion's "time frame." We can see that "extending" the "time frame" demonstrates the idea of "invalidat[ing]" the "projection" somewhat, but not "entirely," as the provided text requires. This choice also creates the opposition required by the word "but" between the idea of "<u>invalidat[ing]</u> her projection entirely" and "almost certainly extend[ing] its time frame." "Extend[ing] its time frame" means that "her projection" is still partially true, just that it will happen over a different period of time from what she said in her original "assertion," and being partially true is opposed to the idea of being "invalidate[d] entirely," again, as the word "but" would require. So (D) is correct.

<u>**Test 2, Module 2, Question 4**</u>   **TYPE: TEXT COMPLETION**

The prompt will be a short passage containing a blank. The correct answer will always be restated or demonstrated by key phrases in the provided text. See "What about Text Completion Questions?" on p. 66.

Subjective Phrases to Ignore: "most"

A   Direct Contradiction: The text says that Tsang "produce[d] a piece that critics found truly (blank)," and that the critics "praised Tsang" for doing something "creatively." So the word in the blank should restate the idea of doing something "creatively" and being "praised" for it. This choice would says the "critics" found the piece to be "restrained," but nothing in the provided text talks about holding something back, or being understated or subdued, or anything else that we could call "restrained"—in fact, it describes doing something with a "massive curtain," and doing anything on a "massive" scale is kind of the opposite of being "restrained." So (A) is wrong.

B ✓   Correct: As we saw in our discussion of (A), the text says that critics "praised Tsang" for doing something "creatively." "Prais[ing] Tsang" for doing something "creatively" directly demonstrates the idea that the critics "found" the work to be "inventive," because both "creative[]" and "inventive" describe making something new. So (B) restates the idea that "critics" found Tsang's work to be "creative[]," which means (B) is correct.

C   Plausible but not in the Text: This choice could be tempting for untrained test-takers who reason that artists and other creative people sometimes do things that are "inexplicable"—that is, things that can't be explained or understood. This might be true in real life, depending on your perspective, but this idea doesn't appear in the provided text—nothing in that text says that critics thought anything about the work couldn't be explained or understood, or that it wasn't clear why Tsang had made some particular choice, or anything like that. So (C) is wrong.

D   Plausible but not in the Text: This choice means basically the same thing as (C), and is wrong for the same reasons.

> **Note**   Notice that the correct answer involved describing something as "inventive," which some test-takers will see as us making a subjective judgment about whether a piece of art, as described in the provided text, is "inventive" or not. But we, as readers, aren't the ones saying the art is "inventive!" In other words, we're not reading the description of the piece, which tells us about "transforming a museum rotunda into a dynamic exhibit by projecting filmed images of Glenn-Copeland onto a massive 84-foot curtain and filling the space with the sounds of his and other voices singing," and then saying "that sounds pretty inventive to me." Instead, the word "creatively" *tells us directly* that the thing that Tsang did was "creative[]," which is the same as being "inventive." So we're not concluding anything based

on our own opinions; we're just answering based on what the text plainly tells us is the case. Remember this on test day—our opinions aren't what matters; what matters is what appears in the text.

The prompt will be a short passage containing a blank. The correct answer will always be restated or demonstrated by key phrases in the provided text. See "What about Text Completion Questions?" on p. 66.

Subjective Phrases to Ignore: "most"

A   **Direct Contradiction:** This choice says "some scientists have suggested that mammals" during a certain era weren't "a very (blank) group," then uses the word "but" to introduce the idea that one person's research "suggests" that those mammals "weren't all ground-dwelling insectivores." The word "but" tells us that the idea that the mammals "weren't all ground-dwelling insectivores" is somehow opposed to the idea that they "were not a very (blank) group." This choice will be tempting for a lot of test-takers, because "insectivores" eat insects, which is an example of being "predatory." But this word would actually result in the opposite meaning required by the provided text! If the passage say that the "mammals" "were not a very predatory group," and then says "but" they "weren't all ground-dwelling insectivores," that would be two consecutive phrases saying that the mammals weren't predatory… but those phrases are connected by the word "but," so the second phrase must be somehow opposed to the first phrase! This choice doesn't meet that requirement, because it doesn't cause the text to demonstrate the kind of relationship required by the word "but." So (A) is wrong.

B   **Confused Relationships:** This choice has the same basic problem as the other wrong answers for this question—it would fail to create the relationship necessitated by the word "but," because it would result in two phrases describing the mammals (that they "were not a very obscure group" and that they "weren't all ground-dwelling insectivores") that aren't opposed to each other the way the word "but" (which connects these two ideas) would require. This choice could be tempting for test-takers who notice the phrase "living in the shadow of dinosaurs," and feel like this demonstrates the idea of being "obscure," and should be a valid answer. But in this case, "living in the shadow of dinosaurs" isn't presented as part of any claim that "scientists" or "paleontologist[s]" "suggest[]" about the mammals, so it's not relevant to this part of the text that discusses what "some scientists" think about the "mammals"; instead, it's just the speaker describing some mammals. This is a very nitpicky distinction, but it's exactly the kind of careful reading we have to do on the SAT—and again, this idea of being "obscure" still doesn't create the opposing ideas in this sentence required by the word "but." With all of this in mind, (B) is wrong.

C ✓ **Correct:** This choice would cause the text to say that "some scientists" think these "mammals" "were not a very diverse group," "but" that those mammals "weren't all ground-dwelling insectivores." So the first phrase would say that they weren't "diverse," and the following phrase would say they "weren't all" one particular thing—that is, "ground-dwelling insectivores." This appropriately demonstrates the relationship required by the word "but" that appears between those two phrases, because the idea of not being "diverse" *is* opposed to the idea of not "all" being one specific thing. This choice causes the text to demonstrate the kind of relationship required by the word "but," so it's correct.

D   **Barely Relevant:** As we saw in our discussions of the other answer choices, the word in the blank needs to result in the phrases before and after the word "but" opposing each other in some way. But the mammals not being very "localized" isn't opposed to the idea that they "weren't all ground-dwelling insectivores," so this choice wouldn't create the relationship required by the word "but." This choice will be tempting for test-takers who notice the idea of a fossil being found in "China," since that's a specific location—but "localized" doesn't just mean that we know something's location; it specifically means that something is *limited* to a certain location. This idea doesn't appear in the text, and this choice doesn't resolve the problem we just discussed related to the word "but." So (D) is wrong.

The prompt asks about the "function" or "structure" of a part of the text. The correct answer must plainly and accurately describe the relevant text, with no interpretation. See "What about "Function and Structure" Questions?" on p. 70.

Subjective Phrases to Ignore: "best"

A   **Literary Interpretation:** The text mentions "Night" twice, but there's nothing specific in the text that demonstrates the idea of either a "rural area" or a "city," as this choice would require. Untrained test-takers will be tempted by this choice, because they'll see that the poem does talk about "Night," and they might decide that "floating dew" is something that would appear in a "rural area," and then kind of conclude that this choice basically says what the text says. But "dew" can appear in a "rural area" or in a "city," so this phrase doesn't necessarily describe either location, and if this choice were correct, the provided text would need to include specific, inarguable words and phrases that describe both a "city" and a "rural area"—something like "tall buildings" and "wide open fields," for example. If that were the case, we could point to those phrases and use them to justify this choice. But it's not, and we can't—so (A) is wrong.

B   Literary Interpretation: This choice, like (A), will be tempting for test-takers who treat this question like a discussion in a literature class, and start picking words and phrases to interpret as describing "nightfall" and "sunrise." But, just as we saw in our discussion of (A) that the poem doesn't contain any specific reference to a "rural area" or to the "city," (B) doesn't contain any specific reference to "sunrise," or to the sun in any capacity, only "Night"—there's no mention of the sun coming up, which this choice would require in order to be correct. So (B) is wrong. (Actually, there's no mention of "nightfall" either—"nightfall" isn't a synonym for "night"; "nightfall" refers to the sun going down and the sky getting dark when night begins, and the passage doesn't include that idea. But even if we didn't realize that, we could still rule this choice out by noticing that "sunrise" isn't mentioned anywhere.)

C ✓ Correct: Unlike (A) and (B), this choice describes something that we can clearly support with specific words and phrases from the text—the poem says that "Night wears a garment," and mentions "her face," over which "she draws a veil." Then it describes "the black of her hair" and her "subtle hands." All of these images—wearing clothes, having a "face," "hair," and "hands"—are things that a person does, and the fact that the poem repeatedly compares "Night" to a "human being" demonstrates the idea of "an extended comparison," as this choice requires. So (C) is correct.

D   Literary Interpretation: This choice will be tempting for the same reasons that (A) and (B) will be tempting, but it's wrong for the same reasons that (A) and (B) are wrong. An untrained test-taker could pick out words and phrases and decide to interpret them as referring to "one season" and "the next," as this choice would require, but there isn't actually any specific reference whatsoever in this text to any season. So (D) must be wrong.

Note   This is a great example of an SAT Reading question where an untrained test-taker will have a hard time picking a choice because it seems like any answer could be correct. And if this were a literature class where we could base our answers on our own interpretation of the text, then we could make an argument in favor of any of these choices, based on that subjective interpretation. But the SAT Reading section has clear rules, and those rules require that we choose an answer based on the literal, specific words that appear on the page—and from that perspective, only (C) is correct. Keep this in mind on test day.

| Test 2, Module 2, Question 7 | TYPE: FUNCTION AND STRUCTURE |

The prompt asks about the "function" or "structure" of a part of the text. The correct answer must plainly and accurately describe the relevant text, with no interpretation. See "What about "Function and Structure" Questions?" on p. 70.

Subjective Phrases to Ignore: "best"

A ✓ Correct: This choice mentions "a claim about labor relations in a particular industry made earlier in the text." We can see that, before the underlined portion, the text says that "food processing companies… suppl[ied] United States armed forces" with food, and that "increased production quotas" gave employees "greater bargaining power." This is "a claim about labor relations"—that is, that the employees in this industry had "greater bargaining power" because of "increased… quotas"—and it's "in a particular industry"—that is, "food processing"—just as this choice requires. The underlined text describes "employees insist[ing] on more favorable benefits," and the employers agreeing, because they were "anxious to fulfill the contracts"—so we can say that the underlined text "elaborates" on the "claim" from earlier, because it provides more information about what the "employees" wanted, how "employers" responded, and why they responded that way—which demonstrates "elaborat[ion]," as this choice requires. So (A) is correct.

B   Plausible but not in the Text: Untrained test-takers will have a hard time choosing between (A) and (B), because these choices almost seem to say the same thing if we don't read them carefully enough. But if we do read closely, we can see that (B) mentions a "trend" in the "economy" at the time, while the "example" only talks about the "food processing" industry—nothing in the text indicates that what was going on in the "food processing" industry was also happening in the economy as a whole at the time, as the phrase "trend in the… economy" would require. It might be true in real life that what's discussed in the passage was part of a "trend" at that time, for all we know, but we have to answer SAT Reading questions based on the provided text, and not on what might be true in real life. The text doesn't tell us that this "example" in "food processing" indicates anything about the "economy" in general, so (B) is wrong.

C   Plausible but not in the Text: "Not[ing] a possible exception" would mean that the underlined text described something that was the opposite of a "narrative" from earlier in the text, but the underlined text isn't any kind of counter-example to anything else that appears in the text. The passage tells us that "Mexican American women made crucial contributions to the labor movement," and that "increased production quotas" gave workers "greater bargaining power," and that "employees" wanted "more favorable benefits", and that "employers… were anxious to fulfill the contracts," so they "complied." Nowhere in there is the idea of a "counter-example" to anything, so (C) is wrong. Some untrained test-takers who attempt to answer this question based on outside knowledge will be tempted by this choice, because they might see what's described in the passage as an "exception" to other situations where employees had less bargaining power; but whether this is true in real life has no bearing on the answer we pick, because we have to pick an answer based on what appears on the page. Since the passage doesn't tell us the underlined text is an "exception" to anything, we can't say that it's an "exception" to anything. Again, (C) is wrong.

D   **Wrong Part of the Passage:** This choice might be tempting, because the passage does describe some of the workers as "Mexican American women," which seems like a demonstration of "provid[ing] further details about the identities of the workers," as this choice would require. But the *underlined text* doesn't provide that detail, as the prompt requires; in fact, the underlined text doesn't provide any details whatsoever about "the identities of the workers," so (D) can't be correct. Remember on test day that we have to base our answer to a question of this type on *the underlined text*, and not just on any phrase in the sentence.

Test 2, Module 2, Question 8   TYPE: FUNCTION AND STRUCTURE

The prompt asks about the "function" or "structure" of a part of the text. The correct answer must plainly and accurately describe the relevant text, with no interpretation. See "What about "Function and Structure" Questions?" on p. 70.

Subjective Phrases to Ignore: "best"

A   **Wrong Part of the Passage:** This choice will be tempting, because "The St. John River… hyacinths" *is* "an extended description of a location," and the underlined portion *does* say that John "loved to wander down to the water's edge." But the *underlined sentence* isn't an "extended description" of anything, as this choice would require. Remember that we have to answer SAT Reading questions of this type based on the underlined sentence—so (A) is wrong.

B   **Wrong Part of the Passage:** Like (A), this choice will be tempting because it does mention an idea from the provided text. That text says "perhaps ten-year-old John was puzzling to the folk there in the Florida woods"—which *does* restate the idea in this choice that "some residents of John's town are confused by his behavior." But the prompt asks about the "underlined sentence," and that underlined sentence doesn't restate the idea from this choice—so like (A), (B) is wrong.

C   **Literary Interpretation:** The text does call John "imaginative" and "fond of day-dreams"—but this choice is still wrong for at least two reasons. For one, this choice requires the text to "compare[]" John's "imagination[]" to those of "other children," but the provided text doesn't make any such comparison—in fact, it doesn't mention any other children at all. Second, the description of John as being "imaginative" and "fond of day-dreams" doesn't even appear in the "underlined sentence," as the prompt would require. So (C) is wrong.

D ✓   **Correct:** The underlined sentence describes how John would "cast[]" "dry twigs" into the river and "watch them sail away" to "the wide world," and that he "wanted to follow them." The idea of wanting to "follow" something into "the wide world" specifically demonstrates the idea that John wanted "to experience a larger life outside the Florida woods," as this choice requires—so (D) is correct.

Test 2, Module 2, Question 9   TYPE: GENERAL PASSAGE

The prompt asks for information from the passage. The answer must be restated or demonstrated by specific phrases in the text. See "What about General Passage Questions?" on p. 69.

A   **Literary Interpretation:** The only mention of "Hallward" in the passage is that he "was speaking to" Dorian, but that "Dorian" wasn't "catching the meaning of his words." The text doesn't say anything about Dorian being interested in Hallward's (or anyone else's) opinion of the painting, or wanting to hear from Hallward about anything. So (A) is wrong. This choice could be tempting for a couple of reasons. For one, a test-taker who didn't read carefully enough might get confused about who painted the painting, and think that this choice says the *painter* wants to know the *subject's* opinion of the painting. This idea still doesn't appear in the text, so as trained test-takers, even if we made this mistake, we should still know that this choice was wrong—but a lot of untrained test-takers will decide that it's reasonable to assume that a painter wants to know what people think of his painting, and will want to pick (A) on that basis. This choice might also be tempting for an untrained test-taker who reads about how much Dorian likes the painting and just assumes that he must want to ask other people what they think of it too—but again, since that idea isn't restated or demonstrated in the provided text, we know it must be wrong.

B ✓   **Correct:** This choice is correct, because the idea that Dorian is "delighted by what he sees in the portrait" is demonstrated repeatedly in the passage—it says that "when he saw" the painting, "his cheeks flushed… with pleasure," and "a look of joy came into his eyes." Then it says Dorian "stood there motionless and in wonder," and that "the sense of his own beauty came on him like a revelation." All of these phrases demonstrate the idea that Dorian "is delighted by what he sees in the portrait," so (B) is correct.

C   **Literary Interpretation:** This choice will be tempting for untrained test-takers, because, as we saw in our discussion of (B), Dorian clearly likes the portrait. In a literature class discussion, some test-takers might use this observation as the basis for an argument that says Dorian "prefers portraits to other types of paintings," as this choice says. But on the SAT, we can only make that statement if the provided text specifically tells us or shows us that Dorian likes portraits, in general, more than other types of paintings. No other painting of any kind is even mentioned in the passage, so (C) can't possibly be correct on the SAT.

D   Barely Relevant: The text never mentions anything about Hallward's "talent as an artist," or what Dorian thinks of Hallward "as an artist." This choice will be tempting for some untrained test-takers precisely because the passage doesn't make a clear statement on this topic; those untrained test-takers will conclude that, because the passage doesn't tell us how Dorian feels about "Hallward's talent as an artist," we can say that Dorian is "uncertain" about it. But as trained test-takers, we know that we can only say Dorian is "uncertain" about this topic if the passage specifically says he's "uncertain" about it, not just because the passage leaves open the possibility that he feels that way. As we just discussed, the passage never says one way or another what Dorian thinks about "Hallward's talent as an artist," and it definitely never says Dorian is "uncertain" about it. So (D) is wrong.

<hr>

Test 2, Module 2, Question 10   **TYPE: DATA**

The passage includes a figure. The question asks for the choice that uses data from the figure to accomplish a certain goal. The right answer will describe the data accurately and plainly accomplish the goal. See "What about "Data" Questions?" on p. 69.

<hr>

Subjective Phrases to Ignore: "best"

A ✓ Correct: The prompt asks for the choice that "describes data" that "support Charles and Stephens's claim," so we need to check the provided text to find out what that claim is. When we do that, we see that "Charles and Stephens claim that the likelihood of voting is driven in part by potential voters' confidence in their assessments of candidates." Then the passage restates that claim as "the more informed voters are about politics, the more confident they are at evaluating… candidates" and "the more likely they are to vote." This choice says that "at each point on the political orientation scale, high-information voters were more likely than low-information voters to vote." The phrase "political orientation" appears in the title of the graph, and also below the graph; the graph shows 7 pairs of columns rated for different political orientations. We see the phrase "high information" and "low information" in the key at the bottom of the figure; it tells us that light gray columns correspond to "low information" voters and that dark gray columns correspond to "high information" voters. Finally, we see the label on the left side of the graph says "probability of voting," where taller columns correspond to a higher likelihood of voting. So this choice says that in every pair of columns, the darker bar in the pair (which represents high-information voters) is taller than the lighter bar in the pair (which represents low-information voters). This choice accurately describes the provided data, and it also demonstrates the claim from the passage that "the more informed voters are about politics… the more likely they are to vote," because—as we just discussed—the graph shows that every darker column is taller than its corresponding lighter column, which means, in every pair of columns, high-information voters were more likely to vote than low-information voters. This choice exactly describes the information in the graph and demonstrates the claim from the prompt, so we know (A) is correct.

B   Barely Relevant: This choice will be tempting for untrained test-takers, because it *does* accurately describe the data. When we read the graph, we can see that the only column whose value is lower than 50 on the "Probability of voting" axis is the light gray column above the "4" on the "Voters' political orientation" axis—and below that axis, we can see that "4" corresponds to the "independent" political orientation, and, as we saw in our discussion of (A), we know that the light gray column represents data for "low-information voters," as described in this choice. So the statement in (B) is accurate—but it doesn't "support Charles and Stephens's claim," as the prompt requires! As we saw in our discussion of (A), that claim is that "the more informed voters are about politics… the more likely they are to vote," but one data point telling us that low-information independents had a voting probability less than 50% doesn't demonstrate that idea. The "claim" we need to support is based on comparing "more informed voters" to less informed voters, but the statement in this choice only mentions data for "low-information voters"; we can't know how that data relates to the claim without comparing it to data for better informed voters, which this choice doesn't do. So we can't say the statement in this choice "support[s]" the "claim," even though it accurately describes the data, which means (B) is wrong.

C   Confused Relationships: This choice has the same problem as (B), and is wrong for the same reason—it describes the data accurately, as represented in the graph, but this information doesn't "support" the "claim" that "the more informed voters are about politics… the more likely they are to vote." This choice will be tempting because it *does* describe a situation where people are more likely to vote, but in this case it shows that "the closer low-information voters are to the ends of the political orientation scale, the more likely they are to vote." Being "closer… to the ends of the political orientation scale," as this choice requires, isn't the same as being "more informed," as the claim mentioned in the prompt requires. Just as we saw in our discussion of (B), this choice only mentions information related to low-information voters without comparing them to high-information voters, so it doesn't impact the claim mentioned in the prompt, which has to do with comparing the behavior of low-information voters to that of high-information voters. So (C) is wrong.

D   Barely Relevant: As we saw in our discussion of the other answer choices, the "claim" we need to "support" is that "the more informed voters are about politics… the more likely they are to vote." This choice doesn't actually even mention anyone's probability of voting, so we know it can't support that claim; it just talks about the political orientation of high-information and low-information voters. So (D) is wrong.

The passage includes a figure. The question asks for the choice that uses data from the figure to accomplish a certain goal. The right answer will describe the data accurately and plainly accomplish the goal. See "What about "Data" Questions?" on p. 69.

Subjective Phrases to Ignore: "best"

A   Barely Relevant: The prompt asks us for the choice that "describes data… that weaken the student's conclusion." In order to answer this question, we need to read the passage to find out what the "student's conclusion" was. The passage says "the student concluded that the reduction in the spider population count in the enclosure with lizards by day 30 was entirely attributable to the presence of the lizards." This choice describes the graph accurately; the key tells us that the light gray column represents the population in the enclosure without lizards, and the dark gray column represents the population in the enclosure with lizards. We can see that the columns that correspond to day 1 are the same height. But this statement doesn't "weaken the student's conclusion," as the prompt requires—that conclusion relates to the "reduction in the spider population in the enclosure with lizards by day 30," but this statement only talks about that population at the beginning of the experiment. Knowing that both enclosures started with the same spider population doesn't tell us anything about how or why those population reduced in either enclosure by day 30. So this statement isn't related to the student's claim, and can't weaken it—which means (A) is wrong.

B ✓ Correct: This choice describes the data accurately, because we can see that the light gray column, which the key tells us represents the spider population in the enclosure with "no lizards," did "substantially decline[] by day 30," from more than 80 spiders to between 40 and 50 spiders. This choice also "weaken[s] the student's conclusion," as the prompt requires, because the student "concluded" that the decreased spider population "in the enclosure with lizards by day 30" could be attributed completely to "the presence of the lizards." But this choice points out that the spider population in the enclosure without lizards *also* decreased, so there must have been some reason other than lizards that this population decreased as well—this demonstrates the opposite of the "student's conclusion," which means it weakens that conclusion, just as the prompt requires. So (B) is right.

C   Barely Relevant: This choice has the same problem as (A), and is wrong for the same reason—it makes an accurate statement about the data, but that statement doesn't "weaken the student's conclusion," as the prompt requires. That conclusion says that the decrease in spider population in the enclosure with lizards was entirely because of the lizards, but pointing out which period of time saw the biggest population drop in that enclosure doesn't weaken or strengthen that conclusion, or have any impact on it. So (C) is wrong.

D   Confused Relationships: This choice has the same problem as (B) and (C). Some test-takers will be tempted by this choice if they don't read carefully enough, and they think that the student's conclusion basically said that lizards decreased the spider population (instead of saying specifically that the population decreased *only* because of lizards), and if the test-taker thought the prompt asked for a statement that *supported* that conclusion, rather than weakened it. But if we read the passage and this choice carefully, as trained test-takers we can see that pointing out that the spider population in the lizard enclosure was lower than in the non-lizard enclosure has no bearing on whether the decrease in the lizard enclosure was *only* due to lizards—this statement could be true whether only lizards decreased that population, or something else did too. So (D) is wrong.

The passage presents some claim or hypothesis. The prompt typically asks us to choose the "finding" that, "if true," would support or weaken the argument. Supporting statements will demonstrate the idea in the claim, and weakening statements will demonstrate the opposite of the idea in the claim. See "What about "If True" Questions?" on p. 71.

Subjective Phrases to Ignore: "most strongly"

A ✓ Correct: The prompt asks us for the choice that "support[s] the team's conclusion." When we check the passage, we can see that "the team concluded that cattle were likely raised closer to human settlements, whereas sheep and goats were allowed to roam farther away." If we look earlier in the passage, we can see that this conclusion is based on the idea that "the team determined that wild plants made up the bulk of sheep's and goats' diets, while the cattle's diet consisted largely of millet, a crop cultivated by humans." This choice says that "the cattle's diet also consisted of wheat, which humans widely cultivated." The passage tells us that the team's conclusion is based partially on the fact that they found that "the cattle's diet consisted largely of millet, a crop cultivated by humans." This choice tells us about another part of their diet which was also "cultivated" by "humans." So this is additional evidence that is similar to the evidence already mentioned in the passage that supports the conclusion; this similar evidence of cattle eating food cultivated by humans must also support the conclusion, as the prompt requires. So (A) is right.

B   Direct Contradiction: This choice would actually *weaken* the argument. The passage says that "the cattle's diet consisted largely of millet," which was "cultivated by humans," whereas sheep and goats ate mostly "wild plants." Based on this, the team concluded that cattle were probably raised "closer to human settlements" and sheep and goats "were allowed to roam farther away." But this choice says that sheep and goats also ate "small portions of millet." So this would *weaken* the argument, because this evidence suggests that sheep and goats lived somewhat near people, like the cattle, since the diet of the sheep and goats included food that the passage tells us was "cultivated by humans," like the cattle's diet. This choice does the opposite of what the prompt asks, so (B) is wrong.

C   **Barely Relevant:** This choice has no bearing on the "conclusion" from the passage; nothing in the passage connects the idea of needing "larger amounts of food and a greater variety of nutrients" to the conclusion in the passage that "cattle were likely raised closer to human settlements, whereas sheep and goats were allowed to roam farther away." Untrained test-takers will be tempted by this choice, because it's kind of open-ended and creates an opportunity for someone to make some assumptions and/or incorporate some outside knowledge, and decide that this choice somehow *does* support the conclusion—but again, that would be based on information that's not actually present in this answer choice or the passage, which can't be the basis for picking a right answer on the SAT. So (C) is wrong.

D   **Direct Contradiction:** This choice is similar to (B), because it would actually *weaken* the argument. If the diets of "sheep, goats, and cattle"—that is, all animals mentioned in the prompt—changed "based on what the farmers in each Bronze Age settlement could grow," that would indicate that sheep and goats, as well as cattle, "were likely raised closer to human settlements," since their diets contained food that came from people. Notice how the idea of "farmer[s]" "grow[ing]" food in this choice restates the idea of "humans" "cultivat[ing]" crops from the passage. This choice is the opposite of what the prompt asks for, so it's wrong.

Test 2, Module 2, Question 13	TYPE: IF TRUE

The passage presents some claim or hypothesis. The prompt typically asks us to choose the "finding" that, "if true," would support or weaken the argument. Supporting statements will demonstrate the idea in the claim, and weakening statements will demonstrate the opposite of the idea in the claim. See "What about "If True" Questions?" on p. 71.

Subjective Phrases to Ignore: "most directly"

A   **Barely Relevant:** The prompt asks us which choice "support[s]" the "claim." When we check the provided text, we find that the "claim" is that "endothermy would have enabled mosasaurs to include relatively cold polar waters in their range." This choice makes a comparison between how easy it is to determine "Mosasaurs' likely body temperatures" as opposed to "the body temperatures of nonendothermic Late Cretaceous marine reptiles." But this comparison doesn't tell us anything about "endothermy... enabl[ing] mosasaurs" to swim in "cold polar waters." In other words, difficulty in determining the "likely body temperatures" of "nonendothermic... reptiles" doesn't change whether the claim in the passage is likely to be true or not, because there's no logical connection between these ideas. Similarly, the passage never mentions any other "marine reptiles," so we have no basis for thinking that a statement about those reptiles would impact the claim. This choice might be tempting for untrained test-takers who use it as a jumping-off point for making their own interpretations and assumptions that might support the claim—but we can't pick an answer on the SAT Reading section based on our own interpretations and assumptions. We have to pick an answer choice based on what appears on the page, and this choice doesn't impact the claim, so it's wrong.

B   **Direct Contradiction:** As discussed above, the claim is that "endothermy... enabled mosasaurs" to swim in "relatively cold polar waters." But this choice says that "fossils of both mosasaurs and nonendothermic marine reptiles have been found in roughly equal numbers... near the poles." If both mosasaurs *and* "nonendothermic" reptiles were found "near the poles," this would *weaken* the claim, since the claim says that "endothermy" made it possible for mosasaurs to swim near the poles, but this choice demonstrates that "reptiles" that *weren't* endothermic were also able to swim "in equal numbers" in the same region. So (B) does the opposite of what the prompt requires, which means it's wrong.

C ✓   **Correct:** This choice says that "mosasaur fossils have been found... near the poles... while relatively few fossils of nonendothermic marine reptiles have been found in those locations." The idea that fossils of mosasaurs, which the text tells us were "endothermic," have been found "near the poles" demonstrates the idea that "relatively cold polar waters" were "in their range," as the claim states. The fact that "relatively few fossils of nonendothermic marine reptiles have been found" near the poles supports the idea that it was "endothermy" that "enabled mosasaurs" to have polar waters in their range, because it shows that "reptiles" without "endothermy" were scarce in that same area. This choice demonstrates the idea that it was "endothermy" that made it possible for polar waters to be in mosasaurs' range, as the prompt requires—so (C) is right.

D   **Confused Relationships:** Untrained test-takers might like this choice at first glance, because they might guess that higher "seawater temperatures... throughout mosasaurs' range" would have some impact on the claim in the passage about "cold polar waters" being in mosasaurs' range, and they might reason that this choice goes along with the idea of mosasaurs swimming in the "polar waters." But the claim actually describes the "polar waters" as "relatively cold"—that is, cold compared to other water—so even if water temperatures were "higher throughout" their range, that doesn't impact the statement about polar waters being "relatively cold," just as the claim says. Also, the claim specifically mentions "endothermy" as the thing that made it possible for mosaurs to swim in "relatively cold polar water," but this choice doesn't say anything about being "endothermic" or not—so this choice can't impact the claim, which means it's wrong.

The passage presents some claim or hypothesis. The prompt typically asks us to choose the "finding" that, "if true," would support or weaken the argument. Supporting statements will demonstrate the idea in the claim, and weakening statements will demonstrate the opposite of the idea in the claim. See "What about "If True" Questions?" on p. 71.

Subjective Phrases to Ignore: "most directly"

A   **Barely Relevant:** This prompt asks us to pick the choice that "support[s] the researchers' hypothesis." When we look for the hypothesis in the passage, we can see that the "researchers hypothesized that a decline in the population of dusky sharks... led to a decline in the population of eastern oysters." (The passage also tells us that the sharks eat cownose rays, and the cownose rays eat the oysters.) This choice tells us that when there are fewer of "dusky sharks' prey other than cownose rays," there are fewer dusky sharks. This fails to support the hypothesis, as the prompt requires, for at least two reasons: first, it specifically tells us what happens when there are declines in "dusky sharks' prey" that are *not* "cownose rays"—remember that the passage told us cownose rays eat eastern oysters—so the "dusky sharks' prey" mentioned in this choice has no connection to the eastern oyster population that we're aware of. Second, even if the information in this choice *did* apply to "cownose rays" as well, this choice would make a connection between the idea of fewer cownose rays and fewer sharks, as opposed to *more* cownose rays and fewer sharks—we'll see in our discussion of (D) that this is basically the opposite of what we're looking for. But again, this choice doesn't even tell us about cownose ray populations anyway. This choice isn't relevant to the hypothesis, so it's wrong.

B   **Barely Relevant:** This choice tells us that there tend to be more eastern oysters where "both dusky sharks and cownose rays" are present, compared to areas with "only dusky sharks." In other words, the presence of the rays, in addition to the sharks, results in more eastern oysters. This doesn't actually impact the hypothesis, because that hypothesis ties "a decline in the population of dusky sharks" to a "decline in the population of eastern oysters"—in other words, fewer sharks leading to fewer oysters. This choice *does* mention the "abundance" of eastern oysters when the sharks are around, but only in relation to the presence or absence of rays—*not* to the size of the shark population increasing or decreasing! In the scenario described in this choice, we don't know anything about whether there were more or fewer sharks in areas with "greater" "eastern oyster abundance"; we just know that sharks were present. If we don't know the numbers of sharks present, we can't see how those numbers related to the numbers of eastern oysters present, which means this situation doesn't impact the hypothesis, and (B) is wrong.

C   **Direct Contradiction:** This choice would *weaken* the hypothesis, not support it, as the prompt requires. The hypothesis says that "a decline in... sharks... led to a decline in... oysters," but this choice says that rays were eating "substantially" more oysters *before* the shark population declined. We can't say that "a decline in... sharks... led to a decline in... oysters," as the hypothesis does, if the "decline in... oysters" happened *before* the "decline in... sharks," as this choice says. So (C) is wrong.

D ✓   **Correct:** This choice says that the "abundance" of rays has "increased" as the "abundance" of "sharks" has "decreased." This supports the hypothesis in the passage, as the prompt requires, because that hypothesis said that a decline in sharks led to a decline in oysters; the passage tells us that cownose rays eat oysters, so the idea from this choice that fewer sharks leads to more rays—that is, more of something that eats oysters—would lead us to expect that more oysters would get eaten by the rays, and there would be a "decline in the population of eastern oysters in the region," just as the hypothesis states. So (D) is right.

The passage presents some claim or hypothesis. The prompt typically asks us to choose the "finding" that, "if true," would support or weaken the argument. Supporting statements will demonstrate the idea in the claim, and weakening statements will demonstrate the opposite of the idea in the claim. See "What about "If True" Questions?" on p. 71.

Subjective Phrases to Ignore: "most directly"

A   **Barely Relevant:** The prompt asks for the choice that would "weaken the claim made by people who favor the traditional view of voter behavior." When we look at the passage, we can see that the claim is that "voting in an election does not change a voter's attitude toward the candidates in that election." This choice says that, "whether subjects" voted or not, their "attitudes toward the winning candidate two years after a given election were strongly predicted" by their "general political orientation." This choice doesn't weaken the claim, because it has no connection to the claim—it doesn't mention how the subjects felt about the candidates in the first place, so we have no idea whether their "attitudes toward the winning candidate two years after a given election" represented a change from how they felt before the election. Instead, it only tells us about their attitudes at one point in time, "two years after a given election." Again, this choice doesn't talk about attitudes changing or staying the same, so it doesn't impact the claim—which means it's wrong.

B   Barely Relevant: This choice will be tempting for some untrained test-takers, because the prompt asks for the choice that "weaken[s]" the claim, and this statement about non-voters having "significantly more positive attitudes" toward winning candidates two years after an election might seem like a kind of opposite statement, compared to the claim made in the passage. But the claim in the passage was about whether voting changes a "voter's" attitude—this statement only talks about changes in non-voters' attitudes, so it can't impact the claim in the passage, which means it must be wrong.

C ✓   Correct: The claim from the passage says that "voting in an election does not change a voter's attitude toward the candidates in that election," but this choice says "subjects who voted in a given election held significantly more polarized attitudes toward the winning candidate two years later" compared to subjects who didn't vote. The phrase "significantly more polarized" directly demonstrates a "change" in "voter's attitude" for the subjects who did vote, but not in the ones who didn't—so this choice demonstrates the opposite of the claim in the passage, which means it weakens that claim, as the prompt requires. So (C) is right.

D   Confused Relationships: This choice has the same basic problem as (A)—it only tells about certain subjects' attitudes at one point in time (in this case, "two years after a given election"). The claim we need to "weaken" has to do with "a voter's attitude" "chang[ing]." We can't know whether an attitude changed if we only know what that attitude was at one point in time—so this choice can't impact the claim, which means (D) is wrong.

Test 2, Module 2, Question 16   **TYPE: DATA**

The passage includes a figure. The question asks for the choice that uses data from the figure to accomplish a certain goal. The right answer will describe the data accurately and plainly accomplish the goal. See "What about "Data" Questions?" on p. 69.

Subjective Phrases to Ignore: "best"

A   Barely Relevant: The choice asks for data that "support" the "conclusion." When we check the text, we can see that "the team… concluded that spray coating holds promise for improving the power conversion efficiency of ETLs in perovskite solar cells." This choice accurately describes the data, because every column in the graph shows a "power conversion efficiency greater than 10%." But nothing in the provided text indicates that performing above 10% indicates anything in particular about a process "hold[ing] promise," as the "conclusion" requires—and beyond that, the comments in this choice relate to both "spin coating" and "spray coating," so they don't say anything specifically about "spray coating" at all, as the prompt requires. So (A) is wrong.

B ✓   Correct: This choice says that the "lowest performing ETL applied through spray coating" (represented by the lighter gray column on the left) "had a higher power conversion efficiency than the highest performing ETL applied through spin coating" (represented by the darker gray column on the right). We can see that this is an accurate statement, because the columns on the left are labeled "lowest performing," and the key tells us that the light gray column represents "spray coating"—and that column *is* taller than the darker gray ("spin coating") column on the right, which is labeled "highest performing." This demonstrates the idea that the "spray coating holds promise," as the prompt requires, because the passage tells us that "spin coating" is "often" used, and the data mentioned in this choice show that the worst-performing "spray coating" had higher efficiency than the best-performing "spin coating," which is already in use. If "spray coating" is more efficient than something that is already widely used, this demonstrates the idea that "spray coating holds promise for improving… efficiency." So (B) is right.

C   Direct Contradiction: This choice inaccurately describes the data, so we know it's wrong—we can see in the graph that "the highest performing… spray coating" had a power conversion efficiency between 16% and 18%, while "the highest performing… spin coating" had a power conversion efficiency between 12% and 14%.

D   Direct Contradiction: This choice has the same problem as (C), because it makes a false statement about the graph. The "lowest" performing "ETLs applied through spray coating" had an efficiency of almost 16%, while the "highest performing ETLs applied through spray coating" had an efficiency between 16% and 18%. This isn't a "substantial difference," as (D) says, so we know (D) is wrong.

Test 2, Module 2, Question 17   **TYPE: IF TRUE**

The passage presents some claim or hypothesis. The prompt typically asks us to choose the "finding" that, "if true," would support or weaken the argument. Supporting statements will demonstrate the idea in the claim, and weakening statements will demonstrate the opposite of the idea in the claim. See "What about "If True" Questions?" on p. 71.

Subjective Phrases to Ignore: "most directly"

A   Direct Contradiction: This choice asks us for the choice that "support[s] the journalist's claim." When we read the passage, we can see that a "journalist[]" is only mentioned once, when the passage says that "according to an arts journalist… Enwezor sought to remedy this deficiency, not by focusing solely on modern African artists, but by showing how their work fits into the larger context of global modern art and art history." We can go back in the passage to see what "this deficiency" refers to, and we find that it says that "in New York City in the 1980s… Enwezor encountered few works by African artists in exhibitions," so we know this is the "deficiency" that "Enwezor sought to remedy." The "journalist's claim" is that Enwezor wanted to "show[] how" work by

African artists "fits into the larger context of global modern art and art history." But this choice just describes an "art exhibition[]" devoted to a Black artist," which isn't the same as putting African art "into the larger context of global modern art and art history," as we'll see in our discussion of (B). In fact, this choice does the *opposite* of what the claim in the passage says, because that claim says Enwezor wanted to achieve his goals "not by focusing solely on modern African artists," but this choice describes "focusing solely" on one African artist. This choice will be tempting for untrained test-takers who read the passage and just come away with the broad impression that Enwezor wanted to showcase African art, and who overlook the phrase about African art "fit[ting] into the larger context of global modern art and art history." So (A) is wrong.

B ✓ Correct: This choice specifically demonstrates the idea from our discussion of (A) of fitting African art into "the larger context of global modern art and art history" when it describes "works by African artists… together with pieces by major figures from other countries," as the "claim" in the passage requires. So (B) is correct.

C Confused Relationships: This choice will be very tempting for untrained test-takers, because it *does* mention art, and history, and Europe, and Africa, which are all ideas that appear in the "journalist's claim." But that claim talks about "fit[ing]" African art "into the larger context of global modern art and art history," whereas this choice talks about how events in European and African history "influenced" *African* art specifically—this choice doesn't even mention any non-African art or artists, so it can't demonstrate the idea of African art in "the larger context of global modern art." So (C) is wrong.

D Direct Contradiction: This choice has the same basic problem as (A) and (C) in that it only talks about work by African artists, whereas the claim specifically requires the idea of African art alongside art from other parts of the "glob[e]," and "not… focusing solely on modern African artists." So (D) is wrong.

Test 2, Module 2, Question 18 — TYPE: SAT WRITING

- Vertical Scan Results: Each choice is a different form of a verb.
- Vertical Scan Notes: We need to decide whether the verb form should be a participle, infinitive, and/or past-tense.
- Key Features in Surrounding Text: The underlined phrase is the main verb of the sentence, and it's the action done by the plural noun "people," so it needs to be conjugated in the third-person plural.

Concepts in the question:

- Independent and Dependent Clauses: Choices would create and/or join clauses. An independent clause can stand on its own as a sentence, and a dependent clause can't. Remember rules for joining clauses related to periods, semi-colons, colons, commas, and conjunctions. (See page 82.)
- Verb Tense/Conjugation: Choices include different forms of the same verb. Look at the surrounding text to find the verb's subject. Also, look for other clues that could indicate the proper tense or form of the verb in the blank. (See page 77.)

ANSWER CHOICE ANALYSIS

A Incorrect: This choice is an infinitive—it isn't in the third-person plural, as our analysis above requires. This choice would leave the sentence without a main verb or an independent clause, which isn't acceptable on the SAT. So (A) is wrong.

B ✓ Correct: This is a third-person plural verb form, which is exactly what needs to go in the blank, as we saw in our analysis above. So (B) is correct. (Note that this is actually the only conjugated verb form in the answer choices, so as soon as we realized that we needed a conjugated verb form, we could eliminate every other choice.)

C Incorrect: This choice is a participle, and like (A), it would leave the sentence without a main verb or an independent clause, which isn't acceptable on the SAT. So (C) is wrong.

D Incorrect: This choice has the same basic problem as (A) and (C), and is wrong for the same reasons—so (D) is wrong.

Test 2, Module 2, Question 19 — TYPE: SAT WRITING

- Vertical Scan Results: Each choice has the same first word, while some also include a comma and/or the word "but."
- Vertical Scan Notes: We need to decide whether "but" and/or a comma should appear after "lifelike."
- Key Features in Surrounding Text: The phrase "while… lifelike" is a dependent clause that appears before the independent clause "others look… 1990s." When a dependent clause appears before an independent clause, there should be a comma between the two clauses.

Concepts in the question:

- Commas: Commas can be used between clauses, to form comma sandwiches, in a list of 3 or more items, and before reported speech. They can't appear for no reason. Review the training for the relevant details. (See page 86.)

- **Independent and Dependent Clauses:** Choices would create and/or join clauses. An independent clause can stand on its own as a sentence, and a dependent clause can't. Remember rules for joining clauses related to periods, semi-colons, colons, commas, and conjunctions. (See page 82.)

A   Incorrect: This choice is missing the comma that the SAT requires when a dependent clause appears before an independent clause. It also adds the word "but," which doesn't follow the rules we learned in the SAT Writing Toolbox: we know that we can join two independent clauses with a comma and then a conjunction like "but," but that doesn't apply here, for two reasons: this choice omits that comma, and "while many… lifelike" is a *dependent* clause, not an independent clause. So (A) is wrong.

B   Incorrect: This choice is missing the comma that the SAT requires between a dependent clause and an independent clause when the dependent clause appears first. So it's wrong.

C ✓   Correct: This choice adds a comma after the dependent clause "while… lifelike" and before the independent clause "others… 1990s," which follows the SAT's standards for a dependent clause appearing before an independent clause, as we learned in the SAT Writing Toolbox in this Black Book. So (C) is correct.

D   Incorrect: This choice includes the comma that should appear after "lifelike," for reasons discussed above, but it also adds the word "but," which creates the problem we saw in our discussion of (A). So (D) is wrong.

Test 2, Module 2, Question 20   **TYPE: SAT WRITING**

- **Vertical Scan Results:** Each choice is a different form of a verb.
- **Vertical Scan Notes:** We need to decide which form "to suggest" should be in.
- **Key Features in Surrounding Text:** We can see that the blank in the passage is a verb being done by "Zufall." Earlier in the passage, we see the phrase "Zufall advised." The blank appears in the phrase "in addition, Zufall (blank)." Since this phrase tells us about something "Zufall" did "in addition" to her last action, and there's no indication of a change in time frame, we should use the same form for this verb as the form of the verb "advised."

Concepts in the question:

- **Parallelism:** The surrounding text includes phrasing and/or grammatical structures that should be mirrored by what appears in the blank. (See page 93.)
- **Verb Tense/Conjugation:** Choices include different forms of the same verb. Look at the surrounding text to find the verb's subject. Also, look for other clues that could indicate the proper tense or form of the verb in the blank. (See page 77.)

A ✓   Correct: This choice matches the form of the verb "advised," so this choice is correct, for the reasons discussed above.

B   Incorrect: This choice is in the present tense, but "Zufall" did the action in the blank "in addition" to the action "advised," and nothing in the text indicates that the action of this verb should be in a different tense from the past-tense verb "advised." So (B) is wrong. See the analysis above for more.

C   Incorrect: Some untrained test-takers will have a hard time choosing between (A), (C), and (D), because they'll realize that a past-tense verb form is appropriate, and they won't be able to choose between these three. But as we saw above, the form of the verb should match the form "advised," which tells us that (A) is right, not (C). Beyond that, no other verb in the passage is in the same form as (C) or (D), which also tells us these choices aren't acceptable. So, again, (C) and (D) are wrong.

D   Incorrect: See the discussion of (C) above.

Test 2, Module 2, Question 21   **TYPE: SAT WRITING**

- **Vertical Scan Results:** Each choice is the same two words with different (or no) punctuation between them.
- **Vertical Scan Notes:** We need to decide whether a semi-colon, period, comma, or no punctuation should appear between "fungi" and "producing."
- **Key Features in Surrounding Text:** "Beatrix Potter… fungi" can stand on its own as a sentence, but "producing… London" is a participial phrase that *can't* stand on its own as a sentence. Instead, this phrase describes "Beatrix Potter," the first noun phrase in the independent clause from this sentence, which means this phrase should be separated from the rest of the sentence with a comma.

Concepts in the question:

- **Avoid Dangling Participles:** When a phrase starting with an -ing/-ed/-en word is joined to the main sentence by a comma, the first noun phrase in the independent clause of that sentence is described by the -ing/-ed/-en word. (See page 90.)

- Independent and Dependent Clauses: Choices would create and/or join clauses. An independent clause can stand on its own as a sentence, and a dependent clause can't. Remember rules for joining clauses related to periods, semi-colons, colons, commas, and conjunctions. (See page 82.)

A   Incorrect: This choice would use a semi-colon to separate one group of words that can stand on its own as a sentence from another group of words that can't stand on its own as a sentence, which isn't acceptable on the SAT. So (A) is wrong.

B   Incorrect: This choice has the same basic problem as (A), and it's wrong for the same reason.

C   Incorrect: This choice is missing the comma that we see in the right answer (D), which means it fails to satisfy the requirements for participial phrases we discussed above. So (C) is wrong.

D ✓   Correct: This choice would use a comma to separate a participial phrase from the sentence containing the idea it describes, which follows the SAT's standards, as discussed above. So (D) is correct.

Test 2, Module 2, Question 22   TYPE: SAT WRITING

- Vertical Scan Results: All choices are long phrases expressing similar ideas with different wording.
- Vertical Scan Notes: We have to pick the choice that would be correctly modified by the participial phrase that appears before the blank.
- Key Features in Surrounding Text: The phrase in the blank is the beginning of the independent clause in this sentence, so we know the first noun phrase in the blank must be the thing that is being modified by the comma-separated participial phrase "in assessing the films of Japanese director Akira Kurosawa." That means the first noun phrase in the right answer will be the thing that is "assessing the films."

Concepts in the question:

- Avoid Dangling Participles: When a phrase starting with an -ing/-ed/-en word is joined to the main sentence by a comma, the first noun phrase in the independent clause of that sentence is described by the -ing/-ed/-en word. (See page 90.)

A ✓   Correct: The first noun phrase in this choice is "many critics," and we can say that "many critics" were what was "assessing the films." So this choice is correct. See the discussion above for more.

B   Incorrect: The first noun phrase in this choice is "Kurosawa's use," and we can't say that "Kurosawa's use" was what was "assessing the films." So this choice is wrong.

C   Incorrect: The first phrase in this choice is "there are many critics," and we can't say that "there are many critics" was what was "assessing the films." So this choice is wrong.

D   Incorrect: The first noun phrase in this choice is "the focus," and we can't say that "the focus" was what was "assessing the films." So this choice is wrong.

Test 2, Module 2, Question 23   TYPE: SAT WRITING

- Vertical Scan Results: Each choice has the same words with different punctuation.
- Vertical Scan Notes: We have to decide whether a comma or semi-colon should appear after "basic," "2009," and/or "network."
- Key Features in Surrounding Text: The underlined phrase is part of a list of three things, which are "the world's first Indigenous-language instructional app, Chickasaw Basic, in 2009," and "an online television network, Chickasaw TV, in 2010," and "a Rosetta Stone language course in Chickasaw, in 2015." Because each item in the list is a phrase involving commas, we know that this is a complex list, as discussed in the SAT Writing Toolbox, and each item should be separated from the next item by a semi-colon. We can also see that each item on the list has a description of something, then a comma, then that thing's name, then a comma, then the year that thing was produced. So the right answer should include a comma after "Basic" (because that's the end of the name "Chickasaw Basic"), a semi-colon after "2009" (because each item in the list ends with a year, so this is the end of one item on the list), and a comma after "network" (because this is the description "an online television network," which is followed by its name "Chickasaw TV" immediately after the blank).

Concepts in the question:

- Commas: Commas can be used between clauses, to form comma sandwiches, in a list of 3 or more items, and before reported speech. They can't appear for no reason. Review the training for the relevant details. (See page 86.)

- **Complex List:** A complex list is a list of items where at least one item is a phrase that includes a comma. Items in a complex list must be separated from each other by a semi-colon. (See page 86.)
- **Parallelism:** The surrounding text includes phrasing and/or grammatical structures that should be mirrored by what appears in the blank. (See page 93.)
- **Semicolons:** Semicolons can be used to separate two sets of words that could each stand on their own as complete sentences, or to separate items in a complex list. (See page 86.)

ANSWER CHOICE ANALYSIS

A   Incorrect: This choice doesn't satisfy the analysis above, so it's wrong—see the discussion above for more.

B   Incorrect: This choice doesn't satisfy the analysis above, so it's wrong—see the discussion above for more.

C ✓ Correct: This choice satisfies the analysis above, so it's right—see the discussion above for more.

D   Incorrect: This choice doesn't satisfy the analysis above, so it's wrong—see the discussion above for more.

Test 2, Module 2, Question 24 — TYPE: SAT WRITING

- **Vertical Scan Results:** Each choice is the same two words with different punctuation between them.
- **Vertical Scan Notes:** We have to decide whether a colon, dash, comma, or no punctuation should appear between "Springs" and "to."
- **Key Features in Surrounding Text:** The dash earlier in the sentence sets off the beginning of the phrase "in this case, the porous rocks of the hills around Hot Springs," which provides additional information relevant to the sentence, but which can be removed and still leave behind an acceptable sentence..

Concepts in the question:

- **Colons:** A colon can only be placed after a group of words that could be a sentence on its own. Everything after the colon must be a demonstration or example of the idea before the colon. (See page 85.)
- **Commas:** Commas can be used between clauses, to form comma sandwiches, in a list of 3 or more items, and before reported speech. They can't appear for no reason. Review the training for the relevant details. (See page 86.)
- **Independent and Dependent Clauses:** Choices would create and/or join clauses. An independent clause can stand on its own as a sentence, and a dependent clause can't. Remember rules for joining clauses related to periods, semi-colons, colons, commas, and conjunctions. (See page 82.)

ANSWER CHOICE ANALYSIS

A   Incorrect: This choice would make the relationship between the infinitive clause "to collect in a subterranean basin" and the rest of the sentence unclear—contrast this with choice (C), which would make it clear in the sentence that "rainwater percolates downward… to collect…. So (A) is wrong. See the discussion of (C) for more.

B   Incorrect: This choice would cause the colon to be followed by the phrase "to collect in a subterranean basin," which wouldn't be an example or explanation of whatever was stated in the sentence leading up to the colon—so this choice wouldn't follow the SAT's standards for colon usage, which makes (B) wrong.

C ✓ Correct: This choice would create a "dash sandwich" ("in this case.. Hot Springs"): a phrase, set off from a sentence by dashes at its beginning and end, that provides additional information about something in the sentence. This phrase can be removed, leaving a sentence that's grammatically acceptable on the SAT. So (C) is correct.

D   Incorrect: This choice would be acceptable if the dash after "earth" were a comma, because then this would create a comma sandwich, which functions the same as the dash sandwich described in our analysis of (C)—but this kind of "sandwich" needs the same punctuation on either end, so it can't start with a dash and end with a comma. So (D) is wrong.

Test 2, Module 2, Question 25 — TYPE: SAT WRITING

- **Vertical Scan Results:** Each choice includes the same word followed by different punctuation; two choices include a second word.
- **Vertical Scan Notes:** We have to decide whether a semi-colon, comma, no punctuation, and/or the word "while" should appear after "varied."
- **Key Features in Surrounding Text:** "the number… varied" can stand on its own as a sentence, and "some shoppers… only six" is an elaboration on what appears in the sentence up to that point. Also, "some shoppers… only six" can stand on its own as a sentence.

Concepts in the question:

- Colons: A colon can only be placed after a group of words that could be a sentence on its own. Everything after the colon must be a demonstration or example of the idea before the colon. (See page 85.)
- Independent and Dependent Clauses: Choices would create and/or join clauses. An independent clause can stand on its own as a sentence, and a dependent clause can't. Remember rules for joining clauses related to periods, semi-colons, colons, commas, and conjunctions. (See page 82.)

ANSWER CHOICE ANALYSIS

A ✓ Correct: This choice appropriately uses a colon to separate a group of words that can stand on its own as a complete sentence from an elaboration on what is expressed in that group of words—so (A) is correct.

B Incorrect: This choice would separate two groups of words that can stand on their own as complete sentences with a comma, which isn't acceptable on the SAT. So (B) is wrong.

C Incorrect: This choice would cause the word "while" to appear in a sentence that doesn't demonstrate the necessary meaning of that word—in order for "while" to be appropriate on the SAT, either the sentence would have to describe something happening during the time that something else was happening, or an idea expressed in the dependent clause that included the word "while" would have to be somehow opposed to an idea that appears in the independent clause it was connected to—but neither of these is the case here. So (C) is wrong.

D Incorrect: This choice has the same problem with the word "while" that we saw in (C), and is wrong for that reason.

Test 2, Module 2, Question 26 — TYPE: SAT WRITING

- Vertical Scan Results: Each choice has the same words with different punctuation.
- Vertical Scan Notes: We have to decide whether a comma or semi-colon should appear after "Lagos," and whether a comma, colon, or no punctuation should appear after "*Marriage.*"
- Key Features in Surrounding Text: This sentence includes a list of three items, each of which is its own phrase that contains commas—also known as a "complex list." Those three items are "*The Joys of Motherhood,* a novel about the changing roles of women in 1950s Lagos," "*A Kind of Marriage,* a television play about the private struggles of a newlywed couple in Nigeria," and "*Head Above Water,* her autobiography." Each item is the italicized name of a work, followed by a comma, followed by a description of that work, and each item should be separated from the previous item by a semi-colon. So "Lagos" should be followed by a semi-colon, since that word is the last word in the first item on the list, and "*Marriage*" should be followed by a comma, because that's the last word in the title of the work, and every item in the list has a comma separating the title of the work from the description that immediately follows it.

Concepts in the question:

- Colons: A colon can only be placed after a group of words that could be a sentence on its own. Everything after the colon must be a demonstration or example of the idea before the colon. (See page 85.)
- Commas: Commas can be used between clauses, to form comma sandwiches, in a list of 3 or more items, and before reported speech. They can't appear for no reason. Review the training for the relevant details. (See page 86.)
- Complex List: A complex list is a list of items where at least one item is a phrase that includes a comma. Items in a complex list must be separated from each other by a semi-colon. (See page 86.)
- Parallelism: The surrounding text includes phrasing and/or grammatical structures that should be mirrored by what appears in the blank. (See page 93.)
- Semicolons: Semicolons can be used to separate two sets of words that could each stand on their own as complete sentences, or to separate items in a complex list. (See page 86.)

ANSWER CHOICE ANALYSIS

A Incorrect: This choice doesn't satisfy the analysis above, so it's wrong—see the discussion above for more.

B ✓ Correct: This choice satisfies the analysis above, so it's right—see the discussion above for more.

C Incorrect: This choice doesn't satisfy the analysis above, so it's wrong—see the discussion above for more.

D Incorrect: This choice doesn't satisfy the analysis above, so it's wrong—see the discussion above for more.

Test 2, Module 2, Question 27 — TYPE: LOGICAL TRANSITION

The choices are different transition phrases like "however," "instead of," or "for example." The right answer must reflect the relationship between the concepts before and after the blank. See "What about Logical Transition Questions?" on p. 71.

Subjective Phrases to Ignore: "most"

A   ✓   Correct: The text mentions the "divergent experiences" of a "couple," which necessarily describes a situation where one person has one experience, while the other person has a different experience. Then the text tells us that "Ifemelu moves to the United States" and "(blank) Obinze travels to London"—note that "moves" and "travels" are both in the present tense. The word "meanwhile" correctly demonstrates that these two people are having two separate, "divergent experiences" at the same time, just as the text describes. So (A) is right.

B   Literary Interpretation: This choice would require the action described after the blank to be something that happened in spite of what is described in the previous sentence—but that idea doesn't appear in the text. This choice might be tempting for untrained test-takers who imagine that Ifemelu doesn't want Obinze to travel to a different country, but Obinze does it "nevertheless." But again, this idea doesn't actually appear in the text, so we can't use this idea as the basis for picking an answer choice. That means (B) is wrong.

C   Confused Relationships: This choice will be tempting for some test-takers, because the text tells us about two things happening: where Ifemelu went, and then where Obinze went. But the text simply describing two things happening isn't a justification for using the word "secondly" to introduce the second thing; instead, the word in this choice would need to appear after a phrase that described something happening "firstly," and would need to be followed by some second point or idea. That doesn't appear in the text, so (C) is wrong.

D   Confused Relationships: This choice would be appropriate if the text after the blank somehow reinforced or offered additional support for the idea in the previous sentence, but that's not the case here. Instead, the text before the blank tells us what one character does, while the text after the blank tells what another character does. This doesn't demonstrate the relationship necessitated by the phrase "in fact," so (D) is wrong.

Test 2, Module 2, Question 28   TYPE: LOGICAL TRANSITION

The choices are different transition phrases like "however," "instead of," or "for example." The right answer must reflect the relationship between the concepts before and after the blank. See "What about Logical Transition Questions?" on p. 71.

Subjective Phrases to Ignore: "most"

A   Direct Contradiction: This is basically the opposite of what should appear in the blank. As we see in our discussion of (B), the first sentence mentions "a number of surprising adaptations," and the following sentence tells us about one such adaptation. That adaptation doesn't "contrast" with the idea in the previous sentence; instead, it's an *example* of that idea. So (A) is wrong.

B   ✓   Correct: The first sentence tells us about "a number of surprising adaptations," and the sentence containing the blank provides an example of one such adaptation. This exactly demonstrates the meaning of the phrase "for example," so (B) is correct.

C   Barely Relevant: This choice would require the information in the second sentence to describe some separate thing happening at the same time as the information in the first sentence, but that's not the case—the first sentence just tells us something that "organisms" have done, and the second sentence tells us what one specific organism can do. So (C) is wrong.

D   Confused Relationships: This choice will be tempting because this word indicates some kind of logical connection between the idea of the "adaptations" mentioned in the first sentence, and the information about tadpole shrimp in the second sentence. But the information about the shrimp in the second sentence isn't the logical result or the effect of the information in the first sentence. Instead, as discussed above, the second sentence provides an example of the idea mentioned in the first sentence. So (D) is wrong.

Test 2, Module 2, Question 29   TYPE: LOGICAL TRANSITION

The choices are different transition phrases like "however," "instead of," or "for example." The right answer must reflect the relationship between the concepts before and after the blank. See "What about Logical Transition Questions?" on p. 71.

Subjective Phrases to Ignore: "most"

A   Confused Relationships: This choice would require the text after the blank to tell us something that happens in place of whatever is described in the text before the blank, but that's not the case—instead, as we see in our discussion of (D), the text after the blank provides additional information that's related to an idea from earlier in the passage.

B   Confused Relationships: This choice will be tempting for some untrained test-takers, because the information before the blank and the information after the blank are closely related, and someone who doesn't carefully read until the end of the passage might think that the text after the blank is an example of what comes before the blank. But it isn't—the information after the blank is additional information related to what comes before the blank. So (B) is wrong.

C   Confused Relationships: This would require the text after the blank to provide a clearer, more direct, or more concrete statement related to what came before the blank—but that's not the case here. So (C) is wrong.

D ✓   Correct: The first two sentences tell us when "the Twentieth Amendment" requires that the "presidential inaugurations" happen, and the third sentence provides more, related information about when that "amendment requires... senators and representatives to be sworn in." The text after the blank provides additional information related to the previous topic, which demonstrates the meaning of the phrase "in addition." So (D) is right.

The choices are different transition phrases like "however," "instead of," or "for example." The right answer must reflect the relationship between the concepts before and after the blank. See "What about Logical Transition Questions?" on p. 71.

Subjective Phrases to Ignore: "most"

A   Confused Relationships: This choice will be tempting for test-takers who focus on the relationship between the first sentence and the third sentence, ignoring the second sentence, because the first sentence makes a broad statement about something an author does, while the third sentence tells us about a "specific[]" instance of the author doing that thing. But this word appears between the second and third sentences, and describes the relationship between *those* two sentences—rather than describing the relationship between the first sentence and the third sentence. So (A) is wrong—see the discussion of (D) for more.

B   Barely Relevant: This choice would be appropriate if the text after the blank told us about something that was the logical result of the information before the blank, but that isn't the case. So (B) is wrong—see our explanation of (D) for more.

C   Literary Interpretation: This choice would make sense if the information after the blank was something that happened in spite of the information before the blank, but this isn't the case. This choice will be tempting for untrained test-takers who attempt to read into the provided text and decide that one character is doing something the other character doesn't want, but that character does it anyway, or something—but these ideas don't appear in the text, so we can't use them as the basis for picking any particular answer choice. With this in mind, we can see that (C) is wrong.

D ✓   Correct: The first sentence tells us that an author "interweaves... characters'... stories with... historical narratives." The second sentence tells us about the author fitting one character's story into a "historical narrative[]," then the third sentence starts with the blank, and tells us about the author fitting *another* character's story into a "historical narrative[]." So the third sentence provides additional information that is "similar[]" to the information in the second sentence, which exactly demonstrates the meaning of the word "similarly." So (D) is correct.

The passage presents a bulleted list of notes, then tells us a goal related to presenting that information. The correct answer will be the only one that demonstrates the ideas in the provided goal. See "What about Notes Questions?" on p. 71.

Subjective Phrases to Ignore: "most"

A ✓   Correct: The prompt wants us to pick the choice that "emphasize[s] the distance covered by the Philadelphia and Lancaster Turnpike." This choice specifically tells us that "the Philadelphia and Lancaster Turnpike" is 62 miles long, just as the prompt requires. So (A) is correct.

B   Off by One or Two Words: As we saw in our discussion of (A), the prompt wants us to pick a choice that "emphasize[s] the distance covered by the Philadelphia and Lancaster Turnpike." This choice mentions that turnpike, but never mentions the distance it covers. So (B) fails to satisfy the prompt, which means it's wrong.

C   Off by One or Two Words: This choice has the same problem as (B), and is wrong for the same reasons. See our discussion of (A) for more.

D   Off by One or Two Words: This choice has the same problem as (B) and (C), and is wrong for the same reasons. See our discussion of (A) for more.

The passage presents a bulleted list of notes, then tells us a goal related to presenting that information. The correct answer will be the only one that demonstrates the ideas in the provided goal. See "What about Notes Questions?" on p. 71.

Subjective Phrases to Ignore: "most"

A   Barely Relevant: The prompt wants us to pick the choice that "emphasize[s] the aim of the research study." This choice tells us about how some "data" was "collected" as part of the study, but it doesn't say anything about what that study was supposed to accomplish, which the phrase "the aim of the research study" would require. So (A) is wrong.

B   Off by One or Two Words: This choice will be tempting for some test-takers, because they will reason that what "Terada wondered" is closely related to what the "study" was intended to do. But a person wondering something isn't the same as "the aim" of a "study"; having an "aim" requires that someone has a goal in mind, which isn't described in this choice. So (B) is wrong.

C ✓ **Correct:** This choice tells us what Terada "set out to determine," which literally demonstrates an "aim," and the phrase "to determine whether some of the Moon's oxygen was coming from Earth" specifically tells us what that aim was, as the prompt requires. So (C) is right.

D **Confused Relationships:** This choice will be tempting, because it tells us what the study "determined." But the "aim" of something is what you *intended* to do in the *beginning*, whereas what you "determine[]" is what you figure out by the *end* of the study. This is a nitpicky distinction that probably wouldn't be necessary in most classroom situations, but it's exactly the kind of distinction we need to make on test day. So (D) is wrong.

Test 2, Module 2, Question 33   TYPE: NOTES

The passage presents a bulleted list of notes, then tells us a goal related to presenting that information. The correct answer will be the only one that demonstrates the ideas in the provided goal. See "What about Notes Questions?" on p. 71.

Subjective Phrases to Ignore: "most"

A **Literary Interpretation:** The prompt asks for the choice that "present[s] the study and its methodology." This choice will be tempting for some test-takers because it provides information related to a study—but these are the *findings* of a study, not its methodology. The methodology of a study would be the way the researchers went about *getting* these findings, but that's not mentioned in this choice, so (A) is wrong.

B ✓ **Correct:** This choice "presents the study" when it says that Yuan was "seeking to understand how ducklings swimming in a line behind their mother save energy," and it tells us the methodology of the study when it describes what Yuan did to pursue this goal: "us[ing] computer simulations to study the effect of the mother duck's wake." This demonstrates exactly what the prompt asked for, so (B) is correct.

C **Literary Interpretation:** This choice will be tempting for some test-takers, because it seems to describe an aspect of the "methodology" of the study, as the prompt requires—but this information is too vague to be the "methodology," because it doesn't provide any details about *how* Yuan "studied the physics," which the word "methodology" requires! Also, it doesn't "present the study," as the prompt requires; notice that the correct choice, (B), tells us about the study when it says what Yuan was "seeking to understand"; that idea is missing from this choice. So (C) is wrong.

D **Literary Interpretation:** This choice is similar to (A), and is wrong for the same reason—it tells us about some findings, but doesn't describe the "study," or the "method[s]" used in the study.

TEST 3, MODULE 1

Test 3, Module 1, Question 1   TYPE: TEXT COMPLETION

The prompt will be a short passage containing a blank. The correct answer will always be restated or demonstrated by key phrases in the provided text. See "What about Text Completion Questions?" on p. 66.

Subjective Phrases to Ignore: "most"

A ✓ **Correct:** The text says tells us about a "writing system," and then says that by a certain point, "over 90 percent of the Cherokee people could read and write it." This literally demonstrates "<u>widespread</u> use," so we know that (A) is correct.

B **Plausible but not in the Text:** This choice will attract a lot of untrained test-takers who think the word "careful" results in a sentence that sounds pretty good, and who assume coming up with this system (and/or learning and using it) probably requires people to be "careful"—but that idea doesn't appear in the text, so (B) must be wrong.

C **Barely Relevant:** This choice would require the provided text to restate or demonstrate the idea that someone did something they didn't mean to do—but that idea doesn't appear anywhere, so (C) must be wrong.

D **Direct Contradiction:** As we see in our discussion of (A), this choice is actually the *opposite* of what's demonstrated in the text: the provided text tells us that "over 90 percent of the Cherokee people" used the "script," which is basically the opposite of "<u>infrequent</u> use," as this choice would require. So (D) is wrong.

Test 3, Module 1, Question 2   TYPE: TEXT COMPLETION

The prompt will be a short passage containing a blank. The correct answer will always be restated or demonstrated by key phrases in the provided text. See "What about Text Completion Questions?" on p. 66.

Subjective Phrases to Ignore: "most"

A ✓ **Correct:** The text refers back to the phrase "other researchers readily (blank) her work as ground-breaking" using the phrase "this recognition." This choice would cause the text to say "other researchers readily <u>acknowledged</u> her work as ground-breaking."

"Acknowledg[ing]" something literally demonstrates the idea of "recognition." This choice demonstrates an idea from the relevant text, so (A) must be correct.

B   **Confused Relationships:** This choice will be tempting for test-takers who aren't sure of the meaning of "ensured," and think that it would cause the text to mean something like "other researchers <u>confirmed</u> that her work was ground-breaking." But that's not what this choice would say; in fact, it's not really clear what it would mean to "ensure" something "as" something else. In any case, to "ensure" something would basically mean to make sure it happens, and the idea of making sure that something happens isn't restated or demonstrated in the text—so (B) can't be right.

C   **Direct Contradiction:** This is basically the opposite of the right answer. It might be tempting for untrained test-takers who misread some part of the text and thought there was a negating word like "not" in there somewhere, or who assume that "other researchers" would feel competitive and "den[y]" any value in Nuttall's work. But this idea doesn't appear in the text, so (C) is wrong.

D   **Confused Relationships:** In order for this choice to be right, the text would have to include the idea of someone thinking that something demonstrated less of some characteristic than was really accurate, but the text never says anything was seen one way, and then found to be much better than that, or anything else along those lines. It's also not really clear what it would mean to "underestimate[]" something as "ground-breaking"; this would imply that the "work" was really even better than "ground-breaking," which is already a strongly positive word. Again, it's not clear what this would mean—but whatever it would mean isn't demonstrated in the text, so we know (D) is wrong.

Test 3, Module 1, Question 3   TYPE: TEXT COMPLETION

The prompt will be a short passage containing a blank. The correct answer will always be restated or demonstrated by key phrases in the provided text. See "What about Text Completion Questions?" on p. 66.

Subjective Phrases to Ignore: "most"

A ✓   **Correct:** The text mentions "laws," and then says that "officials (blank) those laws by devising policies and administering services in accordance with them." This choice would cause the sentence to say that "officials <u>implement</u> those laws by devising policies and administering services in accordance with them." To "implement" something means to put it into practice, and "devising policies and administering services in accordance with" laws is the same as putting "those laws" into practice—so the phrase after the word "by" demonstrates the idea of "implement[ing]" "laws," as (A) would require, which means (A) is correct.

B   **Literary Interpretation:** This choice might tempt untrained test-takers who read this passage about "officials," and make some connection between the idea of people in power and "presum[ing]" to do things. But this choice would require the text to say something about someone supposing that something is true, or making an assumption, or daring to do something that might be against social rules or expectations. But none of that appears in the text, so (B) can't be right.

C   **Confused Relationships:** The provided text describes people "generat[ing] laws," and some test-takers might think that this restates the phrase "improvise those laws," which this choice would create. But to "improvise" something isn't the same as just creating or making something—the word "improvise" specifically contains the idea of doing something without any preparation or notice ahead of time; this idea isn't present in the text. Also, the word "by" tells us that the phrase after "by" must be an explanation of how "officials (blank) those laws," and this choice fails to put a word in the blank that makes this the case (unlike (A)). For either of these reasons, (C) can't be right.

D   **Confused Relationships:** This choice will be tempting for test-takers who assume that laws created by one group are probably similar to other laws created by other groups, and who feel like "mimic" reflects that idea. But the passage doesn't contain that idea, and this choice wouldn't make the text say that, anyway—this choice would say that the "chief and... officials <u>mimic</u>" the same "laws" mentioned earlier in the text that their own tribe made. This doesn't really make any sense and, again, isn't present in the text—the text doesn't talk about anyone copying or duplicating anything, or doing anything we could called "mimic[king]." So (D) is wrong.

Test 3, Module 1, Question 4   TYPE: TEXT COMPLETION

The prompt will be a short passage containing a blank. The correct answer will always be restated or demonstrated by key phrases in the provided text. See "What about Text Completion Questions?" on p. 66.

Subjective Phrases to Ignore: "most"

A   **Direct Contradiction:** This choice will be tempting for test-takers who read the text, get the general idea that the passage is describing something that's complex, and feel like this choice reflects that idea—but this word specifically describes something that *can't* be read or made sense of; this idea directly contradicts the text after the colon, which provides a bunch of details about the "Three Sisters" (if the system were "indecipherable," we wouldn't be able to know all the details that appear after the colon). Beyond that, the idea of something that can't be read or understood doesn't appear in the text, so (A) must be wrong.

B   Plausible but not in the Text: This choice will be tempting for test-takers who know that some plants can be "ornamental"—that is, for the purpose of decorating something—or who think that the passage is talking about a "web" that's decorative. But this idea of being an "ornament[]" doesn't appear anywhere in the passage, so we know (B) is wrong.

C   Literary Interpretation: A lot of untrained test-takers might assume that the information in this passage is "obscure"—that it comes from some little-known source, or isn't known by many people, or something along those lines. But we could only pick a choice like this if that idea were present in the text, and it's not. So (C) is wrong.

D ✓ Correct: This choice creates the phrase "<u>intricate</u> web of relations," and then it describes a bunch of different ways that these three plants relate to each other. This depiction of multiple things connected in multiple ways literally demonstrates the idea of an "<u>intricate</u> web of relations," so we know (D) is correct.

Test 3, Module 1, Question 5	TYPE: TEXT COMPLETION

The prompt will be a short passage containing a blank. The correct answer will always be restated or demonstrated by key phrases in the provided text. See "What about Text Completion Questions?" on p. 66.

Subjective Phrases to Ignore: "most"

A   Literary Interpretation: The text says that "artisans… typically (blank)… techniques that have been passed down," and then goes on to say "but they don't strictly observe every tradition." The word "but" tells us that the idea that they "don't strictly observe every tradition" is somehow opposed to the previous idea that the "artisans… typically (blank)… techniques that have been passed down." We can see that "techniques that have been passed down" restates the idea of "tradition," so we know that "they don't strictly observe" must also be the opposite of "artisans… typically (blank)," and, by extension, "observe" must mean the same thing as "typically (blank)." But the phrase "experiment with" doesn't restate the idea of "observ[ing]," and the passage doesn't describe anyone "experiment[ing] with" anything. Some test-takers will think "experimenting" is demonstrated by the idea of "now us[ing] air-conditioning motors instead of handheld bellows," but "experimenting" isn't the same thing as using technology, or doing something differently from the way it used to be done; "experimenting" specifically means trying something new when you're not sure what the results will be, and the passage doesn't describe that. So again, (A) is wrong.

B ✓ Correct: This choice creates the phrase "artisans… typically <u>adhere to</u>… techniques that have been passed down… but they don't strictly observe every tradition." Note that "<u>adhere to</u>… techniques that have been passed down" restates the phrase "observe… tradition," and the idea of "typically adher[ing]" is opposed to the idea that "they don't strictly observe every tradition," as the word "but" requires, in accordance with the logic we discussed in our analysis of (A). This choice creates a phrase that is restated in the relevant text, so (B) is correct.

C   Direct Contradiction: Like (A), this choice will be tempting for test-takers who focus on the idea of "now us[ing] air-conditioning motors instead of handheld bellows," since that sounds like an "improve[ment]." But this choice would fail to create the relationship required by the word "but." If we inserted this choice in the provided text, the word "but" would make "us[ing] air-conditioning motors" a *counter-example* to the idea of "improv[ing] on… techniques that have been passed down," rather than an example of that. So (C) is wrong.

D   Plausible but not in the Text: This choice will definitely tempt untrained test-takers who try to answer based on "real-world" assumptions, and who decide that "the bronze- and brass-casting techniques" mentioned in the passage would be something challenging that "artisans" would have to "grapple with"—that is, a difficult task they would attempt to take on. But that idea isn't stated or demonstrated in the text, and we can't pick an answer choice based on an assumption. Beyond that, this choice would fail to create a sentence that demonstrates the opposing relationship required by the word "but," as we saw in our discussion of (A). So (D) is wrong.

Test 3, Module 1, Question 6	TYPE: TEXT COMPLETION

The prompt will be a short passage containing a blank. The correct answer will always be restated or demonstrated by key phrases in the provided text. See "What about Text Completion Questions?" on p. 66.

Subjective Phrases to Ignore: "most"

A ✓ Correct: This choice says "some economic historians (blank) that…" and then, after a dash, explains this statement by saying "they assumed that…." Later, the text refers to what the historians "assumed," and what they "(blank)," as "this supposition." So we know the word in the blank must mean the same thing as "suppos[e]" and "assume[]." This choice restates both of those words, so we know that (A) is correct.

B   **Confused Relationships:** This choice can mean something like "intentionally say or create something false." Some test-takers will like this idea, because they'll feel like it is demonstrated by the "economic historians" thinking something that ended up being "disprove[d]." But being wrong isn't the same thing as "contriv[ing]." In order for this choice to be correct, the text would have to describe someone being deliberately deceptive—this ideas doesn't appear in the text, so (B) can't be right.

C   **Direct Contradiction:** As we saw in our discussion of (A), the text refers to the action in the blank as an "assum[ption]" and a "supposition." To "question[]" something is basically the opposite of "assum[ing]" or "suppos[ing]" something, because "question[ing]" means wondering whether something is true, instead of saying that you think it *is* true. So this choice is the opposite of what should go in the blank, and (C) is wrong.

D   **Literary Interpretation:** The passage tells us that a "supposition" made by "economic historians" was "disprove[n]," and some untrained test-takers might pick this choice because they assume those "historians" "regret[]" being wrong. But that idea isn't present in the text—and even if it were, this choice wouldn't cause the text to say "historians <u>regretted</u>" being wrong. Instead, it would make the text say the historians "<u>regretted</u> that… households… experienced an economy of scale…" which doesn't really make any sense, and certainly isn't restated or demonstrated elsewhere in the text. So (D) can't be right.

Test 3, Module 1, Question 7   **TYPE: TEXT COMPLETION**

The prompt will be a short passage containing a blank. The correct answer will always be restated or demonstrated by key phrases in the provided text. See "What about Text Completion Questions?" on p. 66.

Subjective Phrases to Ignore: "most"

A   **Direct Contradiction:** The text tells us about an artist, then mentions "tension among his (blank) influences," and then, after a colon, lists three different influences. This choice would cause the text to call the "influences" "complementary." But there's nothing about the "influences" mentioned in the text to suggest that they're "complementary" to one another—that there's some kind of harmony or agreement among them. In fact, the idea that they're "complementary" contradicts the information in the text that there is "tension among" those "influences." This choice contradicts an idea that's present in the text, so we know it must be wrong.

B   **Direct Contradiction:** This choice contradicts what's present in the text, because it would call the "influences" "unknown," and then immediately list out those influences. The text can't tell us what the "influences" are if those influences are "unknown," so (B) can't be right.

C ✓   **Correct:** This choice would call the "influences" "disparate." The idea that the "influences" are "disparate," or different from each other, is demonstrated by the idea that there is "tension among" those "influences." This choice creates a phrase that's restated in the relevant text, so (C) is correct.

D   **Barely Relevant:** In order for this choice to be correct, the text would have to state or demonstrate the idea that the "influences" can be swapped out with each other, because that's what "interchangeable" means—but the idea of being able to remove one influence and put another influence in its place isn't mentioned anywhere, and wouldn't even really make sense. So (D) is wrong.

Test 3, Module 1, Question 8   **TYPE: TEXT COMPLETION**

The prompt will be a short passage containing a blank. The correct answer will always be restated or demonstrated by key phrases in the provided text. See "What about Text Completion Questions?" on p. 66.

Subjective Phrases to Ignore: "most"

A   **Literary Interpretation:** The word "though" tells us that there is some kind of opposition between the idea that "there have been many studies of the effect of high altitude on blood chemistry" and the idea that "there is a (blank) studies of the effect on blood chemistry of living in locations below sea level." Saying that there is a "<u>quarrel about</u> studies of the effect on blood chemistry of living in locations below sea level" doesn't cause the text to demonstrate the relationship required by the word "though." Some test-takers will like this choice because they'll feel like there must be some conflict between the people who do the one kind of study and the people who do the other kind of study, and that this choice restates that idea—but that idea isn't in the text, and this choice wouldn't cause the text to say that, anyway. Instead of saying there is a quarrel between two groups of people, it would say that there was a "quarrel about" the second kind of study, without explaining who was involved in the quarrel, or why they were quarreling. This choice wouldn't demonstrate the kind of relationship required by the word "though," so (A) must be wrong. See the discussion of (B) for more.

B ✓   **Correct:** This choice would cause the text to say "though there have been many studies about" one topic, "there is a <u>paucity of</u> studies" on another topic—that is, not many studies on that other topic. The idea of there being a lot of studies about one thing but not very many studies about another thing exactly demonstrates the opposing relationship required by the word "though," so (B) is correct.

C   Direct Contradiction: This choice would cause the text to express the opposite of the relationship required by the word "though"—instead of saying that there was a lot of one kind of study and not many of another kind, as we saw in the correct answer, (B), the text would say that there was a lot of one kind of study, and also a "profusion of" another kind of study—that is, a lot of that other kind of study, too. This is the opposite what should go in the blank, so it's wrong.

D   Barely Relevant: This choice would cause the text to say that "studies of the effect on blood chemistry of living in locations below sea level" have a similarity to real life. This choice doesn't restate or demonstrate anything in the text, and doesn't create the kind of opposing relationship between two ideas required by the word "though." This choice will probably be most tempting for test-takers who don't know what "verisimilitude" means, and who don't feel sure of the other choices, and decide that their best shot is the choice with the unknown word.

Test 3, Module 1, Question 9	TYPE: MAIN IDEA

The prompt asks about the "main purpose" or "main idea" (or some similar phrase) of the text. The correct answer must be directly restated or demonstrated in the passage, with no interpretation. See "What about "Main Idea/Main Purpose" Questions?" on p.69.

Subjective Phrases to Ignore: "best"

A   Literary Interpretation: The text does mention a "long-expected guest," and some test-takers will associate the idea of having a guest with "worr[ying]." But the passage never mentions anyone worrying about anything, so (A) can't be right.

B   Off by One or Two Words: This choice might tempt test-takers who notice the phrase "she seldom went out now," which tells us that someone used to go out more often than she does now. This would be an example of a "character[]... chang[ing] over time," as this choice requires. But this choice mentions "characters," plural, "chang[ing] over time," which would require the text to tell us how at least one more character "changed over time." That information doesn't appear in the text, so (B) must be wrong.

C   Confused Relationships: This choice would require a clear difference between the level of "activity indoors" and the "stillness outside" to justify the word "contrast," but that doesn't appear in the text—it mentions a woman who is "stately and calm," and another woman "coming in from the garden"; outside there are "robins" singing and the sun going down. No particular phrase indicates that there was a lot of activity inside or "stillness outside," and both would be required for this choice to be right. So (C) is wrong.

D ✓   Correct: The text "depict[s] the setting" by telling us what "Miss Pyne" and "Martha" are doing in the house, and describing the "bright cool evening," and telling us about the "golden robins" and the "sun... going down behind the apple-trees," and so on. We also know "the characters await a visitor's arrival," because the text tells us that "Miss Pyne sat by the window watching" when it "was almost time for the carriage," and that the house "stood wide open to the long-expected guest." Each part of this answer is demonstrated in the text, so we know (D) is correct.

Test 3, Module 1, Question 10	TYPE: FUNCTION AND STRUCTURE

The prompt asks about the "function" or "structure" of a part of the text. The correct answer must plainly and accurately describe the relevant text, with no interpretation. See "What about "Function and Structure" Questions?" on p. 70.

Subjective Phrases to Ignore: "best"

A   Barely Relevant: This choice can't be right, because "the work of Nance and colleagues" isn't even mentioned until the next sentence, and this sentence doesn't talk about how anyone "in the field" received anything. So (A) must be wrong.

B   Barely Relevant: The underlined sentence doesn't present any findings whatsoever; it simply tells us something that "astronomers" aren't "confident" about, and tells us why. So (B) is wrong.

C ✓   Correct: The underlined sentence "identifies a problem," as this choice requires, when it says that figuring out "when this will happen" ("this" refers to when "Betelgeuse" will "explode," as mentioned in the previous sentence) "depends on internal characteristics of Betelgeuse that are largely unknown." We know this problem is "the problem that Nance and colleagues attempted to solve but did not" when we read the third sentence, which says that "Nance and colleagues" "investigated whether acoustic waves in [Betelgeuse] could be used to determine internal stellar states," but they "concluded that this method could not sufficiently reveal Betelgeuse's internal characteristics" to make this possible—note that the "method... not... reveal[ing]" Betelgeuse's internal characteristics" restates the idea that Nance and colleagues "did not" "solve" "the problem" of the "internal characteristics of Betelgeuse" being "largely unknown," as this choice requires. With all of this in mind, we can see that (C) is correct.

D   Wrong Part of the Passage: This choice will be tempting for some test-takers, because the third sentence does tell us about something that "Nance and colleagues" were unable to do, which might seem related to "a serious limitation of the method used by Nance and colleagues." But this question asks about the *second* sentence, which doesn't mention any method or any limitation of any kind. So (D) is wrong.

The prompt asks for information from the passage. The answer must be restated or demonstrated by specific phrases in the text. See "What about General Passage Questions?" on p. 69.

A   Literary Interpretation: This choice will be tempting for some test-takers because the text says that "Elinor" "counteract[ed]" her mother, and describes "knowledge" that Elinor had but "which her mother had yet to learn." This demonstrates some differences between Elinor and her mother, and some untrained test-takers will assume this means they "argue[d]." But we know we can't assume things on the SAT; we have to pick answers based on what appears on the page, and the passage never mentions them (or anyone else) arguing about anything. Beyond that, the text doesn't mention Elinor "fail[ing] to change" anyone else's mind. For either of these reasons, (A) is wrong.

B   Literary Interpretation: The text does say that Elinor's "feelings were strong," which some test-takers might understand to mean that she was "sensitive," as this choice requires—but having "strong" "feelings" isn't the same as being sensitive, because being sensitive includes the idea of being very attuned to and/or affected by what happens around you, particularly in regard to other people's feelings and actions. A person can have "strong" "feelings" and be very sensitive, or not sensitive at all, or anything in between. So the text doesn't actually state or demonstrate that Elinor is "sensitive," as this choice requires—and even if it did, it doesn't describe her as "overly" sensitive, or sensitive "with regard to family matters," both of which would be required by this choice. So (B) is wrong. This is a great example of a choice that will seem like a possible right answer to an untrained test-taker, because the passage does mention "family matters" and "feelings"—but if we as trained test-takers think carefully about what this choice specifically says, we can see very clearly that it's wrong.

C   Literary Interpretation: The passage describes Elinor's mother as "impruden[t]," and says that when Elinor "counteract[s]" her mother, it is "to the advantage of them all"—that is, it's better for everybody when Elinor works against her mother. The passage also mentions that Elinor "knew how to govern" her "strong" "feelings," which was a skill "her mother had yet to learn." A lot of test-takers will read this passage and make their own personal judgment that Elinor's mother is "a bad role model," as this choice says, and then decide to go with this answer choice. But as trained test-takers, we know we can't approach the test this way. We can't answer this question as though the prompt said "what do you, personally, think is true?" and as though this answer choice said "Elinor's mother is a bad role model." We have to remember that the prompt asked us "what is true about Elinor," and the choice says "Elinor thinks her mother is a bad role model." When we remember this, we can see that the text never says her mother is a bad role model, and more importantly it never says that *Elinor* thinks her mother is a bad role model, which this choice requires. So (C) is wrong, regardless of our own impressions of Elinor's mother.

D ✓   Correct: The passage describes Elinor as having "effectual" "advice," "a strength of understanding," a "coolness of judgment," and other good qualities that demonstrate "matur[ity]." It says that "her feelings were strong; but she knew how to govern them," which also demonstrates maturity. The text also specifically says that she was "the counselor of her mother," and that she "counteract[ed]" her mother's "impudence"; "counteract[ing]" "impudence" literally demonstrates "matur[ity]." Finally, it says the she did these things "though only nineteen"—the phrase "though only" tells us that Elinor is unexpectedly young to have these qualities, which restates that she is "remarkably mature for her age," as this choice requires. So (D) is right.

The prompt asks about the "main purpose" or "main idea" (or some similar phrase) of the text. The correct answer must be directly restated or demonstrated in the passage, with no interpretation. See "What about "Main Idea/Main Purpose" Questions?" on p.69.

Subjective Phrases to Ignore: "best"

A   Plausible but not in the Text: This choice will be tempting for untrained test-takers because it says that living in a home like the one described in the passage "can be rejuvenating," which restates the part of the passage that says the effect of the house is "invigorating." But this choice *also* says that "it is unsustainable," which the text never says. Many untrained test-takers will like this choice, because they'll read this passage and think that living in the home it describes sounds "unsustainable" *to them*—but as trained test-takers, we know we can't pick an answer choice based on our own opinions. The text doesn't say living in the house is "unsustainable," as this choice would require, so (A) is wrong. Remember that we can't pick an answer choice just because it *partially* restates or demonstrates ideas from the text; if it includes ideas that aren't in the text, it's wrong.

B   Off by One or Two Words: The text says that living in the home described in the passage is "invigorating" and associated with "significant health benefits," which some test-takers will decide means that it "create[s] a physically stimulating environment." But the passage definitely never says living in this kind of space is the "most effective way" to create that kind of environment, which this choice would require. In fact, it never says anything is the "most effective way" to do anything. So (B) is wrong.

C   Barely Relevant: The only thing the text says about Yamaoka is that he spent "four years" living in the "apartment building" described in the passage, and that he "reported significant health benefits." The text says nothing about whether Yamaoka has ever "supported… conceptual artists" in any other situation. So (C) is wrong. Some test-takers will assume that a "filmmaker" probably wants to support other artistic people, so this statement is probably true—but as trained test-takers, we know we can't make assumptions like that on the SAT.

D ✓ Correct: This choice describes "the design of the apartment building" as "impractical," which is directly restated in the first sentence in the passage ("an apartment building"… that's "more fanciful than functional"). Then it says this design "may improve the well-being of the building's residents," which is directly demonstrated by the fact that Yamaoka spent "four years there" and "reported significant health benefits." Every part of this choice is restated or demonstrated in the relevant text, so it's right.

Test 3, Module 1, Question 13   **TYPE: QUOTATION**

The prompt will make a claim about a literary work, then ask which quotation "illustrates the claim." The right answer will plainly demonstrate the ideas in the provided claim. See "What about Quotation Questions?" on p. 70.

Subjective Phrases to Ignore: "best"

A   Barely Relevant: The prompt asks for the choice that "illustrate[s] the student's claim." When we look at the text, we can see that the student claims that "some historians… have evaluated Patrice Lumumba… primarily as a symbol rather than in terms of his actions." This choice doesn't specifically mention Lumumba being viewed as a symbol, nor does it tell us how his "actions" are viewed, or should be viewed. This choice doesn't demonstrate the ideas in the "claim," so it's wrong. See the note below for more.

B   Barely Relevant: This choice has the same problem as (A), and it's wrong for the same reason; it makes a statement about Lumumba, but doesn't talk about people viewing him as a symbol, or how people see his actions. See the note below for more.

C ✓ Correct: This choice says that "Lumumba's practical accomplishments can be passed over quickly," which directly demonstrates the idea of not evaluating Lumumba "in terms of his actions," as the prompt and the claim require. This choice also says that Lumumba "warrants scholarly attention" "mainly as the personification of Congolese independence," which directly demonstrates the idea from the claim of Lumumba being "evaluated… as a symbol." Notice how the phrase "practical accomplishments" from this choice demonstrates the word "actions" from the "claim," and the phrase "personification" from this choice demonstrates the word "symbol" from the "claim." This choice exactly demonstrates the "claim," so (C) is correct.

D   Barely Relevant: This choice has the same problem as (A) and (B), and is wrong for the same reason. It doesn't mention anything about him being seen as a symbol, or about his actions being overlooked. See the note below for more.

> **Note**   Each wrong answer choice for this question was fairly similar; it made a statement that would have been very open to interpretation for untrained test-takers, which might make those choices difficult to eliminate at first. But as trained test-takers, when we read the correct answer, we should recognize immediately that this choice very specifically meets the requirements of the prompt: it clearly demonstrates Lumumba being "evaluated" as a "symbol," and not based on "his actions." On test day, if you start to work through the answer choices on a question, and you're having trouble evaluating those choices, don't get stuck—just read each choice and move on, and keep reading until something clicks. Either you'll see a clearly wrong or clearly right choice, and get back on track—or you won't, and you can decide to move on to the next question and come back to this question in a later round.

Test 3, Module 1, Question 14   **TYPE: DATA**

The passage includes a figure. The question asks for the choice that uses data from the figure to accomplish a certain goal. The right answer will describe the data accurately and plainly accomplish the goal. See "What about "Data" Questions?" on p. 69.

Subjective Phrases to Ignore: "most effectively"

A   Direct Contradiction: The passage ends with a semi-colon, and then the phrase "for instance, (blank)." We know that whatever appears in the blank should be an example of what's described earlier in that sentence. The beginning of that sentence says "in some regions, female farmers were found to be especially prominent" in farming certain crops, and that they were "even… the majority of farmers" raising certain crops. This choice *would* be an example of that idea—because it talks about two instances where women were "the majority of farmers" growing certain crops in certain regions—but this choice doesn't accurately describe the graph. This choice says that "most of the farmers" growing "cereal" and "non-root vegetables in south Ondo were women." We can see that most of the farmers growing non-root vegetables in south Ondo *were* women, as this choice states, because the black column representing the percentage of farmers growing non-root vegetables in south Ondo who were female shows a value over 50. But the same isn't true of cereals—the dark gray column representing the percentage of farmers growing cereal in south Ondo who were female was between 35 and 40—this is less than 50, so we can't say "most" farmers growing cereals in south Ondo were women. This choice describes the graph inaccurately, so it must be wrong.

B   Direct Contradiction: We can see that this choice makes an inaccurate statement about the data, because the light gray column that represents the percentage of farmers growing root crops in central Ondo who were women is smaller than the dark gray column that represents the percentage of farmers growing cereals in central Ondo who were women. Even if the statement in this choice were true, though, it still wouldn't be an example of the idea in the last sentence of the passage, as the prompt requires, because both of these percentages are below 50, so neither is an instance of "the majority of farmers" cultivating a certain crop being women, and comparing the two percentages to each other isn't related to whether or not either percentage is a "majority." For any of these reasons, (B) is wrong.

C ✓ Correct: This choice accurately describes the data, and it makes a statement that's an example of the idea from the last sentence of the passage, as the prompt requires. The fact that "most of the farmers" who grew "non–root vegetables in north and south Ondo were women" directly demonstrates that "female farmers" were "the majority of farmers" raising certain crops "in some regions," as stated in the passage. So (C) is right.

D Confused Relationships: This choice accurately describes the data, but it's not an example of the idea from the last sentence in the passage. The idea that "women across the three regions of Ondo mainly cultivated cereals" in "relatively equal proportion" isn't an example of female farmers being "the majority of farmers" raising certain crops in certain regions. In fact, "female farmers" weren't "the majority of farmers" raising "cereals" in any region from the graph. So (D) must be wrong.

| Test 3, Module 1, Question 15 | TYPE: IF TRUE |

The passage presents some claim or hypothesis. The prompt typically asks us to choose the "finding" that, "if true," would support or weaken the argument. Supporting statements will demonstrate the idea in the claim, and weakening statements will demonstrate the opposite of the idea in the claim. See "What about "If True" Questions?" on p. 71.

Subjective Phrases to Ignore: "most directly"

A Confused Relationships: The prompt asks for the choice that "weaken[s]" the claim. When we read the passage, we can see that the claim is that "host stars (such as the Sun) and their planets (such as those in our solar system) are composed of the same materials," and that the planets have "equal or smaller quantities of the materials that make up the host star." This choice only talks about the "materials" that make up "stars," with no mention of what "materials" "planets" are made of. So this statement doesn't say anything about whether the materials making up those stars' "planets" is the "same" as the material that makes up the stars, which means this choice has no bearing on the "claim," and (A) is wrong.

B Confused Relationships: Like (A), this choice only talks about "materials" that make up "stars" (in this case, the stars are a "host star" and "the Sun"—notice that the passage tells us specifically that the Sun is a "host star," and that we don't need to know this outside information ahead of time). Since the claim has to do with planets and stars being made of "the same materials," a statement that only talks about the materials that make up stars isn't relevant. So (B) is wrong too.

C ✓ Correct: The claim says that "planets" have "equal or smaller quantities of the materials that make up the host star." But this choice describes "some rocky planets" with "considerably higher" "iron" "than… their host star" has. The statement in this choice demonstrates the exact opposite of what the claim in the passage says, which means this choice weakens that claim, just as the prompt requires. So (C) is right.

D Confused Relationships: This choice has the same basic problem as (A) and (B), except that while those choices only make statements about stars, this choice only makes a statement about planets. The claim in the passage specifically talks about planets and stars being made of "the same materials," so a statement that only discusses the materials making up planets doesn't impact that statement. So (D) is wrong.

| Test 3, Module 1, Question 16 | TYPE: IF TRUE |

The passage presents some claim or hypothesis. The prompt typically asks us to choose the "finding" that, "if true," would support or weaken the argument. Supporting statements will demonstrate the idea in the claim, and weakening statements will demonstrate the opposite of the idea in the claim. See "What about "If True" Questions?" on p. 71.

Subjective Phrases to Ignore: "most directly"

A Direct Contradiction: The prompt asks us for the choice that "support[s] Paredes's argument." When we read the passage, we find out that "Paredes's argument" is that "while some Spanish influence is undeniable, Mexican American folklore is mainly the product of the ongoing interactions of various cultures in Mexico and the United States." This choice might be tempting for test-takers who get confused about which "argument" the correct answer should "support," or about whether they should be "support[ing]" or weakening the argument, because this choice actually "support[s]" the *other* argument in the passage, which says that "Mexican American folklore derived largely from the folklore of Spain." Again, since this choice describes aspects of Mexican American folklore that "originat[ed] in… Spain," this choice supports the *other* argument in the passage, and actually weakens "Paredes's argument" that "Mexican American folklore is mainly the product of the ongoing interactions of various cultures in Mexico and the United States," which is the opposite of what the prompt requires. So (A) is wrong.

B   Barely Relevant: "Paredes's argument" is that "Mexican American folklore is mainly the product of… cultures in Mexico and the United States." This choice doesn't tell us anything about what the folklore is "the product of"; it only tells us that folklore from different regions "had similar elements." This could be true whether that folklore had roots in Mexico, as "Paredes… argued," or in Spain, as others argued, or in some other place. This choice doesn't impact Paredes's argument, so it's wrong.

C   Barely Relevant: This choice has the same basic problem as (B)—the argument in question makes a statement about which cultures influenced "Mexican American folklore," but this choice doesn't say anything about any culture influencing folklore, only that "most" of the "folklore" "collected" by the "ethnographers" mentioned in the passage "was previously unknown to scholars." This statement can be true regardless of which cultures influenced that folklore. So (C) is wrong.

D ✓   Correct: The passage talks about one argument that says "Mexican American folklore derived largely from the folklore of Spain," and that Spain "ruled Mexico from the sixteenth to early nineteenth centuries." On the other hand, "Paredes's argument" said that "Mexican American folklore" is "the product of ongoing interactions of various cultures in Mexico and the United States." This choice mentions folklore "of a clearly recent origin." If the origin of the folklore is "recent," then it couldn't be the result of an influence from previous centuries, like "Spa[nish]" "rule[]"—but it *could* be the result of interactions that are "ongoing," like those mentioned in Paredes's argument from the passage. So this choice supports "Paredes's argument," as the prompt requires, which means that (D) is right. (Notice that "ongoing" demonstrates the idea of something "recent," while something from "the sixteenth to early nineteenth centuries" demonstrates the opposite of "recent.")

Test 3, Module 1, Question 17   TYPE: MOST LOGICALLY COMPLETES

The passage ends with a blank, and the answer choices are relatively long phrases. The right answer will restate or demonstrate an idea in the provided text. See "What about "Most Logically Completes" Questions?" on p. 68.

Subjective Phrases to Ignore: "most"

A ✓   Correct: The text tells us that "some Euro-American farmers… used agricultural techniques developed by the Haudenosaunee… centuries earlier," and that "few of those farmers had actually seen Haudenosaunee farms firsthand." Then it says "barring the possibility of several farmers of the same era independently developing [Haudenosaunee] techniques," the facts indicate "(blank)." If these different farmers are using the same techniques, and "few" of one group saw the farms of the other group, and we're "barring the possibility" of different farmers" "developing" these "techniques" "independently," then the Haudenosaunee farmers must have influenced the Euro-American farmers in some way—this directly demonstrates "barring" the idea that the techniques were developed "independently." This choice says that the "Euro-American farmers" "learned the techniques from other people who were more directly influenced by Haudenosaunee practices." This choice demonstrates the idea that few of the "Euro-American farmers" saw "Haudenosaunee farms firsthand," but that they still didn't come up with their techniques "independently," as the prompt requires—instead, they learned from other people who "directly" learned "Haudenosaunee practices." This choice demonstrates all the requirements mentioned in the passage, so it's right.

B   Direct Contradiction: The text tells us that "Euro-American farmers in the northeastern United States used agricultural techniques developed by the Haudenosaunee (Iroquois) people." If the crops those "Euro-American farmers" grew "were not well suited to Haudenosaunee farming techniques," then we wouldn't expect them to use those techniques, which contradicts what the text tells us. This choice doesn't "logically complete" the text, as the prompt requires; it provides additional information that calls ideas from the text into question. This is basically the opposite of what the prompt asks for, so (B) is wrong.

C   Barely Relevant: This choice doesn't have any clear connection to the statements in the passage. The passage already tells us that these "techniques" had spread somewhat from the farmers that came up with them to some other farmers, so for all we know, those techniques could have been "widely used" elsewhere as well, or not. This choice will be tempting for untrained test-takers who use it as a jumping-off point for an argument based on assumptions connected to the idea that farming techniques used in other regions could make their way from one community to another, or something along those lines—but no idea like that appears in this choice, so (C) must be wrong. Contrast this with (A), which specifically describes different groups of farmers learning these techniques from each other.

D   Direct Contradiction: This choice is similar to (B), because it calls statements from the passage into question. If "Euro-American farmers only began to recognize the benefits of Haudenosaunee farming techniques late in the nineteenth century," then it's not clear why the text would say they used these techniques "in the early nineteenth century." So this choice is wrong for the same reasons that (B) is wrong.

Test 3, Module 1, Question 18   TYPE: MOST LOGICALLY COMPLETES

The passage ends with a blank, and the answer choices are relatively long phrases. The right answer will restate or demonstrate an idea in the provided text. See "What about "Most Logically Completes" Questions?" on p. 68.

Subjective Phrases to Ignore: "most"

A Confused Relationships: The passage mentions "artifacts" in "Kuulo Kataa" "from the thirteenth century CE," and says those artifacts might indicate "that the settlement was founded before or around that time." The passage also mentions "other evidence" that Kuulo Kataa was founded in the "fourteenth century," not the thirteenth century. The sentence with the blank requires us to decide what would be "impl[ied]" "if both the artifact dates and the fourteenth century CE founding date are correct." So we need an answer choice that demonstrates "both the artifact dates and the fourteenth century CE founding date" being correct. The idea in this choice that "fourteenth century" artifacts "are more commonly recovered" than "thirteenth century" artifacts doesn't have any impact on the idea that Kuulo Kataa was founded in the fourteenth century CE but contains artifacts from the thirteenth century CE; it's the presence of "artifacts" from the "thirteenth century" at all that seems to conflict with "a fourteenth century… founding date," not the relative frequency with which they're found. This choice doesn't account for how the "artifact dates" and "fourteenth century CE founding date" can both be correct, as the prompt requires, so (A) is wrong.

B ✓ Correct: This choice says that "the artifacts originated elsewhere" and came to Kuulo Kataa afterward. This makes it possible for the artifacts to date from before the founding of Kuulo Kataa, which addresses the apparent contradiction created by artifacts that are older than the settlement where they were "recovered." So "both the artifact dates and the fourteenth century CE founding date" can be "correct," as the provided text requires, which means (B) is right.

C Literary Interpretation: This choice will be tempting for test-takers who read this statement, and then assume some additional information about those "people from a different region" bringing older artifacts along with them when they founded Kuulo Kataa. But this choice doesn't actually include that information, so we can't use that information as a basis for picking this choice. The statement in this choice, alone, doesn't address the apparent contradiction in the passage between "the artifact dates and the fourteenth century CE founding date," so (C) is wrong. Contrast this with the correct answer, (B), which specifically describes the artifacts "originat[ing] elsewhere."

D Barely Relevant: This choice will be tempting for test-takers who think that the presence in Kuulo Kataa of "artifacts dating to the fourteenth century CE" confirms the "fourteenth century… founding date." But this information doesn't have any impact on the presence of the artifacts from the thirteenth century, so this choice doesn't address the idea in the sentence with the blank about "the artifact dates" being "correct." So (D) is wrong.

Test 3, Module 1, Question 19 — TYPE: MOST LOGICALLY COMPLETES

The passage ends with a blank, and the answer choices are relatively long phrases. The right answer will restate or demonstrate an idea in the provided text. See "What about "Most Logically Completes" Questions?" on p. 68.

Subjective Phrases to Ignore: "most"

A Literary Interpretation: This choice will be tempting for test-takers because the passage only describes *A. thaliana* demonstrating "temperature-sensitive accelerated flowering," and no other plant. But this passage not telling us about any other plant having this capability isn't the same as the passage saying that no other plant has this capability, as the word "unique" would require! The passage never tells us that only *A. thaliana* is capable of "temperature-sensitive accelerated flowering," so we can't pick a choice that says this is the case. That means (A) is wrong.

B Confused Relationships: The text does tell us that the "unmodified plants," which still have "the protein ELF3," are the ones that "exhibited accelerated flowering," while the "altered plants" that had their ELF3 "replaced" didn't exhibit this trait. But flowers with ELF3 "exhibit[ing] accelerated flowering" and those without it not exhibiting that trait isn't the same as those flowers "increase[ing] ELF3 production as temperatures rise." We don't know whether the flowers increase production of the protein in any particular situation, or whether the protein is always there in the same quantities and only activates at certain temperatures, or what. The text never describes "ELF3 production" at all, and certainly never talks about "ELF3 production" increasing in any particular situation. So (B) can't be correct.

C ✓ Correct: The text tells us that the two groups of plants "showed no difference in flowering at 22° Celsius," and then describes the "unmodified plants," which still have "the protein ELF3," "exhibit[ing] accelerated flowering" "at 27° Celsius," while the "altered plants" that had their ELF3 "replaced" didn't exhibit this trait. This directly demonstrates the idea that the "ELF3 enables *A. thaliana* to respond to increased temperature," because the unmodified *A. thaliana* plants with ELF3 responded to the increase in temperature to 27° Celsius by "exhibit[ing] accelerated flowering," while the "altered" *A. thaliana* plants without ELF3 didn't "respond to increased temperatures," and didn't exhibit this ability. So (C) is correct.

D Literary Interpretation: This choice will be tempting for test-takers who notice that the passage only talks about plants flowering at or above 22° Celsius—but the passage doesn't say it's not possible for them to flower at lower temperatures, it just mentions them flowering at these temperatures. We can't say that something is impossible just because the passage doesn't mention it happening. This choice has the same basic problem as (A); it mentions a phenomenon from the text, but then says that phenomenon can *only* happen the way it's described in the text, even though the text doesn't specify that. So (D) is wrong.

- Vertical Scan Results: Each choice is a different from of the same verb.
- Vertical Scan Notes: We have to decide whether a past-tense form, infinitive, or participle of the verb "to provide" is appropriate.
- Key Features in Surrounding Text: The underlined phrase is the main verb in a dependent clause whose action is being done by the relative pronoun "which," which refers to "handbook." So the verb should be conjugated to agree with the third-person singular noun "handbook."

Concepts in the question:

- Independent and Dependent Clauses: Choices would create and/or join clauses. An independent clause can stand on its own as a sentence, and a dependent clause can't. Remember rules for joining clauses related to periods, semi-colons, colons, commas, and conjunctions. (See page 82.)
- Verb Tense/Conjugation: Choices include different forms of the same verb. Look at the surrounding text to find the verb's subject. Also, look for other clues that could indicate the proper tense or form of the verb in the blank. (See page 77.)

ANSWER CHOICE ANALYSIS

A ✓ Correct: As we saw in our analysis above, the verb should be conjugated for the relative pronoun "which," which refers to "handbook." This choice is the appropriately conjugated form "provided," which creates the phrase "…Handbook, which provided…." This choice satisfies our reasoning above, so it's correct.

B Incorrect: This choice doesn't satisfy our reasoning above; it would leave the dependent phrase "which… Venus" without a main verb, which isn't acceptable in an SAT Writing question. So (B) is wrong.

C Incorrect: This choice has the same basic problem as (B), and is wrong for the same reason.

D Incorrect: This choice has the same basic problem as (B) and (C), and is wrong for the same reason.

> **Note** Some test-takers will look at choice (A) and get hung up on whether the verb should be in the past-tense—but once we notice that a conjugated verb form must appear in the blank, and we see that (A) is the only option with a conjugated verb form, we know that (A) must be right, and we don't need to worry about its tense.

- Vertical Scan Results: Each choice starts with the same word; some choices add a comma and/or the word "but" after that word.
- Vertical Scan Notes: We need to decide whether the word "value" by itself should appear in the blank, or whether a comma and/or the word "but" should also appear.
- Key Features in Surrounding Text: "Typically… value" can stand on its own as a sentence, and "when… literary scholars" can also stand on its own as a sentence.

Concepts in the question:

- Commas: Commas can be used between clauses, to form comma sandwiches, in a list of 3 or more items, and before reported speech. They can't appear for no reason. Review the training for the relevant details. (See page 86.)
- Independent and Dependent Clauses: Choices would create and/or join clauses. An independent clause can stand on its own as a sentence, and a dependent clause can't. Remember rules for joining clauses related to periods, semi-colons, colons, commas, and conjunctions. (See page 82.)

ANSWER CHOICE ANALYSIS

A ✓ Correct: This choice would use a comma and the conjunction "but" to separate two independent clauses, which follows the grammar and punctuation rules we discussed in the SAT Writing Toolbox earlier in this section. So (A) is right.

B Incorrect: This choice would cause two groups of words that can each stand on their own as sentences ("typically… value" and "when… literary scholars") not to be separated by anything—not a period, or a semi-colon, or a comma and a conjunction or relative pronoun. This isn't acceptable in an SAT Writing question, so (B) is wrong.

C Incorrect: This choice results in a comma splice, because it would cause two groups of words that can each stand on their own as sentences ("typically… value" and "when… literary scholars") to be separated by a comma, which isn't acceptable in an SAT Writing question. So (C) is wrong.

D   Incorrect: This choice is similar to the right answer (A), except it's missing a comma—and we know from our training that we have to use both a comma *and* a conjunction to separate two independent clauses, not just the conjunction. So (D) is wrong.

- Vertical Scan Results: Each choice includes the same two words, with a comma, period, the word "and," or nothing appearing between the two words.
- Vertical Scan Notes: We have to decide whether a comma, period, the word "and," or nothing should appear between "percent" and "such."
- Key Features in Surrounding Text: "After the… percent" can stand on its own as a sentence, and "such taxes… up" can stand on its own as a sentence.

Concepts in the question:

- Comma Splice: A comma can't join two groups of words that could each be sentences on their own. (See page 83.)
- Independent and Dependent Clauses: Choices would create and/or join clauses. An independent clause can stand on its own as a sentence, and a dependent clause can't. Remember rules for joining clauses related to periods, semi-colons, colons, commas, and conjunctions. (See page 82.)

ANSWER CHOICE ANALYSIS

A   Incorrect: This choice results in a comma splice, because it would separate two groups of words that can each stand on their own as sentences with a comma, which isn't acceptable on the SAT. So (A) is wrong.

B   Incorrect: This choice isn't acceptable, because it would separate two groups of words that can each stand on their own as sentences with only the conjunction "and." We know from our training that this would be okay if there were a comma before "and," but that comma is missing from this answer choice—so (B) is wrong.

C ✓ Correct: This choice separates two groups of words that can each stand on their own as sentences with a period, which is acceptable in an SAT Writing question. So (C) is correct.

D   Incorrect: This choice would result in two groups of words that can each stand their own as sentences with nothing between them—no period, or semi-colon, or comma and conjunction—which is unacceptable in an SAT Writing question. So (D) is wrong.

- Vertical Scan Results: Each choice is the same two words with a comma, semi-colon, period, or no punctuation between the two words.
- Vertical Scan Notes: We have to decide which punctuation, if any, should appear between "added" and "whenever."
- Key Features in Surrounding Text: "Specifically… added" can stand on its own as a sentence, but "whenever…clocks" can't stand on its own as a sentence. "Whenever… clocks" is a prepositional phrase that comes immediately after the verb "added."

Concepts in the question:

- Commas: Commas can be used between clauses, to form comma sandwiches, in a list of 3 or more items, and before reported speech. They can't appear for no reason. Review the training for the relevant details. (See page 86.)
- Independent and Dependent Clauses: Choices would create and/or join clauses. An independent clause can stand on its own as a sentence, and a dependent clause can't. Remember rules for joining clauses related to periods, semi-colons, colons, commas, and conjunctions. (See page 82.)

ANSWER CHOICE ANALYSIS

A   Incorrect: This choice inserts a comma between a verb and its preposition, which doesn't follow any of the standards for comma usage that we discussed in the SAT Writing Toolbox. So (A) is wrong. (Remember that if we don't have a specific reason to include a comma, we should omit it.)

B   Incorrect: This choice would result in a semi-colon separating one group of words that can stand on its own as a sentence from another group of words that can't, which isn't acceptable on the SAT. So (B) is wrong.

C   Incorrect: This choice would result in a period separating one group of words that can stand on its own as a sentence from another group of words that can't—that is, from a sentence fragment—which isn't acceptable on the SAT. So (C) is wrong.

D ✓ Correct: This choice allows the verb "added" to be immediately followed by its preposition "whenever" with no punctuation in between them. Nothing in the SAT Writing Toolbox tells us that any punctuation should appear between these two words, so we know (D) is right.

- Vertical Scan Results: Each choice is a different form of the same verb.
- Vertical Scan Notes: We have to decide whether a singular, plural, past, or present form of "enhance" is appropriate.
- Key Features in Surrounding Text: The underlined phrase is the verb being done by *A Sheaf Gleaned in French Fields*, which the sentence tells us is "a volume of English translations of French poems." So the subject of the verb is a singular noun, which requires a singular verb form.

Concepts in the question:

- Intervening Phrase: A distracting phrase appears between words that need to agree with each other grammatically. Identify pairs of words that need to agree with each other, and ignore phrases that appear between those words. (See page 92.)
- Verb Tense/Conjugation: Choices include different forms of the same verb. Look at the surrounding text to find the verb's subject. Also, look for other clues that could indicate the proper tense or form of the verb in the blank. (See page 77.)

ANSWER CHOICE ANALYSIS

A ✓ Correct: This is the only singular verb form in the answer choices, so we know (A) must be correct, based on our analysis above.

B   Incorrect: This is a plural verb form, but as we discussed above, the blank must be a verb form conjugated for a singular subject. So (B) is wrong.

C   Incorrect: This choice has the same problem as (B), and is wrong for the same reason.

D   Incorrect: This choice has the same problem as (B) and (C), and is wrong for the same reason.

> **Note**   This question included a lot of confounding text to obscure the fact that the subject of the verb was singular— including the descriptive noun phrase "a volume of English translations of French poems," and also the publication year in parentheses. The title of the work itself was a bit confusing, since it ended with the plural noun phrase "French Fields." But if we read carefully, we can see that the subject of the verb is the title of a book (and is singular), which means we can confidently pick the only choice that is a singular form of the given verb.

- Vertical Scan Results: Each choice is the same two words with commas, semi-colons, or neither after each word.
- Vertical Scan Notes: We have to decide whether a comma or semi-colon should appear after "nickname," and whether a comma, semi-colon, or no punctuation should appear after "however."
- Key Features in Surrounding Text: "Scott-Heron… godfather nickname" can stand on its own as a sentence whether "however" would be part of that sentence or not, but "feeling that… preferred" can't stand on its own as a sentence, whether the word "however" is included in that phrase or not. "Feeling that… preferred" is a participial phrase that describes "Scott-Heron," which is the first noun phrase in the independent clause of the sentence where it appears, and which needs to be separated from that independent clause with a comma.

Concepts in the question:

- Avoid Dangling Participles: When a phrase starting with an -ing/-ed/-en word is joined to the main sentence by a comma, the first noun phrase in the independent clause of that sentence is described by the -ing/-ed/-en word. (See page 90.)
- Independent and Dependent Clauses: Choices would create and/or join clauses. An independent clause can stand on its own as a sentence, and a dependent clause can't. Remember rules for joining clauses related to periods, semi-colons, colons, commas, and conjunctions. (See page 82.)

ANSWER CHOICE ANALYSIS

A   Incorrect: This choice would fail to use a comma to separate the participial phrase "feeling that… preferred" from the independent clause containing the phrase it describes, which isn't acceptable on the SAT. So (A) is wrong.

B   Incorrect: This choice would cause a semi-colon to separate one group of words that can stand on its own as a sentence ("Scott-Heron… godfather nickname, however") from another group that can't ("feeling that… preferred"), which isn't acceptable on the SAT. So (B) is wrong.

C ✓ Correct: This choice solves the problem from (A) by including the comma between the participial phrase "feeling that… preferred" and the independent clause that starts with the noun phrase it describes, and this choice doesn't create any other problems—so (C) is correct.

D   Incorrect: This choice has the same problem as (B), and is wrong for the same reason.

- **Vertical Scan Results:** Each choice includes the same two words, with a comma, semi-colon, period, and/or the word "and" between them.
- **Vertical Scan Notes:** We have to decide which punctuation should appear between "quilts" and "the," and whether "and" should appear between them.
- **Key Features in Surrounding Text:** "When… quilts" can stand on its own as a sentence, but "the stitching… fabric" can't. "The stitching… fabric" is a noun phrase that tells us more about the "quilts."

Concepts in the question:

- **Commas:** Commas can be used between clauses, to form comma sandwiches, in a list of 3 or more items, and before reported speech. They can't appear for no reason. Review the training for the relevant details. (See page 86.)
- **Independent and Dependent Clauses:** Choices would create and/or join clauses. An independent clause can stand on its own as a sentence, and a dependent clause can't. Remember rules for joining clauses related to periods, semi-colons, colons, commas, and conjunctions. (See page 82.)
- **Descriptive Noun Phrase:** A comma-separated noun phrase describes the nearest phrase in the sentence where it appears. (See page 88.)

ANSWER CHOICE ANALYSIS

A   **Incorrect:** This choice is incorrect because, in an SAT Writing question, we should use only a comma to separate a descriptive phrase like "the stitching… fabric" from the word it describes ("quilts"), not a comma and the word "and." So (A) is wrong.

B ✓   **Correct:** This choice correctly uses a comma to separate the word "quilts" from the noun phrase "the stitching… fabric" that describes it. So (B) is correct.

C   **Incorrect:** This choice would cause a semi-colon to separate one group of words that can stand on its own as a sentence from another group that can't, which isn't acceptable on the SAT. So (C) is wrong.

D   **Incorrect:** This choice would cause a period to separate one group of words that can stand on its own as a sentence from another group that can't (that is, from a sentence fragment), which isn't acceptable on the SAT. So (D) is wrong.

The choices are different transition phrases like "however," "instead of," or "for example." The right answer must reflect the relationship between the concepts before and after the blank. See "What about Logical Transition Questions?" on p. 71.

Subjective Phrases to Ignore: "most"

A ✓   **Correct:** The passage starts by saying that "most conifers… are evergreen." Then it explains that this means "they keep their green leaves or needles year-round." The next sentence starts with "however," and says "not all conifer species are evergreen." Finally, the sentence with the blank says that "larch trees, (blank) lose their needles every fall." So the text demonstrates the idea that "larch trees" are an example of a "conifer species" that isn't "evergreen" (we know this because the text tells us that evergreens "keep their… needles year-round," but larch tress "lose their needles every fall"). That's exactly what this choice requires, since the phrase "for instance" introduces an example of what was previously mentioned in the text. So (A) is right.

B   **Direct Contradiction:** This choice would say that "larch trees… lose their needles every fall" in spite of something, or even though something else is true, which isn't an idea that's reflected in the text. It would indicate that "larch trees… los[ing] their needles" was something opposed to the fact that "not all conifer species are evergreen"—instead of being an *example* of that fact, as we saw in our discussion of (A). This is basically the opposite of what should go in the blank, so it's wrong.

C   **Confused Relationships:** This choice would be appropriate if the sentence where it appeared was just some additional information about a different topic. But that's not the case here—this sentence is an example of the idea from the previous sentence, as we saw in our discussion of (A), so the correct answer needs to reflect that relationship. This choice doesn't do that, so (C) is wrong.

D   **Confused Relationships:** This choice will be tempting, because the information in this sentence seems to go along with the information from the previous sentence. But in order for "in addition" to be appropriate, this sentence would specifically need to build on something from the previous sentence with more of the same kind of information. For example, if this sentence said something like "not all conifer species live in cold climates, either," then a phrase like "in addition" would be appropriate. But we can't introduce an example with a phrase like "in addition" unless it's preceded by another example, and we're saying this example is "in addition" to the previous one. That's not the case here, so (D) is wrong.

The passage presents a bulleted list of notes, then tells us a goal related to presenting that information. The correct answer will be the only one that demonstrates the ideas in the provided goal. See "What about Notes Questions?" on p. 71.

Subjective Phrases to Ignore: "most"

A ✓ **Correct:** We need the choice that "describe[s] the rocking chair to an audience unfamiliar with Sam Maloof." This choice very clearly demonstrates these requirements: the phrases "sleek, contoured armrests and seat" and "walnut rocking chair" "describe the rocking chair," just as the prompt requires, and the phrase "American woodworker Sam Maloof" is appropriate for "an audience unfamiliar with Sam Maloof," as the prompt also requires, because it provides basic introductory information about Sam Maloof. So (A) is right.

B **Literary Interpretation:** This choice will be tempting for some test-takers, because it does tell us about Sam Maloof, as the prompt requires, and it does give us some info about the chair—but it doesn't "describe the... chair," as the prompt requires. That would require telling us something about the physical characteristics of the chair, but that's not present in this choice. So (B) is wrong.

C **Literary Interpretation:** Like (B), this choice tells us about Sam Maloof, but it doesn't contain any description of the chair, as the prompt requires—in fact, this choice doesn't even mention the chair. So (C) must be wrong.

D **Literary Interpretation:** This choice is a description of the chair, as the prompt requires, but it doesn't contain any information about Sam Maloof, which the prompt also requires—remember from our training that if the prompt of a "Notes" question requires us to pick an answer for an audience unfamiliar with a person, then the right answer must provide basic introductory information about that person. This choice doesn't satisfy all the requirements of the prompt, so it's wrong.

The passage presents a bulleted list of notes, then tells us a goal related to presenting that information. The correct answer will be the only one that demonstrates the ideas in the provided goal. See "What about Notes Questions?" on p. 71.

Subjective Phrases to Ignore: "most"

A **Literary Interpretation:** The prompt asks for the choice that "emphasize[s] the decline in unique apple varieties in the U.S." and also "specif[ies] why this decline occurred." We know the correct answer must meet both of these requirements. This choice tells us that the "Lost Apple Project" is trying to find some "apple varieties" that have been lost, which does mention the idea of "apple varieties" being "lost," but it doesn't "specify why this decline occurred," as the prompt requires. The word "specify" necessarily requires details (or "specifics") to be included, but "a shift in agricultural practices in the mid-1900s" doesn't include any details— it doesn't tell us what that shift was, or why it happened. So (A) is wrong.

B **Literary Interpretation:** This choice tells us that there was a decline in "apple varieties... grown in the US," but it doesn't include any information about "why this decline occurred," as the prompt requires. So (B) is wrong.

C ✓ **Correct:** This choice mentions "the loss of thousands of varieties" of apples, which "emphasize[s] the decline in unique apple varieties in the U.S.," as the prompt requires. This choice also "specif[ies] why this decline occurred" when it tells us that "since the rise of industrial agriculture, US farmers have mainly grown the same few unique apple varieties." This choice meets all the requirements of the prompt, so it's right.

D **Barely Relevant:** This choice might seem to meet the requirements of the prompt, if we don't read carefully—but it doesn't actually mention apples at all! This choice only talks about "agriculture," but the prompt specifically asks for a choice that talks about "the decline in unique apple varieties." So (D) can't be right.

The passage presents a bulleted list of notes, then tells us a goal related to presenting that information. The correct answer will be the only one that demonstrates the ideas in the provided goal. See "What about Notes Questions?" on p. 71.

Subjective Phrases to Ignore: "most"

A **Literary Interpretation:** The prompt asks for the choice that "introduce[s] the artist's 1983 poetry collection." This choice mentions "*Precario/Precarious* (1983)," and we might know from reading the notes that this is a "poetry collection"—but this choice doesn't actually tell us this was a poetry collection (or even provide any information about the work except its name and publication year), so we can't says that it "introduce[s]" the "poetry collection," as the prompt requires. So (A) is wrong.

B **Barely Relevant:** This choice mentions the artist's name, and says she has written "numerous poetry collections," but it doesn't mention any specific "poetry collection," and certainly not the one from 1983 mentioned in the prompt. So (B) must be wrong.

C ✓ **Correct:** This choice "introduce[s] the artist's 1983 poetry collection" by telling us the work's name, publication year, and that it's "a collection of poetry by the multidisciplinary artist Cecilia Vicuña." This exactly demonstrates the idea of "introduc[ing]" something, as required by the prompt, by telling us basic information about that thing. So (C) is right.

D **Barely Relevant:** This choice does provide basic information about something related to the artist, as the prompt requires—but it tells us about her "first solo art exhibition" "in 1971," not her "1983 poetry collection." This choice never even mentions that poetry collection, so it must be wrong.

Test 3, Module 1, Question 31   **TYPE: NOTES**

The passage presents a bulleted list of notes, then tells us a goal related to presenting that information. The correct answer will be the only one that demonstrates the ideas in the provided goal. See "What about Notes Questions?" on p. 71.

Subjective Phrases to Ignore: "most"

A **Confused Relationships:** The prompt asks for the choice that "emphasize[s] the study's methodology." This choice just provides information about where "student policies of 132 medical schools" can be found, which isn't any kind of "methodology." So (A) is wrong. This choice will be tempting for some test-takers because it mentions information that's relevant to Terry Kind's study, but the information in this choice itself isn't a "methodology" of any kind, as the prompt requires. (As we'll see in our discussion of (B), the information from this choice would be helpful in carrying out the methodology of the study—that is, in examining the student policies of a lot of schools—but this choice doesn't mention that process; instead, it only tells us where some documents can be found.)

B ✓ **Correct:** This choice tells us that "Terry Kind and her team examined the student policies of 132 medical schools," and that this is what the researchers did in order "to find out how many medical schools have guidelines about student social media use." Describing what researchers did in order to achieve the goal of a study is the same as telling us that study's "methodology," as the prompt requires. So (B) is right.

C **Confused Relationships:** This choice provides information related to the study, but it's not the study's methodology, it's the *findings* of the study—that is, it's what the researchers found out after applying the methodology. So (C) is wrong.

D **Confused Relationships:** This choice will be tempting for some test-takers, because it tells us the goal of the study—but it doesn't tell us *how* "Terry Kind and her team" went about achieving that goal, which is what a "methodology" is, as we saw in our discussion of (B). This choice doesn't meet the requirements of the prompt, so it's wrong.

Test 3, Module 1, Question 32   **TYPE: NOTES**

The passage presents a bulleted list of notes, then tells us a goal related to presenting that information. The correct answer will be the only one that demonstrates the ideas in the provided goal. See "What about Notes Questions?" on p. 71.

Subjective Phrases to Ignore: "most"

A **Barely Relevant:** The prompt asks us for the choice that "emphasize[s] the duration and purpose of Cohen's and Rodrigues's work." This choice does mention "the Gullah Museums," which the notes tell us were founded by Cohen and Rodrigues, but this choice itself doesn't actually tell us that Cohen and Rodrigues had anything to do with them. The choice also doesn't say anything related to "the duration" of their work, so it must be wrong (note that "for centuries" refers to the length of time that "the Gullah people" have "lived in the region," not how long the museums have been open).

B **Confused Relationships:** This choice will be tempting, because it does tell us about "Cohen's and Rodrigues's work," as the prompt requires, and it does mention the "duration" of something, which appears in the prompt—but the prompt wants a choice that mentions the "duration" of "Cohen's and Rodrigues's work," while this choice mentions the duration of the Gullah people's presence in the U.S. So (B) is wrong.

C ✓ **Correct:** This choice tells us that "Louise Miller Cohen and Vermelle Rodrigues have worked to preserve Gullah culture through their museums," which exactly demonstrates the idea of the "purpose of Cohen's and Rodrigues's work," as required by the prompt, and it also tells us that they have done this work "since 2003," which tells us the "duration" of the work, as required by the prompt. This choice meets all the requirements in the prompt, so it's right.

D **Barely Relevant:** This choice provides some general information about "Gullah culture," but that information doesn't tell us anything about either the "duration" or "purpose" of "Cohen's and Rodrigues's work." So (D) must be wrong.

Test 3, Module 1, Question 33   **TYPE: NOTES**

The passage presents a bulleted list of notes, then tells us a goal related to presenting that information. The correct answer will be the only one that demonstrates the ideas in the provided goal. See "What about Notes Questions?" on p. 71.

Subjective Phrases to Ignore: "most"

A ✓ **Correct:** The prompt asks for the choice that "emphasize[s] the aim of the research study." This choice states that the "researchers... wanted to know if woodland expansion is related to changes in climate." The thing that "researchers" "want[] to know" is the "aim" of a "research study," so this choice exactly demonstrates what the prompt requires. That means (A) is right.

B **Confused Relationships:** This choice tells us the *results* of the study, but the prompt asks for the *aim* of the study. So (B) is wrong. This choice will be tempting for test-takers who have a hard time making the distinction between what researchers want to find out about at the *beginning* of a study, and what they end up learning *after* the study.

C **Confused Relationships:** This choice is similar to (B), and is wrong for the same reasons—it tells us what the researchers found out, rather than what they set out to learn.

D **Confused Relationships:** This choice describes the methodology that the researchers used—that is, what they actually did to find out the information they were looking for. But the prompt asked for the choice that told us the "aim of the research study," and this choice doesn't include that information. So (D) is wrong.

TEST 3, MODULE 2

| Test 3, Module 2, Question 1 | TYPE: TEXT COMPLETION |

The prompt will be a short passage containing a blank. The correct answer will always be restated or demonstrated by key phrases in the provided text. See "What about Text Completion Questions?" on p. 66.

Subjective Phrases to Ignore: "most"

A **Direct Contradiction:** The text tells us about "a viburnum plant experiencing insect damage." Then it mentions "a (blank) viburnum plant, on the other hand." The phrase "on the other hand" tells us that this "viburnum plant" is somehow the opposite of the one "experiencing... damage." But a plant that is "struggling" would be the same as one "experiencing... damage," not the opposite, as the phrase "on the other hand" would require. So this is basically the opposite of what we need in the blank, which means (A) is wrong.

B **Confused Relationships:** This choice will be tempting for some test-takers, because—if we don't think carefully enough— the idea of a plant that is "beneficial" might seem to be the opposite of a plant that's "experiencing... damage," as the phrase "on the other hand" requires. But let's think carefully about what the word "beneficial" would mean in this sentence! "Beneficial" *doesn't* mean "doing well" or "in good shape." "Beneficial" means "providing something good for something else." So "beneficial" could potentially describe a plant whether that plant is "experiencing... damage" or not. That means this choice doesn't actually demonstrate the idea of a plant that is somehow the opposite of the one "experiencing... damage," as the phrase "on the other hand" requires, which means (B) must be wrong.

C **Barely Relevant:** This choice will be tempting for untrained test-takers who just think this choice makes an okay-sounding sentence, or who attempt to interpret the text and end up concluding that the idea of something being "simple" is generally positive, and should work in the blank for that reason. But we have to answer based on the actual meaning of the words in the answer choices, and being "simple" isn't necessarily the opposite of "experiencing... damage," as the phrase "on the other hand" requires." So (C) is wrong.

D ✓ **Correct:** As we saw in our discussion of the other answer choices, the phrase "on the other hand" tells us that the word in the blank should describe a "viburnum plant" that is somehow the opposite of one that is "experiencing... damage." A "<u>healthy</u> viburnum plant" would be the opposite of one that is "experiencing... damage," as the phrase "on the other hand" requires, so (D) is correct.

| Test 3, Module 2, Question 2 | TYPE: TEXT COMPLETION |

The prompt will be a short passage containing a blank. The correct answer will always be restated or demonstrated by key phrases in the provided text. See "What about Text Completion Questions?" on p. 66.

Subjective Phrases to Ignore: "most"

A **Direct Contradiction:** The underlined phrase tells us about Cole's attitude toward "his two passions." This choice would say that he is "indifferen[t] to" them, which is the opposite of how someone feels about a "passion[]." So (A) is wrong.

B ✓ **Correct:** This choice would say that Cole has "<u>enthusiasm for</u> his two passions," which demonstrates exactly how people feel about their "passions"—by definition, a "passion[]" is something we have strong positive feelings about, which is the same as having "enthusiasm," as we see in this choice. So (B) is right.

C **Literary Interpretation:** This choice might be tempting for some test-takers who decide that someone's "passions" would be of "concern" to them, or something along those lines. But "concern about his two passions" would mean that Cole was somehow worried about those passions, which doesn't demonstrate how people feel about their "passions," and which isn't restated or demonstrated in the text. So (C) is wrong.

D   Barely Relevant: This choice would says that Cole feels "<u>surprise at</u> his two passions." The word "surprise" doesn't demonstrate how people feel about "passions," and the idea of "surprise" isn't restated or demonstrated elsewhere in the passage—so (D) is wrong.

Test 3, Module 2, Question 3   **TYPE: TEXT COMPLETION**

The prompt will be a short passage containing a blank. The correct answer will always be restated or demonstrated by key phrases in the provided text. See "What about Text Completion Questions?" on p. 66.

Subjective Phrases to Ignore: "most"

A   Direct Contradiction: The passage tells us that the "novelist… declines to (blank) the conventions" of her "genre," then refers to this situation as "this willingness to thwart expectations and avoid formulaic plots and themes." The word "this" tells us that the phrase "this willingness to thwart expectations and avoid formulaic plots and themes" refers back to "declin[ing] to (blank) the conventions" of her "genre." So we need a phrase in the blank that satisfies this requirement. This choice would cause the text to say the "novelist… declines to <u>question</u> the conventions" of her "genre." If anything, "declin[ing] to <u>question</u> the conventions" would mean that she goes along with those "conventions," which would pretty much be the opposite of "thwart[ing] expectations and avoid[ing] formulaic plots and themes,"—because "conventions" are the things that are normally done, and would be in line with the "expectations" of readers, as opposed to "thwart[ing]" them. So (A) is wrong.

B   Direct Contradiction: This choice will be tempting for some test-takers who feel like Jemisin's decisions as a novelist are a "react[ion]" to other works of "science fiction"—that she sees what other authors are doing, and decides to do something different. But that's actually kind of the opposite of what this choice would cause the passage to say—with this choice, the passage would say that she "declines to <u>react to</u> the conventions" of the genre. If anything, Jemisin *is* "react[ing]" to those conventions, by choosing not to follow them—but either way, the idea of "declin[ing] to <u>react to</u>… conventions" isn't restated or demonstrated anywhere in the passage, so this choice must be wrong.

C   Direct Contradiction: This choice will be tempting for some test-takers, because if they don't read too carefully, they'll think this choice would cause the text to say something like "Jemisin ignores the conventions of science fiction and just writes whatever she wants," which kind of sounds like being willing to "thwart expectations and avoid formulaic plots and themes," as the passage describes. But this choice would specifically say that she "declines to <u>perceive</u> the conventions" of her genre—that she specifically chooses not to even *be aware* of them. We know this choice must be wrong for a couple of reasons. First, the text doesn't restate or demonstrate the idea of Jemisin choosing not to be aware of conventions (or anything else). Second, the text says "she has suggested" her readers like her work "because of this willingness to thwart expectations and avoid formulaic plots and themes." The word "this" tells us that Jemisin is discussing how she "thwart[s] expectations" and "avoid[s] formulaic plots and themes." The fact that she's discussing these ideas, and that she can "thwart" and "avoid" them, means she must be aware of them—that she must "perceive" them—which is the opposite of what this choice would require. So (C) is wrong.

D ✓   Correct: As we saw in our discussion above, the word "this" tells us that the phrase describing the author's "willingness to thwart expectations and avoid formulaic plots and themes" refers back to the way she "declines to (blank) the conventions" of her "genre." This choice would cause the first sentence to say she "declines to <u>conform to</u> the conventions" of her "genre," which restates the idea of "thwart[ing] expectations and avoid[ing] formulaic plots and themes." Both phrases basically say the author doesn't do what people expect authors in her genre to do. Notice especially how "expectations" and "formulaic plots and themes" demonstrate the idea of "conventions." So (D) is right.

Test 3, Module 2, Question 4   **TYPE: TEXT COMPLETION**

The prompt will be a short passage containing a blank. The correct answer will always be restated or demonstrated by key phrases in the provided text. See "What about Text Completion Questions?" on p. 66.

Subjective Phrases to Ignore: "most"

A   Literary Interpretation: We can see that the underlined phrase tells us how Pico feels about the "natural world." The passage mentions "the centrality of nature within his tribe's traditional beliefs" as well as "his distaste for being in wilderness settings himself." This choice would say the poem "portrays his <u>responsiveness to</u> the natural world." Some untrained test-takers might assume that someone whose tribe sees nature as "central[]" to their "beliefs" would be "responsive[]" to nature, but this passage doesn't actually restate or demonstrate the author "respon[ding]" to the natural world, or to anything else. So (A) is wrong. Remember, we can't just pick a choice because the resulting sentence would sound "okay" to some people in real life—we have to pick the choice that restates or demonstrates relevant ideas from the provided text.

B ✓   **Correct:** This choice would cause the text to mention Pico's "<u>ambivalence toward</u> the natural world." This is exactly demonstrated by Pico's two opposite feelings mentioned in the text: the idea that "the natural world" is "central[]" to "his tribe's traditional beliefs," and also that he has a "distaste for being in wilderness settings." This choice is demonstrated in the provided text, so it's right.

C   **Literary Interpretation:** This choice will be tempting for test-takers who focus on the idea that Pico feels "distaste for being in wilderness settings," but feeling "distaste" for something isn't the same as renouncing something, or stating that you're going to give it up forever. In order for this choice to be correct, the text would specifically have to say that Pico pledged never to go in the woods again, or that he has permanently given up on seeing any value in the natural world, or something along those lines—but nothing like this appears in the text. So (C) is wrong.

D   **Literary Interpretation:** This choice is somewhat similar to (C) in that it focuses on one of the two opposing ideas related to Pico's feelings about nature, and it makes a statement that might at first seem similar to what appears in the text, but that actually isn't restated or demonstrated anywhere in that provided text. While (C) is related to Pico's "distaste for being in wilderness settings," this choice will probably attract the attention of untrained test-takers who focus on the idea that "nature" is "central[]" to the "beliefs" of Pico's tribe, and who think that this is basically the same as Pico having "<u>mastery over</u> the natural world," as this choice would require. But having important beliefs related to nature isn't the same as having "mastery over" nature. In order for this choice to be correct, the text would have to say something like "Pico could bend nature to his will" or "there was nothing Pico couldn't do out in the wild." This idea isn't stated or demonstrated anywhere in the text, so (D) is wrong.

Test 3, Module 2, Question 5   TYPE: MAIN IDEA

The prompt asks about the "main purpose" or "main idea" (or some similar phrase) of the text. The correct answer must be directly restated or demonstrated in the passage, with no interpretation. See "What about "Main Idea/Main Purpose" Questions?" on p.69.

Subjective Phrases to Ignore: "best"

A ✓   **Correct:** We know the poem discusses "the repetitiveness inherent in human life" because it mentions how "grey lives reprise their span"—the word "reprise" describes something being repeated over again, and the idea of "lives repris[ing]" restates the idea of "repetitiveness" "in human life." The idea of "repetit[ion]" is also demonstrated by the use of the word "same" twice in the poem, which shows us that something that has happened before is now happening again. The text also demonstrates how life "can be… rewarding," as this choice requires, when it talks about "new roads," "a new beating of the drum," "fresh seeing," and "the new sun," as well as how life can be "challenging" when it mentions "backs bending" and "sad feet… drum[ming]." This choice is demonstrated in the text, so it's right.

B   **Literary Interpretation:** This choice will be tempting for untrained test-takers, because the text does mention "day" and "night," and people doing various activities. But the text never specifies which activities are done at which times, never "question[s]" anything, and never talks about whether anything is "memorable" or not, all of which this choice would require—so (B) is wrong.

C   **Literary Interpretation:** This choice will also be tempting for untrained test-takers, because, as we saw in our discussion of (A), the text does mention ideas related to positive as well as negative experiences in human life, which may seem connected to the ideas of "joy" and "sadness," as mentioned in this choice. But in order for this choice to be correct, the passage would have to refer to the idea that "joy" is "experienced" more than "sadness is," and the passage would *also* have to "refute" that idea. But nothing in the passage even mentions the idea of one emotion being "more common[]" than another, or of anything happening "more commonly" than anything else, which this choice would require. So (C) is wrong. (Some untrained test-takers might try to figure out whether the writer says something happens "more commonly" than something else by counting how many times something gets mentioned, or something like that, but that wouldn't actually tell us how "commonly" something is "experienced," as this choice requires; the text would have to directly state or show that one thing happens more than something else, which it doesn't do.)

D   **Barely Relevant:** The text does discuss some "experiences" that people have, but it doesn't make any distinction between "experiences of individuals" and "experiences of their communities," as this choice would require, so it can't possibly talk about how these separate kinds of experiences relate to one another. So (D) is wrong.

Test 3, Module 2, Question 6   TYPE: MAIN IDEA

The prompt asks about the "main purpose" or "main idea" (or some similar phrase) of the text. The correct answer must be directly restated or demonstrated in the passage, with no interpretation. See "What about "Main Idea/Main Purpose" Questions?" on p.69.

Subjective Phrases to Ignore: "best"

A ✓   **Correct:** We know that the play will "involve only a small number of people" because the intro to the provided text tells us it will be "stag[ed] at home with… friends and family," and Tom says it will be "nothing but a little amusement among ourselves" with "no audience, no publicity." We also know "the play will be inoffensive," as the prompt requires, because the text says it will be "in the elegant written language of some respectable author"—notice how the words "elegant" and "respectable" demonstrate the idea of being "inoffensive." So (A) is right.

B   Confused Relationships: This choice will be tempting for some untrained test-takers who misunderstand the last sentence and think that Tom is saying that the actors will be "chattering in words of [their] own" instead of "in the elegant written language of some respectable author." But Tom is saying that they *will* be speaking in the "language" of the "author," not in "words of [their] own"—and even in the incorrect, opposite interpretation, the text still wouldn't say anything about the play happening in a way that *Tom* didn't intend, as this choice requires; it would say that the actors would be performing the play in a way that the *author* didn't intend, since they would use the words of the actors and not the words of the author (and, again, this isn't even what Tom is saying). Nothing in the text states or demonstrates that Tom "originally" planned to perform the play one way, and then something about that changed—so (B) is wrong.

C   Literary Interpretation: This choice might be tempting for some untrained test-takers who read the passage and assume that "Tom" and his "friends and family" won't do a great job with the play. But this idea isn't stated in the text—simply stating that the play is "a little amusement among ourselves" with "no audience" isn't the same as saying the people involved can't "successfully stage a play," as this choice requires. For all we know, some of these people are professional actors who "successfully stage… play[s]" all the time, but they're just taking a more casual approach to this play; the text doesn't tell us either way, so we don't know—which means (C) must be wrong.

D   Direct Contradiction: This choice is the opposite of what appears in the text, because Tom specifically says "we want no audience, no publicity"—and there is no mention whatsoever of anyone "promot[ing]" the play, as this choice would require. So (D) is wrong.

Test 3, Module 2, Question 7 — TYPE: FUNCTION AND STRUCTURE

The prompt asks about the "function" or "structure" of a part of the text. The correct answer must plainly and accurately describe the relevant text, with no interpretation. See "What about "Function and Structure" Questions?" on p. 70.

Subjective Phrases to Ignore: "best"

A ✓ Correct: The text "presents a claim about Mitchell," as this choice requires, when it says that Mitchell "uses images she creates for her album covers to emphasize ideas expressed in her music." Then it "gives an example supporting that claim" when it talks about the "cover of her album" that was "a striking self-portrait" similar to a Van Gogh painting, and how on that album Mitchell sings about Van Gogh's "legacy," and how she "feels a strong artistic connection to Van Gogh." So the text tells us directly that this painting was an "image[] she create[d] for her album cover[]," and the passage even reinforces that this image "emphasize[s]" an "idea[] expressed in her music" (as the earlier claim states) when it refers to something expressed in a song from the album as "an idea that is reinforced by her imagery on the cover." So the text definitely provides an "example" "supporting" the "claim" that it "presents," just as this choice requires—which means (A) is right.

B   Plausible but not in the Text: Some untrained test-takers will be tempted by this choice, since the text says that Mitchell "feels a strong artistic connection to Van Gogh." But the text certainly never mentions Mitchell "influenc[ing]" any "other artists," as this choice would require—it doesn't even mention any other artists, other than Van Gogh—so (B) is wrong. Remember that we can't pick a choice like this one just because we assume that Mitchell must have "influence[d]" "other artists" in real life; we must always pick an answer choice based specifically on what the text says, and this text never talks about Mitchell influencing anyone.

C   Plausible but not in the Text: This choice is wrong for a few reasons. For one thing, it never "notes" any "difference between" Mitchell and Van Gogh. We might know some differences between these two people in real life, but the text never "notes" any such difference—in order for this idea to be restated or demonstrated in the text, that text would have to say something like "while Mitchell is a musician and painter, Van Gogh focused only on painting" or "Mitchell liked to paint in this one style, while Van Gogh painted in this other style," or something like that. Nothing like that appears in the text, so we can't say the text "notes a difference between them." We can see that the text also never says that there is "a similarity between" the "two artists." It does mention that Mitchell painted something that "closely resembles" a Van Gogh painting, but that's a similarity between two *paintings*, not between two artists. So even though the text does mention some things that are similar to other things, and even though we might know about some differences between people mentioned in the text, that text never actually *says* that Mitchell and Van Gogh are similar to each other, or different from each other, as this choice requires. So (C) is wrong.

D   Off by One or Two Words: This choice will be very tempting for some test-takers, because the text does mention the "title song" of the album *Turbulent Indigo*, and how that song relates to Van Gogh, whose painting inspired the album cover—this is an example of one of the songs from the album "relat[ing] to the album's cover," as this choice requires. But this choice says the text "describes the songs," plural—and the text doesn't do that. The passage only mentions a single song, not multiple songs, as this choice would require. So we can't say the text "describes the songs" on the album, which means (D) is wrong.

The question will ask what the author of one passage would think about some aspect of the other passage. The answer must always be directly stated in the text, with no guessing or assumption from the test-taker. See "What about Paired Passages?" p. 70.

Subjective Phrases to Ignore: "most likely"

A   Literary Interpretation: This choice may be tempting because Text 1 says that a "team reported" something that "support[s] the presence of exoplanets with continental crusts," and some test-takers will interpret that to mean that the idea of "exoplanets with continental crusts" is something new. But just saying that someone found evidence to support something isn't the same as saying that, before this evidence, people widely believed that thing didn't exist, as this choice would require. Neither text specifically mentions the idea of people "widely believ[ing]" anything, as this choice would require, so (A) can't be right.

B   Literary Interpretation: In order to restate or demonstrate the idea of something being "premature," the text would have to say that it happened too early, or that researchers should wait until more data is available, or that there hasn't been enough time to conclude something, or something else along those lines—but Text 2 doesn't mention any such idea, so we can't say that anyone in Text 2 would call anything "premature." That text also doesn't say that "trying to determine what kinds of crusts white dwarf exoplanets had" is something that "researchers have only just begun," as this choice would require. For either reason, (B) is wrong.

C ✓ Correct: Text 1 describes a study whose findings "support the presence of exoplanets with continental crusts similar to Earth's." Text 2 mentions "studies" that "have concluded that certain exoplanets had continental crusts"—we know that the study from Text 1 made this conclusion, so what Text 2 says about those studies tells us how "Putirka and Xu" feel about "the conclusion presented in Text 1," as the prompt requires. Text 2 says that Putirka and Xu "argue" that "those studies unduly emphasize" certain things (note that if you think a study does something "unduly," this demonstrates the idea that you find the results of that study "questionable," as this choice requires). Text 2 goes on to say that the studies "don't adequately account for different minerals made up of various ratios of" certain elements; the idea of not "adequately account[ing]" for something restates the idea of "an incomplete consideration," as this choice requires. Finally, the "different minerals made up of various ratios of those elements" as well as "the possibility of rock types not found on Earth that contain those minerals" mentioned in Text 2 are the "potential sources of the elements detected in white dwarf atmospheres," as this choice requires. So every part of (C) is demonstrated in the text, which means (C) is right.

D   Barely Relevant: This choice will be tempting for test-takers who notice the word "puzzling," and who understand that Putirka and Xu from Text 2 disagree with "the conclusion presented in Text 1," but who don't read carefully enough to understand why. This choice talks about how it's "unusual to successfully detect lithium and sodium," but Text 2 never says that it's "unusual" to "detect" those elements "successfully"—in fact, Text 2 never even mentions sodium at all. Instead, Text 2 questions the conclusion that the presence of "lithium and other individual elements" means those elements come from "the types of rock found on Earth," when they might come from "rock types not found on Earth that contain those minerals." So (D) is wrong.

The prompt asks for information from the passage. The answer must be restated or demonstrated by specific phrases in the text. See "What about General Passage Questions?" on p. 69.

A ✓ Correct: The prompt asks why "ecologists" are "worried about Pando," and the text says that "ecologists are worried that its growth is declining in part because of grazing by animals." The phrase "its growth is declining" from the text exactly restates "it isn't growing at the same rate it used to" from this choice, so (A) is right.

B   Direct Contradiction: This will be very tempting for test-takers who misread the provided text and end up making a couple of assumptions. The text says that fences might "prevent deer from eating young trees," so some test-takers will think it's okay to say that the problem is that Pando "isn't producing young trees anymore," as this choice would require, since the text describes something that is interfering with the growth of young trees. But, for one thing, the idea of "deer... eating young trees" doesn't mean that deer are eating *all* the "young trees." Maybe the deer are eating *some* young trees, while other young trees are not getting eaten—so deer could "eat[] young trees" without preventing Pando from still growing some young trees successfully. Beyond that, if we know deer are "eating young trees," that means Pando must still be producing them—they're just getting eaten. This detail alone tells us that this choice is the *opposite* of the truth. Some test-takers will assume that young trees getting eaten is basically the same as not producing young trees, but as trained test-takers, we know that this is exactly the kind of distinction we need to be aware of! With all of this in mind, we know (B) is wrong.

C   Confused Relationships: The text does mention "fences," which will make this choice tempting for some test-takers—but the "fences" are mentioned in the passage as a way to "prevent deer from eating young trees." The text never says that fences are "block[ing]" Pando in any way, so (C) is wrong.

D   Plausible but not in the Text: This is a great example of a choice that will be tempting for untrained test-takers who make a simple assumption—those test-takers will notice that Pando has "47,000... trees that all share a single root system," and think that this sounds like too many trees for one "root system." Based on that assumption (which isn't actually stated anywhere in the text), they'll think it's okay to say this "root system can't support many more new trees," as this choice requires. But that idea doesn't actually appear in the text, and we know that we can only pick answer choices based on what actually appears in the text—so (D) is wrong.

Test 3, Module 2, Question 10   TYPE: GENERAL PASSAGE

The prompt asks for information from the passage. The answer must be restated or demonstrated by specific phrases in the text. See "What about General Passage Questions?" on p. 69.

A   Off by One or Two Words: This question asks why the "discovery" was "significant." The text says that "Bo Wang and others have identified.. remains of... *Terropterus xiushanensis*," the animal mentioned in the prompt. The text describes this event as "a discovery that expands our understanding of the geographical distribution of mixopterids," and it tells us that this "new mixopterid species" lived "over 400 million years ago" on a paleocontinent named "Gondwana." This choice says the fossil is the "first evidence... that mixopterids lived more than 400 million years ago." The text *does* say that the fossil was of a "mixopterid species... that lived over 400 million years ago," but it doesn't say this was the *first* evidence of "mixopterids" doing that, as this choice would require. So (A) is wrong. Notice that just because this was a fossil of a new mixopterid species, and just because that species lived over 400 million years ago, that's not the same as saying this was the *first evidence* of any such species living at that time. For all we know, scientists have already discovered other mixopterid species from that time, and this is just one more.

B   Confused Relationships: The text does tell us that mixopterids were "related to modern arachnids and horseshoe crabs," but it doesn't say that the discovery mentioned in the prompt impacted that knowledge, and it doesn't describe mixopterids being seen as more or less "closely related to modern arachnids and horseshoe crabs" at different times. So (B) is wrong.

C   Plausible but not in the Text: The text doesn't mention the idea of "the evolution of mixopterids," or the evolution of anything, in any way. It also doesn't tell us that any "timeline" was made "more accurate," as this choice would require. This choice will be tempting for test-takers who assume that discovering a new mixopterid species will necessarily impact scientists' understanding of the evolution of mixopterids, and also improve any related "timeline." But neither idea is stated in the text, so we know that (C) is wrong.

D ✓ Correct: The text mentions that "the only existing fossil evidence of mixopterid[s]... came from... the paleocontinent of Laurussia." Then it says there was "a discovery that expand[ed] our understanding of the geographical distribution of mixopterids," and that discovery was "a new mixopterid species" found "on the paleocontinent of Gondwana." So the text directly states that the "discovery of the *Terropterus xiushanensis* fossil" was "significant," as the prompt requires, because it "expand[ed] our understanding of the geographical distribution of mixopterids," since it was found on "Gondwana," a different paleocontinent from "Laurussia," where all previous known species had been discovered. This exactly demonstrates the idea in choice (D) that "the fossil constitutes the first evidence... that mixopterids existed outside... Laurussia", so (D) is correct.

Test 3, Module 2, Question 11   TYPE: IF TRUE

The passage presents some claim or hypothesis. The prompt typically asks us to choose the "finding" that, "if true," would support or weaken the argument. Supporting statements will demonstrate the idea in the claim, and weakening statements will demonstrate the opposite of the idea in the claim. See "What about "If True" Questions?" on p. 71.

Subjective Phrases to Ignore: "most strongly"

A ✓ Correct: We need to pick the choice that "support[s] the scholar's claim." When we look at the passage, we can see that the "scholar asserts that one of Morrison's likely aims... was to strengthen the presence of Black writers" at "Random House[]" when she was an editor there. The text tells us that Morrison was an editor at Random House "from 1967 to 1983." This choice says that "the percentage of authors published by Random House who were Black rose in the early 1970s and stabilized throughout the decade." So the text tells us that Morrison was an editor at Random House throughout the 1970s, and this choice says that during this time, the percentage of Black authors "published by Random House... rose." The idea that the percentage of Black authors published by Random House rose while Morrison was an editor there demonstrates the idea of her "strengthen[ing] the presence of Black writers on the list of Random House's published authors," just as the "claim" requires. Notice that "the percentage of authors published by Random House who were Black rose" from this choice restates the idea of "strengthen[ing] the presence of Black writers on the list of Random House's published authors" from the passage. So (A) is right.

B   Plausible but not in the Text: This choice talks about how Morrison "influence[d]" other authors," but it doesn't mention anything about Random House, or Black writers getting published by Random House, or Morrison's work as an editor. Some untrained test-takers will pick this choice because it sounds like a statement that might be true in real life, but it's not related to the "claim" in the passage, so (B) can't be right.

C   **Barely Relevant:** This choice mentions Morrison writing novels, and it mentions a year that appeared in the passage (1983)—but, like (B), this choice doesn't mention Random House, or Black writers getting published by Random House, or Morrison's work as an editor, so it has no bearing on the "claim" we need to support. So (C) is wrong.

D   **Barely Relevant:** This choice does talk about Morrison's time at Random House, but it doesn't mention Black writers at all, or their "presence... on the list of Random House's published authors." So the statement in (D) isn't related to the "claim," which means it must be wrong.

Test 3, Module 2, Question 12   TYPE: QUOTATION

The prompt will make a claim about a literary work, then ask which quotation "illustrates the claim." The right answer will plainly demonstrate the ideas in the provided claim. See "What about Quotation Questions?" on p. 70.

Subjective Phrases to Ignore: "most effectively"

A ✓   **Correct:** The prompt asks for the quote that "illustrates the claim." When we read the passage, we can see that the claim is "that a society's spiritual well-being depends on the character of its literary culture." This choice demonstrates the idea that "the character of its literary culture" is what a "society's well-being depends on" when it says that "poetry... fortifies or brings anguish," and that it "shores up or demolishes souls" and "gives or robs men of faith and vigor," and finally when it says that "literature gives [a people] the desire and strength for life." All of these things ("souls," "faith," "vigor," "strength for life," etc.) relate to "a society's spiritual well-being," and the "or" statements (that is, the repeated mention of one good outcome and one bad outcome) demonstrate the idea that this well-being "depends on" the "poetry" and "literature" of that society—that is, "on the character" of that society's "literary culture." So (A) is correct.

B   **Literary Interpretation:** This choice does talk about the importance of literature, but it doesn't mention anything about "spiritual well-being," so (B) can't be correct.

C   **Literary Interpretation:** This choice will be tempting, because it does seem to discuss "a society's spiritual well-being," as mentioned in the prompt. But this choice doesn't actually mention literature, or books, or poetry, or anything at all related to reading, so (C) can't be right. A lot of untrained test-takers will pick this choice because they assume, based on the passage and the other choices, that the writer must be talking about "literature." But we have to answer based on what actually appears in each answer choice, and this choice doesn't mention anything related to literature in any way.

D   **Confused Relationships:** In this choice, the author describes a "hardworking and satisfied nation," and tells his readers to "listen to Walt Whitman." Then he connects Walt Whitman's work with ideas like "majesty," "tolerance," "justice," and "joy." This might sound like stating that "a society's spiritual well-being depends on the character of its literary culture," as the passage requires—but this choice is missing a few key ideas. For one, it describes a "nation" as "hardworking and satisfied"; this might seem like a commentary on that "society's spiritual well-being," but it doesn't say that the nation has these qualities *because* of anything Walt Whitman or any other writer did, as the phrase "depends on" from the claim would require. For another, the text says that "majesty," "tolerance," "justice," and "joy" are things that Whitman is "exalt[ed]... to." In other words, these are ways that *Whitman* is elevated, not any "society." Finally, this choice talks about a specific "nation" (which we know from the phrase "this... nation") and a specific person ("Walt Whitman"), but the claim talks about how literature impacts "a society"—that is, societies and cultures in general, not just one person or one country (notice that the phrase "a people" in the correct answer, (A), leaves the discussion open to any people, while the phrase "this... nation" refers to a specific nation). For any of these reasons, (D) is wrong.

Test 3, Module 2, Question 13   TYPE: DATA

The passage includes a figure. The question asks for the choice that uses data from the figure to accomplish a certain goal. The right answer will describe the data accurately and plainly accomplish the goal. See "What about "Data" Questions?" on p. 69.

Subjective Phrases to Ignore: "best"

A   **Direct Contradiction:** The prompt asks for the data that "support[s] Barrett and Rayfield's suggestion." When we read the passage, we can see that the "suggestion" is that "an estimate of dinosaur bite force may be significantly influenced by the methodology used in generating that estimate." This choice incorrectly describes the data, so we know it must be wrong—it says that "body-mass scaling... produced the lowest estimated maximum bite force," when in fact it produced the *highest* estimated maximum bite force, at 235,000 newtons. It also says that "muscular and skeletal modeling... produced the highest estimated maximum," when in fact it produced the second highest estimated maximum bite force, at 63,000 newtons. Again, this means (A) must be wrong.

B   Barely Relevant: This choice accurately describes the data, but it doesn't relate to the "suggestion" mentioned in the prompt. That "suggestion" was that the "methodology used" to "generat[e]" an "estimate" "significantly influence[s]" that estimate, but this choice only discusses one type of methodology. We can't evaluate whether using different methodologies influences estimates of bite force by only considering one methodology—so (B) must be wrong.

C ✓ Correct: As we saw in our discussion above, the "suggestion" we need to "support" says that the "methodology used" to "generat[e]" an "estimate" "significantly influence[s]" that estimate. This choice talks about how "bite force estimates produced by Bates and Falkingham and by Cost et al." were "similar to each other." When we check the table, we can see that these two groups, who got "similar" results, used the same method: "muscular and skeletal modeling." This choice goes on to point out that the results "produced by Meers and by Gignac and Erickson each differed substantially from any other estimate." When we check the table, we can see that Meers was the only one who used "body-mass scaling," while Gignac and Erickson were the only ones who used a different method, "tooth-bone interaction analysis." The idea that groups using the same method got results that "were similar to each other" while groups that used different methods got "substantially" "differe[nt]" estimates demonstrates the idea from the "suggestion" in the passage that "estimate[s] of dinosaur bite force may be significantly influenced by the methodology used." This "support[s]" the "suggestion," as the passage and prompt require. So (C) is right.

D   Direct Contradiction: This choice does the *opposite* of what the prompt requires, because the "suggestion" that the prompt asks us to "support" is that "estimate[s] of dinosaur bite force may be significantly influenced by the methodology used in generating that estimate"—but this choice points out a difference between results found by two different groups using the "same method," as this choice specifies, and the table confirms. Some test-takers will point out that the difference is fairly small relative to some other differences between results we can see in the table; this is true, but even so, this choice can't "support" the "suggestion" about differences in results when using different methods, because it only talks about the results of one method, as we saw in our discussion of (B). So with all this in mind, we know (D) is wrong.

Test 3, Module 2, Question 14   TYPE: DATA

The passage includes a figure. The question asks for the choice that uses data from the figure to accomplish a certain goal. The right answer will describe the data accurately and plainly accomplish the goal. See "What about "Data" Questions?" on p. 69.

Subjective Phrases to Ignore: "most effectively"

A ✓ Correct: The prompt asks for the choice that "support[s] the research team's conclusion." When we read the passage, we can see that this "conclusion" is that "tools made with seafloor shells" "were likely more challenging to obtain." When we check this choice against the table and the "conclusion," we can see the leftmost column is labeled "depth of tools found below surface in cave." For each depth in that column, the number of "clamshells that Neanderthals collected from the beach," as represented in the middle column, is larger than the number of "clamshells that Neanderthals harvested from the seafloor," as represented in the rightmost column. This choice says that this data "suggests that shells were easier to collect from the beach than to harvest from the seafloor"—this is accurate, since Neanderthals consistently "collected" more clamshells "from the beach" than they did "from the seafloor." The idea in this choice that "shells were easier to collect from the beach than to harvest from the seafloor" directly restates the "conclusion" we want to "support" that "tools made with seafloor shells" "were likely more challenging to obtain." So we know that (A) must be correct.

B   Barely Relevant: This choice accurately describes the provided data, and it makes a statement that sounds like it could be true in real life. But this statement isn't related to the "conclusion" that we need to "support," because that "conclusion" compares the "challeng[e]" in "obtain[ing]" tools from the "beach" as opposed to the "seafloor," and this choice doesn't make any distinction between shells from these two different places. So (B) is wrong.

C   Direct Contradiction: This choice would provide an alternate interpretation of the relevant data, saying that more clamshells were "collected from the beach," not because doing so was less "challenging," but because Neanderthals "preferred... clamshells from the beach," since they were more "durab[le]." But that contradicts the statement from the passage that "Neanderthals prized the tools made with seafloor shells" because they were "sturdy," while those on the beach were "thin"—and even if it didn't, as stated, this choice would *contradict* the conclusion (the one that the prompt asked us to support) that "tools made with seafloor shells" "were likely more challenging to obtain" by providing a different reason that more were collected "from the beach" than "from the seafloor" (again, that different reason is "that Neanderthals preferred clamshells from the beach because of their durability"). For either reason, (C) is wrong.

D   Barely Relevant: Any information related to "the size of clam populations chang[ing] over time" doesn't impact the "conclusion" in the passage, because nothing indicates that a difference in "the size of clam populations" is related to how "challenging" it is "to obtain" shells from the beach, as opposed to the seafloor, which is what the conclusion we need to support talks about. So (D) is wrong. This is a great example of a statement that some untrained test-takers will use as a jumping-off point to make some assumptions about a possible connection between "clam populations" and the conclusion in the prompt—but no such conclusion is spelled out on the page, so this choice can't be right.

The passage includes a figure. The question asks for the choice that uses data from the figure to accomplish a certain goal. The right answer will describe the data accurately and plainly accomplish the goal. See "What about "Data" Questions?" on p. 69.

Subjective Phrases to Ignore: "best"

A   **Plausible but not in the Text:** The prompt asks for the choice that "support[s]" the "hypothesis." When we check the passage, we can see that the "hypothesis" is that "because Arctic ground squirrels hibernate alone, they would likely exhibit longer bouts of torpor and shorter arousal episodes than Alaska marmots." This choice inaccurately describes the data, because it says that "the Alaska marmots' arousal episodes lasted for days," which isn't true: in the column labeled "Alaska marmots," we can see that the bottom cell, which tells us the "duration per episode," says that the average duration of an "arousal episode" was 21.2 hours, which is less than one day—which can't be called "days," as this choice says. This choice will be very tempting, for a couple of reasons. For one, the idea of the marmots having longer "arousal episodes" than the squirrels *does* "support the researcher's hypothesis," as the prompt requires, and the table *does* show that the marmots have longer "arousal episodes." Also, it would be easy for an untrained test-taker who wasn't reading carefully enough to misread the graph and think that the 11 in the table, which indicates the *number* of "arousal episodes," was actually the *length* of those episodes in days, since the data point right above it is measured in days. But this isn't the case, and as stated earlier, we know (A) must be wrong because it makes an inaccurate statement about the data. See the note below for more on reading this table.

B   **Barely Relevant:** This choice accurately describes the data, but it doesn't support the hypothesis—that hypothesis talked about aspects of marmot and squirrel behavior that were different, but this choice describes something about their behavior that was the same—that they "both maintained torpor for several consecutive days per bout." So (B) can't be right.

C ✓   **Correct:** This choice accurately describes the data, because it says that "marmots had shorter torpor bouts" than squirrels, and we can see in the table that the "duration per bout" row shows that marmots had an average duration of 13.81 days per torpor bout, which is shorter than the 16.77 days per torpor bout that squirrels experienced, on average. This choice also says that marmots had "longer arousal episodes" than the squirrels; we can see that this is true, because the "duration per episode" row shows that marmots had an average duration of 21.2 hours per arousal episode, which is longer than the 14.2 hours per arousal episode that squirrels experienced, on average. The statement from this choice that says "marmots had shorter torpor bouts" exactly restates the idea from the hypothesis that squirrels "would likely exhibit longer bouts of torpor," and the part of this choice that says marmots had "longer arousal episodes" than the squirrels had exactly restates the idea from the hypothesis that the squirrels would have "shorter arousal episodes" than the marmots. So (C) supports the hypothesis, and (C) is correct.

D   **Barely Relevant:** This choice describes the data accurately, but it doesn't impact the "hypothesis" that we need to "support." That hypothesis talks about a difference between marmot and squirrel behavior, but this choice only talks about what marmots do—so it can't possibly impact that hypothesis. So (D) is wrong.

Note   This is an excellent example of an SAT Reading question made *much* more difficult by unusual words and phrases, and by a difficult-to-read table. First, the similar multi-word noun phrases "Alaska marmots" and "Arctic ground squirrels" can make it hard to keep straight which animal we're talking about—imagine how much easier this would be if the animals were just "cats" and "dogs," or another pair of animal names that were familiar, concise, and distinct from each other. Next, the frequent repetition in the answer choices of the phrases "torpor bout" and "arousal episode" can be extremely challenging to sort through, especially combined with the repeated comparisons of things being longer or shorter than other things. Finally, the table is strange—you have a row listing the numbers of "torpor bouts" experienced by the animals, and then a row below that listing their average duration, measured in days—then below that is a row for "arousal episodes," below which is *their* average duration, measured in *hours*. It would be very easy for someone to confuse the *number* of bouts or episodes with the *duration* of each of those events, and it would also be easy to get confused about which numbers are measured in hours as opposed to days. But the big takeaway here is that if we know how the test works, we can see through all of these little difficulties by expecting them ahead of time, and knowing that this is just an example of the College Board trying to distract us from the fact that the right answer must always appear plainly on the page, and that if we read carefully, we can find it. Note, for example, that as weird as the table is, the row labeled "duration per bout" makes it clear that it's talking about the "torpor bouts," since the word "bout" is only used in conjunction with "torpor," while the row labeled "duration per episode" makes it clear that it's talking about the "arousal episodes," since the word "episode" is only used in conjunction with "arousal." So no matter what unusual words, phrases, or figures we encounter, if we stick to our training and read carefully, we know that we can find the correct answer with certainty.

The passage ends with a blank, and the answer choices are relatively long phrases. The right answer will restate or demonstrate an idea in the provided text. See "What about "Most Logically Completes" Questions?" on p. 68.

Subjective Phrases to Ignore: "most"

A   Confused Relationships: The text tells us that "the protocol" "ensur[es]" that Indigenous communities are compensated when their agricultural resources and knowledge... are utilized by agricultural corporations," and that one shortcoming of this agreement is that "corporations" can "insist that their agreements with communities... remain confidential." The sentence with the blank says that "the protocol may have the unintended effect of (blank)." This choice mentions "diminishing the monetary reward" corporations might get from these agreements. This choice has a couple of problems—for one thing, the text doesn't mention anything related to the idea of any "monetary reward" "diminishing." For another, the text tells us that the purpose of the protocol is to "ensure[e] that Indigenous communities are compensated," and it says nothing about worrying whether "corporations" get enough of a "monetary reward," as this choice states—in other words, the protocol has no "inten[tion]" related to "corporations" getting any certain amount of money, so a "diminish[ed]... monetary reward" for "corporations" can't be called an "unintended effect." So (A) is wrong—although this choice will be tempting for test-takers who don't read carefully enough, and think that this choice is talking about the *Indigenous communities* getting "diminishing... reward[s]," and not the "corporations."

B   Barely Relevant: The text *does* mention "research that corporations conduct," as this choice requires, but it doesn't restate or demonstrate the idea of anything "limit[ing]" that "research." This is the kind of choice that might be appealing to untrained test-takers who try to generate an argument related to the prompt based on their own assumptions, but we know that we have to pick a choice based on what appears in the text, and nothing in the text relates to the idea of "limiting... research." So (B) is wrong.

C ✓   Correct: The passage tells us that the purpose of "the protocol" is to "ensur[e]" that Indigenous communities are compensated when their agricultural resources and knowledge... are utilized by agricultural corporations." Then the passage tells us that one "shortcoming" of the protocol is that companies can make these arrangements "confidential." The next sentence is the one that contains the blank, and it starts with the word "therefore"—this word tells us that what this last sentence says must be the logical result of the previous sentence that mentions that the "agreements... remain confidential." So the blank in this last sentence has to describe an "unintended effect" of the "the protocol" that results from the "agreements" being "confidential." As trained test-takers, we know that an "unintended effect" of "the protocol" must be something that goes against the goals of "the protocol," as stated in the passage—and as we just discussed, we know that it must be the result of the agreements being "confidential." This choice satisfies all these requirements, because "preventing independent observers from determining" something demonstrates what happens when something is "confidential," and the idea that those observers can't tell "whether the agreements guarantee equitable compensation for Indigenous communities" demonstrates the idea of an "unintended effect" of "the protocol": the passage tells us that the point of the protocol was to make sure that "Indigenous communities are compensated," but the "confidential" nature of the agreements under the protocol makes it hard to tell whether those "Indigenous communities" are actually getting "equitable compensation." So this choice restates or demonstrates the relevant ideas from the passage, and relates those ideas to each other the same way the passage does. That means (C) is right.

D   Confused Relationships: This choice could be tempting, because it mentions ideas from the passage like "Indigenous communities," and "methods for harvesting plants," and "corporate partners." But this choice relates those ideas to one another in ways that don't appear in the provided text: the passage never discusses "Indigenous communities... learning new methods" for agriculture, or learning anything "from their corporate partners," as this choice would require. So (D) can't be right.

The passage ends with a blank, and the answer choices are relatively long phrases. The right answer will restate or demonstrate an idea in the provided text. See "What about "Most Logically Completes" Questions?" on p. 68.

Subjective Phrases to Ignore: "most"

A   Literary Interpretation: This choice will be tempting for test-takers who notice the phrase "Native Hawaiians and other Indigenous peoples were cultivating the plant centuries before..." But that sentence doesn't say they were "cultivating the plant centuries before" people in South America were! It says they were "cultivating the plant centuries before seafaring first occurred" between "them" and "South America." The passage doesn't actually give us any concrete information about when the plant was first cultivated in either Polynesia or South America; it does say people have only been in Polynesia for three thousand years, so the plant wasn't cultivated in Polynesia more than three thousand years ago, but it doesn't provide any similar timeline for South America that could be the basis for a comparison. (Notice that the text says "the domestic sweet potato... descends from a wild plant native to South America." Some test-takers might take this to mean definitively that the plant was cultivated in South America first, which would allow us to eliminate this choice for that reason—but in case you saw the phrase and wondered why I didn't bring it up, I wanted to point out that the "wild" ancestor of the plant in question being "native to South America" doesn't mean the plant itself must have first been cultivated—that is, grown by humans—there. But as discussed, we can eliminate (A) anyway because the text doesn't provide a basis for the comparison in this choice.) So (A) is wrong.

B   Direct Contradiction: This choice might seem reasonable to a test-taker who focuses on the idea from the text that "Polynesia was peopled only in the last three thousand years." Based on this idea, we might assume that "Polynesian peoples" must have "acquired the sweet potato from South American peoples" within that time frame. But this assumption contradicts another statement in the text that says "Native Hawaiians and other Indigenous peoples were cultivating the plant centuries before seafaring first occurred" between Polynesia and South America—that is, people in Polynesia were growing the plant before they had contact with the people of South America, so they couldn't have "acquired" it from them, as this choice states. So (B) is wrong.

C ✓   Correct: The passage tells us that "Native Hawaiians and other Indigenous peoples were cultivating the plant centuries before seafaring first occurred" between Polynesia and South America. In other words, they cultivated the plant before people were able to travel between these two locations. The text also says that "Polynesian varieties" of the plant "diverged from South American ones over 100,000 years ago," and that "Polynesia was peopled only in the last three thousand years." So we know that Polynesian varieties of the plant "diverged from South American ones" before people even lived in Polynesia, and we know that people couldn't have carried the plant from one place to the other. All of this demonstrates the idea that "human activity likely played no role in the introduction of the sweet potato in Polynesia," just as this choice requires. So (C) is right.

D   Direct Contradiction: This choice might be tempting for test-takers who focus on the first sentence of the passage, which says "the domestic sweet potato... descends from a wild plant native to South America." But this choice actually *contradicts* that statement by saying "Polynesian sweet potato varieties likely descend from a single South American variety that was *domesticated* [emphasis added], not wild." This choice might also be tempting for test-takers who don't read carefully and think that the text says people in South America domesticated sweet potatoes and then brought them to Polynesia—but as we saw in our discussion of the other choices, that's not the case. So (D) can't be correct.

Test 3, Module 2, Question 18   TYPE: SAT WRITING

- Vertical Scan Results: Each choice is a different form of the same verb.
- Vertical Scan Notes: We need to decide whether we need a past, present, or future form of the verb "to reach."
- Key Features in Surrounding Text: The other conjugated verbs in the sentence are "travel" and "are," which are in the present tense. Nothing in the text indicates that the action in the blank happens in a different time frame from those verbs.

Concepts in the question:

- Parallelism: The surrounding text includes phrasing and/or grammatical structures that should be mirrored by what appears in the blank. (See page 93.)
- Verb Tense/Conjugation: Choices include different forms of the same verb. Look at the surrounding text to find the verb's subject. Also, look for other clues that could indicate the proper tense or form of the verb in the blank. (See page 77.)

ANSWER CHOICE ANALYSIS

A   Incorrect: This is a future tense form of the verb, but none of the other verb tenses in the text are in the future, and nothing in the text indicates that the action in the blank should be happening in the future. So (A) is wrong.

B ✓   Correct: This is a present-tense verb form, which matches the tense of the other verbs in the sentence ("travel" and "are"), and is appropriately conjugated for its plural noun subject "they." So (B) is correct.

C   Incorrect: This is a past tense form of the verb, but none of the other verb forms in the text are in the past, and nothing in the text indicates that the action in the blank should be happening in the past. So (A) is wrong.

D   Incorrect: As we saw in our discussion of (B), the correct answer should be a present tense verb form, and this choice *is* in the present tense—but it doesn't match "travel" or "are." No other action in the sentence is expressed with a combination of a helping verb like "are" and a noun form ending in "-ing" like "reaching"—but there *is* another verb form like the correct answer (B), "reach," which is "travel," as discussed above. Choice (B) copies a structure already present in the provided text, so that choice is right, but (D) doesn't—so (D) is wrong.

Test 3, Module 2, Question 19   TYPE: SAT WRITING

- Vertical Scan Results: Each choice is a different form of the same verb.
- Vertical Scan Notes: We have to decide whether an infinitive, participle, or conjugated form of the verb "to explain" is appropriate.

- Key Features in Surrounding Text: The phrase in the blank is the action being done by the subject noun "study," and it's the main verb in the independent clause "a recent study (blank) why"—remember from our training that when a colon appears in an SAT Writing question, an independent clause must appear before that colon. So the verb in the blank should be conjugated to agree with the singular noun "study."

Concepts in the question:

- Colons: A colon can only be placed after a group of words that could be a sentence on its own. Everything after the colon must be a demonstration or example of the idea before the colon. (See page 85.)
- Independent and Dependent Clauses: Choices would create and/or join clauses. An independent clause can stand on its own as a sentence, and a dependent clause can't. Remember rules for joining clauses related to periods, semi-colons, colons, commas, and conjunctions. (See page 82.)
- Verb Tense/Conjugation: Choices include different forms of the same verb. Look at the surrounding text to find the verb's subject. Also, look for other clues that could indicate the proper tense or form of the verb in the blank. (See page 77.)

ANSWER CHOICE ANALYSIS

A ✓ Correct: This is the only answer choice that's conjugated to agree with the singular subject "study," resulting in an acceptable independent clause before the colon—so it's correct.

B Incorrect: As we saw in our analysis above, the right answer needs to be a singular verb form to match the singular subject "study," but this choice is a participle that isn't conjugated at all. So (B) is wrong.

C Incorrect: This choice has the same basic problem as (B), and is wrong for the same reason.

D Incorrect: As we saw in our analysis above, the right answer needs to be a conjugated singular verb form to match the singular subject "study," but this choice is an infinitive that isn't conjugated at all. So (D) is wrong.

Test 3, Module 2, Question 20   **TYPE: SAT WRITING**

- Vertical Scan Results: Each choice is a different form of the same verb.
- Vertical Scan Notes: We have to decide whether a plural, singular, past, or present tense form of "to outline" is appropriate.
- Key Features in Surrounding Text: The subject of the verb in the blank is "that," which refers to "document"—so we need to choose a singular verb form to agree with "document."

Concepts in the question:

- Verb Tense/Conjugation: Choices include different forms of the same verb. Look at the surrounding text to find the verb's subject. Also, look for other clues that could indicate the proper tense or form of the verb in the blank. (See page 77.)

ANSWER CHOICE ANALYSIS

A Incorrect: As we saw in our analysis above, the word in the blank needs to be a singular verb form to agree with the singular subject "document." But this is a plural verb form, so we know (A) is wrong.

B Incorrect: This is a plural verb form like (A), and is wrong for the same reason.

C ✓ Correct: As we saw in our analysis above, the word in the blank needs to be a singular verb form to agree with the singular subject "document." This choice is the only singular verb form, so it's the right answer.

D Incorrect: This is a plural verb form like (A) and (B), and is wrong for the same reason.

Test 3, Module 2, Question 21   **TYPE: SAT WRITING**

- Vertical Scan Results: Each choice is the same two words with different punctuation between them.
- Vertical Scan Notes: We need to decide whether a colon, period, semi-colon, or comma should appear between "decade" and "while."
- Key Features in Surrounding Text: "For instance... decade" can stand on its own as a sentence. "The rougheye... centuries" is an independent clause that can stand on its own as a sentence, but the word "while" at the beginning turns it into a dependent clause. So the spot in the blank where the punctuation goes separates an independent clause from a dependent clause.

Concepts in the question:

- Colons: A colon can only be placed after a group of words that could be a sentence on its own. Everything after the colon must be a demonstration or example of the idea before the colon. (See page 85.)

- **Commas:** Commas can be used between clauses, to form comma sandwiches, in a list of 3 or more items, and before reported speech. They can't appear for no reason. Review the training for the relevant details. (See page 86.)
- **Independent and Dependent Clauses:** Choices would create and/or join clauses. An independent clause can stand on its own as a sentence, and a dependent clause can't. Remember rules for joining clauses related to periods, semi-colons, colons, commas, and conjunctions. (See page 82.)
- **Semicolons:** Semicolons can be used to separate two sets of words that could each stand on their own as complete sentences, or to separate items in a complex list. (See page 86.)

ANSWER CHOICE ANALYSIS

A   **Incorrect:** This choice would result in a colon followed by something that doesn't illustrate or exemplify the statement made in the independent clause before the colon, which isn't acceptable on the SAT. So (A) is wrong.

B   **Incorrect:** This choice would separate an independent clause from a dependent clause with a period, which isn't acceptable on the SAT, because a dependent clause can't stand on its own as a sentence. So (B) is wrong.

C   **Incorrect:** This choice would separate an independent clause from a dependent clause with a semi-colon, which isn't acceptable on the SAT, because a semi-colon separates two groups of words that can each stand on their own as a sentence, and a dependent clause can't stand on its own as a sentence. (We can also use semi-colons in complex lists, but the provided text doesn't contain any lists.) So (C) is wrong.

D ✓   **Correct:** Without a comma, the sentence would say that the "calico rockfish... can survive for a little over a decade" *during the time that* "the rougheye rockfish... boasts a maximum life span of about two centuries." In other words, it would describe "the rougheye rockfish" in the process of "boast[ing] a maximum life span of about two centuries," and "while" that fish is "boast[ing]," the "calico rockfish" is in the process of "surviv[ing] for a little over a decade." This doesn't make any sense, and it also fails to provide the sentence with a clear example after the phrase "for instance" of "the life spans of rockfish vary[ing] greatly by species." With the comma added, as we see in this choice, it's clear that the comma and "while," together, separate these two ideas and express the difference between them—that one fish lives for a certain amount of time, and the other lives for a much longer time, which is an example of "the life spans of rockfish vary[ing] greatly by species," as the phrase "for instance" requires. So (D) is right. See the note below for more.

Note   The explanation for the right answer in this question is a little on the nitpicky side, even for an SAT question—but when we focus on all the wrong answer choices, we see that we can eliminate them fairly easily, as long as we're familiar with the SAT Writing Toolbox. Colons, periods, and semi-colons have limited and specific uses in SAT Writing questions, and we can see that none of those uses applies in this question. So even if we felt a little unclear on why, precisely, the comma in choice (D) was acceptable in the provided text, we should have been able to pick that choice after eliminating the other three. If you're able to apply your training and feel confident about eliminating all the wrong answer choices, then you don't have to be totally certain why the right answer is right—remember this on test day.

Test 3, Module 2, Question 22   TYPE: SAT WRITING

- **Vertical Scan Results:** Each choice is the same series of words with commas appearing in different places.
- **Vertical Scan Notes:** We have to decide whether commas should appear after "energy," "collected," "panels," and/or "day."
- **Key Features in Surrounding Text:** "Powered with <u>energy collected by solar panels during the day</u>" is a participial phrase that describes "the blinking LEDs," which is the first noun phrase in this sentence's independent clause—so that participial phrase should be set off from the independent clause that contains "the blinking LEDs" with a comma. The phrase "collected by solar panels" describes the "energy," and no comma should appear between this phrase and the word it describes. The phrase "during the day" tells when the "energy" is "collected," and, again, no comma should appear between "during the day" and the action it modifies.

Concepts in the question:

- **Avoid Dangling Participles:** When a phrase starting with an -ing/-ed/-en word is joined to the main sentence by a comma, the first noun phrase in the independent clause of that sentence is described by the -ing/-ed/-en word. (See page 90.)
- **Commas:** Commas can be used between clauses, to form comma sandwiches, in a list of 3 or more items, and before reported speech. They can't appear for no reason. Review the training for the relevant details. (See page 86.)

ANSWER CHOICE ANALYSIS

A   Incorrect: This choice fails to satisfy our analysis above; as a result, among other problems, it would say that "during the day the blinking LEDs keep lions away at night," which is nonsensical, since it's not possible to do something "during the day" "at night." So (A) is wrong.

B   Incorrect: This choice fails to satisfy our analysis above by leaving out the one comma that should appear in the underlined phrase—the one that separates the participial phrase "powered with… day" from the independent clause that begins with the noun phrase that the participial phrase modifies ("the blinking LEDs"). So (B) is wrong.

C ✓ Correct: This choice would use a comma to separate the participial phrase "powered with <u>energy collected by solar panels during the day</u>" from the independent clause that contains the phrase it describes ("the blinking LEDs"), as required by our analysis above. So (C) is correct.

D   Incorrect: Among other problems, this would create the comma-separated participial phrase "collected by solar panels during the day," which would have to describe the first noun phrase in that sentence's independent clause, which is "the blinking LEDs." It doesn't make sense to say that "the blinking LEDs" are "collected by solar panels during the day," so this phrase can't describe "the blinking LEDs," which is one reason we know that (D) is wrong.

Test 3, Module 2, Question 23   TYPE: SAT WRITING

- Vertical Scan Results: Each choice is the same word with a comma and/or a conjunction after it.
- Vertical Scan Notes: We have to decide whether or not a comma and/or the word "but" should appear after "(Ru)."
- Key Features in Surrounding Text: Everything from the beginning of the sentence through "(Ru)" can stand on its own as a sentence, and everything after the blank ("the alloy… NiCoCr") can also stand on its own as a sentence. We know that we can join two groups of words that can each stand on their own as sentences with a comma and then a conjunction like "but."

Concepts in the question:

- Commas: Commas can be used between clauses, to form comma sandwiches, in a list of 3 or more items, and before reported speech. They can't appear for no reason. Review the training for the relevant details. (See page 86.)
- Independent and Dependent Clauses: Choices would create and/or join clauses. An independent clause can stand on its own as a sentence, and a dependent clause can't. Remember rules for joining clauses related to periods, semi-colons, colons, commas, and conjunctions. (See page 82.)

ANSWER CHOICE ANALYSIS

A   Incorrect: This choice would result in a run-on sentence—that is, two groups of words that can each stand on their own as sentences with no punctuation, conjunction, or relative pronoun between them. This isn't acceptable on the SAT, so (A) is wrong.

B   Incorrect: This choice would insert the word "but" between two sets of words that can stand on their own as sentences. We know from our training that when we use a conjunction like "but" to join two independent clauses, a comma must appear before the word "but." This choice doesn't include that comma, so (B) is wrong.

C   Incorrect: This choice creates a comma splice, because it would separate two groups of words that can each stand on their own as sentences with a comma, which isn't acceptable on the SAT. So (C) is wrong.

D ✓ Correct: This choice would separate two independent clauses with a comma followed by the conjunction "but," which is acceptable on the SAT. So (D) is right.

Note   Notice that this question includes terminology and conventions related to chemistry, like "NiCoCr" and "(Ni)" and "ruthenium"—and that one of those terms ("(Ru)") even appears in each answer choice. A lot of untrained test-takers will give up on this question before they even start it because they'll feel uncomfortable with the subject matter, and they'll assume they need to have some familiarity with chemistry to understand what's going on here. In reality, we don't have to know what any of these terms mean—we can apply our SAT Writing training whether we've heard of any of this stuff or not. On test day, remember that we don't need outside subject matter knowledge to answer real SAT questions, so we should never be intimidated by the subject of any passage.

Test 3, Module 2, Question 24   TYPE: SAT WRITING

- Vertical Scan Results: Each choice is a different form of the same verb.
- Vertical Scan Notes: We have to decide whether a present, past, singular, and/or plural form of "to be" is acceptable.
- Key Features in Surrounding Text: The subject of the verb is the singular noun "Josephine St. Pierre Ruffin," so we need a singular verb form in the blank. Note that the plural noun "leaders" right before the blank isn't the subject of the verb; it's part of the prepositional phrase "among the clubs' leaders." (This question involves a slightly unusual word order; the right answer may become clearer if we treat the sentence as though it were written like this: "Josephine St. Pierre Ruffin (blank) among

the clubs' leaders…." Remember that we always need to read sentences on SAT Writing questions carefully, so we can figure out how the different words and phrases in those sentences relate to one another.)

Concepts in the question:

- **Intervening Phrase:** A distracting phrase appears between words that need to agree with each other grammatically. Identify pairs of words that need to agree with each other, and ignore phrases that appear between those words. (See page 92.)
- **Verb Tense/Conjugation:** Choices include different forms of the same verb. Look at the surrounding text to find the verb's subject. Also, look for other clues that could indicate the proper tense or form of the verb in the blank. (See page 77.)

ANSWER CHOICE ANALYSIS

A ✓ **Correct:** As discussed above, the verb in the blank should be singular, and this choice is the only singular verb form. So (A) is right.

B **Incorrect:** As discussed above, the verb in the blank should be singular, but this choice is plural. So (B) is wrong.

C **Incorrect:** This choice has the same problem as (B), and is wrong for the same reason.

D **Incorrect:** This choice has the same problem as (B) and (C), and is wrong for the same reason.

Test 3, Module 2, Question 25　　　　**TYPE: SAT WRITING**

- **Vertical Scan Results:** Each choice is a long phrase involving similar words ordered in different ways.
- **Vertical Scan Notes:** We need to pick the choice that begins with a phrase that can be described by the phrase before the blank.
- **Key Features in Surrounding Text:** The participial phrase "uncovering fragments of a 2,000-year-old reindeer training harness in northern Siberia" must describe the first noun phrase in that sentence's independent clause, and each answer choice will be the first half of the independent clause in the relevant sentence. So the noun phrase at the beginning of the right answer choice must be something that can be "uncovering fragments… in northern Siberia."

Concepts in the question:

- **Avoid Dangling Participles:** When a phrase starting with an -ing/-ed/-en word is joined to the main sentence by a comma, the first noun phrase in the independent clause of that sentence is described by the -ing/-ed/-en word. (See page 90.)
- **Independent and Dependent Clauses:** Choices would create and/or join clauses. An independent clause can stand on its own as a sentence, and a dependent clause can't. Remember rules for joining clauses related to periods, semi-colons, colons, commas, and conjunctions. (See page 82.)

ANSWER CHOICE ANALYSIS

A ✓ **Correct:** This choice would cause "researcher Robert Losey" to be the first noun phrase in the sentence's independent clause, which makes sense, because we can say that a person is "uncovering fragments… in northern Siberia." So (A) is right.

B **Incorrect:** This choice would result in a sentence that said "researcher Robert Losey's argument" was "uncovering fragments… in northern Siberia." We can't say an "argument" was "uncovering fragments… in northern Siberia," so (B) is wrong.

C **Incorrect:** This choice would result in a sentence that said "domestication" was "uncovering fragments… in northern Siberia." We can't say "domestication" was "uncovering fragments… in northern Siberia," so (C) is wrong.

D **Incorrect:** This choice would result in a sentence that said "the argument researcher Robert Losey has made" was "uncovering fragments… in northern Siberia." We can't say "the argument" was "uncovering fragments… in northern Siberia," so (D) is wrong.

Test 3, Module 2, Question 26　　　　**TYPE: SAT WRITING**

- **Vertical Scan Results:** Each choice is the same two words with different punctuation (or the word "and") between them.
- **Vertical Scan Notes:** We need to decide whether a comma, period, the word "and," or nothing should appear between "tombs" and "built."
- **Key Features in Surrounding Text:** "Archaeologist Laila Nehmé… tombs" can stand on its own as a sentence, and "built into… nature" can stand on its own as a sentence.

Concepts in the question:

- **Comma Splice:** A comma can't join two groups of words that could each be sentences on their own. (See page 83.)

- **Independent and Dependent Clauses:** Choices would create and/or join clauses. An independent clause can stand on its own as a sentence, and a dependent clause can't. Remember rules for joining clauses related to periods, semi-colons, colons, commas, and conjunctions. (See page 82.)

ANSWER CHOICE ANALYSIS

A ✓ **Correct:** This choice would use a period to separate two groups of words that can each stand on their own as sentences, which is acceptable on the SAT. So (A) is right.

B **Incorrect:** This choice creates a comma splice, because it would use a comma to separate two groups of words that can each stand on their own as sentences. This isn't acceptable on the SAT, so (B) is wrong.

C **Incorrect:** This choice would insert the word "and" between two sets of words that can each stand on their own as sentences. We know from our training that when we use a conjunction like "and" to join two independent clauses, a comma must appear before the word "and." This choice doesn't include that comma, so (C) is wrong.

D **Incorrect:** This choice would result in a run-on sentence: two groups of words that can each stand on their own as sentences with no punctuation, conjunction, or relative pronoun between them. This isn't acceptable on the SAT, so (D) is wrong.

Test 3, Module 2, Question 27 — TYPE: SAT WRITING

- **Vertical Scan Results:** Each choice is the same three words with commas appearing in different places.
- **Vertical Scan Notes:** We have to decide whether or not a comma should appear after "compound" and/or "oxide."
- **Key Features in Surrounding Text:** The noun phrase "aluminum oxide" is an example of a "chemical compound." When we have a noun phrase followed immediately by another noun phrase that's an example of that first noun phrase, no comma appears between those two noun phrases. Also, "to make a glassy solid…" is an infinitive clause appearing after an independent clause, and no comma should appear between those two clauses.

Concepts in the question:

- **Commas:** Commas can be used between clauses, to form comma sandwiches, in a list of 3 or more items, and before reported speech. They can't appear for no reason. Review the training for the relevant details. (See page 86.)
- **Independent and Dependent Clauses:** Choices would create and/or join clauses. An independent clause can stand on its own as a sentence, and a dependent clause can't. Remember rules for joining clauses related to periods, semi-colons, colons, commas, and conjunctions. (See page 82.)

ANSWER CHOICE ANALYSIS

A **Incorrect:** This choice fails to satisfy our analysis above, so it's wrong.

B **Incorrect:** This choice fails to satisfy our analysis above, so it's wrong.

C **Incorrect:** This choice fails to satisfy our analysis above, so it's wrong.

D ✓ **Correct:** As we saw in our analysis above, the right answer shouldn't include any commas, so (D) is correct.

Test 3, Module 2, Question 28 — TYPE: LOGICAL TRANSITION

The choices are different transition phrases like "however," "instead of," or "for example." The right answer must reflect the relationship between the concepts before and after the blank. See "What about Logical Transition Questions?" on p. 71.

Subjective Phrases to Ignore: "most"

A ✓ **Correct:** The second sentence tells us that "archaeologists have known of the lines since the 1920s," when someone "spotted" them, and then says archaeologists "have been studying" them ever since. The past-tense verbs "spotted" and "have been studying" in this sentence tell us about things happening in the past. The sentence that contains the blank uses only present-tense verb forms ("are aided" and "capture"). We need something in the blank to signal this shift in tense; that shift from discussing the past to discussing the present demonstrates the relationship required by the word "currently" from this choice, so (A) is correct.

B **Confused Relationships:** This choice would be appropriate if the sentence where the blank appears discussed similarities and/or differences between something in the previous sentence and something in this sentence. But that's not the case—both this sentence and the previous sentence talk about things archaeologists are doing, and they don't compare anything to anything else. So (B) is wrong.

C **Confused Relationships:** This choice would require this sentence to express an idea that's happening in spite of the idea in the previous sentence, or with no regard for the idea in the previous sentence, but that's not the case here—the previous sentence talks about something archeologists did in the past, and this sentence talks about something they're doing now, with no indication that the second idea is in any way in conflict with the first idea. So (C) is wrong.

D   Confused Relationships: This choice would require this sentence to express an idea that's somehow opposed to the idea in the previous sentence, but that's not the case here—so (D) is wrong.

The choices are different transition phrases like "however," "instead of," or "for example." The right answer must reflect the relationship between the concepts before and after the blank. See "What about Logical Transition Questions?" on p. 71.

Subjective Phrases to Ignore: "most"

A   Confused Relationships: This choice would be appropriate if it introduced a sentence that described something that somehow took the place of the thing described in the previous sentence, or that happened in place of something from the previous sentence. But that's not the case—instead, the previous sentence and this sentence both explain reasons why "Archaeologist Sue Brunning" says the "burial site" was probably for a "king." So (A) is wrong.

B   Confused Relationships: This choice would only be appropriate if this sentence expressed something that was happening in spite of the idea in the previous sentence. But that's not the case—see our discussion of (D) for more.

C   Confused Relationships: This choice would express the idea that the information in this sentence provided further details and/or examples related to the idea in the previous sentence, but that's not the case—see our discussion of (D) for more.

D ✓   Correct: The first sentence tells us that "archaeologist Sue Brunning explains why the... burial site" was probably for a "king." The next sentence starts with "first," then provides one reason to support this assertion, and the following sentence provides a second reason to support this assertion. This choice would appropriately cause that last sentence to begin with the word "second," which reflects the idea that this sentence contains the second of two things, right after a sentence starting with "first." So (D) is right.

The choices are different transition phrases like "however," "instead of," or "for example." The right answer must reflect the relationship between the concepts before and after the blank. See "What about Logical Transition Questions?" on p. 71.

Subjective Phrases to Ignore: "most"

A   Confused Relationships: This choice would be appropriate if this sentence described something that happened after the thing described in the previous sentence, but that's not the case; instead, these are just two sentences discussing animals' relative brain sizes, with no indication of anything happening in sequence. So (A) is wrong.

B   Confused Relationships: This choice would indicate that the second sentence provides an additional piece of information to reinforce the information in the previous sentence, but that's not the case—the previous sentence describes a trend, and this sentence says what "should" be true based on that previous sentence. So (B) is wrong—see the discussion of (D) for more.

C   Direct Contradiction: This choice would require the second sentence to express something that is true in spite of the idea in the previous sentence, but that's not the case—in fact, that's basically the opposite of the relationship between this sentence and the previous sentence. See the discussion of (D) for more.

D ✓   Correct: The first sentence says that "the more diverse... an animal's behaviors, the larger and more energy demanding the animal's brain tends to be." The sentence containing the blank makes a statement that "should" be true, based on the idea from the previous sentence—that animals who only perform "basic actions" (which is the opposite of "diverse... animal[] behaviors" from the previous sentence) should "allocate fewer resources to growing and maintaining brain tissue"—that is, have smaller brains (which is the opposite of "larger and more energy demanding... brain[s]" from the previous sentence). In other words, the first sentence says that animals with more diverse behaviors tend to have bigger brains, and this choice would make the second sentence say that, based on this idea from the first sentence, animals with simpler behaviors should have smaller brains. This demonstrates the relationship required by the word "thus," because "thus" introduces a conclusion that is the logical result of the idea from the previous sentence. So (D) is correct.

The choices are different transition phrases like "however," "instead of," or "for example." The right answer must reflect the relationship between the concepts before and after the blank. See "What about Logical Transition Questions?" on p. 71.

Subjective Phrases to Ignore: "most"

A ✓   Correct: The first sentence tells us that "Larlarb typically custom fits garments to each actor" when making costumes for movies. The following sentence tells us that she "had a factory reproduce" a "spacesuit" for a movie, and that the result "lack[ed] a tailor-made quality." So the second sentence expresses an idea that's the opposite of the idea in the first sentence—instead of "custom"-

making costumes, she had a "factory" make them, and the result wasn't "tailor-made." This opposition appropriately demonstrates the relationship required by the word "nevertheless," so (A) is correct.

B   Direct Contradiction: This choice would be correct if the second sentence expressed the logical result of the idea from the previous sentence, but it doesn't—as we saw in our discussion of (A), the second sentence tells us something that's the opposite of what's expressed in the first sentence. So (B) is wrong.

C   Direct Contradiction: This choice would be appropriate if the second sentence provided additional information that was similar to the information in the first sentence, but, as we discussed above, the information in the second sentence is the opposite of what appears in the first sentence.

D   Direct Contradiction: This choice has basically the same problem as (C), and is wrong for that reason.

Test 3, Module 2, Question 32　　　　　　　　　　**TYPE: NOTES**

The passage presents a bulleted list of notes, then tells us a goal related to presenting that information. The correct answer will be the only one that demonstrates the ideas in the provided goal. See "What about Notes Questions?" on p. 71.

Subjective Phrases to Ignore: "most"

A   Direct Contradiction: The prompt asks for the choice that "emphasize[s] a similarity between the two books by Shaun Tan." This choice does mention "two books by Shaun Tan," but it doesn't mention any similarity between them. Instead, it mentions a *difference* between them—that one contains fewer short stories than the other. So (A) is wrong.

B   Direct Contradiction: Like (B) this choice mentions both books, but tells us about a difference between the two books: they have different publication years. The prompt asks for a choice that "emphasize[s] a similarity," so (B) is wrong.

C   Direct Contradiction: This choice has the same problem as (A) and (B), and is wrong for the same reason: it tells us about a difference between the books, but the prompt asked for a "similarity."

D ✓ Correct: This choice names "Shaun Tan's books" and says they "both describe surreal events occurring in otherwise ordinary places." This statement about what they "both" do demonstrates the idea of a "similarity between the two books," as the prompt requires, so (D) is right.

Test 3, Module 2, Question 33　　　　　　　　　　**TYPE: NOTES**

The passage presents a bulleted list of notes, then tells us a goal related to presenting that information. The correct answer will be the only one that demonstrates the ideas in the provided goal. See "What about Notes Questions?" on p. 71.

Subjective Phrases to Ignore: "most"

A ✓ Correct: The prompt asks for the choice that "emphasize[s] the aim of the research study." This choice tells us what the "researchers wanted to know," which exactly demonstrates "the aim of the research study," as the prompt requires. So (A) is right.

B   Confused Relationships: This choice provides the *results* of the research study—that is, what the researchers found out after conducting the study. But the prompt asked for the "aim," which is what they wanted to know when they started. So (B) is wrong.

C   Confused Relationships: This is the conclusion that the researchers came to at the end of the study—but the prompt asked for the "aim" of the study, which is what they wanted to know when they started. So (C) is wrong.

D   Confused Relationships: This choice describes how the "researchers" went about finding the information they wanted— that is, their methodology. But that's not the "aim of the research study," as the prompt requires. The "aim" is what they want to find out, not how they go about finding it. So (D) is wrong.

TEST 4, MODULE 1

Test 4, Module 1, Question 1　　　　　　　　　　**TYPE: TEXT COMPLETION**

The prompt will be a short passage containing a blank. The correct answer will always be restated or demonstrated by key phrases in the provided text. See "What about Text Completion Questions?" on p. 66.

Subjective Phrases to Ignore: "most"

A   Barely Relevant: The passage says that the spacecraft "(blank) a sample of the surface, gathering pieces of it to bring back to Earth." As trained test-takers, we know that the right answer should create a phrase that restates "gathering pieces... to bring back to Earth." This choice might be tempting for test-takers who assume that the spacecraft had to "attach[]" itself to the asteroid as part of the process described in the passage, but that idea isn't actually present in the text, so it can't be the basis for choosing the right answer. Another problem with this argument is that the verb in the blank doesn't describe what the spacecraft did to the surface of the asteroid; it describes what the spacecraft did with "a sample of the surface," so the previous logic wouldn't even work anyway. Choice (A) doesn't restate a relevant idea from the text, so it's wrong.

B ✓ **Correct:** This choice results in the phrase "<u>collected</u> a sample of the surface," which is exactly restated by the subsequent phrase "gathering pieces of [the surface] to bring back." So (B) is correct.

C **Barely Relevant:** Like (A), this choice might be tempting for test-takers who imagine the process of the spacecraft getting to the asteroid, and they assume that at one point the spacecraft must have "followed" the asteroid, so they decide that maybe this choice could work. But that's not what "followed a sample of the surface" would mean—and aside from that, we know as trained test-takers that the right answer has to be restated or demonstrated in the text, and the provided text doesn't tell us about anything "follow[ing]" anything else. So (C) is wrong.

D **Direct Contradiction:** This choice is basically the opposite of the right answer, because it would describe putting something back on the asteroid, as opposed to "gathering pieces... to bring" somewhere else, which is what the text describes. So (D) is wrong.

<hr>

▍Test 4, Module 1, Question 2	TYPE: TEXT COMPLETION

The prompt will be a short passage containing a blank. The correct answer will always be restated or demonstrated by key phrases in the provided text. See "What about Text Completion Questions?" on p. 66.

<hr>

Subjective Phrases to Ignore: "most"

A ✓ **Correct:** This choice would cause the text to say that "the Moon's surface may not accurately <u>reflect</u> early impact events," which exactly restates the idea in the provided text that says "evidence of early impacts may no longer be present" on the Moon. So (A) is correct.

B **Barely Relevant:** This choice might be tempting for untrained test-takers who misunderstand the text and think that it says the moon no longer experiences "impact events." Even if that idea were present in the text—which it isn't—that's not what the phrase "may not accurately <u>receive</u> early impact events" would even mean. It's not clear what it would mean to "not accurately receive" something, but the idea of "not receiving" something isn't restated or demonstrated in the text, so we know (B) is wrong.

C **Confused Relationships:** Some untrained test-takers might be interested in this choice if they misunderstand the text and think that it says that researchers can't "evaluate early impact events" because those events don't leave much "of an impression." But the action in the blank is being done by "the Moon's surface," not human researchers, so this concept doesn't apply. Nothing in the text talks about the "the Moon's surface" "evaluat[ing]" anything, as this choice would require, so (C) is wrong.

D **Literary Interpretation:** A lot of test-takers will have a hard time choosing between (A) and (D), but we can be sure (D) is wrong for a couple of reasons. For one, to "mimic" something means to copy or imitate something—the Moon isn't capable of copying or imitating anything, because it's not a living thing, and it can't actively do anything. For another, "evidence" left behind after an impact can't be called "mimic[ry]" of that "impact." "Mimic[king]" an impact event would mean copying the actual event of something striking the moon, not leaving behind evidence that shows something happened in the past. So "the Moon's surface" can't "mimic" anything, and the passage doesn't demonstrate anything that could be called "mimic[king]" anyway. That means (D) is wrong.

<hr>

Note Notice that in order to realize that (D) was wrong, we had to think carefully about what the word "mimic" can and can't mean, and also consider what exactly it would mean to "mimic early impact events," in a way that we wouldn't typically need to do in a classroom setting. This is another great example of the important difference between classroom skills and SAT skills.

<hr>

▍Test 4, Module 1, Question 3	TYPE: TEXT COMPLETION

The prompt will be a short passage containing a blank. The correct answer will always be restated or demonstrated by key phrases in the provided text. See "What about Text Completion Questions?" on p. 66.

<hr>

Subjective Phrases to Ignore: "most"

A ✓ **Correct:** The provided text says that "handedness... typically is easy to observe in humans." Then it says that "this trait is present but less (blank) in many others animals," and that "researchers" use "tasks" "to reveal individual animals' preferences for a certain hand or paw." This choice would cause the text to say that "handedness" "is present but less <u>recognizable</u> in... other animals." The phrase "but less <u>recognizable</u>" would complete the comparison between "handedness" being "easy to observe in humans" and this trait not being as easy to observe in animals—this idea is demonstrated by the information later in the text that says "researchers often employ tasks specially designed to reveal individual animals' preferences for a certain hand or paw." That is, the researchers can't just "observ[e]" the "handedness" of the animal, as they might with "humans"; they have to use "special[]" "tasks... to reveal" the animal's "handedness," because that "trait is... less <u>recognizable</u>" (notice how the phrase "preferences for a certain hand or paw" restates "handedness, a preferential use of either the right or left hand," and notice that the idea that something would need

<hr>

to be "reveal[ed]" demonstrates the idea that it's "less <u>recognizable</u>"). So this choice creates a phrase that's demonstrated in the provided text, which means that it's right.

B   **Plausible but not in the Text:** This choice would create the phrase "but less <u>intriguing</u>"; that might be tempting for untrained test-takers who personally think this topic isn't very intriguing, or who assume that "handedness" in animals just isn't something researchers are probably very interested in. But as trained test-takers, we know we can't base our answers on our own opinions or assumptions; we have to pick an answer choice based on the provided text, and nothing in the text restates or demonstrates the idea of "handedness" being "less <u>intriguing</u> in... other animals." So (B) is wrong.

C   **Plausible but not in the Text:** Like (B), this choice might be tempting for test-takers who just assume that "handedness" is less of a big deal for animals than for people, and who pick this choice based on that assumption. But we can't use assumptions as the basis for picking an answer choice on the SAT, and the text doesn't restate or demonstrate the idea of anything being "less <u>significant</u>" than anything else. So (C) is wrong.

D   **Plausible but not in the Text:** This choice has the same basic problem as (B) and (C), and is wrong for the same reason.

Test 4, Module 1, Question 4   **TYPE: TEXT COMPLETION**

The prompt will be a short passage containing a blank. The correct answer will always be restated or demonstrated by key phrases in the provided text. See "What about Text Completion Questions?" on p. 66.

Subjective Phrases to Ignore: "most"

A   **Direct Contradiction:** The phrase "by no means" tells us that what's in the blank is the *opposite* of what it is "to recognize the influence of... Bosch on... Banisadr[]." The word "indeed" tells us that the sentence "Banisadr himself cites Bosch as an inspiration" restates the idea from the previous sentence, so "it is by no means (blank) to recognize the influence of... Bosch on... Banisadr[]" should restate the idea that "Bosch" is an "inspiration" to "Banisadr." This choice doesn't meet that requirement, because the phrase "it is by no means <u>substantial</u> to recognize the influence of... Bosch on... Banisadr[]" doesn't restate or demonstrate the idea that "Bosch" inspired "Banisadr." In fact, it's not really clear what that phrase would mean, but if anything it would indicate that "the influence of... Bosch on... Banisadr" is unimportant, or even not real. This choice will be tempting for some test-takers who notice the idea later in the text of something else having "a far greater impact on Banisadr's work," and who think it makes sense to say that Bosch's "influence" on Banisadr wasn't "substantial" by comparison—but the idea of something else have a "greater impact" doesn't change the fact that the provided text tells us directly that "Banisadr himself cites Bosch as an inspiration," and that this choice would contradict the provided text for the reasons mentioned above. Again, (A) is wrong.

B   **Barely Relevant:** This choice could be tempting for test-takers who imagine a scenario where one artist doesn't want to "recognize the influence" of another artist for some personal or creative reason—but no such idea appears in the text, and we can't pick answer choices just because we can imagine a situation where they're plausible. So (B) is wrong.

C ✓   **Correct:** This choice would cause the text to say that "it is by no means <u>unimportant</u> to recognize the influence of... Bosch on... Banisadr[]," which restates the idea from the following sentence that "Banisadr himself cites Bosch as an inspiration" (notice that the phrase "it is by no means <u>unimportant</u>" means the same thing as "it is important"). This also demonstrates the kind of relationship required by "however" later in the sentence, which introduces the idea that a certain "poem... may have had a far greater impact on Banisadr's work." With this choice in the blank, the text says that it's not "<u>unimportant</u> to recognize the influence of... Bosch on... Banisadr[]," "however," something else "had a far greater impact." The idea that something influenced Banisadr, but something else "had a far greater impact" demonstrates the kind of opposition required by the word "however." With all of this in mind, we can see that (C) is correct.

D   **Direct Contradiction:** This choice would directly contradict the text; since the text says that "Banisadr himself cites Bosch as an inspiration," we can't say that "it is by no means <u>appropriate</u> to recognize the influence of... Bosch on... Banisadr[]." This choice would say that Bosch *didn't* influence Banisadr, which, again, contradicts the statement in the text that "Banisadr himself cites Bosch as an inspiration." So (D) is wrong.

Test 4, Module 1, Question 5   **TYPE: MAIN IDEA**

The prompt asks about the "main purpose" or "main idea" (or some similar phrase) of the text. The correct answer must be directly restated or demonstrated in the passage, with no interpretation. See "What about "Main Idea/Main Purpose" Questions?" on p.69.

Subjective Phrases to Ignore: "best"

A ✓   **Correct:** The "old man" in the passage says of the picture that it "don't belong in here"—that is, in his shop. Immediately after, the phrase "and yet" introduces an opposite feeling—that "the old man was secretly proud of his acquisition." The idea that he feels the picture doesn't "belong" in his shop, and that he was "proud" of it at the same time, demonstrates that he has "conflicted feelings," as stated in (A). So (A) is correct.

B   Literary Interpretation: This choice will be tempting for untrained test-takers who try to interpret the text, or to make assumptions about how they would feel in the old man's place. The text describes "the person he got the new picture from" as "persuasive," and mentions what that person "claimed" he was doing, and what "he called" the price for the picture—which indicate that this person wasn't trustworthy. But thinking someone isn't trustworthy isn't the same as resenting that person, and as we saw in our discussion of (A), "the old man" was "proud" of the picture he got from that person. If he "resent[ed]" that person, the text would have to restate or demonstrate the idea that he had bad feelings toward that person as a result of their deal—but this idea doesn't appear in the text, so (B) is wrong.

C   Confused Relationships: The passage does mention some "items" in the shop: "views of the city… pictures of cats and dogs… flaming bits of landscape." But it never says that he "prizes" any of them, let alone that he "prizes" them "most highly." Some untrained test-takers might like this choice because the text says the old man is "secretly proud" of the picture, which might sound like a description of something "highly prize[d]." But someone can be "proud" of something without it being what that person "most highly prizes," as this choice requires—plus this choice mentions "items," plural, "that the shop owner most highly prizes," and the picture is only one item that the passage indicates the old man has positive feelings about. So for any of these reasons, (C) is wrong.

D   Off by One or Two Words: This choice will be very tempting to a lot of test-takers, because the passage says "the picture failed to fit in with the rest of the shop," and "the old man" says the picture doesn't "belong" in his shop. This might seem to support the statement in this choice about "differences between the new picture and other pictures in the shop." But this choice also says that the passage "explain[s]" those "differences," and this idea of "explain[ing]" the differences doesn't actually appear in the text! In fact, the text provides no details whatsoever about the "new picture," so we don't know anything about what makes the "new picture" different from the "other pictures" in the shop. *Saying* that a picture is different from other pictures, as the passage does, isn't the same as *explaining the differences* between that pictures and the other pictures, which this passage doesn't do. So (D) is wrong.

Test 4, Module 1, Question 6   **TYPE: FUNCTION AND STRUCTURE**

The prompt asks about the "function" or "structure" of a part of the text. The correct answer must plainly and accurately describe the relevant text, with no interpretation. See "What about "Function and Structure" Questions?" on p. 70.

Subjective Phrases to Ignore: "best"

A   Confused Relationships: This choice will attract some untrained test-takers, because the first half of the choice is accurate—the speaker does "assess[]" the "natural phenomenon" of the tree, calling it "a most beautiful thing." Then she asks a couple of questions when she says "Why… are you black? And why are you pointing upwards?" But asking a question isn't the same as *questioning* something—to question an idea means to doubt it. And her questions aren't related to *her assessment*, as this choice requires. She doesn't ask "is it really beautiful?" or "am I right to feel this way?" or anything else that we could call "question[ing] the accuracy of her assessment." So (A) is wrong.

B ✓ Correct: The speaker says she saw "a most beautiful thing, slim and still, against a gold, gold sky, a straight black cypress, sensitive, exquisite, a black finger pointing upwards." This exactly demonstrates the idea of "describ[ing] a distinctive sight in nature"—the words "beautiful," "slim," "still," "gold," "straight," "black," "sensitive," and "exquisite" all "describe[]" the scene, as this choice requires; we also know it's a "distinctive sight," because she calls it a "most beautiful thing," and we know it's "in nature" because it's a tree "against" the "sky." So we can see the text demonstrates everything in the first half of this choice. The second half of the choice says she "ponders what meaning to attribute to that sight." This is demonstrated by the speaker asking "why… are you black? And why are you pointing upwards?" Asking why the tree is the way it is, and why it does what it does, is the speaker wondering "what meaning" to attribute to what she sees. So every part of (B) is demonstrated in the text, which means (B) is right.

C   Confused Relationships: The first half of this choice is accurate—the speaker does "present[] an outdoor scene"—but the second half of this choice doesn't appear in the text. This choice will be tempting for test-takers who get confused and think that the speaker is talking about a person's "black finger," and that the speaker asks why the person is "pointing" the finger "upwards." But the text tells us that the "black cypress" is the "black finger." With that in mind, we can see that no "human" is part of what the author has "seen," and no "human behavior occur[s]" anywhere in the "outdoor scene," as this choice would require—which means (C) must be wrong.

D   Literary Interpretation: As with the other wrong answer choices, the first half of this choice is accurate, because the speaker does "examine[] her surroundings." But the speaker never says anything about her own "emotional state." This is a great example of the kind of statement that could be part of a discussion in a high school English classroom; we could almost always discuss a poem in class and interpret some aspect of the text as commenting on the author's "emotional state." But on the SAT, we can't make a statement like this unless the literal words on the page specifically discuss the emotions that the speaker is feeling. This passage doesn't say anything about the author's emotions, so (D) can't be right. (Note that some test-takers will think that the word "sensitive" could describe the speaker's "emotional state"—but nothing in the poem indicates that this word describes any person, let alone the speaker. Again, as we saw in our discussion of (C), no person is described at all. "Sensitive" could, in some other context, describe a person's "emotional state," but that's not what it's doing in this poem.)

The prompt asks about the "function" or "structure" of a part of the text. The correct answer must plainly and accurately describe the relevant text, with no interpretation. See "What about "Function and Structure" Questions?" on p. 70.

Subjective Phrases to Ignore: "best"

A   **Confused Relationships:** This choice will be extremely tempting for many test-takers, because the speaker *does* ask a "question[]" about something that other people feel—that is, some feel that he "seek[s] to destroy institutions," about which he asks "what... have I in common with them? Or... with the destruction of them?" He then describes something he wants to "establish" in many places, which he calls "the institution of the dear love of comrades"; some test-takers might see this as related to his "worldview." But even though a lot of untrained test-takers will think this choice is very appealing, we as trained test-takers can see multiple concrete reasons why it's definitely wrong. First, what the speaker "questions" isn't actually an "attitude." He says people think he "seek[s] to destroy institutions," but thinking a certain thing is true isn't the same as having any particular "attitude," which would be more of an established way of thinking about a certain subject. Also, the second half of the text talks about something he wants to do, which is likely to be related to "his worldview," but which isn't actually his worldview—someone's worldview isn't a *goal* of theirs; instead, it's the way they tend to view things, which the speaker doesn't describe. Finally, and most glaringly, this choice describes the "attitude" mentioned earlier as "increasingly prevalent." The word "increasingly" *requires* the text to say that the attitude had some level of prevalence at one point, and that level of prevalence has increased. That idea certainly doesn't appear anywhere in the text, and for any of these reasons, we know (A) is wrong.

B   **Plausible but not in the Text:** A lot of test-takers will try to apply outside knowledge about Walt Whitman to this question—especially if they're aware that he spent a lot of his time in the woods, often alone—because they'll use that awareness as a justification for the phrase "isolation from others" in this choice. Also, since the text talks about "the dear love of comrades," they might decide it makes sense to say that he seems to value time with "comrades," so he probably "regrets his isolation from others" that he has experienced at other times in his life. But as trained test-takers, we know we can't use outside knowledge on the SAT, and the text never says anything at all about the speaker experiencing "isolation," let alone that he regrets any such "isolation." For that reason alone, we can eliminate (B).

C   **Literary Interpretation:** The passage starts with the speaker saying "it is charged against me that I seek to destroy institutions." The idea that something is "charged" against him might sound like the author is "conced[ing]" a "shortcoming[]," as this choice requires. But there are a few problems with this: for one, this choice mentions "shortcomings," plural, so the text would need to demonstrate the speaker "conced[ing]" at least two separate "shortcomings." For another, simply saying that other people say something about you isn't the same as "conced[ing]" that their "charge[]" is a "shortcoming[]" of yours, as this choice would require. The speaker only says "it is charged against me that..."; he doesn't say the "charge[]" is valid. In fact, he questions that "charge[]," by asking "What indeed have I in common with [institutions]?— Or what with the destruction of [institutions]?" Finally, this choice says the speaker "boasts of his many achievements." The text does describe Whitman "establish[ing]" an "institution" in many places, which might seem like "boast[ing]" of "many achievements," as this choice would require—but he's actually saying what he "will" do in the future. So this is a goal of his that hasn't happened, not an achievement that has happened in the past (we can't call something that might happen in the future an "achievement[]," as this choice would require), and at any rate, this choice mentions "achievements," plural, which means the text would have to describe at least two separate achievements. For any of these reasons, we know (C) is wrong.

D ✓   **Correct:** The phrase "criticism leveled against him" exactly restates the "charge[] against me" that Whitman mentions in the first line, and he addresses that "charge[]," which he says is that he "seek[s] to destroy institutions," by saying he is "neither for nor against institutions." So we can see that the first half of this choice is directly restated and demonstrated in the text. Then, Whitman says he "will establish... the institution of the dear love of comrades," which we can call an "ambition" of his, because it's something he says he "will" do, and we can say it's a "grand" ambition because he says he wants to do it in many, many places: "in the Mannahatta... and in every city of These States, inland and seaboard, and in the fields and woods, and above every keel... that dents the water." So the text demonstrates the speaker "announc[ing] a grand ambition of his," as this choice requires, which means that every part of this choice is restated and demonstrated in the provided text, and (D) is correct.

The prompt asks about the "function" or "structure" of a part of the text. The correct answer must plainly and accurately describe the relevant text, with no interpretation. See "What about "Function and Structure" Questions?" on p. 70.

A   Plausible but not in the Text: This choice refers to "the hypothesis that Chang and colleagues had set out to investigate," but the passage doesn't mention any such "hypothesis," or say that "Chang and colleagues" were "investigat[ing]" anything. All we know from the passage is that they were "monitoring mimosa trees." So (A) is wrong.

B ✓ Correct: The sentence in question is a "generalization," because it talks about "evolutionary links," "predators and their prey," and "centuries and continents" in general terms, without mentioning any specific examples of any of these things. We know that this generalization is also "exemplified by the discussion of the mimosa trees and *B. terrenus*" in the passage, because the text tells us that the "beetle" (which we're told is a "predator," since it "preys on" the "seeds" of the "mimosa tree") and the "mimosa tree" (which is its "prey," as we just mentioned) were "link[ed]" "in East Asia" prior to "1785," as described in the text. Then, they were "link[ed]" again "centuries" later in "2001" in "North America" (a different "continent"), where the mimosa tree was now growing, and where the beetles had just been introduced. There, "within a year" of their introduction, beetles had "attacked" "93 percent of the [mimosa] trees." This description of the beetles preying on the mimosa trees in East Asia prior to 1785, and then in North America after 2001, exactly demonstrates the idea of "links between predators and prey... persist[ing] across centuries and continents." So (B) is correct.

C   Confused Relationships: This choice might be appealing, because, as we saw in our discussion of (B), the underlined sentence does make a statement that "is exemplified" by the information about the trees and the beetles. But even if we call the underlined sentence an "explanation for the findings of Chang and colleagues," which isn't exactly accurate, that still wouldn't make that sentence an "*alternative* explanation," [emphasis added], as this choice requires, because if that were the case, then the text would have to provide a primary explanation "for the findings," and *then* include this underlined statement as an "alternative." No such primary explanation appears in the text, so (C) can't be right.

D   Confused Relationships: This choice might be tempting because the underlined sentence kind of sounds like a clarification of an idea from the text—but when we read carefully, we can see that the underlined sentence only talks about "links between predators and prey... persist[ing]." It never discusses "why" any "species... spread to new locations," and it doesn't even mention any specific species or location. Beyond that, no other part of the text explains why species spread from one place to another; the text simply states that the tree and the beetle were in East Asia, and that later on they were in North America, with no explanation of "why" that happened. (Note that the sentence "*B. terrenus* was introduced in southeastern North America" only tells us *what* happened, it doesn't tells us *why* this happened—and even if it did, the prompt asks about the third sentence, not about this statement, so that statement isn't relevant to this question anyway.) With all of this in mind, we know that (D) is wrong.

Test 4, Module 1, Question 9   **TYPE: PAIRED PASSAGES**

The question will ask what the author of one passage would think about some aspect of the other passage. The answer must always be directly stated in the text, with no guessing or assumption from the test-taker. See "What about Paired Passages?" p. 70.

A   Confused Relationships: The prompt asks us how "Graeber and Wengrow (Text 2)" would respond to the ""conventional wisdom" presented in Text 1." When we read Text 1, we can see that the "conventional wisdom" is "that human social systems evolved in stages," starting with "hunter-gatherers" who had "equal status" with each other, then evolving into "groups with hierarchical structures." This choice will be tempting for test-takers who see that the texts disagree with each other, and who notice that both of them mention phrases like "hierarchical systems" and "decentralized collective societies," but who aren't clear about what exactly the texts disagree on. As we'll see in our discussion of (B), the disagreement isn't over whether "hierarchical systems" or "decentralized collective societies" are more important, as this choice would require; instead, it's over whether "human social systems" evolved in a sequence of stages (as described in Text 1), or whether they shifted back and forth, from one form to another and back again, over time (as described in Text 2). So (A) is wrong.

B ✓ Correct: As we saw in our discussion of (A), the "conventional wisdom" from Text 1 is that "human social systems evolved in stages," starting with "hunter-gatherers" with "equal status," then evolving into "groups with hierarchical structures." Text 2 says "humans have always been socially flexible, alternately forming systems based on hierarchy and collective ones with decentralized leadership," and says that "some hunter-gatherers adjusted their social structures seasonally," which could mean existing as "small groups" sometimes, and as "communities that included esteemed individuals" at other times. This exactly demonstrates the idea from this choice that "Graeber and Wengrow" from Text 2 would "disput[e] the idea that developments in social structures have followed a linear progression through distinct stages," since the "conventional wisdom" in Text 1 says "human social systems evolved in stages," while the ideas in Text 2 are the opposite of this kind of "linear progression"—notice particularly that words like "alternately" and "seasonally" specifically express the idea of things repeatedly changing, and then changing back, as opposed to being "linear." So (B) is right.

C   Direct Contradiction: Text 2 doesn't mention agriculture at all, but it does talk about "evidence… as far back as 50,000 years ago" that there were "communities that included esteemed individuals," while Text 1 mentions a "shift to agriculture about 12,000 years ago"—so if anything, Text 2 specifically talks about "hierarchical roles" from long before the "shift to agriculture." So this choice is basically the opposite of what the passage says, and we know it's wrong.

D   Direct Contradiction: The "earliest" mention in either text of any "form[] of social structure" appears in Text 2, and it relates to "hunter-gatherers" from "50,000 years ago." So if anything, "Graeber and Wengrow" from Text 2 are the ones who would *agree* with the "assumption" mentioned in this choice, not "challeng[e]" it, as this choice requires—which means this choice is basically the opposite of what appears in the text. So (D) is wrong.

Test 4, Module 1, Question 10   TYPE: MAIN IDEA

The prompt asks about the "main purpose" or "main idea" (or some similar phrase) of the text. The correct answer must be directly restated or demonstrated in the passage, with no interpretation. See "What about "Main Idea/Main Purpose" Questions?" on p.69.

Subjective Phrases to Ignore: "best"

A   Plausible but not in the Text: This choice mentions ideas from the text ("Mary," the "garden," "work"), but mixes up how they relate to each other. The text actually says Mary was *doing* work in the garden, not "avoid[ing]" it: "she worked and dug and pulled up weeds steadily." This choice will tempt test-takers who get confused about how the ideas in the passage relate to each other, and/or who just think it sounds plausible that a "young girl" would hide in a garden to "avoid… chores." But as trained test-takers, we know we can't pick a choice just because it "sounds plausible" in real life, and we know that (A) is wrong.

B   Direct Contradiction: This choice is similar to (A)—it sounds plausible in real life, but actually describes the opposite of what the text says; the text says that Mary "worked and dug and pulled up weeds steadily, only becoming more pleased with her work every hour instead of tiring of it." So she didn't "get[] bored… pulling… weeds"; in reality, she "only [became] more pleased" with it. So (B) is wrong.

C   Confused Relationships: The only mention of "play" in the passage is that "her work" in the garden (which we're told included digging and "pull[ing] up weeds") "seemed to her like… play." There's no restatement or demonstration of Mary making room in the garden to play; all she does in the garden, according to the passage, is "work" in the garden. So (C) is wrong.

D ✓ Correct: The phrase "Mary feels very satisfied" from this choice is exactly restated by the phrase in the passage that describes Mary as "pleased with her work," and the passage says she felt this way when "she worked and dug and pulled up weeds" in the garden, which restates the phrase "when she's taking care of the garden" from this choice. So this choice is exactly restated in the passage, which means it's correct.

Test 4, Module 1, Question 11   TYPE: GENERAL PASSAGE

The prompt asks for information from the passage. The answer must be restated or demonstrated by specific phrases in the text. See "What about General Passage Questions?" on p. 69.

A   Plausible but not in the Text: Some test-takers will assume this choice must make a true statement, because they reason that "becom[ing]" anything, including "increasingly vigorous," must happen during "the passage" of some amount of "time." But we can't just assume that this is true if the text doesn't actually say something like "as time goes on, the mind gets stronger and stronger," or something like that (and even if it did say that, the text would also have to include the idea that this makes the mind "like a flower," as the prompt requires). But none of this appears in the text, so (A) is wrong. (Incidentally, notice that the text also describes a situation where the mind "beginneth… to languish," so even if someone tried to argue that the "passage of time" must be part of the process of becoming "vigorous," it must also be part of the process of "languish[ing]," which is the opposite of being "vigorous"—so it's not the mere "passage of time" that determines the outcome here, but something else, as we'll see in our discussion of (C). Again, (A) is wrong.)

B   Confused Relationships: This choice will be tempting for untrained test-takers, because the passage mentions "rain" as something that causes a "flower" to "unfold[] its gleaming foliage," and then says this is similar to the way the speaker's "tender mind flourish[es], if it be fed." But "rain" is an example of *weather*—not an example of "changes in the weather," as this choice requires—and the text doesn't restate or demonstrate the idea that weather changing gives strength to both "the human mind" and "flower[s]," as this choice would require. Beyond that, the text also describes a situation with dry weather (without "dew and rain"), and in that situation, the flower "languishes," which is the opposite of giving the flower "strength," as this choice requires. So we know we can't simply say that "weather," let alone "changes in the weather," give "strength" to both "the human mind" and "flower[s]," which means (B) is wrong. See the discussion of (C) for more.

C ✓ Correct: The text says that a "flower unfolds its… foliage… if the dew and the rain draw it forth." Then it says "so doth my tender mind flourish, if it be fed with the sweet dew of the fostering spirit." We can see that the "flower unfold[ing] its… foliage…" and the "mind flourish[ing]" both demonstrate the idea of "thriv[ing]" from this answer choice, and the idea that this "thriv[ing]" only happens to the flower "if the dew and the rain draw it forth," and to the mind "if it be fed with the sweet dew of the fostering spirit," demonstrates that both the mind and the flower "require[] proper nourishment." So every idea in this answer choice is demonstrated in the relevant text. Note that we don't need to interpret the text or understand the biology of flowers to know that a "flower unfold[ing] its gleaming foliage" is an example of the plant "thriv[ing]," because the word "so" in the phrase "so doth" specifies that the previous statement about the flower is the same as the subsequent statement about the "mind," which "flourish[es], if it be fed"—since "so" can mean something like "in this way" or "in the same way." This lets us know that the "mind flourish[ing], if it be fed" is like the "flower unfold[ing]... if the dew and the rain draw it forth," and we know that "flourish" means basically the same thing as "thrive" from this choice. With all of this in mind, we know (C) is right.

D   **Direct Contradiction:** This is actually the opposite of what the text describes—as we saw in our discussion of (C) above, both the mind and the flower "thrive" when given "nourishment," while the text specifies that a flower "born upon dry earth"—which is the only thing in the text we could call a "challenging circumstance[]"— will "languish," not "persevere[]," as this choice would require. So (D) is wrong.

Test 4, Module 1, Question 12   **TYPE: MAIN IDEA**

The prompt asks about the "main purpose" or "main idea" (or some similar phrase) of the text. The correct answer must be directly restated or demonstrated in the passage, with no interpretation. See "What about "Main Idea/Main Purpose" Questions?" on p.69.

Subjective Phrases to Ignore: "best"

A   **Literary Interpretation:** This choice will be tempting for untrained test-takers, because the text does describe Buck being unsocial. But this choice requires that the text specifically restate or demonstrate the idea that Buck became "less social since he began living with Thornton"—in other words, that he used to be more social, but then he started living with Thornton and became less social. We know right away that this choice must be wrong, because the text never says anything about how Buck was before "living with Thornton," so we have no basis to make the comparison—we can't know if he's "less social" now that he lives with Thornton, because we have no idea what he was like before he lived with Thornton. So (A) can't be right. Some test-takers will read a choice like this and imagine that Buck must have gotten attached to Thornton and protective of him, and that he was probably more open to other people before he met Thornton, because they know some dogs in real life who were that way—but as trained test-takers, we know that we can't ever answer an SAT Reading question based on some dogs we know in real life, or on anything outside of the text that appears on the page.

B   **Literary Interpretation:** This choice could be tempting, because the text does describe Buck "avoid[ing]" "humans": he "walk[s] away" from people who are "demonstrative," and he "refused to notice" two other people. But the text also shows that he doesn't avoid "Thornton," who "held" him; it's only "the rest of mankind" that "was as nothing." We can't say that "Buck" "avoid[s]" "humans" if the text specifically describes him being close to a human. Also, this choice would require the text to say that "Buck mistrusts humans." Untrained test-takers might assume a dog like Buck would "mistrust humans," but that idea doesn't appear in the text—it doesn't say that Buck thinks humans will do him harm, or that he doubts their intentions, or anything else we could call "mistrust[ing]." It just says he's "cold" to "humans," and "walk[s] away" from them, and "refuse[s] to notice them." So (B) is wrong.

C   **Confused Relationships:** This choice could be tempting for untrained test-takers, because the text mentions "Hans and Pete"— who are described as "Thornton's partners"—giving Buck "favors." But this isn't the same as saying that "Buck has been especially well liked by most of Thornton's friends," as this choice requires. For one thing, the phrase "especially well liked" would require the text to demonstrate the idea that Thornton's friends like Buck not just a lot, but specifically *more* than they like other things, in order to justify the word "especially." The fact that "Hans and Pete" gave him "favors" isn't sufficient to demonstrate this idea; even if giving him "favors" means they like him, it doesn't mean they "especially" like him. Also, the text calls "Hans and Pete" Thornton's "partners," but never says they're his "friends," as this choice would require. Finally, the phrase "most of Thornton's friends" *requires* the text to say that more than half of Thornton's friends feel this way, because that's what "most" means—even if Hans and Pete are Thornton's friends, we can't say that "most" of his friends like Buck just because two of them do. For any of these reasons, (C) is wrong.

D ✓   **Correct:** The text starts by saying "Thornton alone held [Buck]" and "the rest of mankind was as nothing." Buck allowing Thornton to hold him demonstrates that Buck had some "regard" for "Thornton" (we also know this from the fact that "Buck refused to notice" "Hans and Pete" "till he learned they were close to Thornton"), and the phrase "the rest of mankind was as nothing" specifies that Buck has no "regard" for "any other person." This exactly demonstrates the statement in this choice, so (D) is correct.

The passage includes a figure. The question asks for the choice that uses data from the figure to accomplish a certain goal. The right answer will describe the data accurately and plainly accomplish the goal. See "What about "Data" Questions?" on p. 69.

Subjective Phrases to Ignore: "most effectively"

A ✓ Correct: This is the only choice that makes an accurate statement about the graph, so it must be correct. It also completes the sentence in the passage that mentions one state's number of organic farms by mentioning another state's number of organic farms.

B   Direct Contradiction: This choice makes an inaccurate statement about the graph, because the graph shows that New York had between 1,000 and 1,200 organic farms, not "fewer than 800 organic farms," as this choice would require. So (B) is wrong.

C   Direct Contradiction: This choice makes an inaccurate statement about the graph; Wisconsin *does* have "between 1,200 and 1,400 organic farms" as this choice states, according to the graph, but Iowa has between 600 and 800, not "between 1,200 and 1,400," as this choice would require. So (C) is wrong.

D   Direct Contradiction: This choice makes an inaccurate statement about the graph, because the graph shows that Pennsylvania had around 800 organic farms, not "more than 1,200 organic farms," as this choice would require. So (D) is wrong.

Note Some test-takers will get hung up wondering whether choice (A) appropriately completes the sentence in the provided text, but once we check all the answer choices and see that (B), (C), and (D) all make inaccurate statements about the graph, we know we can mark (A) and move on.

The passage presents some claim or hypothesis. The prompt typically asks us to choose the "finding" that, "if true," would support or weaken the argument. Supporting statements will demonstrate the idea in the claim, and weakening statements will demonstrate the opposite of the idea in the claim. See "What about "If True" Questions?" on p. 71.

Subjective Phrases to Ignore: "most directly"

A   Off by One or Two Words: The prompt asks for the choice that "support[s]' the "hypothesis." When we read the text, we can see that the "hypothesis" is that "females are attracted to the specific sound made by the males of their own subspecies, and that over time" this will create "further genetic and anatomical divergence between the subspecies." This choice will be tempting for some test-takers because it does mention a physical difference between the two subspecies, which could be an example of "anatomical divergence between the subspecies," an idea that appears in the "hypothesis." But that hypothesis specifies that there will be not just "divergence," but "*further* [emphasis added] genetic and anatomical divergence." A difference between the species isn't the same as "further… divergence" between them; in order to justify the word "further," this choice would have to describe these feathers becoming increasingly narrower over time. This idea doesn't appear in this choice, so (A) is wrong.

B ✓ Correct: This choice describes a sound made by "migratory male[s]" that gets "progressively higher pitched relative to" the sound "made by the feathers of nonmigratory males" "over several generations." This exactly demonstrates the idea from the hypothesis that "over time" there will be "further genetic and anatomical divergence between the subspecies." Notice that the phrase "relative to that made by nonmigratory males" demonstrates the idea of "divergence between the subspecies," and the phrase "progressively higher pitched" demonstrates the idea of "further genetic and anatomical divergence." So every part of (B) demonstrates an idea from the "hypothesis," and we can see that (B) is correct.

C   Off by One or Two Words: This choice has the same basic problem as (A)—it describes something that's "different," but that difference isn't growing over time, so we can't say that it's an example of "further… divergence" "over time," as the hypothesis requires. So (C) is wrong.

D   Direct Contradiction: This is the *opposite* of what the prompt asks for. The "hypothesis" we need to "support" talks about "further… divergence between the subspecies" "over time," but this choice talks about something that "remained… the same over several generations." So (D) is wrong.

The passage includes a figure. The question asks for the choice that uses data from the figure to accomplish a certain goal. The right answer will describe the data accurately and plainly accomplish the goal. See "What about "Data" Questions?" on p. 69.

Subjective Phrases to Ignore: "most effectively"

A   Confused Relationships: The phrase "for example" tells us that the text that follows this phrase is an "example" of the text that preceded it. The sentence before the phrase "for example" says "material in slower-moving SPC or AST dust has a lower rate than the same material in faster-moving HTC or OCC dust." The given text mentions the "ablation rate for iron from AST dust" (which the text tells us is an example of "slower-moving dust"), so to complete the example of the idea from the previous sentence, we need to compare the data for "the same material in faster-moving... dust." This choice *does* use data for the same material, "iron," but it tells us about iron's ablation rate in SPC dust, which the text tells us is "slower-moving," like the "AST dust" already mentioned in this sentence. So this choice wouldn't make the comparison, required by the provided text, between ablation rates for the "same material" in "faster-moving... dust" and "slower-moving... dust," which means (A) is wrong.

B   Confused Relationships: As we saw in our discussion of (A), the comparison in the sentence with the blank should be between ablation rates of the *same material* in faster-moving dust and slower-moving dust, but this choice would compare the rates for different materials—the rate for "sodium" to the rate for "iron." So (B) must be wrong.

C ✓   Correct: As we saw in our discussion of (A), the passage tells us that this example needs to be a comparison between a "material in slower-moving SPC or AST dust" (which already appears in the last sentence), and "the same material in faster-moving HTC or OCC dust" (which is what appears in this choice—namely, "iron" in "HTC dust"). So this choice appropriately completes the example of the idea from the second-to-last sentence by comparing the "ablation rate for iron from AST dust" to the "ablation rate" "for iron from HTC dust." Also, this choice does show that the rate is higher in the "faster-moving dust," as the statement in the second-to-last sentence requires—and we can see that this choice accurately reports the data from the table, as well. For all these reasons, (C) is right.

D   Confused Relationships: This choice basically combines the problems from (A) and (B), because it tells us the rate for a different material (sodium) through slower-moving dust (AST). So (D) is wrong.

Test 4, Module 1, Question 16   **TYPE: QUOTATION**

The prompt will make a claim about a literary work, then ask which quotation "illustrates the claim." The right answer will plainly demonstrate the ideas in the provided claim. See "What about Quotation Questions?" on p. 70.

Subjective Phrases to Ignore: "best"

A ✓   Correct: The prompt asks us for the "quotation" that "illustrates" the "claim." When we read the text, we can see that the "claim" is "this can be difficult for artists who are often used to having sole control over their work." When we check earlier in the text, we can see that the word "this" refers to "art collectives" that "involve some collaboration among the artists." This quotation says "we had a hard time sharing credit and responsibility for our work," which exactly restates the idea from the claim that collectives "can be difficult for artists who are often used to having sole control over their work." Notice that "had a hard time" from this choice restates the phrase "be difficult" from the text, and the idea of "[having] a hard time sharing credit and responsibility" for their work from this choice restates the idea of being "used to having sole control over their work" from the text. So (A) is right.

B   Literary Interpretation: This choice demonstrates the idea of artists "work[ing] together," which appears in the passage. But it doesn't restate or demonstrate the idea that "work[ing] together" was "difficult" for any of the artists, as the "claim" requires; this choice doesn't actually mention any kind of problem or difficulty at all. So (B) must be wrong.

C   Direct Contradiction: This choice illustrates the opposite of the "journalist's claim," because that claim talks about "work[ing] together" being "difficult" for artists, but this quote only mentions "support" from the collective, which "encourages... individual expression rather than limits it." So this choice only describes something good about the collective, while the claim talks about a "difficult" aspect of the collective, which means (C) is wrong.

D   Barely Relevant: This choice has the same basic problem as (B) and (C)—it doesn't mention anything "difficult" about artists working in the collective together, whereas the "claim" that the "quotation" should "illustrate" says working in an "art collective[]" "can be difficult." So (D) must be wrong.

Test 4, Module 1, Question 17   **TYPE: DATA**

The passage includes a figure. The question asks for the choice that uses data from the figure to accomplish a certain goal. The right answer will describe the data accurately and plainly accomplish the goal. See "What about "Data" Questions?" on p. 69.

Subjective Phrases to Ignore: "most effectively"

A ✓   Correct: The sentence with the blank says "the student... was surprised to discover that (blank)," so we know that whatever goes in the blank should be "surpris[ing]." The passage tells us that the student grew "one nonmycorrhizal species," which we're told is "a species that doesn't benefit from and may even be harmed by mycorrhizal fungi." The table tells us that "broccoli" is the plant that's not a "mycorrhizal host"—that is, it's the plant that "doesn't benefit from and may even be harmed by mycorrhizal fungi." This choice would say that the "broccoli grown in soil" with "fungi" had a "slightly higher average mass" than "broccoli grown in soil" without "fungi." This demonstrates something unexpected, as the word "surprised" in the provided text requires, because the passage says a "nonmycorrhizal" species like "broccoli" shouldn't "benefit from... mycorrhizal fungi," and might even be "harmed" by it—but in this case, the broccoli in the experiment grew larger in "soil containing fungi." So (A) is right.

B   Barely Relevant: This choice doesn't describe anything that would be "surpris[ing]," according to the passage. In fact, the comparison made in this choice isn't really relevant to the passage at all, because this choice compares the average masses of two *different* plants—corn and broccoli. In order to consider their relative sizes in light of the information from the text, we would need to compare each plant grown in soil with "fungi" to *the same plant species* grown in soil without "fungi." Comparing two different plant species grown in similar conditions doesn't tell us anything about how the presence or absence of "fungi" in the soil impacts the way either species grows. So (B) must be wrong.

C   Direct Contradiction: This choice actually reports something that would be *expected* based on the passage, not "surpris[ing]" as the last sentence requires. The table tells us that "marigolds" are "mycorrhizal hosts," and the passage says "mycorrhizal hosts" "benefit from mycorrhizal fungi." So the information in this choice that "marigolds grown in soil" with "fungi had a much higher average mass than marigolds grown in soil" without "fungi" is exactly what we would expect, which means it's not "surpris[ing]," as the provided text requires. So (C) is wrong.

D   Direct Contradiction: This choice makes an inaccurate statement about the data in the table, so we know it must be wrong. We can look in the rightmost column of that table to see that broccoli, not corn, "had the highest average mass" of all the plants "grown in soil" without "fungi." Again, this means (D) is wrong.

Test 4, Module 1, Question 18   TYPE: MOST LOGICALLY COMPLETES

The passage ends with a blank, and the answer choices are relatively long phrases. The right answer will restate or demonstrate an idea in the provided text. See "What about "Most Logically Completes" Questions?" on p. 68.

Subjective Phrases to Ignore: "most"

A ✓ Correct: The passage mentions "artworks" that "depict a female figure fishing with a cupid nearby," and that some scholars say "the figure is the goddess Venus," because she is associated with "cupids" "in Roman culture." But someone else says "cupids may have also been associated with fishing." If this is true, then the cupids might only be in the "artworks" because they're associated with "fishing"—and not because "Venus" appears in the "artworks." In other words, the "associat[ion] with fishing" provides an alternate explanation for the cupids' presence in the artworks (other than the female figure being Venus, who cupids are also "linked with"). This alternate explanation demonstrates the idea that "cupid" appearing "near the female figure" doesn't necessarily mean "the figure is Venus," just as this choice says. So (A) is right.

B   Confused Relationships: This choice takes several ideas from the text and mixes them up—the passage does mention "Venus" being connected to "a cupid," and "cupids" being connected to "fishing," but the text doesn't make any direct connection between "Venus" and "fishing," as this choice would require—instead, it discusses whether "a female figure fishing with a cupid nearby" is "Venus" or not. As we saw in our discussion of (A), the figure might be Venus, or might not. This isn't a basis for saying "Venus was often depicted fishing," as this choice would require—in fact, based on the text, we're not certain she was *ever* depicted fishing. So (B) is wrong.

C   Confused Relationships: As we saw in our discussion of (A), the "cupid... near the female figure" doesn't mean the figure *can't* be Venus, as this choice would require; it only means that the figure doesn't *have* to be Venus. The passage tells us that the reason people think she might be Venus is because of the presence of a cupid, but the passage also tells us there's another reason for a cupid to be there—because cupids are "associated with fishing," and someone in the "artworks" is fishing. So, again, the figure might be Venus, or might not, which means (C) is wrong.

D   Direct Contradiction: This is the opposite of what the text states; the cupid *wouldn't* be difficult to account for, because the text specifically tells us another reason why a "cupid" would be nearby (even "if the figure is not Venus," as this choice states), which is that cupids are "associated with fishing," and someone in the "artworks" is fishing. So (D) is wrong.

Test 4, Module 1, Question 19   TYPE: SAT WRITING

- Vertical Scan Results: Each choice is different versions of the same two words.
- Vertical Scan Notes: We have to decide whether "people" and/or "stories" should be plural and/or possessive.
- Key Features in Surrounding Text: The provided text talks about "ghostwriters" who write "stories" that belong to "other people." So the word "stories" should be plural, and the "stories" belong to "people." That means "people" should be in a possessive form. Nothing in the text belongs to "stories," so "stories" shouldn't be possessive.

Concepts in the question:

- Possessive and/or Plural: Choices include nouns ending in "-s," with or without an apostrophe before or after the "-s." The provided text will indicate which nouns should show ownership, and which shouldn't. (See page 79.)

ANSWER CHOICE ANALYSIS

A ✓   Correct: This is the only choice that includes a possessive form of "people," and a non-possessive form of "story." So (A) is correct. See the analysis above for more.

B   Incorrect: This choice is the opposite of the right answer, because "peoples" isn't possessive, and "story's" is. So (B) is wrong. See the analysis above for more.

C   Incorrect: This choice is wrong because "peoples" isn't possessive. See the analysis above for more.

D   Incorrect: This choice is wrong because "story's" is possessive. See the analysis above for more.

- Vertical Scan Results: Each choice is a different version of the same verb.
- Vertical Scan Notes: We have to decide whether a past or present form of "survive" is appropriate, among other things.
- Key Features in Surrounding Text: Every verb in the text is in the present tense ("is," "helps") and nothing indicates that this verb happens in a different time frame—so the right answer should be in the present tense as well.

Concepts in the question:

- Parallelism: The surrounding text includes phrasing and/or grammatical structures that should be mirrored by what appears in the blank. (See page 93.)
- Verb Tense/Conjugation: Choices include different forms of the same verb. Look at the surrounding text to find the verb's subject. Also, look for other clues that could indicate the proper tense or form of the verb in the blank. (See page 77.)

ANSWER CHOICE ANALYSIS

A   Incorrect: This verb is in the past tense, but every other verb in the sentence is in the present tense, and nothing indicates that this verb should happen in a different time frame from the other verbs. So (A) is wrong.

B   Incorrect: This choice has the same basic problems as (A), and is wrong for the same reason.

C   Incorrect: As we saw in our discussion above, there is nothing in the provided text to indicate that this verb form should be anything but the present tense, and nothing in the text justifies the presence of "would" in this choice. So (C) is wrong.

D ✓   Correct: This choice is the only present tense verb form, which means it's the only one that satisfies our reasoning above. So (D) is right.

     Note   Many untrained test-takers approach SAT Writing questions by mentally inserting each answer choice into the blank, and then just asking themselves which option "sounds best" to them. But as trained test-takers, we know that we need to select answers based on applying the rules in the SAT Writing Toolbox to the specific words and phrases that appear in the question. In this case, there's nothing in the text we can point to that justifies using anything but the present tense in the blank, so we can eliminate (A), (B), and (C) with confidence, and pick the correct answer, (D). Remember on test day that we never answer based on how anything "sounds" to us; we only ever pick answer choices based on the SAT's rules and standards.

- Vertical Scan Results: Each choice is the same three words with different punctuation.
- Vertical Scan Notes: Every choice has a dash after "ran," so we know that first dash is part of the right answer. We have to decide whether a dash, comma, period, or nothing should appear between "fast" and "during."
- Key Features in Surrounding Text: "Defying all… fast" can stand on its own as a sentence, and "during the… Olympics" can stand on its own as a sentence.

Concepts in the question:

- Comma Splice: A comma can't join two groups of words that could each be sentences on their own. (See page 83.)
- Independent and Dependent Clauses: Choices would create and/or join clauses. An independent clause can stand on its own as a sentence, and a dependent clause can't. Remember rules for joining clauses related to periods, semi-colons, colons, commas, and conjunctions. (See page 82.)

ANSWER CHOICE ANALYSIS

A   Incorrect: This choice would use a dash to separate two groups of words that can each stand on their own as sentences, which isn't acceptable on the SAT. So (A) is wrong.

B   Incorrect: This choice would result in two groups of words that can each stand on their own as sentences not having any punctuation, conjunction, or relative pronoun between them, which isn't acceptable on the SAT. So (B) is wrong.

C   Incorrect: This choice creates a comma splice, because it would cause two groups of words that can each stand on their own as sentences to be separated by a comma, which isn't acceptable on the SAT. So (C) is wrong.

D ✓   Correct: This choice would separate two groups of words that can each stand on their own as sentences with a period, which is acceptable on the SAT. So (D) is right.

Test 4, Module 1, Question 22   TYPE: SAT WRITING

- Vertical Scan Results: Each choice is a different version of the same verb.
- Vertical Scan Notes: We have to decide whether "to be" should be past, present, singular, or plural.
- Key Features in Surrounding Text: When we ignore the intervening phrase "representing the mountain itself," we can see that the subject of the verb is the singular noun "triangle." So this verb should be singular as well. Only one choice is singular, so we can pick the right answer choice based on this issue alone.

Concepts in the question:

- Intervening Phrase: A distracting phrase appears between words that need to agree with each other grammatically. Identify pairs of words that need to agree with each other, and ignore phrases that appear between those words. (See page 92.)
- Verb Tense/Conjugation: Choices include different forms of the same verb. Look at the surrounding text to find the verb's subject. Also, look for other clues that could indicate the proper tense or form of the verb in the blank. (See page 77.)

ANSWER CHOICE ANALYSIS

A   Incorrect: As discussed above, the verb form needs to be singular, but this is a plural verb form. So (A) is wrong.

B   Incorrect: This choice has the same problem as (A), and is wrong for the same reason.

C   Incorrect: This choice has the same problem as (A) and (B), and is wrong for the same reason.

D ✓   Correct: This is the only singular verb form, so it's the only choice that can agree with the singular subject "triangle." That means (D) is right.

Note   This is a classic pattern in SAT Writing questions involving verb forms—several choices are in different tenses, and some test-takers will focus on that issue and get distracted by the fact that the verb form needs to be singular, and only one choice is singular. Once we notice this, we can ignore the tense issue and just pick the only choice that agrees in number with its subject.

Test 4, Module 1, Question 23   TYPE: SAT WRITING

- Vertical Scan Results: Each choice is the same word with different punctuation, and two choices include an additional word.
- Vertical Scan Notes: We have to decide whether a comma, semi-colon, or nothing should appear after "sampler," and whether "later" and a comma should appear at the end of the choice.
- Key Features in Surrounding Text: "In 2004… sampler" can stand on its own as a sentence, and "in 2014… pillars" can stand on its own as a sentence, whether "later" appears at the beginning of that sentence or not.

Concepts in the question:

- Commas: Commas can be used between clauses, to form comma sandwiches, in a list of 3 or more items, and before reported speech. They can't appear for no reason. Review the training for the relevant details. (See page 86.)
- Independent and Dependent Clauses: Choices would create and/or join clauses. An independent clause can stand on its own as a sentence, and a dependent clause can't. Remember rules for joining clauses related to periods, semi-colons, colons, commas, and conjunctions. (See page 82.)
- Semicolons: Semicolons can be used to separate two sets of words that could each stand on their own as complete sentences, or to separate items in a complex list. (See page 86.)

ANSWER CHOICE ANALYSIS

A   Incorrect: This choice would result in two groups of words that can each stand on their own as sentences not having any punctuation, conjunction, or relative pronoun between them, which isn't acceptable on the SAT. So (A) is wrong.

B ✓   Correct: This choice would separate two groups of words that can each stand on their own as sentences with a semi-colon, which is acceptable on the SAT. So (B) is right.

C   Incorrect: This choice creates a comma splice, because it would cause two groups of words that can each stand on their own as sentences to be separated by a comma, which isn't acceptable on the SAT.

D   Incorrect: This choice has the same problem as (C), and is wrong for the same reason.

This question will throw off some test-takers, because they won't know what the word "sampler" means, and because they'll wonder whether including the word "later" changes whether the text from that point on can stand on its own as a sentence or not. But all we need to know about the word "sampler" is that it's a noun, and the object of the verb "craft." We can be sure it's a noun, because the text describes it as "10-by-13-inch," and anything with physical dimensions has to be a noun. Also, the presence or absence of the word "later" doesn't change the fact that the text after the blank contains an independent clause, and can be its own sentence. Once we clear those words up, this is a fairly straightforward SAT Writing question. Remember that the College Board loves to include slightly unusual words or phrases in an effort to fluster you—don't let them succeed! Keep your training in mind, and if you *do* get flustered, don't stress about skipping the question you're on and coming back to it later.

Test 4, Module 1, Question 24   **TYPE: SAT WRITING**

- Vertical Scan Results: Each choice is a long phrase involving similar words ordered in different ways.
- Vertical Scan Notes: We need to pick the choice that begins with a phrase that can be described by the phrase before the blank.
- Key Features in Surrounding Text: The participial phrase before the blank says "Named… as one of the greatest achievements…." So whatever noun phrase appears first in the following independent clause has to be something that can be "named" as an "achievement[]."

Concepts in the question:

- Avoid Dangling Participles: When a phrase starting with an -ing/-ed/-en word is joined to the main sentence by a comma, the first noun phrase in the independent clause of that sentence is described by the -ing/-ed/-en word. (See page 90.)

ANSWER CHOICE ANALYSIS

A   Incorrect: According to our analysis above, this choice would say that "Julian" was "named" as an "achievement," but a person can't be an "achievement." So (A) is wrong.

B   Incorrect: This choice has the same problem as (A), and is wrong for the same reason.

C ✓   Correct: According to our analysis above, this choice would say that "Julian's 1935 synthesis" was "named" as an "achievement," which makes sense—even if we're not familiar with the word "synthesis," the phrase "Julian's 1935" tells us that this was something Julian did at a certain time, and something that a person does can be called an "achievement." So (C) is right.

D   Incorrect: This choice will be very tempting for some test-takers, but it ultimately has the same problem as (A) and (B)—it calls something an "achievement" that can't be called an "achievement." The "alkaloid physostigmine" itself isn't the "achievement," it's some physical object or substance. An "achievement" is something that a person *does*—like the "synthesis" from choice (C), the correct answer—not a physical thing, as we see in this choice. In everyday conversation we might not make this distinction, but on the SAT this is exactly the kind of thing that separates right answers from wrong answers. So (D) is wrong.

Note   Each choice contains the phrase "the alkaloid physostigmine." Some test-takers will feel like they can't pick the right answer if they don't know what this phrase means, but in fact all we need to know about this phrase is that it describes something that can be "synthesized"—and for that matter, all we need to know about the word "synthesized" is that it's an action a person can do, as we saw in our discussion of (C). Never assume that you can't answer a question because of the presence of an unknown word or phrase! Occasionally this can cause a problem, but more often than not, such a word or phrase has no impact on your ability to find the right answer. Just stay calm and apply your training.

Test 4, Module 1, Question 25   **TYPE: SAT WRITING**

- Vertical Scan Results: Each choice contains the same words with different punctuation.
- Vertical Scan Notes: We have to decide whether there should be a comma, semi-colon, or nothing after "species" and "nonnative."
- Key Features in Surrounding Text: The underlined phrase is part of a complex list of three things: "growing diverse plant species, both native and nonnative," "fostering scientific research," and "educating the public about plant conservation." The phrase "both native and nonnative" is a descriptive phrase that modifies "diverse plant species." We know that a semi-colon needs to appear between the different items on the list, and that the descriptive phrase "both native and nonnative" should be separated from the thing it describes by a comma.

Concepts in the question:

- **Commas:** Commas can be used between clauses, to form comma sandwiches, in a list of 3 or more items, and before reported speech. They can't appear for no reason. Review the training for the relevant details. (See page 86.)
- **Complex List:** A complex list is a list of items where at least one item is a phrase that includes a comma. Items in a complex list must be separated from each other by a semi-colon. (See page 86.)

A   Incorrect: This choice does separate the phrase "both native and nonnative" from "diverse plant species" with a comma, but it uses a comma instead of a semi-colon to separate "growing diverse plant species, both native and nonnative" from "fostering scientific research," so it doesn't satisfy our reasoning above. That means (A) is wrong.

B ✓   Correct: This choice satisfies our reasoning above: it separates the phrase "both native and nonnative" from "diverse plant species" with a comma, and it uses a semi-colon to separate "growing diverse plant species, both native and nonnative" from "fostering scientific research." So (B) is right.

C   Incorrect: This choice switches the placement of the comma and semi-colon that we saw in the right answer, (B), which would make it unclear how the phrase "both native and nonnative" is related to the rest of the sentence. So (C) is wrong.

D   Incorrect: This choice fails to separate "both native and nonnative" from the thing it describes with a comma, and it uses a comma instead of a semi-colon to separate "growing diverse plant species, both native and nonnative" from "fostering scientific research." So (D) is wrong.

Test 4, Module 1, Question 26   **TYPE: SAT WRITING**

- **Vertical Scan Results:** Each choice is the same words with different punctuation.
- **Vertical Scan Notes:** We have to decide whether a comma, semi-colon, or nothing should appear after "single-handedly" and after "however."
- **Key Features in Surrounding Text:** "Okinaka doesn't… single-handedly" can stand on its own as a sentence, whether or not the word "however" appears at the end, and "all historical… culture" can also stand on its own as a sentence, whether or not the word "however" appears at the beginning. If "however" is connected to the independent clause before the blank, then it refers to the relationship between that independent clause and the sentence before it, but if "however" is connected to the independent clause after the blank, then it refers to the relationship between that independent clause and the independent clause before the blank. (If that doesn't make sense, right now, just keep reading—and if you're still not clear on this walkthrough after you read it, maybe read the whole thing through a second time.)

Concepts in the question:

- **Commas:** Commas can be used between clauses, to form comma sandwiches, in a list of 3 or more items, and before reported speech. They can't appear for no reason. Review the training for the relevant details. (See page 86.)
- **Independent and Dependent Clauses:** Choices would create and/or join clauses. An independent clause can stand on its own as a sentence, and a dependent clause can't. Remember rules for joining clauses related to periods, semi-colons, colons, commas, and conjunctions. (See page 82.)

A ✓   Correct: This choice would separate two groups of words that can each stand on their own as sentences with a semi-colon, which is acceptable on the SAT. It would also appropriately connect the word "however" to the first of the two independent clauses affected by this blank—this results in "however" reflecting the opposition between the idea in the first sentence that "Okinaka" has a certain "task[]," and the idea in the following independent clause that he doesn't perform this task "single-handedly." So (A) is correct.

B   Incorrect: This choice would separate two groups of words that can each stand on their own as sentences with a semi-colon, which is acceptable on the SAT. However, unlike the correct answer (A), this choice would connect the word "however" to the second of the two independent clauses affected by this blank. The word "however" requires that the two ideas it connects must be opposed to each other in some way, but the independent clauses before and after the blank don't demonstrate this relationship. The previous clause says "Okinaka doesn't make such decisions single-handedly," and the following clause says the decisions involve "a group of nine other experts." These clauses express similar, related ideas, with no opposition between them that would justify the word "however" connecting them. So (B) is wrong.

C   Incorrect: This choice creates a comma splice, because it would cause two groups of words that can each stand on their own as sentences to be separated by a comma, which isn't acceptable on the SAT.

D   **Incorrect:** This choice would result in two groups of words that can each stand on their own as sentences not having any punctuation, conjunction, or relative pronoun between them, which isn't acceptable on the SAT.

> **Note**   Most test-takers who are comfortable with these question types won't have much trouble eliminating (C) and (D). The challenge in this question is that it contains the added wrinkle of deciding whether the semi-colon should appear before or after the word "however." We know that the word "however" signals some kind of difference or opposition between the clause where it appears and the previous clause, so in order to choose between (A) and (B), we have to think about whether that opposition exists between the first sentence and the clause before the blank, or between the clause before the blank and the clause after the blank. After we take this extra step, we can select the right answer, as discussed above.

Test 4, Module 1, Question 27   TYPE: LOGICAL TRANSITION

The choices are different transition phrases like "however," "instead of," or "for example." The right answer must reflect the relationship between the concepts before and after the blank. See "What about Logical Transition Questions?" on p. 71.

Subjective Phrases to Ignore: "most"

A   **Confused Relationships:** This choice would be appropriate if this sentence told us something that happened in place of something else from the previous sentence—for example, if the last sentence ended with something like "everyone said the bill would fail," then this sentence could say "instead, the bill passed." But that's not the case, and (A) is wrong.

B   **Confused Relationships:** This choice would be appropriate if this sentence described some additional information that was similar to the information in the previous sentence, but that's not the case. So (B) is wrong.

C ✓   **Correct:** The text mentions a bill "introduced" "in 1968," and then says the bill was "resubmitted" for "fifteen years." The sentence with the blank says what happened with the bill "in 1983." The word "finally" appropriately reflects the fact that this sentence describes something that happened after a long period of time. So (C) is right.

D   **Confused Relationships:** This choice has the same basic problem as (B), and is wrong for the same reason.

Test 4, Module 1, Question 28   TYPE: LOGICAL TRANSITION

The choices are different transition phrases like "however," "instead of," or "for example." The right answer must reflect the relationship between the concepts before and after the blank. See "What about Logical Transition Questions?" on p. 71.

Subjective Phrases to Ignore: "most"

A   **Confused Relationships:** This choice would only be appropriate if the previous sentence contained a word or phrase like "firstly." If that were the case, then "secondly" could introduce an additional, similar idea related to the idea introduced by "firstly." But this isn't present in the provided text, so (A) is wrong.

B   **Confused Relationships:** This choice would work if the idea in this second sentence were the logical result of what was mentioned in the first sentence—but that's not the case, as we'll see in our discussion of (D). So (B) is wrong.

C   **Direct Contradiction:** This choice would be appropriate if this sentence included an additional idea that reinforced an idea in the previous sentence, but that's not the case—in fact, this sentence contains an idea that is the *opposite* of what appears in the previous sentence. So (C) is wrong.

D ✓   **Correct:** The first sentence says that "geoscientists have long considered Hawaii's Mauna Loa volcano to be Earth's largest shield volcano." The sentence with the blank then introduces an opposing idea—that a different "shield volcano is significantly larger." The word "however" reflects this opposing relationship between one volcano being seen as the biggest, but another one actually being larger—so (D) is right.

Test 4, Module 1, Question 29   TYPE: LOGICAL TRANSITION

The choices are different transition phrases like "however," "instead of," or "for example." The right answer must reflect the relationship between the concepts before and after the blank. See "What about Logical Transition Questions?" on p. 71.

Subjective Phrases to Ignore: "most"

A ✓   **Correct:** The second sentence says that "Coleridge-Taylor emphasized his mixed-race ancestry." The following sentence provides one example of that: "he referred to himself as Anglo-African." The next sentence, which is the one with the blank, mentions another example of that idea: "he incorporated… African music into his… compositions." This choice appropriately reflects the idea that this sentence provides another example of "Coleridge-Taylor emphasiz[ing] his mixed-race ancestry" on top of the one in the previous sentence. So "in addition" in choice (A) is correct.

B   Direct Contradiction: This choice would indicate that this sentence contains some information that it unexpected, given the information in the previous sentence. But that's not the case—in fact, this sentence contains an additional example along the same lines as the example from the previous sentence, as we saw in our discussion of (A). So (B) is wrong.

C   Direct Contradiction: This choice has basically the same problem as (B), and is wrong for the same reason.

D   Confused Relationships: This choice would indicate that that the idea in this sentence is true in spite of the idea in the previous sentence, but as we saw in our discussion of (A), this sentence just provides another example like the one in the previous sentence. So (D) is wrong.

Test 4, Module 1, Question 30	TYPE: LOGICAL TRANSITION

The choices are different transition phrases like "however," "instead of," or "for example." The right answer must reflect the relationship between the concepts before and after the blank. See "What about Logical Transition Questions?" on p. 71.

Subjective Phrases to Ignore: "most"

A ✓   Correct: This choice indicates that the idea in this sentence is a logical conclusion based on the idea in the preceding sentence. This is accurate because the previous sentence says the "dish," which has a name meaning "unwinding," "inspired a sense of calm," and this sentence says that "the researchers," who knew that "dishes were… named after their… effects," "theorized" that this dish was named after its effect. The "theor[y]" in this sentence that the dish got its name because it helped people "relax" is the logical result of the fact in the previous sentence that the dish's name meant "unwinding," and the dish "inspired a sense of calm." So "therefore" reflects the relationship between the ideas before and after the blank, and (A) is right.

B   Direct Contradiction: This choice would work if this sentence expressed an idea that was a different option from what was proposed in the previous sentence—but as we saw in our discussion of (A), that's not the case. So (B) is wrong.

C   Direct Contradiction: This choice would be correct if this sentence expressed an idea that was true in spite of what appears in the previous sentence, but that's not the case—so (C) is wrong.

D   Confused Relationships: This choice will be tempting for some test-takers who don't think carefully about what the word "likewise" means, and just like this choice because they have a vague sense that this word can connect two related ideas. But "likewise" would introduce new, additional information that's similar to what comes before this sentence, which isn't what appears in the text. In this case, as we saw in our discussion of (A), the information in this sentence contains a conclusion based on the idea in the previous sentence, which demonstrates a relationship between those two sentences that "likewise" doesn't express. So (D) is wrong.

Test 4, Module 1, Question 31	TYPE: NOTES

The passage presents a bulleted list of notes, then tells us a goal related to presenting that information. The correct answer will be the only one that demonstrates the ideas in the provided goal. See "What about Notes Questions?" on p. 71.

Subjective Phrases to Ignore: "most"

A   Direct Contradiction: The prompt tells us that we need to pick the choice that "emphasize[s] a difference between baking soda and baking powder." This choice might be tempting for some test-takers, because it does mention both "baking soda and baking powder." But this choice actually tells us something *similar* about them, which is that they're both "leavening agents." So this choice does the opposite of what the prompt requires, and it's wrong.

B   Direct Contradiction: This choice has the exact same problem as (A), and is wrong for the same reason—it tells us something that is true about both "baking soda and baking powder," instead of a "difference" between them, as the prompt requires. So (B) is wrong.

C   Barely Relevant: This choice tells us some specific information about "baking soda," but it doesn't even mention "baking powder," so it can't "emphasize a difference between baking soda and baking powder," as the prompt requires. So (C) is wrong.

D ✓   Correct: This choice tells us that "baking soda needs to be mixed with an acidic ingredient" in order "to produce carbon dioxide," but that "baking powder does not." The idea that baking soda does something but "baking powder does not" exactly demonstrates a "difference between baking soda and baking powder," as the prompt requires. So (D) is right.

Test 4, Module 1, Question 32	TYPE: NOTES

The passage presents a bulleted list of notes, then tells us a goal related to presenting that information. The correct answer will be the only one that demonstrates the ideas in the provided goal. See "What about Notes Questions?" on p. 71.

Subjective Phrases to Ignore: "most"

A   Off by One or Two Words: The prompt tells us to find the choice that "describe[s] *Unwoven Light* to an audience unfamiliar with Soo Sunny Park." This choice *does* "describe *Unwoven Light*" when it mentions that the work "included a chain-link fence and iridescent tiles made from plexiglass." But we know from our training that if the right answer mentions Soo Sunny Park, then it must also introduce her, since the prompt tells us the "audience" is "unfamiliar with Soo Sunny Park." This choice fails to do that, so (A) is wrong.

B   Confused Relationships: This choice will be tempting for some test-takers, because it provides some information about Soo Sunny Park (as the prompt requires when it tells us the "audience" is "unfamiliar with Soo Sunny Park"), and it also mentions *Unwoven Light*. But mentioning something isn't the same as "describ[ing]" it, and this choice doesn't provide any description of "*Unwoven Light*," as the prompt requires—so (B) is wrong.

C   Off by One or Two Words: This choice is basically similar to (A); it provides some details about *Unwoven Light* but doesn't tell us anything about Soo Sunny Park. So (C) is wrong.

D ✓   Correct: This choice provides basic information about "Soo Sunny Park," as the prompt requires when it tells us the "audience" is "unfamiliar with Soo Sunny Park": it calls her "Korean American artist Soo Sunny Park." This choice also describes *Unwoven Light* when it says that in this work, "light formed colorful prisms as it passed through a fence Park had fitted with iridescent tiles." This choice meets all the requirements of the prompt, so (D) is correct.

Test 4, Module 1, Question 33	TYPE: NOTES

The passage presents a bulleted list of notes, then tells us a goal related to presenting that information. The correct answer will be the only one that demonstrates the ideas in the provided goal. See "What about Notes Questions?" on p. 71.

Subjective Phrases to Ignore: "most"

A   Off by One or Two Words: The prompt asks for a choice that "present[s] Tan's research to an audience unfamiliar with Angkor Wat." This choice tells us about "Tan's research," as the prompt requires, but it mentions Angkor Wat without providing any information about what Angkor Wat is, as though the reader is already familiar with it—this fails to meet the prompt's requirement about presenting information "to an audience unfamiliar with Angkor Wat," so (A) is wrong. (Remember from our training that when the prompt tells us to pick a choice for an audience that's unfamiliar with some concept, any mention of that concept must include basic introductory information.)

B   Barely Relevant: This choice tells us about a technique that Tan used in his research, but we can't say it "present[s]" that research, as the prompt requires, because we know from the notes that the research was done with images of Angkor Wat, and Angkor Wat isn't even mentioned. So (B) is wrong.

C ✓   Correct: This choice "present[s] Tan's research" when it tells the reader that "Tan revealed hundreds of images hidden on the walls of Angkor Wat" by "using a novel digital imaging technique." It also tells us that "Angkor Wat" is "a Cambodian temple"; this accounts for the idea from the prompt that the "audience" is "unfamiliar with Angkor Wat" by providing some basic introductory information about what "Angkor Wat" is. This choice satisfies all the requirements of the prompt, so it's right.

D   Barely Relevant: This choice addresses the idea from the prompt about presenting information to an "audience unfamiliar with Angkor Wat" by telling the reader what Angkor Wat is, but this choice doesn't tell us anything about "Tan's research," as the prompt requires. In fact, it doesn't even mention Tan at all. So (D) is wrong.

TEST 4, MODULE 2

Test 4, Module 2, Question 1	TYPE: TEXT COMPLETION

The prompt will be a short passage containing a blank. The correct answer will always be restated or demonstrated by key phrases in the provided text. See "What about Text Completion Questions?" on p. 66.

Subjective Phrases to Ignore: "most"

A   Confused Relationships: This choice will be tempting for some test-takers who feel like the idea of "produc[ing]" something is related to the discussion in the text about "market[s]," and "consumers," and "revenues," etc. But this text doesn't actually restate or demonstrate the idea of anyone "produc[ing]" anything—in fact, it specifically talks about the "resale market," which depends on selling things that already exist. Beyond that, inserting this word into the provided sentence wouldn't even describe "produc[ing]" goods for sale; instead, it would result in the phrase "analysts <u>produce</u> that revenues...," which doesn't even really have any clear meaning. So (A) is wrong.

B   Direct Contradiction: The idea that "revenues will more than double" demonstrates the "continued growth" which the text says the "analysts" are "expecting to see." The word "denied" would indicate that the "analysts" *don't* think that "revenues will more than double," but again, the provided text specifically says the "analysts" are "expecting to see continued growth." So this choice would cause the text to contradict itself, which means it's wrong. Beyond that, nothing in the text restates or demonstrates the idea of the "analysts" (or anyone else) "den[ying]" anything. See the discussion of (D) for more.

C   **Barely Relevant:** In order for this choice to be correct, the text would specifically have to tell us or show us that the "analysts" were "worried" that "revenues" would "more than double." But this idea doesn't appear in the text—as we saw in our discussion of the other answer choices, the only thing we're told about the analysts is that they're "expecting to see continued growth." Nothing in the provided text restates or demonstrates anyone "worr[ying]" about anything, so (C) is wrong.

D ✓   **Correct:** The sentence containing the blank starts with the phrase "expecting to see continued growth," which describes "analysts," and the "analysts" are the ones doing the action in the blank. This choice would cause the text to say that "analysts predicted that revenues will more than double by 2028." This exactly demonstrates the idea that those analysts "expect[] to see continued growth." To "predict" something means to say what you think will happen—that is, what you "expect[]"; the analysts "expect" that "continued growth" will happen, and "revenue… more than doubl[ing]" is an example of "continued growth." So this choice demonstrates a relevant idea from the provided text, which means (D) is correct.

Test 4, Module 2, Question 2	TYPE: TEXT COMPLETION

The prompt will be a short passage containing a blank. The correct answer will always be restated or demonstrated by key phrases in the provided text. See "What about Text Completion Questions?" on p. 66.

Subjective Phrases to Ignore: "most"

A   **Direct Contradiction:** This choice will be appealing to test-takers who feel like the word "conceptualize" sounds relevant to a discussion of scientists addressing a "problem." "Conceptualize" means something like "form an idea or concept of something," and this choice would cause the text to say that "it may be possible to conceptualize this problem…." But the problem is *already* "conceptualize[d]" in the text itself in the phrase "it is difficult to transmit biomolecules through the layers of the plant cell wall," and the people mentioned in the text couldn't even work on the problem if it weren't "conceptualize[d]" already—so it doesn't make any sense to say something "may be possible" when we can clearly see that it *is* possible. Beyond all of that, nothing in the text restates or demonstrates the idea of "conceptualiz[ing]" a "problem by transmitting molecules through carbon nanotubes," as this choice would require; in fact, it's not even clear what that could mean. With all of this in mind, (A) is wrong.

B   **Direct Contradiction:** As we'll see in our discussion of (D), the text demonstrates the idea of resolving the "difficult[y]" mentioned earlier in the text, which is essentially the opposite of "neglect[ing]" the problem, as this choice would require—so (B) is wrong.

C   **Direct Contradiction:** This choice is fairly similar to (A); the text itself already "illustrate[s]" the problem by describing it in the phrase "it is difficult to transmit biomolecules through the layers of the plant cell wall." So saying that "it may be possible to illustrate this problem" would contradict the fact that the problem is already "illustrate[d]" earlier in the text. We can't say it "may be possible" when we know for sure it's possible, because the text itself does that. Like (A), this choice also has the problem that the idea of "illustrat[ing]" a "problem by transmitting molecules through carbon nanotubes" isn't restated or demonstrated anywhere in the text, and doesn't even have a clear meaning in English. So (C) is wrong.

D ✓   **Correct:** The text tells us that it is "difficult to transmit biomolecules through the layers of the plant cell wall." Then it tells us that "transmitting molecules through carbon nanotubes" is possible, and that "carbon nanotubes… can cross cell walls." The idea that it's hard to "transmit biomolecules" "through… the cell wall," but that "it may be possible" to "transmit[] molecules through carbon nanotubes" that can "cross cell walls" demonstrates the idea of "overcom[ing]" the "problem" from earlier in the text, exactly as this choice requires. So (D) is correct.

Test 4, Module 2, Question 3	TYPE: TEXT COMPLETION

The prompt will be a short passage containing a blank. The correct answer will always be restated or demonstrated by key phrases in the provided text. See "What about Text Completion Questions?" on p. 66.

Subjective Phrases to Ignore: "most"

A   **Plausible but not in the Text:** This choice might be tempting for test-takers who don't read carefully and just imagine that scientists looking at "particles" might "select[]" some of them for some purpose, but we can't pick this choice unless the text specifically restates or demonstrates the idea of choosing something—and it doesn't. So (A) is wrong.

B ✓   **Correct:** The text says that the physicists "(blank) what is invisible to the naked eye," and then says "they closely examine the behavior of subatomic particles," which are "the smallest detectable parts of matter." The colon between "(blank) what is invisible to the naked eye" and "they closely examine the behavior of subatomic particles" tells us that these phrases restate each other; the word "inspecting" from this choice exactly restates the phrase "closely examine," so (B) is right. (Also notice that "what is invisible to the naked eye" restates "subatomic particles, the smallest detectable parts of matter.")

C   **Plausible but not in the Text:** In another context, physicists might "creat[e]" things, as this choice requires—but nothing in the provided text restates or demonstrates the idea of anyone creating anything. So (C) must be wrong.

D   **Plausible but not in the Text:** This choice is similar to (A) and (C), because it includes a verb that sounds kind of related to what "physicists" probably do sometimes in their work. But, like (A) and (C), (D) is wrong because the text never restates or demonstrates the concept from this choice—nothing in the text talks about anyone "deciding" anything. Instead, the text demonstrates the idea of "<u>inspecting</u> what is invisible to the naked eye" when it mentions "closely examin[ing] the behavior of subatomic particles," as we saw in our discussion of (B).

Test 4, Module 2, Question 4	TYPE: TEXT COMPLETION

The prompt will be a short passage containing a blank. The correct answer will always be restated or demonstrated by key phrases in the provided text. See "What about Text Completion Questions?" on p. 66.

Subjective Phrases to Ignore: "most"

A   **Plausible but not in the Text:** In order for this choice to be correct, the text would have to specify that the "clavicle and shoulder bones" of the "early hominin" were not as good as those of "modern apes," as the phrase "surpassed by" from this choice requires. Some untrained test-takers might assume that "modern" "bones" would "surpass[]" "3.6-million-year-old" bones in some way, but this idea isn't actually present in the text—so (A) is wrong.

B ✓   **Correct:** The text says the "clavicle and shoulder bones" of the "early hominin" were "(blank) the clavicle and shoulder bones of modern apes that are frequent climbers," and that this "suggest[ed]" that the "early hominin" "had adapted to life in the trees." This choice would cause the text to say that the bones of the "early hominin" were "comparable" to those of "frequent climbers." The "suggest[ion]" that the hominin "had adapted to life in the trees" demonstrates the idea that "these bones" were "comparable" to those of "frequent climbers." So this choice results in a phrase that demonstrates a relevant idea from the text, which means it's right.

C   **Direct Contradiction:** This choice might be tempting for untrained test-takers who assume that the older bones were different from and unrelated to the bones of "modern apes." But as we saw in our discussion of (B), they were actually *similar* to one another, which means (C) is basically the opposite of the right answer.

D   **Plausible but not in the Text:** This choice will be tempting for test-takers who try to use outside knowledge about evolution and related species to justify the idea that one set of bones was "obtained from" the other set, but there are several problems with this idea. For one, this choice would say the older bones were "obtained from" the newer bones, which isn't possible, since the newer bones didn't exist when the older bones developed. For another, even if one set of bones evolved from another set, this isn't the same as saying it was "obtained from" the other set. Finally, and most importantly, the text doesn't restate or demonstrate the idea of anything being "obtained from" anything else. So (D) is wrong.

Test 4, Module 2, Question 5	TYPE: TEXT COMPLETION

The prompt will be a short passage containing a blank. The correct answer will always be restated or demonstrated by key phrases in the provided text. See "What about Text Completion Questions?" on p. 66.

Subjective Phrases to Ignore: "most"

A   **Barely Relevant:** The text says that a character in a certain author's book is a poet, and that being a poet in a book written by that author "is not (blank)." Then it tells us that "nearly a dozen of the characters that populate [this author's] novels are poets or writers." The colon in between these phrases tells us that they restate each other. Not being "infallible" means that someone isn't perfect, and can make mistakes—but the idea of people making mistakes or not making mistakes doesn't appear in the text, and doesn't necessarily describe what a "poet" is or isn't. So (A) is wrong.

B ✓   **Correct:** This choice would say that being a poet in this author's books "is not <u>atypical</u>," which is exactly demonstrated by the following statement that "nearly a dozen of the characters that populate his novels are poets or writers." In other words, characters the are "poets or writers" are common, or "not <u>atypical</u>." So (B) is right.

C   **Plausible but not in the Text:** This choice might be tempting for test-takers who feel like being a "poet" is not a great way to make money in real life, which is what the phrase "is not <u>lucrative</u>" would mean. But we can't answer based on something we think is true in real life; instead, we have to answer based on what appears on the page, and the provided text never tells us that poets don't make a lot of money—in fact, the text never even mentions money. So (C) is wrong.

D   **Plausible but not in the Text:** Some test-takers might think that the novel mentioned in the text sounds like it's exciting, or that being a poet sounds exciting, or that something else connected to the provided text could be called "not <u>tedious</u>." But the text never actually says anything is or isn't boring, or "tedious," so (D) can't be the right answer.

The prompt will be a short passage containing a blank. The correct answer will always be restated or demonstrated by key phrases in the provided text. See "What about Text Completion Questions?" on p. 66.

Subjective Phrases to Ignore: "most"

A   Literary Interpretation: This choice would work if something in the provided text indicated that Jeyifous confirmed the worth or authenticity of the "new images," as the word "validated" would require—but this idea doesn't appear in the text. Some test-takers will be tempted by this choice because they imagine a situation where images in an "exhibition" would be "validated," but we can't pick this choice unless that idea actually appears in the text—and, again, it doesn't. So (A) is wrong.

B ✓   Correct: The text describes how Jeyifous "photographed… models and layered… photos over… images of… cells, resulting in" a certain kind of "portraiture." This exactly demonstrates the fact that Jeyifous "created" the "series of new images," as this choice would require—so (B) is right.

C   Confused Relationships: This choice will tempt test-takers who assume that some aspect of this undertaking "challenged" Jeyifous, or that the work itself "challenged" some belief, or something along those lines. But that idea doesn't appear in the text, and even if it did, this choice would cause the text to say that Jeyifous "<u>challenged</u> a series of new images," which doesn't even really make sense. So (C) is wrong.

D   Confused Relationships: The provided text mentions a "series of… posters from the 1970s," so test-takers who don't read carefully might assume this choice refers to "restor[ing]" that older series. But this choice would cause the text to say Jeyifous "<u>restored</u> a series of new images," not the old posters—and the text doesn't mention anyone restoring those old posters (or anything else) anyway. The text tells us that Jeyifous "based" his series on that older series, but that's not the same as "restor[ing]" images; "restor[ing]" them would mean repairing and renewing them, which isn't described in the text. With all of this in mind, we know (D) is wrong.

The prompt will be a short passage containing a blank. The correct answer will always be restated or demonstrated by key phrases in the provided text. See "What about Text Completion Questions?" on p. 66.

Subjective Phrases to Ignore: "most"

A ✓   Correct: This choice would cause the text to say "Sumner was a <u>proponent of</u> increasing the opportunity for Black students to study psychology," which is exactly demonstrated by the fact that he "help[ed] to found the psychology department at… a historically Black university," as we're told later in the text. So (A) is correct.

B   Confused Relationships: This choice might sound vaguely similar to (A), but the idea that "Sumner was a <u>supplement to</u> increasing the opportunity for Black students to study psychology" doesn't really have any clear meaning. This choice might be tempting for test-takers who read the phrase "in addition" and feel like they're getting "supplement[al]" information about Sumner; but even if that's true, that's not what the sentence "Sumner was a <u>supplement to</u> increasing the opportunity for Black students to study psychology" would mean. So (B) is wrong.

C   Confused Relationships: This choice would be tempting for students who get confused about some of the relationships expressed in the sentence and think that someone else helped found the "psychology department at Howard University," and that Sumner was a student there afterward—in other words, that he was the "beneficiary" of somebody *else* being the kind of "proponent" we saw in our discussion of (A). But when we read carefully, we see that the reverse is basically true—that Sumner "help[ed]" create "opportunit[ies]," and that others were the "beneficiar[ies]" of those "opportunit[ies]." So (C) is wrong.

D   Direct Contradiction: It's not really clear what being "a <u>distraction</u> for increasing… opportunity" would mean; if anything, this choice might make it sound like Sumner somehow worked *against* "increasing the opportunity for Black students to study psychology," which is the opposite of what we saw in the right answer (A). Either way, we know the text doesn't restate or demonstrate the idea of anyone being a "distraction" of any kind, so (D) must be wrong.

The prompt will be a short passage containing a blank. The correct answer will always be restated or demonstrated by key phrases in the provided text. See "What about Text Completion Questions?" on p. 66.

Subjective Phrases to Ignore: "most"

A   Confused Relationships: This choice will be tempting for some untrained test-takers who try to incorporate outside knowledge about how monarchs inherit their position from their parents, and who feel like "reciprocate" reflects that process. But as trained test-takers, we know that we can't use outside knowledge like that to answer SAT questions, and we recognize that the idea of anyone inheriting a throne doesn't appear in the text, and we also know that "reciprocate" wouldn't really describe this situation anyway; the word "reciprocate" necessarily involves the idea of doing something for someone who has done something for you, which is not how inheritance works, and which doesn't appear in the text, regardless. For any of these reasons, we know (A) is wrong.

B   Literary Interpretation: To "annotate" means "to make notes on." Some untrained test-takers might imagine historians making notes about some of the ideas that appear in this passage, but the provided text doesn't restate or demonstrate any "monarch" making notes on "his right to hold the throne," as this choice would require—so (B) is wrong.

C ✓   Correct: The text mentions that "questions of legitimacy" might impact the "reign" of a "monarch." To "buttress" something means to strengthen or support it, and this choice would cause the text to mention "factors that allowed the monarch to <u>buttress</u> his right to hold the throne." Strengthening one's "right" to do something exactly demonstrates what a monarch would do if the "legitimacy" of that right was "question[ed]," so (C) is correct.

D   Plausible but not in the Text: We might know that some monarchs in real life choose to give up their right to hold the throne, and the phrase created by this choice ("<u>disengage</u> his right to hold the throne") sounds like it might describe that idea—but we can't answer SAT questions based on outside knowledge, and that idea doesn't appear in the text (nor does the idea of anyone "disengag[ing]" anything else). So (D) can't be the right answer.

Test 4, Module 2, Question 9	TYPE: FUNCTION AND STRUCTURE

The prompt asks about the "function" or "structure" of a part of the text. The correct answer must plainly and accurately describe the relevant text, with no interpretation. See "What about "Function and Structure" Questions?" on p. 70.

Subjective Phrases to Ignore: "best"

A   Barely Relevant: The underlined sentence doesn't mention any "physical feature of female cuckoos," and no physical feature of any bird "is described later in the text." So we know (A) is wrong.

B   Barely Relevant: The underlined sentence does mention "nests," but those are "nests of other bird species," not "cuckoo nests," as this choice would require—and this sentence doesn't say anything about the "appearance" of those nests, anyway, and no "cuckoo nests" are even "mentioned earlier in the text." For any of these reasons, (B) is wrong.

C ✓   Correct: The previous sentence tells us that some "females lay their eggs in other nests, next to another bird species' own eggs," which demonstrates the idea of "the behavior discussed in the text" from this choice. This sentence specifies that "female cuckoos... lay[] eggs in the nests of other... species," which demonstrates "female cuckoos carry[ing] out" the previously mentioned behavior, as this choice requires. Finally, the idea that "female cuckoos" do this "when those birds are out looking for food" is the "detail" about the way "female cuckoos carry out the behavior" that this choice mentions. So every part of this choice is demonstrated in the text, which means (C) is right.

D   Wrong Part of the Passage: This choice will be tempting for students who get mixed up about which sentence we're discussing. The *following* sentence talks about what the "noncuckoo parents" do after the female cuckoo lays eggs in their nest, but the underlined sentence, which is the one the prompt asks about, doesn't mention "other birds react[ing]" to anything the "female cuckoo" does. So (D) is wrong.

Test 4, Module 2, Question 10	TYPE: GENERAL PASSAGE

The prompt asks for information from the passage. The answer must be restated or demonstrated by specific phrases in the text. See "What about General Passage Questions?" on p. 69.

A ✓   Correct: The text says that "researchers" "measur[ed] cats' levels of surprise based on their ear and head movements." The phrase "measur[ed] cats' levels of surprise" in the text directly restates "determine the level of surprise displayed by the cats" in the prompt, and the phrase "based on their ear and head movements" in the text restates the idea that the researchers "watched how each cat moved its ears and head" from this choice. So (A) exactly restates the relevant information from the text and the prompt, which means it's correct.

B   Off by One or Two Words: This choice will be tempting for test-takers who don't read carefully, and don't notice that this choice mentions "the voice of a stranger." The text never says anything about the cats "react[ing]" to a stranger's voice; instead, it only mentions "recordings of their owners' voices." Choice (B) contradicts the text, so we know it's wrong.

C   Barely Relevant: This choice might be tempting for test-takers who just assume that at some point the cat would "physically interact[] with its owner," but that's never described in the text—in fact, the text only talks about "recordings of their owners' voices," and never even says the cats and owners were physically in the same place, let alone "physically interact[ing]" with each other. So (C) is wrong.

D   Barely Relevant: This choice is similar to (C), because it describes something that an untrained test-taker might assume was part of the experiment—but the text never describes any "cat mov[ing] around the room," so (D) must be wrong.

The passage presents some claim or hypothesis. The prompt typically asks us to choose the "finding" that, "if true," would support or weaken the argument. Supporting statements will demonstrate the idea in the claim, and weakening statements will demonstrate the opposite of the idea in the claim. See "What about "If True" Questions?" on p. 71.

Subjective Phrases to Ignore: "most directly"

A ✓   Correct: The prompt asks us for the choice that "weaken[s]" the "hypothesis." When we read the text, we can see that the hypothesis was "that a slightly acidic soil environment is more beneficial for the growth of… choy sum." The text tells us that some plants were grown in soil with "acidic" "coffee grounds," while others were grown in "neutral" soil without the acidic coffee grounds. This choice says the choy sum "in the soil without coffee grounds" were "taller" than the choy sum "in the mixture of soil and coffee grounds." This would weaken the hypothesis, because it would show that the plants grown *without* the acidic "coffee grounds" grew better than the plants in the "acidic soil environment" *with* the "coffee grounds"; this situation demonstrates the opposite of "a slightly acidic soil environment" being "more beneficial" for plants, as the hypothesis would require. Since the prompt asked for the choice that would *weaken* the hypothesis, (A) is right.

B   Direct Contradiction: We need a choice that would *weaken* the hypothesis that an "acidic soil environment" is better for choy sum than a "neutral soil environment." But this would *support* that hypothesis, because it would show that the plants in the "neutral soil" didn't grow as well as the plants in the "acidic" soil with the "coffee grounds," exactly as the hypothesis predicts. So (B) is wrong.

C   Direct Contradiction: This choice has the same basic problem as (B): instead of *weakening* the hypothesis that an "acidic soil environment" is better for choy sum than a "neutral soil environment," as the prompt requires, this choice provides an example of the plants in "acidic soil" growing better than the plans in the "neutral soil," just as the hypothesis predicts. In this case, the plants in "neutral soil" took a lot longer to sprout. So (C) is wrong.

D   Direct Contradiction: This choice has the same problem as (B) and (C), and is wrong for the same reason—"fewer… seeds" "sprout[ing]" in the neutral soil than in the "acidic soil" *supports* the hypothesis that the plants benefit from the acidic soil, but the prompt asks for a choice that *weakens* the hypothesis. So (D) is wrong.

> **Note**   A key detail for evaluating the answer choices is remembering that the soil *with* coffee grounds was the acidic soil, and the soil *without* coffee grounds was the neutral soil. The College Board loves to put you in situations where you need to remember these kinds of details to find the right answer. Also, notice that if you overlooked the word "weaken" and thought you were supposed to find a choice that "supported" or "strengthened" the hypothesis, any of the wrong answers would have been appealing. Always remember to read carefully on test day!

The prompt will make a claim about a literary work, then ask which quotation "illustrates the claim." The right answer will plainly demonstrate the ideas in the provided claim. See "What about Quotation Questions?" on p. 70.

Subjective Phrases to Ignore: "most effectively"

A   Literary Interpretation: The prompt asks us which choice "illustrates the claim." The claim in the text says that "Mansfield frequently contrasts the character's pleasant appearance with her unpleasant attitude." This choice describes the teenager not liking "flowers on a table." Some test-takers might be unsure whether this could be an example of the "unpleasant attitude" described in the provided text, but trained test-takers will know that we can eliminate this choice either way, because the choice definitely doesn't include any mention of her "appearance," "pleasant" or otherwise, as the text would require—so (A) is wrong.

B ✓   Correct: As we saw in our discussion of (A), we need a choice that "illustrates" the "claim" that "Mansfield frequently contrasts the character's pleasant appearance with her unpleasant attitude." This choice mentions "her lovely nose," which demonstrates "the character's pleasant appearance," and also how she "shook the poor little puff as though she loathed it," which demonstrates "her unpleasant attitude"—notice how the word "loathe" specifies that she has a distinctly negative feeling toward something, with justifies the phrase "unpleasant attitude." This choice demonstrates every part of the "claim" from the passage, so we know (B) is right.

C   Literary Interpretation: This choice is similar to (A)—some untrained test-takers will wonder whether the girl not being able to "stand this place a moment longer" and "jump[ing] up and turn[ing] away" are examples of an "unpleasant attitude," but trained test-takers will realize that this doesn't matter, because the choice doesn't mention her "appearance" at all, as the "claim" requires, so it must be wrong.

D   Literary Interpretation: This choice has the same problem as (A) and (C)—it describes behavior that might indicate an "unpleasant attitude," but doesn't describe the girl's "appearance" at all, so it can't support the claim that the author "contrasts" her "pleasant appearance with her unpleasant attitude." So (D) is wrong.

Test 4, Module 2, Question 13   TYPE: DATA

The passage includes a figure. The question asks for the choice that uses data from the figure to accomplish a certain goal. The right answer will describe the data accurately and plainly accomplish the goal. See "What about "Data" Questions?" on p. 69.

Subjective Phrases to Ignore: "most effectively"

A   Direct Contradiction: This prompt asks for "data" that "illustrate[s] the claim." When we read the provided text, we can see that the "claim" is that "a general measure may not fully reflect uncertainty about specific areas of policy." Looking back in the text, we can see that "general measure" refers to a measure for "general economic policy uncertainty." We can eliminate this choice without even thinking about any of that, though, because it makes an inaccurate statement about the data; it says that "general economic policy uncertainty… differed from uncertainty about tax and public spending policy by a large amount in 2009." When we check the columns that correspond to 2009, we can see that all three of them are very close in height, and none of them "differ[s]" from any other "by a large amount." So (A) must be wrong.

B   Direct Contradiction: Like (A), this choice is wrong because it makes an inaccurate statement about the data. This choice says that "general economic policy uncertainty was substantially lower than uncertainty about tax and public spending policy each year from 2005 to 2010"—that is, for every year represented on the graph. We can use the provided key to determine that the black column represents uncertainty about "general economic policy," and the darker gray column (the first one in every group of three columns) represents uncertainty about "tax and public spending policy." The black column was only "substantially lower" than the dark gray column in 2010, and was actually *higher* than the dark gray column in 2006, 2007, and 2009. So again, (B) is wrong.

C   Direct Contradiction: Like (A) and (B), this choice makes an inaccurate statement about the data. It says that "general economic policy uncertainty reached its highest level" on the graph the same year that the other two measures "reached their lowest levels." We can see that the black column representing "general economic policy" was at its highest in 2010, and that the dark gray column representing "tax and public spending policy" actually reached its *highest* value that year, not its lowest value, as this choice would require. So (C) must be wrong.

D ✓   Correct: We can look at the graph and see that the black column representing "general economic policy" was "substantially lower" than the light gray column representing "trade policy" in 2005, just as this choice claims, and the black column representing "general economic policy" was "substantially higher" than the light gray column representing "trade policy" in 2010, just as this choice claims. This is the only choice that accurately describes the data, so we already know it must be the right answer, but we can also see that it "illustrate[s] the claim," as the prompt requires, because the measure of uncertainty about "general economic policy" being very different from measures of other specific kinds of uncertainty exactly demonstrates the idea in the claim that "a general measure may not fully reflect uncertainty about specific areas of policy." So again, (D) is correct.

Test 4, Module 2, Question 14   TYPE: IF TRUE

The passage presents some claim or hypothesis. The prompt typically asks us to choose the "finding" that, "if true," would support or weaken the argument. Supporting statements will demonstrate the idea in the claim, and weakening statements will demonstrate the opposite of the idea in the claim. See "What about "If True" Questions?" on p. 71.

Subjective Phrases to Ignore: "most strongly"

A   Literary Interpretation: The prompt asks for the claim that "support[s]" the "hypothesis." We can read the provided text and see that the "hypothesis" is that the "debate-driven approach," which the text tells us is "framing… issues in terms of two… perspectives," "can strip issues of their complexity and… can be less informative than the presentation of multiple perspectives" to an "audience." This choice talks about how "knowledgeable" the "participants perceived" the "commentators" to be, but the "hypothesis" has nothing to do with how the "participants" "perceive[] commentators." Instead, it has to do with how "informative" the different approaches are—whether commentary is "informative" depends on how much people actually learn from it, not whether the people doing the commentary seem "knowledgeable." This choice doesn't include any information that tells us how "informative" anything is, so it's not relevant to the hypothesis.

B   Literary Interpretation: This choice has the same problem as (A), and is wrong for the same reason.

C ✓   Correct: The idea that "participants who watched the panel correctly answered more questions about the issue than those who watched the debate" specifically demonstrates that the "panel," which presented "multiple perspectives," was more "informative" than the "debate," which presented two "opposing views," just as the "hypothesis" states. So (C) is the correct answer. Notice that "participants… correctly answer[ing] more questions" after watching the "panel" demonstrates the idea that the "panel" was "informative," because the participants would have to be more "inform[ed]" to "answer more questions" "correctly," whereas participants "perceiv[ing] commentators as more knowledgeable" doesn't demonstrate that those commentators were actually more "informative," as we saw in (A) and (B). Also notice that the information about the "single commentator" isn't relevant to the hypothesis, so it doesn't impact our reasoning about this choice.

D   Barely Relevant: The "hypothesis" has to do with how "informative" the presentation of "two... perspectives" is compared to "the presentation of multiple perspectives." But the "single commentator" isn't an example of either of these options, so comparing how informative the "debate" was to how informative the "single commentator" was doesn't tell us anything about the "hypothesis." That means (D) is wrong.

Test 4, Module 2, Question 15 — TYPE: QUOTATION

The prompt will make a claim about a literary work, then ask which quotation "illustrates the claim." The right answer will plainly demonstrate the ideas in the provided claim. See "What about Quotation Questions?" on p. 70.

Subjective Phrases to Ignore: "most effectively"

A   Direct Contradiction: The prompt asks for a "quotation" that "illustrate[s] the claim." When we read the provided text, we can see that the claim is that King Lear "later expresses regret for his actions." The idea in this choice that King Lear is "more sinned against than sinning" means that people have done bad things to him (he's been "sinned against") more than he himself has done bad things (or been "sinning"). So this choice doesn't express any kind of "regret," as the "claim" would require—if anything, he's expressing the *opposite* of regret by emphasizing the bad others have done over the bad things he's done. So (A) is wrong.

B   Confused Relationships: The idea of the storm ("tempest") not giving King Lear a chance to think about ("ponder") "things" that "would hurt [him] more" doesn't demonstrate any kind of "regret," as the "claim" requires, so (B) is wrong. Notice that we don't have to understand every word in this choice to know it's wrong; we know that "regret" refers to feeling bad about something one has done in the past, but this choice says the tempest "will not give" him leave to think about things that "would" hurt him more—in other words, he's talking about what *won't* happen in the future, not wishing something in the past were different. Some test-takers might think the mention of "things would hurt me more" could refer to feelings of regret, but the idea of something "hurt[ing]" King Lear isn't the same as saying he regrets anything; to demonstrate "regret," as the "claim" requires, would necessarily require expressing the idea that he wishes he didn't do something that he did. This idea doesn't appear in this choice, so we know (B) is wrong. See the discussion of (C) for more.

C ✓ Correct: We know that in this choice, King Lear "expresses regret for his actions," as the "claim" requires, because he says his head "let folly in" and "judgement out." "Folly" is the same as foolishness, or lack of judgment, and the idea of exercising foolishness and a lack of judgment is stated again by the idea that he "let... judgement out." So King Lear is saying that he did something foolish (without "dear judgement")—this demonstrates "regret for his actions," as the "claim" requires, so (C) is right. (Notice that the detail that King Lear is "striking his head" while saying the phrase "beat at this gate" demonstrates the idea that King Lear is saying he "let... folly in" to his mind, and "judgement out" of it.)

D   Confused Relationships: This choice will be tempting for untrained test-takers, because it includes the idea of King Lear doing something bad: he says "I will do such things" that "shall be the terrors of the earth!" But the "claim" says King Lear "expresses regret," and a person necessarily feels "regret" *after* doing something in the *past*, not about things that person "will do" in the *future*—everything King Lear says in this quote is about the future ("I will do..." "they shall be..."). Beyond that, "regret" for something doesn't just mean thinking that an action is bad; it specifically means *wishing that you didn't do* something, which doesn't appear in this text either (and again, wouldn't even really make sense about something in the future that hasn't happened yet). For either of these reasons, (D) is wrong.

Test 4, Module 2, Question 16 — TYPE: MOST LOGICALLY COMPLETES

The passage ends with a blank, and the answer choices are relatively long phrases. The right answer will restate or demonstrate an idea in the provided text. See "What about "Most Logically Completes" Questions?" on p. 68.

Subjective Phrases to Ignore: "most"

A ✓ Correct: The text tells us that "Shakespeare's tragedies address broad themes that still appeal to today's audiences," and are "produced widely around the world." Then it says "but understanding Shakespeare's so-called history plays can require a knowledge of several centuries of English history"—notice how the word "but" specifically tells us that something about the "history plays" is different from what we were told about the "tragedies," and that "requir[ing] a knowledge of... English history" is the opposite of "address[ing] broad themes that... appeal to today's audiences." This choice would cause the final sentence to say "consequently, many theatergoers... today... find Shakespeare's history plays less engaging than the tragedies." This exactly demonstrates the idea that the "tragedies address broad themes that still appeal to today's audiences," while the "history plays," which "can require a knowledge of... English history," do not. So every part of (A) demonstrates ideas from the text, which means (A) is right.

B   Barely Relevant: The text discusses whether "Shakespeare's" "plays... still appeal to today's audiences," but never actually mentions anything related to "twentieth-century plays." So the comparison in this choice between "Shakespeare's tragedies" and "twentieth-century plays" isn't relevant to the text, and (B) is wrong.

C   Off by One or Two Words: Some test-takers will be tempted by this choice, since the text mentions that the "broad themes" "address[ed]" in "Shakespeare's tragedies... still appeal to today's audiences," and then discusses *Romeo and Juliet* as an example. But simply mentioning an example of a play that's "thematically accessible" isn't the same as saying that play is the "*most* thematically accessible... traged[y] [emphasis added]*," as this choice would require. Nothing in the text specifies that *Romeo and Juliet* is more "thematically accessible" than any other of "Shakespeare's tragedies," so (C) can't be correct.

D   Literary Interpretation: This choice will be tempting for a lot of test-takers because of the sentence in the provided text that says "understanding Shakespeare's... history plays can require a knowledge of... English history." But that part of the provided text refers to *understanding* the "history plays," not "prefer[ring]" them, as this choice would require. For all we know, "experts in English history" might understand the "history plays" better than anyone else, but still prefer the "tragedies." The text doesn't actually restate or demonstrate the idea of anyone "prefer[ring]... history plays" because they know a lot about "English history," as this choice would require—so (D) is wrong.

Note   This is an excellent example of at least two important aspects of SAT training. For one, all three wrong answer choices are exactly the kind of statement that would be perfectly acceptable as part of a classroom discussion in almost any high school or college Literature class—but on the SAT, they're clearly wrong, because they restate or demonstrate ideas that don't appear in the provided text. For another, this question shows us how the College Board can take something like a discussion of Shakespeare (which most people would see as something that involves a lot of interpretation and opinion) and apply the rules and standards of the SAT to come up with a question that has one clearly right answer, and three clearly wrong answers. Keep these ideas in mind on test day.

Test 4, Module 2, Question 17	TYPE: MOST LOGICALLY COMPLETES

The passage ends with a blank, and the answer choices are relatively long phrases. The right answer will restate or demonstrate an idea in the provided text. See "What about "Most Logically Completes" Questions?" on p. 68.

Subjective Phrases to Ignore: "most"

A   Barely Relevant: The text talks about "turkeys" in one area "descend[ing]" from "turkeys" in another area, but this has nothing to do with "similar[]" "terrains" between any two places; in other words, the existence of "similar[]" "terrains" doesn't cause animals to be descended from each other. Beyond that, the text doesn't discuss "terrain" at all. This choice might be tempting for test-takers who assume that if related animals live in two different places, those places must have "similar[]" "terrains"—but this idea doesn't appear in the text, so we can't use it as the basis for picking an answer choice. (Beyond that, this choice includes the added idea that these two places had "greater similarities" to each other "in the past than they do today," which also isn't supported by anything in the text.) With all of this in mind, we know that (A) is wrong.

B ✓   Correct: The text tells us that "Ancestral Puebloans" were in a certain area in "1500 B.C.E.," and they had "systems for farming... turkeys." Then they "abandon[ed] established villages" "in the late 1200s C.E." "Turkey remains" at "one such village," compared to "modern turkey populations in the Rio Grande Valley," showed that the Rio Grande turkeys "descended" from the "village" "turkeys," with "shared genetic markers only after 1280"—in other words, the Rio Grande turkeys only showed genetic similarity to the village turkeys after 1280, which is "in the late 1200s C.E.," which, as the text tells us, is when the "Ancestral Puebloans" "abandon[ed] established villages." The statement in this choice that "Ancestral Puebloans migrated to the Rio Grande Valley in the late 1200s and carried farming practices with them" is demonstrated by the fact that their turkeys' descendants are in the Rio Grande Valley (the provided text tells us that raising those turkeys was one of their "systems for farming," which restates "farming practices" in this choice), and by the fact that "genetic markers only after 1280" indicate that the "Rio Grande" turkeys' genetic connection to the "village" turkeys only starts "after 1280" (which demonstrates this choice's statement that the "migrat[ion]" happened "in the late 1200s"). So (B) is correct. (Notice that we don't needs to know exactly what "shared genetic markers" are to answer this question. The word "genetic" is enough to tell us that we're talking about the turkeys' "genes," and the word "shared" tells us the turkeys had "genes" in common with the other turkeys—that is, they were related. The fact that the markers appeared "only after 1280" tells us that these two populations didn't have anything in common until after 1280. We can understand this much without knowing exactly what "shared genetic markers," are, and that's all we need to understand to find the right answer.)

C   Confused Relationships: This choice will be tempting for test-takers who notice that the Ancestral Puebloans had "systems for farming crops and turkeys," and then decide this phrase means that "crops and turkeys" were their "primar[y]" food sources at the time, and who think that the phrase "shared genetic markers appearing only after 1280" means there were no turkeys in the Rio Grande Valley until 1280. But there are several problems with this line of reasoning. For one, this choice mentions "Indigenous peoples living in the Rio Grande Valley," not "Ancestral Puebloans;" we aren't told anything about the farming practices of the "Indigenous peoples living in the Rio Grande Valley," specifically, so we don't know what they planted, cultivated, or ate "before 1280." Also, the fact that the turkey population in the Rio Grande Valley only showed "shared genetic markers" with the Ancestral Puebloans' turkeys after 1280 doesn't mean that there were no turkeys in that valley before 1280; it only means that any turkeys in that valley before 1280 weren't related to the Ancestral Puebloans' turkeys. So the Indigenous peoples there might have had turkeys before 1280, or they might not have; we can't say based on the text. For any of these reasons, (C) is wrong.

D   **Plausible but not in the Text:** This choice will be tempting for test-takers who assume that the "Ancestral Puebloans of Mesa Verde" learned the "farming practices" of other people at some point. This might be true in real life, or it might not; we don't know, and the text doesn't tell us either way. We can only pick an answer choice on the SAT Reading section based on what appears in the text, and the text doesn't restate or demonstrate the idea of the "Ancestral Puebloans... adopt[ing]" anybody else's "farming practices." So (D) is wrong.

The passage ends with a blank, and the answer choices are relatively long phrases. The right answer will restate or demonstrate an idea in the provided text. See "What about "Most Logically Completes" Questions?" on p. 68.

Subjective Phrases to Ignore: "most"

A   **Literary Interpretation:** In order for this choice to be correct, the text would have to restate or demonstrate the idea that it was hard to "find valid data about the behavior of politicians who do not currently hold office." But that idea doesn't appear in the provided text—the only thing that the text says is difficult is "ensuring that the experiment has an appropriate control group" (which, by the way, is pretty much exactly what we see restated in the correct answer, (D)). The text never says that finding data about any particular person is a "struggle," so (A) can't be right. See the discussion of (D) for more.

B   **Direct Contradiction:** This choice will be tempting for test-takers who feel like the situation described in the passage has no solution, and that the "only" way to "conduct" [a] "valid stud[y]" is with "people who have previously held office rather than people who presently hold office." But there are several problems with this choice. First, the text never says that the "challenge" it talks about is impossible to overcome, and that "researchers" will just have to come up with some other kind of study, like the one described in this choice. Second, even if it were impossible, that doesn't mean the option in this choice is the "only" way to "conduct valid studies." Third, nothing in the text restates or demonstrates the idea of "conduct[ing]... studies with people who have previously held office." Instead, the provided text only talks about "researching whether holding elected office changes a person's behavior," which necessarily must involve a person "holding elected office"—in fact, the text directly states "researchers must compare people who hold elected office with people who do not hold office...." So this choice, if anything, is the opposite of what the text says, and the opposite of the right answer, which means (B) is wrong.

C   **Direct Contradiction:** The text mentions the need to find an "appropriate control group," then elaborates on that by telling us that "researchers must compare people who hold elected office with people who do not hold office but who are otherwise similar to the office-holders." The idea from this choice of "select[ing] a control group of people who differ from office holders in several significant ways" is the *opposite* of what the text says "researchers must" do, so we know (C) is wrong.

D ✓   **Correct:** The passage starts by saying "one challenge when researching whether holding elected office changes a person's behavior is the problem of ensuring that the experiment has an appropriate control group." The phrase "the problem of ensuring that the experiment has an appropriate control group" directly restates the idea in this choice that researchers "will find it difficult to identify a group of people who can function as an appropriate control group for their studies." This choice is directly restated in the text, so it's right.

- **Vertical Scan Results:** Each choice is the same phrase with variations on the first word and the last word in the phrase.
- **Vertical Scan Notes:** We need to decide whether "story" and "immigrant" should be singular, plural, and/or possessive.
- **Key Features in Surrounding Text:** Nothing in the sentence belongs to "story," so the right answer shouldn't include a possessive form of "story." The "stories" belong to the "immigrants," but this relationship is already expressed by the phrase "of the," and nothing appears directly after "immigrants" for "immigrants" to possess. So the right answer shouldn't include a possessive form of "immigrant," either.

Concepts in the question:

- **Possessive and/or Plural:** Choices include nouns ending in "-s," with or without an apostrophe before or after the "-s." The provided text will indicate which nouns should show ownership, and which shouldn't. (See page 79.)

ANSWER CHOICE ANALYSIS

A   Incorrect: As we saw in our discussion above, the correct answer shouldn't include any possessive forms—but this choice includes the possessive form "story's," so (A) is wrong.

B   Incorrect: As we saw in our discussion above, the correct answer shouldn't include any possessive forms—but this choice includes the possessive forms "story's" and "immigrants'," so (B) is wrong.

C ✓   Correct: As we saw in our discussion above, the correct answer shouldn't include any possessive forms. This choice is the only one that meets that requirement, so (C) is correct.

D   Incorrect: As we saw in our discussion above, the correct answer shouldn't include any possessive forms—but this choice includes the possessive forms "stories'" and "immigrant's," so (D) is wrong.

Note   This question was a little tricky, because the "immigrants" were the ones that the "stories" belonged to—but we still didn't need a possessive form of "immigrants," because the phrase "of the" expressed that possession already. However, we didn't even really need to do this extra bit of analysis anyway, because once we realized that nothing belonged to the "stories," we could eliminate every wrong answer choice, since only (C), the correct answer, didn't include a possessive form of "stories." On test day, if you find yourself unsure whether an answer choice meets a certain standard, consider checking the answer choice against other standards—you may be able to eliminate it (or verify it) for another reason.

Test 4, Module 2, Question 20   **TYPE: SAT WRITING**

- Vertical Scan Results: Each choice is the same word with different punctuation after it.
- Vertical Scan Notes: We have to decide whether a comma, dash, colon, or nothing should appear after "of."
- Key Features in Surrounding Text: "Of healing, self-discovery, and memory" is a prepositional phrase, and nothing in our training tells us that any punctuation should appear after the preposition and before the rest of that phrase. Remember that we only include punctuation if our training tells us that there's a reason for it; otherwise, we leave it out.

Concepts in the question:

- Colons: A colon can only be placed after a group of words that could be a sentence on its own. Everything after the colon must be a demonstration or example of the idea before the colon. (See page 85.)
- Commas: Commas can be used between clauses, to form comma sandwiches, in a list of 3 or more items, and before reported speech. They can't appear for no reason. Review the training for the relevant details. (See page 86.)

ANSWER CHOICE ANALYSIS

A ✓   Correct: As we saw in our discussion above, no punctuation should appear between the preposition "of" and the rest of the prepositional phrase. That means (A) is right.

B   Incorrect: This choice would insert punctuation somewhere without any valid reason from the SAT Writing Toolbox, so (B) is wrong.

C   Incorrect: This choice has the same problem as (B), and is wrong for the same reason.

D   Incorrect: This choice has the same problem as (B) and (C), and is wrong for the same reason.

Test 4, Module 2, Question 21   **TYPE: SAT WRITING**

- Vertical Scan Results: Each choice is the same word with punctuation and/or a second word added after that word.
- Vertical Scan Notes: We need to decide whether a comma and/or "that" should appear after "company."
- Key Features in Surrounding Text: Nothing in the surrounding text creates a situation that would require a comma in the underlined phrase, as taught in the section on commas in the SAT Writing Toolbox earlier in this book.

Concepts in the question:

- Commas: Commas can be used between clauses, to form comma sandwiches, in a list of 3 or more items, and before reported speech. They can't appear for no reason. Review the training for the relevant details. (See page 86.)

ANSWER CHOICE ANALYSIS

A   Incorrect: Omitting the word "that" leaves the verb phrase "specializes in the creation and promotion of stories told from diverse perspectives for children and young adults" without anything to connect it to the main sentence, or to indicate who or what is doing the action "specializes." So (A) is wrong.

B ✓   Correct: This choice would use the relative pronoun "that" to connect the verb phrase "specializes in the creation..." to the phrase that's doing the "specializ[ing]," which is "company." We know from our training that we don't include commas (or other punctuation) unless we have a specific reason to do so, as found in the SAT Writing Toolbox—this phrase is not one of those situations from our training that would require a comma (or any other punctuation), so no punctuation should appear in this phrase. That means (B) is right.

C   Incorrect: This choice creates a comma splice, because it would separate two groups of words that can each stand on their own as sentences ("In 2011… Literary" and "a book…. adults") with a comma, which isn't acceptable on the SAT. So (C) is wrong.

D   Incorrect: This choice is similar to (B), except it makes the mistake of inserting a comma between the noun "company" and the relative pronoun "that." As we saw in our discussion of the correct answer, (B), we should only include a comma (or any other punctuation) if we have a specific reason to do so, and this phrase doesn't meet any of the requirements for inserting a comma, as discussed in the "Commas" section of the SAT Writing Toolbox. So (D) is wrong.

Test 4, Module 2, Question 22   TYPE: SAT WRITING

- Vertical Scan Results: Each choice is the same noun phrase with different punctuation.
- Vertical Scan Notes: We have to decide whether a comma should appear after "carbon-13," and/or after "(^{13}C)."
- Key Features in Surrounding Text: The word "carbon-13" is a noun phrase that describes "rare carbon isotope," and "(^{13}C)" tells us that "carbon-13" can also be written as "^{13}C." We know this because after the blank, this sentence uses "^{13}C" to refer to this isotope in the phrase "higher ^{13}C levels in corn and cane sugar." So "carbon-13" is a descriptive noun phrase that should be set off from the surrounding text with commas, and (^{13}C), which tells us more about "carbon-13," should immediately follow "carbon-13," and should also be set off from the rest of the text—but because "(^{13}C)" is already set off with parentheses, (^{13}C) doesn't need to be set off with its own set of commas.

Concepts in the question:

- Commas: Commas can be used between clauses, to form comma sandwiches, in a list of 3 or more items, and before reported speech. They can't appear for no reason. Review the training for the relevant details. (See page 86.)
- Descriptive Noun Phrase: A comma-separated noun phrase describes the nearest phrase in the sentence where it appears. (See page 88.)

ANSWER CHOICE ANALYSIS

A   Incorrect: As we saw in our discussion above, the entire phrase "carbon-13 (^{13}C)" should be set off with commas on either end, but this choice doesn't meet that requirement. So (A) is wrong.

B   Incorrect: This choice has the same problem as (A), and is wrong for the same reason.

C   Incorrect: This choice has the same problem as (A) and (B), and is wrong for the same reason. Note that "(^{13}C)" doesn't need to be set off with commas because it's already set off with parentheses.

D ✓   Correct: This choice meets the requirements we discussed above, which means it's correct.

Test 4, Module 2, Question 23   TYPE: SAT WRITING

- Vertical Scan Results: Each choice is the same two words with different punctuation or the word "so" between them.
- Vertical Scan Notes: We have to decide whether a comma, period, the word "so," or nothing should appear between "walls" and "with."
- Key Features in Surrounding Text: "In 2010… walls" can stand on its own as a sentence, and "with the… paintings" can stand on its own as a sentence.

Concepts in the question:

- Comma Splice: A comma can't join two groups of words that could each be sentences on their own. (See page 83.)
- Independent and Dependent Clauses: Choices would create and/or join clauses. An independent clause can stand on its own as a sentence, and a dependent clause can't. Remember rules for joining clauses related to periods, semi-colons, colons, commas, and conjunctions. (See page 82.)

ANSWER CHOICE ANALYSIS

A   Incorrect: This choice creates a comma splice, because it would cause two groups of words that can each stand on their own as sentences to be separated by a comma, which isn't acceptable on the SAT. So (A) is wrong.

B   Incorrect: This choice would result in two groups of words that can each stand on their own as sentences not having any punctuation, conjunction, or relative pronoun between them, which isn't acceptable on the SAT. So (B) is wrong.

C Incorrect: This choice would use the conjunction "so" to separate two groups of words that can each stand on their own as sentences. We know from our training that we can join two such groups of words with a *comma* and *then* a conjunction like "so," but this choice omits that comma. So (C) is wrong.

D ✓ Correct: This choice would separate two groups of words that can each stand on their own as sentences with a period, which is acceptable on the SAT. So (D) is right.

Test 4, Module 2, Question 24   **TYPE: SAT WRITING**

- Vertical Scan Results: Each choice is a different form of the same verb.
- Vertical Scan Notes: We need to decide whether the infinitive or a participle form of "to forge" is appropriate.
- Key Features in Surrounding Text: Everything from the beginning of the text through the word "bacteria" can stand on its own as a sentence, and no comma appears after the word "bacteria."

Concepts in the question:

- Independent and Dependent Clauses: Choices would create and/or join clauses. An independent clause can stand on its own as a sentence, and a dependent clause can't. Remember rules for joining clauses related to periods, semi-colons, colons, commas, and conjunctions. (See page 82.)

ANSWER CHOICE ANALYSIS

A ✓ Correct: If we insert this choice, we would get "Charpentier and… Doudna… re-created and then reprogrammed the so-called 'genetic scissors'… to forge a tool that is revolutionizing the field…." The phrase "to forge a tool that is revolutionizing the field…" is an infinitive clause, which can appear directly after a group of words that can stand on its own as sentence, with no comma between them. So (A) is correct.

B Incorrect: This word could begin a participial phrase—but that phrase would need to be separated from the rest of the sentence by a comma, and no comma appears in the text before the blank. So (B) is wrong.

C Incorrect: This choice would create the verb phrase "forged a tool that is revolutionizing the field of gene technology." The sentence already tells us that the subjects of the sentence "re-created and then reprogrammed" something; if we want to add another verb phrase, we need to use a word like "and" at the beginning of this phrase to create the phrase "and forged a tool that is revolutionizing the field of gene technology." The word "and" doesn't appear before the blank, so (C) can't be right.

D Incorrect: This choice basically tries to solve the problem we saw in our discussion of (B) by applying the solution needed in (C)—instead of adding the comma needed before "forging" in (B), this choice adds the word "and" that needed to appear before "forged" in (C). But the result doesn't fix the problem from (B), and (D) is still wrong.

Test 4, Module 2, Question 25   **TYPE: SAT WRITING**

- Vertical Scan Results: Each choice is a long phrase involving similar words ordered in different ways.
- Vertical Scan Notes: We need to pick the choice that begins with a phrase that can be described by the phrase before the blank.
- Key Features in Surrounding Text: The text says that "bioswales" "absorb and divert stormwater." The last sentence in the provided text starts with the participial phrase "by reducing the runoff flowing into city sewers," and each answer choice is an independent clause. With this in mind, we know the first noun phrase in the right answer choice needs to be something that can "reduc[e]… runoff."

Concepts in the question:

- Avoid Dangling Participles: When a phrase starting with an -ing/-ed/-en word is joined to the main sentence by a comma, the first noun phrase in the independent clause of that sentence is described by the -ing/-ed/-en word. (See page 90.)

ANSWER CHOICE ANALYSIS

A Incorrect: This choice would say that "the mitigation" is the thing that was "reducing the runoff." This will be tempting for test-takers who don't think carefully about what exactly that means—but if we do think carefully, we know that "reducing the runoff" *is* "the mitigation," it's not an *action* that the "mitigation" *does*. We can't describe "the mitigation" as doing the action of "reducing the runoff," so (A) is wrong.

B ✓ Correct: This choice would correctly say that "the bioswales" are the thing that was "reducing the runoff," which is demonstrated in the part of the text that says "bioswales… absorb and divert stormwater." So (B) is correct.

C   Incorrect: This choice has the same basic problem as (A); it would say that "the bioswales' mitigation" is the thing that is "reducing the runoff," but "mitigation" is an abstract concept that can't "reduc[e] runoff." So (C) is wrong—see our discussion of (A) and (B) above for more.

D   Incorrect: This choice would say that "both street flooding and the resulting pollution of nearby waterways" is the thing that was "reducing the runoff"—which doesn't cause the sentence to demonstrate an idea from earlier in the text like choice (A) does, and which doesn't even really make sense. In fact, "reducing the runoff" is the thing that *prevents* the "flooding" and "pollution," so this choice would basically contradict itself. That means (D) is wrong.

Test 4, Module 2, Question 26   TYPE: SAT WRITING

- **Vertical Scan Results:** Each choice is the same two words with different punctuation between them.
- **Vertical Scan Notes:** We have to decide whether a colon, semi-colon, period, or nothing should appear between "continents" and "geological."
- **Key Features in Surrounding Text:** "A study… continents" can stand on its own as a sentence. "Geological structures… above" *can't* stand on its own as a sentence, and this phrase illustrates an idea from the independent clause "a study… continents." So these two groups of words should be separated by a colon.

Concepts in the question:

- **Colons:** A colon can only be placed after a group of words that could be a sentence on its own. Everything after the colon must be a demonstration or example of the idea before the colon. (See page 85.)
- **Independent and Dependent Clauses:** Choices would create and/or join clauses. An independent clause can stand on its own as a sentence, and a dependent clause can't. Remember rules for joining clauses related to periods, semi-colons, colons, commas, and conjunctions. (See page 82.)

ANSWER CHOICE ANALYSIS

A   Incorrect: This choice would cause the phrase "geological structures… above" not to be connected to the rest of the sentence with any appropriate punctuation or conjunction. So (A) is wrong.

B ✓   Correct: This choice would use a colon to separate a group of words that can stand on its own as a sentence from a phrase that illustrates an idea mentioned before the colon, which is acceptable on the SAT. So (B) is right.

C   Incorrect: This choice would separate one group of words that *can* stand on its own as a sentence from another groups of words that *can't* stand on its own as a sentence with a semi-colon, which isn't acceptable on the SAT—a semi-colon must separate two groups of words that can each stand on their own as sentences. So (C) is wrong.

D   Incorrect: This choice has the same basic problem as (C), and is wrong for the same reason; this choice has a period instead of a semi-colon, but the same rule applies. On the SAT, a period must separate two groups of words that can each stand on their own as sentences, so (D) is wrong.

Test 4, Module 2, Question 27   TYPE: LOGICAL TRANSITION

The choices are different transition phrases like "however," "instead of," or "for example." The right answer must reflect the relationship between the concepts before and after the blank. See "What about Logical Transition Questions?" on p. 71.

Subjective Phrases to Ignore: "most"

A ✓   Correct: This choice appropriately expresses the idea that what this sentence says happened "after[]" the action in the previous sentence. We know this is the case because this sentence says the CEO "acknowledged what happened and apologized," and it's only possible to do these actions *after* something happens, as the word "afterward" requires. So (A) is right.

B   Literary Interpretation: This choice might be tempting for an untrained test-taker who doesn't think carefully enough about what it would mean, and decides it means basically the same thing as (A). But this choice would require the second sentence to provide another piece of information similar to what was in the last sentence (for example, another way that the rocket failed), which isn't the case; also, this choice fails to demonstrate the sequential relationship between the action of the first sentence and the action of the second sentence that we saw in our discussion of (A). So (B) is wrong.

C   Confused Relationships: This choice would be appropriate if this sentence provided additional information to reinforce or emphasize the idea from the previous sentence (like "Indeed, the booster barely ignited at all," or something similar), but that's not the case. So (C) is wrong.

D   Confused Relationships: This choice would be appropriate if this sentence described another situation that was similar to the one from the previous sentence (like another time that a rocket failed, for example), but that's not the case. So (D) is wrong.

The choices are different transition phrases like "however," "instead of," or "for example." The right answer must reflect the relationship between the concepts before and after the blank. See "What about Logical Transition Questions?" on p. 71.

Subjective Phrases to Ignore: "most"

A ✓ Correct: The first sentence tells us that "contaminated" "soil" "can be removed from the ground" and put in a "landfill." This sentence tells us something else that can be done with "contaminated soil": it "can be detoxified" with "plants." This choice appropriately reflects the idea that this sentence describes another option or a different possibility from the one mentioned in the previous sentence. So (A) is right.

B   Confused Relationships: This choice will be tempting for untrained test-takers who don't pay close enough attention and think that the second sentence just explains the idea from the first sentence in more detail. If that were the case, this choice would be right—but as we saw in our discussion of (A), the second sentence provides an alternative to the option presented in the first sentence. So (B) is wrong.

C   Confused Relationships: This choice has the same basic problem as (B), and is wrong for the same reason.

D   Confused Relationships: This choice would be appropriate if this sentence described the logical outcome of the idea in the previous sentence, but that's not the case—see our discussion of (A) for more. So (D) is wrong.

The passage presents a bulleted list of notes, then tells us a goal related to presenting that information. The correct answer will be the only one that demonstrates the ideas in the provided goal. See "What about Notes Questions?" on p. 71.

Subjective Phrases to Ignore: "most"

A   Confused Relationships: The prompt asks for the choice that "explain[s] an advantage of the Hanke-Henry calendar." This choice mentions a *difference* between "the Hanke-Henry calendar" and "the Gregorian calendar," but it doesn't tell us any way that "the Hanke-Henry calendar" is *better* than other calendars, which the word "advantage" from the prompt requires. So (A) is wrong.

B   Off by One or Two Words: This choice will be tempting, because it says that "the Hanke-Henry permanent calendar... solve[s] a problem with the Gregorian calendar," which might sound to an untrained test-taker like "explain[ing] an advantage" of "the Hanke-Henry calendar," as the prompt requires. But just saying that something "solves a problem" isn't the same as "explain[ing] an advantage" of that thing. In order to "explain an advantage of the Hanke-Henry calendar," this choice must actually tell us what that advantage is—what problem, specifically, it solves. This choice doesn't do that, so we know it's wrong.

C ✓ Correct: This choice tells us that "the Hanke-Henry calendar supports more predictable scheduling than does the Gregorian calendar." The phrase "supports more predictable scheduling" directly "explain[s] an advantage of the Hanke-Henry calendar," as the prompt requires. So (C) is right.

D   Barely Relevant: This choice does provide some information about "the Hanke-Henry calendar," but it doesn't mention any "advantage" that this calendar has over any other calendar, which the prompt requires. So (D) is wrong.

The passage presents a bulleted list of notes, then tells us a goal related to presenting that information. The correct answer will be the only one that demonstrates the ideas in the provided goal. See "What about Notes Questions?" on p. 71.

Subjective Phrases to Ignore: "most"

A   Barely Relevant: The prompt asks for the choice that "present[s] the influence theory...." This choice mentions that something was "influential," but doesn't say anything about "the influence theory," so we can't say this choice "presents" that theory, as the prompt requires—so (A) is wrong.

B   Barely Relevant: This choice mentions "the influence theory"—but doesn't actually provide any details about the influence theory, as the phrase "present the influence theory" from the prompt requires. It also mentions "the Haudenosaunee Confederacy" without explaining what that is, which fails to meet the requirement from the prompt of addressing "an audience unfamiliar with the Haudenosaunee Confederacy." So (B) is wrong.

C ✓ Correct: This choice *does* "present the influence theory," as the prompt requires—it directly explains to us that "the influence theory holds that... the Great Law of Peace... influenced the US Constitution." It also does this without mentioning "the Haudenosaunee Confederacy," which satisfies the requirement in the prompt of accounting for "an audience unfamiliar with the Haudenosaunee Confederacy." So (C) is correct.

D   Barely Relevant: This choice is similar to (A) because it includes a form of the word "influence," which might make it seem relevant to the prompt—but this choice doesn't actually say anything about "the influence theory," as the prompt would require. It also mentions "the Haudenosaunee Confederacy" without explaining what it is, which violates the requirement in the prompt of accounting for "an audience unfamiliar with the Haudenosaunee Confederacy." For either reason, (D) must be wrong.

Test 4, Module 2, Question 31   TYPE: NOTES

The passage presents a bulleted list of notes, then tells us a goal related to presenting that information. The correct answer will be the only one that demonstrates the ideas in the provided goal. See "What about Notes Questions?" on p. 71.

Subjective Phrases to Ignore: "most"

A ✓   Correct: The prompt tells us to find the choice that "emphasize[s] how hot the Sun is relative to nearby stars." This choice specifies that "the Sun is hotter than most but not all of the stars within 10 parsecs of it." This exactly demonstrates the requirement from the prompt by telling us "how hot the Sun is relative to nearby stars," so (A) is right.

B   Literary Interpretation: This choice tells us how hot the Sun is, and that it's "a G star." It also tells us the classifications of some other stars near the Sun—but it doesn't relate the temperature of the Sun to the temperatures of those other stars, as the phrase "how hot the Sun is relative to nearby stars" requires. So this choice fails to satisfy the prompt, and it's wrong.

C   Literary Interpretation: This choice tells us about the "surface temperatures" of some stars within a certain range of the Sun— but it never tells us whether the Sun is hotter or cooler than those stars, or says anything else about how hot the Sun is. So we can't say that it tells us "how hot the Sun is relative to nearby stars," as the prompt requires, which means (C) is wrong.

D   Literary Interpretation: This choice is similar to (B), and is wrong for the same reason—it tells us how hot the sun is, and it tells us the classifications of some stars near the Sun, but it doesn't compare the heat of the sun to the heat of the other stars. So (D) is wrong.

> **Note**   Note that an untrained test-taker could make an argument for any of the wrong answers above by *referring to additional information in the provided notes,* but that none of the wrong answers says "how hot the Sun is relative to nearby stars" *in the answer choice itself.* Remember that the right answer to a Notes question must satisfy the requirements of the prompt *without* requiring the reader to refer back to the notes.

Test 4, Module 2, Question 32   TYPE: NOTES

The passage presents a bulleted list of notes, then tells us a goal related to presenting that information. The correct answer will be the only one that demonstrates the ideas in the provided goal. See "What about Notes Questions?" on p. 71.

Subjective Phrases to Ignore: "most"

A ✓   Correct: The prompt asks for the choice that "introduce[s] Cathryn Halverson's book to an audience already familiar with the *Atlantic Monthly.*" This choice introduces Halverson's book *Faraway Women and the "Atlantic Monthly"* by telling us basic information regarding the subject matter of the book—the book "discusses female authors whose autobiographies appeared in the magazine in the early 1900s." This choice also doesn't provide any basic information about "the *Atlantic Monthly,*" and refers to it ("the magazine") as though the reader already knows what it is, which fulfills the prompt's requirement about "an audience already familiar with the *Atlantic Monthly.*" So (A) meets every requirement in the prompt, which means it's right.

B   Barely Relevant: This choice fails to assume the "audience [is] already familiar with the *Atlantic Monthly,*" as the prompt requires, because it mentions "a magazine called the *Atlantic Monthly*"—as though the reader doesn't know the *Atlantic Monthly* is a magazine—and then provides some information about the magazine. This choice also doesn't even mention the name of Halverson's book, let alone any basic information about the book, as the phrase "introduce Cathryn Halverson's book" in the prompt would require. So (B) is wrong.

C   Direct Contradiction: Like (B), this choice introduces the *Atlantic Monthly,* which means it doesn't meet the prompt's requirement about assuming the "audience [is] already familiar with the *Atlantic Monthly.*" So (C) is wrong.

D   Confused Relationships: This choice will be tempting for test-takers who know that it mentions information about Halverson's book from the notes, and feel like that qualifies as an "introduc[tion]"—but this choice itself doesn't actually "introduce" her book, as the prompt would require; it doesn't tell us the name of the book, or any basic information about it. In fact, it doesn't even mention any book. So (D) is wrong.

Test 4, Module 2, Question 33   TYPE: NOTES

The passage presents a bulleted list of notes, then tells us a goal related to presenting that information. The correct answer will be the only one that demonstrates the ideas in the provided goal. See "What about Notes Questions?" on p. 71.

Subjective Phrases to Ignore: "most"

A   Confused Relationships: The prompt asks for the choice that "emphasize[s] a similarity between the two ways a magnificent frigatebird acquires food." But this choice only mentions one way that the bird "acquires food": by "snatch[ing] prey from the surface" of the water. So (A) is wrong.

B ✓ Correct: This choice refers to the idea that the bird has "two ways of acquiring food," and tells us that "neither… requires the bird to dive into the water." This shared characteristic exactly demonstrates the idea of "a similarity between the two ways" the bird "acquires food," as the prompt requires—so (B) is right.

C   Direct Contradiction: This choice actually tells us about a *difference* between the "two ways" the bird "acquires food," because if "only one" way is called "kleptoparasitism," then the other way *isn't* called "kleptoparasitism"—which, again, is an instance of the "two ways" being different, not "similar[]," as the prompt requires. So (C) is wrong.

D   Confused Relationships: This choice *does* describe "the two ways a magnificent frigatebird acquires food"—but it doesn't specify any way that these two methods are "similar[]," as the prompt requires! Some test-takers might be tempted by this choice because they feel like the idea of "snatching prey from the water" is similar to the idea of "tak[ing] food… by force." But in order for us to say that this choice "emphasize[s] a similarity," as the prompt requires, the choice *itself* must say that the two things are similar (contrast this with the right answer, (B), which specifies something that "neither" of the bird's "two ways of acquiring food requires"). This choice doesn't restate or demonstrate the idea of any two things being similar, so we know that (D) is wrong.

Part 7: Math Section Training and Walkthroughs

In part 6, we just saw how to attack the SAT Reading and Writing section by relying on literal reading, objectivity, and our awareness of the College Board's limited standards for grammar and punctuation. Now, we'll build on this foundation to address the SAT Math section. You'll see how we combine our awareness of the test's unique design with our existing math knowledge and our reading skills, which will allow us to find correct answers quickly and efficiently.

In this part, you'll learn the following:

- why the SAT Math section is unlike the math tests you take in high school
- why the SAT Math section had to be designed in a particular way to make its results useful for colleges
- the single biggest secret of the design of the SAT Math section
- the two critical components of success on the SAT Math section
- all of the basic math ideas that you'll need on test day
- how truly powerful the digital SAT's provided calculator can be
- the ways that variables, coefficients, exponents, and constants can affect the output of a function
- what backsolving is, why it helps some test-takers a lot, and how to apply it in ways most people aren't aware of
- why it's so important to consider every answer choice on the SAT Math section—and how it can save you time
- the unwritten rules of the SAT Math section
- why formulas matter much less on test day than most people would expect
- why every real SAT Math question can potentially be answered in under 30 seconds
- the hidden patterns of the SAT Math section, and how they can help you attack and check questions efficiently
- the 3 major types of approaches to an SAT Math question, along with the advantages and drawbacks of each
- the recommended 7-step "Math Path" for attacking questions quickly and effectively on test day
- how to deal with "student-produced response" questions
- why it can be important not to think about "showing your work" on test day
- why the "order of difficulty" really doesn't exist
- how to apply these concepts to every math question from four Official SAT Practice Tests
- and more…

SAT Math Training

> *The essence of mathematics is not to make simple things complicated, but to make complicated things simple.*
> S. Gudder

Overview and Important Reminders for SAT Math

The Math questions on the SAT are a very mixed bag. The current version of the SAT features several different areas of math; almost everything you could study in high school math is on there except calculus, advanced trig, and advanced statistics. On top of that, an individual question can combine concepts from multiple areas of math, which often makes the questions hard to classify.

Some test-takers cover all the basics of SAT Math before they reach high school, and some take geometry as seniors and never even have classes in algebra. For the first type of person, SAT Math concepts are almost forgotten; for the second type, they're just barely familiar.

In short, nobody I've ever met has felt completely comfortable with all the math on the SAT when they began training, for a variety of reasons. Don't let this bother you!

But that's not all—mastering the key mathematical concepts that can appear on the SAT still won't guarantee a high score. In fact, you probably know some people who are "math geniuses" who still don't make perfect scores on the SAT Math section. You might even be one of those people yourself.

For those people—and for most test-takers, actually—there's something missing when it comes to SAT Math. There's a key idea that they haven't realized yet.

What idea is that? It's the fact that the SAT Math test isn't primarily a math test... at least, not in the sense that you're probably used to. You need more than just mathematical knowledge to do well on the SAT Math section. Think of it as a bunch of problem-solving exercises. Actually, the better you get at SAT Math, the more you'll come to realize it's just a game—and the more you come to see it as a game, the better you'll get at it.

The truth is that SAT Math is primarily a test of your knowledge and application of mathematical definitions and properties, and your ability to identify patterns and "shortcuts" that most untrained test-takers won't be looking for. The calculations themselves generally aren't complicated—even on so-called "hard" questions—as you'll see when we go through some real test questions in the walkthroughs at the end of this section. The main thing that really makes most SAT Math questions difficult is understanding what they're asking you to do in the first place.

So trained test-takers do better on "SAT Math" partly because they focus on looking for the most efficient ways to set problems up, rather than automatically trying to use formulas. Unfortunately, most test-takers never realize how different SAT Math is from school math, so they spend too much time trying to find complicated solutions to the problems on the SAT, the way they might on a regular math test in high school. This is very frustrating, and results in lower scores. It's like trying to cook a soufflé with a hammer.

Studying this Black Book will help you learn and practice the techniques that trained test-takers use to score well on the SAT Math section. More importantly, you'll come to see the SAT "Math" test for what it really is: a reading and problem-solving test that happens to involve numbers!

The "Big Secret" of SAT Math

Before we go any further, it's important that you be in the right frame of mind when you approach SAT Math questions. As I've mentioned a couple of times so far, most SAT Math questions aren't really "math" questions at all, at least not in the way you probably think of math questions. You need to understand why this is.

Put yourself in the College Board's position for a moment. If you're the College Board, your goal is to provide colleges and universities with useful, reliable data on their applicants' abilities. It wouldn't really make sense to have those applicants take a traditional test of advanced math, for two reasons:

- Not all applicants will have taken the same math classes, so a traditional test wouldn't be able to distinguish students who had never had a chance to learn a certain type of math from students who had learned it, and were bad at it.

- More importantly, the high school transcript already does a pretty good job of indicating a student's ability to answer traditional math questions.

So a traditional test of advanced math wouldn't let the College Board provide very useful data to colleges and universities. And it wouldn't make any sense to come up with a traditional test of *basic* math, either, because far too many test-takers would do very well on that, and the results would be largely meaningless.

The College Board's solution to this problem is actually kind of clever. They make sure that SAT Math questions only cover relatively basic math topics, but they cover those topics in non-traditional ways. In doing so, the College Board can be fairly certain that every test-taker has the potential to answer every question correctly—but only by applying their math skills in ways that might not be taught in a typical classroom setting, which keeps the results of the test interesting for colleges and universities.

In fact, let me say that last part again, in all caps, and centered, because it's super important:

SAT MATH QUESTIONS TEST RELATIVELY BASIC MATH IDEAS IN STRANGE WAYS.

That idea is the thing that most test-takers don't realize. It's the thing that causes so many people to spend so much time practicing math for the SAT with so little result. The way to get better at SAT Math isn't to learn advanced math, because most SAT Math isn't very advanced. The way to get better is to learn to take apart SAT Math questions so you can understand which basic ideas are involved in each question.

For this reason, you'll often find that the most challenging SAT Math questions can't be solved with any of the formulas you normally use in math class. In general, SAT Math questions avoid formal solutions. If anything, you might even say that answering SAT Math questions is kind of a creative process, because we never know exactly what the next question will involve, even though we can know the general rules and principles underlying its design.

The Two Critical Components of SAT Math Success

Since the SAT Math section is all about basic math ideas presented in strange ways, there are two key areas of knowledge we'll need to do well on the test:

- basic knowledge of arithmetic, geometry, trigonometry, and algebra (including some basic graph-related ideas), and
- a thorough understanding of the SAT's unwritten rules, patterns, and quirks.

So you will need *some* math knowledge, of course, but you won't need anything like calculus or advanced trig or stats, and you won't have to memorize tons of formulas. Like I keep saying (and will continue to say), it's much more important to focus on understanding how the test is designed than to try to memorize formulas.

In a moment we'll go through the Math Toolbox, which is a list of math concepts that the SAT is allowed to incorporate when it makes up questions. After that, we'll get into the SAT's unwritten rules of math question design.

SAT Math Toolbox

In a moment, we'll talk about how to attack the SAT Math section from a strategic perspective. But first, it's important to make sure we know all the mathematical concepts the SAT is allowed to test (don't worry, there aren't that many of them).

This concept review is designed to be as quick and painless as possible—our goal here isn't to learn all of these ideas from scratch, but to review them on the assumption that you've already learned most of them in a classroom setting at some point. If you feel that you'd like a little more of an explanation for a certain topic, the best thing to do is ask somebody who's good at math (a teacher, parent, or friend) to spend a little time explaining any problem areas to you. None of this is super advanced, so you don't need an expert.

The ideas in this Toolbox might seem easier to you than the actual SAT Math section. That's because the difficulty in SAT Math usually comes from the setup of each problem, not from the concepts that the problem involves. The concepts in this review are the same concepts you'll encounter in your practice and on the real test, but the real test often makes questions look harder than they really are by combining and disguising the underlying concepts in the questions.

For SAT Math, it's not that important to have a *thorough* understanding of the underlying concepts. All you need is a quick, general familiarity with a few relatively basic ideas. So that's all we'll spend time on.

Please note that this list is similar in some ways to lists of math concepts provided by the College Board, but my list is organized a little differently and presents the material in more discrete units. In addition, my list explains things in plainer language, omits some concepts that are redundant in College Board sources, and makes fewer assumptions about what you already know, making it easier to study. (This is also a good time to point out that the College Board occasionally provides some math questions that *don't* appear in official full-length SATs—instead, they appear in practice materials that are meant to sharpen your general math skills. These College Board math questions that appear outside of an official SAT Practice Test are often significantly more advanced, academic, and challenging than real SAT Math questions will be, and I recommend you avoid them. The College Board probably provides these additional practice questions in an attempt to make untrained test-takers believe that the SAT Math section covers more challenging concepts than it really does. So stick to the SAT Math questions you encounter in official SAT Practice Tests from the College Board!)

As you're going through this list, you may see concepts that aren't familiar. Before you let yourself get confused, make sure you've read this list through TWICE. You'll probably find that a lot of your confusion clears itself up on the second reading. You may also see concepts that seem very familiar, basic, and boring. I would still recommend that you read through the whole list TWICE. A lot of the critical subject matter on the SAT Math section *is* pretty basic and boring, and it's helpful to review that material so that you're completely comfortable with it—you may even clear up an important misunderstanding that you didn't realize you had.

Also, please try to remember that the material in the Math Toolbox is pretty dry and technical, and that it shouldn't be the focus of the proper strategic approach to the SAT. It's just a set of basic ideas that need to be refreshed before we get into the stuff that's more important from a test-taking perspective.

Properties of Integers

An **integer** is any number that can be expressed without a fraction, decimal, percentage sign, or symbol.

Integers can be **positive** or **negative**.

Zero is an integer.

> These numbers are integers: $-99, -6, 0, 8, 675$
>
> These numbers are NOT integers: $\pi, 96.7, \frac{3}{4}$

There are **even** integers and there are **odd** integers.

Only integers can be odd or even—a fraction or symbolic number is neither odd nor even.

Integers that are even can be divided by 2 without having anything left over.

Integers that are odd have a remainder of 1 when they're divided by 2.

> These are even integers: $-6, 4, 8$
>
> These are odd integers: $-99, 25, 671$

Some integers have special properties when it comes to addition and multiplication:

- Multiplying any number by 1 leaves the number unchanged.

- Dividing any number by 1 leaves the number unchanged.

- Multiplying any number by 0 results in the number 0.

- Adding 0 to any number leaves the number unchanged.

- Subtracting 0 from any number leaves the number unchanged.

- It's impossible, for purposes of SAT Math, to divide any number by 0.

Word Problems

SAT **word problems** are typically simple descriptions of real-life situations. An SAT word problem about a real-life situation might look like this:

> "Joe buys two balloons for three dollars each, and a certain amount of candy. Each piece of candy costs 25 cents. Joe gives the cashier ten dollars and receives 25 cents in change. How many pieces of candy did he buy?"

To solve SAT word problems, we sometimes have to transform them into math problems. These are the steps we follow to make that transformation:

- Identify key phrases and translate them into mathematical symbols for operations and variables. Use these symbols to connect the numbers that appear in the problem.
- After the word problem has been translated into numbers and symbols, solve it like any other SAT Math problem.

> In the phrase "two balloons for three dollars each," the *each* part means we have to *multiply* the two balloons by the three dollars in order to find out how much total money was spent on the two balloons.
> $2 \times \$3.00 = \$6.00$. Six dollars were spent on the two balloons if they cost three dollars each. The sentence "Joe gives the cashier ten dollars and receives 25 cents in change" tells us that we need to *subtract* 25 cents from 10 dollars to find out the total cost of the balloons and candy—that's $\$10.00 - \$0.25 = \$9.75$. If the total cost was $\$9.75$ and the balloons were $\$6.00$, then the cost of the candy must have been $\$9.75 - \$6.00$, or $\$3.75$. If Joe spent $\$3.75$ on candy, and each piece of candy cost 25 cents, then we can *divide* $\$3.75$ by 25 cents to get $\frac{\$3.75}{\$0.25}$, or 15. So Joe bought 15 pieces of candy.

Word problems on the SAT Math section can also occasionally avoid calculations altogether, and be based more heavily on the kinds of careful reading we need to do on the other parts of the SAT. Remember that careful reading is always the single most important skill on every section of the SAT!

(Also note that sometimes, word problems on the SAT can include a function, and answering the question might require us to understand how a certain variable relates to the real-life scenario described in the word problem. We'll discuss scenarios like that in "Special Technique:" on page 275.)

Number Lines

A **number line** is a simple diagram that arranges numbers from least to greatest.

The positions on a number line can be labeled with actual numbers or with variables.

> This number line shows all the integers from −6 to 4:

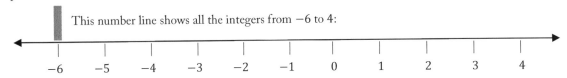

To determine the distance between two numbers on a number line, just subtract the number to the left from the number to the right.

> On the number line above, the distance between 1 and 3 is two units, which is the same thing as saying that $3 - 1 = 2$.

A number's **absolute value** is the distance of that number from zero on the number line.

> −4 and 4 both have an absolute value of 4. We signify the absolute value of a number with vertical lines on either side of the number: $|-4| = |4| = 4$

Basic Operations

You'll have to do basic operations (addition, subtraction, multiplication, division) with integers, fractions, and decimals.

These are examples of basic operations on integers:

$3 + 4 = 7$ $5 - 2 = 3$

$3 \times 7 = 21$ $8 \div 4 = 2$

These are examples of basic operations on fractions:

$$\frac{1}{2} + \frac{3}{2} = 2 \qquad\qquad \frac{4}{3} - \frac{2}{3} = \frac{2}{3}$$

$$\frac{3}{2} \times \frac{1}{2} = \frac{3}{4} \qquad\qquad \frac{7}{4} \div \frac{1}{4} = 7$$

(We discuss performing basic operations on fractions in more detail in "Fractions and Rational Numbers" below.)

These are examples of basic operations on decimals:

$$2.3 + 3.19 = 5.49 \qquad\qquad 9.3 - 6.3 = 3$$

$$1.24 \times 3.5 = 4.34 \qquad\qquad 8.7 \div 10 = 0.87$$

Squares and Square Roots

To **square** a number, multiply the number by itself.

Five squared is five times five, or 5×5, or 5^2, or 25.

To find the **square root** of a number, find the amount that has to be multiplied by itself in order to generate the number.

> The square root of 25 is the amount that yields 25 when it's multiplied by itself. As we just saw, 5 squared is equal to 25. So a square root of 25 is 5.

When you square any number, the result is always positive. This is because a positive number times a positive number gives a positive result, and so does a negative number times a negative number. So any real number multiplied by itself must be positive.

A **radical expression** uses the $\sqrt{}$ symbol to indicate the square root of a given number.

> $\sqrt{7}$ is a radical expression that indicates the square root of 7.

Radical expressions on the SAT are always positive.

Fractions and Rational Numbers

A **fraction** is a special type of number that represents parts of a whole.

Fractions are written this way:

$$\frac{\text{[number of parts being described in the situation]}}{\text{[number of parts that the whole is divided into]}}$$

The number above the fraction bar is called a **numerator**.

The number under the fraction bar is called a **denominator**.

> Imagine that we're sharing a six-pack of soda cans. I really like soda, so I drink five of the cans. In this situation, I've had five of the six cans that make up the six-pack—I've had $\frac{5}{6}$ of the six-pack.

When the numerator of a fraction is less than the denominator, the value of the fraction is less than 1.

When the numerator of a fraction is greater than the denominator, the value of the fraction is greater than 1.

When the numerator of a fraction is equal to the denominator, the value of the fraction is 1.

> $\frac{1}{2}$ is equal to one half, which is less than 1. $\frac{6}{3}$ is equal to 2, which is greater than 1. $\frac{9}{9}$ is equal to 1.

Any integer can be thought of as having the denominator 1 already underneath it.

> 7 is the same thing as $\frac{7}{1}$.

A **reciprocal** is what you get if you switch the numerator and the denominator of a fraction.

> The reciprocal of $\frac{2}{3}$ is $\frac{3}{2}$. The reciprocal of 7 is $\frac{1}{7}$. (Remember that all integers can be thought of as having the denominator 1.)

To multiply two fractions, first multiply their numerators and write that amount as the numerator of the new fraction; then, multiply their denominators and write that amount as the denominator of the new fraction.

> $$\frac{4}{7} \times \frac{9}{13} = \frac{36}{91}$$

To divide fraction a by fraction b, we actually multiply fraction a by the RECIPROCAL of fraction b.

$$\frac{4}{7} \div \frac{9}{13} = \frac{4}{7} \times \frac{13}{9} = \frac{52}{63}$$

Fraction a is equal to fraction b if you could multiply the numerator in a by a certain number to get the numerator in b, and you could also multiply the denominator in a by the same number to get the denominator of b.

$\frac{3}{5}$ is equal to $\frac{18}{30}$ because $3 \times 6 = 18$ and $5 \times 6 = 30$. Here's another way to write this: $\frac{3}{5} \times \frac{6}{6} = \frac{18}{30}$. Note

that $\frac{6}{6}$ is the same thing as 1 (six parts of a whole that's divided into six parts is the same thing as the whole

itself). So all we really did here was multiply $\frac{3}{5}$ by 1, since $\frac{6}{6} = 1$, and we know that multiplying $\frac{3}{5}$ by 1 will

give us an amount equal to $\frac{3}{5}$.

We can **reduce a fraction** when the numerator and denominator can both be evenly divided by the same number—we divide the numerator and denominator by that number. The resulting reduced fraction is equal in value to the original fraction.

The fraction $\frac{15}{25}$ can be reduced because both 15 and 25 can be evenly divided by 5. When we divide the

numerator and denominator by 5, we get $\frac{3}{5}$. The reduced fraction $\frac{3}{5}$ is equal to the original fraction $\frac{15}{25}$.

Order of Operations (PEMDAS)

When an expression involves multiple types of operations, the rules of math require us to perform them in a certain order, called the order of operations . Many students learn the proper order by memorizing the acronym **PEMDAS**, which stands for Parentheses, Exponents, Multiplication, Division, Addition, Subtraction.

This is the order in which we must perform the operations in an expression. Any PEMDAS operations that don't appear in an expression are omitted when we evaluate that expression.

Imagine we have to evaluate the following expression: $1 + (9 - 3) \times 7 - 6^2 \div 2$

PEMDAS tells us that we first do the operation within the Parentheses:

$$1 + \underline{(9 - 3)} \times 7 - 6^2 \div 2 = 1 + \underline{6} \times 7 - 6^2 \div 2$$

Next, we address the Exponent expression:

$$1 + 6 \times 7 - \underline{6^2} \div 2 = 1 + 6 \times 7 - \underline{36} \div 2$$

Then we do any Multiplication in the equation:

$$1 + \underline{6 \times 7} - 36 \div 2 = 1 + \underline{42} - 36 \div 2$$

Then we do the Division:

$$1 + 42 - \underline{36 \div 2} = 1 + 42 - \underline{18}$$

Next we do any Addition:

$$\underline{1 + 42} - 18 = \underline{43} - 18$$

Finally, we do any Subtraction that might be in the equation:

$$\underline{43 - 18} = \underline{25}$$

That gives us the simplified value of the expression:

25

Ratios, Proportions, and Percentages

Ratios, proportions, and percentages are all ways to express a relationship between two numbers.

A **ratio** is often written as a pair of numbers with a colon between them; it can also be expressed as a fraction.

If you make 5 dollars for every 1 dollar Bob makes, then the ratio of *your pay* to *Bob's pay* is $5 : 1$, or $\frac{5}{1}$.

A **proportion** is two ratios or fractions set equal to one another.

> If you make 5 dollars for every 1 dollar Bob makes, and your boss makes 10 dollars for every 2 dollars you make, then the proportion $\frac{5}{1} = \frac{10}{2}$ shows that the same relationship exists between your pay and Bob's pay as between your boss's pay and your pay.

A **percentage** is a special fraction where one number is compared to 100.

To determine a percentage, start with a fraction, then divide the top number by the bottom number, and multiply the result by 100%.

> If Bob makes 1 dollar for every 5 dollars you make, then the fraction that compares Bob's pay to your pay is $\frac{1}{5}$. If we divide 1 by 5 and multiply by 100%, then we can see that Bob makes 20% of what you make, because $1 \div 5 \times 100\% = 20\%$.

Converting among Fractions, Decimals, and Percentages

Because fractions, decimals, and percentages are all ways to express a portion of a whole unit, it can be helpful to know how to express the same value as a fraction, decimal, or percentage.

To make a fraction into a decimal, divide the numerator by the denominator (feel free to use your calculator). Remember that your decimal expression will be less than 1 if the numerator is smaller than the denominator, and greater than 1 if the numerator is larger than the denominator.

> For example, $\frac{3}{16} = 3 \div 16 = 0.1875$

To make a fraction into a percentage, divide the numerator by the denominator, then multiply by 100 and add a percent symbol.

> For example, $\frac{3}{5} = 3 \div 5 = 0.6$, and $0.6 \times 100\% = 60\%$

To make a percentage into a fraction, just give the percentage a denominator of 100, drop the percent sign, and then simplify if necessary.

> For example, 47% is the same as $\frac{47}{100}$.

To make a percent value into a decimal expression, just divide the percentage by 100 and drop the percent sign.

> For example, 3% is the same as 0.03, because $3 \div 100 = 0.03$

To make a decimal into a percentage, we multiply the decimal expression by 100 and then add the percent sign.

> For example, 0.895 is the same as 89.5%, because $0.895 \times 100\% = 89.5\%$

Making a decimal value into a fraction can be a little more complicated, and it doesn't come up very often on the SAT, although the ability to think of a decimal in terms of a roughly equivalent fraction can be helpful sometimes when we're approximating (for example, it may be useful to realize that 0.78 is approximately $\frac{3}{4}$ or $\frac{4}{5}$).

Toward that end, it helps to be able to recognize some decimal expressions and their equivalent fractions:

- $0.1 = \frac{1}{10}$
- $0.2 = \frac{1}{5}$
- $0.\overline{3} = \frac{1}{3}$
- $0.\overline{6} = \frac{2}{3}$
- $0.\overline{1} = \frac{1}{9}$
- $0.25 = \frac{1}{4}$
- $0.5 = \frac{1}{2}$
- $0.75 = \frac{3}{4}$

Remember that you can use your calculator to confirm the fraction equivalent of a decimal expression if you need to for some reason.

> For example, if you see the value 0.125, and you think it's equal to $\frac{1}{8}$, but you're not sure, then you can just divide 1 by 8 on a calculator and make sure you're right.

Distance = Rate × Time ($d = rt$), a.k.a. The Distance Formula

(The concepts behind the distance formula can appear on the SAT in different forms, so read this carefully even if you feel comfortable with the distance formula.)

A **rate** is a ratio that tells us how often one event happens in relation to another event happening. Rates are usually (but not always) expressed in terms of time. For example, if someone walks at a rate of 3 miles per hour, then that person walks 3 miles every time 1 hour passes.

To find the distance traveled by an object, we can multiply the rate at which the object travels by the time that the object spends traveling at that rate. As we just saw, this relationship is expressed by the distance formula, $d = rt$.

What is the distance covered by a car traveling at 60 miles per hour for 2 hours?

$d = rt$ (distance formula)

$d = (60)(2)$ (plug in $r = 60$ mph and $t = 2$ hours)

$d = 120$ (simplify)

So a car traveling at 60 miles per hour for 2 hours will cover 120 miles.

We can use the same formula to find out how long an object takes to cover a certain distance at a certain rate of speed:

How long does it take a car traveling at 40 miles per hour to go 10 miles?

$d = rt$ (distance formula)

$10 = (40)t$ (plug in $d = 10$ miles and $r = 40$ mph)

$\frac{10}{40} = t$ (divide both sides by 40)

$\frac{1}{4} = t$ (reduce)

So a car traveling at 40 miles per hour will cover 10 miles in $\frac{1}{4}$ hours.

We can also use this formula to find out the speed of an object that covers a certain distance in a given time.

How fast does a car travel if it covers 200 miles in 4 hours?

$d = rt$ (distance formula)

$200 = r(4)$ (plug in $d = 200$ miles and $t = 4$ hours)

$50 = r$ (divide both sides by 4)

So a car that goes 200 miles in 4 hours travels at an average speed of 50 miles per hour.

The same relationship can be used to discuss the rates at which other processes happen, not just the rate of movement of an object. We just use the variables in the following way:

- We make d equal to the total amount of whatever ends up getting done.
- We make r equal to the rate at which that activity gets done.
- We make t equal to the amount of time it takes to get that activity done.

Brandon can mow 14 lawns in a week. How long will it take him to mow 168 lawns?

$d = rt$ (distance formula)

$168 = (14)t$ (plug in $d = 168$ lawns and $r = 14$ lawns per week)

$\frac{168}{14} = t$ (divide both sides by 14)

$12 = t$ (reduce)

So it will take Brandon 12 weeks to mow 168 lawns.

(Notice in the example above that the d value was equal to the total number of lawns that got mowed, and the r or "rate" value was the number of lawns Brandon could mow in a week.)

Maritza can write 3 chapters of her book in one month. How many chapters can she write in eight months?

$d = rt$ (distance formula)

$d = (3)(8)$ (plug in $r = 3$ chapters per month and $t = 8$ months)

Facebook.com/QuestPreparation   Youtube.com/QuestPrep

$$d = 24 \qquad \text{(simplify)}$$

So Maritza can write 24 chapters in eight months.

(Notice in the example above that the d value was equal to the total number of chapters Maritza wrote, and the r or "rate" value was the number of chapters Maritza could write in a month.)

Unit conversion

On the SAT, we occasionally encounter questions that require us to convert data from one unit of measure to another unit of measure.

Joe has 500 grams of sugar. If there are 1000 grams in a kilogram and approximately 0.45 kilograms in a pound, about how many pounds of sugar does Joe have?

First, we convert from grams to kilograms. We are told that 1000 grams corresponds to 1 kilogram, and we want to figure out how many kilograms 500 grams corresponds to. So we set up an equation using these ratios:

$$\frac{1000\text{ g}}{1\text{ kg}} = \frac{500\text{ g}}{x\text{ kg}} \qquad \text{(set ratios equal to one another)}$$

$$1000x = 500 \qquad \text{(cross-multiply)}$$

$$x = \frac{500}{1000} = \frac{1}{2} \qquad \text{(divide both sides by 1000 to isolate } x\text{)}$$

So 500 grams is equal to $\frac{1}{2}$ kilogram, or 0.5 kilograms. Now we need to convert kilograms to pounds. We are told that 0.45 kilograms corresponds to approximately 1 pound, and we want to figure out how many pounds 0.5 kilograms corresponds to. So we set up an equation using these ratios:

$$\frac{0.45\text{ kg}}{1\text{ lb}} = \frac{0.5\text{ kg}}{x\text{ lb}} \qquad \text{(set ratios equal to one another)}$$

$$0.45x = 0.5 \qquad \text{(cross-multiply)}$$

$$x \approx 1.11 \qquad \text{(divide both sides by 0.45 to isolate } x\text{)}$$

So 500 grams is equal to approximately 1.11 pounds.

Note that we can be expected to know the relationships between common, everyday units like minutes, hours, and days—there are 60 minutes in an hour and 24 hours in a day, for example—but any relevant information about more obscure units will be provided by the College Board.

Converting length measurements to square units

Some SAT questions will provide a unit conversion for a measure of *length* (like "1 foot = 12 inches"), and then ask you to convert the measure of an *area* from one unit to another (like converting 9 *square* feet into *square* inches). When this happens, you must remember to *square* each measure. So an area that's 1 foot wide by 1 foot long has an area of 1 square foot, because $1 \times 1 = 1$. But if we convert that area to square inches, we find that one square foot *isn't* equal to 12 square inches—it's equal to 12×12 square inches, or 144 square inches! So 9 square feet would be $9 \times 12 \times 12$ square inches, or 1,296 square inches. The College Board likes to throw in this little wrinkle, so watch out for it on test day.

Algebra

For our purposes, **algebra** is the process of using variables like x to stand for unknown numbers in mathematical expressions, and then manipulating those expressions to find the values of one or more of those unknown numbers.

Using equations

On the SAT, an **equation** is a statement that involves an algebraic expression and an equals sign.

$5x = 20$ is an equation, because it involves the algebraic expression $5x$ and an equals sign.

Solving an equation means figuring out the value of the variable in the equation. We solve equations just like you learned in algebra class—by performing the same operations on both sides of the equation until the variable is left by itself on one side of the equation, and the value of that variable is on the other side of the equation.

Here's an example of solving for x in an algebraic equation:

$$5x = 20 \qquad \text{(example equation)}$$

$$\frac{5x}{5} = \frac{20}{5} \qquad \text{(divide both sides by 5 to isolate } x)$$

$$x = 4 \qquad \text{(simplify)}$$

On the SAT, it can often be useful to **cross-multiply**. When we encounter an equation on the SAT with one fraction on either side of the equals sign, we can multiply the denominator of each side by the numerator of the other side and end up with two expressions that must be equal. Let's look at an example without variables first:

Imagine the equation $\frac{9}{15} = \frac{3}{5}$. We know this equation is true because we can reduce $\frac{9}{15}$ to $\frac{3}{5}$ by dividing the numerator and denominator of $\frac{9}{15}$ by 3. Notice that when we cross-multiply—that is, multiply the numerator on the left side of the equation by the denominator on the right side of the equation, and vice-versa—we end up with two expressions that are equal to each other:

$$9 \times 5 = 3 \times 15, \;\; \text{or} \;\; 45 = 45.$$

This can be a handy shortcut when dealing with an equation involving variables, if the equation has one fraction on each side:

$$\frac{12}{x} = \frac{20}{5} \qquad \text{(given equation)}$$

$$12(5) = 20(x) \qquad \text{(cross-multiply)}$$

$$60 = 20x \qquad \text{(simplify)}$$

$$3 = x \qquad \text{(divide both sides by 20)}$$

Solving an equation for one variable "in terms of" another variable means isolating the first variable on one side of the equation so that the other side of the equation is an expression involving the other variable.

What if we have the equation $4n - 7 = 2a$, and we want to solve for n in terms of a?

$$4n - 7 = 2a \qquad \text{(original equation)}$$

$$4n = 2a + 7 \qquad \text{(add 7 to both sides to isolate the term involving } n)$$

$$n = \frac{2a + 7}{4} \qquad \text{(divide both sides by 4 to isolate } n \text{ completely)}$$

Systems of Equations

A **system of equations** contains two or more equations with the same variables.

A solution to a system of equations is a set of values that creates a valid statement when plugged into each equation in the system. The easiest way to solve a system of equations algebraically is usually to solve one equation in terms of one variable, like we just did before. Then we plug the expression we found into the second equation, and solve.

Imagine that we need to solve the following system of equations—that is, to find an (x, y) pair that satisfies both equations:

$$x + y = 5$$

$$2x - y = 7$$

First, we'll isolate the y in the first equation, giving us that equation in terms of y. We can do that by subtracting x from both sides, which gives us $y = 5 - x$. Now that we know y is the same thing as $5 - x$, we just plug in $5 - x$ wherever y appears in the second equation:

$$2x - (5 - x) = 7 \qquad \text{(plug } y = 5 - x \text{ into second equation)}$$

$$2x - 5 + x = 7 \qquad \text{(distribute negative sign)}$$

$$3x - 5 = 7 \qquad \text{(simplify)}$$

$$3x = 12 \qquad \text{(add 5 to both sides)}$$

$$x = 4 \qquad \text{(divide both sides by 3)}$$

Now that we know $x = 4$, we plug that back into either original equation, and we'll be able to solve for y:

$$(4) + y = 5 \qquad \text{(plug } x = 4 \text{ into first equation)}$$

$$y = 1 \qquad \text{(subtract 4 from both sides)}$$

So the solution to the system of equations above is $x = 4$ and $y = 1$, or $(4, 1)$.

When we graph a system of equations, each solution to the system is a point of intersection of the graphs of those equations. This is the graph of the system of equations from the example above:

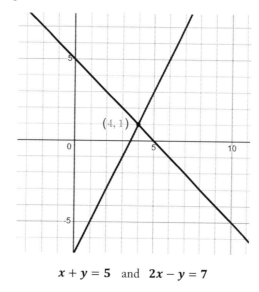

$$x + y = 5 \quad \text{and} \quad 2x - y = 7$$

The point of intersection in the graph is $(4, 1)$, which is the solution of the system of equations.

We'll discuss the following in more detail after the Math Toolbox when we focus on the strategic side of SAT Math, but it's such an important idea that I'll mention it now too: using the provided graphing calculator to find points of intersection in a system of equations is an *incredibly powerful* technique on the SAT Math section. There are a lot of SAT Math questions involving systems of equations that can be solved in several minutes by writing out a lot of algebra, or that can be solved in about 5 seconds by graphing them in the provided calculator and then finding the information you need from the resulting graph.

In order to find these solutions, you'll still need to read the question carefully and take the time to *understand* the relevant concepts, to make sure you know what information to look for in the graph—but the graphing calculator can save you a ton of time and mental energy when used properly. Again, we'll discuss this more in the section called "Special Technique: Using The Surprisingly Powerful Digital SAT Calculator" on page 280, and we'll also see examples of this idea at work in the SAT Math walkthroughs later in this section.

We can also solve a system of equations by adding the equations in the system together in order to eliminate one of the variables. Basically, we stack the two equations on top of each other so that corresponding variables are lined up vertically, and then we add them to get rid of one of the variables, and find the value of the remaining variable. Once we know the value of one variable, we can just plug that value into either equation to find the value of the remaining variable, as we did above.

That may sound a little confusing if you're not familiar with this technique, so let's just look at an example.

If we have the following system of equations:

$$2x - 3y = 12$$

$$x + 3y = 3$$

Then we can add the equations together to get rid of the y-term, like this:

$$2x - 3y = 12$$

$$+ \quad x + 3y = 3$$

$$3x \qquad = 15$$

In the above example, we added $2x$ to x and got $3x$, we added $-3y$ and $3y$ which canceled out the y-term, and we added 12 and 3 to get 15. The result was the equation $3x = 15$. We can divide both sides of that equation by 3 to find that $x = 5$, and then we can plug $x = 5$ into either equation to solve for y. If we plug $x = 5$ into the second equation, we get $(5) + 3y = 3$, then $3y = -2$, then $y = -\frac{2}{3}$. So the solution to this system of equations is $\left(5, -\frac{2}{3}\right)$.

In the example above, notice that this approach only worked because one equation included $-3y$ and the other included $3y$, so adding the equations together canceled out those y-terms. What if you're trying to solve a system of equations that doesn't have terms that cancel out this way?

For one thing, if both equations included the same term (like $3y$, for example), then we could have just *subtracted* the second equation from the first—the exact same process as above, just subtracting each term from the one above it, instead of adding them.

But we won't always be able to just add or subtract the given equations, as they are, to cancel out one of the terms. Another option we have is to multiply one (or both) of the equations by a number, and *then* add or subtract to get rid of one of the variable terms.

If we have the following system of equations:

$$8x - y = 8$$

$$2x + 2y = 20$$

Then we might notice that we can't just add them together, or subtract one from the other, to cancel out either variable. But if we multiply every term in the first equation by 2, then we get this:

$$16x - 2y = 16$$

$$2x + 2y = 20$$

Now we can add the equations together to cancel out the y-term. If we do that, we get this result:

$$16x - 2y = 16$$

$$+ \quad 2x + 2y = 20$$

$$18x \qquad = 36$$

Now we have the equation $18x = 36$, so we know that $x = 2$. If we plug $x = 2$ into the second equation, we get $2(2) + 2y = 20$, then $2y = 16$, then $y = 8$. So the solution to this system of equations is $(2,8)$.

Inequalities

On the SAT, inequalities are statements that show a particular amount is greater than or less than a second amount. They use these symbols:

- The symbol $<$ means "less than."
- The symbol $>$ means "greater than."
- The symbol $\leq$ means "less than or equal to."
- The symbol $\geq$ means "greater than or equal to."

You solve an inequality the same way you solve an equation, with one difference: when you multiply or divide both sides by a *negative* number, you have to switch the direction of the inequality symbol:

$$-\frac{x}{4} \leq 10 \qquad \text{(example inequality)}$$

$$-x \leq 10(4) \qquad \text{(multiply both sides by 4)}$$

$$-x \leq 40 \qquad \text{(simplify)}$$

$$x \geq -40 \qquad \text{(multiply by } -1 \text{ and switch direction of inequality symbol)}$$

When we graph an inequality, we end up with a shaded region on the side of the line that contains all the points that are solutions to the inequality.

This is the graph of $y \leq 2x - 5$. The shaded region represents all the (x, y) coordinates that are solutions of the inequality.

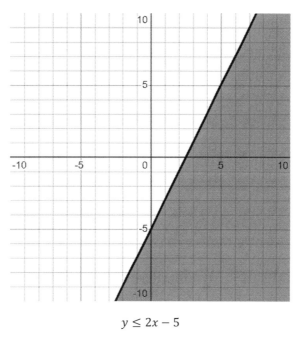

$$y \leq 2x - 5$$

We can check whether a particular point is a solution of an inequality by plugging that point into that inequality. If the result is a valid statement, then the point is a solution of the inequality.

Is the point $(10, 2)$ a solution for $y \leq 2x - 5$?

$y \leq 2x - 5$	(given inequality)
$2 \leq 2(10) - 5$	(plug in $(10, 2)$)
$2 \leq 20 - 5$	(simplify)
$2 \leq 15$	(simplify)

Plugging $(10, 2)$ into the inequality gives us a valid statement. So $(10, 2)$ is a solution of $y \leq 2x - 5$.

We've already discussed systems of equations in this toolbox. We can also have a **system of inequalities** . When we graph a system of inequalities, the solution region will be the set of points in the coordinate plane that satisfy both inequalities.

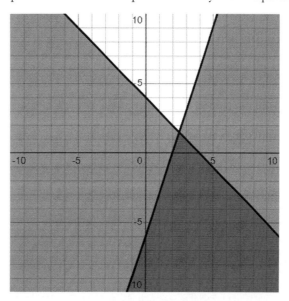

The above graph represents the following system of inequalities:

$$y \leq 4 - x$$

$$y \leq 3x - 6$$

The bottom-middle area of the graph where the two shaded regions overlap is the solution region of this system of inequalities. Each of the points in that double-shaded region satisfies both inequalities.

We can check whether a particular point is a solution to a system of inequalities by plugging that point into each of the inequalities in the system. If the point satisfies all the inequalities, then the point is a solution to the system of inequalities. If the point fails to satisfy any the inequalities, then the point isn't a solution to the system of inequalities.

Is the point $(2, 1)$ a solution for the following system of inequalities?

$$y \leq 4 - x$$

$$y \leq 3x - 6$$

First, let's plug $(2, 1)$ into the first inequality.

$y \leq 4 - x$	(first inequality)
$1 \leq 4 - 2$	(plug in $(2, 1)$)
$1 \leq 2$	(simplify)

When we plug $(2, 1)$ into the first inequality, we get a valid statement. So $(2, 1)$ is a solution of the first inequality. Now let's plug $(2, 1)$ into the second inequality.

$y \leq 3x - 6$	(second inequality)
$1 \leq 3(2) - 6$	(plug in $(2, 1)$)
$1 \leq 6 - 6$	(simplify)
$1 \leq 0$	(simplify)

When we plug $(2, 1)$ into the second inequality, we get an invalid statement. So $(2, 1)$ isn't a solution of the second inequality, which means it isn't a solution of the system of inequalities.

Exponents

An exponent of a number indicates that we multiply the number by itself a certain number of times.

a^3 is an example of an exponential expression. It's equal to $a \times a \times a$. The 3 in this example is the "exponent," and the a is called the "base."

Exponents can be positive or negative.

When an exponent is positive, we multiply the base by itself as many times as the exponent indicates, just like we did in the above example.

When an exponent is negative, we treat it just like a positive exponent EXCEPT that we take the *reciprocal* of the final amount, as demonstrated in the following example:

$$a^5 = a \times a \times a \times a \times a$$

$$a^{-5} = \frac{1}{a^5}$$

We can multiply exponent expressions by each other when the bases are identical. To do that, we just add the exponents:

$$(a^2)(a^3) = (a \times a)(a \times a \times a) = a \times a \times a \times a \times a = a^5$$

$$(a^7)(a^{-4}) = a^3$$

We can also divide exponent expressions when they have the same base. For that, we just subtract the exponents:

$$\frac{a^8}{a^2} = a^{(8-2)} = a^6$$

We can raise exponential expressions to other exponents by multiplying the first exponent by the second one:

$$(a^4)^5 = a^{20}$$

When we raise a number to a fractional exponent, the denominator of the fraction denotes the root of the base in the expression:

$$a^{\frac{1}{2}} = \sqrt{a}$$

$$a^{\frac{1}{3}} = \sqrt[3]{a}$$

When fractional exponents include numerators other than 1, the numerator determines the exponent to which the base is raised, and the denominator indicates the root of the expression to be taken.

$$a^{\frac{5}{3}} = \sqrt[3]{(a^5)} = \left(\sqrt[3]{a}\right)^5$$

a raised to the $\frac{5}{3}$ exponent is equal to the cube root of a raised to the fifth power. Notice that it doesn't matter whether the cube root of a is found first and the result is raised to the fifth power, or a is raised to the fifth power and the cube root of the result is found; the value of the expression is the same either way.

Note that raising any number to an exponent of zero gives you the number 1.

$$a^0 = 1$$

Polynomials

On the SAT, a **polynomial** is an expression that includes multiple terms, at least one of which contains a variable.

The following are examples of polynomials:

$5x + 3$

$x^2 - 2x + 9$

$4ab^2 + 5a$

Remember that a **variable** is a letter, like x or a, that's used to represent a value. In different expressions, a variable can have different values. For example, in one expression, x can be equal to 100, while in another expression, x can be equal to 12.

A **constant** is a number like 3 or 11 or 716.9234 that has a set, defined value that can't change. The constant 7 is always equal to 7, regardless of the expression where the 7 appears.

A **coefficient** is a constant that appears immediately before a variable in a polynomial to indicate that the variable is being multiplied by the amount of the coefficient. So in the expression $8 + 2y$, we know that 8 is a constant, y is a variable, and 2 is the coefficient of y.

When we write a polynomial, we list the terms in decreasing order of the exponent of the variable. That may sound complicated, so let's look at an example:

$$x^4 + 3x^3 + 5x^2 - 2x + 4 = 0$$

We started with the x-term raised to the fourth power, then followed with the one raised to the third power, then the one that was squared, then the x-term without an exponent (which is the same as x^1), then the constant with no x-term (which is the same as an x^0 term, since any number raised to the power of zero is equal to 1).

The **degree** of a variable in a polynomial refers to the highest exponent to which that variable is raised in the expression. So $x^3 + 5x^2 - x - 7$ is a third-degree polynomial, because the highest exponent of an x-term in the polynomial is 3.

Operations on polynomials

Polynomials can be added, subtracted, multiplied, and divided, but sometimes there are special considerations.

When we add or subtract polynomials, we simply combine like terms.

Let's add the polynomials $5x + 3$ and $x^2 - 2x + 9$:

$5x + 3 + x^2 - 2x + 9$ \qquad (original expression)

$x^2 + (5x - 2x) + (3 + 9)$ \qquad (group like terms)

$$x^2 + 3x + 12 \qquad \text{(simplify)}$$

As you can see, we combined the following kinds of terms:

- the x^2 terms (there was only one, in this case)

- the x terms ($5x$ and $-2x$)

- the constants (3 and 9)

Notice that you can only add or subtract like terms during this process.

Let's add the polynomials $2x^3 + 4x^2$ and $x + 7$:

$$2x^3 + 4x^2 + x + 7 \qquad \text{(given expression)}$$

In this case, nothing can be combined, because there are no like terms. So we just write the sum including all the terms from both polynomials, as shown above.

We can multiply a polynomial by another quantity by multiplying each term in the polynomial by that quantity.

$$3y(5x + 6) \qquad \text{(given expression)}$$

$$(3y \times 5x) + (3y \times 6) \qquad \text{(multiply the } 3y \text{ by } 5x \text{ and by 6)}$$

$$15xy + 18y \qquad \text{(simplify)}$$

Note that multiplying one term by each of two or more terms in parentheses is called **distribution**.

$$3(x + 7) \qquad \text{(given expression)}$$

$$3x + 21 \qquad \text{(distribute the 3)}$$

A **binomial** is a polynomial with two terms.

We can multiply one binomial by another binomial using the **FOIL** technique, which you've probably encountered in your math classes. "FOIL" stands for First, Outer, Inner, Last, and the technique works as we see in the following example.

Let's multiply $2x + 5$ by $x - 1$:

$$(2x + 5)(x - 1)$$

First, we multiply the first two terms of each polynomial together (the "F" in FOIL stands for "first"). That gives us $2x(x)$, or $2x^2$.

Next, we multiply the outer two terms together (the "O" in FOIL stands for "outer"). That gives us $2x(-1)$, or $-2x$.

Next, we multiply the two inner terms together (the "I" in FOIL stands for "inner"). That gives us $5(x)$, or $5x$.

Last, we multiply the last two terms of each polynomial together (the "L" in FOIL stands for "last"). That gives us $5(-1)$, or -5.

Now that we have all the terms, we simply add them together (combining like terms, as always):

$$2x^2 + (-2x) + 5x + (-5)$$

$$2x^2 + 3x - 5$$

On the SAT, we can also divide a polynomial by another quantity if each term of the polynomial has a factor in common with the quantity we're dividing by. Simply divide each term of the polynomial individually.

Let's divide $14ab + 2b$ by $2b$:

$$\frac{14ab+}{2b}$$ (given expression—note that $2b$ is a factor of both terms in the numerator)

$$\frac{14ab}{2b} + \frac{2b}{2b}$$ (rewrite as the sum of two fractions with a common denominator)

$$7a + 1$$ (simplify)

Factoring polynomials

On the SAT, factoring polynomials means taking a polynomial and breaking it into two expressions that can be multiplied together to get the original polynomial.

On the SAT, there are two important factoring situations you'll need to be able to recognize:

- common factors
- FOIL in reverse

Recognizing **common factors** involves noticing that each term in a polynomial has a common factor that can be factored out.

If we have a polynomial like $(3x + 9)$, we can see that both $3x$ and 9 are divisible by 3. That means we can divide a 3 out of each term in the polynomial and end up with the factors 3 and $(x + 3)$, because $3(x + 3) = 3x + 9$.

Another way to factor polynomials is to do **FOIL in reverse**. This might sound intimidating, but it gets easy when you're used to it.

Suppose we need to factor the expression $6x^2 - 7x - 3$ into two binomials. We can reverse-FOIL this expression. The product of the first terms of each polynomial will have to be $6x^2$, so we'll start by just picking two x terms that meet this requirement to try out, like $3x$ and $2x$:

$$(3x+?)(2x+?)$$

We also know the last terms will have to multiply together to equal -3, so they must be either -1 and 3 or 1 and -3. We'll just try one pair (reverse-FOILing often involves some trial and error).

$$(3x + 1)(2x - 3)$$

Then we multiply out our binomials to see if we've reverse-FOILed correctly:

$$(3x + 1)(2x - 3)$$ (our guess for the factorization)

$$6x^2 - 9x + 2x - 3$$ (FOIL the two binomials)

$$6x^2 - 7x - 3$$ (simplify)

In this case, we got it right on the first try; if you don't, of course, you can look at what didn't work and try other pairs of factors. Problems like this on the SAT aren't too common, and the factors usually aren't too hard to figure out. This gets a lot easier with a little bit of practice.

Completing the square

Note: Before we discuss this topic, I want to make something very clear: you don't have to know how to use this technique for the SAT Math section. There are questions where you *can* use this technique to find the answer, but there is always a different, easier, faster way to answer those questions—usually involving the graphing function of the provided SAT calculator, as we'll discuss in the section called "Special Technique: Using The Surprisingly Powerful Digital SAT Calculator" on page 280. We'll see examples of this in the walkthroughs.

For that reason, I basically don't ever recommend using this technique against real SAT Math questions, unless you just can't think of any other approach. I'm only including this in the training because it comes up a couple of times in the walkthroughs, and some students will want to know how it works. But if this never feels comfortable to you, it's not something you need to worry about in an SAT context. With that in mind, let's proceed.

Sometimes it can be useful to rewrite a polynomial expression as an equivalent polynomial that includes a squared binomial, which is a technique called "completing the square." This is especially true when completing the square allows us to produce standard versions of certain equations (like those for circles and parabolas) that can give us useful information about key features of the relevant shape. (If this isn't making sense to you yet, just keep reading.)

We complete the square by adding the same amount to both sides of a given equation so that one side becomes a polynomial expression that can be expressed as the square of a binomial; we then reverse-FOIL that expression so that we can write it as the square of a binomial, and then finish the process by re-isolating the other variable. Again, if that doesn't make sense, just keep reading.

Let's complete the square so that we can create an expression of the equation $y = x^2 + 6x + 15$ that involves a squared binomial.

$y = x^2 + 6x + 15$ (original polynomial, not expressed as the square of a binomial)

$y - 15 = x^2 + 6x$ (subtract the constant on the right side from both sides)

$y - 15 + 9 = x^2 + 6x + 9$ (find half the coefficient of x, square the result, and add that number to both sides of the equation)

$y - 6 = (x + 3)^2$ (combine like terms on the left side of the equation, and reverse-FOIL the right side of the equation to generate the squared binomial)

$y = (x + 3)^2 + 6$ (add or subtract any constants on the left to both sides, as necessary, to isolate y again)

So when we complete the square with the equation $y = x^2 + 6x + 15$, the result is $y = (x + 3)^2 + 6$. This equation is now in the format of the vertex form of a quadratic equation, which is $f(x) = a(x - h)^2 + k$, where the vertex of the parabola is at (h, k). We now know that when we graph $y = (x + 3)^2 + 6$, the vertex of the resulting parabola is at $(-3, 6)$. Of course, if we needed to know the vertex of this equation to answer an SAT Math question, we could have found that a lot faster by using the provided graphing calculator, as mentioned above. Again, this technique is very inefficient on SAT Math questions, but we're discussing it here just because some readers will wonder about it.

Solving Quadratic Equations by Factoring

Note: In just about any situation where factoring a quadratic equation could help you answer an SAT Math question, it's quicker and easier to use your graphing calculator, as we discuss in the section called "Special Technique: Using The Surprisingly Powerful Digital SAT Calculator" on page 280. I'm mainly discussing this topic here for the sake of completeness, and because leaving it out might confuse people. So go ahead and read it, but plan to use primarily the techniques we'll discuss in the aforementioned SAT calculator training when you see this kind of question in practice and on test day.

A quadratic equation is an equation that involves three terms:

- one term is a variable expression raised to the power of 2.
- one term is a variable expression not raised to any power.
- one term is a constant.

$x^2 + 3x = -2$ is a quadratic equation because it involves a term with x squared, a term with x, and a constant.

One way to answer SAT questions that involve quadratic equations is by factoring. See the discussion of factoring polynomials above if you need a refresher on that general idea. (Graphing and the quadratic formula are two other ways to answer SAT questions that involve quadratic equations, in case you were wondering.)

To solve a quadratic equation by factoring, we have to make one side of the equation equal to zero, and then factor the other side of the equation (the quadratic part).

$x^2 + 3x = -2$ (given quadratic equation)

$x^2 + 3x + 2 = 0$ (add 2 to both sides to make the right side equal to 0)

$(x + 1)(x + 2) = 0$ (reverse-FOIL left side of equation)

Now that we know $(x + 1)(x + 2) = 0$, what else do we know? We know that one of those two factors has to equal zero—either $x + 1 = 0$, or $x + 2 = 0$. How do we know this? Remember that the only way to multiply two numbers and get zero is if one of the numbers *is* zero. So if we can multiply $x + 1$ by $x + 2$ and get zero, then either $x + 1$ is zero or $x + 2$ is zero.

Once we've factored, we solve for the variable by creating two small sub-equations in which each factor is set equal to zero.

$$x + 1 = 0 \ \text{ or } \ x + 2 = 0$$

$$x = -1 \ \ \text{ or } \ x = -2$$

So in the equation $x^2 + 3x = -2$, x can equal either -1 or -2.

Quadratic equations can have multiple solutions, as we've just seen.

Quadratic formula

Note: This topic is similar to the "completing the square" topic that we discussed above, because you *can* use it to answer SAT Math questions, but you never *have* to—it's always possible to use a simpler, more straightforward approach to those questions instead of using the quadratic formula. I only bring it up here because it comes up in the walkthroughs and official College Board explanations, and some students will want to see it explained—but you definitely shouldn't waste time focusing on this topic, even if you're not super comfortable with it. Instead, just read this section, and then continue moving through this toolbox and the rest of your training.

The general quadratic equation is $ax^2 + bx + c = 0$. As we've discussed elsewhere, it's sometimes possible to determine the value of x in such a quadratic equation through reverse-FOILing, or other types of factoring—but those approaches aren't always easy to apply.

We can *always* find the solutions to a quadratic equation using the quadratic formula, which is as follows, given the general quadratic format of $ax^2 + bx + c = 0$:

$$x = \frac{-b \pm \sqrt{b^2 - 4ac}}{2a}$$

Find the solutions to the equation $3x^2 + 10x - 2 = 0$.

$x = \frac{-b \pm \sqrt{b^2 - 4ac}}{2a}$ (quadratic formula)

$x = \frac{-(10) \pm \sqrt{(10)^2 - 4(3)(-2)}}{2(3)}$ (plug in $a = 3$, $b = 10$, and $c = -2$)

$x = \frac{-10 \pm \sqrt{124}}{6}$ (simplify)

$x = \frac{-10 \pm 2\sqrt{31}}{6}$ (factor $\sqrt{4}$ out of the expression under the radical)

$x = \frac{-5 \pm \sqrt{31}}{3}$ (reduce)

So the two solutions are $x = -\frac{5}{3} + \frac{\sqrt{31}}{3}$ and $x = -\frac{5}{3} - \frac{\sqrt{31}}{3}$.

(Notice in the example above that we find the a, b, and c values by comparing the given equation to the general quadratic equation. In this case, when we compare the given equation $3x^2 + 10x - 2 = 0$ to the general quadratic equation $ax^2 + bx + c = 0$, we can see that $a = 3$, $b = 10$, and $c = -2$.)

Functions

Concepts related to functions appear frequently on the SAT. Make sure you're thoroughly comfortable with this topic before test day, and see the question walkthroughs later in this Black Book for examples of how these concepts are tested in real questions.

A **function** is a type of equation that allows us to enter one value (often called x) and generate another value (often called y, or $f(x)$).

The values we enter into the function can be referred to as **inputs** or x-values (if the function is written in terms of x).

The values generated by the function can be referred to as **outputs** or y-values (if the function is written in terms of y) or $f(x)$ values (if the function is called f and is written in terms of x-values).

There are many different ways we can write a function, but one of the most common on the SAT is probably by using $f(x)$:

$$f(x) = x + 3$$

Even though the most common way that functions are expressed on the test is in terms of f and x, any other two letters can also be used, as in the following examples:

$$g(h) = h + 3$$

$$E(\theta) = \theta + 3$$

$$r(N) = N + 3$$

All of these functions express the same relationship; they just use different letters as variables.

In the example function above, the function $f(x)$ is equal to $x + 3$. In other words, for any x-value that we enter into the function above, we find $f(x)$ by adding 3 to the x-value. For example, entering $x = 8$ will produce an $f(x)$ value of 11. We could write this in the following way: $f(8) = 11$.

The expression in parentheses immediately after the f is the thing we'll be plugging into the function:

- If the expression in parentheses after the f is a variable, such as x, then we're using it to represent the idea of *any* value being plugged into the function.

$$f(x) = x + 3 \qquad \text{(equation defining function } f\text{)}$$

- If the expression in parentheses after the f is a specific value, such as 8, then the notation describes the idea of that specific value being plugged into the function.

$$f(8) = 8 + 3 \qquad \text{(plug in } x = 8\text{)}$$
$$f(8) = 11 \qquad \text{(add 3 and 8 to find } f(8)\text{)}$$

A function is **undefined** when the function includes a fraction whose denominator is equal to 0.

The function $f(x) = \frac{1}{x-3}$ is undefined at $x = 3$ because $f(3) = \frac{1}{(3)-3}$ which is equal to $\frac{1}{0}$, and dividing by 0 results in an undefined value.

Linear functions

The xy-coordinate plane has 4 quadrants numbered $I, II, II,$ and IV.

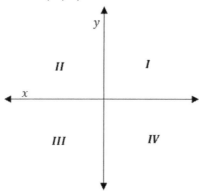

The **origin** is the point where the x-axis and y-axis intersect. The coordinate pair that corresponds to the origin is $(0, 0)$.

A **point** can be plotted on the xy-coordinate plane in (x, y) notation if we make the x number the horizontal separation between the point (x, y) and the origin $(0, 0)$, and then we make the y value the vertical separation between (x, y) and $(0, 0)$.

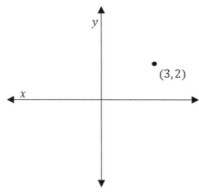

The above graph shows the point $(3, 2)$ on the xy-coordinate plane. (Notice, in the graph above, that point $(3, 2)$ is 3 units to the right of the origin and 2 units above the origin.)

A **linear function** is a function whose (x, y) value pairs form a straight line when they're plotted as points on a graph.

$f(x) = x - 1$ is linear, because all the (x, y) pairs that it generates form a straight line when plotted on a graph.

Here are some (x, y) pairs for the function $f(x) = x - 1$:

x	y
-2	-3
-1	-2
0	-1
1	0
2	1
3	2

When we plot the (x, y) pairs from a linear function, we can see they fall in a straight line:

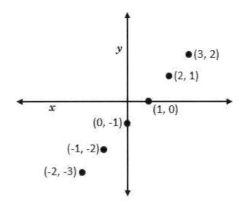

As you can see, we've only plotted six specific points based on the (x, y) coordinates we got for six specific values of x. But we can draw a line connecting these plotted points, and the line will represent all possible (x, y) pairs that satisfy $f(x) = x - 1$.

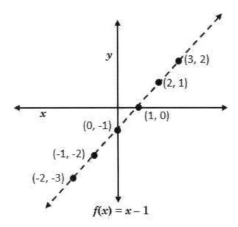

The slope of a function is a fraction that expresses a measurement of how far up or down the line travels for a given distance that it travels from left to right:

- The number of units traveled up goes in the numerator of the slope fraction. (A negative number in the numerator indicates that the line travels down as it goes from left to right, and a zero in the numerator—in other words, a slope of zero—indicates that the line is horizontal.)
- The number of units traveled from left to right is the denominator of the slope fraction.

For this reason, the slope fraction is often described as "rise over run"—the number of units traveled up (the "rise"), divided by the number of units traveled from left to right (the "run").

If the slope of a line is $\frac{1}{3}$, then the line travels 1 unit up for every 3 units it travels from left to right, because the numerator, or "rise," is 1, and the denominator, or "run," is 3.

This means we can calculate the slope between two points on a function graph by finding the vertical distance between them, and dividing it by the horizontal distance between them:

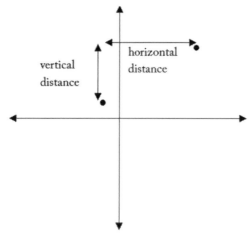

The vertical distance between the two points is the difference between the y-values of the points, and the horizontal distance between them is the difference between their x-values.

> The slope between the points $(5, 3)$ and $(19, 8)$ is equal to $\dfrac{8-3}{19-5}$, or $\dfrac{5}{14}$.

By convention, we take the values from the left-most point and subtract them from the values of the right-most point, but it doesn't actually matter which order you subtract in, as long as you use the same order for the coordinates in both the numerator and denominator, and you keep track of any minus signs.

> If we switch the order of subtraction for the points from the previous example, we get $\dfrac{3-8}{5-19}$, or $\dfrac{-5}{-14}$, which is still equal to $\dfrac{5}{14}$.

As we discussed earlier, a line with a positive slope is slanted upward as we read from left to right, and a line with a negative slope is slanted downward as we read from left to right:

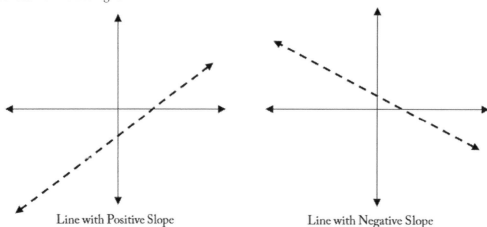

Line with Positive Slope   Line with Negative Slope

We can also describe a function with a positive slope as "increasing" and a function with a negative slope as "decreasing."

The **y-intercept** is the y-value of the function where $x = 0$, and is also the point where the graph of the function crosses the y-axis.

An **x-intercept** of a function is a point where the graph of the function crosses the x-axis, which is also a point where the y-value of the function is equal to 0.

Two linear functions with the same slope and different y-intercepts are **parallel**.

Two lines are **perpendicular** when their slopes are the opposite reciprocals of one another. When this happens, the lines cross each other at a 90° angle.

> 2 and $-\dfrac{1}{2}$ are examples of perpendicular slopes

The slope of a **horizontal** line is 0, because the "rise" is always zero, and 0 divided by any number is 0.

The slope of a **vertical** line is **undefined**, because the "run" is always zero, and any number divided by 0 is undefined.

You'll never have to draw your own graph of a function on the SAT, because the format of the test makes that impossible. Instead, you'll need to use your understanding of a provided graph in the question to figure out a certain value, or you'll be able to graph one or more functions from the prompt with the provided calculator, and then use those graphs to find the information that satisfies the prompt—see the walkthroughs later in this Black Book for examples of these ideas in action.

Slope-intercept form

We can easily find the slope of a line when the equation of the line is in something called **slope-intercept form**, which looks like this:

$$y = mx + b$$

The variables in slope-intercept form represent the following aspects of the graph:

- y and x represent the values in an (x, y) coordinate pair of any point on the graph
- m represents the slope, often in fraction form
- b represents the y-intercept

So when a line is in slope-intercept form, the coefficient of x is the slope of the line.

> For the function $y = 4x - 7$, the slope of the line is 4, and the y-intercept is $(0, -7)$.

> For the function $y = \frac{x}{5} + 1$, the slope is $\frac{1}{5}$, and the y-intercept is $(0, 1)$. (Remember $\frac{x}{5}$ is the same as $\frac{1}{5}x$.)

Point-slope form

When we know the slope of a line, m, and a point on that line, (x_1, y_1), we can create an equation for that line using **point-slope form**, which looks like this:

$$y - y_1 = m(x - x_1)$$

> For the line with slope $m = 2$ that contains the point $(1, 6)$, an equation using point-slope form is $y - 6 = 2(x - 1)$.

Translation

Some SAT Math questions will talk about "translating" or "shifting" a graph in a certain direction. This refers to the idea of the entire graph moving a certain number of units up, down, left, or right.

When this happens, we can find any point on the translated graph by taking the corresponding point from the original graph and translating that point as described in the prompt.

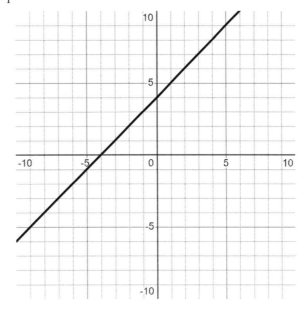

> This is the graph of function j. Function k is the result of translating function j down three units. What is the value of $k(1)$?

> We can see that $j(1) = 5$, because the graph of j travels through $(1,5)$. If k is just j translated down three units, then k must travel through $(1,2)$, which means $k(1) = 2$.

Evaluating a function

When we evaluate a function like $f(x)$, we determine the output when we plug in a certain x value. The two most common ways to evaluate a function are:

- to plug an x value into the function itself, or
- to look at a graph of the function and see which y value corresponds to the desired x value.

We'll look at both methods.

We can evaluate $f(x) = 2x + 4$ when $x = 5$ by plugging $x = 5$ into the given function:

$f(x) = 2x + 4$ \qquad (given function)

$f(5) = 2(5) + 4$ \qquad (plug in $x = 5$)

$f(5) = 14$ \qquad (simplify)

So if we evaluate $f(x) = 2x + 4$ when $x = 5$, we find that $f(5) = 14$.

Below is the graph of $g(x)$:

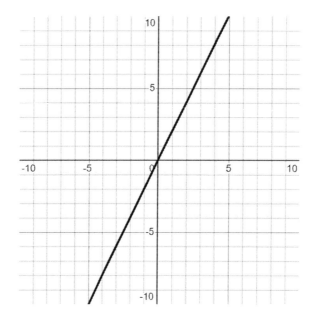

We can evaluate $g(2)$ by finding the value of $g(x)$ when $x = 2$. We can see that when $x = 2$, the y-value on the graph is 4. So we know that $g(2) = 4$.

(Notice that when we have a graph of $g(x)$, we can evaluate $g(x)$ without actually knowing what expression $g(x)$ is equal to.)

An **equivalent form** of a function or equation is basically another way to write the same function or equation. Both forms of the function or equation will be satisfied by the exact same set of (x, y) coordinates, which means they produce identical graphs. Any function or equation can have many different equivalent forms.

$y = (x + 4)(x - 1)$ and $y = x^2 + 3x - 4$ are equivalent forms of the same equation, because they're both satisfied by the same sets of (x, y) coordinates, and both produce the same graph, which looks like this:

\qquad Facebook.com/QuestPreparation \qquad Youtube.com/QuestPrep

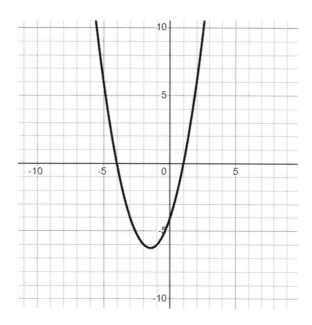

Quadratic functions

For our purposes, a **quadratic function** is an exponential function where the x variable has an exponent of 2.

$f(x) = x^2 + 2x - 1$ is a quadratic function.

Quadratic functions are NEVER linear. Instead, they are **exponential**. The graph of an exponential function is always a curve, not a straight line.

Again, the SAT never requires you to draw a graph by hand. It will only ask you to use given graphs to answer questions, or it will ask a question that allows you to use the provided graphing calculator to find the answer to the prompt.

Parabolas

The graph of a quadratic function is a parabola. Some parabolas extend infinitely up, and some parabolas extend infinitely down.

The graph of $f(x) = x^2$ extends up infinitely, and looks roughly like this:

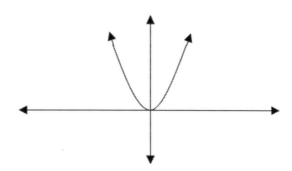

The graph of $f(x) = -(x^2)$ extends down infinitely, and looks roughly like this:

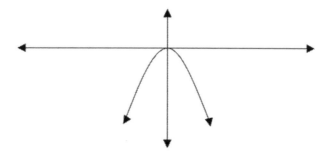

When a parabola "opens down," its highest point or **maximum value** is the (x, y) pair that has the greatest y value.

When a parabola "opens up," its lowest point or **minimum value** is the (x, y) pair that has the lowest y value.

The general equation of a parabola is $y = a(x - h)^2 + k$, where (h, k) is the vertex of the parabola.

This is the graph of $y = 3(x - 2)^2 + 4$, which opens up and has a vertex at $(2, 4)$.

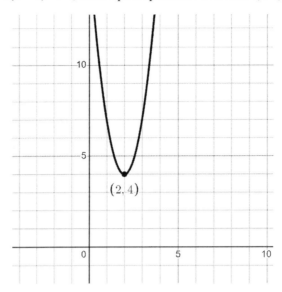

$(2, 4)$

Angles in the Plane

Degrees are the units that we use to measure how "wide" or "big" an angle is.

This is a 45-degree angle:

This is a 90-degree angle, also called a "right angle:"

This is a 180-degree angle, which is the same thing as a straight line:

You will also (less commonly) see angles measured in radians. Radians are just another way to measure the size of an angle, and are usually expressed using π. $360° = 2\pi$ radians (this conversion is provided in the SAT Math reference sheet that you'll have on test day).

Congruent angles are just angles with the same measures. So if one angle has a measure of 30° and another angle has a measure of 30°, those two angles are congruent.

Sometimes angles have special relationships. Three types of special relationships that appear often on the SAT are vertical angles, supplementary angles, and complementary angles.

Vertical angles are the pairs of angles that lie across from each other when two lines intersect. In a pair of vertical angles, the two angles have the same degree measurements as each other (in other words, they are congruent).

Angles $\angle ABC$ and $\angle DBE$ are a pair of vertical angles, so they have the same degree measurements as each other. Angles $\angle ABD$ and $\angle CBE$ are also a pair of vertical angles, so they have the same measurements as each other as well.

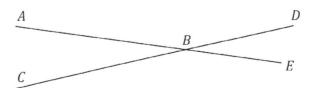

Supplementary angles are pairs of angles whose measurements add up to 180 degrees. When supplementary angles are next to each other, they form a straight line.

∠ABC and ∠ABD are a pair of supplementary angles, because their measurements together add up to 180 degrees—together, they form the straight line CD.

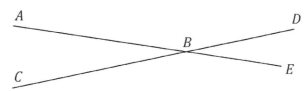

Complementary angles have measures that add up to 90°.

In the figure below, ∠AXB and ∠BXC are complementary, because the sum of the measures of the two angles is 90°.

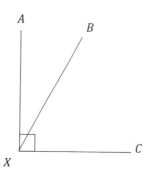

A transversal is the result when a line crosses two parallel lines, as we can see in the diagram below.

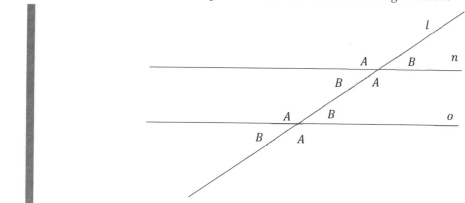

In the above diagram,

- n and o are parallel
- all angles labeled A are equal to one another
- all angles labeled B are equal to one another
- $A + B = 180°$

We can see that each angle labeled A lies across from another angle labeled A, and that each pair of angles labeled A is a set of vertical angles. Similarly, each angle labeled B lies across from another angle labeled B, and each pair of angles labeled B is a set of vertical angles.

Also, because lines n and o are parallel, we know that that line l crosses line n at the same angle that line l crosses line o. For this reason, we know that the angles labeled A in the top intersection are equal to the angles labeled A in the bottom intersection, and also that the angles labeled B in the top intersection are equal to the angles labeled B in the bottom intersection.

There are special terms for the relationships among the various angles created by a transversal, but we don't need to know those on the SAT, beyond what we've already discussed in this section.

Triangles

The SAT loves to ask about triangles.

The sum of the measures of the angles in any triangle is 180 degrees.

In any triangle, the longest side is always opposite the biggest angle, and the shortest side is always opposite the smallest angle.

In an equilateral triangle, all the sides are the same length, and all the angles measure 60 degrees each.

In the equilateral triangle ΔEQI below, all the sides are of equal length, and all the angles are 60 degrees.

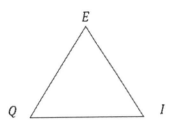

In an **isosceles triangle**, two of the three sides are the same length, and two of the three angles are the same size as each other.

In the isosceles triangle ΔISO below, side $\overline{IS}$ is the same length as side $\overline{SO}$. Also, $\angle SIO$ and $\angle SOI$ have the same degree measurement as each other.

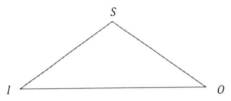

A **right triangle** is a triangle that includes a ninety-degree angle as one of its three angles.

A special relationship exists between the measurements of the sides of a right triangle: If you take the lengths of the two shorter sides (the "legs") and square each one, and then add those two squares together, the resulting amount is the square of the length of the longest side (the "hypotenuse").

In the right triangle below, $a^2 + b^2 = c^2$.

The expression of this relationship, $a^2 + b^2 = c^2$, is called the "**Pythagorean Theorem**." You'll never need to know this term to answer an SAT question, but you will probably have to use this relationship occasionally.

A "**Pythagorean triple**" is a set of three numbers that can be the lengths of the sides of a given right triangle. Memorizing four of these sets will make your life easier on the SAT.

$\{3, 4, 5\}$ is a Pythagorean triple because $3^2 + 4^2 = 5^2$

$\{1, 1, \sqrt{2}\}$ is a Pythagorean triple because $1^2 + 1^2 = \sqrt{2}^2$

$\{1, \sqrt{3}, 2\}$ is a Pythagorean triple because $1^2 + \sqrt{3}^2 = 2^2$

$\{5, 12, 13\}$ is a Pythagorean triple because $5^2 + 12^2 = 13^2$

When we multiply each number in a Pythagorean triple by the same number, we get another Pythagorean triple.

If we know $\{3, 4, 5\}$ is a Pythagorean triple, then we also know $\{6, 8, 10\}$ is a Pythagorean triple, because $\{6, 8, 10\}$ is what we get when we multiply every number in $\{3, 4, 5\}$ by 2.

In a $\{1, 1, \sqrt{2}\}$ right triangle, the angle measurements are 45°, 45°, 90°.

In a $\{1, \sqrt{3}, 2\}$ right triangle, the angle measurements are 30°, 60°, 90°.

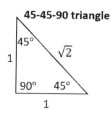

45-45-90 triangle

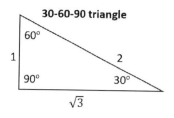

30-60-90 triangle

Two triangles are **similar triangles** if they have all the same angle measurements.

Between two similar triangles, the ratio between the lengths of any two corresponding sides is the same as between the lengths of any other two corresponding sides.

> Triangles $\triangle ABC$ and $\triangle DEF$ below are similar. Side $\overline{AB}$ has length 8, and corresponding side $\overline{DE}$ has length 24, so every other side measurement in $\triangle DEF$ must also be three times the corresponding side in $\triangle ABC$, just as the length of $\overline{DE}$ is three times the length of $\overline{AB}$.

 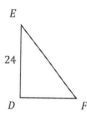

Two triangles are **congruent triangles** if they have all the same angle measurements *and* the same side lengths.

The formula for the **area of a triangle** is given in the front of every real SAT Math section. That formula is $A = \frac{1}{2}bh$, which means that the area of a triangle is equal to one half the length of the base of the triangle multiplied by the height of the triangle.

In every triangle, the length of each side must be less than the sum of the lengths of the other two sides. (Otherwise, the triangle wouldn't be able to "close," because the longest side would be too long for the other two sides to touch.)

> You can see in this diagram that the longest side is longer than the two shorter sides combined, which means the two shorter sides are too far apart to connect and "close" the triangle.

Rectangles

Rectangles are 4-sided shapes where all the angles measure 90°. In a rectangle, if you know the lengths of the sides, then you can always figure out the length from one corner to the opposite corner by using the Pythagorean theorem.

> In the rectangle below, all angles are right angles, and we can use the Pythagorean theorem to determine that the diagonal $\overline{AC}$ must have a length of 13, since $5^2 + 12^2 = 13^2$.

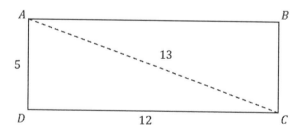

Squares

Squares are special rectangles where all the sides have equal length.

Area

The **area** of a two-dimensional figure is the amount of two-dimensional space that the figure covers.

Area is always measured in square units.

All the area formulas you need for the SAT appear in the beginning of each Math section, so there's no need to memorize them—you just need to know how to use them, which we'll see in the walkthroughs later in this section.

Perimeters (Squares, Rectangles, Circles)

The perimeter of a two-dimensional object is the sum of the lengths of its sides, or, for a circle, the distance around the circle.

To find the perimeter of a non-circle, just add up the lengths of its sides.

The perimeter of a circle is called the circumference—see the following section on circles for more information.

Circles

A circle is the set of points in a particular plane that are all equidistant from a single point, called the **center**.

Circle O has a center at point O, and consists of all the points in one plane that are 5 units from the center:

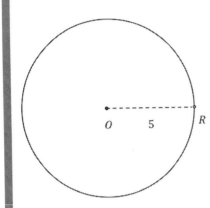

A radius is a line segment drawn from the center point of a circle to the edge of the circle.

In circle O above, $\overline{OR}$ is a radius because it runs from the center of the circle (O) to the edge of the circle at point R.

All the radii of a circle have the same length, since all the points on the circle are the same distance from the center point.

A diameter is a line segment drawn from one edge of a circle, through the center of the circle, all the way to the opposite edge.

$\overline{LR}$ is a diameter of circle O because it starts at one edge of the circle, stretches through the center of the circle, and stops at the opposite edge of the circle.

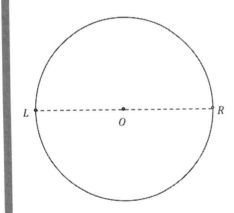

Because a diameter can be broken into two opposite radii, a diameter always has a length equal to twice the radius of the circle.

A diameter of a circle is the longest line segment that can be drawn through the circle.

The perimeter of a circle is called the **circumference** .

The formulas for area of a circle ($A = \pi r^2$) and circumference of a circle ($C = 2\pi r$) appear in the beginning of all real SAT Math sections, so there's no need to memorize them if you don't already know them. (In each formula, r represents the radius of the circle.)

An arc is a portion of a circle that is measured in degrees, like an angle. We can measure an arc by drawing radii to the endpoints of the arc, and then measuring the angle formed by the radii at the center of the circle.

Circle O has a 135° arc $\overset{\frown}{YZ}$, whose measure we can find by measuring the angle formed by radius YO and radius ZO.

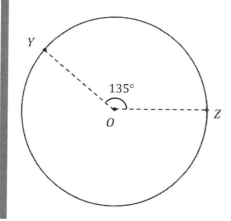

A **central angle** is an angle whose vertex is the center of a circle and whose sides are radii of that circle

In the previous figure, $\angle YOZ$ is a central angle whose measure is 135°.

A **sector** of a circle is a portion of that circle's area defined by a central angle. We can find the area of a sector by dividing the central angle by 360°, then multiplying the result by the total area of the circle.

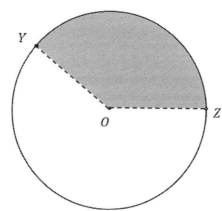

In the above figure, $\angle YOZ$ is a central angle whose measure is 135°. The radius of circle O is 5. The area of the sector is $\frac{135°}{360°}$ multiplied by $\pi(5)^2$, or 9.375π (remember that the area of a circle is given by $A = \pi r^2$).

The **standard equation for a circle** with a center at the origin and a radius of r is $x^2 + y^2 = r^2$

The above equation is for a circle with a center at the origin. A circle whose center isn't at the origin can be expressed like this:

$$(x - h)^2 + (y - k)^2 = r^2$$

The circle described by the above equation will have a center at (h, k).

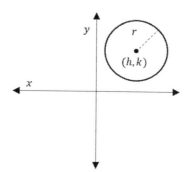

Solid Geometry
On the SAT, solid geometry may involve cubes, rectangular solids, prisms, cylinders, cones, spheres, or pyramids.
All necessary volume formulas will be given to you, so there's no need to memorize them.

The surface area of a solid is the sum of the areas of its faces (except for spheres or other "rounded" solids, whose surface areas won't be tested on the SAT unless a question provides a formula for finding their surface areas).

Statistics

The **mean** or **arithmetic mean** of a set of numbers is the result you get when you add all the numbers in the set together and then divide the result by the number of numbers in the set.

> The average of $\{4, 9, 92\}$ is 35, because $\frac{4+9+9}{3} = 35$.

The **median** of a set of numbers is the number that appears in the middle of the set when all the numbers in the set are arranged from least to greatest.

> The median of $\{4, 9, 92\}$ is 9, because when we arrange the three numbers from least to greatest, 9 is in the middle.

If there is an even number of elements in the set, then the median of that set is the arithmetic mean of the two numbers in the middle of the set when the elements of the set are arranged from least to greatest.

> The median of $\{4, 9, 11, 92\}$ is 10, because the number of elements in the set is even, and 10 is the average of the two numbers in the middle of the set (which are 9 and 11).

The **mode** of a set of numbers is the number that appears most frequently in the set.

> The mode of $\{7, 7, 23, 44\}$ is 7, because 7 appears more often than any other number in the set.

The **range** of a set of numbers is the difference between the highest number in the set and the lowest number in the set.

> The range of $\{7, 7, 23, 44\}$ is 37, because 44 is the largest number in the set, 7 is the smallest, and $44 - 7 = 37$.

On a graph that shows a set of data points, the **line of best fit** is a line that demonstrates the trend in the data. In the sample figure below, the points represent actual data, while the dashed line is a line of best fit that demonstrates the *trend* in the data:

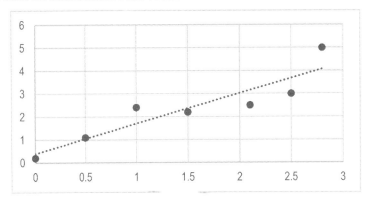

On the SAT, you'll never have to calculate a line of best fit, but you will need to understand that the line of best fit shows us the overall trend in the data—it doesn't represent *actual* data.

Probability

The **probability** of an event is a fraction from 0 to 1 that describes how likely the event is to happen. If the fraction is closer to 1, the event is *more* likely to happen; if the fraction is closer to 0, the event is *less* likely to happen.

To construct this fraction, you first calculate the total number of possible outcomes and place this number in the denominator of the fraction; then, you determine the number of outcomes that satisfy the given requirements, and place this number in the numerator of the fraction. The result looks like this:

$$\frac{number\ of\ desired\ outcomes}{number\ of\ possible\ outcomes}$$

Example:

> The probability of rolling a 3 on a normal 6-sided die is $\frac{1}{6}$. There are 6 possible outcomes, so 6 goes in the denominator of the fraction. Out of those 6 outcomes, we only want one—the one where a 3 comes up—so 1 goes in the numerator.

The probability of rolling an odd number on a normal 6-sided die is $\frac{3}{6}$. Again, there are 6 possible numbers we might roll, so 6 is our denominator. But now, since we want any odd number, the numbers 1, 3, and 5 all satisfy the requirements of our event, so there are 3 possible outcomes that we'll be happy with—that means 3 goes in the numerator. (Notice that we can reduce the probability of $\frac{3}{6}$ to $\frac{1}{2}$.)

Probability questions often involve rolling dice or flipping coins. Note that if a question mentions a "fair die" or a "fair coin," that just means a die or coin where landing on any side is equally likely.

Probability fractions can be manipulated just like any other fractions.

To find the probability of two or more events happening in a sequence, we just find the probability of each event by itself, and then multiply them by each other.

The probability of rolling two sixes on two normal 6-sided dice is $\frac{1}{36}$, because the probability of rolling a six on either die is $\frac{1}{6}$, and $\frac{1}{6} \times \frac{1}{6} = \frac{1}{36}$.

Trigonometry

The trigonometry that you need on the SAT is very basic and limited. The most important things you need to know are the three basic trigonometric ratios. You've probably learned these three basic ratios in math class with the acronym "SOHCAHTOA."

"SOH" stands for Sine = Opposite / Hypotenuse

"CAH" stands for Cosine = Adjacent / Hypotenuse

"TOA" stands for Tangent = Opposite / Adjacent

Given a right triangle:

The **hypotenuse** is the side that's opposite the right angle.

The **opposite** side is the side across from the angle whose sine, cosine, or tangent we're evaluating.

The **adjacent** side is the side that's next to the angle we're evaluating (the side that isn't the hypotenuse).

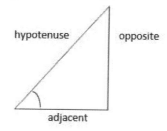

Conclusion

We've just covered all the math concepts that the College Board will allow itself to cover on the SAT. As I mentioned at the beginning of the Toolbox, it's important to keep in mind that simply knowing these concepts is not enough to guarantee a good SAT Math score. It's much more important to focus on the design of the SAT Math section, and to learn to take apart challenging questions, which we'll discuss in the coming pages.

The Basics of Surveys and Sampling

Some SAT Math questions may discuss surveys and samples, so it's important for you to have a basic understanding of how those things work.

Scientists test a sample of something when they want to know some information about a larger whole, but they don't have the time or resources to test the entire whole. The basic idea behind sampling is that we assume the properties of the sample are roughly the same as the properties of the whole.

For example, if we want to know what the water is like in a certain lake, then we might dip a bucket in the lake, and test the water in the bucket—in this case, the lake would be the "whole," and the water in the bucket would be the "sample."

As another example, if we wanted to know the opinions of the people in a whole state, we might survey the opinions of a hundred people who live in that state. Here, the state would be the "whole," and the hundred people we asked would be the "sample."

One thing to keep in mind with sampling is that a sample won't necessarily perfectly represent the whole that it's taken from. The bucketful of water might not be exactly like the water in the rest of the lake, and the hundred people who were surveyed might not reflect the opinions of everyone from the state where they live.

So surveys and samples have what's called a "margin of error" that reflects how close the result of testing the sample likely is to the real number that the scientists would find if they applied the same test to the whole. You won't have to calculate a margin of error on the SAT, but you will need to understand what a margin of error is in the context of the results of a survey or sample.

> If a survey of people in a certain town finds that 30% of people in that town want to elect a marmot to city council, and the survey has a margin of error of 6%, that means that the real percentage of people in that town who want a marmot on the city council is probably anywhere from 6% *less* than the number that was found to 6% *more* than the number that was found.
>
> In this case, that translates to anywhere from 24% to 36% of the population wants a marmot on the city council—again, because the survey found that 30% of people want a marmot on the city council, and the 6% margin of error tells us that the real percentage is probably anywhere from 6% less than 30% to 6% greater than 30%.

In real life there are a lot of other things to keep in mind related to surveys and sampling, but this covers what you'll need to know about this topic on the SAT.

Special Technique: Interpreting Mathematical Models of Real-life Situations

The College Board generally includes a few questions per test that ask us to identify the role of a particular variable or constant in an equation that models a real-life situation. For example, a question might tell you that the total cost, C, to rent a car for d days is represented by the equation $C = 45d + 10$. Then the question might ask what a particular part of that equation represents (such as the number 45 in this example).

In this section, we'll discuss the most effective ways to answer these kinds of questions. We'll start with a little background on the math ideas involved, and then we'll address SAT-specific issues that will be relevant on test day.

Math Background

Before we can discuss the ways that different parts of an equation interact, we need to have a quick discussion about the basic differences among variables, coefficients, and constants. You may have covered some of these topics in your math classes, but we need to discuss them as precisely as we can, so I'll go through a quick refresher now to make sure we're on the same page. We'll use the example equation we just mentioned for reference:

$$\overset{\text{Variable}}{C} = \underset{\text{Coefficient}}{45}\overset{\text{Variable}}{d} + \underset{\text{Constant}}{10}$$

- A variable is a placeholder (typically represented by a letter like x or y) that can have different values in an equation . In the example above, C and d are variables; the rest of the equation demonstrates the relationship that must exist between any valid (C, d) pair that satisfies the equation. In this example, the provided text tells us that C represents the total cost of renting the car, while d represents the length of the rental in days.
- A coefficient is a numerical value that's multiplied by a variable. In the example above, the number 45 is a coefficient; it indicates that the value represented by d in this equation is multiplied by 45. (Remember that even when an equation includes a term like $\frac{x}{4}$, we can think of that as the variable x multiplied by a coefficient of $\frac{1}{4}$, because $\frac{x}{4} = \frac{1}{4}x$.)
- A constant is an unchanging numerical value that's added to (or subtracted from) an expression. In the example above, the number 10 is a constant; it indicates that we add 10 to the expression $45d$ in this equation.

The role of variables in mathematical models

A variable in a mathematical model takes the place of a real-world quantity; the whole purpose of this type of model is to show us the unchanging relationship among real-world quantities that are represented by variables.

Mathematical models are often written so that they seem to have a clear "output" variable, and a clear "input" variable. The output variable is usually isolated on one side of the equation, and the input variable can be found on the other side of the equation, along with any necessary coefficients and constants that show us how the input variable can be used to produce the output variable.

Let's take another look at our previous example formula for the cost in dollars of renting a car, $C = 45d + 10$, where the variables correspond to the following real-world values:

- C is the total cost of the rental, in dollars
- d is the number of days that the car is rented

This formula is telling us that we can find the overall cost of renting the car if we multiply the number of days (d) by 45, and then add that result to the number 10. In this case, the equation is expressed in a format that isolates C on one side of the equation, so the output variable is C (the overall cost of the rental) and the input variable is d (the number of days of the rental).

The role of coefficients in equation models

Coefficients in an equation are used to indicate that we need to take a value represented by a variable and multiply or divide it by a consistent amount.

Coefficients often indicate a consistent, repeated increment, such as a daily, monthly, or yearly increase in a number. In our example equation that models the cost of a car rental, $C = 45d + 10$, the coefficient 45 is multiplied by the variable d. So for every additional day, d, of the car rental, the cost of the rental in dollars, C, increases by 45.

The role of constants in equation models

Constants are used to reflect scenarios in which a value always needs to be adjusted up or down by a certain unchanging amount. For this reason, constants are often used to represent things like one-time costs in a model involving money. In our example equation that models the cost of a car rental, $C = 45d + 10$, the constant 10 represents a one-time cost charged by the car rental company. This means the car rental company will add a single $10 charge to the cost of a car rental no matter how long the rental is—whether the car is rented for 1 day or 20 days, the one-time $10 charge will be part of the cost.

A Few More Examples of Equation Models with Variables, Coefficients, and Constants

Let's take a quick look at a few more examples of equation models so you can see these ideas at work in other situations.

Cost of an international phone call

The cost of an international phone call could be modeled by the equation $P = 2m + 3$, where P represents the cost of the phone call in dollars and m is the length of the call in minutes. We multiply the variable m by the coefficient 2, and then add the result to the constant 3 to find the value of the variable P. In plain English, this model tells us that the cost of an international phone call is $3 to start plus an additional $2 per minute—so a 5-minute phone call will cost 13 dollars, because $2(5) + 3 = 13$.

Number of members joining a new gym

The number of members joining a new gym in its first month of business could be modeled by the equation $M = 5d$, where M represents the total number of members and d is the number of days since the gym has opened. We multiply the variable d by the coefficient 5, and the result is the number of members the gym has, M. In plain English, this model tells us that in its first month of business, a new gym adds 5 new members every day—so, after 9 days, the gym will have 45 members, because $5(9) = 45$.

True temperature compared to measured temperature

The temperature of a room could be modeled by the equation $T = r - 10$, where T represents the true temperature of the room and r is the temperature reading given by a faulty thermometer in the room. We subtract the constant 10 from the variable r, and the result is the true temperature of the room, T. In plain English, this model tells us that a faulty thermometer gives us a reading that's 10 degrees warmer than the actual temperature of the room—so when the thermometer shows a reading of 81 degrees, the temperature in the room is actually 71 degrees, because $(81) - 10 = 71$.

Applying this Knowledge on Test Day

The prompt for a questions about an equation model typically describes some kind of real-life situation, provides an equation to model that real-life situation, and then asks a question like:

- "Which of the following is the best interpretation of the y-intercept of the graph in this context?"
- "Which of the following is the best interpretation of the number 12 in this context?"

When you answer these questions, keep in mind the stuff we've talked about so far:

- Variables are placeholders to represent numbers that can be plugged into the equation to produce a result.
- Coefficients indicate that a variable is always multiplied by the same amount; they often apply when we're modeling something connected to recurring costs, consistent ratios, and so on.
- Constants indicate that an expression needs to be adjusted up or down by a fixed, one-time amount. They're often used to model things like one-time costs or a starting value.

These ideas will help you to understand how the relationships among the variables in the equation are used to model the situation described in the prompt. For examples of how this approach can be used on test day, see the walkthroughs for the following questions:

- SAT Practice Test #1, module 1, question 3 (find the walkthrough on page 302 of this Black Book)
- SAT Practice Test #1, module 1, question 8 (find the walkthrough on page 306 of this Black Book)
- SAT Practice Test #1, module 1, question 17 (find the walkthrough on page 316 of this Black Book)
- SAT Practice Test #1, module 2, question 1 (find the walkthrough on page 330 of this Black Book)

Graphs of Linear Equation Models

Let's further discuss these ideas in the context of the car rental equation we analyzed earlier in this article. That equation was $C = 45d + 10$, and it tells us the cost, C, in dollars of renting a car for d days.

When we graph that equation, we get the following (note that the scales on the two axes are different from one another):

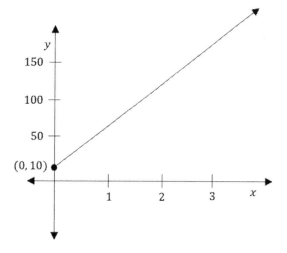

We might notice that the equation $C = 45d + 10$ looks a lot like the slope-intercept form of an equation, $y = mx + b$. In fact, if we substitute y for C and x for d—to reflect the idea that we've graphed C on the vertical axis and d on the horizontal axis—we get $y = 45x + 10$. This lets us see right away that the slope of the line is 45, and the y-intercept is $(0, 10)$. (For more on slope-intercept form, see "Slope-intercept form" on page 263 in the Math Toolbox in this Black Book.)

(We'll find that equation models on the SAT are often written in $y = mx + b$ form, or can be easily rewritten in that form. That makes determining the slope and y-intercept quick and easy. But equation modeling questions on the SAT don't just ask for the slope or y-intercept of a line. Instead, they ask what that slope or y-intercept *represents*.)

In this example:

- d is the input variable, so d-values are plotted on the horizontal axis of the graph,
- C is the output variable, so C-values are plotted on the vertical axis of the graph,
- 45 is the slope of the line, which represents the daily increase in the cost of the rental—each day, the cost increases by \$45—and
- 10 is the y-intercept, which represents the one-time cost applied to each rental, without considering the daily rate—each rental includes a single charge of \$10, regardless of duration.

Conclusion

We need to get comfortable understanding which specific components of equation models correspond to the different aspects of the real-life situations modeled by those equations. This concept will definitely come up on test day in a variety of ways.

Please review this section carefully until it feels comfortable—and most importantly, make sure to review the selected SAT practice questions listed above, and to work through other real SAT practice questions from the College Board that involve equation modeling to see how these ideas will appear on the test.

Special Technique: Backsolving

One common tactic for trying to beat multiple-choice math questions in school is called "backsolving." This is basically when a question asks you to find the value of a variable, but instead of setting up a formal algebraic solution and then arriving at one of the answer choices on your own, you just take numbers from the answer choices and plug them into the prompt to see which choice results in a valid equation.

Many test-takers are aware that backsolving exists, but most don't realize the extent to which we can use it on this test, so I strongly recommend that you pay attention to this section, even if you think you're already familiar with backsolving!

There are two main kinds of backsolving that we can do:

- Backsolving when there are no variables in the answer choices
- Backsolving when the answer choices include variables

Backsolving When There are No Variables in the Answer Choices

This type of backsolving is useful on some questions that ask for the value of a variable in a given expression. We can often just take the numbers from the answer choices and plug them into the given equation to see which one makes a true statement.

You can see an example of this type of backsolving in SAT Practice Test #1, module 1, question 4. This question gives us the function $g(x) = x^2 + 9$, and then asks for the value of x when $g(x) = 25$. We can use backsolving to answer this question by plugging each answer choice in for x in the expression $x^2 + 9$. The answer choice that makes the expression equal to 25 is the correct answer. To see the full solution, read the walkthrough of this question on page 303.

Here are a few more examples of official SAT questions whose solutions can involve this type of backsolving:

- SAT Practice Test #1, module 2, question 10 (my walkthrough is on page 338 of this Black Book)
- SAT Practice Test #1, module 2, question 12 (my walkthrough is on page 342 of this Black Book)
- SAT Practice Test #1, module 2, question 16 (my walkthrough is on page 344 of this Black Book)

Backsolving when the Answer Choices Include Variables

This type of backsolving can get a little more complicated, but it's still a valuable tactic on some questions. When the answer choices are expressions involving variables, we can pick an arbitrary value to plug in for the variable in the expressions from the answer choices, and see which expression gives the result that the question is looking for.

You can see an example of this type of backsolving in SAT Practice Test #1, module 2, question 11. That question gives us an expression involving x and asks us to pick the choice with an equivalent expression. One way to solve this question is as follows:

1. Choose an arbitrary value for x.
2. Plug this arbitrary value into the original expression from the prompt, and determine the numerical value of the expression.
3. Plug the same x-value into each expression in the choices, and determine the numerical values of each expression.
4. See which choice produces the same numerical value as the expression in the prompt. That choice is the right answer.

(For the full solution to this question, read its walkthrough on page 339 in this Black Book.)

There are two things we must keep in mind when backsolving like this:

1. Any value we decide to pick for the variable must meet the requirements given in the question.

    For example, if the question says x must be greater than 6, then we have to pick a value greater than 6 for x; we can't pick 5. If the question requires a negative integer, then we have to pick a negative integer. And so on. You get the idea—if the number we use to backsolve doesn't meet the requirements given by the prompt, then our conclusions won't be reliable. This might seem like a silly thing to point out, but I bet you'd be surprised how many times I've seen trained test-takers miss a question because they accidentally tried to backsolve with a number that didn't meet the written requirements of the prompt.

2. We should generally avoid picking numbers that are likely to result in false positives.

    Depending on how a question is set up, and on what number we decide to use for backsolving, it can sometimes happen that more than one answer choice will give us a result that matches the result from the expression in the prompt, just by sheer coincidence, even when two expressions aren't algebraically equivalent. I call these coincidental matches "false positives."

To understand how we might get a false positive, consider the following algebraic expressions:

x $2x$ x^3

If we plugged 0 into these expressions as x, we'd get the same result for all three, even though the expressions themselves aren't algebraically equivalent for all values of x. If we plugged 1 into all three expressions as x, then the first and third expressions would produce the same result as one another. On the other hand, if we plugged in 2, 3, 4, 5, or most other numbers, we'd get three different results from the three different expressions.

Generally speaking, we're more likely to produce false positives on the SAT Math section when we backsolve with 0, 1, and -1, so we should avoid picking those numbers when we backsolve.

But don't worry too much if you accidentally do create a false positive in your backsolving—that is, if you find that more than one answer choice is equivalent to the expression from the prompt. You can fix the problem by picking another value to backsolve with, and then plugging *that* value into each answer choice. The correct choice will be the only one whose value matches the value from the prompt, no matter which valid number is used to backsolve. (By the way, the odds are usually pretty small that you would pick two numbers in a row that would coincidentally give you a false positive when you backsolve with them.)

Since running into a false positive means you'll have to do all your backsolving work again with different numbers, you can potentially save time on test day by avoiding false positives in the first place. Again, the easiest way to prevent these kinds of issues is to make a habit of avoiding 0, 1, and -1 when picking an arbitrary number for backsolving.

Here are a few more examples of official SAT questions that can be backsolved, and that have variable expressions in the choices:

- SAT Practice Test #1, module 2, question 19 (my walkthrough is on page 347 of this Black Book)
- SAT Practice Test #2, module 2, question 15 (my walkthrough is on page 395 of this Black Book)
- SAT Practice Test #3, module 1, question 25 (my walkthrough is on page 434 of this Black Book)

Catching and Fixing Common Mistakes by Evaluating Every Answer Choice

As trained test-takers, we understand the importance of avoiding small mistakes on the SAT, and we know that the College Board often designs wrong answers to attract people who make those mistakes. There are two major types of mistakes that a test-taker could be likely to make when backsolving, and there's a single technique that can help us eliminate both.

The first mistake is to backsolve with a number that happens to have a unique property relative to the question, and results in more than one answer seeming to be correct (in other words, getting one or more "false positives"). We discussed ways to avoid this situation in general above, but it can still come up on some questions even if you don't backsolve with -1, 0, or 1. If there are two or three answer choices that coincidentally all work out to the same result during your backsolving, then you run the risk of selecting a wrong answer.

The second type of potential mistake is to make a small error in your calculations while you're backsolving. As you might imagine, this can easily cause an incorrect answer to seem correct (or vice-versa) if you don't realize your mistake.

We can greatly reduce the likelihood of both kinds of mistakes by making sure that we *always evaluate all the answer choices whenever we backsolve!* This will give us a better chance of noticing when more than one answer choice seems to work out to the target value. For example, if a trained test-taker is working through a backsolving solution and finds that (B) seems to be correct, she shouldn't just stop working on the question and pick (B) as her answer! She should continue to evaluate (C) and (D). If she finds that more than one choice results in the desired value, then she knows she needs to re-evaluate her work—it might be that she's picked a number that results in a false positive, or it might just be that she's miscalculated. In either case, one of the best ways to try to find the correct answer is to retry the backsolving with a different number plugged in. If the initial mistake was choosing a bad number, then choosing a new number will usually solve the problem, because it's unlikely that two consecutive numbers will both result in false positives; if the initial mistake was a miscalculation, then the test-taker will often avoid that mistake on a second approach with new values.

It's very important to commit to the idea of testing out every answer choice whenever you backsolve! This is why you'll always see me go through every answer choice whenever I use a backsolving approach in the walkthroughs in this Black Book. Remember that even the best test-takers still make mistakes sometimes—they're just good at catching them and fixing them, using techniques like this one.

What if none of the answer choices seems to work?

Of course, another type of error in the backsolving process could lead us to think that all of the answer choices are wrong, if we make a mistake when we're working with the choice that's actually correct. When this happens, we do basically the same thing we would do if we thought all the choices were wrong for any other question on the SAT: we realize that we must have made a mistake, and we decide whether it makes more sense to try again, skip the question for the time being, or guess on it.

As always, it's important to remember that our mistake might be a simple miscalculation, but it could also be something else. We might have misread something, or we might even have been wrong to think the question could be backsolved in the first place.

Conclusion

Backsolving can be a very useful technique, and it can be applied in a lot of different ways on real SAT Math questions from the College Board. The best way to get more comfortable with backsolving is to see it in action before trying it yourself, so make sure you read this Black Book's walkthroughs of the listed example questions above for both types of backsolving.

Be sure to keep the possibility of backsolving in mind when we discuss the Math Path in a few pages.

Special Technique: Using The Surprisingly Powerful Digital SAT Calculator

You probably already realize that the SAT calculator is going to be helpful for certain questions involving functions, systems of equations, and things like that—but it can actually do a lot more than most test-takers realize. Before we get into that, let's cover some basic SAT calculator facts:

- For the digital SAT, every test-taker gets access to the same calculator. This calculator was developed by a company called Desmos (which has no affiliation with this Black Book), and it's built right into the test-taking software.

- Like any piece of software, this calculator has its own interface that takes a little time to get used to. In my opinion it's pretty intuitive and well-executed—but even so, it's critical that you get completely comfortable using this calculator by practicing with it before test day.

- You can practice with the SAT calculator by downloading the College Board's free Bluebook app—for more on that application, see "Only Work with Questions from the College Board!" on page 16 of this Black Book. If you open a practice test or test preview in that app, you'll be able to use the calculator as long as you're working on an SAT Math section (the "test preview" will allow you to use the calculator without a time limit, so this is what I recommend you do if you're getting comfortable with the calculator, or using it to answer practice SAT questions).

Now let's get down to the nitty gritty. Here's a list of the most useful stuff this calculator can do for you, in no particular order:

The SAT Calculator can graph stuff, which has more applications than you might realize.

You can enter an equation or function in the calculator and see a graph of that expression, whether that equation has one variable or two variables. One of the most convenient aspects of this calculator is that <u>you don't have to solve equations in terms of y before graphing them!</u> It doesn't matter if the provided equation looks like $y = 3x + 1$ or $\frac{x^2}{y+2} = 78(2y)^x$, you can just enter it exactly as it appears right into the calculator to get the graph. This is a huge timesaver from earlier graphing calculators that required equations to be in terms of y before they were graphed.

Note that it's probably a good idea to enter equations into the calculator using the variables x and y, even if those equations appear in the question using other variables; you'll just need to keep straight which variables correspond to one another in the question you're working on. For example, if a question asks about the equation $3t = p^2 + 6$, you can enter it into the SAT calculator as $3y = x^2 + 6$. You'll just need to remember when choosing your answer which variable corresponds to which (in this case, that y corresponds to t and x corresponds to p). The SAT calculator *can* use other variables, but certain variables will trigger the calculator to incorporate other functionalities, and some variables won't work in combination with certain other variables—so basically, you'll either need to memorize which variables and/or combinations of variables to avoid, or you can just get in the habit of sticking with x and y. This isn't a huge deal, but it's yet another reason why it's critical to practice with the calculator before test day.

Graphing Individual Equations

One of the most basic things you can do is to enter a function and see which x values correspond to which y values. The SAT will ask about this basic idea in a lot of different ways, but finding the solution typically comes down to a similar process; you just have to make sure that you select the answer choice that corresponds to the specific thing the prompt asks for.

We can see this idea in action is question 4 from module 1 of SAT Practice Test #1, which asks which x-value produces a $g(x)$ value of 25 in the function $g(x) = x^2 + 9$. We can answer this by entering $y = x^2 + 9$ into our calculator to see what the x-value is when $y = 25$ (note that we swapped y in for $g(x)$). When we do that, we can see that $g(x) = 25$ when $x = 4$. For a full explanation of that question, see its walkthrough on page 303 of this Black Book.

Graphing Systems of Equations

We can use this same approach to find information related to systems of equations; we just end up entering two equations instead of one. The SAT likes to come up with different ways to ask us about systems of equations, but they almost always come down to figuring out the (x, y) point where the two equations intersect. The question might ask for that point specifically, or it might ask for us to find the point of intersection and then find $x + y$, or $x - y$, or even just the x or y value where the lines intersect—regardless, it's our job to find that point of intersection and then make sure we read the prompt carefully enough to know what the College Board wants for an answer.

We can see an example of this idea in question 10 from module 1 of SAT Practice Test #1. That question provides us with two equations and says their solution is (x, y), then asks us for the value of x. So all we need to do is enter those two equations into our graphing calculator, find the point of intersection, and select the answer choice that corresponds to the x-value from that point of intersection. For more on that question, take a look at its walkthrough on page 308 of this Black Book.

Graphing Circles and Quadratic Equations

Sometimes SAT Math questions will ask about circles, or minimum or maximum values of quadratic equations. One way to answer those questions will typically involve fairly complex algebraic approaches that require you to memorize aspects of the standard equations for those shapes, and then you'll have to complete the square to get the provided equation into that standard equation so you can then apply your memorized knowledge to find the answer… or you can just enter the equation, exactly as it was provided, into your graphing calculator, and use the resulting graph to answer the question. This graphing approach usually takes about 5 seconds and involves no algebra on your part whatsoever.

For an example of this idea at work in a question related to circles, see the walkthrough of question 23 from module 2 of SAT Practice Test #1 on page 352. For an example of this idea at work in a question related to quadratic equations, see the walkthrough of question 13 from module 1 of SAT Practice Test #2 on page 365.

Graphing Inequalities, Including Systems of Inequalities.

Just as the calculator can graph equations and systems of equations, it can also graph inequalities and systems of inequalities. You can see an example of this in the walkthrough for question 19 from module 1 of SAT Practice Test #3 on page 427.

The SAT Calculator can do algebra for you.

This use of the SAT calculator is so powerful that, frankly, I'm surprised it's allowed. You can enter an equation involving one variable directly into the calculator, and you'll get a graph that tells you the solution(s) to that equation. For example, question 14 from module 1 of SAT Practice Test #1 provides the equation $z^2 + 10z - 24 = 0$, and asks for one of the solutions to the given equation. We can swap z for x, then enter that equation right into the SAT calculator to get this:

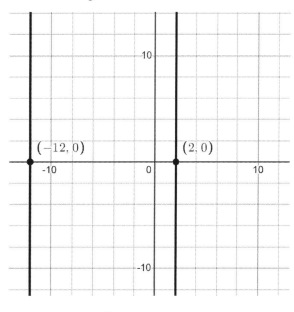

$$x^2 + 10x - 24 = 0$$

The vertical lines at $x = -12$ and $x = 2$ tell us that the 2 solutions are -12 and 2. Once again, all we had to do here to find the answer was enter the provided equation directly into the calculator to get the answer. You can see the full walkthrough for that question on page 313.

The SAT Calculator can label points

This little detail can be surprisingly helpful—you can enter an (x, y) coordinate pair like $(3,8)$ into your calculator, and the calculator can plot and label that point. It can often be useful to know whether a certain function goes through a certain point, either because the test asks for that information directly, or because you use your training to figure out that you can confirm or eliminate a choice based on whether it travels through that point. Instead of trying to eyeball the line and the point, you can just plot that point right on the graph and see what you need to see much more quickly and easily.

For an example of this approach in action, see the walkthrough for question 15 from module 1 of SAT Practice Test #2 on page 367.

Things to Keep in Mind When Using the SAT Calculator

Viewing window adjustments

A graph can only help you if you're able to read the relevant information off that graph. Most test-takers are pretty comfortable zooming in and out of images on a touch screen, but it's a little different navigating around a graph generated by the SAT calculator. The best way to get used to it is just to do it in the Bluebook app, as mentioned above and discussed on page 16 in this Black Book.

Also, most SAT Math questions where you'll use a graph involve values under 20 where you don't need to adjust the viewing window much, if at all—but occasionally you'll encounter functions that model real life situations with values in the 100s or even 10,000s. When that happens, it will be useful for you to set the viewing window directly, instead of just scrolling and zooming.

In the top right of the SAT calculator, you can see a little wrench. If you click on that wrench, you can enter the minimum and maximum x and y-values you want shown on the graph. For example, if a question provides a function and the answer choices mention outputs as high as 20,000, it might be a good idea to adjust the viewing window for the graphing calculator so that the minimum y-value is 0 and the maximum is something like 25,000, just to make sure you can see everything you need to see. Of course, you may do that and find you want to adjust the viewing window further; there's not one right value to choose, and you don't have to pick a perfect viewing window on your first try. As you do this more and more, the process will get more intuitive.

You may also find that having a very different scale for the x-values compared to the y-values makes sense. If a model talks about a factory that makes thousands of light bulbs every day, for example, and asks how many bulbs are produced in 3 days, where x represents the number of days and y represents the number of light bulbs, it might make sense for the x-values to range from 0 to 5 while the y-values range from 0 to 10,000.

For a real-life example of a graph with this kind of viewing window, see the walkthrough for question 5 from module 1 of SAT Practice Test #2 on page 359.

Practice makes perfect.

Once more, this calculator is a really powerful tool, and learning to use it is a really important part of your preparation—and you absolutely must get comfortable using it before test day. The best way to do that is just to practice with the calculator when answering real SAT Math questions, and also to use it as you go through the walkthroughs. If I show you a solution that involves graphing, don't just look at my graph; actually enter the relevant expressions into the SAT calculator yourself, then adjust the window, if needed, to see what you need to see to find the answer—that way, you'll get comfortable with this whole process. The reason I keep repeating this idea is that it's an absolutely critical part of your success on the SAT Math section.

Unwritten Rules of SAT Math

The rules for SAT Math problems are pretty much the same whether you're looking at multiple choice questions or student-produced response questions.

SAT Math Rule 1: You Need to Know the Words in Order to be Certain of the Answer.

On the Reading and Writing section of the SAT, you can usually "fake" your way past a few exotic words in a particular question by using the "bad connection" technique, as we discussed on page 64 of the Reading and Writing section training of this Black Book. But if an SAT Math question asks you about the minimum of a function, for example, then there's typically no way to answer the question without knowing what "minimum" and "function" mean, because SAT Math questions typically don't provide you with context in the way that questions on the rest of the SAT might. You pretty much have to know the terminology, which is why we discussed all those concepts in the Math Toolbox. If you're practicing with real SAT questions from the College Board and you run into a math term you're not familiar with, and it keeps you from answering a question with confidence, then it's a good idea to make sure you learn what the term means, because there's a chance you could see it again on test day. (Sometimes we only need a general understanding of the term, as we see in question 24 from module 2 of SAT Practice Test #3. In that question, we need to understand the term "standard deviation." As you can see in the walkthrough for that question on page 461 of this Black Book, you don't actually have to be able to calculate standard deviation, or even have a detailed understanding of the concept—but you still need a rough idea of what the term means in order to answer the question correctly.)

SAT Math Rule 2: Formulas aren't as Important as you Probably Think.

While memorized formulas can play a small role in the SAT Math section, you'll find that most of the difficulty you encounter on the SAT Math section is related to things like reading carefully and making sure you avoid small errors in calculation. Also remember that the test provides a resource box for the Math section which contains a lot of the formulas that might be relevant to the questions you'll encounter—in fact, that resource box contains every formula related to area or volume that the SAT can require you to know. So if you're looking at a real SAT question that asks you to work with the area or volume of a figure, then there must be some way to work out the answer using only the area or volume formulas in that resource box.

SAT Math Rule 3: SAT Calculations are Usually Relatively Easy.

In advanced high school math problems, finding the solution to a single problem might involve complex graphs, obscure trigonometric concepts, and numbers like e and i. Complex problems tend to have complex answers.

On the SAT, the solution is much more likely to be a plain old number like 2, because the actual calculations that we do for an SAT Math question are usually basic (such as multiplying two single-digit integers, or using algebra to isolate a variable in an equation involving only a few terms). The most challenging part of an SAT Math question will typically be figuring out what the prompt is asking you to do in the first place; actually doing the relevant calculations usually isn't too hard after that.

(If that sounds a little confusing right now, don't worry—it'll make a lot more sense after we look at some examples of real SAT Math questions together in a few pages.)

Some questions will be very easy all around.

Every SAT Math section contains a small number of questions that are very, very straightforward, especially questions near the beginning of a module, and (frequently, but not always) questions with no answer choices. For example, question 7 from module 2 of SAT Practice Test #2 (which has no answer choices) provides the equation $x + 40 = 95$ and then asks for the value of x.

For many test-takers, a question like this is incredibly easy. In fact, it might be so easy that it will make them stop and think "Wait a minute, is this really it? Am I missing something?" Then they might double-check everything, or even start to doubt themselves and wonder whether there's something else going on that they're just not seeing. This is probably what the College Board wants, incidentally: to throw you off your rhythm and make you flustered.

But as trained test-takers who have worked through a number of modules, we'll know that some SAT Math questions are just… not that challenging. It might be a simple equation like the one above, it might be a question that just asks you to read a value off of a graph, or it might be something else equally simple and straightforward. When it happens, just read carefully (as always), find the answer that the prompt asks for, re-check everything as you would for any other question, and move on.

SAT Math Rule 4: Limited Subject-Matter.

In the Math Toolbox on page 243, we went over every single mathematical concept you'll need for test day. You'll probably find that you're familiar with most of them—if not all of them—and that the rest are relatively straightforward to learn. Once you know these concepts, you can rest assured that they will be enough to answer *every single real SAT Math question*, even if that might not seem to be the case when you first read the question. In fact, we'll often find that what actually makes a challenging question hard is the process of figuring out how the question relates back to the limited list of relatively basic math concepts that the College Board allows itself to cover on the SAT, and not the math you'll need to do once you figure that first part out.

SAT Math Rule 5: 30 Seconds or Less.

Perhaps the most important rule of all, from a strategic perspective, is that EVERY SINGLE REAL SAT MATH QUESTION can be answered in less than 30 seconds if we find the most efficient possible solution.

But this doesn't mean that you're going to get the question wrong if it takes you longer, or even that you should be trying to answer each question in under 30 seconds! It just means that you aren't going about answering the question in the easiest way if your solution takes you longer than half a minute. When you're looking for a way to solve the problem, just remember that answering every single question *can* be simple, no matter how complicated the question may seem at first. When we run into questions we can't figure out initially—which is guaranteed to happen to everyone—we need to train ourselves so that our instincts are to look for ways to make things simpler, not more complex.

SAT Math Rule 6: Questions Provide all Necessary Information to Find a Correct Answer with Total Certainty

In order for the SAT Math section to serve its purpose and generate reliable data on test-takers' performances every year, the answer to each question has to be totally objective and beyond dispute—just as we saw with the Reading and Writing section. That means each SAT Math question must include all the information necessary for a test-taker to choose the correct answer choice with total certainty, no matter how much it might sometimes seem like the only way to find the answer is with a lucky guess.

So the key thing to keep in mind is that SAT Math questions will always provide you with all the information you need to find the right answer with total certainty, assuming you know the concepts in the SAT Math Toolbox.

SAT Math Rule 7: Wrong Answers are There for a Reason.

The College Board doesn't just randomly generate the wrong answers that it offers you on every multiple-choice question; instead, wrong answers are the result of certain mistakes that the College Board thinks untrained test-takers will make on a particular question.

Imagine that you try to solve an SAT Math question and end up with the number 15 as your answer. Then you look at the answer choices and see that they only include 10, 12, 18 and 24. In that case, you'd know right away that you had made a mistake on the question—because the answer you found wasn't one of the choices—and you'd be able to start over and try again to solve the question correctly. From the College Board's standpoint, this would be like letting you get away with a free mistake, because you'd be able to realize you'd done something wrong, and you'd have a chance to fix it.

To keep that from happening, the College Board does its best to include wrong answers that try to anticipate the mistakes you're likely to make. So to continue the example above, if the College Board realized that a common mistake on that question would result in test-takers thinking 15 was the correct answer, then the College Board would make 15 one of the wrong answer choices. That way students who thought 15 was the answer would probably mark that answer and move on, never realizing they had made a mistake.

This might seem mean-spirited on the part of the College Board, but we can actually use it to our advantage as trained test-takers. Since the College Board tries to come up with wrong answers to tempt us into making mistakes—and since it has to do this in standardized, repetitive ways, just like everything else it does—then we can learn to use the concepts and relationships that appear in the answer choices to get an idea of what the question is actually asking about.

This will make a lot more sense after we talk about common patterns that we'll encounter in the answer choices, and after we go through some solutions to real SAT Math questions together. We'll cover some of those common patterns starting on the next page, and then we'll see them in action as we discuss hundreds of math questions from official SAT Practice Tests later in this Black Book.

SAT Math Rule 8: When in Doubt, Try The SAT Calculator.

I've mentioned a few times already that the SAT Calculator is really, really powerful—in fact, there was a whole article about it back on page 280. I included this rule partially as an excuse to mention this concept to you again because I want to make sure you know that understanding everything the SAT calculator can do for you on test day will raise your SAT Math score *significantly*.

I also want to mention that one specific benefit of using this calculator is that it can help you when you're stuck on an SAT Math question and not sure how to proceed—whether you're halfway through a solution and you realize that you don't know where to go from there, or you haven't even been able to get started in the first place.

When you find yourself in this situation, consider whether you can try to graph any of the given expressions in the prompt, and/or the expressions in the answer choices. Being able to visualize those expressions can help clear up confusion more often than you might think, and sometimes will even give you the solution outright.

So when you find yourself stumped—whether in practice, or on test day—remember this incredibly powerful tool, even if you're not really sure in the moment how exactly it's going to help. (Of course, if you try this and you're still stuck, just move on to another question as normal.)

Wrong Answer Choice Patterns of SAT Math Questions

Most of the hidden patterns on the SAT Math section involve using the answer choices to help you determine the most efficient ways to answer questions and check your work—remember that small mistakes can kill your chances of a good score, even if you have a very good grasp of math! Before we get into these patterns, I'd like to take a moment to remind you why they're a part of the SAT.

As we discussed in "The "Big Secrets" of the SAT: Simplicity, Repetition, Weirdness, and Details" on page 12 of this Black Book, it's important to remember that the SAT isn't a normal test. It has a very specific purpose and must, therefore, follow very specific rules to make sure that questions are designed to test the same skills in the same underlying ways from test to test, without actually repeating the questions word-for-word. It's also important to remember that the SAT is predominantly a multiple-choice test, and that the multiple-choice format only requires a test-taker to separate right answers from wrong answers, rather than requiring you to produce correct answers on your own. This means that the relationships among right answers and wrong answers must remain constant for all real SAT tests, because changing those relationships would involve changing the nature of the multiple-choice questions, and breaking the standardization rules of the test.

So you'll definitely want to keep these things in mind as we discuss the patterns in the SAT Math section, and as you encounter real SAT Math questions in the future.

You'll find that some of the answer-choice patterns on an SAT Math question can be easily identified before you start working on a question, such as the "Halves and Doubles" pattern or the "Opposites" pattern. On the other hand, some patterns can only be identified after you've started working on a question, such as the "Right Approach, Wrong Step" pattern. We'll discuss the pre-solution patterns first, and then tackle the post-solution patterns afterward.

Pre-Solution Patterns

These patterns reflect relationships in the answer choices that we can notice before we've even tried to attack the question.

Hidden pattern 1: Halves and doubles

Very often, one of the wrong answer choices will be twice as much as the right answer, or half as much as the right answer. This is especially true when the problem involves multiplying or dividing an amount by 2, but we'll often observe this pattern even on questions where finding the answer has no obvious connection to the idea of multiplying or dividing by 2. If you solve a problem and get an answer like 18, a wrong answer choice like 36 or 9 might make you more confident that you're probably right.

But remember that this pattern is an indication that you're *probably* right, not a confirmation that you're *definitely* right! Also, it's important not to get it backwards—in the same hypothetical example, the right answer might be 36 or 9, and the wrong answer might be 18, rather than the other way around. Be very aware of this useful pattern, but don't rely on it exclusively to pick an answer. For this reason, if you notice that some answer choices are half as much as other choices, then you should be especially on guard against any mistakes that might cause you to be off by a factor of 2 while you plan (and execute) your attack on the question.

Hidden pattern 2: "Opposites"

You'll sometimes encounter questions with answer choices that are opposites of each other.. For example, a question might have choices like 9 and -9, or $\frac{1}{3}$ and $-\frac{1}{3}$.

Untrained test-takers commonly lose track of negative signs (or misremember rules related to negative values) when they're doing their calculations, which can cause them to come up with an answer that's the opposite of the correct answer. So you'll commonly see two answer choices that are opposites of one another, and the correct answer is slightly more likely to be one of those two choices than it is to be an answer choice whose opposite isn't present in the provided choices.

But these types of opposites aren't the only "opposites" that you should look out for on test day! You might also see any of the following kinds of opposites:

- a pair of choices that are reciprocals of one another, such as $\frac{r}{k}$ and $\frac{k}{r}$
- a pair of choices that include commonly confused concepts, such as sine and cosine
- a pair of choices that could be thought of as complements or supplements of one another, such as 35° and 55° (which add up to 90°), or 20% and 80% (which add up to 100%)

For the purposes of this pattern, any pair of answer choices like this can be thought of as "opposites," because they all reflect an attempt by the College Board to get us to confuse two concepts that might seem easily interchangeable if we aren't paying close enough attention.

If you see this pattern in a set of answer choices, you should be especially careful to double-check your work for any mistake that could result in choosing the "opposite" of the correct answer. Such mistakes could involve things like multiplying an expression by -1 instead of 1, or going in the wrong direction on a number line, or confusing the numerator and denominator of a fraction, and so on.

As with any pattern in the answer choices, seeing a pair of opposites doesn't guarantee that one of the opposites is correct, but noticing this pattern can often help alert you to potential mistakes that you'll want to avoid while you figure out your solution. You'll see several examples of how this pattern can influence our thinking in the question walkthroughs later in this Black Book.

Hidden pattern 3: The first and last terms in a series are often wrong answers.

Sometimes the answer choices in a math question will include a series. These series might be pretty easy to recognize in some cases, such as 7, 8, 9, 10. In other cases, the series might be less obvious, and it might be related to a concept in the question: if the question is talking about dividing some quantity by 4, then the answer choices might contain the series 3, 12, 48, because each number in the series is one fourth of the next number in the series.

The College Board seems to include series in the answer choices when it hopes that you'll make a mistake and repeat a step in the solution one time too many or too few, ending up with one of the wrong answers in the series. In other words, if a question involves finding the perimeter of a triangle with sides of 5 units each, then the answer choices might include the series 10, 15, 20, because the College Board is hoping you'll either add 5 one time too few (ending up with 10) or one time too many (ending up with 20).

For this reason, when a series is involved in the answer choices, we'll typically find that the correct answer isn't the first or last number in the series. The College Board seems to like to put the correct answer near the middle of the series in order to allow you to make a mistake in either direction and still find a wrong answer that reflects your mistake.

Remember, as with the other patterns in this section, that this isn't an unbreakable rule. So I'm not saying that we'll never, ever find the right answer at the beginning or the end of a series; sometimes we will. I'm just saying that it's more common to find it in one of the middle positions of a series, and that it helps to be aware of that. Again, we'll see examples of how to use this pattern in the walkthroughs later in this section.

Hidden pattern 4: Wrong answers try to imitate right answers.

The College Board likes to create wrong answers that incorporate elements of correct answers, probably in an attempt to make it harder for you to eliminate answer choices on the basis of a partial solution. In other words, if you're working on a question where the answer choices are all algebraic expressions, and you figure out that the right answer should include the expression $2r$ along with some other stuff, then you'll often find that a majority of the answer choices include $2r$. This way, the College Board can try to force you to figure out the rest of the question in order to identify the correct answer.

While this can be an annoying thing for the College Board to do, you'll find that you can actually use it to your advantage in many cases: after you think you've solved a question, if you see that the wrong answers seem to include a lot of the elements in common with the choice that you like, then you can often take that as a good sign that you've thought about the question correctly. (Notice I said, "often," and not "always!")

Similarly, if you're having trouble deciding how to start attacking a question, then an expression or idea that appears often in the answer choices can give you a hint about how to set up your solution! For example, if most or all of the choices involve dividing by 3, that's a strong hint that a correct solution will involve dividing by 3; if most or all of the choices include a radical expression, that's a strong hint that a correct solution will involve finding the square root of something.

Noticing this kind of imitation among the answer choices can also help remind you to stay sharp and avoid any mistakes related to the common elements of the choices, because those common elements indicate that the College Board is expecting untrained test-takers to make mistakes related to those concepts! So, for example, if you see that some answer choices involve adding 4 and some involve subtracting 4, then you know that the College Board expects some test-takers to get confused on how to handle the number 4 in their solution—which lets you know that *you* should pay special attention to that issue.

We'll see several examples of this, and of the other SAT Math patterns, when we go through some questions from real SAT tests in a few pages.

Post-Solution Patterns

These patterns are just as useful for trained test-takers as the pre-solution patterns are, but they can usually only be identified with certainty after we've done some calculations for a particular question. (We should also note that, on some questions, any of the pre-solution patterns we just discussed might also only really be noticeable after you've finished the solution, so they can all be thought of as potential post-solution patterns too, depending on the circumstances.)

Hidden pattern 5: Right approach, wrong step.

One of the ways that the SAT will try to confuse you is by giving you a problem that involves multiple steps, and then making one of the wrong answers a number that you'd get if you attempted a valid solution, but then accidentally stopped after one of the earlier steps, before your solution was complete. For example, a problem might ask you to find the price of erasers by giving you the prices for different combinations of pencils and erasers. The problem might require you to figure out the price of pencils in order to find the price of erasers, and one of the wrong answers would be the price of pencils.

Because this type of wrong answer *is* actually a number that you find in the process of solving the math problem, seeing it can reassure you that you've approached the question correctly—but you can usually only realize that this kind of wrong answer is present after you've already gone through a few steps of a valid approach to the question.

This wrong answer pattern is an important reminder that you always need to read SAT Math questions carefully, to be sure that the answer you select is actually what the question asks for, and not just a number you find on the way to the real answer!

Hidden pattern 6: The right answer to the wrong question.

This answer choice pattern takes advantage of situations where the test-taker gets mixed up about what the question is asking, either through careless reading or through losing track of the steps in a question.

A classic example of this type of choice is when a question about the *area* of a figure includes an answer choice that's the *perimeter* of the figure. In this case, we can imagine that a test-taker who gets caught up in executing the solution to the question might not realize that he mixed up area and perimeter when he read the question. The answer he ends up with seems right to him, *but it's the right answer to the wrong question.*

Other examples of this kind of thing could include an answer choice that provides the y-intercept of a graph when the question asked for the x-intercept, or an answer choice that provides the mean of a set of numbers instead of the median, and so on.

Of course, when you think an answer choice is following this pattern, you should check to make extra sure that you've identified the answer choice that actually reflects what the prompt is asking for.

Don't worry if this sounds a little vague right now. We'll see several examples of it when we go through real SAT questions from the College Board in a few pages.

Understanding the Major Types of Approaches to SAT Math Questions

As we'll see repeatedly in the various walkthroughs in this Black Book, one of the most important aspects of approaching the SAT like a trained test-taker is the realization that the SAT doesn't really test your abilities the same way they might get tested in high school and college, which means that we'll often find that the most effective way to approach an SAT question is very different from the kinds of approaches you can use on questions in school.

This idea is perhaps most important on the Math section of the SAT, because the types of formulas and techniques we might use in a math class often can't be applied at all to an SAT Math question. In fact, we'll see that most SAT Math questions can be successfully approached in more than one way, and some of the most effective approaches for a particular question might include some combination of graphing something on your calculator, remembering and applying the definition of a term, backsolving with values from the answer choices, and so on.

As it turns out, there are three general types of ways to approach SAT Math questions, and it can be useful for you to be aware of all of them, even though you'll only need to come up with *one* successful approach for each question you see on test day. These three general types of approaches are the following:

- concrete approaches
- abstract approaches
- test-smart approaches

Let's explore each type in more detail, and see some examples of them.

Concrete

Generally speaking, concrete approaches to an SAT Math question involve the idea of actually testing out or observing specific mathematical situations that are described in a question, and then picking the answer choice that fits with what you've observed in your test. Concrete approaches typically include things like the following, which we'll discuss in more detail below:

- backsolving
- calculator graphing

Using a concrete approach can often allow you to find a correct answer to an SAT Math question even if you don't completely remember or understand all the details of the math concepts that appear in the question.

One reason that SAT Math questions often lend themselves to concrete approaches is that the test's format means the College Board can't check your work in the way that a teacher might check it in class—your answer sheet only reflects your final answer to a question, not the process that you used to get there. So, for example, if a question asks you to find a solution to a system of equations, the College Board has no way of knowing whether you found the correct answer through a formal algebraic approach, or by graphing the equations on your calculator and seeing where they intersect—which is much faster for most people. So when you're trying to decide how to attack a question, remember that the SAT doesn't care whether you use the same formal algebraic approach that you might have to use in math class.

Concrete approaches can also be especially well-suited to multiple-choice questions, because questions in that format often provide us with a set of answer choices that we can test against the prompt to see which one is valid, instead of requiring us to generate answers ourselves; most test-takers find it easier to check whether a choice could be correct than to go through the mental work of finding a correct answer completely on their own. So, for example, if a multiple-choice question asks us to find a possible value of x in a given equation, it's often easier to plug in the values from each answer choice to find the choice that works, rather than formally working out the algebra to generate the correct value, as you'd have to do in a math class.

For these reasons, concrete approaches to SAT Math questions are often attractive to test-takers who lack confidence in their math abilities. But there is a potential drawback to concrete approaches: they generally take longer than other kinds of approaches, because they typically involve working through every single answer choice to make sure we've identified the correct one with no false positives (see the article "Special Technique: Backsolving" on page 278 of this Black Book for more details on this idea). Concrete solutions also tend to require a test-taker to do more calculations than the other approaches require, even if the calculations we use for concrete approaches are less advanced than the math ideas we'd apply in abstract or test-smart solutions, which we'll discuss soon.

With that in mind, let's discuss the two major types of concrete approaches in a little more detail.

Backsolving

Backsolving is the process of testing concrete values against an algebraic expression in a question's prompt, which allows us to identify the correct answer choice without actually going through a formal algebraic solution. (Backsolving is probably one of the most well-known "tricks" for multiple-choice math questions, but most test-takers don't realize all the ways backsolving can be applied, or all the ways it can go wrong if you're not careful. The best-known form of backsolving is the process of plugging the number from each answer choice back into an algebraic expression from the prompt to see which choice results in a valid statement, instead of formally solving that algebraic expression. But we can also sometimes use backsolving even when the answer choices are all algebraic expressions themselves. That's why I included an entire article on how to backsolve effectively on page 278, and I strongly recommend you read it.)

Calculator graphing

Many questions on the SAT Math section address topics like the x- and y-intercepts of functions, solutions to systems of equations, or other aspects of a function that can be easily found with the provided SAT graphing calculator if we input the function from the prompt. This approach can even save you a lot of time and algebra when tackling equations with just one variable—for a complete discussion of this incredibly important topic, please read the article on the SAT calculator called "Special Technique: Using The Surprisingly Powerful Digital SAT Calculator" on page 280.

Now that we've discussed some concrete approaches to SAT Math questions, we can talk about approaching questions in ways that are not so concrete.

Abstract

Abstract approaches to SAT Math questions involve applying generalized mathematical reasoning, rather than working out specific instances of a given situation, as we'd do in a concrete approach. Abstract approaches usually require less time to execute than concrete approaches do—in fact, we'll sometimes find that we can apply an abstract approach without actually writing down any calculations at all. The trade-off for this speed improvement over concrete approaches is that abstract approaches generally require a test-taker to be a little more comfortable with math as an academic subject.

There are two common types of abstract approaches, which we'll discuss here in order to give you a sense of how abstract approaches work in general:

- understanding equations
- definitions and attributes

Understanding equations

Some SAT Math questions ask us about equations in a way that allows us to find the correct answer by thinking about the relationships among the components of the equation without actually calculating anything in the equation. (Remember that formulas and functions are equations.) For an example of this approach at work, see the third solution in the walkthrough for question 23 from module 1 of SAT Practice Test #2, which is on page 377 of this Black Book.

Definitions and attributes

Sometimes the key to approaching a question in an abstract way lies in the specific definitions or attributes of a mathematical concept, and keeping these definitions and attributes in mind allows us to see the correct answer right away, often without picking up our pencils or using our calculators. To see this in action, review the second solution in the walkthrough for question 9 from module 1 of SAT Practice Test #1, which is on page 307 of this Black Book.

As I mentioned above, abstract approaches are faster than concrete approaches, but they require a bit more confidence with math as a subject. But some questions allow for approaches that are even faster; I call this last type of approach a "test-smart" approach.

Test-Smart

A test-smart approach to an SAT Math question is one in which we combine our knowledge of math (and possibly some basic calculations) with an awareness of the limitations of the SAT's design and patterns. This can sometimes let us see quickly that the correct answer to a question must have a particular type of appearance, such as including an x-term with a negative coefficient, or be in a particular range of the number line, etc., and that only one choice fits that requirement—which means that choice must be correct. Some test-smart solutions are so quick that we can't even really list out steps for them, because the act of noticing the possibility of the test-smart solution reveals the answer to the question. For an example of this kind of test-smart approach, consider the second solution in the walkthrough of question 23 from module 1 of SAT Practice Test #1, which starts on page 321 of this Black Book.

Now that we've discussed the major types of approaches to SAT Math questions, let's consider a real SAT question from the College Board that can be approached in each of these three ways.

An Example of an Official SAT Question that Allows all 3 Types of Approaches: SAT Practice Test #1, Module 1, Question 8

This question describes a situation where a teacher creates an assignment worth 70 points, with some questions worth 1 point, and some worth 3 points, and then asks for the equation that represents this situation. My walkthrough for this question starts on page 306 of this Black Book.

- The first solution in my walkthrough is a concrete one, in which we come up with a number of 1-point questions and 3-point questions that satisfies the requirements in the prompt, then plug those values into each equation to see which one is valid.

- My second solution is abstract: we analyze the equations in the answer choices and think about which one accurately reflects the ideas in the prompt.

- Finally, in my third solution, we realize that a certain pair of numbers that meets the requirements in the prompt is very easy to come up with and to check in every answer choice, and we use those values to eliminate each wrong answer choice quickly and easily.

Conclusion and Progression

As you may have noticed in the example we just saw, I generally tend to organize my walkthroughs for SAT Math questions so that concrete approaches are presented before abstract approaches, and test-smart approaches are presented last of all. To be clear, it's not that every question lends itself easily to all three types of solutions; it's just that, in general, I present the more concrete solutions first, and then transition into more abstract solutions last, where applicable.

I do this because I want my readers to have the best chance of understanding each approach, and how the approaches relate to each other. Concrete approaches are generally the easiest types of approaches for most people to understand; abstract approaches basically involve realizing in a general way what the concrete approaches are showing us in specific instances. Finally, test-smart approaches represent a level of applied abstract thinking that combines math principles with the design of the SAT. By generally handling more concrete approaches for a given question earlier than more abstract approaches, the walkthroughs can help test-takers who don't feel comfortable with the higher-level approaches develop the kind of confident understanding of the test that allows them to come up with faster solutions on test day.

The Recommended Math Path

Now that we've explained the rules and patterns that you'll find on the SAT Math section, we can look at the process that I recommend for those questions. I call it the "Math Path," mostly because that rhymes.

The Math Path is a set of guidelines whose purpose is to help us figure out how to attack tough questions. You won't need to use it on every question, and you can modify it as you keep practicing. I'm teaching it to you because it's a good way to keep all the elements of SAT Math questions in mind. If you practice with these ideas, you'll find that implementing them becomes second nature, and you won't need to make a point of always following every single step on every single question.

Here's a high-level list of the seven steps on the Math Path, and then I'll go into each step in more detail:

1. Read the prompt carefully and identify what the prompt is asking for.

2. Consider diagrams, if there are any.

3. Read and analyze the answer choices, if there are any.

4. Think about which areas of math might be involved.

5. Look for a 30-second solution.

6. Carry out your solution.

7. Re-check your work, paying attention to post-solution patterns. Consider using a different approach to re-solve the question.

Now let's take a closer look at each step.

1. Read the Prompt Carefully and Identify what the Prompt is Asking For.

This might sound kind of strange, but if you asked me to pick the single mistake that costs people the most points on the Math part of the SAT, I'd say it's the mistake of not reading carefully.

In fact, we should really think of the entire SAT, including the Math section, as an extended test of reading skills. Most of what we do on the Math section will depend on our ability to notice key phrases and details in each question—which, ultimately, comes down to our ability to read what's on the page and catch what it actually says.

(By the way, because of the way SAT Math works, if you know the meanings of every word and concept in a particular question, then you know enough math to be able to answer that question. Trust me on this—we'll see proof of it as we continue.)

At some point, the prompt will specify exactly what it wants from us when we choose the correct answer. (This will usually, but not always, appear in the last sentence of the prompt.) We need to make sure we know what the question is asking us to figure out because this will determine and direct all our other decisions as we work on the question.

We must always keep in mind what the question is actually asking for! We'll often find that the College Board deliberately tries to confuse untrained test-takers with wrong-answer choices that reflect the values of expressions that are relevant to the question, but that aren't the expressions we were asked to find. (For example, a question might mention the variables x and y, and then ask us for the value of y, while providing a wrong answer that reflects the value of x instead.)

In high school math classes, we often don't need to make a special effort to keep our minds focused on what a question is asking for, because most math classes give you homework and tests that involve batches of questions all asking you to do basically the same thing for each question. But on the SAT Math section, it's unlikely that two consecutive questions would ask you to solve the same kind of problem in the same way, so it's very important that we always make sure we know what each question is asking us to do. Never lose sight of that.

2. Consider Figures, if There are Any.

There are a couple of important things we should always keep in mind when an SAT Math question includes a figure:

1. The figure is part of the prompt, so we should read it as carefully as we read the rest of the prompt.

   Whether the figure is a graph, table, chart, diagram, or anything else, it's part of the prompt, and it might contain information we need to find the right answer—so be sure to read any labels, values, symbols, etc. just as carefully as you would read any other part of the prompt.

2. Look out for information that's left out of the figure, but included in the text underneath it.

   Sometimes figures (especially diagrams) will omit certain information that's then provided in the *text* of the question. That information will probably be the basis for the first step in the solution to the question. For example, in question 5 from module 2 of SAT Practice Test #1, the provided diagram only shows a triangle whose side lengths are labeled with variables; when we look below the diagram, we see in the prompt that $a = 4$, and that $b = 5$. These two pieces of information are the first things we need to consider when finding the most efficient approach to the question—see the walkthrough for this question on page 333 of this Black Book if you'd like the rest of the solution.

3. Read and Analyze the Answer Choices, if there are Any.

Most untrained test-takers ignore the answer choices in a Math question until they're basically done with the question. They typically read a question, try to figure out the answer on their own, and then look for the answer they found (or a similar answer) in the answer choices. Now, if you could successfully do that for every question over the course of an entire test without making a single mistake, it's true that you wouldn't miss any questions. But so many questions become so much easier to answer when we consider the answer choices as part of the question from the very beginning.

Remember that the College Board likes to play little "games" in the answer choices of the SAT Math section. We talked about some of those games a moment ago when we covered the hidden patterns of these answer choices on page 285. For example, the wrong answers will sometimes include elements of the right answer, or sometimes they'll form a series, and so on. In some cases, simply noting that all the answer choices are one-digit numbers can be enough to help you realize how to approach a question.

So after you read the prompt and any figures, look over the answer choices and see what kind of options the SAT is giving you. Try to figure out why the test is presenting the answer choices that way—look at the values in the choices, but also look at the *relationships among those values*, and try to think about how those relationships might be important to the question.

I said earlier that it's important to remember that every SAT Math question can be answered in less than 30 seconds each if we're really on our game. Often, a large part of finding these extremely fast solutions involves thinking about how the answer choices relate to the question from the very beginning, because noticing some of these relationships can help us realize that it's possible to attack a question in a way that's different from how we would be forced to attack the question in a traditional math class.

So remember to think of the entire question, including the answer choices, as one big system of ideas. We'll see several examples of how this works when we look at some real SAT questions from the College Board in a few pages.

Make a quick mental note of the similarities, differences, and other relationships among the answer choices.

The College Board wants untrained test-takers to be able to find answer choices that reflect likely mistakes in attacking the question. Sometimes, the College Board provides wrong answers that reflect simple mistakes in reading or calculation; other times, the mistakes may reflect more fundamental errors, like confusing the definitions of "mean" and "median."

As we just discussed, we'll often find it useful to compare a question's answer choices to one another *before we start trying to figure out how to answer the question*. There are multiple reasons for this:

- Noting the *similarities* in the answer choices can help us realize which math concepts are likely to be involved in the ideal approach to the question. For example, if all the choices are algebraic expressions with two variables, then we know that a valid solution to the question must ultimately result in an expression with two variables. If all the answer choices include radical expressions, then we know that our solution must include the idea of taking the square root of some value. We'll see several examples of this kind of thing in the walkthroughs in a few pages.

- Noting the *differences* can help us realize what kinds of simple mistakes the College Board thinks an untrained test-taker would be likely to make. For example, if two answer choices contain fractions that are reciprocals of one another, then we know the College Board probably thinks that some test-takers will make a small mistake that causes them to switch the numerator and denominator of the correct fraction. Again, we'll see examples of these kinds of issues in the walkthroughs.

- Noting other relationships can make us aware of the best ways to approach a question, and help alert us to specific issues for that question. For example, if you notice the halves-and-doubles pattern in the answer choices, then you should be aware that solving the question might involve multiplying or dividing by 2.

(For more on this idea of comparing answer choices to one another, please see "The Vertical Scan: A Key Tactic for Trained Test-Takers" on page 45 of this Black Book.)

4. Think About Which Areas of Math Might be Involved.

Now that you've read the question and the answer choices, and considered the figure if there is one, you should have a pretty good idea of which specific math terms and concepts are mentioned in the question.

Many test-takers overlook the fact that the solution to a question can only involve concepts that are immediately related to the concepts in the question. (This idea sounds kind of obvious once it's pointed out, but it's something that people often don't realize on their own: everything in math proceeds in a step-by-step fashion, with each step building on the previous one.)

When most people get stumped on the SAT Math section, they panic and try to call to mind every single math concept they know in the hope that one of those concepts will miraculously reveal the answer. This usually doesn't work, because it overwhelms the test-taker and prevents him from focusing on the specific issues related to the question. So instead of panicking and mentally flailing around, we want to narrow our focus and confine our thought process to two types of ideas:

- the concepts mentioned directly in the question, and
- the concepts that are directly related to the concepts mentioned in the question.

For example, if an SAT Math question involves words like "degrees" and "radius" and "center," then it must be a question about circles, and we know that the SAT is only allowed to ask us about a limited set of circle-related concepts (look back at the portion of the SAT Math Toolbox that focused on circles on page 270 if you don't remember what they are). That means that the solution to the question must somehow involve those circle-related concepts, so we should focus our attention on them.

If necessary, identify the "bridge" concepts that connect what the prompt is asking for to the ideas you've found in the question.

In some situations, the math concepts that you've noticed in the question may not directly address what the prompt asked you to find in the first place. For example, the prompt may have asked you about the y-intercepts of two different functions, without explicitly reminding you that the y-intercept of a function appears where x in the function is set equal to zero. In this scenario, the "bridge" concept would be the idea of setting x equal to zero in order to find the y-intercept: coming up with an effective solution to the question requires you to remember the bridge concept and realize that it's relevant.

If we wanted to be really technical, we could say that every single SAT Math question involves a bridge concept in the sense that solving every question requires us to realize *something* that's not directly spelled out on the page. But in many cases, the bridge concept is fairly obvious. For example, if a question gives us an algebraic equation and asks us to solve for a variable, then the bridge concept is the idea that we can transform the equation in a series of steps that each involve modifying both sides of the equation in the same way, until the variable is isolated on one side of the equation. Most test-takers don't need to be reminded of a bridge concept like that, because they automatically know that they can solve for a variable in that way.

But we'll sometimes find that the bridge concepts are less obvious, and we may need to spend a few seconds trying to identify the concept that relates the ideas in the prompt (and/or the figure) to the answer choices.

Note things to look out for!

As trained test-takers, we know that one of the most important aspects of maximizing our score on a standardized test is the idea of avoiding mistakes (or catching them and correcting them after we've made them).

The Math section of the SAT will provide us with a lot of opportunities to make small mistakes like the following:

- confusing the numerator and denominator of a fraction
- solving for the wrong variable in a question that involves more than one variable
- reducing a fraction incorrectly
- misreading the label on an axis of a graph
- ...and so on.

These kinds of mistakes can easily cause us to miss questions even when we fully understand what the questions are asking us to do.

So one of the easiest and most straightforward ways to improve your SAT Math score is to get in the habit of identifying the aspects of a question that might cause you to make a mistake... *before* you make the mistake, so you can avoid it in the first place.

Again, one of the best ways to do this is to pay attention to answer choice patterns (if a question has answer choices, of course). For example, if you notice that two choices are opposites, then there's a good chance that some untrained test-takers might misunderstand the question in a way that causes them to pick the opposite of the right answer. You can also notice potential pitfalls in a question when you read the prompt—for example, if a question mentions more than one variable, then you know that it's important to keep the variables separate in your mind, and to remember which variable (if any) the prompt is asking you about, because some untrained test-takers will make the mistake of finding the wrong variable.

5. Look for a 30-Second Solution.

In this step, we try to use everything we've already figured out to help us string together the right basic math ideas that will let us connect the prompt to the correct answer choice. And don't forget—the fastest solutions will take you less than 30 seconds to work out.

If you can't think of a fast, efficient way to find the correct answer with total certainty, then consider saving the question for a later pass, as we discussed earlier in this Black Book, in the section called "Time Management On Test Day" on page 36; if you've already passed on the question multiple times, or if you only have a few minutes left on the section, then consider guessing.

Of course, as I said before, you can still get the question right even if you can't find a solution in under 30 seconds. But it's a good idea to get in the habit of looking for fast, simple solutions, because practicing this mindset will train you to approach SAT Math questions like a trained test-taker. A lot of the difficulty that people have on the SAT Math section comes from expecting to have to carry out the more complex, formal solutions that we'd expect in a classroom situation; test-takers who use this approach tend to overlook the kinds of small details in a question that we can use to pursue a simpler solution.

6. Carry Out Your Solution.

After you have read the prompt, the figure, and the answer choices, and thought about what the College Board is presenting to you and how it fits with what you know about the design of the SAT, and you've decided on a straightforward solution, you've finally earned the right to go ahead and solve the problem. If you try to solve the problem without going through the earlier steps—especially if it's a more challenging problem—then there's a very good chance you'll make exactly the kind of mistake the College Board is hoping you'll make.

This is one more way that SAT Math questions differ from the math questions you encounter in school. In school, the questions on a math test are basically just like the questions you've been doing for homework and the questions your teacher has been doing in lectures, so you build up a kind of instinctive, automatic approach to school math, in which you memorize formulas and then automatically apply certain formulas in certain situations.

But that won't work on the SAT Math section, where questions are often specifically written so that formulas are of little help. If you read a math question on the SAT and dive right into it without thinking about it first, you're probably doing something wrong, and you'll probably end up choosing the wrong answer. Don't try to solve the problem until you've read it and thought about how it fits the SAT's patterns and rules.

7. Re-check Your Work, Paying Attention to Post-Solution Patterns. Consider Using a Different Approach to Re-solve the Question.

Checking your work is critical, because one of the easiest ways to lose points on the SAT Math section is to make a small mistake even though you fully understand the question.

One of the best ways to guard against mistakes is to look at all the choices you think are wrong and see if you can figure out why some of them were included. In other words, if you can figure out the mistakes that the College Board wanted you to make to arrive at some of the wrong choices, then there's a pretty good chance that you've handled the question correctly. But if you look back over the wrong answers and you don't have any idea why any of them are there, that can be a sign that you misunderstood the question, and you may have fallen for one of the test's tricks. Be especially on the lookout for hidden patterns like the ones we talked about on page 285.

Another good way to check your work is to see if you can figure out a different way to arrive at the same result you found originally. For example, if you originally found a y-intercept for a function by graphing it on your calculator, then you could re-confirm that value by plugging it in for y in the original function and making sure that $x = 0$ in the resulting equation.

Of course, another way to check your work is just to re-do exactly the same steps you've already completed, which is what most people do when they check their work in a math class. This approach can be effective, but it's not my favorite way to guard against errors: many people will have a hard time identifying small mistakes they've just made if they go back through their work only a few seconds later, because they're still in the same frame of mind that they were in when they made the mistake in the first place. This is why I prefer to approach a question in a different way when I'm checking for mistakes, rather than just walking back through the same steps I used in my initial approach. On the SAT, these alternative approaches can often include things like considering patterns in the answer choices, using a calculator to backsolve, and so on; we'll see a lot of situations where we can solve the same question with multiple approaches in the walkthroughs starting in a few pages.

If you're fully satisfied that you know why your answer is right (ideally including understanding why at least one or two of the other answer choices are present as wrong answers), then you can mark your answer and move on to the next question. If you're not completely sure that you've figured out the correct answer, consider saving the question until a later pass, as we discussed in "Time Management On Test Day" on page 36. If you decide that it's time to guess on the question, remember the ideas we discussed in "Guessing on the SAT" on page 33.

Closing Thoughts on the SAT Math Path

You shouldn't try to solve SAT Math questions without reading them carefully and setting them up first, taking into account all of the aspects of the SAT's design that make these questions different from traditional math questions. Taking a few seconds to get your bearings will make answering the question a lot easier. Remember to keep the solution to every problem as simple as possible, and remember that you shouldn't be looking for formulaic approaches in most cases.

It may feel like the process we've just gone over is pretty long or complicated, especially for questions that seem obvious when you first look at them. But it's important to remember that you don't have to use this process on every question—only on the ones that you're having trouble figuring out at first. And you can modify the process as you see fit, depending on the question and your own preferences.

The important thing is to be aware of all the elements involved in the Math Path and try to implement them in your practice sessions, so they can become second nature when you see challenging questions on the test. This will allow you to use these ideas naturally, when you need them, instead of turning the Math Path into a rote system that you force yourself to follow even when you can answer a question without it.

I'll list the steps here one more time for reference:

1. Read the prompt carefully and identify what the prompt is asking for.

2. Consider figures, if there are any.

3. Read and analyze the answer choices, if there are any.

4. Think about which areas of math might be involved.

5. Look for a 30-second solution.

6. Carry out your solution.

7. Re-check your work, paying attention to post-solution patterns. Consider using a different approach to re-solve the question.

As I said, this process will allow you to break down any official SAT Math question you run into on test day, and figure out the most effective and efficient way to attack it. But I know from experience that some readers will have lingering questions about some aspects of the process, so we'll address those below.

What about Student-Produced Response Questions?

Many students wonder if the student-produced response questions require a different approach from the multiple-choice questions. For the most part, the Math Path process that we just discussed is the process I would follow for the student-produced response questions as well (with the obvious exception that we won't have any answer choices to consider in deciding how to attack the question).

There are a few special considerations we should keep in mind for these questions, though.

Make sure you know how to enter mixed numbers and decimals.

The College Board has fairly particular rules about entering mixed numbers (that is, numbers like $4\frac{1}{2}$ that include both a whole number and a fraction) and decimals. It is **very important** that you get familiar with these rules before test day, otherwise you could end up getting all the math right and being wrong anyway because you didn't enter the result correctly.

First, we need to know that **we can't enter mixed numbers as answers** . At all. Really. We have to change them to improper fractions (for example, enter $4\frac{1}{2}$ as $\frac{9}{2}$, since these expressions are equivalent), or enter their decimal equivalents ($4\frac{1}{2}$ would be 4.5). Either option is equally valid.

Second, we need to know how to enter longer decimal expressions correctly. To quote the SAT Math instructions for the digital SAT, "if your answer is a decimal that doesn't fit in the provided space, enter it by truncating or rounding at the fourth digit." "Truncating" just means cutting it off at the fourth digit—for example, 3.666666666... would be truncated as 3.666, while it would be rounded as 3.667, although either answer is equally acceptable. What we *can't* do is enter a number like 3.666666666... as 3.6, or 3.7, or 3.67, or anything else that doesn't follow the rule we just discussed.

These are the two rules that will probably cause the most problems for most test-takers, but you should familiarize yourself with all the rules for student-produced response questions. You can find those rules in the instructions for the SAT Math section in the Bluebook app (note that these instructions differ slightly for the paper test, so you'll need to see them in the Bluebook app specifically).

If the question refers to the possibility of multiple solutions, make sure you understand why.

The student-produced response format allows the College Board to ask more open-ended math questions, which is one of the reasons it exists on the SAT in the first place. So be aware that you might see questions that allow more than one valid solution. Such a question will often use a phrase like "one possible value," as in, "If x has a value between 3.9 and 4, what is one possible value of x?"

If you realize that you're dealing with a question that refers to the possibility of more than one valid response, make sure you can figure out why. In other words, if you can only think of one possible answer for such a question, then you've probably misunderstood it in some fundamental way, which means there's a very good chance that the answer you're thinking of is wrong.

I'm not saying that you actually need to work out more than one solution in order to know that you've got the question right! I'm just saying that you need to understand where other solutions might come from.

For example, consider Question 6 from module 2 of SAT Practice Test #4. The prompt asks us for "one possible solution to the given equation." When we look at the question, we should be able to tell that there are two possible values of x, because the equation involves x inside an absolute value bracket. On the other hand, if we read the phrase "one possible value" in the prompt and couldn't understand how the question might have more than one solution, then we'd know that we misunderstood the question. (See my walkthrough of this question on page 496 of this Black Book for more.)

Don't be afraid to guess, but don't expect much to come of it.

Of course, you should never leave a question blank on the SAT, since there's no penalty for guessing. On the other hand, since there are essentially infinite ways to answer a student-produced response question, the chance of guessing right is relatively small.

If you do decide to guess on a student-produced response question, make that decision as quickly as you can so you don't waste any more time on the question than necessary. If you have a rough idea of what the answer might be, guess that, and move on—your chance of being correct on a random guess is basically zero anyway.

What about Showing Your Work?

Lots of test-takers experience significant difficulty on the SAT Math section for a reason that might seem strange to a lot of people: they try to approach each question in a formalized way that would satisfy a math teacher.

But by now we know that the SAT doesn't reward the same things that school rewards, and the SAT Math section is no exception.

The bottom line is that the SAT doesn't care what kind of work you do to arrive at the answer that you choose. The SAT only cares if the answer that you choose is correct. That's it.

This fact has two very important implications for us as test-takers. First, it means that we can, and should, get in the habit of looking for the fastest, most direct route to the answer, even if that route doesn't involve solving a formal equation (or writing anything down at all!). Second, it means that we have to make sure we don't make any small mistakes in our solution that might lead us to mark the wrong answer even if our overall approach is formally sound, because the College Board will never know what our approach was. For the College Board, a wrong answer is a wrong answer no matter how solid the approach to the question was, and a right answer is a right answer no matter what you did to arrive there (as long as you don't cheat, of course).

In the parts of this book where I provide solutions to real SAT Math questions from the College Board, you'll often see that the approach I recommend wouldn't be acceptable to most math teachers, because it's not formal. This isn't because I'm not good at math; it's because I'm very, very good at *SAT Math*, and in SAT Math we have no obligation to use a formal approach. In fact, we're usually better off avoiding formal math whenever possible, because the most efficient approaches to many questions involve taking advantage of the flaws in the SAT's design, as we'll see in the walkthroughs.

So try to get in the habit of finding the most direct approach to a question that you possibly can, and remember that the only thing that matters to the College Board is that you mark the correct answer without cheating!

What about the "Order of Difficulty?"

Test-takers are often encouraged to believe that the questions on the SAT Math section get harder as the section goes on—the conventional wisdom is that you should expect to be able to cruise through the early questions in a section, and you should expect more of a challenge later in the section. Even though this idea can be somewhat accurate in a very generalized sense, I would recommend ignoring it in your training.

At this point, I'm sure you're starting to realize that every SAT question deserves our full attention and respect on test day, because it's very easy to make small mistakes in our approach and end up choosing the wrong answer, even if we fully understand all the concepts in what seems to be an "easy" question. At the same time, you're probably also beginning to see that it's often possible to find very efficient solutions if we're aware of the test's design limitations, even when we're answering a "hard" question.

When we combine those two ideas, we see that we should always watch out for test questions trying to trick us into small mistakes, and we should always be aware of the possibility of an easier way to answer every question. Once we're in that frame of mind, worrying about the so-called "order of difficulty" makes no sense. Every question becomes both an opportunity to find a clever solution and a challenge to make sure we avoid small mistakes.

(By the way, when I work with students who are trying to score a perfect 800 on the SAT Math section but who might be missing a few questions per test, I find that they often miss questions in the first half of a section because of small mistakes—usually because they've been incorrectly taught that those questions are always "easy" and that they don't have to worry so much about them.)

So here's the bottom line: you should ignore the idea of an order of difficulty, because it serves no purpose. Instead, treat each question as a separate event. Don't be afraid of any question, and don't take any question for granted, either.

The Adaptive SAT

Some tutors and guidance counselors especially make a big deal out of the question of the "order of difficulty" in the context of the adaptive digital SAT—the current version of the SAT takes a look at your performance on the first module of a section, and then adjusts the difficulty (as defined by them) of the second module of the section accordingly.

But once again, this shouldn't impact the way you approach the test! It doesn't change the fact that your job is always to do your best to answer the question in front of you, and that you should be aware that you could potentially make a small mistake on any question (no matter how "hard" the question is or in which part of which module it appears), and that there's always the potential for a quick and straightforward solution for any question (no matter how "hard" the question is or in which part of which module it appears). For more on this topic, see "How The Digital SAT Impacts Our Approach" on page 54.

SAT Math Quick Summary

This is a one-page summary of the major relevant concepts. Use it to evaluate your comprehension or jog your memory. For a more in-depth treatment of these ideas, see the rest of the section.

The Big Secret of SAT Math Questions

SAT Math tests relatively simple things in relatively strange ways.

Sat Math Training Summary

- The concepts in the SAT Math section must be limited because of standardization. No calculus or advanced stats—just arithmetic, algebra, geometry, and very basic trig and statistics. Refer to the SAT Math Toolbox if necessary.

- Focus on the definitions and properties of the concepts in each question, not primarily on formulas. The College Board provides all the formulas related to area and volume that you'll be required to use.

- SAT Math is usually simpler than it looks, and each question can be done in 30 seconds or less if you find the fastest solution. If your solution is very complicated, you're probably doing the question wrong.

- Look for shortcuts, things that cancel out, equivalent terms, etc., especially when expressions involve fractions and radicals.

- If you're comfortable with all the concepts in the Math Toolbox of this Black Book, then every question contains all the information you need to answer it, even if it doesn't seem that way at first glance. If you understand every word in the question, then you know enough to figure out the right answer.

Some common wrong answer patterns include choices that are:

- half or double the right answer

- the opposite of the right answer (or its reciprocal, or complement, etc.)

- in a series with the right answer

- a number that you get on an earlier step of the right approach to the question

- the right answer to the wrong question

- similar in appearance to the right answer

I recommend a step-by-step process called the Math Path for questions that are hard to figure out. Here's a simplified version:

1. Read the question carefully, and consider the words in the question. This is the most important step.

2. Read any figures just as carefully as you read the rest of the prompt.

3. Consider answer choices (if there are any)—analyze their relationships with each other and with the question.

4. Which areas of math are involved? What can the SAT test in those areas? (Math Toolbox.)

5. In light of steps 1 - 4, look for a solution—ideally one that would take 30 seconds or less.

6. Execute your solution.

7. Check your work using the answer choices and/or alternate solutions. Remember that small, avoidable mistakes cost most people more points than any other single thing does.

Remember:

- Always think about the question as a whole system of ideas—prompt, figures, answer choices, and so on—before you actually start solving it.

- Ignore the idea of an "order of difficulty." You can make careless mistakes on any question, and every question has a simple, direct solution.

See the walkthroughs in this Black Book for demonstrations of all these ideas.

Math Question Walkthroughs

Now that we've thoroughly discussed the right approach to the SAT Math section in general terms, we'll go through all the SAT Math questions in four real SAT Practice Tests from the College Board, so you can see this approach in action against official SAT questions. (See "Only Work with Questions from the College Board!" on page 16 of this Black Book for details on why official questions are so important, and where to get them for free. And if you'd like to see some video demonstrations of these ideas, go to www.SATprepVideos.com for a selection of demonstration videos that are free to readers of this book.)

Sample Math Walkthrough

My SAT Math walkthroughs are roughly similar to the SAT Reading and Writing walkthroughs we saw earlier in this Black Book, though the Math ones have a few more components. As with the Reading and Writing walkthroughs, you don't need to worry about copying my approach exactly when you attack a question on your own. Instead, the walkthroughs are presented in a format that lets us do the following:

- show the ideal thought process for attacking a question, from the initial assessment, through one or more solutions, ending with checking the result and observing any relevant post-solution patterns in the answer choices (But remember that you only need to find one solution on test day! I just show multiple solutions to help you understand that SAT Math questions can be attacked in a variety of ways.)

- allow you to focus on the specific information you're interested in for a particular question, while also letting you read through the entire walkthrough easily if you prefer

- present each walkthrough so it can stand on its own as a full explanation of the question, while still making it easy to refer back to relevant parts of the training for more details if you want a refresher

- show how simple the reasoning and calculations are for most SAT Math questions, and how important it is to avoid small mistakes

Here's a diagram of a sample walkthrough, with the key elements of the walkthrough explained on the next page:

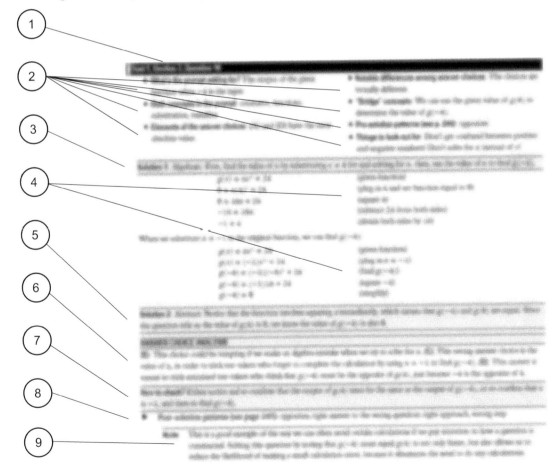

Explanation of Walkthrough Elements

The elements of the walkthrough are presented in an order that reflects the "Math Path" from page 291 of this Black Book:

1. This shows the test, module, and question number of the question being analyzed in the walkthrough. You can use this information to locate the relevant question in the College Board's free online practice tests, available from the College Board's website or from QuestPrep.com/Practice.

2. This area of the walkthrough reflects steps 1-4 of the "Math Path" on page 291 of this Black Book; in other words, this part of the walkthrough shows the kinds of things that a trained test-taker might notice initially, while she was deciding on the best way to attack the question. This part of the walkthrough reflects the following ideas:

   - the specific thing that the prompt is actually asking for

   - the math concepts in the prompt, figure, and/or answer choices

   - the notable features of the answer choices (you could choose to use a vertical scan to pick these out, as described on page 45 of this Black Book)

   - the patterns in the answer choices that might be observable before we attempt a solution

   - a list of potential mistakes and pitfalls to look out for before we begin our solution

3. This Item reflects step 5 in the "Math Path" on page 291 of this Black Book: it names the first solution that the walkthrough will explore. It begins with a simple one- or two-word description of the type of solution that's being discussed (such as "backsolving" or "graphing"), and then proceeds to a one- or two-sentence description of the steps that would be taken for the solution. As you become more comfortable with SAT Math, you may be able to understand the entire solution just from this Item. (In Item 4, this simple description will be fleshed out at length.)

4. In this Item, which reflects step 6 in the "Math Path" on page 291 of this Black Book, we spell out the specific steps for the solution from Item 3. These steps allow you to follow along with the exact process that would lead to the answer to the question according to the approach in Item 3.

5. Here you'll find a different potential solution to the question from the one in Item 3, also reflecting step 5 in the "Math Path" on page 291 of this Black Book. Just like the description in Item 3, this description will begin with a one- or two-word rough classification of the type of solution being proposed (such as "abstract" or "test-smart"), followed by a one- or two-sentence description of the solution. This Item will be followed by another set of relevant steps, if applicable, just as Item 4 provides the steps for the solution in Item 3. Note that you only need to find one solution on test day! We just go through multiple solutions in the walkthroughs so you can come to understand how each question can be attacked in multiple ways.

6. After all the solutions are presented, along with their various steps, Item 6 discusses the wrong answer choices, and indicates likely errors that might have led to some or all of them.

7. This Item provides a quick indication of a way to check over our work to catch any mistakes we might have made.

8. This Item notes any answer choice patterns that might only be noticeable after we've executed a solution. Items 6, 7, and 8 all reflect Step 7 in the "Math Path" on page 291 of this Black Book.

9. If I feel that something is noteworthy about the question but I can't fit it in the rest of the walkthrough, then I'll note that at the end of the walkthrough. Be sure to pay attention to these notes when they appear, as they'll often contain useful information about what a particular question can teach us generally about future SAT questions.

Note that some walkthroughs are missing some of the items in this list! If one of the Items above isn't relevant to a particular question, then it's omitted.

Remember that the ultimate goal of these walkthroughs is to help you see multiple ways that I might attack each question, and how I recommend you do the same. Also notice that the walkthroughs always begin by pointing out all the key details of the question that will help you figure out the most efficient solution to apply—this is very important to keep in mind on test day!

As always, feel free to modify my approach as you see fit, as long as your modifications still bring you the results you want.

Test 1, Module 1, Question 1

- What's the prompt asking for? 10% of 470.
- Math concepts in the prompt: percentages
- Elements of the answer choices: Each answer choice is an integer ranging from 37 to 460.
- Notable features of the answer choices: Two answer choices are two-digit integers, and two are three-digit integers. Both two-digit answers have the same ones digit.
- Pre-solution patterns (see p. 285): wrong answers try to imitate right answers
- Things to look out for: Take the right percentage of the right number—don't subtract 10% of 470, or add or subtract the number 10 from anything.

Solution 1: Concrete: Enter "10% of 470" into the SAT calculator.

The result will be "10% of 470 = 47." So the right answer is (B).

Solution 2: Algebra: Convert 10% to a decimal expression, and multiply the result by 470.

$$470 \times 10\% \quad \text{(provided equation)}$$
$$470 \times 0.1 \quad \text{(convert percentage to decimal)}$$
$$47 \quad \text{(simplify)}$$

So the right answer is (B).

ANSWER CHOICE ANALYSIS

(A): This is the result if we find 10% of 470, and then subtract 10 from the result. **(C):** This is the result if we reduce 470 by 10%, rather than finding 10% of 470 as the prompt requires. **(D):** This is the result of subtracting 10 from 470.

How to check? Verify that $47 \times 10 = 470$. Try an alternate approach above. Try to figure out which mistakes could lead to some of the wrong answer choices, and verify that you haven't made any such mistakes.

▶ Post-solution patterns (see page 286): the right answer to the wrong question

Test 1, Module 1, Question 2

- What's the prompt asking for? The equation whose solution is the same as the solution for the given equation.
- Math concepts in the prompt: algebra, variables, equations, coefficients
- Elements of the answer choices: Each answer choice is an equation that starts with "$4x =$."
- Notable features of the answer choices: Every answer choice is $4x$ set equal to a different integer.
- "Bridge" concepts: The solution for these equations is the x-value that we can plug in to make the equation a true statement, so the right answer will be the choice whose x-value matches the x-value in the provided equation.
- Pre-solution patterns (see p. 285): halves and doubles; wrong answers try to imitate right answers
- Things to look out for: Don't just find the value of x and pick the answer where that value appears—make sure you understand what the question is asking for!

Solution 1: Concrete/backsolving: Solve for x in the provided equation. Then plug that x-value into each answer choice and see which one results in a valid equation.

$$4x + 6 = 18 \quad \text{(given equation)}$$
$$4x = 12 \quad \text{(subtract 6 from both sides)}$$
$$x = 3 \quad \text{(divide both sides by 4 to isolate } x)$$

Now we can plug $x = 3$ into each answer choice to see which one results in a valid equation.

$$4(3) = 108 \quad (x = 3 \text{ plugged into equation from (A))}$$
$$12 \neq 108 \quad \text{(simplify)}$$

So plugging $x = 3$ into the equation from (A) resulted in an invalid equation, which means (A) is wrong. Let's check (B).

$$4(3) = 24 \quad (x = 3 \text{ plugged into equation from (B))}$$
$$12 \neq 24 \quad \text{(simplify)}$$

Plugging $x = 3$ into the equation from (B) resulted in an invalid equation, which means (B) is wrong. Now we'll check (C).

$$4(3) = 12 \quad (x = 3 \text{ plugged into equation from (C))}$$

$$12 = 12 \qquad \text{(simplify)}$$

When we plug $x = 3$ into the equation from (C), we get a valid equation, which means (C) is correct. We know from our training that it's important to check every answer choice to help us catch any potential mistakes, so we're going to check (D) too.

$$4(3) = 3 \qquad (x = 3 \text{ plugged into equation from (D)})$$
$$12 \neq 3 \qquad \text{(simplify)}$$

We can see that plugging $x = 3$ into the equation from (D) resulted in an invalid equation, which means (D) is wrong.

After checking each answer choice, we can see that (C) is correct.

Solution 2: Concrete/graphing: Enter the given equation as-is directly into your graphing calculator. Then, do the same with each answer choice. The graph of the correct answer will show the same x-value as the graph of the given equation.

Let's start with the graph of the given equation:

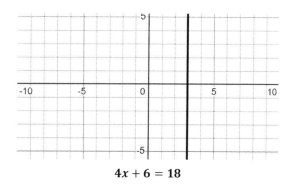

$$4x + 6 = 18$$

Now let's graph the answer choices:
(A) $4x = 108$

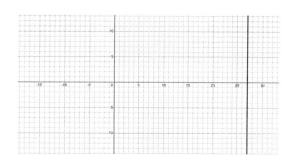

(B) $4x = 24$

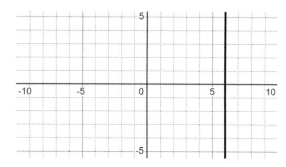

(C) $4x = 12$

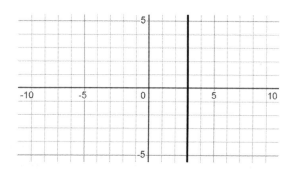

(D) $4x = 3$

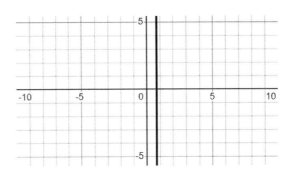

We can see that (C) matches the graph of the given equation, so (C) is correct.

Solution 3: Test-smart: Each answer choice has $4x$ on the left side of the equation. If we subtract 6 from both sides of the given equation, then the left side of the given equation will match the answer choices, and the right side must match the correct answer as well.

$4x + 6 = 18$	(given equation)
$4x = 12$	(subtract 6 from both sides)

After subtracting 6 from both sides, we can see that this expression is equal to (C), which means (C) is the right answer.

ANSWER CHOICE ANALYSIS

(A): This is the result if we accidentally subtract 6 from the left side of the given equation and then *multiply* the right side by 6, instead of subtracting 6 from the right side. **(B):** This is the result if we accidentally subtract 6 from the left side of the given equation and then *add* 6 to the right side, instead of subtracting 6 from the right side. **(D):** When we solve for x in the given equation, we find that $x = 3$. Some untrained test-takers will forget what the prompt actually asks for, and just pick the answer choice that says something is equal to 3—if they do that, they'll pick this choice, and be wrong. Remember to double-check what the prompt is actually asking for before you decide on an answer choice!

How to check? Verify that plugging $x = 3$ into the provided equation and into your answer choice results in a true statement in both cases. Try an alternate approach above. Try to figure out which mistakes could lead to some of the wrong answer choices, and verify that you haven't made any such mistakes.

▶   Post-solution patterns (see page 286):   the right answer to the wrong question

Note   This is a great example of an SAT Math question that tries to take advantage of your classroom instincts. In most high school math classrooms, when a question presents us with an algebraic expression containing one variable, our job will be to find the value of that variable. But that's not what this questions asks for! Many students will struggle with this question, not because they can't handle the math skills involved, but because they're not used to reading carefully and paying close attention to what math questions are actually asking for. Keep this in mind as you continue to prepare!

Test 1, Module 1, Question 3

- What's the prompt asking for? The inequality that represents the situation described in the prompt.

- Math concepts in the prompt: word problems, variables, money, rates, inequalities

- Elements of the answer choices: Each answer choice is an inequality ending in "≤ 75."

- Notable features of the answer choices: Every answer choice is a different inequality, all involving t, 10, and/or 25 on the left side, and all set less than or equal to 75.

- "Bridge" concepts: The service fee is a one-time fee, and shouldn't be multiplied by anything. The per hour rental fee should be multiplied by the number of hours for which the surfboard is rented.

- Pre-solution patterns (see p. 285): wrong answers try to imitate right answers

- Things to look out for: Don't forget to account for the service fee *and* the rental fee! Don't confuse the service fee and the rental fee! Remember that the service fee is the same no matter how long the surfboard is rented, but the rental fee is per hour, and should be multiplied by the number of hours!

Solution 1: Careful reading: Convert the phrases in the prompt into a mathematical expression.

a $25 service fee and a $10 per hour rental fee

The text doesn't tell us that the $25 fee ever changes for any reason, or is ever impacted by anything else, so we can just leave that as 25. The $10 fee is "per hour," which means it needs to be multiplied by the number of hours. The prompt tell us that t is the number of hours the surfboard is rented. The word "and" means we're adding the service fee and the rental fee together. Let's change our statement accordingly.

$$25 + 10t$$

The prompt tells us the person renting the surfboard will "spend a maximum of $75." This is the same as saying that the total of the above expression will not be more than $75, which is the same as saying it will be less than or equal to $75. Again, let's update our statement with this information.

$$25 + 10t \leq 75$$

This matches answer choice (D), and we can see that (D) is correct.

Solution 2: Abstract: Consider how each answer choice relates to the information in the prompt. Eliminate each choice that fails to account for everything described in the prompt, and confirm that the remaining choice accurately reflects the ideas in the prompt.

(A) This choice multiplies the number of hours t by 10. That makes sense, because the prompt tells us that part of the total cost to rent the surfboard is "a $10 per hour rental fee," so multiplying the number of hours by 10 would tell us the hourly fee. But this inequality doesn't account for the $25 service fee, so it can't be right.

(B) We can probably tell this choice is wrong for a couple of reasons. First, the number 10 isn't being multiplied by anything. The prompt tells us that part of the total cost to rent the surfboard is "a $10 per hour rental fee," which means each additional hour should increase that hourly rental fee by another $10. But this inequality includes a flat $10 no matter what t is. Along similar lines, this choice multiplies t by 25. The only mention of 25 in the prompt is the "$25 service fee," but nothing tells us that this service fee increases according to the number of hours of the rental. As we'll see in our discussion of (D), this choice is the same as the right answer, but the 25 and the 10 are switched; this choice would be tempting for test-takers who understood the question and knew how to find the right answer but didn't keep accurate track of the numbers in the problem, or for test-takers who mixed up the concepts of a service fee and an hourly fee.

(C) This choice combines the errors in (A) and (B); it multiplies t by 25 (the amount of the service fee) instead of by 10 (the amount of the per hour rental fee), and it only accounts for one of the two fees from the prompt.

(D) This choice correctly adds the service fee of $25 to the product of the $10 hourly fee and the number of hours of the rental, t. In other words, it represents a total cost of $10 for each hour the surfboard is rented, plus an unchanging $25 service fee. It also sets this total equal to or less than $75, which demonstrates the idea of "spend[ing] a maximum of $75 to rent the surfboard"— although in this case, if we used our Vertical Scan (as described on page 45), we would notice that *every* choice ends with "≤ 75," so we know this will be part of the right answer no matter what, and we can focus on everything to the left of the inequality sign. With all of this in mind, we know (D) is correct.

How to check? Verify that your answer choice accounts for both the service fee and the rental fee. Try an alternate approach above. Try to figure out which mistakes could lead to some of the wrong answer choices, and verify that you haven't made any such mistakes.

Test 1, Module 1, Question 4

- What's the prompt asking for? The value of x for which $g(x) = 25$.

- Math concepts in the prompt: functions, variables, exponents

- Elements of the answer choices: Each answer choice is an integer ranging from 4 to 13.

- Notable features of the answer choices: Three answer choices are single-digit integers, and one answer choice is a double-digit integer.

- "Bridge" concepts: We can plug the right answer in for x in the provided function, and the result will be 25.

- Things to look out for: Don't forget that x will be squared, and 9 will be added to the result!

Solution 1: Concrete/graphing: Graph the provided function and find the input of the point where the output is 25.

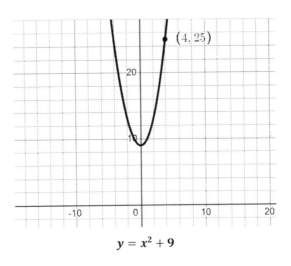

$$y = x^2 + 9$$

We can see that $g(4) = 25$, so (A) is correct.

Solution 2: Concrete/backsolving: Plug in each answer choice for x, and pick the choice that results in a $g(x)$ value of 25.

$g(x) = x^2 + 9$	(given equation)
$g(4) = 4^2 + 9$	(plug in $x = 4$ from (A))
$g(4) = 25$	(simplify)

After testing the value from (A), we can see that $g(4)$ results in a value of 25, which means (A) looks like it's correct. We know that catching our mistakes on the SAT is an important test-taking strategy, and one great way to do that is to make sure we always check each answer choice when we execute a backsolving approach like this one. So we'll go ahead and plug in the values from the other choices as well. If we seem to find another right answer, we'll know we made a mistake somewhere; if we don't, and we double-check our math for (A), we can feel confident that we've found the right answer.

$g(5) = 5^2 + 9$	(plug in $x = 5$ from (B))
$g(5) = 34$	(simplify)

This value produced 34, not 25, so (B) isn't the right answer. Let's try (C).

$g(9) = 9^2 + 9$	(plug in $x = 9$ from (C))
$g(9) = 90$	(simplify)

Plugging in the value from (C) gave us 90, not 25 as the prompt required. Let's check (D).

$g(13) = 13^2 + 9$	(plug in $x = 13$ from (D))
$g(13) = 178$	(simplify)

The value from (D) gave us 178, so (D) isn't right either. After checking each answer choice, we can see that (A) is correct.

Solution 3: Algebra: Set $g(x)$ equal to 25, and then solve for x.

$25 = x^2 + 9$	(given equation with $g(x)$ set equal to 25)
$16 = x^2$	(subtract 9 from both sides)
$4 = x$	(take the square root of both sides)

We can see that (A) is the correct answer.

ANSWER CHOICE ANALYSIS

(B): This choice would be correct if $g(x)$ were equal to x^2, instead of $x^2 + 9$. **(C):** This is the y-intercept for $g(x)$—that is, the value of the function when $x = 0$. This choice might be tempting for test-takers who got confused about what the question was asking about.

How to check? Plug $x = 4$ into the provided function and verify that the result is 25. Try an alternate approach above. Try to figure out which mistakes could lead to some of the wrong answer choices, and verify that you haven't made any such mistakes.

▶ Post-solution patterns (see page 286): the right answer to the wrong question

Test 1, Module 1, Question 5

- What's the prompt asking for? The probability of rolling a 2 if the die is rolled one time.

- Math concepts in the prompt: probability

- Elements of the answer choices: Each answer choice is a fraction with a denominator of 14.

- Notable features of the answer choices: Every answer choice has a different numerator and the same denominator.

- Pre-solution patterns (see p. 285): halves and doubles; opposites

- Things to look out for: Make sure you find the probability of rolling a 2, rather than the probability of <u>not</u> rolling a 2!

Solution 1: Concrete: Construct a probability fraction using the information in the prompt.

We construct a probability fraction by making the numerator the number of desired outcomes and the denominator the number of possible outcomes. In this case, there is one desired outcome—rolling a 2—and 14 possible outcomes—the 14 sides of the die. So our probability fraction looks like this:

$$\frac{1}{14}$$

So (A) is correct.

ANSWER CHOICE ANALYSIS

(B): This choice might be tempting for test-takers who think the specific number to be rolled is what goes in the numerator of the fraction, or who don't read the question carefully enough and think the "2" in the prompt indicates that 2 different numbers will satisfy the prompt. **(C):** This choice combines the errors in (B) and (D), because it's the probability of rolling any value *except* for 2 specific values on the die described in the prompt. **(D):** This would be the probability of rolling any value *except* 2 on the 14-sided die.

How to check? Double-check that you constructed your probability fraction correctly. Try to figure out which mistakes could lead to some of the wrong answer choices, and verify that you haven't made any such mistakes.

▶ Post-solution patterns (see page 286): the right answer to the wrong question

---

Test 1, Module 1, Question 6

- What's the prompt asking for? The rate in posters per hour that the printer makes the posters.
- Math concepts in the prompt: word problems, rates, unit conversion

- "Bridge" concepts: In an hour, the printer must make 60 times as many posters as the printer makes in a minute.
- Things to look out for: Don't reverse the relationship between the number of posters printed in a minute and the number of posters printed in an hour!

Solution 1: Concrete: Think about how many posters the printer must make in 60 minutes, based on the output in one minute.

There are 60 minutes in an hour, so if a printer makes 42 posters per minute, the printer must makes 60 times that amount in an hour. $60 \times 42 = 2,520$, so the printer makes 2,520 posters per hour, and the right answer is 2,520.

How to check? Verify that your answer is 60 times the number of posters produced in a minute.

Test 1, Module 1, Question 7

- What's the prompt asking for? The value of $f(x)$ when $x = 4$.
- Math concepts in the prompt: functions, plugging in values

- "Bridge" concepts: We can plug 4 in for x in the function to find the value of $f(x)$ when $x = 4$.
- Things to look out for: Don't just find the value of $7(4)$, make sure to add 2 to the result!

Solution 1: Concrete/graphing: Graph the provided function, and find the value of the function when $x = 4$.

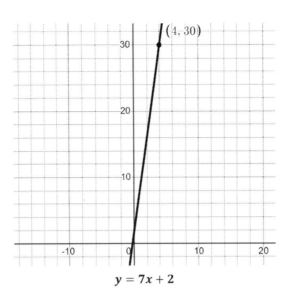

$$y = 7x + 2$$

We can see that $f(4) = 30$, so the answer is 30.

Solution 2: Algebra: Plug $x = 4$ into the provided function.

$$f(x) = 7x + 2 \qquad \text{(given equation)}$$
$$f(4) = 7(4) + 2 \qquad \text{(plug in } x = 4 \text{ from the prompt)}$$
$$f(4) = 28 + 2 \qquad \text{(simplify)}$$
$$f(4) = 30 \qquad \text{(simplify)}$$

Again, we can see that $f(4) = 30$, so the answer is 30.

How to check? Try an alternate approach above.

Test 1, Module 1, Question 8

- What's the prompt asking for? The equation that represents the situation described in the prompt, where x is the number of questions worth 1 point and y is the number of questions worth 3 points.

- Math concepts in the prompt: word problems, equations, variables

- Elements of the answer choices: Each answer choice is an equation involving x and y and ending in "$= 70$."

- Notable features of the answer choices: Each answer choice is a different equation involving an expression with $x, y, 3$ and/or 4, set equal to 70.

- "Bridge" concepts: The expression involving x should represent all the points from the 1-point questions, and the expression involving y should represent all the points from the 3-point questions, and the sum of these expressions should be equal to 70.

- Pre-solution patterns (see p. 285): wrong answers try to imitate right answers

- Things to look out for: Don't get confused about what x represents and what y represents!

Solution 1: Concrete: Think of an x-value and a y-value that would result in a total of 70 points. Plug those values into the provided equations, and eliminate any answer choices that result in an invalid equation.

If there are 10 questions worth 3 points, then $y = 10$, and the 3-point questions account for 30 of the 70 total points. That leaves 40 points for the 1-point questions to account for. If 40 points come from 1-point questions, there must be 40 1-point questions. So when $y = 10, x = 40$.

Now that we have a valid (x, y) pair, we can plug those values into the equation from each answer choice and eliminate each one that isn't equal to 70.

$$4xy = 70 \qquad \text{(equation from (A))}$$
$$4(40)(10) = 70 \qquad \text{(plug in } x = 40 \text{ and } y = 10)$$
$$1,600 \neq 70 \qquad \text{(simplify)}$$

We can eliminate (A), because it doesn't produce a true statement when $x = 40$ and $y = 10$. Let's try (B).

$$4(x + y) = 70 \qquad \text{(equation from (B))}$$
$$4(40 + 10) = 70 \qquad \text{(plug in } x = 40 \text{ and } y = 10)$$
$$200 \neq 70 \qquad \text{(simplify)}$$

We can eliminate (B), because it doesn't produce a true statement when $x = 40$ and $y = 10$. Let's try (C).

$$3x + y = 70$$ (equation from (C))

$$3(40) + (10) = 70$$ (plug in $x = 40$ and $y = 10$)

$$130 \neq 70$$ (simplify)

We can eliminate (C), because it doesn't produce a true statement when $x = 40$ and $y = 10$. Let's try (D).

$$x + 3y = 70$$ (equation from (D))

$$(40) + 3(10) = 70$$ (plug in $x = 40$ and $y = 10$)

$$70 = 70$$ (simplify)

(D) is the only choice that produces a valid equation when $x = 40$ and $y = 10$, so (D) is correct.

Solution 2: Abstract: Consider how each answer choice relates to the information in the prompt. Eliminate each choice that fails to account for everything described in the prompt, and confirm that the remaining choice accurately reflects the ideas in the prompt.

(A) This choice multiplies the number of 1-point questions by the number of 3-point questions—which already doesn't reflect anything in the prompt—and then multiplies that total by the sum of the two possible point values (1 and 3). This choice involves values from the prompt, but doesn't reflect any of the relationships described in the prompt, so it's wrong. Test-takers who picked this choice probably misread or misunderstood some fundamental aspect of the prompt, which will likely be cleared up by reading the explanations for the other answer choices.

(B) This choice represents the idea of adding up the total number of questions (that is, the sum of the number of 1-point questions, x, and the number of 3-point questions, y) and multiplying the result by 4. But that would tells us the total number of points if all the questions were worth 4 points, not if some questions were worth 1 point and the other questions were worth 3 points. So (B) is wrong.

(C) This choice multiplies the number of 1-point questions, x, by 3, and then adds that result to the number of 3-point questions, y. But that would tell us the number of points if 1-point questions were worth 3 points and 3-point questions were worth 1 point, which is the reverse of what's described in the prompt—in other words, this is the right answer except the x and y are switched. Mixing up the variables like this is exactly the kind of simple mistake we should expect the College Board to try to trick us into making, so it's exactly the kind of mistake we need to watch out for, in practice and on test day. So (C) is wrong.

(D) This choice is just like (C) except the x and y are switched—which, as we saw in our discussion of (C), means it's correct. The left side of this equation includes x by itself, which accounts for 1 point for each of the 1-point questions, and $3y$, which accounts for 3 points for each of the 3-point questions. Those values are added together and set equal to 70, just as the prompt describes (note that every choice sets the expression on the left equal to 70, which means we can just focus on the left side of the expression to find the right answer). This choice demonstrates all of the ideas in the prompt, so (D) is correct.

Solution 3: Test-Smart: Realize that $x = 70$ and $y = 0$ must be valid solutions for the correct answer. Plug those values into each answer choice and eliminate any choice that doesn't produce a valid equation.

If the assignment is worth 70 points, and all those points come from 1-point questions, then it would be true that $x = 70$ and $y = 0$.

(A)	$4(70)(0) = 0$	($x = 70$ and $y = 0$ plugged into expression from (A))
(B)	$4(70 + 0) = 280$	($x = 70$ and $y = 0$ plugged into expression from (B))
(C)	$3(70) + 0 = 210$	($x = 70$ and $y = 0$ plugged into expression from (C))
(D)	$70 + 3(0) = 70$	($x = 70$ and $y = 0$ plugged into expression from (D))

When we plug in $x = 70$ and $y = 0$—which, as discussed above, will result in an assignment worth 70 points, according to the information in the prompt—we see that only choice (D) produces a value of 70. So we know (D) is correct.

ANSWER CHOICE ANALYSIS

(A): This could be the result if a test-taker wasn't sure how to solve the question and just ended up trying to combine different numbers and variables that appear in the prompt. **(C):** This would be the result if a test-taker attempted a valid solution but got confused about what x represents and what y represents.

How to check? Try an alternate approach above. Try to figure out which mistakes could lead to some of the wrong answer choices, and verify that you haven't made any such mistakes.

Test 1, Module 1, Question 9

- What's the prompt asking for? Measure of angle Q.
- Math concepts in the prompt: right triangles, similar triangles, angles
- Elements of the answer choices: Each answer choice is an angle measure in degrees ranging from 37° to 143°.

- Notable features of the answer choices: (A) and (B) add up to 90°. (A) and (D) add up to 180°. (B) and (C) add up to 180°.
- "Bridge" concepts: If the triangles are similar, as the prompt tells us, and angle M corresponds to angle Q, as

the prompt tells us, then the measure of angle Q is equal to the measure of angle M.

- Pre-solution patterns (see p. 285): opposites
- Things to look out for: Don't mix up which angles correspond to each other between the two triangles!

Don't assume that your solution must involve the idea that these are right triangles! Don't assume that the right answer must be the measure of the angle that isn't provided in the prompt (that is, the angle that isn't 90° or 53°)!

Solution 1: Concrete: Sketch the triangles as described in the prompt, and use the sketch to find the measure of angle Q.

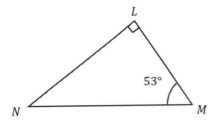 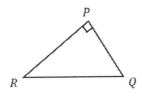

We know that similar triangles have the same angle measures, and the prompt tells us that "L and M correspond to P and Q, respectively," which means that M corresponds to Q, and the measure of angle M will be equal to the measure of angle Q. The prompt tells us that the measure of angle M is 53°, which means the measure of angle Q is also 53°. So the answer is (B).

Solution 2: Abstract: Notice that angle M corresponds to angle Q, and use this information to answer the question.

Once we realize that the triangles are similar, and that angle M corresponds to angle Q, we know that their angle measures must be equal, which means the answer is (B), 53°.

ANSWER CHOICE ANALYSIS

(A): This is the measure of the angle in each triangle that isn't the 90° angle or the 53° angle, but that's not what the question asks for! **(C):** This is the sum of the measures of angles P and R, not the measure of angle Q. **(D):** This is the sum of the measures of angle Q and the right angle, not the measure of angle Q alone.

How to check? Verify that angles M and Q should have the same measure according to the prompt, and that the measure of angle M is 53°. Try an alternate approach above. Try to figure out which mistakes could lead to some of the wrong answer choices, and verify that you haven't made any such mistakes.

▶ Post-solution patterns (see page 286): the right answer to the wrong question

> **Note** Many test-takers will read this prompt too quickly and assume that they need to use the fact that the sum of a triangle's angle measures must be 180° to find the measure of the angle whose size isn't provided—that is, the angle that isn't 90° or 53°. But that's not what the prompt asks for! The presence of the right angle and the fact that the sum of a triangle's angle measures must be 180° aren't relevant to this question. The prompt asks us for the measure of angle Q in one triangle, and tells us that angle Q corresponds to angle M in a similar triangle, and that the measure of angle M is 53°. All we need to know is that corresponding angles in similar triangles have the same angle measures, and based on that we can pick the right answer, (B). Remember never to make assumptions about what a question is asking for, and always to read carefully and make sure you understand what the prompt wants you to do!

Test 1, Module 1, Question 10

- What's the prompt asking for? The value of x in the (x, y) solution to the given system of equations.
- Math concepts in the prompt: systems of equations, variables
- Elements of the answer choices: Each answer choice is an integer ranging from 1 to 45.
- Notable features of the answer choices: (C) is 3 times as much as (B), and (D) is three times as much as (C).

- "Bridge" concepts: We can solve the system of equations, and the x-value of that solution will be the right answer.
- Pre-solution patterns (see p. 285): first and last terms in a series are often wrong answers
- Things to look out for: Don't accidentally choose the value of y! Remember that the (x, y) solution must satisfy both of the provided equations!

Solution 1: Graphing: Graph the equations and find the point of intersection. The correct answer is the x-value of that point.

Facebook.com/QuestPreparation   Youtube.com/QuestPrep

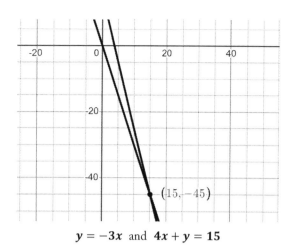

$$y = -3x \text{ and } 4x + y = 15$$

We can see that the lines intersect at $(15, -45)$, so $x = 15$, and the answer is (C), 15.

Solution 2: Concrete: Plug each value from the answer choices in for x in both provided equations, then solve for y. The right answer will produce the same y-value in both equations.

$y = -3x$	$4x + y = 15$	(given equations)
$y = -3(1)$	$4(1) + y = 15$	($x = 1$ from (A) plugged into both equations)
	$4 + y = 15$	(simplify)
$y = -3$	$y = 11$	(simplify)

Plugging $x = 1$ into both equations resulted in two different y-values, so 1 isn't the x-value in the (x, y) solution to the given system of equations. Let's try (B).

$y = -3(5)$	$4(5) + y = 15$	($x = 5$ from (B) plugged into both equations)
	$20 + y = 15$	(simplify)
$y = -15$	$y = -5$	(simplify)

Plugging $x = 5$ into both equations resulted in two different y-values, so 5 isn't the x-value in the (x, y) solution to the given system of equations. Let's try (C).

$y = -3(15)$	$4(15) + y = 15$	($x = 15$ from (C) plugged into both equations)
	$60 + y = 15$	(simplify)
$y = -45$	$y = -45$	(simplify)

Plugging $x = 15$ into both equations resulted in the same y-value for each one, so 15 is the x-value in the (x, y) solution to the given system of equations, which means (C) is correct. Let's try (D) to help make sure we haven't made any mistakes or overlooked anything.

$y = -3(45)$	$4(45) + y = 15$	($x = 45$ from (D) plugged into both equations)
	$180 + y = 15$	(simplify)
$y = -135$	$y = -165$	(simplify)

Plugging $x = 45$ into both equations resulted in two different y-values, so 45 isn't the x-value in the (x, y) solution to the given system of equations. After plugging in each x-value from the answer choices, we can see that the correct answer is (C).

Solution 3: Algebra: Plug $y = -3x$ from the first equation into the second equation, and solve for x.

$4x + (-3x) = 15$	(value of y from first equation plugged into second equation)
$x = 15$	(simplify)

So $x = 15$, and the answer is (C).

ANSWER CHOICE ANALYSIS

(B): This is one third of the correct answer. **(D):** This choice is three times the correct answer, and it's the absolute value of y in the (x, y) solution to the system of equations.

How to check? Plug $x = 15$ into either equation, solve for y, then plug that (x, y) pair into the other equation to make sure it results in a valid statement. Try an alternate approach above. Try to figure out which mistakes could lead to some of the wrong answer choices, and verify that you haven't made any such mistakes.

▶ Post-solution patterns (see page 286): the right answer to the wrong question

Test 1, Module 1, Question 11

- What's the prompt asking for? The equation that's a linear model for the data in the provided figure.
- Math concepts in the prompt: equations, linear models, scatterplots, slope
- Elements of the answer choices: Each answer choice is an equation in $y = mx + b$ form involving y, $1.9x$, and 10.1.
- Notable features of the answer choices: Each answer choice starts with "$y =$" followed by either $-1.9x$ or $1.9x$, which is then followed by either -10.1 or $+10.1$.

- "Bridge" concepts: The graph of the correct answer would be a line that goes more or less through the dots in the provided scatterplot.
- Pre-solution patterns (see p. 285): opposites; wrong answers try to imitate right answers
- Things to look out for: Don't mix up which value in the equations corresponds to slope, and which corresponds to the y-intercept! Don't get confused about what positive versus negative slope looks like on a graph! Don't get confused about what a positive versus negative y-intercept looks like on a graph!

Solution 1: Concrete/graphing: Graph each choice and see which line looks roughly like the scatterplot.

(A) $y = -1.9x - 10.1$

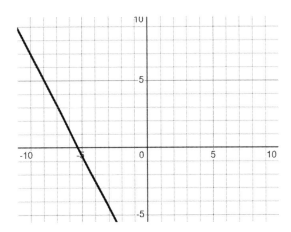

(B) $y = -1.9x + 10.1$

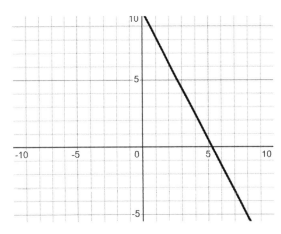

(C) $y = 1.9x - 10.1$

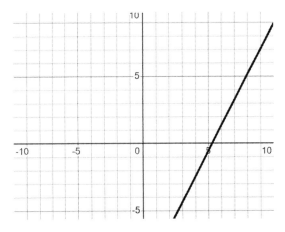

(D) $y = 1.9x + 10.1$

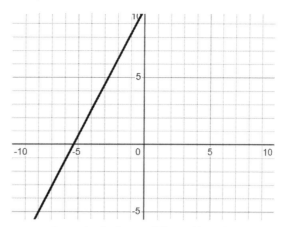

When we graph each answer choice, we can see that only the line in (B) would go through the points in the provided scatterplot, so (B) is right.

Solution 2: Abstract: Think about the slope and y-intercept that the answer must have, based on our understanding of slope-intercept form and the provided figure. Pick the answer choice that meets these requirements.

When we do a vertical scan, we can see that these choices are the four possible combinations of two different elements: either $-1.9x$ or $1.9x$ first, then either -10.1 or $+10.1$ after that.

If we remember our discussion of slope-intercept form from the SAT Math Toolbox, we can recognize that the number multiplied by x is the slope. The choices give us either 1.9 or -1.9 for the slope—the same number, just positive or negative. When we look at the scatterplot we can see that the y-values get lower from left to right, which means the slope is negative. So the right answer must involve $-1.9x$, not $1.9x$, because the line that would model the provided data must have a negative slope.

(Even if we didn't remember slope-intercept form, we could see that in the provided scatterplot, as the x-value increases, the y-value decreases, and we could still use that information to conclude that the number multiplied by x must be negative.)

That leaves either $+10.1$ or -10.1. Again, if we remember slope-intercept form, we know this value is the y-intercept. A linear model of the provided scatterplot would cross the y-axis at a positive y-value, so the y-intercept must be positive. Of the two choices, we know $+10.1$ must be correct.

(Again, even if we didn't remember slope-intercept form, we could see in the provided scatterplot that when $x = 0$, y must be positive, so we could still draw the same conclusion that the correct answer should include $+10.1$, not -10.1.)

With all of this in mind, we know the right answer must be (B).

ANSWER CHOICE ANALYSIS

(A): This choice is the same as the right answer, but with a negative y-intercept instead of a positive one. **(C):** This is the right answer, but with the positive and negative signs of the slope and y-intercept switched. **(D):** This choice is the same as the right answer, but with a positive slope instead of a negative one.

How to check? Verify that the answer you picked has a negative slope and a positive y-intercept. Try an alternate approach above. Try to figure out which mistakes could lead to some of the wrong answer choices, and verify that you haven't made any such mistakes.

Test 1, Module 1, Question 12

- What's the prompt asking for? The number of x-values where $f(x) = 0$

- Math concepts in the prompt: functions, polynomials, variables, constants, graphs, zeros

- Elements of the answer choices: The answer choices are the numbers one through four.

- "Bridge" concepts: When $f(x) = 0$, the graph will cross the x-axis.

- Pre-solution patterns (see p. 285): halves and doubles; first and last terms in a series are often wrong answers

- Things to look out for: Remember that your answer will be the *number* of x-values that satisfy the prompt, not an actual x-value that satisfies the prompt!

Solution 1: Abstract: Think about what happens to the graph of a line when $f(x) = 0$, and use that understanding, along with the provided graph, to determine the number of x-values for which $f(x) = 0$.

When $f(x) = 0$, that's the same as saying that plugging a given x-value into a function produces an output of 0. On the graph of such a function, an x-value that produces an output of 0 is a point directly on the x-axis. This means that when we graph a function, every x-value where $f(x) = 0$ is a point where the graph touches or crosses the x-axis.

We can see in the provided graph that the line crosses the x-axis three times, so there must be three values of x where $f(x) = 0$, which means the answer is (C), three.

ANSWER CHOICE ANALYSIS

(A): This is the absolute value of one of the x-values where $f(x) = 0$. **(B):** This is the number of times when the *slope of the function* is zero, but that's not what the prompt asks for. **(D):** This is one of the x-values where $f(x) = 0$.

How to check? Try to figure out which mistakes could lead to some of the wrong answer choices, and verify that you haven't made any such mistakes.

▶   Post-solution patterns (see page 286): the right answer to the wrong question

---

Test 1, Module 1, Question 13

- What's the prompt asking for? The number of cupcakes that Vivian bought in the situation described in the prompt.

- Math concepts in the prompt: word problems, money, multiplication

- "Bridge" concepts: If we figure out the total cost of the packages of party hats, we can find the total money spent on cupcakes, and then use the cost of each cupcake to find out how many cupcakes Vivian bought.

- Things to look out for: Don't confuse the cost of hats with the cost of cupcakes!

Solution 1: Concrete: Figure out the total cost of the party hats. Subtract the result from the total money spent. The remaining amount is the total money spent on cupcakes; divide that by the cost per cupcake to find the answer.

Using the information in the prompt, we can see that Vivian bought 10 packages of party hats, and that each package of party hats cost \$3. 10 packages of party hats at \$3 each would be $10 \times \$3$, or \$30, so Vivian must have spent \$30 on party hats.

The prompt also tells us that she spent \$71, and that she spent all that money on party hats and cupcakes. If she spent \$30 on party hats, then she must have spent the remainder of the money on cupcakes. Since $\$71 - \$30 = \$41$, she must have spent \$41 on cupcakes.

The prompt says that each cupcake cost \$1. If she spent \$41 on cupcakes, and each cupcake cost her \$1, she must have bought 41 cupcakes. So the correct answer is 41.

Solution 2: Abstract: Turn the information in the prompt into an equation, and solve for the number of cupcakes.

The first sentence tells us that the cost of party hats and cupcakes is equal to \$71, so let's start with that:

$$\text{cost of party hats} + \text{cost of cupcakes} = 71$$

The next sentence mentions that packages of party hats cost \$3—let's use the variable h to represent the number of packages of party hats—which means that each additional package of party hats increases the money that Vivian spent by \$3. We can represent this idea with the expression $3h$.

$$3h + \text{cost of cupcakes} = 71$$

That same sentence tells us that cupcakes are \$1 each (we'll use c to represent the number of cupcakes). Using the same logic as above, we can represent this cost as $1c$, which is the same as c.

$$3h + c = 71$$

The third sentence tells us that Vivian bought 10 packages of party hats. That means our h-value is 10, so we can add this information to our expression:

$$3(10) + c = 71$$

And then we can simplify that expression:

$$30 + c = 71$$
$$30 + c - 30 = 71 - 30$$
$$c = 41$$

So Vivian bought 41 cupcakes, and the answer is 41.

How to check? Work backwards—use your answer for the number of cupcakes, figure out how much money that number of cupcakes would cost, then add that amount to the money spent on packages of party hats, as described in the prompt. See if the result is \$71, as the prompt requires. Try an alternate approach above. Try to figure out which mistakes the College Board might hope you would make in finding your solution, and verify that you haven't made any such mistakes.

Note   This is a great example of a question where you can sometimes get started on your solution even when you're not totally sure yet how you're going to get all the way to the answer. You might read the prompt and have a vague idea that it contains all the information you need, without being totally sure which steps to take. In a situation like this, many trained test-takers will recognize that the prompt tells us Vivian bought 10 packages of party hats, and that each package of party hats cost \$3 each. Using that information, we can see that Vivian spent \$30 on party hats. From there, it becomes clearer that we can use what we just learned to figure out how much money she spent on cupcakes, and then from there we can determine how many cupcakes she bought, since the prompt tells us that each cupcake cost $1. So remember that even if you aren't certain how to execute your solution right away, as long as you can use the provided information in a question to figure *something* out—in this case, the money Vivian spent on party hats—you'll often find that whatever you figured out makes your path to the right answer more obvious.

Test 1, Module 1, Question 14

- What's the prompt asking for? One of the solutions to the given equation.

- Math concepts in the prompt: equations, polynomials, variables, exponents

- "Bridge" concepts: A solution to the equation is a z-value that will cause the expression on the left to equal zero.

- Things to look out for: The phrase "one of the solutions" tells us that there is more than one solution to this equation—make sure this fits with your understanding of the question and your approach! Don't make a mistake related to sign!

Solution 1: Graphing: Graph the provided equation, swapping z for x. The graph will show a vertical line for every x-value that's a solution to the equation.

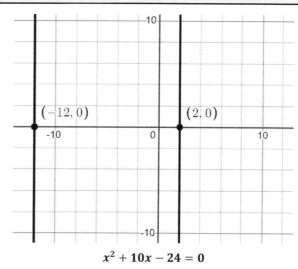

$$x^2 + 10x - 24 = 0$$

We can see that the given equation is true when $z = 2$ or $z = -12$. The question asks for "one of the solutions to the given equation," so the correct answer can be either 2 or -12.

Solution 2: Algebra: Factor the provided equation by reverse-FOILing. Use the factors to find the z-values that satisfy the given equation.

$z^2 + 10z - 24 = 0$	(given equation)
$(z + 12)(z - 2) = 0$	(reverse-FOIL—see the discussion of this step below)
$z + 12 = 0 \qquad z - 2 = 0$	(set each factor equal to 0)
$z = -12 \qquad z = 2$	(isolate z)

We can see that the expression will be true when either $z = -12$ or $z = 2$. The question asks for "one of the solutions to the given equation," so the correct answer is either 2 or -12.

Let's discuss the reverse-FOIL step for a moment, because some test-takers won't be comfortable with that. When we reverse-FOIL, we're going to end up with two parenthetical expressions multiplied together, and each of those expressions will be a variable (in this case "z"), a plus sign or minus sign, and then a constant, which we can think of like this:
$$(z \pm \, ?)(z \pm \, ?)$$
In this case, we can see that the last term in the provided polynomial is "-24." Because that number is negative, we know that it must be the result of multiplying a positive number and a negative number, which means the constant in one of the factors is a positive number, and the constant in the other factor is a negative number (again, because these are the two numbers we multiply together to get -24, and we can only get a negative number if one number being multiplied is negative and the other is positive). So let's update our expression:
$$(z + \, ?)(z - \, ?)$$
Since the two constants multiplied together equal -24, they must be factors of 24. Also, since the coefficient of z in the middle term of the provided polynomial is 10, then the sum of these numbers is 10—remember, one of these numbers is negative, and the other is positive, so we can also think of 10 as the difference between their absolute values.

(If you're not super comfortable with math, that might not sound helpful, but keep reading and it should start to make more sense.)

Let's think of numbers we can multiply together to get 24. Here are some:

$$24 \times 1 \qquad 12 \times 2 \qquad 8 \times 3 \qquad 6 \times 4$$

Now that we know some numbers that equal 24 when multiplied together, we should ask ourselves whether any of them have a difference of 10. When we do that, we see that 12 and 2 have a difference of 10. It looks like 12 and 2 are our missing numbers, so now we just need to figure out whether we should be adding 10 and subtracting 2, or the other way around—that is, whether the factored expression should be:

$$(z + 12)(z - 2)$$

Or:

$$(z + 2)(z - 12)$$

In the given polynomial, the z-term is "$+ 10z$," not "$- 10z$." Since it's a positive value, it must be that the larger of the two numbers (12) is added, while the smaller of the two numbers (2) is subtracted. That gives us:

$$(z + 12)(z - 2)$$

This might seem like a lot, but once you get used to it you can usually do it fairly quickly. You're pretty much just thinking of factors that multiply out to the third term in the polynomial, and add up to the coefficient of the second term in the polynomial; after that it's just a matter of keeping the plus and minus signs straight. Also, once you've got your result, you can pretty quickly multiply it out to make sure you did it right.

For more on all this, see "Factoring polynomials" in the Math Toolbox on page 257. Also, notice that the graphing approach above avoids all of this algebra anyway, and make sure that you become really comfortable using the SAT calculator before test day (see "Special Technique: Using The Surprisingly Powerful Digital SAT Calculator" on page 280 for more.)

How to check? If you did FOIL in reverse, multiply out the factors you found to verify that the result is the original polynomial that you factored. Try an alternate approach above. Try to figure out which mistakes the College Board might hope you would make in finding your solution, and verify that you haven't made any such mistakes.

Test 1, Module 1, Question 15

- **What's the prompt asking for?** The number of cells per milliliter there will be 15 hours after the initial observation.

- **Math concepts in the prompt:** word problems, doubling, time

- **Elements of the answer choices:** Each answer choice is an integer ranging from 1,500,000 to 9,600,000.

- **Notable features of the answer choices:** (C) is three times as much as (A). (D) is four times as much as (B).

- **"Bridge" concepts:** We can take the initial number of cells per milliliter and double it the number of times described in the prompt to find the answer.

- **Things to look out for:** Don't mix up which numbers are doubling, or how many times they double in the given time period!

Solution 1: Concrete: Start with the number of cells per milliliter from the prompt, then double that number as described.

The prompt tells us that there were 300,000 cells per milliliter to start with, and that "the number of cells per milliliter doubles every 3 hours." It wants to know the number of cells per milliliter 15 hours after the initial observation, so let's think through this process three hours at a time.

at 0 hours:	300,000	(initial number of cells per milliliter)
at 3 hours:	600,000	(double the initial 300,000 cells per milliliter)
at 6 hours:	1,200,000	(double the 600,000 cells per milliliter after 3 hours)
at 9 hours:	2,400,000	(double the 1,200,000 cells per milliliter after 6 hours)
at 12 hours:	4,800,000	(double the 2,400,000 cells per milliliter after 9 hours)
at 15 hours:	9,600,000	(double the 4,800,000 cells per milliliter after 12 hours)

So, after doubling every three hours for 15 hours, the initial 300,000 cells per milliliter will be 9,600,000 cells per milliliter, which means (D) is correct.

Solution 2: Abstract: Create a mathematical expression that represents the situation from the prompt, and use it to find the answer.

If the number of cells per milliliter doubles every 3 hours over the course of 15 hours, that's the same as doubling 5 times, because $\frac{15 \text{ hours}}{3 \text{ hours}} = 5$. Doubling 5 times is the same as multiplying by 2 five times, which is the same as multiplying by 2^5. So the answer is $300,000 \times 2^5$, which is 9,600,000. So the answer is (D).

ANSWER CHOICE ANALYSIS

(A): This is the result of starting at zero and adding 300,000 cells per milliliter 5 times, rather than starting with 300,000 cells per milliliter and *doubling* that initial value 5 times. **(B):** This is the result of doubling the initial value every *5* hours for 15 hours, instead of every *3* hours for 15 hours. **(C):** This is the result of starting at zero and adding 300,000 cells per milliliter 15 times.

How to check? Make sure you doubled the initial number the correct number of times. Verify that you doubled the amount each time, rather than just adding 300,000 each time. Try an alternate approach above. Try to figure out which mistakes could lead to some of the wrong answer choices, and verify that you haven't made any such mistakes.

▶ Post-solution patterns (see page 286): the right answer to the wrong question

Test 1, Module 1, Question 16

- **What's the prompt asking for?** The expression that's equivalent to $6x^8y^2 + 12x^2y^2$.

- **Math concepts in the prompt:** polynomials, variables, exponents, equivalent expressions

- **Elements of the answer choices:** Each answer choice is a variable expression starting with $6x^2y^2$.

- **Notable features of the answer choices:** Each answer choice is $6x^2y^2$ multiplied by a different expression involving an exponent of x.

- **Pre-solution patterns** (see p. 285): wrong answers try to imitate right answers

- **Things to look out for:** Keep track of the number of xs and ys that should be multiplied together! Verify whether any given variable term should be added to, or multiplied by, the expression!

Solution 1: Algebra: Multiply out each expression in the answer choices. The one that matches the given expression is the right answer.

(A)	$6x^2y^2(2x^6) = 12x^8y^2$	(expression from (A) multiplied out)
(B)	$6x^2y^2(x^4) = 6x^6y^2$	(expression from (B) multiplied out)
(C)	$6x^2y^2(x^6 + 2) = 6x^8y^2 + 12x^2y^2$	(expression from (C) multiplied out)
(D)	$6x^2y^2(x^4 + 2) = 6x^6y^2 + 12x^2y^2$	(expression from (D) multiplied out)

When we multiply out each choice, we can see that (C) is equivalent to the provided expression, which means (C) is right.

Solution 2: Test-smart: Use the vertical scan to determine that we can factor out $6x^2y^2$ from the given expression to make that expression look the same as the right answer.

When we use the vertical scan to evaluate the differences and similarities among the answer choices, we can see that every answer choice is $6x^2y^2$ multiplied by an expression in parentheses. If we haven't realized it already, this should be a hint that the equivalent expression will be a factored version of the provided expression where we factor out the same term from each of the two terms being added together in the provided expression—that is, from $6x^8y^2$ and $12x^2y^2$. We can verify this by checking that $6x^2y^2$ can be factored out from each of those terms in the provided expression, and it can—each term includes a constant that's divisible by 6, and an exponent expression divisible by both x^2 and y^2.

(Note that this is an excellent example of the value of the vertical scan and the importance of looking at the answer choices before you start solving a problem. An untrained test-taker might immediately start trying to figure out what to factor out of $6x^8y^2 + 12x^2y^2$, and then spend valuable time determining that $6x^2y^2$ can be factored out of that given expression—but if he had just checked the answer choices from the beginning, he would see that every choice is $6x^2y^2$ multiplied by something, so $6x^2y^2$ *must* be the expression that gets factored out. Always remember to consider the answer choices before you start your solution to an SAT Math question!)

Now that we know we need to factor $6x^2y^2$ out of the provided expression, we can look at the constant (6), the x-term (x^2), and the y-term (y^2), and see how each of those would factor out of each corresponding component of both $6x^8y^2$ and $12x^2y^2$. We'll start with factoring $6x^2y^2$ out of $6x^8y^2$, which is the same as dividing $6x^8y^2$ by $6x^2y^2$.

$$\frac{6x^8y^2}{6x^2y^2}$$
(first term in the provided expression divided by the number we're factoring out of that expression)

$$x^6$$
(simplify)

When we do that, we can see that the 6 and the y^2 cancel each other out, and the remaining $\frac{x^8}{x^2}$ reduces to x^6. Now let's repeat this process with the second term in the provided expression, which means dividing $12x^2y^2$ by $6x^2y^2$.

$$\frac{12x^2y^2}{6x^2y^2}$$
(second term in the provided expression divided by the number we're factoring out of that expression)

$$2$$
(simplify)

In this case, the x^2 and the y^2 cancel out, leaving $\frac{12}{6}$, which reduces to 2.

Now that we've factored $6x^2y^2$ from each of those terms, which gave us x^6 and 2, we just multiply $6x^2y^2$ by the sum of x^6 and 2, which gives us $6x^2y^2(x^6 + 2)$. This matches (C), and (C) is the correct answer.

ANSWER CHOICE ANALYSIS

(A): This is the correct answer, except with 2 multiplied by x^6 instead of added to it. **(D):** This choice would be correct if it were true that $6x^2y^2(x^4)$ were equal to $6x^8y^2$, but that's not how multiplying exponents works—instead, $6x^2y^2(x^4) = 6x^6y^2$.

How to check? Try an alternate approach above. Try to figure out which mistakes could lead to some of the wrong answer choices, and verify that you haven't made any such mistakes.

Test 1, Module 1, Question 17

- **What's the prompt asking for?** The best interpretation of what x represents in the equation from the prompt.

- **Math concepts in the prompt:** word problems, modeling, equations, variables

- **Elements of the answer choices:** Each answer choice describes an idea from the situation in the prompt.

- **Notable features of the answer choices:** Two answer choices talk about the "average number of trees per hectare," while the other two talk about the "total number of trees." Two answer choices mention the park, and two mention the residential area.

- **Pre-solution patterns (see p. 285):** wrong answers try to imitate right answers

- **Things to look out for:** Don't confuse x with y! Remember that the prompt asks for the interpretation of x, not the expression $2x$ from the equation!

Solution 1: Careful reading: See how the provided equation relates to the situation described in the prompt. Consider how each answer choice would fit into that equation as x, if it were correct. Eliminate each choice that contradicts the relationships described in the prompt, and confirm that the remaining choice accurately reflects the ideas in the prompt.

If (A) were right, that would mean the given equation multiplies the average number of trees per hectare in the park by 2 as part of the process of finding the "total number of trees in the neighborhood." That makes sense, because part of figuring out how many trees are in the neighborhood would be figuring out how many trees are in the park, and we could do that by multiplying the average number of trees per hectare in the park by the number of hectares in the park. For example, if there were 15 trees per hectare of park, and the park was 2 hectares, we would multiply 15 by 2 to find that there are 30 trees in the park. Choice (A) looks good, but let's check the other choices.

If (B) were right, that would mean the given equation multiplies the average number of trees per hectare in the residential area by 2. But the prompt tells us that the residential area is 35 hectares, so multiplying the average number of trees per hectare in the residential area by 2 wouldn't really tell us anything relevant—we would need to multiply it by 35, not 2, to figure out the total number of trees in the residential area, since the residential area is 35 hectares. This choice doesn't seem to make sense; let's look at (C).

(C) says the "total number of trees in the park," but if that were true, that would mean the provided equation multiplies the total number of trees in the park by 2. There's nothing in the prompt to indicate that doubling the total number of trees in the park would help us find the total number of trees in the neighborhood (it doesn't say there are two parks that are the same size, or anything like that), so this choice doesn't make sense. Let's check (D).

(D) has the same basic problem as (C); it would cause the provided equation to take the total number of trees in one of the areas and then double that number, and nothing in the provided text indicates that we need to do that to find the total number of trees in the neighborhood.

After considering each answer choice, we can see that (A) is correct.

Solution 2: Abstract: Analyze the prompt and the provided equation to figure out what x must represent.

The variable x is multiplied by 2. In the provided text, 2 is only mentioned in connection with the size of the park, not the residential area—so we can eliminate (B) and (D), because they only mention the residential area, and not the park. Of the remaining choices, one says x is the average number of trees per hectare in the park, while the other says x is the total number of trees in the park. Again, x is multiplied by 2, the number of hectares in the park—we would need to multiply the average number of trees per hectare in the park by the number of hectares in the park to find the total number of trees in the park, as (A) would require, but we wouldn't need to multiply "the total number of trees in the park" by anything to find the total number of trees in the park. So because x is multiplied by 2, we can eliminate the choice that mentions "the total number of trees," which is (C).

After eliminating (B), (C), and (D), we can see that (A) is right.

ANSWER CHOICE ANALYSIS

(B): This is what y represents. **(C):** This is what $2x$ represents. **(D):** This is what $35y$ represents.

How to check? Try an alternate approach above. Try to figure out which mistakes could lead to some of the wrong answer choices, and verify that you haven't made any such mistakes.

▶ Post-solution patterns (see page 286): the right answer to the wrong question

Test 1, Module 1, Question 18

- What's the prompt asking for? The equation that represents the relationships shown in the graph.
- Math concepts in the prompt: word problems, line graphs, variables, x-values, y-values
- Elements of the answer choices: Each answer choice is an equation involving x and y.
- Notable features of the answer choices: Two answer choices are in slope-intercept form, and the other two

are in standard form. The constants 8, 12, and 480 appear in most or all of the choices.
- "Bridge" concepts: The graph of the right answer will be the line in the provided figure.
- Pre-solution patterns (see p. 285): wrong answers try to imitate right answers
- Things to look out for: Don't confuse x and y!

Solution 1: Graphing: Graph each choice. The result that matches the provided graph is the correct answer.

(A)

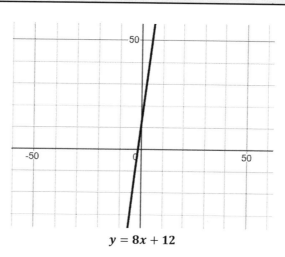

$$y = 8x + 12$$

(B)

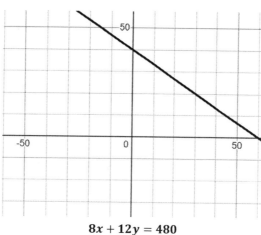

$$8x + 12y = 480$$

(C)

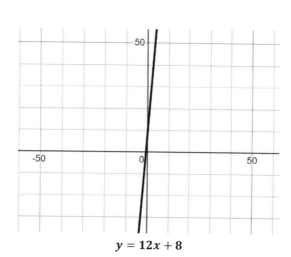

$$y = 12x + 8$$

(D)

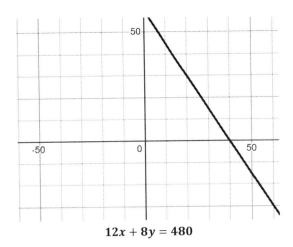

$$12x + 8y = 480$$

We can see that (B) matches the provided graph, so (B) is correct (notice that (B) includes points at (0,40) and (60,0), just like the provided graph).

Solution 2: Concrete: Find an (x, y) value from the provided graph, and plug it into the provided equations. Eliminate any choice that doesn't contain that point.

The graph has a point at $(0, 40)$, so we know the correct answer will have a valid solution where $x = 0$ and $y = 40$.

(A)	$(40) = 8(0) + 12$	$40 \neq 12$	($x = 0$ and $y = 40$ plugged into the equation from (A))
(B)	$8(0) + 12(40) = 480$	$480 = 480$	($x = 0$ and $y = 40$ plugged into the equation from (B))
(C)	$(40) = 12(0) + 8$	$40 \neq 8$	($x = 0$ and $y = 40$ plugged into the equation from (C))
(D)	$12(0) + 8(40) = 480$	$320 \neq 480$	($x = 0$ and $y = 40$ plugged into the equation from (D))

When we plug $(0, 40)$ into each equation in the answer choices, only (B) results in a valid equation. So (B) is correct.

ANSWER CHOICE ANALYSIS

(A): We can eliminate this choice because it would result in a line with a positive slope, but we can see that the line in the graph has a negative slope. **(C):** This choice has the same problem as (A). **(D):** This is the right answer with the coefficients of x and y switched.

How to check? Pick a point from the provided graph, and verify that the (x, y) coordinates of that point are a solution to the equation in the choice you picked. Try an alternate approach above. Try to figure out which mistakes could lead to some of the wrong answer choices, and verify that you haven't made any such mistakes.

Test 1, Module 1, Question 19

- What's the prompt asking for? How many times greater the area of circle B is than the area of circle A.
- Math concepts in the prompt: circles, radii, variables, constants
- Elements of the answer choices: Each answer choice is an integer ranging from 43 to 1,849.
- Notable features of the answer choices: (B) is twice as much as (A). (C) is the sum of (A) and (B). (D) is (A) squared.

- "Bridge" concepts: We can us the formula for the area of a circle to make the comparison that the prompt asks for. We don't need to know the value of n to answer the question.
- Pre-solution patterns (see p. 285): halves and doubles
- Things to look out for: Make sure to use the formula for area, not circumference! Make sure you square the relevant expressions correctly!

Solution 1: Concrete: Pick a value for n, then calculate the areas of the two circles with that n- value and find the ratio of the area of circle B to the area of circle A.

The prompt says "n is a positive constant," so we can pick any positive constant for this value. Let's say $n = 4$. So the radius of circle A must be $3(4)$, or 12, and the radius of circle B must be $129(4)$, or 516. We can use these radii to find the area of each circle, and then compare those areas as described in the prompt.

$A = \pi r^2$	(formula for area of a circle)
$A = \pi(12)^2$	(plug in $r = 12$ to find the area of circle A)
$A = 144\pi$	(simplify)

So the area of circle A is 144π. Let's find the area of circle B.

$A = \pi r^2$	(formula for area of a circle)

$$A = \pi(516)^2$$ (plug in $r = 516$ to find the area of circle B)
$$A = 266{,}256\pi$$ (simplify)

So the area of circle B is $266{,}256\pi$. We can find the ratio of the area of circle B to the area of circle A by creating a fraction with the area of circle B in the numerator and the area of circle A in the denominator.

$$\frac{266{,}256\pi}{144\pi}$$

We can cancel out π, which leaves:

$$\frac{266{,}256}{144}$$

When we reduce that fraction, we get 1,849, which is choice (D). So (D) is correct.

Solution 2: Algebra: We can use the provided radii to find the area of each circle, and then compare those areas to each other to find the answer.

$$A = \pi r^2$$ (formula for area of a circle)
$$A = \pi(3n)^2$$ (plug in $r = 3n$ to find the area of circle A)
$$A = \pi 9n^2$$ (simplify)

So the area of circle A is $\pi 9n^2$. Let's find the area of circle B.

$$A = \pi r^2$$ (formula for area of a circle)
$$A = \pi(129n)^2$$ (plug in $r = 129n$ to find the area of circle B)
$$A = \pi 16{,}641n^2$$ (simplify)

So the area of circle B is $\pi 16{,}641n^2$. We can find the ratio of the area of circle B to the area of circle A by creating a fraction with the area of circle B in the numerator and the area of circle A in the denominator.

$$\frac{\pi 16{,}641n^2}{\pi 9n^2}$$

Both π and n^2 cancel out, which leaves:

$$\frac{16{,}641}{9}$$

When we reduce that fraction, we get 1,849, which is choice (D). So (D) is correct.

Solution 3: Test-smart: We can compare the squares of the radii of the two circles to find the answer to the question.

If we know that the formula for the area of a circle is $A = \pi r^2$, then we can find the ratio of the areas of two different circles by comparing the squares of the their radii (multiplying the square of each radius by π doesn't change the ratio between the two squared radii, so we don't need to consider π in making this comparison).

In this case that gives us $\frac{(129n)^2}{(3n)^2}$, which is equal to $\frac{16{,}641n^2}{9n^2}$, which reduces to 1,849. So we can see that (D) is correct.

ANSWER CHOICE ANALYSIS

(A): This is the ratio of the radius of circle B to the radius of circle A, not the ratio of their *areas*, as the prompt requires. **(B):** This is the result of *doubling* the ratio of the radius of circle B to the radius of circle A, rather than *squaring* it.

How to check? Double-check that you made the comparison between the *areas* of the circles, and not some other measurement. Try an alternate approach above. Try to figure out which mistakes could lead to some of the wrong answer choices, and verify that you haven't made any such mistakes.

▶ Post-solution patterns (see page 286): the right answer to the wrong question

Test 1, Module 1, Question 20

- What's the prompt asking for? The maximum data value in the data set.
- Math concepts in the prompt: data, frequency tables, maximum

- "Bridge" concepts: The maximum value in a data set doesn't change depending on how many of that maximum data value there are.
- Things to look out for: Make sure you understand what the question is asking, and what the numbers in the table represent!

Solution 1: Careful reading: Read the table and find the highest value in the table.

The lefthand column is labeled "Data value." The maximum value in that column is 14. So the answer is 14.

How to check? Reread the prompt to make sure you haven't overlooked anything. Try to figure out which mistakes the College Board might hope you would make in finding your solution, and verify that you haven't made any such mistakes.

> **Note** This is a great example of an SAT Math question that seems really simple... and *is* really simple. This will probably happen at least a couple of times on test day—just reread the prompt carefully, make sure you understand what it's asking, mark the down the correct answer, and move on. Don't assume the question has to be complex!

- **What's the prompt asking for?** The value of r in the provided equation.
- **Math concepts in the prompt:** circles, diameters, endpoints, equations, variables
- **"Bridge" concepts:** The provided endpoints must lie on the graph of the circle. Also, r is the radius of the circle.
- **Things to look out for:** Don't mix up the x and y values! Don't make a mistake related to sign!

Solution 1: Concrete: Plug the coordinates of the endpoints into the provided equation, then solve for r.

We know that the endpoints of a circle's diameter must lie on that circle, by definition. So $(2, 4)$ and $(2, 14)$ are both coordinate pairs that must satisfy the provided equation. We can plug either of these (x, y) coordinate pairs into that equation and solve for r. We'll use $(2, 4)$, just because lower numbers tend to make calculations easier.

$$(x - 2)^2 + (y - 9)^2 = r^2 \qquad \text{(provided equation)}$$
$$(2 - 2)^2 + (4 - 9)^2 = r^2 \qquad \text{(plug in } x = 2 \text{ and } y = 4\text{)}$$
$$(0)^2 + (-5)^2 = r^2 \qquad \text{(simplify)}$$
$$25 = r^2 \qquad \text{(simplify)}$$
$$5 = r \qquad \text{(simplify)}$$

So r is 5, and the answer is 5.

Solution 2: Definitions and properties: Use your understanding of the standard equation of a circle to relate the length of the diameter described in the prompt to the r-value we need to find.

If we're familiar with the standard equation of a circle, we know that the r-value in the provided equation is the radius of the circle. We should also know that the radius of a circle is half the diameter of that circle. The prompt tells us a diameter of the circle has endpoints at $(2, 4)$ and $(2, 14)$. We can tell that these endpoints are 10 units apart, because they both have an x-value of 2, and the difference between their y-values is $14 - 4$, which is 10. If the diameter is 10, then the radius must be 5, which means r is 5, and the correct answer to this question is 5.

How to check? After you find the r-value, plug the (x, y) values from either endpoint into the resulting equation and verify that it results in a true statement. Try an alternate approach above. Try to figure out which mistakes the College Board might hope you would make in finding your solution, and verify that you haven't made any such mistakes.

> **Note** This is a great example of a question where we can quickly find the answer whether we're comfortable with the subject matter or not—if we recognize the standard equation of a circle, then we know the r-value we need to find is the radius, and we can find that value using the length of the diameter. If we don't recognize that equation, we can still just plug the provided values into the provided equation and solve for r, whether we realize what r signifies or not.

- **What's the prompt asking for?** The measure of angle T in degrees.
- **Math concepts in the prompt:** angles, radians, π, degrees
- **Elements of the answer choices:** Each answer choice is an integer ranging from 75 to 390.
- **Notable features of the answer choices:** (C) is the sum of (A) and (B). (D) is twice as much as (C).
- **Pre-solution patterns (see p. 285):** halves and doubles
- **Things to look out for:** Remember that 360° is the same as 2π radians, not π radians! Remember to keep track of the denominators when working with fractions!

Solution 1: Concrete: Convert the provided angle measures to degrees, then add the results.

The provided reference sheet tells us that 360° is the same as 2π radians, which means 180° must be the same as π radians. We can use this information to convert the provided angle measures to degrees, and then answer the question.

The prompt tells us that the measure of angle R is $\frac{2\pi}{3}$ radians. That's the same as $\frac{2}{3}$ of π radians, and π radians is 180°, as we just established—so $\frac{2}{3}$ of π radians must be the same as $\frac{2}{3}$ of 180°, which is 120°. So the measure of angle R in degrees is 120°.

The prompt tells us that the measure of angle T is $\frac{5\pi}{12}$ radians larger than that of angle R, so we need to convert this value to degrees as well, and add it to the value we just found to calculate the measure of angle T.

Using the same process we used to convert the measure of angle R, we can realize that $\frac{5\pi}{12}$ radians is the same as $\frac{5}{12}$ of π radians. Since π radians is 180°, $\frac{5}{12}$ of π radians must be the same as $\frac{5}{12}$ of 180°, which is 75°. So the measure of angle T in degrees is 75° greater than the measure of angle R, which we already found to be 120°. That means the measure of angle T is 120° + 75°, or 195°, and (C) is correct.

Solution 2: Concrete: Add the provided fractions, then convert the result to degrees.

We want to add two fractions; one has a 3 in the denominator and one has a 12 in the denominator. In order to add these two fractions, we need them to have the same denominator. We can multiply the first fraction by $\frac{4}{4}$ so that it will have a 12 in its denominator; the result will be $\frac{2\pi}{3} \times \frac{4}{4}$, which is the same $\frac{8\pi}{12}$.

Now we know the first fraction is equivalent to $\frac{8\pi}{12}$. The prompt tells us that the measure of angle T, which is what we're trying to find, is $\frac{5\pi}{12}$ radians greater than the measure of angle R. So we can add $\frac{8\pi}{12}$ radians to $\frac{5\pi}{12}$ radians to get the measure of angle T. $\frac{8\pi}{12} + \frac{5\pi}{12} = \frac{13\pi}{12}$, so the measure of angle T is $\frac{13\pi}{12}$ radians.

$\frac{13}{12}$ radians is the same as $\frac{13}{12}$ of π radians, and π radians is 180°, as we just established in the previous solution—so $\frac{13}{12}$ of π radians must be the same as $\frac{13}{12}$ of 180°, which is 195°. So the measure of angle T in degrees is 195°, and the answer is (C).

Solution 3: Test-smart: Use your understanding of radians and degrees to approximate the sum of the two given values, and eliminate every choice that isn't close to that approximation.

In order to answer this question, we need to add $\frac{2\pi}{3}$ radians and $\frac{5\pi}{12}$ radians. $\frac{2\pi}{3}$ is a little more than half of π, and $\frac{5\pi}{12}$ is a little less than half of π, so adding these fractions together should give us a value around π. π radians is the same as 180°, so the answer should be around 180°. The only answer that's right around 180° is the right answer, (C), 195°.

ANSWER CHOICE ANALYSIS

(A): This is $\frac{5\pi}{12}$ radians in degrees. **(B):** This is the measure of angle R (that is, $\frac{2\pi}{3}$ radians) in degrees. **(D):** This is double the right answer; this would be correct if it were true that π radians = 360°.

How to check? Try an alternate approach above. Try to figure out which mistakes could lead to some of the wrong answer choices, and verify that you haven't made any such mistakes.

▶ Post-solution patterns (see page 286): right approach, wrong step; the right answer to the wrong question

Test 1, Module 1, Question 23

- What's the prompt asking for? The area of the town in square yards.
- Math concepts in the prompt: area, square miles, square yards, unit conversion
- Elements of the answer choices: Each answer choice is an integer ranging from 404 to 13,505,536.

- Notable features of the answer choices: The increase in size from one choice to the next in substantial.
- "Bridge" concepts: If 1 mile = 1,760 yards, then 1 square mile = 1,760² square yards, or 3,097,600 square yards.
- Things to look out for: Don't conclude that 1 square mile = 1,760 square yards!

Solution 1: Concrete: Figure out how many square yards are in a square mile, then multiply the result by the number of square miles to find the area of the town.

If 1 mile is equal to 1,760 yards, then one square mile must be equal to 1,760 × 1,760, or 3,097,600 square yards.

If one square mile is 3,097,600 square yards, then 4.36 square miles must be 4.36 × 3,097,600 square yards, or 13,505,536 square yards. So (D) is correct.

Solution 2: Test-smart: Note that even one square mile is more than one million square yards, so multiple square miles must also be more than one million square yards. Eliminate each choice that is less than one million square yards.

As part of finding this answer, we'll need to square 1,760 to find out how many square yards are in a square mile. 1,000 squared is 1,000,000, so 1,760 squared must be more than 1,000,000. If just one square mile is more than 1,000,000 square yards, then 4.36 square miles must be even more than that—the only answer that's greater than 1,000,000 is (D), so (D) must be right.

(A): This is the number of yards in a mile divided by the area of the town in square miles. This represents two errors—thinking that there are 1,760 square yards in a square mile, and dividing the number of square yards in a square mile by 4.36, instead of multiplying. **(B):** This would be the answer if there were 1,760 square yards in a square mile, rather than 3,097,600 square yards in a square mile. **(C):** This is the result if you find the number of square yards in a square mile and then *divide* the result by 4.36, instead of *multiplying* it by 4.36.

How to check? Verify that you squared the right value. Try an alternate approach above. Try to figure out which mistakes could lead to some of the wrong answer choices, and verify that you haven't made any such mistakes.

▶   Post-solution patterns (see page 286):   the right answer to the wrong question

Test 1, Module 1, Question 24

- What's the prompt asking for? The x-intercept of line k.

- Math concepts in the prompt: lines, (x, y) coordinate pairs, translation

- Elements of the answer choices: Each answer choice is an (x, y) coordinate pair with a negative fraction for an x-value and zero for a y-value.

- Notable features of the answer choices: The x-value in two choices has a denominator of 6, while one choice has an x-value with a denominator of 3, and one choice has an x-value with a denominator of 2.

- "Bridge" concepts: If we know multiple points on line k, we can use them to find the x-intercept of line k.

- Things to look out for: Keep track of which line is which, and whether it's being translated up or down! Remember to find the x-intercept of line k, not the y-intercept of line k!

Solution 1: Concrete: Use the three provided (x, y) coordinate pairs to find three points that lie on line k. Use those points to find the slope and x-intercept of line k.

In order to find the x-intercept of line k, we need to find the slope of line k, and use that information along with the provided points to figure out where line k crosses the x-axis.

The prompt tells us that the provided points correspond to line h, and that "line k is the result of translating line h down 5 units." If line k is line h translated down 5 units, that's the same as saying that every point on line k can be found by subtracting 5 from the y-value of a point on line h. So let's find the three points on line k that correspond to the three provided points on line h by subtracting 5 from each of those y-values. That gives us the following three points:

$$(18, 125), (23, 155), (26,173)$$

Now that we have three points from line k, let's find the slope of that line. The slope of a line is its "rise" over its "run,"—that is, slope is a fraction with the distance the line travels vertically between two points in its numerator, and the distance the line travels horizontally between those two points in its denominator. That's the same as the difference between the two y-values of any two points on the line over the difference between the two x-values of those same points.

So we can calculate the slope of this line with any two points on the line; I'll take the first two points above for no particular reason.

$$\frac{155 - 125}{23 - 18} = \frac{30}{5} = 6$$

So the slope of the line is 6. That means for every unit the line travels to the right, it travels 6 units up. It also means that for every unit the line travels left, it travels 6 units down. From the point $(18, 125)$, line k needs to travel 125 units down to get to the x-axis (remember that we're finding the x-intercept, which is where the line crosses the x-axis).

If the lines travels 6 units down for every 1 unit left, we can set up the following proportion to figure out how many units to the left will correspond to traveling 125 units down:

$$\frac{6}{1} = \frac{125}{x}$$

Now we can cross multiply to find the value of x:

$$6x = 125$$
$$x = \frac{125}{6}$$

So line k will cross the x-axis $\frac{125}{6}$ units to the left of $(18, 125)$. We can convert 18 to sixths by multiplying it by $\frac{6}{6}$, which gives us $\frac{18}{1} \times \frac{6}{6} = \frac{108}{6}$.

Now let's subtract $\frac{125}{6}$ from $\frac{108}{6}$ to find the x-value that's $\frac{125}{6}$ to the left of $x = 18$:

$$\frac{108}{6} - \frac{125}{6} = -\frac{17}{6}$$

So line k crosses the x-axis at $\left(-\frac{17}{6}, 0\right)$, and the correct answer is (D).

Solution 2: Concrete: Use point-slope form and the information in the prompt to find the x-intercept of line k.

    If we know point-slope form, we can find the slope as described in the previous solution (which is 6), and subtract 5 from each y-value in the provided table to get three points from line k (although we only need one). Then we can use one of those points and the slope to get an equation for line k in point-slope form. We'll use $(18, 125)$.

$$y - y_1 = m(x - x_1) \qquad \text{(point-slope form)}$$
$$y - 125 = 6(x - 18) \qquad \text{(plug in } m = 6, x_1 = 18, \text{ and } y_1 = 125\text{)}$$

    Now that we have an equation for line k, we can set y equal to zero and solve for x (remember that the x-intercept is the point where the line crosses the x-axis, which is a point where $y = 0$, by definition).

$$y - 125 = 6(x - 18) \qquad \text{(equation we found for line } k\text{)}$$
$$0 - 125 = 6(x - 18) \qquad \text{(plug in } y = 0\text{)}$$
$$-125 = 6(x - 18) \qquad \text{(simplify)}$$
$$-125 = 6x - 108 \qquad \text{(simplify)}$$
$$-17 = 6x \qquad \text{(add 108 to both sides)}$$
$$-\frac{17}{6} = x \qquad \text{(divide both sides by 6)}$$

So $x = -\frac{17}{6}$ when $y = 0$, which means line k crosses the x-axis at $\left(-\frac{17}{6}, 0\right)$, and the correct answer is (D).

Solution 3: Graphing: Graph the equation and find where it crosses the x-axis.

    Once we find the equation of line k in point-slope form in the previous solution, we can simply graph line k by entering $y - 125 = 6(x - 18)$ into the provided calculator. Then, we can use the graph to find where the line crosses the x-axis.

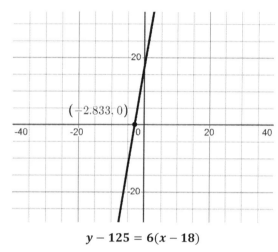

$$y - 125 = 6(x - 18)$$

    At this point, we might notice that the answer choices are fractions, but the x-value of the coordinates of the point on the graph above is a decimal expression. To address this, we can just use our calculator to find decimal approximations of each point in the answer choices.

(A) $\left(-\frac{26}{3}, 0\right) = (-8.666, 0)$

(B) $\left(-\frac{9}{2}, 0\right) = (-4.5, 0)$

(C) $\left(-\frac{11}{3}, 0\right) = (-3.666, 0)$

(D) $\left(-\frac{17}{6}, 0\right) = (-2.833, 0)$

When we do this, we can see that the answer is (D).

ANSWER CHOICE ANALYSIS

(A): This would be the result if line h were moved *left* 5 units, instead of *down* 5 units. **(C):** This is the x-intercept of line h.

How to check? Try an alternate approach above. Try to figure out which mistakes could lead to some of the wrong answer choices, and verify that you haven't made any such mistakes.

Test 1, Module 1, Question 25

- What's the prompt asking for? The value of c in the situation described in the prompt.

- Math concepts in the prompt: graphs, polynomials equations, intersection, variables

---

- Elements of the answer choices: Each answer choice is a negative number ranging from $-\frac{481}{4}$ to $-\frac{9}{2}$.
- Notable features of the answer choices: (A), (B), and (C) form a series where each choice is $\frac{81}{4}$ more than the previous choice.
- "Bridge" concepts: If the provided equation is a parabola that opens up or down, then a horizontal line that intersects the parabola at one point must intersect that parabola at its vertex.
- Pre-solution patterns (see p. 285): first and last terms in a series are often wrong answers
- Things to look out for: Don't make a small mistake related to sign!

Solution 1: Graphing: We can graph the provided equation to find its vertex; this is the only point where a horizontal line like $y = c$ could possibly intersect that equation at one point.

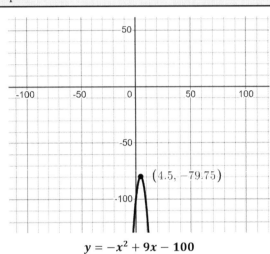

$$y = -x^2 + 9x - 100$$

When we graph the provided equation, we can see that the vertex is at $(4.5, -79.75)$. We can divide out the answer choices to find their decimal equivalents, which gives us this:

(A) $-\frac{481}{4} = -120.25$

(B) -100

(C) $-\frac{319}{4} = 79.75$

(D) $-\frac{9}{2} = 4.5$

So the vertex is at $\left(\frac{9}{2}, -\frac{319}{4}\right)$, which means a horizontal line at $y = -\frac{319}{4}$ would intersect the graph at one point, and the correct answer is (C).

Solution 2: Graphing: Graph the provided equation along with $y = c$, using each answer choice as c. The right answer will be the one that intersects the provided equation at only one point.

If we're not sure we understand this question, or we don't realize that the graph of the provided equation will be a parabola, we could start by graphing the provided equation, and then graphing $y = c$ with each c-value provided in the answer choices—that is, each of the following equations:

(A) $y = -\frac{481}{4}$ and $y = -x^2 + 9x - 100$

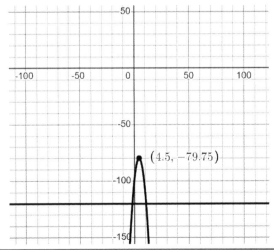

(B) $y = -100$ and $y = -x^2 + 9x - 100$

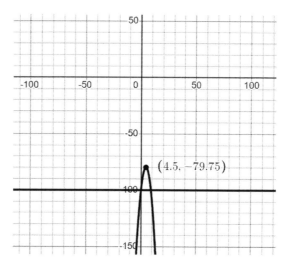

(C) $y = -\frac{319}{4}$ and $y = -x^2 + 9x - 100$

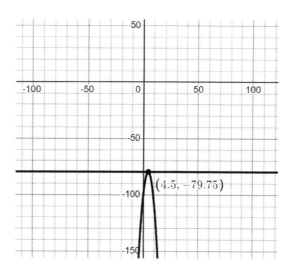

(D) $y = -\frac{9}{2}$ and $y = -x^2 + 9x - 100$

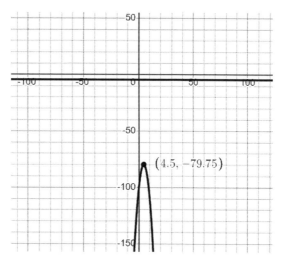

When we do this, we see that only one of those lines intersects the provided equation at "exactly" one point: $y = -\frac{319}{4}$, which means (C) is correct.

ANSWER CHOICE ANALYSIS

(D): This is the opposite of the x-coordinate of the point of intersection, but we need to find the y-coordinate of that point.

How to check? Try an alternate approach above. Try to figure out which mistakes could lead to some of the wrong answer choices, and verify that you haven't made any such mistakes.

▶ Post-solution patterns (see page 286):

Note As you can see in the official College Board explanation for this question, it's also possible to find the answer using the quadratic formula. I didn't include that solution here for several reasons. For one, you can already find that solution for free in the College Board's explanations. For another, it doesn't really help anybody—in my experience, students who are already comfortable using that approach don't benefit from seeing it written out again, and students who aren't comfortable with it aren't going to get comfortable just because they saw somebody use the quadratic formula. Most importantly, the solutions above are so quick and easy (because they take advantage of the powerful graphing calculator that almost every SAT-taker will have on test day) that it seems unhelpful to point out an unnecessarily slow and complicated solution. I strongly recommend that you get used to these graphing approaches, because they can make the process of solving an otherwise challenging and potentially time-consuming question straightforward and quick.

Test 1, Module 1, Question 26

- **What's the prompt asking for?** The point that lies on the graph of each of the provided equations.
- **Math concepts in the prompt:** systems of equations, variables, graphs
- **Elements of the answer choices:** Each answer choice is an (x, y) coordinate pair featuring fractions and r.
- **Notable features of the answer choices:** (B), (C), and (D) all include r as one of the coordinates. (A) is the only choice that includes $\frac{r}{5}$.

- **"Bridge" concepts:** Graphing the two provided equations produces the exact same line, so any point on one line must also be a point on the other line.
- **Pre-solution patterns (see p. 285):** wrong answers try to imitate right answers
- **Things to look out for:** Don't make a small algebra mistake!

Solution 1: Graphing: We can graph the provided equations to see what we can learn. Then we can plug the provided coordinate pairs into the equations to see which pair is a solution for both equations.

Let's start by graphing the provided equations.

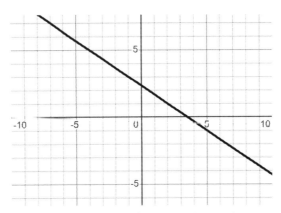

$$2x + 3y = 7 \text{ and } 10x + 15y = 35$$

We can see that these two graphs are identical; that is, they produce the same line. So the right answer is the coordinate pair that produces a point on that line when any real number is plugged in for r.

With that in mind, we can pick any real number value for r, and plug it into the coordinate pairs in each answer choice. Then we can plug the resulting (x, y) coordinate pair into the equation for either line (remember that we found out that both graphs describe the same line) and eliminate any choice whose coordinate pair doesn't lie on the graph of the provided equations.

Let's use $r = 2$, since r is a real number (as the prompt requires) and lower numbers tend to make the math a little simpler.

(A) $\left(\frac{r}{5} + 7, -\frac{r}{5} + 35 \right)$ $\qquad$ $\left(\frac{(2)}{5} + 7, -\frac{(2)}{5} + 35 \right)$ $\qquad$ $\left(7\frac{2}{5}, 34\frac{3}{5} \right)$

We see that plugging $r = 2$ into the coordinate pair from (A) produced $\left(7\frac{2}{5}, 34\frac{3}{5} \right)$. Let's plug that coordinate pair into $2x + 3y = 7$.

$$2x + 3y = 7 \qquad 2\left(7\frac{2}{5}\right) + 3\left(34\frac{3}{5}\right) = 7 \qquad 118.6 \neq 7$$

When we plugged $x = 7\frac{2}{5}$ and $y = 34\frac{3}{5}$ into the first provided equation, the result wasn't a true statement—so $\left(7\frac{2}{5}, 34\frac{3}{5}\right)$ doesn't lie on the graph of the provided equations, and (A) is wrong. Let's check (B).

(B) $\qquad\left(-\frac{3r}{2}+\frac{7}{2}, r\right) \qquad\qquad \left(-\frac{3(2)}{2}+\frac{7}{2}, (2)\right) \qquad\qquad \left(\frac{1}{2}, 2\right)$

We see that plugging $r = 2$ into the coordinate pair from (B) produced $\left(\frac{1}{2}, 2\right)$. Let's plug that coordinate pair into $2x + 3y = 7$.

$$2x + 3y = 7 \qquad\qquad 2\left(\frac{1}{2}\right) + 3(2) = 7 \qquad\qquad 7 = 7$$

Plugging $r = 2$ into the coordinate pair from (B) produced $\left(\frac{1}{2}, 2\right)$. When we plugged $x = \frac{1}{2}$ and $y = 2$ into the first provided equation, the result was a true statement—so $\left(\frac{1}{2}, 2\right)$ does lie on the graph of the provided equations, and (B) appears to be right. Let's check the remaining choices to help make sure we didn't make a mistake.

(C) $\qquad\left(r, \frac{2r}{3}+\frac{7}{3}\right) \qquad\qquad \left((2), \frac{2(2)}{3}+\frac{7}{3}\right) \qquad\qquad \left(2, \frac{11}{3}\right)$

We see that plugging $r = 2$ into the coordinate pair from (C) produced $\left(2, \frac{11}{3}\right)$. Let's plug that coordinate pair into $2x + 3y = 7$.

$$2x + 3y = 7 \qquad\qquad 2(2) + 3\left(\frac{11}{3}\right) = 7 \qquad\qquad 15 \neq 7$$

Plugging $r = 2$ into the coordinate pair from (C) produced $\left(2, \frac{11}{3}\right)$. When we plugged $x = 2$ and $y = \frac{11}{3}$ into the first provided equation, the result wasn't a true statement—so $\left(2, \frac{11}{3}\right)$ doesn't lie on the graph of the provided equations, and (C) is wrong. Finally, let's check (D).

(D) $\qquad\left(r, -\frac{3r}{2}+\frac{7}{2}\right) \qquad\qquad \left((2), -\frac{3(2)}{2}+\frac{7}{2}\right) \qquad\qquad \left(2, \frac{1}{2}\right)$

We see that plugging $r = 2$ into the coordinate pair from (D) produced $\left(2, \frac{1}{2}\right)$. Let's plug that coordinate pair into $2x + 3y = 7$.

$$2x + 3y = 7 \qquad\qquad 2(2) + 3\left(\frac{1}{2}\right) = 7 \qquad\qquad 5.5 \neq 7$$

Plugging $r = 2$ into the coordinate pair from (D) produced $\left(2, \frac{1}{2}\right)$. When we plugged $x = 2$ and $y = \frac{1}{2}$ into the first provided equation, the result wasn't a true statement—so $\left(2, \frac{1}{2}\right)$ doesn't lie on the graph of the provided equations, and (D) is wrong.

After checking each answer choice, we can see that (B) is correct.

Solution 2: Graphing: We can use an r-value to generate a coordinate pair for each answer choice, then graph the points we found along with the provided equations to see which coordinate pair lies on the graph.

Instead of using algebra to check each coordinate pair from the previous solution, we could also check them by graphing the provided equation $2x + 3y = 7$, along with each coordinate pair, and eliminating each point that doesn't lie on the line. Again, we'll use the coordinate pairs we found for each answer choice from the previous solution.

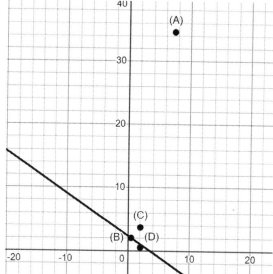

We can see that only the point from choice (B) lies on the line, so (B) must be correct.

Solution 3: Graphing/Test-smart: We can plug the (x, y) coordinate pairs from the answer choices in for x and y in one of the given equations; the right answer will make that equation a true statement.

As we saw in the previous solution, when we graph the two provided equations, we see that they form the same line; they are equivalent. So we can just focus on one equation; let's pick the first equation.

$$2x + 3y = 7$$

The prompt asks for the point that would lie on the graph of this line "for each real number, r." Each answer choice is an (x, y) coordinate pair, with both x and y expressed in terms of r. If the right answer is a coordinate pair that lies on the graph of the provided equation, then we can plug the x and y values from that answer into the provided equation to produce a true statement.

If we're very careful with our parentheses, we can take the $2x + 3y$ part of the first equation, then plug the x-coordinate and y-coordinate from each answer choice in for x and y, respectively, then set that $2x + 3y$ part of the equation equal to y, and graph the result—the right answer will produce the line $y = 7$.

(Note that because the SAT calculator works best with equations involving x and y, we'll use x for r.)

(A) $2\left(\frac{x}{5} + 7\right) + 3\left(-\frac{x}{5} + 35\right) = y$

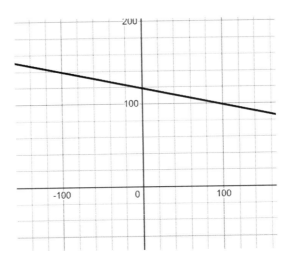

(B) $2\left(-\frac{3x}{2} + \frac{7}{2}\right) + 3(x) = y$

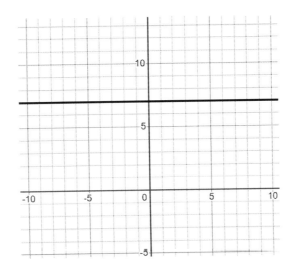

(C) $2(x) + 3\left(\frac{2x}{3} + \frac{7}{3}\right) = y$

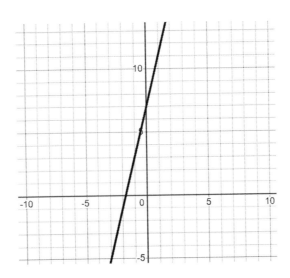

(D) $2(x) + 3\left(-\frac{3x}{2} + \frac{7}{2}\right) = y$

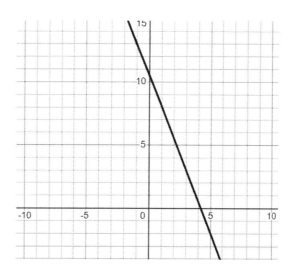

We can see that the graph of (B) produced the line $y = 7$, which means the coordinate pair in (B) causes $2x + 3y$ to be equal to 7 for all real numbers. So (B) is correct.

(If this solution didn't make sense to you, don't dwell on it. Take a second look at it, and if it doesn't help, just move on and continue with your training. You don't have to understand every solution in this book to get an elite or even perfect SAT Math score.)

ANSWER CHOICE ANALYSIS

(D): This is the right answer with the x and y coordinates switched.

How to check? Try an alternate approach above. Try to figure out which mistakes could lead to some of the wrong answer choices, and verify that you haven't made any such mistakes.

Test 1, Module 1, Question 27

- What's the prompt asking for? The value of k in the situation described in the prompt.
- Math concepts in the prompt: perimeter, equilateral triangles, variables, square roots

- "Bridge" concepts: We can use the provided information to find the height of the triangle. Then we can set that height equal to $k\sqrt{3}$ and solve for k.
- Things to look out for: Don't make a small algebra mistake!

Solution 1: Geometry: Use the provided information to find the length of each side of the triangle, and then its height. Then set that height equal to $k\sqrt{3}$ and solve for k.

If the perimeter of an equilateral triangle is 624 centimeters, then the length of each side must be $\frac{624}{3}$, or 208 centimeters, because an equilateral triangle has three sides of equal length, by definition. Let's sketch an equilateral triangle with these dimensions:

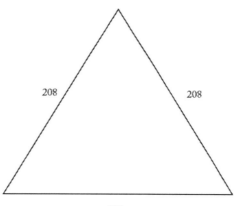

The prompt told us that the triangle's height is $k\sqrt{3}$ centimeters, so we can add that to our diagram as well:

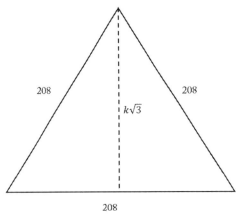

We know that the angles of a triangle add up to 180°, and that an equilateral triangle has three equal angles, so each angle in this triangle must be $\frac{180°}{3}$, or 60°. We also know that the height we drew in must meet the base of the triangle at a 90° angle, by definition. So let's add these angle measures to the diagram too.

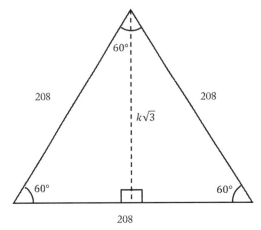

If we focus on the right half of the triangle, we may notice that it's a 30°: 60°: 90° triangle, which has side lengths in the ratio $1: \sqrt{3}: 2$. We may also realize that we know two of its side lengths—the hypotenuse is 208 centimeters, and the base is half of 208 centimeters, or 104 centimeters (since the base is one of the sides of the original equilateral triangle cut in half by the height we drew in).

The ratio of the length of the shorter leg of a 30°: 60°: 90° triangle to the longer leg of a 30°: 60°: 90° triangle is $1: \sqrt{3}$—we might remember that, but if we don't, we can find that info in the math reference material provided by the College Board. Either way, the shorter leg of this 30°: 60°: 90° triangle is 104 centimeters, so the longer leg—which is the height we're looking for—must be $104\sqrt{3}$ centimeters.

That means the height of $k\sqrt{3}$ centimeters is equal to $104\sqrt{3}$ centimeters, so $k\sqrt{3} = 104\sqrt{3}$, and $k = 104$, and the answer is 104.

(Notice that the prompt asked for the value of k, *not* the height of the triangle! So the answer is 104, and not $104\sqrt{3}$. This is exactly the kind of simple mistake the College Board is hoping you'll make on test day. Always make sure you know which value the prompt is asking for, and be sure that your answer addresses *that* question.)

How to check? Try to figure out which mistakes the College Board might hope you would make in finding your solution, and verify that you haven't made any such mistakes.

TEST 1 - MODULE 2

Test 1, Module 2, Question 1

- What's the prompt asking for? The amount of money that Tilly earns for $39w$ hours of work.
- Math concepts in the prompt: money, variables
- Elements of the answer choices: Each answer choice is an expression involving p and 39.
- Notable features of the answer choices: Every choice includes p and 39, but each choice combines these values in a different way. One answer choice involves division, one involves multiplication, one involves addition, and one involves subtraction.
- "Bridge" concepts: If Tilly earns p dollars in w hours, then she must make $39p$ dollars in $39w$ hours.
- Pre-solution patterns (see p. 285): wrong answers try to imitate right answers
- Things to look out for: Don't overthink this question!

Facebook.com/QuestPreparation *Youtube.com/QuestPrep*

Solution 1: Algebra: Consider the situation described in the prompt, and pick the choice that represents that situation.

If Tilly earns p dollars for every w hours of work, then she must make p dollars in w hours, by definition. In $39w$ hours, she must make 39 times as many dollars as she makes in w hours, which is the same as $39 \times p$, or $39p$. So the answer is (A).

ANSWER CHOICE ANALYSIS

(B): This is the amount of money Tilly would earn in $\frac{w}{39}$ hours.

How to check? Reread the prompt to verify that you understand the prompt and what it's asking for. Try to figure out which mistakes could lead to some of the wrong answer choices, and verify that you haven't made any such mistakes.

Test 1, Module 2, Question 2

- What's the prompt asking for? The function m that models the number of minutes it will take Juan to ride x miles at 5.7 minutes per mile.

- Math concepts in the prompt: word problems, rates, functions, models, variables

- Elements of the answer choices: Each answer choice is a function involving x and 5.7.

- Notable features of the answer choices: Every choice combines x and 5.7 in a different way. One answer choice involves division, one involves multiplication, one involves addition, and one involves subtraction.

- "Bridge" concepts: If Juan rides one mile every 5.7 minutes, he must ride x miles in $5.7x$ minutes.

- Pre-solution patterns (see p. 285): wrong answers try to imitate right answers

- Things to look out for: Don't overthink this question! Don't mix up what m and x represent!

Solution 1: Concrete: Pick a number for x, and think about how many minutes it would take Juan to ride that many miles. Then, plug that value into the function from each answer choice to see which one produces the right answer.

If it takes Juan 5.7 minutes to ride his bike one mile, it must take him three times that, or 17.1 minutes, to ride three miles. Let's plug $x = 3$ into each function to see which one produces a value of 17.1

(A) $m(x) = \frac{x}{5.7}$ $m(3) = \frac{(3)}{5.7} \approx 0.53$

(B) $m(x) = x + 5.7$ $m(3) = (3) + 5.7 = 8.7$

(C) $m(x) = x - 5.7$ $m(3) = (3) - 5.7 = -2.7$

(D) $m(x) = 5.7x$ $m(3) = 5.7(3) = 17.1$

Only (D) produces the correct value, so (D) is the right answer.

Solution 2: Careful reading: Think carefully about the situation described in the prompt, and figure out how to represent that situation with mathematical terms.

If it takes Juan 5.7 minutes to ride his bike one mile, then it must take him an additional 5.7 minutes to ride each additional mile beyond that. This is the same as saying that we can multiply 5.7 minutes by the number of miles Juan rides to find the total number of minutes it would take Juan to ride that distance, which is the same as saying Juan will ride x miles in $5.7x$ minutes.

This is what we see in choice (D), so (D) is correct.

ANSWER CHOICE ANALYSIS

(A): This would be the answer if Juan rode his bike at $\frac{1}{5.7}$ minutes per mile.

How to check? Reread the prompt to verify that you understand the prompt and what it's asking for. Try an alternate approach above. Try to figure out which mistakes could lead to some of the wrong answer choices, and verify that you haven't made any such mistakes.

Test 1, Module 2, Question 3

- What's the prompt asking for? The value of y in the solution to the system of equations.

- Math concepts in the prompt: systems of equations, variables, (x, y) coordinate pairs

- Elements of the answer choices: Each answer choice is an integer ranging from -3 to 30.

- Notable features of the answer choices: (A) is negative, while the remaining choices are positive.

- Things to look out for: Don't mix up x and y! Don't make a simple mistake related to sign!

Solution 1: Concrete/graphing: We can graph the two equations to find the (x, y) coordinate pair where they intersect. The correct answer will be the y-value of that coordinate pair.

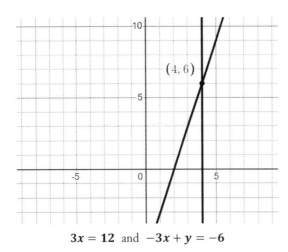

$$3x = 12 \text{ and } -3x + y = -6$$

When we graph these two equations, we can see they intersect at (4,6). So the y-value of their point of intersection is 6, and the answer is (B).

Solution 2: Algebra: Solve for x, then use that value to find y.

We can solve for x in the first equation like this:

$3x = 12$	(first equation)
$x = 4$	(divide both sides by 3)

Now we can plug $x = 4$ into the second equation and solve for y:

$-3x + y = -6$	(second equation)
$-3(4) + y = -6$	(plug in $x = 4$)
$-12 + y = -6$	(simplify)
$y = 6$	(add 12 to both sides)

So $y = 6$, and the answer is (B).

Solution 3: Algebra: Add the equations to find the value of y directly.

We can add the two equations together like this:

$$
\begin{aligned}
3x \quad\;\; &= 12 \\
-3x + y &= -6 \\
\hline
y &= 6
\end{aligned}
$$

Again we can see that $y = 6$, and the answer is (B).

ANSWER CHOICE ANALYSIS

(A): This is the value of y we would find if we made a mistake and thought that $x = 1$. **(C):** This would be the result if we tried to plug $3x = 12$ from the first equation into the second equation and made a mistake related to sign.

How to check? Plug your y-value into the second equation along with $x = 4$ to verify that you get a valid result. Try an alternate approach above. Try to figure out which mistakes could lead to some of the wrong answer choices, and verify that you haven't made any such mistakes.

Test 1, Module 2, Question 4

- What's the prompt asking for? The speed of the car, in miles per hour, 5 seconds after it began to accelerate.

- Math concepts in the prompt: word problems, equations, speed, acceleration

- Elements of the answer choices: Each answer choice is an integer ranging from 40 to 55.

- **"Bridge" concepts:** We can find the answer by plugging $t = 5$ in to the provided equation.

- Pre-solution patterns (see p. 285): wrong answers try to imitate right answers

- Things to look out for: Don't make a simple algebra mistake!

Solution 1: Concrete: We can plug $t = 5$ into the provided equation to find the speed s of the car 5 seconds after it began to accelerate.

$s = 40 + 3t$	(provided equation)
$s = 40 + 3(5)$	(plug in $t = 5$)
$s = 55$	(simplify)

So after 5 seconds of acceleration, the car travels at 55 miles per hour. That means (D) is correct.

Solution 2: Concrete/graphing: We can graph the provided equation, and find the value of s when $t = 5$.

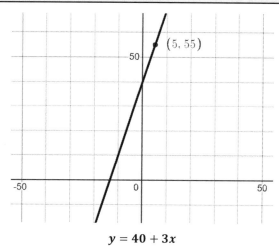

$$y = 40 + 3x$$

When $t = 5$, $s = 55$. So the answer is (D), 55. (Notice that we switched t for x and s for y, since the SAT calculator tends to work better with the variables x and y.)

ANSWER CHOICE ANALYSIS

(A): This is the speed of the car when it starts accelerating, at $t = 0$. **(B):** This would be the speed of the car 1 second after it begins to accelerate. **(C):** This choice would be correct if the provided equation were $s = 40 + t$.

How to check? Try an alternate approach above. Try to figure out which mistakes could lead to some of the wrong answer choices, and verify that you haven't made any such mistakes.

Test 1, Module 2, Question 5

- What's the prompt asking for? The expression that represents the value of c.
- Math concepts in the prompt: right triangles, variables
- Elements of the answer choices: Each answer choice includes 4 and 5.
- Notable features of the answer choices: Three answer choices are radical expressions. One choice involves exponents.

- "Bridge" concepts: We can use the Pythagorean theorem to relate the provided values to each other and answer the question.
- Pre-solution patterns (see p. 285): wrong answers try to imitate right answers
- Things to look out for: Don't get confused about which expressions to square and which expressions to put under a radical! Don't mix up which side is which length!

Solution 1: Algebra: Plug the provided values into the Pythagorean theorem and solve for c.

The Pythagorean theorem tell us that $a^2 + b^2 = c^2$, where a and b are the side lengths of a right triangle, and c is the hypotenuse of that right triangle. (We may remember this equation, or if we don't, then we can find it in the math reference information provided by the College Board.)

For this situation, we can plug in $a = 4$ and $b = 5$, which gives us the following:
$$4^2 + 5^2 = c^2$$
Now let's take the square root of both sides:
$$\sqrt{4^2 + 5^2} = c$$
This is the same as the expression in (D), so (D) is the right answer.

Solution 2: Concrete/Test-smart: Calculate the value of each answer choice and use what you know about right triangles to eliminate any choice that can't be right.

Let's find the value of each answer choice:
- (A): $4 + 5 = 9$
- (B): $\sqrt{(4)(5)} \approx 4.47$
- (C): $\sqrt{4 + 5} = 3$
- (D): $\sqrt{4^2 + 5^2} \approx 6.40$

We know that the hypotenuse of a right triangle must be longer than either of the legs of the right triangle. That eliminates (B) and (C), because both of those values are less than the length of side b, which is 5.

We also know that any side of a triangle must be less than the sum of the lengths of the other two sides, which means the length of c must be less than $4 + 5$, or 9. So (A) can't be correct.

That only leaves (D) as a possible length for c, so (D) is the right answer.

ANSWER CHOICE ANALYSIS

(A): This would be the right answer if the Pythagorean theorem were $a + b = c$, instead of $a^2 + b^2 = c^2$. **(B):** This would be the right answer if the Pythagorean theorem were $ab = c^2$, instead of $a^2 + b^2 = c^2$. **(C):** This would be the right answer if the Pythagorean theorem were $a + b = c^2$, instead of $a^2 + b^2 = c^2$.

How to check? Try an alternate approach above. Try to figure out which mistakes could lead to some of the wrong answer choices, and verify that you haven't made any such mistakes.

Test 1, Module 2, Question 6

- What's the prompt asking for? The solution to the given equation.
- Math concepts in the prompt: equations, variables

- "Bridge" concepts: The solution is the x-value that makes the equation a valid statement.
- Things to look out for: Don't overthink this question!

Solution 1: Concrete/graphing: We can graph the provided equation to find its solution.

When we enter the provided equation—exactly as it is—into our calculator, we get the following graph:

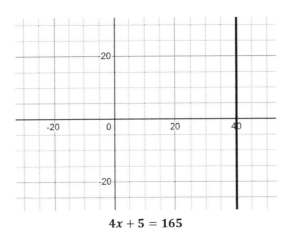

$$4x + 5 = 165$$

We can see a vertical line at $x = 40$, so the answer is 40.

Solution 2: Algebra: Use algebra to isolate x.

$4x + 5 = 165$	(provided equation)
$4x = 160$	(subtract 5 from both sides)
$x = 40$	(divide both sides by 4)

So $x = 40$, and the answer is 40.

How to check? Plug the x-value you found back into the original equation to make sure it results in a valid statement. Try an alternate approach above. Try to figure out which mistakes the College Board might hope you would make in finding your solution, and verify that you haven't made any such mistakes.

Note This is a great example of an SAT Math question that's so straightforward, it almost seems like a trick. As trained test-takers, we know that the College Board likes to include questions like this one sometimes, probably for that exact reason—it makes you start to doubt yourself, to the point that you might make a small mistake, or at least waste some time wondering whether you're missing anything. But as long as we read carefully and we understand what the question is asking, we can go ahead and answer it with confidence, and move on.

Test 1, Module 2, Question 7

- What's the prompt asking for? The value of x in the x-intercept of the graph.

- Math concepts in the prompt: graphs, x-intercepts, parabolas

- "Bridge" concepts: x is the x-coordinate of the point where the line touches the x-axis.

- Things to look out for: Don't overthink this question!

Solution 1: Concrete: Look at the provided graph, find the x-intercept, and mark down the x-value of that point.

The x-intercept of a graph is the point where that graph touches the x-axis. We can see that the provided graph touches the x-axis at $(7,0)$, so $x = 7$, and the answer is 7.

How to check? Try to figure out which mistakes the College Board might hope you would make in finding your solution, and verify that you haven't made any such mistakes.

Note Like the previous question, this one seems almost *too* straightforward. Again, we just reread the prompt carefully, make sure we understand it, answer the question, and move on.

Test 1, Module 2, Question 8

- What's the prompt asking for? The y-intercept of the graph of $y = f(x)$ in the xy-plane.

- Math concepts in the prompt: functions, fractions, y-intercepts

- Elements of the answer choices: Each answer choice is a coordinate pair where one value is zero.

- Notable features of the answer choices: All four answer choices include 0. Two answer choices include -2, and two include $\frac{1}{10}$.

- "Bridge" concepts: The y-intercept is the point where the graph crosses the y-axis.

- Pre-solution patterns (see p. 285): wrong answers try to imitate right answers

- Things to look out for: Don't mix up which part of the function tells us about its slope, and which part tells us about its y-intercept! Don't make a small algebra mistake!

Solution 1: Concrete/graphing: We can graph the function to find its y-intercept.

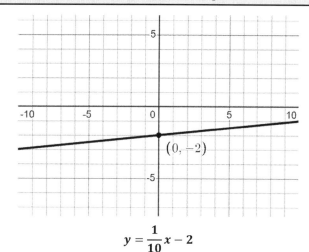

$$y = \frac{1}{10}x - 2$$

When we graph the function, we can see that its y-intercept is $(0, -2)$, which means (B) is correct.

Solution 2: Algebra: The y-intercept occurs where $x = 0$, so find $f(0)$.

We can plug in $x = 0$ to find the y-value of the y-intercept of the graph.

$$f(x) = \frac{1}{10}x - 2 \qquad \text{(provided function)}$$
$$f(0) = \frac{1}{10}(0) - 2 \qquad \text{(plug in } x = 0\text{)}$$
$$f(0) = -2 \qquad \text{(simplify)}$$

So when $x = 0$, $y = -2$. That means the y-intercept of the graph is at $(0, -2)$, and (B) is correct.

Solution 3: Test-smart/properties and definitions: Notice that the function is already in $y = mx + b$ format, and use that information to find the y-intercept.

When a function is in $y = mx + b$ format, we know that b tells us the y-intercept of that function. In this case b is -2, so the y-intercept is at $(0, -2)$, and (B) is correct.

ANSWER CHOICE ANALYSIS

(A): This is the right answer with the x- and y-values switched. **(C):** This is the result if we think the slope of the line is its y-intercept. **(D):** This is the result if we combine the errors from (A) and (C).

How to check? Verify that plugging in $x = 0$ produces a y-value of -2. Try an alternate approach above. Try to figure out which mistakes could lead to some of the wrong answer choices, and verify that you haven't made any such mistakes.

▶   Post-solution patterns (see page 286): the right answer to the wrong question

Test 1, Module 2, Question 9

- What's the prompt asking for? The equation that defines function g, as described in the prompt.

- Math concepts in the prompt: functions, exponents, graphs, translation

- Elements of the answer choices: Each answer choice is a function involving $7x^3$ and 2.

- Notable features of the answer choices: Every answer choice includes $7x^3$, with 2 being added, or subtracted, or used to divide some part of the expression.

- "Bridge" concepts: Every $g(x)$ value will be 2 units less than the corresponding $f(x)$ value.

- Pre-solution patterns (see p. 285): wrong answers try to imitate right answers

- Things to look out for: Don't get confused about how shifting the function 2 units down should impact $f(x)$!

Solution 1: Concrete/graphing: We can graph the provided function, then graph each function in the answer choices. The correct answer will be the graph that's the same as $f(x)$ shifted down 2 units.

Let's start by graphing the provided function:

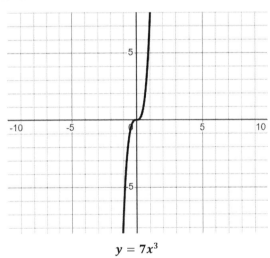

$$y = 7x^3$$

Now we can graph each function in the answer choices.

(A)

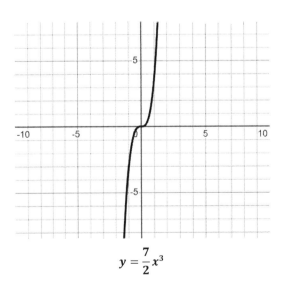

$$y = \frac{7}{2}x^3$$

(B)

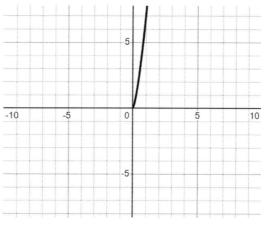

$$y = 7x^{\frac{3}{2}}$$

(C)

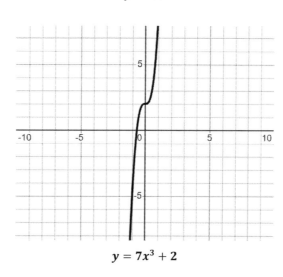

$$y = 7x^3 + 2$$

(D)

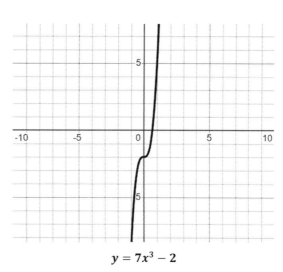

$$y = 7x^3 - 2$$

We can see that the only choice that's the same as $f(x)$ shifted down 2 units is (D). So (D) is correct.

Solution 2: Abstract: Think about how to represent mathematically the idea of moving $f(x)$ down 2 units.

The y-value of a coordinate pair is the value that tells us how far up or down a point should be, so shifting the graph of a function down 2 units is the same as subtracting 2 from every y-value in that function.

So we need a function that results in a $g(x)$ value that is two *less* than the original function $f(x)$. Since $f(x)$ was equal to $7x^3$, $g(x)$ must be equal to 2 less than that, or $7x^3 - 2$. So it must be the case that $g(x) = 7x^3 - 2$, which means (D) is correct.

ANSWER CHOICE ANALYSIS

(A): This choice would be correct if the prompt told us $g(x)$ would be half the value of $f(x)$. **(C):** This would be the result of shifting $f(x)$ 2 units *up*, not two units *down*, as the prompt requires.

How to check? Verify that you didn't mix up $f(x)$ and $g(x)$. Try an alternate approach above. Try to figure out which mistakes could lead to some of the wrong answer choices, and verify that you haven't made any such mistakes.

▶ Post-solution patterns (see page 286): the right answer to the wrong question

Test 1, Module 2, Question 10

- **What's the prompt asking for?** The ordered pair that's a solution for the given system of equations.

- **Math concepts in the prompt:** systems of equations, coordinate pairs, exponential expressions

- **Elements of the answer choices:** Each answer choice is a coordinate pair with an x-value of 3.

- **Notable features of the answer choices:** Every choice has an x-value of 3 and a different y-value.

- **Pre-solution patterns (see p. 285):** wrong answers try to imitate right answers

- **Things to look out for:** Don't mix up x and y! Don't overlook the exponent in the second equation!

Solution 1: Concrete/graphing: We can graph both equations and find their point of intersection.

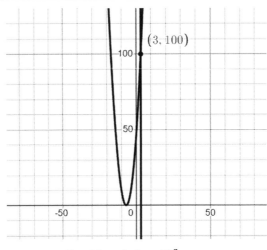

$$x + 7 = 10 \text{ and } (x + 7)^2 = y$$

When we graph both equations, we can see that they intersect at the point $(3, 100)$. So $(3, 100)$ is the solution to the system of equations, and the answer is (A).

Solution 2: Concrete/backsolving: Plug the (x, y) pairs from the answer choices into the system of equations to find which one produces a valid statement for both equations.

(A) $(3) + 7 = 10$ $\qquad$ $10 = 10$

$\quad$ $((3) + 7)^2 = (100)$ $\qquad$ $100 = 100$

When we plugged $(3, 100)$ from (A) into the system of equations, we got two valid statements, so (A) looks right. Let's check the remaining choices to help make sure we didn't make a mistake.

(B) $(3) + 7 = 10$ $\qquad$ $10 = 10$

$\quad$ $((3) + 7)^2 = (3)$ $\qquad$ $100 \neq 3$

When we plugged $(3,3)$ from (B) into the system of equations, the second equation was invalid. So (B) is wrong—let's check (C).

(C) $(3) + 7 = 10$ $\qquad$ $10 = 10$

$\quad$ $((3) + 7)^2 = (10)$ $\qquad$ $100 \neq 10$

When we plugged $(3,10)$ from (C) into the system of equations, the second equation was invalid. So (C) is wrong—let's check (D).

(D) $(3) + 7 = 10$ $\qquad$ $10 = 10$

$\quad$ $((3) + 7)^2 = (70)$ $\qquad$ $100 \neq 70$

When we plugged $(3,70)$ from (D) into the system of equations, the second equation was invalid. So (D) is wrong. After checking each answer choice, we can conclude that (A) is correct.

Solution 3: Algebra: Solve for x in the first equation, then plug that value into the second equation to find y.

We can solve for x in the first equation like this:

$$x + 7 = 10 \qquad\qquad\qquad \text{(first equation)}$$

$$x = 3 \qquad \text{(subtract seven from both sides)}$$

Now we can plug $x = 3$ into the second equation and solve for y.

$$(x + 7)^2 = y \qquad \text{(second equation)}$$
$$(3 + 7)^2 = y \qquad \text{(plug in } x = 3)$$
$$10^2 = y \qquad \text{(simplify)}$$
$$100 = y \qquad \text{(simplify)}$$

We found that $x = 3$ and $y = 100$, so the solution to the system of equations is $(3, 100)$, and (A) is correct.

Solution 4: Test-smart: Notice that every answer choice has an x-value of 3, which means we know $x = 3$. Plug this value into the second equation and solve for y.

$$(x + 7)^2 = y \qquad \text{(second equation)}$$
$$(3 + 7)^2 = y \qquad \text{(plug in } x = 3)$$
$$10^2 = y \qquad \text{(simplify)}$$
$$100 = y \qquad \text{(simplify)}$$

If $x = 3$ and $y = 100$, then the solution to the system of equations is $(3, 100)$, and (A) is correct.

ANSWER CHOICE ANALYSIS

(B): This could be the result of solving for x and then getting confused about which variable you solved for. **(C):** This would be the result of overlooking the exponent in the second equation.

How to check? Plug your answer back into the given equations to make sure that each one makes a valid statement. Try an alternate approach above. Try to figure out which mistakes could lead to some of the wrong answer choices, and verify that you haven't made any such mistakes.

Test 1, Module 2, Question 11

- What's the prompt asking for? The expressions that's equivalent to $(7x^3 + 7x) - (6x^3 - 3x)$.

- Math concepts in the prompt: polynomials, variables, exponents

- Notable features of the answer choices: Every answer choice includes an x^3 term and an x term, with -13, 10, and 4 appearing in different positions.

- "Bridge" concepts: We can combine the provided terms into an expression with just 2 terms.

- Pre-solution patterns (see p. 285): wrong answers try to imitate right answers

- Things to look out for: Remember not to combine terms with different exponents! Don't make a simple mistake related to sign!

Solution 1: Concrete/backsolving: Pick a value for x and plug it into the given expression. Then, plug that same x-value into the expression in each answer choice. Eliminate every choice that doesn't produce the same result you found when plugging x into the given expression.

Let's evaluate the given expression when $x = 3$.

$$(7x^3 + 7x) - (6x^3 - 3x) \qquad \text{(given expression)}$$
$$(7(3)^3 + 7(3)) - (6(3)^3 - 3(3)) \qquad \text{(plug in } x = 3)$$
$$(7(27) + 21) - (6(27) - 9) \qquad \text{(simplify)}$$
$$(189 + 21) - (162 - 9) \qquad \text{(simplify)}$$
$$(210) - (153) \qquad \text{(simplify)}$$
$$57 \qquad \text{(simplify)}$$

So when $x = 3$, the given expression is equal to 57. Now let's plug $x = 3$ into each expression from the answer choices.

(A)	$x^3 + 10x$	$(3)^3 + 10(3)$	57
(B)	$-13x^3 + 10x$	$-13(3)^3 + 10(3)$	-321
(C)	$-13x^3 + 4x$	$-13(3)^3 + 4(3)$	-339
(D)	$x^3 + 4x$	$(3)^3 + 4(3)$	39

After plugging $x = 3$ into the expression from each answer choice, we can see that only (A) produces the same value that we got when we plugged $x = 3$ into the provided expression. So (A) is right.

Solution 2: Concrete/graphing: We can set the provided equation equal to y and graph the result, then repeat that process for each answer choice. The correct answer will be the one whose graph matches the graph of the provided equation.

Let's set the provided equation equal to y and graph the result:

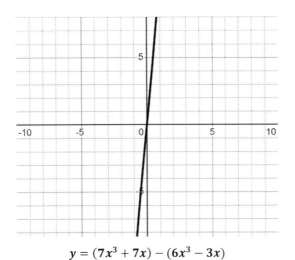

$$y = (7x^3 + 7x) - (6x^3 - 3x)$$

Let's do the same for the expressions in each of the answer choices:

(A)

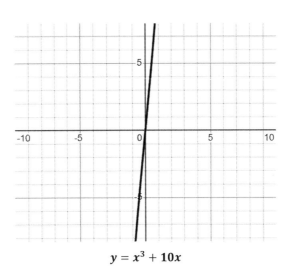

$$y = x^3 + 10x$$

(B)

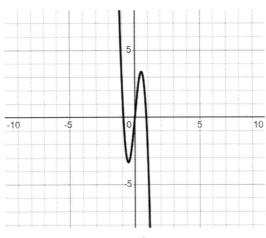

$$y = -13x^3 + 10x$$

(C)

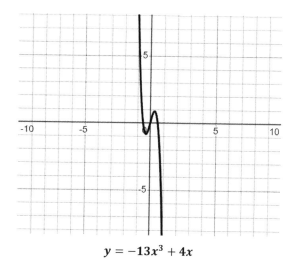

$$y = -13x^3 + 4x$$

(D)

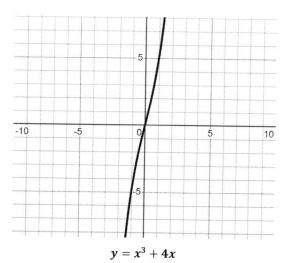

$$y = x^3 + 4x$$

We can see that only the graph of (A) is the same as the graph of the expression from the prompt, so (A) must be correct.

Solution 3: Algebra: Distribute the implied 1 to $(7x^3 + 7x)$ and the implied -1 to $(6x^3 - 3x)$ to get rid of the parentheses, then combine like terms.

We can simplify the provided expression by removing the parentheses. We can think of removing the first set of parentheses as distributing the implied "1" multiplied by that expression. (In other words, if the expression in the parentheses were being multiplied by 5, for example, and it looked liked $5(7x^3 + 7x)$, then we could get rid of the parentheses by distributing the 5. But the expression in the parentheses isn't being multiplied by anything, which is the same as being multiplied by 1. This is basically the same as just removing the parentheses, but some test-takers feel hesitant to do that without understanding why.) Here's what that looks like:

$$(7x^3 + 7x) - (6x^3 - 3x) \qquad \text{(given expression)}$$
$$7x^3 + 7x - (6x^3 - 3x) \qquad \text{(distribute 1 to first parenthetical expression)}$$

Now we need to deal with the second set of parentheses. That expression is being subtracted, which is the same as multiplying by an implied -1. So in order to get rid of those parentheses, we need to distribute -1 to that parenthetical expression, which is the same as multiplying $6x^3$ by -1 and $-3x$ by -1. That looks like this:

$$7x^3 + 7x - 6x^3 + 3x \qquad \text{(distribute } -1)$$

Now we can just combine like terms.

$$x^3 + 10x \qquad \text{(simplify)}$$

So the answer is (A).

ANSWER CHOICE ANALYSIS

(B): This is the result of accidentally combining $-7x^3$ and $-6x^3$, instead of $7x^3$ and $-6x^3$. **(C):** This is the result of accidentally combining $-7x^3$ and $-6x^3$, instead of $7x^3$ and $-6x^3$, and also accidentally combining $7x$ and $-3x$ instead of $7x$ and $3x$. **(D):** This is the result of accidentally combining $7x$ and $-3x$ instead of $7x$ and $3x$.

How to check? Try an alternate approach above. Try to figure out which mistakes could lead to some of the wrong answer choices, and verify that you haven't made any such mistakes.

Test 1, Module 2, Question 12

- What's the prompt asking for? The value of n when $p(n)$ is equal to 56.

- Math concepts in the prompt: functions, exponents

- Elements of the answer choices: Each answer choice is a numerical value ranging from 2 to 8.

- Notable features of the answer choices: Three choices are integers and one is a fraction.

- Things to look out for: Remember that the 3 in the function is an exponent, not a coefficient!

Solution 1: Concrete/graphing: We can graph the provided function and find the point where $p(n) = 56$. The n-value of that point will be the answer. (Remember that it's a good idea to use x and y in the provided calculator, which means we graph $y = 7x^3$.)

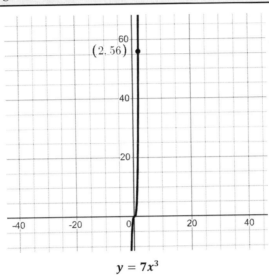

$$y = 7x^3$$

When we graph the provided function, we see that it contains the point $(2, 56)$, which means that when $p(n) = 56, n = 2$. So the correct answer is (A).

Solution 2: Concrete/backsolving: Plug in each answer choice for n. The one that produces a $p(n)$ value of 56 will be the correct answer.

$p(n) = 7n^3$	(given function)
$p(2) = 7(2)^3$	(plug in $n = 2$ from (A))
$p(2) = 7(8)$	(simplify)
$p(2) = 56$	(simplify)

So when $n = 2$, $p(n) = 56$. (A) looks like it's right, but let's check the remaining choices to make sure we haven't made a mistake or overlooked anything.

$p(n) = 7n^3$	(given function)
$p\left(\frac{8}{3}\right) = 7\left(\frac{8}{3}\right)^3$	(plug in $n = \frac{8}{3}$ from (B))
$p\left(\frac{8}{3}\right) = 7\left(\frac{512}{27}\right)$	(simplify)
$p\left(\frac{8}{3}\right) \approx 132.74$	(simplify)

We can see that when $n = \frac{8}{3}$, $p(n) \approx 132.74$. So (B) isn't right; let's check (C).

$p(n) = 7n^3$	(given function)
$p(7) = 7(7)^3$	(plug in $n = 7$ from (C))
$p(7) = 7(343)$	(simplify)
$p(7) = 2,401$	(simplify)

We can see that when $n = 7$, $p(n) = 2,401$. So (C) isn't right; let's check (D).

$p(n) = 7n^3$	(given function)
$p(8) = 7(8)^3$	(plug in $n = 8$ from (D))
$p(8) = 7(512)$	(simplify)

$$p(8) = 3,584 \qquad \text{(simplify)}$$

So when $n = 8$, $p(n) = 3,584$. So (D) isn't right either. After checking every answer choice, we can see that (A) is correct.

Solution 3: Algebra: Set $p(n)$ equal to 56, and then solve for n.

$$p(n) = 7n^3 \qquad \text{(given function)}$$
$$56 = 7n^3 \qquad \text{(set } p(n) \text{ equal to 56)}$$
$$8 = n^3 \qquad \text{(divide both sides by 7)}$$
$$2 = n \qquad \text{(take the cube root of both sides)}$$

So when $p(n) = 56$, $n = 2$. That means (A) is correct.

ANSWER CHOICE ANALYSIS

(B): This choice would be correct if it were true that $p(n) = 7n(3)$, instead of $p(n) = 7n^3$. **(D):** This choice would be correct if it were true that $p(n) = 7n$, instead of $p(n) = 7n^3$.

How to check? Plug your value into the function and verify that the resulting $p(n)$ value is 56. Try an alternate approach above. Try to figure out which mistakes could lead to some of the wrong answer choices, and verify that you haven't made any such mistakes.

▶ Post-solution patterns (see page 286): the right answer to the wrong question

Test 1, Module 2, Question 13

- What's the prompt asking for? The value of x.
- Math concepts in the prompt: parallel lines, intersection, variables, transversals, angle measures

- "Bridge" concepts: The sum of 110 and x must be 180.
- Things to look out for: Remember that the measures of the two angles must add up to 180, not 90 or 360!

Solution 1: Geometry: Use your understanding of transversals to answer the question.

Since lines s and t are parallel, line c must cross them at the same angle. That means the labeled 110° angle in the provided figure where c crosses t is the same size as the corresponding angle where c crosses s. Let's add that measurement to the figure.

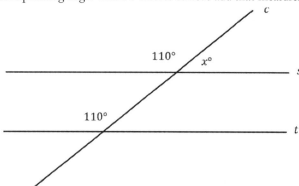

We can see that the 110° angle and the x° angle must add up to 180°, because together they form a straight line. This is the same as saying that $110° + x° = 180°$. When we subtract 110° from both sides, we get $x = 70°$. So the answer is 70.

How to check? Try to figure out which mistakes the College Board might hope you would make in finding your solution, and verify that you haven't made any such mistakes.

Test 1, Module 2, Question 14

- What's the prompt asking for? The mean of the provided data
- Math concepts in the prompt: data values, integers, mean

- "Bridge" concepts: The mean of the data is the result when the all the values are added together and the result is divided by the number of values.
- Things to look out for: Be careful when adding or counting a series of numbers that you don't overlook or double count any!

Solution 1: Algebra: To find the mean of the data, add up all the values in the set and then divide by the number of values.

$$\frac{6 + 8 + 16 + 4 + 17 + 26 + 8 + 5 + 5 + 5}{10} = 10$$

The sum of all the values is 100, and there are 10 values. 100 divided by 10 is 10, so the answer is 10.

How to check? Verify that you've added the numbers correctly, and divided by the right number of values. Try to figure out which mistakes the College Board might hope you would make in finding your solution, and verify that you haven't made any such mistakes.

Test 1, Module 2, Question 15

- What's the prompt asking for? The best interpretation of the number 5 in the situation described in the prompt.

- Math concepts in the prompt: word problems, functions, exponents, modeling

- Elements of the answer choices: Each answer choice is a phrase describing some aspect of the situation from the prompt.

- Notable features of the answer choices: Three answer choices mention "the number of employees," and the remaining one mentions "the number of years the restaurant has been open." Choices mention the idea of an estimated number, an increase in a number, and a percent increase in a number.

- Pre-solution patterns (see p. 285): wrong answers try to imitate right answers

- Things to look out for: Remember to read both the prompt and each answer choice very carefully! Don't pick an answer choice that includes an idea that doesn't appear in the prompt!

Solution 1: Careful reading: See how the provided equation relates to the situation described in the prompt. Consider how each answer choice would fit into that equation as 5, if it were correct. Eliminate each choice that contradicts the relationships described in the prompt, and confirm that the remaining choice accurately reflects the ideas in the prompt.

(A) When the restaurant opened, $t = 0$, since the prompt tells us that "t is the number of years since the restaurant opened"—at the time that the restaurant opened, the number of years since opening would be zero. When $t = 0$, the provided function (which represents "the estimated number of employees at a restaurant") would be $E(0) = 5(1.8)^0 = 5$. So it's true that the number 5 would be "the estimated number of employees when the restaurant opened," as this choice says. (A) looks right, but let's check the other choices.

(B) The prompt tells us that "t is the number of years since the restaurant opened." So each year, t increases by one. The impact on provided function $E(t) = 5(1.8)^t$ when t increases by one is that the exponent of 1.8 increases by one, which means the expression is multiplied by 1.8 one additional time. Multiplying a value by 1.8 isn't the same as increasing that number by 5, as this choice would require. So (B) is wrong.

(C) The prompt says that "t is the number of years since the restaurant opened," and nothing indicates that $t = 5$. So (C) is wrong.

(D) As we saw in our discussion of (B), each year the estimated number of employees is multiplied by 1.8 one additional time. This isn't the same as the estimated number of employees increasing by 5% each year, and nothing in the provided information supports the idea of anything increasing by 5%—so (D) must be wrong.

After considering each choice, we can see that (A) must be correct.

Solution 2: Abstract: Analyze the prompt and the provided equation to figure out what 5 must represent.

The prompt tells us that $E(t) = 5(1.8)^t$, and this expresses "the estimated number of employees at a restaurant, where t is the number of years since that restaurant opened." So $E(t)$ is that estimated number, which is found by taking the value 5 and multiplying it by $(1.8)^t$. We can see that as t increases, 5 will be multiplied by a larger and larger number. In other words, 5 is the starting number, and we find the change in $E(t)$ as times goes on by multiplying 5 by $(1.8)^t$. We can see that this means 5 is the estimated number of employees when the restaurant opened—that is, when $t = 0$—which means (A) is correct.

ANSWER CHOICE ANALYSIS

(B): This choice describes the change in E when t increases by one. **(C):** The prompt tells us that this is what t represents.

How to check? Try an alternate approach above. Try to figure out which mistakes could lead to some of the wrong answer choices, and verify that you haven't made any such mistakes.

▶ Post-solution patterns (see page 286): the right answer to the wrong question

Test 1, Module 2, Question 16

- What's the prompt asking for? The minimum value of the given function.

- Math concepts in the prompt: functions, exponents, minimum values

- Elements of the answer choices: Each answer choice is an integer ranging from 0 to 3,025.

- Notable features of the answer choices: Each answer choice has one more digit than the previous answer choice. (C) is twice as much as (B). (A), (B), and (C) form a series where each choice is 55 more than the previous choice. (D) is (B) squared.

- "Bridge" concepts: The minimum value of the function is the least possible value of $g(x)$.

- Pre-solution patterns (see p. 285): halves and doubles; first and last terms in a series are often wrong answers

- Things to look out for: Don't overlook the fact that x is squared! Don't mistake the exponent for a coefficient!

Solution 1: Concrete/graphing: We can graph the provided function to find the lowest value for $g(x)$.

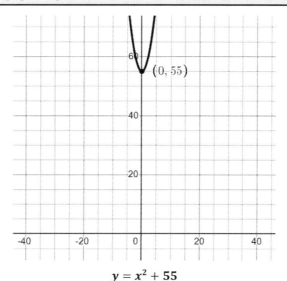

$$y = x^2 + 55$$

When we graph the function, we can see that the lowest value for $g(x)$ is 55, so (B) is correct.

Solution 2: Concrete: Set $g(x)$ equal to each answer choice, and solve for x. The smallest value that produces a real value for x will be the right answer..

(A) $(0) = x^2 + 55$

$-55 = x^2$

$\sqrt{-55} = x$

When we plug 0 from choice (A) in for $g(x)$, we find that x must be equal to the square root of a negative number. So no real value of x results in a $g(x)$ value of 0, which means (A) is wrong. Let's check (B).

(B) $(55) = x^2 + 55$

$0 = x^2$

$0 = x$

When we plug 55 from choice (B) in for $g(x)$, we find that $x = 0$. This is the lowest remaining answer choice after eliminating (A), and we can see that it *is* a value of the given function, since it's the result of plugging in $x = 0$, a real value of x. So (B) appears to be correct. Let's check the remaining choices to help make sure we didn't make a mistake.

(C) $(110) = x^2 + 55$

$55 = x^2$

$\sqrt{55} = x$

When we plug 110 from choice (C) in for $g(x)$, we find that $x = \sqrt{55}$. So choice (C) *is* a value of the given function, but (B) is too, and (B) is lower—so (C) can't be the minimum value of the function, as the prompt requires. Let's check (D).

(D) $(3,025) = x^2 + 55$

$2,970 = x^2$

$\sqrt{2,970} = x$

When we plug 3,025 from choice (D) in for $g(x)$, we find that $x = \sqrt{2,970}$. So choice (D) *is* a value of the given function, but (B) is too, and (B) is lower—so (D) can't be the minimum value of the function, as the prompt requires.

We found that (B) was lowest value of the given function, so (B) must be correct.

Solution 3: Abstract: Consider the provided function and think about the minimum value it could produce.

If we try to imagine the lowest possible value for $g(x)$, we can see that $g(x)$ is determined by two things: x^2 and 55. The 55 value won't change because it's a constant, so the only thing can change is the value of x^2. The value of x^2 will be positive for any non-zero number, because multiplying two negative numbers or two positive numbers will result in a positive number. So the lowest possible value for x^2 will occur when $x = 0$, at which point $x^2 = 0$ as well. When $x = 0$ and $x^2 = 0$, $g(x) = 0 + 55 = 55$. So the minimum value for $g(x)$ is 55, and (B) is correct.

(A): This is the x-value that produces the lowest $g(x)$ value, but that's not what the question asked for. This would also be the right answer if the function were $g(x) = x^2$. **(C):** This would be the correct answer if the lowest possible value for x^2 were 55, for some reason. **(D):** This would be the result if a test-taker wasn't sure what to do and plugged $x = 55$ into x^2.

How to check? Try an alternate approach above. Try to figure out which mistakes could lead to some of the wrong answer choices, and verify that you haven't made any such mistakes.

▶ Post-solution patterns (see page 286): the right answer to the wrong question

Test 1, Module 2, Question 17

- **What's the prompt asking for?** The choice that best models how the value of the investment changes over time.

- **Math concepts in the prompt:** word problems, functions, models, percentages, increasing value

- **Elements of the answer choices:** Each answer choice is a two-word phrase describing the function.

- **Notable features of the answer choices:** Each answer choice is a combination of either the word "decreasing" or "increasing" first, and either the word "exponential" or "linear" second.

- **Pre-solution patterns (see p. 285):** opposites; wrong answers try to imitate right answers

- **Things to look out for:** Read the prompt carefully, and think carefully about the behavior it describes!

Solution 1: Careful reading: Read the prompt carefully to determine whether the function that models the situation in the prompt would be "decreasing" or "increasing," and "exponential" or "linear."

The prompt tells us that the value of the investment "increases by 0.49% of its value the previous year." If it "increases" by a certain positive percentage of its value, then the model must be increasing, as opposed to decreasing. That eliminates (A) and (B); now we have to determine whether a model of the investment's value would be "exponential" or "linear."

A linear model would change by the same amount each year, while an exponential model would change by a different amount each year. The prompt tells us that the value of the investment "increases by 0.49% of its value the previous year." Since the yearly change is based on a percentage of the investment's value the previous year, and since that value increases every year, the yearly change must increase every year as well—that means the model of the investment must be exponential, not linear. That eliminates (D), and leaves (C) as the correct answer.

(A): We know this choice is wrong because the prompt directly states that the value "increases." **(B):** This choice has the same problem as (A). **(D):** We know the function can't be linear because it changes by a different amount each year.

How to check? Try to figure out which mistakes the College Board might hope you would make in finding your solution, and verify that you haven't made any such mistakes.

Test 1, Module 2, Question 18

- **What's the prompt asking for?** The value of k in the situation described in the prompt.

- **Math concepts in the prompt:** word problems, populations, percentage, variables, multiplication

- **Elements of the answer choices:** Each answer choice is a decimal value ranging from 0.07 to 1.7.

- **Notable features of the answer choices:** Every answer choice ends in a 7. Two choices are greater than 1 and two are less than one. Two choices include .07, and

two include .7. (C) is one more than (A), and (D) is one more than (B).

- **"Bridge" concepts:** We can multiply the 2015 population by k to find the 2016 population.

- **Pre-solution patterns (see p. 285):** wrong answers try to imitate right answers

- **Things to look out for:** Make sure your answer choice reflects the idea that the population grew by 7%!

Solution 1: Concrete: Pick a number for the population, and figure out what that number would be if it grew by 7%. Multiply the number you picked for the population by each value in the answer choices. The one that produces the same value you found when you figured out what the population would be if it grew by 7% is the correct answer.

If "the 2016 population is k times the 2015 population," as the prompt tells us, that means we can multiply the 2015 population by k to get the 2016 population. So multiplying the 2015 population by k should be the same as a 7% increase over the 2015 population.

Let's make up a number for the 2015 population—we'll say that it was 100. 7% of 100 is 7, so the 2016 population would have been $100 + 7$, or 107. Now let's multiply 100 by k using each answer choice as the k-value described in the prompt, and see which one produces a result of 107.

(A) $100 \times 0.07 = 7$
(B) $100 \times 0.7 = 70$
(C) $100 \times 1.07 = 107$
(D) $100 \times 1.7 = 170$

Only (C) produced the correct value, so (C) is right.

Solution 2: Abstract: Read each answer choice carefully, and think about what would happen if we multiplied the population by that amount. Eliminate each choice that doesn't result in the population growing by 7%.

If "the 2016 population is k times the 2015 population," as the prompt tells us, that means we can multiply the 2015 population by k to get the 2016 population. In other words, if we multiply the 2015 population by k, that should be the same as a 7% increase over the 2015 population. With this in mind, let's consider each answer choice.

(A) If we multiply the 2015 population by 0.07, which is less than 1, the result will be a decrease in population—but we're looking for a 7% *increase*. So (A) must be wrong.

(B) This choice has the same problem as (A)—it would result in a *decrease* in population, not an increase. (B) is wrong too.

(C) If we multiply the 2015 population by 1.07, we would get the 2015 population *plus* the result of multiplying that population by 0.07. Multiplying something by 0.07 is the same as finding 7% of something, so this choice would give us 7% more than the 2015 population, which is what the prompt asked for.

(D) If we multiply the 2015 population by 1.7, we would get a result that's 70% greater than the 2015 population—this is significantly more than the 7% increase described in the prompt, so (D) is wrong.

After considering each answer choice, we can see that (C) is correct.

ANSWER CHOICE ANALYSIS

(A): This choice represents 7% of the population, not an *increase* of 7%, as the prompt requires. **(B):** This choice represents 70% of the population. **(D):** This choice represents the population growing by 70%, not by 7% as the prompt requires.

How to check? Try an alternate approach above. Try to figure out which mistakes could lead to some of the wrong answer choices, and verify that you haven't made any such mistakes.

▶   Post-solution patterns (see page 286):   the right answer to the wrong question

Note   Test-takers who are comfortable with percentages will be able to tell pretty quickly that increasing by 7% is the same as multiplying by 1.07—but if you aren't so comfortable with this topic, the techniques above can help you avoid falling for the wrong answer choices, which are specifically designed to catch people who get mixed up reading the prompt and/or finding the answer.

Test 1, Module 2, Question 19

- **What's the prompt asking for?** The expression that's equivalent to $a^{\frac{11}{12}}$ when $a > 0$.

- **Math concepts in the prompt:** variables, fractional exponents, inequality

- **Elements of the answer choices:** Each answer choice is a radical expression involving a raised to an exponent.

- **Notable features of the answer choices:** Each choice includes a^{132} under a radical sign representing a different root of that expression.

- **Pre-solution patterns (see p. 285):** wrong answers try to imitate right answers

- **Things to look out for:** Don't get confused about the right way to express fractional exponents as radicals! Don't mix up the numerator and the denominator of the exponent!

Solution 1: Concrete/backsolving: Pick a value for a, and plug it into the provided expression. Then plug that same a-value into the expression from each answer choice. Eliminate any answer choice that doesn't produce the same result you got when you plugged that a-value into the provided expression.

Let's say that $a = 5$. We can use the provided calculator to evaluate the given expression when $a = 5$, then we can evaluate each expression in the answer choices when $a = 5$ to see which one matches the value of the expression from the prompt.

$a^{\frac{11}{12}}$ (given expression)

$5^{\frac{11}{12}}$ (plug in $a = 5$)

$$\approx 4.372 \qquad \text{(evaluate using calculator)}$$

Now let's find out the value of the expressions from the answer choices when $a = 5$. (When entering these values into the calculator, note that $\sqrt[12]{a^{132}}$ is the same as $a^{\frac{132}{12}}$.)

(A) $\quad \sqrt[12]{a^{132}} \qquad\qquad \sqrt[12]{(5)^{132}} = 5^{\frac{132}{12}} = 48{,}828{,}125$

(B) $\quad \sqrt[144]{a^{132}} \qquad\qquad \sqrt[144]{(5)^{132}} = 5^{\frac{132}{144}} \approx 4.372$

(C) $\quad \sqrt[121]{a^{132}} \qquad\qquad \sqrt[121]{(5)^{132}} = 5^{\frac{132}{121}} \approx 5.788$

(D) $\quad \sqrt[11]{a^{132}} \qquad\qquad \sqrt[11]{(5)^{132}} = 5^{\frac{132}{11}} = 244{,}140{,}625$

Choice (B) gives us the same value as the original expression when we use the calculator to evaluate it when $a = 5$, so (B) is correct.

Solution 2: Graphing: We can set the expression in the prompt equal to y and graph it. Then we can do the same with the expression from each answer choice, and see which answer choice's graph matches the graph of the expression from the prompt.

We start by graphing the given expression:

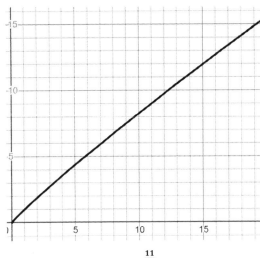

$$y = x^{\frac{11}{12}}$$

Then we graph each choice:

(A)

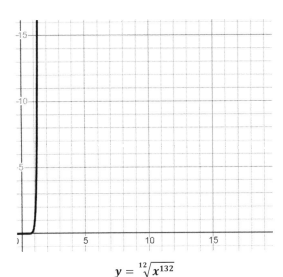

$$y = \sqrt[12]{x^{132}}$$

(B)

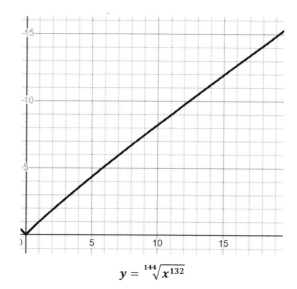

$$y = \sqrt[144]{x^{132}}$$

(C)

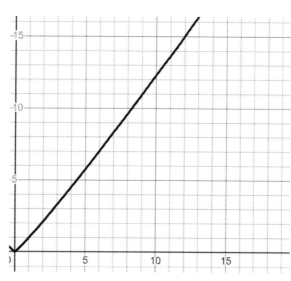

$$y = \sqrt[121]{x^{132}}$$

(D)

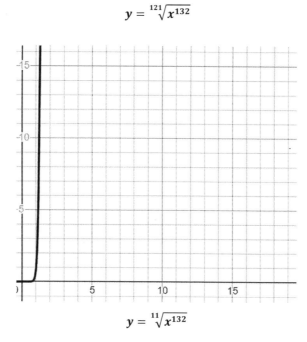

$$y = \sqrt[11]{x^{132}}$$

We can see that the graph of choice (B) matches the graph of the provided expression, so (B) is correct. (Note that the prompt says $a > 0$, so we don't care what the graph does to the left of the y-axis.)

Solution 3: Test-smart: Compare the numerator to the denominator of the original expression, and eliminate any answer choice whose root and exponent don't reflect a similar relationship.

In the provided expression, the numerator of the exponent is slightly smaller than the denominator of the exponent. That means the root in the correct answer must have a slightly larger value than the exponent that a is being raised to. In every choice, a is raised to a power of 132. The only choice with a root that's greater than 132 is (C), with a root of 144. So only (B) can be correct.

ANSWER CHOICE ANALYSIS

(C): This choice would be correct if 132 and 121 were swapped.

How to check? Try an alternate approach above. Try to figure out which mistakes could lead to some of the wrong answer choices, and verify that you haven't made any such mistakes.

Test 1, Module 2, Question 20

- What's the prompt asking for? The greatest number of attendees the party can have without exceeding the budget, as described in the prompt.

- Math concepts in the prompt: word problems, money
- Things to look out for: Make sure you read the question carefully and understand what it's asking for!

Solution 1: Concrete: Figure out how much of the budget can go toward paying for attendees, and then figure out how many attendees that amount of money can cover.

We can subtract the one-time fee of $35 from the budget of $200 to find out how much money the event planner has left over to pay the $10.25 cost per attendee. $200 − $35 = $165, which means the event planner can spend $165 on the per-attendee fee.

We can divide $165 by $10.25 to find out how many times the event planner can pay the $10.25 fee with $165:

$$\frac{\$165}{\$10.25} \approx 16.1$$

So the planner can pay for approximately 16.1 attendees with $165. We need to round this number down to 16, because there must be a whole number of attendees, and if we rounded up we would exceed the budget, which the prompt says we can't do. So the answer is 16.

Solution 2: Algebra: Convert the words and phrases in the prompt into a mathematical expression relating all the values in the prompt, then use that expression to answer the question.

The cost we're trying to calculate is the following:
$$\text{onetime fee} + \text{total cost for all attendees} \leq \$200$$
The onetime fee is $35, so let's add that to our expression:
$$\$35 + \text{total cost for all attendees} \leq \$200$$
The total cost for all attendees will be the number of attendees multiplied by the $10.25 fee for each attendee, since each attendee will incur a cost of $10.25. Let's use x as the number of attendees.
$$\$35 + \$10.25x \leq \$200$$
We can subtract $35 from both sides:
$$\$10.25x \leq \$165$$
Now we divide both sides by $10.25 to see how many attendees the event planner can pay for with $165:
$$x \leq 16.1$$
The event planner can pay for a little more than 16 attendees. We have to round this number down to 16, because there must be a whole number of attendees, and rounding up would exceed the budget, which the prompt tells us not to do. Again, we see the answer is 16.

How to check? Use the value you found to determine the total money spent on attendees, then add that result to the onetime fee. Make sure the total is less than $200, but not by enough that the difference could pay for more attendees. Try an alternate approach above. Try to figure out which mistakes the College Board might hope you would make in finding your solution, and verify that you haven't made any such mistakes.

Test 1, Module 2, Question 21

- What's the prompt asking for? The positive value of $x - 1$.
- Math concepts in the prompt: equations, variables, absolute value

- "Bridge" concepts: Because $4x - 4$ appears in absolute value brackets in the given equation, $x - 1$ will have a positive value and a negative value.
- Things to look out for: Make sure your solution accounts for the idea that $|4x - 4|$ must have both a positive and negative value!

Solution 1: Algebra: Account for the positive and negative values of the absolute value expression, find the two possible values of $x - 1$, and use the positive one to answer the question.

If $|4x - 4| = 112$, then it must be true that $4x - 4 = 112$ *or* $4x - 4 = -112$. Let's solve each of these equations for x, and then find "the positive value of $x - 1$" as the prompt requires.

$4x - 4 = 112$	(one of the possibilities, given that $|4x - 4| = 112$)
$4x = 116$	(add 4 to both sides)
$x = 29$	(divide both sides by 4)
$x - 1 = 28$	(find $x - 1$, as the prompt requires)

Now let's account for the other possibility of the absolute value equation.

$4x - 4 = -112$	(the other possibility, given that $|4x - 4| = 112$)
$4x = -108$	(add 4 to both sides)
$x = -27$	(divide both sides by 4)
$x - 1 = -28$	(find $x - 1$, as the prompt requires)

We found two values of $x - 1$, 28 and -28. We can see that "the positive value of $x - 1$" is 28, so the answer must be 28.

Solution 2: Test-smart: Notice that you can simplify the initial expression by dividing it by 4, then use that simplified expression to answer the question.

We might notice that the prompt asks us for $x - 1$, and the provided expression involves $|4x - 4|$, which is the absolute value of 4 times what the prompt asks for. Let's see what happens when we divide the provided expression by 4. When we do that, we get:

$$|x - 1| = 28$$

If $|x - 1| = 28$, then it must be true that $x - 1 = 28$ *or* $x - 1 = -28$. The prompt asks us for "the positive value of $x - 1$," which is 28—so the correct answer is 28.

How to check? Verify that your approach accounts for both a positive and negative value for $x - 1$. Try an alternate approach above. Try to figure out which mistakes the College Board might hope you would make in finding your solution, and verify that you haven't made any such mistakes.

Test 1, Module 2, Question 22

- What's the prompt asking for? The volume of the space in the cube <u>not</u> taken up by the sphere, to the nearest cubic inch.

- Math concepts in the prompt: cubes, edges, spheres, radii, volume

- Elements of the answer choices: Each answer choice is an integer ranging from 149,796 to 310,800.

- Notable features of the answer choices: (A), (B), and (C) all begin with 1, but (C) begins with 3.

- "Bridge" concepts: We can find the answer by subtracting the volume of the sphere from the volume of the cube.

- Things to look out for: Don't confuse the edge length with the radius length! Don't mistake the radius for a diameter! Don't accidentally find areas instead of volumes!

Solution 1: Geometry: Use the formulas provided by the College Board to find the volume of the cube and the sphere, then subtract the volume of the sphere from the volume of the cube.

Let's start by finding the volume of the cube—remember that the formula for the volume of a cube is in the provided reference sheet from the College Board.

$V = lwh$	(volume of a rectangular prism)
$V = 68^3$	(plug in 68 for l, w, and h)
$V = 314,432$	(simplify)

Next we need to subtract the volume of the sphere to find "the volume of the space in the cube <u>not</u> taken up by the sphere," as the prompt asks. So the next step is to find the volume of the sphere. Once again, we can find the formula we need in the provided reference sheet.

$V = \frac{4}{3}\pi r^3$	(volume of a sphere)
$V = \frac{4}{3}\pi (34)^3$	(plug in $r = 34$)
$V = \frac{4}{3}\pi (39,304)$	(simplify)
$V \approx 164,636$	(simplify)

Now we can subtract the volume of the sphere from the volume of the cube:

$$314{,}432 - 164{,}636$$

(volume of cube minus volume of sphere)

$$149{,}796$$

(simplify)

So the volume of the space in the cube not taken up by the sphere is 149,796 cubic inches, and the answer is (A).

(B): This is the approximate volume of the sphere. **(D):** This is the approximate result if we subtract the *area* of a *circle* with radius 34 inches from the volume of the cube, rather than subtracting the *volume* of a *sphere* with radius 34 inches.

How to check? Try an alternate approach above. Try to figure out which mistakes could lead to some of the wrong answer choices, and verify that you haven't made any such mistakes.

▶ Post-solution patterns (see page 286): right approach, wrong step; the right answer to the wrong question

Test 1, Module 2, Question 23

- What's the prompt asking for? The diameter of the circle with the given equation.
- Math concepts in the prompt: circles, diameter, equations
- Elements of the answer choices: Each answer choice is an integer ranging from 4 to 32.
- Notable features of the answer choices: The answer choices are in a series where each choice is twice as much as the previous choice.

- **"Bridge" concepts:** In the standard equation of a circle, the number to the right of the equals sign is the radius of the circle squared.
- Pre-solution patterns (see p. 285): halves and doubles; first and last terms in a series are often wrong answers
- Things to look out for: Remember that in the standard equation for a circle, 16 in the given equation corresponds to r^2, not r! Remember that the question asks for the *diameter* of the circle, not its radius!

Solution 1: Graphing: Graph the provided equation and find the diameter of the circle.

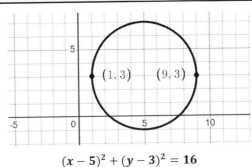

$$(x - 5)^2 + (y - 3)^2 = 16$$

When we graph the provided equation, we can see that the circle stretches from $(1, 3)$ to $(9, 3)$, which means the diameter of the circle is 8, and (B) is correct.

Solution 2: Properties and definitions: Use your understanding of the standard equation of a circle to find the answer.

If we recognize the standard equation for a circle, we would know that 16 is equal to r^2, which means the radius is 4, and the diameter must be 8. Again, that means (B) is correct.

(A): This is equal to the radius of the circle, not its diameter **(C):** This is the square of the radius, not the diameter. It's also twice the diameter. **(D):** This would be the answer if the radius of the circle were 16 instead of 4.

How to check? Verify that the question asked about the diameter, and that you found the diameter. Try an alternate approach above. Try to figure out which mistakes could lead to some of the wrong answer choices, and verify that you haven't made any such mistakes.

▶ Post-solution patterns (see page 286): right approach, wrong step; the right answer to the wrong question

Test 1, Module 2, Question 24

- What's the prompt asking for? The equivalent form of f that shows the value of k as the coefficient or base.
- Math concepts in the prompt: exponential functions, variables, constants, bases
- Elements of the answer choices: Each answer choice is a function involving raising 1.6 to an exponent.

- Notable features of the answer choices: Each answer choice is a function composed of some constant multiplied by 1.6 raised to a different exponent involving an x-term.

- "Bridge" concepts: We can plug $x = 1$ into the function to find k, and then we can pick the choice where that k-value is a coefficient or a base.

- Pre-solution patterns (see p. 285): wrong answers try to imitate right answers

- Things to look out for: Notice that every exponent in the answer choices is different!

Solution 1: Concrete: Read the question carefully, try to figure out what it means, and use that information to find the answer (this solution is kind of based on not really knowing what the question is asking for in the first place, because that's how a lot of test-takers will feel after they read this prompt, so don't worry if the description for this solution seems kind of vague).

The prompt tells us that "the value of $f(1)$ is k, where k is a constant." Then it asks us to find the answer choice that "shows the value of k as the coefficient or the base."

This is kind of a weird question, by the way—but we'll discuss that more in the note below. For now, let's focus on solving it.

If $f(1)$ is k, as the prompt says, that means plugging in $x = 1$ results in k. If k is also "the coefficient or the base," that means this k-value—which, again, we get when $x = 1$—must be either the coefficient or the base in the correct answer.

Another way to think of this is to say that when we plug $x = 1$ into the right answer, that resulting $f(1)$ value (which the prompt tells us is k) must be the same as either the coefficient or the base in the correct answer. Even if we're a little unclear on what this means, let's plug $x = 1$ into each function and see what we get.

(A) $f(1) = 50(1.6)^{1+1}$ $= 50(1.6)^2$ $= 128$
(B) $f(1) = 80(1.6)^1$ $= 80(1.6)$ $= 128$
(C) $f(1) = 128(1.6)^{1-1}$ $= 128(1.6)^0$ $= 128$
(D) $f(1) = 204.8(1.6)^{1-2}$ $= 204.8(1.6)^{-1}$ $= 128$

Every choice equaled 128—which makes sense, since the prompt tells us these are all "equivalent forms" of the same function f, so plugging in the same value *should* produce the same result. But now we know that $f(1) = 128$, which means k must equal 128. The only choice where 128 appears is (C), where it's the coefficient of $(1.6)^{x-1}$. In other words, choice (C) includes k as the coefficient, as the prompt requires, which means (C) must be correct.

Solution 2: Test-smart: Find the k-value described in the prompt, and pick the answer choice where that k-value appears as a coefficient or a base.

If we understand what the question is asking, we know that each of these functions is equivalent to the others, so we can find $f(1)$ (which the prompt tells us is k), by plugging $x = 1$ into any of the functions. When we do that we learn that $k = 128$. The prompt asks us to find the choice where k is "the coefficient or the base," which means k, or 128, must appear in the function. Only (C) includes 128, which is k, which means (C) must be correct.

ANSWER CHOICE ANALYSIS

(A): This choice would be correct if the prompt said that $f(-1)$ was k, instead of $f(1)$. **(B):** This choice would be correct if the prompt said that $f(0)$ was k, instead of $f(1)$. **(D):** This choice would be correct if the prompt said that $f(2)$ was k, instead of $f(1)$.

How to check? Reread the prompt to verify that you know what it's asking for, and that your answer satisfies that requirement. Try an alternate approach above. Try to figure out which mistakes could lead to some of the wrong answer choices, and verify that you haven't made any such mistakes.

▶   Post-solution patterns (see page 286): the right answer to the wrong question

Note   This is a great example of the way that an SAT Math question can ask something we may have never seen in a math question before, but if we understand each word in the question and think carefully about what those words mean, we can still find the answer with certainty. We may not have ever seen a question that asks for an "equivalent form[]" of a function that shows a certain value "as the coefficient or the base," but we can still use our understanding of each of those words to find the right answer. Remember this on test day—even if you see something you've never seen before, just take the question one word at a time and one concept at a time, and try to make progress.

Test 1, Module 2, Question 25

- What's the prompt asking for? The equation that represents the model described in the prompt.

- Math concepts in the prompt: word problems, models, populations, percentages, time

- Elements of the answer choices: Each answer choice is an equation that starts with "$n =$."

- Notable features of the answer choices: Each answer choice includes a function set equal to either the value 72 or 180, and that value is multiplied by either 1.5 or 2.5 raised to an exponent of t.

- "Bridge" concepts: When $t = 1$, the squirrel population must be 180.

- Pre-solution patterns (see p. 285): wrong answers try to imitate right answers

- Things to look out for: Notice that the squirrel population was 180 at the end of 2016, not at the end of 2015! Notice that a 150% increase is the same as multiplying by 2.5, not by 1.5!

Solution 1: Concrete: Plug $t = 1$ into each answer choice, and eliminate each one that doesn't produce a value of 180.

The prompt tells us that t is the number of years after the end of 2015, and it tells us that there were 180 squirrels in the population "at the end of 2016." The end of 2016 is one year after the end of 2015, so that means when $t = 1$, the number of squirrels in the population n was 180. We can plug $t = 1$ into each provided equation to see which one produces a population of 180 squirrels.

    (A) $n = 72(1.5)^{(1)}$ $= 108$
    (B) $n = 72(2.5)^{(1)}$ $= 180$
    (C) $n = 180(1.5)^{(1)}$ $= 270$
    (D) $n = 180(2.5)^{(1)}$ $= 450$

After checking each choice, we can see that only the equation in (B) reflected a squirrel population of 180 after 1 year, as the prompt required—so (B) must be correct.

Solution 2: Careful reading: Use the information in the prompt to eliminate wrong answer choices.

As we saw in our previous solution, we can learn from the prompt that when $t = 1$, the squirrel population is 180. Since the prompt tells us that the squirrel population grows each year, it must be true that when $t = 0$, the squirrel population is less than 180. That eliminates (C) and (D), because each of those choices would result in a squirrel population of 180 when $t = 0$.

So we only have (A) and (B) left. The prompt mentions the squirrel population increasing by 150%. That's the same as multiplying by 2.5, not by 1.5—multiplying by 1.5 would reflect a 50% increase, not a 150% increase. So we know the right answer will involve multiplying by 2.5, not 1.5, which is enough for us to eliminate (A). That leaves only (B), the correct answer.

Solution 3: Test-smart: Use the fact that the population is 180 when $t = 1$ to eliminate wrong answer choices.

Once we understand that the population must be 180 squirrels after one year (when $t = 1$), we can eliminate (C) and (D), because each one would result in a number larger than 180 when $t = 1$. We can also eliminate (A) because when $t = 1$ choice (A) would involve multiplying a number (72) that's less than half of 180 by a number (1.5) that's less than 2, which must result in a number *less than* 180 when $t = 1$, which contradicts the prompt. That leaves only (B), the correct answer.

ANSWER CHOICE ANALYSIS

(A): This choice would reflect the idea of the squirrel population increasing by 50% each year, not by 150%. **(C):** This choice combines the errors from (A) and (D). **(D):** This choice would be correct if the population were 180 in 2015, not in 2016, as the prompt tells us.

How to check? Plug $t = 1$ into the choice you selected and verify that the result is 180. Try an alternate approach above. Try to figure out which mistakes could lead to some of the wrong answer choices, and verify that you haven't made any such mistakes.

▶   Post-solution patterns (see page 286): the right answer to the wrong question

---

Test 1, Module 2, Question 26

- **What's the prompt asking for?** The pair of equations that represents a pair of perpendicular lines.

- **Math concepts in the prompt:** systems of equations, perpendicular lines, constants

- **Elements of the answer choices:** Each answer choice is a system of equations involving x, y, a, and b.

- **Notable features of the answer choices:** The first equation in each choice includes some combination of $10x, 5x$, and $7y$. The second equation includes some combination of ax and by, with different signs and sometimes a coefficient of 2.

- **"Bridge" concepts:** The slopes of perpendicular lines are the opposite reciprocals of each other.

- **Pre-solution patterns (see p. 285):** halves and doubles; wrong answers try to imitate right answers

- **Things to look out for:** Don't make a small mistake related to sign! Don't mix up the 4 different variables in this question! Don't confuse the properties of perpendicular lines with those of parallel lines!

Solution 1: Concrete: Find the slopes of the provided equations in terms of a, b, and x. Use the fact that the slopes of perpendicular lines are the negative reciprocals of each other to figure out enough about a and b to determine which system of equations in the answer choices has lines that are perpendicular to each other too. (If this doesn't make sense to you yet, just keep reading through the explanation.)

If two lines are perpendicular to one another, their slopes are opposite reciprocals of each other. Let's find the slope of each line from the given equations and see what we can figure out. There are various ways to find the slope of a line; we'll do it by solving each equation for y to put it in slope-intercept form.

$$5x + 7y = 1 \qquad \text{(first equation)}$$
$$7y = -5x + 1 \qquad \text{(subtract } 5x \text{ from both sides)}$$
$$y = -\frac{5}{7}x + \frac{1}{7} \qquad \text{(divide both sides by 7)}$$

In slope-intercept form, the coefficient of x is the slope of the line. So the slope of the first line is $-\frac{5}{7}$. Now let's find the slope of the second line in terms of a and b.

$$ax + by = 1 \qquad \text{(second equation)}$$
$$by = -ax + 1 \qquad \text{(subtract } ax \text{ from both sides)}$$
$$y = -\frac{a}{b}x + \frac{1}{b} \qquad \text{(divide both sides by } b)$$

So the slope of the second line in terms of a and b is $-\frac{a}{b}$. At this point in the solution, a lot of test-takers still won't be totally sure how they're going to find the answer to the question. But now that we've found the slopes of the two provided equations, it probably makes sense to try to find the slopes of the equations in all the other answer choices. We'll start with (A).

$$10x + 7y = 1 \qquad \text{(first equation from (A))}$$
$$7y = -10x + 1 \qquad \text{(subtract } 10x \text{ from both sides)}$$
$$y = -\frac{10}{7}x + \frac{1}{7} \qquad \text{(divide both sides by 7)}$$

So the slope of the first equation in (A) is $-\frac{10}{7}$. Let's find the slope of the second equation.

$$ax - 2by = 1 \qquad \text{(second equation from (A))}$$
$$-2by = -ax + 1 \qquad \text{(subtract } ax \text{ from both sides)}$$
$$y = \frac{a}{2b}x - \frac{1}{2b} \qquad \text{(divide both sides by } -2b)$$

So the slope of the second equation in (A) is $\frac{a}{2b}$. Is this the opposite reciprocal of $-\frac{10}{7}$? Well, we know from our analysis of the provided pair of equations that $-\frac{5}{7}$ and $-\frac{a}{b}$ must be opposite reciprocals (again, we know that because we're told those lines are perpendicular to one another, and we know that perpendicular lines have slopes that are opposite reciprocals of one another).

Let's think this through. If $-\frac{5}{7}$ is the opposite reciprocal of $-\frac{a}{b}$, what's the opposite reciprocal of $-\frac{10}{7}$? In $-\frac{10}{7}$, the numerator is twice as much as the numerator in $-\frac{5}{7}$. So in the opposite reciprocal of $-\frac{10}{7}$, the denominator must be twice as much as the denominator in $-\frac{a}{b}$. That means the opposite reciprocal of $-\frac{10}{7}$ in terms of a and b would be $-\frac{a}{2b}$. That's not the same as the slope of this line, which was $\frac{a}{2b}$, so the graphs of these equations aren't perpendicular to one another, and (A) is wrong. Let's check (B).

The first equation in (B) is the same as the first equation in (A), so we already know the slope of the first equation is $-\frac{10}{7}$. Now let's find the slope of the second equation.

$$ax + 2by = 1 \qquad \text{(second equation from (B))}$$
$$2by = -ax + 1 \qquad \text{(subtract } ax \text{ from both sides)}$$
$$y = -\frac{a}{2b}x + \frac{1}{2b} \qquad \text{(divide both sides by } 2b)$$

So the slope of the second equation in (B) is $-\frac{a}{2b}$. As we saw in our discussion of (A), this *is* the opposite reciprocal of $-\frac{10}{7}$. Again, we know this because we figured out from the provided equations that $-\frac{5}{7}$ is the opposite reciprocal of $-\frac{a}{b}$, and we can see that $-\frac{10}{7}$ is the same as $-\frac{5}{7}$ with the numerator doubled, so its opposite reciprocal must be $-\frac{a}{b}$ with the *denominator* doubled—which is the same as $-\frac{a}{2b}$. So (B) appears to be correct; let's check the remaining answer choices to make sure we haven't overlooked anything or made a mistake.

Again, the first equation in (C) is the same as the first equation in (A) and (B), so we already know the slope of the first equation is $-\frac{10}{7}$. Now let's find the slope of the second equation.

$$2ax + by = 1 \qquad \text{(second equation from (C))}$$
$$by = -2ax + 1 \qquad \text{(subtract } 2ax \text{ from both sides)}$$
$$y = -\frac{2a}{b}x + \frac{1}{b} \qquad \text{(divide both sides by } b)$$

So the slope of the second equation in (C) is $-\frac{2a}{b}$. Using the same analysis we just used on (A) and (B), we can see that this isn't the opposite reciprocal of $-\frac{10}{7}$. Finally, let's check (D).

$$5x - 7y = 1 \qquad \text{(first equation from (D))}$$
$$-7y = -5x + 1 \qquad \text{(subtract } 5x \text{ from both sides)}$$
$$y = \frac{5}{7}x - \frac{1}{7} \qquad \text{(divide both sides by } -7)$$

So the slope of the first equation in (D) is $\frac{5}{7}$. The second equation in (D) is the same as the second equation from the prompt, so we know the slope of the second equation in (D) must be $-\frac{a}{b}$. We know from our analysis of the two equations in the prompt that the negative reciprocal of $-\frac{a}{b}$ is $-\frac{5}{7}$, not $\frac{5}{7}$. So (D) is wrong.

After considering each answer choice, we can see that (B) is correct.

Solution 2: Test-smart: Compare the equations in the answer choices to the equations from the prompt to figure out which one must be a pair of perpendicular lines.

As we saw in the solution above, the slopes of the two provided lines are $-\frac{5}{7}$ and $-\frac{a}{b}$. In both cases, the slope is a negative fraction with the coefficient of x in the numerator and the coefficient of y in the denominator.

The first three answer choices have the same first equation, which is the same as the first equation in the prompt, except the coefficient of x is doubled from 5 to 10. If the coefficient of x is doubled, that means that means the slope of that line must have a numerator which is twice as much as the numerator of the slope fraction of the line from the prompt (again, because the numerator of the slope fraction is that coefficient of x). This means the slope of the first line in (A), (B), and (C) must be $-\frac{10}{7}$.

In order for the other equation to have a slope that's the opposite reciprocal of the slope of a line with double the coefficient of x, that other equation must have double the coefficient of y—because we doubled the numerator of the first slope fraction, so now we need to double the denominator of its reciprocal in the other slope fraction. (Again, as we just discussed, the denominator of that slope is the coefficient of y.)

With all of this in mind, we know that a line whose slope is the opposite reciprocal of the slope of $10x + 7y = 1$ must be $ax + 2by = 1$ (once more, because the coefficient of x in the given first equation was doubled from 5 to 10, so we need to double the coefficient of y from the given second equation from b to $2b$). This is what we see in (B), so we know that (B) is correct.

(If this didn't make sense to you, read through it one more time. Take it phrase by phrase and idea by idea, checking the relevant equations as you go. If it still doesn't make sense, don't worry—you don't have to understand every solution to every question; you should just aim to understand at least one solution, and to find the kinds of approaches that you're most comfortable with so you have the best shot at each question on test day.)

ANSWER CHOICE ANALYSIS

(A): This choice is the same as the right answer, except the coefficient of y in the second equation is negative, not positive. **(C):** This choice is the same as the right answer, with the coefficient of ax and by in the second equation switched. **(D):** This choice has the same second equation as the one we saw in the prompt, but its first equation has a minus sign, not a plus sign, as we saw in the prompt. We know this choice must be wrong because $ax + by = 1$ can't be perpendicular to both $5x + 7y = 1$ from the prompt and $5x - 7y = 1$ from this choice.

How to check? Try an alternate approach above. Try to figure out which mistakes could lead to some of the wrong answer choices, and verify that you haven't made any such mistakes.

> **Note** Some students will see the provided equations and feel like they can't find the slope of a line that includes the variables a, b, x, and y. We might not typically see something like this in a classroom situation, but we can still manipulate the provided equations just as we normally would—we'll end up finding a slope with variables in it, but that doesn't mean we can't use it to find the answer to the question. An important part of your SAT Math preparation is learning to get comfortable attempting a solution even when the prompt involves something you haven't seen before. Just focus on what you *do* know, apply that knowledge to the task in front of you, and you'll typically find that your solution will start to come together and make sense.

Test 1, Module 2, Question 27

- **What's the prompt asking for?** The least possible value of n.
- **Math concepts in the prompt:** equations, constants, exponents, variables, inequalities

- **"Bridge" concepts:** The question is asking for the maximum value of the given equation in an unusual way.
- **Things to look out for:** Don't make a simple mistake related to sign! Make sure you read the prompt carefully and understand what it's asking for!

Solution 1: Concrete/graphing: Make c equal to y, and then graph the resulting equation.

We can make c equal to y, and then graph the resulting equation:

$$x^2 - 34x + y = 0$$

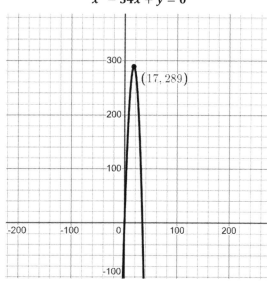

$(17, 289)$

The maximum y-value of that graph will be the lowest n-value for which there are no real solutions when $c > n$, as the prompt requires. In other words, when y is *greater* than the greatest y-value on the graph, the equation has "no real solutions"—because we're talking about y-values that don't appear on the graph (remember that we changed the c from the prompt to y because it's typically easier to use x and y in the SAT's graphing calculator). If this doesn't make much sense to you, don't worry; just keep reading.

We can see that the maximum y-value in that graph is 289—in other words, there are no coordinate pairs in that graph with a y-value greater than 289, which means that the original equation has no real solutions when c is more than 289 (again, we turned c into y when we graphed the equation). So the least possible value of n is 289, and the answer is 289.

How to check? Reread the question and make sure you understand what it's asking. Try to figure out which mistakes the College Board might hope you would make in finding your solution, and verify that you haven't made any such mistakes.

Note There's another way to approach this question that you can find in the College Board's free explanations. That approach is very algebra-intensive and requires you to remember some facts about quadratic equations. I find that most students don't think that approach is very helpful, either because they already understand it, or because they are completely uncomfortable with it. I would encourage you to get used to looking for graphical solutions like the one above on test day, because those solutions are the quickest, easiest, and cleanest in the vast majority of situations.

TEST 2 - MODULE 1

Test 2, Module 1, Question 1

- What's the prompt asking for? The model year for which the percent of cars for sale is the smallest.

- Math concepts in the prompt: word problems, line graphs, percentages, years

- Elements of the answer choices: Each answer choice is a year ranging from 2012 to 2015.

- "Bridge" concepts: The answer will be the year that corresponds to the smallest value on the graph.

- Pre-solution patterns (see p. 285): first and last terms in a series are often wrong answers

- Things to look out for: Make sure you note which year lines up with which value on the graph!

Solution 1: Concrete: Read the graph to find the information required by the prompt.

When we read all the labels related to the graph, we can see that the vertical axis shows the "Percent of cars for sale," and it ranges from 0% to 15%. The value that is the lowest against that vertical axis is the one for 2014. So the answer is (C), 2014.

ANSWER CHOICE ANALYSIS

(A): This year is tied for the *greatest* percent, not the smallest.

How to check? Double-check the prompt and graph. Try to figure out which mistakes could lead to some of the wrong answer choices, and verify that you haven't made any such mistakes.

▶ Post-solution patterns (see page 286): the right answer to the wrong question

Note This question is very straightforward; don't let that throw you off. We often see questions like this in the SAT Math section, especially near the beginning of a module.

Test 2, Module 1, Question 2

- What's the prompt asking for? The probability of selecting a bead that has a defect
- Math concepts in the prompt: word problems, fractions, probability
- Elements of the answer choices: Every answer choice is a fraction that includes 1 and 29; some include zeros as well.

- Notable features of the answer choices: (B) is 100 times greater than (A). (D) is 10 times greater than (C).
- Pre-solution patterns (see p. 285): wrong answers try to imitate right answers
- Things to look out for: Think carefully about how to construct a probability fraction! Think carefully about which quantity is the desired outcomes, and which quantity is the possible outcomes!

Solution 1: Probability: Use the information in the prompt to construct a probability fraction.

To construct a probability fraction, we put the number of desired outcomes in the numerator, and the number of possible outcomes in the denominator, like this:

$$\frac{\text{number of desired outcomes}}{\text{number of possible outcomes}}$$

In this case, the desired outcome (that is, the outcome we're being asked about) is "selecting a bead that has a defect." The prompt tells us that this happens 29 times in the given sample size. So 29 is the numerator of our fraction.

The "number of possible outcomes" in the given sample size is 100, because the 29 beads with defects from the prompt were selected from 100 beads; in other words, those 29 beads came from a group of 100 beads, any one of which could possibly be chosen. So 100 is the denominator of our fraction.

That means the probability fraction the question asks about is $\frac{29}{100}$, and the correct answer is (C).

ANSWER CHOICE ANALYSIS

(B): This is the probability of picking any one bead from the 29 defective beads. **(D):** This is ten times the correct answer.

How to check? Try to figure out which mistakes could lead to some of the wrong answer choices, and verify that you haven't made any such mistakes.

Test 2, Module 1, Question 3

- What's the prompt asking for? The value of x.
- Math concepts in the prompt: parallel lines, intersecting lines, variables, transversals, angle measures
- Elements of the answer choices: Each answer choice is an integer ranging from 33 to 147.

- Notable features of the answer choices: (A) and (B) add up to 90°. (A) and (D) add up to 180°. (B) and (C) add up to 180°.
- "Bridge" concepts: The sum of the two angle measures must be 100°.
- Things to look out for: Don't get confused about whether the angles should add up to 90° or 180°!

Solution 1: Concrete/geometry: Use your understanding of transversals to determine the relationship between the 33° angle and x.

Since lines m and n are parallel, line t must cross them at the same angle. That means the labeled 33° angle in the provided figure where t crosses n is the same size as the corresponding angle where t crosses m. Let's add that measurement to the figure.

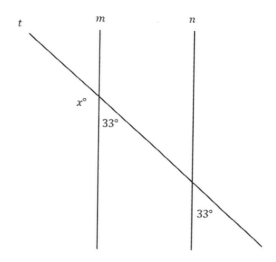

We can see that the 33° angle and the $x°$ angle must add up to 180°, because together they form a straight line. This is the same as saying that $33° + x° = 180°$. When we subtract 33° from both sides, we get $x = 147°$. So the answer is (D), 147.

ANSWER CHOICE ANALYSIS

(A): This is the value of the labeled angle from the diagram. **(B):** This would be the answer if the two angles added up to 90° instead of 180°. **(C):** This is the measure of the labeled angle, plus 90°.

How to check? Verify that your answer added to 33° is equal to 180°. Try to figure out which mistakes could lead to some of the wrong answer choices, and verify that you haven't made any such mistakes.

▶   Post-solution patterns (see page 286): right approach, wrong step; the right answer to the wrong question

Test 2, Module 1, Question 4

- What's the prompt asking for? The y-intercept of the graph.
- Math concepts in the prompt: y-intercept, line graphs
- Elements of the answer choices: Each answer choice is a coordinate pair where one of the values is zero.
- Notable features of the answer choices: Each answer choice includes either a positive or negative 6 or 8, and a zero.

- "Bridge" concepts: The y-intercept of the graph is the point where the line crosses the y-axis.
- Pre-solution patterns (see p. 285): opposites; wrong answers try to imitate right answers
- Things to look out for: Don't confuse x and y! Don't make a simple mistake related to sign!

Solution 1: Concrete: Find the information to answer the question in the provided graph.

We can see that the line crosses the y-axis at $(0, 8)$, so the answer is (D).

ANSWER CHOICE ANALYSIS

(A): The is the opposite of the right answer in two ways—it includes -8 instead of 8, and 8 appears as a y-value instead of an x-value. **(C):** The line appears to have a y-value of 6 on the far left side of the graph, but that's not what the prompt asks about.

How to check? Verify that you haven't gotten x and y mixed up. Try to figure out which mistakes could lead to some of the wrong answer choices, and verify that you haven't made any such mistakes.

Test 2, Module 1, Question 5

- What's the prompt asking for? The total cost to lease a car when the monthly payment is $400.
- Math concepts in the prompt: word problems, functions, money, monthly payments
- Elements of the answer choices: Each answer choice is a dollar amount ranging from $13,000 to $37,400.
- Notable features of the answer choices: Two answer choices start with 13, and three end with 400.

- "Bridge" concepts: The answer will be the value of the function when $x = 400$.
- Pre-solution patterns (see p. 285): wrong answers try to imitate right answers
- Things to look out for: Don't make a simple algebra mistake! Don't forget to account for the $1,000 from the function in the total cost!

Solution 1: Concrete: Plug in $x = 400$ to find the total cost to lease a car when the monthly payment is $400.

The prompt tells us that the provided function $f(x)$ tells us the total cost, in dollars, to lease a car for 36 months. Then it tells us that x in that function "is the monthly payment, in dollars." So we can plug in the monthly payment the prompt asks about for x to find the total cost, as the prompt requires. That monthly payment is $400, so w'll find the answer by plugging $x = 400$ into the provided function.

$$f(x) = 36x + 1{,}000 \qquad \text{(provided function)}$$
$$f(400) = 36(400) + 1{,}000 \qquad \text{(plug in } x = 400\text{)}$$
$$f(400) = 14{,}400 + 1{,}000 \qquad \text{(simplify)}$$
$$f(400) = 15{,}400 \qquad \text{(simplify)}$$

So the total cost to lease a car for 36 months with a monthly payment of $400 is $15,400, and the answer is (C).

Solution 2: Concrete/graphing: We can graph the provided function, then find the $f(x)$ value when $x = 400$.

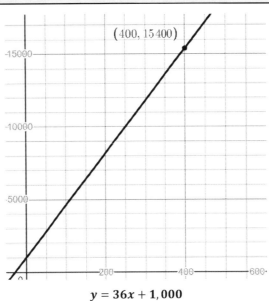

$$y = 36x + 1{,}000$$

We can see that when $x = 400$, $f(x) = 15{,}400$. So the answer is $15,400, and choice (C) is correct.

ANSWER CHOICE ANALYSIS

(A): This would be the result if we accidentally *subtracted* $1,000 from $14,400, instead of adding it. **(D):** This is the result of thinking that plugging $x = 400$ into $36x + 1{,}000$ produces the expression $36{,}400 + 1{,}000$.

How to check? Try an alternate approach above. Try to figure out which mistakes could lead to some of the wrong answer choices, and verify that you haven't made any such mistakes.

Test 2, Module 1, Question 6

- What's the prompt asking for? The perimeter of the square described in the prompt.
- Math concepts in the prompt: squares, perimeter, side length

- "Bridge" concepts: The perimeter of the square is the sum of the lengths of its sides.
- Things to look out for: Don't confuse perimeter and area! Don't make a mistake adding up the side lengths!

Solution 1: Geometry: Sketch the square described in the prompt, and add up the lengths of its sides.

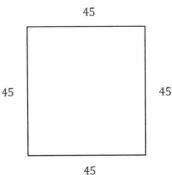

$$45 + 45 + 45 + 45 = 180$$

So the sum of the lengths of the four sides is 180, and the answer is 180.

Solution 2: Abstract: Use your knowledge of squares to find the perimeter based on the provided information.

Squares have 4 sides of equal length. If one side length is 45, then the perimeter is 45×4, or 180. That means the answer is 180.

How to check? Try an alternate approach above. Try to figure out which mistakes the College Board might hope you would make in finding your solution, and verify that you haven't made any such mistakes.

Note Like many SAT Math questions with no answer choices, this one is pretty straightforward. The fact that there aren't any answer choices probably makes it more likely that some untrained test-takers will accidentally solve for the *area* of the square, instead of its perimeter, and they'll be less likely to notice their error since they won't see the perimeter in the answer choices. Keep the possibility of this kind of error in mind on test day when you see questions with no answer choices.

Test 2, Module 1, Question 7

- What's the prompt asking for? The positive solution to the given equation.
- Math concepts in the prompt: equations, fractions, variables
- "Bridge" concepts: The answer will be a positive value for x that makes the given equation true.

- Things to look out for: Make sure your understanding of the question and your solution account for the idea that this equation has multiple solutions! Don't make a simple mistake related to sign!

Solution 1: Concrete/graphing: We can enter this equation into the provided graphing calculator to find the values for x that are solutions to the given equation.

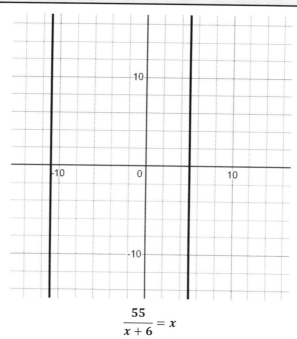

$$\frac{55}{x + 6} = x$$

When we do that, the results are $x = -11$ and $x = 5$. The prompt asks us for "the positive solution to the given equation," and the only positive solution is 5, so the answer is 5.

Solution 2: Algebra: Solve for x, and find the positive x-value that's a solution to the equation.

$\frac{55}{x+6} = x$	(provided equation)
$55 = x(x + 6)$	(multiply both sides by $(x + 6)$)
$55 = x^2 + 6x$	(simplify)
$0 = x^2 + 6x - 55$	(subtract 55 from both sides)
$0 = (x - 5)(x + 11)$	(reverse-FOIL)
$x - 5 = 0$ or $x + 11 = 0$	(set each factor equal to zero)
$x = 5$ or $x = -11$	(simplify)

So the solutions to the equation are $x = 5$ and $x = -11$. The prompt asks us for "the positive solution to the given equation," and the only positive solution is 5, so the answer is 5.

How to check? Try an alternate approach above. Try to figure out which mistakes the College Board might hope you would make in finding your solution, and verify that you haven't made any such mistakes.

Test 2, Module 1, Question 8

- **What's the prompt asking for?** The time in seconds that it would take for the object in the prompt to travel 108 centimeters.
- **Math concepts in the prompt:** speed, time, distance
- **Elements of the answer choices:** Each answer choice is an integer ranging from 9 to 972.

- **"Bridge" concepts:** We can find the time it takes the object to travel 108 centimeters by dividing that distance by the object's speed.
- **Things to look out for:** Don't get confused about how the speed and distance relate to one another! Don't make a simple algebra mistake!

Solution 1: Abstract: Read the prompt and think about how the speed relates to the distance, and use that information to answer the question.

If an object travels at 12 centimeters per second, we can find out how long it takes that object to travel 108 centimeters by figuring out how many 12-centimeter chunks make up a distance of 108 centimeters, because we know each span of 12 centimeters takes a second for the object to travel it.

This is the same as dividing 108 by 12. When we do that, we get $\frac{108}{12} = 9$. So 12 centimeters goes into 108 centimeters 9 times, and the object will travel 108 centimeters in 9 seconds. That means the answer is (A).

Solution 2: Algebra: Use $d = rt$ to solve for the time it would take the object to cover 108 centimeters at 12 centimeters per second.

If we know the formula $d = rt$, or $distance = rate \times time$, we can plug in the provided values and solve for time.

$d = rt$	(distance formula)
$108 = 12t$	(plug in $d = 108$ and $r = 12$)
$\frac{108}{12} = t$	(divide both sides by 12)
$9 = t$	(simplify)

So it will take the object 9 seconds to travel 108 centimeters, and (A) is correct.

Solution 3: Test-smart: Use your understanding of $d = rt$ to eliminate each wrong answer choice.

When we multiply the given speed by the right answer (which is the time spent traveling at that speed), the result must be 108. Multiplying 96 by 12 will give us a result much greater than 108, and so will any number larger than 96—so we can eliminate (B), (C), and (D), which means (A) is correct.

ANSWER CHOICE ANALYSIS

(B): This is $108 - 12$, which combines two numbers from the prompt, but not in a way that answers the question. **(C):** This is $108 + 12$, which combines two numbers from the prompt, but not in a way that answers the question.

How to check? Try an alternate approach above. Try to figure out which mistakes could lead to some of the wrong answer choices, and verify that you haven't made any such mistakes.

Test 2, Module 1, Question 9

- **What's the prompt asking for?** The statement that correctly compares the mean of data set X to the mean of data set Y.
- **Math concepts in the prompt:** data, mean
- **Notable features of the answer choices:** Each choice makes a different comparison between the two data sets.

- **"Bridge" concepts:** Data set Y is the same as data set X, except Y has one additional data point (27) that's higher than any other data point.
- **Pre-solution patterns (see p. 285):** opposites
- **Things to look out for:** Don't confuse X and Y!

Solution 1: Concrete: Calculate the mean of each data set, and make the comparison.

The mean of a data set is the sum of the values in the data set divided by the number of values in the set. So the mean of data set X is:

$$\frac{5 + 9 + 9 + 13}{4} = \frac{36}{4} = 9$$

And the mean of data set Y is:

Facebook.com/QuestPreparation   Youtube.com/QuestPrep

$$\frac{5 + 9 + 9 + 13 + 27}{5} = \frac{63}{5} = 12.6$$

So the mean of data set Y is greater than the mean of data set X, and (B) is correct.

Solution 2: Abstract: Think carefully about the differences between the data sets, and about how those differences impact the mean of each set.

We can see that data set Y is identical to data set X except it includes one additional number, 27, that's greater than any other value in the set. Whatever the mean of data set X is, adding a number that's higher than every value in data set X must increase that mean, so the mean of data set Y must be greater than the mean of data set X, and (B) is correct.

ANSWER CHOICE ANALYSIS

(A): This is the opposite of the right answer.

How to check? Try an alternate approach above. Try to figure out which mistakes could lead to some of the wrong answer choices, and verify that you haven't made any such mistakes.

Test 2, Module 1, Question 10

- What's the prompt asking for? The approximate amount of propellant the rocket burned each second after launch, on average.

- Math concepts in the prompt: word problems, average, burn rate, subtraction

- Elements of the answer choices: Each answer choice is an integer ranging from 4,995 to 104,895.

- "Bridge" concepts: We can find the amount of propellant burned per second by finding the total amount of propellant burned, and then dividing that amount by the number of seconds it took to burn.

- Things to look out for: Make sure to use the right value for the amount of fuel that burned in the 21 seconds!

Solution 1: Concrete: Find the amount of fuel that burned, then divide the result by the 21 seconds that the fuel took to burn.

In order to find the average amount of propellant the rocket burned per second over the course of the 21 seconds, we need to know the total amount of propellant the rocket burned over that period of time. We can find that amount by subtracting the amount of remaining propellant from the initial amount of propellant.

The prompt tells us the rocket started with 467,000 kg of propellant and was left with 362,105 kg of propellant after the 21 seconds. So it burned 467,000 − 362,105, or 104,895 kg of propellant.

Now we divide this amount by the number of seconds the rocket took to burn that much propellant; the result will be how much of the propellant the rocket burned each second.

$$\frac{104,895 \text{ kg}}{21 \text{ s}} = 4,995$$

So the rocket burned 4,995 kg of fuel per second, and (A) is correct.

Solution 2: Test-smart: Use the provided information to approximate the answer, and eliminate all choices that aren't close to your approximation.

Once we notice that 467,000 kg is a little more than 100,000 kg more than 362,015 kg, we can realize that the number we're looking for is a little more than 100,000 kg divided by just over 20, which will be right around $\frac{100,000}{20}$, which is right around 5,000. Only one answer choice is anywhere near 5,000, and that's the correct answer, (A).

ANSWER CHOICE ANALYSIS

(B): This would be the rate if 362,105 kg burned in 21 seconds. **(C):** This would be the rate if 467,000 + 362,105 kg burned in 21 seconds. **(D):** This is the total amount of fuel that burned in 21 seconds.

How to check? Multiply your answer by 21 to verify that the result is the difference between 467,000 and 362,105. Try an alternate approach above. Try to figure out which mistakes could lead to some of the wrong answer choices, and verify that you haven't made any such mistakes.

▶ Post-solution patterns (see page 286): right approach, wrong step; the right answer to the wrong question

Test 2, Module 1, Question 11

- What's the prompt asking for? The value of $16x + 8$.
- Math concepts in the prompt: equations, variables

- Elements of the answer choices: Each answer choice is an integer ranging from 40 to 60.

- Notable features of the answer choices: (A), (B), and (C) form a series where each choice is 8 more than the previous choice.
- "Bridge" concepts: We can use the value of x in the given equation to find the value of the expression the prompt asks about.

- Pre-solution patterns (see p. 285): first and last terms in a series are often wrong answers
- Things to look out for: Don't make a simple mistake related to sign! Don't make a simple algebra mistake! Don't overlook "+2" from the provided equation!

Solution 1: Algebra: Solve for x in the provided equation, then use that x-value to answer the question.

$$4x + 2 = 12 \qquad \text{(given equation)}$$
$$4x = 10 \qquad \text{(subtract 2 from both sides)}$$
$$x = 2.5 \qquad \text{(divide both sides by 4)}$$

Now we can plug $x = 2.5$ into $16x + 8$ to find the answer to the question.

$$16x + 8 \qquad \text{(expression whose value we need to find)}$$
$$16(2.5) + 8 \qquad \text{(plug in } x = 2.5)$$
$$40 + 8 \qquad \text{(simplify)}$$
$$48 \qquad \text{(simplify)}$$

So the answer is (B), 48

Solution 2: Test-smart: Find the value of $16x + 8$ using the value of $4x + 2$ directly, without finding the value of x.

If we notice that $16x + 8$ is 4 times as much as $4x + 2$, we can just multiply the value of $4x + 2$ by 4 to find the value of $16x + 8$. The prompt tells us that $4x + 2 = 12$, so $16x + 8$ must be 4 times as much as 12, or 48. So (B) is correct.

ANSWER CHOICE ANALYSIS

(A): This is value of $16x$, not $16x + 8$. **(C):** This would be the answer if the provided equation was $4x = 12$.

How to check? Try an alternate approach above. Try to figure out which mistakes could lead to some of the wrong answer choices, and verify that you haven't made any such mistakes.

▶ Post-solution patterns (see page 286): the right answer to the wrong question

Test 2, Module 1, Question 12

- What's the prompt asking for? The height in meters from which the object was kicked.
- Math concepts in the prompt: word problems, equations, height, time
- Elements of the answer choices: Each answer choice is a numerical value ranging from 0 to 9.

- Notable features of the answer choices: Three answer choices are integers, and one is a decimal expression. Each non-zero choice appears in the provided equation.
- Things to look out for: Don't confuse h and t! Think carefully about how the situation in the prompt relates to the equation!

Solution 1: Concrete/graphing: We can graph the equation and check the value of h the moment the object was kicked, when $t = 0$.

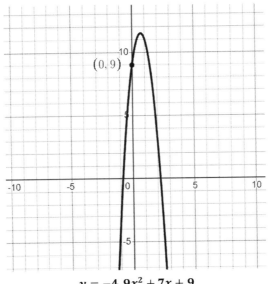

$$y = -4.9x^2 + 7x + 9$$

We can see that when $t = 0$, $h = 9$, so (D) is correct.

Solution 2: Algebra: Find the value of h when $t = 0$.

The prompt asks about "the height... from which the object was kicked." The height from which the object is kicked must be the height where the object is at the moment it's kicked—in other words, 0 seconds after it's been kicked, when $t = 0$.

If we plug $t = 0$ into the provided equation, we get $h = -4.9(0)^2 + 7(0) + 9$, or $h = 9$. So the "height, in meters, from which the object was kicked" must be 9, and the answer is (D).

ANSWER CHOICE ANALYSIS

(A): This is the t-value we need to plug in to find the right answer. **(B):** This is a coefficient from the provided equation. **(C):** This is a coefficient from the provided equation.

How to check? Try an alternate approach above. Try to figure out which mistakes could lead to some of the wrong answer choices, and verify that you haven't made any such mistakes.

▶ Post-solution patterns (see page 286): right approach, wrong step; the right answer to the wrong question

Test 2, Module 1, Question 13

- What's the prompt asking for? The value of x for which $f(x)$ reaches its minimum.

- Math concepts in the prompt: functions, parabolas, minimum

- "Bridge" concepts: The answer will be the x-value that produces the smallest possible $f(x)$ value when plugged into the given equation.

- Things to look out for: Don't make a small mistake related to sign! Remember that you need to find the x-value from the coordinate pair that corresponds to the minimum of the function!

Solution 1: Graphing: We can graph this function to find its minimum value.

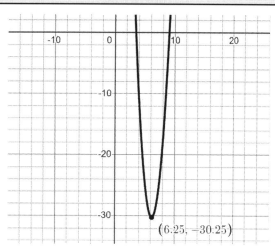

$$y = 4x^2 - 50x + 126$$

We can zoom in on the minimum value to see that it occurs at $(6.25, -30.25)$. The prompt asked "for what value of x does $f(x)$ reach its minimum?" That means the right answer is the x-value from that coordinate pair. So the answer is 6.25 (note that 6.25 and $\frac{25}{4}$ are both acceptable ways to enter the answer).

How to check? Verify that you've entered the equation into the graphing calculator correctly. Try to figure out which mistakes could lead to some of the wrong answer choices, and verify that you haven't made any such mistakes.

Note There's also a more formal, formulaic way to find the minimum value of the function, which you can see in the College Board's explanation for this question. I didn't include it here because students who are already comfortable with that approach won't benefit further from seeing it here, and in my experience students who aren't comfortable with it will still be uncomfortable with it after reading such a solution. Above all else, the graphing solution is so quick and easy that I *strongly* encourage you to get comfortable answering a question like this by using the provided calculator, instead of wasting precious time on test day writing out avoidable algebra.

- What's the prompt asking for? The maximum number of large candles the owner can purchase while staying within the budget and maintaining the discounted pricing.

- Math concepts in the prompt: money, prices, discounts, budget

- "Bridge" concepts: The business owner can't just spend all the money on large candles; the owner must buy enough small candles as well to meet the minimum order of 200 candles required for the discount.

- Things to look out for: Remember that your solution needs to account for both the budget and the discount.

Solution 1: Algebra: Create a system of inequalities based on the prompt, and solve it for the answer to the question.

Let's use s to represent the number of small candles purchased by the business owner and l to represent the number of large candles purchased by the business owner.

The prompt tells us that "the owner must purchase a minimum of 200 candles." That's the same as saying the sum of the number of small candles and the number of large candles must be at least 200, or $s + l \geq 200$.

The prompt also tells us that the owner has \$2,200 to purchase candles, and asks us for "the maximum number of large candles the owner can purchase to stay within the budget." Staying within the budget means the total cost of all the candles must be no more than \$2,200. That's the same as saying the total cost of the large candles and small candles must be at most \$2,200, or $\$4.90s + \$11.60l \leq \$2,200$.

(Note that we represented the total money spent on small candles with $\$4.90s$, which is the cost for each small candle multiplied by the number of small candles purchased, and we represented the total money spent on large candles with $\$11.60l$, which is the cost for each large candle multiplied by the number of large candles purchased. We added these together to represent the total amount of money spent on candles, and set that amount equal to or less than \$2,200 to represent the idea of spending no more than \$2,200 total on candles.)

We've created the following system of inequalities:

$$s + l \geq 200$$
$$\$4.90s + \$11.60l \leq \$2,200$$

We can solve for s in terms of l in one inequality, and then plug the resulting value into the other inequality to find the value of l.

$s + l \geq 200$	(first inequality we created)
$s \geq 200 - l$	(subtract l from both sides)

Now we can plug $200 - l$ in for s in the other equation.

$\$4.90s + \$11.60l \leq \$2,200$	(second inequality we created)
$\$4.90(200 - l) + \$11.60l \leq \$2,200$	(plug in $200 - l$ for s)
$\$980 - \$4.90l + \$11.60l \leq \$2,200$	(distribute the \$4.90)
$\$980 + \$6.70l \leq \$2,200$	(combine like terms)
$\$6.70l \leq \$1,220$	(subtract \$980 from both sides)
$l \leq 182.089$	(divide both sides by \$6.70)

So the number of large candles that the owner can buy must be less than 182.089 in order to be able to afford at least 200 candles total, and to avoid spending more than \$2,200 total. The largest whole number that's less than 182.089 is 182, so the answer is 182.

Solution 2: Concrete/graphing: Once we get the system of inequalities from the previous solution, we can graph them to find the answer.

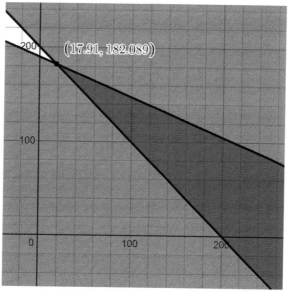

$$s + l \geq 200 \quad \text{and} \quad \$4.90s + \$11.60l \leq \$2,200$$

The inequalities intersect at $(17.91, 182.089)$. We can see that the maximum whole number of large candles the owner can purchase while staying within the budget and maintaining the discounted pricing is 182, so the answer is 182.

How to check? Verify that purchasing 182 large candles leaves enough money to purchase at least 18 small candles. Try an alternate approach above. Try to figure out which mistakes the College Board might hope you would make in finding your solution, and verify that you haven't made any such mistakes.

Test 2, Module 1, Question 15

- What's the prompt asking for? The equation that defines f.

- Math concepts in the prompt: linear functions, inputs and outputs

- Elements of the answer choices: Each answer choice is a function with an x-term.

- Notable features of the answer choices: Each choice is a different combination of 4, 8, 12, and x.

- "Bridge" concepts: We can use the provided inputs and outputs to test the different answer choices.

- Pre-solution patterns (see p. 285): wrong answers try to imitate right answers

- Things to look out for: Don't mix up the inputs and outputs! Don't make a simple algebra mistake!

Solution 1: Concrete: Find $f(0)$ and $f(1)$ for the function in each answer choice. Eliminate any choice where $f(0) \neq 8$ or $f(1) \neq 12$.

(A)	$f(0) = 12(0) + 8$	$= 8$	$f(1) = 12(1) + 8$	$= 20$
(B)	$f(0) = 4(0)$	$= 0$	$f(1) = 4(1)$	$= 4$
(C)	$f(0) = 4(0) + 12$	$= 12$	$f(1) = 4(1) + 12$	$= 16$
(D)	$f(0) = 4(0) + 8$	$= 8$	$f(1) = 4(1) + 8$	$= 12$

Choice (D) is the only function for which $f(0) = 8$ and $f(1) = 12$, so (D) is correct.

Solution 2: Concrete/graphing: We can graph each choice and eliminate each one where $f(0) \neq 8$ or $f(1) \neq 12$.

(A)

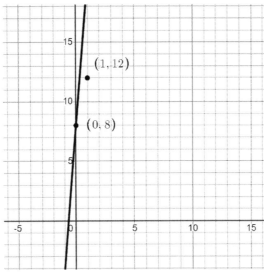

$y = 12x + 8$

(B)

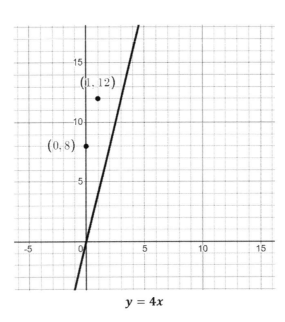

$y = 4x$

(C)

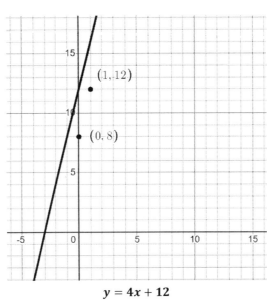

$y = 4x + 12$

(D)

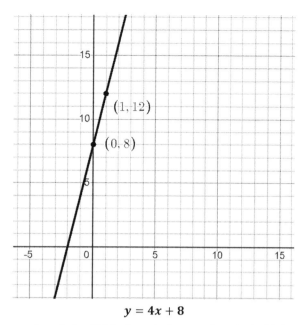

$$y = 4x + 8$$

When we check the graphs, we can see that choice (D) is the only function for which $f(0) = 8$ and $f(1) = 12$, so (D) is correct.

Solution 3: Test-smart. Quickly check the choices using the provided information, and eliminate each choice that fails to meet the requirements from the prompt.

When we plug in $x = 0$, we can quickly see that (B) and (C) won't produce a result of 8, so we can eliminate them. Then we can just check (A) and (D) by plugging in $x = 1$, at which point we can eliminate (A) and see that (D) is correct.

ANSWER CHOICE ANALYSIS

(A): For this choice $f(0) = 8$ but $f(1) \neq 12$. **(B):** This choice doesn't meet either requirement from the prompt. **(C):** For this choice, $f(0) = 12$, but the prompt tells us that $f(0) = 8$ and $f(1) = 12$.

How to check? Plug $x = 0$ and $x = 1$ into the function from the choice you picked to verify that the results satisfy the requirements in the prompt. Try an alternate approach above. Try to figure out which mistakes could lead to some of the wrong answer choices, and verify that you haven't made any such mistakes.

Test 2, Module 1, Question 16

- What's the prompt asking for? The choice that is the best interpretation of $f(14) = 1{,}176$.

- Math concepts in the prompt: functions, area of a rectangle, width, length

- Notable features of the answer choices: Each answer choice makes a different statement relating the width of the rectangle to its area or length.

- "Bridge" concepts: In $f(14) = 1{,}176$, the width of the rectangle is 14 and the area of the rectangle is 1,176.

- Pre-solution patterns (see p. 285): wrong answers try to imitate right answers

- Things to look out for: Don't mix up the relationships among the concepts and values in the prompt!

Solution 1: Careful reading: Compare the statements made in the prompt to the statements made in the answer choices, and eliminate each choice that makes a statement that is inconsistent with the information in the prompt.

The prompt tells us that in the function $f(w)$, w is the width of a rectangle in feet. In evaluating $f(14)$, it must be the case that $w = 14$, which means the width of the rectangle is 14 feet. That eliminates (C) and (D), because they both say the width of the rectangle is 1,176 feet. This leaves us with (A) and (B), which both correctly say that the width of the rectangle is 14 feet.

The prompt tells us that $f(w)$ gives us the *area* of a rectangle, so the value of $f(14)$ must be the area when $w = 14$. If $f(14) = 1{,}176$, then 1,176 must be the area of the rectangle when its width is 14. This eliminates (B), which says 1,176 is the *length* of the rectangle. So we know that choice (A) is correct.

ANSWER CHOICE ANALYSIS

(B): This would be correct if the output of the function were the *length* of the rectangle, rather than its area. **(C):** This choice makes the mistake from (B), and also reverses the input and output values of the function we're asked about. **(D):** This choice reverses the input and output values of the function we're asked about.

Test 2, Module 1, Question 17

- What's the prompt asking for? The length of arc QR.
- Math concepts in the prompt: circles, circumference, diameters, arc length
- Elements of the answer choices: Each choice is an even 2-digit integer multiplied by π.
- Notable features of the answer choices: (A), (B), and (D) form a series where each choice is twice as much as the previous choice. (A), (B), (C), and (D) form a series where each choice is 24π more than the previous choice.

- "Bridge" concepts: We can use the provided information to figure out which portion of the circumference corresponds to arc QR.
- Pre-solution patterns (see p. 285): halves and doubles; first and last terms in a series are often wrong answers
- Things to look out for: Don't mix up the start and end points of the difference arcs! Don't get confused about which arc length you need to find!

Solution 1: Geometry: Use your understanding of circles, diameters, and circumference to figure out which portion of the circumference corresponds to the length of arc QR.

If $\overline{PR}$ and $\overline{QS}$ are diameters, then by definition they must cross circle O at its widest point, and they must divide the circle in half—that is, an equal portion of the area and circumference of circle O must lie on either side of diameter $\overline{PR}$, and the same must be true on either side of $\overline{QS}$.

The prompt tells us that the circumference is 144π. Since arc PS and arc PQ together make up everything on one side of diameter $\overline{QS}$, then together they must account for half the circumference of the circle, or 72π (since $\frac{144\pi}{2} = 72\pi$). Let's add that to the diagram.

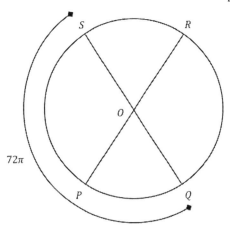

The prompt also tells us that "the length of arc PS is twice the length of arc PQ." So the length of arc PS must be $\frac{2}{3}$ the length of arc QS, or 48π, and the length of arc PQ must be $\frac{1}{3}$ the length of arc QS, or 24π. Let's add this information to the diagram too.

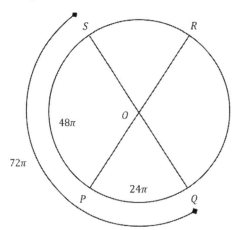

From this point, there are several ways we can tell that arc QR is the same length as arc SP. One way to tell is that since $\overline{PR}$ and $\overline{QS}$ are both diameters of the circle, each must pass through the center of the circle, and each must bisect the other—so exactly half of each diameter lies to the left of point O, and exactly half of each diameter lies to the right of point O. Furthermore, the diameters must form

---

vertical angles where they cross, so central angle ∠SOP is equal to central angle ∠ROQ. In other words, arc PS is essentially a mirror image of arc QR, so if arc PS has a length of 48π, then arc QR must have a length of 48π as well. So the answer is (B), 48π.

ANSWER CHOICE ANALYSIS

(A): This is the length of either arc PQ or arc SR. **(C):** This is the length of either arc PR or arc SQ. **(D):** This the length of the portion of the circumference that is *not* arc QR.

How to check? Try to figure out which mistakes could lead to some of the wrong answer choices, and verify that you haven't made any such mistakes.

▶   Post-solution patterns (see page 286):   right approach, wrong step; the right answer to the wrong question

Test 2, Module 1, Question 18

- What's the prompt asking for? The number of people in the group that were children in the situation described in the prompt.

- Math concepts in the prompt: word problems, money

- Elements of the answer choices: Each answer choice is an integer ranging from 3 to 18.

- Notable features of the answer choices: (B) is half of (D); (C) is the sum of (A) and (B).

- Pre-solution patterns (see p. 285): halves and doubles

- Things to look out for: Read carefully! Make sure you don't switch the numbers related to adults and the numbers related to children!

Solution 1: Concrete: Calculate the total revenue that would result from groups with the given number of children for each choice, based on the provided information. Pick the one whose revenue is 1,440 dollars.

Since we know that each group has a total of 21 people, we can use the given number of children in each answer choice to calculate the number of adults for that group. From there, we can use the number of children and adults, along with the information in the prompt, to find the total revenue for that group.

(A)   If 3 people were children, then 18 were adults. $3(60) + 18(80) = 1,620$
(B)   If 9 people were children, then 12 were adults. $9(60) + 12(80) = 1,500$
(C)   If 12 people were children, then 9 were adults. $12(60) + 9(80) = 1,440$
(D)   If 18 people were children, then 3 were adults. $18(60) + 3(80) = 1,320$

Only choice (C) results in a revenue of $1,440 for the whole group, so (C) is correct.

Solution 2: Algebra: Create a system of equations based on the information in the prompt, then use that system of equations to answer the question.

Let's use a to represent the number of adults and c to represent the number of children. The prompt tells us that there were 21 people in the group, which means the number of adults plus the number of children was equal to 21. This is the same as saying $a + c = 21$.

The prompt also tells us that the company's revenue is $80 per adult; that means we can find the total revenue from all adults by multiplying the amount of revenue per adult by the number of adults, which is the same as $80a$. Similarly, the prompt tells us that the company's revenue is $60 per child; we can find the total revenue from all children by multiplying the amount of revenue per child by the number of children, which is the same as $60c$. The prompt says that for the group in question, the total revenue was $1,440, which is the same as saying that $80a + 60c = 1,440$.

Now we have the following system of equations:

$$a + c = 21$$
$$\$80a + \$60c = \$1,440$$

To find the value of c, we can solve the first equation for a in terms of c, and then plug the result into the second equation and solve for c.

$a + c = 21$	(first equation)
$a = 21 - c$	(subtract c from both sides)

Now we can plug $a = 21 - c$ into the second equation and solve for c.

$\$80a + \$60c = \$1,440$	(second equation)
$\$80(21 - c) + \$60c = \$1,440$	(plug in $a = 21 - c$)
$\$1680 - \$80c + \$60c = \$1,440$	(distribute the $80)
$\$1680 - \$20c = \$1,440$	(combine like terms)
$\$1680 - \$20c = \$1,440$	(subtract $1,440 from both sides)
$\$240 - \$20c = \$0$	(subtract $1,440 from both sides)
$\$240 = \$20c$	(add $20c to both sides)
$12 = c$	(divide both sides by $20)

So there were 12 children in the group, and the answer is (C).

Solution 3: Graphing: Once we have the system of equations, we can graph both equations and find their point of intersection.

We'll use x for a and y for c, which gives us this:

$$x + y = 21$$
$$\$80x + \$60y = \$1,440$$

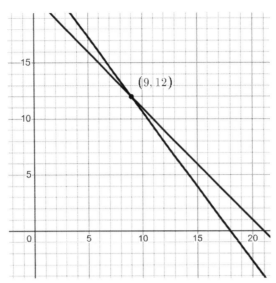

We can see that the graphs intersect at $(9, 12)$. We used y for the c-value, so the y-coordinate tells us the number of children in the group that represented a total revenue of $1,440. That means there were 12 children in that group, and the answer is (C).

ANSWER CHOICE ANALYSIS

(A): This would be the number of children in a group where *the adults alone* accounted for 1,440 dollars in revenue. **(B):** This is the number of *adults* in the group that had a revenue of 1,440 dollars, not children, as the prompt asked for. **(D):** This is the number of adults that would account for 1,440 dollars in revenue alone, without counting the revenue for the children.

How to check? Try an alternate approach above. Try to figure out which mistakes could lead to some of the wrong answer choices, and verify that you haven't made any such mistakes.

▶   Post-solution patterns (see page 286):   right approach, wrong step; the right answer to the wrong question

Test 2, Module 1, Question 19

- What's the prompt asking for? The value of $a + b$.
- Math concepts in the prompt: functions, graphs, x-intercepts, y-intercepts
- Elements of the answer choices: The answer choices are integers ranging from 21 to 35.
- Notable features of the answer choices: (A), (B), and (D) form a series where each choice is 7 more than the previous choice.

- "Bridge" concepts: The x-intercept of the line is the point where the line crosses the x-axis. The y-intercept of the line is the point where the line crosses the y-axis.
- Pre-solution patterns (see p. 285): first and last terms in a series are often wrong answers
- Things to look out for: Don't confuse x and y! Don't confuse a and b! Remember that the prompt asks for the value of $a + b$!

Solution 1: Concrete/graphing: We can graph the provided function to find its intercepts.

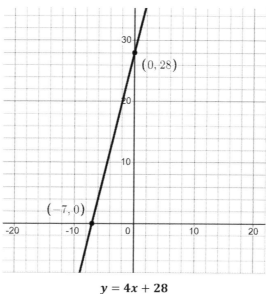

$$y = 4x + 28$$

We can see that the graph has an x-intercept at $(-7, 0)$ and a y-intercept at $(0, 28)$. That means $a = -7$ and $b = 28$, so $a + b = -7 + 28 = 21$, and the answer is (A), 21.

Solution 2: Algebra: Use the provided function to find its x-intercept and y-intercept, then use this info to answer the question.

In the equation $y = 4x + 28$, we can find the x-intercept by setting y equal to zero and solving for x.

$y = 4x + 28$	(graph of the function h when $y = h(x)$)
$0 = 4x + 28$	(set y equal to zero to find the x-intercept)
$-28 = 4x$	(subtract 28 from both sides)
$-7 = x$	(divide both sides by 4)

So the x-intercept is at $(-7, 0)$, which means the a-value described in the prompt is -7. Now we can find the y-intercept by setting $x = 0$ and solving for y.

$y = 4x + 28$	(graph of the function h when $y = h(x)$)
$y = 4(0) + 28$	(set x equal to zero to find the y-intercept)
$y = 28$	(simplify)

So the y-intercept is at $(0, 28)$, which means the b-value described in the prompt is 28.

If $a = -7$ and $b = 28$, then $a + b = -7 + 28 = 21$, and the answer is (A).

ANSWER CHOICE ANALYSIS

(B): This is the value of b, not the value of $a + b$. **(D):** This is the value of $b - a$, and would also seem to be the value of $a + b$ to an untrained test-taker who made a mistake and found that $a = 7$, instead of $a = -7$.

How to check? Try an alternate approach above. Try to figure out which mistakes could lead to some of the wrong answer choices, and verify that you haven't made any such mistakes.

▶ Post-solution patterns (see page 286): right approach, wrong step; the right answer to the wrong question

---

Test 2, Module 1, Question 20

- What's the prompt asking for? The smallest possible value of b.

- Math concepts in the prompt: polynomial expressions, factors, constants

- "Bridge" concepts: There must be multiple possible values for b; we need to find the smallest one.

- Things to look out for: Don't make a simple algebra mistake!

Solution 1: Concrete/graphing: We can set this equation equal to y and then graph it to see where it crosses the x-axis. We can use each of those points to determine the factors of the given expression, and then use those factors to answer the question.

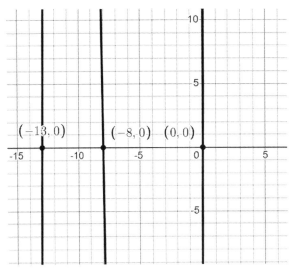

$$y = 2x^3 + 42x^2 + 208x$$

We can see that the zeros of the graph are $(-13, 0)$, $(-8, 0)$, and $(0, 0)$. That means its factors must be $x + 13$, $x + 8$, and x. The prompt tells us that one factor is $x + b$, and that b is a positive constant, so the two possible values of b are 13 and 8. The prompt asks for the smallest possible value of b, so the answer is 8.

Solution 2: Algebra: Factor the expression, and use those factors to answer the question.

When the College Board presents an expression like this, two situations are highly likely—either we won't actually need to factor the expression, or there will be something about the expression that makes it easier to factor than we might expect at first glance.

If we look for something easy to factor out, we might notice that each term can be divided by $2x$. That means we can factor out $2x$, like this:

$$2x^3 + 42x^2 + 208x \qquad \text{(provided expression)}$$
$$2x(x^2 + 21x + 104) \qquad \text{(factor out } 2x\text{)}$$

Now we have the expression $x^2 + 21x + 104$, which we can factor by reverse-FOILing. We can see that in order to do this, we need to think of two numbers that add up to 21 and that equal 104 when multiplied together. Let's try some to see what we get (for a refresher on reverse-FOILing, go take a look at page 257 in the SAT Math Toolbox in this Black Book).

$$10 \times 11 = 110$$
$$9 \times 12 = 108$$
$$8 \times 13 = 104$$

Now that we know 8 and 13 add up to 21 and multiply out to 104, we can finish reverse-FOILing:

$$x^2 + 21x + 104 \qquad \text{(expression we want to reverse-FOIL)}$$
$$(x + 8)(x + 13) \qquad \text{(result of reverse-FOILing)}$$

So the factors of $2x^3 + 42x^2 + 208x$ are $2x$, $x + 8$, and $x + 13$. The prompt tells us one factor of the given expression is $x + b$, and that b is a positive constant, so b must be either 13 or 8. The prompt asks for "the smallest possible value of b," so the answer is 8.

How to check? Try an alternate approach above. Try to figure out which mistakes the College Board might hope you would make in finding your solution, and verify that you haven't made any such mistakes.

Test 2, Module 1, Question 21

- What's the prompt asking for? The value of a.
- Math concepts in the prompt: systems of equations, constants, real solutions
- "Bridge" concepts: If the system has exactly one distinct real solution, then these lines must touch at exactly one point.

- Things to look out for: Make sure that the value you find for a only allows for one real solution to the system of equations!

Solution 1: Concrete/graphing: We can graph the provided equations, and use what we learn to figure out how to proceed with our solution.

Even if we're not sure how to proceed, we can graph the two provided equations to see what we can learn. We don't know the value of a, so let's just leave it out for now and see what we can figure out. That means we're graphing the following equations:

$$y = -1.5$$
$$y = x^2 + 8x$$

Facebook.com/QuestPreparation   Youtube.com/QuestPrep

When we do that, we get this result:

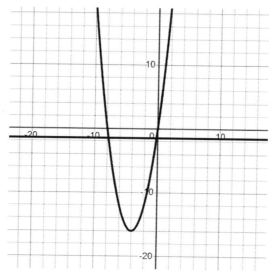

Now that we see the graph, this question might start to make a little more sense. In order for this system of equations to have "exactly one distinct real solution," it must be the case that the horizontal line $y = -1.5$ touches the parabola from the other equation at the vertex of that parabola.

(We know this must be true because if the horizontal line $y = -1.5$ is above the vertex, then it will cross the parabola at two points, which would mean the system has two real solutions, and if that horizontal line is below the vertex, it won't cross the parabola at all, which would mean the system would have no real solutions; either of these cases would contradict the statement in the prompt that "the system has exactly one distinct real solution." Again, the only way for the system to have one distinct real solution would be for $y = -1.5$ to touch the vertex of the parabola.)

We can see in the graph that the y-coordinate of the vertex of the parabola is -16. That vertex needs to move up 14.5 units to touch $y = -1.5$ at exactly one point. In order to make this happen, we would need to add 14.5 to $x^2 + 8x$ in the equation $y = x^2 + 8x$. That means $a = 14.5$, and the answer is 14.5. (Note that we can also enter this answer as $\frac{29}{2}$.)

Note that once we figure this out, we can change the second equation in our calculator to $y = x^2 + 8x + 14.5$ to confirm that this causes the graphs to intersect at exactly one point—the resulting graph looks like this:

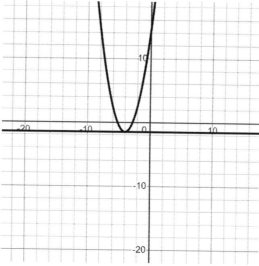

Again, we can see that the answer is 14.5, or $\frac{29}{2}$.

How to check? Verify that you've entered everything into the calculator correctly. Try to figure out which mistakes the College Board might hope you would make in finding your solution, and verify that you haven't made any such mistakes.

Note A lot of test-takers will see this question and not really be sure how to approach it. When that happens, one of the first things you should consider doing is trying to graph something from the question, and seeing if that clears anything up. In this case, we can leave off the a-value in the second equation, then graph both equations. When we consider the results in light of the prompt, we can see how moving that second equation vertically could result in a situation where the system has one real solution, just as the prompt requires. Remember on test day that the provided calculator is a very powerful tool—particularly the graphing functionality—and it can often help you to solve complex SAT Math questions in seconds.

- What's the prompt asking for? The table of values that represents $y = f(x) - 3$.

- Math concepts in the prompt: functions, tables of values

- Elements of the answer choices: Each answer choice is a table of values displaying x inputs and y outputs for a function.

- Notable features of the answer choices: Each table of values from the answer choices has the same 3 x-values $(-6, -5, 4)$ with different y-values.

- "Bridge" concepts: If $y = f(x) - 3$, then each y-value must be 3 less than the result when x is plugged into $f(x)$.

- Pre-solution patterns (see p. 285): opposites; wrong answers try to imitate right answers

- Things to look out for: Don't make a simple mistake related to sign! Don't confuse $f(x) - 3$ with $x - 3$!

Solution 1: Concrete: Plug the three x-values that appear in all four tables into $f(x) - 3$ and eliminate each choice whose y-values don't match the results.

Once we notice that each table has the same three x-values, we know we can check each answer choice by just plugging in those three values. Once we find $f(x)$ for each of those x-values, we can subtract three from each $f(x)$ value to account for the fact that $y = f(x) - 3$, as detailed in the prompt.

$$f(-6) = \quad (-6+6)(-6+5)(-6-4) = \quad (0)(-1)(-10) = 0$$
$$f(-5) = \quad (-5+6)(-5+5)(-5-4) = \quad (1)(0)(-9) = 0$$
$$f(4) = \quad (4+6)(4+5)(4-4) = \quad (10)(9)(0) = 0$$

So we got the following coordinate pairs after plugging $x = -6$, $x = -5$, and $x = 4$ into $y = f(x)$:
$$(-6, 0) \quad (-5, 0) \quad (4, 0)$$

Subtracting 3 from each y-value gives us:
$$(-6, -3) \quad (-5, -3) \quad (4, -3)$$

This matches the table in (B), so (B) is correct.

Solution 2: Concrete/graphing: We can graph the provided function, then find $f(x)$ for each provided x-value. Finally, we can subtract 3 from each $f(x)$ value we found and see which answer choice matches the result.

Let's start by graphing the provided function $f(x) = (x+6)(x+5)(x-4)$.

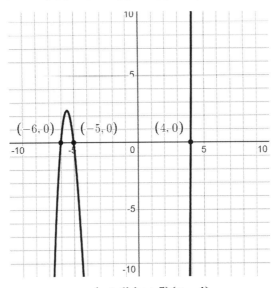

$$y = (x + 6)(x + 5)(x - 4)$$

Now we can check each x-value, see what the corresponding $f(x)$-value is, and then subtract 3 from that result to account for the idea that $y = f(x) - 3$.

We can see that $f(-6) = 0$, $f(-5) = 0$, and $f(4) = 0$. So there are points on the graph of the original function at $(-6, 0)$, $(-5, 0)$, and $(4, 0)$. When we subtract 3 from each of those y-values, we're left with the points $(-6, -3)$, $(-5, -3)$, and $(4, -3)$. So (B) is correct.

Solution 3: Test-smart: Notice that the provided x-values would each cause $f(x)$ to equal zero, and use this information to figure out the y-values that should appear in the table from the correct answer.

If we notice that the x-values in each table correspond with the zeros of the provided function (that is, $x = -6$ will cause $(x + 6)$ to equal zero, $x = -5$ will cause $(x + 5)$ to equal zero, and $x = 4$ will cause $(x - 4)$ to equal zero), then we know that $f(x)$ for all three x-values will be zero, and subtracting 3 from each of those zeros (which we need to do, because $y = f(x) - 3$) will give us -3. So the right answer must have -3 for each y-value, which means (B) is correct.

ANSWER CHOICE ANALYSIS

(A): This is the table of values for $y = x - 3$. **(C):** This is the table of values for $y = x + 3$. **(D):** This is the table of values for $y = f(x) + 3$.

How to check? Try an alternate approach above. Try to figure out which mistakes could lead to some of the wrong answer choices, and verify that you haven't made any such mistakes.

Test 2, Module 1, Question 23

- **What's the prompt asking for?** The equation that defines q, if $q(0) = 14$.
- **Math concepts in the prompt:** functions, percent decrease, variables
- **Elements of the answer choices:** Each answer choice is a function with an expression raised to an exponent of x.

- **Notable features of the answer choices:** Each choice involves the numbers 0.55, 14, and/or 1.45, combined in different ways.
- **"Bridge" concepts:** Decreasing by 45% is the same as being multiplied by $(1 - 0.45)$, or 0.55.
- **Pre-solution patterns** (see p. 285): wrong answers try to imitate right answers
- **Things to look out for:** Think carefully about what happens when a number decreases by 45%!

Solution 1: Concrete/graphing: Graph each choice and eliminate each one that doesn't decrease.

The prompt tells us that "the value of $q(x)$ decreases" with "every increase in the value of x by 1." So any choice whose graph doesn't decrease must be wrong, and can be eliminated.

(A)

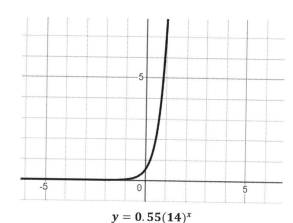

$$y = 0.55(14)^x$$

(B)

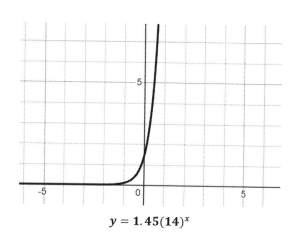

$$y = 1.45(14)^x$$

(C)

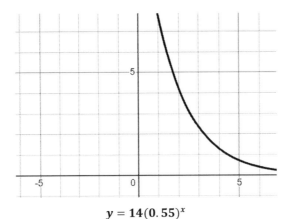

$$y = 14(0.55)^x$$

(D)

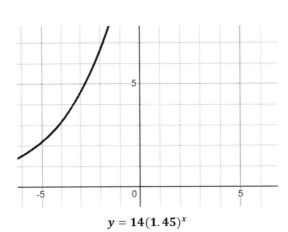

$$y = 14(1.45)^x$$

We can see that only (C) decreases, as the prompt requires. So (C) must be right.

Solution 2: Concrete: Use the information in the prompt to test the answer choices. Eliminate each choice that isn't consistent with the information in the prompt.

The prompt tells us that $q(0) = 14$. Let's start by plugging $x = 0$ into each answer choice to see what we get.

    (A) $q(0) = 0.55(14)^0 = 0.55(1) = 0.55$

    (B) $q(0) = 1.45(14)^0 = 1.45(1) = 1.45$

    (C) $q(0) = 14(0.55)^0 = 14(1) = 14$

    (D) $q(0) = 14(1.45)^0 = 14(1) = 14$

So we can eliminate (A) and (B), since $q(0) \neq 14$ for those two choices. That leaves us with (C) and (D).

The prompt tells us that "the value of $q(x)$ decreases by 45%" when x increases by 1. Decreasing by 45% is the same as multiplying by $(1 - 0.45)$, or 0.55. Choice (C) reflects this idea, because it involves 0.55 raised to an exponent of x, which means each time x increases by one, that expression will be multiplied by 0.55 one additional time—which is the same as decreasing by 45%, as the prompt describes.

On the other hand, (D) involves multiplying the expression by 1.45, which is the same as *increasing* by 45%—not *decreasing* by 45%, as the prompt requires.

So we can see that (C) satisfies the requirements in the prompt and (D) doesn't, which means (C) is correct.

Solution 3: Abstract: Think carefully about what would cause the value of the function to decrease as x increases, and eliminate any choices that don't satisfy this reasoning.

(A), (B), and (D) all involve raising a number larger than 1 to an exponent of x, so as x increases, (A), (B), and (D) will all increase. But the prompt asked for a function where the value of $q(x)$ *decreases* as x gets larger. Only (C) will *decrease* as x *increases*, so only (C) can be correct.

(Notice that (C) involves raising a number less than 1—that is, 0.55—to an exponent of x, which means that every time x increases by 1, the value of $q(x)$ will get multiplied by 0.55 one additional time, which will cause that value to decrease, as the prompt requires).

ANSWER CHOICE ANALYSIS

(A): This is the right answer with 0.55 and 14 switched. **(B):** This choice combines the errors from (A) and (D). **(D):** This function demonstrates the idea of *increasing* by 45%, not *decreasing* by 45%.

How to check? Verify that the answer you picked will decrease as x increases. Try an alternate approach above. Try to figure out which mistakes could lead to some of the wrong answer choices, and verify that you haven't made any such mistakes.

▶ Post-solution patterns (see page 286): the right answer to the wrong question

Test 2, Module 1, Question 24

- What's the prompt asking for? The equation that defines function f.

- Math concepts in the prompt: graphs, functions

- Elements of the answer choices: Each choice is a function in $y = mx + b$ format.

- Notable features of the answer choices: Each answer choice is the same except for the last term.

- "Bridge" concepts: Each choice has the same slope and a different y-intercept. The provided graph is of

$y = f(x) + 14$, so every y-value in $y = f(x)$ will be 14 less than in the provided graph.

- Pre-solution patterns (see p. 285): wrong answers try to imitate right answers

- Things to look out for: Don't mix up y-intercepts and x-intercepts! Don't misread the graph! Remember that the graph shows $f(x) + 14$, *not* $f(x)$!

Solution 1: Concrete: Figure out a point that must lie on $f(x)$, based on the provided graph of $f(x) + 14$, then test the equations in the answer choices to see whether they contain that point or not.

The prompt provides a graph of $y = f(x) + 14$. In other words, every point on the provided graph has a y-value which is the result of adding 14 to $f(x)$.

That means we can find a point from the provided graph, subtract 14 from the y-value of that point, and the result will be a point that lies on the graph of the function we need to find in the answer choices.

We can see that the point $(0, 2)$ lies on the provided graph. That means the point $(0, 2 - 14)$, or $(0, -12)$, must lie on $f(x)$, which is the same as saying that $f(0) = -12$. So we can find $f(0)$ for each of the functions in the answer choices, and eliminate each one that doesn't produce a value of 12.

$$\text{(A)} \quad f(0) = -\tfrac{1}{4}(0) - 12 = \quad 0 - 12 = \quad -12$$
$$\text{(B)} \quad f(0) = -\tfrac{1}{4}(0) + 16 = \quad 0 + 16 = \quad 16$$
$$\text{(C)} \quad f(0) = -\tfrac{1}{4}(0) + 2 = \quad 0 + 2 = \quad 2$$
$$\text{(D)} \quad f(0) = -\tfrac{1}{4}(0) - 14 = \quad 0 - 14 = \quad -14$$

Choice (A) is the only function for which $f(0) = -12$, so (A) is correct.

Solution 2: Concrete/graphing: Add 14 to each function in the answer choices to see which one produces the function whose graph is provided.

The prompt tells us that the provided graph is the graph of $y = f(x) + 14$, and then asks us to choose the answer choice that defines function f. That means we can add 14 to the end of the correct answer to get the function whose graph is provided in the prompt.

So let's add 14 at the end of every function in the answer choices, and then graph them to see which one matches the provided graph.

$$\text{(A)} \ f(x) + 14 = -\tfrac{1}{4}x - 12 + 14 \qquad f(x) + 14 = -\tfrac{1}{4}x + 2$$

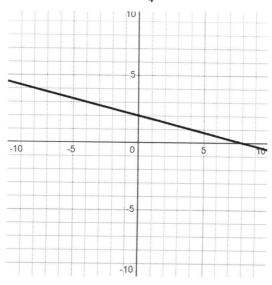

(B) $f(x) + 14 = -\frac{1}{4}x + 16 + 14 \qquad f(x) + 14 = -\frac{1}{4}x + 30$

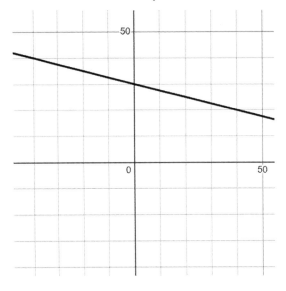

(C) $f(x) + 14 = -\frac{1}{4}x + 2 + 14 \qquad f(x) + 14 = -\frac{1}{4}x + 16$

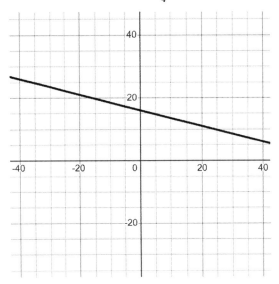

(D) $f(x) + 14 = -\frac{1}{4}x - 14 + 14 \qquad f(x) + 14 = -\frac{1}{4}x$

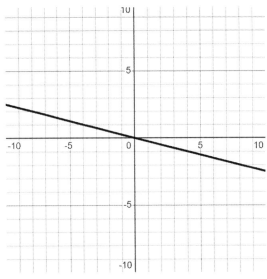

Only choice (A) matches the provided graph, so (A) is correct.

Solution 3: Test-smart: Use your understanding of slope-intercept form and the provided graph to figure out which is the only choice whose function would result in the correct y-intercept after 14 is added to it.

If we're familiar with slope-intercept form, we can tell that each answer choice is in slope-intercept form. That means the constant at to the end of each function in the answer choice is the y-intercept of that function.

We can see that the y-intercept of $y = f(x) + 14$ in the provided graph is $(0, 2)$. If that graph is the result of adding 14 to each value in $f(x)$, then the y-intercept of $f(x)$ must be 14 units *less* than the y-intercept in the graph from the prompt. So the y-intercept of $f(x)$ must be $2 - 14$, or -12.

The only choice with a y-intercept of -12 is (A), so (A) is the right answer.

ANSWER CHOICE ANALYSIS

(B): This choice would be the result if the provided graph were the function $f(x)$, and we were supposed to find the choice that was $f(x) + 14$, and not the other way around. **(C):** This choice matches the provided graph—but that graph is of $f(x) + 14$, and the prompt wants us to find the function f. **(D):** This choice might be tempting for test-takers who thought the provided graph showed $f(x) = -\frac{1}{4}x$, and/or who misunderstood the prompt and assumed that the right answer should include "-14."

How to check? Verify that your solution involved moving the graph 14 units in the correct direction. Try an alternate approach above. Try to figure out which mistakes could lead to some of the wrong answer choices, and verify that you haven't made any such mistakes.

▶ Post-solution patterns (see page 286): the right answer to the wrong question

Test 2, Module 1, Question 25

- **What's the prompt asking for?** The value of $\tan W$.
- **Math concepts in the prompt:** right triangles, similar triangles, tangent, trigonometry
- **Elements of the answer choices:** Each answer choice is a fraction with 5, 12, and/or 13 in the numerator and denominator.
- **Notable features of the answer choices:** Two answer choices have 5 in the numerator, two have 12 in the numerator, and two have 13 in the denominator. 5 appears three times and 12 appears three times.

- **"Bridge" concepts:** If Triangles RST and UVW are similar, and T corresponds to W, then $\tan T$ is the same as $\tan W$.
- **Pre-solution patterns (see p. 285):** opposites; wrong answers try to imitate right answers
- **Things to look out for:** Don't mix up the different labels for the vertices! Don't confuse tangent with sine or cosine!

Solution 1: Geometry: Draw right triangle RST as described in the prompt, and label the sides according to the provided information. Then find the tangent of the vertex that corresponds to W.

Let's start by drawing the right triangle described in the prompt.

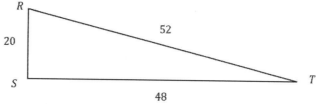

The prompt asks us about the tangent of an angle in another triangle that is similar to triangle RST. We know that a similar triangle will have the same angle measures as triangle RST, and that its sides will be in the same proportion as the sides of triangle RST, by definition. So let's just redraw the above triangle, substituting S for V, T for W, and R for U (we know that R must correspond to U, even though the prompt doesn't say so, because those are the only vertices not accounted for in the prompt, so the only possibility is that they correspond with each other).

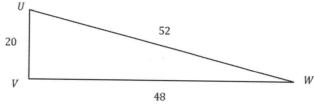

Note that we aren't given the side lengths for triangle UVW, but we *do* know that this triangle is similar to triangle RST, so we know the sides of triangle UVW are in the same *proportion* as the sides of triangle RST. Since the question asks about tangent, which is a ratio of one side length to another, we don't need to know the exact length of any side, as long as the side lengths we use are in the right proportion.

So this all comes down to the idea that we can answer the question using the same side lengths from the original triangle, because we know that they're in the right proportion to one another, and that's all we need to know to answer this question.

We know from SOHCAHTOA that $tangent = \frac{opposite}{adjacent}$, so the tangent of W is equal to the length of the side opposite W, which is 20, divided by the length of the side adjacent to W, which is 48.

That means $\tan W = \frac{20}{48}$. This number isn't in the answer choices, but $\frac{20}{48}$ reduces to $\frac{5}{12}$, which is the correct answer, (B).

Solution 2: Test-smart: Use your understanding of tangent and $5:12:13$ right triangles, along with the information in the prompt, to find the right answer.

If we notice that the given side lengths are in the proportion of $5:12:13$, and/or if we notice that each answer choice includes two of these three numbers, then we know that we're being asked about a right triangle with sides in that ratio. Since the question asks about tangent, which is $\frac{opposite}{adjacent}$, we know the right answer will be a ratio involving 5 and 12, but not 13, since 5 and 12 correspond to the two legs of the triangle (one of which must be opposite W, and one of which must be adjacent to W), while 13 corresponds to the hypotenuse of the triangle, which isn't part of the tangent ratio.

That means the tangent fraction must be either $\frac{5}{12}$ or $\frac{12}{5}$, depending on whether the shorter side is opposite W (and therefore in the numerator of the fraction), or whether the shorter side is adjacent to W (and therefore in the denominator of the fraction).

The prompt tells us that T corresponds to W. We can tell from the listed side lengths that T must be opposite the shortest side, RS, since that side doesn't include the point T. So the side opposite T is the shortest side, which means the side opposite W is the shortest side, which means the numerator in $\tan W$ must be 5, because that corresponds to the length of the shortest side of the triangle. That leaves 12 as the adjacent side proportion in the denominator of the fraction (again, because 13 corresponds to the hypotenuse of the triangle, which isn't part of the tangent ratio), so the adjacent side must be 12.

So $\tan W = \frac{5}{12}$, and (B) is right.

ANSWER CHOICE ANALYSIS

(A): This is $\sin W$. **(C):** This is $\cos W$ **(D):** This is the reciprocal of the right answer.

How to check? Verify that you used the correct trigonometric identity, that you didn't confuse which vertices correspond to each other, and that you labeled the sides of the triangles correctly. Try an alternate approach above. Try to figure out which mistakes could lead to some of the wrong answer choices, and verify that you haven't made any such mistakes.

▶ Post-solution patterns (see page 286): the right answer to the wrong question

> **Note** This question technically involves trigonometry, but it's far simpler than most classroom trig questions, and really depends on your understanding of similar triangles. The only thing we needed to remember from trigonometry to answer this question was SOHCAHTOA.

Test 2, Module 1, Question 26

- **What's the prompt asking for?** The amount of paint in gallons needed to paint the walls of the room twice, in terms of P and w.

- **Math concepts in the prompt:** word problems, variables

- **Elements of the answer choices:** Each answer choice is an equation that equates P to an expression involving w.

- **Notable features of the answer choices:** (C) is half of (A), and (D) is half of (B). (A) and (C) involve division, while (B) and (D) involve multiplication. Two choices involve 220, while one involves 110 and one involves 440.

- **"Bridge" concepts:** If a gallon of paint will cover 220 square feet, then it will cover 110 square feet twice. Two gallons will be required to cover 220 square feet twice.

- **Pre-solution patterns (see p. 285):** halves and doubles; opposites; wrong answers try to imitate right answers

- **Things to look out for:** Make sure your answer accounts for the idea of painting the room *twice!*

Solution 1: Concrete: Read the prompt carefully and come up with a w-value and corresponding P-value that satisfy the requirements in the prompt. Plug that w-value into the equation from each answer choice, and eliminate each choice that doesn't produce the correct P-value.

Let's imagine that the room has 220 square feet of wall area, which means that $w = 220$. We can reason that if one gallon of paint will cover 220 square feet, then we will need one gallon of paint to cover a room with 220 square feet of wall area—and we will need *two* gallons of paint to cover that 220 square foot area *twice*, as the prompt requires.

Based on this reasoning, we know that when $w = 220$—that is, when we paint a room whose wall area is 220—then P should equal 2—that is, we'll need two gallons of paint to paint the walls of that room twice.

With this in mind, let's plug $w = 220$ into each answer choice. We can eliminate any choice that doesn't produce a P-value of 2.

(A) $P = \frac{w}{110}$ $= \frac{(220)}{110}$ $= 2$

(B) $P = 440w$ $= 440(220)$ $= 96,800$

(C) $P = \frac{w}{220}$ $= \frac{(220)}{220}$ $= 1$

(D) $P = 220w$ $= 220(220)$ $= 48,400$

After checking each answer choice, we can see that only (A) resulted in a P-value of 2, so (A) must be correct.

Solution 2: Abstract: Reason through the prompt and construct an expression the reflects the relationships in the prompt.

For every 220 square feet of wall area, one gallon of paint will be needed to paint that area *once*. We can think of this like breaking up the wall area into 220 square foot chunks—every 220 square foot chunk will require one gallon of paint to be painted once.

Breaking up that area into 220 square foot chunks is the same as dividing that area by 220. The prompt tells us that the area is w square feet, so we would need to divide w square feet by 220 to find out how many gallons of paint we would need to paint that wall area once. That's the same as $\frac{w}{220}$.

But the prompt asks us how much paint we need to paint the surface *twice*, and so far we've only considered painting it once! We need twice as much paint to paint it twice, which is the same as $2 \times \frac{w}{220}$, which is the same as $\frac{2w}{220}$, which reduces to $\frac{w}{110}$. So (A) is correct.

ANSWER CHOICE ANALYSIS

(B): This choice might be tempting for test-takers who mixed up what P and w represent, among other errors. **(C):** This is how much paint we would need to paint the surface *once*, not *twice* as the prompt requires. **(D):** This choice would be the result of a set of errors similar to the ones we saw in (B).

How to check? Plug in a value for w and make sure the results are consistent with the information in the prompt. Try an alternate approach above. Try to figure out which mistakes could lead to some of the wrong answer choices, and verify that you haven't made any such mistakes.

▶ Post-solution patterns (see page 286): the right answer to the wrong question

Note Many test-takers will be completely comfortable with the math concepts in this question, but they'll overlook the very last word in the prompt: "twice." If that happens, they'll get the question wrong—not because they couldn't handle the math, but because they didn't read carefully enough! Remember, once again, that careful reading is the most important skill across the whole SAT.

Test 2, Module 1, Question 27

- What's the prompt asking for? The value of a.
- Math concepts in the prompt: variables, percent greater, percent less
- "Bridge" concepts: We can start by finding the value of b, and then use that to find the value of a.

- Things to look out for: Think carefully about what it means for a number to be 110% greater than another number! Don't make a simple algebra mistake!

Solution 1: Concrete: Use the only provided constant to make the percent changes described in the prompt and find the value of a.

Let's start with the only constant in the prompt, and work from there. We're told that b is "90% less than 47." Being 90% *less than* something is the same as being 10% *of* something—when you remove 90% of something, you're left with 10% of that thing. So b must be 10% of 47. We can find that by multiplying 47 by 0.10, which gives us 4.7. So $b = 4.7$.

The prompt tells us that a is "110% greater than the number b." Let's think about this carefully. The phrase "110% greater than" is NOT the same as the phrase "110% of." 110% *of* something is just 10% more than that thing. But something that is 110% greater than a number is 100% greater—that is, greater by 100%, or *twice* as much as the original number—*plus* an *additional* 10%. We would find 110% of a number by multiplying that number by 2.1, because that reflects the idea of being 100% greater—that is, twice as much—plus an additional 10%.

So a number 110% greater than 4.7 is the same as 4.7×2.1, which is 9.87. So the answer is 9.87.

How to check? Make sure your solution correctly accounted for the idea of a number being 110% greater than another number. Try to figure out which mistakes the College Board might hope you would make in finding your solution, and verify that you haven't made any such mistakes.

Note A lot of test-takers will approach this question as though it said "110% of the number b," rather than "110% greater than the number b." But these are two different ideas! "110% greater than the number b" doesn't mean 10% more than b—it means *twice as much* as b, and then an additional 10% beyond that! This is probably easier to realize if we think about how "100% greater" means twice as much of something. A lot of capable math students miss SAT Math questions involving percentages, not because they can't handle the calculations involved, but because they misunderstand the provided text and don't actually realize what the question is asking for. So whenever you see an SAT Math question involving percentages, take an extra second to make sure you understand which percentage of which value you actually need to find.

TEST 2 - MODULE 2

Test 2, Module 2, Question 1

- What's the prompt asking for? The best estimate of the total number of Spanish club students who intend to enroll in the study program.

- Math concepts in the prompt: word problems, surveys, percentages

- Elements of the answer choices: Each answer choice is an integer ranging from 11 to 55.

- Notable features of the answer choices: (C) is four times as much a (A), and (D) is five times as much as (A). (D) is the sum of (A) and (C).

- "Bridge" concepts: If 20% of the sample intended to enroll, then the "best estimate" "based on the survey" would be that 20% of the 55 people in the club also intend to enroll.

- Pre-solution patterns (see p. 285): wrong answers try to imitate right answers

- Things to look out for: Think carefully about what the question is asking for!

Solution 1: Concrete: Use the information from the survey to find the estimated percentage of the 55 students who intend to enroll in the study program.

If 20% of those surveyed said they intended to enroll in the study program, then we can estimate that 20% of the class intends to enroll in that program. 20% of the class is 20% of 55, which is 55×0.2, which is 11. So (A) is correct.

ANSWER CHOICE ANALYSIS

(B): This is the percentage from the prompt, but we need to multiply this percentage by the number of students in the club to find the answer. **(C):** This is the number of students *not* expected to enroll, based on the information in the prompt. **(D):** This is the total number of students in the club.

How to check? Verify that you've read the prompt correctly. Try to figure out which mistakes could lead to some of the wrong answer choices, and verify that you haven't made any such mistakes.

▶ Post-solution patterns (see page 286): the right answer to the wrong question

Test 2, Module 2, Question 2

- What's the prompt asking for? The equation that represents the situation described in the prompt.

- Math concepts in the prompt: word problems, rates, time, distance, $d = rt$

- Elements of the answer choices: Each answer choice is an equation involving r and w.

- Notable features of the answer choices: Each answer choice involves either $3w$ and $5r$ or $\frac{1}{3}w$ and $\frac{1}{5}r$ on the left side, and either 14 or 112 on the right side.

- "Bridge" concepts: The right answer should express the idea of adding the distance Jay covers while walking to the distance he covers while running, with the result equal to 14.

- Pre-solution patterns (see p. 285): opposites; wrong answers try to imitate right answers

- Things to look out for: Don't mix up the walking speed and running speed! Don't mix up w and r! Make sure you understand how the provided information fits into the $d = rt$ formula, if you use it!

Solution 1: Careful reading: Read the prompt carefully and figure out how to express the information it contains in terms of w and r.

If Jay walks at 3 miles per hour for w hours, we can find the total distance he walks by multiplying 3 by w—the distance he walks in one hour multiplied by the number of hours he spends walking at that speed. So the distance he walks is given by $3w$.

Similarly, if Jay runs at 5 miles per hour for r hours, we can represent the distance he runs by multiplying 5 by r. So the distance he runs is given by $5r$.

We can add these values together to find the total distance he walks in w hours and runs in r hours, which looks like this: $3w + 5r$. The prompt tells us this value is equal to 14, which gives us this expression:

$$3w + 5r = 14$$

So (A) is right.

Solution 2: Algebra: Use $d = rt$ to find the distance Jay walks and the distance Jay runs, and then add these values together and set the result equal to the total distance he covered.

We know that $d = rt$, which means distance is equal to the rate of speed multiplied by the time spent traveling at that speed. In this case, the distance Jay walks can be expressed in this way:

$$d = rt \qquad \text{(distance = rate} \times \text{time)}$$
$$d = 3w \qquad \text{(plug in 3 for the rate of speed and } w \text{ for the time)}$$

So the distance Jay walks is equal to $3w$. Let's repeat the process to find the distance he runs.

$$d = rt \qquad \text{(distance = rate} \times \text{time)}$$
$$d = 5r \qquad \text{(plug in 5 for the rate of speed and } r \text{ for the time)}$$

We can add these distances together to find the total distance Jay covered:

$$3w + 5r$$

Then we can set this expression equal to 14, since the prompt tells us he traveled 14 miles:

$$3w + 5r = 14$$

So (A) is correct.

Solution 3: Test-smart: Use your understanding of the question to eliminate wrong answer choices.

Once we realize that the correct answer should end with "= 14," because the total distance is 14 miles, we can eliminate (C) and (D). Once we realize that we'll be multiplying something by 3 and 5, and not dividing anything by 3 and 5, we can eliminate (B). That leaves only the correct answer, (A).

ANSWER CHOICE ANALYSIS

(B): This could be the result if someone got confused about how the rate of speed and the time relate to each other, and accidentally divided the time by the rate of speed. **(C):** This choice combines the errors from (B) and (D). **(D):** This is the right answer, except the expression is set equal to 112, instead of 14. 112 would be the result if we added 3 and 5 to find a total speed of 8, and then assumed that Jay traveled at that speed for 14 hours. But we can't add speeds that way, and Jay didn't travel for 14 hours, as we saw in the prompt and in our solutions above.

How to check? Try an alternate approach above. Verify that you didn't mix up the relationships among speed, time, and distance. Try to figure out which mistakes could lead to some of the wrong answer choices, and verify that you haven't made any such mistakes.

Test 2, Module 2, Question 3

- What's the prompt asking for? The equation that best represents the line of best fit.

- Math concepts in the prompt: scatterplot, variables, line of best fit

- Elements of the answer choices: Each answer choice is the equation of a line.

- Notable features of the answer choices: Each choice starts with "$y =$" followed by either 2.8 or -2.8, then followed by either $+1.7x$ or $-1.7x$.

- "Bridge" concepts: The right answer should have the same slope and y-intercept as the line in the graph.

- Pre-solution patterns (see p. 285): opposites; wrong answers try to imitate right answers

- Things to look out for: Remember the properties of positive versus negative slope, and positive versus negative y-intercepts! Don't get confused about which part of the provided equations relates to slope and which part relates to y-intercept!

Solution 1: Graphing: Graph each choice and see which one looks like the scatterplot.

(A)

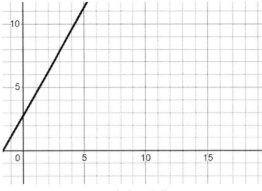

$$y = 2.8 + 1.7x$$

(B)

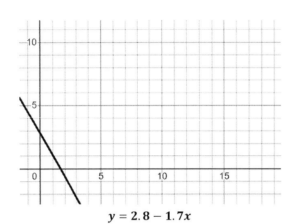

$$y = 2.8 - 1.7x$$

(C)

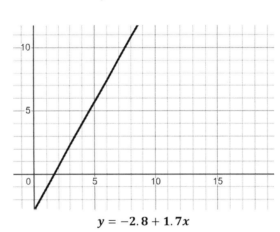

$$y = -2.8 + 1.7x$$

(D)

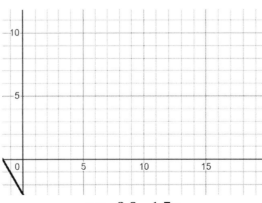

$$y = -2.8 - 1.7x$$

When we graph each answer choice, we can see that only (A) looks like the provided line, so (A) is right.

Solution 2: Answer choice analysis: Consider the elements of the answer choices, and eliminate each choice that doesn't meet the requirements of the prompt.

When we do a vertical scan, we can see that these choices are the four possible combinations of two different elements: either 2.8 or −2.8 first, then either +1.7x or −1.7x after that.

If we remember our discussion of slope-intercept form from the SAT Math Toolbox, we can recognize that each of these choices is in slope-intercept form—that is, $y = mx + b$ form—with the mx and b parts switched. So in each choice the 2.8 or −2.8 part is the y-intercept of the line, and the +1.7x or −1.7x part is the slope.

The choices give us either 2.8 or −2.8 for the y-intercept—the same number, just positive or negative. When we look at the scatterplot we can see that the line intercepts the y-axis at a positive value, so the y-intercept must be positive. So the right answer must involve 2.8, not −2.8.

That leaves either +1.7x or −1.7x. Again, if we remember slope-intercept form, we know the coefficient of x is the slope of the line. The line is angled up reading from left to right, which means it has a positive slope—so the right answer must include +1.7x, not −1.7x.

So the right answer involves 2.8 and +1.7x. With all of this in mind, we know the right answer must be (A).

Solution 3: Test-smart: Use your understanding of slope-intercept form to eliminate each choice that doesn't match the graph.

If we recognize that every answer choice is (basically) in slope-intercept form, and we can see that the line in the provided graph has a positive slope and a positive y-intercept, then we know the right answer choice must be the only choice with a positive slope and a positive y-intercept, which is (A).

ANSWER CHOICE ANALYSIS

(B): This choice has a negative slope, but the line in the graph has a positive slope. **(C):** This choice has a negative y-intercept, but the line in the graph has a positive y-intercept. **(D):** This choice has a negative slope and a negative y-intercept, which is the opposite of what appears in the graph.

How to check? Verify that you haven't made a mistake related to sign. Try an alternate approach above. Try to figure out which mistakes could lead to some of the wrong answer choices, and confirm that you haven't made any such mistakes.

Test 2, Module 2, Question 4

- What's the prompt asking for? The value of $f(0)$.
- Math concepts in the prompt: graphs, functions, hyperbolas
- Elements of the answer choices: Each answer choice is a numerical value from −3 to 3.
- Notable features of the answer choices: (A) is the opposite of (D). (A), (B), and (D) form a series where each choice is 3 more than the previous choice. The number 3 appears in 3 of the 4 choices.

- "Bridge" concepts: The value of $f(0)$ will be the y-value of the graph when $x = 0$.
- Pre-solution patterns (see p. 285): opposites; first and last terms in a series are often wrong answers; wrong answers try to imitate right answers
- Things to look out for: Make sure you read the graph carefully! Make sure you think carefully about what $f(0)$ represents!

Solution 1: Careful reading: Read the prompt, then read the graph to find the value of $f(x)$ when $x = 0$.

The prompt tells us that the figure is "the graph of $y = f(x)$," so we know that that $f(0)$ must be the y-value we get when we plug in $x = 0$ (this is also the y-intercept). We can find that by locating the 0 on the x-axis (that is, on the horizontal axis), and then seeing which y-value corresponds to an x-value of 0. In this case, the function has a point at $(0, 3)$, which means when $x = 0, y = 3$. So $f(0)$ is 3, which means (D) is correct.

ANSWER CHOICE ANALYSIS

(A): This is the opposite of the right answer. **(B):** This is the x-value whose corresponding y-value we needed to find.

How to check? Try to figure out which mistakes could lead to some of the wrong answer choices, and verify that you haven't made any such mistakes.

Note A lot of test-takers will be intimidated by this question at first glance because it involves the graph of a hyperbola. But when we actually read the question, we see that all we have to do is read the correct value off the graph; the shape of the graph and the equation of the line have no impact on our solution whatsoever. Remember this on test day: even if a question looks a little strange or hard, take the time to read the prompt and find out what it's actually asking you to do. Very frequently, SAT Math questions that look advanced actually rely on very basic math skills.

- **What's the prompt asking for?** The expression that's equivalent to the provided expression, where the variables involved are positive.

- **Math concepts in the prompt:** equivalent expressions, variables, exponents, multiplication

- **Elements of the answer choices:** Each answer choice involves m, q, and z raised to different exponents and multiplied together.

- **Notable features of the answer choices:** Each variable is raised to a different exponent in each answer choice.

- **"Bridge" concepts:** We can multiply the given expressions to combine like terms and get a result that looks like one of the answer choices.

- **Pre-solution patterns (see p. 285):** wrong answers try to imitate right answers

- **Things to look out for:** Don't forget the rules about combining exponents! Make sure to deal with the exponents of the different variables separately!

Solution 1: Algebra: Use your understanding of the rules for combining exponents to simplify the expression from the prompt, then pick the answer choice that matches the simplified expression.

All of these terms are variables being multiplied together, so we can just drop the parentheses, like this:
$$(m^4 q^4 z^{-1})(m q^5 z^3) = m^4 q^4 z^{-1} m q^5 z^3$$

It doesn't matter what order things are multiplied in, which means we can move around the variables so similar variables are next to each other, like this:
$$m^4 q^4 z^{-1} m q^5 z^3 = m^4 m q^4 q^5 z^{-1} z^3$$

Finally, we can combine the exponential expressions with the same base by combining them into one expression and adding their exponents together.
$$m^4 m q^4 q^5 z^{-1} z^3 = m^5 q^9 z^2$$

So the answer is $m^5 q^9 z^2$, and (B) is correct.

Solution 2: Test-smart: Pick any one variable's exponent from the provided expression, figure out what its simplified form should be, and eliminate each choice that doesn't contain that exponent.

Once we notice that each answer choice has a different exponent for each variable, we can realize that we can find the right answer by finding the correct exponent for just one variable with certainty. If, for example, we can confidently multiply m^4 by m to get m^5, then we can be sure the right answer will contain m^5. Only (B) contains m^5, so (B) has to be right.

ANSWER CHOICE ANALYSIS

(A): This would be the result if we *multiplied* the exponents by each other for corresponding variables, instead of adding them together.

How to check? Imagine writing out each exponent expression as a series of variables multiplied together (e.g., $m^4 = m * m * m * m$), as an extra check to make sure that your solution follows the rules of exponents. Try an alternate approach above. Try to figure out which mistakes could lead to some of the wrong answer choices, and verify that you haven't made any such mistakes.

- **What's the prompt asking for?** The median of the provided data.

- **Math concepts in the prompt:** data, median

- **"Bridge" concepts:** The median is the middle value when the values are ordered least to greatest (or the average of the two middle values when there's an even number of values).

- **Things to look out for:** Remember to find the median, and not the mean, mode, or range!

Solution 1: Properties and definitions: Use your understanding of median to answer the question using the provided data.

The median is the number in the middle when the numbers in a set are ordered from least to greatest. If the set has an even number of numbers, the median is the average of the two middle numbers.

We can see that the numbers in the provided data set are ordered from least to greatest. We can also count up the numbers to find that there are 9 numbers. That means that 5th number will be the middle number, which will be the median. The 5th number in the sequence is 79, so the answer is 79.

How to check? Verify once more that you found the median, and not the mean, mode, or range. Try to figure out which mistakes the College Board might hope you would make in finding your solution, and verify that you haven't made any such mistakes.

- What's the prompt asking for? The value of x.
- Math concepts in the prompt: equations, algebra
- "Bridge" concepts: The right answer will result in a valid statement when plugged into the given equation.

- Things to look out for: Don't make a simple mistake related to algebra or sign!

Solution 1: Concrete: Isolate x to find its value.

We can subtract 40 from both sides to get x.

$$x + 40 = 95$$
$$x = 55$$

(provided equation)
(subtract 40 from both sides)

So $x = 55$, and the answer is 55.

Solution 2: Concrete/graphing: We can enter the equation exactly as it is into our graphing calculator. The graph will be a vertical line that corresponds to the x-value that solves the equation.

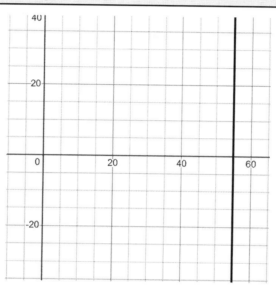

$$x + 40 = 95$$

We can see that the value of x is 55, so the answer is 55.

How to check? Try an alternate approach above. Try to figure out which mistakes the College Board might hope you would make in finding your solution, and verify that you haven't made any such mistakes.

Note This will be a very easy question for many test-takers, but it's still possible to make mistakes on easy questions! Treat it like any other SAT Math question: read it carefully, apply your training to find the answer, check your work, and move on.

Test 2, Module 2, Question 8

- What's the prompt asking for? The value of $x + y$, where (x, y) is the solution to the provided system of equations.
- Math concepts in the prompt: systems of equations, variables, addition
- Elements of the answer choices: Each answer choice is an integer ranging from -17 to 17.
- Notable features of the answer choices: (A) is the opposite of (D), and (B) is the opposite of (C). 13 appears twice in the answer choices, and 17 appears twice in the answer choices.

- "Bridge" concepts: The solution to the given system of equations is the (x, y) pair that results in a valid statement when plugged into each equation. It's also the point where the graphs of the two equations intersect.
- Pre-solution patterns (see p. 285): opposites; wrong answers try to imitate right answers
- Things to look out for: Don't make a simple mistake related to algebra or sign! Remember that the prompt asked for the value of $x + y$!

Solution 1: Concrete/graphing: We can graph the equations to see where they intersect, and then use that information to find $x + y$.

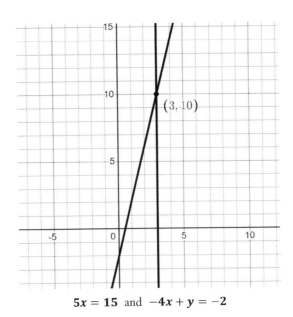

$$5x = 15 \text{ and } -4x + y = -2$$

The graphs intersect at $(3, 10)$, so $x + y = 3 + 10 = 13$. That means the answer is (C).

Solution 2: Algebra: Solve for x in the first equation, use that value to find y, and then add the two values together to find the answer.

We can solve for one variable, then plug that value into the other equation to find the value of the other variable. Let's solve for x in the first equation; that equation only has an x-value and no y-value, which should make the math simpler.

$5x = 15$	(first equation)
$x = 3$	(divide both sides by 5)

Now let's plug $x = 3$ into the other equation and solve for y.

$-4x + y = -2$	(second equation)
$-4(3) + y = -2$	(plug in $x = 3$)
$-12 + y = -2$	(simplify)
$y = 10$	(add 12 to both sides)

Now we know the solution to the given system of equations is $(3, 10)$, which means $x + y = 3 + 10 = 13$. So the answer is (C).

Solution 3: Test-smart: Add the equations to find $x + y$ directly.

We can add the two equations to find $x + y$.

$$
\begin{array}{rl}
5x & = 15 \\
-4x + y & = -2 \\
\hline
x + y & = 13
\end{array}
$$

So $x + y = 13$, and (C) is correct.

ANSWER CHOICE ANALYSIS

(A): This choice combines the errors from (B) and (D). **(B):** This is the opposite of the right answer. This choice could be tempting for a test-taker who made any of several mistakes related to sign in finding the values of x and y. **(D):** This is four more than the right answer; selecting this choice could easily be the result of reading -2 as $+2$ in the provided second equation (or making a similar mistake related to sign).

How to check? Verify that plugging your (x, y) solution into each provided equation results in a valid statement. Try an alternate approach above. Try to figure out which mistakes could lead to some of the wrong answer choices, and verify that you haven't made any such mistakes.

Test 2, Module 2, Question 9

- **What's the prompt asking for?** The approximate number of gallons of gasoline used to drive each mile in the situation described in the prompt.

- **Math concepts in the prompt:** word problems, function models, distance

- **Elements of the answer choices:** The answer choices are numerical values that range from 0.05 to 242.0.

- **Notable features of the answer choices:** One choice is an integer, and the rest are decimal expressions. The largest answer choice is significantly larger than the smallest answer choice.

- **"Bridge" concepts:** We can relate the given function to the ideas in the prompt to find the answer.

- Things to look out for: Think carefully about the situation described in the prompt, and how that situation relates to the given function!

Solution 1: Careful reading: Figure out how the numbers and variables in the provided function relate to the ideas in the prompt.

The prompt tells us that m represents the number of miles driven, and that the function g tells us the number of gallons of gasoline remaining from a full gas tank after a car drives m miles. When we look at $g(m)$, we can see that m is multiplied by -0.05. In other words, every time m increases by one, the number of gallons of gasoline in the tank is reduced by 0.05. That's the same as saying that the car uses 0.05 gallons of gas to drive each mile, which means (A) is correct.

ANSWER CHOICE ANALYSIS

(B): This is the number of gallons of gas in the car when the car hasn't driven any miles—that is, when $m = 0$ and the gas tank is full. **(C):** This is the number of miles the car can travel using one gallon of gas, but that's not what the question asked for. **(D):** This is the total number of miles the car can travel on a full tank of gas.

How to check? Try to figure out which mistakes could lead to some of the wrong answer choices, and verify that you haven't made any such mistakes.

▶ Post-solution patterns (see page 286): the right answer to the wrong question

Test 2, Module 2, Question 10

- What's the prompt asking for? The equation that correctly expresses x in terms of b and y.
- Math concepts in the prompt: equations, variables, fractions
- Elements of the answer choices: Each answer choice is x set equal to an expression involving b and y, along with either 77, or 7 and 11.
- Notable features of the answer choices: Two answer choices include fractions, and two don't. Three choices include 77, and the other includes 7 and 11.

- "Bridge" concepts: We can manipulate the given equation to isolate x.
- Pre-solution patterns (see p. 285): wrong answers try to imitate right answers
- Things to look out for: Don't get mixed up as you multiply and divide the provided equation by different variables to find the answer!

Solution 1: Algebra: Manipulate the provided equation until x is alone on one side of the equation. Then pick the answer choice that matches the result.

We can manipulate the given expressions to get x by itself on one side of the equation.

$$\frac{1}{7b} = \frac{11}{y}$$ (provided equation)

$$\frac{y}{7b} = 11x$$ (multiply both sides by y)

$$\frac{y}{77b} = x$$ (divide both sides by 11)

So the answer is (C).

Solution 2: Test-smart: Think about what features the expression equal to x must have, and eliminate any answer choices that don't meet this requirement.

Once we notice that we'll need to solve the equation by multiplying both sides by y—which will leave x on one side of the equation, equal to a fraction with y in the numerator and b in the denominator on the other side—we know the right answer will include a fraction with y in the numerator and b in the denominator. Only (C) meets this requirement, so (C) is right.

We can actually simplify this approach even further—once we think about solving for x and realize that x will be equal to an expression with b in its denominator, we can rule out (A), (B), and (D), leaving only the correct answer, (C).

ANSWER CHOICE ANALYSIS

(A): This choice could be the result of a mistake during cross-multiplication while trying to isolate x. **(D):** This choice includes x on one side of the equation, and every other number in the provided expression multiplied together on the other side.

Test 2, Module 2, Question 11

- What's the prompt asking for? A possible value of x.
- Math concepts in the prompt: equations, intersection, variables
- Elements of the answer choices: Each answer choice is a numerical value ranging from $-\frac{76}{5}$ to 76.
- Notable features of the answer choices: One answer choice is a fraction, and the others are integers. Two answer choices are negative, and two are positive.

- "Bridge" concepts: The phrase "a possible value of x" tells us that more than one x-value is possible. This is because x in the second equation is squared, and x^2 will produce the same value whether x is positive or negative.
- Things to look out for: Don't make a simple mistake related to algebra or sign! Remember that the question asks for the value of x, not the value of y!

Solution 1: Concrete/graphing: We can graph these two equations to see where they intersect.

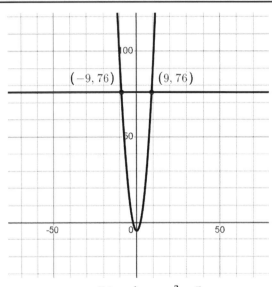

$$y = 76 \quad \text{and} \quad y = x^2 - 5$$

We can see that the two graphs intersect when $x = -9$ and when $x = 9$. So the answer is (B), -9.

Solution 2: Algebra: Plug the provided y-value into the second equation and solve for x.

The first equation is just a y-value, so we can plug that into the second equation to see what we get.

$y = x^2 - 5$	(second equation)
$76 - x^2 - 5$	(plug in $y = 76$)
$81 = x^2$	(add 5 to both sides)
$9 = x \quad$ or $\quad -9 = x$	(take the square root of both sides)

So x can equal 9 or -9. Only -9 appears in the answer choices, so (B), -9, is correct.

ANSWER CHOICE ANALYSIS

(A): This choice could be the result of an algebra error when attempting the second solution above. **(C):** This number appears in the second equation, but this value isn't what the question asks for. **(D):** This is the y-value of the point of intersection, but the prompt asked for the x-value.

How to check? Plug your answer into the second equation to make sure the resulting y-value is 76. Try an alternate approach above. Try to figure out which mistakes could lead to some of the wrong answer choices, and verify that you haven't made any such mistakes.

▶ Post-solution patterns (see page 286): the right answer to the wrong question

Test 2, Module 2, Question 12

- What's the prompt asking for? The choice that could be the value of x.
- Math concepts in the prompt: systems of inequalities, variables

- Elements of the answer choices: Each answer choice is an integer ranging from -9 to 9.
- Notable features of the answer choices: (A) is the opposite of (D). (B) is the opposite of (C). Two answer choices are negative, and two are positive. The number 5 appears in two answer choices, and the number 9 appears in two answer choices.

- Pre-solution patterns (see p. 285): opposites; wrong answers try to imitate right answers
- Things to look out for: Don't make a simple mistake related to algebra or sign! Remember that you're dealing with inequalities, not equations!

Solution 1: Concrete: Plug the values from each answer choice into the provided inequalities and eliminate any choice that doesn't result in a valid statement.

In order for the point $(x, 53)$ to be a solution for the provided system of inequalities, it must be the case that plugging $(x, 53)$ into both of the provided inequalities results in a true statement.

The first inequality is $y > 14$. For the point $(x, 53)$, $y = 53$, which is greater than 14. So we already know $(x, 53)$ causes the first inequality to make a true statement, which means we can focus on the second inequality as we test each answer choice. Let's plug each value from the answer choices into the second inequality to see which one results in a true statement (remember that we're testing the point $(x, 53)$, so we can plug 53 in for y in the second inequality).

$$4x + (53) < 18 \qquad \text{(second inequality, with } y \text{ equal to 53)}$$

Let's test (A):

$$4(-9) + 53 < 18 \qquad \text{(plug in } x = -9 \text{ from (A))}$$
$$-36 + 53 < 18 \qquad \text{(simplify)}$$
$$17 < 18 \qquad \text{(simplify)}$$

This results in a true statement, so (A) seems to be right. Let's check the other choices to help make sure we haven't made any mistakes. We'll continue with (B):

$$4(-5) + 53 < 18 \qquad \text{(plug in } x = -5 \text{ from (B))}$$
$$-20 + 53 < 18 \qquad \text{(simplify)}$$
$$33 < 18 \qquad \text{(simplify)}$$

This isn't a true statement, so (B) appears to be wrong. Let's check (C):

$$4(5) + 53 < 18 \qquad \text{(plug in } x = 5 \text{ from (C))}$$
$$20 + 53 < 18 \qquad \text{(simplify)}$$
$$73 < 18 \qquad \text{(simplify)}$$

Again, this statement isn't true. Finally, let's check (D):

$$4(9) + 53 < 18 \qquad \text{(plug in } x = 9 \text{ from (D))}$$
$$36 + 53 < 18 \qquad \text{(simplify)}$$
$$89 < 18 \qquad \text{(simplify)}$$

After checking every answer choice, we can see that (A) is correct.

Solution 2: Concrete/graphing: Graph the system of inequalities, then graph the four coordinate pairs created using each x-value from the answer choices. Pick the one that can be a solution to the system of inequalities.

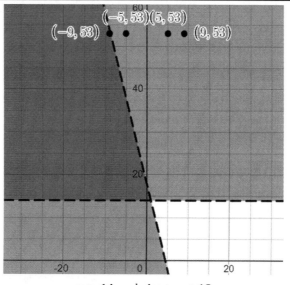

$$y > 14 \text{ and } 4x + y < 18$$

We can see that $(-9, 53)$ is the only choice that satisfies both inequalities, so (A) is right.

Solution 3: Test-smart: Think about the properties of inequalities in the context of the prompt, and realize what must be true about the right answer.

Once we understand that the correct answer must cause the left half of the second inequality to be less than 18, we can be sure that (A) must be right. Each answer choice is greater than the choice before it, so if (D) could be a value of x, then the same would have to be true of (C), (B), and (A), since all those values are less than (D). Similarly, if (B) or (C) were correct, the other, lower values would also have to be correct. We know that on the SAT, only one choice can be right, and only (A) wouldn't require other choices to be right too. So the lowest value, (A), is correct. (Note that this analysis won't work on just *any* inequality. In this case, the expression on the left of the less-than sign was $4x + 53$, so smaller x-values would make the expression smaller, and larger x-values would make that expression larger. If that expression included fractions, negative numbers, or other concepts, this might not have been the case.)

ANSWER CHOICE ANALYSIS

(D): This is the opposite of the right answer.

How to check? Plug the value you found back into the provided inequalities to verify that the result is a valid statement in both cases. Try an alternate approach above. Try to figure out which mistakes could lead to some of the wrong answer choices, and verify that you haven't made any such mistakes.

Test 2, Module 2, Question 13

- What's the prompt asking for? The number of seeds that sprouted.
- Math concepts in the prompt: word problems, percentages
- "Bridge" concepts: The answer will be 80% of 300.
- Things to look out for: Don't make a simple algebra mistake! Don't overthink this question!

Solution 1: Concrete: Multiply the number of seeds by the percentage that sprouted to find the number of seeds that sprouted.

80% of 300 is the same as 300×0.8, which is the same as 240. So the answer is 240. Some test-takers may find this to be more intuitive if they realize that 80% of the seeds sprouting means that for every 100 seeds, 80 seeds sprouted. There were 300 seeds, which is three sets of 100 seeds, so three sets of 80 seeds sprouted, which—again—is the same answer, 240 seeds.

How to check? Try to figure out which mistakes the College Board might hope you would make in finding your solution, and verify that you haven't made any such mistakes.

Test 2, Module 2, Question 14

- What's the prompt asking for? The value of x where $f(x) = 8$.
- Math concepts in the prompt: functions, variables
- "Bridge" concepts: We can find the answer by setting 8 equal to $4x$.
- Things to look out for: Don't make a simple algebra mistake! Don't overthink this question!

Solution 1: Graphing: Graph the provided function and find the x-value for which $f(x) = 8$.

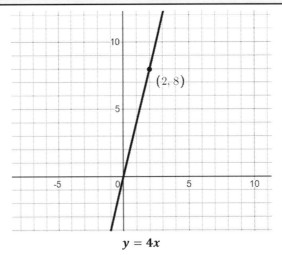

$y = 4x$

We can see that $f(x) = 8$ when $x = 2$. So the answer is 2.

Solution 2: Algebra: Set $4x$ equal to 8 and solve for x.

If $f(x) = 4x$, and $f(x) = 8$, it must be the case the $4x = 8$. We can divide both sides of $4x = 8$ by 4 to find that $x = 2$. So the answer is 2.

How to check? Try an alternate approach above. Try to figure out which mistakes the College Board might hope you would make in finding your solution, and verify that you haven't made any such mistakes.

Test 2, Module 2, Question 15

- **What's the prompt asking for?** The expression that's equivalent to the provided expression, where $x > 7$.
- **Math concepts in the prompt:** polynomials, fractions, variables, inequalities
- **Elements of the answer choices:** Each answer choice is a fraction with variables in the numerator and/or denominator.
- **Notable features of the answer choices:** Two answer choices have a binomial in the numerator and a single digit integer for a denominator, while the other two have a trinomial in the numerator and a binomial for a denominator.
- **"Bridge" concepts:** The right answer will be a simplified version of the expression in the prompt.
- **Pre-solution patterns (see p. 285):** wrong answers try to imitate right answers
- **Things to look out for:** Don't make a simple algebra mistake when simplifying the provided expression!

Solution 1: Concrete: Plug an x-value into the provided expression. Then, plug the same x-value into the expression from each answer choice. Eliminate each answer choice that doesn't produce the same result you got from the provided expression.

If we're not sure how to tackle this question, one approach is just to plug a value for x into the given expression, and then find the value of that expression. Then we plug that same x-value into the expression from each answer choice, and eliminate any choice that doesn't have the same value as the one we found in the given expression.

Remember that any time we pick values for a variable, we need to make sure our values follow any rules for that variable provided in the question. In this case, the question says $x > 7$. So we'll use $x = 8$.

$$\frac{8x(x-7)-3(x-7)}{2x-14} \qquad \text{(provided expression)}$$

$$\frac{8(8)((8)-7)-3((8)-7)}{2(8)-14} \qquad \text{(plug in } x = 8\text{)}$$

$$\frac{64(1)-3(1)}{16-14} \qquad \text{(simplify)}$$

$$\frac{61}{2} \qquad \text{(simplify)}$$

So when we plug in $x = 8$, the original expression is equal to $\frac{61}{2}$. Now let's plug $x = 8$ into the expression from each answer choice and eliminate each one that doesn't produce a value of $\frac{61}{2}$.

(A) $\quad \dfrac{x-7}{5} \qquad\qquad\qquad\qquad\qquad = \dfrac{8-7}{5} \qquad\qquad\qquad\qquad = \dfrac{1}{5}$

(B) $\quad \dfrac{8x-3}{2} \qquad\qquad\qquad\qquad\qquad = \dfrac{8(8)-3}{2} \qquad\qquad\qquad\qquad = \dfrac{61}{2}$

(C) $\quad \dfrac{8x^2-3x-14}{2x-14} \quad = \dfrac{8(8)^2-3(8)-14}{2(8)-14} \quad = \dfrac{512-24-14}{16} \quad = \dfrac{474}{2} \quad = 237$

(D) $\quad \dfrac{8x^2-3x-77}{2x-14} \quad = \dfrac{8(8)^2-3(8)-7}{2(8)-14} \quad = \dfrac{512-24-77}{16-14} \quad = \dfrac{411}{2}$

After plugging $x = 8$ into each expression in the answer choices, we found that only (B) produced a value of $\frac{61}{2}$, like we saw in the provided expression. So (B) is correct.

Solution 2: Algebra: Simplify the provided expression until it matches an expression from the answer choices.

First, let's multiply out the expression in the numerator:

$$\frac{8x^2-56x-3x+21}{2x-14} \qquad \text{(provided expression with numerator multiplied out)}$$

$$\frac{8x^2-59x+}{2x-14} \qquad \text{(simplify)}$$

At this point, it would be great if something canceled out in an obvious way that would make our expression look like one from the answer choices, but it doesn't seem to. Let's see if we can factor anything—we can start by trying to reverse-FOIL the numerator:

$$\frac{(8x-3)(x-7)}{2x-14}$$

(reverse-FOIL the numerator)

In order to simplify the fraction further, we would need to factor out either $(8x - 3)$ or $(x - 7)$ from the top and bottom of this fraction. We might notice that we can rewrite the denominator like this:

$$\frac{(8x-3)(x-7)}{2(x-7)}$$

(factor $(x - 7)$ out of the denominator)

Now the $(x - 7)$ expressions cancel out, leaving us with:

$$\frac{8x - 3}{2}$$

This is equal to the correct answer, (B).

Solution 3: Test-smart: Simplify the provided expression by factoring.

If we notice that the numerator involves two expressions being multiplied by $(x - 7)$, and we notice that we can factor out $(x - 7)$ from the denominator to make it $2(x - 7)$, then we can end up with a fraction like this one:

$$\frac{8x(x - 7) - 3(x - 7)}{2(x - 7)}$$

From here, we can factor $(x - 7)$ out of each term to end up with:

$$\frac{8x - 3}{2}$$

This is equal to the correct answer, (B).

ANSWER CHOICE ANALYSIS

(A): This choice could be the result of a mistake in attempting to factor the provided expression and/or reducing the resulting fraction. **(C):** This choice could be the result of an algebra error when trying to simplify the equation. **(D):** This choice could be the result of an algebra error when trying to simplify the equation.

How to check? Try an alternate approach above. Try to figure out which mistakes could lead to some of the wrong answer choices, and verify that you haven't made any such mistakes.

Test 2, Module 2, Question 16

- What's the prompt asking for? The slope of line r.
- Math concepts in the prompt: equations, perpendicular lines, slope
- Elements of the answer choices: Each answer choice is a numerical value ranging from -9 to 9.
- Notable features of the answer choices: (A) is the opposite of (D). (B) is the opposite of (C). Two answer choices are negative, and two are positive. Two answer choices are fractions, and two are integers.

- "Bridge" concepts: The slopes of perpendicular lines are opposite reciprocals of one another.
- Pre-solution patterns (see p. 285): opposites; wrong answers try to imitate right answers
- Things to look out for: Be careful finding the opposite reciprocal of the slope of p! Remember that the lines are *perpendicular*, not *parallel!*

Solution 1: Concrete/graphing: We can graph the provided equation and use our understanding of perpendicular lines to figure out the slope of r.

When we graph the provided equation, we get this:

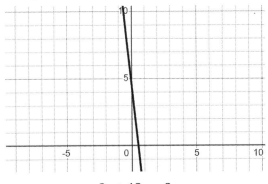

$$2y + 18x = 9$$

Facebook.com/QuestPreparation Youtube.com/QuestPrep

The positioning of the line makes it a little hard to just look at the graph and determine the exact slope, but we can still figure out the answer anyway.

If we know that perpendicular lines have slopes that are the opposite reciprocals of each other, and we can see that the slope of line p is negative, then we know that the slope of line r must be positive. So we can eliminate (A) and (B).

The remaining choices are $\frac{1}{9}$ and 9. Even if the graph makes it hard to determine the exact slope of the line just from counting the number of units the line moves down (the "rise") for every unit it moves to the right (the "run"), we can still determine the right answer here in a couple of different ways. For one, if we try to determine the "rise" over the "run" of line p visually, we can see it's somewhere around $-8, -9,$ or -10. Remember that we want the negative reciprocal of that value, so that would leave us with $\frac{1}{8}, \frac{1}{9},$ or $\frac{1}{10}$. Between (C) and (D), we know the answer must be (C).

Another way to determine the right answer is to realize that the slope of the line in the graph is pretty steep, which means it moves several units down for every unit it moves to the right—its absolute value must be greater than 1. A perpendicular slope would have to be relatively flat, then, moving several units to the right for every unit it moves up or down—its absolute value must be a fraction less than 1. So the slope of r must be a fraction less than 1, which means that between (C) and (D), (C) must be correct.

Solution 2: Algebra: Find the slope of p, then find the opposite reciprocal of that slope.

We know from our training that when two lines are perpendicular, their slopes are opposite reciprocals of each other. Since line r is perpendicular to line p, we can find the slope of line r by first finding the slope of line p, then finding the opposite reciprocal of the slope of line p.

The prompt tells us that line p is defined by $2y + 18x = 9$. We can solve for y to put this equation into slope-intercept form, which will tell us the slope of the line.

$$2y + 18x = 9 \qquad \text{(slope of line } p\text{)}$$
$$2y = -18x + 9 \qquad \text{(subtract } 18x \text{ from both sides)}$$
$$y = -9x + \frac{9}{2} \qquad \text{(divide both sides by 9)}$$

When the equation of a line is in slope-intercept form, the coefficient of x is the slope of the line. So the slope of line p is -9. But that's not what the question asked us to find!

If the slope of line p is -9, then the slope of perpendicular line r must be the opposite reciprocal of -9, which is $\frac{1}{9}$. So (C) is correct.

ANSWER CHOICE ANALYSIS

(A): This is the slope of line p. This would be the right answer if the lines were *parallel*, rather than perpendicular. **(B):** This is reciprocal of the slope of p, but we need to find the *opposite* reciprocal of that slope. **(D):** This is opposite of the slope of p, but we need to find the opposite *reciprocal* of that slope.

How to check? Verify that the question asked about a *perpendicular* line, and that you answered accordingly. Try to figure out which mistakes could lead to some of the wrong answer choices, and verify that you haven't made any such mistakes.

▶   Post-solution patterns (see page 286): right approach, wrong step; the right answer to the wrong question

---

Test 2, Module 2, Question 17

- What's the prompt asking for? The best interpretation of the y-intercept of the graph of the given function.
- Math concepts in the prompt: word problems, function models, time, inequality, graphs, y-intercept
- Elements of the answer choices: Each answer choice is a sentence related to the ideas in the prompt.
- Notable features of the answer choices: Two choices mention a "minimum estimated number of coupons the

company sent to their customers during the 5 years," and two mention an "estimated number of coupon the company sent to their customers at the end of 1998." Two choices include the number 1,428, and two choices include the number 8,000.

- Pre-solution patterns (see p. 285): wrong answers try to imitate right answers
- Things to look out for: Read the prompt and each answer choice very carefully!

Solution 1: Graphing: We can graph the equation and use the y-intercept to find the answer.

When we graph the equation, we get this:

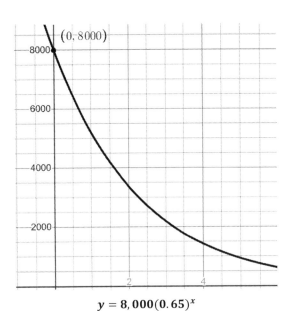

$$y = 8,000(0.65)^x$$

We can see that the y-intercept is at $(0, 8000)$, which occurs when $t = 0$. The prompt tells us that "t represents the number of years since the end of 1998." If $t = 0$, then there have been 0 years since the end of 1998, which means $f(0)$ must tell us the number of coupons the company sent to its customers at the end of 1998—that is, 8,000 coupons. So (D) is correct.

Solution 2: Algebra: Use your understanding of the y-intercept along with the information in the prompt to answer the question.

The y-intercept of the graph is the point where $t = 0$. The prompt tells us that "t represents the number of years since the end of 1998." If $t = 0$, then there have been 0 years since the end of 1998, which means $f(0)$ must tell us the number of coupons the company sent to its customers at the end of 1998.

If we plug $t = 0$ into the provided equation, we get the following:

$$f(t) = 8,000(0.65)^t \qquad \text{(provided function)}$$
$$f(0) = 8,000(0.65)^0 \qquad \text{(plug in } t = 0\text{)}$$
$$f(0) = 8,000(1) \qquad \text{(simplify)}$$
$$f(0) = 8,000 \qquad \text{(simplify)}$$

So the number of coupons the company sent to its customers at the end of 1998 was 8,000, which is exactly what choice (D) says. So (D) is correct.

ANSWER CHOICE ANALYSIS

(A): This choice combines the errors from (B) and (C). **(B):** This choice mentions the idea of 8,000 coupons, which is correct, but that number of coupons was sent out at the end of 1998, not over the whole 5 year period. **(C):** This choice mentions the right year, but provides the number of coupons that corresponds to 2002, not 1998.

How to check? Verify that $t = 0$ corresponds to 1998. Try an alternate approach above. Try to figure out which mistakes could lead to some of the wrong answer choices, and verify that you haven't made any such mistakes.

Test 2, Module 2, Question 18

- What's the prompt asking for? The measure of $\angle T$.
- Math concepts in the prompt: similar triangles, angle measures, equations
- Elements of the answer choices: Each answer choice is an angle measure ranging from 2° to 40°.
- Notable features of the answer choices: (B) is half of (C), and (C) is half of (D). (C) is the product of (A) and (B). (D) is the product of (A) and (C).

- "Bridge" concepts: The prompt tells us that Z corresponds to T, so the measure of $\angle Z$ must be equal to the measure of $\angle T$.
- Pre-solution patterns (see p. 285): halves and doubles; first and last terms in a series are often wrong answers; wrong answers try to imitate right answers
- Things to look out for: Don't mix up which parts of each triangle correspond to one another!

Solution 1: Geometry: Sketch the two triangles and label them according to the information from the prompt. Then, use your understanding of similar triangles to answer the question.

Let's start by drawing these two triangles. Notice that the prompt tells us that the triangles are similar, and that $X, Y,$ and Z correspond to $R, S,$ and T, respectively. (Note that we don't have to draw these triangles exactly to scale or anything, as long as any labels in our drawings match the information provided in the prompt.)

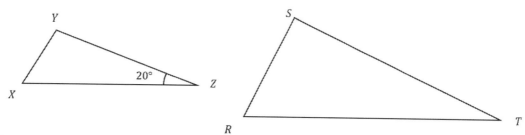

We know from our training that when triangles are similar, corresponding angles are equal. We can see that $\angle Z$ corresponds to $\angle T$; since the measure of $\angle Z$ is 20°, the angle of $\angle T$ must also be 20°. So (C) is right.

Solution 2: Test-smart: Ignore the unnecessary information in the prompt and use your understanding of similar triangles to answer the question.

The prompt tells us that the triangles are similar, the measure of $\angle Z$ is 20°, and Z corresponds to T. So the measure of $\angle T$ must be the same as the measure of $\angle Z$, which is 20°. That means (C) is right.

ANSWER CHOICE ANALYSIS

(A): This choice could be the result of using the fact that $2XY = RS$ to attempt an algebraic solution, and getting off track. **(B):** This is half of the right answer; this choice could be tempting for test-takers who attempt an algebraic solution as discussed in our analysis of choice (A). **(D):** This is twice the right answer, and could be tempting for test-takers who think that since the side lengths of triangle RST are twice the size of the side lengths of triangle XYZ, $\angle T$ should also be twice the size of $\angle Z$—but this isn't how similar triangles work.

How to check? Double-check that Z corresponds to T in the similar triangles. Try an alternate approach above. Try to figure out which mistakes could lead to some of the wrong answer choices, and verify that you haven't made any such mistakes.

Note   This is a great example of a very simple SAT Math question that a lot of smart test-takers will still get wrong. We know from our training that the College Board loves to present simple things in ways that make them look more complicated. In this case, they did that by including the phrase "and $2XY = RS$." This information is completely irrelevant to the question, but a lot of test-takers will think the fact that this statement appears means they need to include this information in their solutions; they'll end up halving or doubling the right answer, and then getting this question wrong. As trained test-takers, we know to focus on what the question actually asks us, and then to find the most direct route to the answer. Remember this on test day.

Test 2, Module 2, Question 19

- What's the prompt asking for? The choice that could be the second equation in the system of equations described in the prompt.

- Math concepts in the prompt: systems of equations with no solution

- Elements of the answer choices: Each answer choice is an equation involving x and y.

- Notable features of the answer choices: Two answer choices start with $-6x$, and the other two start with $-12x$. Two answer choices end with 18, one with 22, and one with 36.

- "Bridge" concepts: If a system of linear equations has no solution, then the line graphs of those equations must be parallel—that is, they must have the same slope—and they must not have any points in common.

- Pre-solution patterns (see p. 285): halves and doubles; wrong answers try to imitate right answers

- Things to look out for: Don't make a simple mistake related to algebra or sign! Don't confuse perpendicular with parallel!

Solution 1: Concrete/graphing: If the system has no solutions, that means the graphs of the two equations never touch each other. We can graph the provided equation along with each of the equations from the answer choices; the graph of the right answer will be the one that never touches the graph of the equation from the prompt.

(A)

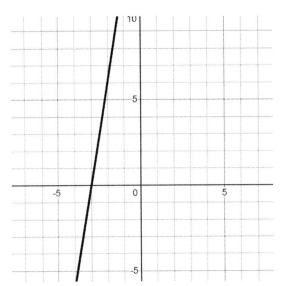

$-6x + y = 18$ and $y = 6x + 18$

(B)

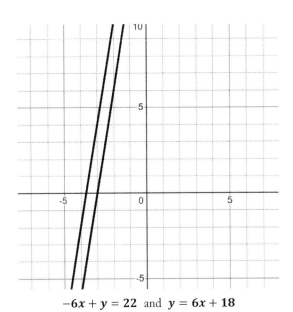

$-6x + y = 22$ and $y = 6x + 18$

(C)

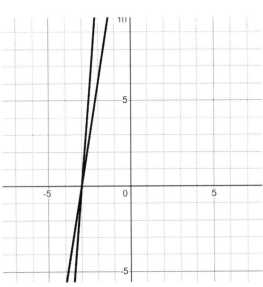

$-12x + y = 36$ and $y = 6x + 18$

(D)

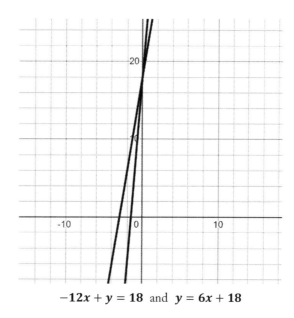

$$-12x + y = 18 \text{ and } y = 6x + 18$$

We can see that the graph of (B) doesn't touch the graph of the equation from the prompt, so (B) is correct. (Note that the graph of choice (A) was the same line as the graph of the provided equation, so it looks like there's only one line—but in reality, it's two lines on top of each other, and *every point* on both lines is a solution to the system of equations, because every point lies on both lines.)

Solution 2: Concrete: Find the slope of the given line, and the slope of each line from the answer choices. Eliminate each choice that doesn't have the same slope as the given line. Use your understanding of systems of equations to eliminate any remaining answer choices.

If a system of two linear equations has no solution, that means the graphs of those two lines never touch each other. In order for the graphs of two lines not to touch each other, they must be parallel to each other. So we can eliminate each choice whose slope isn't parallel to the slope of the line provided in the prompt.

This will probably be easiest to determine by putting every answer choice into slope-intercept form; that way we can easily see the slope of each line (remember: in slope-intercept form, the slope of a line is the coefficient of x).

(A)	$-6x + y = 18 =$	$y = 6x + 18$	(add $6x$ to both sides)	The slope is 6.
(B)	$-6x + y = 22 =$	$y = 6x + 22$	(add $6x$ to both sides)	The slope is 6.
(C)	$-12x + y = 36 =$	$y = 12x + 36$	(add $12x$ to both sides)	The slope is 12.
(D)	$-12x + y = 18 =$	$y = 12x + 18$	(add $12x$ to both sides)	The slope is 12.

The slope of the provided equation is 6, since that equation is in slope-intercept form and the coefficient of x is 6. So we can eliminate each answer choice whose slope isn't 6. Choices (C) and (D) have a slope of 12, which we know because we put them in slope-intercept form, and each one has a coefficient of 12 for x. That means (C) and (D) are both wrong.

We're left with (A) and (B), two choices that have a slope of 6. We know that each SAT Math multiple choice question has only one right answer, so unless we made a mistake, either (A) or (B) must be wrong.

When we take a second look at the equation from the prompt, we might notice that choice (A) in slope-intercept form is identical to the provided equation. In other words, the provided equation and (A) are the same equation, and would produce the same line. In that case, every point on the graph of the provided equation would be the same as every point on the graph of choice (A)—so a system of linear equations with these two lines would have *infinite* solutions, not *no* solution, as the prompt requires.

That means we can eliminate (A), which leaves the correct answer, (B)—the equation in (B) has the same slope as the equation in the prompt, but it isn't the same line. That means it would be parallel to that line, but not touch that line. A system of equations with these two lines would have no solution, as the prompt requires.

ANSWER CHOICE ANALYSIS

(A): This choice has the same slope as the right answer, but this choice is the same exact line as the given equation. A system of equations with the given equation and this equation would have *infinite* solutions, not no solution as the prompt requires, because every point on either line would also be a point on the other line—again, because they're the same line. **(D):** This choice has the same y-intercept as the given equation, but that's not what the prompt asks for.

How to check? Try an alternate approach above. Try to figure out which mistakes could lead to some of the wrong answer choices, and verify that you haven't made any such mistakes.

- What's the prompt asking for? The area of the rectangle described in the prompt.
- Math concepts in the prompt: area, rectangles, side lengths
- "Bridge" concepts: The area of a rectangle is its length multiplied by its width.
- Things to look out for: Don't make a simple algebra mistake! Don't mix up area and perimeter!

Solution 1: Concrete: Use the formula for the area of a rectangle to answer the question.

The area of a rectangle can be found by multiplying its length by its width. The prompt tells us that the length of the rectangle is 34 cm and the width of the rectangle is 29 cm. That means we can find its area by multiplying 34×29, which gives us 986. So the answer is 986.

How to check? Try to figure out which mistakes the College Board might hope you would make in finding your solution, and verify that you haven't made any such mistakes.

Note As simple as this question is, some test-takers will get it wrong because they'll absent-mindedly find the perimeter instead of the area. Always remember to verify that the answer you find is what the question actually asks for!

- What's the prompt asking for? The value of $x - y$, given that the solution to the system of equations is (x, y).
- Math concepts in the prompt: systems of equations, coordinate pairs, variables
- "Bridge" concepts: The solution to the given system of equations is the (x, y) pair that results in a valid statement when plugged into each equation. It's also the point where the graphs of the two equations intersect
- Things to look out for: Don't make a simple mistake related to algebra or sign!

Solution 1: Concrete/graphing: We know from our training that a solution to a system of two equations is a point where the graphs of those two equations intersect. We can graph these two equations to find their point of intersection, and use that information to answer the question.

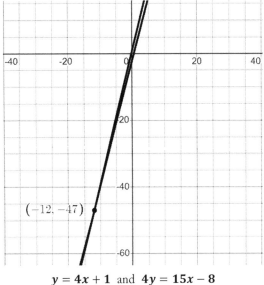

$$y = 4x + 1 \text{ and } 4y = 15x - 8$$

The graphs intersect at $(-12, -47)$. So $x - y$ is the same as $-12 - (-47)$, which is 35. So the answer is 35.

Solution 2: Algebra: Plug the given value of y in the first equation into the second equation to find x. Then use that x-value to find y, and use the values of x and y to answer the question.

We can solve one of the equations in terms of one variable, then plug that value into the other equation and solve for the other variable. When we have the value of that second variable, we can plug that into either equation to find the value of the first variable.

The first equation is already solved for y, so we can just plug $y = 4x + 1$ into the second equation.

$$4y = 15x - 8 \qquad \text{(second equation)}$$
$$4(4x + 1) = 15x - 8 \qquad \text{(plug in } y = 4x + 1)$$

$$16x + 4 = 15x - 8 \qquad \text{(simplify)}$$
$$x + 4 = -8 \qquad \text{(subtract } 15x \text{ from both sides)}$$
$$x = -12 \qquad \text{(subtract 4 from both sides)}$$

So $x = -12$. We can plug this in to either equation to find the value of y; let's plug it in to the first equation because it seems like the math will be slightly simpler that way.

$$y = 4x + 1 \qquad \text{(first equation)}$$
$$y = 4(-12) + 1 \qquad \text{(plug in } x = -12\text{)}$$
$$y = -48 + 1 \qquad \text{(simplify)}$$
$$y = -47 \qquad \text{(simplify)}$$

So the solution to the system of equations is $(-12, -47)$, which means $x - y$ is $-12 - (-47)$, or 35. That means the answer is 35.

How to check? Plug your x- and y-values back into the provided equations to make sure they result in true statements. Try an alternate approach above. Try to figure out which mistakes the College Board might hope you would make in finding your solution, and verify that you haven't made any such mistakes.

Test 2, Module 2, Question 22

- **What's the prompt asking for?** The number of distinct real solutions the given equation has.

- **Math concepts in the prompt:** equations, solutions, variables

- **Elements of the answer choices:** Each answer choice is a phrase describing a certain number of solutions.

- **Notable features of the answer choices:** Three answer choices say there is at least one solution, while one says there are no solutions.

- **"Bridge" concepts:** A distinct real solution is a number you can plug in for x that makes the equation true.

- **Things to look out for:** Remember that just finding a solution isn't enough of a reason to pick (A), and not being able to find a solution isn't enough of a reason to pick (D). You need to pick an answer choice because you were able to determine that the choice is correct!

Solution 1: Concrete/graphing: We can set the expression equal to y, and then graph it.

The given equation is $5x^2 + 10x + 16 = 0$. We can set it equal to y, which gives us $5x^2 + 10x + 16 = y$. If we graph that equation, then every x-value that produces a y-value of 0 will be a solution to the equation.

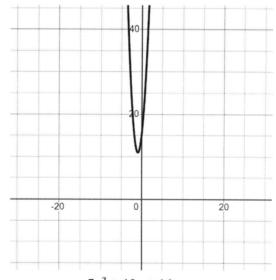

$$5x^2 + 10x + 16 = y$$

Every time $y = 0$—that is, every time the graph crosses the x-axis—represents a real solution to the given equation, because when $y = 0$, the given equation is true. The graph above never crosses the x-axis, which means there is no real x-value for which $y = 0$, which means there are no real solutions for the given equation. So the answer is (D), zero.

(Note that we can also enter the equation just as it is into the graphing calculator—that is, set equal to zero instead of y. The result would be a completely blank graph, because no x-value makes the equation true. Some test-takers might get confused when they see a blank graph, and they might think they did something wrong, so the approach above can be helpful because it does produce a graph, and we can interpret that graph to find the answer—but either way can work, depending on your level of comfort with this kind of solution.)

ANSWER CHOICE ANALYSIS

(A): This choice could be tempting for test-takers who attempt to factor the provided equation and make a mistake. **(B):** This choice has the same issue as (A). **(C):** This choice may be tempting for test-takers who get confused about what a "real solution" would be in this context.

How to check? Try to figure out which mistakes could lead to some of the wrong answer choices, and verify that you haven't made any such mistakes.

Note   As you can see in the official College Board explanation for this question, it's also possible to find the answer using the quadratic formula. I decided not to include that solution because you can already find it for free in the College Board's explanations, and because, in my experience, it doesn't really help anybody—students who are already comfortable using that approach don't benefit from seeing it written out again, and students who aren't comfortable with it aren't going to get comfortable just because they saw somebody use the quadratic formula again. Most importantly, the graphing solution is so quick and easy that it seems unhelpful to point out an unnecessarily slow and complicated solution. I strongly recommend that you get used to these graphing approaches, because they can save you a ton of time on test day.

Test 2, Module 2, Question 23

- What's the prompt asking for? The area of the park in square miles.
- Math concepts in the prompt: word problems, area, unit conversion
- Elements of the answer choices: Each answer choice is a decimal expression ranging from 1.96 to 6,740.8.
- Notable features of the answer choices: The first two choices are less than 10, and the other two choices are in the thousands. (A) is (C) divided by 1,760, and (B) is (D) divided by 1,760.
- "Bridge" concepts: If 1 mile = 1,760 yards, then 1 *square* mile = $1,760^2$ *square* yards, or 3,097,600 square yards.
- Things to look out for: Remember the difference between yards and square yards!

Solution 1: Concrete: Find the number of square yards in a square mile, then divide the number of square yards in the park by that value.

We can find the area of the park in square miles by finding out how many square yards are in one square mile, and then dividing the area of the park in square yards by that number. Note that the prompt provides the relationship between *miles* and *yards*, but this isn't the relationship we need to answer the question! We have to know how many *square* yards are in a *square* mile.

If 1 mile is 1,760 yards, then 1 *square* mile must by 1,760 yards *squared*, or 1,760 × 1,760, or 3,097,600 square yards. So there are 3,097,600 square yards in a square mile.

Now we can divide the area of the park in square yards by the number of square yards in a square mile to find the area of the park in square miles:

$$\frac{11,863,808 \text{ square yards}}{3,097,600 \text{ square yards}/\text{square mile}} = 3.83 \text{ square miles}$$

So the answer is (B), 3.83.

Solution 2: Concrete: Find the number of square yards in a square mile, then compare the result to the ratio of the park's area in square yards to the park's area in square miles.

In order to find this answer, we have to know how many square yards are in a square mile. As we saw in the previous solution, there are 3,097,600 square yards in a square mile.

The ratio of the area of the park in square yards the area of the park in square miles (which we'll call x) must be the same as the ratio of the number of square yards in a square mile to the number of square miles in a square mile (which is one, of course). With this in mind, we can set up the following proportion:

$$\frac{11,863,808}{x} = \frac{3,097,600}{1}$$

Now we can solve for x:

$\frac{11,863,808}{x} = \frac{3,097,600}{1}$	(proportion we just set up)
$11,863,808 = 3,097,600x$	(cross-multiply)
$\frac{11,863,808}{3,097,600} = x$	(divide both sides by x)
$3.83 = x$	(simplify)

So there are 3.83 square miles in 11,863,808 square yards, and (B) is right.

(A): This is the result of finding the right answer, then finding its square root. **(C):** This is the square root of the park's area in square yards. **(D):** This is the result if we forget to account for the change from yards and miles to *square* yards and *square* miles, and think 1 square mile = 1,760 square yards.

How to check? Multiply your answer by the number of square yards in a square mile (3,097,600) to make sure the result is 11,863,808. Try an alternate approach above. Try to figure out which mistakes could lead to some of the wrong answer choices, and verify that you haven't made any such mistakes.

▶   Post-solution patterns (see page 286):   the right answer to the wrong question

Test 2, Module 2, Question 24

- What's the prompt asking for? The equation that represents a circle that intersects the y-xais at exactly one point.

- Math concepts in the prompt: circles, y-axis, equations, intersection

- Elements of the answer choices: Each answer choice is a standard equation of a circle.

- Notable features of the answer choices: Two answer choices include $x - 8$; two include $y - 9$; and $y - 8$, $y - 4$, $x - 4$, and x each appear once. Every expression is equal to 16.

- "Bridge" concepts: In order for a circle to intersect the y-axis at exactly one point, only the very edge of the circle must touch the y-axis—in other words, the y-axis must be one radius away from the center of the circle.

- Pre-solution patterns (see p. 285): halves and doubles; wrong answers try to imitate right answers

- Things to look out for: Don't make a simple mistake related to algebra or sign! Don't get confused about which part of the standard equation of a circle represents which part of the circle!

Solution 1: Concrete/graphing: We can graph each circle in the answer choices to see which one intersects the y-axis at exactly one point.

(A)

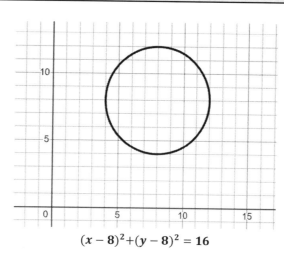

$$(x - 8)^2 + (y - 8)^2 = 16$$

(B)

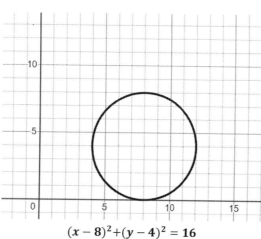

$$(x - 8)^2 + (y - 4)^2 = 16$$

(C)

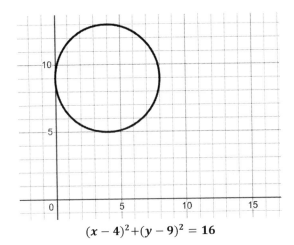

$$(x - 4)^2 + (y - 9)^2 = 16$$

(D)

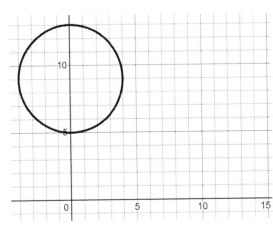

$$x^2 + (y - 9)^2 = 16$$

We can see that only the graph of choice (C) touches the y-axis at only one point, so (C) is correct.

Solution 2: Geometry: Use your understanding of the standard equation of a circle to determine the center and radius of each circle in the answer choices, and then use that information to answer the question.

If we remember that the standard equation for a circle is $(x - h)^2 + (y - k)^2 = r^2$, where (h, k) is the center of the circle and r is the radius of the circle, then we can learn the center and radius of each circle fairly quickly and easily.

For example, for choice (A), the equation is $(x - 8)^2 + (y - 8)^2 = 16$. When we compare this to the standard equation for a circle, which is $(x - h)^2 + (y - k)^2 = r^2$, we can see that $h = 8, k = 8$ and $r^2 = 16$. So the center of the circle represented by the equation in (A) is $(8, 8)$, and the radius is 4.

Using the same process, we can tell that the following is true of the circles whose equations appear in the answer choices:

(A)   Center of the circle: $(8, 8)$ Radius: 4
(B)   Center of the circle: $(8, 4)$ Radius: 4
(C)   Center of the circle: $(4, 9)$ Radius: 4
(D)   Center of the circle: $(0, 9)$ Radius: 4

We can see that each of these circles has a radius of 4. With a radius of 4, a circle's center would have to be 4 units away from the y-axis to touch it at exactly one point.

The center of circle (A) is 8 units from either axis, not 4, so (A) can't be right.

The center of circle (B) is 8 units from the y-axis, not 4, so (B) is wrong too.

The center of circle (C) is 4 units from the y-axis. With a radius of 4, that means this circle would touch the y-axis at exactly one point. (C) looks correct, but we'll check the final answer choice to minimize the chance of an error.

The center of circle (D) would lie on the y-axis, which means it would touch the y-axis in two places, not "exactly one," as the prompt requires. So (D) is wrong.

After considering each answer choice, we can see that (C) is the right answer.

(A): This choice would be correct if the circle's radius were 8 instead of 4. **(B):** This choice touches the x-axis at one point, rather than the y-axis. **(D):** The center of this circle is on the y-axis, but that's not what the prompt asked for.

How to check? Try an alternate approach above. Try to figure out which mistakes could lead to some of the wrong answer choices, and verify that you haven't made any such mistakes.

▶ Post-solution patterns (see page 286): the right answer to the wrong question

Note A lot of test-takers feel a little rusty when it comes to equations for circles, and they get intimidated by questions like this one. But this is just another example of why the calculator for the digital SAT is so powerful, since you can enter these equations directly into that calculator and find the right answer, even if you've never heard of the standard equation of a circle. Remember this on test day!

Test 2, Module 2, Question 25

- **What's the prompt asking for?** The additional piece of information that's sufficient to determine whether triangle *ABC* is congruent to triangle *DEF*.

- **Math concepts in the prompt:** congruent triangles, angles

- **Elements of the answer choices:** Each choice is a piece of information related to triangles, except for (D), which says that no additional information is necessary.

- **Notable features of the answer choices:** One choice mentions an angle measure, and two choices mention side lengths.

- **"Bridge" concepts:** Congruent triangles have the same corresponding angle measures *and* the same corresponding side lengths.

- **Things to look out for:** Remember the difference between similar triangles and congruent triangles!

Solution 1: Geometry: Sketch the triangles described in the prompt, and label them with the information in the prompt. Consider the piece of information from each choice to see whether it's enough to determine that the triangles are congruent.

Let's draw the triangles described in the prompt.

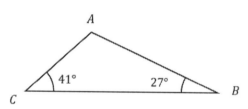
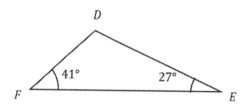

Now that we've done that, it might be even easier to tell that these triangles must have all the same angle measures, because if we know two of the three angle measures in a triangle, then we can figure out the third one—in this case, it's $180° - 41° - 27°$, or $112°$.

(We didn't need to calculate the missing third angle measure to answer this question; I just did it to show that we can be sure that if two triangles have the same two corresponding angle measures, the third angle measure must correspond as well.)

So these triangles have the same angle measures, which means they must be similar. Similar triangles always have sides in the same proportion—that is, if one side of the first triangle is twice as long as its corresponding side in the second triangle, then every side in the first triangle must be twice as long as its corresponding side in the second triangle, for example.

The prompt asked which additional piece of information was sufficient to tell whether triangle *ABC* was *congruent* to triangle *DEF*. In order to answer this question, it's important to make a distinction between similar triangles and congruent triangles. Similar triangles have all the same corresponding angle measures as each other, while congruent triangles have all the same corresponding angle measures *and* side lengths as each other. We've already determined that these triangles are at least similar—that is, they have the same corresponding angle measures. Now we need to figure out which answer choice provides sufficient information for us to know whether their corresponding side lengths are equal too.

(A) is wrong, because figuring out the measure of angle *A* doesn't give us any information about how the side lengths of these two triangles compare. Besides, as stated above, we already know all three corresponding angle measures on these two triangles are the same based on the provided information, and that just tells us these triangles are *similar*, not *congruent*, as the prompt requires. So (A) is wrong.

(B) does provide us information about a side length, but only one side of one triangle. This isn't enough for us to determine whether corresponding side lengths on the two triangles are equal to each other. So (B) is wrong too.

(C) would tell us the lengths of two corresponding sides on the two triangles—that is, *B* corresponds to *E*, and *C* corresponds to *F*, so it must be the case that *BC* corresponds to *EF*. This *is* enough information for us to tell whether the triangles are congruent, because if the length of *BC* is equal to the length of *EF*, then all three corresponding side lengths must be equal to one another—because we already know the triangles are similar, and side lengths of similar triangles are in proportion to one another. In that case, the two triangles would be congruent. On the other hand, if the length of *BC isn't* equal to the length of *EF*, then the triangles can't have equal corresponding side lengths, and they can't be congruent. So (C) would give us the information we need to tell whether the triangles are congruent, which means (C) is right.

(D) is wrong for the reasons we just discussed in our analysis of (C)—the provided information is only enough to determine that the triangles are *similar*, not whether they're *congruent*. In order to tell whether they're congruent, we need to know at least one set of corresponding side lengths, again, as discussed in (C). So (D) is wrong.

ANSWER CHOICE ANALYSIS

See the solution above for analysis of the answer choices.

How to check? Verify that the question asked about congruent triangles, not similar triangles. Try to figure out which mistakes could lead to some of the wrong answer choices, and verify that you haven't made any such mistakes.

▶ Post-solution patterns (see page 286): the right answer to the wrong question

Test 2, Module 2, Question 26

- **What's the prompt asking for?** The smallest possible difference between the mean of data set *A* and the mean of data set *B*.

- **Math concepts in the prompt:** data sets, integers, histograms, mean, frequency

- **Elements of the answer choices:** Each answer choice is an integer ranging from 0 to 23.

- **Notable features of the answer choices:** 1 appears in two answer choices, and 0 appears in two answer choices.

- **"Bridge" concepts:** We can't use the figures to determine the exact difference between the means of the two sets of data, but we can use them to find a *range* of possible differences.

- **Pre-solution patterns (see p. 285):** wrong answers try to imitate right answers

- **Things to look out for:** Read the data carefully! Make sure your solution accounts for the idea that there are multiple possible differences between the means of the data sets! Don't make the mistake of thinking the histograms are identical!

Solution 1: Careful reading: Read the prompt and the figures carefully, then use your understanding of histograms and mean to answer the question.

When we look closely at the figures, we can see that the histogram for Data Set B is just like the histogram for Data Set A, except each column is moved one interval to the left—that is, A has no integers greater than or equal to 10 but less than 20, while B has 3; A has 3 integers greater than or equal to 20 but less than 30, while B has 4; A has 4 integers greater than or equal to 30 but less than 40, while B has 7; A has 7 integers greater than or equal to 40 but less than 50, while B has 9, and A has 9 integers greater than or equal to 50 but less than 60, while B has 0.

Again, the histogram for Data Set B is kind of like taking each column from the histogram for Data Set A, picking it up, and then setting it down one interval to the left.

The prompt asks for "the smallest possible difference" between the means of the two sets, so we should think about the smallest change that could cause a number to move from one column to the next. (Remember that we're being asked about integers, so we're not talking about fractional or decimal expressions—only whole numbers.)

Let's consider the first two intervals. The greatest number that could appear in the first interval would be 19, because it's greater than or equal to 10 but less than 20—and the next-highest integer, 20, would be in the second column, which is for integers greater than or equal to 20 but less than 30. So the highest number that can appear in the first column is 19, and the lowest number that can appear in the second column is 20. That difference of one is what separates these numbers into their two columns.

So if we're trying to figure out the smallest possible difference between the means of these two data sets, that would occur when the difference between the numbers in the set is as small as possible. The smallest way to move each data point from one interval to the next lowest interval would be for that data point to be the smallest it could be for its current interval, and then to subtract one, which would move it to the interval to its left. In other words, the values in Data Set A would all have to be 20s, 30s, 40s, and 50s, and then to create Data Set B, we would have to subtract 1 from each of those values to make them 19s, 29s, 39s, and 49s.

The result is two data sets where each value from the first data set is one more than the corresponding value in the second data set. If one data set is identical to another except that every value is one more than a corresponding value in the other, then the means of those two sets must differ by one as well. So (B) is correct.

ANSWER CHOICE ANALYSIS

(A): This choice would be correct if the two figures were identical, but in reality the figure for Data Set *B* is the same as the one for Data Set *A*, *except* every column is moved one slot to the left. **(C):** This would be the right answer if a value had to increase by 10 to move one column to the right, but we can see in the prompt that this isn't the case. **(D):** This is the smallest possible difference between the *sums* of the two data sets, not their means, as the prompt requires.

How to check? Reread the prompt and the figures to verify that your understanding of both is accurate. Try to figure out which mistakes could lead to some of the wrong answer choices, and verify that you haven't made any such mistakes.

▶   Post-solution patterns (see page 286): the right answer to the wrong question

Test 2, Module 2, Question 27

- What's the prompt asking for? The value of d, according to the information in the prompt.

- Math concepts in the prompt: right triangles, side lengths, hypotenuse, radical expressions, variables, integers

- "Bridge" concepts: We can find the hypotenuse of the triangle, and then use that value to find d.

- Things to look out for: Remember that the prompt doesn't ask for the length of the hypotenuse—it asks for the value of d in the expression from the prompt!

Solution 1: Geometry: Sketch and label the triangle according to the information in the prompt, then use your understanding of right triangles and the Pythagorean theorem to create an expression you can solve for d.

Let's start by drawing the triangle in question, and labeling the sides according to the information in the prompt.

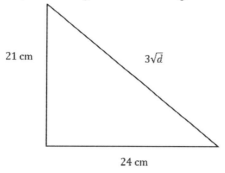

The Pythagorean theorem tells us that $a^2 + b^2 = c^2$, where a and b are the lengths of the legs of a right triangle, and c is the length of the hypotenuse of the right triangle. For our triangle, that means the following must be true:

$$21^2 + 24^2 = (3\sqrt{d})^2$$

We can solve this equation for d to find the answer to this question.

$21^2 + 24^2 = (3\sqrt{d})^2$	(Pythagorean theorem with values from the prompt)
$441 + 576 = 9d$	(simplify)
$1{,}017 = 9d$	(simplify)
$113 = d$	(divide both sides by 9)

So $d = 113$, and the answer is 113.

Solution 2: Concrete/graphing: Once you set up the equation from the previous solution, use the graphing function of your calculator to find the value of d.

We can actually avoid the algebra here once we set up the equation, and simply enter the equation we found, $21^2 + 24^2 = (3\sqrt{d})^2$, into the provided calculator. We switch the d for an x, because the calculator works best with the variables x and y, so we need to enter $21^2 + 24^2 = (3\sqrt{x})^2$.

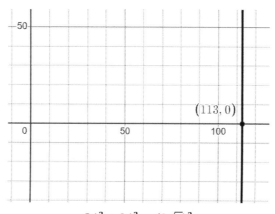

$$21^2 + 24^2 = (3\sqrt{x})^2$$

When we do that, we can zoom out and see a vertical line at $x = 113$, which is the correct answer. Of course, this approach depends on entering the equation into the calculator correctly, so make sure you get in plenty of practice with the calculator before test day.

How to check? Try an alternate approach above. Try to figure out which mistakes the College Board might hope you would make in finding your solution, and verify that you haven't made any such mistakes.

Note This is a great example of how the College Board can take a straightforward question about finding the hypotenuse of a right triangle and make it a bit more complicated by incorporating a variable in a radical expression whose value we need to find—but even when that happens, we can still keep calm and apply our SAT Math training to find the answer.

TEST 3 - MODULE 1

Test 3, Module 1, Question 1

- What's the prompt asking for? The solution to the given equation.
- Math concepts in the prompt: equations, variables
- Elements of the answer choices: Each answer choice is an integer ranging from 28 to 4,032.

- "Bridge" concepts: The solution to the equation is the number that makes the equation true when we plug it in for k.
- Things to look out for: Don't make a simple algebra mistake!

Solution 1: Concrete/graphing: We can graph the provided equation to find the value of k. Remember to use x instead of k, because the SAT calculator works best using the variables x and y.

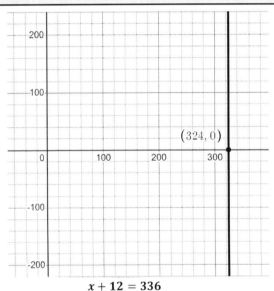

$$x + 12 = 336$$

When we zoom out, we can see a vertical line at $x = 324$. So (B) is right.

Solution 2: Algebra: Isolate k to answer the question.

We can solve the provided equation for k.

$$k + 12 = 336 \qquad \text{(given equation)}$$
$$k = 324 \qquad \text{(subtract 12 from both sides)}$$

So $k = 324$, and (B) is correct.

ANSWER CHOICE ANALYSIS

(A): This would be the answer if the left side of the equation was $12k$, rather than $k + 12$. **(C):** This would be the answer if the left side of the equation was $k - 12$, rather than $k + 12$. **(D):** This would be the answer if the left side of the equation was $\frac{k}{12}$, rather than $k + 12$.

How to check? Plug the answer you found back into the original equation and verify that it results in a valid statement. Try an alternate approach above. Try to figure out which mistakes could lead to some of the wrong answer choices, and verify that you haven't made any such mistakes.

▶ Post-solution patterns (see page 286): the right answer to the wrong question

---

- What's the prompt asking for? The value of $f(2)$.
- Math concepts in the prompt: functions, exponents, variables
- Elements of the answer choices: Each answer choice is an integer ranging from 20 to 24.
- Notable features of the answer choices: The choices are the integers from 20 to 24, excluding 22.

- "Bridge" concepts: $f(2)$ is the result that we get when we plug $x = 2$ into the given function.
- Pre-solution patterns (see p. 285): wrong answers try to imitate right answers
- Things to look out for: Don't make a simple algebra mistake! Notice that x is raised to an exponent of 3, not 2!

Solution 1: Concrete/graphing: We can graph the provided function to find the value of y when $x = 2$.

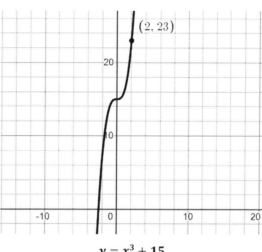

$$y = x^3 + 15$$

After graphing the function, we can see that when $x = 2$, $y = 23$. We can see this either from reading the graph directly, or clicking the settings wheel icon above the function in the SAT calculator, then clicking the table icon to create a table. Then we can read the table to find the relevant value. Either way, we can see that the answer is (C), 23.

Solution 2: Algebra: Plug $x = 2$ into the given function to find the answer to the question.

We can find $f(2)$ by plugging $x = 2$ into $f(x)$.

$$f(x) = x^3 + 15 \qquad \text{(given function)}$$
$$f(2) = 2^3 + 15 \qquad \text{(plug in } x = 2\text{)}$$
$$f(2) = 8 + 15 \qquad \text{(simplify)}$$
$$f(2) = 23 \qquad \text{(simplify)}$$

So the answer is (C).

ANSWER CHOICE ANALYSIS

(A): This would be the result if the function were $f(x) = x + 3 + 15$, rather than $f(x) = x^3 + 15$. **(B):** This would be the result if the function were $f(x) = 3x + 15$, rather than $f(x) = x^3 + 15$. **(D):** This would be the result if the function were $f(x) = 3^x + 15$, rather than $f(x) = x^3 + 15$.

How to check? Try an alternate approach above. Try to figure out which mistakes could lead to some of the wrong answer choices, and verify that you haven't made any such mistakes.

▶ Post-solution patterns (see page 286): the right answer to the wrong question

---

- What's the prompt asking for? The equation that represents the total cost, c, in dollars, to rent the tent with insurance for d days.
- Math concepts in the prompt: word problems, money, renting, onetime fees, function modeling

- Elements of the answer choices: Each answer choice is an equation with c set equal to an expression involving d.
- Notable features of the answer choices: Two choices include $d + 10$, and two include $d + 11$. Two choices feature parentheses, and two don't. Every choice includes 10 and 11.

- Pre-solution patterns (see p. 285): wrong answers try to imitate right answers
- Things to look out for: Don't mix up c and d or 10 and 11!

Solution 1: Concrete: Pick a value for d, and use the prompt to figure out what the total cost c would be to rent the tent for that number of days. Then plug your d-value into each answer choice and eliminate any choice whose resulting c-value doesn't match what you found.

Let's think through the total cost of renting the tent with insurance for 5 days. The prompt tells us that renting the tent costs $11 per day, so 5 days of renting the tent must cost $5 \times \$11$, or $55.

The prompt also says there's a onetime $10 fee for insurance. So we can add $10 to $55, which gives us a total cost of $65 to rent the tent with insurance for 5 days.

Now we know that when $d = 5$, c should be $65, so we can plug $d = 5$ into the equation in each answer choice, and then eliminate any choice that doesn't produce a c-value of $65.

(A) $c = 11((5) + 10)$ $= 11(15)$ $= 165$
(B) $c = 10((5) + 11)$ $= 10(16)$ $= 160$
(C) $c = 11(5) + 10$ $= 55 + 10$ $= 65$
(D) $c = 10(5) + 11$ $= 50 + 11$ $= 61$

When we plug $d = 5$ into each equation, only the equation in (C) produces a result of $c = 65$. So (C) is correct.

Solution 2: Careful reading: Read the prompt and figure out how to represent the ideas from the prompt in terms of c and d. Pick the answer choice that demonstrates your reasoning.

If renting the tent costs $11 per day, and d is the number of days that Sean rents the tent, then the total cost of that daily rental fee must be $11d$—that's the cost to rent a tent for a day multiplied by the number of days that the tent is rented.

But that isn't the only cost described in the prompt. We're also told that there's a "onetime insurance fee of $10." If it's a onetime fee, then it stays the same no matter how many days the tent is rented. So we shouldn't multiply that $10 by anything; instead, we should just add it to the total rental cost of $11d$ that we just figured out.

That means the total cost of renting the tent, with insurance, for d days must be $11d + 10$. If the total cost is represented by c, then we can say $c = 11d + 10$. So (C) is right.

ANSWER CHOICE ANALYSIS

(A): This would be the right answer if the parentheses were removed. **(B):** This choice combines the errors from (A) and (D). **(D):** This choice is the right answer, except the 10 and 11 are reversed.

How to check? Verify that you used the right numbers for the rental cost and the onetime fee. Try an alternate approach above. Try to figure out which mistakes could lead to some of the wrong answer choices, and verify that you haven't made any such mistakes.

Test 3, Module 1, Question 4

- What's the prompt asking for? The value of x in the diagram.
- Math concepts in the prompt: parallel lines, variables, transversals, angle measures
- Elements of the answer choices: Each answer choice is an integer ranging from 13 to 154.

- Notable features of the answer choices: (A), (B), and (C) form a series in which each choice is twice as much as the previous choice.
- "Bridge" concepts: Since m and n are parallel, we can use the given angle measure to find the value of x.
- Pre-solution patterns (see p. 285): halves and doubles
- Things to look out for: Remember that x and 26 should add up to 180, *not* 90!

Solution 1: Geometry: Use your understanding of transversals to figure out what x and 26 must add up to, then solve for x.

Since lines m and n are parallel, line l must cross them at the same angle. That means the labeled 26° angle in the provided figure where l crosses n is the same size as the corresponding angle where l crosses m. Let's add that measurement to the figure.

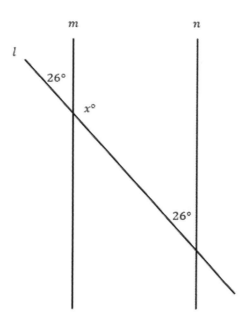

We can see that the 26° angle and the $x°$ angle must add up to 180°, because together they form a straight line. This is the same as saying that $26° + x° = 180°$. When we subtract 26° from both sides, we get $x = 154°$. So the answer is (D), 154.

Solution 2: Test-smart: Evaluate the answer choices in light of what we know about x, and eliminate choices accordingly.

Once we start the solution above and realize that the angle in question must have a value greater than 90°, we can eliminate (A), (B), and (C), and choose (D).

ANSWER CHOICE ANALYSIS

(A): This is half of the given angle measure. **(B):** This is equal to the given angle measure; sometimes angles in transversals have equal measures, but that isn't the case here. **(C):** This is twice the given angle measure.

How to check? Add your answer to 26 to verify that the sum is 180. Try an alternate approach above. Try to figure out which mistakes could lead to some of the wrong answer choices, and verify that you haven't made any such mistakes.

▶   Post-solution patterns (see page 286): the right answer to the wrong question

---

Test 3, Module 1, Question 5

- **What's the prompt asking for?** The equation that represents the situation described in the prompt.
- **Math concepts in the prompt:** word problems, money, down payment, monthly payments
- **Elements of the answer choices:** Each answer choice is an equation involving p.
- **Notable features of the answer choices:** Each answer choice starts with either $16p$ or $37p$, followed by either a plus sign or a minus sign, followed by either 16 or 37, ending with an equals sign and the number 165.

- **"Bridge" concepts:** We can check each answer choice against the ideas in the prompt to see which one satisfies the prompt.
- **Pre-solution patterns (see p. 285):** opposites; wrong answers try to imitate right answers
- **Things to look out for:** Remember which cost in the prompt is monthly, and which is a onetime down payment! Think carefully about how to represent each relationship in the prompt mathematically!

Solution 1: Careful reading: Read the prompt and think carefully about how to express the money John paid for the microscope in an equation. Eliminate any choices that don't match your reasoning.

If John made a down payment, then that amount of money shouldn't be multiplied by anything, because that payment was only made once. (Note that even if we don't know what a down payment is, the prompt says he made "a down payment," which tells us it was only one payment.)

So the $37, which was the amount of the down payment, shouldn't be multiplied by anything, since it only happened once. Based on that, we can eliminate (B) and (D).

That leaves (A) and (C). The only difference between (A) and (C) is that (A) *subtracts* 37 from $16p$, while (C) *adds* those values together. The prompt says that John paid "a total of $165" by making a $37 payment "plus" p monthly payments, so an equation that "represents this situation," as the prompt requires, would need to add the $37 and the $16p$ expression, not subtract one from the other. So we can eliminate (A), which means that (C) is right.

Solution 2: Abstract: Build an equation that represents the situation in the prompt using key phrases from the prompt.

The prompt tells us that John paid "a total of $165 for a microscope." So we can start with an equation like this.

$$\text{total payment for microscope} = \$165$$

Then the prompt tells us John paid the total by paying "a down payment of $37 plus p monthly payments of $16 each," so we can adjust our equation accordingly.

$$\text{down payment of } \$37 + p \text{ monthly payments of } \$16 \text{ each} = \$165$$

The down payment is just $37; it's not multiplied by anything or anything like that. So we can simplify our equation a little.

$$\$37 + p \text{ monthly payments of } \$16 \text{ each} = \$165$$

If there were p monthly payments, and each payment was $16, then we could find the total amount of those payments by multiplying 16 by p, which gives us $16p$. That gives us the following:

$$\$37 + \$16p = \$165$$

This is equal to the expression in (C), so (C) is correct.

ANSWER CHOICE ANALYSIS

(A): This choice reflects the idea that the total of the monthly payments is $37 *more* than the price of the microscope, which doesn't appear in the prompt. **(B):** This choice combines the mistakes from (A) and (D). **(D):** This choice reverses the amount of money for the down payment and the monthly payment.

How to check? Try an alternate approach above. Try to figure out which mistakes could lead to some of the wrong answer choices, and verify that you haven't made any such mistakes.

Test 3, Module 1, Question 6

- What's the prompt asking for? The value of y in the given equation when $x = 8$
- Math concepts in the prompt: equations, variables

- "Bridge" concepts: We can plug $x = 8$ into the given equation to find the value of y that the prompt asks for.
- Things to look out for: Don't mix up x and y! Don't make a simple mistake related to algebra or sign!

Solution 1: Concrete: Plug $x = 8$ into the given equation to find the answer.

We can plug $x = 8$ into the provided equation to find the answer to this question.

$y = 5x + 10$	(provided equation)
$y = 5(8) + 10$	(plug in $x = 8$)
$y = 40 + 10$	(simplify)
$y = 50$	(simplify)

So the answer is 50.

Solution 2: Concrete/graphing: We can graph the provided equation and then find the y-value when $x = 8$.

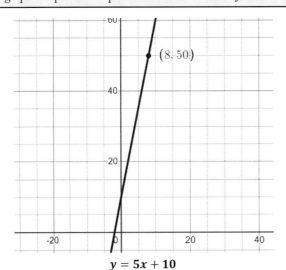

$$y = 5x + 10$$

We can see that when $x = 8$, $y = 50$. So the answer is 50.

How to check? Try an alternate approach above. Try to figure out which mistakes the College Board might hope you would make in finding your solution, and verify that you haven't made any such mistakes.

Test 3, Module 1, Question 7

- **What's the prompt asking for?** The number of cans collected by group 6.
- **Math concepts in the prompt:** reading bar graphs, distribution

- **Things to look out for:** Make sure you answer using the data for group 6, and not some other group!

Solution 1: Careful reading: Read the prompt and the bar graph carefully to find the answer.

In order to answer this question, we need to read all the labels on the graph. We can see that the x-axis is labeled with the word "Group," and the y-axis is labeled with the phrase "Number of cans." So we should be able to find group 6 along the x-axis, and then read how many cans group 6 collected from the y-axis.

When we find the "6" on the axis labeled "Group," we can see that the corresponding column extends to the line that's labeled "40" on the axis labeled "Number of cans." So Group 6 collected 40 cans, and the answer is 40.

How to check? Try to figure out which mistakes the College Board might hope you would make in finding your solution, and verify that you haven't made any such mistakes.

Note We know that the College Board frequently includes SAT Math questions with no answer choices that are pretty straightforward, especially near the beginning of a module. Some test-takers will feel like there must be some more complicated aspect of the question that they're missing, but as trained test-takers, we just carefully read whatever's in front of us, and then apply our training to find the right answer—whether that question is very straightforward, a little more complicated, or anything in between.

Test 3, Module 1, Question 8

- **What's the prompt asking for?** The probability that a student from the chart selected at random voted for a lion.
- **Math concepts in the prompt:** word problems, voting, tables, probability, randomness
- **Elements of the answer choices:** Each answer choice is a fraction ranging from $\frac{1}{9}$ to $\frac{2}{3}$.

- **Notable features of the answer choices:** Three answer choices have a 1 in the numerator, and the other has a 2. The denominator of each choice is different.
- **"Bridge" concepts:** We need to compare the number of votes cast for a lion to the total number of votes.
- **Things to look out for:** Think carefully about what a desired outcome and a possible outcome is in this scenario! Make sure you read the table carefully!

Solution 1: Probability: Use the prompt and the table to figure out the number of desired outcomes and the number of possible outcomes, and use that information to construct a probability fraction and answer the question.

In order to create the probability fraction this question asks for, we need to know the number of desired outcomes and the number of possible outcomes. Then we can construct a probability fraction like this:

$$\frac{\text{number of desired outcomes}}{\text{number of possible outcomes}}$$

The desired outcome is picking "a student whose vote for a new mascot was for a lion." So we need the total number of students who cast votes for "Lion." At the top left of the table, we can see the label "Mascot," and underneath that, we can find the label "Lion." So the row labeled "Lion" tells us how many students voted for a lion.

Near the top right, we can see the word "total." This column tells us the total number of votes for the mascot choices in each labeled row. We can read across the row labeled "Lion" to see where it intersects with the column labeled "Total" to find the total number of votes for a lion, which was 20. So 20 total students voted for "Lion," which means the number of desired outcomes is 20. Now we just need the number of possible outcomes.

The number of possible outcomes is the 80 students who voted, because that's the pool of people we're choosing from—we know that because the sentence above the table says that the table provides info "for 80 students," and the sentence below the table asks about a situation where "one of these students is selected at random"—that is, one of the 80 students. So our probability fraction is $\frac{20}{80}$. That doesn't match any other answer choices, but it does reduce to $\frac{1}{4}$, which is (C). So (C) is correct.

ANSWER CHOICE ANALYSIS

(B): This would be the result if someone accidentally added the 20 lion votes to the 80 total votes in the denominator and created the fraction $\frac{20}{100}$, or if someone mistakenly reduced $\frac{20}{80}$ to $\frac{1}{5}$.

How to check? Verify that you read the correct values off the table. Try to figure out which mistakes could lead to some of the wrong answer choices, and verify that you haven't made any such mistakes.

Test 3, Module 1, Question 9

- **What's the prompt asking for?** The best interpretation of the slope of the graph.
- **Math concepts in the prompt:** word problems, graphs, onetime fees, hourly rates, slope
- **Elements of the answer choices:** Each answer choice is a phrase related to the ideas in the prompt.
- **Notable features of the answer choices:** Each choice is a different aspect of what the electrician charges.
- **"Bridge" concepts:** The slope must tell us about something that increases as x increases.
- **Things to look out for:** Think carefully about how the provided graph relates to the situations described in the prompt!

Solution 1: Careful reading: Consider each answer choice in light of the prompt and eliminate each one that doesn't fit logically with the idea of slope.

(A) The electrician's hourly rate tells us how much the electrician charges per hour of work. We can also think of this as the amount the electrician's total charge increases every hour—because each hour that the electrician works, the total charge increases by that hourly rate. Similarly, the slope of the graph is the rate of increase of the value represented by the line—for each additional x hours of work, the electrician earns an additional y dollars. So the slope of the graph does appear to be the electrician's hourly rate, which would make (A) correct, but let's check each answer choice to make sure we haven't made a mistake.

(B) The slope of the graph tells us how much the electrician's total charge increases as time goes on, but a onetime fee doesn't change, no matter how much time the electrician works. So it doesn't make sense to say the slope, which represents the change in a value, is the electrician's onetime fee, which doesn't change. So (B) is wrong.

(C) The slope of the graph is the change in the total charge as x increases—that is, as the electrician works more and more hours. It doesn't represent any maximum value, and nothing in the prompt even indicates that there *is* a maximum value—as far as we know, if the electrician keeps on working and working, the total charge will just keep increasing, with no maximum. So (C) is wrong.

(D) This choice will be tempting for some test-takers, because they will look at the line and think "well, this line tells me what the electrician charges, so (D) seems right." But (D) would be right if the question asked about what a *point* on the line represents—that is, the total charge y when the electrician works x hours. Instead, the question asks us about the *slope* of the line, which is the change in y as x increases (and which, incidentally, is constant for the whole line, while the total amount that the electrician charges changes with x). So (D) is wrong.

After considering each answer choice, we can see that (A) is right.

ANSWER CHOICE ANALYSIS

See the solution above for answer choice analysis.

How to check? Try to figure out which mistakes could lead to some of the wrong answer choices, and verify that you haven't made any such mistakes.

Test 3, Module 1, Question 10

- **What's the prompt asking for?** The length of one side of square Y.
- **Math concepts in the prompt:** squares, side lengths, perimeter
- **Elements of the answer choices:** Each answer choice is an even integer ranging from 6 to 24.
- **Notable features of the answer choices:** One answer choice is a single digit, and the rest are double digits. 1 and 4 appear twice in the answer choices; every other numeral appears once. (D) is the sum of (B) and (C).
- **"Bridge" concepts:** If the perimeter of square Y is 2 times the perimeter of square X, then each side of square Y must be twice as long as each side of square X.
- **Things to look out for:** Don't mix up X and Y! Don't confuse perimeter and area!

Solution 1: Geometry: Draw and label square X according to the information in the prompt. Use your sketch and your understanding of perimeter to answer the question in the prompt.

Let's draw square X, incorporating the information from the prompt.

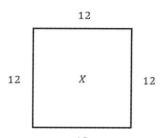

The perimeter of square X is the sum of the lengths of its sides, so its perimeter must be $12 + 12 + 12 + 12$, or 48.

The prompt tells us that the perimeter of square Y is twice the perimeter of square X. We just found that the perimeter of square X was 48, so the perimeter of square Y must be twice that, or 96.

If the perimeter of square Y is 96, then each side must be one fourth of 96. So each side is $\frac{96}{4}$, or 24 cm long. So (D) is correct.

Solution 2: Test-smart: Think about what doubling the perimeter of a square must do to each side length of that square, and use this information to answer the question.

If the perimeter of square Y is twice as much as the perimeter of square X, then each side of square Y must also be twice as much as each side of square X. We know this is true because if the sum of the four sides of square Y is twice as much as the sum of the four sides of square X, it must be the case that each of the four sides of square Y is twice as long as each side of square X.

Since square X has sides that are 12 cm long, square Y must have sides that are 24 cm long. So (D) is correct.

ANSWER CHOICE ANALYSIS

(A): This would be the right answer if the perimeter of square X were twice as large as the perimeter of square Y, and not the other way around. **(B):** This is 2 less than the side length of square X. This choice might be tempting for a test-taker who misread the question. **(C):** This is the result of adding 2 to the side length of square X, rather than doubling that side length.

How to check? Try an alternate approach above. Try to figure out which mistakes could lead to some of the wrong answer choices, and verify that you haven't made any such mistakes.

▶ Post-solution patterns (see page 286): the right answer to the wrong question

Test 3, Module 1, Question 11

- What's the prompt asking for? The equation of the line described in the prompt.
- Math concepts in the prompt: equations, coordinate pairs, parallel lines
- Elements of the answer choices: Each answer choice is an equation involving y, x, and either 5 and/or 7.
- Notable features of the answer choices: Two answer choices include $5x$ and two include $7x$. One choice ends in $+5$, one ends in $+7$, and the other two don't have a constant added to the x-term.

- "Bridge" concepts: A line parallel to $y = 7x + 4$ will have the same slope as that line. Also, if a line passes through $(0,5)$, then the y-intercept of that line is $(0,5)$.
- Pre-solution patterns (see p. 285): opposites; wrong answers try to imitate right answers
- Things to look out for: Don't mix up slope and y-intercept! Don't mix up "parallel" and "perpendicular!"

Solution 1: Concrete/graphing: We can graph the provided equation, and then graph every answer choice to see which one meets the requirements of the prompt.

(A)

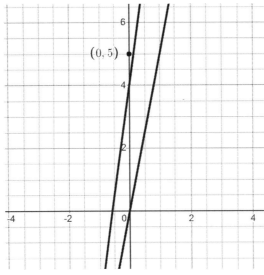

$y = 5x$

(B)

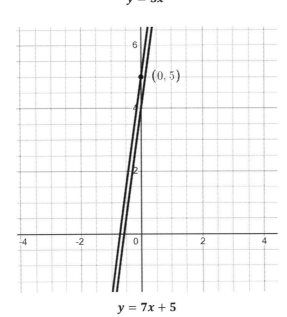

$y = 7x + 5$

(C)

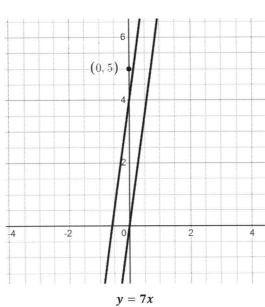

$y = 7x$

(D)

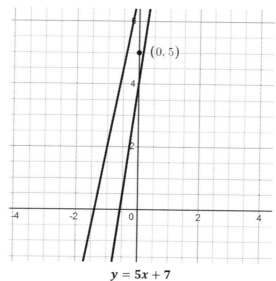

$$y = 5x + 7$$

We can eliminate (A) and (D) because neither is parallel to the graph of the provided equation. We can also eliminate (C), because it passes through the origin, not through $(0, 5)$, as the prompt requires—that leaves only (B), which is parallel to the graph of the provided equation, *and* which also passes through $(0, 5)$. Choice (B) meets all the requirements in the prompt, so (B) is correct.

Solution 2: Concrete: Figure out the slope and y-intercept the right answer should have, then determine the slope and y-intercept of each answer choice. Eliminate each choice that doesn't meet the requirements you found.

If we're familiar with slope-intercept form, then we can see that the provided equation and each answer choice is in this form, which looks like $y = mx + b$, where m is the slope and b is the y-intercept.

The prompt asks for the equation of the line that's parallel to the graph of the given equation. Parallel lines have the same slope, and, using our understanding of slope-intercept form, we can see that the slope of the line for the provided equation is 7. So the slope of the line in the correct answer must also be 7, in order for the lines to be parallel.

Also, if a line passes through the point $(0, 5)$, that means it crosses the y-axis at $(0, 5)$, which the same as saying its y-intercept is 5. With this in mind, we can quickly determine the slope and y-intercept for the graph of each equation in the answer choices.

(A)	Slope = 5	y-intercept = 0
(B)	Slope = 7	y-intercept = 5
(C)	Slope = 7	y-intercept = 0
(D)	Slope = 5	y-intercept = 7

The only choice with a slope of 7 that passes through the point $(0, 5)$ is (B), and (B) is correct.

ANSWER CHOICE ANALYSIS

(A): This choice has the wrong slope and the wrong y-intercept. **(C):** This choice has the right slope, but the wrong y-intercept. **(D):** This choice switches the slope and y-intercept.

How to check? Verify that your choice meets the requirements in the prompt. Try an alternate approach above. Try to figure out which mistakes could lead to some of the wrong answer choices, and verify that you haven't made any such mistakes.

Test 3, Module 1, Question 12

- What's the prompt asking for? The equation that defines h, according to the information in the prompt.

- Math concepts in the prompt: functions, inputs and outputs

- Elements of the answer choices: Each answer choice is a function involving x and/or 41.

- "Bridge" concepts: We can use the inputs and outputs from the prompt to test an equation and see if it could define h.

- Pre-solution patterns (see p. 285): wrong answers try to imitate right answers

- Things to look out for: Don't make a simple mistake related to algebra or sign! Don't get confused about which numbers in the prompt are inputs and which ones are outputs!

Solution 1: Concrete: Plug the inputs from the prompt into the equation in each answer choice, and eliminate each choice whose outputs don't match the ones in the prompt.

According to the prompt, the right answer will produce an $h(0)$ value of 41 and an $h(1)$ value of 40. So if we plug $x = 0$ into the right answer, the result will be 41, and if we plug $x = 1$ into the right answer, we'll get 40. Let's plug these values into each answer choice to see what we get.

(A) $\quad h(0) = -(0) + 41 = 41 \qquad h(1) = -(1) + 41 = 40$

(B) $\quad h(0) = -(0) = 0 \qquad\qquad h(1) = -(1) = -1$

(C) $\quad h(0) = -41(0) = 0 \qquad\quad h(1) = -41(1) = -41$

(D) $\quad h(0) = -41 \qquad\qquad\quad h(1) = -41$

After checking each answer choice, we can see that only (A) has an $h(0)$ value of 41 and an $h(1)$ value of 40, so (A) is correct.

Solution 2: Graphing: We can graph each answer choice to see which one goes through the point $(0, 41)$ and $(1, 40)$.

(A)

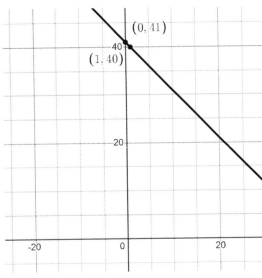

$$y = -x + 41$$

(B)

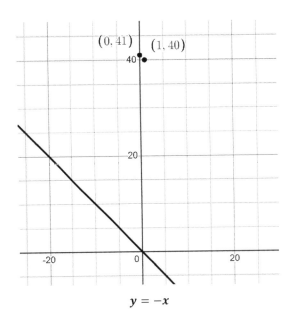

$$y = -x$$

(C)

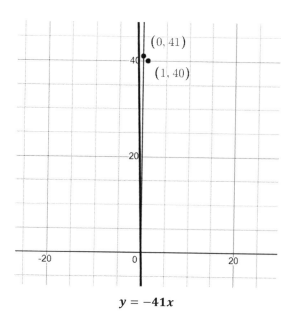

$$y = -41x$$

(D)

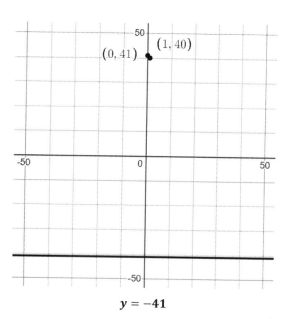

$$y = -41$$

We can see that only the graph of (A) passes through these points, so (A) is correct.

ANSWER CHOICE ANALYSIS

(B): This choice has the right slope, but the wrong y-intercept. **(C):** This choice could be tempting for a test-taker who knows the right equation should involve x, 41, and a negative sign, but who gets confused about how to connect those elements.

How to check? Try an alternate approach above. Try to figure out which mistakes could lead to some of the wrong answer choices, and verify that you haven't made any such mistakes.

Test 3, Module 1, Question 13

- **What's the prompt asking for?** The time it takes to double the number of bacteria in the population.

- **Math concepts in the prompt:** word problems, functions, time, doubling

- **"Bridge" concepts:** We can use the provided function to figure out how much time it will take for the population to double.

- **Things to look out for:** Don't make a simple algebra mistake! Find the time it takes for the population *double*, not to be raised to a power of 2!

Solution 1: Concrete/graphing: We can graph the provided function to see how many minutes it takes for $f(t)$ to double.

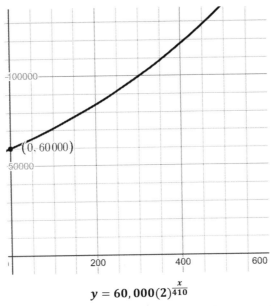

$$y = 60,000(2)^{\frac{x}{410}}$$

We can see that at 0 minutes, $f(t) = 60,000$. If we can figure out the t-value that causes $f(t)$ to equal twice that much, or 120,000, we'll have the right answer. The easiest way to do this with the graphing calculator is probably just to graph $y = 120,000$ and see where the two lines intersect.

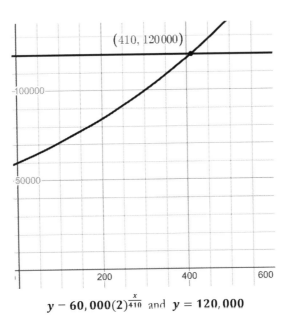

$y = 60,000(2)^{\frac{x}{410}}$ and $y = 120,000$

When we do that we can see that they intersect at $(410, 120,000)$, which means that $f(t)$ doubles from 60,000 to 120,000 in 410 minutes. So the answer is 410.

Solution 2: Abstract: Carefully analyze the function and the prompt, and think about what would have to happen for the value of the function to double.

We need to find out how long it takes for $f(t)$ to double. When we look at the provided function, we might notice that it involves multiplying by 2. Then we might notice that the 2 is raised to a power of $\frac{t}{410}$. So $f(t)$ will double every time the function involves multiplying by 2 an additional time, which will happen every time $\frac{t}{410}$ increases by one.

In other words, at $t = 0$, $\frac{t}{410}$ will equal $\frac{0}{410}$, which means the 2 will be raised to a power of 0. We know $2^0 = 1$, so 60,000 will be multiplied by 1. $\frac{t}{410}$ will increase from 0 to 1 when $t = 410$, because $\frac{410}{410} = 1$. At that point, 2 will be raised to a power of 1, and since $2^1 = 2$, then 60,000 will be multiplied by 2—that is, the function will be double the amount it was when $t = 0$. When t increases by another 410 to 820, $\frac{t}{410}$ will increase from 1 to 2, because $\frac{820}{410} = 2$. So 2 will be raised to a power of 2, and $f(t)$ will be multiplied by 2^2, or 4—so the function will be twice as much as it was when t was equal to 410.

We can reason that every time 410 minutes passes, the 2 in $f(t)$ will be raised to an exponent that is greater by one, which is the same as saying $f(t)$ will be multiplied by 2 every 410 minutes. So the answer is 410.

How to check? Try an alternate approach above. Try to figure out which mistakes the College Board might hope you would make in finding your solution, and verify that you haven't made any such mistakes.

Test 3, Module 1, Question 14

- What's the prompt asking for? The value of $g(0)$.
- Math concepts in the prompt: functions, factors, translating graphs, inputs and outputs
- "Bridge" concepts: If we can figure out $f(0)$, we can use the information in the prompt to figure out $g(0)$.

- Things to look out for: Don't confuse g and f! Remember that $g(x)$ is 4 units *up* from $f(x)$, not *down* from $f(x)$! Don't make a simple algebra mistake!

Solution 1: Concrete/graphing: We can graph the provided function to find $f(0)$.

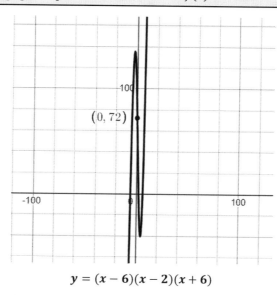

$$y = (x - 6)(x - 2)(x + 6)$$

When we do that, we can see that $f(0) = 72$. If $y = g(x)$ is the result of translating the graph of $y = f(x)$ up four units, then $g(x)$ must be 4 units greater than $f(x)$, which means $g(0)$ must be 4 more than $f(0)$, which means $g(0) = 72 + 4$, or 76. So the answer is 76.

Solution 2: Concrete: Find $f(0)$, then use that value, along with the information in the prompt, to find $g(0)$.

We can plug 0 into the given equation to find $f(0)$.

$$f(x) = (x - 6)(x - 2)(x + 6) \quad \text{(given function)}$$
$$f(0) = ((0) - 6)((0) - 2)((0) + 6) \quad \text{(plug in } x = 0)$$
$$f(0) = (-6)(-2)(6) \quad \text{(simplify)}$$
$$f(0) = 72 \quad \text{(simplify)}$$

So $f(0) = 72$. As we saw in our last solution, if $y = g(x)$ is the same as $y = f(x)$ moved up 4 units, and $f(0) = 72$, then $g(0)$ must be 4 more than that, or 76. So the answer is 76.

How to check? Verify that you understood where $f(x)$ moved to become $g(x)$. Try an alternate approach above. Try to figure out which mistakes the College Board might hope you would make in finding your solution, and verify that you haven't made any such mistakes.

Test 3, Module 1, Question 15

- What's the prompt asking for? The number of hours the candle has been burning if 6 ounces of wax remain in the candle, according to the information in the prompt.
- Math concepts in the prompt: word problems, rates, time
- Elements of the answer choices: Each answer choice is an integer ranging from 3 to 44.

- Notable features of the answer choices: Two choices have one digit, and two have two digits. The two-digit integers both end with 4. (A) is half of (B).
- "Bridge" concepts: We can use the provided information to figure out how long it would take for 11 ounces of wax to burn.
- Pre-solution patterns (see p. 285): halves and doubles

- Things to look out for: Don't mix up what 4 and 6 represent in the prompt! Don't make a simple algebra mistake!

Solution 1: Concrete: Use the provided information to figure out how many ounces of the wax burned away, then multiply that amount by 4 hours per ounce.

If 6 ounces of wax remain in the candle, then the candle has lost 11 ounces of wax while burning, because $17 - 6 = 11$.

The prompt tells us that the amount of wax in the candle decreases by one ounce for every 4 hours it burns. If the candle has lost 11 ounces of wax, and if each of those ounces represents 4 hours of burning, then the candle must have been burning for 11×4 hours, or 44 hours. So the answer is (D).

Solution 2: Test-smart: Think about how long it would take for the whole candle to burn. Use this information to approximate the answer, and then eliminate any choice that doesn't fit with this approximation.

Based on the information in the prompt, we can determine that the whole candle would burn away in 17×4 hours, or 68 hours, since the candle is made of 17 ounces of wax and each ounce takes 4 hours to burn. If we realize that the candle is more than half gone, then we know that it must have been burning for more than half of 68 hours. Only (D) is more than half of 68, so (D) must be correct.

ANSWER CHOICE ANALYSIS

(B): This would be the answer if 6 ounces had burned away, not "remained," *and* if it took one hour to burn an ounce of wax, neither of which is the case. **(C):** This is how long it would take for 6 ounces of wax to burn—but the prompt didn't say that 6 ounces had burned; it said that 6 ounces were *left*.

How to check? Try an alternate approach above. Try to figure out which mistakes could lead to some of the wrong answer choices, and verify that you haven't made any such mistakes.

▶ Post-solution patterns (see page 286): the right answer to the wrong question

Test 3, Module 1, Question 16

- What's the prompt asking for? The equation that correctly expresses k in terms of j and m.
- Math concepts in the prompt: equations, variables
- Elements of the answer choices: Each answer choice is k set equal to an expression involving m and $14j$.
- Notable features of the answer choices: Three choices include a fraction with 5 as the denominator; one choice has no fraction.

- "Bridge" concepts: We can manipulate the provided expression to isolate k and find the answer to the question.
- Pre-solution patterns (see p. 285): wrong answers try to imitate right answers
- Things to look out for: Don't make a simple mistake related to algebra or sign!

Solution 1: Algebra: Manipulate the expression to isolate k, then pick the matching answer choice.

$14j + 5k - m$	(given equation)
$5k = m - 14j$	(subtract $14j$ from both sides)
$k = \frac{m - 14j}{5}$	(divide both sides by 5)

So the answer is (A).

ANSWER CHOICE ANALYSIS

(B): This would be the result of making an algebraic error on the third step in the solution above and only dividing m by 5, and not dividing the whole expression $m - 14j$ by 5. **(C):** This choice results from accidentally putting the minus sign in front of m, instead of in front of $14j$. **(D):** This mistake is similar to the one in (B), with the added error of multiplying by 5 instead of dividing by 5.

How to check? Try to figure out which mistakes could lead to some of the wrong answer choices, and verify that you haven't made any such mistakes.

Test 3, Module 1, Question 17

- What's the prompt asking for? The value of $\sin(J)$ if $\sin(F) = \frac{308}{317}$.
- Math concepts in the prompt: similar triangles, right triangles, angle measures, sine, fractions

- Elements of the answer choices: Each answer choice is a fraction involving 75, 317, and/or 308.
- Notable features of the answer choices: 317 is the numerator of two fractions and the denominator of

two fractions. 308 is the numerator of one fraction and the denominator of one fraction. 75 is the numerator of one fraction and the denominator of one fraction.

- "Bridge" concepts: The prompt tells us that the triangles are similar, and that angle F corresponds to angle J. With that in mind, we know that $\sin(F)$ must be equal to $\sin(J)$.

- Pre-solution patterns (see p. 285): wrong answers try to imitate right answers
- Things to look out for: Don't mix up the different side lengths! Don't mix up which vertices on one triangle correspond to which vertices on the other triangle!

Solution 1: Geometry: Sketch and label the triangles described in the prompt. Then, use the information in the prompt to find $\sin(J)$.

Let's draw the two triangles described in the prompt. Notice that the prompt tells us that the triangles are similar, and that angle F corresponds to angle J, and that G and K are both right angles. (Note that we don't have to draw these triangles exactly to scale or anything, as long as any labels in our drawings match the information provided in the prompt, and we don't get confused about which points correspond to each other.)

The prompt tells us that $\sin(F) = \frac{308}{317}$. We know from SOHCAHTOA that the sine of an angle is equal to the length of the side opposite that angle divided by the length of the hypotenuse. So we can label the side opposite angle F as 308 units long, and the hypotenuse as 317 units long.

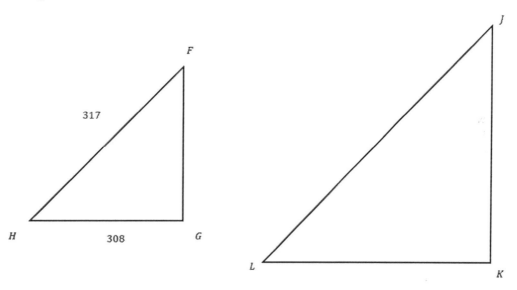

The prompt tells us that these two triangles are similar. That means their corresponding angles are equal, and their corresponding sides are in proportion to one another. In this case, we can see that the hypotenuse of the second triangle corresponds to the hypotenuse in the first triangle, and that side LK in the second triangle corresponds to side HG in the first triangle. So we can't know the specific lengths of the hypotenuse and side LK in the second triangle based on the provided information, but we can know that the same proportion exists between the second triangle's hypotenuse and LK as the one that exists between the first triangle's hypotenuse and HG. That means that the ratio of the side opposite angle J to the second triangle's hypotenuse is the same as the ratio of the side opposite angle F to the first triangle's hypotenuse, which means $\sin(J)$ must be equal to $\sin(F)$, which means $\sin(J) = \frac{308}{317}$. So the correct answer is (B).

Solution 2: Test-smart: Notice that the triangles are similar, and angle F corresponds to angle J, which means that $\sin(F)$ must be equal to $\sin(J)$, and use that info to answer the question.

If triangle FGH is similar to triangle JKL, then that means the triangles have the same corresponding angle measures, and their corresponding sides are all in the same proportion to one another. If angle F corresponds to angle J, then $\sin(F)$ must be equal to $\sin(J)$, and if $\sin(F) = \frac{308}{317}$, then $\sin(J) = \frac{308}{317}$. So the correct answer is (B).

ANSWER CHOICE ANALYSIS

(A): This is $\cos(J)$, but the prompt asks for $\sin(J)$. **(C):** This is the reciprocal of the right answer. **(D):** This is the reciprocal of (A).

How to check? Verify that you used the right trigonometric ratio. Try an alternate approach above. Try to figure out which mistakes could lead to some of the wrong answer choices, and verify that you haven't made any such mistakes.

▶ Post-solution patterns (see page 286): the right answer to the wrong question

---

- What's the prompt asking for? The smaller of the two integers described in the prompt.
- Math concepts in the prompt: multiplication, addition, positive integers
- Elements of the answer choices: Each answer choice is an integer ranging from 7 to 78.
- Notable features of the answer choices: (A) is half of (B). (C) is half of (D). (C) is "11 greater than twice" as much as (B). (A) times (D) equals 546. (B) times (C) equals 546.
- Pre-solution patterns (see p. 285): halves and doubles
- Things to look out for: Don't overlook the word "twice" in the prompt! Don't choose the *larger* of the two integers!

Solution 1: Concrete: Find the value that's "11 greater than twice" each integer in the answer choices, and multiply the resulting number by that answer choice. The choice that produces a value of 546 will be the right answer.

The prompt describes a "first integer" that's "11 greater than twice the second integer." Then it asks us about the "smaller" integer. The smaller integer must be the second one, because we have to double it and add 11 to it in order to get the first integer. So the answer to this question is the second integer described in the prompt.

We can treat each answer choice as the second, smaller integer: we can double it and add 11 to the result to find its corresponding first integer, and then multiply the two integers together. The right answer will produce 546.

(A) 7	$(7 \times 2) + 11 = 25$	$7 \times 25 = 175$
(B) 14	$(14 \times 2) + 11 = 39$	$14 \times 39 = 546$
(C) 39	$(39 \times 2) + 11 = 89$	$39 \times 89 = 3{,}471$
(D) 78	$(78 \times 2) + 11 = 167$	$78 \times 167 = 13{,}026$

We can see that only (B) produces a result of 546 as the prompt requires, so (B) is right.

Solution 2: Abstract: Turn the words and phrases in the prompt into a system of equations, and then solve the system of equations. Mark the answer choice that corresponds to the smaller value you found.

We can turn the information in the prompt into a series of equations, and then find their solution. Let's call the two integers we're looking for x and y.

The prompt tells us that the product of two positive integers is 546. That's the same as saying $xy = 546$, so this is our first equation. Then the prompt tells us that the first integer is 11 greater than twice the second integer. We can write that like this:

$$\text{first integer} = 11 \text{ greater than twice the second integer}$$

We'll call the first integer x and the second integer y (it doesn't matter which one is which; either way the answer we choose will be the smaller of the two).

$$x = 11 \text{ greater than twice } y$$

"11 greater than" is the same as just adding 11, and "twice y" is the same as $2y$, so let's adjust our equation accordingly.

$$x = 11 + 2y$$

Okay, now we have our system of equations:

$$xy = 546$$
$$x = 11 + 2y$$

From here, there are a few ways we can solve for x and y. The quickest and easiest way is probably to graph our equations and find their point of intersection, which looks like this:

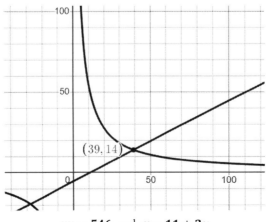

$$xy = 546 \text{ and } x = 11 + 2y$$

We can see they intersect at $(39, 14)$, which means our two integers are 39 and 14. The smaller of the two integers is 14, so (B) is correct. (Note that the graphs also intersect in the bottom left area of the graph, where x and y are negative—but the prompt tells us we're worried about "two positive integers," so the graphs intersecting when x or y is negative doesn't affect our solution.)

Solution 3: Test-smart: Reason through the information in the prompt to determine the properties that the integer we're looking for must have, and then eliminate the choices that don't have those properties.

The prompt tells us that the product of the two integers is 546, which is even. In order for the product of two integers to be even, at least one of the two integers must be even. We're told that the larger integer is the result of doubling the smaller integer and adding 11—this is guaranteed to produce an odd number, because doubling any integer produces an even result by definition, and adding 11 to an even number produces an odd result. So the large integer will definitely be odd, which means the smaller integer—our correct answer—must be even. (Again, we know this because otherwise the product of the two integers can't be the even number 546.)

That eliminates (A) and (C). Between (B) and (D), we can see that (D) is far too large—even 78^2 is in the thousands, so if we multiply 78 by a number more than twice as much as 78, the result will be a lot more than 546. That leaves only (B) as a possible correct answer, so (B) is right.

Solution 4: Test-smart: See if two of the choices have the mathematical relationship described in the prompt. If they do, test to see whether their product is 546. If so, the smaller value is the right answer.

We might guess that if the prompt asks us for the *smaller* of two integers, then one wrong answer will be the *larger* of the two integers. With that in mind, we might notice that (C) is the result when we double (B) and add 11—that is, $2(14) + 11 = 39$. If we continue our hunch and then multiply (B) and (C) together, we find that their product is 546. So the two integers described in the prompt are 14 and 39, and the smaller integer is 14, so the answer is (B).

ANSWER CHOICE ANALYSIS

(A): This is half of the right answer. **(C):** This is the larger of the two integers that the prompt talks about. **(D):** This is twice as much as the larger of the two integers the prompt talks about.

How to check? Make sure you picked the smaller of the two integers. Try an alternate approach above. Try to figure out which mistakes could lead to some of the wrong answer choices, and verify that you haven't made any such mistakes.

▶ Post-solution patterns (see page 286): right approach, wrong step; the right answer to the wrong question

Test 3, Module 1, Question 19

- What's the prompt asking for? The point that is a solution to the given system of inequalities.
- Math concepts in the prompt: systems of inequalities, solutions, (x, y) points
- Elements of the answer choices: Each answer choice is a coordinate pair involving 0 and either 14 or −14.
- Notable features of the answer choices: Two answer choices include 0 as an x-value, and two answer choices include 0 as a y-value. Two answer choices include −14, and two answer choices include 14.
- "Bridge" concepts: A solution to an inequality results in a valid statement when plugged in to that inequality.
- Pre-solution patterns (see p. 285): opposites; wrong answers try to imitate right answers
- Things to look out for: Don't mix up x and y! Don't make a simple mistake related to algebra or sign! Remember that these are inequalities, not equations!

Solution 1: Concrete/graphing: We can graph the provided inequalities and the points from the answer choices to see which point is a solution.

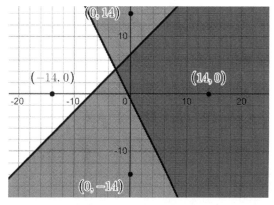

$$y \le x + 7 \text{ and } y \ge -2x - 1$$

We can see that only $(14, 0)$ from choice (D) is valid for both inequalities, so (D) is correct.

Solution 2: Concrete: Test each choice by plugging it in to the given system of inequalities. Eliminate every choice that results in an invalid statement when plugged in to either inequality.

We can plug the x and y-values from each answer choice into the provided inequalities to see which choice works for both.

(A) $(0) \leq (-14) + 7$ $(0) \geq -2(-14) - 1$
        $0 \leq -7$ $0 \geq 27$

(A) doesn't work for either inequality, so (A) is wrong. Let's look at (B).

(B) $(-14) \leq (0) + 7$ $(-14) \geq -2(0) - 1$
        $-14 \leq 7$ $-14 \geq -1$

(B) works for the first inequality, but not the second—so (B) is wrong too. Let's look at (C).

(C) $(14) \leq (0) + 7$ $(14) \geq -2(0) - 1$
        $14 \leq 7$ $14 \geq -1$

(C) works for the second inequality, but not the first—so (C) is wrong too. Let's check (D).

(D) $(0) \leq (14) + 7$ $(0) \geq -2(14) - 1$
        $0 \leq 21$ $0 \geq -29$

(D) produces a valid statement for both inequalities, so (D) is correct.

ANSWER CHOICE ANALYSIS

(A): This would be the right answer if the x-value were positive, not negative. **(B):** This choice combines the errors from (A) and (C). **(C):** This would be the right answer if the x and y values were switched.

How to check? Try an alternate approach above. Try to figure out which mistakes could lead to some of the wrong answer choices, and verify that you haven't made any such mistakes.

Test 3, Module 1, Question 20

- What's the prompt asking for? The smallest solution to the given equation.
- Math concepts in the prompt: equations, radical expressions, exponents, variables
- "Bridge" concepts: The phrase "smallest solution" tells us that this equation has multiple solutions. We can square both sides, get all the x terms on one side of the equation, and then manipulate that expression as needed to answer the question.
- Things to look out for: Don't make a simple mistake related to algebra or sign! Notice that the equation has more than one solution, and make sure your understanding of the question and your solution are in line with that idea!

Solution 1: Concrete/graphing: We can graph the provided equation to find its solutions; the smallest solution will be our answer.

When we enter the provided equation—exactly as it is—into our calculator, we get the following graph:

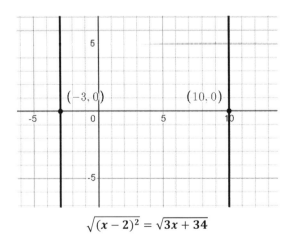

$$\sqrt{(x - 2)^2} = \sqrt{3x + 34}$$

We can see a vertical line at $x = -3$ and $x = 10$, so these are the two solutions to this equation. The smallest solution is $x = -3$, so the answer is -3.

Solution 2: Algebra: Manipulate the equation until 0 is on one side, and an expression with all the other terms is on the other side. Then factor the nonzero expression and use the results to answer the question.

We can create an equation with an expression involving x on one side and 0 on the other side, and then go from there.

$$\sqrt{(x - 2)^2} = \sqrt{3x + 34}$$ (provided equation)

$$(x - 2)^2 = 3x + 34 \qquad \text{(square both sides)}$$
$$x^2 - 4x + 4 = 3x + 34 \qquad \text{(FOIL the left side)}$$
$$x^2 - 7x + 4 = 34 \qquad \text{(subtract } 3x \text{ from both sides)}$$
$$x^2 - 7x - 30 = 0 \qquad \text{(subtract 34 from both sides)}$$
$$(x - 10)(x + 3) = 0 \qquad \text{(reverse-FOIL)}$$

We know that the above equation will be true when $x - 10 = 0$ or when $x + 3 = 0$, which will be the case when $x = 10$ or when $x = -3$. The "smallest solution," as the prompt requires, is $x = -3$, so the answer is -3.

How to check? Make sure you picked the smallest solution. Try an alternate approach above. Try to figure out which mistakes the College Board might hope you would make in finding your solution, and verify that you haven't made any such mistakes.

Test 3, Module 1, Question 21

- **What's the prompt asking for?** The store's cost for the shirt.

- **Math concepts in the prompt:** word problems, money, discounts, percentages, cost

- **"Bridge" concepts:** We can start with the regular price for the shirt, then apply the percentages according to the information in the prompt to find the store's cost.

- **Things to look out for:** Don't mix up which percentage relates to the sale price and which relates to the store's cost! Don't get confused about whether you're finding a certain percentage *of* a number, or a percentage *greater* or *less than* that number!

Solution 1: Careful reading: Start with the regular price of the shirt. Then, carefully read the prompt to find the sale price of the shirt based on the regular price, and then find the store's cost for the shirt based on the sale price.

Let's start by finding the sale price of the shirt. If the sale price of the shirt is 80% *less than* the regular price, that's the same as 20% *of* the regular price, because $100\% - 80\% = 20\%$. The regular price is \$11.70, and $\$11.70 \times 0.2 = \$2.34$. So the sale price is \$2.34.

The prompt also tells us that the sale price of the shirt is 30% greater than the store's cost. 30% greater than the sale price is the same as 130% of the sale price, because $100\% + 30\% = 130\%$. If we call the store's cost for the shirt x, then we can set up this equation:
$$1.3x = \$2.34$$
(Again, we know the equation above is true because the prompt tells us that the sale price of the shirt, which is \$2.34, is 30% greater than the store's cost.) We can divide both sides by 1.3 to get the value of x, which is 1.8. So the answer is 1.8, which we can also enter as $\frac{9}{5}$.

How to check? Try to figure out which mistakes the College Board might hope you would make in finding your solution, and verify that you haven't made any such mistakes.

Note The College Board loves to ask questions involving percentages, and they're hoping you'll find the *wrong* percentage because you didn't read carefully enough. For example, this question includes the phrase "80% less than the regular price." This means the regular price, minus 80% of itself—in other words, 20% of the regular price. But some untrained test-takers will understand this phrase to mean "80% *of* the regular price"—in other words, the regular price with a 20% discount. Think carefully about the differences between these ideas, and read carefully on test day to make sure you avoid misunderstanding prompts involving percentages!

Test 3, Module 1, Question 22

- **What's the prompt asking for?** The mass of the sample described in the prompt.

- **Math concepts in the prompt:** word problems, density, kilograms per cubic meter, cubes, length, volume

- **Elements of the answer choices:** Each answer choice is an integer ranging from 588 to 1,107.

- **Notable features of the answer choices:** Three choices are 3-digit integers, and one is a 4-digit integer.

- **"Bridge" concepts:** We can use the edge length of the cube to find its volume, and then we can use the density of the oak to find the cube's mass.

- **Things to look out for:** Remember that the cube's *edge length* is 0.90 meters, but this isn't the same as the cube's *volume!*

Solution 1: Geometry: Use the edge length of the cube to find its volume, and then use the density of the oak to find the cube's mass.

The prompt tells us that the oak has a density of 807 kilograms per cubic meter. In other words, every cubic meter of the oak has a mass of 807 kilograms. That means if we can figure out how many cubic meters of oak are in the sample, we can multiply that number by 807 to find the mass of that sample.

The prompt tells us that the sample is a cube, and each edge of the cube is 0.90 meters long. We can find the volume of a cube by multiplying its length, width, and height together.

$$V = lwh \qquad \text{(formula for volume of a cube)}$$
$$V = (0.9)(0.9)(0.9) \qquad \text{(plug in 0.9 for all values)}$$
$$V = 0.729 \qquad \text{(simplify)}$$

So the volume of the cube is 0.729 cubic meters. We can multiply this volume by the provided density to find out the mass of the cube. The result is 0.729×807, which is equal to 588.303. The prompt asks for the mass "to the nearest whole number," so the answer is 588, and (A) is correct.

Solution 2: Test-smart: Think about what we know about the right answer based on the information in the prompt, and then eliminate each choice that isn't consistent with your conclusions.

If the density of the oak is 807 kilograms per cubic meter, then one cubic meter of oak would have a mass of 807 kilograms, by definition. Also, a cube with sides 1 meter long would have a volume of one cubic meter, by definition.

If a cube has edges of 0.9 meters, that cube must have a volume of *less* than one cubic meter, so its mass must be *less* than 807 kilograms. That eliminates (C) and (D).

Once we understand that we don't just multiply 807 by 0.9 to find the answer—because we have to multiply 0.9 by itself multiple times to find the volume of the cube—we know the mass must be *less than* 90% of 807. 90% of 807 is approximately 726, so the right answer is less than 726. Only (A) is less than 726, so (A) is right.

ANSWER CHOICE ANALYSIS

(B): This would be the answer if the cube in question had 90% of the volume of one meter cubed, but it doesn't—it has $90\% \times 90\% \times 90\%$ of that volume, or 72.9% of that volume, as we saw in solution 1 above. **(C):** This is the sum of 807 and 90, two numbers that appear in the prompt—but that's not what the prompt asked for. **(D):** This is $807 \div 0.729$, rather than 807×0.729.

How to check? Try an alternate approach above. Try to figure out which mistakes could lead to some of the wrong answer choices, and verify that you haven't made any such mistakes.

▶   Post-solution patterns (see page 286):   right approach, wrong step; the right answer to the wrong question

---

Test 3, Module 1, Question 23

- What's the prompt asking for? The choice that could describe the function.

- Math concepts in the prompt: functions, percentage, variables

- Elements of the answer choices: Each answer choice is a two word phrase.

- Notable features of the answer choices: Two answer choices start with "decreasing," and two start with "increasing." Two answer choices end with "exponential," and two end with "linear."

- "Bridge" concepts: If the function gets bigger as x increases, it's increasing; if the opposite is true, it's decreasing. If the graph of the function is a straight line, the function is linear; if the graph is a curve, the function is exponential.

- Pre-solution patterns (see p. 285): opposites; wrong answers try to imitate right answers

- Things to look out for: Think carefully about what it means for a function to be decreasing as opposed to increasing, and exponential as opposed to linear!

Solution 1: Concrete/graphing: We can take the information provided in the prompt and turn it into an equation, which we can then graph. Then we can use that graph to pick the right answer choice.

Let's start by replacing the word "equals" with "=."
$$f(x) = 201\% \text{ of } x$$
201% of x is the same as $2.01x$, so we can make that substitution as well.
$$f(x) = 2.01x$$
Now we can set $f(x)$ equal to y and graph this function:

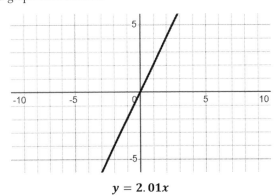

$$y = 2.01x$$

We can see that the graph is a straight line, which means its linear, and that it travels up moving from left to right, which means that it's increasing. So (D) is correct.

Solution 2: Careful reading: Read the prompt, and think carefully about what it tells us about the function. Reason whether the function should be increasing or decreasing, and whether it should be linear or exponential.

If $f(x)$ is 201% of x, then as x gets bigger, $f(x)$ must also get bigger. So the function is increasing, which eliminates (A) and (B).

Also, if $f(x)$ is 201% of x, then every time x increases by 1, $f(x)$ must increase by 2.01. In other words, $f(1) = 2.01$, $f(2) = 4.02$, $f(3) = 6.03$, and so on. The fact that $f(x)$ increases by the same amount every time x increases by 1 tells us that the graph of this function is a straight line, not a curve—if the function were exponential, $f(x)$ would have to increase by a progressively smaller or larger amount each time x went up by 1. So the function is linear, which means we can eliminate (C). That leaves only the correct answer, (D).

ANSWER CHOICE ANALYSIS

(B): This choice would be correct if the function were decreasing instead of increasing. **(C):** This choice would be correct if function were exponential instead of linear.

How to check? Try an alternate approach above. Try to figure out which mistakes could lead to some of the wrong answer choices, and verify that you haven't made any such mistakes.

Test 3, Module 1, Question 24

- What's the prompt asking for? The equation that could define function g if $g(x) = f(x + 4)$.

- Math concepts in the prompt: functions, equations, graphs, curves

- Elements of the answer choices: Each answer choice is a function that includes a fraction with 6 in the numerator.

- Notable features of the answer choices: $x + 4$ is the denominator of two answer choices, $x + 8$ is the denominator of one answer choice, and x is the denominator of one answer choice.

- "Bridge" concepts: $g(x)$ must be $f(x)$ moved four units to the left.

- Pre-solution patterns (see p. 285): halves and doubles; first and last terms in a series are often wrong answers

- Things to look out for: Don't make a simple mistake related to algebra or sign!

Solution 1: We can graph the function in each answer choice to see which one produces a graph that is 4 units to the left of the provided graph.

If $g(x) = f(x + 4)$, that means every x-value plugged into $g(x)$ produces the corresponding $f(x)$ value for an x-value that's 4 units greater. In other words, $g(0) = f(4), g(1) = f(5), g(2) = f(6)$, and so on. This is the same as taking every $f(x)$ value and moving it 4 units to the left, which means that $g(x)$ is just $f(x)$ moved 4 units to the left. Let's graph each answer choice and find the one that's the same as the provided graph moved four units left.

(A)

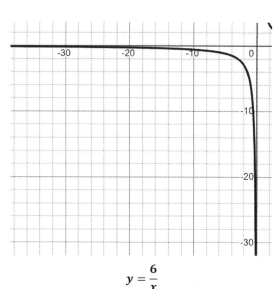

$$y = \frac{6}{x}$$

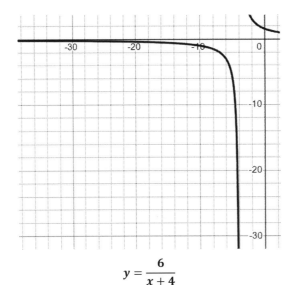

$$y = \frac{6}{x + 4}$$

(C)

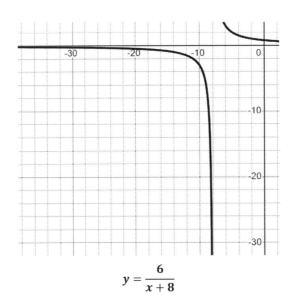

$$y = \frac{6}{x + 8}$$

(D)

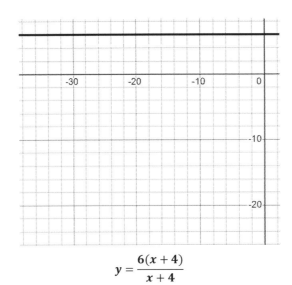

$$y = \frac{6(x + 4)}{x + 4}$$

We can see that the graph of choice (C) is just the provided graph moved 4 units to the left, so (C) is correct.

Solution 2: Concrete: Find a coordinate pair that you know must be part of $g(x)$, and test it in every function from the answer choices. Eliminate each choice that fails this test.

If $g(x) = f(x + 4)$, then it must be the case that every (x, y) coordinate pair in $f(x)$ can be thought of as a coordinate pair from $g(x)$ with 4 added to the x-value. So if we can see a coordinate pair in the provided graph, we can subtract 4 from the x-value in that coordinate pair to find a valid coordinate pair from $g(x)$. Once we have a coordinate pair we know is part of $g(x)$, we can plug that into the functions in the answer choices and eliminate any choice that results in a false statement.

We can see that $(-10, -1)$ is a point on $f(x)$. Since the prompt tells us that $g(x) = f(x + 4)$, we can subtract 4 from x to find the (x, y) pair that must be part of $g(x)$. With this in mind, we know that $(-14, -1)$ is a point on the graph of $g(x)$. We can plug these values into each function from the answer choices and eliminate any choice that doesn't produce a true statement.

(A) $\quad g(x) = \dfrac{6}{x} \qquad\qquad (-1) = \dfrac{6}{(-14)} \qquad\qquad\qquad\qquad\qquad\qquad -1 \neq \dfrac{3}{-7}$

(B) $\quad g(x) = \dfrac{6}{x+4} \qquad (-1) = \dfrac{6}{(-14)+4} \qquad\qquad -1 = \dfrac{6}{-1} \qquad -1 \neq \dfrac{3}{-5}$

(C) $\quad g(x) = \dfrac{6}{x+8} \qquad (-1) = \dfrac{6}{(-14)+8} \qquad\qquad -1 = \dfrac{6}{-6} \qquad -1 = -1$

(D) $\quad g(x) = \dfrac{6(x+4)}{x+4} \qquad (-1) = \dfrac{6((-1\ )+4)}{(-14)+4} \qquad -1 = \dfrac{6(-10)}{-10} \qquad -1 \neq 6$

After plugging $(-14, -1)$ into each of the provided functions, we found that only (C) produced a true statement, so (C) is correct.

Solution 3: Algebra: Use a couple of (x, y) coordinate pairs from the provided graph to find the values of a and b. Use these values to define $f(x)$, and use the result to define $g(x)$.

We can find the values of a and b by finding a couple of (x, y) coordinate pairs from the provided graph, plugging those values in for x and y, solving one of those equations for a, plugging that value into the other equation to solve for b, and then plugging that b-value into either equation to find a. I know that might sound like a lot, and it might be a little confusing, but let's take it one step at a time.

We can see that one point on the provided graph is $(-10, -1)$. So let's plug $x = -10$ and $y = -1$ into the function from the prompt that defines $f(x)$.

$\qquad y = \dfrac{a}{x+b}$ $\qquad\qquad\qquad\qquad\qquad$ (provided equation)

$\qquad (-1) = \dfrac{a}{(-10)+b}$ $\qquad\qquad\qquad\quad$ (plug in $x = -10$ and $y = -1$)

$\qquad -1(-10 + b) = a$ $\qquad\qquad\qquad\quad$ (multiply both sides by $(-10 + b)$)

$\qquad 10 - b = a$ $\qquad\qquad\qquad\qquad\qquad$ (simplify)

Now we can plug in another value—we can see that the line in the provided graph also travels through $(-7, -2)$, so let's use $x = -7$ and $y = -2$.

$\qquad y = \dfrac{a}{x+b}$ $\qquad\qquad\qquad\qquad\qquad$ (provided equation)

$\qquad (-2) = \dfrac{a}{(-7)+b}$ $\qquad\qquad\qquad\qquad$ (plug in $x = -7$ and $y = -2$)

$\qquad -2(-7 + b) = a$ $\qquad\qquad\qquad\qquad$ (multiply both sides by $(-7 + b)$)

$\qquad 14 - 2b = a$ $\qquad\qquad\qquad\qquad\quad$ (simplify)

We can take the a-value from the first equation and plug it into the second equation, then solve for b.

$\qquad 14 - 2b = a$ $\qquad\qquad\qquad\qquad\quad$ (second equation we found)

$\qquad 14 - 2b = 10 - b$ $\qquad\qquad\qquad\quad$ (plug in $a = 10 - b$ from first equation))

$\qquad 14 = 10 + b$ $\qquad\qquad\qquad\qquad\quad$ (add $2b$ to both sides)

$\qquad 4 = b$ $\qquad\qquad\qquad\qquad\qquad\qquad$ (subtract 10 from both sides)

Now we know that $b = 4$. We can plug this value into either equation and solve for a. I'll use our first equation because the math looks like it would be pretty simple.

$\qquad 10 - b = a$ $\qquad\qquad\qquad\qquad\qquad$ (our first equation)

$\qquad 10 - 4 = a$ $\qquad\qquad\qquad\qquad\qquad$ (plug in $b = 4$)

$\qquad 6 = a$ $\qquad\qquad\qquad\qquad\qquad\qquad$ (simplify)

Now we know that $a = 6$ and $b = 4$, so the provided function is $f(x) = \frac{6}{x+4}$. At this point, some test-takers might notice this function is choice (B), and they might be tempted to pick that choice. But we just found $f(x)$, and the question asked us which equation could define g!

The prompt tells us that $g(x) = f(x + 4)$. So we can find $g(x)$ by plugging $x + 4$ into the $f(x)$ expression we just found. The result is $g(x) = f(x + 4) = \frac{6}{(x+4)+4} = \frac{6}{x+8}$. So $g(x) = \frac{6}{x+8}$, and (C) is right.

ANSWER CHOICE ANALYSIS

(A): This is $f(x - 4)$, not $f(x + 4)$. **(B):** This is $f(x)$, not $g(x)$

How to check? Try an alternate approach above. Try to figure out which mistakes could lead to some of the wrong answer choices, and verify that you haven't made any such mistakes.

▶   Post-solution patterns (see page 286):   the right answer to the wrong question

▍Test 3, Module 1, Question 25

- **What's the prompt asking for?** The expression that's equivalent to the expression in the prompt.

- **Math concepts in the prompt:** equivalent expressions, polynomials, fractions, exponents

- **Elements of the answer choices:** Every answer choice is a fraction with a polynomial in the numerator and a polynomial in the denominator.

- **Notable features of the answer choices:** (A) and (D) have the same denominator. (C) and (D) have the same numerator.

- **"Bridge" concepts:** We can manipulate the provided equations until they look like the given equation. Also, any x and y values we plug into the given expression will produce the same result when we plug them into an equivalent expression.

- **Pre-solution patterns (see p. 285):** wrong answers try to imitate right answers

- **Things to look out for:** Don't make a simple mistake related to algebra or sign! Don't mix up x and y!

Solution 1: Concrete: Pick values for x and y, plug them into the given expression, and find its value. Then plug the same x and y-values into the expression from each answer choice and eliminate any choice that doesn't produce the same value.

Let's use $x = 2$ and $y = 3$.

$$\frac{y+12}{x-8} + \frac{y(x-8)}{x^2y-8xy}$$ (provided expression)

$$\frac{(3)+12}{(2)-8} + \frac{(3)((2)-8)}{(2)^2(3)-8(2)(3)}$$ (plug in $x = 2$ and $y = 3$)

$$\frac{15}{-6} + \frac{(3)(-6)}{4(3)-48}$$ (simplify)

$$\frac{5}{-2} + \frac{-1}{12-4}$$ (simplify)

$$\frac{5}{-2} + \frac{-18}{-36}$$ (simplify)

$$\frac{5}{-2} + \frac{1}{2}$$ (simplify)

$$-2$$ (simplify)

So when $x = 2$ and $y = 3$, the given expression has a value of -2. That means when we plug $x = 2$ and $y = 3$ into the expression from the correct answer, that expression will also have a value of -2. Let's do that.

(Note that the algebra is fairly simple and repetitive, so I will omit some steps for the sake of brevity.)

(A) $\dfrac{xy+y+4}{x^3y-16x^2y+64xy}$ $\dfrac{(2)(3)+(3)+4}{(2)^3(3)-16(2)^2(3)+6\ (2)(3)}$ $\dfrac{6+7}{24-192+384}$ $\dfrac{13}{216}$

(B) $\dfrac{xy+9y+12}{x^2y-8xy+x-8}$ $\dfrac{(2)(3)+9(3)+1}{(2)^2(3)-8(2)(3)+2-8}$ $\dfrac{6+27+12}{12-48}$ $\dfrac{45}{-42}$ $-\dfrac{15}{14}$

(C) $\dfrac{xy^2+13xy-8y}{x^2y-8xy}$ $\dfrac{(2)(3)^2+13(2)(3)-8(3)}{(2)^2(3)-8(2)(3)}$ $\dfrac{18+78-24}{12-48}$ $\dfrac{72}{-36}$ -2

(D) $\dfrac{xy^2+13xy-8y}{x^3y-16x^2y+64x}$ $\dfrac{(2)(3)^2+13(2)(3)-8(3)}{(2)^3(3)-16(2)^2(3)+6\ (2)(3)}$ $\dfrac{18+78-24}{24-192+384}$ $\dfrac{72}{216}$ $\dfrac{1}{3}$

When we plug $x = 2$ and $y = 3$ into each expression in the answer choices, we find that only (C) produces a value that matches the value we found when we plugged those values into the provided expression. So only (C) could be equivalent to the given expression, which means (C) is correct.

Solution 2: Algebra: Manipulate the given expression until it looks like one of the answer choices.

Since every answer choice is a single fraction, rather than multiple fractions added together, it makes sense to try to modify the provided fractions so they have the same denominator, and then we can add them together to make one fraction.

The denominator of the first fraction is $x - 8$, and the denominator of the second fraction is $x^2y - 8xy$. We know that the College Board likes to make expressions like this seem more intimidating than they really are, and that there are often expressions that can cancel out, or be factored out, or something along those lines. With this in mind, we might realize that $x - 8$, the denominator of the first fraction, can be factored out of the denominator of the second fraction, like this:

$$x^2y - 8xy = xy(x - 8)$$

So we can make the denominator of the second fraction $(x - 8)xy$, like this:

$$\frac{y + 12}{x - 8} + \frac{y(x - 8)}{xy(x - 8)}$$

Now we might notice that the only difference between the two denominators is that the second one is the first one multiplied by xy. We can make the first denominator the same as the second denominator by multiplying the first fraction by $\frac{xy}{xy}$. This is the same as multiplying by 1, since $\frac{xy}{xy}$ must reduce to 1, so it doesn't change the value of the first fraction, but it does change its denominator to match the denominator of the second fraction. Let's do that.

$$\left(\frac{xy}{xy}\right)\frac{y+12}{x-8} + \frac{y(x-8)}{xy(x-8)} \qquad \text{(multiply first fraction by } \tfrac{xy}{xy}\text{)}$$

$$\frac{xy^2+12xy}{xy(x-8)} + \frac{y(x-8)}{xy(x-8)} \qquad \text{(simplify)}$$

Now the two fractions have the same denominator, so we can add them together:

$$\frac{xy^2+12xy}{xy(x-8)} + \frac{y(x-8)}{xy(x-8)} \qquad \text{(provided fractions with common denominator)}$$

$$\frac{xy^2+12xy \quad (x-8)}{xy(x-8)} \qquad \text{(simplify)}$$

$$\frac{xy^2+12xy+xy-8y}{x^2y-8xy} \qquad \text{(distribute the } y \text{ in the numerator)}$$

$$\frac{xy^2+13xy-8y}{x^2y-8xy} \qquad \text{(simplify)}$$

This expression matches choice (C), so (C) is correct.

Solution 3: Test-smart: Think about what features the right answer must have, and eliminate any choices that don't have those features.

Once we realize that the denominator of the second fraction can be factored into $xy(x - 8)$, and that we can make the first fraction have the same denominator as the second one (as we saw in our previous solution), we know that the right answer will have the same denominator as the second fraction—again, because we know we're going to change the denominator of the first fraction to match the denominator of the second fraction, and then add both fractions together. The result will be one fraction that will have the same denominator as the second fraction from the original expression. Only (C) has that same denominator, so (C) is correct.

(We may realize that the denominator could change if we're able to cancel out some terms from that denominator during our solution—but if that were the case, we'd end up with a simpler denominator, while choices (A), (B), and (D) all have a denominator that is more complex than $x^2y - 8xy$. Again, we can see that (C) must be right.)

ANSWER CHOICE ANALYSIS

(A): This choice is the result of making various algebra errors when trying to combine the two fractions in the given equation. **(B):** The denominator of this fraction is the result of just adding the two denominators in the given expression straight across, which isn't a valid way to combine denominators. **(D):** This choice has the same numerator as the right answer, but the wrong denominator.

How to check? Try an alternate approach above. Try to figure out which mistakes could lead to some of the wrong answer choices, and verify that you haven't made any such mistakes.

- What's the prompt asking for? The number of votes by which Angel Cruz would be expected to win, according to the poll, if 6,424 people vote in the election.

- Math concepts in the prompt: word problems, surveys, random sampling, data tables

- Elements of the answer choices: Each answer choice is an integer ranging from 163 to 5,621.

- Notable features of the answer choices: (A) has three digits, and the other choices have four digits.

- "Bridge" concepts: The proportion of people in the poll who preferred Angel Cruz should be roughly the same as the proportion of voters in the election who vote for Angel Cruz.

- Things to look out for: Don't just find the margin by which Angel Cruz was ahead in the poll! Remember that the question asked for the number of votes by which Angel Cruz would expect to win the election, *not* the number of total votes Angel Cruz would be expected to get!

Solution 1: Algebra: Use the information in the poll to find the percentage of voters that would be expected to vote for each candidate, and use that information to answer the question.

The prompt tells us that 803 voters were polled, and the table labeled "Poll Results" tells us that 483 voters said they preferred Angel Cruz. So Angel Cruz got 483 out of 803 votes. We can express this proportion as $\frac{483}{803}$, which means Angel Cruz got about $\frac{483}{803}$ of the votes in the poll. If 6,424 people vote in the election, as the prompt states, then we would expect Cruz to get $\frac{483}{803}$ of those votes as well. $6,424 \times \frac{483}{803} = 3,864$, so we would expect Cruz to get about 3,864 votes.

But that's not what the prompt asked for! We also need to know how many voters would be expected to vote for Terry Smith, and then we need find the difference between these two numbers. Terry Smith got 320 votes in the poll, so we would expect Smith to get $\frac{320}{803}$ of the 6,424 votes cast in the election. $6,424 \times \frac{320}{803} = 2,560$.

The difference between these numbers is $3,864 - 2,560$, or $1,304$. So (B) is correct.

Solution 2: Test-smart: Find the margin by which Angel Cruz won the poll as a fraction of the people who were polled, and multiply that fraction by the number of voters in the election.

In the poll, Angel Cruz got 163 more votes than Terry Smith, because $483 - 320 = 163$. This difference represents $\frac{163}{803}$ of the votes cast in the poll. So we would expect Cruz to win by a proportional margin in the actual election. The prompt tells us that 6,424 people vote in the election. We can multiply 6,424 by $\frac{163}{803}$ to find the number of votes by which Cruz is expected to win. The result is $6,424 \times \frac{163}{803}$, which is the same as 1,304. So (B) is correct.

ANSWER CHOICE ANALYSIS

(A): This is the margin by which Angel Cruz won the *poll*, not the margin by which Cruz would be expected to win the election. **(C):** This is the *total number of votes* Angel Cruz would be expected to receive in the election, not the margin by which Cruz would be expected to win. **(D):** This is the difference between the expected number of voters and the number of people who participated in the poll.

How to check? Double-check that your answer addresses what the prompt asks. Try an alternate approach above. Try to figure out which mistakes could lead to some of the wrong answer choices, and verify that you haven't made any such mistakes.

▶ Post-solution patterns (see page 286): right approach, wrong step; the right answer to the wrong question

- What's the prompt asking for? The length of the radius of the circle described in the prompt.

- Math concepts in the prompt: graphs, circles, radii, equations

- "Bridge" concepts: We can find the length of the radius through graphing or algebra.

- Things to look out for: Don't make a simple algebra mistake!

Solution 1: Concrete/graphing: We can graph the provided equation to find the radius of the circle.

When we graph the provided equation, we end up with this:

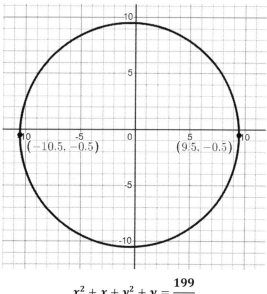

$$x^2 + x + y^2 + y = \frac{199}{2}$$

At first it might be hard to determine the radius, because the highest, lowest, leftmost, and rightmost point on this circle don't fall on coordinates with whole numbers, which makes it hard to eyeball the full diameter of the circle (which we can then use to find the radius). But if we zoom in a little on the left edge of the circle, we can see that the value that is farthest to the left is $(-10.5, -0.5)$. If we repeat this process on the right, we can see that the value farthest to the right is $(9.5, -0.5)$.

So the diameter of the circle stretches from -10.5 to 9.5, which is 20 units long. That means the diameter of the circle is 20 units. The radius of a circle is half its diameter, so the radius is 10 units, and the answer is 10.

Solution 2: Algebra: Manipulate the given equation until it's in the form of the standard equation for a circle, then use your understanding of the standard equation for a circle to determine the circle's radius.

If we want to find the answer using the provided equation, then we need to put that equation into the standard equation for a circle—which is $(x - h)^2 + (y - k)^2 = r^2$, where (h, k) is the center of the circle, and r is the radius of the circle. Let's focus on the x-terms first.

We need to get $x^2 + x$ into the form $(x - h)^2$, which we can do using a process called "completing the square." To do this, we find half of the coefficient of x, square it, and then add it to the expression—in this case, the coefficient of x is 1, so we take half of 1, which is $\frac{1}{2}$, and square it, which gives us $\frac{1}{4}$.

When we add that to $x^2 + x$, we get $x^2 + x + \frac{1}{4}$, which we can now express as a square, like $(x - h)^2$. In this case, that square is $\left(x + \frac{1}{2}\right)^2$.

Note that we added $\frac{1}{4}$ to $x^2 + x$, which is on the left side of the equation that was provided in the prompt. Since we added $\frac{1}{4}$ to the left side of the equation, we need to add it to the right side of the equation as well. With all of this in mind, we now have this expression:

$$\left(x + \frac{1}{2}\right)^2 + y^2 + y = \frac{199}{2} + \frac{1}{4}$$

Now we need to get $y^2 + y$ into the form $(y - k)^2$, which is going to be pretty much exactly what we just did with $x^2 + x$. We need to add the square of half the coefficient of y—that coefficient is 1, half of 1 is $\frac{1}{2}$, and the square of $\frac{1}{2}$ is $\frac{1}{4}$, just as we saw before with $x^2 + x$. The result of adding $\frac{1}{4}$ is that we end up with $y^2 + y + \frac{1}{4}$. We can now express that as a square, like $(y - k)^2$, which is $\left(y + \frac{1}{2}\right)^2$.

Again, since we added $\frac{1}{4}$ to the left side of the given equation, we need to add $\frac{1}{4}$ to the right side as well. Now our equation looks like this:

$$\left(x + \frac{1}{2}\right)^2 + \left(y + \frac{1}{2}\right)^2 = \frac{199}{2} + \frac{1}{4} + \frac{1}{4}$$

Adding $\frac{1}{4}$ and $\frac{1}{4}$ gives us $\frac{1}{2}$, and adding $\frac{1}{2}$ to $\frac{199}{2}$ gives us $\frac{200}{2}$, which is the same as 100. So now our equation looks like this:

$$\left(x + \frac{1}{2}\right)^2 + \left(y + \frac{1}{2}\right)^2 = 100$$

We know from the standard equation of a circle, which again is $(x - h)^2 + (y - k)^2 = r^2$, that 100 in the equation above corresponds to r^2—that is, to the length of the radius squared. If $100 = r^2$, then $r = 10$, and the answer is 10.

How to check? Verify that the question asked for the radius (and that you found the radius), as opposed to the diameter. Try an alternate approach above. Try to figure out which mistakes could lead to some of the wrong answer choices, and verify that you haven't made any such mistakes.

TEST 3 - MODULE 2

Test 3, Module 2, Question 1

- **What's the prompt asking for?** The number of harvested potatoes that Isabel saved to plant next year.
- **Math concepts in the prompt:** word problems, integers, percentages
- **Elements of the answer choices:** Each answer choice is an even 2-digit integer ranging from 66 to 86.
- **Notable features of the answer choices:** (A), (B), and (D) form a series where each choice is 10 more than the previous choice.

- **"Bridge" concepts:** We can answer the question by finding 10% of 760.
- **Pre-solution patterns (see p. 285):** first and last terms in a series are often wrong answers; wrong answers try to imitate right answers
- **Things to look out for:** Don't get confused about what percentage you need to find!

Solution 1: Concrete: Find 10% of 760.

The prompt tells us that Isabel saved 10% of her 760 potatoes. 10% of 760 is the same as 760×0.1, which is equal to 76. So the answer is (B).

ANSWER CHOICE ANALYSIS

(A): This is 10% of the potatoes, minus ten. **(C):** This is 10% of the potatoes, increased by 10% (and then rounded up to the nearest whole number). **(D):** This is 10% of the potatoes, plus ten.

How to check? Try to figure out which mistakes could lead to some of the wrong answer choices, and verify that you haven't made any such mistakes.

Test 3, Module 2, Question 2

- **What's the prompt asking for?** The y-intercept of the graph.
- **Math concepts in the prompt:** y-intercepts, graphs
- **Elements of the answer choices:** Each choice is an (x, y) pair involving 0 and/or 2.
- **Notable features of the answer choices:** Two choices start with zero, and two end with zero. Two choices start with two, and two end with two.

- **"Bridge" concepts:** The y-intercept is the point where the graph of the line crosses the y-axis.
- **Pre-solution patterns (see p. 285):** opposites; wrong answers try to imitate right answers
- **Things to look out for:** Make sure you read the graph accurately!

Solution 1: Concrete: Find the y-intercept of the provided graph.

The y-intercept of the graph is the point where the graph crosses the y-axis. We can see that the graph crosses the y-axis at $(0, 2)$, so the answer is (B).

ANSWER CHOICE ANALYSIS

(A): This is the right x-value, twice. **(C):** This is the right answer with the x and y values switched. **(D):** This is the right y-value, twice.

How to check? Try to figure out which mistakes could lead to some of the wrong answer choices, and verify that you haven't made any such mistakes.

Test 3, Module 2, Question 3

- **What's the prompt asking for?** The length in centimeters that's equivalent to 51 meters.
- **Math concepts in the prompt:** length, equivalency, unit conversion
- **Elements of the answer choices:** Each answer choice is a numerical expression involving 51.

- **Notable features of the answer choices:** Two choices are decimal expressions less than one, and two are integers in the thousands.
- **"Bridge" concepts:** We can use the provided conversion to answer the question.

- Pre-solution patterns (see p. 285): wrong answers try to imitate right answers
- Things to look out for: Count zeros and/or decimals carefully so you don't end up off by a factor of 10 or

100! Think carefully about whether your answer should be greater than or smaller than 51!

Solution 1: Multiplication: Use the provided conversion to find out how many centimeters are in 51 meters.

The prompt asks us to express 51 meters in centimeters. The prompt tells us that 1 meter is the same as 100 centimeters, so 51 meters must be the same as 51×100 centimeters, which is 5,100 centimeters. So the answer is (C).

ANSWER CHOICE ANALYSIS

(B): This is how many meters are in 51 centimeters, not how many centimeters are in 51 meters. **(D):** This would be correct if the question asked about 510 meters, or if there were 1,000 centimeters in a meter.

How to check? Double-check the zeros in your answer to make sure you're not off by a factor of 10. Try to figure out which mistakes could lead to some of the wrong answer choices, and verify that you haven't made any such mistakes.

▶ Post-solution patterns (see page 286): the right answer to the wrong question

---

Test 3, Module 2, Question 4

- What's the prompt asking for? How many feet the bus will be from the marker 2 seconds after passing the marker.
- Math concepts in the prompt: word problems, speed, $d = rt$, distance, time
- Elements of the answer choices: Each answer choice is an even integer ranging from 30 to 90.
- Notable features of the answer choices: (A), (C), and (D) form a series where each choice is 30 more than the previous choice. (A) is half of (C). (A), (C), and (D) are multiples of 30.
- "Bridge" concepts: We can plug in $t = 2$ to find the answer.
- Pre-solution patterns (see p. 285): halves and doubles; first and last terms in a series are often wrong answers
- Things to look out for: Don't make a simple algebra mistake!

Solution 1: Concrete: Plug in $t = 2$ and solve for d to find the answer.

The prompt says that the given equation tells us "the distance, d, in feet from a road marker, that a bus will be t seconds after passing the marker." Then it asks for the distance from the marker that the bus will be 2 seconds after passing the marker. If we're finding the distance 2 seconds after the bus passes the marker, then $t = 2$. So let's find d when $t = 2$.

$$d = 30t \qquad \text{(given equation)}$$
$$d = 30(2) \qquad \text{(plug in } t = 2\text{)}$$
$$d = 60 \qquad \text{(simplify)}$$

So when $t = 2$, $d = 60$. That means the correct answer is (C).

Solution 2: Abstract: Read the prompt carefully and think about how far the bus will travel in two seconds.

If we're comfortable interpreting equations, we can see that the provided equation tells us that every second, the bus travels another 30 feet away from the marker. After 2 seconds, the bus will travel 60 feet, so the answer is (C).

ANSWER CHOICE ANALYSIS

(A): This is the distance after 1 second, and it's also the speed of the bus in feet per second. **(B):** This is the result of adding 2 to 30, instead of multiplying 30 by 2. **(D):** This is the distance after 3 seconds.

How to check? Try an alternate approach above. Try to figure out which mistakes could lead to some of the wrong answer choices, and verify that you haven't made any such mistakes.

▶ Post-solution patterns (see page 286): the right answer to the wrong question

---

Test 3, Module 2, Question 5

- What's the prompt asking for? The expression that's equivalent to the expression in the prompt.
- Math concepts in the prompt: variable expressions, equivalency
- Elements of the answer choices: Each choice is a two-digit integer multiplied by w.
- "Bridge" concepts: We can simplify the provided expression and pick the choice that matches it.

- Things to look out for: Don't make a simple mistake related to algebra or sign!

Solution 1: Concrete: Pick a value for w. Plug that value into the provided expression, and then plug it into each expression from the answer choices. The output of the correct answer choice will match the output from the provided expression.

Let's pick a value for w. We'll say $w = 3$. We can plug $w = 3$ into the given expression to find its value, and then we can plug $w = 3$ into each expression from the answer choices to find their values. After that, we can eliminate each choice whose expression doesn't have the same value as the given expression when $w = 3$.

$20w - (4w + 3w)$	(given expression)
$20(3) - (4(3) + 3(3))$	(plug in $w = 3$)
$60 - (12 + 9)$	(simplify)
$60 - 21$	(simplify)
39	(simplify)

Now let's plug $w = 3$ into the expression from each answer choice and eliminate each one that doesn't equal 39.

(A)	$10w$	$10(3) = 30$
(B)	$13w$	$13(3) = 39$
(C)	$19w$	$19(3) = 57$
(D)	$21w$	$21(3) = 63$

Only (B) has a value of 39 when $w = 3$, just like the given expression, so (B) must be correct.

Solution 2: Algebra: Simplify the provided expression, and pick the answer choice that matches the result.

Let's use algebra to simplify the expression.

$20w - (4w + 3w)$	(given expression)
$20w - 7w$	(simplify expression in parentheses)
$13w$	(simplify)

So the expression is equal to $13w$, and the answer is (B).

ANSWER CHOICE ANALYSIS

(C): This would be the result of subtracting $4w$ and then adding $3w$. **(D):** This would be the result if a test-taker accidentally ended up adding $4w$ and then subtracting $3w$.

How to check? Plug a value in for w in your chosen expression and in the provided expression, and make sure they both produce the same result. Try an alternate approach above. Try to figure out which mistakes could lead to some of the wrong answer choices, and verify that you haven't made any such mistakes.

Test 3, Module 2, Question 6

- What's the prompt asking for? The value of $18 + 3x$.
- Math concepts in the prompt: equations, variables, binomials

- "Bridge" concepts: We can find the value of x in the given equation and use that to find the value the prompt asks us for.
- Things to look out for: Don't make a simple mistake related to algebra or sign!

Solution 1: Algebra: Solve for x, and use that value to find $18 + 3x$.

Let's solve for x, and then plug that value into $18 + 3x$.

$6 + x = 9$	(provided equation)
$x = 3$	(subtract 6 from both sides)

Now we can plug $x = 3$ into the expression in question.

$18 + 3x$	(provided expression)
$18 + 3(3)$	(plug in $x = 3$)
$18 + 9$	(simplify)
27	(simplify)

So the answer is 27.

Solution 2: Test-smart: Use the value of $6 + x$ to find the value of $18 + 3x$ directly.

If we noticed that $18 + 3x$ is three times as much as $6 + x$, and that $6 + x = 9$, then we can find the value of $18 + 3x$ by multiplying 9 by 3 (again, because $6 + x = 9$, and $18 + 3x$ is three times as much as $6 + x$). The result is 27, so the answer is 27.

How to check? Try an alternate approach above. Try to figure out which mistakes the College Board might hope you would make in finding your solution, and verify that you haven't made any such mistakes.

Test 3, Module 2, Question 7

- What's the prompt asking for? The value of x where y reaches its minimum.
- Math concepts in the prompt: equations, variables, minimum y-values

- Things to look out for: Don't make a simple mistake related to algebra or sign! Note that the question doesn't ask for the minimum y-value—it asks for the x-value that *corresponds* to the minimum y-value!

Solution 1: Concrete/graphing: We can graph this equation to find its minimum value.

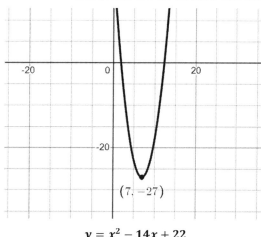

$$y = x^2 - 14x + 22$$

We can see that this graph reaches its minimum value at $(7, -27)$. The prompt asks for the x-value for which y reaches its minimum, so the answer is the x-coordinate from that pair, which means the answer is 7.

Solution 2: Algebra: Use the formula for the x-value that corresponds to the minimum y-value for an equation written in this form.

When an equation is in the form $y = ax^2 + bx + c$, we find the minimum y-value with the expression $x = -\frac{b}{2a}$. In this case, $a = 1$ and $b = -14$, so $x = -\frac{-14}{2(1)}$, which is equal to $\frac{14}{2}$, which is equal to 7. So the answer is 7.

How to check? Try an alternate approach above. Try to figure out which mistakes the College Board might hope you would make in finding your solution, and verify that you haven't made any such mistakes.

Note This is a great example of a question where we can find the answer by remembering a specific obscure formula and applying it perfectly (as we saw in Solution 2), or by just graphing the provided equation and reading the answer right off the graph (as we saw in Solution 1). I know I say this a lot, but please remember that the SAT Math calculator is a very powerful tool that can save you a lot of time on test day if you learn to use it correctly—so please take the time to do that!

Test 3, Module 2, Question 8

- What's the prompt asking for? The expression that's equivalent to $9x^2 + 5x$.
- Math concepts in the prompt: binomials, exponents, variables
- Elements of the answer choices: Each answer choice is an expression involving different combinations of 9, 5, 1, and x added and/or multiplied together.
- Notable features of the answer choices: $(9x + 5)$ appears in two answer choices. Each choice starts with a different x-term.

- "Bridge" concepts: Each answer choice is two expressions multiplied together, so we can factor the given expression to see which answer choice it matches.
- Pre-solution patterns (see p. 285): wrong answers try to imitate right answers
- Things to look out for: Don't make a simple algebra mistake!

Solution 1: Concrete: Pick a value for x, plug it into the given expression, and find the value of that expression. Then plug the same x-value into the expression from each answer choice, and eliminate any choice that doesn't produce the same value as the given expression does.

Let's pick a value for x. We'll say $x = 2$. We can plug $x = 2$ into the given expression to find its value, and then we can plug $x = 2$ into each expression from the answer choices to find their values. After that, we can eliminate each choice whose expression doesn't have the same value as the given expression does when $x = 2$.

$$9x^2 + 5x \qquad \text{(given expression)}$$
$$9(2)^2 + 5(2) \qquad \text{(plug in } x = 2\text{)}$$
$$9(4) + 10 \qquad \text{(simplify)}$$
$$36 + 10 \qquad \text{(simplify)}$$
$$46 \qquad \text{(simplify)}$$

Now let's plug $x = 2$ into the expression from each answer choice and eliminate each one that doesn't equal 46.

(A)	$x(9x + 5)$	$(2)(9(2) + 5)$	$= (2)(18 + 5)$	$= 46$
(B)	$5x(9x + 1)$	$5(2)(9(2) + 1)$	$= 5(2)(18 + 1)$	$= 190$
(C)	$9x(x + 5)$	$9(2)((2) + 5)$	$= 9(2)(7)$	$= 126$
(D)	$x^2(9x + 5)$	$(2)^2(9(2) + 5)$	$= 4(18 + 5)$	$= 92$

Only (A) has a value of 46 when $x = 2$, just like the given expression, so (A) must be correct.

Solution 2: Concrete: Simplify the expression in each answer choice, and see which one matches the provided expression.

We can multiply out the expressions in the answer choices to see which one matches the given expression.

(A)	$x(9x + 5)$	$9x^2 + 5x$
(B)	$5x(9x + 1)$	$45x^2 + 5x$
(C)	$9x(x + 5)$	$9x^2 + 45x$
(D)	$x^2(9x + 5)$	$9x^3 + 5x^2$

We can see that (A) matches the given expression, so (A) is correct.

Solution 3: Algebra: Factor the given solution and pick the answer choice that matches the result.

When we look at $9x^2$ and $5x$, we can see that their only common factor is x. When we factor x out of $9x^2$, we get $9x$. When we factor x out of $5x$, we get 5. That leaves us with this expression:

$$x(9x + 5)$$

This matches choice (A), and (A) is correct.

Solution 4: Test-smart: Think about the properties the factored expression must have, and pick the only choice that meets the requirements you come up with.

Once we realize that the only thing we can factor out of the given expression is x, we know that (A) must be correct, because only (A) factors out just the x from the given expression—the other choices try to factor out $5x$, $9x$, and x^2, respectively. So (A) must be right.

ANSWER CHOICE ANALYSIS

(C): This choice is the right answer with x and $9x$ reversed. **(D):** This choice is equivalent to $9x^3 + 5x^2$, not $9x^2 + 5x$.

How to check? Try an alternate approach above. Try to figure out which mistakes could lead to some of the wrong answer choices, and verify that you haven't made any such mistakes.

Test 3, Module 2, Question 9

- What's the prompt asking for? The measure of angle *A*.

- Math concepts in the prompt: triangles, angle measures

- Elements of the answer choices: Each answer choice is an angle measure ranging from 21° to 111°.

- "Bridge" concepts: the sum of the angle measures of a triangle must be 180°, so we can use two of the angle measures of a triangle to find the third.

- Things to look out for: Don't get confused about how the provided angle measures relate to the third angle measure!

Solution 1: Concrete: Subtract the given angle measures from 180° to find the third angle measure.

We know that the sum of the measures of the angles of a triangle must be 180°. If we know the measures of two of a triangle's angles, we can subtract those measures from 180° to find the measure of the third angle. Let's do this, using the angle measures from the prompt:

$$180° - 52° - 17° = 111°$$

So the measure of angle *A* is 111°, and the answer is (D).

Solution 2: Test-smart: Think about the properties the right answer must have, and pick the only choice that meets the requirements you come up with.

Once we realize that the three angle measures must add up to 180°, and we see that the provided angle measures add up to less than 90°, we know that the third angle measure must be greater than 90°. Only (D) is greater than 90°, so (D) is correct.

ANSWER CHOICE ANALYSIS

(B): This is the difference between the provided angle measures. **(C):** This is the sum of the provided angle measures.

How to check? Try an alternate approach above. Try to figure out which mistakes could lead to some of the wrong answer choices, and verify that you haven't made any such mistakes.

Test 3, Module 2, Question 10

- What's the prompt asking for? The value of y.
- Math concepts in the prompt: systems of equations, exponents, intersection
- Elements of the answer choices: Each answer choice is an integer and a multiple of 8 ranging from 8 to 72.
- Notable features of the answer choices: (A), (B), and (D) form a series where each choice is 3 times more than the previous choice. (A) is the square root of (C). (D) is the sum of (A) and (C).
- "Bridge" concepts: The value of x is given to us directly in the first equation.
- Pre-solution patterns (see p. 285): first and last terms in a series are often wrong answers
- Things to look out for: Don't mix up x and y!

Solution 1: Concrete/graphing: We can graph these two equations to find their point of intersection, and we can pick the answer choice that corresponds to the y-value of that point.

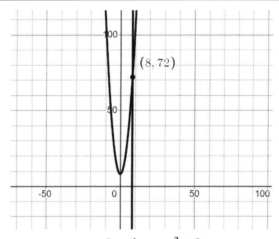

$$x = 8 \text{ and } y = x^2 + 8$$

We can see that the graphs intersect at $(8, 72)$. The y-value from that coordinate pair is 72, so the answer is (D).

Solution 2: Plug the x-value from the first equation into the second equation and solve for y.

The first equation is just $x = 8$, so we can plug $x = 8$ into the second equation to find the corresponding value of y.

$y = x^2 + 8$	(second equation)
$y = (8)^2 + 8$	(plug in $x = 8$)
$y = 64 + 8$	(simplify)
$y = 72$	(simplify)

So the y-value of the coordinate pair where these two equations intersect is 72, and the answer is (D).

ANSWER CHOICE ANALYSIS

(A): This is the x-value of the point of intersection, not the y-value. **(C):** This would be right if the second equation were $y = x^2$ instead of $y = x^2 + 8$.

How to check? Try an alternate approach above. Try to figure out which mistakes could lead to some of the wrong answer choices, and verify that you haven't made any such mistakes.

▶ Post-solution patterns (see page 286): right approach, wrong step; the right answer to the wrong question

Test 3, Module 2, Question 11

- What's the prompt asking for? The equation that best represents the line of best fit.
- Math concepts in the prompt: scatterplots, x and y, lines of best fit

- Elements of the answer choices: Each answer choice is the equation of a line.
- Notable features of the answer choices: Each choice starts with "$y =$" followed by either 13.5 or -13.5, then followed by either $+0.8x$ or $-0.8x$.
- "Bridge" concepts: The right answer should have the same slope and y-intercept as the line in the graph.

- Pre-solution patterns (see p. 285): opposites; wrong answers try to imitate right answers
- Things to look out for: Remember the properties of positive versus negative slope, and positive versus negative y-intercepts! Don't get confused about which part of the provided equations relates to slope and which part relates to y-intercept!

Solution 1: Concrete/graphing: Graph each choice and pick the one that looks like the line of best fit in the provided figure.

(A)

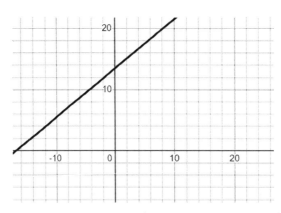

$$y = 13.5 + 0.8x$$

(B)

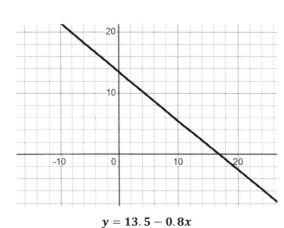

$$y = 13.5 - 0.8x$$

(C)

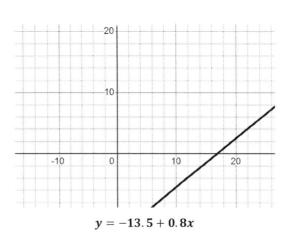

$$y = -13.5 + 0.8x$$

(D)

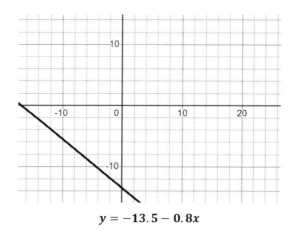

$$y = -13.5 - 0.8x$$

When we graph each answer choice, we can see that only (B) looks like the provided graph, so (B) is right.

Solution 2: Answer choice analysis: Consider the elements of the answer choices, and eliminate each choice that doesn't meet the requirements of the prompt.

When we do a vertical scan, we can see that these choices are the four possible combinations of two different elements: either 13.5 or -13.5 first, then either $+0.8x$ or $-0.8x$ after that.

If we remember our discussion of slope-intercept form from the SAT Math Toolbox, we can recognize that each of these answer choices is in slope-intercept form—that is, $y = mx + b$ form—with the mx and b parts switched. Even though those parts are switched, we can still tell very quickly what the slope and y-intercept of each equation would be.

So in each equation, the number that's not multiplied by x is b, the y-intercept of the line. That means the y-intercept must be either 13.5 or -13.5 (we know this because these are the only possible values for the y-intercept that appear in the answer choices). We can see that the y-intercept of the line is positive, so we can eliminate (C) and (D), since those choices would have a negative y-intercept of -13.5.

(Even if we didn't remember slope-intercept form, we could see in the provided graph that when $x = 0$, y is positive, so we could still draw the same conclusion that the correct answer should include 13.5, not -13.5.)

Now let's consider the remaining answer choices—the only difference between (A) and (B) is that (A) includes $+0.8x$, while (B) includes $-0.8x$. As we discussed earlier, we know that the coefficient of x is the slope of the line for each equation. Choice (A) includes $+0.8x$, which means it would have a positive slope, while choice (B) includes $-0.8x$, which means it would have a negative slope. We can see that the provided graph has a negative slope, which means we can eliminate (A), and (B) must be correct.

Solution 3: Test-smart: Use your understanding of slope-intercept form to eliminate each choice that doesn't match the provided graph.

If we recognize that every answer choice is in slope-intercept form, and we can see that the line in the provided graph has a negative slope and a positive y-intercept, then we know the right answer choice must be the only one with a negative slope and a positive y-intercept, which is (B).

ANSWER CHOICE ANALYSIS

(A): This choice has a positive slope, but the line in the graph has a negative slope. **(C):** This choice has a positive slope and negative y-intercept, which is the opposite of what appears in the graph. **(D):** This choice has a negative y-intercept, but the line in the graph has a positive y-intercept.

How to check? Verify that your choice has a positive y-intercept and a negative slope, like the line in the provided graph. Try an alternate approach above. Try to figure out which mistakes could lead to some of the wrong answer choices, and verify that you haven't made any such mistakes.

Test 3, Module 2, Question 12

- What's the prompt asking for? The value of x for which $f(x) = 48$.

- Math concepts in the prompt: functions, radical expressions

- Elements of the answer choices: Each answer choice is an even integer ranging from 6 to 64.

- Notable features of the answer choices: (A) is the square root of (C). (B) is the square root of (D).

- Things to look out for: Don't make a simple algebra mistake! Remember that $f(x) = 8\sqrt{x}$, not $8x$!

Solution 1: Concrete/graphing: We can graph the provided function, find the point where $y = 48$, and then look for the corresponding x-value.

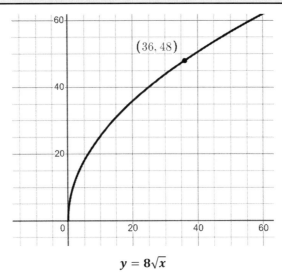

$$y = 8\sqrt{x}$$

We can see that $y = 48$ when $x = 36$, so the answer is (C).

Solution 2: Calculator: Plug in 48 for $f(x)$ in the provided function and enter the resulting equation in your calculator.

We can set the function equal to 48, like this:

$$f(x) = 8\sqrt{x} \qquad \text{(given function)}$$
$$48 = 8\sqrt{x} \qquad \text{(set } f(x) = 48\text{)}$$

We can enter this equation into our graphing calculator to find the x-value when $f(x) = 48$.

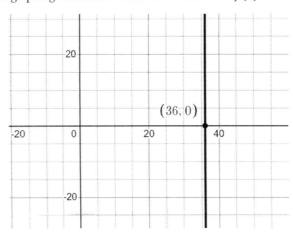

$$48 = 8\sqrt{x}$$

This graph shows a vertical line where $x = 36$, so the answer is (C).

Solution 3: Algebra: Plug in 48 for $f(x)$ in the provided function and solve for x algebraically.

We can set the function equal to 48, and then solve for x:

$$f(x) = 8\sqrt{x} \qquad \text{(given function)}$$
$$48 = 8\sqrt{x} \qquad \text{(set } f(x) = 48\text{)}$$
$$6 = \sqrt{x} \qquad \text{(divide both sides by 8)}$$
$$36 = x \qquad \text{(square both sides)}$$

So $f(x) = 48$ when $x = 36$, and (C) is correct.

ANSWER CHOICE ANALYSIS

(A): This would be the answer if the function were $f(x) = 8x$. **(B):** This would be the answer if the function were $f(x) = 6x$. **(D):** This would be the answer if the function were $f(x) = 6\sqrt{x}$.

How to check? Plug your answer in for x in the provided function and verify that the result is 48. Try an alternate approach above. Try to figure out which mistakes could lead to some of the wrong answer choices, and verify that you haven't made any such mistakes.

▶ Post-solution patterns (see page 286): the right answer to the wrong question

Test 3, Module 2, Question 13

- What's the prompt asking for? The measure of ∠RSO.
- Math concepts in the prompt: circles, centers, points, triangles, angle measures

- "Bridge" concepts: Two sides of triangle ORS are radii of the circle, so those two sides must have the same length, which makes triangle ORS an isosceles triangle.
- Things to look out for: Make sure you keep track of which points and angles the prompt is talking about!

Solution 1: Geometry: Sketch and label the circle, points, and triangle described in the prompt. Use that sketch and your understanding of circles and triangles to answer the question.

Let's draw the situation described in the prompt.

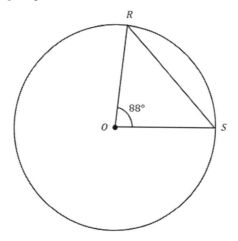

Since the question asks for the measure of ∠RSO, we know that we must have enough information to find the measure of that angle. If we try to think of everything we can tell about triangle ORS, we might realize that sides OR and OS are both radii of circle O—that means their lengths must be equal to one another, which means triangle ORS must be an isosceles triangle.

If ORS is isosceles, then angle R and angle S must have equal measures. If we call their measures x, we can set up this equation (remember that the sum of the three angle measures of any triangle must be 180°):

$$180° = 88° + 2x$$

We can solve that equation for x to find the value of ∠RSO.

$180° = 88° + 2x$	(equation we just found)
$92° = 2x$	(subtract 88° from both sides)
$46° = x$	(divide both sides by 2)

So the measure of ∠RSO is 46°, and the answer is 46.

How to check? Try to figure out which mistakes the College Board might hope you would make in finding your solution, and verify that you haven't made any such mistakes.

Test 3, Module 2, Question 14

- What's the prompt asking for? The sum of the solutions to the given equation.
- Math concepts in the prompt: equations, solutions

- Things to look out for: Don't make a simple mistake related to algebra or sign! Remember that the question asks for the sum of the solutions!

Solution 1: Graphing: We can enter this equation, as-is, into our graphing calculator to find the solutions.

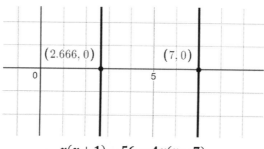

$$x(x + 1) - 56 = 4x(x - 7)$$

The graph produces two vertical lines: one at $x = 2\frac{2}{3}$, and one at $x = 7$. We can add these values together to get $9\frac{2}{3}$. The College Board's policy on entering a mixed number like $9\frac{2}{3}$ is to "write it as an improper fraction," which in this case would be $\frac{29}{3}$, or its "decimal equivalent." The College Board wants repeating decimals to be "truncate[d]… or round[ed] at the fourth digit," which in this case would be 9.666 or 9.667. So the acceptable answers to this question would be $\frac{29}{3}$, 9.666, or 9.667.

How to check? Try to figure out which mistakes the College Board might hope you would make in finding your solution, and verify that you haven't made any such mistakes.

Note As we can see in the College Board's free explanations for these practice questions, we can also solve this question using the quadratic formula. That approach would require us to multiply out the expressions on both sides of the equals sign, get all the different terms on one side of the equals sign and zero on the other, then plug the appropriate values into the quadratic formula, simplify that formula, and finally find the factors we're looking for. Or we can just enter the provided equation into our graphing calculator, find the two solutions instantly, and add them together as the prompt requires. The non-calculator solution is *so much more difficult* that even including it seems like a waste of time for your preparation. As I've said in our discussions of some other real SAT Math questions, there are so many real SAT Math questions that are pretty intimidating and difficult without the calculator, and pretty quick and easy with the calculator. You don't get bonus points for doing it the hard way. Please get comfortable executing these kinds of solutions with your calculator before test day.

Test 3, Module 2, Question 15

- What's the prompt asking for? The value of $5x$.
- Math concepts in the prompt: systems of equations, solutions, variable expressions
- Elements of the answer choices: Each answer choice is an integer ranging from 5 to 24.
- Notable features of the answer choices: (A) is twice as much as (C). (B) is 3 times as much as (D).

- "Bridge" concepts: We can solve the system of equations to find the value of x, then multiply the result by 5 to find $5x$.
- Pre-solution patterns (see p. 285): halves and doubles
- Things to look out for: Don't make a simple algebra mistake!

Solution 1: Concrete/graphing: We can graph these equations to see where they intersect.

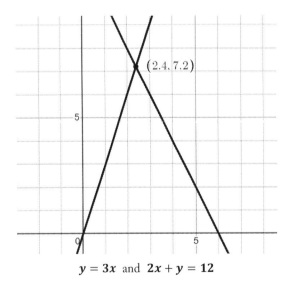

$$y = 3x \text{ and } 2x + y = 12$$

The point of intersection for these graphs is $(2.4, 7.2)$. So $x = 2.4$, and $5x = 5(2.4) = 12$. That means (C) is correct.

Solution 2: Algebra: We can solve the system of equations algebraically and then use the resulting x-value to answer the question.

We can plug $y = 3x$ from the first equation into the second equation and solve for x, then use that value to solve for $5x$.

$2x + y = 12$	(second equation)
$2x + (3x) = 12$	(plug in $y = 3x$ from the first equation)
$5x = 12$	(simplify)
$x = \frac{12}{5}$	(divide both sides by 5)

So $x = \frac{12}{5}$, which means $5x = 5\left(\frac{12}{5}\right) = 12$. So (C) is correct.

Solution 3: Test-smart: We can answer the question directly by plugging $y = 3x$ into the second equation.

When we plug $y = 3x$ from the first equation into the second equation, we get the answer to the question:

$$2x + (3x) = 12 \qquad \text{(plug in } y = 3x \text{ from the first equation)}$$
$$5x = 12 \qquad \text{(simplify)}$$

So we don't have to find the value of x first and then multiply it by 5, since the question asks for the value of $5x$ and we happened to find the value of $5x$ on our way to finding the value of x. You may have noticed in our previous solution that one of the steps was finding the value of $5x$; we could have stopped at that point and known the answer. Again, (C) is correct.

ANSWER CHOICE ANALYSIS

(A): This is the value of $10x$.

How to check? Try an alternate approach above. Try to figure out which mistakes could lead to some of the wrong answer choices, and verify that you haven't made any such mistakes.

Test 3, Module 2, Question 16

- What's the prompt asking for? The volume of the cube.
- Math concepts in the prompt: cubes, edge length, volume
- Elements of the answer choices: Each answer choice is an integer ranging from 164 to 68,921.

- "Bridge" concepts: We can find the volume of a cube by cubing its edge length.
- Things to look out for: Don't just find the area of a square with sides 41 inches long!

Solution 1: Geometry: Use the formula for the volume of a cube to find the answer.

We can find the volume of a cube by multiplying its height, width, and length. Since it's a cube, each of those dimensions is the same—in this case, 41 inches.

$$V = lwh \qquad \text{(volume equation)}$$
$$V = (41)(41)(41) \qquad \text{(plug in 41 for each dimension)}$$
$$V = 68,921 \qquad \text{(simplify)}$$

So the correct answer is (D).

ANSWER CHOICE ANALYSIS

(A): This is the perimeter of a square with sides 41 inches long. **(B):** This is the area of a square with sides 41 inches long. **(C):** This is the surface area of the cube—that is, the sum of the areas of all 6 faces of the cube.

How to check? Verify that you found the volume of the cube and not some other measure. Try to figure out which mistakes could lead to some of the wrong answer choices, and verify that you haven't made any such mistakes.

▶   Post-solution patterns (see page 286): the right answer to the wrong question

---

Test 3, Module 2, Question 17

- What's the prompt asking for? The function that best models the population of Lowell m months after the census.
- Math concepts in the prompt: word problems, function models, population
- Elements of the answer choices: Each answer choice is a function involving 90,000 multiplied by an expression that's raised to an exponent involving m.
- Notable features of the answer choices: (A) includes $\frac{90,000}{12}$, while the other choices include 90,000. (B) and (C) involve $\frac{1.06}{12}$, while the other choices involve 1.06.

The exponent in (A) and (B) is m, while the exponent in (C) and (D) is $\frac{m}{12}$.

- "Bridge" concepts: We need to figure out how changing the unit of time from years to months will impact the function.
- Pre-solution patterns (see p. 285): wrong answers try to imitate right answers
- Things to look out for: Remember that we're switching from years to months, not vice versa! Think carefully about the parts of the function that will (and will not) be impacted by changing the unit of time!

Solution 1: Concrete: Come up with corresponding values for t to plug in to the given function and the provided functions, and pick the choice that matches the results from the given function.

We're told that the provided function and the functions in the answer choices model the same thing—the population of Lowell a certain amount of time after a census. The only difference between them is that the provided function $p(t)$ measures the time in *years*, while the functions in the answer choices $r(m)$ measure that time in *months*.

If the functions in the answer choices model the same thing as the provided function, then we can plug a value into the provided function, and then plug an equivalent value into each of the answer choices, and eliminate any answer choices that don't produce the same result.

In order for this to work, we just have to make sure that the value we use in the provided function is the same amount of time as the value we use in the functions in the answer choices. In other words, if we use $t = 1$ in the provided function, that's one year—so we would need to plug $m = 12$ into the answer choices, because that would be 12 months, which is the same as 1 year.

Let's use $t = 3$ for 3 years in the provided function, and then we'll plug $m = 36$ for 36 months into the functions in the answer choices, since 3 years is the same as 36 months. We'll start with plugging $t = 3$ into the provided function $p(t)$.

$$p(t) = 90{,}000(1.06)^t \qquad \text{(function from the prompt)}$$
$$p(3) = 90{,}000(1.06)^3 \qquad \text{(plug in } t = 3\text{)}$$
$$p(3) = 90{,}000(1.191016) \qquad \text{(simplify)}$$
$$p(3) = 107{,}191.44 \qquad \text{(simplify)}$$

So $p(3) = 107{,}191.44$. Now we can plug $m = 36$ into each function from the answer choices (again, because the functions in the answer choices measure time in months, and 36 months is equal to 3 years, which is the value we used in the function from the prompt).

(A) $r(m) = \frac{90{,}000}{12}(1.06)^m$ $\qquad$ $r(36) = \frac{90{,}000}{12}(1.06)^{36}$ $\qquad$ $r(36) \approx 61{,}104.39$

(B) $r(m) = 90{,}000\left(\frac{1.06}{12}\right)^m$ $\qquad$ $r(36) = 90{,}000\left(\frac{1.06}{12}\right)^{36}$ $\qquad$ $r(36) = 1.03 \times 10^{-33}$

(C) $r(m) = 90{,}000\left(\frac{1.06}{12}\right)^{\frac{m}{12}}$ $\qquad$ $r(36) = 90{,}000\left(\frac{1.06}{12}\right)^{\frac{36}{12}}$ $\qquad$ $r(36) = 62.03$

(D) $r(m) = 90{,}000(1.06)^{\frac{m}{12}}$ $\qquad$ $r(36) = 90{,}000(1.06)^{\frac{36}{12}}$ $\qquad$ $r(36) = 107{,}191.44$

Only choice (D) matches the value we found for $p(3)$, so (D) is the correct answer.

Solution 2: Concrete/graphing: We can graph the provided function and the functions from the answer choices, adjusting the units of time accordingly. The graph from the answer choices (again, adjusted for different units of time) that matches the graph of the provided function will be the correct answer.

We can graph the provided function $p(t)$, like this:

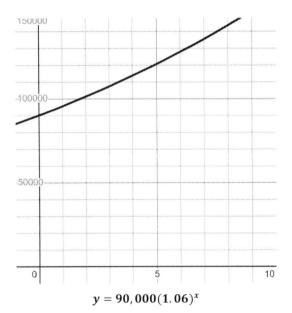

$$y = 90{,}000(1.06)^x$$

Now we can graph the functions from the answer choices. There are 12 months in a year, so the graph of the right answer should be like the graph of the function $p(t)$ from the prompt, *except* the value of the function from the prompt for a given value of x should correspond to the value of the function from the correct answer for $12x$—for example, $p(1)$ should be the same as $r(12)$, $p(3)$ should be the same as $r(36)$, and so on. Again, this is because $p(t)$ uses t-values measured in years, while $r(m)$ uses m-values measured in months, and there are 12 months in a year.

In order to account for the difference in units, I've adjusted the viewing window in the following graphs so that the x-axis is 12 times *greater* than the x-axis in the above graph. So while the above graph shows x-values as high as 10, the below graphs show x-

values as high as 120. Because of this adjustment, the graph that matches the graph of the given function should look exactly like the above function.

With this in mind, let's take a look at the graphs of the answer choices:

(A)

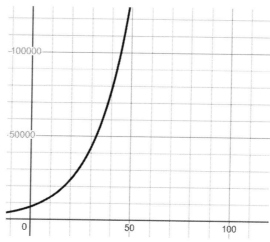

$$y = \frac{90,000}{12}(1.06)^x$$

(B)

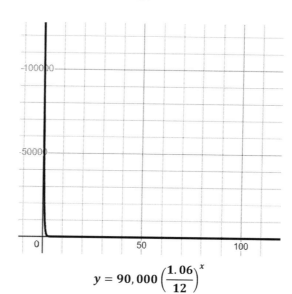

$$y = 90,000 \left(\frac{1.06}{12}\right)^x$$

(C)

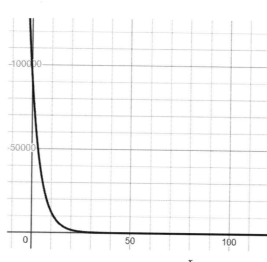

$$y = 90,000 \left(\frac{1.06}{12}\right)^{\frac{x}{12}}$$

(D)

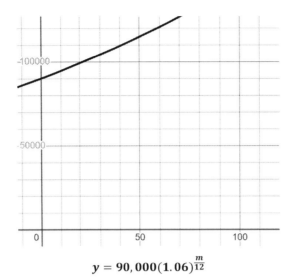

$$y = 90{,}000(1.06)^{\frac{m}{12}}$$

We can see that the graph of (D) is the same as the graph of $p(t)$, except each r-value is produced by an m-value that's 12 times greater than the t-value that produces a corresponding p-value. So (D) is correct.

Solution 3: Abstract: Think carefully about how changing from years to months should impact the function, and pick the choice that satisfies your reasoning.

Let's look at the provided function and think about how it would change if t represented months instead of years. The only appearance of t in the given function is in the exponent above 1.06. If t needed to represent months and we didn't make any change to the function, then 1.06 would be raised to an exponent that was 12 times too big—after 1 year, for example, 1.06 would be raised to an exponent of 12 (for 12 months) instead of 1, and after 5 years 1.06 would be raised to an exponent of 60 (for 60 months) instead of 5, and so on.

So if changing the units from years to months means we're raising 1.06 to an exponent that's 12 times too big, then we need to divide that exponent by 12. That way after a year we'd be raising 1.06 to an exponent of $\frac{12}{12}$, or 1, and after 5 years we'd be raising 1.06 to an exponent of $\frac{60}{12}$, or 5, and so on.

Only (C) and (D) divide the exponent of 1.06 by 12, so we can eliminate (A) and (B).

The only difference between (C) and (D) is that (C) divides 1.06 by 12, and (D) doesn't. There's no reason to divide 1.06 by 12—the only interaction between 1.06 and t in the original equation was that 1.06 was raised to an exponent of t, and we already addressed that issue. So (C) makes an unnecessary change to the function, which means we can eliminate it, and the remaining answer is the correct answer, (D).

ANSWER CHOICE ANALYSIS

(A): This choice fails to account appropriately for the idea of dividing the unit of time by 12. **(B):** This choice has the same basic problem as (A). **(C):** This choice has the right exponent but unnecessarily divides 1.06 by 12.

How to check? Try an alternate approach above. Try to figure out which mistakes could lead to some of the wrong answer choices, and verify that you haven't made any such mistakes.

Test 3, Module 2, Question 18

- What's the prompt asking for? The value of y.
- Math concepts in the prompt: systems of equations
- Elements of the answer choices: Each answer choice is an integer ranging from -2 to 18.
- Notable features of the answer choices: (A) is the only negative answer choice. (B) is half of (C).
- "Bridge" concepts: The solution to the given system of equations is the (x, y) pair that results in a valid statement when plugged into each equation. It's also the point where the graphs of the two equations intersect.
- Pre-solution patterns (see p. 285): halves and doubles
- Things to look out for: Don't make a simple mistake related to algebra or sign! Don't mix up x and y!

Solution 1: Concrete/graphing: We can graph these equations to find their point of intersection.

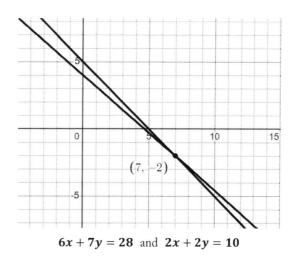

$$6x + 7y = 28 \text{ and } 2x + 2y = 10$$

We can see that the graphs intersect at $(7, -2)$, so the y-value at their point of intersection is -2, and the answer is (A).

Solution 2: Algebra: Solve for x in one equation, then plug that x-value in to the other equation to find the value of y.

Let's start with the second equation, because the algebra looks like it might be a little easier (though either equation is fine).

$2x + 2y = 10$	(second equation)
$2x = 10 - 2y$	(subtract $2y$ from both sides)
$x = 5 - y$	(divide both sides by 2)

So $x = 5 - y$. Let's plug this x-value into the first equation, and solve for y.

$6x + 7y = 28$	(first equation)
$6(5 - y) + 7y = 28$	(plug in $x = 5 - y$)
$30 - 6y + 7y = 28$	(distribute the 6)
$30 + y = 28$	(simplify)
$y = -2$	(subtract 30 from both sides)

So $y = -2$, and the answer is (A).

Solution 3: Test-smart: We can find y directly by adding the equations if we multiply the second equation by 3 first.

We may notice that if we multiply the second equation by 3, we can just subtract the second equation from the first equation and we'll be left with the value of y.

$$\begin{array}{r} 6x + 7y = 28 \\ - \quad 6x + 6y = 30 \\ \hline y = -2 \end{array}$$

So the answer is (A), -2.

ANSWER CHOICE ANALYSIS

(B): This is the x-value of the solution to the system of equations. **(D):** This is the result if we attempt Solution 3 above but forget to multiply 10 by 3 as well.

How to check? Verify that you picked the y-value of the solution, not the x-value. Try an alternate approach above. Try to figure out which mistakes could lead to some of the wrong answer choices, and verify that you haven't made any such mistakes.

▶ Post-solution patterns (see page 286): the right answer to the wrong question

Test 3, Module 2, Question 19

- What's the prompt asking for? The inequality that shows the possible values of x.

- Math concepts in the prompt: minimum values, inequalities, variables

- Elements of the answer choices: Each answer choice is an inequality that relates the value of x to an expression involving n.

- Notable features of the answer choices: Each choice features $6n$, 12, and a minus sign. Two choices include

$6n - 12$, and two include $12 - 6n$. Two choices use a $\leq$ sign, and two use a $\geq$ sign.

- Pre-solution patterns (see p. 285): opposites; wrong answers try to imitate right answers

- Things to look out for: Don't make a simple mistake related to algebra or sign! Remember that you're dealing with inequalities, not equations!

Solution 1: Answer choice analysis: Use the information in the prompt to eliminate incorrect choices by focusing on the differences among the answer choices.

When we look at the answer choices, we can see that the only differences among them are that two choices ((A) and (C)) begin with "$x \leq$," while the other two begin with "$x \geq$," and that two choices ((A) and (B)) involve the expression "$6n - 12$," while the other two involve the expression "$12 - 6n$." Let's consider these two issues one at a time.

When we consider whether the "greater than or equal to" sign or the "less than or equal to" sign is appropriate, we can notice that either option acknowledges that x can be equal to the expression—the question is just whether x can also be greater than that expression or less than that expression.

The prompt tells us that the expression is "the minimum value of x." The word "minimum" tells us that x can't be any less than that expression—that's what "minimum" means. So x can be equal to that expression, or greater than that expression, but it can't be less than that expression. That means the correct answer should start with "$x \geq$," which means (A) and (C) are wrong.

Now we just need to figure out whether the expression after the inequality symbol should be "$6n - 12$" or "$12 - 6n$." The prompt says the expression is "12 less than 6 times another number n." To find "12 less than" something, we need to subtract 12 *from* that thing, as opposed to starting with 12 and then subtracting something from 12. So the expression should involve subtracting 12 from something else, and it shouldn't involve subtracting something from 12. That eliminates (D), and leaves only the correct answer, which is (B).

Solution 2: Careful reading: Turn the phrases in the prompt into an inequality, and pick the choice that matches the result.

Let's take the sentence from the prompt that describes the relationship between x and n, and turn it into an inequality.

the minimum value of x is 12 less than 6 times another number n

Let's start by writing "6 times another number n" as $6n$.

the minimum value of x is 12 less than $6n$

Next we can probably see that "12 less than $6n$" is $6n - 12$, so let's make that change.

the minimum value of x is $6n - 12$

Now we need to think about what "the minimum value of x" means. Well, if it's the minimum value of x, then x *can* be equal to that expression. But "minimum" means smallest, so that means x could be bigger than that value too—x just can't be smaller than that value, or else it wouldn't be true that the expression is the "minimum value of x."

So if x can be equal to that expression, and it can be greater than that expression, it must be true that x can be greater than or equal to that expression, which we can write as "$x \geq$."

$$x \geq 6n - 12$$

So the answer is (B).

ANSWER CHOICE ANALYSIS

(A): This is the right answer except the inequality sign is reversed. **(D):** This is the right answer with 12 and $6n$ reversed.

How to check? Try an alternate approach above. Try to figure out which mistakes could lead to some of the wrong answer choices, and verify that you haven't made any such mistakes.

Test 3, Module 2, Question 20

- What's the prompt asking for? The mean of data set C.
- Math concepts in the prompt: word problems, data sets, heights, mean
- "Bridge" concepts: We can use the mean from each of the smaller data sets to find the total of the heights from each of those sets, and then use that information to answer the question.
- Things to look out for: Don't just find the mean of the two means given in the prompt! Remember to account for the fact that each set represents a different number of buildings!

Solution 1: Algebra: Use the provided information to find the sums of all the heights in data sets A and B, and then use that information to find the mean of data set C.

We find the mean of a data set by adding up the values in that set and then dividing them by the number of values in that set.

If we want to find the mean of data set C (which we'll call x), then we need to find the sum of all the values in data set C, and divide that by the total number of values in data set C, like this:

$$\frac{\text{sum of the values in C}}{\text{number of values in C}} = x$$

The prompt tells us that data set C is composed of "the heights of the 125 buildings from data sets A and B." That means that the sum of the values in C is equal to the sum of the values in A and the sum of the values in B added together. This phrase also tells us directly that there are 125 values in C. We can adjust our equation accordingly.

$$\frac{\text{sum of the values in A} + \text{sum of the values in B}}{125} = x$$

Now we just need to find the sum of the values in A and the sum of the values in B, and we'll have our answer. Let's start by focusing on the sum of the values in A.

In order to find the mean of data set A, we would have to find the sum of the 75 values in that set, and then divide that result by 75; the prompt tells us that result was 32. Let's write that out in an equation:

$$\frac{\text{sum of the values in A}}{75} = 32$$

With this in mind, we can multiply the mean of data set A by 75 to find the sum of the values in A.

$$sum\ of\ the\ values\ in\ A = 32 \times 75 = 2{,}400$$

So even though we don't know the individual values in data set A, we can figure out that the sum of those values must be 2,400.

Now let's repeat that process with data set B. The prompt tells us that data set B is composed of the heights of 50 buildings—which means it contains 50 values—and that the mean of that set is 62 meters. Let's write that out like we did for data set A.

$$\frac{\text{sum of the values in B}}{50} = 62$$

Just as with data set A, we can multiply the mean of the set by the number of values in the set to find the sum of the values in B.

$$sum\ of\ the\ values\ in\ B = 62 \times 50 = 3{,}100$$

Now we know that the sum of the values in A was 2,400, and the sum of the values in B was 3,100. We can insert those values into the equation we found at the beginning of this explanation:

$$\frac{\text{sum of the values in A} + \text{sum of the values in B}}{125} = x \qquad \text{(equation we found earlier for the mean of C)}$$

$$\frac{2{,}400 + 3{,}100}{125} = x \qquad \text{(plug in sum of values in A and sum of values in B)}$$

$$\frac{5{,}500}{125} = x \qquad \text{(simplify)}$$

$$44 = x \qquad \text{(simplify)}$$

So the answer is 44.

How to check? Try to figure out which mistakes the College Board might hope you would make in finding your solution, and verify that you haven't made any such mistakes.

Test 3, Module 2, Question 21

- **What's the prompt asking for?** The x-coordinate of the x-intercept of the resulting graph.

- **Math concepts in the prompt:** line graphs, translation, x-intercept

- **"Bridge" concepts:** The x-intercept of $9x - 10y = 19$ after it's translated down 4 units will be the same as the x-coordinate of $9x - 10y = 19$ when $y = 4$.

- **Things to look out for:** Remember that we're being asked about the graph after it was translated *down*, not *up!* Remember to answer the question based on the translated version of the equation, not the equation given in the prompt!

Solution 1: Concrete/graphing: We can graph the provided equation and use what we learn to work toward the solution.

Let's start by graphing the provided equation.

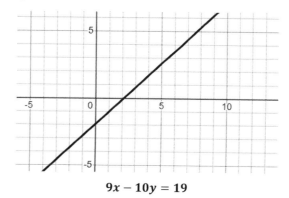

$$9x - 10y = 19$$

The prompt asks us for the x-coordinate of the x-intercept when the graph "is translated down 4 units in the xy-plane." When the graph is moved down 4 units, the graph will cross the x-axis at the same point that the original graph will cross a horizontal line 4 units *above* the x-axis. (If that doesn't make sense, it may help to think of this like moving the x-axis up 4 units to see where that axis would cross the original graph after that graph was translated down 4 units.)

A horizontal line that's 4 units higher than the x-axis would be a line at $y = 4$. Let's add that to our graph.

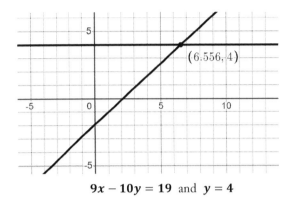

$$9x - 10y = 19 \text{ and } y = 4$$

We can see that the original graph crosses a line 4 units above the x-axis at $(6.556, 4)$. That means if we moved the original graph down 4 units, it would cross the x-axis at $(6.556, 0)$. The question asks for the x-coordinate of the x-intercept of that graph, so the answer is 6.556. (Note that 6.555, 6.556, and $\frac{59}{9}$ are all acceptable ways to enter this answer.)

Solution 2: Algebra: Get the provided equation into slope-intercept form, then use the result to find the equation of the same line translated down 4 units. Use that equation to answer the question.

We can think of translating the graph of a line down 4 units as moving that line's y-intercept down 4 units. Let's put the provided equation into slope-intercept form, and then we'll lower its y-intercept by 4. Finally, we'll find the x-intercept of the new line so we can answer the question.

$9x - 10y = 19$	(provided equation)
$9x = 10y + 19$	(add $10y$ to both sides)
$9x - 19 = 10y$	(subtract 19 from both sides)
$\frac{9}{10}x - \frac{19}{10} = y$	(divide both sides by 10)
$y = \frac{9}{10}x - \frac{19}{10}$	(switch sides of the equation for clarity)

So the original equation in slope-intercept form is $y = \frac{9}{10}x - \frac{19}{10}$. Remember that slope-intercept form means the equation for a line is in $y = mx + b$ form, where m is the slope and b is the y-intercept. With this in mind, we can see that the y-intercept for this line is $-\frac{19}{10}$. If we translate the line down 4 units, that means the y-intercept of the line must move down 4 units, which means the resulting y-intercept must be 4 less than $-\frac{19}{10}$. 4 less than $-\frac{19}{10}$ is $-\frac{19}{10} - 4$, which is the same as $-\frac{19}{10} - \frac{40}{10}$, which is $-\frac{59}{10}$.

We can switch out this new y-intercept in the original equation to find the equation of the line after it's translated down 4 units. The result is $y = \frac{9}{10}x - \frac{59}{10}$.

We can find the x-intercept of the graph of this new equation by plugging in $y = 0$ and solving for x (we know this because when $y = 0$, the graph must be touching the x-intercept).

$y = \frac{9}{10}x - \frac{59}{10}$	(equation of the line that we translated down 4 units)
$0 = \frac{9}{10}x - \frac{59}{10}$	(set $y = 0$ to find the x-intercept)
$\frac{59}{10} = \frac{9}{10}x$	(add $\frac{59}{10}$ to both sides)
$59 = 9x$	(multiply both sides by 10)
$\frac{59}{9} = x$	(divide both sides by 9)

So the x-value of the x-intercept of the given line when it's translated down 4 units is $\frac{59}{9}$, which means the answer is $\frac{59}{9}$ (notice that this is approximately equal to the 6.556 value we found in our last solution).

Note that once we had the equation $y = \frac{9}{10}x - \frac{59}{10}$, we could also graph that equation to find its x-intercept, instead of doing the above algebra:

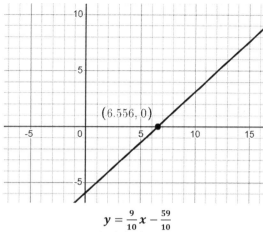

$$y = \frac{9}{10}x - \frac{59}{10}$$

Again, we can see that the x-value of the x-intercept is 6.556 (which we can enter as 6.555, 6.556, or $\frac{59}{9}$).

How to check? Try an alternate approach above. Try to figure out which mistakes the College Board might hope you would make in finding your solution, and verify that you haven't made any such mistakes.

Note   Another way to account for the idea of translating this equation down 4 units would be to plug in $y + 4$ for y in the original equation—adding 4 to y reflects the idea that when the graph is moved *down* 4 units, we would have to add 4 to y for any given value of x to get the same (x, y) pair from the original equation. This is kind of counter-intuitive for a lot of test-takers who might end up substituting $y - 4$ instead of $y + 4$, and then get the question wrong—the solutions above tend to make it easier to keep track of whether we're moving the line up or down, so we avoid that situation.

Test 3, Module 2, Question 22

- What's the prompt asking for? The equation that represents the relationship described in the prompt.
- Math concepts in the prompt: relationships between variables, world problems
- Elements of the answer choices: Each answer choice is an equation with y set equal to an expression involving $4, 200, x$, and an exponent.
- Notable features of the answer choices: Each choice mixes up the same 3 elements as either the first value,

the second value being multiplied by the first value, or the exponent that the second value is being raised to.
- "Bridge" concepts: We can use the phrases in the prompt to relate $4, x$, and 200 to each other.
- Pre-solution patterns (see p. 285): wrong answers try to imitate right answers
- Things to look out for: Think carefully about the relationships expressed in the prompt, and make sure your answer choice reflects those relationships!

Solution 1: Concrete/graphing: Use information from the prompt to test each answer choice. Eliminate each choice that fails the test.

The prompt tells us that when $x = 0, y = 200$. That means the graph of the right answer must have a point at $(0, 200)$. Let's start by graphing each answer choice and eliminating any choice that doesn't contain the point $(0, 200)$.

(A)

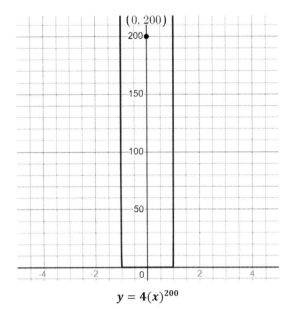

$$y = 4(x)^{200}$$

(B)

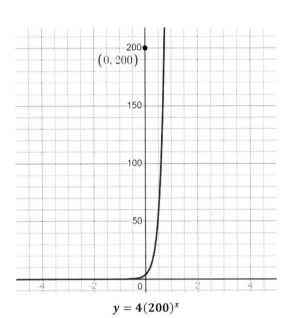

$$y = 4(200)^x$$

(C)

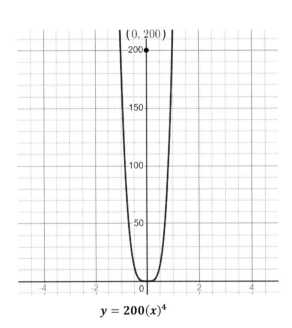

$$y = 200(x)^4$$

(D)

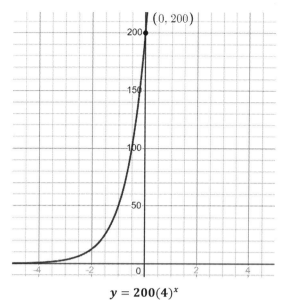

$$y = 200(4)^x$$

After graphing each answer choice, we can see that only choice (D) contains the point $(0, 200)$, so (D) must be correct.

Solution 2: Concrete: Use information from the prompt to test each answer choice. Eliminate each choice that fails the test.

The prompt tells us that when $x = 0, y = 200$. That means when we plug $x = 0$ into the correct answer, the resulting y-value must be 200. Let's plug $x = 0$ into the equation from each answer choice and eliminate each one that doesn't produce a y-value of 200.

(A)	$y = 4(x)^{200}$	$y = 4(0)^{200}$	$y = 4(0)$	$y = 0$
(B)	$y = 4(200)^x$	$y = 4(200)^{(0)}$	$y = 4(1)$	$y = 4$
(C)	$y = 200(x)^4$	$y = 200(0)^4$	$y = 200(0)$	$y = 0$
(D)	$y = 200(4)^x$	$y = 200(4)^{(0)}$	$y = 200(1)$	$y = 200$

Only (D) has a point at $(0, 200)$, so (D) is correct.

Solution 3: Abstract: Think carefully about the ideas expressed in the prompt, and pick the only choice that reflects those ideas accurately.

The prompt tells us that "for every increase of 1 in the value of x, the value of y increases by a factor of 4." In other words, every time x goes up by 1, y gets multiplied by 4 an additional time. This is the same as saying we multiply y by 4 x times, which is the same as saying that we raise 4 to an exponent of x—that way, each time x goes up by 1, we multiply by 4 an additional time, just as the prompt says.

So the right answer must include 4^x. We can see that only (D) includes 4^x, so (D) must be correct.

To make extra sure, we can plug in the provided values from the prompt to make sure that when $x = 0, y = 200$.

$y = 200(4)^x$	(equation from (D))
$y = 200(4)^0$	(plug in $x = 0$)
$y = 200(1)$	(simplify)
$y = 200$	(simplify)

Choice (D) is the only choice that accurately reflects the information in the prompt, and we've confirmed that for choice (D), when $x = 0, y = 200$. So (D) is correct.

ANSWER CHOICE ANALYSIS

(A): This choice combines the errors from (B) and (C). **(B):** This choice is right answer with 4 and 200 reversed. **(C):** This choice raises x to an exponent of 4, instead of the other way around.

How to check? Try an alternate approach above. Try to figure out which mistakes could lead to some of the wrong answer choices, and verify that you haven't made any such mistakes.

Test 3, Module 2, Question 23

- What's the prompt asking for? The value of k.
- Math concepts in the prompt: equations, solutions, constants, radical expressions

- Elements of the answer choices: each answer choice is an even integer ranging from 8 to 40.

- Notable features of the answer choices: (B), (C), and (D) form a series where each choice is twice as much as the previous choice.
- "Bridge" concepts: We can find the solutions to the given equation and use them to find the value of k in the given expression.

- Pre-solution patterns (see p. 285): halves and doubles; first and last terms in a series are often wrong answers
- Things to look out for: Don't make a simple mistake related to algebra or sign! Remember that the prompt isn't asking for a solution to the equations—it's asking for the value of k!

Solution 1: Graphing: We can enter the provided equation into our graphing calculator to find solutions for x.

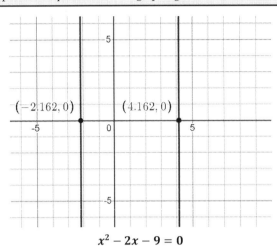

$$x^2 - 2x - 9 = 0$$

We can see that there is a vertical line at $x = -2.162$, and at $x = 4.162$. The prompt describes "one solution," so it might be the case that either of these solutions is the one described in the prompt. Let's plug each value into $x = 1 + \sqrt{k}$ to find the corresponding k-value.

$x = 1 + \sqrt{k}$	(solution to the provided equation expressed as $1 + \sqrt{k}$)
$-2.162 = 1 + \sqrt{k}$	(plug in $x = -2.162$)
$-3.162 = \sqrt{k}$	(subtract 1 from both sides)
$9.998 = k$	(square both sides)

Let's repeat this with the other x-value from the graph.

$x = 1 + \sqrt{k}$	(solution to the provided equation expressed as $1 + \sqrt{k}$)
$4.162 = 1 + \sqrt{k}$	(plug in $x = 4.162$)
$3.162 = \sqrt{k}$	(subtract 1 from both sides)
$9.998 = k$	(square both sides)

The result for both x-values is the same k-value that's very close to 10. We know that calculators aren't perfect and have to round off very long decimal expressions (like square roots of numbers that aren't perfect squares), and that working with those rounded-off expressions (like -2.162 and 3.162) can produce results that are very slightly off from their true values. So we can compare this result to the answer choices and see that $k = 10$, which means (B) is correct.

Solution 2: Concrete: Test each answer choice by using it as k in the given expression, then plug the result into the given equation to see which one produces a valid statement.

We can plug each answer choice in for k in the provided solution from the prompt, and then plug the result into the provided equation to see which one produces a valid statement. (I recommend using the provided calculator to evaluate each of the below expressions.)

(A) $x = 1 + \sqrt{8}$	$\left(1 + \sqrt{8}\right)^2 - 2\left(1 + \sqrt{8}\right) - 9 = 0$	$-2 = 0$
(B) $x = 1 + \sqrt{10}$	$\left(1 + \sqrt{10}\right)^2 - 2\left(1 + \sqrt{10}\right) - 9 = 0$	$3.552 \times 10^{-15} = 0$
(C) $x = 1 + \sqrt{20}$	$\left(1 + \sqrt{20}\right)^2 - 2\left(1 + \sqrt{20}\right) - 9 = 0$	$10 = 0$
(D) $x = 1 + \sqrt{40}$	$(1 + \sqrt{40})^2 - 2(1 + \sqrt{40}) - 9 = 0$	$30 = 0$

We can eliminate (A), (C), and (D) because they produce invalid equations. When we consider (B), we can see that the resulting equation says that 0 is equal to a tiny, tiny decimal—if we write out that value that's in scientific notation above, we get 0.000000000000003552. This is due to an imperfection with the calculator, since square roots of imperfect squares, expressed as decimals in a calculator, have to get rounded off at some point. We know that the result of (B) must really be $0 = 0$, which means that when $k = 10$, the expression $1 + \sqrt{k}$ is a solution for the provided equation, and (B) is correct.

(C): This is double the right answer.

How to check? Try an alternate approach above. Try to figure out which mistakes could lead to some of the wrong answer choices, and verify that you haven't made any such mistakes.

Test 3, Module 2, Question 24

- **What's the prompt asking for?** The statements that must be true.
- **Math concepts in the prompt:** dot plots, data sets, distributions of values, median, standard deviation
- **Elements of the answer choices:** Each choice mentions statement I and/or statement II, or neither statement.
- **Notable features of the answer choices:** The choices are all possible combinations of including or excluding each statement.

- **"Bridge" concepts:** We can use our understanding of median and standard deviation to evaluate the statement and answer the question.
- **Pre-solution patterns (see p. 285):** wrong answers try to imitate right answers
- **Things to look out for:** Read the figures and the statements carefully! Think carefully about the meaning of "median" and "standard deviation"!

Solution 1: Careful reading: Evaluate each statement based on the information in the figures.

Let's consider each of the statements separately.

Roman numeral I says that the medians of the two sets are equal. The median of a data set is the number in the middle when the values in that set are ordered from least to greatest. We can see that the medians of data sets A and B are both 13 in at least two different ways.

For one, we could count out the total number of dots in each set, which is 17. The value in the middle will be the 9th one, so we can just count the dots starting from the left to see which column contains the 9th dot. In either case, it will be the "Value" column labeled "13," which means the median is 13.

The other way we can tell is by carefully looking at the dot plots and seeing that each one is symmetrical, and that the value in the middle is 13—that is, each dot plot has the "Value" column labeled "13" in the middle, and each one has an equal number of dots on either side of that 13 column, so the middle value when the values in the set are ordered from least to greatest will be 13 for data set A as well as data set B.

That means the first statement is true. Now let's consider the second statement.

Roman numeral II says that the standard deviations of the sets are equal. Remember that we never need to calculate the standard deviation of a set of data on the SAT, but we very rarely may need to understand what a standard deviation is. We can think of the standard deviation of a data set as a measure of the tendency of the values in that data set to be close to or far from the mean of that set.

When we compare the dot plots, we can see that the only difference between them is that data set A has one less value at 10 and 16 (the least and greatest values) and two more values at 13 (the mean value), and that data set B has one more value at 10 and 16 (the least and greatest values) and two fewer values at 13 (the mean value).

So we can see plainly that the values in A tend to be closer to the mean than the values in B do (again, because A literally has two more values that are equal to the mean, while B has an additional value each in the columns with the least and greatest values, respectively), which means these two data sets must have different standard deviations. That means the second statement is false.

So the correct answer is (A).

ANSWER CHOICE ANALYSIS

(B): This is the opposite of the right answer.

How to check? Try to figure out which mistakes could lead to some of the wrong answer choices, and verify that you haven't made any such mistakes.

Note Even if we aren't exactly sure what "standard deviation" means, we've got a good shot at figuring out enough about the term to be able to answer this question anyway. We probably know that "standard" means something like "regular" or "normal," and "to deviate" from something means "to be different" from that thing, or "to move away" from it. This suggests that "standard deviation" means something like "being different from the normal thing." (Of course, this definition isn't exactly precise, and might not be very helpful in a math classroom. But we'll see how this kind of definition can be useful on this question, and how this general type of thinking can be helpful on the rest of the SAT.) Now let's think about the data in the dot plots. We can see that the values for Data Set A are identical to the values in Data Set B, except that Data Set A has two more values in the middle of the set (13), and one fewer each of the minimum (10) and maximum (16) values of the set. So the values in Data Set A don't "deviate" as much from that "standard" value of 13 as the values in Data Set B do—again, because A has two more values right in the middle of the dot plot, while B has more of the greatest and least values in the range. That means Roman numeral II must not be true. Also notice that the College Board could have made this question much more challenging by making it harder to compare the two data sets. If the data sets weren't identical aside from the two values changed from the middle of the set to the least and greatest values of the set, we might have actually had to calculate the standard deviation for each set to find the right answer. But the question was intentionally designed so that calculations wouldn't be necessary, and anyone with a general understanding of the term "standard deviation" could read the dot plots and find the correct answer.

Test 3, Module 2, Question 25

- What's the prompt asking for? The length of one leg of the triangle described in the prompt.

- Math concepts in the prompt: isosceles triangles, right triangles, radical expressions, perimeter, length

- Elements of the answer choices: Two choices are integers, and the other two are the same integers multiplied by $\sqrt{2}$.

- Notable features of the answer choices: Two choices include 47, and the other two include 94. Two choices include $\sqrt{2}$. (A) is half of (C), and (B) is half of (D).

- "Bridge" concepts: An isosceles right triangle has a 90° angle and two legs of equal length. The other two angles in the triangle have the same measure, which means they must both be 45°.

- Pre-solution patterns (see p. 285): halves and doubles; wrong answers try to imitate right answers

- Things to look out for: Find the length of the correct part of the triangle!

Solution 1: Concrete: Use the Pythagorean theorem to test each side length and see which one results in a triangle with a perimeter of $94 + 94\sqrt{2}$ inches.

An isosceles right triangle is a triangle with a 90° angle and with two legs of equal length. The Pythagorean theorem tells us that the sum of the squares of the lengths of the legs of a right triangle is equal to the square of the hypotenuse.

In this case, if we know the length of one of the legs, then we also know the length of the other leg (since, as we just discussed, the legs must be the same length). If we know the length of both legs, we can square each length, add them together, and find the square root of the result to get the length of the hypotenuse of that triangle. At that point, we'll know the lengths of the two sides and the hypotenuse of that triangle, and we can add those three values to find the perimeter.

So we can test each answer choice by figuring out what the perimeter of the isosceles right triangle would be if that answer were correct, and then eliminating any choice that doesn't result in a perimeter of $94 + 94\sqrt{2}$ inches.

Since we'll be using our calculator to find decimal approximations of the square roots we'll use, let's find the decimal approximation of the perimeter given in the prompt. When we enter $94 + 94\sqrt{2}$ into our calculator, we get approximately 226.94. So we're looking for the answer choice that would produce a triangle with a perimeter of approximately 226.94. Now let's test each choice, starting with (A).

First, we need to use the given leg length in (A) along with the Pythagorean theorem to find what the length of the hypotenuse of a right isosceles triangle would be if one of the leg lengths was 47 inches.

$a^2 + b^2 = c^2$	(Pythagorean theorem)
$47^2 + 47^2 = x^2$	(plug in 47 from (A) for both leg lengths)
$4{,}418 = x^2$	(simplify)
$66.47 \approx x$	(take the square root of both sides)

Now we know that a right isosceles triangle with legs 47 inches long would have a hypotenuse of approximately 66.47 inches. The perimeter of that triangle would be the sum of those three sides, which is $47 + 47 + 66.47$, or 160.47. This isn't equal to 226.94, so (A) is wrong. Let's repeat this process with (B).

$a^2 + b^2 = c^2$	(Pythagorean theorem)
$(47\sqrt{2})^2 + (47\sqrt{2})^2 = x^2$	(plug in $47\sqrt{2}$ from (B) for both leg lengths)
$8{,}836 = x^2$	(simplify)
$94 = x$	(take the square root of both sides)
$47\sqrt{2} + 47\sqrt{2} + 94 \approx 226.94$	(perimeter using value from (B))

Using the value from (B), we get an approximate perimeter of 226.94, which is equal to our decimal approximation of the perimeter from the prompt. So (B) appears to be the correct answer, but we'll still check (C) and (D) to help catch any mistakes we might have made.

$a^2 + b^2 = c^2$	(Pythagorean theorem)
$(94)^2 + (94)^2 = x^2$	(plug in 94 from (C) for both leg lengths)
$17{,}672 = x^2$	(simplify)

$$132.94 \approx x \qquad \text{(take the square root of both sides)}$$
$$94 + 94 + 132.94 \approx 320.94 \qquad \text{(perimeter using value from (C))}$$

Using the value from (C), we get an approximate perimeter of 320.94, which isn't equal to our decimal approximation of the perimeter from the prompt. So (C) isn't right; let's check the remaining answer choice.

$$a^2 + b^2 = c^2 \qquad \text{(Pythagorean theorem)}$$
$$(94\sqrt{2})^2 + (94\sqrt{2})^2 = x^2 \qquad \text{(plug in } 94\sqrt{2} \text{ from (D) for both leg lengths)}$$
$$35{,}344 = x^2 \qquad \text{(simplify)}$$
$$188 = x \qquad \text{(take the square root of both sides)}$$
$$94\sqrt{2} + 94\sqrt{2} + 188 \approx 453.87 \qquad \text{(perimeter using value from (D))}$$

Using the value from (D), we get an approximate perimeter of 453.87, which isn't equal to our decimal approximation of the perimeter from the prompt. So (D) isn't right either. After checking each choice, we can see that (B) must be correct.

Solution 2: Test-smart: Use your knowledge of 45°: 45°: 90° triangles to test each side length and see which one results in a triangle with a perimeter of $94 + 94\sqrt{2}$ inches.

If we recognize that an isosceles right triangle is a 45°: 45°: 90° triangle, then we know that its sides are in the ratio $1 : 1 : \sqrt{2}$. Once we realize that, we can pretty quickly figure out the side lengths and perimeter of the triangle that would be produced with the side length from each answer choice.

(A) side ratio: $47 : 47 : 47\sqrt{2}$	perimeter: $47 + 47 + 47\sqrt{2} =$	$94 + 47\sqrt{2}$
(B) side ratio: $47\sqrt{2} : 47\sqrt{2} : 94$	perimeter: $47\sqrt{2} + 47\sqrt{2} + 94 =$	$94 + 94\sqrt{2}$
(C) side ratio: $94 : 94 : 94\sqrt{2}$	perimeter: $94 + 94 + 94\sqrt{2} =$	$188 + 94\sqrt{2}$
(D) side ratio: $94\sqrt{2} : 94\sqrt{2} : 188$	perimeter: $94\sqrt{2} + 94\sqrt{2} + 188 =$	$188 + 188\sqrt{2}$

We can see that choice (B) would produce a right isosceles triangle with the perimeter from the prompt, so (B) is correct.

Solution 3: Test-smart: Use your understanding of triangles and a decimal approximation of the perimeter from the prompt, as well as decimal approximations of the value of each answer choice, to eliminate each answer choice that can't satisfy the requirements in the prompt.

We can enter the perimeter provided in the prompt into our calculator to find a decimal approximation of that perimeter. The result is approximately 226.94.

If each side of the triangle were equal in length—that is, if this were an equilateral triangle—then we could find the approximate length of each side by dividing the 226.94 by 3. The result would be approximately 75.65.

That would be each side length if this were an *equilateral* triangle, which it isn't. Instead, it's an isosceles right triangle, and we have to find the length of one of the legs. In a right triangle, the hypotenuse must be the longest side, by definition, so the length of each leg must be shorter than the length of the hypotenuse, which means the length of each leg must be *less than* one third of the perimeter of the triangle. In this case, that means the length of each leg must be less than 75.65, which means we can eliminate any choice greater than 75.65.

That eliminates (C), and also (D), since (D) takes a value greater than 75.65 and multiplies it by a value greater than 1, which must produce a result greater than 75.65.

We can see that (A) is less than 75.65, and if we find a decimal approximation of (B), we find that it's approximately equal to 66.47, so that choice also meets the requirement we just figured out.

Let's think about the remaining choices, (A) and (B), in light of what we know about triangles. We know that the longest side of a triangle must be shorter than the sum of the other two sides, or else the two shorter sides can't meet to form a triangle.

If we know the perimeter of a right triangle, we can subtract the lengths of its two legs to find the length of the hypotenuse of that triangle. For choice (A), that would mean subtracting 47 twice (once for each leg) from 226.94, our decimal approximation of the triangle's perimeter from the prompt. The result is $226.94 - 47 - 47$, which is equal to 132.94.

So if each leg of the isosceles right triangle were 47 inches long, then the hypotenuse of that triangle would be approximately 132.94 inches long—but that's impossible, because 132.94 is more than the sum of the lengths of the other two legs (that sum is $47 + 47$, or 94), which means these dimensions would produce a "triangle" whose shorter legs are too far from each other to meet and actually form a triangle. That means (A) can't be right.

This leaves only (B); let's test (B) the same way we just tested (A) to make sure (B) would result in side lengths that could make up a triangle. Again, we start with our decimal approximation of the length of the perimeter, and subtract each leg length. Our decimal approximation for the leg length in (B) is 66.47, so that would be $226.94 - 66.47 - 66.47$, which is equal to 94.

So if each leg of the isosceles right triangle were 66.47 inches long, then the hypotenuse of that triangle would be approximately 94 inches long. That's not a problem, because 94 is less than the sum of the lengths of the two legs (which is approximately 132.94).

After considering each answer choice and applying some basic understanding of triangles, we were able to eliminate (A), (C), and (D), which leaves only (B), the right answer.

Test 3, Module 2, Question 26

- What's the prompt asking for? The value of c.
- Math concepts in the prompt: equations, constants, solutions
- Elements of the answer choices: Each answer choice is an integer ranging from -53 to 3.
- Notable features of the answer choices: Two choices are negative, one is positive, and one is zero. 3 appears in two choices and 5 appears in two choices.

- "Bridge" concepts: When the equation has only one solution, that means only one x-value will make the equation a valid statement.
- Things to look out for: Think carefully about what the prompt is asking for! Remember to try your graphing calculator if you're not sure how to proceed!

Solution 1: Concrete/graphing: Graph the provided equation, using y for c. Find the y-value that corresponds to exactly one x-value.

The prompt provides us with an equation involving the variable x and the constant c, then tells us that the given equation "has exactly one solution," and asks for the value of c.

This is the same as saying that we need to find the value of c for which only one x-value is a solution of the given equation. We can find this by graphing the given equation in our calculator, using y in place of c (remember that our calculator works best in terms of x and y, not c, but that we can change variables in SAT questions to x and y as long as we keep track of what they represent).

The result of the graph of $-9x^2 + 30x + y = 0$ appears below:

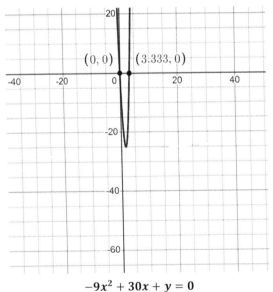

$$-9x^2 + 30x + y = 0$$

This graph shows us every solution at a given y-value for the equation $-9x^2 + 30x + y = 0$. In other words, when $y = 0$, there are two x-value solutions, which are $x = 0$ and $x = 3.333...$, because $(0, 0)$ and $(3.333..., 0)$ are both coordinate pairs that cause the left side of the equation to be equal to 0. Similarly, when $y = -53$, as we see in choice (D), there are no real solutions, because there is no point on the graph with a y-value of -53.

The only y-value with exactly one x-value solution is -25, the minimum point of the graph, because only one point on the line has a y-value of -25. In other words, when y (which we substituted for c in the given equation) is -25, there's only one x-value that's a solution to the given equation, just as the prompt requires. So -25 is the correct answer, and (C) is right.

If you're having trouble visualizing this, it may help to look at the graph of $-9x^2 + 30x + y = 0$ along with graphs of all the other c-values from the answer choices (remember that we're using y in place of c, so that would be the graphs of $y = 3$ from (A), $y = 0$ from (B), $y = -25$ from (C), and $y = -53$ from (D)).

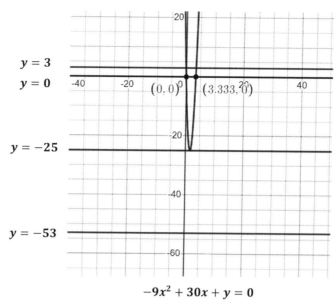

$$-9x^2 + 30x + y = 0$$

We can see that $y = 3$ crosses the graph of the provided equation at two points, which means there are two x-value solutions on that graph when $y = 3$, so (A) can't be right. The same is true of $y = 0$ from (B)—it crosses the graph of the provided equation in two places, so the equation has two solutions when $y = 0$. The line $y = -25$ from (C) only touches the graph of the provided equation at one point, though—that means when $y = -25$, only one x-value is a solution to the provided equation, just as the prompt requires. Finally, the graph of $y = -53$ from (D) doesn't touch the graph of the provided equation at all, so there are no x-values that are solutions when $y = -53$.

Again, we can see that (C) must be correct.

ANSWER CHOICE ANALYSIS

(A): When $c = 3$, the equation has two solutions. **(B):** When $c = 0$, the equation has two solutions. **(D):** When $c = -53$, the equation has zero solutions.

How to check? Try to figure out which mistakes could lead to some of the wrong answer choices, and verify that you haven't made any such mistakes.

Test 3, Module 2, Question 27

- What's the prompt asking for? The value of p.
- Math concepts in the prompt: equations, fractions, variables, polynomials

- "Bridge" concepts: If a linear system of equations has no solution, that means the lines in that equation are parallel—that is, their slopes are the same.
- Things to look out for: Don't make a simple mistake related to algebra, sign, or fractions!

Solution 1: Algebra: Find the slopes of the given lines, set them equal to one another, and solve for p.

When a system of linear equations has no solution, that means the two lines are parallel. One way to compare the slopes of two lines is to put them in slope-intercept form, which is the same $y = mx + b$ form. Let's do that with the provided equations and see what happens.

$$\frac{3}{2}y - \frac{1}{4}x = \frac{2}{3} - \frac{3}{2}y \qquad \text{(first equation)}$$

$$3y - \frac{1}{4}x = \frac{2}{3} \qquad \text{(add } \tfrac{3}{2}y \text{ to both sides)}$$

$$3y = \frac{1}{4}x + \frac{2}{3} \qquad \text{(add } \tfrac{1}{4}x \text{ to both sides)}$$

$$y = \frac{1}{12}x + \frac{2}{9} \qquad \text{(divide both sides by 3)}$$

In $y = mx + b$ form, the slope of the line is the coefficient of x. In this case, the coefficient of x is $\frac{1}{12}$, so the slope of the first line is $\frac{1}{12}$. Let's put the second line in slope-intercept form and see what the value p would have to be for that line to have the same slope as the first line.

$$\frac{1}{2}x + \frac{3}{2} = py + \frac{9}{2} \qquad \text{(second equation)}$$

$$\frac{1}{2}x - 3 = py \qquad \text{(subtract } \frac{9}{2} \text{ from both sides)}$$

$$py = \frac{1}{2}x - 3 \qquad \text{(switch sides for clarity)}$$

$$y = \frac{1}{2p}x - \frac{3}{p} \qquad \text{(divide both sides by } p\text{)}$$

Again, the slope of this line is the coefficient of x, so the slope of the second line is $\frac{1}{2p}$. In order for the lines to be parallel, their slopes must be equal, so let's set the slopes of the two lines equal to each other, and solve for p.

$$\frac{1}{12} = \frac{1}{2p} \qquad \text{(slope of the first line set equal to the slope of the second line)}$$

$$2p = 12 \qquad \text{(cross-multiply)}$$

$$p = 6 \qquad \text{(divide both sides by 2)}$$

So the two lines have the same slope when $p = 6$, which means they're parallel when $p = 6$, and therefore have no solution, as the prompt requires. So the answer is 6.

How to check? Verify that you marked down the value of p, and not the slope of the lines. Try to figure out which mistakes the College Board might hope you would make in finding your solution, and verify that you haven't made any such mistakes.

TEST 4 - MODULE 1

Test 4, Module 1, Question 1

- What's the prompt asking for? The number of students that chose activity 3.
- Math concepts in the prompt: reading bar graphs
- Elements of the answer choices: Each answer choice is a two-digit integer ranging from 25 to 50.
- Notable features of the answer choices: (A) is half of (D).

- "Bridge" concepts: We can read the answer off the graph.
- Pre-solution patterns (see p. 285): halves and doubles
- Things to look out for: Make sure you understand the prompt and read the right part of the graph to find the answer!

Solution 1: Concrete: Read the graph to find the number of students who chose activity 3.

The vertical axis is labeled "Number of students," and there are horizontal lines extending off that axis labeled with the numbers 5, 10, 15, and so on. The horizontal axis is labeled "Activity," and we can see that the activity columns are labeled 1, 2, 3, 4, and 5.

The activity column labeled "3" extends upward, just short of the horizontal line labeled "40." So the number of students who chose activity 3 must be slightly less than 40. The only answer choice between 30 and 40 is (B), so (B) must be correct.

ANSWER CHOICE ANALYSIS

(C): This is a little less than 50, but the right answer is a little less than 40. (D): This is the highest value in the graph.

How to check? Try to figure out which mistakes could lead to some of the wrong answer choices, and verify that you haven't made any such mistakes.

Test 4, Module 1, Question 2

- What's the prompt asking for? What percentage 75 is of 300.
- Math concepts in the prompt: percentages
- Elements of the answer choices: Each answer choice is a percentage and a multiple of 25.
- Notable features of the answer choices: (A), (B), and (C) form a series where each choice is 25 more than the previous choice. (A), (C), and (D) form a series

where each choice is 3 times as much as the previous choice.
- "Bridge" concepts: 300 multiplied by the right answer will be 75.
- Pre-solution patterns (see p. 285): first and last terms in a series are often wrong answers
- Things to look out for: Don't get confused about what percentage you're finding of what number!

Solution 1: Concrete: Multiply 300 by each percentage in the answer choices to find which one produces a result of 75.

(A) $300 \times 25\% = 300 \times 0.25 = 75$

(B) $300 \times 50\% = 300 \times 0.50 = 150$

(C) $300 \times 75\% = 300 \times 0.75 = 225$

(D) $300 \times 225\% = 300 \times 2.25 = 675$

Only (A) produced a result of 75, so (A) is correct.

Solution 2: Algebra: Calculate the percentage of 300 represented by 75.

We can answer this question by setting up the following proportion:

$$\frac{75}{300} = \frac{x}{100}$$ (proportion showing 75 relates to 300 as x relates to 100)

$$7{,}500 = 300x$$ (cross multiply)

$$25 = x$$ (divide both sides by 300)

So $\frac{75}{300}$ is equal to $\frac{25}{100}$, which means 75 is 25% of 300. So (A) is right.

Solution 3: Test-smart: Think about the properties the right answer must have, and pick the only choice that meets the requirements you come up with.

50% of 300 is 150. 75 is less than 150, so the answer must be less than 50%. Only (A) meets this requirement, and (A) is correct.

ANSWER CHOICE ANALYSIS

(C): 75 is 75% of 100, not 300. **(D):** If we ignore the percent sign, this is $300 - 75$, and also 75% of 300.

How to check? Reread the prompt and verify that you found the right percentage of the right number. Try an alternate approach above. Try to figure out which mistakes could lead to some of the wrong answer choices, and verify that you haven't made any such mistakes.

▶   Post-solution patterns (see page 286):   the right answer to the wrong question

---

Test 4, Module 1, Question 3

- What's the prompt asking for? A solution to the given equation.

- Math concepts in the prompt: exponents, fractions, equations

- Elements of the answer choices: Each answer choice is an even integer ranging from 6 to 900.

- Notable features of the answer choices: Three answer choices end with a zero. (C) is half of (D).

- "Bridge" concepts: We can solve for x to find the answer.

- Pre-solution patterns (see p. 285): halves and doubles

- Things to look out for: Don't make a simple algebra mistake!

Solution 1: Concrete: We can plug each value in for x to see which choice results in a valid equation.

(A) $\dfrac{6^2}{25} = 36$ $\dfrac{36}{25} = 36$ $36 \neq 900$

(B) $\dfrac{30^2}{25} = 36$ $\dfrac{900}{25} = 36$ $900 = 900$

(C) $\dfrac{450^2}{25} = 36$ $\dfrac{202{,}500}{25} = 36$ $202{,}500 \neq 900$

(D) $\dfrac{900^2}{25} = 36$ $\dfrac{810{,}000}{25} = 36$ $810{,}000 \neq 900$

Only (B) produces a valid equation, so (B) is correct.

Solution 2: Concrete/graphing: We can enter the equation directly into our graphing calculator to find the answer.

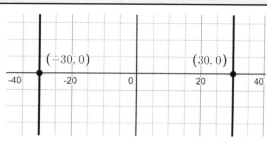

$$\frac{x^2}{25} = 36$$

We can see that there's a vertical line at $x = -30$ and $x = 30$. Only 30 appears in the answer choices, so (B) is correct.

Solution 3: Algebra: Solve the provided equation for x.

$$\frac{x^2}{25} = 36 \qquad \text{(provided equation)}$$
$$x^2 = 900 \qquad \text{(multiply both sides by 25)}$$
$$x = \pm 30 \qquad \text{(take the square root of both sides)}$$

So $x = 30$ or $x = -30$. That means (B) is correct.

ANSWER CHOICE ANALYSIS

(A): This would be the answer if the provided equation were $x^2 = 36$, instead of $\frac{x^2}{25} = 36$. **(D):** This is the value of x^2, not x. This would be the answer if the provided equation were $\frac{x}{25} = 36$, instead of $\frac{x^2}{25} = 36$.

How to check? Plug your answer into the provided function and verify that it results in a true statement. Try an alternate approach above. Try to figure out which mistakes could lead to some of the wrong answer choices, and verify that you haven't made any such mistakes.

▶ Post-solution patterns (see page 286): the right answer to the wrong question

Test 4, Module 1, Question 4

- **What's the prompt asking for?** The equation that represents the situation described in the prompt.
- **Math concepts in the prompt:** multiplication, addition, variables, equations
- **Elements of the answer choices:** Each answer choice is an equation involving 8, 3, and x.

- **Notable features of the answer choices:** (A), (C), and (D) are set equal to 83. Two choices include $8x$.
- **Pre-solution patterns (see p. 285):** wrong answers try to imitate right answers
- **Things to look out for:** Read the prompt carefully and make sure your answer accurately reflects the ideas in the prompt!

Solution 1: Careful reading: Analyze the answer choices and eliminate each one that doesn't accurately reflect the ideas in the prompt.

(A) would multiply 8 and x by 3, but the phrase "3 more than" from the prompt describes *adding* 3 to something, not multiplying anything by 3. So (A) can't be right.

(B) would set the equation equal to $8x$, not "equal to 83," as the prompt requires, and would express the idea of 3 being added to 83, not 3 being added to "8 times a number x," as the phrase "3 more than 8 times a number x" requires. So (B) is wrong.

(C) would multiply x by 3 and add 8 to the result, instead of "multiplying 8 times a number x" and then finding "3 more than" that, as the prompt requires.

(D) includes "8 times a number x," which is $8x$, and adds 3 to that value, as "3 more than" requires, and then sets that "equal to 83," again, as the prompt says. This choice is exactly what the prompt says, so (D) is correct.

Solution 2: Careful reading: Convert the phrases in the prompt into an equation

Let's start with the sentence from the prompt, and turn it into an equation.

$$\text{3 more than 8 times a number } x \text{ is equal to 83}$$

We can start by changing "is equal to 83" into "= 83."

$$\text{3 more than 8 times a number } x = 83$$

Now let's change "8 times a number x" into "$8x$."

$$\text{3 more than } 8x = 83$$

"3 more than" is the same as adding 3 to something, so let's add 3 to $8x$.

$$8x + 3 = 83$$

This is equal to (D), and (D) is the right answer.

ANSWER CHOICE ANALYSIS

(A): This would be 3 *times* 8 times a number being equal to 83, not 3 *more than* 8 times a number. **(B):** This choice would be the right answer, except the "+3" is on the wrong side of the equals sign. **(C):** This would be *8* more than *3* times a number being equal to 83, not *3* more than *8* times a number.

How to check? Try an alternate approach above. Try to figure out which mistakes could lead to some of the wrong answer choices, and verify that you haven't made any such mistakes.

- What's the prompt asking for? The best interpretation of 25 in the context of the prompt.
- Math concepts in the prompt: functions, word problems, money
- Elements of the answer choices: Each answer choice is a sentence about the situation in the prompt involving the number 25.
- Notable features of the answer choices: Three choices mention 25 as an amount of money, and one mentions 25 as a number of deposits.

- "Bridge" concepts: The right answer will make a true statement about the number 25 in the situation described in the prompt.
- Pre-solution patterns (see p. 285): wrong answers try to imitate right answers
- Things to look out for: Remember to read both the prompt and each answer choice very carefully! Don't pick an answer choice that includes an idea that doesn't appear in the prompt!

Solution 1: Concrete/graphing: We can graph the provided equation and use what we learn to work toward the solution.

Let's graph the provided function.

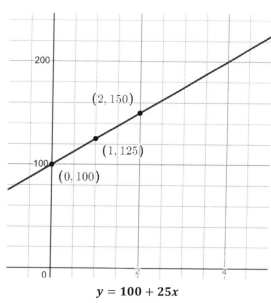

$$y = 100 + 25x$$

If the statement in (A) were true, then every time t increases by 1—that is, each time Hana makes a monthly deposit—the value of the function would increase by 25. We can check the graph to see that this is true: each time t increases by 1, $f(t)$ increases by \$25. So (A) appears to be correct.

"Before any monthly deposits" from (B) would mean at the point when Hana has made 0 monthly deposits—that is, when $t = 0$. But we can see on the graph that when $t = 0$, the value of the function is \$100, not \$25—so (B) must be wrong.

"After 1 monthly deposit" from (C) must be when $t = 1$ (remember that the prompt tells us that the function represents how much money is in Hana's bank account "after t monthly deposits"). We can see on the graph that when $t = 1$, the value of the function is \$125, not \$25. So (C) is wrong.

There's nothing in the prompt or on the graph to suggest that Hana made "a total of 25 monthly deposits," or any other specific number of deposits, as (D) would require. So (D) must be wrong.

After considering each answer choice, we can see that only (A) can be correct.

Solution 2: Abstract: Analyze the prompt and the provided function to figure out what 25 must represent.

The number 25 in the function is multiplied by t. The prompt tells us that the function gives the amount of money in Hana's bank account "after t monthly deposits." In other words, if Hana has made 6 monthly deposits, then t would have to be 6, if Hana made 100 monthly deposits, then t would have to be 100, and so on.

So we multiply 25 by the number of monthly deposits Hana makes. That means each time she makes a monthly deposit, the value of the function (which the prompt tells us is "the amount, in dollars" in the bank account) must increase by 25. That's what choice (A) says, so (A) must be correct.

ANSWER CHOICE ANALYSIS

(B): Before making any deposits, Hana had \$100 in her bank account, not \$25. **(C):** After 1 monthly deposit, Hana had \$125 in her bank account, not \$25. **(D):** The prompt doesn't tell us anything about the total number of monthly deposits Hana made.

How to check? Try an alternate approach above. Try to figure out which mistakes could lead to some of the wrong answer choices, and verify that you haven't made any such mistakes.

Test 4, Module 1, Question 6

- What's the prompt asking for? The number of pounds of oranges the customer purchased.

- Math concepts in the prompt: word problems, money, multiplication

- "Bridge" concepts: We can use the total amount of money spent and the cost per pound of oranges to determine how many oranges the customer bought.

- Things to look out for: Don't make a simple algebra mistake!

Solution 1: Algebra: Divide the total cost by the price per pound to find the number of pounds of oranges purchased.

The prompt says oranges are $3 per pound. In other words, for every $3 a customer has, that person can buy one pound of oranges. We can answer this question by finding out how many times $3 goes into $27.

$$\frac{\$27}{\$3} = 9$$

So $3 goes into $27 9 times, which means you can buy 9 pounds of oranges for $27 when they cost $3 per pound. The answer is 9.

How to check? Try to figure out which mistakes the College Board might hope you would make in finding your solution, and verify that you haven't made any such mistakes.

Test 4, Module 1, Question 7

- What's the prompt asking for? The original price for 1 storage bin.

- Math concepts in the prompt: word problems, money, discounts

- "Bridge" concepts: We can use the amount of the discount to find the price for the entire purchase, and then use the price for the entire purchase to find the cost of 1 storage bin.

- Things to look out for: Think carefully about how to calculate the original price for the entire purchase! Don't make a simple algebra mistake!

Solution 1: Concrete: Find the total price before the discount, and then divide that total price by 9 to find the cost of each bin.

The prompt asks for "the original price" of 1 storage bin. Let's start by finding the original price of all 9 storage bins.

We're told Nasir spent $27 on 9 bins after a using a coupon, and that the coupon saved $63 off the entire purchase. If Nasir spent $27 after saving $63, then the original price without the coupon would have to be $27 + $63, which is equal to $90.

So the original price for 9 storage bins was $90. That means the price for one of those storage bins must be $\frac{1}{9}$ of that amount, or $\frac{\$90}{9}$, which is $10. The answer is 10.

How to check? Verify that you found the original price for one bin, not all 9 bins. Try to figure out which mistakes the College Board might hope you would make in finding your solution, and verify that you haven't made any such mistakes.

Test 4, Module 1, Question 8

- What's the prompt asking for? The equation that defines $f(x)$.

- Math concepts in the prompt: linear functions, tables of values, inputs and outputs

- Elements of the answer choices: Each answer choice is a function involving x, 3, 29, 32, and/or 35.

- Notable features of the answer choices: (A) has a single-digit coefficient of x, while the other answer choices have a 2-digit coefficient of x. (A) and (C) both end in 29.

- "Bridge" concepts: The function in the correct answer will be the only one that produces the inputs and outputs in the data table.

- Pre-solution patterns (see p. 285): wrong answers try to imitate right answers

- Things to look out for: Don't make a simple algebra mistake!

Solution 1: Concrete: Test the provided inputs from the table in the functions from the answer choices, and eliminate any choice that doesn't produce the corresponding output from the table.

Let's plug $x = 0$ into each answer choice, and we can eliminate each choice where $f(0)$ isn't equal to 29.

(A) $f(0) = 3(0) + 29 = 29$
(B) $f(0) = 29(0) + 32 = 32$
(C) $f(0) = 35(0) + 29 = 29$

(D) $f(0) = 32(0) + 35 = 35$

We can eliminate (B) and (D), because their $f(0)$ values weren't 29. Now let's find $f(1)$ for the remaining two choices, (A) and (C). Remember that, according to the provided table, $f(1)$ should be 32.

(A) $f(1) = 3(1) + 29 = 32$

(C) $f(1) = 35(1) + 29 = 64$

Only (A) has an $f(1)$ value equal to 32, so (A) is correct.

Solution 2: Concrete/graphing: We can graph the functions from the answer choices along with the provided coordinates from the table, and then eliminate any function whose graph doesn't travel through those three points.

(A)

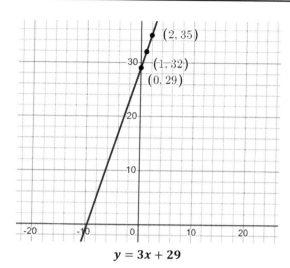

$$y = 3x + 29$$

(B)

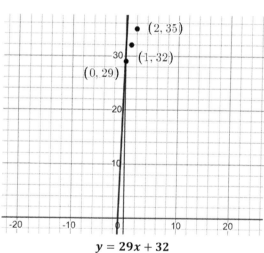

$$y = 29x + 32$$

(C)

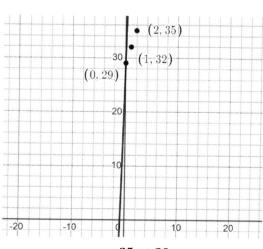

$$y = 35x + 29$$

(D)

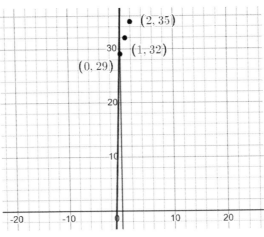

$$y = 32x + 35$$

We can see that only the graph for choice (A) travels through the three provided points, so (A) is correct.

Solution 3: Test-smart: Notice in the table how much $f(x)$ increases when x increases by one, and use that information to evaluate the answer choices.

If we notice that each time x increases by 1, $f(x)$ increases by 3, then we know that the correct equation must involve adding $3x$, because adding $3x$ means each time x goes up by one, the function must increase by 3×1, or 3 (this is the same as saying the slope of the function must be 3).

Only (A) involves adding $3x$, so (A) must be correct.

ANSWER CHOICE ANALYSIS

(C): The graph of this choice includes the point $(0,29)$, but none of the other points from the table.

How to check? Try an alternate approach above. Try to figure out which mistakes could lead to some of the wrong answer choices, and verify that you haven't made any such mistakes.

Test 4, Module 1, Question 9

- What's the prompt asking for? The measure of angle S.
- Math concepts in the prompt: right triangles, similar triangles, corresponding angles, angle measures
- Elements of the answer choices: Each answer choice is an even angle measure ranging from 18° to 162°.
- Notable features of the answer choices: The sum of (A) and (B) is 90°. The sum of (A) and (D) is 180°. (B) is 4 times as much as (A).

- "Bridge" concepts: We can use the measures of angle Q to find the measure of angle T, and then use that information (along with the measure of right angle U) to answer the question.
- Pre-solution patterns (see p. 285): opposites
- Things to look out for: Don't get confused about which angles correspond to one another! Don't get confused about which angle measure you need to find!

Solution 1: Geometry: Label the triangles with the information from the prompt. Use that information to find the measure of angle T, and then use that information to find the measure of angle S.

Let's start by drawing these two triangles, filling in the information we know from the prompt. Since the prompt tells us that the measure of angle Q is 18°, we know that the measure of corresponding angle T must also be 18°, so we'll add both of those measures to our diagram.

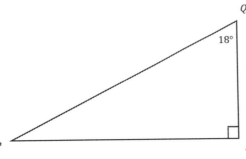
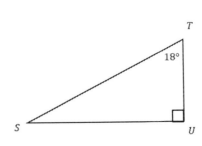

At this point, we may realize that we know two of the three angle measures of right triangle STU. Because this is a right triangle, we know the largest angle is 90°, and we also know that angle T is 18°. We know that the sum of the angle measures of any triangle must be 180°, so we can find the measure of the remaining angle by subtracting the two angle measures we know from 180°. The result is $180° - 90° - 18° = 72°$. So the remaining angle measure, which is the measure of angle S, is 72°. That means the answer is (B).

ANSWER CHOICE ANALYSIS

(A): This is the measure of angle Q, and also the measure of angle T. **(C):** This is the result if we accidentally think angles P and Q (or angles S and T) should add up to 100° instead of 90°, or we make a simple calculation error subtracting 18° and 90° from 180°. **(D):** This is the sum of the measures of angles P and R, and also the sum of the measures of angles S and U.

How to check? Verify that you found the measure of the correct angle, and that the sum of the three angle measures you found for the triangle is 180°. Try to figure out which mistakes could lead to some of the wrong answer choices, and verify that you haven't made any such mistakes.

▶ Post-solution patterns (see page 286): right approach, wrong step; the right answer to the wrong question

Test 4, Module 1, Question 10

- What's the prompt asking for? The equation that's the most appropriate linear model for the data shown.

- Math concepts in the prompt: scatterplots, variables, equations, linear models

- Elements of the answer choices: Each choice is an equation for a line involving x, positive or negative 0.9, and positive or negative 9.4.

- Notable features of the answer choices: Two answer choices start with 0.9, and two start with 9.4. Two include a plus sign, and two include a minus sign. 2 end with $9.4x$, and two end with $0.9x$

- "Bridge" concepts: The graph of the correct answer would be a line that goes more or less through the dots in the provided scatterplot.

- Pre-solution patterns (see p. 285): wrong answers try to imitate right answers

- Things to look out for: Don't mix up which value in the equations corresponds to slope, and which corresponds to the y-intercept! Don't get confused about what positive versus negative slope looks like on a graph! Don't get confused about what a positive versus negative y-intercept looks like on a graph!

Solution 1: Concrete/graphing: We can graph the equations from the answer choices and pick the one that would travel through the data in the scatterplot.

(A)

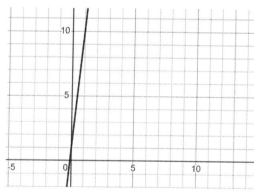

$$y = 0.9 + 9.4x$$

(B)

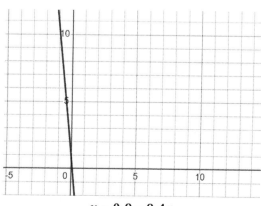

$$y = 0.9 - 9.4x$$

(C)

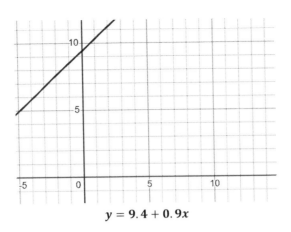

$$y = 9.4 + 0.9x$$

(D)

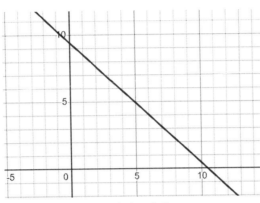

$$y = 9.4 - 0.9x$$

Only choice (D) results in a line that would travel through data shown, so (D) must be correct.

Solution 2: Abstract: Think about the slope and y-intercept that the answer must have, based on our understanding of slope-intercept form and the provided figure. Pick the answer choice that meets these requirements.

If we're familiar with slope-intercept form, which looks like $y = mx + b$, then we can see that each of these choices is basically in that form—the only difference is that mx and b are reversed. We can still see that the coefficient of x is the slope, and the constant that isn't multiplied by anything is the y-intercept.

A line through the data in the provided graph would have a y-intercept of around 10—that is, it would cross the y-axis near $y = 10$. Choices (A) and (B) have y-intercepts of 0.9, while (C) and (D) have y-intercepts of 9.4. So we can eliminate (A) and (B), because their y-intercepts wouldn't be close to 10.

The difference between (C) and (D) is that (C) has a slope of 0.9, while (D) has a slope of -0.9. We can see that a line through the data in the graph would have a negative slope, because those points trend downward from left to right. So we can eliminate (C), which leaves the right answer, (D).

ANSWER CHOICE ANALYSIS

(B): This is the same as the right answer, but with the values for slope and y-intercept switched. **(C):** This choice is the same as the right answer, but with a positive slope instead of a negative one.

How to check? Verify that the answer you picked has a negative slope and a positive y-intercept. Try an alternate approach above. Try to figure out which mistakes could lead to some of the wrong answer choices, and verify that you haven't made any such mistakes.

Test 4, Module 1, Question 11

- What's the prompt asking for? The number of birds the business can care for on a day when it cares for 16 reptiles.

- Math concepts in the prompt: word problems, equation models

- Elements of the answer choices: Each answer choice is an integer ranging from 0 to 80.

- Notable features of the answer choices: (A), (C), and (D) form a series in which each choice is 40 more than the previous choice. (C) is half of (D).

- "Bridge" concepts: We can plug in $r = 16$ and then solve for b to answer the question.

- Pre-solution patterns (see p. 285): halves and doubles; first and last terms in a series are often wrong answers

- Things to look out for: Don't get b and r mixed up! Don't make a simple algebra mistake!

Solution 1: Algebra: Use the provided r-value to solve for b.

We can plug in the provided r-value of 16 and then solve for b to find the number of birds the business can care for on a day that it cares for 16 reptiles.

$2.5b + 5r = 80$	(provided formula)
$2.5b + 5(16) = 80$	(plug in $r = 16$)
$2.5b + 80 = 80$	(simplify)
$2.5b = 0$	(subtract 80 from both sides)
$b = 0$	(divide both sides by 2.5)

So on a day the business can care for 16 reptiles, it can care for 0 birds. That means (A) is correct.

ANSWER CHOICE ANALYSIS

(B): This is the number we needed to multiply r by as part of our solution, but it's not the answer to the question. **(D):** This number appears in the provided equation, but it's not the answer to the question.

How to check? Plug in the value you found along with $r = 16$ to make sure the equation makes a valid statement. Try to figure out which mistakes could lead to some of the wrong answer choices, and verify that you haven't made any such mistakes.

Test 4, Module 1, Question 12

- What's the prompt asking for? The equation of the graph shown.
- Math concepts in the prompt: linear equations, line graphs
- Elements of the answer choices: Each answer choice is the equation of a line in slope-intercept form.
- Notable features of the answer choices: Each equation ends with "−8." The only difference between the equations is whether they feature positive or negative x, or positive or negative $2x$.
- Pre-solution patterns (see p. 285): halves and doubles; opposites
- Things to look out for: Don't make a simple mistake related to sign! Remember what the equation of a line in slope-intercept form tells us about the slope and y-intercept of the line!

Solution 1: Concrete/graphing: We can graph the equations from the answer choices to see which one matches the provided graph.

(A)

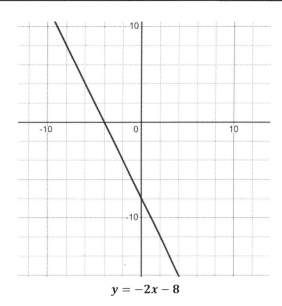

$$y = -2x - 8$$

(B)

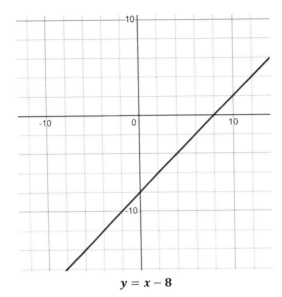

$$y = x - 8$$

(C)

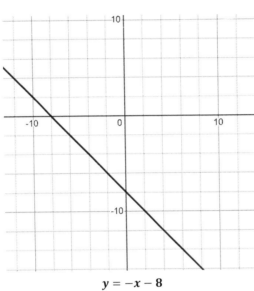

$$y = -x - 8$$

(D)

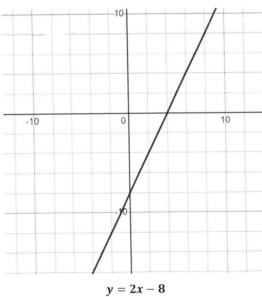

$$y = 2x - 8$$

When we graph each choice, we can see that (C) matches the provided graph. So (C) is correct.

Solution 2: Abstract: We can analyze the provided graph and use what we know about slope-intercept form to determine which choice must be correct.

Each answer choice is in slope-intercept form—that is, each choice is in $y = mx + b$ form, where m is the slope of the line and b is the y-intercept of the line. With this in mind, we can see that each choice has the same y-intercept of -8. So we know the right answer must have a y-intercept of -8, and we can focus on the slope of the line.

The provided graph has a negative slope, so we can eliminate any choice with a positive slope. That means we can eliminate (B) and (D), leaving only (A) and (C).

The difference between (A) and (C) is that (A) involves $-2x$, which means it has a slope of -2, and (C) involves $-x$, which means it has a slope of -1.

We can see that the provided graph passes through $(-8, 0)$ and $(0, -8)$. That means it travels 8 units to the right, and 8 units down. The slope of a line is the same as its "rise" (number of units traveled up or down) over its "run" (number of units traveled to the right). In this case, that's $\frac{-8}{8}$, which is the same as -1. So (C) is correct.

ANSWER CHOICE ANALYSIS

(A): This choice is similar to the right answer, but with a slope of -2. We can see that the line in the graph travels one unit down for every one unit to the right, so the slope must be -1, not -2. **(B):** This choice is similar to the right answer, but with a slope of 1, rather than -1. We can see that the line travels down moving from left to right, which means its slope must be negative. **(D):** This choice combines the problems from (A) and (B).

How to check? Use the provided graph to verify that the answer you picked has the correct slope. Try an alternate approach above. Try to figure out which mistakes could lead to some of the wrong answer choices, and verify that you haven't made any such mistakes.

Note The provided graph might trip up some test-takers for two main reasons. First, the lines are labeled in multiples of 2—that is, 2, 4, 6, 8, etc. instead of 1, 2, 3, 4, etc. So some untrained test-takers might think of the line moving down 2 units and then right 2 units as $-\frac{2}{2}$, and then they might mistakenly reduce that to -2, instead of -1! Second, the scale is a little different horizontally from what it is vertically—even though each line represents 2 units in both directions, the graph is stretched a bit horizontally. This might make it harder to notice right away that the slope is -1; the line looks a little flatter than a typical line with a slope of -1, which might throw off some test-takers. In either case, though, we can avoid a mistake by just remembering to read very carefully, and to be on the lookout for these small errors. Very often on SAT Math questions, it's little, avoidable issues like these—and not a lack of familiarity with advanced, complex math concepts—that stop untrained test-takers from reaching their potential.

Test 4, Module 1, Question 13

- What's the prompt asking for? The value of $\frac{8}{x}$.
- Math concepts in the prompt: equations, fractions, variables

- "Bridge" concepts: We can manipulate the provided expression to find the answer.
- Things to look out for: Don't make a simple algebra mistake! Remember that prompt asks for $\frac{8}{x}$, not x!

Solution 1: Algebra: Solve for x, then use that expression to find the value of $\frac{8}{x}$.

We can solve for x, and then use that value to find the value of $\frac{8}{x}$.

$$\frac{x}{8} = 5 \qquad \text{(provided equation)}$$

$$x = 40 \qquad \text{(multiply both sides by 8)}$$

Now let's plug $x = 40$ into $\frac{8}{x}$.

$$\frac{8}{x} \qquad \text{(value we're asked to find)}$$

$$\frac{8}{40} \qquad \text{(plug in } x = 40\text{)}$$

$$\frac{1}{5} \qquad \text{(simplify)}$$

So the answer is $\frac{1}{5}$, which we can also enter as 0.2.

Solution 2: Test-smart: Notice that we're already given the reciprocal of the value we need to find, and use that information to answer the question.

We're told $\frac{x}{8}$ is equal to 5. $\frac{8}{x}$ is the reciprocal of $\frac{x}{8}$, so $\frac{8}{x}$ must be equal to the reciprocal of 5, which is $\frac{1}{5}$. So the answer is $\frac{1}{5}$ (or 0.2).

How to check? Verify that your answer is the value of $\frac{8}{x}$, *not* x! Try to figure out which mistakes the College Board might hope you would make in finding your solution, and verify that you haven't made any such mistakes.

Note Some test-takers will be on auto-pilot, and they'll just find the value of x—then they'll mark down 40, and get the question wrong! It's easy on the SAT Math section to know all the relevant math and *still* get the question wrong because you didn't read carefully enough, or you forgot some detail of the question. Keep this in mind on test day!

Test 4, Module 1, Question 14

- What's the prompt asking for? The value of y.
- Math concepts in the prompt: system of equations, variables

- "Bridge" concepts: We can find the solution to the given system of equations, and use that information to answer the question.
- Things to look out for: Don't make a simple mistake related to algebra or sign!

Solution 1: Concrete/graphing: We can graph these two equations to find their point of intersection.

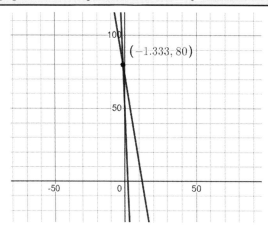

$$24x + y = 48 \text{ and } 6x + y = 72$$

These graphs intersect at $(-\frac{4}{3}, 80)$ The prompt asks for the value of y from that solution, so the answer is 80.

Solution 2: Algebra: Use one equation to find the value of x in terms of y, then use the result to solve for y in the other equation.

We can solve for x in one equation, then plug that value into the other equation and solve for y. Let's start with the second equation, for no particular reason.

$6x + y = 72$	(second equation)
$6x = 72 - y$	(subtract y from both sides)
$x = 12 - \frac{y}{6}$	(divide both sides by 6)

Now we have a value for x. Let's plug that value into the first equation to solve for y.

$24x + y = 48$	(first equation)
$24(12 - \frac{y}{6}) + y = 48$	(plug in $x = 12 - \frac{y}{6}$)
$288 - 4y + y = 48$	(distribute the 24)
$288 - 3y = 48$	(combine like terms)
$288 = 48 + 3y$	(add $3y$ to both sides)
$240 = 3y$	(subtract 48 from both sides)
$80 = y$	(divide both sides by 3)

So in the solution to the given system of equations, $y = 80$. That means the answer is 80.

Solution 3: Algebra: Add the equations to find the value of y directly.

We might notice that if we multiply the second equation by 4, the x-terms of the two equations will be the same. Then, we can subtract the second equation from the first one to get rid of the x-term, and be left with an equation in terms of y, which we can quickly solve for y to answer the question.

If we multiply that second equation by 4, the result is $24x + 4y = 288$. When we subtract that equation from the first equation, we get this:

$$24x + y = 48$$
$$- \underline{(24x + 4y = 288)}$$
$$-3y = -240$$

So we end up with $-3y = -240$, and when we divide both sides by -3, we get $y = 80$. Again, we can see that the answer is 80.

How to check? Try an alternate approach above. Try to figure out which mistakes the College Board might hope you would make in finding your solution, and verify that you haven't made any such mistakes.

Test 4, Module 1, Question 15

- **What's the prompt asking for?** The equation that defines line t.

- **Math concepts in the prompt:** lines, slope, equations, points in the xy-plane

- **Elements of the answer choices:** Each answer choice is the equation of a line in $y = mx + b$ format.

- **Notable features of the answer choices:** Two answer choice include $-\frac{x}{3}$, while one includes $13x$ and another includes $9x$. Two answer choices end with $+10$, while one ends with $+13$ and another ends with $-\frac{1}{3}$.

- **"Bridge" concepts:** We can use the information in the prompt to figure out which equation describes line t.

- **Pre-solution patterns (see p. 285):** wrong answers try to imitate right answers

- **Things to look out for:** Don't make a simple mistake related to algebra or sign! Don't mistakenly think that the point mentioned in the prompt is the y-intercept of the line!

Solution 1: Graphing: We can graph each choice and eliminate each one that doesn't have a slope of $-\frac{1}{3}$ or pass through $(9, 10)$.

(A)

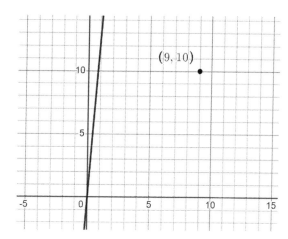

$$y = 13x - \frac{1}{3}$$

(B)

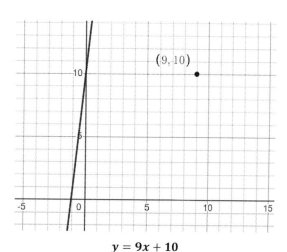

$$y = 9x + 10$$

(C)

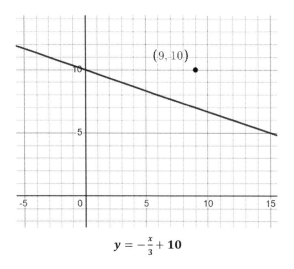

$$y = -\frac{x}{3} + 10$$

(D)

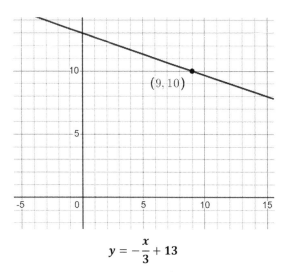

$$y = -\frac{x}{3} + 13$$

After graphing each choice, we can see that only (C) has a slope of $-\frac{1}{3}$ and passes through the point $(9, 10)$. So (D) must be correct.

Solution 2: Careful reading: Analyze the answer choices and eliminate every choice that doesn't meet the requirements of the prompt.

We can see that each answer choice is in slope-intercept format, which means the slope of the line represented by each equation is the coefficient of x. With that in mind, we can quickly determine the slope of each line from the answer choices. The slope of the line from (A) will be 13, the slope of the line from (B) will be 9, and the slopes of the lines from (C) and (D) will both be $-\frac{1}{3}$. So we can eliminate (A) and (B), since they don't have a slope of $-\frac{1}{3}$ as the prompt requires, which leaves us with (C) and (D).

From here, we can see that (C) must be wrong and (D) must be right in a couple of different ways. One way is to notice that (C) has a y-intercept at $(0, 10)$. The only way that a straight line like the one from (C) can pass through the point $(0, 10)$ and $(9, 10)$ (as the prompt requires) is if the line is perfectly horizontal, but we can see that (C) has a slope of $-\frac{1}{3}$, which means the line isn't horizontal. So (C) can't pass through $(9, 10)$ *and* $(0, 10)$, which means it must be wrong.

Another way is to plug $(9, 10)$ into each equation to see which produces a true statement.

(C) $y = -\frac{x}{3} + 10$ $(10) = -\frac{(9)}{3} + 10$ $10 \neq 7$

(D) $y = -\frac{x}{3} + 13$ $(10) = -\frac{(9)}{3} + 13$ $10 = 10$

The equation from (D) produces a true statement when $x = 9$ and $y = 10$, while (C) doesn't—so again, (D) is correct.

ANSWER CHOICE ANALYSIS

(A): This choice is the right answer with the numerical value of the slope and y-intercept switched. **(B):** This choice might be tempting for a test-taker who misunderstands what it means that the line travels through the point $(9,10)$. **(C):** This choice has the right slope, but it doesn't pass through $(9, 10)$.

How to check? Try an alternate approach above. Try to figure out which mistakes could lead to some of the wrong answer choices, and verify that you haven't made any such mistakes.

- What's the prompt asking for? The best interpretation of "$f(5)$ is approximately equal to 243" in this context.

- Math concepts in the prompt: functions, word problems, money, exponents

- Elements of the answer choices: Each answer choice is a sentence about the value of the bank account that includes the numbers 5 and/or 243.

- Notable features of the answer choices: (A) describes an increase over 5 years, (B) mentions a value in 1962, (C) mentions a proportional increase from 1957 to 1962, and (D) mentions an increase that happens every 5 years over a given period.

- "Bridge" concepts: We can read the function, prompt and answer choices carefully, and pick the answer choice that reflects the ideas from the prompt.

- Pre-solution patterns (see p. 285): wrong answers try to imitate right answers

- Things to look out for: Remember that careful reading is the most important skill across the whole test!

Solution 1: Concrete/graphing: Let's graph the provided function and see what it tells us about the statement in each answer choice.

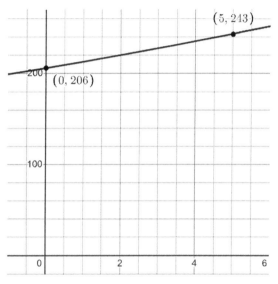

$$y = 206(1.034)^x$$

The prompt tells us that "x is the number of years after 1957." So $f(0)$ would tell us the value of the function 0 years after 1957, which is the same as 1957, while $f(1)$ would tell us the value of the function 1 year after 1957, which is 1958, and so on. With that in mind, we know that $f(5)$ would tell us the value of the function 5 years after 1957, which would be 1962.

We can see in the graph that in 1962 (when $x = 5$), the value of the function is approximately 243, while in 1957 (when $x = 0$), the value of the function is 206. This isn't a difference of 5 dollars, so the statement in (A) is false, and (A) is wrong.

In 1962 (when $x = 5$), the value of the function is approximately 243, which means that the value of the bank account in 1962 is approximately 243 dollars, just as (B) says. So (B) appears to be right, but we'll check the remaining answer choices to help catch any mistakes we might have made.

As we saw in our discussion of (A) and (B), in 1962 (when $x = 5$), the value of the function is approximately 243, while in 1957 (when $x = 0$), the value of the function is 206. The value in 1962 isn't 5 times greater than the value in 1957, so the statement in (C) is false, and (C) is wrong.

We already saw in our discussions of (A) and (C) that the value of the bank account didn't "increase by approximately 243 dollars" in the 5 year period between 1957 and 1962, so the statement in (D) can't be right.

After considering each choice, we can see that (B) is correct.

Solution 2: Abstract: Use the information in the prompt to interpret "$f(5)$ is approximately equal to 243," and pick the answer choice that matches the result.

The prompt tells us that $f(x)$ "models the value, in dollars, of a certain bank account by the end of each year." It also tells us that "x is the number of years after 1957." So $f(5)$ must tell us the value, in dollars, of the bank account 5 years after 1957, which is the same as

---

1962. If "$f(5)$ is approximately equal to 243," then the value of the bank account in 1962 must be approximately 243 dollars, as (B) says. So (B) is right.

ANSWER CHOICE ANALYSIS

(D): This choice might be tempting for test-takers who assume the bank account started out at 0 in 1957, but that idea isn't present in the provided text.

How to check? Try an alternate approach above. Try to figure out which mistakes could lead to some of the wrong answer choices, and verify that you haven't made any such mistakes.

Test 4, Module 1, Question 17

- What's the prompt asking for? The amount that the length of the rectangular region must change to maintain the given ratio if the width of the rectangular region increases by 7 units.

- Math concepts in the prompt: rectangles, length, width, ratios

- Elements of the answer choices: Each answer choice is a sentence that describes a change in the length of the rectangle.

- Notable features of the answer choices: Two choices say the length must increase, while two say it must decrease; two choices mention 24.5 units, while two mention 7 units.

- "Bridge" concepts: We can use the provided ratio to determine how the length must change in the scenario from the prompt.

- Pre-solution patterns (see p. 285): opposites; wrong answers try to imitate right answers

- Things to look out for: Think carefully about what a ratio is! Don't mistakenly think that maintaining the ratio means the perimeter must stay the same! Don't mistakenly think that maintaining the ratio means both dimensions must increase by the same amount!

Solution 1: Algebra: Use the provided information to set up a ratio between the length and width of the new rectangle, then set that ratio equal to the given ratio between the length and width of the original rectangle. Finally, solve for the length of the new rectangle.

Let's say the rectangle's length is 35 and its width is 10. (The prompt didn't give us the actual dimensions of any rectangle, only the ratio of its width to its length, but as long as we use a rectangle with a length and width in the ratio of 35 to 10, we'll be able to find the right answer.) With that in mind, we can set up this equation:

$$\frac{35}{10} = \frac{x}{17}$$

This is the length-to-width ratio of our original rectangle set equal to the same rectangle when its width is increased by 7 and its length is the unknown number x. Now we can solve for x, compare that value to 35, and answer the question.

$$\frac{35}{10} = \frac{x}{17} \qquad \text{(equation we just came up with)}$$

$$595 = 10x \qquad \text{(cross-multiply)}$$

$$59.5 = x \qquad \text{(divide both sides by 10)}$$

So when the width increases by 17, the length increases from 35 to 59.5. This is an increase of 24.5 units, so (B) is correct.

Solution 2: Test-smart: Think about the properties the right answer must have, and pick the only choice that meets the requirements you come up with.

If the ratio of the rectangle's length to its width is 35 to 10, then it must be the case that when one dimension increases, the other increases as well. So we can eliminate (A) and (C).

A ratio of 35 to 10 means that the original length and width are different, and must therefore increase at different rates. So if the width increases by 7 units, the length will increase by a different number of units. That eliminates (D).

So (B) is the right answer.

ANSWER CHOICE ANALYSIS

(A): This would be the right answer if it said "increase" instead of "decrease." **(C):** This would keep the *perimeter* of the rectangle the same, but the resulting rectangle would have a different length to width ratio from the one in the prompt. **(D):** This would result in both dimensions increasing by the same number, but the resulting rectangle would have a different length to width ratio from the one in the prompt.

How to check? Try an alternate approach above. Try to figure out which mistakes could lead to some of the wrong answer choices, and verify that you haven't made any such mistakes.

▶   Post-solution patterns (see page 286):   the right answer to the wrong question

Test 4, Module 1, Question 18

- What's the prompt asking for? The answer choice that defines f.

- Math concepts in the prompt: squares, side lengths, perimeter, area, functions

- Elements of the answer choices: Each answer choice is a function involving the square of a binomial.

- Notable features of the answer choices: Two answer choices involve adding either 44 or 176 to x, and then squaring the result. Two answer choices involve adding either 44 or 176 to $176x$, and then squaring the result.

- "Bridge" concepts: We can read the prompt carefully, and then pick the answer choice with the function that represents the ideas from the prompt.

- Pre-solution patterns (see p. 285): wrong answers try to imitate right answers

- Things to look out for: Don't make a simple algebra mistake! Think carefully about the situation the prompt describes!

Solution 1: Concrete: Think of an x-value, then use the prompt to come up with a corresponding area for square Q. Next, plug that same x-value into the function from each answer choice, and eliminate each choice that doesn't produce the same area for square Q that you just found.

Let's say that $x = 5$, which means P has a side length of 5 inches. If P has a side length of 5 inches, it must have a perimeter of $5 + 5 + 5 + 5$ inches, which is the same as 20 inches. The prompt tells us that "square Q has a perimeter that is 176 inches greater than the perimeter of square P," which means the perimeter of Q must be $20 + 176$ inches, or 196 inches, when $x = 5$.

If the perimeter of Q is 196 inches, we can divide 196 by 4 to find the side length of Q. The result is $\frac{196}{4}$, or 49. If the side length of Q is 49 inches, the area of Q must be 49^2, or 2,401. Now let's plug $x = 5$ into each answer choice and eliminate any choice that doesn't produce a value of 2,401.

(A)	$f(5) = \left((5) + 44\right)^2$	$= 49^2$	$= 2,401$
(B)	$f(5) = \left((5) + 176\right)^2$	$= 181^2$	$= 32,761$
(C)	$f(5) = (176(5) + 44)^2$	$= 924^2$	$= 853,776$
(D)	$f(5) = (176(5) + 176)^2$	$= 1,056^2$	$= 1,115,136$

Only (A) produces an area of 2,401 square inches for square Q when $x = 5$, so (A) is correct.

Solution 2: Careful reading: Analyze the prompt to figure out what properties the right answer must have, and pick the only choice that meets the requirements you come up with.

The area of a square is its side length squared, so the area of square Q must be the side length of Q squared. Each answer choice is a parenthetical expression squared, so we need to find the choice whose parenthetical expression is equal to the side length of Q.

The prompt tells us that "square P has a side length of x inches," and that "square Q has a perimeter that is 176 inches greater than the perimeter of square P." The perimeter of the square is the sum of the lengths of its 4 sides, which is the same as 4 times its side length. If the perimeter of square Q is 176 inches greater than the perimeter of square P, then each side of Q must be one quarter of 176 inches greater than each side of P. So each side of Q is $\frac{176}{4}$ inches, or 44 inches, greater than each side of P.

Since the prompt told us that P has a side length of x inches, Q must have a side length of $x + 44$ inches, which means the area of Q must be $(x + 44)^2$. This is equal to the function in (A), so (A) is correct.

ANSWER CHOICE ANALYSIS

(B): This choice would be correct if *each side* of square Q was 176 inches longer than each side of square P, rather than the whole perimeter being 176 inches greater than the other perimeter, as the prompt tells us. **(C):** This could be the result if a test-taker attempts to express the ideas in the prompt algebraically, and then gets mixed up somewhere along the line. **(D):** This choice could be the result of a mistake similar to the one we saw in our discussion of (C).

How to check? Try an alternate approach above. Try to figure out which mistakes could lead to some of the wrong answer choices, and verify that you haven't made any such mistakes.

▶   Post-solution patterns (see page 286):   the right answer to the wrong question

- What's the prompt asking for? The equation that correctly expresses w in terms of x and y.
- Math concepts in the prompt: equations, fractions, radical expressions, variables
- Elements of the answer choices: Each answer choice is an equation setting w equal to an expression involving x and y.
- Notable features of the answer choices: Two answer choices involve a fractional expression under a radical, and two involve a fractional expression squared.

- "Bridge" concepts: We can manipulate the given equation to isolate w.
- Pre-solution patterns (see p. 285): wrong answers try to imitate right answers
- Things to look out for: Don't make a simple mistake related to algebra or sign! Don't get confused about whether you should be squaring an expression or finding its square root!

Solution 1: Algebra: Manipulate the given expression to isolate w.

$$\frac{14x}{7y} = 2\sqrt{w + 19} \qquad \text{(provided equation)}$$

$$\frac{14x}{14} = \sqrt{w + 19} \qquad \text{(divide both sides by 2)}$$

$$\frac{x}{y} = \sqrt{w + 19} \qquad \text{(cancel out 14 on the left side of the equation)}$$

$$\left(\frac{x}{y}\right)^2 = w + 19 \qquad \text{(square both sides)}$$

$$\left(\frac{x}{y}\right)^2 - 19 = w \qquad \text{(subtract 19 from both sides)}$$

This matches the expression from (C), so (C) is correct.

Solution 2: Test-smart: Think about the properties the right answer must have, and pick the only choice that meets the requirements you come up with.

Once you notice that you're going to have to divide both sides of the given equation by 2 (resulting in $\frac{14x}{14}$ on the left side of the equation, which reduces to $\frac{x}{y}$), and that you're then going to have to square both sides to get rid of the radical (resulting in $\left(\frac{x}{y}\right)^2$ on the left side of the equation), then you know the right answer must include $\left(\frac{x}{y}\right)^2$. Only (C) meets this requirement, so (C) is correct.

ANSWER CHOICE ANALYSIS

(A): This would be the result if a test-taker takes the square root of $\frac{x}{y}$, rather than squaring it. **(B):** This choice combines the mistakes from our discussions of (A) and (D). **(D):** This would be the result if a test-taker multiplies $\frac{14x}{7y}$ by 2, rather than dividing it by 2.

How to check? Try an alternate approach above. Try to figure out which mistakes could lead to some of the wrong answer choices, and verify that you haven't made any such mistakes.

- What's the prompt asking for? The measure of angle *ROS*.
- Math concepts in the prompt: circles, centers of circles, arcs, central angles
- "Bridge" concepts: The degree measure of an arc is equal to the degree measure of its central angle.

- Things to look out for: Don't assume this question must be more complicated than it is! Don't get confused about the properties and definitions of circles involved in this question!

Solution 1: Geometry: Sketch circle O and label it with the information from the prompt.

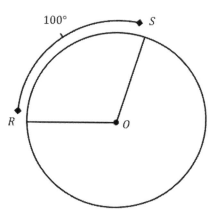

By definition, the degree measure of an arc is equal to the degree measure of its central angle. So the measure of angle *ROS* is equal to the measure of arc *RS*, which means the answer is 100.

How to check? Try to figure out which mistakes the College Board might hope you would make in finding your solution, and verify that you haven't made any such mistakes.

Note Like a lot of SAT Math questions with no answer choices, this one is very straightforward. Don't let that throw you! Just double-check that you read the question correctly, answer it carefully, and move on.

Test 4, Module 1, Question 21

- What's the prompt asking for? The value of $a + b$.
- Math concepts in the prompt: radical expressions, exponential expressions, positive constants, inequality
- "Bridge" concepts: We can simplify the provided expression to find the answer.

- Things to look out for: Don't get confused about the rules related to exponents and radical expressions! Remember that what the prompt actually asks for is the value of $a + b$!

Solution 1: Algebra: Carefully simplify the components of the provided expression, and use the results to find the value of $a + b$.

Let's work through these expressions one piece at a time. $\sqrt[5]{3^5}$ is just 3, and $\sqrt[5]{x^{45}}$ is x^9. So $6\sqrt[5]{3^5 x^{45}}$ is equal to $6 \times 3x^9$, or $18x^9$. Now let's look at the second half of the expression.

$\sqrt[8]{2^8}$ is just 2, and $\sqrt[8]{x}$ is just $x^{\frac{1}{8}}$. So $\sqrt[8]{2^8 x}$ is just $2x^{\frac{1}{8}}$.

So now we've simplified the expression to $18x^9 \times 2x^{\frac{1}{8}}$, but the prompt tells us that we need to get the expression in a form that looks like ax^b. That means we need to combine the two terms in $18x^9 \times 2x^{\frac{1}{8}}$ so that we end up with a constant a multiplied by x raised to another constant b.

We know from our "Exponents" training on page 254 of this Black Book that when we multiply exponent expressions with identical bases (in this case x), we add the exponents. So when we multiply $18x^9$ and $2x^{\frac{1}{8}}$, we get $(18 \times 2)x^{\left(9 + \frac{1}{8}\right)}$, which is $36x^{\frac{73}{8}}$.

Again, the prompt tells us this form is equivalent to ax^b, so $a = 36$ and $b = \frac{73}{8}$. The question asks for $a + b$, which is equal to $36 + \frac{73}{8}$. We can either multiply 36 by $\frac{8}{8}$ to get the equivalent number $\frac{288}{8}$, and then add that to $\frac{73}{8}$ to get $\frac{361}{8}$, or we can evaluate $36 + \frac{73}{8}$ with our calculator and enter the answer as the decimal approximation 45.12 or 45.13. So the answer is $\frac{361}{8}$, or 45.12, or 45.13.

How to check? Double-check that you combined the exponents correctly. Try to figure out which mistakes the College Board might hope you would make in finding your solution, and verify that you haven't made any such mistakes.

Test 4, Module 1, Question 22

- What's the prompt asking for? The area of the triangle described in the prompt.
- Math concepts in the prompt: right triangles, side lengths, radical expressions, area of a triangle
- Elements of the answer choices: Each answer choice involves integers and/or radical expressions.
- Notable features of the answer choices: Two choices are integers, one is an integer multiplied by a radical

expression, and one is an integer multiplied by a radical expression added to a radical expression. (B) is half of (D).

- "Bridge" concepts: We can figure out which side lengths correspond to the legs of the right triangle, and use that information to find the area of that triangle.
- Pre-solution patterns (see p. 285): halves and doubles; wrong answers try to imitate right answers

---

- Things to look out for: Make sure you figure out which side length is the longest! Make sure to use the formula for area of a triangle correctly!

Solution 1: Geometry: Find decimal approximations for the provided side lengths. Remember that the longest side length must be the hypotenuse, and the two shorter sides must be the legs. Sketch and label the right triangle described in the prompt accordingly, and use that information to find the area of the triangle.

We know that it can be helpful to approximate radical expressions as decimals, so let's do that with every value in the prompt.

$$2\sqrt{2} \approx 2.83 \qquad 6\sqrt{2} \approx 8.49 \qquad \sqrt{80} \approx 8.94$$

Now let's sketch this triangle. The prompt doesn't tell us the names of any vertices of the triangle, or name any sides and tell us which side corresponds to which length, or anything like that—but since this is a right triangle, we know that the longest length must be the hypotenuse, and the other two lengths must be the legs of the triangle.

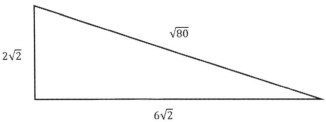

The area of a triangle is equal to one half its base multiplied by its height—in other words, $A = \frac{1}{2}bh$. (If we didn't remember that formula, we could find it in the reference information provided by the College Board.) In this case, $b = 6\sqrt{2}$ and $h = 2\sqrt{2}$.

$A = \frac{1}{2}bh$ (formula for area of a triangle)

$A = \frac{1}{2}(6\sqrt{2})(2\sqrt{2})$ (plug in $b = 6\sqrt{2}$ and $h = 2\sqrt{2}$)

$A = \frac{1}{2}(24)$ (simplify)

$A = 12$ (simplify)

So the area of the triangle is 12, and (B) is right.

ANSWER CHOICE ANALYSIS

(A): This is the result of adding all three side lengths together. **(C):** This is the result of multiplying all three side lengths together. **(D):** This is twice the right answer, which could be the result if someone used bh to find the area of the triangle, rather than $\frac{1}{2}bh$.

How to check? Try to figure out which mistakes could lead to some of the wrong answer choices, and verify that you haven't made any such mistakes.

▶ Post-solution patterns (see page 286): right approach, wrong step; the right answer to the wrong question

---

Test 4, Module 1, Question 23

- What's the prompt asking for? The choice that must be an integer.

- Math concepts in the prompt: polynomial expressions, integer constants, factoring

- Elements of the answer choices: Each answer choice is a fraction involving b, h, k, and/or 45.

- Notable features of the answer choices: Two answer choices have b as the numerator, and two have 45 as the numerator. Two answer choices have h as the denominator, and two have k as the denominator.

- "Bridge" concepts: We can use the fact that h, k, and j are integer constants to figure out which expression in the answer choices must also be an integer constant.

- Pre-solution patterns (see p. 285): opposites; wrong answers try to imitate right answers

- Things to look out for: Remember what an integer is! Don't assume that any fraction with an integer in the numerator and an integer in the denominator must be an integer!

Solution 1: Abstract: Multiply out the provided expression, and use the fact that h, k, and j are integer constants to figure out which expression in the answer choices must also be an integer constant.

Let's start by multiplying out the rewritten parenthetical expression in the prompt.

$$(hx + k)(x + j) \qquad \text{(rewritten parenthetical expression from the prompt)}$$

$$hx^2 + jhx + kx + kj \qquad \text{(result of FOILing)}$$

So according to the prompt, $hx^2 + jhx + kx + kj$ is equal to $4x^2 + bx - 45$. We know that the terms multiplied by different powers of x must correspond to one another, so that means the following are true:

$$hx^2 = 4x^2 \qquad\qquad jhx + kx = bx \qquad\qquad kj = -45$$

The prompt tells us that h, k, and j are integer constants. If $kj = -45$, then it must be true that $-\frac{45}{k} = j$. If $-\frac{45}{k} = j$, and j is an integer constant, then $\frac{45}{k}$ must equal $-j$, which must also be an integer constant. So (D) is the right answer.

ANSWER CHOICE ANALYSIS

(A): The prompt tells us that b is a constant and that h is an integer constant, but that's not enough for us to conclude that $\frac{b}{h}$ is an integer. **(B):** This choice has the same basic problem as (A). **(C):** We know that 45 is an integer and that h is an integer constant, but that's not enough for us to conclude that $\frac{45}{h}$ is an integer.

How to check? Double-check to verify that you haven't mixed up the exponents. Try to figure out which mistakes could lead to some of the wrong answer choices, and verify that you haven't made any such mistakes.

Note This is a great example of an SAT question that just seems kind of weird and intimidating, and can leave a lot of test-takers not even knowing where to start. When that happens, we should just try to think of *anything* we can do to get started—graph an expression, factor something, multiply something out, sketch a shape described in the prompt, etc.—even if we're not sure what good it will do. In this case, it was multiplying out an expression from the prompt; once we did that, some pieces fell into place and we were able to make progress. But realistically, for most test-takers, that won't work every single time: there will be one or more questions on test day where you just can't seem to make any headway on your first attempt. We know from our training that when that happens, we should skip the question, and only come back to it on a later pass when we've already answered the questions that we can get through fairly quickly.

Test 4, Module 1, Question 24

- What's the prompt asking for? The value of x.
- Math concepts in the prompt: systems of equations, constants, line graphs, intersection
- Elements of the answer choices: Each answer choice is an integer ranging from -8 to 8.
- Notable features of the answer choices: Two choices are negative, and two are positive. Two include the numeral 6, and two include the numeral 8. (A) is the opposite of (D), and (B) is the opposite of (C).

- "Bridge" concepts: We can figure out what a needs to be for the equations to intersect at one point, and then figure out what that point of intersection is, and then use that information to answer the question.
- Pre-solution patterns (see p. 285): opposites; wrong answers try to imitate right answers
- Things to look out for: Think carefully about what would cause the graphs of these two equations to intersect at one point!

Solution 1: Concrete/graphing: We can graph the provided equations and use what we learn to work toward the solution.

We can start by graphing the two provided equations. We don't know the value of a, so just leave it out for now. Here's the result:

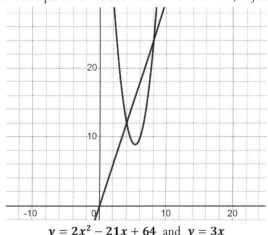

$$y = 2x^2 - 21x + 64 \text{ and } y = 3x$$

Remember that the prompt tells us that the graphs of these two equations intersect at exactly one point. With this in mind, we can imagine how the value a could vertically shift the straight line in the graph above in such a way that it would only touch the graph of the parabola in one place.

You can start playing around with the value of a to move that line down—I started with -5, then went to $-6, -7$, and finally -8.

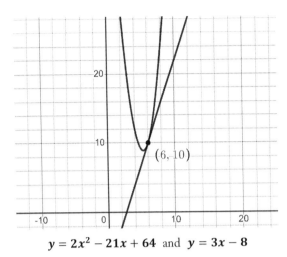

$$y = 2x^2 - 21x + 64 \text{ and } y = 3x - 8$$

When $a = -8$, and the graph of the second line is $y = 3x - 8$, the two graphs touch at exactly one point, and that point is $(6, 10)$. The prompt asks for the value of x from that point, so the answer is (C), 6.

ANSWER CHOICE ANALYSIS

(A): This is a, but that's not what the prompt asked for. **(B):** This is the opposite of the right answer. **(D):** This is the opposite of a.

How to check? Make sure your answer choice was the value of x, which is what the prompt asked for, and not the value of a. Try to figure out which mistakes could lead to some of the wrong answer choices, and verify that you haven't made any such mistakes.

▶ Post-solution patterns (see page 286): right approach, wrong step; the right answer to the wrong question

Note This is another question, like the last one, that will intimidate a lot of test-takers. In this case, even if weren't sure how to find the right answer, we could just try to graph the provided equations to see what we could learn. We left out the a term initially, since we didn't have a value for it—but once we did that, and we thought about the idea of these two equations intersecting at one point, we started to understand what was going on in this question, and we were able to find the right answer without even really doing any calculations. Remember on test day that just because you look at a question and you don't see a path to the answer, that doesn't mean you can't find the answer—and it doesn't even mean that the question must be difficult or complicated once you get started.

Test 4, Module 1, Question 25

- What's the prompt asking for? The perimeter of the triangle.
- Math concepts in the prompt: isosceles triangles, right triangles, hypotenuse, perimeter
- Elements of the answer choices: Each answer choice involves $\sqrt{2}$, and either 29, 58, and/or 116.
- Notable features of the answer choices: Two choices are an integer multiplied by $\sqrt{2}$, and two choices are an integer added to an integer multiplied by $\sqrt{2}$. (A) is half of (B).

- "Bridge" concepts: If we know the hypotenuse of an isosceles right triangle, we can find the lengths of its sides.
- Pre-solution patterns (see p. 285): halves and doubles; wrong answers try to imitate right answers
- Things to look out for: Don't get confused about whether a value you found is the length of one leg, or the length of both legs! Remember that the perimeter of a triangle is the sum of the lengths of all three sides: in this case, the 58 inch hypotenuse, and the two legs!

Solution 1: Algebra: Use the Pythagorean theorem along with the length of the hypotenuse to find the lengths of the legs of the triangle, then add those three lengths to find the perimeter.

In order to find the perimeter of the triangle, we need to know the length of each of its sides. The prompt tells us that its hypotenuse is 58 inches, so we need to find the length of each of the two legs.

An isosceles right triangle has a 90° angle and two sides of equal length. The Pythagorean theorem tells us that the sum of the squares of the lengths of the legs of a right triangle is equal to the square of the hypotenuse—in other words, $a^2 + b^2 = c^2$, where a and b

are the lengths of the legs, and c is the length of the hypotenuse. With this in mind, we can use the provided length of the hypotenuse to find the lengths of the legs.

$$a^2 + b^2 = c^2 \qquad \text{(Pythagorean theorem)}$$
$$a^2 + b^2 = 58^2 \qquad \text{(plug in } c = 58\text{)}$$
$$a^2 + b^2 = 3{,}364 \qquad \text{(simplify)}$$
$$a^2 + a^2 = 3{,}364 \qquad (b = a\text{, since the leg lengths are equal)}$$
$$2a^2 = 3{,}364 \qquad \text{(combine like terms)}$$
$$a^2 = 1{,}682 \qquad \text{(divide both sides by 2)}$$
$$a \approx 41.01 \qquad \text{(divide both sides by 2)}$$

So each leg length is approximately 41.01 inches, which means the perimeter is approximately $58 + 41.01 + 41.01$, or 140.02. The answer choices all use radical expressions, so let's find decimal approximations of those values:

(A) $29\sqrt{2} \approx 41.01$
(B) $58\sqrt{2} \approx 82.02$
(C) $58 + 58\sqrt{2} \approx 140.02$
(D) $58 + 116\sqrt{2} \approx 222.05$

Our answer is approximately equal to (C), and (C) is correct.

Solution 2: Test-smart: Use the length of the hypotenuse along with your understanding of $45°\!:45°\!:90°$ triangles to find the perimeter.

If we recognize that an isosceles right triangle is a $45°\!:45°\!:90°$ triangle, then we know that its sides are in the ratio $1\!:\!1\!:\!\sqrt{2}$. Once we realize that, we can pretty quickly figure out the leg lengths and perimeter of a right isosceles triangle with a hypotenuse of 58 inches.

The hypotenuse of 58 inches corresponds to the $\sqrt{2}$ value in the ratio above, so we can divide 58 by $\sqrt{2}$ to get the length of each side. $\frac{58}{\sqrt{2}} = 29\sqrt{2}$, so each leg is $29\sqrt{2}$ inches long, and the perimeter is $58 + 29\sqrt{2} + 29\sqrt{2}$, which is equal to $58 + 58\sqrt{2}$ inches long. So (C) is correct.

(If we didn't feel comfortable dividing by a radical expression, we could still use our calculators to find decimal approximations of the relevant values. The result would have been $\frac{58}{1.41} \approx 41.13$ which would give us a perimeter of $58 + 41.13 + 41.13$, or 140.26, which would be approximately equal to the decimal approximation of (C). Again, we can see that (C) is correct.)

Solution 3: Test-smart: Find decimal approximations of the answer choices, and use your understanding of triangle perimeters to eliminate each choice that can't possibly be the perimeter of the triangle from the prompt.

We know that, for any triangle, the length of one side can't be greater than the sum of the lengths of the other two sides—otherwise the two shorter sides wouldn't be able to touch and form a triangle.

We know that the hypotenuse is the longest side of any right triangle. For each answer choice, we can subtract the length of the hypotenuse (which we're told is 58), and what's left must be the sum of the lengths of the two shorter sides. We can eliminate any choice where this value is less than 58—again, because if it's less than 58, that means the sum of the two legs is less than the length of the hypotenuse, which is impossible.

The answer choices all use radical expressions, so let's find decimal approximations of those values, then subtract 58 from those approximations:

(A) $29\sqrt{2} \approx 41.01$ $41.01 - 58 = -16.99$
(B) $58\sqrt{2} \approx 82.02$ $82.02 - 58 = 24.02$
(C) $58 + 58\sqrt{2} \approx 140.02$ $140.02 - 58 = 82.02$
(D) $58 + 116\sqrt{2} \approx 222.05$ $222.05 - 58 = 164.05$

Both (A) and (B) produced results less than 58, so we can eliminate those choices.

Since the hypotenuse is the longest side of the triangle, the perimeter of the triangle must be less than 58×3—again, because we know that the hypotenuse is 58 inches long, and we know the other two sides must be less than 58 inches long.

$58 \times 3 = 174$. Choice (D) is greater than this value, so we can eliminate (D) (again, because (D) would result in legs that are longer than the hypotenuse). That leaves only choice (C), which is the correct answer.

ANSWER CHOICE ANALYSIS

(A): This is the length of each leg. **(B):** This is the combined length of both legs. **(D):** This is the answer we would find if we mistakenly multiplied 58 by $\sqrt{2}$ to find the length of each leg, instead of dividing 58 by $\sqrt{2}$ (if we did this, we might catch our mistake by realizing that the leg lengths must be *shorter* than the hypotenuse, so we can't find them by multiplying the length of the hypotenuse by a number greater than 1).

How to check? Try an alternate approach above. Try to figure out which mistakes could lead to some of the wrong answer choices, and verify that you haven't made any such mistakes.

▶ Post-solution patterns (see page 286): right approach, wrong step; the right answer to the wrong question

Test 4, Module 1, Question 26

- **What's the prompt asking for?** The choice that could be the value of $a + b + c$.

- **Math concepts in the prompt:** parabolas, vertices, intersection, equations, constants

- **Elements of the answer choices:** Each answer choice is a negative integer ranging from -23 to -12.

- **"Bridge" concepts:** We can use the standard equation of a parabola, along with the provided vertex and the

fact that the parabola crosses the x-axis, to find the value of $a + b + c$.

- **Things to look out for:** Don't make a simple mistake related to algebra or sign! Think carefully about what the information in the prompt tells us about the parabola!

Solution 1: Algebra: Plug the provided vertex into the standard equation for a parabola, use the result to find $a + b + c$ in terms of a, and use the fact that the parabola opens upward to determine which choice could be the value of $a + b + c$. (If that doesn't make sense, don't worry—just read on.)

The general equation of a parabola is $y = a(x - h)^2 + k$, where (h, k) is the vertex of the parabola. Let's figure out a possible equation for the parabola in the question, and see what we can figure out from there.

We're told the parabola has vertex $(9, -14)$. Based on what we just said about the general equation of a parabola, the equation $y = a(x - 9)^2 - 14$ would have a vertex at $(9, -14)$. Let's try to manipulate that expression so it looks like the $y = ax^2 + bx + c$ form from the prompt.

$$y = a(x - 9)^2 - 14 \qquad \text{(parabola with vertex } (9, -14))$$
$$y = a(x^2 - 18x + 81) - 14 \qquad \text{(FOIL)}$$
$$y = ax^2 - 18ax + 81a - 14 \qquad \text{(distribute the } a)$$

We've now expressed the parabola described in the prompt with the equation $y = ax^2 - 18ax + 81a - 14$. The prompt says this parabola can also be expressed as $y = ax^2 + bx + c$. We know that the terms in each equation with matching exponents of x must correspond, so $ax^2 = ax^2$, $bx = -18ax$, and $c = 81a - 14$, which also means $a = a$, $b = -18a$, and $c = 81a - 14$.

We've now expressed a, b, and c in terms of a, so we can add these expressions together to find $a + b + c$ in terms of a.

$$a + b + c \qquad \text{(expression whose possible value we need to find)}$$
$$a - 18a + 81a - 14 \qquad \text{(plug in } b = -18a \text{ and } c = 81a - 14)$$
$$64a - 14 \qquad \text{(simplify)}$$

We may wonder what to do with this expression, because it doesn't appear in the answer choices. Well, if we look back at the prompt, we see that the parabola in question has a vertex below the x-axis, and it "intersects the x-axis at 2 points." That means it must open upward.

Since this is true, if the equation of that parabola is expressed as $y = ax^2 + bx + c$, then a must be positive, otherwise the parabola will open downward (which would contradict the information in the prompt, as we just discussed). You can test this out in the graphing calculator by graphing $y = x^2$ and $y = -x^2$.

So now we know that $64a - 14$ is equal to $a + b + c$, and we know that a must be positive. Let's set $64a - 14$ equal to the values from each answer choice and see which one results in a positive a value.

(A) $\quad 64a - 14 = -23 \qquad 64a = -9 \qquad a = -\dfrac{9}{64}$

(B) $\quad 64a - 14 = -19 \qquad 64a = -5 \qquad a = -\dfrac{5}{64}$

(C) $\quad 64a - 14 = -14 \qquad 64a = 0 \qquad a = 0$

(D) $\quad 64a - 14 = -12 \qquad 64a = 2 \qquad a = \dfrac{2}{64}$

Only (D) results in an a-value that's positive, which means only (D) is possible for a parabola with vertex $(9, -14)$ that opens upward. So (D) is correct.

ANSWER CHOICE ANALYSIS

(A): This choice results in a negative a-value, but as we discussed above, the a-value needs to be positive. **(B):** This choice has the same basic problem as (B). **(C):** This choice results in an a-value of 0, but as we discussed above, the a-value needs to be positive.

How to check? Try to figure out which mistakes could lead to some of the wrong answer choices, and verify that you haven't made any such mistakes.

> **Note** A lot of students won't know what to do with this question. That's fine! You can be completely lost on a couple of math questions on test day and still get an elite score, as long as you effectively apply your training to all the other questions. The most important thing to do on test day if you encounter a question where you have no idea how to proceed is to not let that question fluster you, or eat up your time—just save it for a later pass, and move on to questions you feel more comfortable with.

Test 4, Module 1, Question 27

- What's the prompt asking for? The value of a.
- Math concepts in the prompt: functions, constants, exponential expressions, y-intercepts, multiplication, variables
- "Bridge" concepts: We can use the provided y-intercept for $y = f(x) - 15$ to find the value of b, and then use the fact that the product of a and b is $\frac{65}{7}$ to find a.

- Things to look out for: Don't make a simple mistake related to algebra or sign! Don't overlook any information in the prompt!

Solution 1: Algebra: Use the provided y-intercept to find the value of b, then plug that value into $ab = \frac{65}{7}$ to find the value of a.

Let's start with the equation whose y-intercept is given in the prompt, and then plug in the expression we're given for $f(x)$. Then we can plug in the coordinates of that y-intercept and see what we learn.

$$y = f(x) - 15 \qquad \text{(provided equation)}$$

$$y = -a^x + b - 15 \qquad \text{(plug in } f(x) = -a^x + b)$$

$$-\frac{99}{7} = -a^0 + b - 15 \qquad \text{(plug in } x = 0 \text{ and } y = -\frac{99}{7})$$

$$-\frac{99}{7} = -1 + b - 15 \qquad \text{(evaluate } a^0)$$

$$-\frac{99}{7} = b - 16 \qquad \text{(simplify)}$$

$$\frac{13}{7} = b \qquad \text{(add 16 to both sides)}$$

The prompt tells us that "the product of a and b is $\frac{65}{7}$," which is the same as $ab = \frac{65}{7}$. Let's solve that equation for a, using the b-value we just found.

$$ab = \frac{65}{7} \qquad \text{(equation described in the prompt)}$$

$$a\left(\frac{13}{7}\right) = \frac{65}{7} \qquad \text{(plug in } b = \frac{13}{7})$$

$$a = \frac{65}{7} \times \frac{7}{13} \qquad \text{(divide both sides by } \frac{13}{7})$$

$$a = \frac{65}{13} \qquad \text{(simplify)}$$

$$a = 5 \qquad \text{(simplify)}$$

So $a = 5$, and the answer is 5.

How to check? Verify that you didn't mix up x and y or a and b. Try to figure out which mistakes the College Board might hope you would make in finding your solution, and verify that you haven't made any such mistakes.

> **Note** Note that the College Board could have provided the equation $ab = \frac{65}{7}$, but they chose to write out "the product of a and b is $\frac{65}{7}$" instead. This is probably because an equation like $ab = \frac{65}{7}$ would have made it more obvious that we could find the value of a if we found the value of b first. Always be on the lookout for important information in the prompt that might be presented in unusual ways!

TEST 4 - MODULE 2

- What's the prompt asking for? The year when the estimated number of chipmunks in the state park was the greatest.
- Math concepts in the prompt: line graphs, word problems, greatest value
- Elements of the answer choices: Each answer choice is a year.

- "Bridge" concepts: The answer will be the year that shows the greatest estimated number of chipmunks.
- Pre-solution patterns (see p. 285): wrong answers try to imitate right answers
- Things to look out for: Don't misread the prompt or the graph! Make sure you match the highest value in the graph to the correct year!

Solution 1: Careful reading: Read the answer off the provided graph.

The vertical axis is labeled "Estimate number of chipmunks." The horizontal axis is labeled "Year." The lines graph reaches its highest vertical point directly above the line that corresponds to 1994 on the "Year" axis. So the answer is (B), 1994.

ANSWER CHOICE ANALYSIS

(A): This is the *lowest* value on the graph, but the prompt asked for the *greatest* value. **(C):** This choice is right next to the year with the greatest value, and could be tempting for test-takers who get confused about which year corresponds to which data point.

How to check? Try to figure out which mistakes could lead to some of the wrong answer choices, and verify that you haven't made any such mistakes.

▶ Post-solution patterns (see page 286): the right answer to the wrong question

Note We shouldn't be surprised to see an early question like this one that's pretty straightforward—just reading a value off a graph. As trained test-takers, we know to read the prompt and answer choices carefully, mark the choice that answers the question in the prompt, and move on.

- What's the prompt asking for? How far the fish swam in miles.
- Math concepts in the prompt: word problems, distance, yards, miles, unit conversion
- Elements of the answer choices: Each answer choice is a numerical value ranging from 0.3 to 6,864.
- Notable features of the answer choices: Two answer choices are decimal expressions less than 3, and two are 4-digit integers.

- "Bridge" concepts: We can divide the number of yards by the number of yards in a mile to find the distance measured in miles.
- Things to look out for: Make sure you keep straight which number should be divided by which number! Make sure your answer makes sense given that a mile is many times longer than a yard!

Solution 1: Concrete: Multiply each answer by 1,760 yards to find out how many yards corresponds to that number of miles. The choice that produces a distance of 5,104 yards is the right answer.

(A) $0.3 \times 1,760 = 528$
(B) $2.9 \times 1,760 = 5,104$
(C) $3,344 \times 1,760 = 5,885,440$
(D) $6,864 \times 1,760 = 12,080,640$

Only (B) produces the correct value, so (B) is the right answer.

Solution 2: Algebra: Divide the number of yards by the number of yards in a mile to find the distance measured in miles.

The prompt tells us that 1 mile = 1,760 yards, so every 1,760 yards the fish swam was the same as one mile. If the fish swam 5,104 yards, we can divide that amount by 1,760 to find how many miles 5,104 yards corresponds to. The result is $\frac{5,104}{1,760} = 2.9$, so (B) is right.

Solution 3: Test-smart: Think about the properties the right answer must have, based on the information in the prompt, and pick the only choice that meets the requirements you come up with.

We know that the fish swam more than 1 mile, since 5,104 is greater than 1,760, so (A) is wrong. We also know that the fish couldn't have swam thousands of miles, as (C) and (D) would require, since every one of those miles would represent more than a thousand yards itself, and those thousands of miles would have to be millions of yards total, far more than the 5,104 yards mentioned in the prompt.

That eliminates (C) and (D), and leaves only the correct answer, (B).

ANSWER CHOICE ANALYSIS

(A): This is $\frac{1,760}{5,104}$, which is the reciprocal of the right answer. **(C):** This is $5,104 - 1,760$, but that's not what the prompt asked for. **(D):** This is $5,104 + 1,760$, but that's not what the prompt asked for.

How to check? Try an alternate approach above. Try to figure out which mistakes could lead to some of the wrong answer choices, and verify that you haven't made any such mistakes.

Test 4, Module 2, Question 3

- What's the prompt asking for? The expression that's equivalent to $12x^3 - 5x^3$.

- Math concepts in the prompt: equivalent expressions, exponential expressions

- Elements of the answer choices: Each answer choice includes a coefficient and x raised to an exponent.

- Notable features of the answer choices: Two choices include 7, and two choices include 17. Two choices include x^6, and two choices include x^3.

- "Bridge" concepts: Both x-terms in the provided expression are raised to the same power, so we can just subtract one from the other.

- Pre-solution patterns (see p. 285): wrong answers try to imitate right answers

- Things to look out for: Think carefully about the rules for adding and subtracting terms raised to an exponent!

Solution 1: Concrete: Pick a value for x, and plug it in to the given expression. Then plug the same x-value into the expressions from the answer choices, and eliminate each choice that doesn't produce the same result.

If we don't feel comfortable working with exponential expressions involving variables, we can pick a value for x and evaluate the given expression. Then we can plug that same x-value into the answer choices to see which one has the same value as the given expression. Let's say $x = 2$.

$12x^3 - 5x^3$	(given expression)
$12(2)^3 - 5(2)^3$	(plug in $x = 2$)
$12(8) - 5(8)$	(simplify)
$96 - 40$	(simplify)
56	(simplify)

So when $x = 2$, the given expression is equal to 56. Now let's plug $x = 2$ into each answer choice to see what we get.

(A)	$7x^6$	$7(2)^6$	$7(64)$	448
(B)	$17x^3$	$17(2)^3$	$17(8)$	136
(C)	$7x^3$	$7(2)^3$	$7(8)$	56
(D)	$17x^6$	$17(2)^6$	$17(64)$	$1,088$

When we plug $x = 2$ into the expression from each answer choice, we can see that only the expression from (C) is equal to 56, which is the same result we get when we plug $x = 2$ into the provided expression. So (C) is correct.

Solution 2: Algebra: Use your understanding of exponents to simplify the given expression. Pick the choice that matches the result.

These are both x^3 terms, so we can just subtract one from the other. The result is $12x^3 - 5x^3 = 7x^3$. So the right answer is (C).

ANSWER CHOICE ANALYSIS

(A): This choice mistakenly adds the exponents together. **(B):** This would be equivalent to $12x^3 + 5x^3$. **(D):** This choice combines the mistakes from (A) and (B).

How to check? Try an alternate approach above. Try to figure out which mistakes could lead to some of the wrong answer choices, and verify that you haven't made any such mistakes.

▶ Post-solution patterns (see page 286): the right answer to the wrong question

---

Test 4, Module 2, Question 4

- What's the prompt asking for? The solution to the given system of equations.

- Math concepts in the prompt: systems of equations, solutions to systems of equations

---

- Elements of the answer choices: Each answer choice is a coordinate pair.
- Notable features of the answer choices: The x-coordinates in each answer choice form a series where each one is one unit more than the previous choice. The y-coordinates in each answer choice form a series where each one is one unit less than the previous choice.

- "Bridge" concepts: The right answer will produce a true statement when plugged into each of the given equations.
- Pre-solution patterns (see p. 285): first and last terms in a series are often wrong answers; wrong answers try to imitate right answers
- Things to look out for: Make sure your choice works in both equations! Don't confuse x and y!

Solution 1: Graphing: We can graph the provided equations to find out where they intersect.

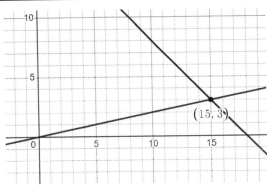

$x + y = 18$ and $5y = x$

We can see that these graphs intersect at $(15, 3)$, so (A) is correct.

Solution 2: Algebra: Plug in $5y$ for x to solve for y in the first equation, then use that y-vaue to solve for x.

The second equation gives us the value of x in terms of y, so let's plug this value into the first equation.

$x + y = 18$ (first equation)
$(5y) + y = 18$ (plug in $x = 5y$ from the second equation)
$6y = 18$ (simplify)
$y = 3$ (divide both sides by 6)

Now we know the value of y, so we can plug that into either equation and solve for x. I'll use the first equation, for no particular reason.

$x + y = 18$ (first equation)
$x + (3) = 18$ (plug in $y = 3$)
$x = 15$ (subtract 3 from both sides)

So the solution to the given system of equations is $(15, 3)$, and (A) is correct.

Solution 3. Test-smart: Analyze the answer choices and pick the only one that produces a true statement in both equations.

We might notice that each of the coordinate pairs from the answer choices satisfies the first equation—in other words, for each pair, the sum of x and y is 18. But there's only one choice where x is also 5 times as much as y, as the second equation requires, and that's (A). So (A) must be right.

ANSWER CHOICE ANALYSIS

(B): This choice works for the first equation, but not for the second equation. **(C):** This choice has the same problem as (B). **(D):** This choice has the same problem as (B) and (C).

How to check? Verify that the x-and y-values in the answer you chose create a true statement when plugged in to both of the provided equations. Try an alternate approach above. Try to figure out which mistakes could lead to some of the wrong answer choices, and verify that you haven't made any such mistakes.

Test 4, Module 2, Question 5

- What's the prompt asking for? The system of inequalities for which the point (8,2) is a solution.
- Math concepts in the prompt: coordinate pairs, systems of inequalities

- Elements of the answer choices: Each answer choice is a system of inequalities comparing x to 0 and y to 0.

- Notable features of the answer choices: Two choices include $x > 0$, while two include $x < 0$. Two choices include $y > 0$, while two include $y < 0$.
- "Bridge" concepts: Both 8 and 2 are greater than 0, so the right answer will be the one where x and y are both greater than 0.

- Pre-solution patterns (see p. 285): opposites; wrong answers try to imitate right answers
- Things to look out for: Think carefully about what it means to be a solution of a system of inequalities! Don't misread a greater-than symbol as a less-than symbol, or vice-versa!

Solution 1: Concrete: Graph each system of inequalities along with the point (8,2) to see which system of inequalities has (8,2) as a solution.

(A)

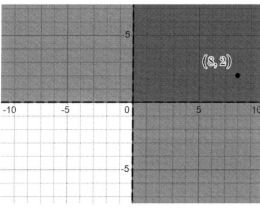

$x > 0$ and $y > 0$

(B)

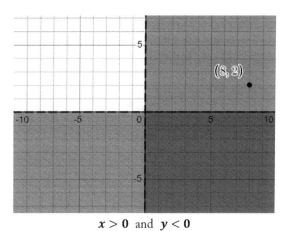

$x > 0$ and $y < 0$

(C)

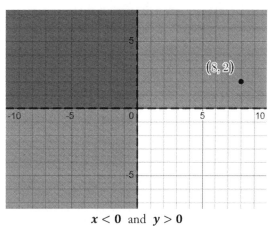

$x < 0$ and $y > 0$

(D)

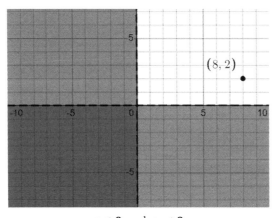

$$x < 0 \text{ and } y < 0$$

We can see that (8,2) is a solution for the system of inequalities from (A), so (A) is correct.

Solution 2: Abstract: Consider the system of inequalities from each answer choice, and think carefully about where (8,2) would appear relative to those systems.

When we look at each answer choice, we can see that each one compares x to 0 and each one compares y to 0—in other words, each choice tells us whether x and y are positive or negative.

We can see that both x and y in the given coordinate pair $(8, 2)$ are positive, so we need to pick the answer choice that says both x and y are greater than 0. Only (A) does that, so (A) is correct.

ANSWER CHOICE ANALYSIS

(B): (8,2) would be a solution for $x > 0$, but not for $y < 0$. **(C):** (8,2) would be a solution for $y > 0$, but not for $x < 0$. **(D):** This is the opposite of the right answer; (8,2) wouldn't be a solution for either of these inequalities.

How to check? Double-check the direction of the inequality symbols in the answer choice you picked. Try an alternate approach above. Try to figure out which mistakes could lead to some of the wrong answer choices, and verify that you haven't made any such mistakes.

Test 4, Module 2, Question 6

- What's the prompt asking for? One possible solution to the given equation.

- Math concepts in the prompt: absolute value, equations, variables, solutions

- "Bridge" concepts: The expression inside the absolute value brackets can be equal to 10 or −10 to make the equation valid.

- Things to look out for: Don't forget to account for the absolute value brackets! Don't make a simple mistake related to algebra or sign!

Solution 1: Concrete/graphing: We can graph the given equation to find its solutions.

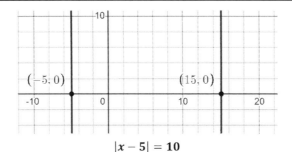

$$|x - 5| = 10$$

We can see a vertical line at $x = -5$ and $x = 15$. So the two possible solutions are −5 and 15, and either answer is correct.

Solution 2: Algebra: Create two equations to account for the absolute value brackets, then solve each one for x.

If $|x - 5| = 10$, then it must be true that $x - 5 = 10$ or $x - 5 = -10$. We can solve each of these equations for x to find the solutions to the given equation. We'll start with $x - 5 = 10$.

$$x - 5 = 10 \quad \text{(equation we just found)}$$
$$x = 15 \quad \text{(add 5 to both sides)}$$

Now let's solve the other equation.

$$x - 5 = -10 \qquad \text{(other equation we just found)}$$
$$x = -5 \qquad \text{(add 5 to both sides)}$$

So $x = 15$ or $x = -5$. That means the two possible solutions are -5 and 15, and either answer is correct.

How to check? Try an alternate approach above. Try to figure out which mistakes the College Board might hope you would make in finding your solution, and verify that you haven't made any such mistakes.

Test 4, Module 2, Question 7

- **What's the prompt asking for?** The total number of people on a company retreat with 7 managers.
- **Math concepts in the prompt:** word problems, function models

- **"Bridge" concepts:** We can plug in $x = 7$ to find the total number of people on the retreat when there are 7 managers.
- **Things to look out for:** Don't make a simple algebra mistake! Don't misunderstand the prompt and think that $f(x) = 7$!

Solution 1: Concrete/graphing: We can graph the provided function, then use it to find the value of y when $x = 7$.

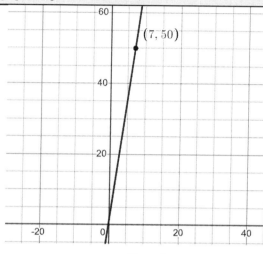

$$y = 7x + 1$$

The prompt tells us that the function "gives the total number of people on a company retreat with x managers." So x is the number of managers, and the output of the function is "the total number of people on a company retreat."

That means if we find the value of y when $x = 7$, we'll know the answer. The graph has a point at $(7, 50)$, so when $x = 7$—that is, when there are 7 managers—we know that $y = 50$—that is, there are 50 total people at the retreat. The answer is 50.

Solution 2: Algebra: Plug $x = 7$ into the provided function to find the answer.

As we saw in our previous solution, the function tells us the total number of people at a company retreat with x managers, and the prompt asks us for the total number of people on a retreat with 7 managers. So we can plug $x = 7$ into the provided function, and the result will be the number of people on a retreat with 7 managers, which is what the prompt asked for.

$$f(x) = 7x + 1 \qquad \text{(provided function)}$$
$$f(7) = 7(7) + 1 \qquad \text{(plug in } x = 7\text{)}$$
$$f(7) = 49 + 1 \qquad \text{(simplify)}$$
$$f(7) = 50 \qquad \text{(simplify)}$$

So when there are 7 managers, there are 50 total people on the retreat. That means the answer is 50.

How to check? Try an alternate approach above. Try to figure out which mistakes the College Board might hope you would make in finding your solution, and verify that you haven't made any such mistakes.

Test 4, Module 2, Question 8

- **What's the prompt asking for?** The table that gives three values of x and their corresponding values of $h(x)$ for the given function h.
- **Math concepts in the prompt:** functions, exponents, tables of values

- **Elements of the answer choices:** Each answer choice is a table of values showing $(x, h(x))$ pairs for a function where $x = 1$, $x = 2$, and $x = 3$.
- **Notable features of the answer choices:** Each choice has a different set of $h(x)$ values.

- "Bridge" concepts: Every $(x, h(x))$ pair in the correct answer choice will make a valid equation when plugged into the provided function.
- Pre-solution patterns (see p. 285): wrong answers try to imitate right answers

- Things to look out for: Don't pick an answer choice just because one $(x, h(x))$ pair works! Don't make a simple mistake related to algebra or sign!

Solution 1: Concrete/graphing: We can graph the provided function, then eliminate any choice whose points don't match up with the graph.

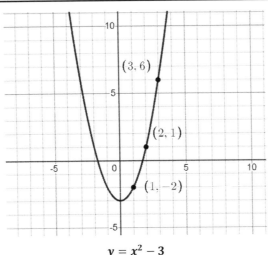

$$y = x^2 - 3$$

We can see that there is a point at $(1, -2)$, which eliminates (A) and (C). There is also a point at $(2, 1)$, which appears on the table for both (B) and (D). Finally, the graph contains a point at $(3, 6)$, which eliminates (D) and confirms (B) as the correct answer.

Solution 2: Concrete: Plug 1, 2, and 3 into the provided function to find their $h(x)$ values, then pick the choice that matches your results.

$h(x) = x^2 - 3$	(provided function)
$h(1) = (1)^2 - 3 = -2$	(result when $x = 1$)
$h(2) = (2)^2 - 3 = 1$	(result when $x = 2$)
$h(3) = (3)^2 - 3 = 6$	(result when $x = 3$)

So $h(x)$ has points at $(1, -2)$, $(2, 1)$, and $(3, 6)$. Those points match the values in (B), so (B) is correct.

ANSWER CHOICE ANALYSIS

(A): These values would work if the function were $h(x) = x + 3$. **(C):** These values would work if the function were $h(x) = 2x - 3$. **(D):** This choice contains the right $h(x)$ values for $x = 1$ and $x = 2$, but not for $x = 3$.

How to check? Try an alternate approach above. Try to figure out which mistakes could lead to some of the wrong answer choices, and verify that you haven't made any such mistakes.

▶ Post-solution patterns (see page 286): the right answer to the wrong question

Test 4, Module 2, Question 9

- What's the prompt asking for? The value of $f(0)$.
- Math concepts in the prompt: functions, exponents
- Elements of the answer choices: Each answer choice is an integer ranging from 0 to 270.
- Notable features of the answer choices: (D) is ten times as much as (C). Two answer choices include 27.

- "Bridge" concepts: A value raised to an exponent of 0 is equal to 1.
- Pre-solution patterns (see p. 285): wrong answers try to imitate right answers
- Things to look out for: Notice that in the provided function 270 isn't being raised to the exponent; (0.1) is being raised to the exponent!

Solution 1: Concrete/graphing: We can graph the provided function and use it to find $f(0)$.

Facebook.com/QuestPreparation   Youtube.com/QuestPrep

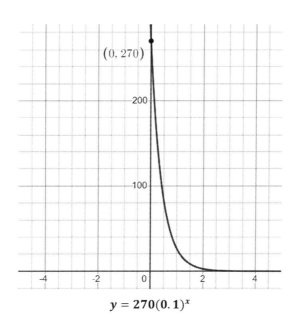

$$y = 270(0.1)^x$$

We can see that there is a point on the graph at $(0, 270)$. So $f(0) = 270$, and the answer is (D).

Solution 2: Algebra: Find $f(0)$ by plugging $x = 0$ into the provided function.

$f(x) = 270(0.1)^x$	(provided function)
$f(0) = 270(0.1)^0$	(plug in $x = 0$)
$f(0) = 270(1)$	(simplify)
$f(0) = 270$	(simplify)

So $f(0) = 270$, and (D) is correct.

ANSWER CHOICE ANALYSIS

(A): This would be the answer if the function were $f(x) = 270(0.1)x$. **(B):** This would be the answer if the function were $f(x) = 270^x$. **(C):** This is the value of $f(1)$.

How to check? Double-check which value is being raised to an exponent. Try an alternate approach above. Try to figure out which mistakes could lead to some of the wrong answer choices, and verify that you haven't made any such mistakes.

▶   Post-solution patterns (see page 286):   the right answer to the wrong question

Test 4, Module 2, Question 10

- What's the prompt asking for? The most appropriate conclusion about the proportion of the population that has the characteristic.

- Math concepts in the prompt: word problems, random sampling, proportions, margins of error

- Elements of the answer choices: Each choice is a sentence that tells us what the proportion is or is likely to be, using the numbers 0.45, 0.49, and/or 0.53.

- Notable features of the answer choices: Three choices give a "plausible" range for the proportion, while one gives an exact value for the proportion.

- "Bridge" concepts: A margin of error can be added to and subtracted from a sampled data point to find the likely range of the relevant value for the whole group the sample was taken from.

- Pre-solution patterns (see p. 285): wrong answers try to imitate right answers

- Things to look out for: Remember the properties of samples and margins of error!

Solution 1: Properties and definitions: Use your understanding of sampling and margins of error to pick the right answer choice.

The margin of error tells us a plausible range for a statistical value—more specifically, we can add the margin of error to an estimate to find the highest plausible value for that statistic, and we can subtract the margin of error from that estimate to find the lowest plausible value for that statistic.

In this case, the estimate is 0.49, and the margin of error is 0.04. So the lowest plausible value for the statistic is $0.49 - 0.04$, or 0.45, and the highest plausible value for the statistic is $0.49 + 0.04$, or 0.53. In other words, "it is plausible that the proportion is between 0.45 and 0.53," exactly as (A) says. So (A) is right.

(C): This was the proportion found in the sample, but this value doesn't mean that the whole population has the same proportion.

How to check? Try to figure out which mistakes could lead to some of the wrong answer choices, and verify that you haven't made any such mistakes.

Test 4, Module 2, Question 11

- What's the prompt asking for? The maximum number of boxes the truck in the prompt can tow in a trailer with a weight of 500 pounds if each box weighs 120 pounds.

- Math concepts in the prompt: word problems, equation models

- Elements of the answer choices: Each answer choice is an integer in the 30s.

- Notable features of the answer choices: The choices are two pairs of consecutive integers.

- "Bridge" concepts: We can use the weight of the trailer and the weight of the boxes, along with the information in the prompt about the truck's capacity, to answer the question.

- Pre-solution patterns (see p. 285): wrong answers try to imitate right answers

- Things to look out for: Don't misread the prompt! Don't forget to account for the weight of the trailer! Don't make a simple algebra mistake!

Solution 1: Concrete: Find the total combined weight of the trailer and boxes using each number in the answer choices. Pick the highest number that doesn't result in a combined weight of more than 4,600 pounds.

The prompt tells us that "the combined weight of the trailer and the boxes it contains" can be "no more than 4,600 pounds." It also tells us that the trailer weighs 500 pounds, and each box weighs 120 pounds. We can multiply the number of boxes by 120 pounds, then add the weight of the trailer to find the combined weight of the trailer and boxes. The answer choice that yields the highest number under 4,600 will be the correct answer.

    (A) $(34 \times 120) + 500 = 4{,}580$ (combined weight of trailer and 34 boxes)
    (B) $(35 \times 120) + 500 = 4{,}700$ (combined weight of trailer and 35 boxes)
    (C) $(38 \times 120) + 500 = 5{,}060$ (combined weight of trailer and 38 boxes)
    (D) $(39 \times 120) + 500 = 5{,}180$ (combined weight of trailer and 39 boxes)

We can see that choice (A) produces the highest total weight that's less than 4,600 pounds, so (A) is correct.

Solution 2: Algebra: Convert the words and phrases in the prompt into a mathematical expression relating all the values in the prompt, then use that expression to answer the question.

We can use the information in the prompt to create an inequality where x is the number of boxes; then we can solve for x.

the combined weight of the trailer and the boxes it contains is no more than 4,600 pounds

"No more than 4,600 pounds" is the same as saying "less than or equal to 4,600 pounds," which is the same $\leq 4{,}600$. So let's make that change.

the combined weight of the trailer and the boxes it contains $\leq 4{,}600$

The weight of the trailer is given as 500 pounds, so let's update our inequality accordingly.

500 and the boxes it contains $\leq 4{,}600$

We're told each box weighs 120 pounds, so the weight of "the boxes it contains" must be the number of boxes multiplied by 120. We'll call the number of boxes x, and we know the word "and" means we're adding the weight of the trailer and the weight of the boxes.

$$500 + 120x \leq 4{,}600$$

Now we can solve for x.

    $500 + 120x \leq 4{,}600$ (inequality we just found)
    $120x \leq 4{,}100$ (subtract 500 from both sides)
    $x \leq 34.17$ (divide both sides by 120)

So the inequality will be true when x is less than or equal to approximately 34.17. We can round down to find the largest whole number of boxes that will result in a valid inequality; the result is 34. So (A) is correct.

Solution 3: Concrete/graphing: Once we found our inequality above, we could have skipped the algebra and just graphed that inequality, then used that graph to find the solution.

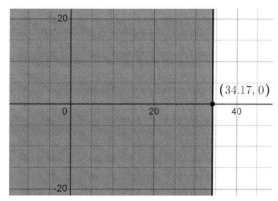

$$500 + 120x \leq 4,600$$

We can see that everything to the left of $x \leq 34.17$ is a solution, so our answer will be the largest whole number less than approximately 34.17. That number is 34, and the answer is (A).

ANSWER CHOICE ANALYSIS

(B): This is the *least* number of boxes that results in a weight that goes *over* the truck's capacity. **(C):** This would be the answer if we didn't need to account for the 500 pound trailer. **(D):** This choice combines the errors from (B) and (C).

How to check? Make sure your solution accounted for the weight of the trailer. Try an alternate approach above. Try to figure out which mistakes could lead to some of the wrong answer choices, and verify that you haven't made any such mistakes.

▶ Post-solution patterns (see page 286): the right answer to the wrong question

Test 4, Module 2, Question 12

- What's the prompt asking for? The positive solution to the given equation.
- Math concepts in the prompt: equations, exponents, positive solutions
- Elements of the answer choices: Each answer choice is an integer or fraction involving 7, 9, and/or 4.
- Notable features of the answer choices: Two answer choices are fractions with a denominator of 4, and two are single-digit integers.

- "Bridge" concepts: There must be at least two solutions to the equation (one positive and one not). Plugging in the right answer will make the given statement true.
- Pre-solution patterns (see p. 285): wrong answers try to imitate right answers
- Things to look out for: Make sure your solution accounts for the idea of more than one solution! Don't make a simple mistake related to algebra or sign!

Solution 1: Concrete/graphing: Put the given equation directly into your graphing calculator to find the solution that the question asks for.

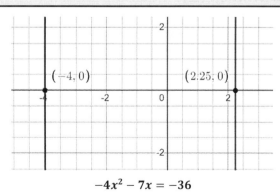

$$-4x^2 - 7x = -36$$

Each vertical line represents a solution to the equation. The vertical line that's to the right of 0 is at $x = 2.25$, which is equal to $\frac{9}{4}$. So (B) is correct.

Solution 2: Concrete: Plug the value from each answer choice into the provided equation to see which one is correct.

$-4x^2 - 7x = -36$	(given equation)
$-4\left(\frac{7}{4}\right)^2 - 7\left(\frac{7}{4}\right) = -36$	(plug in $x = \frac{7}{4}$ from (A))

$$-\frac{49}{4} - \frac{49}{4} = -36 \qquad \text{(simplify)}$$

$$-\frac{98}{4} = -36 \qquad \text{(simplify)}$$

$$-24.5 \neq -36 \qquad \text{(simplify)}$$

This statement isn't true, so (A) is wrong. Let's check (B).

$$-4x^2 - 7x = -36 \qquad \text{(given equation)}$$

$$-4\left(\frac{9}{4}\right)^2 - 7\left(\frac{9}{4}\right) = -36 \qquad \text{(plug in } x = \frac{9}{4} \text{ from (B))}$$

$$-\frac{81}{4} - \frac{63}{4} = -36 \qquad \text{(simplify)}$$

$$-\frac{144}{4} = -36 \qquad \text{(simplify)}$$

$$-36 = -36 \qquad \text{(simplify)}$$

This statement is true, so (B) appears to be correct. Let's check the remaining choices to help make sure we didn't make a mistake.

$$-4x^2 - 7x = -36 \qquad \text{(given equation)}$$

$$-4(4)^2 - 7(4) = -36 \qquad \text{(plug in } x = 4 \text{ from (C))}$$

$$-64 - 28 = -36 \qquad \text{(simplify)}$$

$$-92 \neq -36 \qquad \text{(simplify)}$$

This statement isn't true, so (C) is wrong. Let's check (D).

$$-4x^2 - 7x = -36 \qquad \text{(given equation)}$$

$$-4(7)^2 - 7(7) = -36 \qquad \text{(plug in } x = 7 \text{ from (D))}$$

$$-196 - 49 = -36 \qquad \text{(simplify)}$$

$$-245 \neq -36 \qquad \text{(simplify)}$$

This statement isn't true, so (D) is wrong. After considering each answer choice, we can see that (B) is correct.

ANSWER CHOICE ANALYSIS

(C): This is the absolute value of the negative solution to the equation.

How to check? Try an alternate approach above. Try to figure out which mistakes could lead to some of the wrong answer choices, and verify that you haven't made any such mistakes.

▶ Post-solution patterns (see page 286): the right answer to the wrong question

Test 4, Module 2, Question 13

- What's the prompt asking for? The probability of selecting a red tile.
- Math concepts in the prompt: data tables, distribution, random selection, probability
- "Bridge" concepts: The probability of an event happening can be expressed as a fraction with the number of desired outcomes as the numerator and the number of possible outcomes as the denominator.
- Things to look out for: Be careful when determining what counts as a desired outcome and what counts as a possible outcome! Don't get distracted by the mention of "shape"—the prompt only asks about choosing a certain color!

Solution 1: Probability: Use the information in the prompt to construct a probability fraction.

In order to find the probability fraction that the prompt requires, we need to figure out the number of desired outcomes and the number of possible outcomes for the situation described in the prompt. The number of desired outcomes will be the numerator of our probability fraction, and the number of possible outcomes will be the denominator of our probability fraction.

The prompt tells us about 100 tiles, and then asks "if one of these tiles…" So we know that we're selecting from the group of 100 tiles, which means there are 100 possible outcomes.

The prompt asks about "selecting a red tile," so the number of desired outcomes is the number of red tiles we might possibly choose. The bottom row of the provided table is labeled "total," and the second column of that table is labeled "Red." That row and column intersect at a cell that says "30," so we know there are 30 total red tiles. That means the number of desired outcomes is 30—in other words, there are 30 red tiles we might choose which would meet the prompt's requirement of "selecting a red tile."

So the numerator of our probability fraction is 30, and the denominator of our probability fraction is 100. That means the probability fraction is $\frac{30}{100}$, and our answer can be entered as the equivalent expressions $\frac{3}{10}$ or 0.3 (remember that the prompt says "Express your answer as a decimal or fraction, not as a percent").

How to check? Try to figure out which mistakes the College Board might hope you would make in finding your solution, and verify that you haven't made any such mistakes.

Test 4, Module 2, Question 14

- What's the prompt asking for? The slope of line j.
- Math concepts in the prompt: functions, graphs, parallel lines, slope
- "Bridge" concepts: Parallel lines have the same slope.

- Things to look out for: Don't make a simple algebra mistake! Remember that the lines are parallel, not perpendicular!

Solution 1: Concrete/graphing: Graph the provided function to find its slope.

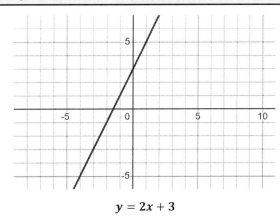

$$y = 2x + 3$$

We can see that for every 2 units the line travels up, it travels 1 unit to the right. That means the slope of f is $\frac{2}{1}$, or 2. If line j is parallel to the graph of $y = f(x)$, then the lines must have the same slope. So the slope of j is also 2, and the answer is 2.

Solution 2: Algebra: Use your understanding of slope-intercept form and parallel lines to answer the question.

If we can recognize that the provided function is in slope-intercept form—that is, $y = mx + b$ form—then we know that the coefficient of x is the slope of the line. So the slope of f is 2.

Parallel lines have equivalent slopes, so the slope of j must also be 2. That means the answer is 2.

How to check? Verify that line j is parallel, not perpendicular, to f. Try an alternate approach above. Try to figure out which mistakes the College Board might hope you would make in finding your solution, and verify that you haven't made any such mistakes.

Test 4, Module 2, Question 15

- What's the prompt asking for? The number of people who voted against the proposal.
- Math concepts in the prompt: word problems, proportions, data
- Elements of the answer choices: Each answer choice is a 4- or 5- digit integer and a multiple of 500.
- Notable features of the answer choices: (A), (B), and (C) form a series where each choice is 7,500 more than the previous choice. (A) is half of (B), and (C) is half of (D).
- "Bridge" concepts: We can use the provided proportion and the difference between the numbers of

voters to find the number of people who voted against the proposal.

- Pre-solution patterns (see p. 285): halves and doubles; first and last terms in a series are often wrong answers
- Things to look out for: Read the prompt carefully! Notice that the 15,000 value in the prompt is neither the number of people who voted for the proposal, nor the number of people who voted against the proposal! Make sure your answer is the number of people who voted against the proposal, not the number who voted for it!

Solution 1: Concrete: Use each answer choice to calculate the number of people who voted for the proposal, and see if the result is 15,000 more than the answer choice, as the prompt requires.

The prompt tells us that "3 times as many people voted in favor of the proposal as people who voted against it." We can use each number from the answer choices as the number of people who voted against the proposal, multiply that number by 3 to find the number of people who voted *in favor* of the proposal (according to that answer choice), and then check to see which answer choice causes the number of people who voted in favor of the proposal to be 15,000 more than the number of people who voted against the proposal.

$$7,500 \times 3 = 22,500$$ (value from (A) multiplied by 3 to find number who voted for)

$$22,500 - 7,500 = 15,000$$ (difference between votes for and against the proposal)

Choice (A) appears to be correct—if 7,500 people voted against the proposal, then 3 times that number, or 22,500, voted for the proposal, and 22,500 is 15,000 more than 7,500, as the prompt requires. Let's check the remaining choices to help make sure we didn't make a mistake.

$$15,000 \times 3 = 45,000$$ (value from (B) multiplied by 3 to find number who voted for)

$$45,000 - 15,000 = 30,000$$ (difference between votes for and against the proposal)

Choice (B) is wrong; if 15,000 people voted against the proposal, then 3 times that number, or 45,000, voted for the proposal, and 45,000 is 30,000 more than 15,000, not 15,000 more, as the prompt requires. Let's take a look at (C).

$$22,500 \times 3 = 67,500$$ (value from (C) multiplied by 3 to find number who voted for)

$$67,500 - 22,500 = 45,000$$ (difference between votes for and against the proposal)

Choice (C) is wrong; if 22,500 people voted against the proposal, then 3 times that number, or 67,500, voted for the proposal, and 67,500 is 45,000 more than 22,500, not 15,000 more, as the prompt requires. Finally, let's check (D).

$$45,000 \times 3 = 135,000$$ (value from (D) multiplied by 3 to find number who voted for)

$$135,000 - 45,000 = 90,000$$ (difference between votes for and against the proposal)

Choice (D) is wrong; if 45,000 people voted against the proposal, then 3 times that number, or 135,000, voted for the proposal, and 135,000 is 90,000 more than 45,000, not 15,000 more, as the prompt requires.

After checking each choice, we can see that (A) is correct.

Solution 2: Abstract: Use the information in the prompt to create two mathematical expressions relating the numbers of voters to each other, and use those expressions to answer the question.

The prompt tells us two statements about the votes for and against the proposal—that 3 times as many people voted for the proposal as people who voted against it, and that 15,000 more people voted for it than voted against it. We can make these statements into a system of two equations, and then find the solution to that system to answer the question.

Let's say x is the number of votes for the proposal, and y is the number of votes against the proposal. If "3 times as many people voted in favor of the proposal as voted against it," that the same as saying $x = 3y$. So that's the first equation in our system of equations.

If "15,000 more people voted in favor of the proposal than voted against it," that's the same as saying $x = y + 15,000$. Now we have our second equation, so our system looks like this:

$$x = 3y$$
$$x = y + 15,000$$

From here, there are a couple of ways we can find the answer. We can graph the two equations, like this:

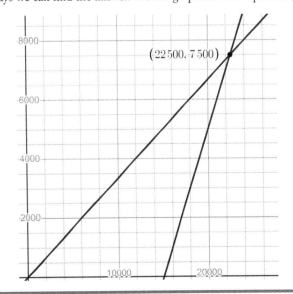

$$x = 3y \text{ and } x = y + 15,000$$

If we do, we can see that the graphs intersect at $(22,500, 7,500)$. That means 22,500 people voted for the proposal, and 7,500 voted against it—so (A) is correct.

We could also plug $x = 3y$ from the first equation into the second equation to get the following:

$3y = y + 15,000$	(x-value from one equation plugged into the other equation)
$2y = 15,000$	(subtract y from both sides)
$y = 7,500$	(divide both sides by 2)

We said that y was the number of votes against the proposal, and that's what the prompt asked for—so the answer is 7,500, and (A) is correct.

ANSWER CHOICE ANALYSIS

(C): This is the number of people who voted for the proposal. **(D):** This would be the result of misreading the prompt and thinking that 15,000 was the number of people who voted for the proposal, and then thinking 3 times as many people voted *against* the proposal as voted for it, instead of the other way around.

How to check? Add 15,000 to the answer you found, and verify that the result is 3 times as much as the answer you found. Try an alternate approach above. Try to figure out which mistakes could lead to some of the wrong answer choices, and verify that you haven't made any such mistakes.

▶ Post-solution patterns (see page 286): the right answer to the wrong question

Test 4, Module 2, Question 16

- What's the prompt asking for? The value of z.
- Math concepts in the prompt: transversals, parallel lines, angle measures, equations
- Elements of the answer choices: Each answer choice is an integer ranging from 3 to 139.
- Notable features of the answer choices: (C) and (D) add up to 180.

- "Bridge" concepts: $x = y$, and $z + y = 180°$.
- Things to look out for: Don't get confused about which variables refer to which angle! Don't get confused about which angle measures are equal, and which ones add up to 180°!

Solution 1: Geometry: Use your understanding of transversals and algebra to find the values of x and y, and use the results to find z.

x and y are the degree measures of two vertical angles. We know from our training that vertical angles have equal measures, by definition, so we can set those two degree measures equal to one another and see what we can learn.

$6k + 13 = 8k - 29$	(measure of x set equal to measure of y)
$13 = 2k - 29$	(subtract $6k$ from both sides)
$42 = 2k$	(add 29 to both sides)
$21 = k$	(divide both sides by 2)

Now that we know the value of k, we can plug it into the expression for either degree measure to find the value of both x and y. Let's use the expression for x, for no particular reason.

$x = 6k + 13$	(measure of each of the vertical angles)
$x = 6(21) + 13$	(plug in $k = 21$)
$x = 126 + 13$	(simplify)
$x = 139$	(simplify)

Now we know that x and y are both equal to 139—but the question asked for the value of z!

The prompt tells us that m and n are parallel, which means t must cross both m and n at the same angle. So the 4 angles created when t crosses m must be equal to the corresponding 4 angles created when t crosses n, like this:

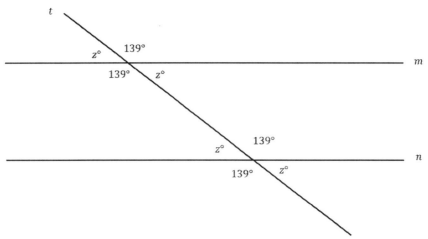

We can see (in several places) that $z°$ and $139°$ are supplementary angles—that is, they add up to a $180°$ angle, which is the same as a straight line. If $z + 139 = 180$, then $z = 41$. So the answer is (C).

ANSWER CHOICE ANALYSIS

(B): This is the value of k. **(D):** This is the value of x, and also the value of y.

How to check? Try to figure out which mistakes the College Board might hope you would make in finding your solution, and verify that you haven't made any such mistakes.

▶ Post-solution patterns (see page 286): the right answer to the wrong question

Test 4, Module 2, Question 17

- What's the prompt asking for? The value of p.
- Math concepts in the prompt: equations with no solution
- Elements of the answer choices: Each choice is a fraction or integer ranging from 0 to 4.
- Notable features of the answer choices: Two choices are integers, and two are fractions.

- "Bridge" concepts: If an equation has no solution, that means there's no x-value we can plug into it to make the equation true.
- Things to look out for: Don't make a simple mistake related to algebra or sign! Think carefully about what it means for an equation to have no solution!

Solution 1: Concrete/graphing: We can graph the given equation in our calculator, using the value from each answer choice as p. The graph that shows no solution will be the right answer.

(A)

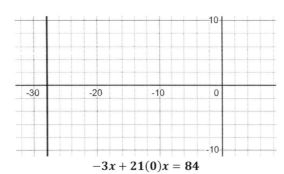

$$-3x + 21(0)x = 84$$

(B)

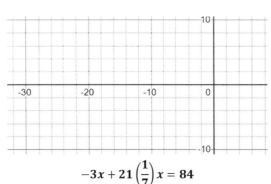

$$-3x + 21\left(\frac{1}{7}\right)x = 84$$

(C)

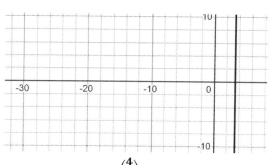

$$-3x + 21\left(\frac{4}{3}\right)x = 84$$

(D)

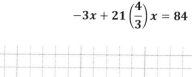

$$-3x + 21(4)x = 84$$

We can see that only (B) shows no solution, so (B) is correct.

Solution 2: Concrete: Plug in each answer choice for p and see which one results in an equation with no solution.

(A) $-3x + 21(0)x = 84$ $\qquad$ $-3x = 84$ $\qquad\qquad$ $x = -28$

(B) $-3x + 21\left(\frac{1}{7}\right)x = 84$ $\qquad$ $-3x + 3x = 84$ $\qquad$ $0 = 84$

(C) $-3x + 21\left(\frac{4}{3}\right)x = 84$ $\qquad$ $25x = 84$ $\qquad\qquad$ $x = \frac{84}{25}$

(D) $-3x + 21(4)x = 84$ $\qquad$ $81x = 84$ $\qquad\qquad$ $x = \frac{28}{27}$

Only (B) resulted in an invalid statement (that is, $0 = 84$), so (B) is the answer.

ANSWER CHOICE ANALYSIS

(A): This choice might be tempting for test-takers who assume the right answer must create a situation where something is divided by 0, but that's not what this choice does.

How to check? Try an alternate approach above. Try to figure out which mistakes could lead to some of the wrong answer choices, and verify that you haven't made any such mistakes.

Note Some test-takers might not be sure what is meant by the sentence "the equation has no solution," and they might not be sure what they're looking for. But even if you weren't sure about that sentence, you could still try either approach above—that is, plugging in each p-value and graphing the result, or plugging in each p-value and simplifying the resulting expression—and you probably would have realized that the right answer was the choice that resulted in no graph, or the one that said $0 = 84$. Remember: you don't have to have a perfect understanding of a question, or a complete roadmap to the answer, to get started on your solution—and often, just getting started *somewhere* can clear a lot of things up.

Test 4, Module 2, Question 18

- What's the prompt asking for? The value of x for which $f(x)$ reaches its minimum.

- Math concepts in the prompt: functions, equations, minimum values

- Elements of the answer choices: Each answer choice is a negative integer or fraction including the numeral 3.

- Notable features of the answer choices: Two choices are integers, and two are fractions with a two for a denominator.

- "Bridge" concepts: The minimum point of the function is the lowest $f(x)$-value produced by plugging in an x-value.

- Pre-solution patterns (see p. 285): wrong answers try to imitate right answers

- Things to look out for: Don't make a simple mistake related to algebra or sign!

Solution 1: Concrete/graphing: We can graph the provided function to find the x-value of the graph's minimum.

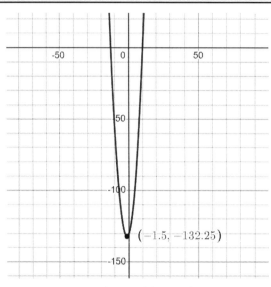

$$y = (x - 10)(x + 13)$$

We can see that the graph reaches a minimum when $x = -\frac{3}{2}$, so (D) is correct.

Solution 2: Concrete: Plug the value from each answer choice into the provided function; the choice that produces the lowest value must be the correct answer.

(A)	$f(-130) =$	$\big((-130) - 10\big)\big((-130) + 13\big) =$	$(-140)(-117) =$	16,380
(B)	$f(-13) =$	$\big((-13) - 10\big)\big((-13) + 13\big) =$	$(-23)(0) =$	0
(C)	$f\left(-\frac{23}{2}\right) =$	$\left(\left(-\frac{23}{2}\right) - 10\right)\left(\left(-\frac{23}{2}\right) + 13\right) =$	$(-21.5)(1.5) =$	-32.25
(D)	$f\left(-\frac{3}{2}\right) =$	$\left(\left(-\frac{3}{2}\right) - 10\right)\left(\left(-\frac{3}{2}\right) + 13\right) =$	$(-11.5)(11.5) =$	-132.25

Choice (D) produces the lowest $f(x)$ value, so (D) must be correct.

ANSWER CHOICE ANALYSIS

(A): This is $f(0)$, which some untrained test-takers might assume would produce the lowest $f(x)$ value.

How to check? Try an alternate approach above. Try to figure out which mistakes could lead to some of the wrong answer choices, and verify that you haven't made any such mistakes.

▶   Post-solution patterns (see page 286): the right answer to the wrong question

---

Test 4, Module 2, Question 19

- What's the prompt asking for? The best interpretation of the vertex of $f(x)$.

- Math concepts in the prompt: function models, time

- Elements of the answer choices: Each choice is a sentence related to the height of the ball.

- Notable features of the answer choices: Two choices mention the ball's minimum height, and two mention the ball's height when it started moving. Two choices mentions 3 inches and two choices mention 7 inches.

- "Bridge" concepts: We can find the vertex of the graph, then use the information from the prompt to figure out what that vertex represents.

- Pre-solution patterns (see p. 285): wrong answers try to imitate right answers

- Things to look out for: Don't mix up x and $f(x)$! Make sure to read the prompt carefully!

Solution 1: Concrete/graphing: Graph the provided equation and use what we learn to eliminate the wrong answer choices.

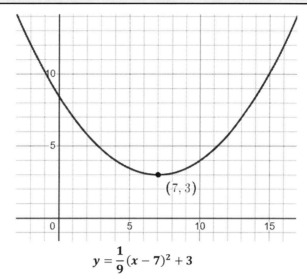

$$y = \frac{1}{9}(x - 7)^2 + 3$$

We can see that the vertex of the graph occurs at the point $(7, 3)$. The prompt tells us that x is the number of seconds after the ball starts moving, and $f(x)$ is the ball's height above the ground, in inches. Every answer choice mentions "height… above the ground," so we know these statements are about the $f(x)$ value, which in this case is 3. So we can eliminate (B) and (D).

(C) includes the phrase "when it started moving," but the prompt tells us that x is the number of seconds "after it started moving." At the point $(7, 3)$, $x = 7$, so we're talking about what's going on 7 seconds *after* the ball started moving—not *when* the ball started moving. So we can eliminate (C) as well.

That leaves only (A), the correct answer.

Solution 2: Concrete/graphing: Graph the provided function, then carefully interpret the vertex in the context of the scenario from the prompt.

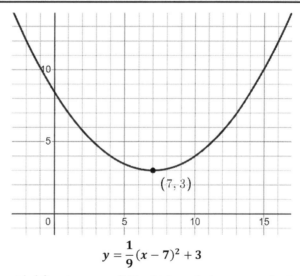

$$y = \frac{1}{9}(x - 7)^2 + 3$$

Once again, when we graph the provided function as we did in the last solution, we see that its vertex is at $(7, 3)$. That coordinate pair means that at 7 seconds after the ball starts moving—remember that the prompt tells us x is the number of seconds after the ball starts moving—the ball is 3 inches above the ground (remember that the prompt tell us $f(x)$ is the ball's height above the ground).

We can see in the graph that this point is the minimum value of the height of the ball. That means the metal ball's minimum height is 3 inches above the ground, just as (A) says. So (A) is right.

ANSWER CHOICE ANALYSIS

(B): This choice would be correct if the vertex were at $(3,7)$ instead of $(7,3)$. **(C):** This choice would be tempting for test-takers who mistakenly assumed that the ball must have started at its lowest point. **(D):** This choice combines the mistakes from (B) and (C).

How to check? Try an alternate approach above. Try to figure out which mistakes could lead to some of the wrong answer choices, and verify that you haven't made any such mistakes.

- What's the prompt asking for? The value of cos(L).
- Math concepts in the prompt: triangles, cosine, right angles

- Things to look out for: Make sure you use the correct trigonometric identity! Don't mix up the different side lengths! Make sure your sketch matches the information from the prompt!

Solution 1: Geometry: Sketch and label the triangle based on the information in the prompt, then use your knowledge of triangles to figure out everything you need to answer the question.

Let's sketch triangle JKL based on the provided information. The prompt says that J is a right angle. Also, we know from SOHCAHTOA that cosine is equal to $\frac{\text{adjacent}}{\text{hypotenuse}}$, so if $\cos K = \frac{24}{51}$, then it must be true that the ratio of the length of the side adjacent to K to the hypotenuse is $\frac{24}{51}$. Let's put all of that in our sketch.

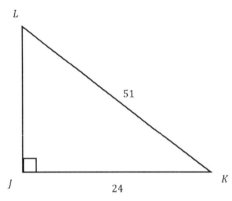

In order to find $\cos L$, we need to know the length of the side adjacent to L (again, because cosine is equal to $\frac{\text{adjacent}}{\text{hypotenuse}}$, and we're missing the length of that adjacent side). If we know the length of the hypotenuse of a right triangle, along with the length of one of its legs, we can use the Pythagorean theorem to find the length of the other leg.

$$a^2 + b^2 = c^2 \qquad \text{(Pythagorean theorem)}$$
$$24^2 + b^2 = 51^2 \qquad \text{(plug in } a = 24 \text{ and } c = 51)$$
$$576 + b^2 = 2{,}601 \qquad \text{(simplify)}$$
$$b^2 = 2{,}025 \qquad \text{(subtract 576 from both sides)}$$
$$b = 45 \qquad \text{(take the square root of both sides)}$$

So the missing side length is 45, which means the side length adjacent to L is 45, so $\cos L = \frac{45}{51}$. This can be reduced and entered as $\frac{15}{17}$, .8824, .8823, or 0.882, according to the College Board's rules for entering fractions or decimal values.

How to check? Verify that you used the right trigonometric identity. Try to figure out which mistakes the College Board might hope you would make in finding your solution, and verify that you haven't made any such mistakes.

- What's the prompt asking for? The greatest possible value of b.
- Math concepts in the prompt: equations, exponents, integers, no real solution, greatest possible value

- "Bridge" concepts: The equation has no real solution when no x-value can make the equation valid.
- Things to look out for: Don't make a simple mistake related to algebra or sign! Remember that b is a positive integer!

Solution 1: Concrete/graphing: We can rewrite the provided equation using y for b, graph the result, and then use that graph to find what the prompt asks for.

When we rewrite the provided equation using y for b, we get this:
$$-x^2 + yx - 676 = 0$$
Now we can graph that equation, which gives us this:

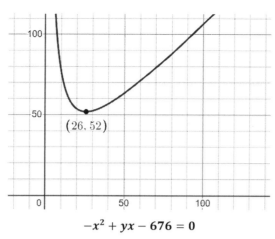

$$-x^2 + yx - 676 = 0$$

We need to figure out the "greatest possible value of b" that causes the equation to have no real solutions, bearing in mind that b must be a positive integer (remember that the y-values in our graph represent different possible values of b).

Every point on the graph must, by definition, correspond to a b-value for which there *is* an x-value solution. Any b-value that doesn't appear on the graph must have no x-value solution—and remember, the prompt asked us to find the greatest b-value where there is no solution. For example, there is no point where $b = 5$ (we know this is true because we can see that the lowest point on the graph has a b-value of 52, and 5 is less than 52), so we know that when $b = 5$, the equation in the prompt has no real solution.

The lowest b-value that *does* have a corresponding x-value is the lowest point on the graph, which is $(26, 52)$. So the lowest b-value on the graph is 52, which means the highest b-value *without* a corresponding x-value—that is, the highest b-value which causes the given equation to have no solution—is the highest integer that's less than 52, which is 51. So the answer is 51. (Remember that the prompt told us that b must be an integer, so an answer like 51.99999 isn't acceptable.)

How to check? Plug the value you found in for b in the given equation, and enter the result into your calculator to verify that the resulting graph shows no solution. Try to figure out which mistakes the College Board might hope you would make in finding your solution, and verify that you haven't made any such mistakes.

Test 4, Module 2, Question 22

- What's the prompt asking for? The number of solutions that the system of three equations will have.
- Math concepts in the prompt: line graphs, systems of equations
- Elements of the answer choices: Each answer choice is a phrase telling us the system will have 0, 1, 2, or infinitely many solutions.

- "Bridge" concepts: A solution to the system of three equations will be a point where all three of the lines intersect.
- Things to look out for: Think carefully about what it means for a system of three equations to have a solution!

Solution 1: Concrete/graphing: We can graph the provided third equation to see whether it passes through the point of intersection of the two lines in the graph, and then use that information to answer the question.

We can see that the two lines in the graph intersect at the point $(8, 2)$. If there is a solution to the system of three equations, then the third equation must pass through that point as well (we know this because a solution to a system of equations is a point where all the lines in that system of equations must intersect, so if two of the lines already only intersect at one point, the only possible way for a system of three equations to have a solution is if the third equation goes through that same point of intersection as well). Let's graph that third equation along with the point of intersection of the other two lines to see what we find out.

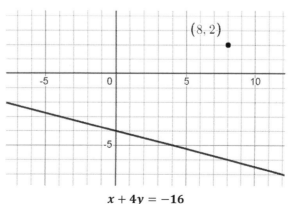

$$x + 4y = -16$$

This line doesn't pass through $(8, 2)$, so there can't be any solution to the system of three equations. So (A) is correct.

Solution 2: Concrete: Plug the point of intersection of the two lines in the graph into the given third equation to see if the new line travels through that point as well.

Instead of graphing the provided equation to see if it passes through the point $(8, 2)$, we could also plug $x = 8$ and $y = 2$ into the provided equation to see if those values result in a true statement.

$$x + 4y = -16 \qquad \text{(provided equation)}$$
$$(8) + 4(2) = -16 \qquad \text{(plug in } x = 8 \text{ and } y = 2)$$
$$16 = -16 \qquad \text{(simplify)}$$

This isn't a true statement, so $(8, 2)$ doesn't lie on the graph of the third equation, which means there is no solution to the system of three equations, and (A) is right.

ANSWER CHOICE ANALYSIS

(B): This is the right answer when only considering the two lines in the provided graph. **(C):** This would be correct if a solution to the system of equations were any point where *two* of the lines intersected, as opposed to all three of the lines.

How to check? Try an alternate approach above. Try to figure out which mistakes could lead to some of the wrong answer choices, and verify that you haven't made any such mistakes.

▶   Post-solution patterns (see page 286): the right answer to the wrong question

Test 4, Module 2, Question 23

- What's the prompt asking for? The value of p.
- Math concepts in the prompt: function models, money, fractional exponents, percentages
- Elements of the answer choices: Each answer choice is an integer ranging from 4 to 64.
- Notable features of the answer choices: (C) and (D) add up to 100.

- "Bridge" concepts: The percent decrease of the value isn't the percentage of the value that remains; it's the percentage of the value that is lost.
- Pre-solution patterns (see p. 285): opposites
- Things to look out for: Make sure you find the *percent decrease* of the value, not the remaining percentage of the value! Notice that x is the number of *months* of use, but the question asks about the decrease each *year!*

Solution 1: Concrete: Find the value of the function after 0 months, and then after 12 months, and find the percent decrease in value over that span.

The prompt tells us that the information in the function is based on x months of use, and asks us about the percentage decrease after 1 year of use—we need to keep in mind that there are 12 months in a year, and make sure that we base our answer on x-values in the function that are 12 units apart.

With that in mind, we can find the value of the function when $x = 0$, and then find the value of the function when $x = 12$, and the result will be two $f(x)$ values that are a year apart. We can find the percent decrease of the second value compared to the first value, and that will be our answer.

$$f(x) = 5{,}470(0.64)^{\frac{x}{12}} \qquad \text{(provided function)}$$

$$f(0) = 5{,}470(0.64)^{\frac{0}{12}} = 5{,}470(1) = 5{,}470 \qquad \text{(value of } f(0))$$

$$f(12) = 5{,}470(0.64)^{\frac{12}{12}} = 5{,}470(0.64) = 3{,}500.8 \qquad \text{(value of } f(12))$$

So after 0 months—that is, when $x = 0$—the value of the function is $5{,}470$, and after 12 months—that is, when $x = 12$—the value of the function is $3{,}500.8$. Now we need to find the percent decrease between those two numbers. To do that, we find the difference between those two numbers, divide that difference by the starting number, and then convert the result to a percentage.

$$5{,}470 - 3{,}500.8 = 1969.2 \qquad \text{(difference between the two values)}$$

$$\frac{1969.2}{5{,}470} = 0.36 \qquad \text{(divide the result by the starting value)}$$

$$0.36 \times 100\% = 36\% \qquad \text{(multiply the result by 100\%)}$$

So there was a 36% decrease in the 12-month period, which means (C) is correct.

Solution 2: Test-smart: Notice what happens to the value in the provided function over the course of a year, and pick the choice that gives the percent decrease over that span.

If we notice that when $x = 0$ we'll be multiplying 5,470 by 1 (because $(0.64)^{\frac{0}{12}} = (0.64)^0 = 1$), and then when $x = 12$ we'll be multiplying 5,470 by 0.64 (because $(0.64)^{\frac{12}{12}} = (0.64)^1 = 0.64$), then we can realize that $f(12)$ must be 64% of $f(0)$, which means that f decreases by 36% from $f(0)$ to $f(12)$ (because $100\% - 36\% = 64\%$). Again, we see that (C) is the correct answer.

ANSWER CHOICE ANALYSIS

(A): This is the approximate percent decrease after one *month*, not after a *year*, as the prompt requires. **(D):** This is the percent of the value *left* after a year, not the *percent decrease,* as the prompt requires.

How to check? Verify that your answer is the percent decrease, not the remaining value. Verify that you correctly accounted for the units of time in the prompt. Try an alternate approach above. Try to figure out which mistakes could lead to some of the wrong answer choices, and verify that you haven't made any such mistakes.

▶   Post-solution patterns (see page 286):   the right answer to the wrong question

Test 4, Module 2, Question 24

- **What's the prompt asking for?** The choice that correctly compares the medians and the ranges of data sets A and B.

- **Math concepts in the prompt:** data sets, dot plots, median, range

- **Elements of the answer choices:** Each answer choice is a sentence that compares the medians and ranges of the two data sets.

- **"Bridge" concepts:** We can use the information in the prompt to figure out how the changes would affect the median and range of the data set.

- **Pre-solution patterns (see p. 285):** wrong answers try to imitate right answers

- **Things to look out for:** Don't mix up sets *A* and *B*! Don't mix up median and range! The answer choices are highly similar—don't misread them!

Solution 1: Concrete: Use the provided information to calculate the median and range for each set, then pick the choice that makes a true statement about the results.

We can calculate the median and range of data set A, then calculate the median and range of data set B, and then make the comparison the prompt asks for.

The median of a set is the number in the middle when the values in that set are ordered from least to greatest (if there is an even number of values, the median is the average of the two middle numbers). The prompt tells us that there are 15 values in data set A, so the 8th value will be the median. We can read the dot plot to see that the first 5 values are 22, and the next 4 values—that is, the 6th through 9th values—are all 23. So the 8th value is 23, which means the median of data set A is 23.

The range of a set of numbers is the lowest number in the data set subtracted from the highest number in the data set. For data set A, the highest number is 26, and the lowest number is 22. $26 - 22 = 4$, so the range of data set A is 4.

Now let's find the corresponding information for data set B, and make our comparison. The prompt tells us that we can find the values in data set B by adding 56 to each of the values in data set A. So all the 22s would become 78s, all the 23s would become 79s, all the 24s would become 80s, all the 25s would become 81s, and all the 26s would become 82s.

The first 5 values will be 78, and the next 4 values will be 79—that is, the 6th, 7th, 8th, and 9th values will be 79. So the 8th value will be 79, which means the median of data set B is 79 (remember that there are 15 values in the set, so the 8th value is the one in the middle).

The highest number in data set B is 82 and the lowest number in data set B is 78, so the range is $82 - 78$, or 4.

We found that the median of data set B is greater than the median of data set A, and the ranges of the two sets are equal. That's what (C) says, so (C) is correct.

Solution 2: Abstract: Think about the properties of median and range in light of the information in the prompt, then pick the choice that makes a true statement.

If we know that the median of a set is the number in the middle when the values in that set are ordered from least to greatest, then we know that increasing every value in that set by the same number must increase the median as well. So the median of B must be greater than the median of A.

If we know that the range of a set is the difference between the greatest number in the set and the smallest number in the set, then we know that increasing every value in that set by the same number won't change the range—the difference between the smallest and greatest number must remain the same. So the range of B must be equal to the range of A.

Our reasoning matches the statements in choice (C), so (C) is correct.

(B): This is the reverse of the right answer.

How to check? Try an alternate approach above. Try to figure out which mistakes could lead to some of the wrong answer choices, and verify that you haven't made any such mistakes.

Test 4, Module 2, Question 25

- What's the prompt asking for? The equation that represents circle B.

- Math concepts in the prompt: equations, circles, translation

- Elements of the answer choices: Each answer choice is an equation for a circle ending in "= 49."

- "Bridge" concepts: If the circle is moved down 2 units, then its center must be moved down 2 units.

- Pre-solution patterns (see p. 285): wrong answers try to imitate right answers

- Things to look out for: Think carefully about what would cause the center of the circle to move down two units! Don't make a simple mistake related to sign!

Solution 1: Concrete/graphing: Graph the provided equation, then graph all the equations from the answer choices to see which one is the original circle moved down two units.

Here's the graph of the provided equation:

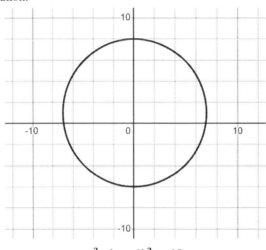

$$x^2+(y-1)^2 = 49$$

Here are the graphs of all the equations from the answer choices:

(A)

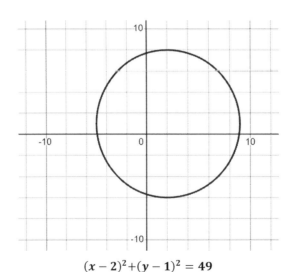

$$(x-2)^2+(y-1)^2 = 49$$

(B)

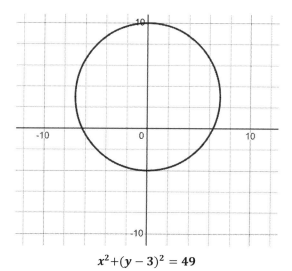

$$x^2 + (y - 3)^2 = 49$$

(C)

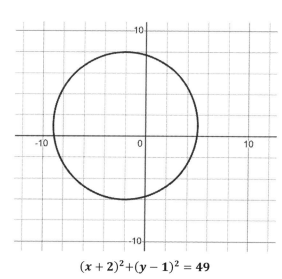

$$(x + 2)^2 + (y - 1)^2 = 49$$

(D)

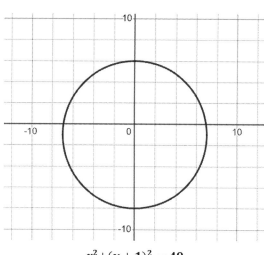

$$x^2 + (y + 1)^2 = 49$$

We can check to see which of the graphs of the answer choices is the original circle moved down two units. The graph of (D) is the original circle moved down two units, so (D) is correct.

Solution 2: Algebra: Use your understanding of the standard equation for a circle to figure out the coordinates of the center of circle *A*, then apply the same analysis to the answer choices to figure out which one has a center that's 2 units lower than the center of A.

If we know that the standard equation for a circle is in the form $(x - h)^2 + (y - k)^2 = r^2$, with a radius of r and its center at (h, k), then we can determine the center and radius of each circle represented by the equations in the answer choices.

(Notice that every answer choice has an r^2 value of 49, which means the radius r of each circle is 7. So we know all these circles are the same size; we just need to find which one is moved down 2 units from circle A's position.)

If a circle shifts down 2 units, it must be the case that the center of that circle shifts down 2 units. So we can determine the center of circle A, and then figure out which answer choice has a center that's 2 units lower than circle A's center.

When we compare the given equation for circle A to the standard equation for a circle $(x - h)^2 + (y - k)^2 = r^2$, we can see that $h = 0$ and $k = 1$, which means the center of circle A is at $(0, 1)$—keep in mind that x^2 is the same as $(x - 0)^2$. Let's use this same process to determine the center of each circle represented by the equations in the answer choices.

(A)	$(x - 2)^2 + (y - 1)^2 = 49$	$h = 2$	$k = 1$	center of the circle is $(2, 1)$
(B)	$x^2 + (y - 3)^2 = 49$	$h = 0$	$k = 3$	center of the circle is $(0, 3)$
(C)	$(x + 2)^2 + (y - 1)^2 = 49$	$h = -2$	$k = 1$	center of the circle is $(-2, 1)$
(D)	$x^2 + (y + 1)^2 = 49$	$h = 0$	$k = -1$	center of the circle is $(0, -1)$

Circle A's center is $(0, 1)$. 2 units below $(0, 1)$ would be $(0, -1)$, which is where choice (D)'s center is. So choice (D) is correct.

ANSWER CHOICE ANALYSIS

(A): This would be correct if circle A were moved *right* 2 units, instead of *down* 2 units. **(B):** This would be correct if circle A were moved *up* 2 units, instead of *down* 2 units. **(C):** This would be correct if circle A were moved *left* 2 units, instead of *down* 2 units.

How to check? Verify that you didn't make an error related to sign. Try an alternate approach above. Try to figure out which mistakes could lead to some of the wrong answer choices, and verify that you haven't made any such mistakes.

▶   Post-solution patterns (see page 286):   the right answer to the wrong question

> **Note**   Notice that knowing the standard equation for a circle was necessary for one of our solutions, but the quicker and easier graphing solution didn't require us to know anything at all about the standard equation for a circle. Remember on test day that the graphing calculator can be a powerful tool even when you're not completely comfortable with the math concepts involved in a given question.

Test 4, Module 2, Question 26

- **What's the prompt asking for?** The side length of each square base.
- **Math concepts in the prompt:** rectangular prisms, height, surface area
- **Elements of the answer choices:** Each choice is an integer ranging from 4 to 16.
- **Notable features of the answer choices:** (A), (C), and (D) are squares. (A), (B), and (D) form a series where each choice is twice as much as the previous choice.

- **"Bridge" concepts:** We can use the heights of the prisms and their combined surface area in terms of K to determine the side length of each square base.
- **Pre-solution patterns (see p. 285):** halves and doubles; first and last terms in a series are often wrong answers
- **Things to look out for:** Make sure you understand the dimensions and position of the objects described in the prompt! Make sure you don't mix up the various dimensions of the prisms!

Solution 1: Concrete: Use the values in the answer choices to calculate the total surface area of each prism on its own, and then calculate the total surface area of the prisms when they're glued together. The correct answer will be the one for which the glued-together surface area is $\frac{92}{47}$ the surface area of each prism individually.

The surface area of a rectangular prism is the sum of the surface areas of each of its sides. We're told in the prompt that the height of the prism is 90 cm; let's call the side length of the square base x.

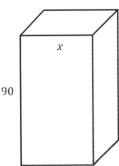

So the prism has 4 rectangular faces with a surface area of $90x$ (because the area of a rectangle is the length of the rectangle multiplied by its width), and two square faces with a surface area of x^2, and the sum of the surface areas of these six faces is the total surface area of the prism. This can be expressed as $4(90x) + 2x^2$, which is the same as $360x + 2x^2$.

The prompt then describes a situation where the prisms "are glued together along a square base." That might be hard to visualize, so let's sketch what that would look like:

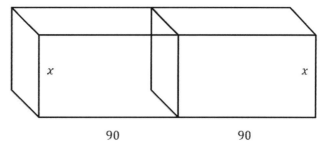

When the two prisms are glued together like this, their total surface area is decreased by twice the area of the square base—since two faces are glued together, one square base from each prism must no longer be on the surface of the object. The total surface area of this object is equal to 8 of the rectangular faces with a surface area of $90x$, and two square faces with a surface area of x^2 (remember that when the two prisms are glued together along the square base, the result still only has two square bases, one at either end). This can be expressed as $8(90x) + 2x^2$, which is the same as $720x + 2x^2$.

Now let's calculate the surface area for the single prism and the glued-together prisms for each answer choice, and see which one causes the glued-together prism to have $\frac{92}{47}$ the surface area of the single prism.

(A) $x = 4$

$360(4) + 2(4)^2 =$	$1{,}440 + 32 =$	$1{,}472$	(area of one prism)
$720(4) + 2(4)^2 =$	$2{,}880 + 32 =$	$2{,}912$	(area of two prisms glued together)

$1{,}472 \times \frac{92}{47} \approx 2{,}881.36$

When $x = 4$, the surface area of the prism is 1,472, and the surface area of the two prisms glued together is 2,912. When we multiplied the surface area of one prism by $\frac{92}{47}$ we got approximately 2,881.36, which wasn't equal to the surface area we found for the two glued-together prisms—so (A) isn't correct. Let's check (B).

(B) $x = 8$

$360(8) + 2(8)^2 =$	$2{,}880 + 128 =$	$3{,}008$	(area of one prism)
$720(8) + 2(8)^2 =$	$5{,}760 + 128 =$	$5{,}888$	(area of two prisms glued together)

$3{,}008 \times \frac{92}{47} = 5{,}888$

When $x = 8$, the surface area of the prism is 3,008, and the surface area of the two prisms glued together is 5,888. When we multiplied the surface area of one prism by $\frac{92}{47}$ we got 5,888, which was equal to the surface area we found for the two glued-together prisms—so (B) appears to be correct. Let's check the remaining choices to help make sure we didn't make a mistake.

(C) $x = 9$

$360(9) + 2(9)^2 =$	$3{,}240 + 162 =$	$3{,}402$	(area of one prism)
$720(9) + 2(9)^2 =$	$6{,}480 + 162 =$	$6{,}642$	(area of two prisms glued together)

$3{,}402 \times \frac{92}{47} \approx 6{,}659.23$

When $x = 9$, the surface area of the prism is 3,402, and the surface area of the two prisms glued together is 6,642. When we multiplied the surface area of one prism by $\frac{92}{47}$ we got approximately 6,659.23, which wasn't equal to the surface area we found for the two glued-together prisms—so (C) isn't correct. Let's check the last answer choice, (D).

(D) $x = 16$

$360(16) + 2(16)^2 =$	$5{,}760 + 512 =$	$6{,}272$	(area of one prism)
$720(16) + 2(16)^2 =$	$11{,}520 + 512 =$	$12{,}032$	(area of two prisms glued together)

$6{,}272 \times \frac{92}{47} \approx 12{,}277.11$

When $x = 16$, the surface area of the prism is 6,272, and the surface area of the two prisms glued together is 12,032. When we multiplied the surface area of one prism by $\frac{92}{47}$ we got approximately 12,277.11, which wasn't equal to the surface area we found for the two glued-together prisms—so (D) isn't correct.

After checking each answer choice, we can see that (B) is correct.

ANSWER CHOICE ANALYSIS

(A): This is half the right answer, and could be tempting for a test-taker who made a mistake involving a 2 at some point in the calculations. **(D):** This choice is double the right answer, and could be appealing for basically the same reason we saw in our discussion of (A).

How to check? Try to figure out which mistakes could lead to some of the wrong answer choices, and verify that you haven't made any such mistakes.

Test 4, Module 2, Question 27

- What's the prompt asking for? The value of p.
- Math concepts in the prompt: integers, percentages
- "Bridge" concepts: "$p\%$ greater than 30" means the amount greater than 30 that something is, expressed as a percentage of 30.

- Things to look out for: Think carefully about what specific percentage the question is asking you for!

Solution 1: Careful reading: Think about exactly what the prompt asks for, then figure out how to find it.

Let's think about what it means to be a certain percent "greater than" another number, as opposed to being a certain percent "of" another number. 30 is 100% *of* 30. But 30 is 0% *greater than* 30, because it isn't greater than 30—they're the same number.

Along similar lines, we can see that 60 is 200% *of* 30—it's twice as big as 30. But 60 is 100% *greater than* 30—it represents what happens when you take 100% of 30, and then add that result to 30.

This question asks us what percent 210 is *greater than* 30. In other words, what percentage of 30 would we add *to* 30 to get 210?

$210 - 30 = 180$, so we would add 180 to 30 to get 210. We can find the percentage that 180 is of 30 by dividing 180 by 30 and multiplying the result by 100%.

$$\frac{180}{30} = 6 \qquad \text{(difference between 210 and 30 divided by 30)}$$

$$6 \times 100\% = 600\% \qquad \text{(multiply result by 100\%)}$$

So 210 is 600% greater than 30, and the answer is 600.

How to check? Double-check which percentage of which number you needed to find to verify that your answer provides that information. Try to figure out which mistakes the College Board might hope you would make in finding your solution, and verify that you haven't made any such mistakes.

Note   This is a classic SAT Math question—the math is fairly simple, but many test-takers will get the wrong answer because they won't read carefully enough, and they'll think the question asks for something it doesn't actually ask for. Remember this lesson on test day: the most important skill on every part of the SAT is careful reading!

Part 8: Closing Thoughts

By now, we've covered everything you need to know for test day. You've seen how the SAT is designed, you know how to exploit that design to maximize your score, and you've seen these ideas applied to four official SAT Practice Tests from the College Board. Now we'll close out this Black Book with some thoughts and observations that may be helpful for some readers… including where to find me online for more advice on test-taking, admissions, career advice, and other challenges facing high school and college students.

In this part of the Black Book, you'll learn the following:

- answers to frequently asked questions relating to the SAT and the process of training for it
- what it means to be an "SAT Machine," and how to become one
- how to shoot for an elite score, or even a perfect score
- what to do if American English isn't your first language
- why every question I've ever been asked about the SAT has basically the same answer
- where to find additional helpful resources online

Frequently Asked Questions

General Questions

"How Long Will I Need to Practice?"

There is no set amount of time that every student should plan to spend practicing. It varies heavily from person to person. Your goal should be to develop a deep understanding of the way the SAT works, not to log an arbitrary number of practice hours. For more on this, see "Things To Think About For Scheduling" on page 30 of this Black Book.

"Where Did You Learn These Strategies?"

I didn't "learn" these strategies in the sense of having some book or tutor explain them to me. These strategies are the result of close analysis of real SAT practice questions to determine which tactics consistently produce right answers. Over the years, I've refined both the strategies themselves and the way that I teach them to students, and I've adapted them to the College Board's occasional format changes—like the one that happened in 2023-2024.

"What's the Best Way to Start Implementing Your Strategies?"

The best way to get started is generally to learn the strategies in an abstract way first, and then to see several sample solutions that implement the strategies against real College Board SAT questions. Finally, it's important to try to implement the strategies yourself, and to try to figure things out on your own as much as you can when you get stuck. For more ideas on specific drills and exercises, please see "Drills and Exercises" on page 28. For a selection of videos that demonstrate the ideas in this book, please visit www.SATprepVideos.com (those sample videos are free to readers of this book).

"Do these strategies work on the ACT? What about other standardized tests?"

All well-designed standardized tests must follow certain rules and patterns when they create their test questions—otherwise the tests wouldn't be standardized. But those particular rules and patterns don't have to be the same for every standardized test. ACT questions have their own standardized design elements that are different from those of SAT questions, but still fairly similar to them.

So the short answer is that the *specific* strategies in this Black Book are aimed at the SAT in particular. Some will work fairly well on other tests, and some won't. But the general idea of analyzing a standardized test in terms of rules and patterns can still be applied successfully against the ACT and other major standardized tests.

If you like the material in this book, and you're also preparing for the ACT, you may be interested in my *ACT Prep Black Book*. For students planning to apply to grad school, I've also written the *GRE Prep Black Book*.

"What if I Want to Score a 1600? What if I Only Need to Score a 1000 (or 1200, or 1400, Etc.)?"

Contrary to popular belief, you don't need to use different strategies to reach different score levels, because the design of the SAT is constant. It would be more accurate to say that in order to score a 1600 you need to be roughly 99% accurate in your execution of the SAT strategies in this Black Book, while in order to score a 1400 you must be roughly 85% accurate, and in order to score a 1000 you must be around 50-60% accurate, and so on.

So scoring higher isn't a question of learning separate strategies; it's a question of becoming more accurate and consistent when applying a fixed set of strategies. For more on how to do these things, see "Being an SAT Machine" on page 523 of this Black Book, and "The Nature of Elite Scores" on page 524.

"What if I Can't Get the Strategies to Work?"

Most students experience difficulty with some of these strategies at some point in their preparation, even if the difficulty is only limited to a single practice question. This can be frustrating, of course—but it's actually a great opportunity to improve your understanding of the test, because the experience of figuring out how to overcome these temporary setbacks can be very instructive, if we let it.

(Bear in mind that this discussion of how to handle difficult questions applies to a *practice situation*. As we discussed in "Part 4: Guessing and Time-Management on Test Day" starting on page 32 of this Black Book, if you're stumped by a question on test day, then you should skip that question and answer easier questions before coming back to the challenging question on a later pass.)

When a strategy doesn't seem to work against a particular question, the first thing to do is to make sure that the practice question is a real SAT question from the College Board. The next thing is to verify that you haven't misread the answer key—I can't tell you how many times a student has reported struggling with a question for a long time, only to realize that he had misread the answer key, and that the correct answer would have made sense the whole time.

Assuming that you're looking at a real College Board question, and assuming that you haven't misread the answer key, the next thing to consider is whether the strategy you're trying to apply is really relevant to the question. Sometimes people mistakenly try to apply a strategy for a Reading question to a grammar-based Writing question, for instance.

If you're pretty sure the strategy you're trying to apply really should work on a particular question, then the issue is probably that you've overlooked some key detail of the question, or that you've misunderstood a word or two somewhere in the question. At this point, it can be a very useful exercise to start over from square one and go back through the question word-by-word, taking nothing for granted and making a sincere effort to see the question with new eyes.

If you do this well, you'll probably be able to figure out where you went wrong and why the question works the way it does. If you make an effort to incorporate the lessons from this experience into your future preparation, then it can be tremendously beneficial to your performance on test day.

On the other hand, if you keep staring at the question and you still can't figure out what the issue is, then I would recommend that you move on to something else for a while—but do make sure you come back to the troubling question at some point and try to work it out, because the standardized nature of the SAT makes it very likely that any troubling strategic issues you run into during practice will reappear on test day, in one form or another.

Of course, you can refer to the troublesome question's walkthrough in this Black Book for extra help in understanding it.

"Which Practice Books Should I Buy?"

I designed this Black Book so the only additional resources you would need are the real PDF practice tests from the College Board, and the College Board's free Bluebook app.

As we've discussed earlier in this book, the digital SAT is adaptive, meaning that your performance on the first module for each section determines which questions you'll see in the second module. The College Board has also released six "paper" practice tests—that is, non-digital, non-adaptive practice tests. (For more on this topic, see our discussion of College Board practice materials for the digital SAT on page 16.) Those paper tests are available for free on the College Board's website at:

https://satsuite.collegeboard.org/digital/digital-practice-preparation/practice-tests/linear

If you don't feel like trying to type all that, you can find links to those same tests at QuestPrep.com/Practice as well.

(Note: The tests at the link above are **not** the same tests available in the College Board Publication *The Official Digital SAT Study Guide*, also called "the Blue Book." Again, for more on this important and potentially confusing topic, read that discussion of College Board practice materials for the digital SAT on page 16 that I just mentioned.)

The walkthroughs in this Black Book correspond to the questions in the first four of those "paper" PDF tests—the ones you can get for free on the College Board's website through the link above. So you will need access to those four tests; you can download the PDFs for free at the link above or at QuestPrep.com/Practice, and then either print them out or just work off your screen.

Again, for more on those practice tests, and why using real practice tests from the College Board is so important, see "Only Work with Questions from the College Board!" on page 16 of this Black Book.

"I'm Having a Hard Time Visualizing Some of Your Techniques. What Can I Do?"

Visit www.SATprepVideos.com, where I've made some sample video solutions available for free to readers of this book, to help you visualize some of the techniques from this book more clearly.

Reading and Writing Questions

"I know you say that the answer to each Reading question is always spelled out on the page, but I found a question where that's not the case. Now what?"

I completely understand that there are some questions where the answer doesn't seem to be on the page somewhere, but I promise you that the issue is always—*always*—some error on the part of the test-taker, not on the part of the test. (This assumes that you're working with a real SAT question published by the College Board, of course. Fake questions from other companies don't have to follow any rules, and the strategies in this Black Book—the strategies for the real SAT—don't always apply to fake questions written by companies like Kaplan, McGraw-Hill, and so on. That's why it's so important to have access to SAT Practice Tests #1-4, as discussed on page 16.)

So if you think you've found a real SAT question that doesn't follow the rules, you need to try to figure out where you've gone wrong. It may be that you haven't read some critical part of the text, or that you misread it, or that you misread an answer choice. It may be that some of the words on the page don't actually mean what you think they mean. It may be a combination of all of the above, or even something else. But, somewhere in there, you've made a mistake.

I know it can be frustrating to hunt back through the question and the text to find your mistake, but I strongly advise you to do so, especially if your goal is to score really high. The process of figuring out your mistake will help you understand the test much better, and greatly improve your future performance. (For more on these ideas, see "The Importance of Details: Avoiding "Careless Errors" on page 14, "How to Train for the SAT—Mastering the Ideas in this Black Book" on page 27, and "The Nature of Elite Scores" on page 524)

"I like my answer to a question better than the College Board's answer. Now what?"

It's normal to feel like the College Board has done a bad job of deciding the correct answer to one of its own questions. But we have to work very hard to overcome that feeling. We need to understand that the SAT is a standardized test with questions and answers that can be reliably predicted because they follow certain rules and patterns. So your job isn't to find the answer choice that seems most satisfactory to you. Your job is to ask yourself, "Which choice will the SAT reward, based on the rules it follows for this type of question?"

"I found a Writing question whose answer doesn't follow the rules of grammar. How can that be?"

Remember that the College Board isn't necessarily following the grammar rules that you learned in school, or even the rules that native speakers of American English follow when they speak or write. Instead, the College Board has its own set of grammar rules. While those rules largely overlap with the current grammar of American English, there may be some points where they differ from what you're used to seeing. Remember that your goal in answering Writing questions isn't to make the sentences sound good to *you*, but to figure out which answer choice the College Board will reward based on the rules and patterns it follows. For more on this, see the part of this Black Book that deals with SAT Writing questions, which starts on page 75.

"What if I don't know the words?"

Sometimes on the SAT, we encounter unfamiliar vocabulary. The first thing to do in this situation is to attempt to answer the question just as we normally would. Often, we're able to do this without any problems, and the unknown word ends up being a non-issue— because we can still either confirm that the right answer is right, or we can concretely eliminate all three wrong answer choices, without knowing the meaning of that one word.

Again, when you encounter an unknown word in an SAT Reading and Writing question, you should first just see if you can figure out the right answer anyway. Many students develop the idea in school that if they see a word they don't know in a test question, they're going to get that question wrong; in school, this is often the case. But when we take the SAT, we'll encounter unfamiliar words, phrases, and concepts all the time, and most of them have no impact on our ability to answer the relevant question. So get comfortable with the idea of working around words you're not familiar with.

If you can't answer the question as normal, then you should skip the question and come back to it on a later pass. Maybe on your next time around, something about the question will click, and you'll be able to figure out the right answer. If not, mark your best guess, move on, and spend your time on questions where you know enough of the words to apply your training effectively.

What you should definitely NOT do is obsess over the question with the unknown word, and spend several minutes trying to answer it anyway, and then get flustered for the rest of the test because you're worried that your vocabulary is inadequate. Everyone should expect to encounter unfamiliar words and concepts on the SAT; the presence of these words and concepts on some questions doesn't have any impact on your ability to answer the large majority of the questions where vocabulary won't be an issue, so make sure to devote your time and energy to those questions. Remember that you can miss a handful of questions on test day and still get an elite SAT score.

One more note—some students *really* get wrapped up in vocabulary issues, and even memorize long lists of vocabulary words in hopes that doing so will improve their SAT performance. This is a bad idea, for a number of reasons:

- We don't know ahead of time which challenging words will appear on the SAT, and trying to guess which difficult words will appear for you on your specific test date isn't possible, so the odds are very much against seeing any word from any given vocab list on test day.

- Even if you see a word from your vocab list on test day, the odds are good that this specific word won't have any impact on your ability to answer that question (assuming that you're comfortable with the training in this Black Book). In other words, you probably could have answered that question even if you hadn't memorized that word's definition ahead of time.

- Memorizing a word and its definition isn't the same as actually being comfortable with reading and understanding that word when it's actually used in a passage—even if you could pick out a word's definition, that doesn't mean you'll necessarily understand that word in a real world situation.

- Memorizing a long list of vocabulary words takes a ton of time and energy. Even if it provides some marginal benefit— which is doubtful—investing that time and energy in actually learning how the test works (as we do in this Black Book) will have an exponentially greater payoff.

So even if you find yourself occasionally encountering unknown words in your practice, resist the urge to memorize vocabulary. It's not going to help your score, but continuing your training and practice with this Black Book, and with real SAT questions, will.

Math Questions

"Which Math Formulas are Most Important for the SAT?"

If I had to pick, I would say that the formulas related to triangles seem to me like they come up most often.
But that answer is kind of misleading, for three reasons:

1. Almost all the geometry formulas you could use on the SAT Math section are provided for you by the College Board, so it's not like you'll need to memorize how to find the area of a circle or anything.

2. In general, the best approach to the SAT Math section doesn't rely primarily on formulas.

3. Many SAT Math questions couldn't be answered with formulas even if we wanted them to be.

For more on how to approach SAT Math, please see the part of this Black Book on SAT Math training, which starts on page 241.

Being an SAT Machine

Trifles make perfection, and perfection is no trifle.
Michelangelo

In this book, I talk a lot about how to answer individual questions. Obviously, that's an important part of beating the SAT.

But you may have noticed that the processes and sample solutions get pretty repetitive pretty quickly. My students often complain, "After a while, doing these questions is just the same thing over and over…"

Some teachers might be insulted by that, but when I hear those magic words I just smile and say, "Exactly!" On a standardized test, when answering questions begins to feel repetitive and automatic, you know you've made a huge improvement.

Standardized Tests Have Standardized Questions

In writing the Black Book, my goal has been to teach you the unwritten rules of the test, so that you know how to attack every real SAT question you'll ever see. Never forget that the SAT is a test with rules and patterns that it has to follow, and once you start to unlock them you almost can't go wrong. It's almost like you turn into an SAT machine.

An SAT Machine at Work

One of the things I often do for students is show them how I would take a section of the test. I don't just show them the processes and strategies I use, although those are definitely important. I also show them the speed and the attitude I use on the test.

When I'm taking the SAT, I have an inner dialogue going on in my head. It's very simple and straightforward. I'm reading each question, thinking briefly about what kind of question it is, then walking myself through the various steps described in these pages. It's all second nature to me, and the layouts of my walkthroughs in this Black Book reflect this style of attack: there's a preliminary set of details I always notice before I start really solving each question, and then I go through my solution, and then I check everything over and make sure I haven't made any mistakes before I move on to the next question. When I think about answer choices, I'm ruthless about cutting them out—as soon as I see something wrong with an answer, it's gone.

Unless I get confused or lose my concentration, I usually finish each section in well under half the allotted time. And it's not because I'm rushing or anything. I just don't waste time thinking about any unnecessary aspects of the questions.

When I take a test, there's no dilly-dallying or second-guessing. I'm prepared, and I know what to expect, because I know the SAT is ALWAYS THE SAME in all the important ways. You'll see this kind of direct, efficient approach reflected in the way I've presented the walkthroughs in this book.

Becoming an SAT Machine

When most untrained test-takers take the SAT, they let their minds wander. They don't realize that every question has one clear answer, so they often waste their time trying to justify every answer choice to themselves. They don't have set processes to rely on. They don't know the recurring rules and patterns to look for in every question. In other words, they don't take advantage of any of the gaping holes in the SAT's armor. They're inefficient and unfocused, and their scores suffer for it.

So what do you do if you want to turn into a machine? The key thing is to remember that every question has one clear answer, and that you can find it. Stick to a game plan—know how to start in on any SAT question and keep going until you either arrive at the answer, decide to skip it for the moment, or use your chosen guessing approach on it. Then just keep working your system all the way through the test. That's it. Don't get distracted. Rely on the SAT to give you the same sorts of questions you've seen before—because it definitely will. It has to.

In a way, taking the SAT is similar to taking a road test for a driver's license. You know in advance which skills you'll be asked to demonstrate and what rules you'll have to follow during the test; what you don't know is the specific situation you'll be in when you demonstrate each skill. Keep this in mind—stay flexible about applying what you know, but never forget that the range of things you can be asked to do on the SAT is very limited.

Also, as weird as it might sound, you should strive for the SAT to be boring and repetitive. Some people want their SAT preparation to feel like academic and educational exploration— but what's the point of that if it doesn't improve your score? Find each answer, and practice finding it as efficiently as possible. You'll be attacking the test in a systematic, methodical way before you know it—and that's the secret to real SAT success. Save the creativity for other areas of your life.

The Nature of Elite Scores

It is not because things are difficult that we do not dare. It is because we do not dare that they are difficult.
Seneca the Younger

Imagine a hypothetical test with 100 questions of varying difficulty on various subjects. If you needed to answer any one question correctly, you could probably find one that seemed to be the easiest for you, and get it right.

Now imagine that you're working on the same imaginary test, and you've answered 90 questions correctly, and you want to get one more of the remaining ten. The odds are good that you've already answered all of the questions that were easiest for you. All that are left are the ones you skipped, and now you're more likely to be stuck than you were when you just started out.

Now imagine that you wanted to get nine of the ten remaining questions, or even all ten. It would only get harder and harder, right?

My point is this: The more you improve on any test, the harder it is to keep improving. The more you succeed with the SAT, the rarer your opportunities for future success become. The more questions you master, the closer you come to having to deal with the questions you dislike most if you want to make any progress.

So making an elite score on the SAT (say, a combined score of 1500 or more) will require most people to put a little extra thought and effort into their preparation. Let's talk about how to do that.

Having the Right Attitude.

Your attitude is an important factor in preparing for the SAT.

Accountability

If you want a good score, *you* have to do it. That may seem fairly obvious, but it's also very important. Every other strategy or attitude will eventually fail you unless you take full accountability for your performance.

The only thing that will help you improve is diligent, intelligent practice. Thinking about nonspecific problems that you cannot fix will only distract you from other weaknesses that you *can* fix. When you conquer all the problems you can pinpoint, one by one, you may be surprised to find out how much progress you can make.

Persistence

You will fail in some way, however small or large, over the course of your SAT preparation. Everyone does. However, failure is as impermanent as you want it to be. If you are willing to work for it, every failure is literally another opportunity to succeed in the future.

Remember to keep working until you achieve the score you want. As your progress becomes more and more difficult, remind yourself that it's only because you've already come so far, and that you can go even farther.

Practicing for the SAT

Performing on the SAT, like any other skill, becomes easier if you practice it.

Choosing Your Pace

You will need some amount of some kind of practice; the kind and amount depend on how well you've done so far, in which areas, and how well you want to do in the future. Refer to "How to Train for the SAT—Mastering the Ideas in this Black Book" on page 27 of this Black Book for more on how to approach your training for the SAT.

You also have to be responsible in your training. If you don't feel like you're practicing enough, or if you're not improving, then you need to think hard about why: you may need to put in more time, review your work more carefully, or go back to basics with the different sections of this book. Just keep working away at it. You get results depending on the quality of the work you put in, so if you want an elite score, remember: Work smarter *and* harder.

Assessing Weakness

As you practice, you will notice certain areas of the test that seem to give you particular trouble. Take note, and work toward a way to improve on those sections. Don't think "I can't do it"—the information you need is there in every question, just learn to see it and use it. Don't be tempted to convince yourself that one question type is just too hard or flawed or has some other problem. You can do them all if you learn to apply the strategies in this book.

When you do start to notice problem areas, see them as places where you have not yet succeeded, not places where you won't or can't succeed. Learn the difference between recognizing weakness and expecting failure.

Making it Count

You can spend all the time in the world practicing, but if it's mindless practice, then you won't improve. Practice actively and intelligently. Don't try to look up every word in the Reading and Writing section and memorize its meaning, but if you feel like you keep seeing a word with which you are unfamiliar (especially in the question prompts), go ahead and look it up, and be sure you understand what it means; you might see it again somewhere.

However, if there is a word in the Math section that you don't understand, look it up every time. This isn't as extreme, since there tend to be fewer unknown words in SAT Math questions than in SAT Reading and Writing questions, but you can't answer an SAT Math question without knowing the vocabulary involved.

Also, feel free to come up with your own tricks while practicing, but if your tricks don't work every time, then don't rely on them. When you've mastered all the techniques, you shouldn't just be right all the time; you should know that you're right, know why you're right, and know why the wrong answers are wrong—every time. Remember: if you're not getting 800s (or whatever your goal is) in practice, you probably won't get them on the real test.

Parting Advice

If you're putting in all this extra effort to reach an elite score, then you must have some larger goal (improving your chances at a particular school, qualifying for a scholarship, or whatever). Keep that goal in mind. Let it motivate you to continue to work even when you don't want to. If you get your score report and you're not satisfied, think of it as a progress report and let your goal keep you working. Repeat this entire process thoroughly in order to optimize your improvement.

At the same time, treat each test as the real thing, because it is. Don't take a test thinking only that it will help you know what to work on later. It will, but always shoot for your goal, or else you might not do as well as you can. Strive to do your best, always.

Advice for Non-Native Speakers of American English

Knowledge, then, is a system of transformations that become progressively adequate.

Jean Piaget

The SAT involves a lot of reading, so it poses special challenges for students who aren't native speakers of American English. There are things we can do to overcome these challenges to some extent.

First, Focus on Questions in Which Language is Not a Problem.

Before we start worrying about building up your vocabulary or grammar knowledge, the most important thing—and the easiest—is to focus on eliminating mistakes in the questions that you can already understand well enough to answer with confidence. It doesn't make sense to try to learn a lot of big words if you haven't reached a point where knowing the words actually helps you to answer a question. So master the strategies in this book as much as you can before you start trying to memorize stuff.

Next, Focus on "Testing" Vocabulary.

Most non-native speakers waste time memorizing the same lists of words that native speakers used to memorize for earlier versions of the SAT, but this is unlikely to improve your score. The only "vocabulary" you should study specifically for the SAT would be the terms in the SAT Math Toolbox (starting on page 243), and any unfamiliar words you encounter repeatedly in question prompts—the kinds of words that actually frame the questions themselves, rather than the words that might show up as answer choices on Reading and Writing questions.

These are the kinds of words that native speakers would normally have few problems with, but that non-native speakers may never have studied specifically. They are absolutely critical if we want to understand what the test is actually asking us—and, most importantly, they are words that you will definitely encounter over and over again as you practice and take the real test.

The best way to discover which parts of "testing" vocabulary need your attention is to mark the unfamiliar words and phrases that you *frequently* encounter in real practice questions—again, pay particular attention to the *prompts* of the question rather than the answer choices, although "testing" vocabulary words can also appear in the answer choices. If you run into a word like "undermine" in 3 or 4 different questions and don't know what it means, then it's a good idea to go online and find the translation in your language.

(Some of these words are discussed in the article called "A Few Important Terms Related To Studies and Experiments" on page 73, so definitely make sure you're familiar with those.)

Then, Focus on SAT Grammar.

Notice that I'm specifically advising you to focus on learning *SAT grammar*, which will be at least a little different from the grammar you learned when you studied English in school. You'll have to make small tweaks to your understanding of "textbook" English to answer every Writing question on the SAT, but, again, those should be easy enough to take care of if you've been studying English for a while.

Conclusion

I hope you've found these tips useful. Remember that the SAT is a unique test, but it's also a very repetitive test, and even a very basic one in a lot of ways. By focusing on the issues I've pointed out above, you should hopefully be able to maximize your score without wasting your time on things that won't really help you.

One Final Piece of Advice
(Or: Every Question I've Ever Been Asked about the SAT Has Basically the Same Answer)

The "paradox" is only a conflict between reality and your feeling of what reality "ought to be."
- Richard Feynman

I've helped a lot of people with a lot of standardized tests, and in a lot of formats. This means I've also gotten a lot of questions from a very wide variety of test-takers. Most of the time those questions are very polite and sincere, but sometimes they're downright accusatory—something along the lines of

You said I could use a certain strategy on this kind of question, but it didn't work and my score went down. What are you, some kind of idiot?

So I wanted to close this book with some words of advice and encouragement for students who are still struggling.

First, the advice: In literally every single instance that I can recall in which a student has become frustrated with an idea in this Black Book, the underlying issue has always—ALWAYS—been that the student overlooked or misunderstood at least one key detail.

Let me say that again.

When you try to apply the ideas in this book to real SAT questions from the College Board and get frustrated by your inability to find correct answers reliably, the reason is nearly always that you've misread or misunderstood some important detail somewhere.

So when a question is giving you trouble, whether during practice or on test day, you must always, always, *always* assume you've made a mistake somewhere, and then set out to find and correct it. You need to develop an instinctive faith in the SAT's rules.

Let me also say, very clearly, that all of us—myself included—will run into situations in which we are completely certain that the College Board has finally made a mistake. No matter how convinced we may be that this is the case, we must remember that *we're* actually the ones who've made the mistake, and go back and re-evaluate our decisions until we figure out where we went wrong.

The most common type of mistake that I see students make is the general mistake of misreading something. Sometimes a question asks us to compare Passage 1 to Passage 2, but we choose the answer that compares Passage 2 to Passage 1 instead. Sometimes the question asks for the area and we find the perimeter. Sometimes we think a minus sign is a plus sign. And so on.

At other times, we may think we know something that actually turns out to be wrong. Once I was talking to a student who incorrectly thought that "taciturn" meant "peaceful" (this is the kind of misunderstanding that often comes from memorizing lists of vocabulary words, by the way). For a while, I thought "pied" meant something like "famous" or "skillful," because of the story *The Pied Piper*. But it turns out that "pied" just refers to something with patches of two or more colors, and I was completely wrong. These kinds of mistakes are harder to figure out during the actual moment of taking the test, because it's usually not possible to realize that something you believe isn't actually correct until after you've chosen the wrong answer, and found out it's wrong.

No matter what the mistake, though, it ultimately comes down to some specific detail (or details) of the question that you've misunderstood in some way. When you can't figure out the answer to a question with certainty, your first instinct must be to take nothing for granted, and expect that you've overlooked or misunderstood something.

Now that I've finished with the advice, let me offer some encouragement. I know how hard it is to stare at a question and feel defeated. I know the frustration of being sure you've answered a question correctly and then finding out later you were wrong. And I know that it's tempting, in those moments, to reject what you've learned and assume the SAT really is unbeatable, like everybody says.

But I'm here to tell you that those moments of frustration are also the moments that offer the most opportunity for progress. When you've wrestled with a question for a while and then you finally figure out how it works and where you went wrong, you learn a tremendous lesson about the test, and about how you've been approaching it. And your score improves.

When you truly figure out a challenging question, you learn something that you'll be able to apply on future questions, because the SAT is standardized. You also develop a stronger trust in the design of the test, which will help you in the future too. More importantly, though, you can learn something about your own problem-solving process, because you can start to figure out which parts of the question kept you from understanding it correctly in the first place; you can also start to reflect on the process you used to uncover and correct that mistake, so you can make that process much smoother in the future.

With the SAT, as with most areas of life, we make the most progress when we're confronted with a difficult situation that we eventually overcome. Good luck!

Thanks for Reading!

I've enjoyed sharing my SAT strategies with you, and I hope you've enjoyed learning how to beat the test, and that you're seeing good results with your practice sessions. It means a lot to me that so many students over the years have trusted me to help them at such an important time in their lives.

If this book has helped you, I would really appreciate it if you could tell your friends about it, or even go on Amazon and leave an honest review, if you'd like to do that.

Thanks again for reading, and I wish you the best of luck—with your preparation, and with everything else in your life.

Also—if you'd like more information from me related to test prep, admissions, and other content, please refer back to "Additional Resources Online" on page 4.

Made in the USA
Middletown, DE
12 August 2024

59015658R00294